TERRYVILLE PUBLIC LIBRARY
3 4028 08698 0860

Y0-ASD-779

Nineteenth-Century Literature Criticism

Guide to Gale Literary Criticism Series

For criticism on	Consult these Gale series
Authors now living or who died after December 31, 1999	*CONTEMPORARY LITERARY CRITICISM (CLC)*
Authors who died between 1900 and 1999	*TWENTIETH-CENTURY LITERARY CRITICISM (TCLC)*
Authors who died between 1800 and 1899	*NINETEENTH-CENTURY LITERATURE CRITICISM (NCLC)*
Authors who died between 1400 and 1799	*LITERATURE CRITICISM FROM 1400 TO 1800 (LC)* *SHAKESPEAREAN CRITICISM (SC)*
Authors who died before 1400	*CLASSICAL AND MEDIEVAL LITERATURE CRITICISM (CMLC)*
Authors of books for children and young adults	*CHILDREN'S LITERATURE REVIEW (CLR)*
Dramatists	*DRAMA CRITICISM (DC)*
Poets	*POETRY CRITICISM (PC)*
Short story writers	*SHORT STORY CRITICISM (SSC)*
Black writers of the past two hundred years	*BLACK LITERATURE CRITICISM (BLC)* *BLACK LITERATURE CRITICISM SUPPLEMENT (BLCS)*
Hispanic writers of the late nineteenth and twentieth centuries	*HISPANIC LITERATURE CRITICISM (HLC)* *HISPANIC LITERATURE CRITICISM SUPPLEMENT (HLCS)*
Native North American writers and orators of the eighteenth, nineteenth, and twentieth centuries	*NATIVE NORTH AMERICAN LITERATURE (NNAL)*
Major authors from the Renaissance to the present	*WORLD LITERATURE CRITICISM, 1500 TO THE PRESENT (WLC)* *WORLD LITERATURE CRITICISM SUPPLEMENT (WLCS)*

ISSN 0732-1864

Volume 90

Nineteenth-Century Literature Criticism

Excerpts from Criticism of the Works of Novelists, Philosophers, and Other Creative Writers Who Died between 1800 and 1899, from the First Published Critical Appraisals to Current Evaluations

Juliet Byington and Suzanne Dewsbury
Editors

Detroit
New York
San Francisco
London
Boston
Woodbridge, CT

STAFF

Lynn M. Spampinato, Janet Witalec, *Managing Editors, Literature Product*
Kathy D. Darrow, *Product Liaison*
Juliet Byington, Suzanne Dewsbury, *Editors*
Mark W. Scott, *Publisher, Literature Product*

Mary Ruby, Patti A. Tippett, *Technical Training Specialists*
Deborah J. Morad, Kathleen Lopez Nolan, *Managing Editors, Literature Content*
Susan M. Trosky, *Director, Literature Content*

Maria L. Franklin, *Permissions Manager*
Edna Hedblad, *Permissions Specialist*
Shalice Shah, *Permissions Assistant*

Victoria B. Cariappa, *Research Manager*
Tracie A. Richardson, *Project Coordinator*
Andrew Guy Malonis, Barbara McNeil, Gary J. Oudersluys, Maureen Richards, Cheryl L. Warnock, *Research Specialists*
Tamara C. Nott, *Research Associate*
Tim Lehnerer, Ron Morelli, *Research Assistants*

Dorothy Maki, *Manufacturing Manager*
Stacy L. Melson, *Buyer*

Mary Beth Trimper, *Composition and Prepress Manager*
Carolyn Roney, *Composition Specialist*

Randy Bassett, *Image Database Supervisor*
Robert Duncan, *Imaging Specialist*
Michael Logusz, *Graphic Artist*
Pamela A. Reed, *Imaging Coordinator*
Kelly A. Quin, *Imaging Editor*

Library of Congress Catalog Card Number
ISBN 0-7876-4545-1
ISSN 0732-1864
Printed in the United States of America

10 9 8 7 6 5 4 3 2 1

Contents

Preface

Since its inception in 1981, *Nineteeth-Century Literature Criticism* (*NCLC*) has been a valuable resource for students and librarians seeking critical commentary on writers of this transitional period in world history. Designated an "Outstanding Reference Source" by the American Library Association with the publication of is first volume, *NCLC* has since been purchased by over 6,000 school, public, and university libraries. The series has covered more than 300 authors representing 29 nationalities and over 17,000 titles. No other reference source has surveyed the critical reaction to nineteenth-century authors and literature as thoroughly as *NCLC.*

Scope of the Series

NCLC is designed to introduce students and advanced readers to the authors of the nineteenth century and to the most significant interpretations of these authors' works. The great poets, novelists, short story writers, playwrights, and philosophers of this period are frequently studied in high school and college literature courses. By organizing and reprinting commentary written on these authors, *NCLC* helps students develop valuable insight into literary history, promotes a better understanding of the texts, and sparks ideas for papers and assignments. Each entry in *NCLC* presents a comprehensive survey of an author's career or an individual work of literature and provides the user with a multiplicity of interpretations and assessments. Such variety allows students to pursue their own interests; furthermore, it fosters an awareness that literature is dynamic and responsive to many different opinions.

Every fourth volume of *NCLC* is devoted to literary topics that cannot be covered under the author approach used in the rest of the series. Such topics include literary movements, prominent themes in nineteenth-century literature, literary reaction to political and historical events, significant eras in literary history, prominent literary anniversaries, and the literatures of cultures that are often overlooked by English-speaking readers.

NCLC continues the survey of criticism of world literature begun by Gale's *Contemporary Literary Criticism* (*CLC*) and *Twentieth-Century Literary Criticism* (*TCLC*).

Organization of the Book

An *NCLC* entry consists of the following elements:

- The **Author Heading** cites the name under which the author most commonly wrote, followed by birth and death dates. Also located here are any name variations under which an author wrote, including transliterated forms for authors whose native languages use nonroman alphabets. If the author wrote consistently under a pseudonym, the pseudonym will be listed in the author heading and the author's actual name given in parenthesis on the first line of the biographical and critical information. Uncertain birth or death dates are indicated by question marks. Single-work entries are preceded by a heading that consists of the most common form of the title in English translation (if applicable) and the original date of composition.

- The **Introduction** contains background information that introduces the reader to the author, work, or topic that is the subject of the entry.

- A **Portrait of the Author** is included when available.

- The list of **Principal Works** is ordered chronologically by date of first publication and lists the most important works by the author. The genre and publication date of each work is given. In the case of foreign authors whose works have been translated into English, the list will focus primarily on twentieth-century translations, selecting those works most commonly considered the best by critics. Unless otherwise indicated, dramas are dated by first performance, not first publication. Lists of **Representative Works** by different authors appear with topic entries.

- Reprinted **Criticism** is arranged chronologically in each entry to provide a useful perspective on changes in critical evaluation over time. The critic's name and the date of composition or publication of the critical work are given at the beginning of each piece of criticism. Unsigned criticism is preceded by the title of the source in which it appeared. All titles by the author featured in the text are printed in boldface type. Footnotes are reprinted at the end of each essay or excerpt. In the case of excerpted criticism, only those footnotes that pertain to the excerpted texts are included. Criticism in topic entries is arranged chronologically under a variety of subheadings to facilitate the study of different aspects of the topic.

- A complete **Bibliographical Citation** of the original essay or book precedes each piece of criticism.

- Critical essays are prefaced by brief **Annotations** explicating each piece.

- An annotated bibliography of **Further Reading** appears at the end of each entry and suggests resources for additional study. In some cases, significant essays for which the editors could not obtain reprint rights are included here. Boxed material following the further reading list provides references to other biographical and critical sources on the author in series published by Gale.

Indexes

Each volume of *NCLC* contains a **Cumulative Author Index** listing all authors who have appeared in a wide variety of reference sources published by the Gale Group, including *NCLC*. A complete list of these sources is found facing the first page of the Author Index. The index also includes birth and death dates and cross references between pseudonyms and actual names.

A **Cumulative Nationality Index** lists all authors featured in *NCLC* by nationality, followed by the number of the *NCLC* volume in which their entry appears.

A **Cumulative Topic Index** lists the literary themes and topics treated in the series as well as in *Classical and Medieval Literature Criticism, Literature Criticism from 1400 to 1800, Twentieth-Century Literary Criticism,* and the *Contemporary Literary Criticism* Yearbook, which was discontinued in 1998.

An alphabetical **Title Index** accompanies each volume of *NCLC*, with the exception of the Topics volumes. Listings of titles by authors covered in the given volume are followed by the author's name and the corresponding page numbers where the titles are discussed. English translations of foreign titles and variations of titles are cross-referenced to the title under which a work was originally published. Titles of novels, dramas, nonfiction books, and poetry, short story, or essay collections are printed in italics, while individual poems, short stories, and essays are printed in roman type within quotation marks.

In response to numerous suggestions from librarians, Gale also produces an annual paperbound edition of the *NCLC* cumulative title index. This annual cumulation, which alphabetically lists all titles reviewed in the series, is available to all customers. Additional copies of this index are available upon request. Librarians and patrons will welcome this separate index; it saves shelf space, is easy to use, and is recyclable upon receipt of the next edition.

Citing *Nineteenth-Century Literature Criticism*

When writing papers, students who quote directly from any volume in the Literary Criticism Series may use the following general format to footnote reprinted criticism. The first example pertains to material drawn from periodicals, the second to material reprinted from books.

Kim McQuaid, "William Apes, Pequot: An Indian Reformer in the Jackson Era," *The New England Quarterly,* 50 (December 1977): 605-25; excerpted and reprinted in *Nineteenth-Century Literature Criticism,* vol. 73, ed. Janet Witalec (Farmington Hills, Mich.: The Gale Group, 1999), 3-4.

Richard Harter Fogle, *The Imagery of Keats and Shelley: A Comparative Study* (Archon Books, 1949), 211-51; excerpted and reprinted in *Nineteenth-Century Literature Criticism,* vol. 73, ed. Janet Witalec (Farmington Hills, Mich.: The Gale Group, 1999), 157-69.

Suggestions are Welcome

Readers who wish to suggest new features, topics, or authors to appear in future volumes, or who have other suggestions or comments are cordially invited to call, write, or fax the Managing Editor:

Managing Editor, Literary Criticism Series
The Gale Group
27500 Drake Road
Farmington Hills, MI 48331-3535
1-800-347-4253 (GALE)
Fax: 248-699-8054

Acknowledgments

The editors wish to thank the copyright holders of the excerpted criticism included in this volume and the permissions managers of many book and magazine publishing companies for assisting us in securing reproduction rights. We are also grateful to the staffs of the Detroit Public Library, the Library of Congress, the University of Detroit Mercy Library, Wayne State University Purdy/Kresge Library Complex, and the University of Michigan Libraries for making their resources available to us. Following is a list of the copyright holders who have granted us permission to reproduce material in this volume of *NCLC*. Every effort has been made to trace copyright, but if omissions have been made, please let us know.

COPYRIGHTED EXCERPTS IN *NCLC*, VOLUME 90, WERE REPRODUCED FROM THE FOLLOWING PERIODICALS:

COPYRIGHTED EXCERPTS IN *NCLC*, VOLUME 90, WERE REPRODUCED FROM THE FOLLOWING BOOKS:

of Chelsea House Educational Communications, Inc. All rights reserved. Reproduced by permission.—Rees, Robert A. From ***Fifteen American Authors Before 1900: Bibliographic Essays on Research and Criticism.*** Edited by Robert A. Rees and Earl N. Harbert. University of Wisconsin Press, 1971. Copyright © 1971 The Regents of the University of Wisconsin. All rights reserved. Reproduced by permission.—Steinecke, Hartmut. From ***Reflection and Action: Essays on the Bildungsroman***. Edited by James Hardin. University of South Carolina Press, 1991. Copyright © 1991 University of South Carolina. Reproduced by permission.—Wagenknecht, Edward. From ***James Russell Lowell: Portrait of a Many-Sided Man***. Oxford University Press, 1971. Copyright © 1971 by Edward Wagenknecht. Used by permission of Oxford University Press, Inc.—Whitaker, Rosemary. From ***Helen Hunt Jackson***. Boise State University, 1987. Copyright 1987 by the Boise State University Western Writers Series. All rights reserved. Reproduced by permission of the publisher and author.—Williams, Carolyn. From ***Transfigured World: Walter Pater's Aesthetic Historicism***. Cornell University Press, 1989. Copyright © 1989 by Cornell University. All rights reserved. Used by permission of Cornell University Press.—Wortham, Thomas. From ***The Transcendentalists: A Review of Research and Criticism***. Edited by Joel Myerson. The Modern Language Association of America, 1984. Copyright © 1984 by The Modern Language Association of America. Reproduced by permission.

PHOTOGRAPHS AND ILLUSTRATIONS APPEARING IN *NCLC*, VOLUME 90, WERE RECEIVED FROM THE FOLLOWING SOURCES:

Coleridge, Hartley, photograph. © Hulton-Getty/Liaison Agency. Reproduced by permission.—Title page from *Poems*, written by Hartley Coleridge, photograph. The University of Michigan Library. Reproduced by permission.—Title page from *Ramona*, by Helen Jackson. Robert Brothers Publishers. Special Collections Library, University of Michigan. Reproduced by permission.—Title page from *Studies in the History of the Renaissance*, by Walter H. Pater. Macmillan and Co., Publishers. Special Collections Library, University of Michigan. Reproduced by permission.—Title page from *The Biglow Papers*, photograph by James Lowell. Special Collections Library, University of Michigan. Reproduced by permission.—Title page from *Wilhelm Meister's Apprenticeship*, by Johann Wolfgang von Goethe. Special Collections Library, University of Michigan. Reproduced by permission.

Hartley Coleridge
1796-1849

English poet, essayist, and critic.

INTRODUCTION

Hartley Coleridge's literary reputation rests principally on one volume of poems and a set of author biographies titled *Biographia Borealis; or, Lives of Distinguished Northerns* (1833). The volume of poetry, titled *Poems: 1833,* is lauded mostly for Coleridge's sonnets, a form at which the author excelled. The brevity of the sonnet form made it a particularly attractive genre for Coleridge, and contemporaries of the poet reported that they had witnessed him write one in a matter of minutes. Expected to be a genius from an early age, Hartley Coleridge, the eldest son of Samuel Taylor Coleridge, was extremely aware that he had fallen short of the literary greatness expected of him, and this deprecatory self-awareness became a common theme in his poetry. The younger Coleridge recognized the failings as his own, though, and openly acknowledged the debt he owed to his father as well as to his father's associates—William Wordsworth and Robert Southey. Hartley Coleridge once remarked in a letter that "If aught of mine be preserved from oblivion, it will be owing to my bearing the name of Coleridge, and having enjoyed . . . the acquaintance of Southey and Wordsworth." Although he never achieved the literary greatness of his mentors, Hartley Coleridge's writing style and his focus on the themes of life and love place him squarely within the tradition of later Romantic poets.

BIOGRAPHICAL INFORMATION

Hartley Coleridge was born in Bristol, England, on September 19, 1796 to Samuel Taylor and Sara Coleridge, and was surrounded by the literary greats of the Romantic era from early in his childhood. His mother's sister was married to the poet Robert Southey who, along with William Wordsworth, served as the Coleridge family guardians for many years. In fact, it was Wordsworth who taught the young Hartley the techniques of poetry, and it is to Wordsworth's work that Hartley's poetry is most often compared. The child Hartley was featured in many of his father's poems, most notably "Frost at Midnight," in which the elder Coleridge declared that he would protect his son from the debilitating influences of city life and let him "wander like a breeze / By lakes and sandy shores. . . ." The young Coleridge also appeared in numerous Wordsworthian poems, including "Ode: Intimations of Immortality." Both poets perceived Hartley as a boy genius who would grow up, unspoiled by city life, to be a successful poet and academic.

A child with a vivid imagination, the young Coleridge seemed to be well on his way to fulfilling the prophecies of his father and mentor when, upon learning of the history of the royal families of England, he created for himself the mythical world of Ejuxria. His parents and all those around him perceived his imagination and strong intellect as evidence of his genius. In accordance with his father's beliefs, Hartley's early education was irregular, and he was left to wander and dream and ponder over the books in his father's study. When he was about eight, Hartley began attending a local school (Ambleside) with his younger brother Derwent. There Hartley remained, frequently seen roaming the countryside in what his brother termed "uncontrolled fits of poetic fancy," until 1815 when, with the assistance of Wordsworth and Southey, he gained admission to Merton College at Oxford. It is obvious from his letters and other papers that the young Coleridge was apprehensive about his reception at college. Having been nurtured all his life with notions of poetic greatness, it is possible that he was unsure of his ability to fulfill this promise. It was as an undergraduate at Oxford that Hartley first showed signs of the alcoholism that would plague him the rest of his life. A frequent and popular attendee of Oxford "wine parties," he would discourse on a wide variety of subjects at these gatherings.

Hartley Coleridge began writing poetry while at Oxford, thrice competing for the coveted Newdigate, the undergraduate prize for English verse. Included in this set is "The Horses of Lysippus," and while these early poems were considered fine examples of technique, detail, and observation, Coleridge's failure to win the Newdigate was a huge disappointment to him. He completed his studies at Merton in 1819, taking a second class degree from Oxford. He was then elected to the coveted position of probationary fellow at Oriel College, and a life of academic study and literary activity seemed assured. It soon became clear, though, that this was not to be—Coleridge continued to spend an enormous amount of time in the company of undergraduate students instead of his fellow scholars and often appeared in the Common room at Oriel inebriated. Because of this and other incidents, Coleridge was expelled from Oriel in 1820. His expulsion had a profound affect on him, and he would later blame many of his other failures on this incident. Following his expulsion from Oriel, Coleridge spent a few years in London, trying to support himself by placing poems and essays in magazines. The work was not enough to support him completely, but a letter written to his brother Derwent during this period reveals that it was around this time that Hartley began thinking seriously about poetry. He declared that "I certainly succeed better in intricate and difficult than in the plainer and simpler textures. The sonnet is my favorite." Although he continued to publish some short poems, some of which appeared in *London Magazine* during the 1820s, it would not be until 1833 that Coleridge would publish an actual volume of poetry.

Since his literary pursuits in London did not provide an adequate means of financial support, in 1823 his father arranged a teaching position for Hartley at Ambleside. Critics contend that it was during his years as a schoolmaster that the younger Coleridge finally developed into a competent, though minor poet of his generation. An example of his work during this time is "The Anemone," a poem that displays his poetic style as well as the themes that would run through all his work. The poem describes the anemone flower, exploring its frailty and smallness. This linking of weakness and size with fear and shame are characteristic themes of Coleridge's work. In 1827 the school at Ambleside closed, leaving Coleridge free to concentrate on his writing again. Publishing success, however, did not happen again until 1832 when the publisher F. E. Bingley of Leeds, with whom Coleridge had been negotiating the publication of his book of poems, asked him to prepare a series of biographies of the "northern worthies." The offer was lucrative because it provided Coleridge with a means to support himself financially; he subsequently moved to Leeds in 1832 to begin work on what would become the *Biographia Borealis.* The series would include biographies on such authors as Andrew Marvell, Richard Bentley, William Congreve, and Roger Ascham, among others. The three-part work was first published in 1832 and later collected into one volume in 1833, the same year that Coleridge also issued his *Poems.*

Although second volumes of both poetry and biographies were planned, Bingley's firm went bankrupt. Coleridge had found the writing dry and distasteful anyway, and the collapse of the firm coupled with his father's declining health led the younger Coleridge back to the Lake District. Except for a brief stint as a schoolmaster during the late 1830s, Coleridge would remain at the Lake District until his own death in 1849, spending his days writing, reading, and wandering the hills. His last published work was an edition of *The Dramatic Works of Massinger and Ford* (1840), and although he attempted to convince the publisher of this work to issue another volume of poems, he did not meet with success.

MAJOR WORKS

Hartley Coleridge wrote numerous poems, essays, and letters during his lifetime, most of which appeared in periodicals and magazines of the time. The only collected works he published during his lifetime are his volume of poetry, titled *Poems: 1833* and his series of biographies, titled *Biographia Borealis.*

The first part of *Poems* consists primarily of a series of thirty-four sonnets. The second part of the book is titled "Thoughts and Fancies" and reveals a change in mood and form, comprised mainly of lyric poetry, addresses to infants, greetings, and translations of other works. Critics have noted a recurring theme of irrecoverable worth, of spent genius, and of unfulfilled heritage in this and other works by Coleridge. According to critic Earl Leslie Griggs, many of the poems in this collection contain an overriding sense of the poet's own weaknesses and lack of consistency. There are also many verses in the collection that reflect the life around him—poems, says Griggs, that are "bubbling over with enthusiasm, and usually composed to celebrate some event important in the lives of country-folk. . . ." Coleridge himself was his own best critic and recognized his limitations—admitting in "Poites apoites": "Not mine the skill in memorable phrase, / The hidden truths of passion to reveal, / To bring to light the intermingling ways, / By which unconscious motives darkling steal."

Coleridge's last collected work was *Essays and Marginalia,* edited by his brother Derwent Coleridge and published, after Hartley's death, in 1851. The collection covers a wide variety of subjects and includes essays, memoirs, and commentaries, many of them originally written for *Blackwood's Magazine.* It is now believed that many of the works in this collection were primarily written to please himself and were not intended for publication. In reviewing this work Eleanor A. Towle remarks that the volume is almost like "Hartley has been thinking aloud and he has put down his thoughts upon paper."

CRITICAL RECEPTION

Coleridge mostly wrote short poems and essays. His verses, though full of beauty, are often termed "detached jewels" due to their brevity and stylistic expertise. His most favored arrangement was the sonnet, and he mastered the technical difficulties of this form. Critics have also noted Hartley Coleridge's indebtedness to his literary masters and teachers Wordsworth and the elder Coleridge. Like their compositions, the younger Coleridge's poetry also explores nature and childhood. However, his focus is more simplistic and his writing is marked with a keen sense of his own failures. Despite this awareness his poetry does not convey any sense of bitterness toward his teachers, and in fact, the 1833 *Poems* contains many pieces addressed to his father and other poetic masters; in comparison to these giants, the younger Coleridge often found himself lacking in talent.

Like the Romantics, Coleridge was charmed by the novelty of everyday things, and Nature served as a symbol of the moral and spiritual world. Although his poems contain simple language and descriptions of ordinary events, like those of his mentor Wordsworth, Coleridge perceived these events as opportunities for the poet to meditate and interpret. The biggest difference between Wordsworth and Hartley Coleridge is the latter's focus on the self. Coleridge also exhibited independence in his use of language and style, and critics have noted that his verse is marked by plays of fancy and humor that are not to be found in Wordsworth's poetry. An example of this type of wordplay is contained in "Address to Certain Gold Fishes," a poem that is lauded as both humorous and reflective. Critics commend this and other poems by Coleridge for their spontaneity, noting the contrast in such lines as "Harmless warriors, clad in mail / Of silver breastplate, golden scale;—" and then "And yet, since on this hapless earth / There's small sincerity of mirth, / And laughter oft is but the art / To drown the outcry of the heart."

As a poet, Hartley Coleridge is most often remembered for his sonnets. Such was his mastery of this difficult form that Samuel Waddington, a contemporary critic, termed him "after Shakespeare our sweetest English sonneteer." Coleridge wrote mostly in the Petrarchan form, a less stylized version than the Shakespearean sonnet that harmonized more fittingly with the simpler spirit of Romantic poetry. Coleridge took liberties even with this form, and Griggs notes that although Coleridge fulfilled the technical requirements for the most part, very often the primary idea in his sonnets runs beyond the required eighth line. A vast majority of Coleridge's other verse is considered standard Romantic fare by many critics. Characterizing his poems as "meditative records of very ordinary incidents," Towle says that like his mentors, Hartley focused on pastoral and individual themes, with Nature as his consoler, bringing peace and healing. Critics, however, have remarked on the spontaneity of Hartley Coleridge's verse in contrast to Wordsworth's poetry, and the former's almost unconscious mastery of the technical forms he used. While many of his poems were left incomplete, the ones that were finished, Griggs calls "nearly faultless. Like delicately cut diamonds, they glisten in the sunshine, paradisiacal emblems of the poet's divine soul." Also in contrast to the work of the other Romantics, Hartley Coleridge's poetry was personal. According to Sister Mary Joseph Pomeroy, his work was almost lyrical, "dealing with the joys, sorrows, hopes, and disappointments of the life he knew; all have a subjective note, and many of them are definite portraits of self."

Coleridge's most noted prose work is the *Biographia Borealis.* The nature of this type of writing was unfamiliar to Coleridge, who mostly wrote poetry in sudden fits of imagination. The structure and restraint imposed by the essay differed from poetry, but Towle notes that Coleridge mostly succeeded in his venture in the interest of "just judgments and historical accuracy." He wanted to present true and realistic pictures of his subjects, hoping to serve both as biographer and historian, and while he often deviated into a discourse on the art of poetry or some other literary definition, Towle calls this collection "the strongest example of a periodic fit of industry." While both Towle and Griggs characterize *Biographia Borealis* as something that does not "greatly contribute to Hartley's literary reputation" (in Towle's words), both agree that Coleridge created complete and interesting accounts of his subjects.

Both Samuel Taylor Coleridge and Wordsworth expected Hartley Coleridge to be a superlative poet. Born at the peak of the Romantic movement and nurtured and taught by its masters, the younger Coleridge, however, did not begin writing until the Victorian era was at hand. By the time he began writing, "political upheaval . . . and changing economic standards had deafened the national ear to strains of the muse," says Herbert Hartman. Sentimentalism was the theme of the oncoming Industrial age, with Sir Walter Scott's novels surpassing Lord Byron's epics. Hartley Coleridge himself recognized this change in the national rhythms, admitting himself to be "a petty man of rhyme, / Nursed in the softness of a female time."

PRINCIPAL WORKS

Biographia Borealis; or, Lives of Distinguished Northerns (biography) 1833

Poems, Vol. I (poetry) 1833

Essays and Marginalia. 2 vols. (poetry and essays) 1851

Poems by Hartley Coleridge. With a Memoir of his Life by his Brother (Derwent Coleridge). 2 vols. (poetry and memoir) 1851

The Complete Poetical Works of Hartley Coleridge (poetry) 1908

Letters of Hartley Coleridge (letters) 1936

CRITICISM

Eleanor A. Towle (essay date 1912)

SOURCE: "Hartley Coleridge as a Poet," in *A Poet's Children: Hartley and Sara Coleridge,* Methuen and Co., 1912, pp. 273-86.

[*In this brief overview of Coleridge's poetry, Towle notes the influence of the Romantics on his work. Nature and memories of childhood are major themes in Coleridge's writing, according to Towle, and the majority of his poems are addressed to children.*]

It is not surprising to find that Hartley Coleridge's poems, collected by his brother Derwent, published in 1851 with a prefatory Memoir, and again recently reissued with some additions in the "Muse's Library," though rich in fancy and felicitous diction, are often the meditative records of very ordinary incidents.

He belonged to a school whereof the teachers, repudiating the artificial canons and sentiments of the eighteenth century, had sought their inspiration at the shrine of truth and in the heart of nature: "and poetry could never again be content to dance in a court dress with Pope, or go through a course of gymnastics with Dryden, or to sit by the fireside with Cowper, or to mount the pulpit with Young."

> The age grew sated with her sterile wit,
> Herself waxed weary on her loveless throne.
> Men felt life's tide, the sweep and surge of it,
> And craved a living voice, a natural tone.

Imagination sought a higher region, a purer air. The office of poetry was not only to allure and captivate, but to instruct and exalt; and, above all, to be the authoritative exponent of beauty both in the moral and physical world.

For the unrestrained and devastating force of passion, destructive of lawful barriers and high ideals, Wordsworth had a severe condemnation and an instinctive repugnance. With reverential delight he had looked into "the face of common things," and found, by reason of his love and reverence, their true interpretation. Moreover, the earnestness and dignity of his intellectual creed impressed itself upon thoughtful and cultivated minds, and led them on to a clearer appreciation of natural grace and truth.

At Wordsworth's side and in the study of his poetry, Hartley (though by no means blind to the defects and limitations of his master) had learned much of the same lore. His verse, both in thought and expression, bears the impress of his close acquaintance with the great poet. Wordsworth himself declared that Hartley's poetry lacked originality: a quality so impossible to define that it is difficult to disprove the assertion; and undoubtedly his lyrics and sonnets, in their painstaking and restrained purity of diction, are a reflection of the circle wherein he had been brought up, though in many instances displaying a pathos and tenderness of feeling peculiarly his own. It was almost by chance that some of his verse was preserved, for though his verbal memory for poetry was remarkable he could rarely remember his own.

The strange visions of his childhood had vanished, he no longer explored the untrodden tracks of unknown continents to meet with the indistinct and fearful shapes of beasts and reptiles, nor unrolled the genealogies of the long line of future kings who were to control the destinies of the world. His brain was not disturbed by metaphysical problems, nor his spirit oppressed by nightmare fantasies; unless it might be when, a solitary wanderer, he escaped for awhile from human companionship and the sheltered precincts of home. He knew nothing of the mystic region where his father's poems had had their birth or of "the finer, more delicately marvellous supernaturalism, the fruits of his more delicate psychology, which Coleridge infuses into romantic narrative." Hartley's Muse was, on the contrary, nourished and sustained by the simplest earthly means. He felt, possibly with justice, that pastoral and individual themes were best suited to his abilities. He loved nature in her mildest, most benignant mood. Though a dweller among the mountains, it was only in times of mental distress and under the pressure of an unconquerable desire to be alone that he fled to their wild recesses or their storm-encircled heights. But for the green flowering meadows, the rushes by the still margin of the lake, the springing delicate fern in the crevice of the rock, the pale clustering primroses, the rose-flushed snow of blossoming orchards, and all the offspring, however lowly, of the "breathing spring"; he had the eye of a poet and the heart of a lover.

His poetry was therefore not imitative in any formal sense of the word, but it was to some extent the result of atmosphere and association.

His moods are very various, tender and gay, descriptive rather than creative: the play of fancy like flickering sunlight, rather than the startling lurid gleams of a storm-tossed imagination. Even in his sadness he catches at each promise of joy, each stirring of gladness in the world around:—

> The little rills
> That trickle down the yellow hills,
> To drive the fairies' water mills.
> And every small bird trilling joyfully
> Tells a sweet tale of hope and love and peace.
> . . . . .
> Such themes I sang—and such I fain would sing,
> Oft as the green buds show the summer near—

But what availeth me to welcome spring,
  When one dull winter is my total year?
When the pure snowdrops couch beneath the snow,
  And storms long-tarrying come too soon at last,
I see the semblance of my private woe,
  And tell it to the dilatory blast.
Yet will I hail the sunbeam as it flies—
  And bid the universal world be glad—
With my brief joy all souls shall sympathise—
  And only I, will all alone be sad.

Thus, though Nature may at times reflect his melancholy, she is more often the consoler, and brings peace and healing in her wings. Still, as he wanders by the quiet waters and seeks the shaded valley or the upland pastures, he can return in spirit to the days to which he refers in one of the first sonnets he ever wrote to "the faithful counsellor of his youth," R. S. Jameson, afterwards Judge Advocate at Dominica:—

When we were idlers by the loitering rills,
  The need of human love we little noted;
Our love was nature and the peace which floated
  On the white mist and dwelt upon the hills.

Moreover, he was pre-eminently a poet of fancy, with no rationalistic prejudices to bid him shun enchanted ground, well fitted to wander with Puck and Oberon in a midsummer dream through the green mazes of a fairy wood; yet his observation is so exact and his quest of truth so dominant that no false lights are thrown upon a subject, and he is even austere in his rejection of meretricious effects. His fresh childlike wondering joy in purity and light and the loveliness of earth finds its expression in the simplest epithets.

But one fault it hath;
It fits too close to life's realities.
In truth to Nature missing truth to Art;
For Art commends not counterparts or copies
But from our life a nobler life would shape,
Bodies celestial from terrestrial raise,
And teach us not jejunely what we are,
But what we may be when the Parian block
Yields to the hand of Phidias.

This Art may need the prophetic vision not granted to Hartley when the dreams of childhood had faded; and the poet's criticism, possibly first suggested by Wordsworth's poetry, recalls his own displeased exclamation when he saw Walter Scott taking notes of scenery: "Nature will not permit you to make an inventory of her charms."

Yet Hartley's minute observation, whether directed to Nature or individuals, was accompanied by a large measure of spiritual insight—more an intuition than a talent. His pictures, subdued in colouring and manifestly true to life, are often mere sketches, recording some trivial passing fancy or quaint conceit that it pleased him to put into verse. There is nothing to dazzle or bewilder, but much to delight and captivate; and his talent was as apparent to a select circle of literary men as it had been to the poet guardians of his childhood. The grace and music of his versification, the elevation and restraint of his diction, appealed to cultivated critics, whilst his sensibility to natural influences brought the sights and sounds of earth before his readers in a few felicitous words:—

The snow
Of sluggard winter bedded on the hill,
And the small trickle of the frozen rill.

. . . . .

The nightingale grew dumb—the cuckoo fled,
And broad-eyed summer glared on hill and plain.

. . . . .

The patient beauty of the scentless rose,
Oft with the Morn's hoar-crystal quaintly glassed,
Hangs a pale mourner for the summer past,
And makes a little summer where it grows.

All these things had a message and a meaning, and he loved them all. At times they were his only solace and refuge, more especially when, after some dark hour of subjection to his fatal infirmity, he shunned alike the companions of his fall and the silent pity of those who loved him best. There were then mysterious absences of which it is probable that only the whispering winds and the babbling streams could have told the story.

At other seasons, though his hearth was lonely his life was by no means solitary. His pleasant though eccentric ways, his humour, and his conversational gifts commended him to many chance acquaintances for whom he was ready to exercise his light impromptu talent of versification. It was the day of extract books and albums, and upon their pages many of his graceful fancies are inscribed. But it was in the innocence and charms of childhood that he found his truest inspiration. To that pure source he ever returned with fresh and inexhaustible pleasure. Without parental experience he had attained to a genuine and discriminating understanding of the infinite possibilities, the distinctions and significance of life in its earlier stages. The opening year with its unstained blossoms, the pale rose of the dawn, were more to him than the wealth and pride of summer or the full splendour of high noonday. At an infant's shrine he was not only a devout but an instructed worshipper. These small magicians could at any moment dispel his melancholy; "these thriftless prodigals of smiles and tears" were quick to arouse his tenderest affections. No other poet, as Professor Dowden observes, has been the laureate of so many baby boys and girls. It is true that he had been brought up amongst those to whom faith in childhood was an integral part of a poet's creed. To his father it was the anchor to which he clung amidst the wreckage of lost beliefs and treasured hopes. The guardians and friends of his own childhood had owned the same allegiance and with unfailing patience awaited the sometimes capricious or tardy fulfilment of early pledges. In his case, as he was well aware, disappointment, crushing and irrevocable, had fallen upon their expectations, and those pledges had been unredeemed. But not even the ever-present sense of personal failure could shake his confidence, and the star of hope still shone with mild and inextinguishable radiance over the birthplace and the cradle. Nor was childhood merely an ideal state of which the customs were strange and the language unfamiliar. He had indeed shrunk from the boisterous spirits or frank insubordination of the ordinary schoolboy and had found his position as a teacher intolerable, but little girls and babies had an especial attraction for him. The helplessness of childhood, the infirmities of age, and the sufferings of dumb animals awakened all his best sympathies and filled him with a passion of pity; and so it comes to pass that a large proportion of his poems are addressed to children, who shall enter heaven at the last great day,

> Alike all blessed, and alike all fair,
> And only God remembers who they were.

He always declared that as an infant he had been perfectly conscious of what was passing around him and much regretted his lack of speech.

Again and again he returns to the theme of the gladness and growth of childhood or to the mysterious state of passive infancy, a condition of "exile perfection to a world forlorn!"

> Sure 'tis a holy and a healing thought
> That fills my heart and mind at sight of thee
> Thou purest abstract of humanity.

He reproved those who would assert that the mind whilst dumb is a blank, and saw in every unconscious look and gesture some revelation of the heaven within. Moreover, like a woman, he dwells with a delight, born of intimate knowledge, upon the minute loveliness of form and movement.

> In the mere sentient life
> Of unremembered infancy, whose speech
> Like secret Love's is only smiles and tears.

When he writes of the strong grasp of a baby's hand, of its attitude in sleep, of its sudden spring of joy, its murmured love-notes and indiscriminating kisses, we are not surprised to hear that he might be found in the house of his friends or by a cottage fireside contentedly nursing a baby by the hour—thus giving practical effect to poetic theories.

Of love poems properly so called he gives few examples.

Though fond of women's society, in youth he had been constrained in their presence and hardly ventured to express wishes he felt must remain unfulfilled. Though in his letters and journals, as well as in his poems, he lays bare with unnecessary frankness the blotted records of his past, he can yet thank Heaven that at least no woman has been involved in the calamities that have wrecked his hopes. At no time does he appear to have felt so far worthy of a woman's love as to strive to win for himself a refuge from loneliness and despondency in the consolatory joys and salutary restraints of domestic life. His fancy may wander free, but he must wake to the consciousness that he is doomed to a solitary existence by his own infirmities.

> "It must be so—my infant love must find
> In my own heart a cradle and a grave.

So he writes in one of his sonnets. And whilst respecting his sentiments one cannot help feeling that love must indeed have been in its infancy or so desirable a self-control might hardly have been attained.

Nevertheless some of his most felicitous verses are inspired by women, never passionate, but graceful and chivalrous, tendered with a half-melancholy yet playful homage from one to whom nearer approach was forbidden, and frequently, like the following stanza, not only beautiful in diction but faithful in portraiture.

> She was a queen of noble Nature's crowning,
> A smile of hers was like an act of grace;
> She had no winsome looks, no pretty frowning,
> Like daily beauties of the vulgar race:
> But if she smiled, a light was on her face,
> A clear cool kindliness, a lunar beam
> Of peaceful radiance, silvering o'er the stream
> Of human thought with unabiding glory;
> Not quite a waking truth, not quite a dream,
> A visitation bright and transitory.
> But she has changed—hath felt the touch of sorrow;
> No love hath she, no understanding friend.
> Oh! grief when heaven is forced of earth to borrow
> What the poor niggard earth hath not to lend.
> But when the stalk is snapt, the rose must bend,
> The tallest flower that skyward rears its head,
> Grows from the common ground and there must shed
> Its delicate petals. Cruel fate, too surely
> That they should find so base a bridal bed,
> Who lived in virgin pride so sweet and purely.
>
> . . . . .
>
> 'Tis vain to say—her worst of grief is only
> The common lot which all the world have known;
> To her 'tis more because her heart is lonely,
> And yet she hath no strength to stand alone—
> Once she had playmates, fancies of her own,
> And she did love them. They are past away
> As Fairies vanish at the break of day—
> And like a spectre of an age departed
> Or unsphered angel woefully astray—
> She glides along—the solitary hearted.

Some charming poems are addressed to his Southey cousins and other girl relations, and one sonnet to **"A Lofty Beauty from her Poor Kinsman,"** demands a place in any review of his poetry.

> Fair maid, had I not heard thy baby cries,
> Nor seen thy girlish sweet vicissitude,
> Thy mazy motions striving to elude,
> Yet wooing still a parent's watchful eyes,
> Thy humours many as the opal dyes,
> And lovely all; methinks thy scornful mood,
> And bearing high of stately womanhood,—
> Thy brow where beauty sits to tyrannize

O'er humble love, had made me sadly fear thee;
For never sure was seen a royal bride,
Whose gentleness gave grace to so much pride—
My very thoughts would tremble to be near thee;
But when I see thee at thy father's side,
Old times unqueen thee, and old loves endear thee.

But multiplied extracts would fail to give a true idea of the variety and scope of his poetic talent, so frequently and easily exercised as by its very facility to persuade him to make light of its claims.

The fugitive character of his poetry, very unequal in merit, and seldom evincing sustained effort, was partly the outcome of abundant but unregulated leisure, and partly the result of a desultory mind. His attempt at a longer consecutive narrative, **"Leonard and Susan,"** has no great interest. It is somewhat prosaic in conception and has no dramatic force, whilst the tragedy is depressingly grim and grey. It would almost seem as if a personal theme could alone evoke the full expression of his poetic gifts. For their development he was eager to recognize the debt he owed to parental influence and education, and it was acknowledged in the Dedicatory Sonnet prefacing the first edition of his ***Poems.***

Father and Bard revered! to whom I owe,
Whate'er it be, my little art of numbers
Thou, in thy night-watch o'er my cradled slumbers,
Didst meditate the verse that lives to show
(And long shall live, when we alike are low)
Thy prayer how ardent, and thy hopes how strong,
That I should learn of Nature's self the song,
The love which none but Nature's pupils know.
The prayer was heard: I 'wandered like a breeze'
By mountain brooks and solitary meres,
And gathered there the shapes and fantasies
Which, mixed with passions of my sadder years,
Compose this book. If good therein there be,
That good, my sire, I dedicate to thee.

As regards literary influences, he was almost overscrupulously anxious to note in an Appendix obligations to other poets or chance reflections of their productions. With a curious mixture of humility and confidence—high hopes of possible attainments easily dashed by a consciousness of weakness and failure—he was inclined to form too low an estimate of his poetry. In respect to metre and diction it may have been the result of close and critical study of great masters in the art, but the motive and the thought was individual and natural. It resembled an air played with executive delicacy upon a fine and intricate instrument. Nevertheless his own lines sincerely represent his conception of his powers and limitations.

No hope have I to live a deathless name
  A power immortal in the world of mind,
A sun to light with intellectual flame
  The universal soul of human kind.

Not mine the skill in memorable phrase
  The hidden truths of passion to reveal,
To bring to light the intermingling ways,
  By which unconscious motives darkling steal.

I have no charm to renovate the youth
  Of old authentic dictates of the heart,—
To wash the wrinkles from the face of Truth,
  And out of Nature form creative Art.

And yet he can claim to have sought and seen the vision and the gleam, and to have spent his life in the unrequited service of

Divinest Poesy!—'tis thine to make
  Age young, youth old—to baffle tyrant Time,
From antique strains the heavy dust to shake,
  And with familiar face to crown new rhyme.

Long have I loved thee—long have loved in vain,
  Yet large the debt my spirit owes to thee,
Thou wreath'dst my first hours in a rosy chain,
  Rocking the cradle of my infancy.

The lovely images of earth and sky
  From thee I learn'd within my heart to treasure;
And the strong magic of thy minstrelsy
  Charms the world's tempest to a sweet sad measure.

Nor Fortune's spite—nor hopes that once have been—
  Hopes which no power of fate can give again—
Not the sad sentence—that my life must wean
  From dear domestic joys—not all the train

Of frequent ill—and penitential harms
  That dog the rear of youth unwisely wasted,
Can dim the lustre of thy stainless charms
  Or sour the sweetness that in thee I tasted.

His personal poems, though they never strike the deeper notes of passion, have been well described as "detaining the fleeting lights of a most affectionate fancy. Those lights might sometimes be called lunar gleams; but they are the moonlight of a warm climate."

Of all the modern poets he may perhaps be said to display the strongest likeness to Charles Turner Tennyson. From the remote Lincolnshire Vicarage, from the man of saintly character and the minister of Christ, there come strains which might almost be mistaken for those of the Vagabond minstrel.

Eleanor A. Towle (essay date 1912)

SOURCE: "Hartley Coleridge's Prose," in *A Poet's Children: Hartley and Sara Coleridge,* Methuen and Co., 1912, pp. 287-97.

[*In the following essay, Towle praises the "robustness and vigour" of Coleridge's biographical sketches, noting his careful and diligent attention to form. The essay also reviews Coleridge's other prose works, including* Essays and Marginalia.]

Selected passages from poems can give but an inadequate, if not misleading idea, of poets whose range and modes of utterance differ as widely as the flight and song of birds. It is even more difficult to convey a true impression of voluminous prose writings by means of extracts.

Hartley Coleridge's pen, when he took it in hand, was ready enough and almost as fluent as his speech; but, like his poems, of a disconnected character; or perhaps it would be more correct to say he chose of set purpose subjects which could be confined to the limits of a biographical notice or an article, probably realizing his incapacity for lengthier narratives or larger themes. "There was some faculty wanting in his mind," so his biographer suggests, "for the completion of any great scheme." His hovering imagination, in the difficulty of self-concentration, imprisoned itself within artificial limits, and his language was not merely true to fact but unaffectedly sincere, his own opinions and predilections being subordinated to the attainment of just judgments and historical accuracy.

His object in compiling the ***Lives of the Northern Worthies*** was to present true and living pictures of the men themselves, only entering upon the proper office of the historian, as apart from that of the biographer, when, as stated in his Preface,

> the acts and accidents of the commonwealth are considered in their relation to the individual, as influences by which his character is formed or modified—as circumstances amid which he is placed—as the sphere in which he moves, or the material he works with. The man, with his works, his words, his affections, his fortunes, is the end and aim of all. . . . There is one species of history which may with great propriety be called biographical, to which we do not remember to have heard the name applied; we mean that wherein an order, institution, or people are invested with personality, and described as possessing an unity of will, conscience and responsibility; as sinning, repenting, believing, apostatizing, etc. Of this, the first and finest example is in the Old Testament, where Israel is constantly addressed, and frequently spoken of as an individual.

And then he adds, that in his present work he professes to do no more than to introduce the reader to the several "Worthies" that may drop in upon him during the course of publication.

The introduction is effected with much pleasant discrimination; and the diversities of circumstances and characters to be portrayed were no obstacles to his task. To dwell long upon one note was ever an uncongenial effort, and the air even when sustained was liable to be lost in its variations. He was as ready to write about the soldier and man of action as about the scholar and divine; though the sketches of Lord Derby and Fairfax are simple narratives affording less scope for reflection and criticism than those of Roger Ascham, Congreve, and William Roscoe.

In writing of the last more especially he wanders off the beaten track into various agreeable by-ways of desultory meditation and suggestion. Roscoe's verse affords an opportunity to descant upon the proper definition of lyrical poetry:

> If there be anything that generally distinguishes the genuine lyrist, it is the nature of his connections and transitions, which do not arise from the necessities of his theme, far less from the arbitrary turns of his convenience, but are determined by the flux and reflux, the undercurrents and eddies of the poetic passion, of that sense of power and joy which a poet feels in the exercise of his art for his own sake; a passion easily mimicked, but not often real, even in those who possess every other requisite of pure poetry.

Roscoe's politics again awaken responsive chords in his own free spirit. In reference to the French Revolution Hartley acknowledges that the "better few while they abhorred oppression and coveted not privilege yet knew in their hearts that 'the wrath of man worketh not the righteousness of God'"; but yet he understood that Roscoe,

> loving liberty as he loved the human race with a soul cheerful as daylight and hopeful as spring, should join the joyful chorus. To see a monarch descended from a long line of sensual despots co-operate with a nation long idolatrous of despotism, in realizing a perfect freedom upon earth—a freedom embodied in laws and institutions which should be the limbs, organs, and senses of the moral will—whose vital heat was universal love, was too great, too glorious, too new a spectacle to give him time for doubt or question. The black and portentous shadow which the past ever throws on the future, fell beyond his sphere of vision.

So Hartley writes of Roscoe's "emotions at the first heavings of that great convulsion, and of the gladness of hopes which he was not quick to relinquish when many years of bloodshed had passed over them."

And then in a note he abruptly quits the subject of Lyrical Poetry and the French Revolution to engage in a dissertation on bookbinding.

> The binding of a book should always suit its complexion. Pages venerably yellow should not be cased in military morocco, but in sober brown Russia. . . . We have sometimes seen a collection of old whitey-brown black-letter ballads so gorgeously tricked out that they remind us of the pious liberality of the Catholics, who dress in silk and gold the images of the saints, part of whose saintship consisted in wearing rags and hair-cloth. The costume of a volume should also be in keeping with its subject, and with the character of its author. How absurd to see the works of William Penn in flaming scarlet and George Fox's Journal in Bishop's purple!

Congreve again is a congenial theme, prompting moral reflections.

> After a certain point," he writes, "there needs no adventitious advantages to conciliate regard to the perfections and achievements of intellect. The danger is that they will be too much prized, too much desired, too much sought for. Already there are many who expect from human knowledge the work of Divine Grace. Science has made man master of matter; it has enabled him to calculate all the revolutions of nature, to multiply his own powers beyond all that was dreamed of spell or talisman; and now it is confidently prophesied that another science is to remove all the moral and political evils of the planet; that by analysing the passions

> we shall learn to govern them; and that, when the science of education is grown of age, virtue will be taught as arithmetic, and comprehended as readily as geometry—with the aid of wooden diagrams. Let us not be deceived. 'Leviathan is not so tamed.' The tree of knowledge is not the tree of life.

And in a rapid survey of Congreve's character he affirms:

> He seems to have been one of those indifferent children of the earth, 'whom the world cannot hate'; who are neither too good or too bad for the present state of existence, and who may fairly expect their portion here." "His comedies," he acutely observes, "are too cold to be mischievous; they keep the brain in too incessant inaction to allow the passions to kindle.

In the midst of the narrative now and again some shaft of criticism or sidelight of personal experience is thrown across the page. In his review of Andrew Marvell's Poems he writes:

> They have much of that over-activity of fancy, that remoteness of allusion which distinguishes the school of Cowley. But though there are cold conceits, a conceit is not necessarily cold. The mind in certain states of passion finds comfort in playing with the echo of a sound.

The ***Lives*** fill a large octavo volume of 632 pages; but the volume is loosely put together. Grave and gay, biographical or critical, they do not greatly contribute to Hartley's literary reputation, though they are the strongest example of a periodic fit of industry. There is, moreover, a robustness and vigour in the style sometimes lacking in his more voluntary and spontaneous writings. He has put himself to school and forms his letters after a correct and approved fashion. It is evidently task-work executed with diligence and care.

The two volumes of ***Essays and Marginalia,*** edited by his brother and published by Moxon in 1851, are more truly representative of the tendencies of his mind, and the style, whilst less studied, is fuller of attractive images and expressive language. The stream of thought no longer flows in an ordered channel, but eddies and ripples in sunlight and shade, full of bright shifting reflections, suddenly turning into sparkling shallows of fancy or profounder depths of wisdom.

According to one of his reviewers, he has caught the trick of Elia's mock gravity. It would be truer to say that a like temperament finds expression in the transforming gleams thrown upon ordinary objects. There are phrases which might have been written by Stevenson, and there are reminiscences of his father's "Table Talk"; but both thoughts and words are Hartley's own, not his by adoption. He had been brought up in a special school of poetry, and though there is at times an imitative quality in his verse, it is rarely, if ever, to be detected in his prose. Indeed, had he desired it, he would have required greater powers of application, and at least some principles of systematized thought, if he would have either moulded his mind or founded its expressions upon those of other writers. His actual mode of writing, here, there, and everywhere, upon the margins of books—jotting down upon any spare piece of paper some grave reflection, apt quotation, or fragment of verse as he sat by the wayside or walked along the road—was an illustration of the manner in which images presented themselves to his mind, each distinct in itself but with no sequence or order.

It would be an interesting, though for the purpose of a Memoir, too long a study, to contrast his paper upon "Hamlet" with his father's lecture upon the same subject; but his observations upon the doctrine of Purgatory with the Ghost for his text are too true to his own fashion of looking at every subject from different points of view, not to be quoted.

> It is not easy to reduce this Ghost to any established creed or mythology. . . . He talks like a good Catholic; though some commentators have taken pains to prove, by chronological arguments, that he must be a Pagan. A Pagan, however, would scarce complain that he was cut off
>
> 'Unhousel'd, disappointed, unaneled.'
>
> And yet would not a true Catholic spirit have requested prayers and masses, rather than vengeance?
>
> Some persons, from these allusions to Popish practices, have inferred that Shakespeare himself was a Papist. If he were, let us hope that before his death he reconciled himself to a Church which, considering the theatrical turn of many of her own ceremonies, deals rather scurvily with players and play-writers. But first, the doctrine of Purgatory does not imply Popery, though the Priesthood have contrived to turn it to excellent account. It is older than Christianity itself; it has been the professed belief of many Protestants, and, it is more than probable, the secret hope of many more; and secondly, on what other hypothesis could the ghost have been introduced with equal effect? A mere shade or Eidolon were too weak a thing to bear the weighty office imposed on this awful visitation. Would men at any time have believed in the descent of an emancipated soul from heaven, to demand vengeance on a wretched body for sending it thither? Or could they have sympathised in the wrongs of a 'goblin damned'? Is not the desire of revenge, even upon an adulterous murderer, one of the imperfections that must be 'burned and purged away'?

And it is not until after some further explorations of side-issues that he comes back to the subject of the Play itself.

In these two volumes we find a medley of subjects jostling one another and finding themselves in strange company. An article on **"Black Cats"** is followed by one on **"Melancholy."** As Ignoramus he discourses on the Fine Arts, and does not think himself above writing a paper upon **"Pins. "** There is a little sermon on **"Pride"** and one on **"Church Sectarianism"**; a chapter upon **"Old Age"**; another on **"Passive Imagination and Insanity"**; there are observations betraying an unclouded spiritual insight, several subtle pieces of analysis; a whole phalanx of moral reflections, and, scattered with a liberal hand across the pages, many execrable puns.

Still there is often a serious strain to be discerned even when, with evident and easy unconcern, he allows some passing fancy to direct his pen.

> "I wish I was a Jew," he writes. ". . . Neither avarice nor amativeness prompt this strange hankering. I envy not the Jew his bargains; I covet not his wife, nor his servant, nor his maid, nor anything that is his, except his pedigree and his *real* property in the Holy Land. . . . The tree of his genealogy is the oak of Mamre. His family memoirs are accounted sacred, even by his worst enemies. He has a portion far away—in the land of imagination, the scene of the most certain truths, and of the wildest fictions. He may at least feed his fancy with the product of his never-to-be-seen acres; and though forbidden to possess a single foot of ground, may rank himself with the landed aristocracy.
>
> "A strange passion possessed the European nations of deriving their origin from the thrice-beaten Trojans. Even the Greeks caught the infection. So enamoured are mankind of a dark antiquity—so averse to consider themselves the creatures of a day—that not content with the hope of a future immortality, they would fain extend their existence through the dusk backward and abysm of time, and claim a share even in the calamities of past generations. How great, then, the prerogative of the Jew whose nation is his own domestic kindred; who needs not to seek his original amid the dust of forgetfulness, and the limitless expanse of undated tradition, but finds it recorded in the Book that teaches to live and to die."

Some short commentaries upon life and its problems bear a stronger stamp of individual conviction:—

> A human ruin is not a ruined temple.
>
> No man is to be trusted when he is wilfully moralizing.
>
> The strength of will in suffering is secure of victory—but action is obliged to borrow hope from contingency; and let a man be never so stout in purpose, he knows not but another as stout may be stronger-limbed, or better-weaponed, or more cunning in fence, or higher in the favour of Destiny; and he whom certain death could not subdue, is oft-times vanquished by the possibility of defeat. . . . Pains of all sorts are intolerable when they make us conscious of weakness. To be weak is miserable.
>
> Power—the power of will felt and manifested—is the proper joy of man, as he is *man*, neither exalted above, or sunk below, his proper nature. If pain, peril, or pangs of death, bring this power into distinct consciousness—then may pain, peril, death, become things of choice and pride.

To turn over the papers of these essays (many of them originally written for "Blackwood's Magazine") is to find oneself, as it were, wandering through the various glades of one wood. The same hand has been at work. Here a space has been cleared, there the undergrowth almost obliterates the track; or, again, we find an unexpected dusky thicket bordering an interspace of sunshine; but the spirit of the wood inhabits them all. Art may have laid its touch upon Nature, but we can discover no traces of artificial culture or restraint. Hartley has been thinking aloud and he has put down his thoughts upon paper, hardly pausing to subject them to mental scrutiny or verbal revision.

"Affectation is the hypocrisy of manners, as hypocrisy is the affectation of morals;" so Hartley wrote, and he knew as little by personal experience of the one as of the other.

Many faults might be discovered by the professional critic, and a student might be reasonably dissatisfied with pages of the ***Essays and Marginalia.*** These last were written merely to please himself and with no idea of publication. Yet their posthumous issue was no unwarrantable intrusion upon his privacy. Hartley's wares were ever freely at the disposal of any passer-by. He would have never desired to put a price upon them.

Moreover, he had an indifference to literary criticism all the more remarkable when taken in conjunction with his earlier sensitiveness to personal slights and censures; and quite at variance with the usual temper of contemporaneous authors.

At a time when reviewers had it in their power to deal death-blows, not only to the reputation of writers but to their very existence; when his father could be made profoundly wretched by disparagement or neglect, and Landor, in bitter resentment, thought it the right and reasonable result of his affection for Southey to break off his friendship with Wordsworth who, using less sententious words than was his custom, had declared "he would not give a shilling a ream for Southey's poetry"; when even Lamb (so happily impervious, as a rule, to more legitimate causes of offence) could feel that Coleridge had in an almost unforgivable manner outraged his feelings and run the risk of destroying their friendship, by writing of him in a poem as "My gentle-hearted Charles"; Hartley took blame and praise with almost equal equanimity; neither depressed by the one, nor unduly elated by the other; having a spirit, as he declared, "That would not be snuffed out by an article."

Sister Mary Joseph Pomeroy (essay date 1927)

SOURCE: "Poetical Influences," in *The Poetry of Hartley Coleridge,* Catholic University of America, 1927, pp. 9-30.

[*In this biographical and critical article Pomeroy traces the influence of Wordsworth, Coleridge, and their Romantic philosophy on Hartley Coleridge's life and writing.*]

The poet child of a poet father, Hartley Coleridge is an interesting exception to the generally acknowledged rule that genius is not inherited.[1] Hartley Coleridge had poetical genius—a genius, perhaps, which did not attain perfect fulfilment, but which enabled him, none the less, to write some poems worthy to take their place among the lasting contributions to English literature.

The name "Coleridge" is a memorable one. In the mind of every schoolboy it is associated with the Ancient Mariner, staggering under the weight of the dead albatross, or holding the wedding guest with "his glittering eye." The more enlightened reader probably thinks of it in connection with

Lamb at the Blue-Coat School, with Southey, in imagination, on the banks of the Susquehanna, or with Wordsworth at Nether Stowey or in the Lake Country. In truth, it is the glow which surrounds the illustrious name of the father that first attracts attention to the son. Hartley realized this, and, in speaking of Richard West and other writers, who, as he remarks, "maintain a sort of dubious, twilight existence, from their connection with others of greater name," he said of himself, "If aught of mine be preserved from oblivion, it will be owing to my bearing the name of Coleridge, and having enjoyed, I fear with less profit than I ought, the acquaintance of Southey and of Wordsworth."[2]

A name may serve to attract attention, but only the personality of the individual can hold the interest. Hartley, once known, holds us by his own charm. After seeing Wilkie's portrait of him as a child of ten, we learn to love the wistfuleyed little boy with his strangely serious face, and, if we pursue this acquaintance through the reading of his poems and essays, we cannot fail to acquire the deepest sympathy for "the little sun-faced man" as Tennyson called him. The men of the Westmoreland dales, among whom Hartley passed the greater part of his life, appreciated him at his true worth, and loved him for his kindly simplicity. And to this day, while the "dalesmen" revere the name of Wordsworth or Southey, they love and cherish the memory of their own poet, Hartley Coleridge.

To know what it was in Hartley Coleridge that claimed the affection of his countrymen, and, indeed, of all who knew him, we must know something of the man and his life. The best place, undoubtedly, to study the man is in his own poetry. Unlike some poets who hide their individuality behind the carefully arranged objectivity of their works, Hartley Coleridge is almost always personal. With few exceptions, all his poems are lyrical, dealing with the joys, sorrows, hopes, and disappointments of the life he knew; all have a subjective note, and many of them are definite portraits of self. In them we may study the play of his emotions: his desponding sadness in periods of self-abasement, his loving hope and triumphant confidence in the face of defeat, find beautiful expression in lines of purest poetry. Our appreciation of this expression is intensified, however, if we can interpret the poems in the light of the circumstances which gave rise to each varying emotion. In this we are aided by a knowledge of the facts of his life.

Hartley Coleridge, the eldest son of Samuel Taylor Coleridge and Sarah Fricker, was born on September 19, 1796, at Kingsdown, Bristol.[3] Coleridge, who was visiting the Lloyds in Birmingham at the time, received the news of his son's birth with forebodings characteristic of his sensitive nature. He has recorded the event in three sonnets. The first describes his feelings when the announcement was made to him:

> When they did greet me father, sudden awe
> Weigh'd down my spirit: I retired and knelt
> Seeking the throne of grace, but inly felt
> No heavenly visitation upwards draw
> My feeble mind, nor cheering ray impart.
> Ah me! before the Eternal Sire I brought
> Th' unquiet silence of confuséd thought
> And shapeless feelings: my o'erwhelméd heart
> Trembled, and vacant tears stream'd down my face.
> And now once more, O Lord! to Thee I bend,
> Lover of souls! and groan for future grace,
> That ere my babe youth's perilous maze have trod,
> Thy overshadowing Spirit may descend,
> And he be born again, a child of God.[4]

The second, composed on the homeward journey, expresses emotions of mingled hope, at the prospect of seeing his son, and fear lest the child should die before he arrived:

> Oft o'er my brain does that strange fancy roll
> Which makes the present (while the flash doth last)
> Seem a mere semblance of some unknown past,
> Mixed with such feelings, as perplex the soul
> Self-questioned in her sleep; and some have said
> We liv'd, ere yet this robe of flesh we wore.
> O my sweet baby! when I reach my door,
> If heavy looks should tell me thou art dead,
> (As sometimes, through excess of hope, I fear)
> I think that I should struggle to believe
> Thou wert a spirit, to this nether sphere
> Sentenc'd for some more venial crime to grieve;
> Did'st scream, then spring to meet Heaven's quick reprieve,
> While we wept idly o'er thy little bier![5]

The third, addressed to a friend, probably Charles Lloyd, who accompanied him from Birmingham to Bristol, and toward whom Coleridge at this time assumed the role of preceptor, gives utterance to the father's melancholy contemplation when he first saw his son:

> Charles! my slow heart was only sad, when first
> I scann'd that face of feeble infancy:
> For dimly on my thoughtful spirit burst
> All I had been, and all my child might be!
> But when I saw it on its mother's arm,
> And hanging at her bosom (she the while
> Bent o'er its features with a tearful smile)
> Then I was thrill'd and melted, and most warm
> Impress'd a father's kiss: and all beguil'd
> Of dark remembrance and presageful fear,
> I seem'd to see an angel-form appear—
> 'Twas even thine, belovéd woman mild!
> So for the mother's sake the child was dear,
> And dearer was the mother for the child.[6]

In a letter to Thomas Poole, written at this time[7] Coleridge announces that he has named the baby David Hartley Coleridge after the man who had won his esteem as a great philosopher. The child, however, was usually known as Hartley, and was later so christened.

The baby Hartley surmounted all obstacles, even his father's ominous forebodings, and at an early age manifested characteristics which led that admiring parent to declare, "That child is a poet, spite of the forehead, 'villainously *low*' which his mother smuggled into his face."[8] Yet some well known lines, written by Coleridge in 1801 and evidently descriptive of his son, show clearly that the child was not always engaged in poetic musing:

A little child, a limber elf,
Singing, dancing to itself,
A fairy thing with red round cheeks,
That always finds, and never seeks,
Makes such a vision to the sight
As fills a father's eyes with light;[9]

In the fall of 1800 the Coleridges moved to Keswick and settled at Greta Hall, which they shared with the owner, Mr. Jackson, and his housekeeper, Mrs. Wilson. Thus does Coleridge describe their new residence in a letter to Thomas Poole: "Our house is a delightful residence, something less than half a mile from the lake of Keswick and something more than a furlong from the town. It commands both that lake and the lake of Bassenthwaite; Skiddaw is behind us; to the left, the right, and in front mountains of all shapes and sizes. The waterfall of Lodore is distinctly visible."[10] Here the father's wish that his son should "learn far other lore" than he himself had learned "in the great city, pent 'mid cloisters dim," where "he saw nought lovely but the sky and stars," was realized. In the Lake Country, Hartley was introduced to the scenes which two years before in the beautiful poem, *Frost at Midnight,* the poet father had predicted would be his:

But *thou,* my babe! shalt wander like a breeze
By lakes and sandy shores, beneath the crags
Of ancient mountain, and beneath the clouds,
Which image in their bulk both lakes and shores
And mountain crags: so shalt thou see and hear
The lovely shapes and sounds intelligible
Of that eternal language, which thy God
Utters, who from eternity doth teach
Himself in all, and all things in himself,
Great universal Teacher! he shall mould
Thy spirit, and by giving make it ask.

Therefore all seasons shall be sweet to thee,
Whether the summer clothe the general earth
With greenness, or the redbreast sit and sing
Betwixt the tufts of snow on the bare branch
Of mossy apple-tree, while the nigh thatch
Smokes in the sun-thaw; whether the eave-drops fall
Heard only in the trances of the blast,
Or if the secret ministry of frost
Shall hang them up in silent icicles,
Quietly shining to the quiet Moon.[11]

Wordsworth, with his sister, Dorothy, had already returned to his native hills. And in 1803 Southey, with his wife and Mrs. Lovell, both sisters of Mrs. Coleridge, joined the Coleridges at Greta Hall. Thus for some years the three poets lived in close union. We can readily imagine what their influence was on the little "faery voyager" whom Wordsworth describes—it now appears almost prophetically—in his poem *To H. C.—Six Years Old:*

O Thou! whose fancies from afar are brought;
Who of thy words dost make a mock apparel,
And fittest to unutterable thought
The breeze-like motion and the self-born carol;
Thou faery voyager! that dost float
In such clear water, that thy boat
May rather seem
To brood on air than on an earthly stream;
Suspended in a stream as clear as sky,
Where earth and heaven do make one imagery;
O blessèd vision! happy child!
Thou art so exquisitely wild,
I think of thee with many fears
For what may be thy lot in future years.

I thought of times when Pain might be thy guest,
Lord of thy house and hospitality;
And Grief, uneasy lover! never rest
But when she sate within the touch of thee.
O too industrious folly!
O vain and causeless melancholy!
Nature will either end thee quite;
Or, lengthening out thy season of delight,
Preserve for thee, by individual right,
A young lamb's heart among the full-grown flocks.
What hast thou to do with sorrow,
Or the injuries of to-morrow?
Thou art a dew-drop, which the morn brings forth,
Ill fitted to sustain unkindly shocks,
Or to be trailed along the soiling earth;
A gem that glitters while it lives,
And no forewarning gives;
But, at the touch of wrong, without a strife
Slips in a moment out of life.[12]

Again in the seventh stanza of the ode on the *Intimations of Immortality,* Wordsworth gives another glimpse of the child Hartley:

Behold the Child among his new-born blisses,
A six years' Darling of a pigmy size!
See, where 'mid work of his own hand he lies,
Fretted by sallies of his mother's kisses,
With light upon him from his father's eyes!
See, at his feet, some little plan or chart,
Some fragment from his dream of human life,
Shaped by himself with newly-learned art;
A wedding or a festival,
A mourning or a funeral;
And this hath now his heart,
And unto this he frames his song:
Then will he fit his tongue
To dialogues of business, love, or strife;
But it will not be long
Ere this be thrown aside,
And with new joy and pride
The little Actor cons another part;
Filling from time to time his "humorous stage"
With all the Persons, down to palsied Age,
That Life brings with her in her equipage;
As if his whole vocation
Were endless imitation.[13]

Nor is the father silent concerning his little son. In a letter to a friend written December 5, 1803, speaking of his family, Coleridge says:

> I have three children, [Berkeley, the second son, died in infancy] *Hartley,* seven years old, *Derwent,* three years, and *Sara,* one year on the twenty-third of this month. *Hartley* is considered a genius by Wordsworth and Southey; indeed by everyone who has seen much of him. But what is of much more consequence and much less doubtful, he has the sweetest temper and most awakened moral feelings of any child I ever saw. He is very backward in his book-learning, cannot write at all, and a very lame reader. We have never been anxious about it, taking it for granted that loving me, and seeing how I love books, he would come to it of his own accord, and so it has proved, for in the last month he has made more progress than in all his former life. Having learnt everything almost from the mouths of people whom he loves, he has connected with his words and notions a passion and a feeling which would appear strange to those who had seen no children but such as have been taught almost everything in books.[14]

As a boy, Hartley had a truly wonderful imagination. This in itself is not remarkable, for most children have lively imaginations. What is astonishing, however, is the facility with which he could find expression for the fancies of his dream world, and the unity which he succeeded in giving to his creations. Having fashioned, at the age of eight, a kingdom called Ejuxria, he ruled over it for many years, directing the activities of his statesmen, grieving at the warlike propensities of his people, and daily announcing to a willing audience—Derwent, Sara, Edith Southey, or adult admirers—the latest account of his nation's progress.

The year 1807 was an eventful one for Hartley. At its commencement he and his father were at Coleorton in Leicestershire at the home of Sir George Beaumont. Here Sir David Wilkie painted the portrait already mentioned, and also used Hartley as the model for the eldest boy in his painting, "The Blind Fiddler." One picture represents a large-eyed, pensive, half-sad little boy with straggling brown hair and a huge white frilled collar—the child "whose fancies from afar are brought"; the other shows a mischievous urchin—the "limber elf"—brandishing a skillet and poker in gleeful mimicry of the old blind player. The truest answer to, "Which is the real Hartley?" is, probably, "Both."

After three months with the hospitable Beaumonts, the two Coleridges, accompanied by Wordsworth, who had been spending the winter at Coleorton Farm House, went to London where they stayed for some weeks at the home of Mr. Basil Montagu. This was Hartley's first introduction to city life. He went to the theater, and also met Sir Humphrey Davy and Walter Scott, who took him on a sight-seeing expedition to the Tower. Later the same year Hartley joined his mother, brother, and sister at Bristol, where they visited Mrs. Coleridge's mother.

The next June (1808) Hartley and Derwent were sent as day scholars to the school of the Rev. Mr. John Dawes at Ambleside. Lodging at Clappersgate, a small hamlet about a mile from the town, they were near Old Brathay, the residence of Charles Lloyd, Coleridge's friend of former days. Thus they were under the maternal eye of kind Mrs. Lloyd, who, in case of need, would have bestowed on Hartley and Derwent the motherly care she lavished on her own large family of five boys and five girls.[15]

Agatha Lloyd who visited her brother, Charles, and met Coleridge and his sons about this time, recorded her impression of Hartley in a letter to her sister-in-law. Speaking of having met Coleridge, she says:

> He has two interesting boys for whom he has a most fatherly affection. Hartley is a child to me *painfully* out of the common way both in *mind* and constitution—should he live, poor fellow, he will be a most interesting character, and I wish, as related his *parents,* he were in more happy circumstances.[16]

The last remark evidently refers to the fact that Coleridge had now separated from his wife, who still remained at Greta Hall, while he lived first with the Morgans at London and at Calne in Wiltshire, and later with the Gillmans at Highgate.

It seems only too true that Hartley was "out of the common way." He never played with his schoolfellows; in fact, he made only one friend at this time, and that not one of his schoolmates, but a young lad of Ambleside, Robert Jameson, to whom he later addressed three beautiful sonnets. The only common bond between Hartley and the boys of Mr. Dawes's school was story telling, an art in which Hartley excelled. Night after night they would listen breathlessly to the wonderful tales—or rather, successive installments of one continuous tale—which he invented for their amusement.

During this period of his life Hartley had constant intercourse with the Wordsworths. He carried on his English studies in Wordsworth's library at Allan Bank and afterwards at Rydal. Dorothy Wordsworth, writing to Mrs. Clarkson at this time, says of Hartley:

> Every time I see Hartley I admire him more. He is very thoughtful, often silent, and never talks as much as he used to do. Both he and Derwent far surpass their schoolfellows in quickness at their books, and both (especially Hartley) are beloved by their schoolfellows, not less than by Mr. Dawes, their master.[17]

He also became acquainted with Professor Wilson of Elleray, and occasionally saw De Quincey, then living at Dove Cottage. "It was so," says his brother,

> rather than by a regular course of study, that he was educated;—by desultory reading, by the living voice of Coleridge, Southey, and Wordsworth, Lloyd, Wilson, and De Quincey,—and again by homely familiarity with town's folk, and country folk, of every degree; lastly, by daily recurring hours of solitude,—by lonely wanderings with the murmur of the Brathay in his ear.[18]

In 1814 Hartley left Rev. Mr. Dawes's school and the following year, aided by Southey and other of his father's friends, he was entered as postmaster at Merton College, Oxford. This was a critical period in poor Hartley's life. Before this time he had lived among understanding friends, who had protected him from his weaknesses. Now cut adrift from home ties, he was unable to meet the rising tide of temptation which rolled in upon him from all sides. The great defect of his nature was an unusual lack of will power. Already this had shown itself in habits of procrastination. As early as 1807 his father, in a letter written on the occasion of Hartley's prospective visit to his uncle, George Coleridge, warns him in these words:

> . . . this power which you possess of shoving aside all disagreeable reflections, or losing them in a labyrinth of day-dreams, which saves you from some present pain, has, on the other hand, interwoven with your nature habits of procrastination, which unless you correct them in time (and it will require all your best exertions to do it effectually), must lead you into lasting unhappiness.[19]

Now it was that the overpowering effect of this weakness was becoming apparent.

The immediate cause of Hartley's failure, as he himself explains it, was his "girlish love of display." Conscious of his unattractive, or, perhaps it would be better to say, unusual and eccentric appearance, and yet craving sympathy and attention with all the ardor of a highly sensitive nature, he sought to gain esteem and applause by means of his mental gifts. Hartley says of himself:

> I had an intense and incessant craving for the notice of females, with a foreboding consciousness that I was never fashioned for a ladies' man. My perverse vanity made me take indifference for absolute aversion, and I fancied that all the antipathy would be changed into beaming, sun-shiny admiration should I appear in the irresistible character of prizeman, as a reciter of intelligible poetry, and it is not unlikely that I should have been an object for a few days of some curiosity to the fair promenaders in Christ Church Meadow; while the dear creatures with whom I was on bowing and speaking terms, might have felt a satisfaction in being known to know me which they had never experienced before.[20]

With this in view he tried for the Newdigate prize, awarded for English verse, and flattered himself that his poem, ***The Horses of Lysippus,*** would bring him the coveted honor. The announcement that not he but another had won the prize was a stunning blow:

> It was almost the only occasion in my life wherein I was keenly disappointed; for it was the only one upon which I felt any confident hope. I had made myself very sure of it, and the intelligence that not I, but Macdonald, was the lucky man, absolutely stupefied me. . . . The truth is, I was *fea*. I sang, I danced, I whistled, I leapt, I ran from room to room, announcing the great tidings, and tried to persuade even myself that I cared nothing at all for my own case. But it would not do. It was bare sands with me the next day. It was not the mere loss of the prize, but the feeling or phantasy of an adverse destiny. I was as one who discovers that his familiar, to whom he has sold himself, is a deceiver. I foresaw that all my aims and hopes would prove frustrate and abortive; and from that time I date my downward declension, my impotence of will, and melancholy recklessness. It was the first time I sought relief from wine, which, as usual in such cases, produced not so much intoxication as downright madness.[21]

This is the same Hartley whom Wordsworth deemed

> Ill fitted to sustain unkindly shocks.

In spite of this overwhelming disappointment, Hartley succeeded in completing his university studies with honor, and, having tried for the Oriel Fellowship, was admitted as Probationary Fellow of Oriel in 1819. At the close of his probationary year, however, he was judged to have forfeited his fellowship, mainly on the grounds of intemperance. The account given by Rannie in his history of Oriel College is as follows:

> Alas! the year of probation ran on, and Coleridge set every convention at defiance. In a non-smoking period of history, he reeked of tobacco; among punctilious colleagues he neglected to dress for dinner, and appeared with a face unshaven for days. Worst of all, the wine he drank unquestionably went to his head. Whatever truth may be in the painful story that he was found one night lying in the gutter in Oriel Street, his ways were too lax for Oriel, and he had to be cast out. On October 17, 1820, the register briefly recorded that the college could be no party to the degradation threatened by the behaviour of Mr. Coleridge, to whom it had lately been intimated that, in spite of frequent admonitions to better behaviour by the Provost and Dean, he had not conducted himself during his year of probation in such a way as to prove himself worthy of admission into the Society. Wherefore the college thought well to vacate his place. This entry was signed by Whately as Dean.[22]

This was a sad decision, but, to Hartley at least, not an unexpected one. He had found the routine of tutorial life irksome, and piqued by a solemnity which ill accorded with his nature, he had, in jest or in earnest, made tactless remarks regarding the government of the University. Unfortunately also his later life offers convincing proof that the charge of intemperance was not unfounded. In May, 1821, Hartley sent the following "short view of his Oxford life" to his brother:

> With few habits but those of negligence and self-indulgence, with principles honest, indeed, and charitable, but not ascetic, and little applied to particulars, with much vanity and much diffidence, a wish to conquer neutralized by a fear of offending, with wavering hopes, uncertain spirits, and peculiar manners, I was sent among men, mostly irregular, and in some instances vicious. Left to myself to form my own course of studies, my own acquaintances, my own habits,—to keep my own hours, and, in a great measure, to be master of my own time, few know how much I went through;—how many shocks I received from within and from without;—how many doubts, temptations, half-formed ill-resolutions passed through my mind. I saw human nature in a new point of view, and in some measure learned to judge of mankind by a new standard. I ceased to look for virtues which I no longer hoped to find, and set perhaps a disproportionate value on those which most frequently occurred. The uncertainty of my prospects cast a gloom on what was before me. I did not love to dwell in the future, and gradually became reconciled to present scenes which at first were painful to me. This was not a good preparatory discipline for Oriel, and, indeed, from the first moment that I thought of offering myself as a candidate, I felt that I was not consulting my own happiness. But duty,

> vanity, and the fear of being shipped off to Brazil, determined me on the trial. You will scarcely believe that, after the first flush of success, I was seized with uneasy melancholy,—triste augurium,—a feeling that I was among strangers, and a suspicion, not yet wholly removed, that my election arose, in a great measure, from the failure of my county opponents, and the vague appearance of talent, rather than from that hearty conviction of my eligibility which, with their views, would have been the only justifying cause of putting me on so severe a trial. My engagement with my pupils contributed (if only by taking up much of my time) to prevent me from falling immediately into Oriel habits; and to tell the truth, I did not much like the state of a probationer, or submit, as I ought to have done, to a yoke of observances which I sincerely think very absurd, and which I hoped that I had escaped by being made a Fellow. I knew, I felt, that I was subjected to a kind of espionage, and could feel no confidence in men who were watching me.
>
> The natural effect of all this on my mind was a tendency to resistance, and I was not bold enough to fight, or prudent enough to make peace. I was induced to fly; to shun the inquiring eyes, which I ought to have met firmly; and to vent my chagrin in certain impotent, but, I dare say, not forgotten, threats of great reformations to take place in the college and university when my unripe fortunes came of age. The complex effect of all this discontent and imprudence was, of course, self-reproach, inconsistency, quickly formed and quickly broken resolutions, just enough caution to lose my reputation for frankness, increasing dread of my consocii, incapability of proceeding in any fixed plan, and an extreme carelessness whenever the painful restraint was removed. You know the consequences.[23]

It was on Samuel Taylor Coleridge, who was then living with the Gillmans at Highgate, that the blow fell most heavily. He went to Oxford to plead with the university authorities for a reversal of their decision, but in vain. A solatium of three hundred pounds was granted to Hartley; the decree of expulsion stood.

In August, 1820, Hartley was in London with Basil Montagu. While there he supported himself by his pen, largely through contributions to the *London Magazine.* After about two years in London, he was persuaded, entirely against his own inclination, to take a school in Ambleside. Hartley had knowledge to impart and could teach in an interesting way, but controlling the conduct of growing boys was beyond him. As Dorothy Wordsworth wrote in 1824, ". . . poor Hartley, he sticks to his school-hours, is liked by his scholars, and is still 'Hartley' among them; even (out of school) the bigger ones address him 'Hartley!' This will give you a notion of the nature of the discipline exercised by him."[24] Hartley continued as a schoolmaster at Ambleside for five or six years, first alone and later as classical assistant to a Mr. Stuart; then this was given up. He had one other experience in school teaching, which seems to have been more successful than the first, when for several months in 1837 he assisted his friend, the Rev. Mr. Isaac Green, in the school of Sedbergh, and in the following year took the place of the Head Master from March to the Midsummer Vacation.

The remainder of his life, with the exception of a short sojourn with a publisher in Leeds, he passed quietly, first with Mrs. Fleming at Grasmere, and from 1837 to his death, with William and Eleanor Richardson at Nab Cottage on Rydal Water. The profits from his pen and an allowance from his mother supplied his simple wants. After his mother's death in 1845, the small bequest which she left him, turned into an annuity, made him independent.

During this period of his life he wrote occasionally for *Blackwood's Magazine* and the *Penny Magazine;* contributed to some annuals, including *The Gem, The Winter's Wreath,* and *The Literary Souvenir;* and published a few books. A biographical work on ***The Worthies of Yorkshire and Lancashire,*** later known as ***Biographia Borealis,*** appeared in 1832, and in the following year, 1833, his ***Poems*** made their first appearance in book form. An "Introduction" to the *Dramatic Works of Massinger and Ford,* edited by Mr. Moxon in 1840, completes the short list of the works of Hartley Coleridge which were published during his lifetime.

In 1847 he delivered a lecture on ***The Final Cause of Poetry,*** and gave two readings of the English poets in the Museum of the Natural History Society of Kendal.

On January 6, 1849, after a short illness, Hartley Coleridge died at Nab Cottage. He was buried on January 11, in the southeast corner of Grasmere churchyard, a place selected for him by Wordsworth as near as possible to the spot reserved for his own last resting place.

Such, briefly, are the facts of Hartley Coleridge's life. What we are chiefly interested to know is what influence such a life had on his poetic production. His infancy, as we have seen, was surrounded by poetry. Hartley has recalled this "fair seed time" of his soul in part of his address to Divinest Poesy in ***Poietes Apoietes:***

> Thou wreath'dst my first hours in a rosy chain
> Rocking the cradle of my infancy.[25]

His childhood, spent in the home of Southey, who thought literature the noblest pursuit of man, and his youth, passed largely under the influence of Wordsworth, who from his own youth had considered himself a spirit "dedicated" to poetry, were not without those fostering influences which would encourage him in the use of the poetical talent he possessed. Thus, in the light of his poetical gifts of nature and circumstance, we are led to expect great poetic achievement. And here we are disappointed. A modern writer has classified Hartley Coleridge as one of a group of "Splendid Failures."[26] The paradox is fitting; his work, standing apart, wears the golden glow of splendor, but, viewed against the rosy-hued background of promise, how quickly it fades to dreary failure!

The explanation of his failure is not far to seek. Hartley directs our attention to the cause in his own sad words, "sought relief from wine." This is but one—although from its nature perhaps the most obvious—of the many manifestations of the real defect of Hartley's nature—weakness of will. This weakness showed itself in varied ways: in his boyish sensitiveness to pain, in his inability to meet an unpleasant situation, and in his benumbing habit of procrastination. Indeed, the beginning of his desire to seek relief in wine can be traced to his inability to face the disappointment of thwarted selflove, as well as to the natural tendency to compensate for unsatisfied love of admiration and sympathy by some gratifying substitution. How much this instability of will may be due to inheritance we can only conjecture. But the remembrance of the fact that heredity had in his case its disadvantages as well as its advantages may make us kinder in our judgments of poor Hartley.

It is his habit of procrastination which best accounts for the small amount of poetry he has left us:

> A heart is mine all things intending,—
> All beginning, nothing ending,—[27]

Many of his poems, as we shall see when we consider his poems of self-description, deal with his woeful want of resolution. It is interesting to notice here, however, what one of his contemporaries has pointed out; namely, that Hartley's weakness of will and self-indulgence did not seem to affect his moral principles:

> One very strong impression, however, with which I always came away from him, may be worth mentioning; I mean, that his moral and spiritual sensibilities seemed to be absolutely untouched by the life he was leading. The error of his life sprung, I suppose, from moral incapacity of some kind—his way of life seemed in some things destructive of self-respect; and was certainly regarded by himself with a feeling of shame, which in his seasons of self-communion became passionate;—and yet it did not at all degrade his mind. It left, not his understanding only, but also his imagination and feelings, perfectly healthy,—free, fresh, and pure.[28]

The poet has said the same of himself:

> Oh! tell them though my purpose lame,
> In fortune's race was still behind,—
> Though earthly blots my name defiled
> They ne'er abused my better mind.[29]

The only explanation for the possible coexistence of a high moral sense and a degrading habit is that, in Hartley's case, principles and practice were completely divorced. Whether this explanation is adequate or not, the fact remains that Hartley Coleridge's friends and acquaintances did not despise him for his weakness. They recognized his need of assistance, and all seemed to wish to help and shield him. Mrs. Wordsworth, in particular, was his kindly angel. It was she who disbursed his little income, supplying him with pocket money, shilling by shilling, and, when the need arose, providing him with new clothes, which she substituted for the old, while Hartley, like Dominie Sampson, was all unconscious of the change.

Mrs. Gordon in her *Memoir* of her father, Professor Wilson, voices the general sentiment of all who knew Hartley, and gives at the same time a graphic description of the small poet:

> Everyone loved Hartley Coleridge; there was something in his appearance that evoked kindliness. Extremely boyish in aspect, his juvenile air was aided not a little by his general mode of dress—a dark blue cloth round jacket, white trousers, black silk handkerchief tied loosely round his throat; sometimes a straw hat covered his head, but more frequently, it was bare, showing his black, thick, short, curling hair. His eyes were large, dark, and expressive, and a countenance almost sad in expression was relieved by the beautiful smile which lighted it up from time to time.[30]

There was something particularly lovable about this "quaint fantastic bard" which made it easy, where he was concerned, to hate the sin and love the sinner.

In considering the influences which affect a writer's work, besides his nature and his immediate environment, we must take into account the period in which he lived. Man is a part of his age. And however secluded his life may be, however rare may be his contacts with the world, still, in some small degree at least, there is an interchange of influence between the individual and his time. Sensibly or insensibly the thoughts, ideals, and enthusiasms of his age have their effect on his thoughts, his ideals, and his enthusiasms.

In Hartley Coleridge's case this influence seems, at first glance, almost imperceptible. The early part of the nineteenth century was one of political and social change. Before Hartley began to write, the Battle of Waterloo had brought to a close the Napoleonic Wars, and England had settled into that period of torpor which followed as a depressing reaction to the extravagances of the French Revolution. Conservatism was the watchword of the day. Yet a note of revolt against this inactivity sounded from time to time. There were many causes for discontent, arising from the changes brought about by the Industrial Revolution of the preceding century, as well as from the heavy taxation necessitated by the war debt, and from the Corn Laws which, coupled with the failure of the crops, made the price of bread prohibitive for many. In addition, the desire of the people for real democracy and a more equal suffrage was growing daily. All this eventually led to sweeping measures of reform, carried out, however, gradually, and often only after bitter struggles. Hartley Coleridge witnessed, during the last twenty years of his life, the Catholic Emancipation Act, the Reform Bill, the abolition of the Corn Laws and of capital punishment for theft, the alleviation of factory conditions, the reform of the Poor Laws, and many other measures marking the beginning of the great reform movement, which continued throughout the entire reign of Victoria. But there is little trace of this political and social upheaval in his poetry; some allusions to political events in ***Leonard and Susan,*** his one long attempt in narrative verse, and in two sonnets, one ***To the Memory of Canning*** and the other on ***Liberty,*** are all.

This apparent indifference to what was going on in the world of affairs was not, however, due to lack of knowledge on Hartley's part. For one of his contemporaries writes that "though in later years living in distant and sequestered scenes, where one might have thought his communion with Nature would have been greater than his worldly information, his knowledge of all that was passing in the bustling haunts of men, of every work that had been recently published, was complete, nay, even it might have seemed, intuitive and miraculous."[31] But Hartley has himself pointed out that his was not a controversial talent:

From May of life to Autumn have I trod
The earth, not quite unconscious of my God;
But apter far to recognize His power
In sweet perfection of a pencill'd flower,
A kitten's gambols, or a birdie's nest,
A baby sleeping on its mother's breast,
Than in the fearful passages of life,—
The battle-field, the never-ceasing strife
Of policy that ever would be wise,
Dissecting truth into convenient lies;
The gallows, or the press-gang, or the press;
The poor man's pittance, ever less and less;
The dread magnificence of ancient crime,
Or the mean mischief of the present time.
Yet there is something in my heart that would
Become a witness to eternal good.
Woe to the man that wastes his wealth of mind,
And leaves no legacy to human kind!
I love my country well,—I love the hills,
I love the valleys and the vocal rills;
But most I love the men, the maids, the wives,
The myriad multitude of human lives.[32]

Thus, though he loved human nature, he did not, like Ebenezer Elliott or Thomas Hood, appear as the champion of any class, for it was not humanity that Hartley Coleridge loved so much as individual human beings.

Although the political and social conditions of his time affected the poetry of Hartley Coleridge very slightly, the state of poetry during that period had a stronger influence. As far as poetry is concerned, the thirty years between 1820-1850 may be termed an interregnum. Before the opening of this period, the great works of high Romanticism had all appeared. Coleridge's poetic flame had died out long before; the death of Keats (1821) was soon followed by that of Shelley and of Byron; Wordsworth alone remained—writing it is true—but producing little of lasting worth. Toward the end of the period Tennyson began to loom large on the poetic horizon, but not until Wordsworth's death did he really become the dominant figure. Hartley Coleridge belongs to a group of transition poets, born between the birth years of Keats and Tennyson, who were fortunate, it may seem, in that they witnessed in their early years the full glory of Romanticism, although they did not follow closely enough to share in its brilliance. This very nearness to their great predecessors was, nevertheless, a disadvantage, for it deprived them of the privilege, later granted to their successors, Browning, Tennyson, and other Victorians, of viewing the great Romanticists from a proper perspective, and thus profiting by their influence. Their age was a time of change; old ideals and customs were crumbling around them, and new ones were not yet established. The poets of the time, Beddoes, Hartley Coleridge, Hood, Horne, Praed, Wade, Wells, and Charles Whitehead, were all lesser luminaries, some surpassing others in power, but none possessing the steady brilliance of a guiding star. The age alone does not make the poet, but this age did much to make Hartley Coleridge and his contemporaries minor poets.

Notes

1. A note of Hartley Coleridge's on "Dryden's Sons" is interesting in this connection: "The *Quarterly Review* carelessly instances the sons of Dryden, as almost the only poetical sons of poets. Has he forgotten Bernardo and Torquato Tasso? It is, however, pretty remarkable that no English poet has made a family. It is said, indeed, that there are descendants of Spenser in existence. Genius is certainly not hereditary, though a certain degree of talent sometimes descends,—oftener in the female than the male. Scribbling is very infectious, and authors have a habit of warning their sons against the trade, which is most wise." *Essays and Marginalia,* II, 33-34.
2. *Ibid.,* II, 109-110, note.
3. Derwent Coleridge in his "Memoir" of his brother, prefixed to his *Poems* (1851) errs in ascribing the birthplace to Clevedon. Cf. James Dykes Campbell, *Samuel Taylor Coleridge,* pp. 51 and 56; Sara Coleridge, *Memoirs and Letters,* p. 34; Joseph Cottle, *Reminiscences of Samuel Taylor Coleridge and Robert Southey,* p. 74.
4. *The Poems of Samuel Taylor Coleridge* (Oxford ed.), pp. 152-153.
5. *Ibid.,* pp. 153-154.
6. *Ibid.,* p. 154.
7. Sept. 24, 1796, *Letters of S. T. Coleridge,* I, 168.
8. Letter of Southey, Aug. 9, 1802, *ibid.,* I, 395.
9. "Christabel," *Poems of S. T. C.,* p. 235, ll. 656-661.
10. Aug. 14, 1800, *Letters of S. T. C.,* I, 335.
11. *Poems of S. T. C.,* p. 242, ll. 54-74.
12. *Poetical Works* (Oxford ed.), p. 88.
13. *Ibid.,* pp. 588-589. Composed 1803 (?1802).
14. Letter to Matthew Coates, *Letters of S. T. C.,* I, 443.
15. Grosvenor (1800-1840), James (1801-1881), Owen (1803-1838), Edward (1804-1865), Arthur, Mary, Sophia, Priscilla, Agatha, Louisa. For an account of this interesting family, see *Charles Lamb and the Lloyds,* ed. E. V. Lucas.
16. January 1809, *Charles Lamb and the Lloyds,* p. 265.
17. *Letters of the Wordsworth Family,* ed. William Knight, I, 514.
18. "Memoir" prefixed to *Poems* (1851), I, lvii.
19. *Letters of S. T. C.,* II, 512.
20. "Memoir" prefixed to *Poems* (1851), I, lxxxiv-lxxxv, note.

21. *Ibid.,* lxxxiii-lxxxiv, note.
22. D. W. Rannie, *Oriel College,* pp. 182-183.
23. "Memoir" prefixed to *Poems* (1851), I, lxxxvii-lxxxviii.
24. Letter to John Kenyon, Nov. 28, 1824, *Letters of the Wordsworth Family,* II, 231.
25. *Poems,* p. 92.
26. Harry Graham, *Splendid Failures,* "Little Hartley," pp. 155-185.
27. *Poems,* p. 283.
28. James Spedding in "Memoir" prefixed to *Poems* (1851), I, cxliii.
29. *Poems,* p. 223.
30. *Christopher North; a Memoir of John Wilson,* p. 312.
31. C. H. Townsend in "Memoir" prefixed to *Poems* (1851), I, cxxix-cxxx.
32. *Poems,* p. 211.

Earl Leslie Griggs (essay date 1929)

SOURCE: "Literary Work," in *Hartley Coleridge: His Life and Work,* University of London Press, 1929, pp. 179-205.

[*This chapter of Coleridge's biography focuses on both his poetry and prose. Griggs notes that Coleridge's poetry, although it falls short of the genius exhibited by his father, overflows with "human emotion." The discussion of Coleridge's prose includes a section on* Northern Worthies, *the author's collection of biographies.*]

I. Poetry

The poets whose names glorify English literature rise above their contemporaries because their poetry is more than a momentary effusion. It is of course a moot question whether a poet must give a philosophy in his poetry, whether he must present ideas or not; but it cannot be doubted that he must be strong enough to have a characteristic attitude towards life. Though his life and work may be marked by an utter disregard for practical problems, this very scorn in itself becomes a fixed principle; though he may agree in nearly every particular with the prevailing thought of his age, he demonstrates clearly his own reaction towards the popular tendencies; though he may present a creed especially revolting to conventional morality, he maintains with an unswerving tenacity what he believes to be true; and though he may change his opinions as he grows older, the very growth of his mind is a revelation of his greatness. Keats ignored the seething political and moral upheavals which moved his contemporaries. Tennyson found himself partially in accord with the popular religious thought of his day. Shelley preached a doctrine of free love which those about him considered blasphemous, and Wordsworth slowly rejected the beliefs of his youth and laid himself open to the criticism of the younger generation; but each of these poets took up some pervading principle which is easily discernible in his work.

Hartley Coleridge wrote to please himself, impelled by a natural poetic instinct. His verse is full of beauty, often expressive of a noble spirit; but the thoughts are all detached jewels, of such varying sizes that it is impossible to string them together. Sometimes he reaches excellence, nay perfection, but never sublimity. There are few great poets; even his illustrious father was a poet only at intervals; and though Hartley's poetry will always be cherished by lovers of beauty, it cannot be granted the highest honours. It is interesting to note, too, that Hartley was at his best in the sonnet. The reason is evident: not having any fixed scheme of things to maintain a mood, and not often being long in a poetic frame of mind, he found the brief sonnet a most fitting vehicle for a fleeting idea. He quickly mastered the technical difficulties of the form, and with very little effort was able to construct a sonnet of considerable excellence. He did not usually tire before he had written fourteen lines,—though many of his unpublished sonnets *are* unfinished—and the metrical restrictions curbed the unorganized impetuosity of his mutable ideas and emotions.

Though Hartley's poems lack the touch of immortal genius, or to use Samuel Taylor Coleridge's phraseology, though they are products of fancy rather than of imagination, they are remarkable manifestations of a sad and wayward spirit. In life Hartley oscillated between effort and relaxation, always with an actual realization of the weakness he could not control; in his poetry he gave expression oftenest to a dignified melancholy, as if he were always trying to redeem himself. The poems of a purely personal nature fall into two distinct groups: those written to assuage the pangs of conscience, tenderly alive with regret for a misspent life; and those written in sheer love of man or nature, bubbling over with enthusiasm, and usually composed to celebrate some event important in the lives of country-folk—a wedding, a birth, a picnic. Most of the religious poems reflect his humble devotion and faith; and good comfort they probably afforded him, in hours of self-reproach.

Those writing personal poems often mar the dignity of the verse by bitterness or by a disregard for others. Hartley withheld every poem suggestive of family discord, or likely to harm anyone else; and in the expression of his own regrets, he always remained restrained and dignified. The sonnet helped to repress any too-intrepid declarations, but more than that Hartley's own spirit held his emotions in check. One reads his poems without being profoundly moved, but with a deep feeling of sympathy with him.

There are in Hartley's poems a few ideas which are frequently repeated. There is, as we have seen, a firm conviction of his weakness, tempered only by a belief in Christian redemption. Hartley lived on, ever lapsing into the habit of intemperance, never being able to break away from his indulgence; yet he was always painfully aware of his wrong-doing, hoping to be able to make new resolutions, never able to resolve. He felt, however, that there is a mercy in God, and intermingled with his self-condemnation is his absolute faith.

Hartley's religious ideas, as they are expressed in his poetry, are simple enough. Nature never became for him an all-pervading power as she did for Wordsworth. Hartley believed in an absolute destiny over the universe—in a God Who would reward and forgive. He found meagre comfort in nature when he sought to alleviate his pain; he saw men and things happy through nature's bounty, but he did not see in her the power to still the restless longings of the soul. In his prose writings he often discussed religion at length, and the ideas naturally became more complicated; but in the poems there is very little beyond mere simple faith. Consider:

> A woeful thing it is to find
> No trust secure in weak mankind;
> But ten-fold woe betide the elf
> Who knows not how to trust himself.
>
> . . . . .
>
> If I am weak, yet God is strong,
> If I am false, yet God is true.
> Old things are past, or right or wrong,
> And every day that comes is new.
> To-morrow then fresh hope may bring
> And rise with healing on its wing."
>
> *Poems,* 218.

In many poems Hartley shows a true appreciation of excellence, whether moral or artistic. In the beautiful sonnets to Wordsworth, or in those to Homer and to Shakespeare, we see his artistic appreciation. The purity of his spirit led him to recognize virtue, and his standard of criticism implied a moral background for the highest poetical achievements. Thus he says, for centuries after Wordsworth's death men and women will love one another, merely because they all cherish his poetry! Of Drayton he writes:

> Hail to thee, Michael! true, painstaking wight,
> So various that 'tis hard to praise thee right;
> For driest fact and finest faery fable
> Employ'd thy genius indefatigable.
> What bard more zealous of our England's glory,
> More deeply versed in all her antique story,
> Recorded feat, tradition quaint and hoary?
> What muse like thine so patiently would plod
> From shire to shire in pilgrim sandal shod,
> Calling to life and voice, and conscious will,
> The shifting streamlet and the sluggish hill?
> Great genealogist of earth and water,
> The very Plutarch of insensate matter.
>
> *Poems,* 320.

Hartley felt his own weakness, or supposed weakness, in poetry, and by his own standards did not judge his work to be imperishable. Seldom did he make ambitious attempts, for of his two long poems one is unfinished and the other does not pretend to be more than an idealization of love, with a hint that modern civilization lays bare the worst

POEMS

BY

HARTLEY COLERIDGE.

> I write, endite, I point, I raze, I quote,
> I interline, I blot, correct, I note,
> I make, allege, I imitate, I feign.
>
> *Drayton.*

> For I, that God of Lov'is Servantes serve,
> Ne dare to love, for mine unlikelinesse,
> Prayin for spede, al should I therefore sterve,
> So ferre am I fro his help in darknesse;
> But nathelesse, if this may doe gladnesse
> To any lovir, and his cause aveile,
> Have he the thanke, and mine be the traveile.
>
> *Chaucer: Troilus and Creseide.*

VOL. I.

LEEDS:
PUBLISHED BY F. E. BINGLEY, CORN-EXCHANGE;
AND BALDWIN AND CRADOCK,
LONDON.
1833.

side of human nature. We can judge Hartley only on what he attempted to do; as he claimed to be only a casual poet, as he never o'erleapt the bounds of simple and frank humanity, he holds a leading place in his class.

We have mentioned again and again Hartley's preference for the sonnet. He usually prefers the Petrarchan form, and he is most careful to fulfil all the technical requirements, though the primary thought often runs beyond the eighth line. His sonnets are almost perfect specimens. It is often evident that they were written spontaneously, the laws of form being followed instinctively. Derwent says Hartley could write a sonnet, a good one, in ten minutes, and that he seldom corrected or even found it necessary to correct the rough draft.[1] The words flow nimbly from his pen, and though occasionally the thought is twisted to fit the rhyme, the product is excellent. And yet, though we would fain suppress it, the feeling arises that the sonnets are sometimes too spontaneous. In a poem so deliberately restrained we do not expect effervescence; and we sometimes find Hartley too much a master of the form, even to be vaguely aware of it. We see, too, the fatigue of the inspiration. In the following unpublished sonnet there is an excellent beginning; but obviously Hartley completed it without a continuance of the inspiration:

Full well I know, my Friends, ye look on me
As living spectre of my Father dead.
Had I not borne his name, had I not fed
On him, as one leaf trembling on a tree,
A woeful waste had been my minstrelsy.
Yet have I sung of maidens newly wed,
And I have wished that hearts too sharply bled
Should throb with less of pain, and heave more free
By my endeavour—still alone I sit,
Counting each thought as Miser counts a penny,
Wishing to spend my pennyworth of wit
On antique wheel of fortune like a Zany.
You love me for my sire to you unknown:
Revere me for his sake, and love me for my own.

If only Hartley had held himself firmly to the task, he might have produced more of his exquisite verse. We have already mentioned that many of the sonnets are unfinished—what true symbols they are of poor Hartley's incomplete life. We all possess a liking for finished poems; but Hartley does not seem to have realized that by earnest application he could have definitely bettered his sonnets.

Yet those sonnets of Hartley's which go into the anthologies of men's memories are nearly faultless. Like delicately cut diamonds, they glisten in the sunshine, paradisiacal emblems of the poet's divine soul. "The soul-animating sonnets of Milton," writes Samuel Waddington in an essay on Hartley Coleridge's poetry, "are more solemn and grand, and those of Keats and Wordsworth may reach a higher level of poetic imagination, yet the fact must be recorded that after Shakespeare our sweetest English sonneteer is Hartley Coleridge."[2]

It must be so,—my infant love must find
In my own breast a cradle and a grave;
Like a rich jewel hid beneath the wave,
Or rebel spirit bound within the rind
Of some old wreathed oak, or fast enshrin'd
In the cold durance of an echoing cave:—
Yea, better thus than cold disdain to brave:—
Or worse,—to taint the quiet of that mind,
That decks its temple with unearthly grace.
Together we must dwell, my dream and I,—
Unknown must live, and unlamented die,
Rather than soil the lustre of that face,
Or drive that laughing dimple from its place,
Or heave that white breast with a painful sigh.

Poems, 62.

Though the sonnet was Hartley's *forte,* he succeeded with other forms. With blank verse he was moderately successful. In ***Leonard and Susan*** the influence of Wordsworth's dignified verse is evident, although Hartley is able to superimpose a sad, swaying rhythm of his own. As the subject matter of the poem is neither exciting nor philosophical, and as it lends itself to satire at only one point, the artist in Hartley led him to adopt a slow and stately verse. The figures of speech spring naturally into being, and though there is a tendency on Hartley's part to make the tale sentimental, the poem is good reading for a dull evening. Turn, for example, to the passage on Susan's death:

For sorrow had become the element,
The pulse, the sustenance of Susan's soul,
And sudden joy smote like the fire of Heaven,
That, while it brightens, slays. A hectic flush,
Death's crimson banner, crossed her marble cheek—
And it was pale again.—The strife is past—
She lies, a virgin corse, in Leonard's arms.

Poems, 14.

The other poems in blank verse need not detain us—they merely indicate a liking for the underlying elements of iambic metre.

Hartley's scholarly tendencies led him to the couplet, rather the heroic couplet of the pseudoclassicists than the romantic one of his contemporaries. He did not exclude *enjambement,* but he did not indulge in it too often: he did not strive for continual balance and conciseness, but felt the merit of an emphatic line; moreover, he did not venture to use the couplet for lyrical expression, but rather to give vent to the vein of satire of which he was not entirely devoid. It is unfortunate that the best of Hartley's verse in heroic couplets is published only in magazines, for he excelled in this kind of verse. He himself said, "I rather think that the couplet and the elegiac quatrain are the metres I manage best." In a poem called the ***Tea Table,*** he writes:

Behold the cups array'd, the table set,
Matrons and Spinsters, all are duly met,
The younger Belles disposed in scatter'd troops
In rows demure, or gaily whispering groups.
The female elders chat the time away—
(I often wonder what they find to say)
Or timely range the fish in painted pools
(Their light exchequers) while their coffee cools.
What various tones from female organs flow
How glibly smooth, or long wishingly slow
The pretty creatures laugh, and weep and rail
In all gradations of the vocal scale
From fell Xantippe's emphasis of brass
To the soft murmur of a melting lass!

Fraser's Magazine, January, 1857.

Hartley's sweetest poems are those lyrics, simple in form and in content, which sing of his joys and sorrows. Here pure inspiration is enough: the firmness of the emotion and the lilt of the music carry along the glowing poet. Just as some of Wordsworth's most enchanting poems (the *Lucy* poems) are lyrics, so are some of Hartley's. His best work was with the sonnet, no one doubts that, but perhaps only in the very best sonnets does his unalloyed spirit burst forth as in many of the lyric verses. The following beautiful poem will serve as an example:

Reply

Ay! well it is, since she is gone,
She can return no more,
To see the face so dim and wan,
That was so warm before.

Familiar things would all seem strange,
And pleasure past be woe;
A record sad of ceaseless change,
Is all the world below.

The very hills, they are not now
The hills which once they were;
They change as we are changed, or how
Could we the burden bear?

Ye deem the dead are ashy pale,
Cold denizens of gloom—
But what are ye, who live to wail,
And weep upon their tomb?

She pass'd away, like morning dew,
Before the sun was high;
So brief her time, she scarcely knew
The meaning of a sigh.

As round the rose its soft perfume,
Sweet love around her floated;
Admired she grew—while mortal doom
Crept on, unfear'd, unnoted.

Love was her guardian Angel here,
But love to death resign'd her;
Tho' love was kind, why should we fear,
But holy death is kinder?

Poems, 72.

In concluding any discussion of Hartley Coleridge's poems, one is always tempted to compare them with those of his father. Samuel Taylor Coleridge possessed a stronger and more virile genius. In the realm of pure imagination, when the unseen glories of the supernatural stood before him, he knew no peer. Hartley Coleridge had a less powerful genius, and he never soared beyond mere fancy. Though in his youth he seems to have possessed a really romantic imagination, which created strange beasts and countries, in manhood he had no such faculty. Samuel Taylor Coleridge has well been termed the father of romantic poetry in England, for it was he who led the way; but his son, Hartley, will be remembered for a few poems, not full of untrammelled imaginative wonders, but overflowing with human emotion and tender self-revelation. And though Hartley possessed the lesser genius, it is interesting to note that there was never any falling-off of his powers, his later poems often being finer than his earlier ones. The genius of Samuel Taylor Coleridge carried him beyond the pre-romantic movement, but Hartley had not "a genius strong enough to wrest and wrench himself out of the transition stage."[3]

II. Prose: Essays and Marginalia

In discussing Hartley's prose work, excepting ***The Northern Worthies,*** one is at once forced into classification. There are two distinct types of essays in the two volumes of prose which Derwent published in 1851: first, the purely critical and religious essays, written as reviews of books, or of persons; and second, the familiar essays, light, witty fancies of the moment, neither instructive nor destructive, neither wise nor foolish; but the two groups often merge into each other. Sometimes it is difficult to discover at what Hartley is aiming, and a serious conclusion may follow a pleasantly meandering fancy; but the suggested classification is usually sound.

Hartley was an excellent critic. His taste was highly cultivated, and he naturally chose works of artistic value. His mind was alert and responsive, and he was able to judge with finesse. The poets and literary men of Hartley's day were not wholly romantic, and they were more moderate in their passionate outbursts than their predecessors. Hartley could not imitate *Christabel,* and he could not give lectures like those of his father on Shakespeare; but he could see with a remarkable lucidity many of the main currents of literature. He read a great deal, despite his statements to the contrary, and he possessed a faculty for the intelligent retention of facts; consequently, when he came to criticize, he brought with him a vast fund of information and a good number of opinions. Even better than his father, he was able to appreciate the worth of the eighteenth century poets; and his sonnets to Homer, Shakespeare, Wordsworth, and Coleridge illustrate the keen perception he possessed.

Nevertheless, Hartley was not at his best in formal criticism; he was too conversational, too discursive for that. Though the world has never been able to decide what it wants for criticism, it generally demands that the critic should show a broad and inclusive philosophy of life, or, at least, that some great principle should underlie his work. Hartley Coleridge was a very talented man; in many respects he was a genius; but he did not possess a soul expansive enough to give him a definite grasp of things. In his criticism he is vivid and interesting; he indicates for us, very successfully indeed, the faults and virtues of a given production; he brings us round to his point of view and is often very convincing; but he does not seem to have been able to organize his thoughts into any plan. The following passage shows a keen perception and a love of strong contrast; but it is no more than a mere passing idea, to be forgotten by its author as quickly as it sprang into being:

> Milton is the most ideal, Spenser the most visionary of poets. Neither of them was content with the world as he found it; but Spenser presents you with a magic picture to exclude it from your sight, Milton produces a pattern to mend it by. After labouring in vain to stamp perfection on an earthly republic, he embodied it in a new World of gods and godlike men. His boldest imaginations have the solemnity, the conscious grandeur of moral truths; his ideals seem more substantial, more real, than any actual reality. He rouses the mind to more than common wakefulness, while Spenser enchants it into an Elysian dream.[4]

Discursiveness neither makes nor unmakes literary criticism; but the permanence of the essays should not rest on digression alone. In a review of Sir Aubrey de Vere's *Julian the Apostate* Hartley's remarks about Shakespeare and his contemporaries[5] are very interesting. To a certain extent they contribute to an understanding of the play being discussed; but in this case, as in others, Hartley leads us too far from the main question, and we find that it is the digression, not the essay proper, which holds our attention. It is very easy for almost any critic to be diverted from his main topic by an inviting by-path; and if Hartley followed the example of the *Biographia Literaria* of his father, either wilfully, or more certainly, because of the resemblance of his mind to that of his father, he had considerable authority in his favour; nevertheless, this weakness greatly interferes with the effectiveness of his criticism and destroys the reader's continuity of thought.

The religious and literary criticism in Volume Two of the ***Essays*** is not on the whole finished work, but represents the spontaneous reaction of Hartley's mind to whatever he was reading. Like his father, he was ever ready to comment or criticize, and the entire volume is scarcely more than a selection of table-talk—in writing. We see quickly the power and amazing activity of Hartley's mind. Here, perhaps, he is most natural, for no critic can be particularly artificial in miscellaneous marginalia. Often his judgment is swayed momentarily by a hidden prejudice; but the criticism as a whole betrays a fair-minded, finely woven, and delicately constructed temperament, ready to love what is good. Hartley's deep religious convictions made him demand a moral basis for his criticism, but withal we find him most appreciative of anything artistic. His love of petty distinctions, of argument for its own sake, often leads him to unnecessary comments; but with a clear understanding he usually finds something interesting to talk about. Had he worked his disconnected jottings into formal essays, he would probably have produced a considerable amount of very readable criticism. Of Richard West, Hartley writes, tempted as always to speak also of himself:

> Some writers maintain a sort of dubious, twilight existence, from their connection with others of greater name. R. West, though an elegant and promising youth, is one of them. He would have been forgotten had he not been the friend of Gray. Jago would have no place among the poets had he not been a favourite of Shenstone. Kirk White will live by the kindness of Southey. If aught of mine be preserved from oblivion, it will be owing to my bearing the name of Coleridge, and having enjoyed, I fear with less profit than I ought, the acquaintance of Southey and of Wordsworth."[6]

Hartley's light essays, in which he attempts to discuss some phase of art, of literature, or of life, and in which Charles Lamb was often his guide, are probably his best prose work; for here the field is broad and unrestricted, and positive proof or formal reasoning is unnecessary. "Pride," says Hartley,

> seems to be involved in the very essence of conscious reflective individuality; it is the peculiar self-love of a rational creature, only subdued by that faith which introduces the creatures into the presence of the Creator, and merges the finite understanding in the infinite Reason;[7]

and then by means of his nimble wit and expansive imagination he produces an essay on one phase of pride. He wrote in a clever and allusive manner, seldom exhausting his subject, always wandering, pleasing himself and his reader by unchanging good-humour, palpable exaggeration, and shrewd insight. He cared not what his subject was; his only interest being in a playful self-revelation.

Hartley's success with this species of writing is due to the fact that the informal essay needs no regularity, no conscious adherence to rule, and is, therefore, exactly compatible with his temperament; and to the fact that he revered Charles Lamb and endeavoured to employ many of his master's tricks of style. The first of these reasons demands no further comment, but it is only fair to Hartley Coleridge to demonstrate the individuality of his own essays, despite their resemblance to those of Charles Lamb. Charles Lamb's nature was, like Hartley's, a combination of melancholy and happiness, and when the circumstances of life came nearest to crushing him, the balance of these two qualities prevented a surrender to madness, or death. When he came, late in life, to write his inimitable familiar essays, he realized fully the tragic circumstances of human existence; but he had found that peace and understanding were the result of gentleness and love. His humour, his ease, and his lightheartedness, therefore, were entirely natural. Herein lies the fundamental difference in the spirit of his and Hartley's essays. Most of Hartley's essays were written when he was a young man, but when he was enduring the pangs of remorse over his unsuccessful trial at Oxford or at Ambleside. Unwilling to expose to the world the sorrow arising from the contemplation of his failures, he affected a light-heartedness. His purpose was to deceive himself, to be happy in spite of a hundred potent reasons why he should not be so. But his pose was not entirely successful, and in spite of his intentions, the marks of artificiality which the familiar essayist tries to conceal are evident. Observe, for example, the forced quality of the following passage:

> I am brief myself; brief in stature, brief in discourse, short of memory and money, and far short of my wishes. In most things, too, I am an admirer of brevity; I cannot endure long dinners. All the delicate viands that sea and land, with all the points 'on the shipman's card,' produce, are not so irresistible a temptation to gluttony, as the ennui of a needless half-hour at table: certain motions of the jaws are undoubtedly infectious: such are laughing, yawning, and eating. Should the nightmare 'and her nine fold,' descend visibly upon the dishes; should indigestion, after the old fashion, assume the shape of Abernethy to admonish me, and gout appear in yet more formidable likeness of a racking toe, the mere dead weight of time would turn the balance of my resolves.[8]

Hartley's affectation goes even farther. Though comparatively young when he wrote for the *London Magazine* or *Blackwood's Magazine,* he nevertheless wrote as if he were old and settled, with a great amount of experience behind him; yet the whimsical manner in which he conversed was obviously intended as an apology for his seeming dogmatism. Elia was never dogmatic; but his humorous remarks were as unaffected as the man himself.

We have already said something about Hartley's style. Its most outstanding characteristics are clearness, rhythm, and artificiality. The clearness of the style is due to a remarkable command of English and a deliberate effort to give pleasure; the rhythm is the product of Hartley's poetical nature, and it is gained by a careful use of words and by a tendency to balance and arrange sentence structure; the artificiality of style is the direct result of a too conscious attempt to disclose the happier and more whimsical side of life. There is, however, for the reader a delight in the rise and fall of Hartley's emotion, in his deft disclosure of fanciful notions. He wrote, not as he lived; but carefully, striving to show, perhaps, the polish and conventionality, the restraint and consciousness, which his life lacked.

III. Prose: *The Northern Worthies*

There are two purposes for biography; it may serve either as a valuable and authentic record for the historian who seeks facts, or as a pleasant literary diversion for the casual reader. The two methods, to be sure, may merge one into the other. In either case it is necessary to examine the inner life, and to discover, if possible, the spiritual forces involved. Biography goes beyond the limits of mere narrative and gives evidence of the biographer's detachment from his subject and of his imaginative sympathy.

Now Hartley Coleridge, whatever may be his merits as an author, wrote his ***Northern Worthies*** without any proper point of view. In each biography he feels that he must give the facts of the man's life, and he proceeds to do so, heaping them on each other in bewildering fashion; but his artistic instinct forces him to do more. He is fond of exploiting his own opinions and often detains us indefinitely, expounding a theory of art or of ethics. He had numerous convictions and maintained a stubborn allegiance to certain fixed dogmas; but his mind never seemed to be able to grasp a scheme for all things, whereby he could arrange in order a fluctuating mass of clever and new ideas. Thus he announces, in his life of Thomas Lord Fairfax, that he will be perfectly unbiassed in describing Fairfax's part in the Revolution; but before we have read very far we feel that Hartley is biassed, despite his unwillingness to be so. We learn of Ascham's scholarly dignity with its influence and power, of Captain Cook's peregrinations to lands afar; we discover the merits and defects of Congreve's dramatic work, the misplaced tenacity of Bentley and his classical opinions; but alas, it is all a jumble of shrewd observations, never consistently followed out! There ensues a chaos of disorder, a sad confusion of criticisms. Such a weakness led Hartley often astray; for throughout the ***Lives*** there are long digressions, interesting enough to be sure, but indicative of a false perspective. We find biography within biography, which, though not always a fault, often arises from an inability to keep to the point. Hartley's genius gave him power to enlarge suggestive opinions on the least provocation; but the power often led him to develop points of secondary importance. In a picture gallery an experienced guide will lead his audience through the maze of paintings with some logical sequence, missing perhaps a few rooms of minor importance, but covering the whole museum in orderly fashion. So we wish biography to be; better the loss of a few details than the loss of a unity of impression.

Yet in observing the general aspects of Hartley Coleridge as a biographer we must not miss his merits. He has an outstanding and characteristic enthusiasm for his subject matter. Save in one or two instances, each biography bears the stamp of this intensity of feeling. He seeks to catch the spirit of the original life, to present to us a living character. He does not content himself with a mere record of facts or with a chronological report, but he tries to fuse together his materials. Many of the details necessary to biography are dull and unimposing; the skill of the author is in the presentation of the facts. Here Hartley is a past master of the art. Just when we are becoming bored with the intricate details of Bentley's quarrels or Cook's journeys, a witty criticism or a shrewd observation carries us away. Hartley may very well have found his job a tedious one, working, as he wrote in a letter, at the rate of twelve pages a day, often with insufficient sources before him; but be it said to his credit that he very seldom shows any lassitude and that the reader very seldom finds his interest flagging.

Hartley's characteristic enthusiasm and his intensity of feeling were the result of his humanity. He loved mankind, and when he studied the life of a man who had been weak or even vicious, he felt too strongly his own aberrations to judge harshly or unsympathetically. He realized, of course, that the first duty of a biographer is to tell the truth; but he knew that judgments are often made on insufficient evidence. Men of the past were to him men of flesh and blood, whose lives were obscured by time; it was his work to present them as living characters, open to the same temptations and emotional crises as his contemporaries. It was natural, therefore, for him to be inspired by his subjects and to be perceptibly moved by their trials and vicissitudes.

The Northern Worthies is a tribute to Hartley's skill as a scholar. The book shows how much he was able to accomplish by honest effort, despite a lack of original sources. Realizing how limited his facilities for work really were, we are often amazed at the fund of information he has acquired. Working often with only one source, he is able to present a logical and readable biography.

Moreover, though Hartley constantly yields to the temptation to wander and digress, he tries to make clear his point of view in each individual case. Usually the accounts are preceded by an introduction, either dealing with the general field of the man's endeavour or of the period in which he lived. These discussions, though sometimes they become digressions, serve to make everything more intense as well as to clarify the reader's hazy ideas of men and times.

Putting aside for the moment any judgment of the merits of the ***Northern Worthies*** as biography, we find two characteristics which make this work interesting: the tendency to generalize, to expand, or to define, and the quality of the style. Improvements in machinery, Hartley says, "have indeed increased wealth, but they have tremendously increased poverty";[9] but he is not content with this mere statement, and proceeds to define:

not that willing poverty which weans the soul from earth, and fixes the desires on high; not that poverty which was heretofore to be found in mountain villages, in solitary dwellings mid-way up the bleak fell side, where one green speck, one garden plot, a hive of bees, and a few sheep would keep a family content; not that poverty which is the nurse of temperance and thoughtful piety—but squalid, ever-murmuring poverty, cooped in mephitic dens and sunless alleys; hopeless, purposeless, wasteful in the midst of want; a poverty which dwarfs and disfigures the body and soul, and renders the capacities and even the acquirements of intellect useless and pernicious, and multiplies a race of men without the virtues which beasts oft-times display—without fidelity, gratitude, or natural affection.[10]

The tendency to define or to expand gives Hartley an opportunity to throw off, as it were, odd fragments of his reflections. The remarks above reveal a tender and sympathetic nature; those in the following passage, which arose from an attempt to distinguish between an ordinary knave and a great one, reveal instead his shrewdness:

It is no doubt easy, for any man that chooses, to be a *knave;* knave enough to ruin himself and his friends, knave enough to lose his character and his soul, but all this a man may do without being a *great* knave, without realizing a fortune of half a million. The common run of small knaves, like small poets, are wretchedly poor, living from hand to mouth upon their shifts or their verses, because they are not the knaves or the poets of nature, but of vanity or necessity. They play off their tricks and their sonnets on the spur of the moment, and are incapable of forming any scheme befitting 'a creature of large discourse, looking before and after.' But the *great* knave despises all epigrams and impromptus, and fugitive pieces of knavery. As the great poet speaks plain prose to his neighbors, writes a letter of business like a man of business, and can see a rose or a pretty milk-maid without committing rhyme or blank [verse] upon either, reserving and consolidating his powers for some great and permanent object, that will rather ennoble his genius, than be ennobled by it. So the truly great knave never throws knavery away; in all but the main point he is minutely honest, and only to be distinguished from the naturally honest man, by the greater anxiety about appearances. But in one thing the great knave differs from the great poet. The poet conceives great ideas of his own, and in the production and development of these ideas his delight consists; he does not readily adopt the ideas of others, far less does he make any use of them. Now the leading faculty of the knave, and it is a faculty none can acquire who is not born with it, is a quiet apprehension of the use to be made of others' labours, others' thoughts, others' inventions.[11]

Hartley is a master of English prose. When under stress, he constructs climactic or balanced sentences which hold the attention of the reader. Sometimes there are evident a certain pride in grammatical correctness and a deliberate attempt to make the words and constructions yield a rich harvest; but there is no obscurity or pomposity, no high-flown phraseology. Like Macaulay, Hartley loved strong contrasts, sweeping generalizations, and colourful exaggeration; and the following passage may well be compared with many similar ones in Macaulay's works:

Fifty thousand subjects of one king stood face to face on Marston Moor. The numbers on each side were not far unequal, but never were two hosts speaking one language of more dissimilar aspects. The Cavaliers, flushed with recent victory, identifying their quarrel with their honour and their love, their loose locks escaping beneath their plumed helmets, glittering in all the martial pride which makes the battle day like a pageant or a festival, and prancing forth with all the grace of gentle blood, as if they would make a jest of death, while the spirit-rousing strains of the trumpets made their blood dance, and their steeds prick up their ears: the Roundheads, arranged in thick dark masses, their steel caps and high crown hats drawn close over their brows, looking determination, expressing with furrowed foreheads and hard-closed lips, the inly-working rage which was blown up to furnace heat by the extempore effusions of their preachers, and found vent in the terrible denunciations of the Hebrew psalms and prophecies. The arms of each party were adapted to the nature of their courage: the swords, pikes, and pistols of the royalists, light and bright, were suited for swift onset and ready use; while the ponderous basket-hilted blades, long halberts, and heavy fire-arms of the parliamentarians were equally suited to resist a sharp attack, and to do execution upon a broken army. The royalists regarded their adversaries with that scorn which the gay and high-born always feel or affect for the precise and sour-mannered: the soldiers of the covenant looked on their enemies as the enemies of Israel, and considered themselves as the elect and chosen people—a creed which extinguished fear and remorse together. It would be hard to say whether there were more praying on one side or swearing on the other, or which, to a truly Christian ear, had been the most offensive. Yet both esteemed themselves the champions of the church, there was bravery and virtue in both; but with this high advantage on the parliamentary side, that while the aristocratic honour of the royalists could only inspire a certain number of *gentlemen,* and separated the patrician from the plebeian soldier, the religious zeal of the Puritans bound officer and man, general and pioneer, together, in a fierce and resolute sympathy, and made equality itself an argument for subordination. The captain prayed at the head of his company, and the general's oration was a sermon.[12]

Certainly with reading and study Hartley had acquired a wide knowledge of words; and the ***Worthies*** shows a careful application of that knowledge. The true literary artist prides himself on his style; and though Hartley's tendency to wander often abruptly breaks the continuity of thought and the unity of impression, his genius and power make his prose very readable.

In the last few years there has been a distinct change in taste, particularly concerning biography. The modern reader seldom has time for long books; and if a book is long it must justify itself by special qualities. The biographies which Hartley wrote could not be popular to-day; they are too long, too digressive, too crammed with observations on life and its problems, to appeal; they lack sufficient information, and there are not enough facts to justify their existence. The modern reader may read through the three volumes of the ***Northern Worthies*** and find them interesting; he may say, as Walter Bagehot says in his *Literary Studies:*

This ***Biographia*** is actually read; a man is glad to take it up, and slow to lay it down; it is a book which is truly valuable, for it is truly pleasing; and which a man

> who has once had it in his library would miss from his shelves, not in the common way, by a physical vacuum, but by a mental deprivation;[13]

but it will necessarily be in spite of his prejudices.

Notes

1. When Hartley *did* revise his poems, they were much improved.
2. *The Poets and the Poetry of the Century,* Miles, A. H., 1898, III, 136.
3. *Cambridge History of English Literature,* Vol. XII, 107.
4. *Essays,* I, 4.
5. Only *Shakespeare and his Contemporaries* is given in the *Essays,* I, 353.
6. *Essays,* II, 110.
7. Ibid., I, 308.
8. *Essays,* I, 47.
9. *Northern Worthies,* 477.
10. Ibid., 477.
11. *Northern Worthies,* 464-5.
12. *Northern Worthies,* 199.
13. *Literary Studies,* 1879, 58.

Herbert Hartman (essay date 1931)

SOURCE: "*Poems* (1833)," in *Hartley Coleridge: Poet's Son and Poet,* Oxford University Press, 1931, pp. 101-15.

[*In this critical overview of* Poems, *Hartman notes the technical skill of Coleridge's sonnets, remarking on the strong influence Wordsworth had on the younger poet.*]

Poems: (*Songs and Sonnets*) by Hartley Coleridge, issued by Bingley at Leeds early in 1833,[1] is the slender octavo volume upon which rests the poetic reputation of the son of S. T. C. 'Some writers', the author wrote a decade later, 'maintain a sort of dubious, twilight existence, from their connection with others of greater name. . . . If aught of mine be preserved from oblivion, it will be owing to my bearing the name of Coleridge, and having enjoyed, I fear with less profit than I ought, the acquaintance of Southey and Wordsworth.' Elsewhere he modestly refers to his 'knack of verse' as entitling him to rank as 'one of the small poets'—and no more. And like Bowles and Lamb, with whom—as poets—he has been appropriately edited, he must be sifted among the minor lyrists of the great Romantic Movement. 'His Muse', said the *Edinburgh Review* after his death, 'never lifted either the trumpet of the moral Prophet, or the lyre of the rapt and mystic Bard . . . she interpreted between him and his neighbours.' Yet for this very reason posterity has seen fit to accord him a special place among his peers. Derivative as is the general tenor of his work, his sonnets have been called among the most perfect in the language,[2] admitting him to the immortal companionship 'even with Shakespeare, Milton, and Wordsworth'. While in all his best poetry he put to such use the disappointment and wistful misdirection of his vagrant life that, for self-portraiture, much of it is unique. The stamp of his bizarre personality—dazzling, tender, fitful, elusive, sad—is upon all his work. Not without reason he has been variously called the dalesmen's laureate, and, towards the end of his days, the laureate of children.

This sole volume of his poems issued during his lifetime embraces (in 157 pages, of which the last 13 are notes) some forty-five sonnets, sixteen stanzaic pieces, thirteen songs, five works in couplets (epistles, Valentines, &c.), five in blank verse (including the long narrative **'Leonard and Susan'**), two translations (***Horace and Petrarch***), an epigram, an epitaph, and a group of album verses. For such mixed fare the reader is duly prepared by the title-page, where Drayton's lines are cited:

> I write, endite, I point, I raze, I quote,
> I interline, I blot, correct, I note,
> I make, allege, I imitate, I feign.

Here, surely, is no young poet overawed with a sense of his own hierophancy, no solicitor of laurels not his due. 'I neither deprecate', he says in the Preface, 'nor defy the censure of the critics. No man can know, of himself, whether he is, or is not, a poet.' And he further recognizes his want of invention, disarming the source-hunter by notes scrupulously acknowledging his debts to other writers. Finally, in his Dedicatory Sonnet to S. T. C., 'Father, and Bard revered', he supinely bestows the credit for his 'little art of numbers' upon his sire.

As one turns the pages, however, it becomes increasingly apparent that in manner and mood Wordsworth at his best, rather than Coleridge at his worst (the S. T. C. 'to turgid ode and tumid stanza dear'), is most frequently his model[3]—the 'mighty Seer' to whom he wrote

> Of Nature's inner shrine thou art the priest,
> Where most she works when we perceive her least.[4]

In his preference for the sonnet (a form within whose limits S. T. C. rarely restrained his genius—and with little success); in his preoccupation with children, lovingly celebrated in birthday sonnets, mannered lyrics, epitaph, and valentine; in the sad overtones of memory, of emotions likewise 'recollected in tranquillity'; in the neo-Platonic vein of preexistence (which Wordsworth himself seems to have absorbed from S. T. C. via Proclus, Fénelon, &c.); and especially in his nature poems, instinct with life in the shadow of Helvellyn and within hearing of the Rotha—more particularly in his love of the lakeland flowers (the flow'rets of that prose idyll, Dorothy's *Journal*)—in all these aspects of Hartley's poetry there is the superscription of Wordsworth. His most ambitious narrative, 'Leonard and Susan', is a brief homely epic confessedly Wordsworthian both in structure and *genre*. Finally, most of his notes, acknowledging lifted phrases and ideas, refer unhesitatingly to the sage of Rydal Mount, his patron, benefactor, and lifelong friend.[5]

The reasons for this discipleship, of course, are not far to seek. Although Hartley learned the habit—if not the art—of versifying as a child from his parent, it was to Wordsworth that he turned, as a young man in his father's absence, for counsel, sympathy, and shelter. Wordsworth's library had been one of his places of refuge from the Ambleside school of his boyhood. The *Ode,* which Hartley as a child partly inspired, he believed to be 'decidedly the finest in any language'. And while in old age, indeed in middle age, he shrank in remorse from contact with the aging, opinionated, spoiled, and often crabbed old Tory that Wordsworth became, Hartley never ceased to venerate the Laureate, uncompanionable as he then seemed. Furthermore, in the widening disparity between S. T. C. and Wordsworth, in temperament, creed, purpose, and aesthetic—familiar first of all in the preface to the second *Lyrical Ballads*—Hartley, whose childhood metaphysics were dissipated in tavern talk, took early his unfilial departure to the side of Wordsworth. In a sonnet to his father he confessed (and from this distance there is an innocent accent of travesty where only reverence was intended)

> Thou walk'dst the earth in penury and pain,
> Thy great Idea was too high a strain
> For my infirmity.

Surely here is a paradox, that the first-born of the Logician, Metaphysician, Bard (Coleridge's life simply reversed Lamb's order), the child of all-but-Pantisocracy, should turn, with congenital atrophy of will and impaired talents, back to the dalesmen's ingle-nooks, the highways and public houses of the vale of Windermere. 'My poetry', wrote the city- and cloister-bred S. T. C. of his early work, 'is crowded and sweats beneath a heavy burden of ideas and imagery'; again, 'I wished to force myself out of metaphysical trains of thought, which, when I wished to write a poem, beat up game of far other kind. Instead of a covey of poetic partridges with whirring wings of music, or wild ducks *shaping* their rapid flight in forms always regular (a still better image of verse), up came a metaphysical bustard, urging its slow, heavy, laborious, earth-skimming flight over dreary and level wastes.'

> But *thou,* my babe! shalt wander like a breeze
> By lakes and sandy shores, beneath the crags
> Of ancient mountains . . .

'As far as regards the *habitats* of my childhood,' Hartley wrote, 'these lines written at Nether Stowey, were almost prophetic.' 'But poets', he hastens to add, 'are *not* prophets.'

Turning once more to the volume of ***Poems*** we find a division of the book into parts: a series of thirty-four sonnets; then a miscellaneous remainder, with a few sonnets interspersed, listed as **'Thoughts and Fancies'**. It is, of course, the former—a sequence only in so far as the majority reflect twilight moods of reverie in a contrite heart—which accord Hartley an indisputably high rank among the English sonneteers. Three or four will serve here to show their excellence.

Wordsworth would seem to be the subject of the fifth:

> What was't awaken'd first the untried ear
> Of that sole man who was all human kind?
> Was it the gladsome welcome of the wind,
> Stirring the leaves that never yet were sere?
> The four mellifluous streams which flow'd so near,
> Their lulling murmurs all in one combined?
> The note of bird unnamed? The startled hind
> Bursting the brake—in wonder, not in fear,
> Of her new lord? Or did the holy ground
> Send forth mysterious melody to greet
> The gracious pressure of immaculate feet?
> Did viewless seraphs rustle all around,
> Making sweet music out of air as sweet?
> Or his own voice awake him with its sound?

Most noteworthy perhaps of all his sonnets in its combination of simple, moving diction and self-portraiture is the following, a fit epitaph for the prematurely grey young poet:

> Long time a child, and still a child, when years
> Had painted manhood on my cheek, was I;
> For yet I lived like one not born to die;
> A thriftless prodigal of smiles and tears,
> No hope I needed, and I knew no fears.
> But sleep, though sleep, is only sleep, and waking,
> I waked to sleep no more, at once o'ertaking
> The vanguard of my age, with all arrears
> Of duty on my back. Nor child, nor man,
> Nor youth, nor sage, I find my head is grey,
> For I have lost the race I never ran:
> A rathe December blights my lagging May;
> And still I am a child, tho' I be old,
> Time is my debtor for my years untold.[6]

How tenderly Hartley could turn to the uses of the sonnet the natural piety that filled, for Wordsworth and himself, 'her best home, the lowly-loving heart', is evident in **'November'**:

> The mellow year is hasting to its close;
> The little birds have almost sung their last,
> Their small notes twitter in the dreary blast—
> That shrill-piped harbinger of early snow;
> The patient beauty of the scentless rose,
> Oft with the Morn's hoar crystal quaintly glass'd,
> Hangs, a pale mourner for the summer past,
> And makes a little summer where it grows:
> In the chill sunbeam of the faint brief day
> The dusky waters shudder as they shine,
> The russet leaves obstruct the straggling way
> Of oozy brooks, which no deep banks define,
> And the gaunt woods, in ragged, scant array,
> Wrap their old limbs with sombre ivy twine.

Finally in this group is his oft-quoted sonnet **'To a Lofty Beauty [Edith Southey], from her Poor Kinsman'**, with its moving conclusion:

For never sure was seen a royal bride,
Whose gentleness gave grace to so much pride—
My very thoughts would tremble to be near thee:
But when I see thee at thy father's side,
Old times unqueen thee, and old loves endear thee.

That Hartley Coleridge was not only a phrase-borrower in the Wordsworth tradition (see, for example, the latter's 'Evening Walk' and notes), but a victim of other conventions as well, is clearly shown in the less distinguished pieces of this sonnet section. There are the familiar apostrophes to love[7] and appeals to Fancy of all the Romantics (poets and poetasters alike); there is a sonnet **'On a Picture of the Corpse of Napoleon lying in State'**; there is a **'Youth, thou art fled'**, followed by **'I thank my God because my hairs are grey!'**; there are sonnets to Wordsworth and Shakespeare; there is the octave-sestet tilt between town and country (his homesickness upon arrival in Leeds); and there is the inevitable translation of Petrarch. *Expectes eadem a summo minimoque poeta.*

'Thoughts and Fancies', the second and longer division of the volume, represents a change of mood as well as of form. Although they were not his happiest exercises, Hartley's occasional verses, his album rhymes, were the medium in which his peculiar fanciful genius was freest to disport. In these indeed he could lead his 'Pegasus a steeple-hunting' and '*make believe* to hang his careless harp upon a willow tree'—in lyric, panegyric, epigram, narrative, love-ditty, medley, translation, and valentine. 'I love albums', he confessed in a note. 'They sometimes procure a sunny look, or a kind word, for some hard-favoured son of the muse, that else might wither in the "shade of cold neglect". Surely there is a moral value in whatever enables a poor man to confer a kindness.' And in one album at least he penned lines (a sonnet to Wordsworth) in august company: Dora Wordsworth's Keepsake was to include both Laureates, both Coleridges, L. E. L., Crabbe, Rogers, Scott, Lockhart, the Lambs, Campbell, Moore, Landor, Hunt, Tennyson, and Matthew Arnold—'a book', wrote the last-mentioned, 'which of world-famous souls Kept the memorial.'[8]

Not all, however, of Hartley's **'Thoughts and Fancies'** are mere album verse. Many are strikingly above that level set by Letitia Landon and his prolific Lakeland neighbour, '*In*felicia' Hemans. Their very variety lifts them above such a category; and only rarely do they incline to what S. T. C. called the 'namby-pamby genus' of his own early verse.[9] Stanzas on conventional themes may abound, often in familiar idiom; but the Coleridge impress of high talent is not long absent, as in the lines 'She was a queen of noble Nature's crowning':

Once she had playmates, fancies of her own,
And she did love them. They are past away
As Fairies vanish at the break of day—
And like a spectre of an age departed,
Or unsphered Angel woefully astray—
She glides along—the solitary hearted.

'When a man is unhappy', the elder Coleridge once put it quite bluntly, 'he writes damn bad poetry, I find.' But through the most barren reaches of his son's verses go dancing elfin lines and images: 'the tip-toe levity of spring', 'unmeet historian of a golden time', 'holy and quiet as a hermit's dream'. From his earliest Miltonizing, through stanzas reminiscent of Spenser and Gray, he tried—too frequently in vain—to disengage his muse from eighteenth-century diction,[10] to get 'beyond the sulphurous bolts of fabled Jove':

Yet write he must, for still he needs must eat—
Retail fantastic sorrow by the sheet—
Sing in his garret of the flowery grove,
And pinch'd with hunger, wail the woes of love.

The **'Thoughts and Fancies'** section of the volume contains many laboured and undistinguished stanzas—half-hearted album verse, sincere but commonplace ditties, pious addresses to infants, New Year and birthday greetings, vapid philosophical epistles, translations of Horace and 'Lines' in the manner of the century before—but amid all these, the Parnassian foothills of any minor poet, several lyrics and fancies lift their heads for the culling. Of these by far the most celebrated is his **'Song'**:

She is not fair to outward view
  As many maidens be,
Her loveliness I never knew
  Until she smil'd on me;
Oh! then I saw her eye was bright,
A well of love, a spring of light.

But now her looks are coy and cold,
  To mine they ne'er reply,
And yet I cease not to behold
  The love-light in her eye:
Her very frowns are fairer far,
Than smiles of other maidens are.[11]

This, the unanimous choice of anthologists, has something of a companion lyric in the concluding stanzas of **'Reply'**:

She pass'd away like morning dew
  Before the sun was high;
So brief her time, she scarcely knew
  The meaning of a sigh.

As round the rose its soft perfume,
  Sweet love around her floated;
Admired she grew—while mortal doom
  Crept on, unfear'd, unnoted.

Love was her guardian Angel here,
  But love to death resign'd her;
Tho' love was kind, why should we fear,
  But holy death is kinder?

Such successful lyrics, however, are few and far between in the entire scope of Hartley Coleridge's poetry. His muse seems more at home among more sportive themes, as in **'A Medley'**, where with changing metre he pursues a substance for his song:

Shall I sing of little rills,
That trickle down the yellow hills,

To drive the Fairies' water-mills? . . .
What if we have lost the creed,
Which thought the brook a God indeed?[12] . . .
Or imagined, in the lymph,
The semblance of a virgin nymph,
With panting terror, flying ever,
From hairy Satyrs' foul endeavour? . . .

—not here, but in the 'happy, happy faith' of his boyhood he chooses still to disport, in the illusions of childhood, in the veracities of fairydom; these, he sings, tell a 'sweet tale of hope, and love, and peace'. These, with their 'momentary fits of laughter', will be his theme. Then suddenly the gay lyric swings characteristically into a grave requiem:

—But what availeth me to welcome spring,
When one dull winter is my total year.

When the pure snow-drops couch beneath the snow,
And storms long tarrying, come too soon at last,
I see the semblance of my private woe,
And tell it to the dilatory blast.

Yet will I hail the sunbeam as it flies—
And bid the universal world be glad—
With my brief joys all souls shall sympathise—
And only I, will all alone be sad.

This sadness, rooted in contrition, overshadows nearly all of Hartley Coleridge's poetry. To this self-debasing sense of irrecoverable worth, of spent genius and unfulfilled heritage, he returns, even in his vagaries, again and again. It is the sole theme wherein are defined for him all the burden and the mystery of life, whose muse, like his father's, was seldom 'wholly un-birdlimed'. Only rarely does the affable side of his nature dispel such melancholy, in occasional bursts of whimsy such as the **'Address to Certain Gold Fishes'**:

Harmless warriors, clad in mail
Of silver breastplate, golden scale . . .
As gay, as gamesome, and as blithe,
As light, as loving, and as lithe,
As gladly earnest in your play,
As when ye gleam'd in far Cathay. . . .

Yet even here (in the humanitarian convention of his forbears) the goldfish, like Mrs. Throckmorton's bullfinch, must be identified with the Romantic School:

And yet, since on this hapless earth
There's small sincerity in mirth,
And laughter oft is but an art
To drown the outcry of the heart;
It may be, that your ceaseless gambols,
Your wheelings, dartings, divings, rambles,
Your restless roving round and round
The circuit of your crystal bound,—
If but the task of weary pain,
And endless labour, dull and vain;
And while your forms are gaily shining,
Your little lives are inly pining![13]

—creatures indeed among whom Horace Walpole's cat might appropriately have been drowned, and over whose bowl S. T. C. in his youth might have shed a glistening Pantisocratic tear.[14]

Of the mass of inconsequential verse that he wrote—New Year's greetings, Valentines, birthday stanzas, reflections, and the like—Hartley was his own best critic. Recognizing his own limitations, acutely aware of his exclusion from the highest order of poets,[15] he penned his own self-searching lines on **'Poietes Apoietes'**:

No hope have I to live a deathless name,
A power immortal in the world of mind,
A sun to light with intellectual flame
The universal soul of human kind.

Not mine the skill in memorable phrase,
The hidden truths of passion to reveal,
To bring to light the intermingling ways,
By which unconscious motives darkling steal.

These, he seems to say, he would leave perforce to Wordsworth and to S. T. C., through whose ministrations divine Poesy rocked the cradle of his infancy. He continues:

I have no charm to renovate the youth
Of old authentic dictates of the heart,—
To wash the wrinkles from the face of Truth,
And out of Nature form creative Art.

Child of the Muse that he was, he had long loved Poesy in vain, for reasons implicit in the closing lines of his address to her:

Nor Fortune's spite, nor hopes that once have been—
Hopes which no power of Fate can give again,—
Not the sad sentence, that my life must wean
From dear domestic joys—nor all the train

Of pregnant ills—and penitential harms
That dog the rear of youth unwisely wasted,
Can dim the lustre of thy stainless charms,
Or sour the sweetness that in thee I tasted.

To restore the balance, however, which properly belongs to any consideration of Hartley's poetic output, the 1833 volume ends with a few miscellaneous sonnets. In this form, his special terrain, the heights to which his halting muse could on occasion ascend are evident in the lines to Homer (the improved version found in Derwent's edition):

Far from the sight of earth, yet bright and plain
As the clear noon-day sun, an 'orb of song'
Lovely and bright is seen amid the throng
Of lesser stars, that rise, and wax, and wane,
The transient rulers of the fickle main;—
One constant light gleams through the dark and long
And narrow aisle of memory. How strong,
How fortified with all the numerous train
Of truths wert thou, Great Poet of mankind,
Who told'st in verse as mighty as the sea,
And various as the voices of the wind,
The strength of passion rising in the glee
Of battle. Fear was glorified by thee,
And Death is lovely in thy tale enshrined.

'What manner of man', asks a critic in the *Temple Bar Magazine,* 'was the writer of these poems? Something may be surmised even from these few and casual relics [i.e. previously unpublished sonnets and notes]. A man of ready sympathy and old-fashioned courtesy; of strong sense and delicate sensibility; affectionate and pious; of pleasant humour and curious learning; well read in English poetry and himself possessed of some poetic gift, a "knack of verse", as he phrased it in the modesty of his later years.'[16] Indeed for such an impression of the man himself one need read no farther than Hartley's own Preface to the Poems:

> 'The thoughts, the feelings, the images, which are the material of poetry, are accessible to all who seek for them; but the power to express, combine, and modify—to make a truth of thought, to earn a sympathy for feeling, to convey an image to the inward eye, with all its influences and associations, can only approve itself by experiment—and the result of the experiment may not be known for years. Such an experiment I have ventured to try, and I wait the result with patience. Should it be favourable, the present volume will shortly be followed by another, in which, if no more be accomplished, a higher strain is certainly attempted.'

Bingley's bankruptcy and Hartley's own indisposition, as we shall see, precluded the supplementary volume of poems during the poet's own lifetime, although two years after his brother's death Derwent edited the miscellaneous verses of his later years. Greater in number and more diversified as they are, the posthumous poems fail to attain the 'higher strain' he promised; like Wordsworth's, Hartley's later work becomes sicklied o'er with piety. Only a few scattered sonnets keep to the level of his earlier work in this form.

For one who in petulant mood wrote

> Oh may all Christian souls while yet 'tis time,
> Renounce the World, the Flesh, the Devil, and Rhyme,

something remains to be said touching his derivative talents. Hartley Coleridge was the child, by birth and association, of the forbears of the Romantic Movement; he was thus a generation too late for innovation, for another gospel, or a new aesthetic. Tiny philosopher that he was in childhood, he early renounced metaphysical speculation and outgrew his taste for the Gothic manner that fired his boyhood dreams. He grew up with and into an era of sentiment and industrialism, when great poetry had passed with the pre-*Waverley* Scott, Wordsworth, S. T. C., Shelley, Keats, and Byron; when political upheaval, the encroachment of science, and changing economic standards had deafened the national ear to strains of the muse. Hartley's ***Poems*** appeared the year after the Reform Bill of 1832—'that huge tapeworm *lie* of some threescore and ten yards', his father called it—when the tidal wave of Romanticism had left the literature of its wake in the charge of poetasters. A spurious sentimentality was in the air. Scott's novels supplanted even Byron's Oriental epics with an incalculably large public, while the annuals teemed with the purlings of Mrs. Hemans, Montgomery, Procter, Joanna Baillie, and the saccharine insipidity of Letitia Landon. Chronologically, Hartley had no choice, admitting himself to be

> —a petty man of rhyme,
> Nursed in the softness of a female time.

The old order was, before his very eyes, yielding place to new; the Victorian era was at hand. With Carlyle fingering the stops of his trumpet, and Dickens becoming a staff reporter for the *Morning Chronicle,* Tennyson (whom Hartley met and admired, enjoying 'the perfume that exhales from [his] pure soul') began writing poetry which he was later to delete. All in all, as he sensed, it was indeed 'a dubious, twilight existence' for the son of Samuel Taylor Coleridge.

Although he has a poetic kinship with the youthful S. T. C. of fugitive pieces and eighteenth-century mannerisms, Hartley disagreed with his father's dictum and practice that 'a great poet must be *implicité,* if not *explicité,* a profound metaphysician'. Returning, after being buffeted about by diverse winds of chance, to 'wander like a breeze' in the Lakeland, he chose the people of Wordsworth's poetry for his companions—and became, far more than the bard himself, their friend and laureate. In their simplicity and goodness, as well as in their readiness to tipple and willingness to listen, he found what he long had sought: a modest folk to live among, freedom from obligation, responsibility, or duty, and a land of windmills to tilt with in the Ejuxria of his solitude. 'The completest originals in the world', he wrote in an essay, 'are your plain, matter-of-fact, every-day folks, that never utter a word but what they mean.' So it was by choice that he would ensconce himself in the ingle-nook of some cottier's house; that he became a familiar figure and byword, a sort of *genius loci* among the sheep-shearers, farmers, and dalesmen.

> Oh! what a faith were this, if human life indeed were but a summer's dream, and sin and sorrow but a beldame's tale, and death the fading of a rainbow, or the sinking of a breeze into quiet air; if all mankind were lovers and poets, and there were no truer pain than the first sigh of love, or the yearning after ideal beauty; if there were no dark misgivings, no obstinate questionings, no age to freeze the springs of life, and no remorse to taint them.

Notes

1. Reissued the same year by John Cross, Leeds; also by Baldwin & Craddock, London.
2. e.g., by Edward Garnett, *Dict. Nat. Biog.*
3. 'somebody has borrowed my Wordsworth and I'm like a Jack Tar without his tobacco pouch'—MS. letter (August 1830).
4. Although, in 1820, he agreed with his parent about the 'unhealthful' nature-worship of Wordsworth—'while the odd introduction of the popular, almost the vulgar, religion in his later publications (the popping in, as Hartley says, of the old man with a beard),

suggests the painful suspicion of worldly prudence' (*Letters,* ed. Allsop, 71).

5. 'It is a pity', Wordsworth wrote to Dyce in December 1833, 'that Mr. Hartley Coleridge's sonnets had not been published before your collection was made, as there are several well worthy of a place in it.' Not the least was that to Wordsworth himself, for celebrating 'the thoughts that make The life of souls, the truths for whose dear sake We to ourselves and to our God are dear' (*Poems,* ed. Colles, 10).
6. First published in the annual *Winter's Wreath* (1831), 322.
7. 'Another source of this silly sameness of love-verses is the notion that a lover must compose as well as dress in the height of the fashion. Hence the endless repetition of stock phrases and similes—the impertinent witticism—the wilful exclusion of plain sense and plain English—the scented, powdered, fringed, and furbelowed coxcombry of quality love-poets.'—'Love-Poetry.'
8. *Dora Wordsworth: Her Book,* ed. F. V. Morley, 1925.
9. *Letters,* i. 54; cf. *Poems,* Oxford ed., i. 45 n. 1.
10. 'Never was there an age which strained so hard after originality as the present—yet it is not an original age. It is indeed somewhat original, to discover that Pope and Dryden were no poets; and so it would be to demonstrate that the moon is made of green cheese.'—*Essays,* i. 71.
11. First printed in *The Gem,* ed. Thomas Hood, i (1829), 21-2. To this annual, Lamb, Scott, John Clare, and others had contributed, along with 'the late John Keats' (Tennyson appeared in the 1831 volume). Hartley wrote to Hood from Bingley's home at Leeds: 'I believe you are neither Whig, Tory, nor Radical High-Churchman, Puritan, or Socinian—that you have a sensible contempt for the whole race of -ologies and isms, with a most kindly disposition towards all -ologists, ists, and inians. . . . If I possess any humour at all—it is of the Shandean school, and not according to the taste of the times,' &c. (MS. letter in the library of the Historical Society of Pennsylvania). Hartley planned to dedicate to Hood a contemplated humorous anthology of his own prose and verse ('I mean would-be humorous').
12. Cf. his note to the song ''Tis sweet to hear the merry lark': 'In fact, nature is very little obliged to the heathen mythology. The constant *anthropomorphism* of the Greek religion sorely perplexed the ancient conceptions of natural beauty. A river is turned into a god, who is still too much of a river to be quite a god. It is a statue of ice in a continual state of liquefaction.' (*Poems,* 1833 ed., 152.)
13. Comparison is inevitable with Rupert Brooke's 'Heaven'—where, all fish trust,

    there swimmeth One
    Who swam ere rivers were begun,
    Immense, of fishy form and mind,
    Squamous, omnipotent, and kind;
    And under that Almighty Fin,
    The littlest fish may enter in . . .

14. 'I call even my Cat Sister in the Fraternity of universal Nature. Owls I respect and Jack Asses I love: for Aldermen and Hogs, Bishops and Royston Crows I have not particular partiality—; they are my Cousins, however, at least by Courtesy,' &c. (S. T. C. to Rev. Wrangham, October 24, 1794. Letter cited by Lowes, *Road to Xanadu,* 573).
15. 'Poetry, as regards small poets, may be said to be, in a certain sense, conventional in its accidents and in its illustrations' (S. T. C., *Letters,* ed. Allsop, 118).
16. J. K. Hudson, 'Hartley Coleridge, with some Unpublished Letters and Verses', *Temple Bar Magazine,* cxxvii (1903), 409-22 (reprinted *Living Age,* ccxxxvii. 574 ff.). 'For myself', Hartley wrote, 'I find it easier to write simply in verse than in prose.'—MS. letter. Again:

    'Easier far
    The minuet step of slippery sliding verse
    Than the strong stately walk of steadfast prose.'

    —MS. blank verse epistle to Sara.

Judith Plotz (essay date 1986)

SOURCE: "Childhood Lost, Childhood Regained: Hartley Coleridge's Fable of Defeat," in *Children's Literature,* Vol. 14, 1986, pp. 133-61.

[*This essay begins with a brief sketch of Coleridge's life, then moves on to provide a reading of "Adolf and Annette," a hitherto unpublished fairy story by the author. Plotz contends that this tale is an allegory of growing up in general and of Coleridge's own "romantic rearing in particular."*]

From all accounts "Li'le Hartley," "poor Hartley" Coleridge, eldest son of Samuel Taylor and Sara Coleridge, was the most beguiling child anyone had ever seen.[1] Yet the pathetic story of his life, from precocious infancy to wasted manhood, is a paradigmatic romantic failure, the failure of the supremely gifted child who does not fulfill the enormous promise of his youth. Romanticism taught us, as—more to the point—it taught Hartley, to regard childhood powers of consciousness and temperament as normative. To be a successful Romantic Child, as Hartley so beautifully was, and then go on to be an adult success "carry[ing] the feelings of childhood into the powers of manhood" (S. T. Coleridge, *Biographia* 1:80-81) by accepting the responsibilities of adulthood without letting go of any of the privileged insights of childhood was a feat not only beyond Hartley's strength, but beyond his real wishes. All Hartley's writings and all Hartley's adult behavior explicitly and implicitly present a child who will not grow up, who refuses adulthood. This pattern is most strikingly manifested in **"Adolf and Annette,"** the fairy story printed below for the first time. In the tale Hartley sets forth with bitter clarity his vision of childhood as paradise, as high success, and of adulthood as hell, as bitterest failure. This essay briefly sketches Hartley's development from boy wonder to ossified boy and then gives a reading of **"Adolf and Annette"** as a parable of growing up in general and of Hartley's romantic rearing in particular.

The eldest child of Samuel Taylor Coleridge, a doting and observant parent (when he was there), the nephew of Southey (in whose household he was reared), the "darling" of the village (S. T. Coleridge, *Letters* 2:1022), Hartley was celebrated in earliest childhood in major romantic works: he is the babe in Coleridge's "Frost at Midnight" and "The Nightingale" as well as the "fairy thing with red round cheeks" in "Christabel"; he is the recipient of Wordsworth's "To H. C. Six Years Old" as well as the alleged inspiration for the "best Philosopher . . . Seer blessed" of the Immortality ode (Hartman 35-41 and Newlyn).

From babyhood, the boy seemed a "piscis rarissima," "a thing sui Generis," "an utter Visionary! like the Moon among thin Clouds . . . in a circle of light of his own making—he alone, in a Light of his own" (S. T. Coleridge, *Letters* 2:960, 802, 1014). Two qualities in the boy struck all observers: his whisking, whirling, almost disembodied joy in nature and his powers of mind. Unlike his earthy, rosy, cake-loving baby brother Derwent, Hartley was an ethereal being, so preoccupied with his thinking that he had to be reminded to eat and even then "put the food into his mouth by one effort, and made a second effort to remember that it was there & to swallow it" (ibid. 2:1022). Most descriptions stress the airy lightness of young Hartley's movements, "like a blossom in a May breeze" (ibid. 2:668), and stress as well his affinity to the spirit of life in nature, likening him to those aspects of the natural world that are most ethereal. Wordsworth's tribute emphasizes the boy's powers of spontaneous joy, his "breeze-like motion and . . . self-born carol" (*Poems* 1:522). Hartley's other boyhood characteristic, his "prodigious and unnatural intellect," was even more striking and earned him the nicknames of "young philosopher" from Lamb (*Letters* 1:180) and "Moses" from Southey (*Letters* 1:241).[2]

Hartley was no knowledge-stuffed homunculus—neither Coleridge nor Southey nor his awe-struck schoolmaster, Mr. Dawes, made any effort to force advanced studies early—but he exhibited a preoccupation with what he called "*thinking of my Thoughts*" (S. T. Coleridge, *Letters* 2:1014), or what his father called "*Thinking* as a pure act & energy . . . *Thinking* as distinguished from *Thoughts*" (S. T. Coleridge, *Notebooks* 1:923), to the exclusion of such bodily joys as eating and playing. Southey reported:

> The boy's great delight is to get his father to talk metaphysics to him—few men understand him so perfectly;—and then his own incidental sayings are quite wonderful. "The pity is," said he one day to his father, who was expressing some wonder that he was not so pleased as he expected with riding in a wheelbarrow,—"the pity is that I'se always thinking my thoughts." (*Letters* 1:241)

At four, Hartley "used to be in an agony of thought, puzzling himself about the reality of existence, as when someone said to him: 'It is not now, but it is to be.' 'But,' said he, 'if it *is* to be, it is'" (Crabb Robinson 1:44). Yet again, Coleridge noted the boy's statement of "some Tale & wild Fancy of his Brain—'It is not yet, but it will be—for it *is*—& it cannot stay always *in* here' (*pressing one hand on his forehead and the other on his occiput*)—'and then *it will be*—because it is not nothing'" (*Notebooks* 3:3547). In boyhood this naive idealist was thus full of high promise. His sayings, his highly elaborated imaginary kingdom (of which a map survives), his nightly episodes of the vast "Tale" which beguiled his schoolfellows, his early powers of reasoning were the wonder of his community. Coleridge reported that Hartley was "considered as a Genius by Wordsworth, & Southey—indeed by everyone who has seen much of him" (*Letters* 2:1022).

Though as he grew up Hartley came to be known as an eccentric boy (a "quizz" he later called himself),[3] dreamily forgetting to eat, wearing peculiar clothes, carelessly picking choice bits of food out of a serving dish, unselfconsciously talking a blue streak to dumb-founded adult visitors, his sweet nature made his parents and his aunt and uncle Southey, all child-lovers, entirely indulgent of his unconventional winning ways. When the nineteen-year-old Hartley went off to Oxford, his mother deemed him so unworldly and impractical that her parting letter contained elaborate instructions on how to pack a trunk and how to address a letter (Stephens 146).

"[It] will be interesting to know what he will be," Coleridge noted of his marvelous boy, "for it is not my opinion, or the opinion of two or three—but all who have been with him, talk of him as of a thing that cannot be forgotten" (*Letters* 1:1014). What he became is soon told. After great success at Mr. Dawes's school in Ambleside, Hartley took a B.A. at Merton College, Oxford, where he dazzled and amused his companions with his Greek, his range of knowledge, and his rambling monologues, unequaled, a contemporary thought, by "any man then living, except his father" (Alexander Dyce, AL, HCP). His election in April 1819 to the coveted Oriel College Fellowship seemed the crown of his brilliant youth. To be a Fellow of Oriel would make Hartley, a man of no private fortune, secure and respectable for life. But the sobersidedness of the Oriel Senior Common Room (John Keble was a Fellow; so was Thomas Arnold) provoked all of Hartley's willful whimsy. In less than a year, against all precedent, for various unspecified offenses involving "sottishness" and consorting with low company, Hartley was stripped of his Fellowship (John Taylor Coleridge, AL, HCP). Contemporaries at Oxford insisted that Hartley's drinking, later in his life to be a grave problem, was modest by Oxford (if not Oriel) standards. It was as much Hartley's unconventional dress, his cavalier omission of routine duties, and his social simplicity as his poor head for alcohol that lost him the Fellowship. The childlike manners, so long cosseted at home, found no such indulgence at Oriel, where John Keble, for example, initially hoped that the puppyish Hartley might "unlearn some of his manifold tricks" but soon came to regard him as an instance of a good head and heart spoiled by a vagrant temperament.[4]

The Oriel disaster, for so Hartley and his family chose to regard it, marked the end of Hartley's attempt to master the world and the beginning of his lifelong pattern of despondency, wandering, and desultory literary activity. After a spell of literary hackwork in London, Hartley yielded to the pressure of his family and drifted back to the Lake District where he remained for the rest of his life. He spent two brief spells as a schoolmaster. In 1824, immediately after his return to the Lakes, he was an assistant to Mr. Dawes; it was then that Dorothy Wordsworth reported he was "liked by his scholars and . . . the biggest address him 'Hartley'! This will give you an idea of the nature of the discipline exercised by him" (*Letters* 1:162-63). For part of 1837 he taught at the Sedburgh School. He also published a volume of poetry in 1833 and at the same time contracted with his Leeds publisher, Bingley, to write a series of biographies of the great and near-great of Lancashire and Yorkshire. While living in Bingley's house in Leeds Hartley succeeded in completing one volume of the promised series, a volume published in 1833 as ***Biographia Borealis,*** but he chaffed at the discipline and, disregarding his written agreement, simply walked out on Bingely, leaving "all his clothes & books behind him, but as happy to return as a boy from school" (James Brancher, AL, HCP). From this time he lived without regular employment, earning a pittance from intermittent journalism, but mostly dependent on the bounty of his family and the kindness of friends. He spent the years from 1822 (when he was 25) until his death in 1849 partly in disorganized study and miscellaneous writing and partly in roaming around the countryside, not always sober, in ironic fulfillment of the "Frost at Midnight" prophecy: "But *thou,* my babe! shalt wander like a breeze / By lakes and sandy shores." He wrote obsessively in his notebooks of lost chances: "Alas that I should have made such little opportunity of seeing . . . [the Isle of Wight]" (marginalia in *Atheneum* of March 27, 1847, HCP); "Alas—what I was [at Calne]! What might I have made of myself!" (marginalia in *London Magazine* of October 1822, HCP). He liked to entertain visitors to the Lakes with wry tales of his wasted life or of his previous incarnations as a louse or a wasp or a donkey.[5] By his middle years, Hartley saw his life as void of any meaning save as a negative example:

> And now my years are thirty-five,
> And every mother hopes her lamb,
> And every happy child alive,
> May never be what now I am.
>
> (**"Written in a Bible,"** ***Complete Poetical Works*** 223)

Though many loved him, no one respected him: in the end Hartley achieved neither fortune nor profession, nor reputation, nor wife, nor child, nor self-respect. Without real love or real work, he remained in manhood what he was in childhood, a glorious (if increasingly elderly) boy.

The form of Hartley's failure was a willed choice of perpetual childhood: "I would be treated as a child / And guided where I go."[6] "He lived as a child," Caroline Fox wrote, "and therefore he was loved as only a child is loved" (Griggs 171).

Physically the role was easy: Hartley was a tiny man, barely five feet tall, who sometimes used the pen name of Tom Thumb, who signed a letter to tall Thomas Poole, "your grateful and sincere little friend" (H. Coleridge, ***Letters*** 18), and who was addicted to self-diminishing anecdotes about his own puniness. He chose a boy's clothes—"a dark blue cloth round jacket, white trousers, black silk handkerchief tied closely round his neck"—and moved with so much lightness of step that even after his dark hair turned white he continued to look like a ghostly boy, "a white-haired apparition wearing in all other respects the semblance of youth with the most delicately grained skin and vividly bright eyes" (de Vere 133). Still more, his behavior was childlike. Children, especially infants, girlish little boys (of big boys he had "an instinctive terror" [H. Coleridge, ***Letters*** 127]), and prepubescent girls were his favorite companions. In his notebooks (those in the Humanities Research Center collection are mostly schoolchildren's soft-covered composition books with horses and alphabets on their covers) he wrote whimsical poems for his young friends—valentines, riddles, songs, attacks on Latin grammar and on teachers with funny names. He shared the children's delight in local fairs and puppet shows.

Hartley invited characterization as a child since he habitually depicted himself in his poetry and in his conversations as a *son,* "a living spectre of my Father dead" ("Full well I know—my Friends—ye look on me," ***New Poems*** 69), that "Father and Bard revered! to whom I owe / What'er it be, my little art of numbers" (**"Dedicatory Sonnet: To S. T. Coleridge,"** ***Complete Poetic Works*** 2). The intimidating father he habitually referred to in his notebooks as a semi-divine "blessed one," *ho makarites,* haunted his consciousness.[7] Hartley's notebooks of the 1840s are full of odd recollections of something his father said in 1807 about volcanoes or Sir Humphrey Davy, recollections of a pun Coleridge made or a literary argument he won against John Pinkerton or a book he recommended, or—more frequent still—recollections of rebukes directed at the boy Hartley thirty or forty years earlier for his bad memory or his lack of pertinacity.

As a poet Hartley's obsession with childhood is obvious. His leading theme is childhood: there are dozens of poems to newborn babies, to two-, three-, or four-year-olds on their birthdays, to his many godchildren, as well as meditations on the mystery of birth and elegiac songs and sonnets about his own infant self and childhood reading. Even his other major subjects, nature and religion, are linked to childhood. The nature poems are all tributes to the greatness of littleness: his theme is the wonder of minimal forms of life such as small animals, birds, fragile flowers, wasps, fleas, microscopic sea creatures:

> But who may count with microscopic eye
> The multitudes of lives, that gleam and flash
> Behind the sounding keel, and multiply
> In myriad millions, when the white oars dash,
> Through waves electric, or at stillest night
> Spread round the bark becalm'd their milky white?
>
> (**"No doubt 'twere Heresy, or something worse,"** Notebook C, HCP).

The religious poems almost all use the metaphor of God as father and man as baby; redemption is depicted as a state of permanently secure childhood. Hartley is the most absolute romantic eulogist of childhood, surpassing even Wordsworth (whom he constantly echoes) in his praise of the child as seer, visionary, and minister of grace. Like Wordsworth and Coleridge, Hartley sees the child's powers of idealism and joyous oneness with nature (qualities for which Hartley himself had been praised and hymned by the two older poets) as essential for all stages of a successful life. Unlike Wordsworth and Coleridge, however, Hartley attributes to infancy as the "breathing image of the life of nature" an immutable strength and absoluteness of Pure Being that makes it utterly distinct from and unassimilable to adulthood (**"The Sabbath-Day's Child,"** ***Complete Poetic Works*** 88). Rather than emphasize the means by which childhood qualities may be carried into adult life, Hartley enjoins the child, "Stay where thou art! Thou canst not better be" (Ibid. 351), and depicts adulthood as a state of steady decline best conveyed through metaphors of impoverishment, death, and even abortion.

Nowhere is Hartley's self-defeating attachment to childhood more clearly depicted than in **"Adolf and Annette,"** his undated fairy story here printed for the first time. The story is about growing up in general and Hartley's coming-of-age in particular.

The story, printed on pages 151-61 [of this issue of *Children's Literature*], follows a familiar fairy-tale pattern. Infant twins, Adolf and Annette, are carried off to safety in their cradle-ark by the same icy flood waters that sweep away their parents' valley cottage. In the safety of the mountains the children are further recipients of nature's bounty. They become wards of nature: they are fed by bees and birds and are protected by a preternaturally beautiful nature spirit, "a lady all of white as if she had been made of sunbeam." In her voice is nature's peace: "Her voice was the voice of the wind when it murmurs low and sweet in a calm cave." She gives them protective parental advice in rhyme and promises the everlasting protection of their parents' spirits on the condition of everlasting docility: "If their good wishes you always obey / Their spirits will guard you for ever and aye." As the children grow up the White Lady is less and less frequently seen. At length she announces her departure to her own "far country" just as Adolf and Annette are on the brink of puberty. Her parting instructions enjoin them to remain good and obedient children: they must not be self-assertive, they must not want anything for themselves alone, they must not go beyond bounds into the valley, they must hope for—but not work for—a reunion with their parents. But the children disobey. Like Adam and Eve in Eden, they grow restless, even selfish. Annette longs to possess for herself a strange red-and-white lily, Adolf an opalescent butterfly; but in their eagerness for possession the children crush the very objects they seek. This omen does not stop Adolf and Annette from yearning after the most forbidden object of all. Discontented with the mountain-top, they look down into the valley: "There it lay, far below the mountain hollows, white and glistening, and 'beautiful exceedingly.'"

Resisting no longer, indeed rationalizing their act as bravery and initiative in search of their parents, the children set out for the valley. Persevering through many perils including a vast cataract like a "white abyss," they reach at last the "glittering valley" where everything gleams as in a dream: the flowerspikes here are "encrusted with shining white crystals," the cottages shine, the ground glistens. In this seeming paradise, the children, hungry and thirsty, reach out to pick the gleaming fruit of a glittering tree: "The white balls tasted like their own tears, only ten times bitterer. . . . For the shining vale was encrusted with thick salt and there was no living leaf or bird or creature or blade of grass therein that had not been turned to salt. Everything was white and shining, but everything, except they two, was dead." Instead of men and women, "strange white forms lay huddled together." Doomed to die as well—for no one can reascend the terrible "white abyss"—the children long for the protected childhood they have thrown away. Suddenly they hear the voice of the White Lady, the hidden voice of nature in the hidden stream, directing them up a hillside toward a few "broad rusty streaks" that are a patch of moorland. Disobedience has almost killed them, so the children hasten to obey her. They mount the hill, finally reaching patches of "brown bare earth," then, blessedly, a patch of moss by a cup-shaped pool. There the White Lady greets the children but warns them that they are forever banished from their mountain home:

> Back to the Mountain I may not lead ye,
> Never again may ye wander there,
> They who have passed through the Shining Valley
> Breathe not again that diviner air.

The children must "travel by common pathways" and have "pain for [their] portion" as they seek "the land where all men dwell." Like *Paradise Lost* the tale ends with the protagonists alive, protected, remorseful, and fallen into permanent exile.

The main lines of Hartley's pattern here are plain. **"Adolf and Annette"** is an autobiographical fairy tale working out the habitual romantic antithesis between innocence and experience, here identified with childhood and adulthood. The mountain is childhood and paradise, the valley independent adulthood and hell, the moorland a state of life-saving semichildhood, safe indeed but tainted by loss of innocence and loss of hope.

Childhood is located in the "blessed heights," the Edenic mountain realm of "diviner air." The mountain landscape is that of the Lake District where Hartley spent his happy youth and sadder maturity. It features valley, lakes, jutting rocks, "short mountain turf," and "rattling sykes" of cold fresh water. (The *OED* notes a "syke" or "sike" as a Scottish or Northern dialect term for a streamlet. One of the illustrative examples cited comes from a poem by Hartley Coleridge.) The mountain is a place of safety where the children are sheltered in "a little hollow place," are soothed by a sound like the wind murmuring in "a calm cave," and feast on ripe berries in "close nooks." In the womblike serenity of this mountain fastness fear is unknown; so are clothes. The Eden is also the realm of natural poetry. Its presiding spirit, the White Lady, is at once the genius of nature, the spirit of poetry, and the surrogate parent. Wonderfully beautiful, she sings a soothing admonitory music which is nature's very voice.

As the realm of childhood innocence, the mountain psychologically is the realm of unselfconsciousness and socially the realm of communal mutuality. The prepubescent Adolf and Annette together embody the presexual completeness of childhood. Their paradise is lost, however, by their decision to grow up, to grow out of the perpetual nonage enjoined by the White Lady. Growing up separates the children from one another and from the possibility of paradise. Adolf's and Annette's efforts to know themselves, to become more individuated and independent, are represented by their separate pursuits of the butterfly and the lily. The images are suggestive, indicating a mixed judgment on the plight of the children. If the lily is a traditional image of innocence, thus apt for Annette, it is also a rather more negative symbol of vulnerability. A similar ambiguity exists about the butterfly, positively a traditional symbol of the soul, negatively of vanity and transience. The flower and the butterfly further hint at and judge each child's developing selfhood. The lily, "rose colored like the dawn," with a heart "like a white dove," suggests Annette's dawning sexuality; the swiftly iridescent butterfly suggests Adolf's ranging curiosity. In reaching for lily and butterfly each is reaching out to possess and to comprehend herself and himself. As they pursue their separate and, they believe, selfish desires, they lose their oneness with each other and their joy in nature. Their desire for individual distinction and their spirit of aspiration are their fall.

This negative judgment on the impulse toward growth is reinforced by the dire imagery of the "white abyss" with its narrow channel and propulsive forces. Seduced by the mocking voice that lures them on, the children choose to be born into the grownup world. They leap into the dangerous white cataract which churns through the ravine and find that they have made an irrevocable descent. Hartley depicts growing up as a descent from life into death, for when Adolf and Annette go down into their parents' adult world they find themselves in the valley of death. The Fall has long since passed in this valley. The postlapsarian calamities of the flood and of the annihilation of Sodom and Gomorrah have occurred—the salt landscape and the human figures turned to salt give mute testimony to that.

Moreover, even adult virtues appear follies in this dead world. What bring the children to the vale of tears are the adult virtues, are those very qualities normally associated both in traditional and Victorian fairy tales with successful mastery of the world: energy, boldness, initiative, self-confidence, and warily selective use of adult guidance. Just as Hartley had dreamed of the glories and paternal praise that were to be his when he descended to his City of the Plain, his Oxford, so do the children strive for the glittering prizes and the imagined parents they believe to be waiting in their "glittering valley." All this effort is vain, producing only a retrospective yearning articulated in a nursery jingle: "For what we have once thrown away, / To have once more we humbly pray." The fruit of all their efforts, Hartley's and the children's, is not knowledge and companionship, but the Sodom apples of despair, appropriate fare for one who explicitly likened himself to "a Dead Sea below the level not only of the Mediterranean but of the Fleet Ditch" (marginalia in *Atheneum* November 10, 1841, HCP). Hartley's tale thus condemns the very impulse toward growth and achievement as leading to self-destruction.

To save Adolf and Annette from the death-in-life that is adulthood, to give his fable a happy ending, Hartley has them elect to resume their earlier, safer, more obedient state, a state resembling Hartley's own protective detention in Grasmere. Here the White Lady promises them life and, vaguely, a journey into the world "where all men dwell." The tale closes, however, before Adolf and Annette move toward that world or even encounter another human being. It closes instead on a note of exhaustion as the White Lady enjoins the children to "abide" and to "come to me, come to me." The tone suggests that the children's vital life is over and that the rest is mere wearisome anticlimax in a simulacrum of childhood security. Hartley's choice of so sad a return to partial childhood for his twin selves indicates how intense is his commitment to the excellence of childhood and how deep his revulsion from the energetic individuality of adult life.

For all Hartley's commitment to childhood, however, his fable also questions the very ideal it largely glorifies. The White Lady, chief artificer of and presider over childhood beatitude, is as sinister as she is glorious. Her threefold identity—as a figure of whiteness, as a figure of admonition, and as a figure of paternal poetry—suggests Hartley's ambivalence toward the very childhood realm he yearns for. In her whiteness the lady is associated not with what is wholesome and lifegiving like the red berries or the green herbs or even the "broad rusty streaks" on the moor, nor with what is richly various like the iridescent butterfly or the rosy lily. She is rather associated with what is deadly, with the white abyss and the salty "shining valley of their vain desire." Further, her lapping love is bound up with things negative—with admonition and with absence. Her addresses to the children consist principally of restraining warnings: "Hush," "Beware," "List to me," "Come to me." Usually present as mere voice, she not only represents the absent parents but herself abandons the children at their most vulnerable time of life. She is thus the source of a rather uneasy security. In this as in other ways, the White Lady seems to be associated with Hartley's father. As a poet who frequently speaks in tetrameter, as a figure whose words are more in evidence than her presence, the White Lady recalls Samuel Taylor Coleridge, who permanently left his family when Hartley was ten. Further, Hartley uses Samuel Taylor Coleridge's words and themes throughout **"Adolf and Annette,"** but especially in connection with the White Lady. Twice the White Lady echoes "Kubla Khan," urging the children to "Beware! Beware!" Both times the echoes occur in lines metrically identical to S. T. Coleridge's "And all should cry Beware! Beware!" As in "Kubla Khan," rushing waters are associated with both life and the icy regions of death. Like *The Ancient Mariner* **"Adolf and Annette"** depicts want in the midst of plenty, thirst in the midst of a salt waste. As in *The Ancient Mariner,* the protagonists endure an experience so horrifying as to make a return to their earlier serenity unthinkable. Echoes from *Christabel* are even more marked. The White Lady owes much to Geraldine: both women are magical, preternaturally bright, white-clad. Both are temporary guardians for the motherless; both are associated with a "far countree" (*Christabel* I 225). The quality Coleridge attributes to Geraldine—that she is "beautiful exceedingly" (*Christabel* I 68)—is by Hartley transferred to the deadly valley which is "white and glistening, and 'beautiful exceedingly.'" There is an echo of *Christabel*'s "So free from danger, free from fear" in the White Lady's parting words to Adolf and Annette: "With much of love and much of fear." The association of **"Adolf and Annette"** with *Christabel,* particularly the association of the seemingly benevolent White Lady with the dangerous Geraldine, suggests an even darker reading for Hartley's tale. Just as his father's *Christabel* can be read in part as the story of a child seduced, abused, and abandoned by those who should protect her, so can **"Adolf and Annette"** be seen as a vision of children doubly betrayed, betrayed both by the world of experience and by their guide to the world of innocence. In the figure of the White Lady who is depicted both as the source of a lovely and sustaining vision of human life and as a seductive abandoner, Hartley seems to be setting forth his heartbroken love and resentment of his father.

Certainly the dominant impulses of **"Adolf and Annette"** are a recoil from adulthood and a desire that childhood last forever. The depiction of the White Lady, however, adds another element. Her equivocal role suggests Hartley's loss of innocence about the very innocence he longs for. Her ominous whiteness suggests Hartley's consciousness that the romantic dream of white innocence may itself be a dangerously self-destructive fantasy. As one who inhabited that dream of perfect childhood, Hartley can write with special authority on themes pervasive in romantic literature. He not only articulates the central romantic assumption of childhood as a state privileged by intuition and imagination,[8] but he criticizes that vision as well. Like Blake in *The Book of Thel* and S. T. Coleridge in *Christabel,* Hartley explores the self-destroying impulse of innocence to shrink back from full knowledge and full experience. A child in so much else, Hartley the artist is mature enough to judge what he loves without ceasing to love it. **"Adolf and Annette"** can properly be read as a late-romantic postscript to the early romantic poetry of innocence, experience, childhood, imagination, and the loss of vision.

Just as **"Adolf and Annette"** resembles the great romantic poems that precede it, so does it resemble the Victorian fairy tales that follow it. Like many works of Victorian children's fantasy, **"Adolf and Annette"** is set in a double universe consisting of one world of childhood and one of maturity. Hartley's childhood realm, as is customary in works of the period, is associated with nature, music, poetry, supernatural beings, helpful animals, and a nonpatriarchal power structure; his child protagonists, like Alice, Mowgli, Jack of *Mopsa the Fairy,* and Diamond of *At the Back of the North Wind,* move through one realm to the other. In their depiction of such a journey, nineteenth-century children's writers tend to adopt one of two attitudes: either a balanced attitude governed, as U. C. Knoepflmacher notes, by "the reality principle" (Knoepflmacher 497)[9] or a regressive attitude governed by nostalgia, loyalty, and imagination. For writers of the first sort—Lewis Carroll, in the Alice books, Molesworth in *Mopsa the Fairy,* Kipling in *The Jungle Books*—the adult world, though certainly more matter-of-fact and constricted than the innocent world, is the destined and largely desirable goal of the child. For such writers the temporary immersion of the reader in fantasy, analogous to the more extended but similarly transient sojourn of the child in childhood, is a refreshing and invigorating respite intended to build strength for the future. For writers of the second kind, however—MacDonald in *At the Back of the North Wind,* Kingsley in *Water Babies,* Barrie in *Peter Pan*—the adult world is a damaging, oppressive place where children do not flourish, at least as children. Only in the realm of imagination, a realm which may look like autism or death to the blurred vision of the adult, can the child thrive.

Hartley Coleridge, whose adult realm is a dead land of salt tears, whose children move from bright mountain to vale of tears only to end as weary, guilty vagrants on the hillside, clearly writes the darker kind of fable of innocence. Moreover, Hartley's fable is further darkened by his children's powerlessness. In most other Victorian fantasies, the magical realm is a realm of at least temporary mastery. In *Phantasmion* (1837), for example, a work by Hartley's sister Sara Coleridge, the hero is a powerful dreamer, whose dreams are a kind of action. In **"Adolf and Annette,"** however, all energy and initiative are depicted as self-destructive or morally wrong. Whether one reads

"Adolf and Annette" as a latterday romantic poem, an early Victorian children's fantasy, or an autobiographical experiment, there are few nineteenth-century works which so sadly and clearly illustrate the power of romantic dreams to act upon a life, and to shape not only fantasies, but a sensibility capable of receiving and reflecting back in poetic images the knowledge of its own defeat.

Notes

1. As an adult Hartley Coleridge was commonly referred to as "Li'le Hartley" (Hartman 129, 131, 140) by the local peasants and as "Poor Hartley" (D. Wordsworth, *Letters* 163, 233, 451, 530) by his disappointed friends and family.
2. Southey wrote of the six-year-old Hartley that "Moses grows up as miraculous a boy as ever King Pharaoh's daughter found his namesake to be. I am perfectly astonished at him, and his father has the same fore-feeling that it is a prodigious and unnatural intellect—and that he will not live to be a man" (Southey 1:241). That Hartley was nicknamed "Moses" is an additional reason for regarding "Adolf and Annette" (with its infants rescued from the waters) as autobiographical.
3. "Autobiography of a Quizz," unpublished fragment, Hartley Coleridge Papers, Humanities Research Center, The University of Texas at Austin. All materials from the Hartley Coleridge Papers are printed here with the kind permission of Joan and Priscilla Coleridge for the Coleridge Estate and of the Humanities Research Center, The University of Texas at Austin. I am most grateful to Joan Coleridge and her daughter for their interest and encouragement. I wish to thank as well the kind assistance of the staff at the Humanities Research Center, particularly that of Ellen Dunlap. The Hartley Coleridge Papers will henceforth be cited as HCP.
4. Keble's increasing vexation with Hartley is evinced throughout the six letters he wrote to John Taylor Coleridge between 1818 and 1822 (six extracts/copies [copied by Sir Bernard Coleridge] HCP).
5. In her 1843 notes on Hartley Coleridge, Sarah Fox notes "that Hartley recalled being present at the siege of Troy: 'I was then an insect which in these days is nameless, and having crawled upon [Helen's] bright yellow hair, I was pointed out to her by Paris, and she crushed me with her pearly nail." On another occasion, Fox notes, Hartley described his earlier incarnation as a clergyman's donkey, a beast so bad-tempered and ungrateful that Hartley was condemned to be reborn as "a man *such as you see me!*" (HCP).
6. The third stanza of "My Times Are in Thy Hands," a manuscript poem (HCP), is a prayer for guidance:

    I would not have the restless will
    That hurries to and fro
    Searching for some great thing to do
    Or secret thing to know
    I would be treated as a child
    And guided where to go.

7. The Greek word *makarites* refers to one who is "blessed," that is, dead. It is cognate with *makar,* "blessed, happy," that is, of the gods as opposed to mortal men. The term, with its association of divinity, imputes an additional grandeur to Samuel Taylor Coleridge. *Ho makarites,* the blessed one, is Hartley's favorite term for his father after Coleridge's death in 1834.
8. For a general account of the high romantic view of childhood privilege, see Judith Plotz, "The Perpetual Messiah: Romanticism, Childhood, and the Paradoxes of Human Development," in *Regulated Children/Liberated Children,* ed. Barbara Finkelstein (New York: Psychohistory Press, 1979), 63-95.
9. Both the article cited and U. C. Knoepflmacher's paper on *Mopsa the Fairy,* "Quest and Loss in the Fantasy World of Victorian Children's Books" (presented at the April 1983 NEVSA Conference), with its illuminating account of Jack's *cheerful* return from fairyland to patriarchy, have been very useful to my thinking about "Adolf and Annette." I am also grateful to Professor Knoepflmacher for his helpful comments on an earlier draft of this paper.

Works Cited

Coleridge, Hartley. *The Complete Poetical Works.* Ed. Ramsay Colles. London: George Routledge and Sons, 1908.

———. *Hartley Coleridge: New Poems.* Ed. Earl Leslie Griggs. 1942; rpt. Westport, Conn.: Greenwood P, 1972.

———. The Hartley Coleridge Papers. Austin: U of Texas, Humanities Research Center.

———. *Letters of Hartley Coleridge.* Ed. Grace Evelyn Griggs and Earl Leslie Griggs. London: Oxford U P, 1936.

Coleridge, Samuel Taylor. *Biographia Literaria.* Ed. James Engell and W. Jackson Bate. 2 vols. *The Collected Works of Samuel Taylor Coleridge* 7. Bollingen Series 75. Princeton: Routledge & Kegan Paul and Princeton U P, 1983.

———. *Collected Letters of Samuel Taylor Coleridge.* Ed. Earl Leslie Griggs. Vols. 1-2. Oxford: Clarendon P, 1956.

———. *Complete Poetical Works of Samuel Taylor Coleridge.* Ed. Ernest Hartley Coleridge. 2 vols. 1912; rpt. Oxford: Clarendon P, 1968.

———. *The Notebooks of Samuel Taylor Coleridge.* Ed. Kathleen Coburn. vols. 1 and 3. Bollingen Series 50. New York: Pantheon, 1957 and 1973.

de Vere, Aubrey. *Recollections of Aubrey de Vere.* London: Edward Arnold, 1897.

Griggs, Earl Leslie. *Hartley Coleridge: Life and Work.* London: U of London, 1929.

Hartman, Herbert. *Hartley Coleridge: Poet's Son and Poet.* London: Oxford U P, 1931.

Knoepflmacher, U. C. "The Balancing of Child and Adult: An Approach to Victorian Fantasies for Children." *Nineteenth-Century Fiction* 37 (1983): 497-530.

Lamb, Charles, and Mary Anne Lamb. *The Letters of Charles and Mary Anne Lamb.* Ed. Edwin W. Marrs, Jr. Vol. 1. Ithaca and London: Cornell U P, 1975.

Newlyn, Lucy. "The Little Actor and His Mock Apparel." *Wordsworth Circle* 14 (1983): 30-39.

Robinson, Henry Crabb. *Henry Crabb Robinson on Books and Their Writers.* Ed. Edith J. Morley. 3 vols. 1938; rpt. New York: AMS P, 1967.

Southey, Robert. *Selections from the Letters of Robert Southey.* Ed. John Wood Warter. 4 vols. London: Longmans, Brown, Green, Longmans, 1856.

Stephens, Fran Carlock. *The Hartley Coleridge Letters: A Calendar and Index.* Austin: U of Texas, Humanities Research Center, 1978.

Wordsworth, William. *The Poem.* Ed. John O. Harden. 2 vols. New Haven and London: Yale U P, 1981.

———, and Dorothy Wordsworth. *The Letters of William and Dorothy-Wordsworth: The Later Years. 1:1821-1830.* Ed. Ernest de Selincourt. Oxford: Clarendon P, 1939.

FURTHER READING

Biography

Reeves, James. "Hartley Coleridge (1796-1849)." In *Five Late Romantic Poets,* edited by James Reeves, pp. 17-25 and 140-46. London: Heinemann, 1974.

> A collection of biographical and critical essays on late romantic poets. Included is a biographical essay on Hartley that also presents a brief overview of his sonnets. Several of his poems are reprinted in the volume.

Criticism

Griggs, Grace Evelyn and Earl Leslie Griggs, eds. *Letters of Hartley Coleridge.* London: Oxford University Press, 1936, 328 p.

> A collection of Hartley Coleridge's letters to his family and friends. The editors claim to have selected letters "which best reveal Hartley Coleridge's mind and personality."

Poston, Lawrence. "'Worlds Not Realized': Wordsworthian Poetry in the 1830s." *Texas Studies in Literature and Language* 28, No. 1 (Spring, 1986): 51-80.

> This essay examines Wordsworth's influence on younger poets of his time and includes a section that discusses Hartley Coleridge's sonnets.

Stephens, Fran Carlock. "Hartley Coleridge and the Brontës." *Times Literary Supplement* (May 14, 1970): 544.

> An overview of the correspondence between Hartley Coleridge and the Brontës. Stephens contends that a letter critiquing a Charlotte Brontë work that was previously attributed to William Wordsworth may actually have been composed by Hartley.

———. *The Hartley Coleridge Letters: A Calendar and Index.* Austin: Humanities Research Center, University of Texas at Austin, 1978, 218 p.

> Compiled as a reference work to assist researchers with the Hartley Coleridge collection at the Humanities Research Center, this book catalogs letters composed and received by the author. Also contains a biographical introduction.

Yarnall, Ellis. *Wordsworth and the Coleridges: With Other Memories Literary and Political.* London: Macmillan, 1909, 331 p.

> A biographical and critical memoir of Sara, Derwent, and Hartley Coleridge by a contemporary author and critic.

Additional coverage of Coleridge's life and career is contained in the following source published by the Gale Group: *Dictionary of Literary Biography,* Vol. 96.

Wilhelm Meisters Lehrjahre

Johann Wolfgang von Goethe

The following entry presents criticism of Goethe's novel, *Wilhelm Meisters Lehrjahre* (1795-1796; *Wilhelm Meister's Apprenticeship*). For information on Goethe's complete career, see *NCLC,* Volume 4; for discussion of Goethe's novel *Die Leiden des jungen Werthers (The Sorrows of Young Werther)* and his drama *Faust,* see *NCLC,* Volumes 22 and 34, respectively.

INTRODUCTION

Essentially a romantic work, *Wilhelm Meisters Lehrjahre* is considered the seminal *Bildungsroman,* or novel of development and maturation, in German literature. An expansion of Goethe's earlier project *Wilhelm Meister's Theatrical Mission,* the *Lehrjahre* details Wilhelm Meister's entry into the theater and subsequent education in the ways of the world as a debt collector for his father and an itinerant actor. Following an intricate plot, *Wilhelm Meisters Lehrjahre* presents not only its protagonist's personal development, but also Goethe's own philosophical and aesthetic views, which are presented via its character's sometimes discursive speeches.

PLOT AND MAJOR CHARACTERS

Goethe's novel is told as a succession of vignettes about the life of a young man in love. As the story begins, the objects of Wilhelm's affections are two-fold, focused both on an actress, Mariane, and the local stage where she performs. With a penchant for versifying rather than for business, Wilhelm determines to scorn his father's disapproval and ask Mariane to marry him while he is away on assignment. Yet his friends are skeptical of the plan and warn him of Mariane's low character. One morning, Wilhelm is shocked to find a man leaving Mariane's house. Jilted by Mariane in favor of Norberg, her protector and lover, Wilhelm decides to accept his father's plan that he travel about collecting debts for the family business; he thus sets out on his adventures. In a nearby town he befriends Philina and Laertes, who become his close companions. While attending an acrobatic show, the three notice that a young girl in the troupe is being poorly treated. Wilhelm rescues the tomboy, Mignon, from the cruelty of her fellows, and she joins him as a devoted follower. Wilhelm then becomes part of a small company of struggling actors. They perform at a nearby castle, where Wilhelm wins the admiration of a countess. The actors then return to their travels and are waylaid by bandits, one of whom wounds Wilhelm before being chased away by a beautiful Amazon. Then follows a period of convalescence for the young man, and for Mignon, who was also injured in the altercation. Time passes, and the acting troupe departs, leaving Wilhelm to pursue his stage career alone after recovering from his wounds. He joins the company of Serlo, a noted actor-manager, in his production of *Hamlet.* Meanwhile, his father has died and Wilhelm, having inherited enough property to support himself, meets Aurelia, Serlo's sister. Some time later, Aurelia dies, but not before asking her friend to take a letter to Lothario, her former lover. Lothario, Wilhelm learns, resides at the nearby castle, and is brother to the countess he had once entertained, as well as a member of a secret society of nobles and intellectuals to which Wilhelm seeks entry. After returning from a mission for Lothario, Wilhelm learns that Mignon has left and is now mortally ill. He locates her and discovers that she is the daughter of an Italian priest who had gone insane with love for his sister. Mignon dies, and Wilhelm again encounters the Amazon, Natalia, who had previously saved him. The two marry and there ends Wilhelm's apprenticeship.

MAJOR THEMES

As a *Bildungsroman, Wilhelm Meisters Lehrjahre* principally sketches the emotional, intellectual, and artistic development of its protagonist, following him from the youthful exuberance of first love to a more mature understanding of his creative capacities and social identity. As it follows Wilhelm on his picaresque quest toward self-fulfillment and awareness of his place in the world, the novel explores the young man's gradual acceptance of responsibility and his instruction in the guiding principles of reason, symbolized, critics note, by Lothario's Society of the Tower. Beyond this overarching theme of education, commentators additionally perceive in *Wilhelm Meisters Lehrjahre* Goethe's concern with the nonlinear representation of time and the recognition of multiple and contradictory sources of truth. The work is also said to reveal Goethe's thoughts on the principles of dramatic art, ideas concentrated in his influential critical discussion of Shakespeare's *Hamlet* in book five of the novel.

CRITICAL RECEPTION

Many critics of *Wilhelm Meisters Lehrjahre* have acknowledged the work's numerous technical flaws, including its inadequately realized characters, meandering plot filled with improbable coincidences, and overall lack of aesthetic unity—the last of these objections having been generally explained by the fact that Goethe paused for several years in his composition of the novel. Most commentators, however, have seen beyond these relatively minor defects and instead focused on its significant impact as the prototypical *Bildungsroman,* a work that essentially defines the salient characteristics of the education novel. Modern critics have also frequently applied the concepts of psychoanalysis to the novel, with many finding this approach useful in examining Wilhelm's forging of a mature identity and in evaluating the work's female characters, particularly the abused Mignon. Several scholars have also commented on the influence of Goethe's friend Friedrich von Schiller upon *Wilhelm Meisters Lehrjahre* and have suggested that the work represents one of the most notable achievements in early German romantic fiction.

PRINCIPAL WORKS

Buch Annette (poetry) 1767
Die Laune des Verliebten (drama) 1767
Neue Lieder (poetry) 1769
Rede Zum Schäkespears Tag (criticism) 1771
Götz von Berlichingen mit der eisernen Hand [first publication] (drama) 1773 *Goetz of Berlichingen with the Iron Hand* 1799
Von deutscher Baukunst (criticism) 1773
Clavigo (drama) 1774 *Clavidgo* (sic), 1798; also published as *Clavigo* 1897
Die Leiden des jungen Werthers (novel) 1774 *The Sorrows of Werter* 1779; also published as *Werter and Charlotte* 1786; *The Sorrows of Young Werther* 1929; and *The Sufferings of Young Werther* 1957
Stella (drama) 1776 *Stella* 1798
Die Geschwister (drama) 1787 *The Sister* published in *Dramatic Pieces from the German,* 1792
lphigenie auf Tauris (drama) 1787 *lphigenia in Tauris* 1793
Der Triumph der Empfindsamkeit [first publication] (drama) 1787
Egmont (drama) 1788 *Egmont* 1841
Faust: Ein Fragment (poetry) 1790
Torquato Tasso (drama) 1790 *Torquato Tasso* published in *Torquato Tasso: A Dramatic Poem from the German with Other German Poetry,* 1827
Versuch die Metamorphose der Pflanzen zu erklären (essay) 1790 *Goethe's Botany: The Metamorphosis of Plants, 1790. Tobler's Ode to Nature, 1782* 1946
Beiträge zur Optik (essay) 1791-92
Der Gross-Kophta (drama) 1792
Der Bürgergeneral [first publication] (drama) 1793
Reineke Fuchs (poetry) 1794 *History of Renard the Fox* 1840; also published as *Reynard the Fox* 1853
Römische Elegien (poetry) 1795 *Goethe's Roman Elegies* 1876?
Wilhelm Meisters Lehrjahre (novel) 1795-96 *Wilhelm Meister's Apprenticeship* 1824
Venezianische Epigramme (poetry) 1796
Xenien [with Friedrich Schiller] (poetry) 1797 *Goethe and Schiller's Xenions* 1896
Hermann und Dorothea (poetry) 1798 *Herman and Dorothea* 1801
Die natürliche Tochter (drama) 1804
Winckelmann und sein Jahrhundert (biography) 1805
Faust (drama) 1808 *Faust* published in *Faust: A Drama by Goethe and Schiller's Song of the Bell,* 1823
Die Wahlverwandtschaften (novel) 1809 *Elective Affinities* published in *Novels and Tales by Göethe,* 1854
Pandora (unfinished drama) 1810
Wanderers Sturmlied (poetry) 1810
Zur Farbenlehre (essay) 1810 *Theory of Colours* 1840; also published as *Goethe's Colour Theory* 1971
Aus meinen Leben: Dichtung und Wahrheit (autobiography) 1811-22 *Memoirs of Goethe: Written by Himself* 1824; also published as *The Autobiography of Goethe: Truth and Poetry from My Own Life* 1848
Des Epimenides Erwachen (drama) 1815
Sonnette (poetry) 1815
Italienische Reise (travel essay) 1816 *Travels in Italy* published in *Goethe's Travels in Italy Together with His Second Residence in Rome and Fragments on Italy* 1885; also translated as *Italian Journey* 1970
Ueber Kunst und Altertum von Goethe 6 vols. (criticism) 1816-32
Zur Morphologie (essay) 1817-23

West-öestlicher Divan (poetry) 1819 *Goethe's West-Easterly Divan* 1877; also published as *West-Eastern Divan* 1914
Wilhelm Meisters Wanderjahre; oder, Die Entsagenden (novel) 1821 *Wilhelm Meister's Travels; or, The Renunciants* published in *German Romance,* 1827
Die Campagne in Frankreich: 1792 (history) 1822 *Campaign in France in the Year 1792* 1849
Trilogie der Leidenschaft (poetry) 1823
Marienbader Elegie (poetry) 1827
Briefwechsel zwischen Schiller und Goethe (letters) 1828 *Correspondence between Schiller and Goethe from 1794 to 1805* 1845
Novelle (novella) 1828 *Goethe's Novel* 1837; also published as *Novella* in *The Sorrows of Young Werther and Novella* 1972
**Wilhelm Meisters Wanderjahre; oder, Die Entsagenden* (novel) 1828 *Wilhelm Meister's Travels: Translated from the Enlarged Edition* 1882
Annalen: Tag-und Jahreshefte (journal) 1830 *Annals; or, Day and Year Papers* 1901
Faust II (drama) 1832 *Goethe's Faust: Part II* 1836
Gespräche mit Goethe in den letzten Jahren seines Lebens: 1823-1832 [with J. P. Eckermann] (conversations) 1837-48 *Conversations with Goethe in the Last Years of His Life* 1839
The Poems of Goethe (poetry) 1846
Goethes sämmtliche Werke 30 vols. (poetry, drama, essays, novels, novellas, short stories, criticism, history, biography, autobiography, letters, librettos) 1848
Goethes sämmtliche Gedichte (poetry) 1869
Goethe's Works 9 vols. (autobiography, drama, poetry, novels, essays, travel essays) 1885
†*Goethes Faust in urspünglicher Gestalt nach der Göch hausenschen Abschrift herausgegeben* (drama) 1888
Wilhelm Meisters theatricalische Sendung (unfinished novel) 1911 *Wilhelm Meister's Theatrical Mission* 1913
Werke 14 vols. (poetry, drama, novels, novellas, short stories, autobiography, biography, criticism, essays, history) 1961-64

*This work is a revision of the earlier *Wilhelm Meisters Wanderjahre; oder, Die Enstagenden.*

†This work is generally referred to as *Urfaust.*

CRITICISM

Frederick Amrine (essay date 1983)

SOURCE: "Comic Configurations and Types in *Wilhelm Meisters Lehrjahre,*" in *Seminar: A Journal of Germanic Studies,* Vol. 19, No. 1, February, 1983, pp. 6-19.

[*In the following essay, Amrine traces comic archetypes, symbols, and themes in* Wilhelm Meisters Lehrjahre.]

I

Goethe himself ranked the ***Lehrjahre*** among the 'most incalculable productions,'[1] yet critics have more often complained that the final sum is drawn all-too-neatly.[2] The ending of the novel, where all the loose ends of the plot are tied up in a flurry of disclosures leading to three marriages, has been felt to be inorganic—something appropriate to a comic novel or even a *Trivialroman,* but very much out of place in the progenitor of a new and complex historical genre. Emil Staiger has gone so far as to suggest a failure of nerve on Goethe's part, a victory of convenience over aesthetic judgment: 'Mit den Vermählungen, die am Schluβ bevorstehen, fallen wir vollends in die Romanschablone einer vorklassischen Literatur zurück. Goethe wolhe fertig werden und lieβ es bei einer Fabel bewenden, die allzu deutlich die Spuren einer klugen Disposition verrät.'[3]

Yet comic elements are to be found not merely at the conclusion, but throughout the ***Lehrjahre***; both the extent and the importance of these elements have been consistently ignored or greatly undervalued. The novel's entire plot-configuration, as well as numerous character types, symbols and themes, correspond closely to Northrop Frye's descriptions of archetypal comic form. By tracing these configurations, types, symbols and themes through the ***Lehrjahre,*** this study will seek to indicate how comic form works as a powerful integrating factor in what is essentially a comic novel.

Other critics have noted comic elements elsewhere in the ***Lehrjahre,*** but have remained content with general assertions about the spirit of the novel, or sought to subsume them beneath another generic designation. The novel's first interpreter found most remarkable in its overall impression 'daβ Ernst und Schmerz durchaus wie ein Schattenspiel versinken und der leichte Humor darüber vollkommen Meister wird.'[4] Friedrich Schlegel also discerned an underlying comic spirit in the novel, calling it a 'heitere Erzählung'[5] and underscoring the third book's 'starke Annäherung zur Komödie' in particular (p. 31). More recently, Joachim von der Thüsen has found comic types and formulas in the novel's opening scene, and Hans Reiss has traced 'Lustspielhaftes' through the whole of the ***Lehrjahre,*** although he finds the comic elements concentrated principally at the beginning and end.[6] Mariane disguising herself as an officer, the 'romantic triangle' of Book One, the ubiquitous 'Versteck- und Rollenspiel,' Philine's playful and flirtatious nature, the incongruity between Wilhelm's illusions and reality, Mignon's sexual ambiguity and the atmosphere of 'Heiterkeit' that pervades the worlds of the itinerant actors and rococo nobility—all these Reiss finds typical of Enlightenment comedy. Moreover, Reiss points out that such amalgamation of genres, the inclusion of dramatic features in prose narratives, is altogether typical of Goethe's age (p. 142). However, even Reiss resists the momentum of his own evidence: he is committed to the notion of *Bildung* as that which ultimately unifies the text (p. 129), and thus concludes that the comic features of the ***Lehrjahre*** 'in no way make it a comic novel' (p. 140).

Yet, as more than one critic has well argued, taking *Bildung* as the structuring principle of the ***Lehrjahre*** proves exceedingly problematical: Wilhelm does not undergo *Bildung* in any clearly defined or programmatic sense of the term (e.g., the 'aesthetic education' leading to a harmonious development and integration of all his powers asserted by earlier interpreters of the novel),[7] while if one understands *Bildung* as mere unspecified development, the notion becomes so vague that few novels would *not* qualify as *Bildungsromane*. One wonders whether the generic term *Bildungsroman* has come to have very much meaning at all when applied to the ***Lehrjahre;*** in any case, the term's validity is dubious enough that it can hardly be used as an excuse for not pursuing other promising interpretations. Indeed, it seems high time for new approaches.

II

Taken as a whole, the plot of the ***Lehrjahre*** exhibits the same 'ternary form' as Northrop Frye's comic modality.[8] Frye's literary modalities (comedy, tragedy, satire and irony, and romance) are 'pregeneric'; that is, they cut across historical genres in the way that tonalities in music transcend but are at the same time shared by different musical forms. Such an approach seems particularly well-suited to a work like the ***Lehrjahre*** that is generically ambiguous in the way described by Reiss above: thus our study of comic form in the ***Lehrjahre*** will employ Frye's masterly work on comedy as its touchstone.

The movement of comedy begins with a temporary thwarting or 'blocking' of the 'comic drive,' which is most commonly that of two lovers striving to become one. Yet comedy need not be romantic: the fundamental comic drive is directed toward union and socialization in the broadest sense, and anything that seeks to thwart this movement (such as a 'humour' in the comedy of manners) can perform the blocking function. The tension of comedy often results from competition between two different societies, one entrenched and the other trying to take form, and the most common form of this struggle is a conflict between the society identified with the 'father' and that of the 'son,' with a romantic attachment usually the bone of contention. This first comic phase has been completed in the ***Lehrjahre*** by the end of book one: Wilhelm's romantic striving to unite with Mariane has been effectively blocked, and his struggle against the bourgeois society of the 'father' (a generic term that fits Norberg, Werner and Melina's 'judges' as well as Wilhelm's own father) leads to a break with that world in favour of the life of an itinerant actor.

The second phase is characterized by 'confusion and sexual license'; Frye also terms it 'the phase of temporarily lost identity' (*NP,* p. 76). The comic action descends into a world of personal, sexual and social ambiguity, a carnivalesque 'Umwertung aller Werte' where 'illusions caused by disguise, obsession, hypocrisy, or unknown parentage' abound (*AC,* p. 170). The worlds of the actors and the *Rokokoadel* in books two through five could hardly be described more accurately: Reiss has touched on some of these elements in the aforementioned study, and I will discuss others further below.[9]

In its third phase, the dialectic of comic form evolves from picaresque chaos into integrations at a higher level in the form of new personal, social and 'dual' identities (*NP,* p. 78; *AC,* pp. 43-4 and 163-5; *SS,* pp. 136-7). The new social identity achieved in comedy's third phase has two major components: a reversal of societal standing, and utopianism. Usually the new society forms around the new 'dual' identity of the hero and his bride. The establishment of a new 'dual' identity in the third phase depends upon a dispelling of the illusions created in the second; this is usually accompanied by a sudden turn in the plot, a revelation that Frye terms 'the comic discovery, *anagnorisis* or *cognitio*' (*AC,* p. 163). Usually the *cognitio* has to do with a revelation concerning the social status of the hero or parentage of the heroine, or both, that renders either or both suddenly marriageable. Comic revelations in the third phase also create or initiate a movement toward a new 'singular' or personal identity on the part of the protagonist. Frye's descriptions of the third phase of comedy's ternary form fit well the events in books seven and eight of the ***Lehrjahre,*** where Wilhelm enters the province of the utopian *Turmgesellschaft,* is united with Natalie, and achieves painful self-knowledge as the mysteries of his own biography are successively revealed.[10]

III

Having sketched in broad strokes the plot of the ***Lehrjahre*** and shown it to reflect comic ternary form, I turn now to consider in greater detail certain archetypal comic figures, symbolic configurations and themes that can be discerned within the ***Lehrjahre.*** Frye has noted that comedy generally develops away from mimetic realism in the direction of symbolism, idealization and convention (*NP,* pp. 8 and 12); part of this tendency is for comic fictions to replace individualized portraits with easily recognizable, standard 'types.' Goethe's 'realistic tic' never allows his characters to become schematic or abstract, yet his complex creations in the ***Lehrjahre*** can nevertheless be seen as embodying the functions of comic 'types'—less so in the realistic-satirical middle books, more so in the first and last books, in which the novel tends toward the 'romantic' side of the comic modality. The most important of these types are the hero and the heroine, the *senex,* the fool and the 'Eros figure.'

Comedy treats its heroes and heroines in two fundamentally different ways, depending whether it is chiefly satirical or romantic in tenor. Satirical comedy tends to surround a 'somewhat dullish pair of technical leads' with blocking characters who become the real focus of attention, while romantic comedy tends much more to focus upon the final scenes of recognition and reconciliation (*AC,* p. 167). In the ***Lehrjahre*** one finds both treatments: in the early and especially the middle books, Wilhelm is very much the dull and uninteresting hero one would expect in this picaresque-satiric phase, while in the last two books he becomes considerably more interesting as his romantic union with Natalie becomes more and more the focal point of the novel. Our attention is no longer diverted by a colourful band of itinerant actors and actresses; even Mignon and the Harfner stand at the periphery, tragic figures unable to find a place in the final comic synthesis. Outwardly, Wilhelm experiences a complicated *anagnorisis* in which many identities are revealed: not only those of the 'schöne Amazone,' Felix, Mignon, Therese, the Harfner and the Abbé, but also, in a way, the identity of Mariane, whose real nature Wilhelm had so long and so tragically mistaken. Yet outer events also call forth self-reflection and memory that were hardly present earlier; Wilhelm's attempts to come to terms with his own past are very much an internalized process of 'recognition and reconciliation,' such as that occasioned by Mignon's death:

> So saβ er neben ihr auf dem Kanapee, auf dem er Natalie zuerst angetroffen hatte. Er dachte mit groβer Schnelle eine Reihe von Schicksalen durch, oder vielmehr er dachte nicht, er lieβ das auf seine Seele wirken, was er nicht entfernen konnte. Es gibt Augenblicke des Lebens, in welchen die Begebenheiten gleich geflügelten Weberschiffchen vor uns sich hin und wider bewegen und unaufhaltsam ein Gewebe vollenden, die wir mehr oder weniger selbst gesponnen und angelegt haben.[11]

In a subtle metamorphosis of the convention, Wilhelm is made to experience an 'inner *anagnorisis*' as well, an often painful dose of self-awareness symbolized by the frequent references to mirror-gazing (e.g. ***HA*** VII, 433, 489, 499 and 505) and, above all, by Wilhelm's reading of his own biography (***HA*** VII, 504-5), in which he is granted a 'narrator's-eye-view' of himself.[12] By the end of the novel, the dullish 'Kaufmannssohn' of the earlier, more realistic books has become not only a comic type, but even an archetypal figure, a 'Königssohn' by virtue of his identification with the 'sick prince' in the rediscovered painting and with 'Saul, der Sohn Kis, der ausging, seines Vaters Eselinnen zu suchen, und ein Königreich fand' (***HA*** VII, 610). Here the comic novel shows its roots in a ritual still evident in Greek Old Comedy, where the victorious hero is crowned king of a newly-formed society. The heroine is an enormously complex and ambiguous function in the novel, yet an analogous progression can be seen in the development of Mariane and Natalie, who might be termed the 'co-heroines.' The heroine of the realistic earlier books becomes an ever more spectral presence as the novel progresses until she 'appears' for the last time, reconciled with Wilhelm's father, in his dream (***HA*** VII, 425-6), while Natalie is so completely idealized (typical bordering on the archetypal) that she can appear in the earlier books only as a dream-like, almost mythical figure.

The blocking action of comedy is, in its archetypal aspect, an Oedipal conflict between father and son:[13] the most important blocking character is thus the father-figure or *senex*. In the ***Lehrjahre,*** this function is again complex and ambiguous: Wilhelm is opposed by no less than four *senex*-figures. The first is of course his own father, who opposes Wilhelm's involvement in the theatrical life, and thus his involvement with Mariane. Here the Oedipal situation is disguised, but present by virtue of a symbol and a surrogate. The father fulfills his Oedipal function symbolically in two ways: by opposing the 'younger' society of the theater; and by selling the painting of 'Der kranke Königssohn,' which depicts the classic Oedipal situation of the son desiring his father's bride. In his conversation with the stranger in book one we learn that it had been Wilhelm's favourite painting, and that he had identified intensely with the sick prince (***HA*** VII, 70). The paternal surrogate, who opposes Wilhelm directly, is Norberg. Norberg conforms perfectly to Frye's description of the father-surrogate fulfilling the function of the *senex:* 'The opponent to the hero's wishes, when not the father, is generally someone who partakes of the father's close relation to established society: that is, a rival with less youth and more money' (*AC,* pp. 164-5). Werner represents the third *senex:* he, too, stands in 'close relation to established society,' and even threatens legal action in his heartless struggle to insulate Wilhelm from Mariane. Moreover, Werner appears as an 'old man' when we meet him again in book eight (***HA*** VII, 498ff.), even though he is, chronologically, a member of Wilhelm's generation. The fourth *senex,* Lothario, also rivals Wilhelm at one point for the same woman, although Wilhelm's desire for Therese is shown at the end to belong to the blocking complication rather than the resolution. Lothario has all the makings of a good *senex:* compared to Wilhelm, he has closer ties to established society, is older and has more money. Yet from another point of view Lothario is also a romantic comic hero freed by *anagnorisis* from the threat of incest that blocks his own desires. Perhaps one should term Lothario a 'temporary *senex*' or a 'pseudo-*senex*' in his relationship to Wilhelm, for while he does not embody this function purely, he does stand in a fatherly relationship to Wilhelm and seems, temporarily at least, to compete with him as a representative of the 'older' society. Although Lothario is certainly a 'father-figure' to Wilhelm, he is more than just a *senex:* Lothario (as well as the Abbé and, to a lesser extent, Jarno) are in a way benevolent father-figures who educate Wilhelm and thus help him toward the fulfillment of his desire. The point is not to make each character in the ***Lehrjahre*** fit neatly into the pigeonhole of a prescribed comic role, but to show that the roles are indeed present in the ***Lehrjahre*** as functions of comic form, however varied, transformed and symbolically removed.

Another important function, particularly in Shakespearean comedy, is that of the fool, which Frye terms a 'spectator role' because the fool stands outside, or is at least not fully identified with the society that he mocks:

> The fool, when technically so, is frequently (Lavache, Touchstone, Feste) said to belong to the older generation, his jokes in a different idiom from what the society of the comedy wants and expects. He is often . . . said to be lustful, more inclined to get girls into trouble than to take responsibility for them afterward. (*NP,* pp. 92-3)

Frye's description fits Friedrich (the Friedrich of book eight, that is) remarkably well. He, too, stands outside, mocks, and is an embarrassment to the comic society of the *Turmgesellschaft.* And while it is true that Friedrich is not a member of the older generation, his way of speaking certainly is: a witty, old-fashioned idiom peppered with Biblical and classical allusions that he happened to have learned while entertaining himself in a Baroque library[14] together with the girl he has 'got into trouble' (***HA*** VII, 555ff.). Friedrich also bears some resemblance to the character type of the 'tricky slave' of classical comedy, whose machinations—like Friedrich's eavesdropping—usually constitute the 'efficient cause' of the comic resolution.[15]

Another comic character type who plays a central role in the consummation of the comic drive toward erotic union is what Frye calls the 'Eros figure' (a potentially confusing term that should not be equated with the Eros-figure in Greek mythology). Frye's 'Eros figure' is 'in himself sexually contained, being in a sense both male and female, and needing no expression of love beyond himself' (*NP*, p. 82). In many Shakespearean comedies, this function is fulfilled by the heroine disguised as a boy (*NP*, p. 83). In the ***Lehrjahre,*** it is fulfilled by Mignon. Mignon is, of course, an extremely complex and ambiguous figure with other important dimensions, yet as one proceeds toward the final books she becomes increasingly identified with this symbolic function. In her study of Mignon and Balzac's Seraphita, Marie Delcourt recalls the ancient myth of the hermaphrodite, whose role, like that of Frye's comic Eros figure, is to bring about and oversee the erotic union: 'Goethe a retrouvé un archétype de la pensée religieuse la plus archaïque, celui de l'être doué des deux puissances, qui n'en exerce aucune, mais qui est invoqué, ainsi que le fut l'Hermaphrodite grec, comme *daimon* tutélaire de l'union sexuelle.'[16] Mignon 'oversees' Wilhelm's night of love with Philine, and it is because of Mignon that Wilhelm travels to Natalie's castle, initiating their comic union (***HA*** VII, 508ff.). Yet Mignon is beyond sexuality in the ways that both Frye and Delcourt describe.[17]

IV

Just as new light is shed upon a mysterious character such as Mignon by viewing her as an archetypal comic figure, new light can be shed upon some of the ***Lehrjahre's*** most important themes, symbols and plot-devices by viewing them within the context of comic form. At first these elements seem unrelated; but when they are viewed under the aspect of comic form, a mutually illuminating and interdependent configuration emerges. To a remarkable extent they correspond to Northrop Frye's catalogue of 'themes' that run throughout Shakespearean romantic comedy: 'The storm at sea, the identical twins, the heroine disguised as a boy, the retreat into the forest, the heroine with the mysterious father, the disappearing ruler: these themes occur so often that in some plays—*Twelfth Night,* for example—a whole group of such formulas is restated' (*NP*, p. 7). Although the source of the list is Shakespearean, these themes and devices are far from unique to Shakespeare: they are recurrent archetypes within a long comic tradition that Shakespeare assimilated and restated in its essence. Goethe knew extremely well both Shakespeare and the comic tradition that Shakespeare knew: thus we need not be surprised that such themes surface together with other comic elements in the ***Lehrjahre.***

One of these themes is not present as such in the ***Lehrjahre:*** 'the storm at sea,' G. Wilson Knight's Shakespearean 'tempest'[18] that symbolizes individual passion and social upheaval. Symbolic drowning, near-drowning or actual drowning occur more frequently in Shakespeare's romances *(Pericles, The Winter's Tale, The Tempest)* than in his comedies, although Viola and her twin brother survive a shipwreck in *Twelfth Night,* and Falstaff is ritually dunked in *The Merry Wives.* Similarly, the symbolic theme of drowning becomes central only in Goethe's romantic ***Wanderjahre,*** where comic form has modulated into romance.[19] Yet it is present at one place in the ***Lehrjahre:*** in Wilhelm's dream at the beginning of book seven, in which Felix falls into a pond and nearly drowns, but is miraculously saved by Natalie. The closely related symbol of fire, however, is to be found in book five, with the same import.

'The disappearing ruler,' pure myth in the literary modes that are not mimetically 'displaced' in Frye's sense, emerges in the ***Lehrjahre*** in the only way possible in more realistic fictions, as a significant image associated with the hero (*AC*, pp. 136-7): I mean of course Wilhelm's association with the 'sick prince' in the painting of the same name. Not only does the painting disappear until book eight (and with it the prince's kingly father), but Wilhelm's 'kingly' father disappears as well, both Wilhelm's actual father, who dies but seems to play the Ghost, and his dramatic 'father,' the man who really performs the elder Hamlet, mysteriously appearing and then disappearing until book eight.

Closely related to 'the disappearing ruler' is 'the heroine with the mysterious father.' A clear variant is again Wilhelm, who becomes 'the *hero* with the mysterious father' when he plays Hamlet. His own father is anything but 'mysterious'—until Wilhelm believes that he has actually returned from the dead to play the Ghost. The novel does not have a single heroine upon whom all would agree, but all the major candidates (I do not consider Philine or the 'schöne Seele' serious contenders) have suitably 'mysterious' fathers: Mariane is an orphan, and her parentage thus a total mystery; Mignon's father long seems to be 'der groβe Teufel' (which is mysterious enough in itself), but is actually the even more mysterious Harfner; Therese's father dies unable to communicate to his daughter the mystery of her parentage; Natalie's upbringing—the office of a father—is entrusted entirely to the Abbé, about whom nobody seems to know much of anything.[20]

The essence of the 'retreat into the forest' is the establishment of a social utopia. The clear analogy to this Shakespearean theme in the ***Lehrjahre*** is the movement of the novel's action into the province of the *Turmgesellschaft.* The society of the *Turmgesellschaft* exhibits many of the most important characteristics of the 'forest world' or 'green world' Frye finds in Shakespearean comedy (e.g., *NP*, p. 141). The forest utopia is 'the place where the upper or purely human world toward which the comic action moves begins to take shape, and around which that world crystallizes' (*NP*, p. 141); one might also say, as has often been said of the *Turmgesellschaft*, a world of enlightened 'Humanität.'[21]

Another theme that 'runs through all the history of comedy' (*AC*, p. 181), that of 'the identical twins' or doubled characters, is almost maddeningly ubiquitous in the ***Lehrjahre***. It seems to be a disease with which the *Turmgesellschaft* and those around it are afflicted. Natalie, the 'schöne Amazone,' is hauntingly similar in appearance to her sister, the Gräfin (***HA*** VII, 240), and their handwriting is so similar that Wilhelm mistakes Natalie's for the Gräfin's (***HA*** VII, 508 and 511). Moreover, the 'schöne Amazone' looks so much like the 'schöne Seele' that Wilhelm mistakes a painting of the aunt for a bad portrait of Natalie (***HA*** VII, 517). Lothario mistakes a cousin for the *Pächterstochter* herself (***HA*** VII, 466), the Abbé has a twin brother (***HA*** VII, 494 and 511), and Mignon dresses as an angel to help celebrate the birthday of twin sisters (***HA*** VII, 514). Even those previously unconnected with the *Turmgesellschaft* become susceptible when they enter into its environs: in Wilhelm's dream, Natalie even 'doubles' Felix as a kind of magic trick (***HA*** VII, 426)! As Lieselotte Dieckmann has noted, these doublings usually have the effect of temporarily blurring or confusing the identity of certain characters.[22] Yet this is but half the effect: the other is the strong establishment of identity that occurs when the ambiguities are clarified, as they are in the final two books. This change in function represents a movement away from the second into the third phase of Frye's ternary comic form, from ambiguity and alienation into the creation of new forms of personal, social and 'dual' identity.[23] The confusion of identity that results from doubling can be harmless (for example Harlequin in the *commedia dell' arte*, who among other things divides himself in two and holds dialogues with himself) or a sinister *Doppelgänger*-experience that can produce insanity (*NP*, p. 78; *SS*, p. 117)—as happens when Wilhelm 'doubles' as the Graf.

'The heroine disguised as a boy' or hermaphrodism, perhaps the most important comic theme in the ***Lehrjahre***, also has a dual function. In the second phase of comedy's ternary form, it contributes to the confusion of identity by creating sexual ambiguity, while in the third, it works as a symbol of union and psychic wholeness to establish new, higher forms of identity. In dramatic comedy, the movement toward resolution is often effected by the heroine disguising herself as a boy (*Twelfth Night* and *As You Like It* spring immediately to mind); in the ***Lehrjahre***, the comic movement is propelled by a whole series of hermaphroditic heroines. The only major female figure who exhibits no sexual ambiguity is Philine—Laertes calls her 'die wahre Eva, die Stamm-Mutter des weiblichen Geschlechts' (***HA*** VII, 100).[24] Beginning with Mariane's entrance in officer's dress on the second page of the novel, all the other heroines contribute either to the sexual ambiguity of the second phase or to the new, trans-sexual identity of the third, or to both at different times. Of the last possibility, the prime example is Mignon. She is first introduced as 'ein junges Geschöpf,' 'das Kind,' 'die Gestalt' (***HA*** VII, 91), and the ambiguity of her sex is preserved throughout the earlier books by pronominal sleight-of-hand, male clothing, and her constant assertion that she wants to be a lad (***HA*** VII, 207, 236-7 and 336). In this second phase, the ambiguity of her identity seems, as Staiger has argued, to be pre-sexual;[25] in the third phase, however, she too exhibits, like the 'Amazonen,' 'eine über das Geschlecht erhabene Menschlichkeit,'[26] a new, 'angelic' identity beyond sexuality that is adumbrated in her song:

> Und jene himmlischen Gestalten,
> Sie fragen nicht nach Mann und Weib,
> Und keine Kleider, keine Falten,
> Umgeben den verklärten Leib.
>
> (***HA*** VII, 516)

Mariane is also initially ambiguous, but shown in the final books (***HA*** VII, 480) to have been a 'true hermaphrodite' when she again donned her 'Offizierstracht' to assert both her individual and a new 'dual' identity by remaining faithful to Wilhelm. Mignon's initial ambiguity, as well as Landrinette's (***HA*** VII, 104) and the Baronesse's (***HA*** VII, 188), contribute to the carnivalesque sexual ambivalence of the second phase, although the earlier, 'low comic' books contain important 'Rückwirkungen' from the third phase, anticipations of the higher forms of identity revealed there. Most important is the apparition of the 'schöne Amazone' (***HA*** VII, 226ff.), who reminds Wilhelm of the 'Mannweiblichkeit' of Tasso's Chlorinde (***HA*** VII, 26-7 and 235). Therese is a 'true amazon' who wears men's clothing and 'can put a hundred men to shame' (***HA*** VII, 439, 446-7 and 454), while even the 'schöne Seele' exhibits 'männlicher[n] Trotz' by demanding complete freedom in the way she conducts her life (***HA*** VII, 379). There are even hints that Wilhelm is on his way to achieving hermaphrodism: his union with Natalie is symbolic rather than erotic, which led Körner to write of him: 'Männlichkeit und Weiblichkeit erscheinen in ihren bedeutendsten Gattungen, und zwischen beiden sehen wir Meister, als eine mittlere Natur—eine Art von Hermaphrodit.'[27] In its highest form, the form in which it is presented in the final books of the ***Lehrjahre***, hermaphrodism represents a merger of comic personal identity and 'dual' identity, a metaphor of psychic wholeness. Schiller's metaphor for the aesthetic condition of balance and inner harmony is Juno Ludovisi, whom he overtly terms a hermaphroditic 'weiblicher Gott' and 'göttliches Weib.'[28] In this highest manifestation, the theme of hermaphrodism is, like comedy itself, a symbol of 'man's quest for wholeness,'[29] a dream of some future time 'quand le désir aura été aboli et avec lui les conséquences de la chute.'[30]

By tracing numerous comic configurations, character types, symbols and themes through the ***Lehrjahre***, this study has attempted to show that the comic ending of the novel is not an inorganic, inartistic appendage, but rather an integral part of a pervasive comic structure. Indeed, it seems impossible to understand the unity of certain themes long held to be central to the novel (hermaphrodism and the 'Königssohn' are the most important) outside of the context of comic form. This approach represents, moreover, an alternative to the problematical notion of *Bildung,* a way of describing the structure of the ***Lehrjahre*** in terms of purely literary categories. Might this not also represent, perhaps, a way of overcoming the ever-more-dubious generic classifications *Bildungsroman, Entwicklungsroman* and *Erziehungsroman*—designations that have tended to isolate the ***Lehrjahre,*** and so many other German novels, from the mainstream of Western literature?

Notes

1. J. P. Eckermann, *Gespräche mit Goethe in den letzten Jahren seines Lebens* (Zürich: Artemis-Verlag, 1948), p. 141 (18 January 1825): 'Es gehört dieses Werk übrigens zu den inkalkulabelsten Produktionen, wozu mir fast selbst der Schlüssel fehlt.'

2. Even Friedrich Schlegel's laudatory review of 1798 expresses misgivings about the unity of the novel as a whole ('Die gewöhnlichen Erwartungen von Einheit und Zusammenhang täuscht dieser Roman eben so oft als er sie erfüllt.') and the ending in particular, which he finds 'fast allgemein seltsam und unbefriedigend' ('Über Goethes Meister,' in *Goethes Wilhelm Meister: Zur Rezeptionsgeschichte der Lehr- und Wanderjahre,* ed. K. Gille (Königsstein/Ts.: Athenäum, 1979), pp. 29-30. Further on, Schlegel goes through strange contortions attempting to defend the 'Willkürlichkeit' of the ending (pp. 36-7).

3. E. Staiger, *Goethe* (Zürich: Atlantis, 1959), 11, 172. Other critics have noted the ending's formulaic comic elements in passing, but then either failed to pursue or retreated from the implications of their presence in the novel. P. Pfaff, for example, sees the resolution of the conflict in the ending as 'Lustspiel,' but fails to elaborate ('Plädoyer für eine typologische Interpretation von "Wilhelm Meisters Lehrjahren",' *Text und Kontext,* 5 [1977], 52), and H. Thomé, who finds in the ending elements of the *commedia dell' arte (Roman und Naturwissenschaft: Eine Studie zur Vorgeschichte der deutschen Klassik* (Frankfurt: Peter Lang, 1978), p. 481). According to Thomé, Goethe turned to comedy at the end of the *Lehrjahre* in order to guarantee a kind of synthesis and harmony he had sought, unsuccessfully, in his scientific studies (p. 482). Yet Thomé expressly denies that these comic elements have any further implications for the *Lehrjahre* as a whole ('Nun sind die "Lehrjahre" gewiß keine "erzählte Komödie",' p. 482). Staiger's judgment is harsh, but perhaps more honest.

4. Schiller, letter to Goethe, 28 June 1796.

5. 'Über Goethes Meister,' p. 24.

6. J. von der Thüsen, 'Der Romananfang in Wilhelm Meisters Lehrjahren,' *DVjs,* 43 (1969), 622-30; H. Reiss, 'Lustspielhaftes in *Wilhelm Meisters Lehrjahre,*' in *Goethezeit: Studien zur Erkenntnis und Rezeption Goethes und seiner Zeitgenossen: Festschrift für Stuart Atkins,* ed. G. Hoffmeister (Bern und München: Francke, 1981), pp. 129-44.

7. K. May argued convincingly against this notion as early as 1957 ('*Willhelm Meisters Lehrjahre,* ein Bildungsroman?' *DVjs,* 31 (1957), 1-37), and H. Eichner, among others, has rejected this view in the strongest terms: 'Bestehen wir also darauf, die "Lehrjahre" als die Darstellung einer Entwicklung zu einem einfachen, wohldefinierten, widerspruchsfreien Bildungsideal zu interpretieren, so kommen wir zu dem Ergebnis, dieser Roman sei Goethe mißglückt. Es fragt sich nur, ob ein solches Verfahren berechtigt ist.' ('Zur Deutung von "Wilhelm Meisters Lehrjahren",' *Jb.d.fr.dt. Hochstifts* 1966, p. 176).

8. See, e.g., *Anatomy of Criticism: Four Essays* (Princeton: Princeton University Press, 1957), p. 171 (hereafter: *AC*). See also Frye's important studies *A Natural Perspective: The Development of Shakespearean Comedy and Romance* (New York: Columbia University Press, 1965) (*NP*) and *The Secular Scripture: A Study of the Structure of Romance* (Cambridge: Harvard University Press, 1976) (*SS*).

9. For a fuller discussion of comic form in the *Lehrjahre* generally, see F. Amrine, 'Goethe's Human Comedy: The Unity of the *Wilhelm Meister*-Novels,' Diss. Harvard 1981, pp. 1-153.

10. The establishment of these new forms of identity is treated at length in Amrine, pp. 99-124.

11. Goethe, *Werke: Hamburger Ausgabe,* vol. VII, 7th ed., ed. E. Trunz (Hamburg: Christian Wegner, 1968), p. 544. Citations of this edition will hereafter be abbreviated '*HA*.'

12. For a fuller discussion of this important moment in the novel, see Amrine, pp. 116-24.

13. N. Frye, 'The Argument of Comedy,' in *English Institute Essays,* 1948, ed. D. Robertson (New York: Columbia University Press, 1949), p. 58.

14. See the commentary by E. Trunz, *HA* VII, 703.

15. N. Frye, 'The Argument of Comedy, p. 59. Thomé also ascribes to Friedrich an important function: rather abstractly, he views Friedrich not as a 'fool,' but as a 'Symbol des Humors' (p. 482).

16. M. Delcourt, 'Deux interpretations romanesques du mythe de l'androgyne Mignon et Seraphita,' *Revue des langues vivantes,* 38 (1972), 239.

17. Cf. H. Ammerlahn, 'Mignons nachgetragene Vorgeschichte und das Inzestmotiv: Zur Genese und Symbolik der Goetheschen Geniusgestalten,' *Monatshefte,* 64 (1972), 15-22. Ammerlahn offers an interpretation of Mignon that is different, yet closely related to that offered here. He sees Mignon as a 'genius-figure born out of the protagonist's longing for the ideal, out of a mental love relationship poetically equated with that between man and woman' (p. 15). Rather different perspectives on Mignon are to be found in two recent studies: W. Gilby, 'The Structural Signifi-

cance of Mignon in *Wilhelm Meisters Lehrjahre,' Seminar,* 16 (1980), 136-150 and H. Ammerlahn, 'Puppe-Tänzer-Dämon-Genius-Engel: Naturkind, Poesiekind und Kunstwerdung bei Goethe,' *The German Quarterly,* 54 (1981), 19-32.

18. G. W. Knight, *The Shakespearean Tempest* (London: Methuen, 1953[3]), *passim.*
19. On the *Wanderjahre* as romance, see Amrine, 'Goethe's Human Comedy,' pp. 154-234, and Amrine, 'Romance Narration in *Wilhelm Meisters Wanderjahre,' The German Quarterly,* 55 (1982), 29-38.
20. The 'schöne Seele,' for example, describes him as 'ein wunderbarer Mann, den man für einen französischen Geistlichen hält, ohne daβ man recht von seiner Herkunft unterrichtet ist' (*HA* VII, 419).
21. A more picaresque variation on this theme is found in the middle books, where the itinerant actors attempt to form a kind of 'anti-society' in parodistic opposition to the 'official' social order. Melina establishes a 'kleine Polizeiverordnung' within the Graf's castle (*HA* VII, 163); later they imagine themselves as a 'Republik' replete with Senate, and finally a 'wandernde Kolonie' and a 'wanderndes Reich' (*HA* VII, 215ff.). Although not purely comic, their society is 'carnivalesque' (in Bakhtin's sense of the term), and thus utopian in its own way.
22. L. Dieckmann, 'Repeated Mirror Reflections: The Technique of Goethe's Novels,' *Studies in Romanticism,* 1 (1961-2), 154-74.
23. Cf. Frye's discussion of the dual nature of this theme in *The Secular Scripture,* p. 117.
24. See W. Larrett, 'Wilhelm Meister and the Amazons. The quest for Wholeness,' *PEGS,* 39 (1968), 31-56.
25. Staiger, p. 166.
26. Staiger, p. 166.
27. Letter to Schiller, 5 November 1796. See Larrett, p. 52.
28. *Ueber die ästhetische Erziehung des Menschen in einer Reihe von Briefen,* letter XV. See Larrett, pp. 53-4. In his book *Goethe the Alchemist: A Study of Alchemical Symbolism in Goethe's Literary and Scientific Works* (Cambridge: Cambridge University Press, 1952), Ronald Gray stresses the hermaphroditical nature of the ultimate alchemical symbol of union, the Philosopher's Stone (p. 34), and speculates elsewhere in the same work that Mignon might have been inspired by Goethe's alchemical studies.
29. Larrett, p. 56.
30. Delcourt, p. 239.

Irene Kacandes (essay date 1990)

SOURCE: "Re-presentations of Time in *Wilhelm Meisters Lehrjahre,*" in *Seminar: A Journal of Germanic Studies,* Vol. 26, No. 2, May, 1990, pp. 95-118.

[*In the following essay, Kacandes analyzes the complex temporal and narrative organization of* Wilhelm Meisters Lehrjahre, *viewing anachrony—dissonance between the order of narration and the actual sequence of events in the storyline—as the structuring principle of the novel.*]

Having just completed the leonine task of reading the whole of ***Wilhelm Meisters Lehrjahre*** in two days, Schiller recorded his immediate impressions in a letter to Goethe (2 July 1796):

> Billig sollte ich . . . heute noch nichts schreiben; denn die erstaunliche und unerhörte Mannigfaltigkeit, die darin im eigentlichsten Sinne versteckt ist, überwältigt mich. Ich gestehe, daβ ich bis jetzt zwar die *Stetigkeit,* aber noch nicht die *Einheit* recht gefaβt habe, obwohl ich keinen Augenblick zweifle, daβ ich auch über diese noch völlige Klarheit erhalten werde, wenn bei Produkten dieser Art die Stetigkeit nicht schon mehr als die halbe Einheit ist . . . Wie ist es Ihnen gelungen, den groβen, so weit auseinandergeworfenen Kreis und Schauplatz von Personen und Begebenheiten wieder so eng zusammenzurücken.[1]

Schiller's amazement at the variety and fullness of the novel as well as his feeling of being overwhelmed—if not stunned—by it are sentiments echoed by the readers who have followed him. The underlying unity which Schiller sensed was there but could not locate has been the topic of much critical debate, from Schiller's and Goethe's own discussions of this novel's poetic qualities to the praises and polemics of Friedrich Schlegel, Novalis, and other *Frühromantiker,* and to contemporary discussions of the novel's "poeticity."[2]

In the search for unity, several scholars point to the presentation of time. Herman Meyer, for example, comments: "Es gibt wohl kaum ein episches Werk, das den Zeitstrom so leibhaftig fühlbar macht . . ." (15; also qtd. in Schumann 154).[3] Consider also Gerhard Storz's description of time in the novel: "Vergangenheit, Zukunft, Gegenwart stehen nicht hintereinander wie in einer linearen Reihe, sie laufen nicht auf getrennten Bahnen nebeneinander, sondern sie greifen ineinander, hängen auf seltsame, ja oft paradoxe Weise zusammen" ("***Wilhelm Meisters Lehrjahre***" 72). Critics' efforts to back up these generalizations, however, tend to follow one of two strategies. Either they cite characters and leitmotifs which appear and reappear at various points in the novel, creating unity through self-reflexivity, or they try to chart or at least follow the "flow" of time, the "*Stetigkeit*" Schiller sensed and commented on in the quotation above.

One of the first critics to attempt the latter was Günther Müller in 1948. His influential study, *Gestaltung-Umgestaltung in '**Wilhelm Meisters Lehrjahren**'* pinpoints several series of consecutive days in the novel and tries to establish the total amount of elapsed time [*Gesamtdauer*]. It was in the course of this work that he outlined the distinction between *Erzählzeit* and *erzählte Zeit*[4]—a point to which I will return. One assiduous attempt by Detlev Schumann to "correct" Müller's calculations for establishing the *Gesamtdauer* of ***Wilhelm Meister*** concludes: "Immerhin: Widersprüche sind da; sie stammen von Goethe selbst" (154). I do not disagree with Schumann's calculations and "corrections," but rather with his interpretation of them. For the critical obsessions with Goethe's "Additionsfehler"[5] and with the chronological plotting of the events of the novel seem to preclude consideration of how Goethe *succeeds* in creating a unifying time structure. Although the story's events may seem to be told mainly chronologically, upon closer examination one will realize that the time structure is highly contrived, anachronous, and carefully manipulated by the narrator for formal and thematic purposes. My goal, then, is to identify the *undermining* of chronology, of *erzählte Zeit,* not to prove that Goethe made "mistakes," but rather with the hope of gaining greater insight into his overall aesthetic design and purpose. I will do this by focusing on the narrator and his strategies of *pre-* and *re*-presentation, aspects of the text which have been largely overlooked.[6]

I would like to begin by considering briefly the difficulties critics have had in establishing the text's overall story time. Their efforts have been frustrated by what are accepted generally as inconsistencies in the novel itself. Such studies presuppose that story time *should* be determinable and add up correctly. After all, one could argue, ***Wilhelm Meister*** is considered the progenitor of the *Bildungsroman*-genre, *Bildung* implies a teleological process, and therefore the *Bildungsroman* presents a chronological series of events in the protagonist's life.[7] Jumps into the past, especially into a different individual's past, such as that related in Book Six of ***Wilhelm Meister,*** the story of the *schöne Seele* or "beautiful soul," are ignored. However, when entire sections of the novel are left unaccounted for, the subject of such studies cannot be "time," as, for example, Schumann's title "Die Zeit in ***Wilhelm Meisters Lehrjahre***" announces, but rather is just the forward motion of the story time. Before proceeding to my own investigation of neglected aspects of the presentation of time, let me linger over two sample "errors" Schumann uncovers.

Utilizing all references to explicit amounts of elapsed time (e.g., the *Polterer*'s statement to Wilhelm about how long ago the acting troupe left Wilhelm's hometown, II/7, 114), series of consecutive days, biological markers (e.g., the pregnancies of Mariane, Frau Melina, and Philine; aging; etc.), and behaviour (e.g., how Jarno and Wilhelm greet one another after a separation, VII/2, 428), Schumann reasons that slightly less than five years pass (149).[8] But among the myriad time indices he considers are many which contradict one another. An obvious example is Werner's description of his two sons as "gescheite Jungen" whom he sees "schon sitzen und schreiben, und rechnen, laufen, handeln und trödeln" (VIII/1, 501). This mature characterization of them conflicts not only with the small amount of objectively calculable time since their parents' wedding, but also relatively with the characterization of Felix, who must be older than they—he was conceived at the beginning of the story time more than three years before Werner's marriage—and yet is described by Werner only moments later as "ein Wurm." Schumann, as did Schiller before him, concludes that this is a mistake (153).[9] Yet even if it is a mistake in "objective" terms, would it not be more useful to ask what purpose such a discrepancy might serve? Might Goethe be trying to indicate something about Werner's personality—i.e., that he projects precocious business acumen onto his own infant offspring while perceiving others' children as less developed than they in fact are? Schumann's preoccupation with chronology prevents him from considering the possibility that this is not an artistic *flaw,* but rather a contradiction which serves an artistic purpose.

Similarly, after calculating that seventeen days pass in Book One, Schumann comments that Wilhelm's query to Mariane, "ob er sich denn nicht Vater glauben dürfe" (I/11, 43), is singularly early (136). Mariane and Wilhelm consummate their love in the ellipsis between the first and second chapters, and only ten days can have passed since then (Schumann 132-37). Mariane could not yet know with certainty that she is pregnant. (Wilhelm assumes an affirmative answer from Mariane's gesture, and Mariane makes a comment on the subject to Barbara the next day [I/12, 45].) It is with regard to this example that Schumann quotes Goethe's statement about "Additionsfehler" mentioned above. Schumann concludes: "Es solle sich nun nicht darum handeln, für alle einzelnen Handlungsphasen des Romans, Kapitel um Kapitel, eine präzise Zeitberechnung durchzuführen" (137). And I would agree with him. But what he then fails to investigate is how Goethe could include precisely such a premature question and not have the reader object—at least not on a first reading or without performing the analytical gymnastics which Schumann does to discover that only ten days can have passed since Wilhelm and Mariane first had intercourse (132-33).[10] Schumann seems oblivious to one of the most interesting aspects of Goethe's art: the purposeful *undermining* of chronology. There is not merely a "discrepancy" between the amount of calculably elapsed time and "inner probability" (Schumann 136), but rather a real *tension* between the two—a tension which the reader may feel less strongly on a first reading of Book One,[11] but one which cannot be missed as (s)he reads on or rereads the beginning. This tension, I suggest, can only be resolved when one collapses chronology and lets all moments of story time reflect on one another. Thus Müller's choice to demonstrate the distinction between *Erzählzeit* and *erzählte Zeit* with ***Wilhelm Meister*** seems a particularly curious one.[12] The development of such a distinction may have been rooted in Müller's reading of similar seemingly contradictory passages as those discussed above. As readers of ***Wilhelm Meister*** ourselves, we can empathize with Schiller's and Müller's (hypothesized) frustrated desire that it should all "add up." And yet, while Müller's distinction has proved to be a powerful analytic tool, I hope to show why undue emphasis on reconstructing a chronological story is tempting, but problematic. Let us approach this larger issue by returning to the specific example at hand: Goethe's creation of a sense that the relationship between Mariane and

Wilhelm *is* sufficiently long standing for conception to have taken place and been confirmed.

The quality of the young lovers' relationship is communicated to the reader, I suggest, through a narrative anomaly which has yet to be categorized by narratologists as far as I know, and which I label "masquerading iterative." I develop my term from Gérard Genette's definition of an iterative as "a single narrative utterance tak[ing] upon itself several occurrences together of the same event (in other words . . . several events considered only in terms of their analogy)" (116). Such narratives are easily identified by their verb tense in French ("imparfait") and English ("iterative," "frequentative," or "progressive"). Although there is no separate tense for the iterative in German, it is distinguishable nonetheless by context and attendant adverbs.[13] Iterative passages are "completely traditional" and serve as "a sort of informative frame or background" for singulative narrative (Genette 116-17). The following excerpt from ***Wilhelm Meister*** appears to be a classic example of the iterative: "Er [Wilhelm] verrichtete des Tags seine Geschäfte pünktlich, entsagte *gewöhnlich* dem Schauspiel, war *abends* bei Tische unterhaltend und schlich, wenn alles zu Bette war, in seinen Mantel gehüllt, sachte zu dem Garten hinaus und eilte, alle Lindors und Leanders im Busen, unaufhaltsam zu seiner Geliebten" (I/3, 15; emphasis added). Although the verbs in the simple past tense could theoretically refer to *unique* events, the adverbs ("gewöhnlich," "abends") mark them as iteratives. One assumes Wilhelm's actions are repeated; this is a pattern of behaviour he has adopted. The context supports this since after the general pattern is established the narrator reports what happened on a particular night ("eines Abends," line 20). Alternation between iterative and singulative is common. This (ostensible) "iterative narrative" communicates the message to the reader that Wilhelm has been spending his nights with Mariane for some time. And yet, this passage is only *masquerading* as an iterative; there are no multiple "similar events" to be narrated once; there is only one event being narrated as if it had happened many times. As of the discourse time of this passage, Wilhelm is following this course of action for the *first* time. By all indications, the "eines Abends" of the next paragraph refers to only the second night of *erzählte Zeit.*

As we recall, the novel opens with an evening rendezvous between Mariane and Wilhelm during which they consummate their love. The next morning Wilhelm is confronted by his mother who communicates to him his father's displeasure at his frequent visits to the theatre (I/2, 11). Toward the conclusion of this conversation Wilhelm asks her where his old puppets are (I/2, 13). The sentences which precede the "iterative" quoted above explain that Wilhelm came up with an arrangement that allowed him to appease his father's wrath (he stops going to Mariane's performances) and yet still enjoy her love (he sneaks out once everyone is asleep). And in the passage following the one quoted above, Wilhelm presents Mariane with the puppets, whose location he (presumably) learned from his mother. It seems unlikely that Wilhelm would have missed a night with Mariane or that he would have retrieved the puppets and not brought them to her at the first opportunity. Thus, as proposed above, the "eines Abends" when he brings the puppets must be the *second* night which Wilhelm spends with Mariane, the only night to which the iterative series can apply.[14]

Since our passage describes a single night, it cannot be an iterative. And yet neither is it an example of what Genette calls the "pseudo-iterative," for in a pseudo-iterative even though the verb tense *is* iterative, "the richness and precision of detail ensure that no reader can seriously believe the event occurs and reoccurs in that manner, several times, without any variation" (121).[15] Our passage has no such detail, *and* its diction is undeniably iterative. Yet it succeeds in functioning as an iterative; when one reads it, one assumes that Wilhelm has made love to Mariane repeatedly. Nothing betrays its deception except careful correlation of other time indices as demonstrated above. Furthermore, one connects this with other iterative passages which also give the impression that the intimate relationship of Wilhelm and Mariane is of extensive duration.

Consider, for example, a passage several chapters later (placed after the conclusion of the narration of the couple's *second* night together): "So brachte Wilhelm seine *Nächte* im Genusse vertraulicher Liebe, seine *Tage* in Erwartung neuer seliger Stunden zu. Schon zu jener Zeit, als ihn Verlangen und Hoffnung zu Marianen hinzog, fühlte er sich wie neu belebt, er fühlte, daβ er ein anderer Mensch zu werden beginne; nun war er mit ihr vereinigt, die Befriedigung seiner Wünsche ward eine reizende *Gewohnheit*" (I/9, 33; emphasis added). The first sentence functions similarly to the passage analyzed above.[16] In the next sentence, even though time is divided into "before" and "now" and is not portrayed in an iterative fashion, Wilhelm's feeling of sempiternal bliss is clearly communicated, contributing indirectly to our understanding that theirs is a long-standing relationship.[17] Thus when Wilhelm asks Mariane a short while later (in both story time and discourse time) if she is pregnant, the reader is not jarred, as Schumann insists, but rather accepts it; the masquerading iterative passages have shaped his/her sense of how long this couple has been together. Far from being "functionally subordinate to singulative scenes" (Genette 116-17), Goethe's "masquerading iteratives" dominate the singulatives here—not in quantity, but in moulding the reader's sense of time.

Nevertheless, there is another time frame in Book One which the iteratives by no means obliterate. The placement of the announcement of Norberg's impending arrival at the beginning of the novel impresses upon the reader the sense of a curtailed period of time.[18] Also, the narrator occasionally does mention the passing of specific days and nights. And finally, the iteratives are, as I have shown, frauds. Rather than conclude that Goethe erred, however, let us ask what purpose these conflicting cues might serve.

The importance of Mariane's pregnancy is clear: in the immediate context of its announcement Wilhelm interprets it as a sign of the couple's great love, and his desire to concretize their relationship through marriage intensifies. Of course, Felix's role in the subsequent unfolding of the plot is also crucial. Hence there is no doubt that Goethe needed to have the question (and the answer) seem plausible. Why then did he just not makes the elapsed time sufficiently great? Another set of considerations makes a sense of imminence desirable. Norberg's impending arrival causes tension and conflict between Barbara and Mariane: Mariane will have to choose. The iteratives, on the other hand, reveal the nature of Wilhelm's love, the nature of Wilhelm as reader of the situation. He loses sight of everything and everyone beyond himself and his own feelings. He senses stability, eternity. But the very existence of the other time scheme highlights Wilhelm's naïveté, egotism, even preposterousness. Not only is Wilhelm ignorant of Norberg's arrival (for that we pardon him), but he, who considers Mariane to be "die Hälfte, mehr als die Hälfte seiner selbst" (I/9, 33), is totally unaware of her precarious emotional state, discussed explicitly by the narrator—ironically enough—immediately after that assertion by Wilhelm (I/9, 34).[19]

On another level, the contradiction between the two time schemes, the external, objective one and the internal, subjective one, reflects the larger contradiction generated by the events of the book between the way things appear to Wilhelm (i.e., Mariane is unfaithful to Wilhelm) and the way things turn out to be (Mariane is true to him). Significantly, the iteratives influence the reader's understanding of time most strongly in the first book, continue to occur in the early books (e.g., in structuring time spent with the actors),[20] but are absent in the last two books. The disappearance of the masquerading iteratives as the novel progresses, then, is linked to Wilhelm's growing ability to place the needs and concerns of others before his own desires; in other words, to become a member of society rather than remain an independent, egotistical sphere of thought and action. The fact that the iteratives prove to be illusive upon closer examination and in relation to the work as a whole is a formal manifestation of the novel's theme: the ultimate falsity of individual perception and the ascendancy of a corporate view. These few observations demonstrate that seeming incongruities in the time scheme must not be labelled "mistakes" and then dismissed, but rather precisely the opposite, that one should focus on them to discover their thematic and formal effects. For masquerading iteratives are only one limited manifestation of a larger strategy in which the narrator sets up chronology as an authority only to wilfully ignore it.

Disagreement among critics about the nature of ***Wilhelm Meister***'s narrator suggests that his true modus operandi has yet to be identified. While Franz Stanzel groups him with such other typical "teller-characters" as the narrators of *Tom Jones, Vanity Fair,* and *Doktor Faustus* (194), other critics have commented that he does not interpret the story he tells.[21] I myself have not found a satisfactory label for him, for the briefest look at his relation to the story he narrates shows both how rarely and briefly he speaks and yet also how extensively he controls the elements of his narrative. When he does speak, however, he often claims the opposite. At the end of Book Five, for example, he places one of Mignon's poems, "das wir früher mitzuteilen *durch den Drang so mancher sonderbaren Ereignisse* verhindert wurden" (V/16, 356; emphasis added). And towards the end of Book Eight he withholds "ein sehr bedeutendes Gespräch, das wir gern, *wenn uns die Begebenheiten nicht zu sehr drängten,* unsern Lesern hier mitteilen würden" (VIII/10, 603; emphasis added). The narrator posits—indeed, almost personifies—the story's events as an external force which controls him and his narrative. They have their own flow which he must not disturb (V/6, 305). Such protestations of servitude should be considered in light of other explicit statements about his activities. The narrator adopts a more aggressive posture, for example, at the beginning of the second book, after Wilhelm's devastating affair with Mariane:

> Jeder, der mit lebhaften Kräften vor unsern Augen eine Absicht zu erreichen strebt, kann, wir mögen seinen Zweck loben oder tadeln, sich unsre Teilnahme versprechen; sobald aber die Sache entschieden ist, *wenden wir unser Auge sogleich von ihm weg . . .*
>
> Deswegen sollen unsre Leser nicht umständlich mit dem Jammer und der Not unsers verunglückten Freundes, in die er geriet . . . , unterhalten werden. Wir überspringen vielmehr einige Jahre und suchen ihn erst da wieder auf, wo wir ihn in einer Art von Tätigkeit und Genuβ zu finden hoffen, wenn wir vorher *nur kürzlich so viel, als zum Zusammenhang der Geschichte nötig ist, vorgetragen haben.* (II/1, 76; emphasis added).

Here the narrator establishes the principles that not everything need be told and that selection lies with the judgment of the observer, not the actor. The narrator controls what we, the readers, will or will not hear about in detail, a familiar "flexing" of the 18th-century narrator's traditional power. He also, however, reveals a duplicitous attitude toward his occupation. While telling us that he will relate "enough" to create a continuity (another bow to an external "reality"), his disdain for the need or obligation to do so is obvious. In fact, I will go so far as to suggest that the narrator tries repeatedly to wean the reader away from interest in a coherent, independent "story" and steer him/her towards the narrator's own construction, i.e., the discourse.[22] The ways in which he does so are subtle and yet so numerous that I will be able to consider only three: how he manipulates the story by appropriation, excision, and transposition.

Although dramatic scenes—usually considered to play the central role in pre-Modernist narrative—do exist in ***Wilhelm Meister,***[23] scrutiny of some of these reveals anomalies. Some episodes which initially appear to be dramatic scenes prove to belong to an a temporal part of the narrator's discourse. The content of letters, songs and poems, manuscripts, and even conversations is often disassociated from the actions and performances which produce and/or receive them and are reproduced as narratorial "digression" (see Genette 94, note 12). Consider the contrast between the narration of the *Harfner*'s performance of a song and Mignon's; first the *Harfner*'s:

> Der Alte schwieg, ließ erst seine Finger über die Saiten schleichen, dann griff er sie stärker an und sang:
>
> "Was hör' ich draußen vor dem Tor,
> Was auf der Brücke schallen?"
> . . .
>
> "Ergeht's euch wohl, so denkt an mich,
> Und danket Gott so warm, als ich
> Für diesen Trunk euch danke."
>
> Da der Sänger nach geendigtem Liede ein Glas Wein . . . ergriff, und es mit freundlicher Miene . . . austrank, entstand eine allgemeine Freude in der Versammlung.
>
> (II/11, 129-30)

Not only the text of the song but a musical score as well were reproduced in the first edition of the novel.[24] Discourse time approximates story time; the reader is given a "recreation" of the *Harfner's* performance analogous to the way "scene" approximates "real" dialogue.[25] Several songs are "reperformed" in the discourse in this manner (cf. II/13, 137; IV/11, 240-41; etc.).

Categorically different, however, is Book Three. Below the chapter heading a poem is printed:

> Drittes Buch
> *Erstes Kapitel*
> Kennst du das Land, wo die Zitronen blühn,
> . . .
> Dahin! Dahin!
> Geht unser Weg: o Vater, laß uns ziehn! (145)

Again, written music was printed for this song in the original edition. But the first sentence of prose relates a (seemingly) irrelevant action of Wilhelm: "Als Wilhelm des Morgens sich nach Mignon im Hause umsah, fand er sie nicht . . ." It is not until the *second* paragraph that any connection between the prose and the poem is hinted:

> Nach Verlauf einiger Stunden hörte Wilhelm Musik vor seiner Türe. Er glaubte anfänglich, der Harfenspieler sei schon wieder zugegen; allein er unterschied bald die Töne einer Zither, und die Stimme, welche zu singen anfing, war Mignons Stimme. Wilhelm öffnete die Türe, das Kind trat herein und sang das Lied, *das wir soeben aufgezeichnet haben.* (III/1, 145; emphasis added)

The explicit mention of the passing of several hours at the beginning of the paragraph parallels in time what is communicated in space: the dissociation of the song from the act which produced it. But even when this event is summarized the diction emphasizes the connection of the song to the *discourse* rather than to the *story.* The adverb *"soeben,"* of course, refers to discourse time,[26] and the relative clause ("das wir soeben aufgezeichnet haben") makes it seem as if the song Mignon sang in the story originated in the discourse rather than vice versa. Even though the concept of "story" is most traditional and comforting, the narrator seems to want to deny its existence to the reader.[27] Although "aufzeichnen" could refer to "recording" what someone else produces (in which case Mignon remains the creative source of the poem), it could also mean the "taking down" of one's own creation (in which case she does not).[28] This example is further complicated by the fact that Wilhelm is said to have translated Mignon's song into German, without being able to recover its full charm (II/1, 146). Is the brilliant poem we in fact read Wilhelm's "imperfect" translation or the narrator's more perfect one? Use of the pronoun "wir" seems to favour the latter supposition, thus again pointing to the hand of the narrator.[29]

Although it is commonplace to assume that authors use "scene" rather than "summary" for special emphasis,[30] in ***Wilhelm Meister*** the most important information is appropriated frequently by the narrator. By incorporating it into his discourse, he formally dissociates its temporal connection to the story, even though a "scenic-like" quality is often retained.[31] The narrator even may leave a marker pointing to what he has annexed. The artistic purpose, I again suggest, is to draw the reader's attention to the disruption of the story and to the authority who can do so. An additional goal seems to be maximal (narratorial) control over the diction, form, and content of important thematic material. The treatment of the "*Roman/Drama*" conversation illustrates this.

The narrator summarizes the group's activity: "Sie sprachen viel herüber und hinüber" (V/7, 307). But rather than quote the discussion and identify it as such—this would be "scene"—the narrator edits it: "und endlich war folgendes *ungefähr das Resultat* ihrer Unterhaltung" (emphasis added). The reader recognizes in the passage which follows (307, line 19, through 308, line 5) the tone of classical "authorial digression." The statements are aesthetic pronouncements which escape the temporality of the story, written in the gnomic present, rather than the subjunctive of indirect discourse. Without any explicit metanarrative comment, however, the narrator then continues with detailed "summary," close to "scene." For example: "So vereinigte man sich auch darüber, daß . . ."; "Diese Betrachtungen führten wieder auf den wunderlichen Hamlet . . ." (308), etc. In this way the narrator masks to a certain extent his earlier personal formulation of the "Resultat ihrer Unterhaltung." Reviewing the entire chapter, one finds: summary, scene (quoted dialogue), summary, atemporal authorial digression, and summary.

The narrator's overt control over what, when, and how the story gets communicated to the reader is also evident in variations of narratorial appropriations in which promised scenes or extended summaries of them are excised, and then deleted altogether (the creation of an ellipsis)[32] or transposed to a later point in the discourse and sometimes then reported as "scene" or, as in the case above, as atemporal discourse. We find an interesting example of excision in Book Two.

A brief summary reports that Friedrich told a "*Märchen*" when asked by the *Stallmeister* about his past.[33] The reader is also informed that Friedrich had repeated this story frequently.[34] The narrator announces, "Wir [gedenken] ein andermal unsre Leser [mit dem Märchen] bekannt zu machen" (II/14, 141). This "andermal" never comes in ***Wilhelm Meister.*** Regardless, the very mention of the event combined with the narrator's promise to tell support the notion of a cadre of external events about which the narrator must report. Yet, as with the appropriations, the excision itself counters the idea. It points rather to the narrator's creative and controlling hand. Pausing to consider why he does not detail Friedrich's *Märchen* at once, but promises its narration at a future point, I conjecture that arousing more curiosity in our minds about Friedrich is useful because he will play the critical role in the end. Thus, excision helps create expectation and desire for another story, another text. Doing so with regard to Friedrich is particularly appropriate since he provides a resolution by similarly pointing to another story (that of Saul, cf. VIII/10, 610). What seems ultimately of greater importance, however, is the effect of narratorial appropriation on the representation of time. In the case of Friedrich's *Märchen,* for example, any subsequent appearance of Friedrich causes the reader to remember this past scene (and others in which he is involved) and its promise of a future revelation about his personal past. In this way the reader brings "Vergangenheit," "Zukunft," and "Gegenwart" together (Storz, "***Wilhelm Meisters Lehrjahre***" 72), as (s)he reads and concomitantly remembers and anticipates, constantly "rewriting" the story being read. When the reader eventually discovers Friedrich's real identity, (s)he realizes there was no need to know the actual content of the *Märchen*; it was clearly a fabrication to disguise his true identity. Thus the ultimate importance of this excision seems to lie in the act of creating a blank.

Far from being directed or restricted by the flow of events, as the narrator sometimes claims, or by adherence to Wilhelm's perspective,[35] or even by desire to create suspense, excisions also serve the narrator's control over the moral and aesthetic influences to which the reader is exposed. Justifying his decision to withhold a song of Philine's on the grounds that "[unsere Leser] es vielleicht abgeschmackt oder wohl gar unanständig finden könnten" (II/11, 130) reveals something about Philine's character, e.g., that she would sing something that might be offensive to somebody. But it also provides us with information about our narrator and his narrative. It is he who would find the song "abgeschmackt" and "wohl gar unanständig"; he is willing and eager to withhold anything that does not serve his didactic or aesthetic goals, or does not interest him or appeal to his taste. Furthermore, the narrator excludes "digressions" while remarking that the reader would find them interesting (e.g., V/6, 305). He skips over conversations he calls "wunderbar" and even "sehr bedeutend" (V/15, 335; VIII/10, 603). Yet, as we have seen, he exposes his own expurgatorial method. The narrator maintains his duplicitous stance of pointing to some outside reality which presumably structures the narrative, while simultaneously pointing to his own ability to manipulate—indeed to create—the only reality which gets communicated to the reader, i.e., the discourse. And, I suggest, his comments when appropriating and then excising story material goad the reader into a parallel activity. Precisely by creating ellipses and calling them "interesting" or "absurd," he piques the reader's desire to know, to fill in the gaps by using his/her imagination. We note the narrator's actions and imagine what might have been sung or said. We realize that *we* create and recreate a text as does this judgmental, autocratic tease of a narrator, eventually realizing that only the text oneself creates exists.

Surely the most significant narratorial manipulation for thematic and formal goals is the transposition of the "Bekenntnisse einer schönen Seele." Towards the conclusion of Book Five, the narrator reports:

> Kurz darauf kam das vom Arzt versprochene Manuskript an. Sie [Aurelie] ersuchte Wilhelmen, ihr daraus vorzulesen, und die Wirkung die es tat, wird der Leser am besten beurteilen können, wenn er sich mit dem folgenden Buche bekannt gemacht hat. Das heftige und trotzige Wesen unserer armen Freundin ward auf einmal gelindert. (V/16, 355)

The order of the events is clear, if incomplete: the manuscript arrives; Aurelie begs Wilhelm to read it to her; [lacuna]; it has an effect on her. The ellipsis of the moment Wilhelm consents and of the reading time and content of the story itself is consequential even though it is obscured by the reference to what lies ahead in the discourse. That future section of the discourse [i.e., Book Six] is the substitute, the equivalent in a restricted sense, of what has been skipped: the perusal and the listening. Even though these actions can be logically deduced from the events that *are* narrated—the narrator even reports later that Aurelie requests rereadings (lines 18-20)—their excision and transposition represent a removal of the *Bekenntnisse* from their story context and a transference to a temporally and spatially independent existence in the discourse. (This is a shift in narrative "levels" from the intradiegetic to the extradiegetic [Genette 228-29].) Located in a separate book, nothing connects the *Bekenntnisse* with the fictive present formally, and structurally there is only the faint anticipation mentioned above. The facts that this section is narrated in the first person singular and that it has no chapter divisions as the other books do also distinguish it.[36] Yet the reader has been given an assignment by the narrator: (s)he is to reconstruct the effect the manuscript has had on Aurelie once (s)he too has been exposed to it. Nonetheless, these instructions are separated from the start of the *Bekenntnisse* by the narration of other events. It is to the last of these "events" that I turn next.

At the conclusion of Book Five the narrator places one of Mignon's poems (another example of a narratorial appropriation). He accounts for his action with the excuse that other more unusual events prevented him from relating it to us sooner. We have already seen that similar manipulations of the narrator are often motivated by structural and/or thematic considerations. For this reason an examination of the poem's content may help explain its placement between Aurelie's reading of the *Bekenntnisse* and their reproduction:

Heiβ mich nicht reden, heiβ mich schweigen,
Denn mein Geheimnis ist mir Pflicht;
Ich möchte dir mein ganzes Innre zeigen,
Allein das Schicksal will es nicht.

Zur rechten Zeit vertreibt der Sonne Lauf
Die finstre Nacht, und sie muβ sich erhellen;
Der harte Fels schlieβt seinen Busen auf,
Miβgönnt der Erde nicht die tiefverborgnen Quellen.

Ein jeder sucht im Arm des Freundes Ruh',
Dort kann die Brust in Klagen sich ergieβen;
Allein ein Schwur drückt mir die Lippen zu.
Und nur ein Gott vermag sie aufzuschlieβen.

(v/16, 356-57)[37]

For one who has already read the conclusion of the novel, the "meaning" of this poem seems obvious. Mignon is referring to the promise she made to the Virgin Mary that she would not talk about her past in exchange for protection (viii/3, 522). But let us pause to consider the poem as it might reveal itself on a first reading. The poem thematizes its form. As an "appropriation" it was "kept silent" until "ein Gott," i.e., the narrator, allowed it expression. Needless to say, its message enhances the mystery which already attends Mignon. It repeats the interdiction against revelation, and yet it also expresses the desire to tell. Most importantly, it promises that disclosure will occur.[38] The narrator's report that Mignon had recited this poem several times causes the reader to recall the past story and consider on what occasions she might have done so. In this way it serves as a link to the narrated past in addition to arousing our curiosity further about Mignon's personal past which is not yet part of the story. It also points to the future when the revelation will occur. But the poem connects with more than an individual's destiny, to more than its own position as a narratorial appropriation. The poem summarizes the anachronous time structure of the novel: pasts suppressed and then revealed, the future foreshadowed. At the proper time, the poem asserts, the sun will drive away the darkness. And that "proper time" has arrived for the novel; the poem heralds solutions to the *Geheimnisse* of the previous books. It does so by pointing to a transposition, to another text.[39] And although Book Six first appears to be the most unrelated anachrony in the novel,[40] it functions as a bridge which connects the past to the future on several levels. As Goethe himself commented: "Das Buch der Bekenntnisse weist vor- und rückwärts, und indem es begrenzt, leitet und führt es zugleich" (as qtd. in Borcherdt 296).

Of the several temporal aspects I have focused on in this essay, it is the nonchronological presentation of events in ***Wilhelm Meister*** which has received the most critical attention. But most scholars limit their investigation of the novel's anachronous structure to the opening *in medias res* and the subsequent flashback to Wilhelm's childhood (cf. Borcherdt 296; Pascal 14; Lämmert 105ff; Blackall 77, 111; and Reiss, *Goethe's Novels* 86). This, too, is predictable, not only because it is exploited by Goethe in a masterly way, but also because its artistic effect is easily contrasted with *Wilhelm Meisters theatralische Sendung,* which is told chronologically. Thus, Eberhard Lämmert, for example, chooses the opening of ***Wilhelm Meisters Lehrjahre*** as his prime example of "aufbauende Rückwendung" in his narratological study, *Bauformen des Erzählens* (105ff). Yet anachronies, both flashbacks and anticipations, abound in every book of the novel; there is no reason to restrict oneself to the opening. Anachrony is not a freak masterstroke, but rather the structuring principle of the novel.[41]

To elucidate the way anachrony can function in the novel, I will briefly explore one example, that of the *Bekenntnisse,* with which we are already somewhat familiar. When a reader approaches Book Six (s)he connects it with Aurelie and to a lesser degree with the doctor who sent her the manuscript. The narrator programs us to consider the Beautiful Soul's story with regard to the effect in had on Aurelie, who in turn was programmed by the doctor to read it as a lesson or parable for herself (v/16, 349-50). We recall that the story not only changed Aurelie's current state of mind, but also caused her to re-evaluate a crucial event of her past. And, indeed, she reverses her attitude toward a former lover. In reading Book Six ourselves, one of the questions on our minds is: What is it in the *Bekenntnisse* that could effect such a radical change of attitude in Aurelie? Thus even though the book is "independent" structurally, it connects to the recent story past (Aurelie) and to the future, since Wilhelm also has been exposed to the *Bekenntnisse* and is on a mission inspired by them. We wonder what will happen when he meets the man from Aurelie's past.

Although the link is not as prominent in the reader's consciousness, the content of Book Six also connects to the main story as told up to this point. For its author was a friend of the doctor. Though this personal connection is slight and less deeply impressed on the reader than the structural connection to Aurelie, this fact is important; as we read this life story it initially appears to be unrelated to the main narrative, but we know it is not. Of course, as we read Books Seven and Eight, it is the connection of the *Bekenntnisse* to Aurelie that fades in our consciousness; their more obvious, vital relevance to the new characters and current events dominates. We even relate the Beautiful Soul to aspects of Books One to Five (besides Aurelie's "conversion"); there is no longer any hesitation about identifying it as a flashback to the main story. Through the Beautiful Soul's uncle we relate her to such diverse characters as Wilhelm's grandfather and the Marchese (and through him to the *Harfner* and Mignon), etc., etc. And, of course, she turns out to be connected to the main characters in Books Seven and Eight, or rather, they turn out to be her nieces and nephews. Even Philine becomes a relative, albeit late in story time and through marriage. The presence of the Beautiful Soul herself is felt not only through the manuscript and her portrait, but more vividly through her living portrait, Natalie (who, as Friedrich insists, supersedes the original [viii/10, 608]). Through her, the Beautiful Soul and her story are ultimately connected to the novel's centre, Wilhelm. The importance of Natalie lies also in the fact that Wilhelm invests her with all the disparate elements of his past and his hopes for the future: "Alle seine Jugendträume knüpften sich an dieses Bild" (IV/9, 235). Furthermore, Natalie provides the model for reading the hidden texts of people's lives. It is she who deciphers Mignon's story, thus enabling Wilhelm to integrate another piece of his own confused past (VIII/3, 522). In sum, the Beautiful Soul anachrony not only brings the various *characters* of the novel into relation, literally and figuratively, but also the *various time levels.*

Although I have merely begun to reveal the multidirectional links of this single anachrony, we recognize that in this example, as in the novel as a whole, the narrator establishes two conflicting structuralizations of time. On the one hand he posits the existence of a chronological, unified story which can and should be told, and on the other, he twists time out of shape. He undermines diachrony by manipulating events so that they engage with one another synchronically rather than sequentially. We may well ask along with Gerhard Storz: "Was wunders, daβ Wilhelm den Offizier im roten Rock (V/15) für Marianne [sic] halten möchte?" ("***Wilhelm Meisters Lehrjahre***" 68).

But perhaps the clearest description of the structure of the novel can be found in a passage describing Wilhelm reading the story of his life, his "Roll of Apprenticeship":

> Er fand die umständliche Geschichte seines Lebens in groβen, scharfen Zügen geschildert; weder einzelne Begebenheiten, noch beschränkte Empfindungen verwirrten seinen Blick, allgemeine liebevolle Betrachtungen gaben ihm Fingerzeige, ohne ihn zu beschämen, und er sah zum erstenmal sein Bild auβer sich, zwar nicht, wie im Spiegel, ein zweites Selbst, sondern wie im Porträt ein anderes Selbst: man bekennt sich zwar nicht zu allen Zügen, aber man freut sich, daβ ein denkender Geist uns so hat fassen, ein groβes Talent uns so hat darstellen wollen, daβ ein Bild von dem, was wir waren, noch besteht, und daβ es länger als wir selbst dauern kann. (VIII/1, 505).

This passage draws our attention once more to the rejection of a chronologically told story and to the rejection of mimesis ("nicht, wie im Spiegel ein zweites Selbst . . ."). It emphasizes, rather, production and re-presentation, the creation of a portrait: an object created in time, but appreciated in its simultaneity. Unity and truth are achieved not by including all details, but by clearing away, by creating some blank spaces. The *Einheit* Schiller sought can be located only in the reader, whose activity parallels that of the narrator. The reader becomes a "groβes Talent" who deconstructs the traditional concept of story and constructs a new "Bild' by conflating past, present, and future in "Produkten dieser Art."

It is immediately upon reading this manuscript that Wilhelm writes *his own* life story. It is significant and appropriate that we, the readers, never see either version.[42]

Notes

1. As quoted in the "Hamburger Ausgabe" of Goethe's *Werke,* 7: 628-29. All references to *Wilhelm Meisters Lehrjahre* refer to this edition and volume and will henceforth be cited in the text by book, chapter, and page number, e.g., V/7, 307.
2. Some of the relevant exchanges between Schiller and Goethe are reprinted in *HA* 620-48. See also reprinted in this volume: Schlegel's comments on the novel (657-75) as well as Novalis's (675-80). For a brief summary of the Romantics' reactions to *Wilhelm Meisters Lehrjahre* see Behler 110-27. Continuing interest in the poetical qualities of the novel is demonstrated by such recent discussions as those of Reiss ("Das 'Poetische' in *Wilhelm Meisters Lehrjahren*") and Kühl ("Das Poetische in Goethes *Wilhelm Meisters Lehrjahre*").
3. Consider also one of the most recent formulations of the unifying element; Behler identifies "Goethe's innovative manner of narration which—through its unique way of foreshadowing, correspondences, symbolization and irony within the work—created a form of unity shaped by the imagination" (114) as the feature which most attracted the *Frühromantiker.*
4. For initial mention of the distinction *Erzählzeit/erzählte Zeit,* see Müller 33. For an attempt to establish the overall elapsed time 65-68, and for discussion of series of subsequent days 68-75. Note that this study was published in the same year as his landmark essay "Erzählzeit und erzählte Zeit," in which *Wilhelm Meister* is the first of three main examples illustrating his narratological distinction *(Mrs. Dalloway* and *The Forsyte Saga* are the others).
5. Goethe's word; as quoted by Schumann 154-55. From letter to Schiller (9 July 1796, rpt. in *HA* 7: 641) in which Goethe admits that he feels like a man, "der nachdem er viele und groβe Zahlen übereinandergestellt endlich mutwillig selbst Additionsfehler machte." But Schumann misconstrues Goethe's statement. Its original context indicates that he was referring to the overall aesthetic effect of *Wilhelm Meister,* not to specific temporal (mis)calculations. Still, critics continue to insist that Goethe was not really in control of the chronology. Consider Meyer's indictment: "dennoch hatte der Dichter selbst von der Gesamtdauer des Geschehens eine unbekümmertundeutliche Vorstellung" (15).
6. I do not imply that the narrator of *Wilhelm Meisters Lehrjahre* has never been examined by critics before; he has—in both older and more recent studies. Of particular note is the doctoral dissertation of Liisa Saariluoma (1985); but I do not think that anyone has yet adequately described his strategies or their importance.
7. Consider Müller's formulation that the *Bildungsroman* "verläuft zeitlich im Sinn des Uhrzeigers vorwärts durch Jahre, wohl auch Jahrzehnte, und sie bringt dabei die Umwelten zusammen mit dem Vorwärtsschreiten des werdenden Ich hervor" (as quoted in Köhn 12). The very idea of *Bildung* as change in status, forward progress, etc., can be deduced from

Dilthey's original comments on the genre even though he never refers to the structuring of time specifically (see Saariluoma 2).

8. This is in contrast to Müller who had argued that *eight* years pass. See *Gestaltung-Umgestaltung* 65-68; also "Erzählzeit und erzählte Zeit" 196.

9. Goethe rewrote this passage at least once in response to a comment from Schiller that Werner's boys could not be as old as they were (originally) portrayed (*HA* 634). The facts that Goethe's attention had already been drawn to the passage and that having made some changes he left the passage the way we read it are further evidence that he wanted Werner's characterization of his sons' maturity to seem hyperbolic.

10. The number of days cannot be ascertained only from the information in Book One. On the contrary, one must first learn that the mysterious figure whom Wilhelm saw leaving Mariane's apartment was Norberg, a fact which Goethe delays imparting to the reader until Book Seven (vii/8, 479), and one must assume that Norberg did in fact return within a fortnight as he announced in the letter to Barbara and Mariane at the beginning of the story. Only then could a reader be sure that this pregnancy is confirmed unbelievably early.

11. The first-time reader's acceptance that the elapsed time is sufficient is also aided by the strong focalization on Wilhelm. In other words, the reader is primarily watching the unfolding of events from Wilhelm's perspective. On the concept of focalization see Genette, esp. 189-94; and Bal's insightful revision of the concept. For the specific feelings of Wilhelm that cause him to believe that Mariane could be pregnant, see my discussion below.

12. Storz also comments on Müller's choice in "Zur Komposition von *Wilhelm Meisters Lehrjahren*" 159.

13. On German's lack of progressive verb forms, see Lockwood 105, 161 and Sparks and Vail 260. Note also that when Eberhard Lämmert discusses the rendering of time in the iterative mode, he lists *adverbial* phrases as its tell-tale sign (84).

14. I am not precluding the possibility that Wilhelm's actions on *subsequent* nights follow this pattern.

15. Note that neither is this Genette's "repeating narrative" in which an event which occurs once is narrated multiple times (114), for this is narrated only once, but in an iterative mode.

16. This, too, would have to be considered a "masquerading" iterative, even though in this instance there are two nights to which it could apply rather than just one. Perhaps one could say this masquerade is less thick.

17. Another way to consider the effect of this passage would be in terms of its focalization. We are tied to *Wilhelm's* perspective. Other critics have noticed this too. Cf. Pascal 26; and Saariluoma, 234. Still, the reader is not totally engulfed by Wilhelm's feelings. Even during a first reading, a word such as "Gewohnheit" can trigger suspicion about the quality of their relationship.

18. Sternberg points out the disproportionate importance of beginnings since first impressions are almost indelible due to what psychologists call the "primacy" effect (93ff).

19. Another sign of Wilhelm's selfish love is his total unawareness of Mariane's lack of interest in his childhood stories. As so many critics remind us, he puts her to sleep with his reminiscences. The quality of his love for her at any point in Book One is suspect when we learn that he assumes she is unfaithful to him on inconclusive evidence, and does not confirm it or confront her with his suspicions even though he believes she is carrying his child.

20. Another section of the novel in which the "masquerading iterative" plays an important role in influencing the reader's sense of elapsed time is at the *Schloβ* (Book Three). Confirming the deception is more difficult, however, since there are fewer "objective" time markers. The purpose, I conjecture, is similar to that in Book One, i.e., that we are caught up in Wilhelm's egotistical perception of himself as centre of the world, as great artist and irresistible lover.

21. Saariluoma 223. Pascal comments that the narrator is not felt as "something 'separate' from the story related" (36), while Blackall seems closer to Stanzel in emphasizing the narrator's ironic distance (111).

22. My point here is similar to one made by Saariluoma, esp. in her chapter "Das Aufgeben der 'Guckkastenillusion': der Leser als Beobachter und Deuter des Geschehens." But while we both stress the reader's need to "construct" the story, Saariluoma emphasizes the issue of visualization via the lack of descriptive passages; she does not discuss the issue of time itself.

23. Scenes in the form of dialogue abound throughout the novel, but particularly in Books Seven and Eight—a point at which, I suggest, the narrator has ideal spokesmen for the ideas he would like to have heard. It is interesting to note that in earlier books only certain characters' own speech is heard frequently, e.g., that of Wilhelm, disguised members of the *Turmgesellschaft,* Jarno, but not Mariane, Philine, Friedrich, etc.

24. See *Wilhelm Meisters Lehrjahre,* ed., Erich Schmidt (Frankfurt am Main: Insel Verlag, 1980), one of the very few subsequent editions in which some of the music of the first edition is reproduced. Jack Stein, in his article "Musical Settings of the Songs from *Wilhelm Meister,*" laments this lack in the vast majority of editions. I agree with his sentiment, since the actual presence of the musical score has a narratological function, reinforcing the sense of discourse as scene.

25. In commenting on the conventional equality between a narrative and story time in a scene, Genette warns that it "cannot serve us as reference point for a rigorous comparison of real durations" (87). The case of a song would be even more obvious than that of dialogue since singing a given text almost always takes longer than speaking it.
26. Genette comments that fictive narrating "is considered to have no duration" (222), but it seems to me that there are hints in *Wilhelm Meister* to the contrary; this "soeben" is an example of one.
27. The story, of course, does not have an existence independent of the discourse which relates it. Sternberg, for example, reminds us that the fabula (story) is "essentially both an abstraction and a reconstitution" (10).
28. The same ambiguity exists with regard to another of the works with which Mignon is associated. Cf v/16, 356, lines 31ff, where the same verb, "aufzeichnen," is used by the narrator.
29. The narrator seems to be a polyglot and skillful translator. In addition to translating Italian, he also translates French! See viii/8, 577.
30. See Genette 109-10. See also Stanzel (191), who cites Otto Ludwig as the first modern critic to build on Plato's distinction between "diegesis" and "mimesis." More familiar to the Anglo-American narratological tradition is the work of Percy Lubbock, following Henry James's compositional principles. Lubbock emphasizes the distinction and superiority of scene over summary: in his terms, of "scenic presentation" over "simple narration" (267 and passim). This assumption also underlies Sternberg's interesting discussion of scenes and "scenic norms" (cf. 19ff). (My thanks to W. J. Lillyman for reminding me of Ludwig's contribution.)
31. These appropriated passages cannot be "scenes"—they clearly are not quoted dialogue, for example, and yet they *are* very often protracted, detailed "summaries." Although Genette implies that "scene" could be something other than dialogue (94), he never specifies another species. It seems to me that the line between this other type of scene and a rich summary is obscure. Therefore although I would label such narratorial appropriations "summary" because the narrator clearly "processes" the material, in general scene and summary can and should be regarded as relative, rather than absolute categories.
32. I borrow the term "ellipsis" from Genette to designate "a nonexistent section of narrative [which] corresponds to some duration of story" (93), and use my own term "excision" to designate specifically the narrator's creation of an ellipsis.
33. It may seem strange that we accept a "fairy tale" as the story of a character's past, but in this novel fictional forms are often used to relate biography. Cf. the songs of Mignon and the *Harfner.* On a rereading, one realizes that Friedrich's response is referred to as a "*Märchen*" because he tells a lie to cover up his true identity. Of course, the lie may have been in the form of a fairy tale as well.
34. This is an example of an aberration in order called "paralipsis" by Genette; a given element is passed over, left unnarrated, even though the time in which it occurred is narrated. Friedrich had told this story on other occasions, probably including some which our narrative covered, but his *Märchen* was "sidestepped" (Genette's term 52). Another example of paralipsis occurs in iii/2, 153. Wilhelm had apparently saved some manuscripts from the purge (ii/2, 81) which we were not told about at the time.
35. See v/14, 334-35, where the narrator only includes the last stanza of a song presumably because that is all Wilhelm remembered. See also ii/13, 136, a version of a poem which Wilhelm supposedly overhears. Such logic, however, does not consistently structure the text. In the example of Philine's song below, surely Wilhelm does hear and enjoy it—and probably remembers it as well!
36. Reiss ("Das 'Poetische'" 122) and others have noted the structural differences between Book Six and the other books; but I do not agree with the many critics who consider it a "foreign body" or "interruption" in the novel (cf. Saariluoma 297; Lienhard 74; Waidson 8; even Storz, "Zur Komposition" 161; he, however, does go on to emphasize its importance in creating unity). Although its narrative structure marks it as different (a first-person text with no subdivisions), as I have already demonstrated and will demonstrate below, this section is connected to the main text on a number of important levels.
37. Music for this poem, too, was printed in the first edition. One wonders if a contradiction was intended between the inclusion of the music and the narrator's comment that it is a poem which Mignon had *recited* (". . . das Mignon mit großem Ausdruck einigemal rezitiert hatte").
38. The novel contains numerous "promises to tell." I have already mentioned several of the narrator's promises. See also Wilhelm's promise to Lothario (viii/10, 607).
39. This poem, it seems to me, has baffled and eluded critics at least as much as Mignon herself eludes her would-be friends. Whereas I believe that it points unflinchingly to what immediately follows it, i.e., Book Six (*as well as* Books Seven and Eight)—note that the poem eases the transition formally in that the first person singular of the poem is followed by the first person singular of Books Six—others have argued that it points *around* Book Six to Books Seven and Eight. Likewise I disagree with the argument that its placement highlights its function as an *autonomous* artwork (Lienhard 73). Furthermore, it is of interest that an article entitled "The Structural Significance of Mignon in *Wilhelm Meisters Lehrjahre*" (Gilby, 1980), does not mention this poem.

40. I use "anachrony" to refer to any event which is narrated in the discourse in a different order from its (hypothesized) place in the sequence of the story. See also Genette 35-36.

41. Storz ("*Wilhelm Meisters Lehrjahre*") describes the anachronic nature of the whole particularly well: "Die Erzählung von Wilhelms Wanderschaft wird nicht nur lang, wie es im Abenteuer-Roman die Linearität der einen, weiter und vorwärts gehenden Bewegung zur Folge hat. Sie wird zugleich rund wie die Welt, und dies geschieht, weil neben der Bewegung nach vorne immer eine solche nach hinten, rückwärts geht. Das Ziel liegt nicht drauβen, am Ende der Erzählung, sondern immer schon in ihr selbst eben als das entstehende Ganze einer Welt" (64). As I mentioned in my introduction, however, he supports this general description with textual evidence such as leitmotif and character, rather than with analysis of the rendering of time.

42. I would like to thank my colleagues in the Departments of German and Comparative Literature who listened to or read versions of this paper. Their comments aided and inspired me.

Works Cited

Bal, Mieke. "Narration et focalisation. Pour une théorie des instances du récit." *Poétique* 29 (1977): 107-27.

Behler, Ernst. "*Wilhelm Meisters Lehrjahre* and the Poetic Unity of the Novel in Early German Romanticism." In *Goethe's Narrative Fiction: The Irvine Goethe Symposium.* Ed. W. J. Lillyman. Berlin, New York: Walter de Gruyter, 1983. 110-27.

Blackall, Eric A. *Goethe and the Novel.* Ithaca: Cornell University Press, 1976.

Borcherdt, Hans Heinrich. *Der Roman der Goethezeit.* Urach and Stuttgart: Port Verlag, 1949.

Genette, Gérard. *Narrative Discourse: An Essay in Method.* Trans. Jane E. Lewin. Ithaca: Cornell University Press, 1980.

Gilby, William. "The Structural Significance of Mignon in *Wilhelm Meisters Lehrjahre." Seminar. A Journal of Germanic Studies* 15-16 (1980): 136-50.

Goethe, Johann Wolfgang Von. *Wilhelm Meisters Lehrjahre.* Vol. 7, *Werke,* "Hamburger Ausgabe." Ed. Erich Trunz. Munich: Verlag C. H. Beck, 1973.

———. *Wilhelm Meisters Lehrjahre.* Ed. Erich Schmidt. Frankfurt am Main: Insel Verlag, 1980.

Köhn, Lothar. *Entwicklungs- und Bildungsroman: Ein Forschungsbericht.* Stuttgart: J. B. Metzlersche Verlagsbuchhandlung, 1969.

Kühl, Kans Ulrich. "Das Poetische in Goethes *Wilhelm Meisters Lehrjahre.*" *Goethe Jahrbuch* 101 (1984): 129-38.

Lämmert, Eberhard. *Bauformen des Erzählens.* Stuttgart: J. B. Metzlersche Verlagsbuchhandlung, 1955, 1972.

Lienhard, Johanna. *Mignon und ihre Lieder gespiegelt in den Wilhelm-Meister-Romanen.* Zürich and Munich: Artemis Verlag, 1978.

Lockwood, W. B. *Historical German Syntax.* Oxford: Clarendon Press, 1968.

Lubbock, Percy. *The Craft of Fiction.* London: J. Cape, 1921.

Meyer, Herman. "Zum Problem der epischen Integration." In *Zarte Empirie. Studien zur Literaturgeschichte. Stuttgart: J.B. Metzlersche Verlagsbuchhandlung, 1963.*

Müller, Günther. "Erzählzeit und erzählte Zeit." *Festschrift Paul Kluckhohn und Hermann Schneider gewidmet zu ihrem 60. Geburtstag.* Ed. by their students in Tübingen. Tübingen: J. C. B. Mohr (Paul Siebeck), 1948. 195-212.

———. *Gestaltung-Umgestaltung in 'Wilhelm Meisters Lehrjahren.'* Halle: Max Niemeyer Verlag, 1948.

Pascal, Roy. *The German Novel. Studies.* Manchester: Manchester University Press, 1956.

Reiss, Hans S. "Das 'Poetische' in *Wilhelm Meisters Lehrjahren.*" *Goethe Jahrbuch* 101 (1984): 112-28.

———. *Goethe's Novels.* Coral Gables, Florida: University of Miami Press, 1969. Saariluoma, Liisa. *Die Erzählstruktur des frühen deutschen Bildungsromans: Wielands 'Geschichte des Agathon', Goethes 'Wilhelm Meisters Lehrjahre.'* Annales Academiae Scientiarum Fennicae Dissertationes Humanarum Litterarum 42. Helsinki: Suomalainen Tiedeakatemia, 1985.

Schumann, Detlev W. "Die Zeit in *Wilhelm Meisters Lehrjahren.*" *Jahrbuch des Freien Deutschen Hochstifts.* Tübingen, 1968. 130-65.

Sparks, Kimberly, and Van Horn Vail. *German in Review.* New York: Harcourt, Brace & World, Inc., 1967.

Stanzel, F. K. *Theorie des Erzählens.* 2nd ed. Göttingen: Vandenhoeck & Ruprecht, 1982.

Stein, Jack. "Musical Settings of the Songs from *Wilhelm Meister.*" *Comparative Literature* 22 (1970): 125-46.

Sternberg, Meir. *Expositional Modes and Temporal Ordering in Fiction.* Baltimore and London: The Johns Hopkins University Press, 1978.

Storz, Gerhard. *"Wilhelm Meisters Lehrjahre."* In *Goethe Vigilien oder der Versuch in der Kunst, Dichtung zu verstehen.* Stuttgart: Klett, 1953. 63-72.

———. "Zur Komposition von *Wilhelm Meisters Lehrjahren.*" In *Das Altertum und jedes neue Gute. Für Wolfgang Schadewaldt zum 15. März 1970.* Ed. Konrad Gaiser. Stuttgart: Verlag W. Kohlhammer, 1970. 157-65.

Waidson, H. M. Introduction. *Wilhelm Meister's Years of Apprenticeship.* By Johann Wolfgang von Goethe. Trans. Waidson. Vol. 1. London: John Calder, 1977. 7-12.

Hartmut Steinecke (essay date 1991)

SOURCE: "The Novel and the Individual: The Significance of Goethe's *Wilhelm Meister* in the Debate about the Bildungsroman," in *Reflection and Action: Essays on the Bildungsroman,* edited by James Hardin, University of South Carolina Press, 1991, pp. 69-96.

[*In the following essay, Steinecke considers* Wilhelm Meisters Lehrjahre *as a seminal Bildungsroman and studies its presentation of the hero's struggle to reconcile himself with reality.*]

If one were to list the most important texts in the history of the novel of the nineteenth century, one work would clearly stand out as the one most frequently mentioned and discussed: ***Wilhelm Meisters Lehrjahre.***[1] This novel is pivotal in the development of the genre in Germany. This fact was seen from the very beginning in critical discussions; dozens of monographs and hundreds of articles deal with the development and meaning of the type of novel that uses Goethe's work as model and for which, for some time now, the term Bildungsroman has been customary.[2] ***Wilhelm Meisters Lehrjahre*** was considered virtually the German equivalent of the social novel as "the medium through which a characteristically German preoccupation can speak with greatest urgency to a wider European public," as Martin Swales wrote in his work *The German Bildungsroman from Wieland to Hesse.*[3] This view is found not only among professional critics. Thomas Mann also repeatedly emphasized that there was only one "typically German" type of novel, that of the autobiographical, confessional Bildungsroman that has as its model ***Wilhelm Meister*** and which represents the single most significant "contribution of Germany to the European art of storytelling" of the nineteenth century.[4] After critical works on the Bildungsroman had swollen for decades in an almost inflationary manner, voices have been heard since the 1960s that express doubt as to how appropriate this concept of the genre might be and how much insight it provides into the literary-historical context of that genre. These objections came precisely from those who worked most intensively with German novels of the nineteenth century. Thus, Friedrich Sengle wrote in an analysis of the Biedermeier period in 1972 that there were—strictly speaking—in this period scarcely any works that one could call Bildungsromane. The whole genre had been so covered in the course of time by "a literary-historical mythology that he of course expected to find little agreement for his skeptical opinion."[5] But others were coming to similar conclusions. Jeffrey L. Sammons in an essay of 1981 extended the search for the Bildungsroman to the entire nineteenth century and in so doing likewise came to a result approaching the discovery that the emperor has no clothes: he found besides ***Wilhelm Meister*** only "maybe two and a half other examples," so that he even speaks of a "phantom genre."[6] Sammons comes to the provocative conclusion that this genre—which has been exposed as a phantom—should be removed from its prominent role in the history of the German novel of the nineteenth century.

Discussion on this question, as controversial as it seems, turns fruitlessly in a hermeneutic circle: the definition is derived from works on which one then tests the appropriateness of the term. Going back to the prototype, ***Wilhelm Meisters Lehrjahre,*** likewise brings no solution, since several scholars in recent years have even doubted that the designation Bildungsroman strikes the mark even with this work.[7]

In dealing with this controversy, we will attempt to avoid literary-historical mythology and will deal first with the historical reception of the term. In this the word *Bildung* plays a role, but the greater context of the discussion on Goethe's work in the nineteenth century will be at the focus of our discussion, because more important from our standpoint than the controversy about the technical term is the fact stated at the outset that ***Wilhelm Meisters Lehrjahre*** was the most important work for the development of the genre in Germany in the nineteenth century and was the model for a large number of novels. For these novels I will use for the time being the neutral term "novels in the ***Wilhelm Meister*** tradition" before the possibility of other designations is discussed.

Even those who have become allergic to the frequent and often undifferentiated use of the concept *Bildung* will not be able to deny that Goethe's novel primarily depicts a course of education. The controversial nature of the interpretation revolves around the question as to what extent the goal of *Bildung* is reached. "Wilhelm Meister's Theatrical Mission," the first, provisional title of the work, marks the first stage of his path toward *Bildung,* and to justify himself Wilhelm writes his unimaginative friend Werner a letter in which he defends his "personal" education as an actor with the goal of becoming a "public person"; in his view this is the only opportunity for a middle-class citizen to compensate for the privileges of birth of the aristocrat. In this connection Wilhelm, in another letter to his friend Werner, formulates his goal in life in a way which many critics view as motto and intention of the novel.

> Let me put it quite succinctly: even as a youth I had the vague desire and intention to develop myself fully, myself as I am.
>
> I have an irresistible desire to attain the harmonious development of my personality such as was denied me by my birth."[8]

Still it is noteworthy that this path of Wilhelm's, which has to do with his training as an actor, turns out only slightly later to be an error.

The further education of Wilhelm, partially directed by the Society of the Tower and partially through accident, leads finally to his being given the Certificate of Apprenticeship *(Lehrbrief).* Its formulations are also frequently cited as evidence to support the thesis of his successful education. But here too it is to be noted that Wilhelm sees this pedagogical instruction as somewhat overdone and comments on it in an annoyed and ironic way. Besides this, the last book of the novel questions the "harmonic" ending of the previous one, so that the conclusion of the novel is hardly unambiguous.

So we see the following: Goethe himself in ***Wilhelm Meister*** has built in warnings about our taking the book to be a description of a successful formation of one's personality; the "irony that hovers over the entire work" (Friedrich Schlegel)[9] does not permit taking individual pedagogical insights and maxims out of context and making them the basis for our interpretation. Nonetheless, it is of course quite possible to integrate these contradictions in the concept of *Bildung;* for after all, Wilhelm learns that going astray is part of one's education.

The controversial interpretations of the role played by *Bildung* in Goethe's novel began with its first readers.[10] Schiller set forth his interpretation in a letter of 8 July 1796; he wrote that Wilhelm was stepping "from an empty, an indefinite ideal into a prescribed active life but without losing his idealism in the process."[11] Christian Gottfried Körner went even further when in a letter to Schiller of 5 November 1796 he praised Wilhelm's development as the "portrayal of a beautiful human character that is formed gradually through the confluence of its inner aptitudes, talents, and by external events. The goal of this education is a perfect equilibrium."[12] Wilhelm von Humboldt contradicted this optimistic interpretation and saw the role of the hero in a more differentiated, more problematic way. In his view Meister's character possessed "complete malleability, but almost devoid of any real goal"; the great merit of the novel was that "it described the world and life just as it is, completely independent of a single individual, and precisely because of this, open for any individuality."[13] Schiller was partially convinced by this argumentation and in a letter to Goethe of 28 November 1796 formulated a position that made a compromise between the extremes.

> Wilhelm Meister is, to be sure, the most necessary but not the most important person; that is one of the peculiarities of your novel—that it doesn't have such a most important person and doesn't need one. *To him* and *around him* everything happens but not really *because* of him. . . .[14]

If one doesn't look too narrowly at the concept of *Bildung*—as is the case with much of the older research—one can recognize in these earliest documents about Goethe's novel a fact that is extremely important for the poetics of the genre: these statements frequently not only have to do with the work itself but also generalize about the genre. That is particularly true of Schiller. He has a very high opinion of ***Wilhelm Meister*** as a work of art—as many of his letters of the years 1794-97 show—but for that reason his criticisms assume added significance. Schiller emphasizes that the "form of ***Meister,*** as indeed every form of the novel . . . is not poetic" and that it is "complete only in the realm of reason," that it is "subject to all the demands of reason," and that it shares "all its limitations." And thus ***Wilhelm Meister,*** with all its undoubted literary qualities, lacks "a certain poetic boldness"; it is characterized by a "strange oscillation between a prosaic and poetic mood."[15]

Novalis, in his fragmentary remarks on Goethe's novel, agrees in some points with this criticism and sharpens Schiller's more cautious objections. That is true above all with regard to the criticism that the book is "unpoetic." For Novalis, ***Wilhelm Meister*** is too rational, too "oeconomisch" [preoccupied with financial matters, ed.], and it treats "merely of ordinary *human* things" and is only "a poeticized bourgeois, domestic story."[16] These reproaches apply not only to Goethe's work but also to the "modern" novel in general—which Novalis here sees realized. And thus he created in his own novel, *Heinrich von Ofterdingen* (published posthumously in 1802), a kind of "anti-***Meister.***" In his remarks on the novel he suggests an alternative concept of the genre in the framework of Romanticism: the novel should bear the stamp of the poetic, the myth, fairy tale, the marvelous.

Although Friedrich Schlegel's ideas about the novel coincide in many respects with those of Novalis, his conclusions go distinctly in another direction. In a review of ***Wilhelm Meister*** of 1798, the first significant published reaction to the work, he emphasizes the role of *Bildung* in Goethe's novel and views it in many respects virtually as the realization of the Romantic ideal of the genre. As congenial as this review may appear to a later observer, it plays only an insignificant role for the judgment of the work by contemporaries. From the perspective of the nineteenth century the significance of the essay resides—as indeed almost the entire early Romantic ***Meister*** criticism—in the fact that Goethe's novel is understood and proclaimed with great emphasis as "timely" and "modern."[17] In the prosaic present, poetry for Schlegel is only possible as a transcendental form in which the conditions for its possible [poetic] existence are also reflected in the work; the concept of a "poetry of poetry" [Poesie der Poesie] is at the very heart of the famous theory of "Progressive Universal Poetry," and its outstanding example in contemporary literature is Goethe's ***Meister.*** Even Schlegel's later negative remarks about this novel reflect a growing skepticism regarding the capacity of the genre "to elevate to poetry a prosaic portrayal of the real present world."[18] In the first phase of the reception of ***Wilhelm Meister***—a period characterized by texts of a high theoretical level—emerges *one* common finding: Goethe's novel is considered the model of the genre, of its potential, but also—and above all—of its limitations.

This line of reception and of the interpretations of Goethe's novel is continued throughout the nineteenth century. Particularly those interested primarily in aesthetic questions discuss the basic criticisms of Schiller and the early Romantics against ***Meister,*** which, in effect, are directed against the genre itself. The collective judgment is somewhat negative, even though Goethe's novel is generally conceded to be the best solution of an insoluble dilemma.

A number of well-known aestheticians and writers of poetics follow this interpretative line. I shall briefly discuss only the most significant one, Hegel. In his *Vorlesungen über die Ästhetik (Lectures on Aesthetics)*[19] he distinguishes the original poetic condition of the world—which brought forth the epic—from the drab modern world which has become prose. The novel as a prose genre is for him the proper and adequate expression of modern bourgeois society. Since the novel, as earlier the epic, is to portray a "totality" and since this totality can be found in our time only in the individual, "the individual event" provides "the center for the whole" in the novel (15:393).

For Hegel the novel thus has the task, on the one hand, of "bringing the prose of real life into its descriptions" and on the other, of avoiding being confined to the "prosaic and everyday." It must "reconquer for poetry, insofar as this is possible, its lost right." "One of the most ordinary and most appropriate collisions to be depicted in the novel is therefore the conflict between the poetry of the heart and the opposing prose of existing conditions as well as the accident of outer circumstances" (15, 393).[20] The individual therefore struggles against current reality with all its rules: "these struggles, however, are in the modern world nothing more than the years of apprenticeship (*Lehrjahre*), the education of the individual through present reality, and they receive through this their true meaning."[21] The terminology, above all the word *Lehrjahre,* makes it clear to what extent Hegel's concept of the genre is based on ***Wilhelm Meister.***

This conflict between the individual and reality can be solved when "the fictional characters, who at first struggle against the ordinary world order, learn to recognize the genuine and substantial in it, and who become reconciled to it and can act effectively in it."[22] That is reminiscent of Goethe, but there is irony in the *Lectures on Aesthetics.* It is more a capitulation of the individual before reality, because the "end of such years of apprenticeship" consists in Hegel's view in the fact

> that he accommodates himself and his wishes and opinions to existing conditions and the reasonableness of them, that he enters into the linkages of the world and gains for himself an appropriate position in it (14:220).[23]

The contrast between the ideals of *Bildung* intended by Goethe, the mastery to which the apprenticeship is to lead as opposed to this picture of middle-class philistinism, is unmistakable. At the same time one can see in this statement Hegel's skepticism about the feasibility of a reconciliation of the individual with reality and thus his skepticism toward the novel as poetic form.

In spite of these reservations Hegel's remarks were taken up immediately by his pupils and were applied directly to literature. Karl Rosenkranz was the first who, under Hegel's influence, in 1827 argued that "*Bildung* was the real object of the novel in general."[24] He considered it self-evident that "*Bildung,*" as in the case of Goethe, "always must have to do with one subject"; the character development of the "interesting subject" was "the life of the novel."[25] Rosenkranz regarded the genre astonishingly positively, indeed pragmatically; he himself attempted to write a novel modeled on ***Wilhelm Meister.*** This shows clearly that Hegel's philosophical reservations about this genre were shared less and less, even by Hegel's pupils. In popular discussion the objections of aestheticians retreated even more. Goethe's exalted reputation among Classicistic critics caused his novel to be praised with fewer and fewer reservations as the very model and proof of the high potential of the genre.

To trace this development I will cite two examples from the period around 1820. I have purposely chosen them from very different areas.

Of all the articles on the novel probably the one exercising the greatest influence in the period was the article in the *Brockhaus Conversations-Lexicon,* which first appeared in 1817 and which remained essentially unchanged for decades. It defines the novel as poetry of reason and of reality, as the appropriate artistic expression in a prosaic epoch:

> [The] . . . life and fate of an *individual* from his birth to his completed *Bildung,* from which, however, the entire tree of humanity, in all its manifold branches in the beautiful time of its maturity and perfection, can be deduced—the apprenticeship of the disciple until he is raised to a master, that is the novel.[26]

It doesn't require an explanation to make clear which type of novel is seen here as the ideal novel of the prosaic age and which work comes closest to this ideal. Goethe's ***Wilhelm Meister*** proves, in the view of the writer, that it was given precisely to the Germans to bring the novel to its zenith because

> in this so idealistically organized Germany with the beautiful and peculiar sensitivity of its inhabitants for the pure education of the individual, without other degrading and limiting considerations, this spirit of the time arose in its most beautiful blossoming.[27]

This is, so far as I know, the most important early example for the connection of this type of novel with characteristics which one felt to be peculiarities of the German character.

As a second example standing for a multiplicity of popular aesthetics and school poetics are the works of the Dorpat professor of aesthetics, Karl Morgenstern.[28] In the center of his deliberations is likewise to be found the contrast of ancient and modern times and the idea that the epic treats the fates of nations while the novel "only has to do with the fate of an individual or with several individuals who interact with him." Since external action in this prosaic age is forbidden, his inner development moves into the focus of interest; thus the novel, according to Morgenstern, shows primarily "people who influence the hero and the surroundings that influence him and the gradual formation of his mind and emotions."[29] The task of the novel is therefore "to lead us into the interior of human souls and to reveal their presentiments, their goals, their struggles, defeats, and victories."[30] From this finding Morgenstern is led "to the concept of the *Bildungsroman,* which is the noblest form of the novel and the form that best captures its nature" (61). He defines it as a novel which

> represents the hero's *Bildung* in its beginning and progress up to a certain stage of perfection. . . . The goal of the writer of such a novel will be to portray in a pleasant, beautiful, and entertaining way the education of an superbly talented person. . . .[31]

It hardly needs mentioning to which model the author is referring.

> As the work of the most general, inclusive portrayal of human *Bildung*, however, ***Wilhelm Meister's Lehrjahre*** by *Göthe*, is the most radiant, a work doubly appealing to us Germans because here . . . the poet gave us, in the hero and in the backdrop and in the surroundings, German life, the German way of thinking and customs in our time. . . .[32]

If one summarizes the articles on the novel in the time around 1820, the following picture emerges: among all the differing views of ***Wilhelm Meister,*** there prevails general agreement that the German novel was fixated philosophically and sociologically on ***Wilhelm Meister*** and on the task of showing developments and problems of an individual in the real, prosaic world. People were in agreement that Goethe had succeeded admirably in achieving precisely this in his ***Meister.*** Critics who think it possible that the novel, in spite of its prose form, can be poetic, therefore recognize in ***Wilhelm Meister*** the most perfect embodiment of the genre. On the other hand, those who do not believe in the realization of this goal must reject ***Meister.*** Goethe's novel is even for these skeptics the work that comes closest to the goal, and yet this novel, with all its extraordinary qualities, shows all the more clearly the necessity of failure. The conviction that the novel has to do with the inner life of the individual is to be found frequently; the concept of *Bildung* plays, to be sure, a certain role in the definition of the genre, but the term Bildungsroman coined by Morgenstern is not taken up by his contemporaries.

Starting in the 1820s, but especially in the period after the July revolution, the interpretation of ***Wilhelm Meister*** that concentrated on the "inner life" and the *Bildung* of the individual diminished in importance. A countermodel was developed first in the historical novel as popularized by Sir Walter Scott and his imitators. The new appreciation of history led to an more positive reevaluation of reality and of the practical world. On the other hand, occupation with individuals, their thought and emotions, the development of their personality, played a lesser role. In many ways, therefore, the hero of the type of Scott's *Waverley* is a direct antipode to that of ***Wilhelm Meister.***

After 1830 the contrasts became even more distinct, as the *Zeitroman* (the epochal novel) and the social novel developed from the historical novel. The individual qualities of the hero retreated even more noticeably in these subgenres, and the society of which he is a part and which conditions and formed him received an ever greater emphasis. In the western European countries this development occurred rapidly, because it could attach to older traditions and reflected contemporary social conditions.

In Germany these novels were also the rage, were much discussed and imitated. But theoreticians, like the novelists, were confronted with two problems: first, the new types of the novel differ in several essential points from the model of the genre which had been derived from ***Wilhelm Meister*** and which just now was becoming the leading type of novel; second, lagging political and economic conditions in Germany proved to be a severe barrier precisely to the development of the types of novels that dealt directly with the realities caused by these backward conditions. For since this malaise was not only the object but also the *condition* of novel writing in this period, in the view of many contemporary writers the genre in Germany had to develop along different lines than in other Western countries.

The designation of the Bildungsroman as the prototype of specifically German development received as early as the 1820s occasionally a new, by no means nationalistic, rather a regretful or reproachful sound. Goethe had already felt this; he complained that German conditions had compelled him in *Wilhelm Meister* to deal with the "most miserable material that can be imagined."[33]

Ludwig Börne ironically confirms Goethe's judgment, saying that the latter had written in his ***Wilhelm Meister*** a "typically German" novel: unfree, narrow, and narrow-minded just like Germany itself; and the hero too, a "lax Wilhelm," given to tears, passive, running after ideals, playing theater instead of exerting himself in a practical way, provided a true picture of the German man.[34] The *Jungdeutschen* [Young Germans] Heinrich Laube, Theodor Mundt, and Ferdinand Gustav Kühne a few years later picked up this criticism and expressed it even more pointedly. Kühne, for example, emphasizes that Goethe's turn to the individual and to his private problems occurred with a conscious neglect of the individual's relationship to public life. At the end of ***Wilhelm Meisters Lehrjahre*** "the *boy* was hardly perfected, not to speak of the man. . . . In order to become a man, a government is necessary, but Goethe didn't know about the idea of a state, he had no idea of how to describe a public civic life, no courage to speak openly of it and to admit that this element was lacking."[35]

Since the German novel had largely followed the Goethean tradition, in Kühne's view the concentration on the private, the interior, the psyche and its development had become even stronger in the following decade. The German novel represented "preferentially and best the well-intentioned, philistine idyll of domesticity" and the "quiet islands of family happiness."[36]

Documents of this kind, in which the contemporary social novel is compared in vigorous images with the outmoded interior novel of the ***Wilhelm Meister*** type, can be found throughout these decades; more characteristic, in fact definitive for an understanding of the time, however, was another tendency: to interpret the Bildungsroman in such a way that it also became the ancestor of the new developments in the genre. Hence, from the 1830s on the emphasis in the interpretation of ***Wilhelm Meister*** shifts: we no longer see so much of the interior life of the individual, the course of his *Bildung* and a goal of this *Bildung* as the central focus, but the world as his *antagonist.* In short, the work is increasingly read and understood as a social novel.

This shift in accent can be seen in the arguments of Mundt and in the novelistic practice of Immermann. Mundt wrote in 1833 that Goethe had with his ***Meister*** "so to speak created a *German standard novel*" (136f.); with this work he had raised the "development of an individual" before the background of a broad portrayal of the period to the "standard theme" of the German novel.[37]

But he warns against treating the fate of an individual as something more important than the portrayal of the "breadth of the world." He turns the charges of Novalis that ***Wilhelm Meister*** was too prosaic, too mercenary, and too bourgeois in a positive direction. Precisely the fact that the novel occupied the center of the "prose of bourgeois life" reveals, in his opinion, the greatness of the work; this striving for an "ideal prose of reality" must be the goal of every *modern novel.*[38]

In the novelistic ***Wilhelm Meister*** tradition the same attitude can be observed most distinctly in Immermann's novel *Die Epigonen* (The Epigones, 1836). Immermann, a passionate adherent of Goethe, repeatedly emphasized the extent to which Goethe's novel had served as a model for the conception and writing of his own novel. The relationship of the two novels is indeed so clear that scarcely any critic failed to point it out: *Die Epigonen* shows the life and fate of an individual hero, his development on the way through the reality of his present—Hermann, its protagonist, is a new Wilhelm.

Even the title of the novel signals, however, that even the general tendencies of the novel have a special meaning and that Hermann is representative of his generation. Even his quite personal fate, his mysterious origin, proves to be representative of the social contradictions of the time, through the tension between the two great historic powers, aristocracy and middle class. In his work there is much reflection about the relationship of the individual to history; it is precisely as a mirror of his time that the individual takes on significance; "never have individuals been more significant than precisely in our days; even the least important one senses the significance of great world events on his innermost being." Today "everyone has taken on historical significance"; only with this understanding could one "write history in family stories."[39]

The representative character of the hero brings with it a diminution of the psychological element and thereby a certain colorlessness. Hermann has a passive role as one who only reacts; his function of linking various social strata by his travels and his struggles takes precedence over any interest in his emotions and personal development; a "maturing" to a "personality" is found only partially in this work; in fact, there is a lack of a precisely described *Bildung* toward which Hermann could develop. Wilhelm has—as Mundt puts it—"the uplifting prospect of some day becoming a *master*[40] either in art or, better, in life. The epigone Hermann is far worse off."[41]

New developments of the time and of society sharpened in other ways understanding of elements of the Goethean novel that earlier interpreters had hardly noticed. For example, in addition to the new attention to the subjective development of the hero, the interest in the portrayal and criticism of society became ever stronger. Shortly after Goethe's death Varnhagen von Ense first pointed to the "socialistic" elements of ***Wilhelm Meister,*** and Karl Rosenkranz and Ferdinand Gregorovius (*Göthe's Wilhelm Meister in seinen socialistischen Elementen entwickelt* [Goethe's ***Wilhelm Meister*** Developed in its Socialistic Elements], 1849) pursued this interpretation farther. The "true socialist" Karl Grün in 1846 even came to the daring conclusion that Wilhelm Meister was a communist. These interpretations were made easier by the fact that the critics not infrequently took ***Wilhelm Meister's Travels***[42] into consideration in their interpretation or read ***Wilhelm Meister's Apprenticeship*** in the light of the ***Wanderjahre.*** Only in a period when one had become more attuned to social problems did one notice, for example, in the continuation (in book 8, chapter 5) of the letter of apprenticeship of the Society of the Tower—which earlier had often been read as a kind of summary of an individualistic program of *Bildung*—doctrines that also described the social responsibility of the individual and his relationship to society in a "socialist" manner (the concept understood in the sense of *Vormärz,* that is, of the period previous to the March revolution of 1848 in Germany), as for example in the formulation:

> All men make up mankind and all forces together make up the world . . . All this . . . lies in the human spirit, waiting to be developed, and not just in one of us, but in all of us.[43]

Why these constant references to Goethe's novel even in works which obviously didn't have much to do with the tradition of the Morgenstern-Hegelian inner-directed Bildungsroman? Probably for some novelists and critics the authority of Goethe and of ***Wilhelm Meister*** in particular, to which they gladly subscribed, played a more important role than the traditional connections and parallels individually. But one series of connections is of a substantive nature: numerous social novels of the *Vormärz* can be seen with some justification to be related to important aspects of Goethe's work that have little or nothing to do with the Bildungsroman.

The changes after the failed revolution of 1848 shifted the critical focus on the novel. The social novel gained in importance and became for decades, even in Germany, the dominant genre. This term described less and less the novel that attempts to portray society in its whole social diversity; the portrayal rather concentrated more and more on a single stratum of society, the bourgeoisie. The disagreement between the novelists Karl Gutzkow and Gustav Freytag is symptomatic of this development. Gutzkow attempted with his nine-volume novel *Die Ritter vom Geiste* (literally, The Knights of the Spirit, 1850-51) in the *Vormärz* tradition to write a work that had as its object the entire spectrum of society. Freytag, on the other hand, concentrated in his *Soll und Haben (Debit and Credit,* 1855) consistently on a portrayal of the middle class. Here only one of the many aspects of this differing emphasis can be discussed: the relationship to ***Wilhelm Meister.*** Both works attempted to be a ***Wilhelm Meister*** for modern times and circumstances. For Gutzkow these circumstances lay in the political and social realm. He had, he emphasized, "so to speak wanted to write a political ***Wilhelm Meister***."[44] This led him to a structural form stressing simultaneity. For Freytag the emphasis lay on the bourgeoisie, and of the two basic elements of the middle class—possessions and *Bildung*—he emphasized the former almost exclusively. And what Novalis had reproached Wilhelm Meister for is true of his hero, Anton Wohlfahrt, in an extreme way: the central significance of the financial element, which completely dominates his education. Since after the middle of the century the middle class placed increasing trust in its own development, Freytag consistently and one-sidedly emphasized the harmonizing aspects of the ***Wilhelm Meister*** model: the process of *Bildung* has reached its zenith when Anton has became the owner of the factory. The overpowering success of this novel, compared with that of Gutzkow, but also with that of the other competing models, indicates the path that the genre would follow in coming decades in Germany. Critics—who helped form public opinion—approved and welcomed this path.

After the middle of the century signs of a new interpretation of the Goethean model of the novel emerge. There is a gradual return to the interpretation of Morgenstern-Hegel with the two closely related focal points of *Bildung* and of the interior of the individual. The ideals of *Bildung* of the classic epoch are reduced in this period virtually to values of the middle class.

The "interior" of the individual moved in the 1850s into the center of the definition of the novel first of all in the philosophical works on aesthetics. Arthur Schopenhauer emphasized that the novelist did not describe great events but "with the least possible use of outer events was to set inner life into the strongest motion."[45] Schopenhauer thus intends largely to eschew the outer totality, the shaping of world and society, deeds and events; he steers the genre toward the inner life of the individual, toward the private sphere. For him it is decidedly true that "The more *inner* life and the less *outer* life a *novel* portrays the more noble and elevated it will be."[46] Similarly the aesthetician Moriz Carriere in his work *Das Wesen und die Formen der Poesie* (The Essence and the Forms of Poetry, 1854) sees the realm of the novel in "emotional development in private life."[47] In his opinion the "circles of private existence" and "the realm of the heart" form the most important objects of the genre.[48] Rudolph Gottschall similarly takes the point of view in his literary history of 1855 [*Die deutsche Nationalliteratur in der ersten Hälfte des 19. Jahrhunderts,* Breslau] and in his *Poetik* of 1858 that the novel is to portray "inner developments," the "dialectic of feelings." The "secrets of spiritual life"; the "content" of the most important "modern novels" is "the inner *'Bildung'* of the individual."[49]

These differing views are summarized, codified, and given some depth in Friedrich Theodor Vischer's *Ästhetik* of 1857. Closely following Hegel's definition of the novel, he develops the idea that the genre has the task of remaining poetic in a prosaic world, and that means seeking a replacement for the lost poetic world. Vischer too finds it primarily in the inner life of the individual, for "somehow, what Schiller had said of ***Wilhelm Meister***" was true of every hero of the novel. The hero goes through his education via "the school of experience."

> The struggles of spirit, of conscience, the deep crises of conviction, of Weltanschauung, which the significant individual goes through, combined with the struggles of emotional life: these are the conflicts, these are the battles of the novel. But naturally they are not merely inner conflicts, they grow out of experience, and the basic conflict is always that of the inexperienced heart which steps into the world with its ideals. . . .[50]

Goethe's work is for Vischer not only the model of the "inner" novel but also remains authoritative for the formation of the hero: the hero is passive, "the rather dependent, only 'processing' focus," and love constitutes "a main element in the maturing of his personality."[51]

Vischer emphasizes that the middle-class novel of this period represents "the actual normal species" of the genre, because "it leads us into the middle stratum of society."[52] Of course, in the view of the aesthetician the burgher is also an individual. Therefore, Vischer can view the historical and the social novel only as a secondary form; the main form and thus the actual novel looks different:

> The hearth of the family is the true center of the universe in the novel, and it takes on its significance only when emotions are united around it, emotions that provide a counterpoint to the hard truth of life.[53]

In his *Ästhetik* Vischer takes up again the old interpretation of ***Wilhelm Meister*** as a Bildungsroman and declares in a programmatic way that its characteristics are peculiarities of the genre in general. It is certainly no accident that he—and this has not been noted in any of the works that deal with the history of this term—also "rediscovered," so to speak, the term Bildungsroman (very probably without knowing Morgenstern). As early as 1839 he defines the Bildungsroman, in a review of Eduard Mörike's novel *Maler Nolten* (The Painter Nolten, 1832), as "the story of the education of a person through life, through love namely; a psychological novel,"[54] but it is significant that this second use of the term, like the first, found no resonance. To be sure, there was a growing number of aestheticians who took up the fight for the "internalized Bildungsroman"; and to be sure there appeared—beginning with Adalbert Stifter's *Der Nachsommer* (*Indian Summer,* 1857) and with the novels of Wilhelm Raabe—works that could have served to demonstrate the significance of this type of novel; but from the standpoint of the genre as a whole and of the development of literature, these tendencies for the time being played only a secondary role.

It is also true a decade later, when for the third time in the nineteenth century it was attempted to introduce the term Bildungsroman for the designation of the type of novel oriented on ***Wilhelm Meister.*** In 1870 Wilhelm Dilthey wrote in his work *Das Leben Schleiermachers,*

> I would like to call the novels which make up the school of Wilhelm Meister . . . "Bildungsromane." Goethe's work shows human cultivation (Ausbildung) in various stages, forms, stages of life.[55]

Although this definition generally is seen as the *locus classicus* of research on the Bildungsroman, there was obviously even at that late date no inclination of literary criticism to use the term and thereby to agree to this narrowing of ***Wilhelm Meister*** interpretation and of the type of novel modeled on it. Only after the turn of the century did the term Bildungsroman emerge more and more frequently in discussion and gradually become widespread. In 1906 Dilthey developed in his book *Das Erlebnis und die Dichtung* (*Experience and Poetry*) his earlier statement in more detail and made more precise what he understood by this kind of novel. The Bildungsroman shows how a youth

> steps into life, seeks related souls, experiences friendship and love, now struggles with the hard realities of the world, and thus made more mature by these manifold life-experiences, finds himself and becomes aware of his task in the world. The task of Goethe was the story of a person who is educating himself for action. . . . These Bildungsromane thus express the individualism of a culture limited to the private sphere. . . . The dissonances and conflicts of life appear as necessary transitional stages of the individual on his path to maturity and to harmony. The 'greatest happiness of earthly children' is the 'personality' as a united and firm form of human existence. Never has this optimism regarding personal development . . . been expressed more cheerfully and optimistically than in Goethe's ***Wilhelm Meister***.. . .[56]

If one regards the history of the reception of ***Wilhelm Meister*** in the discussion of the novel of the nineteenth century, the characteristic nature of the statements of Dilthey and also their historical significance can be more precisely determined.

Dilthey is, of course, a very sensitive interpreter but he is also an idealistic literary scholar of the bourgeois epoch. And so he takes at face value—and that seems to me the key to his ***Meister*** interpretation—Wilhelm's statement that he sought the "harmonic development" of his nature not only as the program of the novel but also as the goal which he reaches at the end of the work. It should be noted that Dilthey, in order to prove his point, takes the quotation out of context and at the same time adds another quotation to his definition; "greatest happiness of earthly children is the personality" is a phrase not found in Goethe's novel but in a poem, in the *West-östliche Divan.* One could say, in short, that Dilthey read ***Wilhelm Meister*** from the vantage point of Schiller and Körner. Whether he understands it the way Goethe did is questionable. He ignores the ironic tone of the book and one-sidedly emphasizes the novel's pedagogical aspect, its harmonic, optimistic side, its tendency to internalize the action and to stress the personal. This interpretation found broad acceptance; with the publication of his essay the view that ***Wilhelm Meister*** was a Bildungsroman—in the sense that it portrays the harmonic cultivation of the individual—began its victory march.

This revival of the classical concept of *Bildung* as understood by Schiller and Goethe was of the greatest importance for the field of German studies [Germanistik] that was developing rapidly in the Wilhelminian period. Dilthey's interpretation emphasizing the harmonic and the private aspects of the novel prevailed in the rapidly growing scholarship on Goethe and in literary histories for quite a long time. In surveying the theoretical-literary discussion about Goethe's novel in the nineteenth century, one could describe the situation this way: with Dilthey begins the narrowing of the view of ***Wilhelm Meister*** to a very specialized type of novel, namely, the Bildungsroman.

In addition to this fixation on one aspect of the novel, a second element entered into the interpretations that is not to be found in Dilthey but which is all too much a part of the spirit of the time in which he wrote: the naively patriotic pride which viewed the novel as "typically German" and that celebrated the Bildungsroman as the sort of novel particularly well-suited for Germans. This idea was promulgated enthusiastically by the more nationalistically inclined Germanists, but the quotations cited at the beginning of this essay show that even significant and sensitive interpreters shared this way of viewing the book, people such as Thomas Mann, who, like a large number of patriotic gymnasial teachers of the Wilhelminian period, praised the "typically German" element in ***Wilhelm Meister*** and in the Bildungsroman.

These interpretations were not new: both the emphasis on *Bildung* and on the "typically German" had been present long before. But the narrowing on these two concepts is new. And this meant that the novel subgenre which one traces to Goethe was itself robbed of essential aspects. The critics of the novel of the nineteenth century—and likewise the great novelists (Immermann, Keller, Raabe, and to a certain extent even Stifter), who, as recent research has determined correctly, did not write Bildungsromane in the sense implied by Dilthey—saw an abundance of characteristics that were lost because of this narrowing: social problems, financial questions, literary expression of ideas of the then-developing liberalism, emphasis on possible conflicts between ego and world, between *Bildungsutopie* and social utopia. Only the most recent ***Wilhelm Meister*** research has again emphasized these aspects: they are therefore, as an analysis of the reception could seem to show, not arbitrary interpretations of these critics, but rather they clearly have their basis in Goethe's novel itself.

To summarize: novels written in the tradition of ***Wilhelm Meister*** were an extremely important factor in the history of the German nineteenth-century novel. The term Bildungsroman is, however, too narrow to include the abundance of forces that influenced both the poetics of the genre and also numerous novels of the century. One could, of course, disengage the concept from the narrow definition of the Dilthey school and define it more broadly, so that it also, in a dialectical way, would include its opposite—the impossibility of *Bildung*—and its parody. But the term then would become far too general. In addition, it has been used so much that it is an ideologically loaded word, and assigning a new meaning to it would be difficult indeed.

I have previously suggested for the novel of the ***Wilhelm Meister*** tradition the term "Individualroman" (individual-novel). Since the reaction of scholars to this suggestion has been rather positive, I would now like to give more precise reasons for using it. The term has the advantage that it is not intellectually laden with interpretations from the past, and that it emphasizes the characteristic of this type of novel generally agreed to be determinant: the role of the individual. Above all, the concept of the individual-novel does not emphasize from the outset—as does the term Bildungsroman—a contrast to the social novel. For in the center of this type of novel is to be found the portrayal of the individual, of his development, of the person as an individual. But that does not imply a restriction to the private sphere, to the inner life of the individual, his psyche, where the epoch and society play only the role of background and foil (as in the artist's novel, in the psychological novel, or in the Bildungsroman, if one views it as narrowly as Dilthey and those of his school). Rather, the social role of the individual and his confrontation with society assumes considerable significance. In this sense description and criticism of society and of reality becomes an essential element even of the individual-novel. It shows what possibilities the society of a period offers the individual for the unfolding of his or her unique personality, or rather which limitations it may place on such development. Precisely since the individual cannot mature in a state of quietude to a harmonically cultivated personality but is exposed to the pressures of society and is tossed around by it, indeed may be deformed by it, the individual-novel broadens its scope and becomes a social novel.

The social novel can also, because of its aim to show the social life of all strata, replace the individual hero by a multiplicity of heros of equal stature and concentrate on a multiplicity of more or less simultaneous events. But it can also illuminate the problems of society through individuals who do not only function as representatives of views and opinions, representatives of groups, that is to say, types, but who can also stimulate the reader's interest as individuals.

And thus, in summary, the type of the individual-novel that was dominant in Germany in the nineteenth century is by no means opposed to the social novel—as interpretations under the rubric of a narrowly understood Bildungsroman have frequently suggested. The difference between the German and the western European novel is, to be sure, recognizable, but this genre in Germany—if one regards it broadly and without allowing one's view to be clouded by literary mythology—by no means took its own unique path.

The controversy about terms and terminology was taken up here only because it has played such an important role in the previous history of research. More important, however, are the characterizations and definitions connected with it. This essay has shown how quite a few aspects of the genre were seen, described, and analyzed in the discussions of critics and aestheticians of the nineteenth century. Since Goethe's novel includes such an abundance of characteristics considered significant in the history of the Bildungsroman, it stimulated novel poetics in a way unlike any other individual-novel of the nineteenth century; as an "individual-novel" it proved to be extremely important not only for the development of the Bildungsroman, but also for that of the social novel in Germany.

Notes

1. This essay appeared in the original German in Hartmut Steinecke, *Romanpoetik von Goethe bis Thomas Mann: Entwicklungen und Probleme der "demokratischen Kunstform" in Deutschland* (Munich: Wilhelm Fink, 1987), 53-75. The English version has been slightly revised and adapted for this volume. Ed.
2. See the state of research summary by Lothar Köhn, *Entwicklungs- und Bildungsroman.* (Stuttgart: Metzler, 1969); Jürgen Jacobs, *Wilhelm Meister und seine Brüder: Untersuchungen zum deutschen Bildungsroman* (Munich: Fink, 1972); Walter H. Bruford, *The German Tradition of Self-Cultivation. 'Bildung' from Humboldt to Thomas Mann* (Cambridge: Cambridge UP, 1975); Martin Swales, *The German Bildungsroman from Wieland to Hesse* (Princeton: Princeton UP, 1978); Michael Beddow: *The Fiction of Humanity: Studies in the Bildungsroman from Wieland to Thomas Mann* (Cambridge: Cambridge UP, 1982); Rolf Selbmann, *Der deutsche Bildungsroman* (Stuttgart: Metzler, 1984).
3. Princeton: Princeton UP, 1978, 160.
4. Thomas Mann, *Gesammelte Werke,* 13 vols. (Frankfurt am Main: S. Fischer, 1974). See 11:702f., and 10:360 ("Die Kunst des Romans").
5. *Biedermeierzeit: Deutsche Literatur im Spannungsfeld zwischen Restauration und Revolution 1815-1848,* 3 vols. (Stuttgart: Metzler, 1971-80). Here see 2:906.

6. "The Mystery of the Missing Bildungsroman, or: What Happened to Wilhelm Meister's Legacy?" *Genre* 14 (1981): 229-46. See Sammons's later article on a similar topic in this volume. Ed.

7. In this discussion foreign literary scholars were mostly in favor of keeping the term (some of the most recent examples being Ivar Sagmo, *Bildungsroman und Geschichtsphilosophie: Eine Studie zu Goethes Roman 'Wilhelm Meisters Lehrjahre'* (Bonn: Bouvier, 1982), 21ff.; Martin Swales, "Utopie und Bildungsroman," in *Utopieforschung: Interdisziplinäre Studien zur neuzeitlichen Utopie,* ed. Wilhelm Voβkamp (Stuttgart: Metzler, 1982), vol. 3, 218-26; Ehrhard Bahr, "'Wilhelm Meisters Lehrjahre' als Bildungsroman," Nachwort der Reclam-Ausgabe (Stuttgart: Reclam, 1982), 643-60; German literary scholars do, however, increasingly voice reservations. See for example Rolf-Peter Janz, "Zum sozialen Gehalt der 'Lehrjahre,'" in *Literaturwissenschaft und Geschichtsphilosophie: Festschrift fur Wilhelm Emrich,* ed. Helmut Arntzen et al. (Berlin, New York: de Gruyter, 1975, 320-340; Stefan Blessin, "Die radikal-liberale Konzeption von Wilhelm Meisters Lehrjahren" in *Die Romane Goethes* (Königstein: Athenäum, 1979), 11-58; Wilhelm Voβkamp, "Utopie und Utopiekritik in Goethes Romanen 'Wilhelm Meisters Lehrjahre' und 'Wilhelm Meisters Wanderjahre.'" in *Utopieforschung,* ed. Voβkamp, 227-49. Concerning this discussion see Selbmann, 63ff.

8. The English quotation is taken here from vol. 9 of *Goethe's Collected Works* (New York: Suhrkamp, 1989), *Wilhelm Meister's Apprenticeship,* 174-75. The original, from Book Five, Chapter III, reads, "Daβ ich Dir's mit *einem* Worte sage: mich selbst, ganz wie ich da bin, auszubilden, das war dunkel von Jugend auf mein Wunsch und meine Absicht. . . . Ich habe nun einmal gerade zu jener harmonischen Ausbildung meiner Natur, die mir meine Geburt versagt, eine unwiderstehliche Neigung." *Goethes Werke,* Hamburger Ausgabe, 11th ed. (Munich: Beck, 1982), 7:290-91.

9. Schlegel, "Über Goethes Meister," in *Charakteristiken und Kritiken I (1796-1801). Kritische Friedrich-Schlegel-Ausgabe,* ed. Ernst Behler (Paderborn, 1958ff) 2:126-46. Quotation on page 137.

10. See concerning subsequent statements the well-researched works of Klaus Friedrich Gille, *"Wilhelm Meister" im Urteil der Zeitgenossen: Ein Beitrag zur Wirkungsgeschichte Goethes* (Assen: van Gorkum, 1971), and Karl Robert Mandelkow, *Goethe in Deutschland: Rezeptionsgeschichte eines Klassikers.* (Munich: Beck, 1980). Vol. 1: *1773-1918.*

11. Schiller to Goethe 8 July 1796. Friedrich Schiller, Nationalausgabe. Begründet von Julius Petersen (Weimar, 1943ff.), 28:254. Wilhelm trete "von einem leeren und unbestimmten Ideal in ein bestimmtes thätiges Leben, aber ohne die idealisierende Kraft dabey einzubüβen."

12. Körner to Schiller, 5 November 1796. Nationalausgabe 36, I, 370. Körner referred to the "Darstellung einer schönen menschlichen Natur, die sich durch die Zusammenwirkung ihrer innern Anlagen und äuβern Verhältniβe allmählich ausbildet. Das Ziel dieser Ausbildung ist ein vollendetes Gleichgewicht."

13. Humboldt to Goethe 24 November 1796. *Briefe an Goethe, Gesamtausgabe in Regestform,* ed. Karl-Heinz Hahn (Weimar: Böhlau, 1981), vol. 2: *1796-1798,* 146: ". . . durchgängige Bestimmbarkeit, ohne fast alle wirkliche Bestimmung . . ."; and "das 'hohe Verdienst' des Romans liege eben darin 'daβ er die Welt u. das Leben ganz wie es ist, völlig unabhängig von einer einzelnen Individualität u. eben dadurch offen für jede Individualität' schildere."

14. Schiller to Goethe, 28 November 1796, NA 29, 16: "Wilhelm Meister ist zwar die nothwendigste aber nicht die wichtigste Person; eben das gehört zu den Eigenthümlichkeiten Ihres Romans, daβ er keine solche wichtigste Person hat und braucht. *An* ihm und *um* ihn geschieht alles, aber nicht eigentlich *seinet*wegen. . . ."

15. Schiller to Goethe, 20 October 1797, NA 29, 149: Schiller stresses that "die Form des Meisters wie überhaupt jede Romanform . . . schlechterdings nicht poetisch [sei]"; "ganz nur im Gebiete des Verstandes [liege]"; "unter allen seinen Forderungen [stehe]" "[und auch] von allen seinen Grenzen [partizipiere]." "[So fehle es dem *Wilhelm Meister* bei allen hohen literarischen Qualitäten im einzelnen] an einer gewissen poetischen Kühnheit"; "[charakteristisch sei ein] sonderbares Schwanken zwischen einer prosaischen und poetischen Stimmung."

16. "Eine poëtisirte bürgerliche und häusliche Geschichte." Novalis, *Schriften,* ed. Richard Samuel, 2d ed. (Stuttgart: Kohlhammer, 1968), vol. 3, *Das philosophische Werk* II, 638ff.

17. Mandelkow, *Goethe in Deutschland,* 50; and on the following, see 52ff.

18. F. Schlegel, *Geschichte der alten und neuen Literatur,* KA 6, 274: "eine prosaische Darstellung der wirklichen Gegenwart zur Poesie zu erheben."

19. Georg Wilhelm Friedrich Hegel, *Vorlesungen über die Ästhetik,* in *Werke in 20 Bänden,* ed. Eva Moldenhauer and Karl Markus Michel (Frankfurt: Suhrkamp, 1970). See especially vols. 13-15. The lectures were written 1818-29.

20. "Eine der gewöhnlichsten und für den Roman passendsten Kollisionen ist deshalb der Konflikt zwischen der Poesie des Herzens und der entgegenstehenden Prosa der Verhältnisse sowie dem Zufalle äuβerer Umstände" (*Werke,* 15:393). Quoted in the original German article by Steinecke, 59.

21. "Diese Kämpfe nun aber sind in der modernen Welt nichts Weiteres als die Lehrjahre, die Erziehung des Individuums an der vorhandenen Wirklichkeit, und erhalten dadurch ihren wahren Sinn," (14:220). Quoted by Steinecke, 59.

22. ". . . die der gewöhnlichen Weltordnung zunächst widerstrebenden Charaktere das Echte und Substantielle in ihr Anerkennen lernen, mit ihren Verhältnissen sich aussöhnen und wirksam in dieselben eintreten" (15:393). Quoted by Steinecke, 59.

23. ". . . daβ sich das Subjekt die Hörner abläuft, mit seinem Wünschen und Meinen sich in die bestehenden Verhältnisse und die Vernünftigkeit derselben hineinbildet, in die Verkettung der Welt eintritt und in ihr sich einen angemessenen Standpunkt erwirbt" (14:220). Cited by Steinecke, 60.

24. "Einleitung über den Roman," in *Aesthetische und Poetische Mittheilungen* (Magdeburg: Heinrichshofen, 1827), 3.

25. Ibid., "Einleitung," 3, 14, 15.

26. "Individuelle Bildungsgeschichte derselben, Leben und Schicksale eines *Einzelnen* von seiner Geburt bis zu seiner vollendeten Bildung, an und mit welchem aber der ganze Baum der Menschheit nach seinen mannichfaltigen Verzweigungen in der schönen Stillstandszeit seiner Reife und Vollendung, deducirt wird, Lehrjahre des Jüngers, bis er zum Meister erhoben ist, das ist der Roman," 399. Cited by Steinecke, 60-61.

27. "In dem so idealisch organisirten Deutschlande mit der schönen wirklich eigenthümlichen Empfänglichkeit seiner Bewohner für reine Ausbildung des Menschen an sich, ohne andre entehrende und beschränkende Rücksichten, sey dieser Geist der Zeit in seiner schönsten Blüthe aufgegangen" 403. Cited by Steinecke, 61.

28. See on related matters Martini's article in this volume. Ed.

29. Karl Morgenstern, "Ueber das Wesen des Bildungsromans," *Inländisches Museum* I (1820), Heft 2, 46-61; Heft 3, 13-27. See here 58-60.

30. "uns in das Innere menschlicher Seelen zu führen, und daselbst ihre Ahnungen, Bestrebungen, Kämpfe, Niederlagen und Siege uns zu offenbaren" 51. Quoted by Steinecke, 61.

31. "des Helden Bildung in ihrem Anfang und Fortgang bis zu einer gewissen Stufe der Vollendung darstellt. . . . An sich gefallende, schöne und unterhaltende Darstellung der Bildungsgeschichte eines ausgezeichnet Bildungsfähigen wird sein objectiver, im Kunstwerke überall sich aussprechender Zweck des Dichters eines solchen Romans seyn . . ." 13. Quoted by Steinecke, 61-62.

32. "Als Werk von der allgemeinsten, umfassendsten Tendenz schönmenschlicher Bildung aber erscheinen im mildesten Glanze *Wilhelm Meister's Lehrjahre* von *Göthe,* doppelt uns Deutsche ansprechend, weil hier . . . der Dichter in dem Helden und der Scene und Umgebung uns deutsches Leben, deutsche Denkart und Sitten unsrer Zeit gab . . ." 15f. Quoted by Steinecke, 62.

33. ". . . den allerelendsten Stoff." Quoted by Steinecke, *Romanpoetik von Goethe bis Thomas Mann* (Munich: Wilhelm Fink, 1987), 25.

34. Börne, *Sämtliche Schriften,* ed. Inge Rippmann and Peter Rippmann, 5 vols. (Düsseldorf & Darmstadt: Melzer, 1964-68), 2:396.

35. ". . . Kaum der Jüngling, geschweige der Mann fertig. . . . Um aber Mann zu werden, dazu gehört ein Staat, den Staat kannte aber Goethe gar nicht, hatte keinen Sinn, ein öffentliches Staatsleben zu schildern, keinen Muth, offen davon zu sprechen und das fehlende Element einzugestehen." In *Literarischer Zodiacus: Journal für Zeit und Leben, Wissenschaft und Kunst* (November, 1835). Cited by Steinecke, 64.

36. ". . . am liebsten und am besten die philisterhaft gutmüthige Idylle der Häuslichkeit." *Literarischer Zodiacus,* 480. Cited by Steinecke, 64.

37. Theodor Mundt, *Kritische Wälder. Blätter zur Beurtheilung der Literature, Kunst und Wissenschaft unserer Zeit,* (Leipzig: Melzer, 1833), 136f., 180, 187. Cited by Steinecke, 64f.

38. Mundt, *Die Kunst der deutschen Prosa. Aesthetisch, literar-geschichtlich, gesellschaftlich* (Berlin: Veit & Comp., 1837), 359. Cited by Steinecke, 65.

39. "Nie sind die Individuen bedeutender gewesen, als gerade in unsern Tagen, auch der Letzte fühlt das Fluβbette seines Innern von groβen Einflüssen gespeist. . . . Jeder Mensch ist eine historische Natur geworden. . . ." Karl Immermann, *Werke in 5 Bänden,* ed. Benno von Wiese et al. (Frankfurt am Main: Athenäum, 1977), 2:508-9. Quoted by Steinecke, 66.

40. Pun on Meister. Ed.

41. ". . . die erhebende Aussicht, einmal *Meister,* entweder in der Kunst, oder, was noch besser, im Leben zu werden. Weit übler ist der Epigone Hermann daran." In "Immermann und das Jahrhundert der Epigonen" (1836), 286. Quoted by Steinecke, 66.

42. See Ehrhard Bahr's essay in this volume on the *Wanderjahre.* See also James Hardin's introduction to *Wilhelm Meister's Travels* in the translation by Thomas Carlyle of the first version of that work (Columbia, SC: Camden House, 1991). Ed.

43. *Goethe's Works* in the Suhrkamp edition (New York, 1989), 9:338. "Nur alle Menschen machen die Menschheit aus, nur alle Kräfte zusammengenommen die Welt . . . alles . . . liegt im Menschen, und muβ ausgebildet werden; aber nicht in einem, sondern in vielen." Hamburg edition of Goethe's *Werke,* 7:552.

44. Gutzkow to Levin Schücking in a letter of 5 August 1850. Quoted in Schücking, *Lebenserinnerungen* (Breslau: Schottländer, 1886), 2:55.

45. ". . . mit dem möglichst geringsten Aufwand von äuβerm Leben das innere in die stärkste Bewegung bringen]." Cited by Steinecke, 69.

46. "Ein *Roman* wird desto höherer und edlerer Art seyn, je mehr *inneres* und je weniger *äußeres* Leben er darstellt." Quoted by Steinecke, 69.

47. ". . . dem Roman die Entfaltung des Gemüths im Privatleben als sein Gebiet." Cited by Steinecke, 69.

48. Cited by Steinecke, 69.

49. Gottschall, *Poetik: Die Dichtkunst und ihre Technik. Vom Standpunkte der Neuzeit* (Breslau: Eduard Trewendt, 1858), 379, 384.

50. "Die Kämpfe des Geistes, des Gewissens, die tiefen Krisen der Ueberzeugung, der Weltanschauung, die das bedeutende Individuum durchläuft, vereinigt mit den Kämpfen des Gefühlslebens: dieß sind die Conflicte, dieß die Schlachten des Romans. Doch natürlich sind dieß nicht blos innere Conflicte, sie erwachsen aus der Erfahrung und der Grundconflict ist immer der des erfahrungslosen Herzens, das mit seinen Idealen in die Welt tritt . . ." *Ästhetik oder Wissenschaft des Schönen,* (Stuttgart: Carl Mäcken, 1857) Part 3, Heft 5, 1308f. Quoted by Steinecke, 70.

51. Ibid., 1308. Cited by Steinecke, 70.

52. Ibid., 1313f. Cited by Steinecke, 70.

53. "Der Heerd der Familie ist der wahre Mittelpunct des Weltbildes im Roman und er gewinnt seine Bedeutung erst, wo Gemüther sich um ihn vereinigen, welche die harte Wahrheit des Lebens mit zarteren Saiten einer erweiterten geistigen Welt wiedertönen." Ibid., 1314. Cited by Steinecke, 70.

54. "Eduard Mörike, Maler Nolten," in *Kritische Gänge, Aesthetik oder Wissenschaft des Schönen,* Tl. 3, Heft 5, 2:7. Cited by Steinecke, 70-71.

55. "Ich möchte die Romane, welche die Schule des Wilhelm Meister ausmachen . . . Bildungsromane nennen. Goethes Werk zeigt menschliche Ausbildung in verschiedenen Stufen, Gestalten, Lebensepochen." Dilthey, *Das Leben Schleiermachers,* in *Gesammelte Schriften,* vol. 13:1, ed. Martin Redeker (Göttingen: Vandenhoeck & Ruprecht, 1970), 299. *Das Leben Schleiermachers* was originally published in 1870.

56. "in das Leben eintritt, nach verwandten Seelen sucht, der Freundschaft begegnet und der Liebe, wie er nun aber mit den harten Realitäten der Welt in Kampf gerät und so unter mannigfachen Lebenserfahrungen heranreift, sich selber findet und seiner Aufgabe in der Welt gewiß wird. Die Aufgabe Goethes war die Geschichte eines sich zur Tätigkeit bildenden Menschen. . . . So sprechen diese Bildungsromane den Individualismus einer Kultur aus, die auf die Interessensphäre des Privatelbens eingeschränkt ist. . . . Die Dissonanzen und Konflikte des Lebens erscheinen als die notwendigen Durchgangspunkte des Individuums auf seiner Bahn zur Reife und zur Harmonie. Und 'höchstes Glück der Erdenkinder' ist die 'Persönlichkeit', als einheitliche und feste Form des menschlichen Daseins. Nie ist dieser Optimismus der persönlichen Entwicklung . . . heiterer und lebenssicherer ausgesprochen worden als in Goethes Wilhelm Meister. . . ." Dilthey, *Das Erlebnis und die Dichtung* 14th ed. (Göttingen: Vandenhoeck & Ruprecht, 1965), 272f. Quoted by Steinecke, 71-72.

Jill Anne Kowalik (essay date 1992)

SOURCE: "Feminine Identity Formation in *Wilhelm Meisters Lehrjahre,*" in *Modern Language Quarterly,* Vol. 53, No. 2, June, 1992, pp. 149-72.

[*In the following essay, Kowalik surveys Goethe's portrayal of the childhood psychosexual development of the female characters in* Wilhelm Meisters Lehrjahre.]

Natalie, the "beautiful soul," and Therese have been treated almost without exception in commentaries on ***Wilhelm Meisters Lehrjahre*** as examples of idealized types, representing static categories or principles of feminine existence. Scholars explicitly or implicitly adopt Schiller's view, expressed in a letter to Goethe dated 3 July 1796: "Es ist zu bewundern, wie schön und wahr die drei Charaktere der *Stiftsdame, Nataliens* und *Theresiens* nuanciert sind. Die zwei ersten sind heilige, die zwei andern sind wahre und menschliche Naturen; aber eben darum, weil Natalie heilig und menschlich zugleich ist, so erscheint sie wie ein Engel, da die Stiftsdame nur eine Heilige, Therese nur eine vollkommene Irdische ist" (It is admirable how subtly the three figures of the canoness [the beautiful soul, J. K.], Natalie, and Therese are so beautifully and truly portrayed. The first two are saintly; the other two have a true and human character; but because Natalie is both saintly and human, she appears as an angel, whereas the canoness is only a saint and Therese only a perfect earthly type).[1]

Schiller arrived at his judgment by ignoring those sections of the novel in which the histories of these characters are recounted. His oversight exemplifies the androcentric ideology of German Classicism, which constructed feminine identity as a timeless, ahistorical existence for which the concept of development or *Bildung* was irrelevant. Kept off the historical stage to play institutionalized "natural" gender roles in the private sphere, women were represented also in theoretical documents on gender as passive, "emotional" creatures whose lives did not and could not contain a dynamic dimension.[2]

In ***Wilhelm Meisters Lehrjahre,*** however, Goethe radically departed from the masculine notion of feminine stasis to offer a detailed and insightful account of the early childhoods—the histories—of the three women whom Schiller idealized. By analyzing Goethe's representation of the interaction between these women as children and their primary caregivers, we can draw some important conclusions about the process of feminine identity formation in late eighteenth-century Germany. This process, as I shall attempt to show, displays certain pathological features of which Goethe, the *Augenmensch* and master observer of human behavior, was keenly aware. I use the term *pathological* here and throughout my essay as a descriptive rather than a normative designation; I am not interested in whether the three women in question are "good," an issue that has obsessed critics for decades. I want instead to examine how their particular adult identities evolved and what their evolution tells us about the social-historical and psychohistorical context in which the novel was produced. Our task is not to assign moralistic labels to its figures but to look into complexities of characterization in order to understand better what the book is actually about.[3]

In my analysis I employ one of several possible psychoanalytic constructs of the personality, namely, the model of psychosexual development proposed by Freud.[4] Although some readers may find it ahistorical to apply an interpretive model developed in the twentieth century to an eighteenth-century text, it is apt for ***Wilhelm Meisters Lehrjahre*** because the work constantly thematizes, as does psychoanalysis itself, the function of the past in the present. Every character in this novel about development has at some point either to come to terms with the past, as Wilhelm has been seen to do, or to be destroyed by it, as the harpist is—indeed, as is his entire family, whose youngest member is celebrated in the *Saal der Vergangenheit* (chamber of the past). While none of the figures I discuss can be said to have been destroyed by her childhood, I shall argue that the contours of their early experience lend their existence a tragic dimension that has not been sufficiently appreciated.

Readers may also harbor the reservation that interpreting the text according to a Freudian model is invariably reductive and simplifies or distorts its dense symbolic structure.[5] Such complaints are rarely heard today with regard to sociocultural readings; few contemporary critics would dispute, for example, that the ***Lehrjahre*** addresses, in any number of controversial ways, the relationship between the aristocracy and the middle class in eighteenth-century Germany. Yet it has not been generally recognized that Goethe likewise deals with the problem of gender identity in this period and that it might well be approached from a psychoanalytic perspective. Thus a Freudian model does not close off but rather allows us access to crucial sections of the novel that have resisted interpretation for almost two centuries.[6]

In the pages that follow I shall be concerned especially with the details of Goethe's presentation. For in the passages that might be dismissed as less significant embellishments of the main plot (if they are mentioned at all), Goethe reveals his ability as a narrator to locate major issues of the ***Lehrjahre*** within the apparently incidental fact or event, the seemingly offhand remark. His narrative strategy enables him not only to integrate important information about the childhood of the three women figures into his text but also, and perhaps most importantly, to represent the attitude of the novel's characters toward this information. While the author is obviously concerned with the etiology of feminine identity, his protagonist is not. Wilhelm is the only character who clearly knew the childhood stories of Natalie, the beautiful soul, and Therese, but his response is silence. He has no comment on the early experience of the woman who was later to become his wife, or on that of her aunt, or on that of Therese, whom he almost married.[7] This curious lacuna exemplifies (and I believe Goethe meant it to exemplify) the male, and specifically the fatherly, neglect of feminine maturation in eighteenth-century Germany, from which all three of the women can be shown to have suffered.

The story of the beautiful soul opens with an erasure: "Bis in mein achtes Jahr war ich ein ganz gesundes Kind, weiβ mich aber von dieser Zeit so wenig zu erinnern als von dem Tage meiner Geburt" (I was quite a healthy child until my eighth year, but I remember as little about that period as I do about the day I was born [***WML,*** p. 358]). The passage refers to what Freud would later term "infantile amnesia," which occurs sometime between the ages of six and eight. The child forgets its own early experiences of sexuality, that is, it forgets nearly everything from its first years, with the possible exception of certain "screen memories" (*Deckerinnerungen*), which for the beautiful soul consist in unspecified recollections that she was not a completely healthy child. Infantile amnesia marks the transition between the Oedipal phase (roughly ages three to five or six) and the period of "latency" that lasts until the rearousal of the child's sexuality during puberty. During this period the child unconsciously carries forward the Oedipal wishes that have already been developed. The experiences recounted by the beautiful soul therefore recapitulate and extend her earlier sexual fantasies. By commencing the narration during a time when previous Oedipal desire is both potent and forgotten, Goethe establishes unconscious repetition as the dominant psychic structure for the beautiful soul. Her life will be informed by a continuous reenactment of her primary, originating erotic encounter with her father.

In the usual course of feminine psychosexual development, daughters both identify with their mothers and become enraged toward them.[8] Identification with the mother predates the Oedipal phase; it is present almost from birth, because the female child naturally views her parent of the same sex as being like herself. During the pre-Oedipal period, the mother is the daughter's primary object of love, just as she is for little boys. Infants of both sexes live in a state of erotic symbiosis with the mother. The daughter's sexual attachment to her mother shifts in the Oedipal phase as the father becomes her love object, but the identification with the mother, which may still contain pre-Oedipal erotic elements, remains. (Little boys stay attached to the love object, mother, but their identification shifts to the father.) As the daughter develops the desire for exclusive possession of her father's love, she becomes enviously aware of her inferior position within the Oedipal triad and feels rage toward her mother as a result. Moreover, she is terrified of being punished should her desire for her father and her angry aggression toward her mother be discovered. Under favorable circumstances, daughters eventually resolve their ambivalence toward the mother as they develop erotic relationships with male peers.[9] But feminine identification with the mother is, Goethe suggests, pathologically complicated in the patriarchy of late eighteenth-century Germany, especially for those daughters, like the beautiful soul, who have intellectual potential.

After mentioning her amnesia, the beautiful soul (who never receives a name because her story is a generic one) describes what happened in her bedroom when she was eight years old. The most significant visitor to sit on her bed was her father, who entertains her with all manner of natural objects from his "Kabinett" (cabinet, i.e., where his collection is held [***WML,*** p. 358]). She seems almost to enjoy her illness and convalescence because in this *nine-month* period her father is drawn more frequently to her bed than he might otherwise have been. She says of this time, "Ich litt und liebte" (I suffered and loved [***WML,*** p. 358]). Because her mother has only told her Bible stories, leaving the narration of romances and fairy tales to an aunt, the beautiful soul knows that she cannot confide in her mother her erotically charged conversations with her father. She therefore creates a surrogate: her invisible friend (also called "das unsichtbare Wesen" [the invisible Being]), whose versified, and therefore "disciplined," conversations (***WML,*** p. 359) she does feel safe in dictating to her mother. She has learned that her erotic attachment to Father is unacceptable to Mother.

Shortly after her illness, she gives up dolls. "Ich verlangte nach Wesen, die meine Liebe erwiderten" (I had a desire for beings who would return my love [***WML,*** p. 359]). With the help of the aunt's fairy tales, she is able to fantasize that she is a princess who marries a "verwünschter Prinz" (a prince who was bewitched), who had previously been a "Schäfchen" (lamb).[10] The beautiful soul says that she derives a lot of pleasure from her father's various animals (***WML,*** p. 359), and she associates them with her magical lamb, which stands also for the Lamb of God, or the invisible Being, or Father. She soon discovers, however, that she might never acquire what she calls "einen so köstlichen Besitz" (such a precious possession [***WML,*** p. 359]). She then consoles herself with the fascinating love stories she finds in books. And she believes that her surrogate friend will compensate her for the love she actually wants from her lamb (cf. ***WML,*** pp. 359-60).

When her mother has her father take her books away, the father secretly returns them. The mother engages in a prohibition vis-à-vis the daughter just as the father tries to deny Wilhelm his visits to the theater. The beautiful soul knows that she and Father are deceiving Mother. The mother eventually realizes her weak position in the triad and allows her daughter to read again, but she tries to channel her reading by denying her seductive works ("verführerische Bücher" [***WML,*** p. 360]). The child, however, merely circumvents the mother and informs herself about sex from the Bible's "bedenkliche Stellen" (questionable passages [***WML,*** p. 360]).

The same sexual curiosity that had motivated her attentive study of the Bible, ("diese Wißbegierde" [***WML,*** p. 360]), eventually leads her into the art of cooking, where she will learn from her mother how animals, that is to say, how women, are cut open and prepared for consumption by men. The child uses these occasions, which she always refers to as "ein Fest" (festival, party [***WML,*** p. 360]), to play with and display to her father animal intestines ("Eingeweide" [***WML,*** p. 360]), which she views as sexual organs. He responds to this kind of play activity by conversing with her as if she were a young student and by calling her his "mißratener Sohn" (misbegotten son [***WML,*** p. 360]). In its context this means the following: "I wish you wouldn't display yourself as my potential sexual partner. I wish you were a boy." Because desire can never be eradicated but only transformed, the beautiful soul takes her father's response to mean: "If I am to fulfill his desire and possess his love, I must identify with him. I must be a boy." From this point on, all of her potentially erotic encounters are necessarily identificatory: Damon, Narziß, and Philo.

In her thirteenth year, for example, the beautiful soul compares her soul to a mirror, which is a familiar Neoplatonic image. She is subsequently attracted to Narziß (Narcissus), whose primary mythic activity is looking at his own reflection. In Narziß she finds her own identity, which is that of a person in love with his or her own reflection. The identification is underlined in their first private moment together: he has a nosebleed, reminiscent of her own "Blutsturz" (coughing up of blood [***WML,*** p. 358]) at the beginning of her remembered life. Later on, after his blood from an injury is washed from her body, she stands gazing at herself in a mirror and acknowledging her own beauty. Still later she meets a man to whom she gives the name Philo, which with respect to sound is the masculine form of the name Phyllis that she gave herself in early adolescence. And Philo had, she says, "im ganzen eine entfernte Ähnlichkeit mit Narzissen" (on the whole a distant similarity to Narcissus [***WML,*** p. 391]).

In her three major encounters with men as partners, the beautiful soul seeks intellectual companionship (which she sometimes receives and sometimes does not) because she believes that it will ultimately result in the fulfillment of her Oedipal wishes for her father. Only in Damon does she believe that she has found her "gewünschtes Schäfchen" (desired lamb [***WML,*** p. 362]). But Damon is a double figure. He has a younger brother who, like Damon himself and like the beautiful soul, is ill. This doubling represents the parental dyad: the older boy, like the father, encourages the identificatory bond with the child, while the younger brother, like the mother, wants to destroy it. This fact did not escape the beautiful soul, who now points out that "die Eifersucht des Jüngeren machte den Roman vollkommen" (the jealousy of the younger boy added the finishing touch to our novel [i.e., love story] [***WML,*** p. 362]). "Phyllis," as she called herself during the affair, can forget the death of both brothers so easily (***WML,*** p. 363), despite her intense involvement with them because she incorporates them. Her independence, both sexual and intellectual, follows from this and prevents her from ever marrying.

Hence neither Narziβ nor Philo, nor the many other men the beautiful soul meets—she has many suitors (cf. ***WML,*** p. 382)—can compete with her invisible friend, with whom she eventually "consummates" her love in an out-of-body experience, which is the logical conclusion of her desire to be a boy, that is, not to be a girl. The experience is set in motion when Philo tells her of his many love affairs, which she associates with David's seduction of Bathsheba and murder of her husband Uriah (cf. ***WML,*** pp. 391-93). She fears that she could commit similar crimes and worries about an ineradicable "Herrschaft der Neigung" (primacy of inclination [***WML,*** p. 393]) within herself. The parallel she draws to David suggests that she is frightened of her desire for illicit sex with the female and elimination of the male competitor, for which she would be punished. These are the Oedipal fantasies of a little boy, but in the beautiful soul they have a somewhat different significance. The "sin" she finds so difficult to conquer is her continuing, unconscious erotic attachment to Mother, which interferes with her relationship to God the Father and places her in a state of perpetual anxiety. Because her father had conveyed to her as a child that her feminine eroticism toward him was unwelcome, the beautiful soul tries throughout her life to cast off her identification with her mother, which is grounded in a powerful pre-Oedipal sexual bond. Her attempts at this explain her lifelong unwillingness to cultivate female friends. At the same time, she is unconsciously enraged at her father for asking her to give up her attachment to her mother and wishes therefore to kill him. When her father finally dies, she says she enjoys "die gröβte Freiheit" (the greatest freedom [***WML,*** p. 414]). The intense ambivalence she feels toward her father—desire for his love along with hatred for him because he will not accept her as a female lover—is eventually overcome, but not resolved, with a compromise. In an ecstatic mystical union with "einem abwesenden Geliebten" (an absent lover [***WML,*** p. 394]), she feels herself to be without her body. She has chosen to repress her feminine identity even at the physical level in a sacrificial merging with Christ on the Cross (***WML,*** p. 394).[11]

Later we find the beautiful soul tending, in a motherly fashion, her sick and elderly father. When her uncle describes her long canceled engagement to Narziβ as an "Aufopferung" (sacrifice), she replies that she was "gern und willig" (happy) to sacrifice her "geliebtes Schaf" (beloved lamb) in favor of the "Gesundheit eines verehrten Vaters" (the health of her dearly respected father [***WML,*** p. 406]). Her refusal to marry has allowed her now to assume, finally, her deceased mother's position. When one of her sisters, who acts as Mother by virtue of her role as the head of the household that they share with their father, dies of a "Brustkrankheit" (chest infection [***WML,*** p. 412), the beautiful soul cannot attend the funeral because she herself suffers from "der alte Schaden auf meiner Brust" (the old wound and damage to my chest [***WML,*** p. 412]). Her psychosomatic identification with her sibling indicates that she no longer wishes to identify with her father, but with her mother, whose imago has been displaced onto her sister. Her original, unresolved wish to occupy Mother's place is manifested in her desire to care for her other sister's children. But her uncle bars her from them, and the beautiful soul consequently suffers the deepest anguish of her life precisely when she would be Mother's most appropriate surrogate.

Patriarchal societies like the one in which the beautiful soul grows to maturity reserve the category of development (*Bildung*) for men. Mothers have been co-opted by the patriarchy because they have internalized the restrictive values of their fathers.[12] Hence mothers are threatened by their daughters' intellectual curiosity, which the patriarchy has banished from the mother's character, for curiosity allows the daughter secret communion with her father. The idea of this communion is threatening for the mother because it reanimates her own unresolved wish for exclusive communion with *her* father. Thus, rather than participate in and enjoy the daughter's intellectual pursuits, the mother seeks to control them in a futile attempt to eliminate a competitor for her husband's (i.e., her "father's") attention.[13] Because the mother cannot identify with her daughter's intellectual inclinations and refuses to let her daughter identify with her as her husband's other lover, the daughter has no choice but to introject the father. She believes that doing so will guarantee her both eros and logos, but she is sorely mistaken. Her father is not threatened by her intellectuality per se, because he is not tempted to identify with his female child. But he *is* threatened by her erotic desire for him, because, paradoxically, it is accompanied by intellectual interests that he cannot share with her mother.

Thus little girls are "shortchanged" in comparison to little boys. For while the mother is able and willing to accept, indeed to arouse, her son's desire as an aspect of his intellectual development (as Kittler and Kaiser have argued in their perceptive but androcentric study of the ***Lehrjahre***), fathers in this patriarchy refuse to do the same for their daughters. Sons therefore eventually resolve their Oedipal conflicts by transferring their eroticism onto peer partners. Daughters, on the other hand, are never allowed to work through and disengage from their Oedipal fantasies, because neither parent will acknowledge to them the acceptability of such childhood desires.

Several recent interpretations of the "Confessions" posit the independence of the beautiful soul as an absolute value in itself and castigate the men who seek to hinder its development and expression.[14] But they ignore the cultural-historical and personal-historical origins of independence in the context of the familial Oedipal configuration. Hence they deny the importance, even the existence, of sexual desire in little girls. Such approaches cannot address, and may even unwittingly reproduce, the patriarchal attitudes represented in the "Confessions." In particular, the repression of unbounded female sexuality is accompanied by life-threatening consequences for women such as Mariane, the Countess, Mignon, and Mignon's mother who experience desire outside the domestic setting. Aurelie, to whom the "Confessions" are read as a form of psychotherapy meant to help her deal with a traumatic sexual rejection and the disintegrating experience of all-consuming desire, does not receive the therapeutic benefit predicted by the doctor. In fact, the story's message of hopelessness kills her. In reviewing the life of a woman who learned to live with unfulfilled or vicariously fulfilled desire, Aurelie is overwhelmed by the patriarchal hostility toward feminine eroticism, which she herself refuses to view as bad or wrong. The history of the beautiful soul, whose Oedipal wishes have not been harmoniously resolved, shows her how harmful it is for a woman to compromise her sexuality, and she dies rather than do so herself.

The secondary literature on the ***Lehrjahre*** often gives one the impression that critics have not really known what to make of the story of the beautiful soul. Interpretations range from the primitive biographical (the beautiful soul is a depiction of Susanna von Klettenberg), to the formalist-technical (book 6 functions as a moment of retardation in the plot), to the social-historical (the beautiful soul represents the conflicts between marriage and independence that women faced in the late eighteenth century). Yet most studies do not show, except in the most superficial way, how book 6 is related to the rest of the novel. It has even been argued that book 6 cannot or should not be integrated into the entire text (Zantop, esp. pp. 87-88). However, as a pedagogical reflection provided to Aurelie and Natalie, who is so often viewed as the ideal of womanhood in the ***Lehrjahre,*** book 6 must be taken as a paradigm of feminine development. Examining the paradigmatic status of the "Confessions" more closely will help us understand the relationship between Natalie and her aunt as more than a vague "harmony" of their souls.

People like the beautiful soul, Natalie tells Wilhelm, resemble ideals that are "nicht zum Nachahmen, sondern zum Nachstreben" (not to be imitated but rather emulated [***WML,*** p. 518]). It has never been noticed that Natalie employs terms fundamental to Karl Philipp Moritz's analysis of imitation in the opening pages of his essay "Über die bildende Nachahmung des Schönen" (1788), written while he and Goethe were together in Rome.[15] Because Natalie, following Moritz, prefers the sublime process of emulation to the base act of imitation (Moritz's word is "nachäffen" [to ape]), she is not interested in replicating the activities of the woman she both resembles and does not resemble in appearance. For example, she does not spend hours in the company of books as her aunt had done; she does not engage in disputations over aesthetics such as her aunt had conducted with the uncle; and she is not given to her aunt's dependence on "das unsichtbare Wesen." As we shall see, the last fact reflects Natalie's different feelings for and relationship to *her* father.

From her earliest years, however, Natalie does pursue what she believes is a creative emulation of the general virtue that she discerns in her aunt's life. The beautiful soul reports that Natalie, as a little girl, liked to appropriate and tailor her aunt's clothing—we could say her aunt's persona—for little girls in need of clothing, which is to say for little girls like herself who were developing a persona. When we encounter Natalie as an adult in book 8, we find her still caring for little girls and displaying her habit by dressing up Mignon. While feminist social historians might see in Natalie's activity merely the static role of the nurturing female, I view her continuing interest in the welfare of little girls as an indication of her development (*Bildung*). From her model Natalie thinks she has learned, first of all, that she can occupy the place of Mother without having to develop a sexual bond to a peer partner, and second, that her autonomy is grounded in her asexual existence. When Wilhelm, standing with her before the portrait of the beautiful soul, praises her aunt's "Reinlichkeit des Daseins" (purity of existence) and the "Selbständigkeit ihrer Natur" (her independence of character)—epithets perfectly appropriate for the Virgin Mother—Natalie agrees. She then observes that "jeder gebildete Mensch weiβ, wie sehr er an sich und andern mit einer gewiseen Roheit zu kämpfen hat" (every well-developed person knows how much he has to battle a certain crudeness in himself and in others [***WML,*** p. 518]). Like the beautiful soul, she has a deep awareness of the danger of desire; we recall her aunt's reference to the "Ungeheuer in jedem menschlichen Busen" (monster in every human breast [***WML,*** p. 420]).

Natalie believes that she has learned how to be an asexual mother from her aunt; but one's gender identity is fixed in a much more fundamental way than through occasional interaction with an aunt in one's youth (i.e., during latency or preadolescence). Natalie may well identify with the beautiful soul, but the cause of her identification almost certainly lies in her much earlier relationship to her parents. The story of her childhood, however, does not exist as a cohesive first-person narrative such as we have in Wilhelm's monologue to Mariane, Therese's report to Wilhelm about her early years, or the beautiful soul's narrative. Natalie's childhood is recounted in the third person because she herself, like Mignon, was so traumatized by the events of her early life that she can neither speak nor write about them. She cannot be conscious of the catastrophe resulting from the death of her parents because it is hidden behind the veil of infantile amnesia; she experienced her loss sometime between the ages of three and five, precisely when she was undergoing the most crucial phase of gender identity formation.

The recollections of her aunt about her own sister's family (***WML,*** pp. 412-20) provide us with the most important body of facts about Natalie's early experience.[16] The beautiful soul tells us that Natalie's father and mother were not happily married and quarreled often. Natalie's mother felt so guilty about it that she asked her sister not to tell their father. Natalie's mother seems to have suffered severe anxiety about the potential loss of love from her own father and thus of his ability to protect her. When he fell seriously ill during her first pregnancy, for example, she suffered a miscarriage. At the time of her husband's death in a riding accident, her daughter Natalie was in the Oedipal phase and still carried a pre-Oedipal identification with her mother. Through her identification Natalie would have absorbed and replicated her mother's anxiety over the loss of her father, Natalie's grandfather, which then actually came to pass when her own father was killed. Natalie's already considerable fears of separation from the father and her feelings of helplessness could only have been intensified as a result.

To make matters worse, Natalie's father had been angry at the birth of his two daughters, according to the beautiful soul; he had hoped instead for sons who could eventually help him administer the family estate. Children perceive the death of a parent as abandonment; Natalie ascribed it—not illogically, given her father's preferences—to the fact that she was not a boy. Furthermore, she assumed that her infantile anger toward her father for preferring boys to girls would cause her father to punish her—by dying and leaving her. Natalie's interpretation of her father's death is one important source of what would become her lifelong guilt over her feminine identity; it explains, for example, why she wears her great-uncle's cape, in which she first appears to us. With the cape she assures herself of the protection of a significant male caregiver, and she is able to hide or deny her female body underneath it.[17]

Her father's rejection of her female identity prior to his death is not the only reason for Natalie's refusal to view herself as a woman. When on the heels of his death her mother also dies after giving birth to Friedrich, Natalie sees firsthand the dangers that await her as a mature woman. But more important than this insight is the issue of her Oedipal guilt. During the Oedipal state of identification with the mother, little girls may wish for the death of the mother in order to occupy her place with the father; they also fear that their aggressive desire vis-à-vis the mother will be found out and punished. When the mother actually dies, the daughter naturally concludes that her wishing has brought it about and that she is being punished by the mother for having had the wish in the first place. Natalie, already in a state of high anxiety and feeling helpless because of the loss of her father, now must cope with the loss of her mother, her last remaining caregiver, and must deal with the fantasy that the death was her fault.

To atone for this horrible crime, which is after all a crime primarily against herself, and to overcome the helplessness that she has introduced into her life, Natalie adopts two strategies. First, she denies her helplessness by becoming utterly self-reliant and self-sufficient. Her aunt reports: "Sie war keinen Augenblick ihres Lebens unbeschäftigt, und jedes Geschäft ward unter ihren Händen zur würdigen Handlung . . . und ebenso konnte sie ruhig, ohne Ungeduld, bleiben, wenn sich nichts zu tun fand. Diese Tätigkeit ohne Bedürfnis einer Beschäftigung habe ich in meinem Leben nicht wieder gesehen" (She was never idle for a moment, and every task was ennobled by her hands . . . yet she could also be patiently still if there was nothing to do. I have never in my life seen such industry that was not driven by need [***WML,*** pp. 417-18]). Second, Natalie projects her helplessness onto other children and then spends the rest of her life as a compulsive caregiver.

Let us observe how Natalie's guilt and subsequent caregiving express themselves in her interaction with one of her charges, Mignon. The girls have heard from peasant children living nearby that angels sometimes visit children in order to punish the bad ones and to present gifts to the good ones. Natalie decides to use the impending birthday of twin girls—the doubling suggests the secret link between Natalie and Mignon—as an occasion to teach the little girls that angels do not really exist. Symbolically, Natalie wants to do away with a magical method of telling who is good and who is bad. Her psychological investment in this process is a reflection of her ambivalence toward herself. She knows that she is bad for having "killed" her mother, but she does not want to be found out; she is afraid that an omniscient force might identify and punish her. So Natalie reverts to her childhood custom of dressing up a little girl, this time as an angel. When Mignon finally appears, holding her lily of purity, the other girls are entertained by the fiction, which they immediately penetrate. But Natalie herself is "überrascht" (surprised [***WML,*** p. 515]) at how angelic Mignon seems. In fact, her astonishment stems from her unacknowledged wish to herself be an angel. Natalie then decides to let Mignon keep her angel's dress and to provide her with similarly feminine clothing. Natalie achieves here a pseudoresolution of her guilt and a vicarious acceptance of her female identity by projecting the entire complex onto Mignon. Mignon, with whom she unconsciously identifies, becomes the angelic woman whom Natalie cannot find within herself.[18]

Although Natalie's dedication to the children is universally praised by the figures in the novel, the narrator has a different opinion. When Natalie is busy telling Wilhelm about all the wonderful things she has done for the little girls, the narrator ironically interrupts her: "Einen umständlichern Bericht, wie Natalie mit ihren Kindern verfuhr, versparen wir auf eine andere Gelegenheit" (We shall present a more circumstantial report of how Natalie treated her children on another occasion [***WML,*** p. 528]). That the occasion never returns is not an oversight on Goethe's part. Natalie's caregiving is the displacement onto other children of her own unacknowledged and therefore unresolvable desire to be taken care of. Because she does not understand that she wants care, attention, and safety, she is not opposed to Wilhelm's abandoning her after their dispassionate engagement.[19]

In 1953 Karl Schlechta went against the grain of traditional views of Natalie by suggesting that "she has no drives [*Triebe*] or passions, no desire or memory"; she only partakes of a "lifeless nature."[20] Hans-Jürgen Schings, responding in 1986 to Schlechta's criticism, tells us that perfect characters are always subjected to the harshest criticism and that in fact Natalie is the embodiment of Spinoza's concept of absolute love. She knows no desire because she is completely unselfish ("vollkommen uneigennützig").[21] While Schlechta's interpretation obviously comes closer to what I have proposed than Schings's, their readings of the text have an important feature in common. Caught in the irrelevant, indeed unaskable, question of whether Natalie is a good or a bad person, neither critic examines the role of Natalie as a literary construct within the text. Although Schlechta is mystified by Philine, who he says gives up her eroticism ("kapituliert") in an opaque ("nicht ganz überschaubar" [p. 226] way, clearly her domestication goes hand in hand with the stories of the beautiful soul and her niece the "beautiful amazon." Schings for his part overlooks the fact that by equating sexual desire with selfishness, he celebrates Natalie's guilt. At issue is not a character but an idea: the fate of female sexuality in Goethe's novel.

The women in the ***Lehrjahre*** who have known intense desire are either killed off (Mariane, Sperata, Mignon, Aurelie) or domesticated (Philine, Lydie); only women who have repressed their sexuality eventually find a role in the Tower Society.[22] Although the question of the novel's utopian dimension has historically been treated in terms of relations among the social classes or in terms of the individual's relationship to the community, it could now also be approached from the standpoint of gender roles.[23] The patriarchal world of the ***Lehrjahre*** seems to include desexualization of its women as a utopian expression of a generalized male wish. Compromised feminine sexuality therefore functions in the novel as the primary virtue of Therese, who will become the consort of the patriarch in the new world created by the Tower Society.

Like Natalie and the beautiful soul, Therese is given a detailed history, which she recounts to Wilhelm as they sit together one day under an oak tree. The first thing Therese mentions about her early years is how much she respected her father and how much she disliked her mother for not appreciating how wonderful her father was. (We learn at the end of the novel, of course, that Therese's mother is *not* her mother. While this fact helps to explain, for example, Therese's observation that her mother did not love her, the question of her biological origin is not relevant to Therese's early feelings about the woman she thought was her mother). Therese's statement to Wilhelm is a clear and rather typical formulation of an Oedipal conflict: she believes that she would have made her father a much better partner than her mother did. The pathology of Therese's childhood is rooted in the fact that her father agrees with her.

Following the breakdown of an initially happy marriage, Therese's mother seeks amusement outside the home with her artistic friends. Seizing the chance to displace her mother, Therese takes over many household duties in an attempt to please her father. Like the beautiful soul, she finds that working with her father allows her to enjoy more of his companionship: "Ich wuchs heran, mit den Jahren vermehrte sich meine Tätigkeit und die Liebe meines Vaters zu mir" (I was growing up, and as the years passed my activities increased, as did my father's love for me [***WML,*** p. 447]). Because Therese is the daughter of a woman to whom her father had been passionately attached and who had capably managed the entire household, we need not view Therese's observation as merely a fantasy about her father's love. She did indeed receive more love as she came to carry out more of the duties that her real mother had assumed (and as she physically matured). In other words, rather than simply accept his daughter's erotically charged feelings for him, Therese's father actively encouraged them, because he was exploiting his child as the replacement for her real mother, whose death soon after Therese's birth he had never accepted (he was "trostlos" [disconsolate] [***WML,*** p. 561]) and with whom he was still in love.[24]

The attention that Therese receives from her father enhances and solidifies her identification with him. "Ich glich meinem Vater an Gestalt und Gesinnungen" (I resembled my father in appearance and attitude [***WML,*** p. 447]), she says, but only after telling Wilhelm of her hostility toward her mother. The identification with the father is most significantly an aspect of Oedipal aggression toward her mother, in which her father unconsciously and inappropriately participates. When Therese's mother and competitor finally leaves the household, she and her father rejoice: "Wir waren nun frei und lebten wie im Himmel" (Now we were free and lived as if in paradise [***WML,*** p. 449]). But Therese's real Oedipal triumph is relatively short-lived. Her father dies, and Therese is left without an inheritance because of a bargain he and his wife had struck before her birth that she knew nothing about. Friends encourage her to contest the will. She refuses because she idealizes her father: "Ich verehrte das Andenken meines Vaters zu sehr" (I respected my father's memory too much [***WML,*** p. 451]).

The idealization is, however, a rationalization. Therese's reluctance to assert her financial rights is based on her unconscious guilt over her relationship with her father. Unlike most daughters, Therese has experienced the fulfillment of her Oedipal fantasies: she has acquired exclusive possession of her father's love. But her success in taking something that she is not supposed to own only arouses in her the most intense terror that she will be devastatingly punished by the mother. Punishment is swift; the father dies. Therese interprets his abandonment of her as the price she must pay for having so grievously transgressed against the mother. Her remorse is infinite.

In reality, Therese never won, but rather lost, the Oedipal battle in a more serious way than any daughter should. She does not know that her father's financial arrangement with his wife reflects his decision to enjoy Therese's mother under the condition that he not provide for his daughter. Hence Therese feels a need to atone for what her father had led her to believe was an Oedipal victory. She becomes compulsively self-sufficient. Her organizational skills are legendary; her household is always in perfect order. And her psyche functions just as smoothly as her home; it is never disrupted by anger, most notably when she is abandoned once again, by Lothario, for abandonment by the male is equivalent in Therese's mind to punishment, which she feels she deserves.[25]

Goethe recapitulates Therese's Oedipal conflicts in the subplot of Lothario's affairs with Lydie and with Therese's mother, using a considerable amount of narrative irony that would be comic were Therese's predicament not so tragic. The original engagement between Lothario and Therese was formed not because they had fallen in love but because both parties shared a devotion to the successful functioning of an estate. Therese is excited by the possibility of such a marriage because it would allow her to reenact, on a much grander scale than before, her relationship with her father. Moreover, she appears to have won out over Lydie, another competitor for Lothario's affection, just as she had earlier displaced her mother in her father's life.

Lydie, who was raised in Therese's family, acts as a surrogate sister to Therese. Ironically, Therese and Lydie have a more symmetrical relationship than they know in that neither of them has a biological link to Therese's supposed mother. From the beginning, Therese is aware of and threatened by Lydie as a sibling competitor for her father's love; hence she easily associates her with her mother. The ever-practical Therese notes that Lydie is "reizend" (charming [***WML,*** p. 448; cf. p. 454]), that she has what Therese views as her mother's frivolous attachment to "Romane" (novels, love stories [***WML,*** p. 460]), and that she became involved not only in her mother's theatrical pursuits but also with her mother's lovers (***WML,*** p. 449). When the mother leaves the home to conduct her libertine activities elsewhere, Lydie accompanies her (***WML,*** p. 451). Finally, just when Therese has lost her father and directly prior to her meeting Lothario, Lydie suddenly and hauntingly reappears, like the ghost of her mother. Similarly, when the engagement between Therese and Lothario is announced, Lydie mysteriously disappears.

Lothario for his part is horrified to discover, soon after his engagement to Therese, that he has had a prior affair with her mother, who lives away from her husband and daughter under the assumed name "Frau von Saint Alban." In the wake of a casual conversation with Therese, during which she unwittingly reveals the identity of Frau von Saint Alban, Lothario suddenly leaves her house, apparently never to return. Because he, like Therese, does not know that his former lover is not Therese's natural mother, he is quick to assume that continuing the engagement would amount to incest.[26] Therese then concludes that her mother has somehow caused Lothario's departure, that she has lost him to her or because of her. Lothario's subsequent diversion with Lydie, who in the meantime has returned, only reinforces Therese's Oedipal anxiety. She responds to Lothario's "unfaithfulness" just as she responded to her father's before: she assumes that she is being punished and atones for her crime by withdrawing into her obsessive perfectionism in the management of her household.

Therese's guilt does not eliminate her desire for her father. Instead, it inspires her to discover a way to possess him that also allows her to hide their relationship. She therefore intensifies her identification with him, for example, by preferring male clothing. She appears to use "defensive identification," in which the bereaved person attempts to deny the loss, and the pain it evokes, by incorporating the personality of the deceased, who then is felt to live on within the bereaved. Having frozen her father's persona inside her, Therese would treat Lothario just as her father had treated his wife: had they married, she says, she would have tolerated his affairs "wenn es nur ihre häusliche Ordnung nicht gestört hätte" (as long as it did not disrupt her domestic order [***WML,*** p. 461]). Her tolerance, far from being an expression of understanding toward Lothario, exemplifies Therese's expectation that she will be continually rejected even as she pursues an essentially narcissistic bond with her father. She is incapable of responding to a man as an autonomous other, as a human being with a sexual identity and boundaries to the self that are distinct from her own. Therese's eventual marriage to Lothario is an asexual merging with a partner who she believes is like her father and therefore exactly like herself.

The beautiful soul, Natalie, and Therese represent three prismatic aspects of feminine character in ***Wilhelm Meisters Lehrjahre.*** While the representation of these desexualized women may open Goethe to the charge of misogyny, I believe that something else is at stake in the novel. In the histories of these women we are given graphic depictions of the failure of the German patriarchy to provide the conditions under which little girls might resolve their conflicts over gender identity. With true psychoanalytic skill, Goethe reveals that growing up female in the eighteenth century had a pathological side with origins in the failure of fathers to understand or accept the needs and desires of their young daughters, who then carried the failure forward by internalizing their fathers' attitudes. All of the women I have discussed unconsciously participate in their own desexualization because, for individual reasons, they paradoxically believe that it will make them more acceptable to their fathers and more likely to triumph in their Oedipal conflict with their mothers. They then rationalize their desexualization by acting out an apparent autonomy that allows them to deny their attachment to their father and their wish for his approval. The pathology is most profound and therefore most tragic for Natalie, whom Schiller and countless readers after him have viewed as the most perfect of these idealized women, because in her sexual purity she affirms her father's perverse patriarchal wish that she had not been born female at all.

Hans Eichner has argued that ***Wilhelm Meisters Lehrjahre*** presents a view of the world that runs counter to the optimism of the Enlightenment. Mastery or maturity ("Meisterschaft") in this world is marked by insight into limitation: some things can be achieved only at the cost of others (esp. pp. 186-92).[27] The figure who best illustrates this principle for Eichner is Natalie: as the embodiment ("Verkörperung") of caritas she cannot have the erotic vitality of a Philine. Eichner is virtually alone among critics in having recognized the compensatory nature of Natalie's character, but he does not understand its cause. Moreover, he does not distinguish between those figures in the novel who learn to understand, even imperfectly, their limitation and those who simply live out its consequences unconsciously.

Wilhelm's psychosexual maturation is overtly thematized with the Hamlet motif and with the painting of the "kranker Königssohn" (the king's son who is ill). The characters in the novel participate in his (imperfect) growth by discussing with him his relationship (or lack thereof) to Hamlet's predicament, or by referring to the existence of the painting and to what it might mean to him. But the sexual development of Natalie, Therese, and the beautiful soul is buried in narratives of early childhood experience whose significance none of the figures in the novel, including the women themselves, appear to have grasped. These women occupy positions of great respect within the Tower Society (despite the uncle's reservations about the beautiful soul or the occasional ironic remarks we hear, for example, from the impish Friedrich about his sister [cf. ***WML,*** p. 565]). The beautiful soul is the spiritual *grande dame* of the group; Therese is the faithful and knowledgeable administrator of a soon-to-be extended household; Natalie single-handedly provides the society's primary emotional support system. Together, their functions are those of an ideal mother. The esteem in which they are held effectively distracts them from (supports their continuing denial of) the compromises they have made with their fathers, on which their apparently satisfying roles in the society are based. They have no knowledge of the early childhood conflicts that so severely damaged them and hence no desire to resolve them or possibility of doing so. These idealized women therefore acquire the dubious honor of incarnating the fundamental, irrevocable loss of eroticism that Freud would later describe as "das Unbehagen in der Kultur" (civilization and its discontents).

Goethe's decision to kill off or domesticate the erotically sensitive women in his novel and to populate the Tower Society with asexual, or rather desexualized, types accounts for every female character in the ***Lehrjahre*** except one: Margarete, the tenant farmer's daughter. She is presented to us in the context of a fairy tale recounted by Lothario to Jarno and Wilhelm over dinner one evening. An analysis of this patriarchal narrative provides a final insight into the representation of female sexuality in the work.

Margarete was a former lover of Lothario's to whom he had been especially attached. Now she is unavailable to him because she is "weit weg verheiratet" (married and living far away [***WML,*** p. 464]). One day Lothario hears that she is visiting her father, who still lives nearby, and decides to seek her out. As he rides away from his estate, he travels through an idyllic natural setting reminiscent of their first meeting, finally reaching the "Zauberwelt" (magical world [***WML,*** p. 465]) where he hopes to find her. Like so many fairy tales, the story is laden with Oedipal themes, but what we especially note is Lothario's reaction. Normally hypersensitive, as we have seen, to the very possibility of incestuous affairs, he is unconcerned about them as he moves through this magical sphere. He becomes immediately fascinated with Margarete's "Muhme" (niece, cousin [***WML,*** p. 466]), who resembles his former lover and whom he first meets instead of her. She is ten years younger than Margarete and thus evokes the image of the woman he remembers. On his first foray into the "Zauberwelt," Lothario is enchanted with multiplying female presences, but he fails to find Margarete herself.

Lothario ends his account at this point, and the other men contribute their own stories of erotic adventure, which the narrator compares to "Gespenstergeschichten" (ghost stories [***WML,*** p. 466]). Lothario then offers the opinion that his marriage to Therese, now apparently impossible, would have been a "Himmel" (paradise), but not one of "schwärmerischen Glücks" (ecstasy [***WML,*** p. 467]). Instead he could have counted on the solid happiness that comes from an ordered life. The interpolation is important because it anticipates the outcome of the fairy tale.

A few days later, Lothario tries a second time to visit Margarete at her father's home, and on this occasion he succeeds. Here again he finds Margarete's "Ebenbild" (likeness [***WML,*** p. 470]), now sitting behind an unambiguously feminine symbol, the spinning wheel, where his lover herself used to sit. Among Margarete's several young children assembled with her is a little daughter who clearly resembles her mother. Lothario later says that in seeing these multiple generations of women, all so charming and similar in appearance, he was cast into a timeless, organic realm where, as if in an orange grove, blossoms and fruit seemed to exist side by side (cf. ***WML,*** pp. 470-71).

The considerable pathos of Lothario's encounter with Margarete and their brief conversation (***WML,*** p. 471) lies in their mutual recognition of an intense desire that is alive but not livable. A man of Lothario's social standing would not have married a woman like Margarete, but this is not Goethe's point in this complex symbolic episode. Lothario can find Margarete only in the "unreal" matriarchal world of vegetative magic and fairy tales. The real patriarchal world to which he returns is one of erotically sterile unions, for which daughters are carefully prepared.

Notes

1. *Der Briefwechsel zwischen Schiller und Goethe,* ed. Emil Staiger (Frankfurt am Main: Insel, 1966), p. 225. All translations of the German are my own. Schiller's praise of these women was not universally repeated in the case of the beautiful soul, although critics continued to view her as a type, albeit a negative one. The most notable contemporary disagree-

ment came from Wilhelm von Humboldt and Friedrich Schlegel. See *Wilhelm Meisters Lehrjahre* ("Hamburger Ausgabe"), ed. Erich Trunz (Munich: Beck, 1981), p. 658 (hereafter cited as *WML*), for Humboldt's letter of 4 December 1794 to Schiller and p. 674 for Schlegel's comments on this figure in his *Athenäum* review. Klaus F. Gille (*"Wilhelm Meister" im Urteil der Zeitgenossen* [Assen: Van Gorcum, 1971], esp. 13-16, 47-50) discusses the early reception of these women. Susanne Zantop ("Eignes Selbst und fremde Formen: Goethes 'Bekenntnisse einer schönen Seele,'" *Goethe Yearbook,* 3 [1986]: 73-92) gives a historical overview of misogynist versus feminist interpretations of the beautiful soul.

2. The most lucid account of women's ahistorical image in late eighteenth-century Germany is Silvia Bovenschen's now-standard work *Die imaginierte Weiblichkeit: Exemplarische Untersuchungen zu kulturgeschichtlichen und literarischen Präsentationsformen des Weiblichen* (Frankfurt am Main: Suhrkamp, 1979), pp. 9-11 and passim. For a discussion of Schiller's androcentric attitudes (but without reference to his discussions of the *Lehrjahre*), see pp. 74-76, 220-56.

3. A dominant trend in *Wilhelm Meister* scholarship has been to reduce one or more members of the feminine triad to "aspects" or "symbols" of Wilhelm's development. This approach was most explicitly defended by Jürgen Rausch ("Lebensstufen in Goethes 'Wilhelm Meister,'" *Deutsche Vierteljahrsschrift,* 20 [1942]: 65-114) and has been continued, for example, by Emil Staiger, *Goethe* (Zurich: Atlantis, 1962), 2:128-74; Hans Eichner, "Zur Deutung von 'Wilhelm Meisters Lehrjahren,'" *Jahrbuch des Freien Deutschen Hochstifts* (1966): 165-96; Peter Pfaff, "Plädoyer für eine typologische Interpretation von 'Wilhelm Meisters Lehrjahren,'" *Text und Kontext,* 5 (1977): 37-55; Ilse Graham, *Goethe: Portrait of the Artist* (Berlin: de Gruyter, 1977), pp. 182-226; Hellmut Ammerlahn, "Goethe und Wilhelm Meister, Shakespeare und Natalie: Die klassische Heilung des kranken Königssohns," *Jahrbuch des Freien Deutschen Hochstifts* (1978): 47-84; Ivar Sagmo, *Bildungsroman und Geschichtsphilosophie: Eine Studie zu Goethes Roman "Wilhelm Meisters Lehrjahre"* (Bonn: Bouvier, 1982); Clark S. Muenzer, *Figures of Identity: Goethe's Novels and the Enigmatic Self* (University Park: Pennsylvania State University Press, 1984); and Monika Fick, *Das Scheitern des Genius: Mignon und die Symbolik der Liebesgeschichten in "Wilhelm Meisters Lehrjahren"* (Würzburg: Königshausen und Neumann, 1987).

4. While there are a few studies that rely wholly or in part on a Freudian model (e.g., Friedrich A. Kittler and Gerhard Kaiser, *Dichtung als Sozialisationsspiel: Studien zu Goethe und Gottfried Keller* [Göttingen: Vandenhoeck und Ruprecht, 1978]; David Roberts, *The Indirections of Desire: Hamlet in Goethe's "Wilhelm Meister"* [Heidelberg: Winter, 1980]; Jochen Hörisch, *Gott, Geld und Glück: Zur Logik der Liebe in den Bildungsromanen Goethes, Kellers, und Thomas Manns* [Frankfurt am Main: Suhrkamp, 1983]; Dorrit Cohn, "Wilhelm Meister's Dream: Reading Goethe with Freud," *German Quarterly,* 62 [1989]: 459-72), I have not been able to locate a single psychoanalytic study of any of the three idealized women. Frederick J. Beharriell's essay "The Hidden Meaning of Goethe's 'Bekenntnisse einer schönen Seele'" (in *Lebendige Form: Festschrift für Heinrich E. K. Henel,* ed. Jeffrey L. Sammons and Ernst Schürer [Munich: Fink, 1970] is unfortunately always cited as a Freudian reading of the "Confessions." Beharriell uses terms such as *sexual neurosis* in a trivial popular sense, however, and displays no understanding of childhood psychosexual development as set forth by Freud. In fact, he does not even discuss the early childhood of the beautiful soul. Some critics have used this essay, quite unfairly, I think, to attack all Freudian approaches to the "Confessions" as reductive (cf. Zantop; Christine Oertel Sjögren, "Pietism, Pathology, or Pragmatism in Goethe's *Bekenntnisse einer schönen Seele,*" *Studies on Voltaire and the Eighteenth Century,* 193 [Oxford: Cheney, 1980], pp. 2009-15; and Lothar Müller, *Die kranke Seele und das Licht der Erkenntnis: Karl Philipp Moritz' Anton Reiser* [Frankfurt am Main: Athenäum, 1987], p. 306).

5. Wilhelm Emrich ("Symbolinterpretation und Mythenforschung: Möglichkeiten und Grenzen eines neuen Goetheverständnisses," *Euphorion,* 47 [1953]: 38-67) rightly attacks the ahistorical quality of Jungian approaches to literary interpretation (which he mistakenly conflates with all psychoanalytic readings) and observes: "Literary studies confront specific historical manifestations and transformations of the human psyche. These differentiated phenomena are what have to be investigated if we are to produce exact, meaningful, and concrete conclusions rather than empty generalizations" (p. 57). But Emrich effectively takes back his insight by reducing all of the symbols in Goethe's texts to expressions of "Goethe's own spiritual conflicts" (p. 55).

6. "'Gender'—as distinct from categories such as 'class,' 'social class,' or 'social standing'—does not as a category have a conceptual [*begriffsgeschichtliche*] tradition" (Bovenschen, p. 14). The best illustration of Bovenschen's point is that the androgynous aspects of the women figures in the *Lehrjahre* have, astoundingly, never been interpreted with respect to historical problems of gender identity. Instead, the entire matter has been reduced to a merely symbolic or mythological theme. The only exception to this rule, to my knowledge, is Ursula R. Mahlendorf's essay "The Mystery of Mignon: Object Relations, Abandonment, Abuse, and Narrative Structure," *Goethe Yearbook,* 7 (forthcoming).

7. In addition to Wilhelm, the figures who are shown to be acquainted with the "Confessions" are the doctor,

Aurelie, and Natalie. Wilhelm is the only figure to whom Therese recounts her story.

8. Sigmund Freud, *The Standard Edition of the Complete Psychological Works,* trans. and ed. James Strachey and Anna Freud, 24 vols. (London: Hogarth, 1962). I have drawn primarily on the following essays: "Three Essays on Sexuality" (vol. 7); "The Sexual Life of Human Beings," "The Development of the Libido and the Sexual Organizations," "Some Thoughts on Development and Regression—Aetiology," and "The Libido Theory and Narcissism" (vol. 16); and "Anxiety and Instinctual Life" and "Femininity" (vol. 22). My reading of Freud has been aided by Erik H. Erikson, *Childhood and Society* (New York: Norton, 1950), esp. chaps. 2, 7; Juliet Mitchell, *Psychoanalysis and Feminism* (New York: Vintage, 1975); Nancy Chodorow, *The Reproduction of Mothering: Psychoanalysis and the Sociology of Gender* (Berkeley: University of California Press, 1978); and Chodorow, *Feminism and Psychoanalytic Theory* (New Haven, Conn.: Yale University Press, 1989). I am also grateful to Jane K. Brown and especially to Ursula R. Mahlendorf for their reactions to my thoughts over the last few years as this essay has taken form.

9. This highly schematic explanation of feminine ambivalence cannot do justice to the complexities of interaction between individual mothers and daughters. Furthermore, ambivalence is probably not confined to the Oedipal phase but appears to begin much earlier. Freud takes note of some special possibilities for "disturbance" in feminine development at the end of his essay "Femininity," pp. 131-35; see also Chodorow, *Reproduction,* chap. 6.

10. My interpretation at this point, where the prince is taken to represent Father, assumes that fairy tales are or can be expressions of the child's sexual wishes, as Bruno Bettelheim has argued in his now-classic study *The Uses of Enchantment: The Meaning and Importance of Fairy Tales* (New York: Knopf, 1976).

11. The three other criminals with whom the beautiful soul identifies during her spiritual crisis following Philo's revelations all reflect her ambivalence toward her father. Without the Father's "unsichtbare Hand" (invisible hand [*WML,* p. 392]) to hold her in check, that is, to block her eroticism, she believes that she could have been responsible for the seduction of a female child by its father confessor, that she could have been a thief (i.e., could have stolen her father from her mother), and that she could have attempted to assassinate the king (her father).

12. Barbara Becker-Cantarino ("'Die Bekenntnisse einer schönen Seele': Zur Ausgrenzung und Vereinnahmung des Weiblichen in der patriarchalen Utopie von 'Wilhelm Meisters Lehrjahren,'" in *Verantwortung und Utopie,* ed. Wolfgang Wittkowski [Tübingen: Niemeyer, 1988], pp. 70-86) offers the best discussion to date of patriarchal structures in the *Lehrjahre.* Her argument that the beautiful soul receives her socialization only through men (p. 73), however, overlooks the complicity of the mother in the socialization of the daughter. Becker-Cantarino locates the first appearance of the invisible friend in the Narziβ episode, when in fact the invisible friend is a bedroom strategy devised by the child to cope with the prohibitions of the mother.

13. As I have already suggested, mothers in a patriarchy, who are of course also daughters, suffer (like their daughters) from unresolved or unresolvable Oedipal fantasies. The mother's competitiveness with and envy for her daughter mean that she has displaced her own mother's imago onto her daughter, a devastating burden for any child to carry.

14. In addition to the studies cited at the end of note 4, see Marianne Hirsch, "Spiritual *Bildung.* The Beautiful Soul as Paradigm," in *The Voyage In: Fictions of Female Development,* ed. Elizabeth Abel, Marianne Hirsch, and Elizabeth Langland (Hanover, N.H.: University Press of New England, 1983), pp. 23-48; and Ulrike Prokop, *Die Illusion vom Groβen Paar,* vol. 1 of *Weibliche Lebensentwürfe im deutschen Bildungsbürgertum, 1750-1770* (Frankfurt am Main: Fischer, 1991), pp. 106-99. Prokop states in her foreword that this book is a psychoanalytic study of three representative female lives: Goethe's mother, his sister Cornelia, and Susanna von Klettenberg. Her treatment of the material is not, however, psychoanalytic but sociological in orientation. Thus she carefully and vividly describes the intellectual, economic, and emotional isolation of these women within the German patriarchy, but she does not provide a psychodynamic investigation of their character. In the case of the "Confessions," which she reductively views as a biography of Klettenberg, Prokop only briefly mentions the early childhood of the beautiful soul (p. 124). My colleague Ehrhard Bahr kindly drew my attention to Prokop's work.

15. See *Moritz: Werke in zwei Bänden* (Berlin: Aufbau, 1973), 2:255-56.

16. In this section of my interpretation, I am indebted to John Bowlby, *Loss: Sadness and Depression,* vol. 3 of *Attachment and Loss* (New York: Basic Books, 1980); Bowlby, "Pathological Mourning and Childhood Mourning," *Journal of the American Psychoanalytic Association,* 11 (1963): 500-541; see also Sol Altschul, ed., *Childhood Bereavement and Its Aftermath* (Madison, Wis.: International Universities Press, 1988). Although Natalie is born into an aristocratic family, her parents appear to have been her primary caregivers, inasmuch as Goethe does not mention any others and wants, moreover, to depict an aristocracy moving toward certain middle-class behavioral patterns.

17. Given the crucial psychological significance of the cape for Natalie, one wonders how she was able to give it up to Wilhelm when he was injured. A sen-

sible answer to this question has been given by Hans-Jürgen Schings ("Wilhelm Meisters schöne Amazone," *Jahrbuch der Deutschen Schillergesellschaft,* 29 [1985]: 141-206), who reminds us that one of Natalie's main activities is to clothe children or others in need (pp. 203-4).

18. Mignon's song on this occasion (*WML,* pp. 515-16) applies just as well to Natalie's inner life as to her own. For example, the line "Zieht mir das weiβe Kleid nicht aus!" (Do not take off my white dress!) expresses Natalie's wish to be free of guilt; the reference to "jene himmlischen Gestalten, / Sie fragen nicht nach Mann und Weib" (those heavenly forms / do not ask whether male or female) captures Natalie's fantasy about a place that would be heavenly because she would not be punished for her sex; "Vor Kummer altert' ich zu frühe" (By worrying I grew old too early) tells us that her "mature" but defensive self-sufficiency damaged her natural growth from child into adult; "Macht mich auf ewig wieder jung!" (Make me eternally young again!) conveys her desire to be a child, which means to be dependent on others.
19. The physically distant quality of their relationship has been well described by Eichner (p. 188 n. 56).
20. *Goethes Wilhelm Meister* (Frankfurt am Main: Klostermann, 1953), p. 57.
21. "Goethes 'Wilhelm Meister' und Spinoza," in Wittkowski, pp. 57-69, esp. pp. 64-65.
22. This grouping of the women in the *Lehrjahre* was first suggested to me by Mahlendorf, "The Mystery of Mignon."
23. Wilhelm Voβkamp ("Utopie und Utopiekritik in Goethes Romanen *Wilhelm Meisters Lehrjahren* und *Wilhelm Meisters Wanderjahren,"* in *Utopieforschung,* ed. Wilhelm Voβkamp [Baden-Baden: Suhrkamp, 1985], 3:227-49) discusses the problematic nature of the concept "utopia" in the novel and also provides additional useful bibliography on the topic. Becker-Cantarino offers an approach to the novel's "utopianism" in terms of gender that is slightly different from my own.
24. To avoid misunderstanding, I stress that Therese's father indulges his own fantasies that his daughter could be his lover; I am not suggesting that incest occurred between them. That fathers have fantasies in the Oedipal situation was generally overlooked by Freud: "In the case of fathers and daughters, Freud claims to distinguish between a daughter's fantasies of seduction and actual seduction by her father, but he ignores the reciprocal possibility—that absence of actual paternal seduction is not the same thing as absence of seductive fantasies toward a daughter or behavior which expresses such a fantasy" (Chodorow, *Reproduction,* p. 160).
25. At the two points in the text where Therese is shown crying over the loss of Lothario, she dismisses one episode (*WML,* p. 443) as the result of an eye infection; the second (WML, p. 458) she cuts short, refusing to give herself over to grief.
26. Lothario's terror of a relationship that is even symbolically incestuous is intimately linked to his promiscuity. Like his sister Natalie, he is a troubled survivor of childhood bereavement. As the oldest of four children, he was probably well into latency or even early adolescence at the time of his parents' death. During this period he would have felt intense ambivalence toward his father that he may not have had an opportunity to resolve. The alternating identification with and fear of his father produce Lothario's ambivalence toward women: his many love affairs are with surrogates for Mother in that Lothario only ever views them as temporarily available to him. He assumes Father's position vis-à-vis the women, and then retreats out of guilt or fear for having done so. When he is confronted "in reality" with the fact that he has slept with "Mother," he bolts.
27. Quite inexplicably, Eichner's interpretation at this point studiously avoids any mention of, though it deals with, the Goethean concept of *Entsagung* (renunciation).

Marc Redfield (essay date 1993)

SOURCE: "Ghostly *Bildung*: Gender, Genre, Aesthetic Ideology, and *Wilhelm Meisters Lehrjahre,*" in *Genre,* Vol. 26, No. 4, Winter, 1993, pp. 377-407.

[*In the following essay, Redfield highlights aesthetic and gender representation in* Wilhelm Meisters Lehrjahre, *evaluating the novel and its relationship to the genre of the Bildungsroman.*]

> For the being of *Geist* has an essential connection with the idea of *Bildung.*
>
> —Gadamer

> Whoever could manage to interpret Goethe's ***Meister*** properly would have expressed what is now happening in literature. He could, so far as literary criticism is concerned, retire forever.
>
> —Friedrich Schlegel

Among the challenges the modern novel offers to genre theory, that of the *Bildungsroman* is remarkable on several counts. Few literary terms have known greater success, both in the academy and in high culture generally, and in any number of national or linguistic contexts. "If a person interested in literary matters commands as many as a dozen words of German," Jeffrey Sammons remarks, "one of them is likely to be: *Bildungsroman*" (229). If this person also commands the staples of Western literary history, she will also know that this subgenre is supposed to have been founded, or at least epitomized, by ***Wilhelm Meister's Apprenticeship,*** is in some way deeply German, but nonetheless also represents "one of the major fictional types of

European realism" (Hirsch 300).[1] At once international and national, "a major fictional type" springing from the historical event of a particular novel, the *Bildungsroman* seems to have inherited the virtues of its nominal father, Goethe, the genius whose life captured for provincial Weimar the full radiance of human potentiality. One would be hard pressed to find another instance of a genre in which particularity and generality appear to mesh so thoroughly. For since the *Bildungsroman* narrates the acculturation of a self—the integration of a particular "I" into the general subjectivity of a community, and thus, finally, into the universal subjectivity of mankind—the genre can be said to repeat, as its identity or content, its own synthesis of particular instance and general form. An equivalent repetition is audible in the signifier itself, which no doubt largely explains why the term "Bildungsroman" is more frequently borrowed than translated: even a dozen words of German suffices to hear an interplay of representation (*Bild*) and formation (*Bildung*), and thus the whisper of a profound homology between pedagogy and aesthetics, the education of a subject and the figuration of a text. The *Bildungsroman,* in short, is a trope for the aspirations of aesthetic humanism.

But if the *Bildungsroman* appears as a figure for a certain aesthetic ideal, it also presents itself as fiction or *Schein* in a less positive sense. For some time now the trend in German studies has been to call the genre's existence into question. Problems begin, appropriately enough, on the level of the signifier itself, since the word "Bildungsroman," purportedly the name of a nineteenth-century genre, was nearly unknown before the early twentieth century—its widespread popularity is, in fact, largely a postwar phenomenon.[2] Generic terms are no doubt usually supposed to lag behind the phenomena to which they refer; but given the "romantic" presuppositions that can be extracted from this particular term, its deferred occurrence raises questions about literary history that rapidly become complex and serious. One might begin to suspect that critics like Lacoue-Labarthe and Nancy have good reason to claim that "a veritable romantic *unconscious* is discernible today, in the most central motifs of our modernity" (15). At the same time, however, one might also begin to suspect that the term *"Bildungsroman,"* like the more notorious label "Romanticism," might have at best an indirect relation to the texts it is supposed to describe. And indeed, unsurprisingly, scholars in German studies have been casting doubt on this word's referential purchase for nearly as long as it has been in wide circulation. As soon as one takes a serious look at the notion of the *"Bildungsroman,"* it begins to unfold such extravagant aesthetic promises that few if any novels can be said to achieve the right to be so defined—possibly not even the five or six German-language novels that, in postwar German studies, have constantly been put forward as this genre's main (and not infrequently its only) representatives.[3] Sammons's well-known article, by no means the first of its sort (see, e.g., Pabst), concludes by wondering whether, among the "legends of literary history," there is one "so lacking in foundation and so misleading as the phantom of the nineteenth-century *Bildungsroman*" (243). Frederick Amrine writes more forgivingly of a "critical fiction" (127)—though like Sammons, Amrine has hard words for members of English departments who appropriate the authority of the term *"Bildungsroman"* without investigating its history or, consequently, its referential difficulties.[4]

But the *Bildungsroman* seems to constitute one of those quagmires of literary study in which increased rigor produces nothing more tangible than increased confusion. On the one hand it is certainly true that under the lens of scholarship this genre rapidly shrinks until, like a figure in Lewis Carroll's Wonderland, it threatens to disappear altogether. Even ***Wilhelm Meister*** has proved resistant to being subsumed under the definition it supposedly inspired: critics with little else in common have registered their sense that at the end of Goethe's novel, Wilhelm "is still a long way from Schiller's theoretically postulated 'beautiful moral freedom'" (Gille 17).[5] As Sammons remarks, "if the status of the model text is problematic, then *a fortiori* the genre itself must certainly be insecure" (237). But on the other hand, Germanists seem all the more ideologically committed to the truth of this "critical fiction" for having examined it and found it ontologically wanting. Monographs on the *Bildungsroman* appear regularly; without exception they possess introductory chapters in which the genre is characterized as a problem, but as one that the critic, for one reason or another, plans either to solve or ignore;[6] and despite the variety of solutions proffered, the definition of the *Bildungsroman* that emerges in study after study usually repeats the self-referential structure of the aesthetic synthesis sketched at the beginning of this essay—which returns one to the beginning of the cycle and necessitates, of course, another book or essay on the *Bildungsroman.* The more this genre is cast into question, the more it flourishes. And though it is certainly poor scholarship to reduce *Bildung* to a vague idea of individual "growth," as common parlance generally does, a more historically and philosophically precise understanding of *Bildung* does not appear either to keep the *Bildungsroman* healthy and alive, or to prevent its corpse from rising with renewed vigor each time it is slain. The popular success of vulgarized notions of the *Bildungsroman* simply repeats, on a grander scale, this genre's indestructibility within the specialized literature, and this is because the content of this genre is never simply a "content," but is always also "Bildung," formation—the formation of the human as the producer of itself as form. Dilthey's seemingly content-oriented definition of the *Bildungsroman* as a "regulated development within the life of the individual," in which each stage of development "has its own intrinsic value and is at the same time the basis for a higher stage" (394), is animated by a formal principle that undermines the content's specificity, as shown clearly in a remark by Robert Musil:

> When one says *"Bildungsroman,"* [Wilhelm] Meister comes to mind. The development of a personal *Bildung.* There is, however, also Bildung in what is at once a narrower and a more extensive sense: with every true experience a cultured man educates himself

> [*bildet sich ein geistiger Mensch*]. This is the organic plasticity of man [*die organsiche Plastizität des Menschen*]. In this sense every novel worthy of the name is a *Bildungsroman*. . . . The *Bildungsroman* of a person is a type [*Typus*] of novel. The *Bildungsroman* of an idea, that's quite simply the novel per se. (572)

The content is thus in an essential sense the form, and the principle of formation is the human: if every novel worthy of the name is a *Bildungsroman,* this is because every human being worthy of the name embodies an essential humanity, an "organic plasticity" that permits the "geistiger Mensch" to produce himself (*sich bilden*). And yet, if the "person" immediately becomes a figure of the "idea"—and the novel a figure for the production of the novel itself—the ongoing debate about the *Bildungsroman* suggests that this power of formalization is less stable—one might also say, less human—than Musil's comments might imply. The idea of this genre persistently drives it in the direction of universality, but since its particularity is constantly in danger of disappearing, "a disturbing dialectic of everything and nothing," as Amrine puts it (124), comes to afflict the notion of the *Bildungsroman* as it vacillates between signifying in vague fashion a narrative in which a protagonist matures (such that "precious few novels would *not* qualify as *'Bildungsromane'*" [122]) and signifying in more rigorous fashion an aesthetic synthesis that threatens to become a sheer mirage. And yet, at once too referential and not referential enough, the *Bildungsroman* nonetheless appears ineradicable from literary criticism. In its nonexistence it is so efficaciously present that Sammons is led to speak more than once of a "phantom genre" (239, 243). And since a tension within the procedures of institutionalized literary studies has generated this ghost, one can hope to learn something about the nature of literary reception by keeping it in view.

Such reflections, however, do not yet fully respond to the question of the *Bildungsroman,* which as an aesthetic genre requires exemplification in a text. Ordinarily we do not think of genres as requiring a model, let alone a visible point of origin; but the *Bildungsroman* is not an ordinary genre: though all generic terms may be considered aesthetic categories, the *Bildungsroman* is the genre *of* aesthetics. In this it differs from a classical genre such as the lyric, for instance, which, for all the aesthetic and ideological investment it has occasioned, bears the traces of multiple and heterogeneous histories. The notion of the *Bildungsroman,* however, has no existence apart from either the post-Romantic history of aesthetics, or the aesthetic formalization that this "genre" takes as its content—in the guise, of course, of the formation of a specific, anthropological subject.[7] As an aesthetic of genre, the *Bildungsroman* must find embodiment in an example; and the burden of such exemplarity has been assigned to ***Wilhelm Meisters Lehrjahre*** ever since Friedrich Schlegel nominated it, with Fichte's philosophy and the French Revolution, as one of the "greatest tendencies of the age," and asserted that it was "so thoroughly new and unique" that "only in itself [*aus sich selbst*] can one learn to understand it" (132). Schlegel, in other words, not only emphasized the text's power to represent "nature or *Bildung* itself . . . in manifold examples" (143), but also insisted on its exemplary force as a text: when reading it we must perform a purely reflective judgment, deriving our generic concept [*Gattungsbegriff*] from the object in its particularity:

> Perhaps one should thus at once judge it and not judge it—which seems to be no easy task. Luckily it is one of those books that judge themselves, and so relieve the critic of all trouble. Indeed, it doesn't just judge itself; it also presents itself [*stellt sich auch selbst dar*]. (133-34)

Critical representations of the text would consequently serve it badly, "apart from the fact that they would be superfluous [*überflüssig*]." In short, as the auto-productive, self-representative text, ***Wilhelm Meister*** would seem the very incarnation of what Lacoue-Labarthe and Nancy call "the literary absolute," and thus would indeed be the exemplary *Bildungsroman.*[8]

WILHELM MEISTER'S

APPRENTICESHIP.

A NOVEL.

FROM THE GERMAN OF

GOETHE.

IN THREE VOLUMES.

VOL. I.

EDINBURGH;

PUBLISHED BY

OLIVER & BOYD, TWEEDDALE-COURT;

AND

G. & W. B. WHITTAKER, LONDON.

1824.

But Schlegel's understanding of the self-sufficient or "self-conscious" text is not what one might expect. A few sentences later we read that the novel "disappoints as often as it fulfills customary expectations of unity and coherence," and that it in fact fails to judge itself insofar as it fails to pass from the level of the particular to that of the general: a failure that signals the return of the formerly "superfluous" reader:

> If any book has genius, it is this one. If this genius had been able to characterize itself in general as well as in particular, no one would have been able to say anything further about the novel as a whole, and how one should take it. Here a small supplement [*Ergänzung*] remains possible, and a few explanations will not seem useless or superfluous [*kann nicht unnütz oder überflüssig scheinen*]. . . . [T]he beginning and the ending of the novel will generally be found peculiar and unsatisfactory, and this and that in the middle of the text will be found superfluous and incoherent [*überflüssig und unzusammenhängend*]. And even he who knows how to distinguish the godlike from artistic willfulness will feel something isolated in the first and last reading, as though in the deepest and most beautiful harmony and oneness the final knotting of thought and feeling were lacking. (134)

The text judges itself but does not judge itself; it accounts for its own particularity but fails to inscribe itself in a genre (*Gattung*). And the reader, initially suspended between judging and not judging, then made *überflüssig* by the text's self-reflexive power, finally becomes a supplement (*Ergänzung*) that is *nicht überflüssig*. This reader, a master reader who "knows how to distinguish the god-like from artistic willfulness," performs an aesthetic judgment and necessarily finds the text wanting. But this magisterial critical stance has been generated by the text's inability to account for itself—a predicament replayed in the lucid incoherence of Schlegel's own theoretical narrative. If the question of the *Bildungsroman* can be said to become that of how ***Wilhelm Meister*** figures the possibility of its own theorization, Schlegel suggests that the difficulties afflicting the idea of this genre might have something to do with the problem of reading.

I

Given the importance, for such questions, of ***Wilhelm Meister***'s representation of art and aesthetic judgment, we might ask first after the relation between the two forms of art most salient in the unfolding of Wilhelm's *Bildung*—theater and portraiture. The two would initially seem to function in opposing ways. The theater is the negative locus of Wilhelm's education: by giving up his dream of becoming an actor he emerges from apprenticeship, a moment of growth registered in his assumption of paternal responsibility toward his son Felix: "His apprenticeship was therefore completed in this sense, for along with the feeling of a father he had acquired the virtues of a solid citizen" (8.1).[9] We shall discuss Wilhelm's acknowledgment of Felix later; for the moment we can focus on his renunciation (*Entsagung*) of the theater, and thus of a desire that has intermittently ruled his life from his infant fascination with marionettes to his climactic assumption of the title role in *Hamlet* in Book V. Though it will be necessary to ask what exactly is being renounced in the name of "theater," and why, the text would at least appear to be allowing its hero to acquire genuine self-knowledge, albeit in the negative mode of knowing what he is not. Meanwhile the unvarying pleasure that Wilhelm takes in contemplating a putatively mediocre painting—a painting of a "sick king's son," which initially forms part of Wilhelm's grandfather's art collection, and then reappears in the possession of the Society of the Tower at the end of the novel—seems to record a hitch in the works of *Bildung,* as Schiller noted in his occasionally anxious remarks to Goethe about this novel.[10] Though the painting is poorly executed, Wilhelm cheerfully affirms at the beginning of his *Bildungsroman* that "the subject is what appeals to me in a painting, not the artistry" (1.17), and near the end of the text he is still sticking to his guns: "He returned eagerly to the picture of the sick prince, still finding it as moving and affecting as ever" (8.3). Like the *schöne Seele,* Wilhelm remains vulnerable throughout his itinerary to the attractions of kitsch, unable to achieve the formal universality of the disinterested subject of aesthetic judgment. Indeed, in his attitude toward the painting Wilhelm would appear neurotically fixated, trapped in the defiles of a repetitive desire that the painting thematizes as oedipal impasse—the sick prince is dying for love of his father's bride. In the case of the theater Wilhelm can give up his narcissistic and oedipal investments, stop playing Hamlet, and start being a father; in the case of the painting he remains a son unable to give up forbidden desire.

However, upon closer inspection, Wilhelm's failure to renounce the painting bears a certain relation to his ability to renounce the theater. The common denominator of both gestures is Wilhelm's inability to preserve aesthetic distance. He is only capable of responding to an aesthetic object when he can identify with its meaning or content; and, as he learns during the premiere of *Hamlet,* he is only capable of good acting when he can identify with the role to such an extent that he is not acting. In giving up the theater Wilhelm thus records his knowledge that he can never give up the particularity of self-interest. His response to the painting confirms this knowledge; and he can thus claim to have undergone a certain ironic *"Bildung"* insofar as he has learned that he will never truly become the universal subject of aesthetics. Since an aesthetic education is always underway toward its own occurrence, to a certain degree it accommodates being refigured as an impossibility, a refiguration that would be ironic in Lukács's sense of irony as compensatory knowledge, as that which "with intuitive double vision, can see where God is to be found in a world abandoned by God" (92). And indeed, Wilhelm's double gesture of renunciation and identification structures a complex dialectic in the course of which the text rigorously explores the possibility of *Bildung* as irony.[11]

The Society of the Tower, it will be recalled, perversely lends its aid to Wilhelm's production of *Hamlet* by providing a Ghost capable of frightening Wilhelm into complete identification with his role. The Abbé justifies this intervention on the dialectical grounds that "error can only be cured through erring" (8.5). The Society of the Tower helps in order to hinder, and hinders in order to help; and

Wilhelm, by acting well when he wasn't acting, learns that he isn't an actor. A genuinely dialectical sublation thus appears to occur, with knowledge emerging *within* error, as the truth of error. But the status of this knowledge is uncertain, as becomes clear when we examine more closely what it is that Wilhelm gives up in giving up the theater. Learning that he is not an actor, he learns that he cannot control the act of identification. Actors such as Serlo or Aurelie enter into their roles knowingly; one could say that, for them, identification is an intentional act. The "self" of an actor, qua actor, resides in his or her ability to intend identification. Wilhelm, the mildly talented amateur, however, identifies blindly with Hamlet because he is frightened by the Ghost: the aesthetic power of his performance is the result of an event over which he has no control. Identification occurs precisely where knowledge and intention are absent. It is therefore slightly misleading to say, as we did above, that Wilhelm cannot give up self-interest. His problem is not that he suffers from an excess or stubbornness of self that prevents him from acting well or judging aesthetically; rather, the opposite is the case: prefabricated roles seize him unpredictably, and without encountering resistance. The actor is always an actor, but Wilhelm, experiencing "Hamlet's" fear, has no identity with which to structure this literary space: the sense of the uncanny that he feels belongs to no one and is in a sense experienced by "no one." And this uncanny moment is precisely the site of pedagogy or *Bildung*. A strange, radical self-loss, which from the "self"'s perspective arrives by accident, must be transformed into self-knowledge: the knowledge that the self cannot intend the occurrence, or construction, of the self—in other words, that the self is not an actor.

This transformation of loss into knowledge occurs as Wilhelm's renunciation or *Entsagung* of the theater, which consequently is a gesture of some complexity. In the first place, Wilhelm is not simply recognizing his own particular limitations: he is simultaneously renouncing an idealized image of the theater. Because acting consists in a power to control identification, the actor provides the illusion of being the aesthetic subject—the subject modeled on the artwork that knows what it does, or on the "literary absolute," in Lacoue-Labarthe and Nancy's sense, which performs itself into existence as the knowledge of its own performance. To the youthful Wilhelm, the stage had thus seemed to offer a middle-class route toward the *sprezzatura* of the aristocrat, and toward the nation as the Aesthetic State, the collective subject of aesthetics. In turning in disillusionment from the theater, Wilhelm recognizes the inessentiality of the theater's aesthetic synthesis: the actor intends identification, but only in the orbit of fiction. When the act of self is known, it is a lie. This insight takes narrative shape as Wilhelm's gradual assessment of the fallibility, or indeed the vulgarity, of his professional colleagues, and as his turn toward the real-life theatrics of a company of genuine aristocrats, the Society of the Tower. The renunciation is thus also a substitution, and the coherence of renunciation depends on the nature of the Society of the Tower's difference from the acting company. The two communities intersect precisely at the point of *Bildung*—Wilhelm's uncanny thespian encounter with the Ghost. In taking up the role of the Ghost, the Society of the Tower acts in order to cure acting, enfolding the craft of the actor in a higher knowledge of a genuine act—the act of imparting knowledge to Wilhelm. Pedagogy thus replaces the theater as the matrix of aesthetics.

Whether Wilhelm has actually acquired knowledge rapidly becomes dubious, however, since the Society of the Tower is more fantastically theatrical than any of Wilhelm's acting companies. Actors at least know that their performance is fictional; the Society of the Tower, seducing Wilhelm with a parody of Masonic ritual, can either be seen as wiser than the actor, or vastly more naive and less genuine. It is for this reason that Schiller registered unhappiness with the idea of the *Turmgesellschaft,* worrying that it might appear "merely a theatrical game and a trick [*Kunstgriff*]" (Seidel 197). Similarly, another writer in the aesthetic tradition, the young Georg Lukács, felt that the appearance of this "fantastic apparatus" introduces "a disruptive dissonance into the total unity of the whole," such that "the miraculous becomes a mystification without hidden meaning, a strongly emphasized narrative element without real importance, a playful ornament without decorative grace" (142). (All the same, "it is quite impossible to imagine ***Wilhelm Meister*** without this miraculous element.") On this account, the Society of the Tower is itself the aesthetic but inessential fiction that the actor performs. Pedagogy, therefore, would be not the negation but the redoubling of acting: the pedagogue, qua pedagogue, acts acting, and then, the day's work done, retires to the theatricality of a Society that, unlike the acting company, *intends* to prefigure the Aesthetic State. If Wilhelm has learned that he is incapable of the aesthetic synthesis of acting and that this synthesis is a sham, both he and his teachers would appear capable of attaining this insight only at the price of entering into a more absurd and literal-minded version of the original delusion. The teacher, in other words, knows how teaching occurs only to the extent that the teaching, like acting, is untrue: Wilhelm may acquire knowledge, but cannot be said to *learn* anything.

The pedagogical plot thus assumes the aspect of a trick, a *Kunstgriff,* and the novel itself becomes the level on which the wise irony of *Bildung* would reside: the text "itself," as a *literary* text, can be said to know the event of itself as text, even if the characters it represents fall short of such aesthetic self-production. On this level too the novel follows out the skewed logic of Wilhelm's predicament by allowing the painting of the sick prince to dictate the terms of the text's closure. Wilhelm's recently-acknowledged son Felix assumes the role of the sick prince: seeing a glass and a bottle of milk, he drinks, not knowing that there is a deadly amount of opium in the milk, since Augustin, the former Harper, has just discovered he is Mignon's incestuous father and has decided to commit suicide. However, the opium is only in the glass, not in the bottle, and the child's bad habit of drinking out of bottles rather than glasses saves him. The doctor speaks of "the luckiest chance [*glücklichsten Zufall*]" and subsequently of divine intervention: "a good spirit guided [Felix's] hand"; Nathalie offers the more dialectical comment that "he has been saved through his bad habit [*Unart*]" (8.10). This revelation transforms into comedy two days of despair, since Felix, afraid of his father's anger, will not confess his poor table manners, and swears he drank from the glass; meanwhile he has been so frightened by the fear of the adults and so pumped full of medicine that for awhile he appears ill—and when, after a few hours, he appears well again, Wilhelm continues for some time to fear that his good health is merely appearance [*Schein*]. Nathalie, meanwhile, swears privately to the Abbé that if Felix dies she will ask Wilhelm to marry her, an oath that Friedrich overhears and subsequently publicizes: "Now that the child lives, why should she change her mind? What one promises in that fashion, one holds to under any circumstance." And he embarrasses Wilhelm and Nathalie into confessing their love for each other by pointing to the painting of the sick prince, and mockingly asking for an unaesthetic, referential reading of it:

> "What was the king's name? . . . What's the name of the old goat-beard with the crown there, pining at the foot of the bed for his sick son? What's the name of the beauty who enters with both poison and antidote [*Gift und Gegengift*] in her demure eyes? What's the name of that bungler of a doctor who at this very moment is seeing the light, who for the first time in his life has the chance to order a rational prescription, a medicine that cures from the ground up [*die aus dem Grunde kuriert*], and is as tasty as it is wholesome?" (8.10)

Wilhelm, thus invited, moves from the position of the child to that of the father, whose illness, in this fantasy, is cured by the discovery that the sick child is not sick. Though the mother's promise of love had seemed to require the child's death, the promise holds without exacting its sacrifice: the child lives in the love that a father receives. These magic gestures of recovery and recompense culminate in Wilhelm's assumption of a unique happiness in the novel's closing words: "I don't know the wealth of a kingdom . . . but I know I have gained a fortune [*Glück*] that I haven't earned, and that I wouldn't exchange for anything in the world."

The novel itself thus "identifies" with the painting's content, as the text's closing tableau repeats and inverts the structure of Wilhelm's obsession, simultaneously replaying the pedagogical gesture of the Society of the Tower. Here Wilhelm is manipulated into post-oedipal love (for Nathalie) rather than oedipal fear (for Hamlet's father's ghost). In a final twist on the Abbé's attempt to "cure error through error," the text cures Wilhelm through his own neurotic fixation on the painting and its deadly oedipal content, a cure imaged in miniature in the text's construction of salvation for Felix through the child's own *Unart*. Given such intricacies of closure, it is hardly surprising that ***Wilhelm Meisters Lehrjahre*** should always have been regarded as a paradigmatically self-conscious novel.[12] Nothing, indeed, could be more self-aware than the text's repetition of Wilhelm's act of identification; however, this is also to say that nothing could be more manifestly fictional than the closing tableau, the "fairy tale, or operetta-like character" of which, as Michael Beddow reminds us, is often remarked. The three promised marriages are all mésalliances between aristocrats (Natalie, Lothario, Friedrich) and commoners (Wilhelm, Therese, Philine), and the novel refuses to offer the slightest indication that these liaisons cut across the grain of the social text[13]—which is fair enough, since the social text has been dissolved into a rush of stylized literary events: Mignon's death and burial, Augustin's multiple and finally successful attempts at suicide, Felix's false death, and what the novel ironically summarizes as "so many terrible and wonderful events coming one after another" as to put the community into a "feverish oscillation." The theatrics of the Society of the Tower are left behind by the text's own performance; and one could thus say that, in closing, the novel imitates not just Wilhelm (who imitates the painting), and not just the Society of the Tower (which imitates this imitation), but also the actor, who knows and controls the production of the self, but only does so in and as a fiction.

The ***Lehrjahre,*** in short, offers itself as a "literary absolute" in Lacoue-Labarthe and Nancy's sense, and consequently as an ironic text in Lukács's sense. *Bildung,* the autoproduction of the self, is strictly speaking impossible, but this impossibility can be sublated into the self-knowledge of the *Roman* that is *Bildung,* the text that builds itself as a self-reflexive structure, a figure (*Bild*) of the fictionality of self-knowledge. This fictionality is figured as the symbolic sacrifice of aesthetics: as the text "identifies" with a poorly-executed painting of its own invention, literature becomes literature in knowing and effecting its own destruction.[14] The literary text's identification with kitsch is a renunciation that negates itself, transforming loss into the "fortune" invoked in the last words of the novel, the *Glück* that, Wilhelm insists, is beyond exchange and cannot be earned. The close of the text is an impossible, absolute gift, which emerges through a gesture of giving so absolute that the gift is precisely that of luck (*Glück*). Schillerian *Bildung* is negated and recuperated as the irony of luck: as the lucky chance that only fiction can reliably provide.[15]

But we have seen that readers of this novel have not always entirely shared its protagonist's happiness; and the grounds of Schiller's concern that the novel is written more "*for* the actor" than "*of* the actor" (Seidel 82) have become clearer. In itself, the "literary absolute," as the ironic knowledge of its own fictionality, is a demandingly ascetic form of aesthetic totalization; but the anxiety it inspires may be traced to the even less comforting status of the "fictional" in these scenes, which is always slipping away from its own knowledge. Fiction's power to posit is unlimited, but what is posited is fictional, bearing within it the insistent question of referential truth that reduces what is posited to "mere" fiction, and spurs the production of another fiction to compensate for the hollowness of the first. The falseness of the theater spurs Wilhelm's renunciation of it, but the result is an even more improbable theatricalization of his life and world; and though the self-conscious fictionality of the text thematizes and absorbs into itself the constant desire for an imperial referent ("What was the king's name?"), a residue of dissatisfaction will always potentially remain, "something isolated in the first and last reading," in Schlegel's words. The *Glück* of fiction at once exceeds the world of exchange and bears the trace of it—though what one exchanges it for is always another fiction. *Entsagung* is thus not a true dialectical process, but rather an act haunted by being an "act," a fiction; and this fictionality cannot be renounced even by a fiction seeking to renounce fictionality via a renunciation of truth.

Consequently, as a figure of *Bildung*—of *Bildung* as the knowledge of the impossibility of *Bildung—Entsagung* becomes illegible. If the knowledge this figure conveys is that the self cannot posit itself, such knowledge can only emerge by annihilating itself: knowledge is knowingly renounced only through a posited homology between knowing and acting that is precisely what knowledge renounces. An ironic spiral results: the act of presupposition (of a homology between knowledge and act) contradicts the knowledge, which confirms the knowledge (of this contradiction), which contradicts it again, and so on. And this ironic spiral is not grounded in an inevitability of intention; rather, the homology between knowledge and act is precisely *fictional,* available only in and as a fiction. Fiction thus becomes (mis)understandable as an incoherent productive force lodged within intention, and within irony as an intentional structure. *Why* such a force should dominate the rhetoric and narrative of ***Wilhelm Meisters Lehrjahre,*** in the guise of *Bildung,* is not yet clear, and to advance further we shall need to look more closely at the text's analysis of the genesis of theatricality. But first we might briefly examine the novel's elaboration of its oedipal allegory, since the figure of fatherhood in the text provides a more lurid, and thus more manifestly unstable, version of the rhetorical difficulty we encounter in the trope of *Entsagung.*

II

The oedipal scenario, as psychoanalysis extracts it from literature, constitutes a dramatic version of the story of identification through the fiction of a renunciation: a story that Lacan captures memorably in his punning interweaving of the "Name" and the "No" of the Father.[16] The male subject becomes the father precisely by not becoming the father: by turning his desire elsewhere so as to desire what the father desires. Since the subject emerges under prohibition, desire is an endless process of substitution; and the psychological subject's successful negotiation of oedipal conflict occurs as the acceptance of loss, just as the ironic subject of aesthetics accepts the endless deferral of aesthetic totalization. This analogy is prompted by the text itself: it is of course no accident that both the painting Wilhelm fetishizes and the play in which he acts feature oedipal narratives as the "content" with which he identifies. Borrowing Hamlet's fear of his ghostly father, and the sick prince's deadly desire for his father's bride, Wilhelm engages himself in the errancy of family romance to the precise extent that, within the orbit of aesthetic judgment, he *fails* to perform one—thus, as we have seen, committing himself to the ironic recuperation of aesthetics through failure. The novel cooperates by negotiating a proper object-choice for him: in an often rambunctious parody of oedipal emplotment, Nathalie replaces the all-too-maternal Mariane, the "mother" of Wilhelm's child—Mariane who is implicitly paired with Wilhelm's own mother in the text's opening chapters, and is ultimately consigned in dream to Wilhelm's dead father ("his father and Mariane seemed to be running away from him. . . . Impulse and desire impelled him to go to their assistance, but the Amazon's [Nathalie's] hand held him back—and how gladly he let himself be held!" [7.1]). The accession to the Name of the Father ("Meister") involves the acceptance of a No that takes the form of a renunciation of the self and its desires, and in this acceptance, which the text figures as Wilhelm's acknowledgment of Felix, the son becomes the father: "Everything he planned was now to mature for the boy, and everything he built was to last for several generations. His apprenticeship was therefore completed in this sense, for along with the feeling of a father [*dem Gefühl des Vaters*] he had acquired the virtues of a solid citizen [*eines Bürgers*]" (8.1). Oedipal identification generates a social identity and a consciousness of historical temporality, and thus provides a model version of negative *Bildung*: though desire always points elsewhere, this lack can be transformed into an index of maturity.

The endlessness of desire, however, which is totalizable precisely *as* an endlessness, and hence as a loss or lack that can be mourned, derives from a less stable epistemological or rhetorical problematic: the transformation of doubt (whether Felix is really Wilhelm's son) into conviction. We recall that by the end of Book VII, Wilhelm has been informed by various authorities—first the duenna Barbara, whom he does not believe; then the Abbé, whom he does—that Mariane, the actress he had abandoned in Book I, and who has since conveniently died, is Felix's mother, and that he, Wilhelm, is the father. Having given up the theater and received his *Lehrbrief* from the Tower, Wilhelm accedes to his overdetermined patronymic—"Meister"—in acceding to fatherhood. "Yes, I feel it," he cries, embracing Felix, "you are mine!" (7.9)—a moment of identification summarized in Friedrich's ironic *mot* late in the novel: "Fatherhood is based entirely and only on conviction; I'm convinced, therefore I'm a father" (8.6). Thus, if Wilhelm's *Bildung* is to occur, it will proceed, like Freud's famous "advance of civilization," under the affirmation that "paternity is a hypothesis, based on an inference and a premiss" (*Moses and Monotheism* 114). The uncertainty of fatherhood is certainly not simply subversive in its effects: it is a topos in Western culture that is regularly associated, as in Freud, with a passage from nature to culture, and from sense-certainty to cognition;[17] if, in Stephen Dedalus's words in *Ulysses,* "paternity may be a legal fiction" (170), this fiction, according to Stephen's parodic reading of *Hamlet,* underwrites theology itself.[18] Fatherhood is founded "upon incertitude," but as a "mystical estate, an apostolic succession" (170); thus, Stephen concludes, Shakespeare lives on in the ghost of Hamlet's father: "But, because loss is his gain, he passes on toward eternity in undiminished personality. . . . He is a ghost, a shadow now . . . a voice heard only in the heart of him who is the substance of his shadow, the son consubstantial with the father" (162).

The tension in Stephen Dedalus's—and Wilhelm Meister's—narrative is between an initial "incertitude," on the one hand, and a dialectical passage from "loss" to "gain" on the other. Uncertainty is not quite the same as loss, and though the dialectical narrative tells the story of the father's "undiminished" survival, the uncertain status of the father renders him "a ghost, a shadow," precisely because this uncertainty can never be entirely stabilized *as* a loss. Like *Ulysses,* ***Wilhelm Meisters Lehrjahre*** routes this tension through the figure of Hamlet's father's ghost. On the one hand, Wilhelm, terrified into his role as Hamlet by the mysterious Ghost, hears in its voice the power of an "undiminished personality": "The voice seemed familiar to everyone, and Wilhelm thought it sounded like that of his own father" (5.11). However, when the Ghost reappears during Wilhelm's initiation into the Society of the Tower, Wilhelm is far less certain he has heard correctly: "he thought he heard his father's voice, and yet not; so confused was he by present reality and past memories" (7.9). Doubt necessarily recurs within oedipal narrative, since this narrative is founded not on a referent but on uncertainty.

For this reason, fathers, for all their omnipresence in ***Wilhelm Meister,*** seem to have no more than a wraith-like grip on the world: Jarno is of uncertain parentage, and his name is strange (3.4); no one knows where the Abbé comes from (6); Lothario's name is a pseudonym (4.16); Nathalie's family is not in the genealogical books (4.11); and so on. Even the identity of the actor playing the ghost of Hamlet's father is in doubt, since the Abbé turns out to have a mysterious twin brother who might or might not have taken the role. And because the father cannot guarantee his own promise to exist, the figure of the ghost drifts away from that of the father, becoming associated more generally with uncertainty itself. Thus, glimpsing the "shadow" of Norberg, the rival who helps bring uncertainty to the paternity of Felix, Wilhelm feels the "uneasiness" of a ghost-effect: "And like a ghost at midnight that scares the wits out of us, and when we regain our composure seems the product of our anxiety and leaves us with doubts whether in fact we ever saw it, a great uneasiness came over Wilhelm" (1.17). Unsure what woman visited him in the night after the production of Hamlet, Wilhelm is relieved at the end of the novel to be told that Philine, and not Mignon, had been the "lovely palpable ghost [*fühlbare Gespenst*]" in his bed (8.6). Similar ghostings proliferate, infecting the production of subjectivity at all levels in this novel.[19]

The duplicity of a ghost-effect that at once enables the Father to survive death and makes it impossible for him to come into existence is represented in ***Wilhelm Meister*** through counterpointed figures of portrait and mirror. The portrait, at least at first glance, represents a stable figurative structure, grounded in a particular referent that it sublimates into a meaning. When Wilhelm obtains his *Lehrbrief* and reads the *Turmgesellschaft*'s account of his life,

> he saw a picture of himself, not like a second self in a mirror, but a different self, one outside of him, as in a portrait [*Porträt*]. One never approves of everything in a portrait, but one is always glad that a thoughtful mind has seen us thus and a superior talent enjoyed portraying us in such a way that a picture survives of what we were, and will survive longer than we will. (8.1)

The subject of *Bildung,* brought to self-consciousness in the gaze of the Other, shoulders its oedipal discomforts ("one never approves of everything") for the sake of an identity that, portrait-like, would sublimate its referent into the historical temporality of a meaning. This, however, is what the text refuses to guarantee; and the "mirror," which Wilhelm distinguishes from the "portrait" in characterizing the narrative of his apprenticeship scroll, registers the volatile nature of all figural relations: the self can duplicate into the "second self" of the mirror because the first self is always possibly a figure masquerading as a referent.[20] In one of the novel's charged moments, Wilhelm, disguised as the count, sees "in the mirror" the real count entering his wife's bedroom: "He saw me in the mirror, as I did him, and before I knew whether it was a ghost or he himself, he went out again" (3.10). The shock of seeing himself redoubled drives the count to forsake the world for a Moravian community; and "you," Jarno tells Wilhelm later, "are the ghost who drove him into the arms of religion" (7.3).

But to be or to see a ghost is precisely not to know whether or not one is or has seen a ghost. Even the "great uneasiness" one feels at such moments is "like a ghost" that "at midnight scares the wits out of us, and when we regain our composure seems the product of our anxiety and leaves us with doubts whether in fact we ever saw it" (1.17): the pathos of a haunting is itself spectral, infected with uncertain theatricality. It is significant that Wilhelm feels drawn to Hamlet's famous meditation on the fictional pathos of the actor ("What's Hecuba to him, or he to Hecuba / That he should weep for her?" [5.6]). The dignified suffering of the oedipal subject, the pathos of *Entsagung,* the labor and patience of the negative, emerge only at the risk of being exposed as fraudulent, just as the transcendental spiral of *Bildung* can occur only at the risk of being exposed as a trick, a *Kunstgriff.* And yet the production of *Bildung,* particularly in its oedipal form, relies upon affect: Wilhelm, we recall, acquires "the feeling of a father [*Gefühl des Vaters*]" in passing out of apprenticeship. The father is a rhetorical effect. And the structure of this rhetorical effect is double: on the one hand it is uncertain, since it can always fail to convince; on the other hand, it can only exist as the obliteration of this uncertainty: unless one is convinced, one is not a father. Fatherhood exists as the repression of its own rhetoricity. Thus fatherhood repeats, more violently, the predicament of *Entsagung:* while the ironic subject of *Bildung* renounces self-knowledge but can only do so knowingly, the subject of paternity comes into being as a "knowledge" that, like Oedipus, blinds itself to itself. While the ironic spiral of knowledge culminates in the text's theatrical assumption of sheer fictionality, the paternal hoax recurs as the constant vacillation of an assertion that cannot know its own impossibility.

Implicitly linking Hamlet's ghost with the picture of the sick prince, Wilhelm insists that in the production of *Hamlet* there be a "lifesize" portrait of Hamlet's father drawn and positioned "so that he looks exactly like the Ghost when it goes out the door. That will be very effective when Hamlet is looking at the Ghost and the queen at the portrait" (5.9). And, after the mysterious Ghost shows up at the opening performance, it is remarked that he had looked exactly like the portrait, as if "he had sat for it himself" (5.12). The portrait precedes its referent, which of course, as a "father," is not a referent but a ghost. Here, in other words, the portrait is revealed to be a trope, a metalepsis dependent for its referent on fiction's power to provide one, just as the father is only persuasive thanks to *Hamlet*'s, or the ***Lehrjahre***'s, rhetorical force. And if we ask after the text's representation of the genesis of this problematic, we need to account for the remaining term in this oedipal scenario: the mother who gazes at the portrait, who is marginalized, half forgotten, and, in the person of Mariane, killed off, but who is also never entirely expelled from the narrative of *Bildung*.

III

The figure of the mother presides over the opening of the novel, though not precisely over the origins of theatricality: Wilhelm cannot decide whether his love for Mariane caused him to love the theater, or vice-versa (4.19), and the reader similarly cannot decide whether Wilhelm loves Mariane or her masculine stage-costume, the "red uniform" and "white vest" that he embraces so eagerly (1.1). Via the language of erotic fetishism, the novel suggests that one can never be certain that desire has not already mimicked itself. And though we discover that a set of marionettes originally gave the child Wilhelm a "taste for the theatre," this taste is uncertainly figurative: since the puppets are kept locked up in the maternal (and, of course, forbidden) space of the kitchen pantry, they literally acquire tastes and smells associated with maternal care (1.2).[21] On the one hand the mother is paired with theatricality as the literal to the figurative; on the other hand, the difference between these two is precisely what cannot be established. This uncertainty means that the very relation between mother and theater, or literal and figurative meaning, is irreducibly theatrical or figurative, since no stabilizing ground of meaning presents itself. However, the drama of uncertainty confronting us here differs slightly from that staged by the tropes of fatherhood or *Entsagung*. In keeping both with bourgeois gender roles and a metaphysical hierarchy that ***Wilhelm Meister*** at least pretends to respect, the mother represents a prelinguistic site of natural origin; and thus in her proximity the text allegorizes the impossible and contradictory referential drive of fiction as the condition of all language. Both fatherhood and renunciation represent the possibility that the referent can be recuperated through negation—that by turning from the father's desire one can become the father; that by giving up self-knowledge one can recover it; that by annihilating the referent in pure fictionality one can obtain the plenitude of *"Glück."* The mother, however, represents not just a referent to be negated in oedipal narrative, but the site of referentiality itself; and the marks of maternal care—the tastes and smells of the pantry—figure the pressure of referentiality precisely as the *undecidability* of the sign.[22] Nourishment, belonging to what Lacan would term the realm of "need," is not language; yet as Cathy Caruth comments apropos the "Blessed Babe" passage in Wordsworth's *Prelude,* "in order to nurse his *mother's breast* the babe first has to read it": gestures of care only become maternal when they are taken as signs (56). There is thus no such thing as the "mother" outside of a signifying system, yet the mother marks the impossibility of closing this system. Language could be said to "prop" itself on nonlinguistic gestures, rather as Freud, in a famous passage, speaks of sexuality "attach[ing] itself to functions serving the purpose of self-preservation" (*Three Essays* 182)—except that what is undecidable is precisely whether marks are nonlinguistic or not.[23] The mother, and the marionettes, figure a non-empirical *materiality* of the sign: the sign's dependence, or "propping," upon an illegibility rather than a presence.[24]

The sign is thus always already theatrical because it can only pretend to be unequivocally a sign. Its possibility entails a radical contingency which must be suppressed if the sign is to be taken *as* a sign, but which leaves its mark in the sign's excessive and insatiable need to refer. The puppets register the material condition of this predicament, which is that of signification as the *inscription,* the violent imposition, of the possibility of reading. As Wilhelm takes up the puppets (1.3), "he was transported [*versetzt*] back to the time when he thought they were alive [*wo sie ihm noch belebt schienen*], when he thought he could bring them alive [*zu beleben glaubte*] by the liveliness [*Lebhaftigkeit*] of his voice and the movements of his hands" (1.2). The puppets, which as material objects are properly speaking neither dead nor alive, represent the "prop" necessary for the imposition of figure as *Schein* or *Bild:* in this sense they are not phenomenal or empirical objects, but rather indicative of an unguaranteed possibility of articulation. Like Mignon's corpse at the end of the novel, they acquire a "Schein des Lebens" by virtue of a rhetorical event that Paul de Man's late work thematizes as catachretic prosopopeia, the disruptive incoherence of which appears in the sentence above as the compressed conjunction of a false constative presupposition (*belebt schienen*) and a fictitious performative act (*zu beleben glaubte*).[25] Henceforth desire can vacillate between the binary oppositions of figurative and literal, life and death, appearance and reality, etc.: once "the appearance of life" has been posited, death can become negation.[26] This dialectic erects itself upon the *taking* of signs as such, figured here as the taking of *bodies:* the body is here the trope of the legible sign, and the marionettes register this body's material support, and hence its ongoing figurative dismemberment. And as critics from Schiller onward have well understood, this predicament leaves its mark in the narrative through the figure of Mignon.[27]

Mignon should indeed, as Eric Blackall claims, be understood as "the spirit of poetry" and the "guiding force of the book," though the consequences of such an insight are not necessarily positive.[28] Mignon, like Wilhelm's grandfather's art collection (and its symbolic complement, the marionettes), comes from Italy, the land of art. Like her father the Harper, she provides the text with a mouthpiece for its famously haunting lyrics; as a corpse she becomes herself a work of art at the end of the novel, lending her body to the "schöne Kunst" of the embalmer (8.5). As befits the "spirit" of poetry, she is deeply associated with the Father's Ghost, and implicated in every turn of Wilhelm's *Bildung.* Hers is the dead father of Hamlet and Wilhelm ("The big devil is dead" [2.4]); the Ghost, she has reason to add, is her "uncle" ("No one understood what she meant, except those who knew that she had called the man she thought was her father 'the big devil'" [5.12]). Knowing the secret of the father, she knows that Felix is Wilhelm's true son: "The ghost told it to me" (7.8). But this is also to say that Mignon is the "riddle" of the text: "Here is the riddle [*Rätsel*]," Philine says, introducing Mignon (2.4); and the legibility of this poetic riddle is never entirely certain. Though Wilhelm is finally told that Philine was the ghost, the *Gespenst,* who came to him in the night after his debut in *Hamlet,* the novel is curiously, even stagily coy in its refusal to provide evidence: "His first guess was that it had been Philine, and yet the charming body he had clasped in his arms did not seem like hers" (5.13). Wilhelm is subsequently "frightened" by a new maturity he sees in Mignon—"she seemed to have grown taller during the night"—and though he persuades himself that his nocturnal visitor must have been Philine after all, the narrator adds, in an atypically theatrical aside, that "we too must share this opinion, because we are not able to reveal the reasons which had made him doubt this and had aroused other suspicions" (5.13). The rationale of this aside—the reason of these "reasons"—is never revealed; the *Rätsel* remains riddled. Mignon thus embodies a remainder of uncertainty within the transcendence of sense perception that is fatherhood.[29] In relation to the gender discriminations that oedipal narratives seek to police, this means that Mignon, a product of the "Gespenst" of incest (8.9), must appear a "hermaphrodite creature" (3.11), the focal point for the text's interest in androgyny.

Thus, what must be expelled from the aesthetic plot, and reintegrated, however problematically, as a "corpse," is Mignon's body. A member of an acrobat's entourage when Wilhelm adopts her, Mignon is associated with bodily deformation as well as with poetic language: when she writes, for instance, her body interferes: "the letters were uneven and the lines not straight. In this too her body seemed to contradict her mind [*dem Geiste zu widersprechen*]" (2.12). And if we examine the figurative resonance of this contradiction, we find that Mignon's crampings of the heart and epileptic seizures return us repeatedly to the puppet theater. Mignon prepares the ground of Wilhelm's *Vaterherz* in a series of curious scenes: accepting him as a surrogate parent, she performs an egg-dance for him like a mechanism [*Räderwerk*] or a clock [*wie ein Uhrwerk*], and Wilhelm, transported by this *Schauspiel,* desires to resuscitate her "with the love of a father" (2.8). A little later, Mignon has a seizure: her body convulses and she falls "as if every limb of her body were broken":

> It was a terrifying sight! "My child," he said, lifting her up and embracing her, "what is it?"—The convulsions persisted, spreading from the heart to the dangling limbs [*schlotternden Gliedern*]; she was just hanging in his arms. (2.14)

Then "all her limbs became alive again"; she clasps his neck "like a lock that springs shut," and when Wilhelm repeats "My child!" she responds "My father! . . . You will be my father!"

The dangling limbs and convulsive, mechanical motions recur later in a scene in which the puppets figure overtly. Wilhelm and his troupe are celebrating a successful premiere of *Hamlet,* and Mignon and Felix, sitting in a chair reserved for the mysterious Ghost, mimic the marionettes:

> The children, who, sitting in the big armchair, stuck out over the table like puppets out of their box, started to put on a little play [*Stück*] of this sort. Mignon imitated the rasping noise very nicely, and they finally banged their heads together and on the edge of the table, in such a manner as actually only wooden puppets can withstand. Mignon was almost frenetically excited . . . she now began to rush around the table, tambourine in hand, hair flying, head thrown back and her limbs flung in the air like one of those maenads whose wild and well-nigh impossible postures still astonish us on ancient monuments. (5.12)

The final simile compresses and repeats, with a *frisson* of orphic dismemberment, the aesthetic trajectory that later in the novel Mignon will follow. And a deforming, disfiguring force will haunt that trajectory, wracking Mignon's body to the moment of death—when once again her "schlotternde Körper" will hang like a puppet's (8.5). Felix as well as Mignon must play out this *Stück,* sitting in the place of the father, for Felix's condition of possibility hangs no less than Mignon's on an act of identification with a puppet—an impossible act that the text registers in one of its most astonishing turns of phrase ("banged their heads together . . . in such a manner as actually only wooden puppets can withstand").[30] The children are not puppets, but they do that which only puppets can do. It is impossible to identify with puppets, but this impossibility "occurs." The story of the child Wilhelm's projection of life onto the marionettes could be told with less manifest strain, since that act of *Belebung* could at least appear to originate in the plenitude of the child's living identity. But

Mignon and Felix's grotesquely inverted repetition of Wilhelm's act underscores the violent, figurative origins of all identities and of all identifications. The children are actors, who intend the identity they posit, and in doing so they reveal the rhetorical precondition of all acting, and all aesthetics, which resides in a prosopopeia irreducible to intentionality: the children, the actor, and the aesthetic text "are" puppets in the sense that they have, impossibly, been made possible by them; and the disruptive materiality of signification that the puppets record is one name for the deadly force inhabiting the body of the "spirit of poetry."[31] The expulsion of this foreign body takes, of course, the form of aestheticization as entombment: once dead, this body will be able to enter the meaningful universe of death and life *as* a body. Mignon thus becomes a beautiful object, a *Schein des Lebens,* through the *schöne Kunst* of the embalmer, as with great ceremony she is encrypted in an antique sarcophagus long devoid of its original inhabitant—a coffin become a commodified artwork, purchased in Italy, the land of art, by Nathalie's uncle. An artwork entombed in art, Mignon is a treasure [*Schatz*] and a portrait, a "beautiful picture of the past [*schöne Gebild der Vergangenheit*]," and is ready to resurface in domesticated form as the sentimental figure of melancholy, *Sehnsucht,* and *Heimweh* that literary history was to make of her.[32]

Death, however, does not lay the ghost to rest. Even before the funeral service has ended (the choir is still busy singing "Unconsumed, in marble it rests; in your hearts it lives and works"), the audience has stopped listening: "no one heard the fortifying message," for everyone has been distracted by the appearance of a story about Mignon's origins. Once again Mignon must be encrypted; but this time, having exhausted other resources, the text can only tell the story of a false burial and a fictional body.[33] The story goes that Mignon, after disappearing from her Italian home, was presumed to have drowned in the local lake; her mother, Sperata, under the influence of a miraculous story, begins to comb the shore for her child's bones, believing that if she could only gather up the entire skeleton and take it to Rome, "the child would appear before the people, in its fresh white skin, on the steps of the high altar of St. Peter's" (8.9). Daily she gathers up animal bones, a deluded reader patiently and madly pursuing reading as the gathering [*légein*] of a body,[34] until public sympathy, in the hope of curing error through error, suggests that "the bones of a child's skeleton should gradually be intermingled with those she already had, to increase her hopes." Sperata experiences great joy as, thanks to yet another dead child, "the parts gradually fitted together." Only a few extremities remain missing when she has a vision of her child, embodied and thus transcendent: "It rose up, threw off the veil, its radiance filling the room, its beauty transfigured, its feet unable to touch the ground, even had they wished to. . . . I will follow my child." Sperata dies, and like Mignon, or Ottilie in the *The Elective Affinities,* her body miraculously resists corruption, and she becomes a religious icon: "There were several cures, which no attentive observer could explain or dismiss as false." Sperata, the exotic, hoodwinked, and sentimentalized peasant mother, has been brought on stage by a fictional power that fiction is powerless to control. She is Schlegel's reader-as-supplement, a reader generated by the slippage of the text that is the production of the text: she is thus at once the figure of a reading, and the figure of the violence with which a text, or a reading, comes into existence—a blind force that is constantly, but always anxiously, misread as the exquisite corpse of a meaning. And if meaning here attains figuration as the body, meaning's materiality is that of scattered bones: minimal units of articulation that, like letters assembled into words, serve as the fragments of a fictional skeleton. This predicament is exemplary precisely to the degree that it is staged and suspect, and in a certain fundamental sense impossible—the impossible generation of identity or meaning out of a tangled pile of articulations, the fragments of marionettes or skeletons. If the *Bildungsroman* rises like a ghost from these scattered bones, this is because of, rather than despite, the impossibility of *Bildung*'s story: a story that can have no origin and no conclusion, since the aestheticization of texts, authors, and bodies must always be done over again to cover up the undoing that composes their possibility.

Thus the story of the puppets becomes the story of Mignon, which in turn becomes the story of a mad, mourning mother, whose incestuous production of her child is reiterated in her deluded labor to re-member or re-produce it. But through the rigor of this figurative sequence ***Wilhelm Meister*** demonstrates that the mother is neither a natural site of meaning nor a deviation from such a site, but is rather the mark of a linguistic predicament, the trace of a randomness within language that can neither be comprehended nor entirely effaced. This readable disjunction within signifying processes is the general condition for all tropes and figures, and can be termed irony. Irony, as the displacement constitutive of language, disarticulates the aesthetic and naturalizing illusion that composes all ideologies, thus opening them to critique by accounting for their occurrence and power. ***Wilhelm Meisters Lehrjahre,*** in other words, in demystifying the Society of the Tower's "portentous words and signs" (8.5), registers the force, as well as the absurdity, of its corporate, multinational cultural ambition. For, as Jarno says, "since property is no longer safe anywhere,"

> from our ancient Tower a Society [*Sozietät*] shall go forth, which will extend into every corner of the globe, and people from all over the world will be allowed to join it. (8.7)

Notes

1. See also Schaffner, and, for a representative study with a more narrowly German focus, Swales. On the history of the term "Bildungsroman," see Martini.

2. The term, according to Martini, makes its earliest appearance around 1819-20 in essays by a professor at the Universität Dorpat, Karl Morgenstern. It then seems to have sunk into oblivion until, fifty years later, Wilhelm Dilthey rather offhandedly introduced

it in *Das Leben Schleiermachers* (1870) to describe "those novels which make up the school of *Wilhelm Meister,*" a definition he later elaborated in a famous passage in *Das Erlebnis und die Dichtung* (1906): "A regular development is observed in the life of the individual: each of the stages has its own intrinsic value and is at the same time the basis for a higher stage. The dissonances and conflicts of life appear as the necessary points of passage [*Durchgangspunkte*] through which the individual must pass on his way to maturity and harmony" (394). The idea of a *Bildungsroman* subsequently caught on, though scholarly studies of it did not begin to appear with great regularity in Germany until the postwar era. Morgenstern's, Dilthey's, and Martini's texts, among others, are conveniently collected in Selbmann.

3. The only novel consistently cited is, of course, *Wilhelm Meister,* though as noted below even this novel has been denied entry into the genre it is usually supposed to have founded or exemplified. Apart from *Wilhelm Meister,* the novels most frequently granted chapters in books on the *Bildungsroman* include: Wieland's *Agathon* (1767); Novalis's *Heinrich von Ofterdingen* (1800); Adalbert Stifter's *Der Nachsommer* (1857); Wilhelm Raabe's *Der Hungerpastor* (1864); Gottfried Keller's *Der grüne Heinrich* (1854/55; 1879/80); and, in the twentieth century, the novels of Hesse and Mann.

4. See also Sammons, 232. The principal target of both critics is Buckley.

5. Cited by Amrine, 125-26. (All translations in this essay are mine unless otherwise noted.) See also Eichner; May (the question of whose title, "'Wilhelm Meisters Lehrjahre,' ein *Bildungsroman?*" is answered negatively: "In the *Lehrjahre,* Goethe has written a novel around the belief that the modern humanistic ideal of harmonious 'Bildung' has to be abandoned" [34]); Saine; Schlechta.

6. This remark may seem cavalier, but is meant seriously and could be justified with many examples, Kontje's remarks at the close of the introductory chapter to his recent *Private Lives in the Public Sphere* being simply more overt than most: "Thus I will not rehearse the tired debate as to whether or not particular texts examined here 'count' as *Bildungsromane.* Obviously I think they do" (17).

7. This is also what distinguishes the question of the *Bildungsroman* from that of other problematic genres such as the *récit* or *Novelle*—or, for that matter, from that of the novel itself.

8. Lacoue-Labarthe and Nancy's definition of the "literary absolute" is complex and nuanced, but may for present purposes be reduced to their claim that it "aggravates and radicalizes the thinking of totality and the Subject" (15) insofar as literature, in producing itself as the reflection on itself, offers itself as exemplary to the Subject. Generally speaking, then, Lacoue-Labarthe and Nancy tend to conceive of literature, and ("Romantic" or "literary") irony as self-reflection, though elements in their argument move in another, more radical direction. For an account and a fine critique of *The Literary Absolute,* see Newmark.

9. Since editions vary and the novel's chapters are generally very short, I have indicated quotations from *Wilhelm Meister* by book and chapter number. The text is that of the Hamburger Ausgabe (abbreviated where necessary *HA*); my translations generally follow those of Blackall.

10. Schiller's correspondence with Goethe during the period 1795-96 has become one of the sacred cows of the modern German canon, because in many respects it provides a bridge between Goethe's novel and one of the founding texts of aesthetic culture, Schiller's *On the Aesthetic Education of Man.* See, for instance, Wilkinson and Willoughby: "We . . . would seek the most adequate fictional counterpart [to the *Aesthetic Education*] in the work that Schiller was receiving in installments while actually engaged on his treatise, namely *Wilhelm Meister*" (cxcv-cxcvi). Schiller's response to the novel, however, is complex and occasionally frankly ambivalent, and merits careful study—not least since these letters compose the first "reading" that *Wilhelm Meister* received, and in a sense can also be understood as the first attempt to read the novel as a *"Bildungsroman."* Often the language of the *Aesthetic Education* is squarely in view: "In him," Schiller writes, for instance, of the character Wilhelm, "dwells a pure and moral image of mankind" (Seidel 189), a claim that echos the typological system of the *Aesthetic Education*: "Every individual man . . . carries in himself, by predisposition and determination, a pure ideal Man, with whose unchanging oneness it is the great task of his being, in all its changes, to correspond" (Letter 4.2, translation modified). But elsewhere more anxious comments appear, many of which resemble the complaints of twentieth-century critics who have had trouble identifying *Wilhelm Meister* as a *Bildungsroman.* I refer here to a moment when Schiller worries that Wilhelm, gazing at aesthetic objects in the Hall of the Past, is "still too much the old Wilhelm, who liked best to linger, in his grandfather's house, by the [portrait of the] sick king's son" (Seidel 208).

11. For a powerful analysis of aesthetics as a structure of ironic postponement, see Lloyd.

12. *Wilhelm Meister* in fact lent its "scènes de marionettes ou de fête au château" to André Gide's famous formulation of the *"mise en abyme"*: see Gide, 41. For a study of Gide's text that (briefly) engages *Wilhelm Meister,* see Dällenbach, 23-24.

13. "The utopian element here is not just that these marriages are proposed in the first place, but that they are envisaged without any issue being made of the socially outrageous character of the unions, even though the narrative has earlier drawn explicit atten-

tion to the 'vast gulf of birth and station' separating Wilhelm from the Countess, Nathalie's sister" (Beddow 139). The present reading will be indirectly questioning Beddow's assurance that the emphatic fictionality of the novel's ending "does not amount to a *radical* ironisation of Wilhelm's represented fulfilment" (139, Beddow's italics).

14. Goethe's writing about Wilhelm Meister and the theater, from the *Theatralische Sendung* (1777-85) to the *Wanderjahre* (1829), pursues a trajectory that ironically repeats Wilhelm's and his text's gestures of *Entsagung*—a reflexive turn typical of the *Bildungsroman* problematic, which at some point necessarily generates the referential question of the "author." If the hero of the *Theatralische Sendung* goes relatively unchastened in his ambition to build a national theater, and the Wilhelm of the *Lehrjahre* is brought to renounce that desire, the protagonist of the *Wanderjahre* will find that the theater has become the only artform to be banned from the Pedagogical Province—primarily because of its ability to attract crowds through "false and unsuitable emotions" (*HA* 8, p. 258). Lest we be tempted to confuse this apparent narrative of *Bildung*-through-*Entsagung* with these texts' (or Goethe's own) vastly complex relation to the theater, we are told that Wilhelm, after listening patiently to the pedagogues' lecture on the evils of drama, "was only half convinced and perhaps somewhat annoyed." Furthermore, "The editor of these pages might himself confess that he has allowed this strange passage [*wunderliche Stelle*] to slip by with some reluctance [*Unwillen*]; for has he not also in various ways expended more life and energy on the theatre than is proper? And is he now to be persuaded that this was an unforgivable error, a fruitless effort?" (ibid.).

15. For a fine reading of the figure of *Glück* and its relation to economic and libidinal exchange in this novel, see Hörisch. The present analysis of fortune, luck, and fiction owes much to Derrida's remarkable analysis of these figures in *Donner le temps.*

16. Lacan's pun exploits the fact that "nom" (name) and "non" (no) are homophones in modern French: see in particular "The Function and Field of Speech and Language in Psychoanalysis," in *Ecrits,* 30-113. For a study of the *Bildungsroman* inspired by Hegel and Lacan, see Smith.

17. For an incisive analysis of the father as a metaphor for the supersensory, see Culler, chapter 9.

18. The *Ulysses* episode in question ("Scylla and Charybdis") begins with an invocation of Goethe's novel: "And we have, have we not, those priceless pages of *Wilhelm Meister.* A great poet on a great brother poet" (151).

19. The ontological uncertainty of identity repeats itself, within the terms of oedipal narrative, as a teasing ambiguity of gender identity. Wilhelm's education at the hands of phallic women begins with Mariane, who on the first page of the novel is dressed as a solider; then there is Therese, who becomes the perfect bourgeoise housewife only by being mannishly independent, and Nathalie, the "Amazon," who when we first meet her is dressed in a man's overcoat. Even the *schöne Seele* begins her career as a tomboy: she is called at one point an "errant son," and later, in becoming a Beautiful Soul against the wishes of her frivolous fiancé, demonstrates a "manly defiance." I discuss the special case of Mignon below; unfortunately, space does not permit an examination of the character most remarkable in this respect: Aurelie, the actress who confuses *Schein* and *Sein* by carrying a real dagger and by mingling her real life with her role as Ophelia—a dark parody of Wilhelm's narcissistic investment in Hamlet. "Smile at me, laugh at my theatrical display of passion!" she cries at Wilhelm; but "the terrifying, half-natural and half-forced state of this woman tormented him too much for that." A moment later Aurelie cuts Wilhelm's hand with the dagger, striking a blow, perhaps, on behalf of the countless damaged and discarded female characters who litter the path of male *Bildung*: "One must mark (*zeichnen*) you men sharply!" (4.20). For a feminist reading of the *Lehrjahre* that discusses Aurelie, see Kowalik.

20. This is one way to understand the frequent redoubling of characters in *Wilhelm Meister.* The Abbé's mysterious twin brother is only one instance of a more general narrative principle, according to which characters no sooner emerge than they divide and multiply: the countess generates a twin sister in Nathalie, Mignon is paired with Felix, etc.

21. The young Wilhelm sneaks into the pantry and discovers the puppets there, and his mother ultimately rewards this mildly erotic transgression by giving the child the puppets, just as she gives the adult Wilhelm the key (1.2, 1.5). The sexual dimension of the episode, obvious enough in the *Lehrjahre,* is made explicit in an explicit in an equivalent scene in Goethe's first version of the novel, *Wilhelm Meisters theatralische Sendung,* where the young Wilhelm's lifting the curtain of the puppet-theater is explicitly compared to falling into sexual knowledge: "Thus at certain times do children become conscious of the difference between the sexes, and their glances through the covers hiding these secrets bring forth wonderful movements in their nature" (*AA,* vol. 8, 532).

22. Of interest in this context would be the unstable place of smell and taste in Kantian aesthetics: see Derrida, "Economimesis."

23. The translation of Freud's term *Anlehnung* as "propping" (in place of Strachey's "anaclisis") was originally suggested by Jeffrey Mehlman as a translation of Jean Laplanche's translation of Freud's term as "étayage" (see Laplanche). Cathy Caruth examines the rhetorical consequences of this moment in Freud's account of the origin of sexuality: see espe-

cially pp. 44-57. In this context it is worth noting that *anlehnen,* like the words Freud once represented as "primal," has two opposing meanings: to lean against, but also to leave ajar.

24. See Chase for a brilliantly original articulation of Julia Kristeva's notion of the "abjection" of the mother with the allegory of meaning-production that a rhetorical reading uncovers: the uncertainty afflicting the sign aligns with the uncertain border between mother and infant, which is the uncertainty that the infant must expel as an "abject" in order to enter the linguistic world of subjects and objects. The scenario Chase describes would clearly hold interest for the reader of *Wilhelm Meister,* given the narrative's reiterated expulsion of maternal figures (Mariane, Wilhelm's mother, Sperata, etc.; as suggested below, Mignon is also in this sense a distorted figure of the "mother").

25. On catachresis and prosopopeia, see in particular de Man, "Hypogram and Inscription," in *The Resistance to Theory,* 27-53. For a reading of Heinrich von Kleist's reading of *Wilhelm Meister,* "On the Marionettentheater" (1810), see de Man's "Aesthetic Formalization in Kleist," in *The Rhetoric of Romanticism,* 263-90. Since this random element in signification is what lies concealed in the post-Kantian commonplace of the non-referentiality of aesthetic form, it is appropriate that the marionettes be complemented by an image of a scattered art collection: Wilhelm's grandfather's, which is broken up and sold around the same time that the puppets make their Christmas appearance in the Meister household.

26. Wilhelm, in other words, will be able to narrate a mini-*Bildungsroman*: the story of his internalization of the puppet-theater's text, of how he reproduced its pathos [*pathetische Rede*] through his good memory [*gutes Gedächtnis*] (1.2). Mariane, appropriately, falls asleep during Wilhelm's story (1.8), for it bores (through) us as the narrative of the disarticulation of narrative. Thus accounting, perhaps, for the addictive tonal blend of sentiment and lighthearted indifference that Goethe achieves in *Wilhelm Meister*—the blend that Schiller, acutely enough, found so disturbing. Pathos has an odd, theatrical status in a novel that, for instance, insists on Mariane's determinative emotional, erotic, and symbolic importance for Wilhelm's development, while granting her very little narrative or descriptive attention before ejecting her from the plot line at the end of Book I.

27. Schiller's first response to a reading of the completed text of *Wilhelm Meister* was to write that "the figure of Mignon looms at the moment most strongly before me" (Seidel 176); and this figure looms her way in interesting fashion through subsequent letters, providing a locus for reflections on pathos and art. As Ammerlahn remarks, "No figure in *Wilhelm Meister* so spoke to the heart and imagination of Goethe's reading public as Mignon; over no other character was so much reflected, conjectured, and written; none has been so frequently imitated, and yet remained so mysterious" ("Wilhelm Meisters Mignon—ein offenbares Rätsel" 89). See also Ammerlahn's more recent study, "Puppe—Tänzer—Dämon—Genius—Engel." For a recent account of the figure of Mignon in literary history, see Tunner. Like these essays—and Schiller's correspondence, and any number of other responses to *Wilhelm Meister*—the present essay represents among other things an attempt to read the "riddle" of Mignon.

28. See Blackall's "Afterword" to his edition of *Wilhelm Meister,* 386. Blackall is invoking a topos in Goethe criticism that, as noted earlier, informs the remarks of the novel's first critic, Schiller, and receives corroboration by countless nineteenth-century readers, from Friedrich Schlegel and Carlyle to Hegel, for whom Mignon's character is "wholly poetic [*schlechthin poetisch*]" (857).

29. The "unnaturalness" of Mignon is frequently invoked in Goethe criticism when the "naturalness" of some other aspect of the novel is in peril: e.g., Beddow: "Both Mignon and the Harper produce, in their solitary and secret predicaments, deeply moving poetry, but their creativity is not for them an experience of human freedom. . . . What little potential humanity they do manage to realise is embodied in the poetry which gives voice to their sense of separation from full humanity. . . . And so Mignon and the Harper take their place among the figures whose destinies develop so differently from Wilhelm's, reminding us that the course of his life, whilst eminently 'natural', is by no means to be taken as normal, in the sense of everyday" (146).

30. Eric Blackall's translation of this sentence is curiously elliptical: "the children started a little game of their own, with Mignon making a rasping noise as puppets do. They banged their heads together as if these were made of wood. Mignon was almost frenetically excited. . . ." The translation of *Stück* ("play" in the sense of theater-piece) as "game," and the elision of Goethe's uncompromising equation of the act of the children with the being of puppets ("Mignon machte den schnarrenden Ton sehr artig nach, und sie stießen zuletzt die Köpfe dergestalt zusammen und auf die Tischkante, wie es eigentlich nur Holzpuppen aushalten können") relieves the scene of much of its figurative density. It is tempting to speculate that once again, the reception of this "spirit of poetry" has exacted a sacrifice. (The passage is accurately represented in Carlyle's translation: see *Wilhelm Meister's Apprenticeship* [London: The Anthological Society, 1901], p. 292.)

31. The figurative language here attached to Mignon recurs in *Die Wahlverwandtschaften,* where Ottilie and her servant Nanni in some ways divide up Mignon's overdetermined role: Ottilie becomes an exquisite corpse, and Nanni, feeling the corpse beckon to her, falls out of a window and lands next to it: "she seemed to be shattered in every limb [*es schien an*

allen Gliedern zerschmettert]." Then "either by chance or providential dispensation" her "dangling limbs [*schlotternden Gliedern*]" touch the corpse and she is resuscitated (*HA* vol. 6, 486). The place of these puppet-metaphors in the rhetorical structure of *Die Wahlverwandtschaften* would require interpretation; for a reading that moves in the direction of the present essay, see Miller.

32. Mignon thus appears in the *Wanderjahre* fully aestheticized as a subject for sentimental exercises in painting by a young artist taken with her story (Book II, ch. 7; *HA* vol. 8, 226ff). See Tunner for a discussion of some of the many literary imitations and invocations of Mignon from Goethe's time to the mid-twentieth century.

33. MacLeod's article was published too late for me to do more than signal here my sense of the congruence between our readings. Though MacLeod understands the figure of androgyny in this text more positively than I do, her interpretation of Mignon's role in the novel is not dissimilar from mine: the arguments being advanced here may be taken as elaborations of MacLeod's claim that "the *Bildungsroman,* whose goal is the education of desire, declares itself as the agent of Mignon's death" (409), and that Mignon is "appropriated aesthetically by the *Turmgesellschaft*—after her elaborately theatrical funeral, she is turned into narrative. The content of the Abbé's narrative is itself revealing, in that it casts the child's story as an incest plot, the only form in which the androgynous Mignon can be rendered intelligible by these purveyors of bourgeois socialization" (411).

34. One thinks here of a well-known passage by Heidegger: "*légein,* being a laying, is also *legere,* that is, reading. We normally understand by reading only this, that we grasp and follow a script and written matter. But that is done by gathering the letters. Without this gathering, without a gleaning in the sense in which wheat or grapes are gleaned, we should never be able to read a single word, however keenly we observe the written signs" (208).

Works Cited

Ammerlahn, Hellmut. "Puppe—Tänzer—Dämon—Genius—Engel: Naturkind, Poesiekind und Kunstwerdung bei Goethe." *The German Quarterly* 54.1 (1981): 19-32.

———. "Wilhelm Meisters Mignon—ein offenbares Rätsel: Name, Gestalt, Symbol, Wesen, und Werden." *Deutsche Vierteljahrsschrift für Literaturwissenschaft und Geistesgeschichte* 42 (1968): 89-116.

Amrine, Frederick. "Rethinking the *Bildungsroman.*" *Michigan Germanic Studies* 13.2 (1987): 119-39.

Beddow, Michael. *The Fiction of Humanity: Studies in the Bildungsroman from Wieland to Thomas Mann.* Cambridge: Cambridge UP, 1982.

Buckley, Jerome H. *Season of Youth: The Bildungsroman from Dickens to Golding.* Cambridge: Harvard UP, 1974.

Caruth, Cathy. *Empirical Truths and Critical Fictions: Locke, Wordsworth, Kant, Freud.* Baltimore: Johns Hopkins UP, 1991.

Chase, Cynthia. "The Witty Butcher's Wife: Freud, Lacan, and the Conversion of Resistance to Theory." *MLN,* 102: 5 (1987): 989-1013.

Culler, Jonathan. *The Pursuit of Signs: Semiotics, Literature, Deconstruction.* Ithaca: Cornell UP, 1981.

Dällenbach, Lucien. *Le récit speculaire: Essai sur la mise en abyme.* Paris: Seuil, 1977.

de Man, Paul. *The Resistance to Theory.* Minneapolis: U of Minnesota P, 1986.

———. *The Rhetoric of Romanticism.* New York: Columbia UP, 1981.

Derrida, Jacques. *Donner le temps I: La fausse monnaie.* Paris: Galilée, 1991.

———. "Economimesis." *Diacritics,* 11:2 (1981): 3-25.

Dilthey, Wilhelm. *Das Erlebnis und die Dichtung: Lessing Goethe Novalis Hölderlin.* Leipzig: Teubner, 1913.

Eichner, Hans. "Zur Deutung von 'Wilhelm Meisters Lehrjahren.'" *Jahrbuch des Freien Deutschen Hochstifts,* 1966. 165-96.

Freud, Sigmund. *Moses and Monotheism. Standard Edition of the Complete Psychological Works.* Vol. 23. Ed. James Strachey. London: Hogarth Press, 1953-74.

———. *Three Essays on Sexuality.* Vol. 7 of *The Standard Edition.*

Gadamer, Hans-Georg. *Truth and Method.* New York: Crossroad Publishing Co., 1982.

Gide, André. *Journal 1889-1939* Paris: Gallimard, 1948.

Gille, Klaus F. *"Wilhelm Meister" im Urteil der Zeitgenossen: Ein Beitrag zur Wirkungsgeschichte Goethes.* Assen: Van Gorcum, 1971.

Goethe, Johann Wolfgang von. *Wilhelm Meister's Apprenticeship.* Ed. and trans. Eric Blackall. New York: Suhrkamp Publishers, 1989.

———. *Sämtliche Werke.* (Artemis-Ausgabe.) Zürich: Artemis Verlag, 1979. [AA]

———. *Werke.* (Hamburger Ausgabe.) Ed. Erich Trunz. Hamburg: Christian Wegner Verlag, 1950. [*HA*]

Hegel, G. W. F. *Aesthetics: Lectures on Fine Art.* Trans. T. M. Knox. Oxford: Clarendon Press, 1975.

Heidegger, Martin. *What is Called Thinking?* Trans. J. Glenn Gray. New York: Harper and Row, 1968.

Hirsch, Marianne. "The Novel of Formation as Genre: Between *Great Expectations* and *Lost Illusions.*" *Genre* 12 (1979): 293-311.

Hörisch, Jochen. *Gott Geld und Glück: Zur Logik der Liebe in den Bildungsromanen Goethes, Kellers und Thomas Manns.* Frankfurt am Main: Suhrkamp, 1983.

Joyce, James. *Ulysses,* The Corrected Text. New York: Vintage Books, 1986.

Kleist, Heinrich von. "Über das Marionettentheater" [1810]. Pp. 338-45 in *Sämtliche Werke und Briefe.* Vol. II. Ed. Helmut Sembdner. Munich: Hanser, 1961.

Kontje, Todd. *Private Lives in the Public Sphere: The German Bildungsroman as Metafiction.* University Park: Pennsylvania State UP, 1992.

Kowalik, Jill Anne. Feminine Identity Formation in *Wilhelm Meisters Lehrjahre," Modern Language Quarterly* 53.2 (June 1992), 149-72.

Lacan, Jacques. *Ecrits: A Selection.* Trans. Alan Sheridan. New York: Norton, 1977.

Lacoue-Labarthe, Philippe, and Jean-Luc Nancy. *The Literary Absolute: The Theory of Literature in German Romanticism.* Trans. Philip Barnard and Cheryl Lester. Albany: SUNY Press, 1988.

Laplanche, Jean. *Life and Death in Psychoanalysis.* Trans. Jeffrey Mehlman. Baltimore: Johns Hopkins UP, 1976.

Lloyd, David, Kant's Examples." *Representations* 28 (1989): 34-54.

Lukács, Georg. *The Theory of the Novel.* Trans. Anna Bostock. Cambridge: MIT Press, 1971.

Macleod, Catriona. "Pedagogy and Androgyny in *Wilhelm Meisters Lehrjahre," MLN,* 108 (1993): 389-426.

Martini, Fritz. "Der Bildungsroman: Zur Geschichte des Wortes und der Theorie." *Deutsche Vierteljahrsschrift für Literaturwissenschaft und Geistesgeschichte,* 35 (1961): 44-63.

May, Kurt. "'Wilhelm Meisters Lehrjahre,' ein Bildungsroman?" *Deutsche Vierteljahresschrift für Literaturwissenschaft und Geistesgeschichte,* 31 (1957): 1-37.

Miller, J. Hillis. "A 'Buchstabliches' Reading of *The Elective Affinities.*" *Glyph* 6 (1979): 1-23.

Musil, Robert. *Tagebücher, Aphorismen, Essays und Reden, in Gesammelte Werke.* Ed. A. Frisé Hamburg: Rowohlt, 1955, vol. II.

Newmark, Kevin. "*L'absolu littéraire:* Friedrich Schlegel and the Myth of Irony." *MLN* 107 (1992): 905-30.

Pabst, Walter. "Literatur zur Theorie des Romans," *Deutsche Vierteljahrsschrift für Literaturwissenschaft und Geistesgeschichte* 34 (1960): 264-89.

Saine, Thomas P. "Über Wilhelm Meisters 'Bildung'." Pp. 63-82 in *Lebendige Form: Interpretationen zur deutschen Literatur.* Eds. Jeffrey Sammons and Ernst Schürer. Munich: Fink, 1970.

Sammons, Jeffrey. "The Mystery of the Missing *Bildungsroman,* or: What Happened to Wilhelm Meister's Legacy?" *Genre,* 14 (1981): 229-46.

Schaffner, Randolph P. *The Apprenticeship Novel: A Study of the "Bildungstroman" as a Regulative Type in Western Literature.* New York: Peter Lang, 1984.

Schiller, Friedrich. *On the Aesthetic Education of Man: In a Series of Letters.* Ed. and trans. Elizabeth M. Wilkinson and L. A. Willoughby. Oxford: Clarendon Press, 1967.

Schlechta, Karl. *Goethes Wilhelm Meister.* Frankfurt am Main: Klostermann, 1953.

Schlegel, Friedrich. "Über Goethes Meister" [1798]. Pp. 126-46 in *Kritische Friedrich-Schlegel-Ausgabe.* Vol. II. Ed. Ernst Behler. Munich: Paderborn, 1967.

Selbmann, Rolf, ed., *Zur Geschichte des deutschen Bildungsromans, Wege der Forschung* Bd. 640. Darmstadt: Wissenschaftliche Buchgesellschaft, 1988.

Seidel, Siegfried, ed. *Der Briefwechsel zwischen Schiller und Goethe.* Vol. I, 1794-1797. Munich: C. H. Beck, 1984.

Smith, John H. "Cultivating Gender: Sexual Difference, *Bildung,* and the *Bildungsroman.*" *Michigan Germanic Studies* 13:2 (1987): 206-25.

Swales, Martin. *The German Bildungsroman from Wieland to Hesse.* Princeton: Princeton UP, 1978.

Tunner, Erika. "'L'Esprit de Mignon': Mignon-Bilder von der Klassik bis zur Gegenwart." *Goethe Jahrbuch,* 106 (1989): 11-21.

Wilkinson, Elisabeth M., and L. A. Willoughby. "Introduction." Schiller, xiiicxcvi.

Ursula Mahlendorf (essay date 1994)

SOURCE: "The Mystery of Mignon: Object Relations, Abandonment, Child Abuse and Narrative Structure," in *Goethe Yearbook,* edited by Thomas P. Saine, Vol. VII, 1994, pp. 23-26.

[*In the following essay, Mahlendorf interprets the figure of Mignon as the embodiment of eroticism and incest in* Wilhelm Meisters Lehrjahre, *seeing her as a symbolic threat to the order of the Bildungsroman.*]

From her first appearance in the novel, the mysterious strange beauty of the child Mignon excites the protagonist's curiosity even as the gender of the "Geschöpf"[1] remains ambiguous. From the beginning, Wilhelm's erotic impulses are awakened in her presence. Compassion with her strange contortions (96) and irresistible attraction to the "geheimnisvollen Zustand" of the child, this "Rätsel" (98), change during that first evening to outrage at her being beaten and abused by the master of the acrobats (103). The air of mystery remains attached to the child's figure until the denouement, when protagonist and reader learn of the mystery's core, that Mignon is the issue of brother/sister incest in an old feudal family. What, then, is the relationship between the ideology of the Meister novel and the insistence of the narrative on mystery, abusive violence, and eroticism?

This particular combination of themes and their undercurrents with regard to the Mignon figure has, of course, not been the focus of the critical literature. To be sure, Mignon's aura of suffering and mystery, her unfathomable yearning have led scholars to interpret her as metaphor of Wilhelm's wounded genius seeking expression in poetry,[2] as metaphor of natural poetry *(Naturpoesie),*[3] or as figure of the divine child,[4] to mention a few of the many interpretations. In their efforts to see Mignon as an ideal, scholars have followed the lead of the Romantic interpreters, all the more so as the novel itself problematizes the response of two characters to her, namely the representative of rationalism, Jarno, and the youthful, emotional protagonist, Wilhelm. Because Wilhelm as a figure engaged the emotions of the Romantics and Jarno alienated them, the Romantics and scholarly readers since then have rejected the overly rational Jarno's negative judgment on and dismissal of the child. Attention to the literal level of the text concerned with Mignon by reading it in terms of a person's behavior and developmental life history will help us to demythologize the figure. The context of the character's appearance, the sequence of events, and actions in which she is involved, as well as her associations with other characters will then be seen as related and interpreted by means of developmental psychoanalytic theory. It is highly significant, for example, that Wilhelm meets Mignon immediately following his encounter with Philine, the representative of eroticism and sexuality in the novel, and that the Mignon action begins with Mignon's abuse by the master of the acrobatic troupe.

If we distinguish, as is usual in film criticism, between story and plot in analyzing the novel's narrative structure, the plot is designed to encapsulate Mignon's mystery while the story gives us the history and prehistory of her life and pathology. The reader's sense of her tragedy is not lessened by this pathology because the novel itself takes the pathology so seriously.[5] But let us begin with the plot. The strategy of plot narration allows none of the persons involved in Mignon's life history access to her whole story, but rather all of them, at considerable intervals, add their fragment—Wilhelm, Natalie, the physician, the Abbé, and finally her uncle, the Marchese, who in turn tells of her grandfather's, her mother's, and her father's relationships. The fragmentation of Mignon's life history by this plot strategy formally renders and communicates to the reader Mignon's own experience of life, which is as discontinuous as the reader's experience of the narrative. Only rarely does the narrator report Mignon's own words, so that the reader must construct her inner life from actions as reported second- or third-hand, from songs attributed to her, from surmises given by those close to her and from the narrator's descriptions. It is striking that the seven sentences devoted to the infant Mignon's relationship to her mother are the only space in the novel given to mother/infant relations, making that relationship a prototype of all object relations in the novel as a whole.

Let us briefly recall the sequence of plot events. The narrator reports Wilhelm's dealings with Mignon until her stay at Natalie's. Then Natalie relates Mignon's history from her abduction by the troupe of acrobats to her meeting with Wilhelm. Enclosed within Natalie's narrative we find the physician's report on Mignon's emotional and physical health, in particular on her heart condition, the symptoms of which only appear in connection with Wilhelm. The narrator then takes up the plot again from Wilhelm's and Mignon's reunion at Natalie's and continues through Mignon's death and interment. In the next chapter, the Abbé reveals the core of the mystery: Mignon's incestuous origins, her infancy, her childhood, and the fate of her mother. Significantly, as we shall see, the narrator's report on the death of her father, the harpist, rounds out the mystery. The sexual and pathological core of the Mignon story appears third-hand as a transcript of confidential talks between the Marchese and the Abbé—a manuscript so explosively dangerous that its reading leads to the death of the harpist, the only direct participant still alive. These narrative plot strategies of shrouding Mignon's being in mystery, of delaying information about her origins, of encapsulating the story of her origins in a secret manuscript, all work together to present the sexual and pathological life histories to the reader as shameful (they can only be told in confidence) and in need of narration from a safe distance (they are so dangerous that direct exposure might harm readers as well as listeners).

But let us look at Mignon's pathology more closely. The plot begins *in medias res* showing the 12- or 13-year-old as she appears to Wilhelm. In every detail, hers is a classical portrait of a long-abused child. All of the physical, social, intellectual and emotional developmental disturbances that have been observed in abused incest children[6] are present: her physical growth is retarded (98), her social behavior alternates between submission ("dabei legte sie jedesmal die Hände an Brust und Haupt und neigte sich tief," 98), wildness and rebellion (her refusal to perform despite threat and punishment). In short, "in alle seinem Tun und Lassen hatte das Kind etwas Sonderbares" (110). She is distrustful of adults (she sizes up Wilhelm "mit einem scharfen schwarzen Seitenblick," 91), and her expression is serious beyond her years ("der Mund . . . zu sehr geschlossen," 99, "düster," 92, 99). Most striking is her language disturbance. She is silent for days on end ("Tage ganz stumm," 110), her speech is broken ("gebrochenes . . . Deutsch," 98, 110), impersonal and abrupt ("Sie heiβen mich Mignon," 98). We might note the conversations between Wilhelm and Mignon (98, 106 or 116), which are always in short phrases and end with "Das Kind war still und nichts weiter aus ihm zu bringen" (146).[7] Her movements are mechanical "wie ein aufgezogenes Räderwerk" (115) and hyperkinetic: she never walks but runs, leaps, or jumps ("Es ging die Treppe weder auf noch ab sondern sprang," 110; "fuhr blitzschnell zur Tür hinaus," 99). The pressure she is under is betrayed by a nervous tic ("mit den Lippen nach einer Seite zuckte," 99). She is obsessively clean ("oft . . . sich wusch, Kleider reinlich . . . obwohl . . . zweifach und dreifach . . . geflickt . . . ," 110), and she punishes herself by her ascetic self-abnegation ("schlief . . . auf der nackten Erde und war durch nichts zu bewegen, ein Bette oder einen Strohsack anzunehmen," 110). She loses herself in service to Wilhelm ("in seinem Dienst war das Kind unermüdet," 110) and in religious devotion. She goes "alle Morgen ganz früh in die Messe" and Wilhelm observes her "in der Ecke der Kirche knien und andächtig beten" (110). Despite Wilhelm's and later Natalie's care for her, her disturbed behavior hardly changes in the course of the novel. Her erratic wild movements (Natalie reproves her for racing Felix and endangering her life just before she dies, 543) as well as her language difficulties (she continues to refer to herself as Mignon, "Mignon klettert und springt nicht mehr," 528) do not disappear. Her strenuous efforts to learn to write and acquire some education fail almost completely ("Buchstaben . . . ungleich und die Linien krumm," 135). She remains the "zwitterhaftes Geschöpf" (193) she was at the beginning, vigorously continues to refuse to be dressed as a girl ("'Nun gar nicht!' rief Mignon," 336), and only relinquishes her boy's dress for that of a theatrical angel, thus demurring from claiming a female gender identity. Yet in song, music and poetry she displays a full and mature emotional expressiveness throughout.

Although designated as a child, preferably with the neuter article all the way through the novel, an erotic aura clings to her. As we have already noted, she is introduced to Wilhelm by Philine, while Wilhelm is still under Philine's spell. In Mignon's desire to be dressed like Wilhelm, the reader soon observes the growth of her identification with him and along with it the development of her passion for him. She insists on being the only one to serve him (107) and it is only for Wilhelm, in a singular show of devotion, that she overcomes her revulsion of performance and dances the egg dance, in a ritual suggestive of fertility and erotic surrender.[8] The development of her love and passion for him finds a disguised, orgasmic release in his embrace on the occasion when he threatens to leave her:

> "Mein Kind!" rief er aus, indem er sie aufhob und fest umarmte, "mein Kind, was ist dir?" Die Zuckung dauerte fort, die vom Herzen sich den schlotternden Gliedern mitteilte; sie hing nur in seinen Armen. Er schloß sie an sein Herz und benetzte sie mit seinen Tränen. Auf einmal schien sie wieder angespannt, wie eins, das den höchsten körperlichen Schmerz erträgt; und bald mit einer neuen Heftigkeit wurden alle ihre Glieder wieder lebendig, und sie warf sich ihm . . . um den Hals, indem in ihrem Innersten wie ein gewaltiger Riß geschah, und in dem Augenblick floß ein Strom von Tränen aus ihren geschlossenen Augen in seinen Busen. [. . .] Ihr ganzes Wesen schien in einen Bach von Tränen unaufhaltsam dahinzuschmelzen. Ihre starren Glieder wurden gelinde, es ergoß sich ihr Innerstes, und in der Verirrung des Augenblickes fürchtete Wilhelm, sie werde in seinen Armen zerschmelzen. . . . (143)[9]

From this point on in the narrative until she bites Wilhelm in maenad-like frenzy (327) and attempts to steal into his bed, a smoldering sexuality drives her that occasionally frightens Wilhelm but that he, and later the physician, deny by calling it a "Neigung" or a "verworrener Zustand" (523). As the explanation of her name indicates,[10] Mignon, the *nameless* child of incestuous passion,[11] is *the* metaphor for repressed sexuality. That this sexuality has infantile characteristics (e.g. her confusion in addressing Wilhelm, as "Vater," "Geliebter," "Beschützer" in her song, 145) finds its explanation in her developmental history, as we will see below.

Mignon's life history retrospectively explains the developmental disturbances and abnormalities we have observed. According to her uncle, most of them existed from infancy. "Ihr [Speratas] Kind wuchs heran und zeigte bald eine sonderbare Natur. Es konnte sehr früh laufen und sich mit aller Geschicklichkeit bewegen, es sang bald sehr artig und lernte die Zither gleichsam von sich selbst. Nur mit Worten konnte es sich nicht ausdrücken, und es schien das Hindernis mehr in seiner Denkungsart als in den Sprachwerkzeugen zu liegen" (586-87). The narrative locates the abnormality not in a physical deficiency but in a mental condition, not in heredity but in the mother/child relationship. The first mention of the mother/infant relation points out that "Sperata war als Mutter in dem kleinen Geschöpf ganz glücklich" (586). As the modifier *ganz* (quite, almost) indicates, Sperata is far from happy. In fact, the absence of her beloved causes her so much uneasiness that the priest who attends her admonishes her to be calm—"für sich und das Kind zu sorgen und wegen der Zukunft Gott zu vertrauen" (586)—which indicates that she was *not* calm. The very next sentences show *how* the attending priest poisons the mother/child relationship by stimulating the mother's ambivalence toward the infant, in which maternal enjoyment struggles with "Abscheu" and death wishes "daß dieses Kind nicht da sein sollte" (587). The word "Abscheu" used for the mother's feeling toward her infant impressively renders the very physical quality of Sperata's rejection.

Soon thereafter the just-weaned two-year-old[12] is separated from her mother. Her relatives cast Mignon out as well and she is given to "guten Leuten" (587), to the kindness of strangers, a fate typical for children of incest until the late eighteenth century.[13] The neglect the child experiences in their hands is evidenced by the fact that Mignon, who can neither speak her mother tongue nor identify herself ("zu jung . . . , um Namen . . . angeben zu können," 522), is allowed to associate with tightrope walkers, to climb, roam freely ("weit; sie verirrte sich, sie blieb aus," 587), and not to return home for days without anyone being much concerned. Given such negligent caretaking of a small (4- to 8-year-old?) female child, it is not surprising that Mignon, on returning from her exploits, does not seek out her caretakers or relatives but rather the "mitleidigen" (519) marble statues in a neighboring villa which express the compassion her relatives lack:

> Es glänzt der Saal, es schimmert das Gemach,
> Und Marmorbilder stehn und sehn mich an:
> Was hat man dir, du armes Kind getan? (145)

We can summarize as follows: Mignon spent her first two years under the cloud of her mother's distress and unease at having been abandoned, only to experience, after weaning, first maternal ambivalence of love and revulsion and then total rejection by mother and relatives. The neglect by her appointed caretakers for a number of years (from two to six or eight years of age) excludes her not only from human warmth and community (note how beautifully Mignon's turning to marble statues for a welcoming response renders this idea) but also from age-appropriate communication and learning. She is left to grow up as a "wild child."[14] The physical and verbal abuse she experiences at the hands of the tightrope walkers from age eight to twelve is only the culmination of the preceding rejection, abandonment, and neglect.

To appreciate what this early experience means, let us look at object relations theory. According to this theory, the totally dependent infant forms its initial relationship to other persons and the world from the mother/infant bond. At the earliest stage, the infant feels at one with the mother, bound to her in a symbiosis. If the mother feels secure in herself and is supported by her husband and family, she will communicate this security and comfort to her infant by her very body language. Even the best of mothers cannot be present for the child and fulfill all its wishes all of the time. Frustrations of the infant's basic needs for contact, touching, food, and comfort are not only inevitable, a certain number of such frustrations are necessary for the infant's growth and differentiation from the mother. However, the "good enough" mother[15] is sufficiently in touch with her infant's needs and maturational level that she can gauge how much separation and frustration the infant can tolerate at any given time. As mother and infant differentiate from one another, a minimally frustrated child will internalize an image of a good mother that will allow the child to bear further separation and to attain satisfaction of its needs when the mother is present. This process of forming a good, reliable and realistic mother image is the basis of a secure sense of self. That is to say, the infant comes to know she is worthwhile (has her needs met appropriately) and that she can obtain care for herself (she can initiate action that will lead to need-satisfaction).

If the mother is stressed (as Sperata is), if the mother is not secure in herself (as Sperata is not, being herself an abandoned child), her relationship with the infant will inevitably be strained. She will not be able to gauge her infant's needs well and an insecure mother/infant bond will result. The child will respond to this insecure bond by clinging to the mother, angrily demanding the secure need-satisfaction the mother is unable to provide. In such cases, it is hardly surprising that the mother feels the demanding infant as a burden and that she responds with hatred and with guilt for feeling the hatred. Ambivalence and guilt may then lead her in one of two alternate directions[16]: either she smothers the child with attention in an attempt to compensate for her hatred and neglect of the child's needs, or she rejects the child altogether and wishes it dead. These death wishes will be unacknowledged or unconscious, especially if the mother feels guilty for having them. This means that the dependent child cannot internalize a realistic image of a good mother. Hence its identity core will be weak and its future relationships to others will be fraught with difficulties. As we have seen, the narrative describes in Sperata's relationship to her infant a sequential reaction from initial ambivalence to complete rejection, with maternal guilt over the rejection playing so large a role that the guilt leads Sperata first to delusion and finally to death.[17]

The consequences for Mignon of the disturbance and disruption of object relations are many. Because no contact other than the very earliest symbiotic one with the mother was ever established, Mignon's later intimate love relationships can be expected to be formed only on the symbiotic level. And this is the way Mignon relates to Wilhelm. Mignon's insistence on being dressed exactly like Wilhelm expresses this symbiotic desire. Once she has formed a symbiotic relationship with Wilhelm, she cannot be without him, is extremely sensitive to his moods, needs and comings and goings. Any separation becomes excruciatingly painful to her, whether it be his making love to another woman, his absence, or his loss to her through marriage. Like a hospitalized infant deprived of her mother's care, she literally wastes away even in the most beneficent surroundings at Natalie's.[18] Therefore, when Wilhelm first sees her at Natalie's after their separation, he observes that "sie sah völlig aus wie ein abgeschiedener Geist" (525). The physician sees this wasting away caused by her yearning: "Die sonderbare Natur des guten Kindes . . . besteht beinahe nur aus einer tiefen Sehnsucht; das Verlangen ihr Vaterland wiederzusehen, und das Verlangen nach Ihnen [Wilhelm] ist . . . das einzig Irdische an ihr" (522). It is not an archetypal "yearning" but the need for a symbiotic bond which causes her decline. Her heart symptoms (from which she suffers only in relation to Wilhelm), her fading away once separated from him, and her very death occur when the symbiotic tie is threatened or disrupted.

Further, since mother and child communicate in the preverbal phase by body language, soundings, gesture, turn-taking games, and establishing common foci of attention that prepare the infant for language, and since these areas were severely stressed in the case of Sperata and her child, Mignon's normal language development was shortchanged.[19] Her difficulties with speaking her mother tongue or later with learning German are not the difficulties of a mentally deficient child or of a foreigner but rather those of a child deprived of early good contact and communication with her mother. She has never been a person to her mother, hence she speaks impersonally and cannot learn to say *I*. Note that when she speaks to Wilhelm at Natalie's, where she has experienced much maternal care, Goethe has her say to Wilhelm: "Mignon klettert und springt nicht mehr" (528). The change in behavior she comments on has not extended to a change in her language. So little has her identity as a female infant been affirmed that she cannot claim either her body as a female (she turns into an ephemeral angel when relinquishing boy's clothing at the end) or her gender role. A maternally deprived child moreover cannot acquire that trust in other persons, that assurance that others mean well by her, which make socialization possible, that is to say, the egosyntonic adaptation to the social customs, mores, and ways of living of the environment. Mignon's behavior alternates between idiosyncratic gesture (note her greetings by subservient gestures) and mechanical imitation (note the references to "clockwork" in the description of the egg dance initially and her slipping into the role of angel and refusing to relinquish it at the end). And because these deficiencies date back to so early a period in life, they cannot be made good: the "critical period"[20] for the development of these capacities is long past when she finally receives some care from such adults as Wilhelm, Therese and Natalie.

Mignon's communication through music, gesture, vivid visual imagery, and her reliance on body language can be interpreted as communication developed in the symbiotic phase or it can be understood in terms of Julia Kristeva's semiotic, as the direct, body-based communication with the mother in the pre-oedipal period.[21] Remaining in the maternal semiotic excludes Mignon from the patriarchal world, from the heritage of the father and the world of the symbolic. Is not incest, after all, brother/sister just as much as mother/son incest, a sign of clinging to the mother in the futile hope that one's unfilled physical needs will be satisfied? Does this not result in the child's rejection of and exclusion from the symbolic realm of the father?[22] And is not therefore Mignon, the daughter of an abandoned mother and the product of incest, doubly excluded from the realm of the father and the symbolic?

In order to prevent an additional threatening incursion of female sexuality into the male realm—we should remember that Sperata herself was the product of unwanted sexuality[23] and excluded from her natal family—Mignon was tattooed with the sign of "ein Kruzifix, von verschiedenen Buchstaben und Zeichen begleitet" (577). Like Mignon's origins as they are narrated in the plot, the mark is hidden in the narrative. We neither know when it was inscribed nor by whom. To be sure, the inscription leads to the (in her case posthumous) *agnitio* (recognition),[24] a favored plot device in fiction concerning abandoned children. But such recognition is usually brought about by tokens or amulets, signs of parental concern for the child's welfare, or by birth marks or accidental, "natural" scars. It is possible to see the sign she bears as having the protective significance usually attributed to amulets or to symbols of the cross. That, at least, is the Abbé's interpretation. He reports that Mignon derived consolation from the image ("Mit welcher Inbrunst küßte sie in ihren letzten Augenblicken [!] das Bild des Gekreuzigten . . . auf ihren . . . Armen," 577).[25] But his interpretation is questionable because Mignon, during her last moments, has no time to kiss the cross, nor is the Abbé present at the occasion. The tattoo "des Gekreuzigten, das auf ihren Armen mit vielen hundert Punkten sehr zierlich abgebildet steht" (577) is a brutal mutilation, a mutilation comparable to the scars on Oedipus's heels, the marks of the exposed, cast off, inevitably doomed child. Both Oedipus and Mignon are children whose infantile sexuality threatens the patriarchy. Mignon's inscription is the sign of her rejection. It seals her permanently into the symbiotic mother/child bond and destines her never to experience a love other than that of the infantile symbiotic relation.

Another consequence of traumatic rejection experienced by Mignon appears in her permanent loss of trust in people and in the splitting of the mother image. The physician reports that, after hearing the acrobats who had abducted her belittling her and joking about their exploit,[26] Mignon had had a vision of the "Mutter Gottes" (522), who assured the child that she would sustain her. Mignon had then sworn "bei sich selbst einen heiligen Eid, daß sie künftig niemand mehr vertrauen, niemand ihre Geschichte erzählen und in der Hoffnung einer unmittelbaren göttlichen Hülfe leben und sterben wolle" (522). The vision (hallucination) is the image of the good mother; it consolidates the split forever. Natalie and the physician reconstruct the contents and the context of the hallucination from isolated remarks of Mignon's, from her songs, and from "kindlichen Unbesonnenheiten, die gerade das verraten, was sie verschweigen wollen" (522). Mignon keeps to her oath of silence and trusts Natalie as little as anyone else. In fact, because her oath and hallucination are likely screen memories of the earlier traumatic loss of trust in the mother repressed in the preverbal phase, the indirect revelations Natalie and the physician observe are the only revelations Mignon can make. The function of the split is the same as it is for other abused and neglected children: to preserve an aspect of the good nurturing mother in order to assure a minimal sense of security for survival's sake.[27] The image of the bad mother is likewise repressed and appears acted out in Mignon's self-punishments, particularly in her refusal to accept a bed or even straw, anything soft and comforting, that is maternal, to rest on. The minimal sense of inner security comes at a high price for Mignon because the child remains bound to the mother image repressed in the preverbal phase. She is therefore condemned to permanent silence and isolation. The psychodynamics of abuse and neglect at this very early age make the damage irremediable.[28] The physical abuse by the master of the acrobatic troupe which we observed at the beginning of the Mignon action subtly prepares the reader to note the other, more hidden signs of violation I have pointed out.

These dynamics of an individual life history must be seen in the larger social and familial context of the novel and its ideological critique of feudalism. Goethe gives considerable attention to the differences in socialization of the children in the feudal family of Mignon and the Marchese, and in Natalie's noble and Wilhelm's bourgeois families. In the case of the Marchese's family, as we know from his narrative, family roles and rules are fixed with no allowance for individual wishes, endowments, and drives. Every member of this feudal, Catholic family is a player in a preordained game. Any deviation from roles or rules dictated by class and church leads into pathology. The grandfather's guilt over his belated passion for his wife without procreative intent forces him to abandon Sperata, Mignon's mother, and to deny her legitimacy.[29] And surely her name is ironic, as her life and that of all persons connected with her ends in hopelessness. Sperata's abandonment leads to her meeting with Augustin in adulthood as a stranger and hence, as in the case of Oedipus and Jocasta, to their inadvertent incest. The feudal family's birth order rules assign to Augustin a role not compatible with his introverted temperament and poetic and scholarly inclinations. But exchanging birth order roles with his younger brother and becoming a monk does not result in greater life satisfaction. His sensitivity, passion, and inclination towards fantasy only increase in his monastic existence and lead him to succumb to the charms of the first and only woman he meets, Sperata.

In Natalie's noble family, roles prescribed by birth order also regulate socialization. But even in the first generation, the individual adjusts to changing circumstances. Thus when the Oheim, the first-born and inheritor of title and estate, loses his wife and child, he adopts the three daughters of his less fortunate brother and helps them to achieve those positions in life most suited to their talents and inclinations. But tragedy strikes again in the second generation and requires the Oheim once more to adapt to changing circumstances. After the death of his married niece and her husband, he adopts their four children and assists them in realizing their individual identities. He is capable of responding to family tragedy and human nature with flexibility. His encouragement of self-development, his loving care and model of public spiritedness produce particularly in Natalie and Lothario a new generation that is flexible enough to relinquish feudal rights and enterprising enough to take a leadership role in a new society.

In Wilhelm's development through the medium of art (the exposure to his grandfather's collection) and the theater (the exposure to French classical as well as Shakespearean drama as actor and dramaturg), the reader can observe a growth towards the capacity to take public responsibility. Thus changed from his bourgeois origins, he comes to share the new nobility's goals and way of life.[30] It is not for nothing that the union of the nobility and the bourgeoisie as exemplified by Wilhelm's and Natalie's marriage is prefigured by the Oheim's and Marchese's acquisition of Wilhelm's grandfather's art collection. The denouement of the novel favors an alliance between the educated bourgeois and the progressive nobility in a new society which rests on education, *Bildung,* and on service to the society at large. In this larger frame, Mignon's fate marks the decadence and end of feudal society. It is not by chance that in death she and the Oheim share the Hall of Remembrance as its first two occupants: she the youngest of a moribund order, he the oldest of a rejuvenated one. This much is conscious on Goethe's part.

But is it not strange that this new society has no room for a living Mignon? Is she so disturbing that she must be eradicated? Let us look at this new society once again. There is no doubt that it is patriarchal. Men like the Oheim and the Abbé have assumed not only the roles of educators but even those of mothers.[31] Lothario, Natalie, the Countess, and Friedrich are raised by their uncle and the Abbé after their mother's early death. In fact, as all of the male characters and all of the admirable women characters (the "schöne Seele," Therese, Natalie) grow up, the fathers are decisive, positive influences who not only guide their intellectual development but even their preparation for female roles. For instance, Therese's father encourages his daughter's playful activities in "Küche, . . . Vorratskammer, . . . Scheunen und Böden" (447) by providing "meinem kindischen Bestreben stufenweise die zweckmäßigsten Beschäftigungen" (447). Her mother neither loves her nor encourages her. On the other hand, mothers in the novel are either dead (those of Felix, Frau Melina, Mignon, Natalie, Lothario, Friedrich, the Countess, Aurelie) or they or rather their surrogates are bad mothers (those of Therese, Lydie, Frau Melina, Felix).[32] There is only one good mother/child relationship mentioned in passing in the entire novel, namely that between Margarete, Lothario's former lover and daughter of a tenant farmer, and her children, that is to say a relationship in a social class separated by a wide gulf from the nobility and the bourgeoisie. Lothario's encounter with Margaret and her children leads him to exclaim, "Es ist nichts reizender, als eine Mutter zu sehen mit einem Kinde auf dem Arme, und nichts ehrwürdiger, als eine Mutter unter vielen Kindern" (470). But note that mother and children here are only the objects of his gaze; he does not interact with them and only speaks briefly to the mother; the class barrier between nobility and peasantry remains firmly in place. It therefore appears that the novel generalizes the unsupportive, pathological relationship of Mignon and her mother to all middle-and upper-class mother/child relationships. Only a few, especially insightful, fathers like the Oheim and the Abbé can provide that nurture and guidance needed to build the new society.

Further and most decisively, only those women can belong to this new society whose sexuality is completely denied (Natalie, Therese) or domesticated by pregnancy and marriage (Philine), or subdued by marriage to a particularly cold and intellectual male as with Lydie to Jarno. The other women involved with Wilhelm are stigmatized as either immoral, hysterical, abnormally sexual, or illegitimate, and they all die—Marianne, Aurelie, Mignon.[33] The price of the new society is the almost total eradication of female sexuality. Female sexuality certainly is not sublimated. It rests together with Mignon's angelically dressed and embalmed remains, a "Schein des Lebens" (577), in a theatrical crypt or is forever postponed in Natalie's waiting for the consummation of her marriage. It is here that we find one of the most serious flaws in the utopianism of German Classicism, a blemish that succeeding generations of critical readers sensed but did not understand in the tastelessness with which Mignon's interment is evoked.[34]

That the novel's ideological point is the victory of a new patriarchy appears in its last and culminating episode, namely the resolution of the harpist's, Mignon's father's story, a play on and an inversion of the Oedipal myth. Note that the allusions to the Oedipal myth run throughout the story of Mignon and the harpist. The Marchese attributes the harpist's madness to a compulsive fear of being murdered by a boy, "denn alle seine Leidenschaften," after being separated from Sperata, "schienen sich in der einzigen Furcht des Todes aufgelöst zu haben" (590). This fear makes him paranoid about Mignon as long as he is not certain of her sex. It leads him to attack Felix, attempting to knife him ("als wenn er ihn opfern wollte") and then burn the remains (330-32). Augustin loses this fear when he obtains a vial of opium, i.e. the means of ending his own life. Having power over his own death, he regains power over his life and reason ("Ich danke diesem Besitz die Wiederkehr meiner Vernunft. [. . .] So habe ich . . . mich durch die Nähe des Todes wieder in das Leben zurückgedrängt," 596-97). He loses this power when, at the end, he discovers the Abbé's manuscript with his own story and realizes that others know his history and therefore have power over him. Deciding to commit suicide, he takes out the vial but then leaves it unguarded. When he believes that Felix has drunk from the deadly vial, he kills himself with a knife. It is a dramatic irony that indirectly, therefore, his delusion becomes reality: he dies by the instrument he had intended to use on Felix; and a powerless boy takes his life.

Together with the physician who has a fine record of exact observations but astonishingly often draws the wrong conclusions from them, past readers have accepted the harpist's delusion about the murderous boy as the nonsensical idea of a madman. But the delusion betrays his unconscious psychodynamics. The delusion dates in fact from the time when he left Sperata and her unborn child. This murderous boy hence becomes the projection of his guilt feelings towards mother and child for having abandoned them. He never knew the sex of the child; but since he identifies with it, he must believe it is male. His feeling of guilt for having abandoned his son then inspires him to draw a further parallel between himself and Laius, the father of Oedipus: abandoning fathers are killed by their sons. One mythical story of incest leads to another, and the reader might recall what we said about Mignon's pre-oedipal relation to her mother earlier: incest with mother or sister means being excluded from the world of the Father and from his inheritance; it means exclusion from the human community of the patriarchy, from the realm of the symbolic, and from *Bildung*. It means imprisonment in the semiotic realm of the mother. And the realm of the mother, as the story of Mignon demonstrates, is equivalent to the rule of female sexuality, which is the antithesis of *Bildung*. The hysterical chaos, its fearful, irrational excess, the lawlessness and speechlessness of the matriarchal sphere lead to insanity, autism and retardation, and back into death. In the Hall of Remembrance death is represented as a goddess, "diese willkürliche und unerbittliche Todesgöttin," and while all of life is subject to "Gesetz," death explicitly has "kein Gesetz" (576). Neither the harpist nor Mignon can be tolerated by the new society because of the stage of development that they represent. Both are too much part of the realm of the archaic matriarchal, which becomes all too easily the archaic realm of the goddess of death.

Notes

1. HA 7:91. Henceforth all citations of this volume will be referenced in my text.
2. Helmut Ammerlahn, "Mignons nachgetragene Vorgeschichte und das Inzestmotiv," *Monatshefte* 64 (1972).
3. In "Uber Goethes Meister" Friedrich Schlegel calls Mignon, Sperata and Augustin "die heilige Familie der Naturpoesie."
4. Alfredo Dornheim, "Goethes Mignon und Thomas Manns Echo: Zwei Formen des göttlichen Kindes im deutschen Roman," *Euphorion* 46 (1952).
5. The reasons for not dismissing her tragedy as mere pathology are manifold, not the least of which are Wilhelm's reaction to Jarno's disparagement of Mignon (193), or Mignon's insightful reply when she declines Wilhelm's wish to have her further her formal education: "Ich bin gebildet genug, . . . um zu lieben und zu trauern" (488).
6. John Money, "Forensic and Family Psychiatry in Abuse Dwarfism: Munchhausen's Syndrome by Proxy, Atonement, and Addiction to Abuse," *Journal of Sex and Marital Therapy* 11,1 (1985): 30-40.
7. The particular features of the language disturbance and the social behavior are very similar to those observed in another "wild child"; cf. Susan Curtiss, *Genie: A Psycholinguistic Study of a Modern Day "Wild Child"* (New York: Academic Press, 1977).
8. Similarly Kurt R. Eissler, *Goethe: A Psychoanalytic Study* (Detroit: Wayne State University Press, 1963) 2:757.
9. The first incident of a clearly sexual nature takes place when Wilhelm has threatened to leave and she seeks refuge in his arms. The description stresses her orgasm-like twitching, convulsions, and final melting in his arms. The second incident is her unsuccessful attempt to sleep with Wilhelm. Cf. also Eissler 2:759ff.
10. Mignon = Freudenknabe; the association with the contemporary Prussian court is surely deliberate. Mignon is not her given name. She does not claim it as hers. "Sie heiβen mich Mignon," she answers to Wilhelm's inquiry (98). The physician, in reporting on her abduction, contradicts himself by claiming on the one hand that she was too young to know her name and on the other hand that she had sworn not to reveal it (522).
11. In this context, the double repression is important in that the incest results from the grandfather's secrecy and inability to acknowledge his sexuality.
12. The average age of weaning in the eighteenth century was two. Cf. *Pediatrics of the Past,* ed. John

Ruhräh (New York: Hober, 1925); Hovolka and Kronfeld, *Vergleichende Volksmedizin* (Stuttgart: Strecker und Schröder, 1909) 2:605. It is of course impossible to reconstruct Mignon's age relative to events from the narrative beyond what can be inferred from normal practice.

13. The Marchese denies the abandonment, but the novel describes how the child Mignon acts out the feeling that she is abandoned. Cf. John Boswell, *The Kindness of Strangers: The Abandonment of Children in Western Europe from Late Antiquity to the Renaissance* (New York: Vintage Books, 1990) 24. Boswell's excellent study clearly establishes that Mignon's fate of expulsion from the family has countless historical parallels.

14. Cf. Curtiss (note 7).

15. Cf. Donald Winnicott, *Playing and Reality* (London: Tavistock Publications, 1971) 11.

16. Cf. Margaret Mahler et al., *The Psychological Birth of the Human Infant: Symbiosis and Individuation* (New York: Basic Books, 1975). Based on clinical studies of well-bonded, ambivalently bonded and rejecting mothers, Mahler gives a detailed account of the three paths the mother/infant relationship can take during the initial individuation/separation phases from 0-18 months. Her examples demonstrate the importance of the mother's positive attitude toward the child and how severe developmental disturbances result from very early stress on and disruption of the mother/infant bond.

17. Cf. Sperata's attempts to resurrect the child she believes to be dead. The prominence and length the narrative gives to the maternal resurrection efforts (eight paragraphs) as compared to the length of the childhood story (four paragraphs) indicates the severity of maternal guilt.

18. It was Renee Spitz who recognized the absence of a specific and constant maternal care-giver in institutionalized children as the reason for hospitalism, that is, the wasting away and dying of an infant even with ample nourishment and physical care: *The First Year of Life: A Psychoanalytic Study of Normal and Deviant Development of Object Relations* (New York: International Universities Press, 1965.)

19. Cf. Jerome Bruner, "The ontogenesis of speech acts," *Journal of Child Language* 2 (1975): 1-19. Bruner demonstrates how important the pre-verbal and early verbal mother/child interaction in turn-taking, segmenting of reality, and language play is to cognitive and language development. Needless to say, for object-relations linguists—as opposed to Lacanians—language development is at first the realm of the mother.

20. John Money in *Venuses, Oenuses: Sexology, Sexosophy and Exigency Theory* (Buffalo, N.Y.: Prometheus Books, 1986) 596 substitutes for the nature/nurture argument about gender differences a paradigm shift to a "three term integration of nature/critical period/nurture. . . . It means that nature and nurture interact at a critical period of development, that the outcome of this interaction is governed by its timing and that the outcome . . . will henceforth be indelible." Similar limitations as to gender development apply to language and other aspects of cognitive/emotional development, a problem studied with autistic and so-called wild or wolf children. Cf. Curtiss.

21. Cf. Sigrid Weigel, *Die Stimme der Medusa: Schreibweisen in der Gegenwartsliteratur von Frauen* (Reinbek bei Hamburg: Rowohlt, 1989) 204ff., whose description of Kristeva's semiotic is useful for interpreting the incest problem. Kristeva's distinction between the semiotic (pre-, early verbal and non-verbal communication) and the symbolic (later, post-oedipal?) language as a system of the patriarchy corresponds roughly to the distinction made by Curtiss between right- and left-hemisphere-based communication.

22. In object relations, bonding theory, and clinical experience, e.g. Winnicott, Mahler, or John Bowlby, *Attachment and Loss* (New York: Basic Books, 1980), 3 vols. it is not too much mother love that holds back the child's development but rather ambivalent and insufficient love. What is described in the Sperata/Mignon relationship is a pathological version of the semiotic or the mother/infant bond.

23. On the abandonment of children of "ill-timed passions," cf. Boswell (note 13) 338, who gives Bertold von Regensburg among others as a possible source for the practice.

24. Cf. Boswell 122. Recognition and recovery of abandoned children in literature was usually, of course, brought about by means of a token, a sign, a "natural" means such as a scar or a mole. In Mignon's case, the artificial, cultural signature is striking.

25. As a protective sign it is like a "linking object," which, like a security blanket, according to Winnicott, *Playing and Reality,* maintains a link with the absent mother.

26. The reference to joking ("scherzten . . . über ihren guten Fang," 522) here is significant. It points to the fact that Mignon feels shame at having been abandoned. Self-blame is characteristic of abandoned and abused children. As a defense mechanism, self-blame preserves an aspect of the parent as "good," that is, reasonable in rejecting the child.

27. Cf. Leonard Shengold, *Soul Murder: The Effects of Childhood Abuse and Deprivation* (New Haven: Yale University Press, 1990).

28. Goethe's description of the abused child, the individual and family psychodynamics, and their consequences are amazingly perceptive and clinically accurate. It does not really matter on whose image Goethe's observations are based. Most likely it is the singer Elisabeth Schmeling, abused by her alcoholic

father, cf. Wolf, *Mignon* (München: Beck, 1909), whom Goethe knew from childhood on. Given the amount of abuse of children in the eighteenth century, it was not hard to observe such dynamics. Unlike his critics and later literary scholars, however, his emotional equilibrium was not so shaken by child abuse that he needed to repress or deny it.

29. Boswell 338 comments on the fear of "dire consequences of ill-timed passions" of married couples in thirteenth-century writing, for instance in the sermons of Bertold von Regensburg.

30. Cf. Dieter Borchmeyer, *Höfische Gesellschaft und Französische Revolution bei Goethe* (Kronberg/Ts.: Athenäum, 1977). Borchmeyer traces Goethe's views concerning the decadence of the feudal system and the rapprochement between bourgeois and aristocratic life style and way of thinking in the course of the *Lehrjahre* in Wilhelm's transformation from *Bürger* into *Citoyen,* from a man confined in the private sphere into a man shouldering public responsibility. Goethe's contemporaries saw the marriages at the end as misalliances and regarded them, at best, as utopian. But Borchmeyer sees the secret societies of the eighteenth century, of which the *Turmgesellschaft* is one, as locales where the educated bourgeois and the nobility-cum-bourgeois could approach each other.

31. The case is similar to that which Gail K. Hart establishes in "A Family without Women: The Triumph of the Sentimental Father in Lessing's *Sara Sampson* and Klinger's *Sturm und Drang,*" *Lessing Yearbook* XXII (1990): 113-32.

32. Felix is raised by the deceitful procuress, old Barbara, during his first three years and then by the passionately irrational Aurelie. Therese/Lydie's and Frau Melina's mothers are substitute mothers, or rather mothers who turn out to be stepmothers. Both harm or attempt to harm their daughters. Wilhelm's mother appears to be the exception until her role in his life is looked at more closely. Though she claims to be the source of his love for the theater by having provided the puppet theater (12), the actual giver and instructor is the lieutenant, a friend of his father's. She permits the boy's interest because his talent is flattering to her. She is given to blaming (12, 14), must be deceived (20) and placated (12-14). She has no role in teaching him anything, and simply disappears from the narrative without a trace.

33. Cf. Sabine Gross, "Scripting the Female Body: Goethe's *Wilhelm Meister,*" paper presented at the Kentucky Foreign Language Conference, Lexington, Ky., April 1990. On the fate of women in eighteenth-century domestic drama, cf. Gail K. Hart, "Voyeuristic Star-Gazing: Authority, Instinct and the Women's World of Goethe's *Stella,*" *Monatshefte* 82, 4 (1990): 405-20.

34. Monika Fick, *Das Scheitern des Genius: Mignon und die Symbolik der Liebesgeschichten in "Wilhelm Meisters Lehrjahren"* (Würzburg: Königshausen und Neumann, 1987) 239 gives a detailed summary of these opinions ("Unsagbarer Kitsch").

Hellmut Ammerlahn (essay date 1997)

SOURCE: "Goethe's *Wilhelm Meisters Lehrjahre*: An Apprenticeship toward the Mastery of Exactly What?" in *Colloquia Germanica,* Vol. 30, No. 2, 1997, pp. 99-119.

[*In the following essay, Ammerlahn discusses Wilhelm's process of mastering his creative imagination in* Wilhelm Meisters Lehrjahre.]

Some 200 years after the publication of ***Wilhelm Meisters Lehrjahre,*** the high regard for Goethe's most influential novel as well as the arguments over its central meaning are thriving unabated.[1] The majority of knowledgeable authors and critics, from Schiller to James Joyce and Thomas Mann, from Friedrich Schlegel to Dilthey and Lukács, are united in their praise of this work. As the artistic pinnacle of Goethe's classical period and as the best known embodiment of the ambiguous prose genre, *Bildungsroman,* this novel according to Hermann Hesse "ist . . . Vorbild und Ideal geblieben, hundertmal nachgeahmt, studiert, umgefühlt [worden], nie wieder erreicht . . ."[2]

Beyond such unison of acclamation, however, uncertainty abounds.[3] Even the most common denominators defining later *Bildungsromane*[4] seem inadequate criteria when judging Wilhelm's own development. Initial subjectivity and self preoccupation? Yes, but why also an unlimited Faustian *Ganzheitsstreben* in Wilhelm's quest? Maturation through conflict and insight? Perhaps, but why primarily in the realms of appearance such as in several types of theater and via two classes of aristocracy? What has aristocratic representation to do with artistic beauty and theatrical illusion with truth? Finally, an active participation in and integration into society? No convincing evidence, unless one finds it where it is hidden, namely in the intricate symbolism and allegory of Wilhelm's relation to the Tower Society. If we disregard these constellations in their figurative importance and take Wilhelm's mood swings, indecisiveness and self-reproaches literally, he cannot but strike us as a vacillating, undefined, even immature character. We have to penetrate the apparently confusing phenomena of life purposefully depicted by Goethe on the *Realebene* to get to the "reality," of the novel which is reached on the *Bedeutungsebene,* the level of meaning, of signification.

To help us out of the labyrinth where we as readers find ourselves no less than the novel's hero, the following questions may be worth pursuing. Why do the members of the Tower Society, secret and elitist as they seem, specifically select the merchant's son, Wilhelm, for their tutelage and guidance?[5] What particular gift worth cultivating does he and only he have in this work? Does Goethe himself feel the need to explore such an asset of his own during the twenty years of writing, thinking and rewriting the novel?

Goethe endows Wilhelm with many endearing traits. So gifted and intelligent that it was for him a "Leichtigkeit, fast in allen lebendigen Sprachen Korrespondenz zu führen" (86),[6] Wilhelm is also shown to be generous, amiable and sociable, warm-hearted, compassionate and moral by nature. But there is one attribute which dominates his life to such an extent that, more often than not, it explains his actions or the lack thereof. It is so predominant that we can symbolically identify Wilhelm with it. This ability is his POWER OF IMAGINATION. Its repercussions pervade the ***Lehrjahre*** as much as they do the ***Theatralische Sendung,*** the fragmentary first version of ***Wilhelm Meister.***[7] In his revision Goethe dropped his original plan of making Wilhelm an actor and the founder of a German national theater. Instead, he explores fundamental features of the process of "Bildung," "Heilung," *and* he pursues his specific inquiry into an artist's concern: namely the possibility of transforming the power of imagination from a given incalculable aptitude to a maturing, more manageable capability approaching mastery.

The *Bildungsroman* now features the author's elaborate analysis of and poetological metatext on creative imagination as a human faculty requiring cultivation, direction and integration just as our other faculties do. On an epistemological and ethical level, ***Wilhelm Meisters Lehrjahre*** represents nothing less than a *Künstlerroman,* the *Bildungsroman* or "inner biography" of the thinking imaginative artist. Goethe decided early on that if he as an artist desired to take his responsibilities toward the arts and to society seriously and to employ his talents effectively for the enhancement of both, he had better become a master in his craft. Goethe's hero, Wilhelm Meister, whom he once called his "geliebte[s] dramatische[s] Ebenbild[.]," is thus not coincidentally surnamed "Meister" (as omen and goal).[8] And it is likewise no coincidence that this fictional younger brother of his, to whom he assumes such a distancing yet loving ironic stance, is christened "Wilhelm" after Shakespeare. Goethe regarded Shakespeare as the paragon among modern poets, as a "großer undeinziger Meister," because he could do both, replicate "das innerste Leben" of nature in his art as well as center his poetic world around an idea or concept.[9]

In the first part of this paper I shall briefly analyze and categorize the various narrative embodiments of Wilhelm's power of "productive imagination" which Goethe intensified rather than reduced in his revision of the novel. In the second part, I shall deal with Goethe's own epistemology as found in his letters and theoretical writings and examine how it explains the necessity of Wilhelm's integration into the Society of the Tower.

I

The following four levels of evidence for "creative imagination" are found in the novel's text: 1. Literal or metaphorical references to Wilhelm's talent. 2. The author's calling attention to Wilhelm's specific productions of a poem, a prologue, a drama or other works. 3. Wilhelm's semi-conscious process of artistic projection and ultimately fully conscious insight into his poetic *Doppelgänger,* especially Mignon and the Harpist, who mirror, diverge from or supplement the title hero's inner world and development. 4. Wilhelm's intuition, creation, translation or distancing "objectification" of Mignon's and the Harpist's songs.

Level 1: As the author *literally* points out in the third chapter of Book I, it is "auf den Flügeln der Einbildungskraft" (14) that Wilhelm "elevates" himself to his first love, an actress whose beauty is enhanced by the limelights of the theater, thus captivating both his heart and his fancy. When Wilhelm tells Mariane one evening about the permanent impact the puppet shows had on him beginning at age ten, his narration emphasizes the metamorphosizing effect of his own creativity: "Meine Einbildungskraft brütete über der kleinen Welt, die gar bald eine andere Gestalt gewann" (23). Symbolically this sentence points forward to the marionette-like figure of Mignon who through her "master," Wilhelm, will also take on different shapes and forms. About his youthful manipulation of the marionettes and his play-acting Wilhelm says to Mariane: "Die größte Freude lag bei mir in der Erfindung und in der Beschäftigung der Einbildungskraft" (24).

Wilhelm's friend Werner likewise observes and speaks to him about his principal impetus, his "dichterische Einbildungskraft" (39). To illustrate Wilhelm's penetrating understanding of Shakespeare in contrast to his as yet inadequate attention to the surrounding reality, his friend Aurelie, the actress of tragedy, *metaphorically* places him among the gods when they deliberated about creating human beings (257). This literary motif of a human being present during divine creation is used by both Goethe and Schiller as a telling characterization of the poet's gift of abiding in higher realms of visual ecstasy and creativity while neglecting earthly and practical concerns.[10]

Equal emphasis is given in ***Wilhelm Meisters Lehrjahre*** to the potential dangers of unrestrained fantasizing. The omniscient author, using critical directness and ironic understatement as well as creating a network of interdigitating symbolic figures and actions in the novel, points to the consequences of Wilhelm's "losgebundene[.] Einbildungskraft" (106). Although directed toward a noble goal, good will and fantasy alone lack the means and skills to be ultimately effective. Two diametrically opposite ventures of Wilhelm's imagination illustrate this. In Book II, the memory of Mariane and inspiration lead Wilhelm impulsively to the liberation and "purchase," i.e., "visual acquisition," of Mignon from the acrobats to become the child of his sick heart and the anchor for his imagination. However, five books later, Wilhelm, disappointed with the theater and rightfully criticized by Jarno on his dilettantic attempts as an actor on the stage, veers to the other extreme. He makes a clandestine marriage proposal to the ultra-practical Theresa who has no imagination at all. Jarno deftly points to Wilhelm's compensatory excesses with the maxim that unaided phantasy can seduce people not only in the realm of thought and images, but push them toward "falsche Tatigkeit" (554).

Level 2: *Direct* references to Wilhelm's productive imagination resulting in a piece of *literature* occur predominantly before his personal and then critical involvement with Shakespeare's *Hamlet.* One of Wilhelm's earliest works is the dramatic poem, "Jüngling am Scheidewege" (37). It is so important for the novel that the poetic paraphernalia Wilhelm assigns to the "muse of tragedy" assume the function of leitmotifs later in ***Lehrjahre.***[11] Recommended as a potential dramatist, the hero in Book III is commissioned by the Count to write the prologue in praise of the Prince. After Wilhelm's jolly river journey with Melina's troupe, the narrator explicitly states: "er komponierte aus dem Reichtum seines lebendigen Bildervorrats sogleich ein ganzes Schauspiel mit allen seinen Akten, Szenen, Charakteren und Verwicklungen" (123f.). This reminds us of what the author records in his autobiography, ***Dichtung und Wahrheit,*** in respect to his own incessant productivity, especially of dramas, during his youth (***HA*** X: 71).

Level 3: Goethe achieves the most intriguing and structurally complex demonstration of Wilhelm's power of imagination with the *creation* of Wilhelm's two so-called *Schutzgeister,* Mignon, the genius child of poetry, and the Harpist, the mythic bard and poetic incarnation of guilt, loneliness and fatalism. They can be called Wilhelm's "Hamlet figures" because, just like Hamlet, the sick prince, Mignon and the Harpist present the dark and tragic foil to Wilhelm's eventual transcendence of what he believes to be his own tragic fate. Just as Hamlet is changed into the brooding prince by the revelations of the ghost, so Wilhelm is changed into a potential Harpist by the traumatic loss of Mariane. She was his first and therefore, according to Goethe, his "absolute" love, whom Wilhelm not only saw as his future wife and partner in a professional acting career, but whom he idealized as his poetic muse.

Wilhelm's analysis in Book IV of Hamlet's pretragic character (and fate, i.e., before Claudius killed Hamlet's father) provides one of the keys for understanding Wilhelm's involvement with Mignon and the Harpist. By reconnecting the travel adventures of the second book of ***Lehrjahre*** to the happy occurrences of the first book, we can see how Wilhelm imaginatively composes the exotic and androgynous figure Mignon from the elements of his pretragic past. In Mignon Wilhelm's love for the marionettes and Mariane crystallizes into a living image in which he finds solace and stability as well as a voice for his longing, for the hope of finding his lost love again. The refuge which a poetically powerful image provides for the suffering heart is a frequent theme in Goethe's works. This theme also applies to the figure of the Harpist, Wilhelm's second so-called *Schutzgeist.* In him Wilhelm creatively encounters a pictorially powerful externalization of his own feeling of tragic loss supposedly inflicted upon him by fate and resulting in extreme inner loneliness. He "adopts" the Harpist into his new family, a constant reminder of his guilt over the abandonment of his love, Mariane. Wilhelm had hastily, and without allowing any explanations, condemned his pregnant fiancee. He had falsely connected phenomena of circumstance apparently supporting suspicions of her disloyalty; he had rushed to judgment based on his worst fears rather than weighing the evidence and looking for the truth.[12]

Tragic or self-inflicted loss can turn creative in an imaginative mind. Goethe, for example, after his own loss of Gretchen, as reported in ***Dichtung und Wahrheit,*** of Käthchen Schönkopf and Friederike Brion, produced a number of fictional disloyal men in his dramas *Götz, Stella, Clavigo* and *Faust.* But while we find in these works the poetic embodiment of the author's self-reproach, among many other themes, in Wilhelm's case we see the process itself at work, the process of dealing with it not only on an emotional and moral, but also on an imaginative and artistic plane.

Level 4: Goethe's ***Lehrjahre*** is unique in that it does not merely contain some of the most heart-rending poetic verse in the songs of Mignon and the Harpist. But Goethe also symbolically depicts these poems' geneses by tracing their diverse elements in Wilhelm's life. Cultural history and the riches of mythology and literature furthermore provide features to which the creative imagination lends depth and evocative power. It is no coincidence that the word *beleben* is a key word throughout the novel. Indeed, we find it emphasized right from the start. In the novel's first book we learn about Wilhelm's double relationship to his marionettes; as a child, he sees them as "alive" and he makes them come alive in his performances. After the terrible loss of Mariane, Wilhelm does the same imaginatively with his past, more unconsciously than consciously creating a living presence out of its elements. Little does it help him that he has sworn to give up all poetic endeavors, just as he has sworn to shun any future embrace by a woman. In the ***Theatralische Sendung*** we still find the seminal sentence which in the ***Lehrjahre*** is conceptually concealed but transformed into symbolic poetry and prose fiction: "so wird der Dichter, um der Dichtung zu entgehen, erst recht zum Dichter" (***TS*** 90).[13]

A comparison of the first with the second version of the novel reveals most convincingly the origin and transformation of Mignon's and the Harpist's lyrical songs. We can distinguish among four tiers (again!) of Wilhelm's association with these songs. On the first tier we have an explicit reference to the fact that the poem was *conceived* and *written* by Wilhelm himself. Mignon's initial song in the ***Sendung*** is a recitation from Wilhelm's heroic pastoral idyll, the "Königliche[.] Einsiedlerin," in which the young poet lets an overwhelming fate demand sworn secrecy of the innermost grievance of his heart, this even to be hidden from the closest of friends: "Heiβ' mich nicht reden, heiβ' mich schweigen" (***TS*** 191). In ***Lehrjahre*** this poem becomes Mignon's next to last song after Wilhelm has left the theater, severed his inner identification with Hamlet's tragic fate, and starts to comprehend the divergent future paths of Mignon and himself. The enormous distance Wilhelm now feels toward this song which expresses absolute resistance to communication, contact and healing can be inferred from the fact that the narrator adds it to the very end of the fifth book, almost as an afterthought. His limp editorial excuse is intentionally transparent: that the novel's events had prevented him from scripting it earlier! The content of this song is then turned upside down in Book VIII, in which Mignon's secret and her past do come to light.

On the second tier of creative association with poetry, Wilhelm is shown as a *translator* of Mignon's pure expression of poesy, which stands for an intuitive mixture of feelings, sounds and images, of native and foreign words. It is characterized by originality, innocence, melody and mood which Wilhelm transforms into communicable poetry, i.e. into a coherent, identifiable language. The most famous song of ***Lehrjahre,*** inspired by Mignon, but written by Wilhelm (and later set to music by a host of composers), expresses longing for love and warmth and the return to Paradise in the mythologically evocative landscape of Italian nature and art: "Kennst du das Land, wo die Citronen blühn" (***TS*** 207).

In his revised and sophisticated "Bildungsroman" plus "artist novel" Goethe again places this poem differently than in the fragment. Now it appears *after* Wilhelm has liberated Mignon and incorporated her into his heart, after he has transformed her in three consecutive stages from an acrobat and marionette to become the living image of his inner longing, his genius child and the personification of his creative imagination. Instead of being called *Gebieter* three times as in the ***Theatralische Sendung,*** Wilhelm in the revised poem is addressed as what he has become for Mignon, what he should be for Mariane and their son Felix: "Geliebter," "Beschützer," "Vater" (145).

A third echelon of association with his doubles via poetry can be seen in the *synchronicity* of Wilhelm's emotions and the corresponding songs of the Harpist and Mignon. When in the second book Wilhelm's jealousy and recollection of an analogous situation in the first book are reawakened by Philine's seductive yet frivolous behavior, he looks for emotional refuge in the Harpist's reclusive domicile, the cheapest room of the cheap inn where they both find tears and songs for their shared deepest grievances. Wilhelm's emotional sufferings are poetically compressed and metaphysically "absolutized" in the Harpist's two songs. One, accusing the heavenly powers of injustice, gives a voice to desperate determinism: "Wer nie sein Brot mit Tränen aβ, / . . . / Der kennt euch nicht, ihr himmlischen Mächte" (136). The other, an inverted love song, depicts the consequences of total loneliness. The Harpist's so-called lover now is personified as pain and suffering; there is nothing to long for but the grave as an escape from the inner turmoil: "Wer sich der Einsamkeit ergibt, / Ach! der ist bald allein; . . ." (137).

Ultimately these songs are Wilhelm's songs that are given a mouthpiece and visual embodiment in the figure of the tragic old bard and balled singer. Less explicit than ***Theatralische Sendung*** in respect to the poetological origin of the Harpist, ***Wilhelm Meisters Lehrjahre*** nevertheless provides ample proof of Wilhelm's "offenbares Geheimnis," e.g. in the following sentence: "Auf *alles,* was der Jüngling zu ihm *sagte, antwortete* der Alte mit der *reinsten Übereinstimmung durch Anklänge,* die *alle verwandten Empfindungen rege machten und der Einbildungskraft ein weites Feld eröffneten*" (138—emphasis added).

Both poetic figures, Mignon and the Harpist, respond in a similar way to an intense emotion of Wilhelm's in the fourth book. Wilhelm has been severely wounded by bandits on the forest meadow and, in the form of an epiphany, receives his first vision of the beautiful Amazon whose appearance initiates the cure of Wilhelm, "our" sick Hamilton prince. During the ensuing convalescence, his longing for her increases to the point where only song can express the deep intensity of his desire for this visualized ideal of wholesomeness. This occasions the only moment in the novel that both of his poetic *Doppelgänger* unite in singing a song of literally "gut-wrenching" and unbounded yearning, "Nur wer die Sehnsucht kennt, / Weiβ, was ich leide!" (240).

Wilhelm's fourth mode of association with poetry, the greatest individuation, i.e., *objectification* of the lyrical voice and its song, is shown in the novel when the paths of the protagonist and his doubles diverge, separate, and no longer reflect each other. I had alluded to such an instance above in Wilhelm's song on the sworn secrecy of the heart sung by Mignon ("Heiβ mich nicht reden"). As Wilhelm is slowly learning to give a life-affirming direction to his imagination, his poetic *Doppelgänger* and their songs reach the greatest identity with each other and the greatest distance from Wilhelm, their fictitious creator. This is, as a rule, found near the end of Mignon's and the Harpist's association with Wilhelm.[14]

In the fifth book, after Wilhelm's recuperative role playing of Hamlet—neither Mignon nor the Harpist ever play roles, whereas Philine constantly does!—the emotional bond with the Harpist is severed. Wilhelm's healthy rejection of the oath of eternal abstinence from sensual love occurs when he does not thwart Philine's love embrace. With it he acknowledges the pleasures of the present moment regenerating his life and giving impetus to an optimistic outlook. He is no longer dominated by the past. After this turning point in Wilhelm's life and during the purging fire, however, the Harpist still threatens the hero's future, symbolically represented in Wilhelm's son, by trying to kill Felix. Failing in this attempt through Mignon's and Wilhelm's intervention, the Harpist goes insane. His song about himself as the pitiful and deranged beggar marks Wilhelm's poetic separation from him. Now and only now is Wilhelm capable of leaving his double by sending the Harpist away to be cured.[15]

Mignon's transformation, however, is harder to achieve. It takes Natalie, the goal and guide of Wilhelm's maturer form of imagination, and her influence. In Natalie's presence Mignon sheds her androgynous nature and literally *appears* in the shape of an earthly angel. The fact that Wilhelm is initiated into the Tower Society at approximately the same time while this, Mignon's penultimate metamorphosis, occurs certainly can not be regarded as a coincidence. When the pragmatic Theresa arrives at Natalie's castle to fulfil Wilhelm's erroneous wish to marry her, this signifies the death stroke for Mignon. But within the symbolic network of the novel it is a necessary death. For Mignon, who has lived as Wilhelm's artist child primarily on the inner stage of her Pygmalion-Father's imagination, now becomes alive in the externalized form of a work of art. Mignon's song, "So laßt mich *scheinen,* bis ich *werde*" (515—emphasis added), precisely expresses this last stage of her appearance in the hero's world of the imagination before she ceases to exist in his mind and heart and is transformed by Wilhelm and his helpers from the Tower Society into a so-called "incorruptible corpse," Goethe's symbol of art.

On a literal level Mignon is interred in a marble casket during an elaborate ceremony; symbolically she is given the form of life-like art in Natalie's castle. Preservation through life-like *Kunst,* art and skill, is mentioned six times in this context! And it occurs in the very same castle which the uncle, founder of the Tower Society, had had built by Italian architects as a model of supreme beauty, of complexity within unity. It epitomizes Goethe's classicism, the consequence of the author's epoch-making two years of "apprenticeship" and "rebirth" in Italy. The youths surrounding Mignon's marble casket in the castle's "Saal der Vergangenheit" sing about Mignon as the "Schatz, das schöne Gebild der Vergangenheit" (578). Whose past? Wilhelm's, of course, but one now "living" on for evermore also in the second realm of art: in the minds and hearts of the novel's readers.[16]

As such a child of poetry and longing living on in the hearts of readers after the publication of the novel, Mignon is known to the Painter who meets Wilhelm in Italy. This occurs in ***Wanderjahre,*** the second of the completed ***Wilhelm Meister*** novels, published some thirty years later. The Painter incorporates Mignon's figure and ambiance into his paintings. Now he and his companions sing Mignon's songs. Here Goethe poetologically preempts 20th-century reception theory, showing how the imaginative poet's work is perceived, assimilated and reproduced by another artist and in a different medium. Thus, according to Goethe's principle of "repeated mirrorings" we encounter yet another dimension of distancing and "objectification" by which the work of art transcends its creator, enters life again and through a new life reflects back on its originator.

In ***Lehrjahre,*** this spiral movement in the relationship of life to art and art to life is aphoristically summarized in the first part of the *Lehrbrief.* Wilhelm receives this certificate as a sign of having completed his apprenticeship upon his initiation into the Tower Society. The *Lehrbrief* begins with the well-known maxim "die Kunst ist lang, das Leben kurz" (496) and, as Jarno confirms, continues to encapsulate insights into the "Ausbildung des Kunstsinnes" (548). As the issues of understanding art, the artist and creative imagination turn out to be major themes of the novel, this document is truly appropriate for an artist's *Bildungsroman* such as Wilhelm's. Interestingly enough, the *Lehrbrief* ends with the word *Meister,* "master", Wilhelm's last name and, we might add, the ultimate goal of his striving.

II

In addition to healing his heart through his engendering, empathizing and formative relationship to Mignon and the Harpist, Wilhelm moves toward "mastering" his "creative imagination" by replacing the theater, the stage where nature and art, truth and illusions are mixed, with the Society of the Tower. Literally and symbolically the "tower"—Lothario's castle has one—is solidly founded, protective of its valuable content, reaches high and possibly far. The Tower Society's leaders attempt to provide those they initiate with a lasting basis, greater overview and orientation, as Wilhelm's increasingly open-eyed approach to his surroundings as well as the Tower Society's consciously drafted collection of life stories demonstrate. Symbolically the enduring and well-founded tower stands as the opposite of the theater's world of make-belief and illusion. The Abbé's insights enable him to confirm Wilhelm's fatherhood of Felix and to identify Theresa's birth mother. The "tower" remains a distrusted secretive realm to outsiders. It is surely not coincidental that none of the actors in the novel, neither Mignon nor the Harpist, neither the Count nor the Beautiful Countess, nor Lydia, Lothario's passionate lover, can be or has been admitted into the self-aware and world-cognizant circle of the Tower members. Their very nature prevents it.

This leaves us with a puzzling question: Why then is Wilhelm deemed worthy of an elaborate initiation ceremony, even though he wavers until the very end of the novel? Not only does he fluctuate between emotional opposites—despair and elation, fear and hope—but he also vacillates in deciding what direction his life should take in the event that Natalie should prove out of reach. Three examples taken from the fifth, seventh and final chapter of the novel's last book will be used to illustrate Wilhelm's indecisiveness. Following that, an excursion into Goethe's epistemology, as found in his theoretical writings and letters, will provide the key for an answer to this question.

After Mignon's death and the expected loss of Theresa to Lothario, Wilhelm is understandably upset. He does not yet grasp the higher significance of these events. Even Jarno's patient revelations about the so-called "secrets" of the Tower Society and its principal members leave him doubtful. He sees nothing but shrewd manipulations by antagonistic forces. Jarno tries to assure Wilhelm that it takes him—because of his great potential—longer to be enlightened about the world and himself, that he is more likely than others to be confused in the course of his development. Wilhelm bears this out when he declares in exasperation that since his initiation into the Tower Society he feels least sure about "was ich kann, will oder soll" (550). No wonder certain critics have pinpointed such behavior as being more typical of the picaresque or adventure novel, claiming that there is no evidence of Wilhelm's maturation.[17]

An even greater despondency overwhelms "our hero" when during certain situations he regards his quest to attain Natalie as hopeless. By the seventh book she has acquired the significance of a *Gestalt aller Gestalten* (445) for him,—an epithet, by the way, which is reserved for only one other person in Goethe's *opus,* namely the paragon of beauty and art, the second Helena in ***Faust II*** (***HA*** III, 1. 8907). As Wilhelm realizes how much he loves and needs Natalie, the prospect of losing her makes him turn into a pitiful anti-hero. He seems to be regressing to the fatalism of the Harpist. Indeed, just moments before the final happy resolution of the novel, in which the love and support of Natalie, her brother Lothario and the other Tower members are bestowed upon him, Wilhelm breaks out into a grand complaint about what he fancies to be the common lot of humans: misery and perdition. Even now—consistent with his character—Wilhelm considers it irrelevant to question more deeply the possible causes for his pessimistic outlook and his images of doom (cf. 607). Here as everywhere else in the novel, Goethe provides hints but leaves it to the reader to discover the solution at his or her level of understanding.

When the author's baffled contemporaries inquired about such weaknesses of his hero, Goethe gave a twofold answer the implications of which seemed to pose another riddle. "Meister," Goethe told Chancellor von Müller, "müsse nothwending [sic] so gärend, *schwankend* und biegsam erscheinen, damit die anderen Charaktere sich an und um ihn entfalten könnten. . . . Er sei wie eine Stange, an der sich der zarte Epheu hinaufranke" (Gräf I, 2: 930—emphasis added). The last part of this statement pertaining to the structure of the work explains why Wilhelm's different environments and the characters he encounters and understands correspond so closely to the stages of his own inner development. The first part of this quote includes a key word synonymous with those verbs which are used in the novel to describe Wilhelm's character. This key term provides us with another venue leading to the epistemological, indeed ontological, explanation for Wilhelm's vacillation in the novel, even within the Tower Society. In Goethe's aesthetic writings we find the very same word as the culmination of verbal concepts describing the nature of the imagination.

While the novel's hero in the first three and a half books ambles, strolls and saunters through life—Goethe's preferred verb here is *schlendern* (141)—, Wilhelm aims for greater direction and purpose after meeting the Amazon, the later Natalie, in the middle of the novel (238). After many fruitful and necessary detours—Goethe uses the term *ausschweifen* (61, 570) to rove, to roam with an unbridled imagination,—Wilhelm is finally integrated into the Tower Society and makes a solemn resolution. He assures Theresa: "Ich überlasse mich ganz meinen Freunden und ihrer Führung . . . es ist vergebens, in dieser Welt nach eigenem Willen zu streben" (594). Why is it futile and even dangerous for Wilhelm, or rather for his particular talent, to roam about unbridled, unaided and according to his "own will"? Is he not a free individual like other human beings? Obviously not on the symbolic and poetological level of the novel. Goethe maintains in ***Lehrjahre*** and explicitly states in ***Wanderjahre***: "die Einbildungskraft sei ohnehin ein vages, unstätes Vermögen" (***HA*** VIII: 249). Although a "göttliches Geschenk" (***HA*** VI: 79), as Werther acknowledges, "gefällt sich [die Einbildungskraft] in dem weiten geheimnißvollen [sic] Felde der Bilder herumzuschweifen . . ."[18] It even "lauert als der mächtigste Feind, sie hat . . . einen unwiderstechlichen Trieb zum Absurden . . . ," as Goethe ascertains in 1805.[19]

The word *schwanken* to waver, the third significant verb, is used by Goethe to characterize Wilhelm's vacillating nature in his answer to Chancellor v. Müller, as quoted above. It connects with the very first line of ***Faust*** where the author in his "Zueignung" addresses the "schwankende Gestalten" evoked by his poetic imagination which are to be shaped into the final version of his drama. It also connects with a major excerpt from his theoretical writings on literature. This Goethean definition reads like a postscript, a conceptual summary of Wilhelm's roaming talent which needs support, guidance and direction and it hints at the reason why it is Natalie and the Tower Society in whom Wilhelm finds the masterly completion of his apprenticeship. Goethe's quote begins with a negative characterization: "Die Einbildungskraft in ihrer ausgedehnten Beweglichkeit scheint zwar kein Gesetz zu haben, vielmehr wie ein wacher Traum hin und her zu schwanken; . . ." Such a description would fit Wilhelm's strange behavior to the very end of the novel, as I have outlined in three examples. Goethe's quote continues with a positive supplement, "aber genau besehen wird sie auf mannigfaltige Weise geregelt: durch Gefühl, durch sittliche Forderungen, . . . am glücklichsten aber durch den Geschmack, wobei die Vernunft ihre edlen Gerechtsame leitend ausübt."[20]

In view of this reflection, is it any wonder that Wilhelm finds the "regulating" goal of his apprenticeship embodied in Natalie and the major personages of the Tower Society? He cannot help but praise the active, multifaceted Lothario and his circle. Only there, he says, has he found clarity, enrichment, and the stability for his own images and thoughts (cf. 443). Another leader in the Tower Society, on the level of Natalie's brother Lothario, is the Abbé whom the novel portrays to be the man of *Vernunft,* i.e., higher intuition and right reason. He emerges as the acknowledged pedagogue and educator of the novel, as the art expert and ultimately as the matchmaker for proper marriages. His "Liebhaberei, manchmal eine Heirat zu stiften" (554), signifies epistemologically, as it did in esoteric alchemy, a knowledgeable agent who finds and combines complementary human capabilities.

When Goethe revised his novel, he not only introduced the picture of the "sick prince" as a major *leitmotif,* but he also invented the attention-provoking chain of emissaries from the Tower Society marking Wilhelm's increasing critical awareness and foreshadowing his happy ending. These emissaries pop up briefly but remain largely opaque to Wilhelm as long as his wavering fancy directs his life exclusively or predominantly. It is especially the Abbé in different embodiments who appears at crucial junctures in Wilhelm's life. As the unknown art expert shortly before Wilhelm's loss of Mariane in Book I, he discusses decisive decision-making vis-à-vis blind belief in fate; as the stowaway country parson on the fancy-free water journey of Melina's troupe in Book II, he alludes to the influence of childhood impressions such as Wilhelm's marionettes on an artist's imagination; and as twin brother to the actor of Hamlet's father's ghost in Book V, he helps Wilhelm to stops identifying with an adopted role, namely that of a tragic hero. Only when Wilhelm has left the realm of the theater, when he has recognized the need to complement his principal asset to give it a lasting foundation and to make it life-enhancing, only then does he find himself a member of the Tower Society. And this not just spontaneously but permanently meaning that he is aware of the circle of higher, i.e. noble human faculties which are symbolically represented by the aristocratic or—regarding the Abbé—clerical members of the Tower. Goethe, the *uomo universale,* strove for such fully developed, cooperative faculties for his person. In the novel the spectrum of human faculties is unfolded into several characters and cooperation among them is advocated. Their tensions, antagonisms, and eventually their mutual assistance become one of the novel's major themes just as it is for Goethe's ***Märchen,*** written in 1795 during the composition of the last books of ***Lehrjahre.***

The framework of this paper does not allow a detailed interpretation of the multilayered symbolism and specific allegory inherent in the Tower.[21] Since I am interested in the philosophical ramifications of the Society, I want to go beyond its humanitarian, economic and political concerns which have received widespread critical attention. But the above references should suffice to answer the question which was posed at the very beginning: Why does the Tower Society, secret and elitist and aristocratic as it appears, specifically select Wilhelm, a mere denizen of the bourgeois "middle class," for its tutelage and guidance? How does he, furthermore, deserve marriage to Natalie, the ideal in the novel, the ultimate aristocrat (Greek: "best" person)? Why is his creative imagination worth cultivating? How can he, who exclusively plays the roles of princes on the stage and is associated with a sick but recuperating prince, assume in the end a pivotal, a princely role within the Tower Society? Does he prove indispensable to the Abbé, Jarno, Lothario and his family? What can he give them that they do not have?

Among Goethe's theoretical statements which support the answer which is inherent in the novel itself, an attachment to a letter directed to Archduchess Maria Paulowna provides a most succinct overview of the interaction of the human faculties of perception, cognition and creativity. Referring to Reinhard's summary of Kant's *Critiques,* Goethe criticizes the philosopher's epistemology for failing to include "imagination" among the human powers of empirical and conscious apperception.[22] Without imagination, the poet claims, an "incurable gap" arises. This short discourse, questionable in respect to Kant is, however, most valuable if we apply its theoretical statements to Goethe's novel ***Wilhelm Meisters Lehrjahre*** in general and to Philine, Natalie and the Tower Society in particular, all of whom would suffer an "incurable gap" without Wilhelm and his principal talent.

Let us briefly point to some of the amazing analogies between Goethe's practice and theory, between the novel and this short treatise.[23] If we reflect upon the implications of Goethe's conceptual discourse here, an additional pathway to understanding previously obscure relationships in the complex and multilayered, yet rationally structured ending of the novel becomes visible. In the last books of ***Lehrjahre,*** Goethe uses both symbolism and allegory to represent his insights into the psychology and epistemology of artistic creativity, as he does constantly in Acts I-III of ***Faust II,*** a work begun in 1800, just four years after the completion of ***Lehrjahre.***

Along with sensation, analytical reason and *Vernunft,* Goethe calls "Phantasie . . . die vierte Hauptkraft unsers geistigen Wesens." And then he summarizes what it does for these other faculties. Imagination "suppliert die Sinnlichkeit, . . . sie legt dem Verstand die Welt-Anschauung vor unter der Form der Erfahrung, sie bildet oder findet Gestalten zu den Vernunftideen. . . ." Would we have a novel without the poet Goethe's intriguing figures and images created by his imagination around Wilhelm the central "rod" and based on guiding ideas of higher intuition? Does not Jarno himself declare that the maxims of the *Lehrbrief* would only make sense to Wilhelm (and any reader) if related to his or her own life's experiences? Goethe concludes the paragraph with an astounding statement that shows only too clearly why Wilhelm's creative imagination is absolutely indispensable, epistemologically and psychologically, in the well-founded circle of developed and far-seeing human faculties symbolically embodied in the Tower Society: Imagination "belebt also die sämtliche Menscheneinheit, welche ohne sie in öde Untüchtigkeit versinken müßte" (***HAB*** III: 385).

Seen from this perspective, Wilhelm reveals himself not as a passive, but rather as the most active figure in the novel. Why is this not readily apparent when we read the work? Because Goethe's "unablenkbare Richtung" has always been, as the friend of his youth, Merck, already noticed, "dem Wirklichen eine poetische Gestalt zu geben" and not, as so many other writers do, to try to make flights of fancy appear real. (***HA*** X: 128). Hidden truths need to be discovered and discerned! In nature and culture, creativity always works well hidden in the center of protective enclosures, e.g. in the roots underground, in the flower bud, the mother's body, the artist's or inventor's head. Only slowly and in its effects does it become obvious. In reference to conceptualizing hidden creative qualities Goethe uses the following metaphor: "Die Quelle kann nur gedacht werden, insofern sie fließt" (***HA*** IX: 228). Thus Wilhelm's creativity is found in the flow of life in the novel. As Goethe had noted in an earlier quote, this abundant life winds itself like ivy around the rod of imagination and in maturing, it becomes cognizant of the creative process and of its needs.

In his autobiographical writings Goethe declared that "immer tätiger, nach innen und außen fortwirkender poetischer Bildungstrieb . . . den Mittelpunkt und die Base seiner Existenz [macht]."[24] In a poem from 1780 he personifies "imagination" as "Meine Göttin" (***HA*** I: 144). But he early on realized that imagination needed guidance by the other human faculties. Goethe's short treatise to Maria Paulowna gives equal emphasis to this insight in the following concepts and metaphors:

> Wenn nun die Phantasie ihren drei Geschwisterkräften solche Dienste leistet, so wird sie dagegen durch diese lieben Verwandten erst ins Reich der Wahrheit und Wirklichkeit eingeführt. Die Sinnlichkeit reicht ihr rein umschriebene, gewisse Gestalten, der Verstand regelt ihre produktive Kraft und die Vernunft gibt ihr die völlige Sicherheit, daß sie nicht mit Traumbildern spiele, sondern auf Ideen gegründet sei. (***HAB*** III: 385)

Goethe located the ultimate "ideas," understood *not* as Kantian modes of thinking, but as creative forces behind all manifestations which we conceptualize as laws and visualize as archetypes, in nature herself. "God-Nature" was and remained for Goethe the dynamic all-inclusive organism, the basis for human striving, for science and the arts. Natalie embodies not only human traits of perfection, reminiscences of Goethe's Spinoza studies, but also several of the morphological laws and principles, the very "ideas" according to which Nature operates and which Goethe believed to have discovered in Italy.[25] It should not surprise us that Wilhelm, after having seen, experienced and recognized Natalie for what she is, cannot live without her. Even before he overcomes his suspicion of the other members of the Tower Society, he finds in Natalie both the foundation and the goal for his creative imagination. He confesses to her: "Ich danke Gott und meinem guten Geist, daß ich diesmal geleitet werde, und zwar von Ihnen" (537).

Likewise it makes sense that Wilhelm and his inheritance, the art collection of his grandfather, which had been sold and which he only now properly appreciates, are united in Natalie's castle. Here he experiences a rebirth, a complete integration into his proper realm of art based on life through the presence of Natalie. Her castle had been built by the Uncle, the founder of the Tower Society and the person in the novel who, as has often been noticed, resembles the mature Goethe the most. Just as Goethe the poet had experienced a rebirth through his studies of the people, the arts and sciences in Italy, he has the Uncle choose Italian architects to erect this "model" of a castle—"etwas Mustermäßiges" (410). It is the Uncle who insists on cultivating the senses as well as the mind in order not to fall for the "Lockungen einer regellosen Phantaise" (408). Goethe's letters from Italy had repeatedly notified his Weimar friends that he had "Gelegenheit gehabt, über mich selbst und andere, über Welt und Geschichte viel nachzudenken," and he concludes: "Zuletzt wird alles im 'Wilhelm' gefaßt und geschlossen." It is noteworthy that the latter applies in particular to the arts when he states: "Ich habe über allerlei Kunst so viel Gelegenheit zu denken, daß mein 'Wilhelm Meister' recht anschwillt."[26] In this respect the novel reveals itself as nothing less than the ironically distanced inner biography of the author's own development as a human being, as an "imaginative" artist and, last but not least, as a thinker.

By the time Goethe seriously got around to revise his novel in 1794, Kant had published his three *Kritik[en]*. With specific reference to Kant, Goethe found it necessary in ***Wilhelm Meisters Wanderjahre*** to call for someone to write "eine Kritik der Sinne," so that the arts in Germany would improve (***HA*** VIII: 287). He did not do that, but he did write, what no one was more qualified to do than he himself: within the framework of one of the most influential and profound novels of world literature Goethe incorporated his self-reflexive 'Critique of Creative Imagination.' It appears as a symbolically encoded metatext in the "Bildungs-" and "Künstlerroman" of his Shakespearean namesake, "William" the potential "Master." The conclusion is unavoidable, as I have tried to show in these all-too-brief references to the novel's cogently structured complexity and comprehensiveness, that Goethe's critique of poetic imagination makes the same demands on intellectual rigor and epistemological scope as are found in any of Kant's three critiques.[27]

While finishing ***Lehrjahre,*** Goethe also wrote the elegy ("Idylle"), **"Alexis und Dora,"** in which Alexis juxtaposes his former passivity of merely seeing Dora's beauty with his present fascination and deep love for her. Surprisingly, he compares these two experiences with two ways of approaching a poetic work. One path is to enjoy its strangely appealing imagery, even though its meaning remains enigmatic. The other path is the search for the poem's not-so-mysterious solution, here pinpointed as the elusive "Wort, das die Bedeutung verwahrt." "Ist es endlich gefunden," Alexis' reflection continues, "dann heitert sich jedes Gemüt auf / Und erblickt im Gedicht doppelt erfreulichen Sinn" (***HA*** I: 185f.). Does this poetological statement, hidden in an elegiac love poem, not also apply to ***Wilhelm Meisters Lehrjahre?*** And can we recognize in the very ending of the novel the *Horen-Märchen's* sequel which, as Goethe stated in a letter to Humboldt, "[er] im Sinne [habe]"? This sequel, Goethe explicitly claimed, "[soll] ganz allegorisch werden." But any "Erinnerung an die [traditionelle?] Allegorie" in this allegorical "fairy tale" would have to be obliterated by "eine sehr lebhafte Darstellung."[28] A vivid presentation is certainly not lacking in the many surprising events of the novel's conclusion. Finally, is it a coincidence that this letter to Humboldt was written in the same month, May of 1796, in which **"Alexis und Dora"** was composed, a copy of which was included in the letter?

Speaking of the relationship of discernment and integration, of "ideas" and "bodies" in the allegory of the Tower, an analogous ironic disguise, differentiation and marvelous complementarity characterize Goethe's and Schiller's correspondence in this regard. Goethe left Schiller's plea for a more explicit enunciation of the novel's—especially the Tower Society's—"main idea" unheeded, since for him poetic symbolism and allegory come closer to life and reality than abstract thought. He consolingly wrote to his philosophical friend who for five years had immersed himself in a study of Kant: "Ich habe zu Ihren Ideen Körper nach meiner Art gefunden; ob Sie jene geistigen Wesen in ihrer irdischen Gestalt wiedererkennen werden, weiβ ich nicht."[29] Schiller, on the other hand, made his most touching remarks about ***Lehrjahre*** after his first readings. He called Goethe's novel a synthesis of beauty and truth imparting "ein Gefühl geistiger und leiblicher Gesundheit." Its poet, having accomplished such a work, became, for Schiller "der einzige wahre *Mensch*" (Schiller's emphasis), the true representative of mankind.[30]

Notes

1. This article is an expanded version of a paper read at the 1996 Annual Conference of the American Society for Eighteenth-Century Studies in a special session arranged by the Goethe Society of North America for the bicentennial commemoration of the publication of Goethe's novel.

2. *Gesammelte Werke in 12 Bänden. Schriften zur Literatur 2* (Frankfurt/Main: Suhrkamp, 1970) 164.

3. For a recent overview of the range, richness and perplexity in the scholarly interpretations of the novel see Benedikt Jeβing, *Johann Wolfgang Goethe* (Stuttgart: Metzler, 1995—Sammlung Metzler, vol. 288) 123-137, 235-240. Other scholars have claimed and traced the development of two major schools of thought regarding *Lehrjahre,* one going back to Schiller and Körner, the other to Novalis. I have addressed these approaches in previous studies and book reviews, e.g. "'Poesy—Poetry—Poetology': Wilhelm 'Meister,' Hamlet und die mittleren Metamorphosen Mignons," *Goethes Mignon und ihre Schwestern. Interpretationen und Rezeption,* ed. Gerhart Hoffmeister (New York: Lang, 1993) 1-25, esp. 1f., 20f. and endnotes 4, 8. To avoid reiteration, the present paper limits the discussion of scholarly positions to recent studies as they pertain to the issues at hand.

4. For a critical survey of the older research literature see Lothar Köhn, "Entwicklungs-und Bildungsroman. Ein Forschungsbericht," *Deutsche Vierteljahrsschrift (DVLG)* 42 (1968): 427ff. and 590ff. Recent compendia dealing with the history of the concept and the genre include: Jürgen Jacobs and Markus Krause, *Der deutsche Bildungsroman: Gattungsgeschichte vom 18. bis 20. Jahrhundert* (München: Beck, 1989), Todd Kontje, *The German Bildungsroman. History of a National Genre* (Columbia, S.C.: Camden House, 1993) and Rolf Selbmann, *Der deutsche Bildungsroman,* 2nd ed. (Stuttgart: Metzler, 1994).

5. The significance of the Tower Society's addition and structural integration into the revised novel cannot be overestimated. It represents, next to the symbolic complexity of Natalie, the most thought-provoking group of educated, wise and therefore authoritative individuals in this work (see second part of this study for their relationship to Goethe's epistemology). Because of my symbolic reading of the novel and Wilhelm Meister's process of "vascillation *cum* maturation," which necessitates the transformation, resp. death of Mignon and the Harpist within the Tower Society's purview, I cannot share its negative assessment by critics such as Rolf Grimmiger, *Die Ordnung, das Chaos und die Kunst* (Frankfurt am Main: Suhrkamp, 1986) 209-230, esp. 222ff. and Günter Saβe, "Die Sozialisation des Fremden. Mignon oder: Das Kommensurable des Inkommensurablen in *Wilhelm Meisters Lehrjahren.*" *Akten des VIII. Internat. Germanisten-Kongresses Tokyo 1990* (München: Judicium, 1991) vol. 11: 103-112.

6. Parenthetical references in the text are to *Goethes Werke. Hamburger Ausgabe in 14 Bänden (HA)*, ed. Erich Trunz (Hamburg: Wegner, 1948ff.) and to *Goethes Briefe, Hamburger Ausgabe in 4 Bänden (HAB)*, ed. Karl Robert Mandelkow and Bodo Morawe (Hamburg: Wegner, 1962ff.). Citations in the text without indication of volume number are to *HA,* vol. VII: *Wilhelm Meisters Lehrjahre,* ed. Erich Trunz, 10th revised ed. (München: Beck, 1981).

7. The traditional view that the two versions differ markedly in the imaginative and artistic potential ascribed to Wilhelm is NOT borne out by the texts. The young Meister, like most artists, starts out by imitating models. The excerpts of Wilhelm's creative dramatic attempts cited in Book II of *Theatralische Sendung* testify to that. Compared to the extraordinary poetic quality of Wilhelm's song of the heart, "Heiβ' mich nicht reden . . ." and those in the later books of the novel, his dramatic versification of emotions and situations (*Belsazar*) are long-winded and unoriginal. Furthermore, in the retrospective of the 1790-s, the French Alexandrine in which "Welch schöner hoher Tag" (Chapter 5) is written had long been superseded. Thus the thought is not far-fetched that Goethe in the novel's revision dropped these samples of Wilhelm's artistic imitations precisely because of their redundancy and NOT because Wilhelm was to be deprived of the creative potential of his imagination. As Hans Reiss (and later critics) clearly recognized, Wilhelm's achievement with these early poetic products, as depicted in *Theatralische Sendung,* is "eindrucksvoll. Den Durchbruch zu einer neuen Dramatik oder Lyrik stellt sie *nicht* dar"

(emphasis added). "Wilhelm Meisters Theatralische Sendung—Ernst oder Ironie?" in: *Jb. d. Dt. Schillergesellschaft* (*JDSG*) 11 (1967): 280.—Regarding the positive as well as negative aspects of dilettantism, see Goethe's und Schiller's "Dilettantismusschema". *Johann Wolfgang Goethe. Gedenkausgabe der Werke, Briefe und Gespräche* (*GA*), ed. Ernst Beutler (Zürich: Artemis, 1948ff.) 14: 729-754 and Hans Rudolf Vaget: *Dilettantismus und Meisterschaft. Zum Problem des Dilettantismus bei Goethe* (München 1971). Like Vaget, I consider Werther to be a dilettante, in contrast, however, not Wilhelm Meister. His developing form consciousness, his critical and dramaturgical treatment of *Hamlet* and finally, his acceptance for initiation into the Tower Society prove otherwise. Symbolically, Mignon's transformation into a work of art in the "Saal der Vergangenheit" is "kunstbewuβte und künstlerisch gekonnte Formgebung," in which Wilhelm (symbolically part of a larger unit, the capabilities of the Tower—see later) participates directly. Also cf. my article, "Puppe-Tanzer-Dämon-Genius-Engel: Naturkind, Poesiekind und Kunstwerdung bei Goethe," in: *The German Quarterly* 54 (1980): 19-32. Vaget, "Die Leiden des jungen Werthers," *Goethes Erzählwerk. Interpretationen,* ed. Paul Michael Lützeler and James E. McLeod (Stuttgart: Reclam, 1985) 59.

8. Letter to Charlotte von Stein, June 24, 1782. Hans Gerhard Gräf, *Goethe über seine Dichtungen,* Part I, vol. 2 (Darmstadt: Wissenschaftliche Buchgesellschaft, 1968) 712.

9. Cf. the early essay "Zum Shakespeares-Tag" in general and the late "Shakespeare und kein Ende" in particular, *HA* XII: 224ff. and 287ff., esp. 294, 296f.

10. Cf. Schiller's poem, "Die Teilung der Erde," *Werke und Briefe,* vol. 1, ed. George Kurscheidt (Frankfurt/M: Deutscher Klassiker Verlag, 1992) 24.

11. Examples: the muse's "chains" reoccur in connection with Melina in Book I, her "mask" has an unintended but symbolically ominous function when the count in Book III sees himself in Wilhelm's disguise, her "dagger" wielded by Aurelie cuts the life line of Wilhelm's hand at the end of Book IV, and it is Natalie who governs the "kingdom" which Wilhelm finally obtains, together with her, at the end of Book VIII.

12. A detailed structural and thematic analysis of these multiple symbolic interrelationships is found in my early article, "Wilhelm Meisters Mignon—ein offenbares Rätsel. Name, Gestalt, Symbol, Wesen und Werden," *DVLG* 42 (1968): 89-116.

13. References in the text marked *TS* are to Harry Maync's original edition of Goethe's *Wilhelm Meisters theatralische Sendung* (Stuttgart: Cotta, 1911).

14. For the Harpist this was also the case at his introduction. Since he enters Wilhelm's bohemian troupe of actors as a ballad singer, his first song, is, of course a ballad which corresponds to his social and poetic role, before he is appropriated more and more by Wilhelm as his tragic double. Yet, as Monika Fick has convincingly shown in her penetrating study of the Harpist, his ballad contains several motifs of Wilhelm's utopia of a bird-like poetic existence which Wilhelm depicts for Werner at the beginning of Book II. In spite of these analogies, Fick repeatedly denies that Wilhelm has creative or artistic abilities; for her he is merely "der Kaufmannssohn mit der korrespondierenden Phantasie." "Destruktive Imagination. Die Tragödie der Dichterexistenz in *Wilhelm Meisters Lehrjahren,*" *JDSG* 29 (1985): 207-247, esp. 212ff., 220, 239.

15. It is interesting to note that Goethe's Harpist, as a hitherto unrecognized forerunner of much more sinister doubles such as found in the works of E. T. A. Hoffmann, Mary Shelley, R. L. Stevenson, Dostoyevski, Maupassant and others, does not overpower his fictitious creator, as most of the above authors' fictitious doubles do. The imagination of Goethe's Wilhelm Meister moves toward cognition and a lasting grasp of reality, while the Harpist only temporarily recovers with the help of his bottle of opium. Thus the positive outcome of the hero's struggle is ontologically inevitable for Goethe. After all, as a scientist and writer Goethe was aiming for and praised the "Phantasie für die Wahrheit des Realen." Cf. Conversations with Eckermann, Dec. 25, 1825, *GA* 24: 165f. This "truth" for Goethe encompasses the tangible phenomena of experience as well as the recognizable laws of nature and the mind.

16. Goethe employs related symbols for the transformation of life into art also in his novel *Die Wahlverwandtschaften* and in *Faust II,* as Wilhelm Emrich has convincingly shown. *Die Symbolik von Faust II. Sinn und Vorformen,* 3rd ed. (Frankfurt: Athenäum, 1964) 355f.

17. Cf. e.g. Klaus-Dieter Sorg, *Gebrochene Teleologie: Studien zum Bildungsroman von Goethe bis Thomas Mann* (Heidelberg: Carl Winter, 1983) 79ff., 97ff.

18. Letter to Behrisch, Nov. 2, 1767. *Der junge Goethe,* ed. Hanna Fischer-Lamberg (Berlin: Walter de Gruyter, 1963) 1: 148.

19. *Tag- u. Jahreshefte, HA* X: 490.

20. "Tausend und ein Tag," *Goethes Werke* (*WA*), publ. under the auspices of Groβherzogin Sophie v. Sachsen, 4 parts in 143 vols. (Weimar, 1889-1919) I, 41, 2:354 (ed. M. Hecker).

21. Epistemological considerations are touched upon in Rosemarie Haas, *Die Turmgesellschaft in "Wilhelm Meisters Lehrjahren." Zur Geschichte des Geheimbundromans und der Romantheorie im 18. Jahrhundert* (Frankfurt/M: Lang, 1975) esp. 51ff. In respect to "Bildung als kognitiv-psychischer Vorgang" see Ivar Sagmo, *Bildungsroman und Geschichtsphilosophie. Eine Studie zu Goethes Roman "Wilhelm Meisters Lehrjahre,"* (Bonn: Bouvier, 1982) esp. 59ff.

22. January 2, 1817. *HAB* III: 384ff. Scholarly research points to Franz Volkmar Reinhard's *Kurze Vorstellung der Kantischen Philosophie* as Goethe's reference here. Cf. discussion and bibliography in "Anmerkungen," *HAB* III: 656. Recent research: Géza von Molnár, *Goethes Kantstudien. Eine Zusammenstellung nach Eintragungen in seinen Handexemplaren der "Kritik der reinen Vernunft" und der "Kritik der Urteilskraft"* (Weimar: Böhlau, 1994), esp. note 8 on p. 21. Far less revealing than Goethe's short treatise to Maria Paulowna, these markings and entries date from 1790-91, i.e. before the major revision of the novel took place. They indicate some common ground in Kant's and Goethe's view regarding the relationship of imagination to "Geist," "Dichtkunst," concepts and good taste (see esp. 116 and 316). For a more detailed analysis of Kant's concepts of "Einbildungskraft" and "Genie" see Hermann Mörchen, *Die Einbildungskraft bei Kant,* 2nd ed. (Tübingen: Niemeyer, 1970) and Jochen Schmidt, *Die Geschichte des Genie-Gedankens in der deutschen Literatur, Philosophie und Politik 1750-1945,* vol. 1 (Darmstadt: Wissenschaftl. Buchgesellschaft, 1985) 354-80.

23. Some readers might question any probing of the epistemological metatext found in the constellations of the novel's principal characters. For them such a systematic analysis amounts to an "abstraction" of the novel's variegated tapestry of life, even though its results unveil a more coherent dimension of the text's richness. Goethe himself approved of a simple and straightforward reading of his work, but repeatedly pointed out that something "higher, something more general," i.e., the laws of mind and nature symbolically depicted in the novel, make for its artistic merit and lasting value (cf. e.g. conversations with Kanzler v. Müller, Jan. 22, 1821; with Eckermann, Dec. 25, 1825).

24. "Selbstschilderung (1)," *HA* X: 529.

25. Hellmut Ammerlahn, "Goethe und Wilhelm Meister, Shakespeare und Natalie: Die klassische Heilung des kranken Königssohns," *Jb. d. Freien Deutschen Hochstifts* 1978: 47-84, esp. 64-73. Hans-Jürgen Schings, "Natalie und die Lehre des †††. Zur Rezeption Spinozas in *Wilhelm Meisters Lehrjahren," Jb. d. Wiener Goethe-Vereins* 89/90/91 (1985/86/87):37-88.

26. Cf. *Italienische Reise, HA* XI: 411 and 366. Similarly the original correspondence to Duke Carl August (e.g. August 11, 1787 and January 25, 1788). See also letter to Ehepaar Herder dated Dec. 13, 1786, *HAB* III: 27.

27. Manfred Engel in his detailed study, *Der Roman der Goethezeit,* vol. 1 (Stuttgart: Metzler, 1993), reaffirms the status of the *Lehrjahre* as a "symbolischer Bildungsroman." Positioning the work as a transition to the genre of the "Transzendentalroman," Engel finds the central theme of Goethe's classical opus to be "die Heilung eines Schwärmers" (317), a theme which he likewise traces in *Werther,* in Moritz' *Anton Reiser* and Tieck's *William Lovell.* Ehrhard Bahr had gone further. He pointed to what might be considered a thematic forerunner of Goethe's novel, Wieland's *Don Sylvio von Rosalva,* in which, according to Bahr, "es . . . nicht nur um die Heilung des schwärmerischen Helden [geht], sondern auch um ein poetologisches Problem, nämlich um die Rolle der echten und unechten Einbildungskraft in der Dichtung." *Erläuterungen und Dokumente. Johann Wolfgang Goethe. Wilhelm Meisters Lehrjahre* (Stuttgart: Reclam, 1982) 149. Hans-Jürgen Schings acknowledges that the completed Wilhelm Meister novels present Goethe's "Gegenthema" to his modern mythological figures of absolute subjectivity, Werther and Faust. After an erudite and circumspect demonstration of the immense knowledge, discipline and artistry Goethe had invested into *Lehrjahre,* Schings conceives it also "zum nicht geringsten Teil, als ein Roman des Glücks." Editor's "Einführung," Johann Wolfgang Goethe. *Wilhelm Meisters Lehrjahre. Ein Roman, Münchener Ausgabe,* vol. 5 (München: Hanser, 1988) 642. For a discussion of Goethe's concept of "Glück" see Gerda Röder, *Glück und glückliches Ende im deutschen Bildungsroman. Eine Studie zu Goethes "Wilhelm Meister."* (München: Hueber, 1968) 87-182, esp. 131, 176ff.; Hellmut Ammerlahn, *Aufbau und Krise der Sinn-Gestalt: Tasso und die Prinzessin im Kontext der Goetheschen Werke* (New York: Lang, 1990) 119ff. and note 93 on p. 120.

28. Letter to Wilhelm von Humboldt, May 27, 1796. Gräf I, 1: 350f. In regard to the utopian elements found in the *Turmgesellschaft,* Goethe's possible reference to it as an allegorical "fairy tale" is not as strange as it might seem on first glance.

29. Letter to Schiller, August 10, 1796. Gräf I, 2: 847. Earlier Goethe had stated that "durch einen mündlichen Kommentar des Abbés" he could easily have provided an explanation in order to give the Tower Society "einen ästhetischen Werth [sic] . . . , oder *vielmehr* ihren *ästhetischen Werth in's Licht zu stellen*" (emphasis added). Letter to Schiller, July 9, 1796. Gräf I, 2: 837. This is in response to and a correction of Schiller's request for an "*ästhetischen* Aufschluβ über den innern Geist . . . jener Anstalten" (Schiller's emphasis). Letter to Goethe, July 8, 1796. Gräf I, 2: 832f., line 41f.

30. Letter to Goethe, Jan. 7, 1795. *HA* VII: 622f. Cf. also Schiller's letter dated July 2, 1796.

John Blair (essay date 1997)

SOURCE: "Monologue and Dialogue in the *Lehrjahre,*" in *Tracing Subversive Currents in Goethe's* Wilhelm Meister's Apprenticeship, Camden House, 1997, pp. 163-83.

[*In the following excerpt from his study of* Wilhelm Meisters Lehrjahre, *Blair focuses on the "multiplicity of voices" and their alternate representations of truth in Goethe's novel.*]

The chapters of this study have viewed the ***Lehrjahre*** as it qualifies or criticizes monolithic or limiting structures within Enlightenment culture—concepts of inheritance, property, legitimacy, propriety, tradition, and notions concerning sexuality. Forces of both authority and transgression are necessary to a vital and balanced system, but authoritative voices in the ***Lehrjahre,*** such as those of the characters who dominate books 7 and 8 of the novel, tend to suppress alternative views, to inhibit movement and interchange. The novel itself presents a multitude of voices and grants many of them—even contradictory ones—credibility. It is open to the play of uncertainty, to alternative meanings, to a complex reality of multiple truths. In this chapter I use the words "monologue" and "dialogue" not only to describe speech behavior—extended theatrical asides on and off the stage, or the tendency to self-indulgent or pedantic lecturing versus mutual, participatory conversation—but also to delineate attitudes toward others' voices or views. In this context "monologue" signifies an authoritative position and its attempt to limit the presence of alternative views. "Dialogue" represents the acceptance or at least recognition of other voices and the recognition of alternative, multiple truths. The ***Lehrjahre*** itself is quite "dialogic" in this sense. It produces or reproduces a "living mix of varied and opposing voices, developing and renewing itself," as Mikhail Bakhtin puts it in a general characterization of the novel (1981, 49). In the ***Lehrjahre,*** culturally dominant principles attempt to overpower alternative voices. Such principles are audible in the abbé's pronouncements, in the description of the abodes and behaviors of Therese and Lothario, and in Wilhelm's prolix remarks on art and the poet. The power of the voice of the dominant culture is particularly ironic when it speaks through Wilhelm since the novel begins with his desire to realize values opposed to those of his more materialistic father. Wilhelm himself appropriates authority and holds forth at length, spouting traditional aesthetic precepts. The voices that the ***Lehrjahre*** calls on in its opposition to such authoritarian tendencies include, in particular, the other major genres, drama and lyric. The role of the poet and the genesis of his art are examined, and the answers suggested provide strong alternatives to Wilhelm's pedantic theoretical remarks and to the aesthetic theories of the uncle and the abbé. Shakespeare's works figure in the novel as a powerful artistic voice that creates a fictional world capable of radically changing readers' perspectives. The reflections and effects of Shakespeare's world highlight ambivalence and multivalence. The images of this world suggest the dissolution of boundaries—particularly that of the ideologically sensitive dichotomy between nature and culture—and so confound the aspirations of any single authoritative voice.

Authority and the One Truth

Authority in its various incarnations in the ***Lehrjahre*** pronounces "truths" and discounts other voices. In Frau Melina's hometown the judge and the community do not listen to her arguments, which are so convincing to Wilhelm and the reader; they unanimously declare her outside of their moral precepts: "a brazen hussy" (***L.*** 26; 1.13). Natalie and her uncle live by rules just as inflexible as these. Her uncle can judge the worth of a person with three brief questions (***L.*** 247; 6). His values and his tastes are set in stone (literally in the "hall of the past"), and have caused him to withdraw from a world where others might have a say (***L.*** 233; 6).[1] The world of books 7 and 8 has grown out of the uncle's life and exhibits a correspondingly fixed set of truths and a strongly negative attitude toward dialogue, toward multivalent contexts and contradictions. The abbé, the uncle's guide and the executor of his ideas after his death, believes in error as a tool and a necessary stage of development, but he also believes in a "right" outcome to development. One merely "unearths" the talents that are already there, excavating that particular individual, who has his or her innate level of productivity: "Even the most minor abilities are there when we are born" (***L.*** 319; 8.3; my translation of "so wird jede, auch nur die geringste Fähigkeit uns angeboren").[2]

This interest in a single truth is reflected in the abbé's detective work, which focuses not only on innate capabilities but on origins. He resolves the mysteries of Felix, Augustin, Mignon, and Therese. The abbé's stories offer a single explanation and attempt to close down the play of uncertainty. His judgments in these cases are lectures; they explicitly stifle dialogue. When Wilhelm's paternity is proclaimed in the initiation ceremony, the abbé warns against questions: "Do not remonstrate with us!" (***L.*** 303; 7.9). The disclosures concerning Therese's past are followed by silence (***L.*** 344; 8.6); and after the story of Augustin and Mignon, Natalie and her sister leave the room, and the rest are silent (***L.*** 363; 8.10).

Naturally these solutions allow the maintenance of the values and judgments to which the abbé ascribes. Jarno remarks that the abbé is not above a bit of matchmaking (***L.*** 339; 8.5). What are these stories but extended "matchmaking," joining not only individuals but cause and effect, expediently marrying situations to felicitous explanations? These stories allow the marriages that finally occur. They also "match" Wilhelm and Felix, doubly associate Wilhelm with the marquis through his assistance to Augustin and Mignon, and supply the various figures' characteristics with appropriate origins. Therese's cleanliness and orderliness are given a genetic base, in keeping with the abbé's theories. Mignon's androgyny, her intuitive relationship to poetry, and her inability to cope with language and the "outside" world are tied to the incest of brother and sister, to a relationship "inside" a closed circle, remote from society and discourse. Augustin's "extremism" relates to his father's absolutism. The abbé attempts to explain the world and to maneuver those parts of it he can influence into a productive and subordinate order. Despite his strong influence both on the present situation and on the education of most of those present, including Wilhelm, he does not quite manage a sovereign position, as his surprise at Wilhelm's proposal to Therese and his difficulty at points in book 8 show. The content of the stories themselves undermines many of the abbé's principles—the church is criticized; all legitimacies are questioned; artists are produced outside of a "high" environment; certainty becomes a shaky proposition—and yet these stories constitute a kind of ritual performance, pronouncing and creating a set of origins for the present circumstances and affirming the possibility of knowledge and authority. The story of Augustin and Mignon reverberates oddly since the abbé uses the lives (and sexuality and poetic production) of those he might otherwise exclude as perverse to support the legitimacy and authority of his own certitude and social vision.[3]

Dwelling in/on Books 7 and 8

In books 7 and 8 Wilhelm and the reader are introduced to a number of living spaces, most notably the estates of Lothario, Therese, and Natalie. Each of these abodes functions as the locus of a particular principle whose domination limits and excludes other voices. They are literally monologic; that is, each is organized in accordance with a single principle. Natalie's (the uncle's) estate has already been discussed.[4] It suffices to remember that it houses exclusively "high" documents and objects and is in fact architecturally (down to the tableware) the sterling example of good taste that the uncle constructed after withdrawing from a world he could not completely control. The principle of Natalie's estate is a prescriptive, comprehensive, and exclusive aesthetic that emphasizes control and consistency. As a world under control, the estate is to a high degree removed from alternative voices.[5] Lothario's and Therese's dwellings similarly reflect a single-voiced principle (productivity and order, respectively) and the attempt to dominate, to exclude, or to suppress voices contrary to their own ideological codes.

Lothario's castle is a paean to productivity and to the power of a leadership that inspires subordination—that is, the reign of one voice. All aesthetic values are sacrificed for comfort and practicality. The irregularity of the original castle is increased by additional structures, and vegetable gardens and orchards cover every available space (*L.* 258; 7.1). The pragmatic and irregular annexes added onto an older, irregularly laid-out castle parallel Lothario's "reforms." On a traditional set of privileges and properties he attempts to add measures that legitimate and insure them. The exclusion of all ornament is echoed by the exclusion of sentiment. Even when Lothario pauses to receive Aurelie's letter, he continues sealing letters for a time before reading it, and he feels that he must excuse his later sentimental reminiscences about his first lover by referring to a general weakness caused by his illness (*L.* 259, 284; 7.1, 7.7). The older parts of the castle, which are inaccessible to Wilhelm, include structures associated with power and exclusion. Lydie reports being held prisoner and comments on these secret parts of the castle; and Therese, Natalie, and Wilhelm support her anxiety (*L.* 261, 283, 328-29; 7.2, 7.6, 8.4). The Tower, a group concerned with the domination by paternal forces of the highest status, clearly excludes women from its secrets entirely. By contrast, the Tower's antithesis, the acting troupe, grants suffrage to women (*L.* 127; 4.2).

Lothario's manner of dealing with Wilhelm on his first arrival exemplifies the silencing of critical voices, and the house itself plays a role in this. Wilhelm intends to criticize Lothario harshly for his seduction of Aurelie and his perfidy to her. Wilhelm is reluctantly admitted into the house, and he must wait in an anteroom for some time before Lothario enters. After a single sentence from Wilhelm, Lothario takes Aurelie's letter and retreats into another room to read it at his leisure, forcing Wilhelm to wait again. Wilhelm is not only unable to recite his diatribe; he is unable to say another word. He is whisked away to a room and instructed in the house regimen (*L.* 259; 7.1). The use of rooms, the control of space and of Wilhelm's comings and goings, has completely disoriented him: "The house in which he found himself was so very strange, that he could not adapt himself to these conditions" (*L.* 259; 7.1). By this time Wilhelm's attitudes have changed. Lothario's behavior and the adept manipulation of space and movement have convinced him of Lothario's authority and his own subservience. He no longer wants to give his sermon: "Lothario had aroused quite unexpected feelings in him" (*L.* 259; 7.1).

Helplessness and subordination characterize Wilhelm during his stay at Lothario's castle. He is disarmed in every sense of the word. He is not allowed to speak. Lothario charms him in no time at all to the point of idolatry. Wilhelm praises Lothario effusively on arriving at Therese's house and declares him worthy of every sacrifice at Natalie's residence (*L.* 271, 328; 7.5, 8.4). Wilhelm's "involvement" with the countess is also used to silence him. Jarno explains that Wilhelm is responsible for the plight of Lothario's sister, the countess, and that Lothario is aware of this (*L.* 264-65; 7.3). Jarno does not mention that he himself and the baroness had played leading roles in plotting both the seduction of the countess and the count's denigration (*L.* 110, 115; 3.10, 3.12).

The second estate Wilhelm visits in book 7, Therese's estate, is dominated by the principle of order. Order rules to such an extent, in fact, that utility is symbolically denied. Wood for the fireplace, whose utility lies in its destruction, takes on a sense of permanence. Ironically, the craft that brings forth this "permanence" neither knows nor values beauty. This world is characterized by the diminutive to a parodic extent, and it is narrow and restrictive (*L.* 272; 5.5; cf. Schlechta 62-64).

Wilhelm is already bored on the afternoon of the first day, and understandably so, for the voice of order ordains a sameness in Therese's environs.[6] Certainly everything about her is antithetical to difference, change, and personal development. She maintains that order and cleanliness were natural to her almost from birth (*L.* 274; 7.6). Wilhelm notes that the breaking off of her engagement to Lothario did not affect her ("keine Veränderung in ihr selbst") and that during his stay on her property, she "remained just the same" (*L.* 281-82; 7.6). The concept of sameness also colors her vision of utopia, for it is only knowing of the existence of people who agree with her that makes the world into a paradise ("populated garden," *L.* 271; 7.5). Therese also celebrates sameness in a description of eye contact with her father: "When I looked into his eyes, it was as it I were peering into my own self" (*L.* 274; 7.6). Here familial identity, physiognomic similarity, a shared sense of moral values, and a love of order converge and suggest intolerance. By comparison, Philine specifically praises the contrast between eye colors ("To look into a pair of beautiful dark eyes doesn't do a pair of blues eyes any harm," *L.* 56; 2.4).

Therese's interest in order and in sameness is advanced by her own extreme loquaciousness. Wilhelm notes her pleasure in speaking during their first meeting: "She said a good deal more about other matters. She seemed altogether to enjoy talking" (*L.* 270; 7.5). After admitting that she has done all the talking, she requests a few remarks from Wilhelm, but only to gain momentum to continue her own narration:

> It's not right that you should just let me talk. You know enough about me already, but I know nothing about you. Tell me something about yourself, while I am gathering strength to tell you about my life and situation.
>
> (*L.* 273; 7.6)

Indeed, two sentences from Wilhelm give her the "strength" to go on for eight pages without interruption (*L.* 273-80; 7.6).

Wilhelm and the Monologue

Wilhelm leaves the mercantile world of his father in search of a more satisfying alternative and later exits the world of the theater with a word of criticism for Lothario's world. He has sought oppositional voices and then intends to be one, but he fails in both these roles. In books 7 and 8 Wilhelm loses all personal power. He denies his past and abdicates all self-determination. His hackles rise a bit against the abbé's suggestions, but he has repeatedly expressed his willingness to submit to Lothario's decision. He has lost his vocation for acting; Augustin and Mignon have died; and he is willing to swear all oaths to marry Natalie, to enter this high and excessively rational world of Natalie's, Therese's, and Lothario's estates. How did Wilhelm become entangled in this realm after his travels through the world of the theater and marketplace? He has consistently exhibited an infatuation with status, authority, and power and a narcissistic belief in the unique validity of his own words. The "voices" of nature, the body, and the socially low have spoken seductively to him, but his socialization has rendered him incapable of responding to them. He searches for a more "whole" life but is hardly capable of perceiving voices from outside himself unless they speak from a position of hierarchical superiority like Jarno, Lothario, Therese, and Natalie.

The ***Lehrjahre*** thematizes Wilhelm's "monologic" tendencies strongly. Wilhelm holds monologues; that is, he speaks at length to himself or to an imagined audience. He often launches into lectures to groups or individuals as well at inappropriate times and without consideration for his listeners, or from a position informed solely by his own socialization and perspective. Most often he speaks about himself and seems unaware of others, and he does this within a novel that provides a large number of varied ideas, perspectives, and events. When this complicated and vital reality does gain entrance into his one-dimensional world—through Philine's seductive attention, for example, or the tumult of the marketplace—he is characteristically paralyzed.[7]

Wilhelm's study of *Hamlet* illustrates his personal tendencies toward a single, narrow and reductive, authoritarian voice even while he attempts to correct it in his approach to the play. He had originally concentrated primarily on Hamlet's soliloquies, and he now describes focusing on fragments of the play as an error (*L.* 127-28; 4.3). In a lecture to the actors, Wilhelm implies that he has corrected his error, that he now has the key to *Hamlet* as a whole. But his present lecture to the actors—both the act of lecturing itself and his lecture's content—suggests continuing self-aggrandizement. His fascination with Hamlet's monologues reminds one of his earlier acting fantasies: while wearing a turban, Oriental costume, sash, and dagger and kneeling on a Persian carpet, he practices acting tragic roles (*L.* 31; 1.15). The suggestion of fantasies of high status is corroborated by his illusory image of the actor:

> How fortunate, he used to think, were actors in former days, when—so he imagined—they had magnificent costumes, suits of armor and weapons and always presented a model of noble behavior, their minds reflecting the noblest and best in attitudes, sentiments, and emotions. (*L.* 31; 1.15)

Wilhelm's "educational" remarks to the actors resemble his earlier illusions of grandeur in that he is playing a status game. He criticizes the aristocracy for an inability truly to experience friendship and the actors for their defamations of the aristocracy. He chides the actors for thanklessness, envy, and egotism (*L.* 124; 4.2). Wilhelm manages to appropriate generosity and graciousness for himself and to criticize both groups at the same time. While talking down to the actors about the problems of status, he has fantasies that involve both his own elevation and the denigration of the actors. He sees himself as Prince Harry from Shakespeare's *Henry IV,* who becomes king in spite of having slummed with unsavory companions (*L.* 123; 4.2). Ironically, while criticizing his own fixation on the role of the prince, Wilhelm has fantasies of aristocratic grandeur.[8] Despite his willingness to take the floor and to give lectures to the group on friendship and generosity, both his friendship and generosity become rhetorical tools in the service of his own status.

Although Wilhelm has lived with the actors, experienced their lot, even become an actor himself, he never really seems fully to comprehend their problems. Early in the ***Lehrjahre*** Herr Melina attempts to explain an actor's life to Wilhelm. From Wilhelm's perspective, Herr Melina belongs to the highest possible sphere because he is an actor, a view that contrasts with the generally denigratory attitude toward actors in the eighteenth century.[9] Herr Melina begins to lose some of this status in his conversation with Wilhelm as soon as he criticizes the social conditions of acting as a profession. In his description of the treatment of actors he uses a series of socially low or animal images—bears, monkeys, and dogs, dancing to the tune of a bagpipe in front of children and "riffraff" (**L.** 28; 1.14)—which are validated in book 3 of the ***Lehrjahre*** when the actors are explicitly compared to horses and dogs being shown to the count (**L.** 104; 3.8). Perhaps because Wilhelm has experienced neither monetary need nor social stigmatism, he is blind to the difficulties of an actor and blind also to the accurate criticisms Herr Melina levels at the theater.

Ironically, for Wilhelm (who is otherwise progressive in his attitudes toward actors), these complaints are the stimulus for a conservative remark alluding to the general syndrome of dissatisfaction with one's appointed place and envy of others' positions (**L.** 28; 1.14). How surprising that Wilhelm should suggest it desirable that people stay in their places! His own monologic perspective does not equip him to notice the irony that this would certainly apply to him as well since his desire to leave the world of the middle class for an acting career constitutes the exact inverse of Herr Melina's intention. When he leaves Herr Melina, he begins an extended derogatory speech, explicitly marked as a monologue:

> *Once he was alone, he vented his feelings in a series of exclamatory outbursts.*
>
> "O, unhappy Melina, the misery that oppresses you, lies not in your profession but in yourself." (**L.** 28; 1.14, my emphasis)

According to Wilhelm, Herr Melina does not have a true vocation ("some inner drive—pleasure—love") that would otherwise inspire him to rise above his circumstances.[10] Certainly the reality of Herr Melina's difficulties has not affected Wilhelm's notions of acting in the least.

Wilhelm continues his monologue—thirty-three lines of elevated text!—with great pleasure, right into bed (**L.** 28-29; 1.14).[11] The narrative puts Wilhelm to bed with explicit fantasies of his own superiority, thus emphasizing his privileged middle-class position, his absolute lack of experience of the situation Herr Melina describes and an inability to appraise it correctly, and his narcissism. Wilhelm's idealized image of an actor's life—"a model of noble behavior" (**L.** 31; 1.15)—does not allow him to see Herr Melina's quotidian difficulties at all, but only the theatrically depicted context of the prisoner's transport and trial.[12] Wilhelm's failure of empathy betrays his limited capacity for dialogue.[13]

Wilhelm's "move" here—appropriation of status for himself while turning an uncomprehending ear to the person across from him—is characteristic. Status necessitates monologue through its dependence on hierarchy, on the inferiority of others, and Wilhelm can create a group less noble than himself by failing to perceive the perspectives of its members. He maintains his own sense of status by failing to notice others' reactions to his pretensions. The ***Lehrjahre*** begins with a monologue with which Wilhelm claims both high status and a privileged perspective for himself.

> It is always pleasant, my dear, to remember old times and our past, but harmless, mistakes. Especially when this occurs as we feel we have achieved a high point from which we can now look about and reflect on the path that brought us to this lofty view. It is pleasant and satisfying to remember the obstacles that we sadly thought were insurmountable, and then compare what we, as mature persons, have now developed into, with what we were then, in our immaturity. (**L.** 5-6; 1.3)

When Wilhelm speaks of having reached "high ground" from which to judge his own past in a sovereign manner, he creates for himself a narrative position that allows a good deal of irony. Since the beginning of his relationship with Mariane, he sees himself as mature: "his duties more compelling, his pastimes more absorbing, his knowledge clearer, his talents much stronger, his purposes more definite" (*L.* 4; 1.3). That his duties—to Mariane and the theater, even the *Nationaltheater*—are "holy" ("heilig") further emphasizes the altitude to which he feels he has risen. The long monologue portraying his youth becomes a vehicle for a depiction of his new clarity and status. He distances himself from the "magic structure" and the "enchantment" of the puppet theater and narrates ironically the attempt to put on a play when no one has distributed parts (**L.** 6, 13; 1.3, 1.8); at the same time, he glorifies his childhood infatuations as the prehistory of his present condition, the story of his development to a potential founder of a national theater.

Wilhelm is so absorbed in his self-congratulatory self-narration that he does not even register the condition of his lover. He fails to notice when she falls asleep, although the narrator brings it to the reader's attention three times (**L.** 10, 13, 15; 1.6, 1.8). She judges these stories and the implications Wilhelm sees in them as too serious (**L.** 10; 1.6). It is, after all, a bit arrogant to read his past as such an important aesthetic development. He arrogates status to himself in a set of terms he deems absolute—based on an aesthetic and artistic calling—and is able to judge rather harshly those less fortunate than himself, such as Herr Melina, whom circumstances allow no pure aesthetic. He gives vent to his criticisms of Herr Melina in self-satisfied monologue and is able to appreciate neither Herr Melina's nor Mariane's difficulties because he is blinded by an illusory sense of his own importance.

Within the larger framework of the novel, the narrator punctures this inflated Wilhelm. When Wilhelm compares the disappearance of the puppet theater to a lost love, the narrator interjects: "His glance at Marianne, drunken with joy, convinced her that he had no fear of ever being in such an unhappy state" (**L.** 6; 1.3, translation modified). The observation that Wilhelm is "drunken with joy" negates both the sovereignty of his perspective and the "high" rationality suggested by the series "duties," "inclinations," "knowledge," "talents," and "intentions" (*L.* 4; 1.3). His present goals and confidence arise in no small part from his relationship with Mariane, which is not at all as secure as he considers it to be. Wilhelm's "drunken" conviction that he could never lose his love, particularly in the context of Mariane's dilemma—her juggling of lovers—both emphasizes the illusory nature of Wilhelm's knowledge of the world and people around him and questions his present image of his own status.

A later image serves as a commentary on this monologue. The narrator refers to the echo as a metaphor for young love:

> Happy youth, happy those first gropings for love, when we converse readily with ourselves, delighting like a child in echoes of our own conversation and satisfied when our invisible partner merely repeats the last syllables of what we have just uttered! (*L.* 30; 1.15, translation modified)

This extended comparison not only explicitly refers to a lack of dialogue; it reverberates ironically with regard to both Mariane and Herr Melina. It is difficult, in view of the quotation's use of an echo in the context of love, not to consider the myth of Narcissus and Echo; the insights this myth affords turn the surface contents of the quotation on its head. On one level Wilhelm is the child, and Mariane is criticized for not listening to, or participating in, Wilhelm's story. She falls asleep while Wilhelm is narrating and contributes little to this conversation. In the myth, however, it is Echo who loves, and whose love remains unrequited by a Narcissus who loves only his own reflected image. Certainly Wilhelm exhibits narcissistic characteristics. He is the exclusive teller of tales in book 1. We do not see him in any real dialogue with Mariane or Barbara. The image of the child who bears the burden of the conversation and is satisfied with murmured echoes, a relatively positive image, becomes narcissistic and negative when viewed in light of these situations.[14] Wilhelm, the "first child of creation" (*L.* 153; 4.16), only perceives what is consonant with his perspective, a very blinkered one. If there is a poetic justice in the novel, it is for this failure, after hearing the "music of the spheres," "every string of *his* soul," and the "melodies of *his* heart," that Iris, the messenger of the gods he has called upon, manages to give him a message from outside himself, in the note from Norberg revealing the presence of Mariane's other lover (*L.* 40; 1.17, my emphasis).

Even where the novel suggests Wilhelm's participation in dialogue, his blindness is also emphasized. The closest Wilhelm comes to actually perceiving another person's perspective is in his relationship to Werner,

> for despite their different attitudes, each of them profited from the other. Werner gave himself credit for being able to restrain in some degree Wilhelm's lively, but occasionally overenthusiastic spirit, and Wilhelm, for his part, had a sense of real triumph when in the heat of his emotion he was able to carry his sober-minded friend with him. (*L.* 32; 1.15)

Their discussions, however, are spiced by a lack of real understanding ("the impossibility of making themselves mutually understood," *L.* 32; 1.15). Wilhelm, at any rate, shows little tendency to allow his friend's muse really to speak to him. In his poem "Youth at the Crossroads" he paints business as an old crone and listens to Werner's defense of commerce more out of fairness than interest or understanding, "for he remembered that Werner used to listen to his speeches without losing his composure" (*L.* 18-19; 1.10). His lack of empathy surprises in light of the passion with which Werner, otherwise described as reserved and phlegmatic, defends commerce, celebrating a very dialogic understanding (*L.* 32-33; 1.15).[15] The movement and exchange of goods from all parts of the world culminate in an image of almost universal understanding; even strangers are touched and participate in the sailor's joy.[16] Wilhelm, far from participating in and empathizing with Werner's enthusiasm, hardly listens and must even suppress irritation.

Images of the Poet

The Wilhelm depicted above fails to see people because of his self-image: he sees himself as an artist partaking in the status of art. Ironically, while superficially elevating art, he diminishes it by perceiving it in terms determined solely by social standing. His various monologues on artists and artworks focus on those characteristics he values at a given time—utility, the unities, organicity—and ignore other "low" qualities: comic, vulgar, and subversive aspects of artworks.[17] Despite his subjective, idiosyncratic appreciation of art, which is tied to his own personal needs and desires, he consistently associates art with exclusively high status.[18] The ***Lehrjahre*** is, however, much more than its protagonist, and it relativizes this monolithic stance with alternative examples—the voices and figures of Augustin, Mignon, Philine, and even an anonymous author.[19] The poems and songs occurring in the ***Lehrjahre*** are alternative voices in the most literal sense. They are inserted texts—generically different both from their contexts and from one another. They betray a variety of aesthetic orientations. With its juxtaposition and appreciation of varied "high" and "low" poetic forms, the ***Lehrjahre*** orchestrates a multivoiced poetic texture that insistently pluralizes literary culture and thus rejects any monologic affirmation of the status quo.

Wilhelm describes his fantasy poet in elevated and exclusive terms that generally agree with the abbé's warning that the artist should avoid low environments at all cost. Although this poet supposedly senses each individual existence and the harmonious interaction of the whole, Wilhelm describes him in exclusively high terms as "teacher, prophet, friend of gods and men" (*L.* 45; 2.2). Not only commerce but even work, plain and simple, is excluded, and Wilhelm describes it, using demeaning animal metaphors, as unworthy of the poet. Although Wilhelm may refer in passing to the working world as a part of his poet's subject matter, his poet is positioned well above not only work but all earthly activity:

> Fate has placed the poet *above all this—like a god.* He sees the whirlpool of passions, the fruitless activity of families and nations, the serious problems born of misunderstandings. (*L.* 45; 2.2, my emphasis)

He chronicles the rise and fall of "families and nations," much like Hamlet's Horatio, but he is above them because he is not involved.

Wilhelm's poet affirms the status quo by illustrating high social standing. The king, hero, lover, and rich man all depend on the poet to allow them to see what and who they are and in what ways they are valuable. Although the merchant, the farmer, and other lower professions might be included theoretically in Wilhelm's description of the poet's function, he seems pointedly less interested in them and the "whole" outside of the court. Wilhelm's poet, then, is an apologist for a romanticized aristocracy, describing the life of the upper classes just as Wilhelm's fantasy actor depicts it. Here the poet not only sings or declaims, but the content of his songs exhibits a monologic perspective concerned with high status. Just as Wilhelm proclaims the glory of the poet as the high of highs, so the poet celebrates the high status of heroes and kings within a harmonious and hierarchical context.

While much of what Wilhelm describes would seem to fit the wandering minstrel Augustin, this figure also contradicts aspects of Wilhelm's image.[20] Wilhelm's ideal poet is above events, while events transform Augustin into a victim. Wilhelm's poet contextualizes to an absolute; he "integrates even the most ordinary occurrence into both past and future" (*L.* 45; 2.2). By contrast, Augustin has lost all sense of context: "I see nothing before me, and nothing behind me . . . but the endless night of loneliness in which I find myself" (*L.* 267; 7.4). Although he sings of a court setting and the inappropriateness of objects of value as a reward for his singing, his song is addressed to a company of actors, and he does need their support (*L.* 73-74; 2.11). He wanders, perhaps in accordance with the weather, like the migration of birds, but his wandering stems from a fear of death (*L.* 361; 8.9). Perhaps most important, Wilhelm's ideal poet participates, at least theoretically, in an exchange with the world. Augustin, like Wilhelm, is blind to the world and out of place in it.

Despite the contradiction between Wilhelm's image of the poet and Augustin's characteristics, the latter clearly represents a poet and can serve—against the views of Wilhelm, the abbé, the marquis, and the uncle—as an example of the development of a poet, and of the constitution of poetry. He is a walking rebuttal to Wilhelm's noble and satisfied singer of the harmony and legitimacy of the moral and political order. That order—represented by his father and the church—has persecuted him; his skills have grown out of suffering and alienation. His songs (and most of the other verse in the novel) do not celebrate the status quo; if they participate in "high" art, it is in opposition to and alienated from the social order.

Augustin's poetic achievement has not resulted from contact with noble people and objects (as the abbé would assume) but rather through experiences including the highs and lows of mysticism, throes of guilt for incest, insanity, years of vagrancy, and alienation. Many of these experiences—not, as the abbé and Augustin's brother would maintain, the historical study of form—constitute the basis for his songs. In contrast to the distanced, harmonious production Wilhelm, the abbé, and the uncle suggest, his songs seem fitted to his present circumstances. His first song, which is not given in the text, suits the situation so well "that he seemed to have composed it at that moment specially for this occasion" (*L.* 72; 2.11). The next two songs mentioned are also direct responses to his audience (*L.* 72-73; 2.11). The other songs are more personal: about his gray hair (*L.* 267; 7.4); about fate, personal guilt, and atonement; about isolation (*L.* 77-88; 2.13); about pain and wandering (*L.* 203; 5.14). His poetry, then, is produced from a myriad of high and low influences and is effective in moving people belonging to various groups. It fulfills Wilhelm's claim of universality for the poet in personal terms, as opposed to Wilhelm's basically monologic images.

Paradoxically, a primary theme of Augustin's songs is alienation, and yet the songs function in dialogue with the listener. The interchange between Augustin and his audience has already been noted. He achieves a more personal "conversation" with Wilhelm:

> We could expend a great number of words and still not be able to convey the charm of the extraordinary conversation which our friend had with the curious stranger. The old man responded, as though agreeing with everything the young man said, by producing music that evoked all sorts of similar feelings and opened up the full range of the imagination.
>
> (*L.* 78-79; 2.13)

While Wilhelm almost certainly reads his problems into the songs, Augustin's songs provide, in addition to an expression of his own personal condition, a multivalent medium of commonality, a sphere in which emotions are produced and discovered. Augustin, in his alienation, produces a means of understanding and dialogue.

Augustin's songs motivate an extended metaphorical clarification, which grants them—and by extension, poetry—personal, multivalent, and multivoiced characteristics. The comparison uses a group of religious people explicitly excluded from the church and its canonical, authoritative, and monologic teachings:

> The leader will adapt to what he is saying the verse of some hymn . . . which inspires the soul to fly in the direction the speaker suggests. Then someone in the group will break in with a different tune, a verse from another hymn. Then a third person will add something from still another hymn, with the result that the community of ideas in these various hymns is evoked, and each individual passage by reason of these associations takes on a new light, as if it had just been composed. A new synthesis is evolved out of familiar ideas and

> hymns and verses for this particular audience, in the enjoyment of which they are edified, quickened and fortified. (*L.* 79; 2.13, translation modified)

The revitalizing "whole" that arises is composed of a number of voices singing pieces of songs and sayings. Each piece takes on a new and individual meaning determined by the moment and by the context. This form of textual dialogue creates new, personal meanings, in contrast to an established religion, which must maintain its one truth. Augustin's textual production—poetry—lies outside of the pragmatic, monologic world of truth defined by authority and fosters the production of personal, immediate, and multiple meanings.

Augustin's songs may be high poetry, but they derive largely from "low" experiences and influences: familial discord, sexuality, alienation, insanity, and wandering all play a role in his poetic production, and this has significance for art in general. Any attempt to harness his person and productivity as an affirmation of a social order interested in utility and control is doomed; his verses spring from conflict with society and undermine its values, at least to the extent that society applauds them.

Mignon, perhaps the personification of poetry, shares with Augustin (in addition to genetic material) low attributes and a poetic voice resistant to appropriation by authority. Her origin, fate, and experiences, like Augustin's, contradict both Wilhelm's and the abbé's theories of the development of the poet and poetic production. Her three songs are all autobiographical or personal (*L.* 82, 216, 316; 3.1, 5.16, 8.2);[21] the third one is so well suited to its specific context that it appears improvised. The first one—"Kennst du das Land, wo die Zitronen blühn" ("Do you know the land where lemon blossoms bloom")—is described as unique, untranslatable, and innocent. During its performance Mignon takes on a number of voices, coloring its repetitions with variation in tone ("solemn grandeur," "somber," "weightiness and mystery," "longing," "entreating and urging," "pressing and full of promise," *L.* 83-84; 3.1). This song, like Augustin's, is about an alienation that references to lover, protector, and father are unable to remedy.[22] The poem's purpose, as we learn from the next poem and from Mignon's history, is to speak about the unspeakable since she has sworn to the Virgin Mary to reveal her origins to no one.

The second poem—"Heiβ mich nicht reden, heiβ mich schweigen" ("Bid me not speak, let me be silent")—deals with this same conflict between revelation and secrecy. Its thematic material and its placement at the end of book 5 suggest that a closer analysis would be rewarding. On one level the poem acts as Mignon's excuse for not revealing her past. On other levels it suggests that ultimate mysteries will remain despite the necessary and natural quality of the reading process. All of nature—according to the second verse—unveils its mysteries at the appointed time; everyone reveals himself to a friend, but some mysteries require divine explication since "only a god may unseal" Mignon's lips. Mignon, despite her desire to reveal herself, cannot. Her poetic talent remains a mystery that cannot be accounted for and, as such, a thorn in the side of the team of "experts" concerned with her condition and origins. The doctor can preserve her body; Natalie can deduce most of her story from fragments; the abbé presides over her funeral and adds a few details to her story; but no one plucks the heart out of her mystery, to paraphrase Hamlet (III.ii.365). Her songs, although they deal with geographic, emotional, and sexual alienation, communicate effectively and at an emotional depth and complexity the Tower cannot fathom.[23] In fact, both Augustin and Mignon and their songs are out of place in the world of books 7 and 8; they constitute embarrassing counterexamples to the abbé's aesthetic and developmental theories and counterforces to his social ideals, all of which depend on the separation of high and low.

Other poetic texts in the ***Lehrjahre*** also support this image of art as repository for voices contrary to the social order, to accepted social norms. Philine performs her songs—"The Shepherd Dressed Himself for the Dance" and "Do Not Sing in Tones Depressing" (*L.* 74, 191-92; 2.11, 5.10)—to good effect in questioning the values of the social order since they present bawdy or erotic content as valid and valuable; and the ***Lehrjahre*** clearly appreciates her songs.[24] It is interesting to note that not a single example of purely affirmative art occurs in the ***Lehrjahre.*** Although the anonymous poem attributed to the pedant in book 3 celebrates the status quo, it remains a mockery of the baron and plays a role in the denigration of the count.[25] Even Wilhelm's artistic production—the play for the count—gains its interest value not from its requested and intended affirmation of the social order (in its praise of the prince) but from the machinations and evasions that allowed the performance of a play entirely divergent from the one the count had commissioned (*L.* 97-101; 3.6-7). Instances of art in the ***Lehrjahre*** negate its use as a legitimation of the status quo, as support for a monolithic, monologic social order—the implicit purpose of the uncle's collections—in favor of a multiplicity of more critical voices. Sadly, at the end of the novel the number of these voices has diminished. Augustin and Mignon are dead, and Philine is silenced by her pregnancy. Their songs have died away.[26] For compensation, the reader can only rely on Friedrich, whose comic voice remains raised in protest.

Nature and Culture in Dialogue through Shakespeare

Shakespeare's works constitute another attempt at a definition of art and another alternative voice in the dialogue of the novel. Certain influential elements of the eighteenth century were shocked by Shakespeare's works because so many voices ran amok in them. During an age when people accepted the *unities* of time, place, and plot, his plays combined voices from different times and places. Against aesthetic dicta that separated comedy and tragedy and delegated class roles to the characters in various genres, he allowed rich and poor, aristocratic and common, educated and vulgar to say their piece.[27] These aspects of Shakespeare's work clearly play a role in the ***Lehrjahre.*** The novel's images of Shakespeare's world go even further, however. They suggest the breakdown of the dichotomy between nature and culture—that is, a final inability to define the natural in any other than provisional terms. Needless to say, such indeterminacy undermines the claims of authoritative voices in favor of a multiplicity of valid perspectives.

Wilhelm's introduction to Shakespeare plays into this tension between nature and the social sphere and, at the same time, illustrates again his tendency toward monologue. The context of this introduction involves both Wilhelm's infatuation with the aristocracy and his conservative attitudes toward literature. The baron has told him of the prince's exclusive preference for French theater, and someone has suggested to Wilhelm that he praise it in the prince's presence (***L.*** 102, 104; 3.8). Following this advice, Wilhelm holds a monologue of sorts. The prince had been ready to leave, and Wilhelm continues at some length (sixteen lines of direct quotation and six of indirect discourse), not knowing that such enthusiasm and depth break aristocratic social codes (***L.*** 104; 3.8). In his subservient quest for status, Wilhelm mirrors himself in his depiction of Racine, whom he describes as an author whose elevated representations of the nobility give the latter their due. Wilhelm's Racine is so dependent on favor that he dies from the king's disapproval (***L.*** 104; 3.8). Wilhelm's kowtowing here is monologic in several senses. He holds forth at length without response. More important, his account praises a canonical dramatist writing in a canonically formulated genre, who depicts, idealizes, and lives for the ruling class. And he attempts to insinuate himself into this same seamless hierarchical world. Naturally the prince nods approval. He leaves to the equivalent of a standing ovation for him personally and for his world's order. The extreme piling up of affirmation—the ludicrous hyperbole—marks this scene as parodic.

Jarno's introduction of Shakespeare into this context interrupts the single-minded affirmation of social class, accepted literary status, and sanctioned aesthetic norms. Wilhelm refers to Shakespeare's works as "strange monstrosities" and implies that his plays are unnatural—that is, improbable and counter to correct behavior (***L.*** 105; 3.8).[28] The French neoclassicists are then "natural" because they obey the three unities, observe class distinctions, treat the aristocracy with respect (*not* in comedies). Shakespeare's work implicitly opposes this monologic merger of class and aesthetic principles. In his *Hamlet* interpretation, Wilhelm later denigrates Rosencrantz and Guildenstern's subordinate behavior, not recalling his own fawning with the prince (***L.*** 180; 5.5). His immediate valorization of Lothario and his own subordination, along with his willingness to deceive Lydie, suggest the behavior he himself criticizes (***L.*** 271; 7.5).[29]

Wilhelm's original judgment of Shakespeare as "unnatural" is immediately inverted when he begins reading him, producing a series of images with aesthetic and political implications. Shakespeare becomes the voice of nature, as is indicated by the first set of metaphors describing Shakespeare's effect on Wilhelm:

> And in a very short while, he was seized, as one would expect, by the torrent of a great genius which swept toward a limitless ocean in which he completely lost and forgot his own self. (***L.*** 105; 3.8)

The power of a river and the expanse of an ocean now characterize Shakespeare. The immensity and incalculable nature of this ocean correspond to a lack of aesthetic rules or limits, in direct contrast to the neoclassical unities. This image of Shakespeare also implicitly questions Wilhelm's fawning praise of Racine, which combined related affirmations of class hierarchy and aesthetic rules.

This move from a stable monologic aesthetic to a multivalent poetic world whose values are in flux has a strong effect on Wilhelm. We have seen him to this point claiming status through the appropriation of every possible "elevated" aesthetic, moral, and political position (and with the moral fervor of soapbox oratory). On reading Shakespeare he forgets himself, loses his bearings, and is swept away. Wilhelm now privileges the antithesis of French drama in terms of both form and content. Wilhelm's hierarchies are subverted, and an extended metaphor, reminiscent of Goethe's "Zauberlehrling" (Sorcerer's Apprentice), describes his complete loss of control:

> There are said to be certain sorcerers who by magic can entice a host of different spirits into their chamber. The conjurations are so powerful that the whole room is filled and the spirits, jostled up to the tiny magic circle that the wizard has drawn, swirl around it and float above his head, constantly changing and increasing in number. Every corner is crammed full, every shelf occupied, eggs keep expanding, and gigantic shapes shrink to toadstools. But unfortunately the necromancer has forgotten the magic word to make this flood of spirits subside. (***L.*** 108; 3.9)

The image of the magician is used earlier in the novel for somewhat ridiculous authority figures (***L.*** 24; 1.13). Here too the magician is an authority figure, overwhelmed by a flood of spirits he purported to control. His space is taken, and he is restricted to a tiny circle. Master and servant exchange roles, and large and small are transformed into their opposites. Wilhelm had depended on authority, from Aristotle through the French neoclassicists to Gottsched, and now this structure is swept away in favor of a nonformulaic aesthetic allowing mixtures of high and low voices and figures. In perceiving these many voices of Shakespeare's world, Wilhelm, often a mouthpiece for authoritarian positions, is appropriately struck dumb for one of the few occasions of the novel.

The magician's loss of power does not apply solely to Wilhelm: the aesthetic shift has political implications. Although Wilhelm retains his idealization of the aristocracy through this experience, the structure of the narrative indicates the significance of this new aesthetic voice to attitudes toward class. In the narrative, references and reactions to Shakespeare alternate with depictions of castle events. Wilhelm's attempt to curry favor with the prince is followed by the introduction of Shakespeare (***L.*** 104-5; 3.8). A description of the incidents associated with the circulation of a denigratory poem against the baron precedes an account of Wilhelm's reactions to reading Shakespeare (***L.*** 106-8; 3.9). The conclusion of the hullabaloo associated with the poem and Wilhelm's symbolic cuckolding of the count are then narrated, succeeded immediately by a more involved account of Shakespeare's effect on Wilhelm (***L.*** 109-13; 3.9-11).

This alternation—or dialogue, if you will—between Wilhelm's earnest Shakespeare reception and events in the castle, which are basically comic, questions the possibility of any natural social or aesthetic order.[30] Both must be negotiated; both are the products of dialogue. Wilhelm later maintains that *Hamlet* is natural, an inviolable, organic whole, a tree composed of its constituent parts. This suggestion summons its antithesis, supplied in Serlo's well-taken objections (***L.*** 177; 5.4). The "organicity" of Shakespeare, or of art in general, can encourage debate, but the ***Lehrjahre*** does not expect any final answers. Shakespeare does offer a new aesthetic model and a new vision of the world. In contrast to neoclassicism, he does not present a world ordered by power exercised from the center, radiating outward from the king through the nobility and middle classes to the peasants. In his world, conflict rages on multiple fronts, and people interact in accordance with a variety of independent goals. In the ***Lehrjahre,*** the introduction of this more complex aesthetic structure, in which a large number of voices contend, supports the novel's requirement of a continual interpretive process that recognizes its own contingency.

Conclusion

This chapter on voices—the voice of authority and its attempt at a kind of *Gleichschaltung,* the voice of the dominant culture through Wilhelm, and the voices of artistic discourses and their relationship to the status quo and to subversion—repeats the themes of this study through the Bakhtinian tropes of monologue and dialogue. The desire for a rule of law and order—aesthetic and moral precepts, truth over superstition, a rational religion—dominates the eighteenth century; it values hierarchy and the status quo and harkens to the voices of power, those that hand down the law and moral teachings from above; it suppresses or fails to hear voices from below. The ***Lehrjahre*** hears these voices and represents them as necessary. Goethe's novel is profoundly aware of a multiplicity of voices—the complex multivalence of the artistic text—which it mobilizes in opposition to Wilhelm's subservience and complicity. Wilhelm's definition of poetry, for example, views the poet as the celebrant of a world of status and power, just as his remarks on the theater early in the novel subordinate it to social utility (***L.*** 52; 2.4). The tendency to conformity that these opinions suggest peaks at the end of the novel in Wilhelm's outright rejection of Philine. The ***Lehrjahre*** offers the reader a different view of poetry, the theater, and the world of the marketplace, all of which are related. Augustin and Mignon present poems that are personal, poems that question social assumptions, thematize alienation while partially alleviating it, and serve as the medium for alternative voices. Shakespeare's plays, like the ***Lehrjahre,*** allow the voices of the high and mighty and the "coarser" voices of the lower class and the marketplace to speak. It is these latter voices that Wilhelm rejects and that Friedrich represents at the end of the ***Lehrjahre.*** Friedrich silences the abbé's authoritative voice and—as if speaking for this *Volksfest* of a novel as a whole—reminds the reader of a whole universe of marginalized voices.[31]

Notes

1. The uncle's Italian parallel, Augustin's father, is so extremely closed to other opinions that he can bear conversation with only one other person, who expressly never contradicts him (*L.* 355; 8.9).
2. The Suhrkamp translation seems quite misleading: "We are born with minimal ability."
3. Jarno labels them, for example, "an itinerant ballad singer and a silly androgynous creature" (*L.* 113; 3.11).
4. See chapter 3 for a discussion of the uncle's estate (and its Italian parallel, that of the marquis).
5. Some elements at the end of the novel—the painting of the sick king's son, Friedrich and his references to the marketplace and (parodically) to erudite works, Wilhelm's sexual confusion, and Felix's "poisoning," for example—do disrupt its smoothly managed pedagogical monologue temporarily.
6. More on Therese and order, particularly relative to her father, in chapter 3.
7. See chapter 1 for more on Wilhelm and paralysis.
8. More on *Henry IV* in chapters 2 and 4.
9. On the status of actors and actresses in the eighteenth century, see Rolf Selbmann 22 and Inge Buck 314.
10. In his valorization of Wilhelm's idealism, Karl Schlechta seems to agree with Wilhelm's judgments, criticizing Herr Melina for never being a real actor and praising Wilhelm for never belonging to or understanding the "common world" (25-26).
11. Anneliese Dick's comments also emphasize Wilhelm's appropriation of a "high" to which he has little right. She sees Wilhelm as a narcissistic young man with shallow ideals who attempts to represent himself as a higher being. She notes that such behavior depends on financial independence (25).
12. See chapter 3 for related material on Herr Melina.
13. For an indication of the importance of dialogue to Goethe, see Peter John Burgard's dissertation, particularly the brief discussion of the power of dialogue in breaking down the authoritative voice in "Der Sammler und die Seinigen," the references to

Goethe's thoughts on dialogue, and on Goethe's criticism of Platonic dialogue as monologue (169-80, 191-94, and 118ff., respectively). I thank Eva Knodt for suggesting this dissertation and lending me her copy.

14. Todd Kontje refers to Wilhelm's monologue in book 1 as "verbal masturbation," citing Kittler's "identification of an indirect reference to the biblical Onan." The Suhrkamp translation—"Wilhelm was convinced that not one word of his narration had been lost" (*L.* 10; 1.7)—obscures this reference. In the German, not one word "fell to the ground" (Kontje 1992, 64, fn. 30).

15. Schiller calls this a masterly apology for commerce (to Goethe, December 9, 1794, *HA* 7.621).

16. See chapter 4 for more on circulation.

17. The exclusion of the comic element from Wilhelm's *Hamlet* interpretation is particularly blatant (see chapter 2).

18. See chapter 4 for a description of Wilhelm's reception of art.

19. The poem credited to the pedant by the count ("O Baron, how I envy you") remains anonymous (*L.* 106; 3.9).

20. Hannelore Schlaffer argues that Wilhelm's fantasy creates the figure of the "true poet" before he appears in the novel as Augustin (42-43). Wilhelm does create a fantasy image resembling Augustin superficially. Augustin and Wilhelm's "poet" differ essentially in term of worldview, mental condition, position in society, and poetic subject matter.

21. Mignon's third poem—"So let me seem till I become"—has been discussed in chapter 1.

22. In addition to remarking on many of the details mentioned here, Oskar Seidlin analyzes the poem in terms of an alienation necessarily tied to death and to the artistic process. He sees the poem as calling forth a rather dark poetic world out of place in the otherwise realistic narrative structure (86, 94).

23. For a brief critique of the morality of the Tower and its associates, see Heinz Schlaffer 219-23.

24. The text of the first song is not printed in the *Lehrjahre.* See chapter 5 for an explication of the second song.

25. See chapter 3 for more on this poem of ridicule.

26. Compare Martina Kieβ 195-96. By contrast, Hellmut Ammerlahn sees Mignon's embalming as a process whereby she becomes a work of art so that Wilhelm may continue to develop (1981, 26-29).

27. See chapter 2 for more on Shakespeare's mixing of genres.

28. As Wilhelm later notes, Shakespeare's Henry V (in *Henry IV*) seems to revel in low environments, and Falstaff is depicted positively, as are both gravedigger and clown in *Hamlet.* Wilhelm uses the behavior of the character Prince Hal as an excuse because he rises to the kingship, denies his low associates, and seems no worse for it (*L.* 123; 4.2). For more on Shakespeare and low culture, see chapter 2.

29. Jane K. Brown does an insightful reading of many of the inserted texts in the *Lehrjahre,* coming to the conclusion that the "theatrical mission of the *Lehrjahre,* then, is to advocate a non-Aristotelian drama *and* a non-Aristotelian novel." She understands "the apparently questionable morality of the *Lehrjahre* . . . at least in part as deliberate violations of the neoclassical demand that literature educate to virtue" (160-62).

30. Another series of alternations concerning Shakespeare occurs in books 4 and 5 of the *Lehrjahre.* Tragic and comic perspectives relating to *Hamlet* engage and qualify one another (see chapter 2).

31. "'You have certainly had great success with the public in providing popular entertainment,' the Abbé replied. 'It seems as if I shall never get to speak today'" (*L.* 373; 8.10). This is a nice irony since he has spoken quite enough, has in fact been one of the dominant voices in the novel, and has had a strong influence on the creation of the world of books 7 and 8.

FURTHER READING

Brown, Jane K. "The Theatrical Mission of the *Lehrjahre.*" In *Goethe's Narrative Fiction: The Irvine Goethe Symposium,* edited by William J. Lillyman, pp. 69-84. Berlin: Walter de Gruyter, 1983.

Studies Goethe's attack on neo-classicism in *Wilhelm Meisters Lehrjahre.*

Cohn, Dorrit. "Wilhelm Meister's Dream: Reading Goethe with Freud." In *German Quarterly* 62, No. 4 (Fall 1989): 459-72.

Argues that Goethe endeavors to portray Wilhelm's dream in Book Seven of *Wilhelm Meisters Lehrjahre* with a great degree of psychological realism, and analyzes the dream itself.

Dürr, Volker O. "The Humanistic Ideal and the Representative Public in *Wilhelm Meister's Apprenticeship.*" In *Papers on Language and Literature* 12, No. 1 (Winter 1976): 36-48.

Contends that *Wilhelm Meisters Lehrjahre* represents Goethe's attempt to align the Bildungsroman's focus on the individual with the theme of maintaining the traditional institutions of social life.

Dye, R. Ellis. "Wilhelm Meister and *Hamlet,* Identity and Difference." In *Goethe Yearbook* IV (1992): 67-85.

Interprets the ironic component of Wilhelm Meister's identification with *Hamlet.*

Flaherty, Gloria. "The Stage-Struck Wilhelm Meister and 18th-Century Psychiatric Medicine." In *MLN* 101, No. 3 (April 1986): 493-515.

Highlights the medical theme in *Wilhelm Meisters Lehrjahre,* claiming that Wilhelm's education concerns "the fundamental health problems that must be faced and solved if any given community is to survive and flourish."

Hatch, Mary Gies. "Mignon: Goethe's Study of Affectional Frustration in Childhood." In *Goethe in the Twentieth Century,* edited by Alexej Ugrinsky, pp. 133-38. New York: Greenwood Press, 1987.

Perceives Mignon as the embodiment of suffering and as a foil to Wilhelm, who represents development through striving.

Hoffmeister, Gerhart, ed. *Goethes Mignon und ihre Schwestern: Interpretationen und Rezeption.* New York: Peter Lang, 1993, 255 p.

Contains three essays in English on the female characters in *Wilhelm Meisters Lehrjahre.*

Jeffers, Thomas. "Forms of Misprison: The Early- and Mid-Victorian Reception of Goethe's *Bildungsidee.*" In *University of Toronto Quarterly* 57, No. 4 (Summer 1988): 501-15.

Surveys misreadings of *Wilhelm Meisters Lehrjahre* by such Victorians as Thomas Carlyle, John Stuart Mill, Matthew Arnold, and Walter Pater.

MacLeod, Catriona. "Pedagogy and Androgyny in *Wilhelm Meisters Lehrjahre.*" In *MLN* 108, No. 3 (April 1993): 389-426.

Examines the numerous transvestite figures in *Wilhelm Meisters Lehrjahre* and the relationship of these androgyne characters to Wilhelm's path toward maturation.

Marchand, James W. "A Milestone in *Hamlet* Criticism: Goethe's *Wilhelm Meister.*" In *Goethe as a Critic of Literature,* edited by Karl J. Fink and Max L. Baeumer, pp. 140-59. Lanham, Md.: University Press of America, 1984.

Probes the psychological understanding of *Hamlet* Goethe presents in *Wilhelm Meisters Lehrjahre* as a turning point in the criticism of Shakespeare's drama.

Molnár, Géza von. "Goethe's Reading of Kant's 'Critique of Esthetic Judgment': A Referential Guide for Wilhelm Meister's Esthetic Education." In *Eighteenth-Century Studies* 15, No. 4 (Summer 1982): 402-20.

Traces the influence of Kant's *Critique of Judgment* on the ethical and esthetic education of Wilhelm Meister.

Saine, Thomas P. "What Time Is It in *Wilhelm Meisters Lehrjahre*?" In *Horizonte: Festschrift für Herbert Lehnert zum 65. Geburtstag,* edited by Hannelore Mundt, Egon Schwarz, and William J. Lillyman, pp. 52-69. Tübingen: Max Niemeyer Verlag, 1990.

Analyzes the central ambiguity of time in *Wilhelm Meisters Lehrjahre.*

———. "Was *Wilhelm Meisters Lehrjahre* Really Supposed to Be a Bildungsroman?" In *Reflection and Action: Essays on the Bildungsroman,* edited by James Hardin, pp. 118-41. Columbia: University of South Carolina Press, 1991.

Questions whether *Wilhelm Meisters Lehrjahre* conforms to the precepts of the Bildungsroman, noting Wilhelm's belief in fate, the central role of family, and the relative lack of "harmonious human development" in the work.

Sammons, Jeffrey L. "The Mystery of the Missing *Bildungsroman,* or: What Happened to Wilhelm Meister's Legacy?" *Genre* 14, No. 2 (Summer 1981): 229-46.

Disputes the assertion that the Bildungsroman was the characteristic subgenre of the nineteenth-century German novel.

Turner, David. "*Wilhelm Meister's Apprenticeship* and German Classicism." In *Periods in German Literature, Vol. II: Texts and Contexts,* edited by J. M. Ritchie, pp. 87-114. London: Oswald Wolff, 1969.

Proposes that, despite certain appearances, *Wilhelm Meisters Lehrjahre* should be considered a work of German Classicism, not Romanticism.

Vazsonyi, Nicholas. "Goethe's *Wilhelm Meisters Lehrjahre:* A Question of Talent." *German Quarterly* 62, No. 1 (Winter 1989): 39-47.

Ponders the link between Wilhelm and the state of the German theater at the end of the eighteenth century.

Additional coverage of Goethe's life and career is contained in the following sources published by the Gale Group: *Dictionary of Literary Biography,* Vol. 94; *DISCovering Authors*; *DISCovering Authors, 3.0*; *DISCovering Authors: British*; *DISCovering Authors: Canadian*; *DISCovering Authors Modules: Dramatists, Most-Studied Authors,* and *Poets*; *Poetry Criticism,* Vol. 5; *Short Story Criticism,* Vol. 38; and *World Literature Criticism.*

Helen Hunt Jackson
1830-1885

Also wrote under the pseudonyms H. H., Saxe Holm, Marah, Rip Van Winkle. American children's author, novelist, essayist, non-fiction writer, and poet.

INTRODUCTION

Known primarily as an author of popular children's books and poems during the late-nineteenth century, Helen Hunt Jackson rarely published under her own name, preferring instead to use such pseudonyms as H. H. and Saxe Holm. Although Jackson was a prolific writer and contributor to magazines and journals, many of her book reviews were unsigned, making it difficult to attribute much of her work. Years after her death, Jackson's fame rests not on the children's books that made her so popular during her lifetime, but on two works written for an adult audience—*A Century of Dishonor* (1881) and *Ramona* (1884). In the 1880s Jackson became a passionate advocate for the Native American cause and both these books reflect her concerns. Jackson's other works include contributions of short stories and essays to various literary and children's magazines, as well as juvenile novels, such as *Nelly's Silver Mine* (1878), that reflected her love for the landscape and life in the western United States.

BIOGRAPHICAL INFORMATION

Jackson was born in 1830, in Amherst, Massachusetts. Her father, Nathan Welby Fiske, was a stern clergyman and professor at Amherst College and her mother, Deborah Vinal, was an educated Bostonian. As a child, Jackson was known for her strong will. After her parents died when she was a teenager, an aunt raised Jackson and her sister. Jackson was educated at the Ipswich Female Academy and then continued her instruction at a school run by John and Jacob Abbott in New York City. She became acquainted with the poet Emily Dickinson during her early years in Amherst and the two remained friends and admirers of each other's work for the rest of their lives. In 1852 Jackson married Lieutenant Edward Bisell Hunt and together they had two sons, one of whom died in infancy. Lt. Hunt died in 1863 following an accident while conducting a scientific experiment, and shortly thereafter Jackson also lost her second son. She was grief-stricken at her loss and eventually moved to Newport, Rhode Island. It was here that she began her lifelong association with the literary world. She began attending meetings of local and visiting writers organized by Thomas Wentworth Higginson. Her contact with these writers and intellectuals rekindled an interest in life and she began writing to support herself financially. She became one of Higginson's protégés and began to contribute poetry and prose to periodicals, including the *New York Independent, Scribner's Monthly,* and the *New York Evening Post.* She went on to publish hundreds of pieces and her work was included in most of the leading journals. In 1870 Jackson issued her first collection of poetry, titled *Verses,* to glowing reviews. In fact, author Ralph Waldo Emerson thought so much of her poetry that he included some of it in the second edition of his anthology *Parnassus* in 1874. After several years in Newport, Jackson traveled to the West in the early 1870s. In 1873, following an illness, she went to Colorado to recover. There she met and married William Sharpless Jackson in 1875. The two had no children, but Jackson was soon consumed with what became her life's crusade. Following a lecture on the suffering and dispossession of Native Americans, Jackson developed an intense interest in their cause and began writing letters and articles on the subject. She devoted the remainder of her life to improving the conditions of Native Americans and exposing the injustices heaped upon this marginalized group. Despite her popularity and acclaim as a poet and children's author, Jackson herself considered *A Century of Dishonor* and *Ramona,* two works that reflected her concern with the Native American cause, her own best legacy. Finally after suffering for several years from an unknown illness, Jackson succumbed to stomach cancer in 1885.

MAJOR WORKS

Jackson began her publishing career in the early 1870s with the publication of several poems and reviews in contemporary literary journals. Her 1870 collection of poetry, *Verses,* derived from these early submissions and was reflective of her grief at losing her sons and her first husband. She followed this publication with two volumes of short stories, in 1874 and 1878. Jackson, like many of her female literary contemporaries, wrote for children, often entertaining them with tales of adventure and mischief. Her short stories are full of her own childhood escapades and Jackson often contributed them to children's magazines including *Riverside Magazine for Young Readers.* In 1876 she collected her children's pieces in one volume, *Bits of Talk, in Verse and Prose, for Young Folks.* In the mid-1870s Jackson also began writing full-length works and her first two novels, *Mercy Philbrick's Choice* and *Hetty's Strange History,* were published in 1876 and 1877 respectively. Both works feature New England settings and hallmark strong characters. A third novel, *Nelly's Silver Mine,* was published in 1878. An adventure story about the fictional March family, the work is based on Jackson's experiences in Colorado. In contrast to many contemporary stories about the West that presented a barbaric view of frontier life, Jackson's work was lauded for its realistic portrayal. Although the book was praised as a "true classic for the nursery," its appeal has not endured and it is now read primarily as a historical curiosity. In contrast, Jackson's poetry for children continued to be popular well after her death. In addition to children's short stories and poetry, Jackson was also known for her "cat stories" which are collected into three publications. The most famous of these, *Letters from a Cat* (1879), relates daily events in the life of a feline. Jackson's other extremely popular cat-related titles include *Mammy Tittleback and Her Family* and *The Hunter Cats of Connorloa.*

During a trip to New York City in the 1870s, Jackson attended a lecture by Ponco Chief Standing Bear on the plight of Native Americans and their suffering and dispossession at the hands of the United States government. Jackson was profoundly affected by this knowledge and she became a passionate advocate working for the cause of Native Americans up until her death. In a letter to her friend Charles D. Warner in 1879, Jackson wrote "I shall be found with 'Indians' engraved on my brain when I am dead. A fire has been kindled within me, which will never go out." Her activism led her to write numerous essays and articles on the subject, which further prompted her research for a non-fiction work to expose the government's maltreatment of these native people. The result was the publication of *A Century of Dishonor.* The work theorizes that contemporary United States government policy regarding Native Americans defied the basic principles of justice. Jackson was so committed to her cause that she mailed copies of the work to all the members of Congress at her own expense. While legislation based on Jackson's work concerning the Mission Indians of California was introduced, and was approved by the Senate, Congress did not pass the bill. In fact, there were many, including Theodore Roosevelt, who criticized her work. Nonetheless, a few years later the Indian Rights Association was formed, and in 1882 Jackson was appointed a commissioner of Indian Affairs, assigned to visit and report on the conditions of Indians in California. Jackson considered *A Century of Dishonor* her best work and though the book went out of print after her death, later students have considered it "one of the soundest and most exhaustive works" on Indian rights. In 1884 Jackson continued her efforts to highlight the plight of Native Americans by the publication of *Ramona,* a romantic novel set against the background of the old Spanish patriarchal life in California. It is the story of Ramona, a half Indian and half Spanish woman and her Indian husband's love in the face of persecution by whites. Ramona, who was designed to represent the best of two races, is considered one of the most memorable female characters in nineteenth-century literature. *Ramona* was the last full-length work issued by Jackson.

CRITICAL RECEPTION

Jackson was a prolific and popular writer at a time when women writers faced hostility and disrespect. Although her poetry is now generally considered dated and her handling of the major themes of life, love, and death frequently interpreted as too sentimental, she was considered one of the best poets in her own time. In fact, at the time of her death, her longtime mentor and friend Higginson rated her poetry as her best contribution to American literature. And while Jackson's poems continued to be anthologized well into the 1970s, most twentieth-century scholarship and criticism of Jackson's writing has focused on *Ramona* and *A Century of Dishonor.* In 1886 Albion W. Tourgee wrote in the *North American Review* that *Ramona* was "unquestionably the best novel yet produced by an American woman." Along with Harriet Beecher Stowe's *Uncle Tom's Cabin,* it was ranked as one of the two great ethical novels of the nineteenth century, and Jackson herself said "If I can do one-hundredth part for the Indian as Mrs. Stowe did for the Negro, I will be thankful." In contrast, most twentieth-century critics consider *Ramona* a great sentimental romance, and while they praise the work for its didactic purpose, many critique it because it offers no constructive remedy. In fact, *Ramona* has become famous primarily because it is a great romance; it has been reprinted over 300 times, attesting to the popularity of the work.

While *Ramona*'s political nature cannot be disputed, some critics have noted that despite its failure to match the social impact of *Uncle Tom's Cabin,* it is nonetheless a better-written work than Stowe's novel. Reviewing *Ramona* in his book *Through Ramona's Country,* George Wharton James noted Jackson's attention to realistic detail. According to James, Jackson used many actual events in the creation of her novel, and although the "hero and heroine are fiction . . . *Ramona* . . . is a work of essential truth." In an essay that traces the factual elements of *Ramona* back to Jackson's *A Century of Dishonor,* critic John R. Byers expresses a similar opinion, calling *Century* "one of the most scathing indictments of the United States Government on the treatment of the Indian population. . . ." Byers further states that *Century* served as the source for *Ramona,* and that the two works share a close relationship, drawing on the same set of facts. In contrast, although *Century* is lauded for its strong and convincing indictment of government policy and practice with regards to Native Americans, most critics agree that the work is "stylistically flawed by hasty writing with little revision." Although Jackson was a popular writer of both prose and poetry in her time, most twentieth-century scholarship focuses on *Ramona.* With this novel and *Century,* says Carol Schmudde, Jackson "put the moral authority" she had gained as a poet and author through her previous works "on the line, and it is for her passionate concern and contribution to her cause that she is most remembered today."

PRINCIPAL WORKS

Bathmendi: A Persian Tale [translated by H. H.] (novel) 1867
Verses [as H. H.] (poetry) 1870
Bits of Travel [as H. H.] (prose) 1872
Bits of Talk about Home Matters [as H. H.] (prose) 1873
Saxe Holm's Stories [as Saxe Holm] (short stories) 1874
The Story of Boon [as H. H.] (novel) 1874
Bits of Talk, in Verse and Prose [as H. H.] (prose) 1876
Mercy Philbrick's Choice [as Anonymous] (novel) 1876
Bits of Travel at Home [as H. H.] (prose) 1878
Nelly's Silver Mine: A Story of Colorado Life [as H. H.] (novel) 1878
Letters from a Cat: Published by Her Mistress for the Benefit of all Cats and the Amusement of Little Children [as H. H.] (short stories) 1879
A Century of Dishonor: A Sketch of the United States Government's Dealings with Some of the Indian Tribes [as H. H.] (nonfiction) 1881
Mammy Tittleback and Her Family: A True Story of Seventeen Cats [as H. H.] (novel) 1881
Report on the Condition and Needs of the Mission Indians of California [by Jackson and Abbot Kinney] (non-fiction) 1883
Ramona: A Story [as Helen Jackson (H. H.)] (novel) 1884
The Hunter Cats of Connorloa [as H. H.] (short stories) 1884
Sonnets and Lyrics (poetry) 1886

CRITICISM

George Wharton James (essay date 1913)

SOURCE: "The Facts and Fictions of *Ramona,*" in *Through Ramona's Country,* Little Brown and Company, 1913, pp. 22-62.

[*In the following excerpt, James explores Jackson's use of actual events in the creation of the fictional world of* Ramona *and praises her descriptions of natural surroundings.*]

There are those in Ramonaland who will tell you that ***Ramona*** is fiction from beginning to end. They will go further. They will denounce the story as untrue to fact, in that it gives too highly colored descriptions of the scenery and too exalted a conception of the Indians. With these critics I take decided issue. As I have shown in the chapter, "A Climatic Wonderland," it is not possible for any one to over-color the descriptions of the natural scenic conditions. And as for the Indians, criticism of them is more often based upon imperfect than adequate knowledge.

Leaving these two great points of ***Ramona*** out of the question, however, there are many facts of detail, which the gifted author most ingeniously wove into her story. Let us, in this chapter, take a survey of these facts, and see how they have been applied.

The description of life in an old time California ranch-house given in the first chapter is the presentation of an eye witness. While the scene is laid at Camulos, it is well known that Mrs. Jackson was there only two hours, while she visited for days at a time at Guajome, the home of Lieutenant Cave J. Couts, where there was just such a retinue of Indians and Mexicans as she so vividly pictures. Mrs. Couts's son, Cave, who now owns Guajome, repeats the story, and thus becomes authority for it, that when his father was a young dashing lieutenant in the First Dragoons, and his regiment was ordered to California from Chihuahua, Mexico, on September 1, 1848, he little dreamed that his fate awaited him in the person of a young and beautiful Spanish lady in the land to which he rode. On the first of April, 1849, he arrived at San Luis Rey. One day a party of San Diegans came to visit the old Mission, and among others was Miss Bandini, the charming, bright, vivacious daughter of Don Juan Bandini, one of the best known dons of Alta California. As the girl and her friends wandered about the building, they climbed upon the parapet over the corridors, and, gaily chatting and laughing, enjoyed themselves as young people will, until, horror of horrors, Miss Bandini slipped and fell headlong to the ground below. Death or a severe injury seemed inevitable, but the young lieutenant, observant of the maid, the glances of whose bright eyes had already penetrated his heart, dashed forward and caught her, thus averting the catastrophe. It was a double fall, however, for both of them, for they then and there fell mutually in love, and, despite all opposition, married. Guajome was built as their home, and there Mrs. Jackson visited Mrs. Couts and saw and learned much of the real life of a California ranch-house.

Cave also tells an interesting story that, one day, he had gone out to see how a band of Indians, who lived on and were dependents of the ranch, had done some work he had allotted to them. They had been both indifferent and lazy, and he was angry with them. Raising his voice he forcefully and roundly abused them for their laziness, and used language with which they were doubtless familiar enough, but which, to a lady of refined temperament, would sound coarse, vulgar, and brutal. Mrs. Jackson happened at that very moment to be coming towards the Indians unperceived by Cave, and she heard much or all of his abusive tirade. Her anger and indignation were as keen as his, but he was the object of them. Roundly she took him to task for swearing at the willing and docile Indians. Firmly and decidedly Cave defended himself, and the result was as near to a quarrel as a lady and gentleman can come. Mrs. Jackson recited the whole circumstances to Mrs. Couts on her return to the ranch, and Cave grimly confesses that his mother sided with her guest, but, nevertheless, he sticks to it that the Indians were lazy and careless and deserved all the "cussing" he gave them on that memorable occasion.

Several other ranches in the neighborhood were visited by Mrs. Jackson at this time, one in particular being historic and famous. Near to Guajome was the Santa Margarita, which, in its palmy days, comprised over a quarter of a million acres. There she saw sheep shearing by the Indians on a large scale, as described in the first chapters of ***Ramona.***

Her pictures of Camulos have already been commented upon. They are historic. Their accuracy is remarkable. Indeed Chapter II contains much valuable information, and more valuable suggestion. The criticisms on the United States Land Commission which, "after the surrender of California, undertook to sift and adjust Mexican land titles" seem to be just. There is no question whatever but that, in many instances, truthful and worthy families were ousted from their legal possession of lands, and that, in other cases, land grabbers and thieves of the worst type were given possession where they had no legal or moral claim.

It is in her remarkable use of such facts as these as *motives* in the minds of her characters that the genius of Mrs. Jackson displayed itself, as well as in her keen observation of other facts which she used in the same manner. For instance, it is true that the Santa Clara Valley road passes at the back of the Camulos ranch-house instead of the front, and that on the hills near-by are crosses. See how these are used in Chapter II to bring out the indignation of the Señora Moreno towards the hated Americans. The house "turned its back on them. She would like always to be able to do the same herself." As for the crosses, how they are made to reveal character: "That the heretics (the Americans) may know, when they go by, that they are on the estate of a good Catholic and that the faithful may be reminded to pray."

Here are fact and fiction,—fact in the statement as to what exists; fiction in the *attribution of motive* in regard to the existence of the fact.

The Indian bowls, described in Chapter II, were made of the soapstone (steatite) or serpentine, found on Santa Catalina Island. The native quarry is still to be seen as left by the aborigines. Unfinished vessels, partially quarried by rude flint tools, remain in the solid rock. As Charles Frederick Holder says: "Here is the old workshop under the blue sky, with its unfinished work, its broken chips and pieces strewn about, the flint tools of the workmen here and there, telling a fascinating story of the possibilities of the human savage when thrown entirely upon the natural resources of a land where the only metals are gold and silver, and where—in place of iron—shell, stone, and wood were used for all purposes."

The trellis work covering the garden walk and the willow trees at the washing place are to be found both at Camulos and Guajome, as, doubtless, at a score of old time ranch-houses in Southern California.

The "carved oaken chairs and benches" (Chapters II and XIX) are a slight stretch of the imagination, or, at least, the reader most probably will deceive himself into imagining them more beautiful and elaborate than any that I have ever found at either Missions or ranch-houses. By the catchword of a clever commercial advertiser, the American people have been led to imagine that the Missions originated a distinctive style of furniture. I have photographed every piece of old furniture now known to exist in the whole chain of Missions from San Diego to Sonoma, and think I know every representative piece. The engraving showing a mission chair is as good as any, except pieces that are avowedly Oriental or European. They are all crude and solid, and such carvings as they bear are rude and of slight artistic merit. Hence it will be seen that the term "Mission," as applied to modern furniture, is a misnomer. It should be called "Craftsman," after its original designer and inventor, Gustav Stickley, the founder and editor of that useful magazine of democratic American art, The Craftsman.

In Chapter II the occupation of San Luis Rey Mission by United States troops is referred to. This is an historic fact. In 1847 the Mormon Battalion,—a branch of Kearny's Army of the West—under the command of Colonel St. George Cooke, was established there for two months, and later on a re-enlisted company occupied it for a short time.

The removal of the statues, etc., by the faithful sacristan here applies to the house at Guajome, though there is every reason to believe that in all of the pillaged Missions some faithful soul was found who did the same thing. The dilapidation of the figures is true to fact. Many are to be found at the various Missions that vividly reveal the rough handling they have suffered. Others have been restored. Here again fact and fiction are skilfully blended,—fact as to the shabby figures of the saints, fiction as to the Señora Moreno's feelings about them: "That one had lost an eye, another an arm, that the once brilliant colors of the drapery were now faded and shabby, only enhanced the tender reverence with which the Señora knelt before them, her eyes filling with indignant tears at the thought of the heretic hands which had wrought such defilement."

The jealousy that existed between the Franciscans and the Catalan priests (see Chapter II) is no fiction, and the possibility of an order being issued forbidding the monks going to and fro in California became an actual fact. The reason is clear to those familiar with this phase of California history. The Franciscans were mainly devout adherents to the throne of Spain. When Mexico threw off her allegiance to Spain, and California became a province of Mexico, the Franciscan priests, (as well as all others), were required to swear allegiance to the new powers. Few of them did so. Some were banished and forcefully removed. Others were allowed to remain on sufferance, though the order of banishment might at any time have been enforced, and, now and again, was threatened, as Mrs. Jackson states.

Then, too, it should be noted that most of the large California ranch-houses belonging to devout Catholics had their own private chapels, where the traveling priests held services as often as they came. This devotion to Mother Church is too apt to be overlooked or forgotten, and in this money-loving and materialistic age it is well to consider the habits of an age that had much good in it we could wish we had not lost.

The description of the Señora's wedding (Chapter II) is a truthful portrayal of such an event, and the beautiful ceremony at the Santa Barbara Mission was seen by many, a few of whom are still living. What a pretty scene, and impressive, when, "on the third day, still in their wedding attire, and bearing lighted candles in their hands, they walked with the monks in a procession, round and round the new tower, the monks chanting, and sprinkling incense and holy water on its walls, the ceremony seeming to all devout beholders to give a blessed consecration to the union of the young pair, as well as to the newly completed tower."

The procession at San Luis Obispo, described in this chapter, is said actually to have occurred. Padre Luis Antonio Martinez was one of the most beloved and well known of the Franciscans. For thirty-two years he labored at San Luis Obispo, commencing his service in 1798, and the cloth of his Indian looms, the flour from his Indian mills, and the mules and horses bred by his Indian *vaqueros* were the best in the territory. Several of the early American traders tell of their dealings with him, and always speak highly of his jolly good nature, and his generosity in trade. He was undoubtedly a bluff, hearty, outspoken man, free in his criticisms of men and affairs, and this led to his banishment. In my *In and Out of the Old Missions* I state that this was for smuggling. While this was one of the charges brought against him, further study has shown that he was tried before a military court on various charges, mainly bearing upon his fidelity to the Spanish throne, and on his open avowal that he was still faithful, and that he had supplied food to the Spanish soldiers when they demanded it of him, he was condemned to exile, placed on board an English vessel, sent to Callao and finally returned to Spain.

The description of the *padre's* procession of poultry is characteristic of the man, and is one of the finest bits of *genre* in words in California (or any other) literature.

The distress and activity of the Señora Moreno (Chapter II) "during the height of the despoiling and plundering of the Missions, under the Secularization Act," were very real facts in several lives. Protestants as a rule are not aware of the deep devotion felt for their church by Catholic women, and to many, in those days, it seemed as if death would be preferable to seeing the ruin of the Missions they had learned to love so well.

In Chapter III the story of Ramona's birth is related and how she came into the Señora's hand, and I have shown in the chapter "Was there a real Ramona" the original of Angus Phail. San Gabriel is described in its own chapter, as is also the subject of the Jewels.

The statement that the fictitious Ramona was sent to the Convent of the Sacred Heart in Los Angeles, has led to the distribution of a photograph of the crude wooden building used in the early days as the home of this Convent with a legend to the effect that this is the "School attended by Ramona in Los Angeles." In Chapter VIII it is said she had one year at school with the nuns, and the sweet simplicity of her life is attributed largely to the early teachings that she had received from the lips of these devoted women. After the Señora had made the discovery, to her so terrible, that Ramona and Alessandro loved each other, she thought of nothing else at first than sending "the shameless hussy" to the nuns for safe keeping and further instruction, and nothing shocked and astounded her more during that heated interview she had with her adopted daughter (Chapter XI) than Ramona's defiance of her when she declared "I can shut you up in the nunnery to-morrow, if I choose."

The vision of the restoration of the Missions seen by Father Salvierderra (see Chapter IV) was shared by many of the monks. It seemed to them incredible that the system they had labored for so many arduous years to build up should be allowed to crumble to pieces so easily, and especially when the awful effect of the change upon the Indians was observed. But things inexplicable are often allowed to go on in this world, and the utter demolition of the Mission system was one of them.

When Mrs. Jackson makes the good old monk reply to Ramona's loving watchfulness (Chapter IV) that he should ride and not walk,—"It was the rule of our order to go on foot,"—she refers to St. Francis's rule; "they (the friars) shall not ride unless compelled through necessity." A California Franciscan friar thus comments on these words, showing how the order interprets the rule as conditions change. "That is all St. Francis says on the subject. We vow this rule, hence it is a great obligation. The term St. Francis uses in Latin means riding on horseback. By implication, because St. Francis insisted that his friars should pass 'through the world in humility and modesty' and above all, because he would have nothing to do with money and forbade his sons to have anything to do with it, the Popes have declared that any kind of conveyance is forbidden save in case of necessity. What degree of necessity is required, is another question. There is a graver necessity required for horseback-riding, as a matter of course. For travelling in wagon, or cars, or ship, no such grave necessity is demanded, as is plain. St. Francis travelled by ship. He was placed on mule-back when ill. The circumstances must decide the matter,—the circumstance of time, which may be pressing, and at our time always is. Father Serra, like his brethren, walked, since they had time; but Serra, in illness, travelled from Cape San Lucas in Lower California to San Diego on horseback or muleback, as is plain, from Palou. It was well said by an old father now dead: 'The first rule of a Franciscan is obedience, the second is common sense.' Hence the rule still stands and is observed literally where possible, and in other cases is regarded as time and other circumstances permit."

The habit of Junipero Serra, the founder of the California Missions, is well known,—his refusal to ride, even when an animal was provided, from Vera Cruz to the city of Mexico; his walking with a diseased leg from La Paz to San Diego up the long weary miles of the peninsula, and his habit of walking, even up to the day of his death.

The description of the wild mustard (Chapter IV) is one of the most realistic, vivid and beautiful pictures in California literature, and only those who saw Ramonaland before the country was cut up into small farms and cultivated can imagine how exquisite a sight it was. To farmers the mustard is a great pest, and they do their best to exterminate it, for it seriously injures their grain crops, but to the outsider, who sees it only from the esthetic standpoint, it is as the lilies of the field which surpassed in gorgeous array even Solomon in all his glory.

The pretty custom of dropping down on the knees, referred to in this same chapter, is still observed by many devout Mexicans and Indians. The reverence to the priest, as an ambassador of God, and the implied request for a blessing is the acknowledgment of a simple soul that he relies upon God and is thankful for all help that can be given. How often has the man and woman of other faiths and no faiths felt an instinctive desire to bow or kneel in the presence of certain men (and women) and crave a blessing at their hands.

In the strong pictures of Margarita's trouble (Chapter IV) over the torn altar cloth, is another fine example of the blending of fact and fiction. The altar cloth at Camulos *is* torn,—*was* torn when Mrs. Jackson saw it in the chapel . . . But all the story about its having been torn by the dog in the artichoke patch, owing to Margarita's disobedience in placing it on the fence to dry, from whence the wind tossed it, is pure fiction.

And the artichoke patch. Many people think the artichoke a French importation of recent date, but the Spaniards and Mexicans of almost a century ago used this delicacy for food in California. To Mrs. Jackson the sight of a patch of these thistle-like growths would naturally be novel and interesting, and hence she could not refuse to use such good descriptive material when placed in her hands.

The old seed-vessels of the artichokes are just as beautiful as described in Chapter IX, and I have seen them used as wreaths for the statues of saints in several places.

At more than one California ranch-house the same inconvenient arrangement (described in Chapter IV) exists as at Camulos, where the dining-room and kitchen are on opposite sides of the courtyard. In those old days, when land and Indians to help were plentiful, no one seemed to give a thought to either conservation of room or energy. "Convenience" was a word not thought of in connection with a house of quality. It was reserved for *gringos* to introduce it, with other of their accursed customs, and apply it to their flats and apartment houses where a score of families herd together in a way unthinkable to the old time Señors and Señoras of Ramona's day.

The beautiful custom of singing a morning hymn was not uncommon in Catholic households (Chapter V) and only those who have been awakened from a sound and healthy sleep by its sweet and solemn strains can know the wonderful impression it makes upon both mind and soul. To me it brought back the days of my childhood when, as soon as breakfast was over, the whole family sat around the old-fashioned English fireplace, and sang "psalms and hymns and spiritual" as well as other songs, before the reading of the Word, and prayer. We may have progressed (!!) in many and material things, but in these means of educating and guarding the soul I am free to confess I am a reactionary and prefer the days that are gone by.

Some express surprise that Mrs. Jackson made of Alessandro a good singer. It was the most natural thing in the world for her to do, for many Indians—men, women, youths, maidens and young children—are fine singers, Miss Natalie Curtis, in her wonderful *Indian's Book,* gives a number of Indian songs, and she and I have listened a hundred times to Indian voices, untutored and uncultured, but rich, sweet, controlled and sensitive to a degree. Several times I have been touched to tears at hearing the Indians sing the songs taught them or their parents by the old *padres,* and none who have ever heard the Acoma Indians, of New Mexico, sing their native thanksgiving songs to Those Above will wonder at Mrs. Jackson's conferring upon her hero a rich, penetrating voice of sweetness and power.

Hence it was nothing out of place to make Alessandro a good singer, with so sweet and restful a voice that he soothed Felipe during his illness (Chapter VI).

At most of the Missions Indian choirs were organized and it was found that men, women, and children speedily learned the European methods of singing. At San Juan Bautista and several other places, orchestras, with violins, violas, etc., were organized, and the Indians taught to use the musical instruments of civilization, upon which many of them became expert performers. In the choir gallery of each Mission—always in the rear of the church—the choristers and orchestra (one or both) met at each service. The music book was a tremendous folio—there are five of them now at the San Luis Rey Mission—large enough to be seen by twenty or more singers standing around it (Chapter XIX). One of the fathers took his place as precentor, in front of the book, which was laid out on a large revolving stand, and thus, with his dusky choir around him, he directed the musical services of the church. Personally I have known several old Indians who were thus honored by being in the choirs under the *padres,* and they could never speak of the joy of those days without tears welling up into their eyes.

Mrs. Jackson refers to the use of the musical instruments in several places, in ***Ramona,*** and Felipe informs Ramona (Chapter V) that Alessandro "plays the violin beautifully . . . the old San Luis Rey music. His father was bandmaster there." Hence it would not be unreasonable to infer that he owned an old violin, given to him by Pablo, his father, for several of the *padres* were themselves accomplished violinists, and there is every reason to believe they brought their instruments with them from Spain. This would lay the foundation for the supposed "pawning" of the violin by Alessandro at the Hartsel store, as told in Chapter XVII.

Another surprise to many readers is that the author makes Pablo (Chapter V) "Father Peyris' right-hand man at the Mission; he kept all the accounts about the cattle; paid the wages; handled thousands of dollars of gold every month." Yet many Indians were made *mayor-domos* at the various Missions during the old *régime,* and not one is known to have defalcated or in any way violated his trust.

Pablo also managed (Chapter VII) "the Mission flocks and herds at San Luis Rey for twenty years, and few were as skilful as he." There was no limit to the trust placed in these superior Indians by the old *padres,* and men never lived who were more worthy of trust than they. Therefore, with this in view, it is natural that Alessandro is made to have had great experience with sheep. Juan Can tells the Señora (Chapter VIII), "I do marvel where the lad got so much knowledge, at his age. He is like an old hand at the sheep business. He knows more than any shepherd I have,—a deal more; and it is not only of sheep. He has had experience, too, in the handling of cattle. Juan José has been beholden to him more than once, already, for a remedy of which he knew not."

All this may be said truthfully today of the sheep-keeping Indians, such as the Navahos. They will herd sheep, and keep them in good condition, under adverse circumstances that would discourage and dishearten white men. Many Navahos own flocks running up into the hundreds, and there are not a few who own thousands. Horses and cattle, too, are owned in large herds.

In regard to the evictions, they have been treated of in another chapter. As Mrs. Jackson says in one of her letters to Mr. Kinney, she placed the Temecula eviction wrongly in point of time, for dramatic effect. Otherwise every slight detail in ***Ramona*** is based upon actual occurrences, and few things in the annals of Irish evictions can surpass some of these details in their hideous cruelty.

In Chapter V the sheep-shearing has actually commenced. Many Indian bands of sheep-shearers used to roam the country, exactly as described in ***Ramona,*** and each one elected its captain. They were generally expert shearers, not to be outdone by Spaniard or Mexican.

Baling machines were unknown in those days, and the baling of the fleeces was done as described in this chapter. No wonder that the heat, dust and stench overpowered the half-sick Felipe, so that he fainted, brought back his illness and thus made it possible for Alessandro, through his singing and playing, to be brought and kept in close association with Ramona.

Then Juan Canito had to break his leg (Chapter VI). I wonder if Mrs. Jackson dreamed that in describing his sensations she was picturing what she herself was to suffer so soon, as her letters reveal.

All through the pages of ***Ramona*** are statements that surprise those who are unfamiliar with the real Indian as he was in the days of the *padres.* Take the faithful watching of Alessandro (Chapter VI) when Felipe was so ill. "Faithful as a dog," may well be paraphrased into "faithful as an Indian," to those who *know.* Never shall I forget the look of sweet tenderness and anxiety that shone in the eyes and face of an old Havasupai Indian, as I stood on the edge of a three thousand foot high precipice and looked down into the gorge at the junction of the Grand and Havasu Canyons. As he put one arm around me, holding onto a rock with the other, he said: "You are *aico*—my white friend—and it makes me cold at the heart to see you run such a risk." And when, afterwards, I talked to him about it, he said: "I love you, my f'end," and putting his hand over his heart, he said, "You my f'end, I your f'end; I feel bad when you put yourself in danger."

The references to the fêtes on the Saints' Days (Chapter VI) are interesting. Every Indian village has its patron saint, San Juan (Saint John) San Esteban (St. Stephen), San Pedro (St. Peter), or some other, and each saint has his own feast day. On the feast day of their particular saint the villages have their great annual *fiesta,* and if one could have seen these *fiestas* in the old days, before the Indians were so spoiled by the evils of our civilization, he certainly would have enjoyed a wonderful experience. In Arizona and New Mexico, in less accessible regions, and where white influences have not so thoroughly penetrated, these *fiestas* could have been witnessed ten, twenty years ago, and I have seen many of them. A service is held in the church—mass, if the priest is there—then the figure of the patron saint is taken down from over the altar, put into a convenient cabinet for carrying, over which a rich canopy is placed, and two or four sturdy Indians carry it aloft, preceded by an acolyte bearing the cross, at the head of the procession. Then come the singers and the great mass of the people. Round the village they go, finally depositing the statue in a temporary shrine near where the rest of the day's events occur. These consist of making thank-offerings to the gods at the shrine, dances (which are always sacred), singing, dramatic representations, racing, feats of horsemanship, the *gallo* race, where a rooster is buried up to the neck in the sand, and a hundred horsemen ride one after another at the highest speed, each leaning from his saddle and trying to pick up the wretched bird by the neck. The successful contestant is then followed by all the rest, laughing, shouting, shrieking, each trying to catch him and wrest the bird, in whole or in part, from him, while the eager spectators climb to the house tops, or any other point of vantage to watch how the good-natured conflict ends.

And one has but to read the annual reports of the Indian agents to the Commissioner of Indian affairs to see how true is the charge that "disorderly whites took advantage of these occasions to sell whiskey and encourage all sorts of license and disturbance." I have been at a Southern California *fiesta* where white men and Mexicans (the latter are just as bad, but no worse, than the former) have sold so much whiskey to the Indians that every man, woman and child was more or less under the influence of liquor, many of them beastly drunk, lying around in their *ramadas* (temporary brush shacks erected for the occasion) and yielding to the grossest sensuality. There is no denying the fact that when Indians *begin* to drink they do not know where to stop, and, while I am a firm believer in and upholder of all just and righteous laws, I am free to confess that it often seems to me that a coat of tar and feathers and being ridden out on a rail would be an impartial and just punishment for the wretches who, for the sake of paltry pelf, debauch the Indians with liquor.

The statues of the saints, referred to above, are several times spoken of by Mrs. Jackson in ***Ramona.*** The Indians regarded them with great veneration and could not bear to see them treated with disrespect. Alessandro is said once to have gone to San Fernando and "there he had seen in a room a dozen statues of saints huddled in dusty confusion." This used to be the fact at San Juan Capistrano before more appreciative priests in a later day took care of them. Mrs. Jackson undoubtedly saw these figures at San Juan and that suggested to her the idea that, in the story, Ramona would be delighted by Alessandro's obtaining one of these neglected statues. This was done and the "saint" brought and placed in their humble Indian home.

When Alessandro was prevailed upon to remain to help take care of Felipe, the band of sheep shearers of which he was the captain decided to vote for the election of a new one. This is the universal habit of election to office, whether a minor and voluntary chieftanship, as in this case, or in the case of the captainship of the village. Each village has its *capitan, alcalde,* (or judge), and sheriff. All are elected subject to the approval of the Indian agent, who, if he is not satisfied with the elected one, either appoints a new officer or orders a new election. Where there is a faction of the Indians opposed to the white man's methods, his schools, his churches, etc.,—*hostiles,* as they are termed,—and the *hostiles* outnumber the *friendlies,* this vetoing power of the agent is often called upon. In some cases, as for instance among the Yumas, the line of demarcation has been so clearly outlined that the two factions would have nothing to do with each other, and a state of open and avowed war has existed. The same has been even more strongly marked in some of the Hopi pueblos of northern Arizona, where United States troops have several times been called upon to aid the agent to quell the disturbances caused by the enmities of the friendly and hostile factions.

At Yuma, the *hostiles,* for years, refused to have any doings with the *friendlies.* Their *powwows* or councils were held separately, and whatever the *friendlies* did was sure to be opposed and criticized by the *hostiles.*

At one time all the villages of one language or *stock* in Southern California elected a head chief, or general, but this was found to work disadvantageously to the plans of the agents, so it was discouraged and finally forbidden. The General, by uniting all the forces of his people, could often circumvent the action of white people of some influence, or could prevail upon the whole tribe to follow some prescribed course of action. Now, there is no head chief. Mrs. Jackson refers to this in Chapter VII.

In my book *What the White Race may Learn from the Indian* I have told of some of the things wherein the Indian race may teach us. Most of these things Mrs. Jackson has presented in the pages of ***Ramona.*** Felipe was a highly cultured gentleman, yet we read (Chapter VII): "If Juan had been told that the Señor Felipe himself had not been more carefully trained in all precepts of kindness, honorable dealing, and polite usage, by the Señora, his mother, than had Alessandro by his father, he would have opened his eyes wide. The standards of the two parents were different, to be sure; but the advantage could not be shown to be entirely on the Señora's side. There were many things that Felipe knew, of which Alessandro was profoundly ignorant; but there were others in which Alessandro could have taught Felipe; and when it came to the things of the soul, and of honor, Alessandro's plane was the higher of the two."

There is nothing in our national treatment of the Indians that has cut them more to the quick than our assumption that they had no honor, no character, no truth. It was bad enough to rob them of their lands, their homes, their hunting grounds, but to rob them of their character and to let it go on record that they were without honor or any spiritual development was an injustice as cruel as it was criminal. In the finer instincts there are many Indians who are far ahead of most white people. In Chapter VII Mrs. Jackson shows Alessandro to be offended when Ramona offered to pay for the messenger that he had sent for his violin, and Felipe exclaims: "You couldn't have offended him more. What a pity! He is as proud as Lucifer himself, that Alessandro."

Yet even Felipe did not understand when (Chapter VII) commenting on the hospitality of Pablo, who "feeds and supports half his village" and who will never see one of his Indians go hungry so long as he has anything," he says: "Of course they have learned it partly from us." The Indians have a standard of generosity or hospitality so far above that of the white man that it cannot be placed in comparison,—it is beyond compare—and it was theirs long before a Spaniard had even trodden the shores of this Continent.

In Chapter VIII is a remark that few white readers of ***Ramona*** would value at its full significance. Alessandro is talking to Juan Canito and says: "My father is many years older than you are, and he rules our people to-day as firmly as ever. I myself obey him, as if I were a lad still." In that truthful statement is an exaltation of the Indian race and a rebuke to our own. We forget that age entitles to reverence. Our youth care nothing for gray hairs and the experience of age, and their irreverence is ghastly and horrible to a truly thoughtful soul. Yet with every Indian, in his natural state, the aged are treated with reverence and respect. Young men and maidens do not flippantly pass by their counsel and advice, nor laugh at their warnings and suggestions.

When it comes to a recognition of the simple and natural laws of health, Mrs. Jackson shows her keen appreciation of the Indians' actual superiority over the white race. Alessandro, desirous of helping Felipe back to health, "meditated a bold stroke." He knew that nowhere, indoors, no matter how well ventilated a room might be, was the air as pure and health-giving as it was outside, where it was vitalized and vivified by the sun and wind. "I should be as ill as the Señor Felipe," he says, "if I had to stay in that room, and a bed is a weakening thing enough to pull the strongest man down. Do you think I should anger them if I asked them to let me bring Señor Felipe out to the veranda and put him on a bed of my making? I'd wager my head I'd put him on his feet in a week."

That is it! The real apostle of the out-of-doors and the healthy life is the Indian. He has lived it for centuries and *knows,* and we are just beginning, with our open-air sleeping porches, our outdoor sleeping places for consumptives, our outdoor athletics and the like to understand that the Indian knows a great deal more about health and how to maintain it than we do.

Languishing for lack of air and the sun though he was, even the keen and loving eyes of the Señora were blind to Felipe's needs, and when Alessandro boldly asked her if he might remove Felipe out of doors for: "With us, it is thought death to be shut up in walls, as he has been so long. Not till we are sure to die, do we go into the dark like that," she hesitated. "She did not share Alessandro's prejudice in favor of fresh air." She even exclaimed the senseless and universal cry of white people, "Surely it is not well to sleep out in the night?" and I doubt not that thousands of readers of ***Ramona*** could not swallow the statement of Alessandro when he replied and *told the strict truth:* "That is the best of all, Señora. I beg the Señora try it. If Señor Felipe have not mended greatly after the first night he have so slept, then Alessandro will be a liar."

And Felipe but responded naturally to the pure instinct within him when he cried out: "That is just what I needed. This cursed bed racks every bone in my body, and I have longed for the sun more than ever a thirsty man longed for water. Bless you, Alessandro. Come here, and take me up in those long arms of yours, and carry me quick. Already I feel myself better." And better he quickly became. Indeed he was soon himself again. The time will come when sensible people will look back upon our civilized(!) sleeping and living habits of to-day with blank amaze. They will be unable to comprehend how we could exist and remain indoors, and especially how we could deprive ourselves of the joy of outdoor sleeping. A house without a place for outdoor sleeping of all its inmates is incomplete, and a hospital without outdoor places for the beds of every patient is a crime and a cruelty. At the St. Helena Sanitarium the hospital bedrooms are connected with large, wide porches by sliding windows, so that every patient's bed, without any trouble, and at a moment's notice, can be wheeled out into the sun and air. *These* are God's remedial and health agents, more than surgeons, physicians, nurses and all the drugs and nostrums of the pharmacy. Yet we have had to learn the lesson from the despised Indians, and we are so obstinate that millions of us in the great United States haven't learned it yet. Those who continue to remain obstinate, however, will soon die off, and then, perhaps, the new generation will see a little more clearly.

As for the rawhide bed, Alessandro does not over-estimate its virtues as compared with the ordinary bed, especially those that sag in the middle after the fashion of a hammock. The harder the bed, in reason, the more comfortable, after a little while to get used to it, and *always* the more healthful.

In Chapter VII Alessandro tells of the speed and strength of the Indian pony or bronco: "They can go a hundred miles in a day, and not suffer." This fact has been a source of surprise to many familiar with the limitations of horses in the Eastern climate. These creatures are so tough that they seem tireless, and their achievements are almost beyond the belief of those who do not know them.

With her ready sympathy with all nature it would not have been possible for Mrs. Jackson to neglect the dove of Southern California. In Ramona's day they were to be found in vast numbers. The sportsman and pot-hunter of the civilized race are rapidly exterminating them. Exquisitely and beautifully the dove is woven into the story. Alessandro, heart-hungry and sick for Ramona, who was locked up by the hard-hearted Señora, was comforted (Chapter X) by Felipe and "the notes of two wood-doves, that at intervals he heard, cooing to each other; just the two notes, the call and the answer, 'Love?' 'Here.' 'Love?' 'Here,'—and long intervals of silence between. That is what my Ramona is like, the gentle wood-dove. If she is my wife my people will call her Majel, the Wood-Dove."

When (Chapter XV) Ramona is trying to get Alessandro to call her by her long used name he finally tells her, at her questioning, why he gave her the name Majella—pronounced Mah-yhel-la, with a soft emphasis on the second syllable—and continues: "The wood-dove's voice is low like yours, and sweeter than any other sound in the earth; and the wood-dove is true to one mate always."

Again, when Ramona was asleep in the solitude of the canyon, and Alessandro sat watching her, the doves sing their sweet messages of comfort to him (Chapter XV).

Joaquin Miller, in one of his sweetest poems gives us:

> Come, listen, O Love, to the voice of the dove,
> Come, harken and hear him say
> There are many To-morrows, my Love, my Love,
> There is only one To-day.
>
> And all day long you can hear him say
> This day in purple is rolled,
> And the baby stars of the milky way
> They are cradled in cradles of gold.
>
> Now what is thy secret, serene gray dove
> Of singing so sweetly alway?
> "There are many To-morrows, my Love, my Love,
> There is only one To-day."
>
> "The Voice of the Dove"

Alessandro (Chapter XIX) introduces Ramona to his people at the village of San Pasquale as Majel, the wood-dove, and with a stroke of finesse that is wonderfully Indian, he commends her by saying: "She is glad to lay down her old name forever, to bear this new name in our tongue."

Even on the last page of the book Mrs. Jackson lovingly dwells upon the call of the wood-dove and Ramona's name, Majella, associating it in Ramona's mind with the loving devotion she gave to her dead Alessandro.

Nothing in the pages of ***Ramona*** is more truthful to fact than the running away of Ramona and Alessandro to be married,—their childlike and simple acceptance of each other. They had no thought of being "compromised" or of any person being so unclean-minded as to think evil of them. Had the novelist been writing of white people such an act would have been construed into a proof of vilest evil. George Eliot, in her *Mill on the Floss,* makes Stephen Guest and Maggie Tulliver, out for a boat-ride, glide so far away on an outgoing tide that they cannot return home, and Stephen, who has long loved Maggie, urges her to go on further and marry him. Maggie yields, but finally decides that a marriage with Stephen would bring much misery to others and she will return home. When she declares this Stephen shows her that by their act the world will believe they are already married, and if they dare to return and say they are unmarried, "you don't know what will be said."

And Maggie's brother sees in this act that which is worse than death,—disgrace, so that when he sees Maggie he greets her: "You will find no home with me. You have disgraced us all. You have disgraced my father's name. You have been a curse to your best friends. You have been base—deceitful; no motives are strong enough to restrain you. I wash my hands of you for ever. You don't belong to me!"

And Tom Tulliver's standard is the generally accepted one of the white race. Think of it. What a conception we have of the honor and purity of our sons and daughters that we *assume*—the whole race takes it as a matter of course—that, given the opportunity to be impure, the crime is as good as committed.

As for me, give me the standard of the Indian, as indicated in the story. I do not want to believe evil of even my enemies, much less my friends, unless I am compelled to do so, and I am grateful to Mrs. Jackson for the lesson thus forcefully read to the white race in the beautiful, simple, exquisite way she treated the elopement of her hero and heroine.

Another touching and beautiful scene in ***Ramona*** is where the oldest woman of San Pasquale is brought to see the new-comer (Ramona) and pass judgment upon her (Chapter XIX). This scene reveals much of Indian character, and Mrs. Jackson's sympathetic and intuitive comprehension of it. Without this comprehension she could not have written as she did. I have seen just such old women, women so withered and shriveled as to be scarcely human, yet when they spoke they uttered words of wisdom, words of serene judgment that were listened to with great respect by their fellow villagers.

When Ramona fled from Camulos she had two of the "large nets which the Indian women use for carrying all sorts of burdens. They are woven out of the fibres of a flax-like plant, and are as strong as iron. The meshes being large, they are very light; are gathered at each end, and fastened to a band which goes around the forehead. In these can be carried on the back, with comparative ease, heavier loads than could be lifted in any other way." The photograph shows one of the Cahuilla Indians carrying one of these nets, to which they give the Spanish name of *red* (pronounced, however, rayd'-ah). Into these Ramona placed Alessandro's violin, her own clothes, food, wine and milk for the journey, and when Alessandro brought her to her horse, Baba, he arranged these, one on each side of the saddle, before Ramona mounted.

There are several canyons which might have been the one Mrs. Jackson had in mind where she made the lovers sleep. . . . Out-of-door sleeping in these places is growing more common each year. In the canyons and on the foothills often grow profusely the *yucca whipplei,* described in Chapter XVI, and which the old Spanish *padres* used to call "Candlesticks of our Lord," because of their exquisite radiance of light and beauty.

The description of Ramona's out-door bed (Chapter XVI) is so much like what Indians have prepared for me in Southern California that I am sure Mrs. Jackson must, at some time during her own trips to the Indians, have had a similar bed for herself. "Before nightfall of this, their first day in the wilderness, Alessandro had prepared for Ramona a bed of finely broken twigs of the manzanita and ceanothus, both of which grew in abundance all through the canyon. Above these he spread layers of glossy ferns, five and six feet long; when it was done, it was a couch no queen need have scorned."

The manzanita is one of the best known shrubs of California. It is plentiful everywhere. With its rich purple brown stems, delicately green leaves and crown of pale foliage, it is exquisitely beautiful, but when, in addition, it is dotted here and there with its clusters of fragrant waxen flowers, like tiny fairy bells, it becomes enchanting. Sometimes it blooms before Christmas, and thus gives to the mountains and canyons the earliest tastes of spring's exuberant beauty. The name is Spanish *manzana,*—apple, and the diminutive *ita,* thus, little apple, so called because of the resemblance its berries have to tiny apples. These red berries give the shrub its botanic name—*arctostaphylos*—or Englished "bearberry." The bears are very fond of them and eat them ravenously, though to our taste they are dry, fibrous and "not worth the trouble of eating." The Indians, however, like them, and eat them both raw and pounded into a flour, from which they make mush. The flavor is pleasantly acid, and they make excellent jelly. On my last visit to the Thomas Ranch, before my good old friend, Charles Thomas, left it to go to reside in Redlands, his daughter, Emma, known and beloved alike by Spaniards, Mexicans, Indians, cowboys, miners, visitors, tourists and residents, gave me a jar of it to bring home. It is a delicious jelly, with a distinctive flavor of the wild mountains and canyons.

It was the ceanothus that Alessandro placed "at the head for Majella's pillow," for it is rich and spicy in odor, and is often called spice-wood. The children also call it "old man." There are a number of varieties of ceanothus, a common one, *integerrimus,* sometimes covering the lower slopes of the Southern California ranges with its white bloom almost like drifted snow. Others grow somewhat taller and have a lilac-tinted bloom, while the commonest of all, perhaps, the *divaricatus,* have a light-blue flower sometimes toned down to almost pure white. The leaves of these shrubs all have the useful quality of saponacity. If one takes a handful of them down to a mountain stream, and there rubs them vigorously as though they were soap, he will find his hands soon covered with a plentiful lather sweetly fragrant like wintergreen. The Indians use it largely, both for themselves and for washing their clothes, and it leaves the hands soft and fragrant, and gives to linen a snowy white appearance.

Capitan, the faithful dog, helped Alessandro watch the sleeping Ramona, and "more than once, spite of all Alessandro could do to quiet him, made the canyon echo with sharp, quick notes of warning, as he heard the stealthy steps of wild creatures in the chaparral."

Chaparral seems to be a general term used in California to describe any thick underbrush. For instance Theodore S. Van Dyke, in one of his books, says of the mountain brooks: "Farther up it divides into smaller brooks, that hiss with speed through winding glens, along whose sides the wild lilac pours forth a rich perfume from panicles of lavender and white; where the mountain mimulus hangs full of golden trumpets; where the manzanita outstretches its red arms full-hung with its little green apple-shaped berries, and the wild mahogany, aglow with a bloom of white or blue, unites with the bright-green cherry to form an almost impenetrable chaparral."

In another place he speaks of "a wall of bright-green chaparral higher than one's head and almost impenetrable," and still again: "The velvet hue that this chaparral gives the hills changes with the sunlight through a dozen shades from pea-green on the sunlit slopes at mid-day to the darkest blue on the shady ones at evening, and is a most restful change for the eye from the brown shimmering plains or bare red hills."

The hill on which the oak trees grew (Chapter XVII) not far from Hartsel's store, was a place well known to Mrs. Jackson. There are many fine live-oak trees covered with acorns and all people familiar with Indians know how large a place the acorn has in their diet. Pounded in a mortar until it is reduced to flour, it is mixed with water, and certain herbs and the bitter taste leached out. A bowl-shaped depression is made and covered or lined with muslin. Into this is poured the acorn flour-mixture. As the water steeps away, a mushy substance is left which is allowed partially to dry. It is then cut into strips and laid out on canvas or on the rocks to dry in the sun. When dry it is either stored away for future use, or pounded up again into flour to be made into mush, acorn-bread, tortillas or other forms of food.

The mountain lion, which Alessandro heard with some fear, while Ramona slept (Chapter XVI) is the *Felis Concolor,* the puma, or panther. It is a member of the cat family, and has all of the feline qualities. Hence the care with which Alessandro loaded his gun and watched the couch of his beloved señorita throughout the night.

I have already referred to the Hartsel store, and its owners. The descriptions given in ***Ramona,*** in Chapter XVII, are true to life.

On leaving Temecula, Ramona and Alessandro came out of the canyon of that name and got their first whiff of the sea, and Alessandro describes the charm of it to his Majella (Chapter XVIII). Mrs. Jackson was here reciting her own experience as she rode out of Temecula Canyon, and her own great fondness for the Pacific.

The lighthouse (Chapter XVIII) is on Point Loma, the point that shuts in the harbor of San Diego. It is a prominent landmark as well as a guide to the sailors. Seen from San Diego, Hotel del Coronado and all the surrounding country, it is a well-known object. Point Loma is where the theosophical headquarters, presided over by Katherine Tingley, are located, and the extensive and elaborate buildings of the brotherhood make of it a most noted place to members throughout the world.

There is little question but that Father A. D. Ubach, was the original of the Father Gaspara of ***Ramona,*** the San Diego priest who married the hero and heroine. In spite of his German name, he was of Spanish birth, for he was born in Barcelona, seventy-three years ago. He belonged to an old and distinguished Catalonian family. When about twenty-three years of age he came to this country and in Missouri continued the studies, begun in youth, for the Catholic ministry. In 1860 he was ordained and came to California, his first pastorates being San Luis Obispo and Watsonville. In 1868 he moved to San Diego and took up his residence in Old Town, in the house before referred to. When the present San Diego was built Father Ubach raised funds and erected a church, part of which stands in the present Catholic church. He also started to build a church in old San Diego but got little further than the foundations, just as related in Chapter XVIII. Mrs. Jackson dealt with this fact in a most sympathetic manner. She wrote, "A few paces off from his door stood the first begun walls of a fine church, which it had been the dream and pride of his heart to see builded, and full of worshippers. This, too, had failed. With San Diego's repeatedly vanishing hopes and dreams of prosperity had gone this hope and dream of Father Gaspara's. It looked now as if it would be indeed a waste of money to build a costly church on this site. Sentiment, however sacred and loving towards the dead, must yield to the demands of the living. To build a church on the ground where Father Junipero first trod and labored, would be a work to which no Catholic could be indifferent; but there were other and more pressing claims to be met first. This was right. Yet the sight of these silent walls, only a few feet high, was a sore one to Father Gaspara,—a daily cross, which he did not find grow lighter as he paced up and down his veranda, year in and year out, in the balmy winter and cool summer of that magic climate."

His faithfulness, unselfishness and devotion to the good of the Indians so commended him to them that in a few short years they gave to him a reverence and obedience little short of hero worship. His word was law among them. They came from as far south as San Rafael on the Peninsula, and from San Juan Capistrano on the north, for in the early years of his pastorate there was no priest at San Luis Rey. He had a peculiar "faculty" in handling even the most turbulent and troublous of the Indians. One secret of his power was that, while slow to make up his mind, he never altered a determination when once arrived at. This gives to any man, who in other things meets their approval, great power, and such, undoubtedly, Father Ubach possessed over the whole of the Indians of his large jurisdiction. Never making his work a burden to their pockets, his parishioners soon came to understand it was their highest good he was seeking and they revered him accordingly. He died in San Diego, in March, 1908, beloved and mourned of all who knew him. Mrs. Jackson's description of him was real and true to life: "Father Gaspara had been for many years at San Diego. Although not a Franciscan, having, indeed, no especial love for the order, he had been from the first deeply impressed by the holy associations of the place. He had a nature at once fiery and poetic; there were but three things that he could have been—a soldier, a poet, or a priest. Circumstances had made him a priest, and the fire and poetry which would have wielded a sword or kindled a verse, had he found himself set either to fight or to sing, had all gathered into added force in his priestly vocation.

"The look of a soldier he had never quite lost—neither the look nor the tread, and his flashing, dark eyes, heavy black hair and beard, and quick, elastic step seemed sometimes out of harmony with his priest's gown. Among the Mission Indians his word was law and their love for him was little short of worship."

The house at old San Diego, described in Chapter XVIII, is the one occupied by the priest on his visits there, and thousands of photographs of it have been sold as "the house where Ramona was married," and likewise, similar thousands have been marked and sold of "the chapel where Ramona was married," and of "the bells that rang when Ramona was married." The old house is there, the chapel is there, and the bells are there, so why not make use of them? So the photographer has utilized them to his profit. But the purchaser of the pictures seems to have forgotten that Ramona was married only in the brain of Mrs. Jackson, and that therefore these real bells can scarcely have rung at a fictitious marriage of a fictitious Ramona to a fictitious Alessandro by a fictitious priest after a fictitious elopement from a fictitious home of a fictitious Señora Moreno. But, all the same, we reproduce the photographs of the house, the chapel, the bells, and the olive trees and palms, all of them at old San Diego, and made of interest to us by their introduction into the story of Ramona. A reason for the error of the statement that Ramona was married at the house of the priest is found in Chapter XVIII.

At several of the Missions the old registers (Chapter XVIII) are to be found, and in all of those where the Missions were founded by Padre Junipero Serra, the revered president of the California Missions, the title page is always in his own hand. It is a striking and distinctive handwriting, and at the close of his signature will be observed his *rubric*. This rubric is found after the signature of all men of his race and day, each one distinctive and individualistic. It acted as a kind of seal,—a personal confirmation of the signature.

The loving power the Franciscans held over the Indians was well understood by Mrs. Jackson, and she makes Father Gaspara, not a Franciscan, comment upon it (Chapter XX). The sorrow of Ramona over the death of Father Salvierderra is not at all overdrawn.

When Felipe goes off in search of Ramona he is made to hear many tales of the devotion of the Indians to their old *padres* (Chapter XXV), and it is an historic fact that Father Sarria died at Soledad of starvation, refusing to leave his Indians to the wolves of secularization.

The devotion of the San Luis Rey Indians to Padre Peyri is truthfully told in Ramona (Chapter XVIII). They would do anything for him, and the true story of their swimming out to the vessel that was to remove him from their sight forever is a pathetic proof of their deep affection.

That Mrs. Jackson viewed the Indians with a calm and rational mind and did not idealize them by refusing to see evil in any of them is evident in several pages of ***Ramona,*** especially in Chapter XVIII where she tells of the wicked Indian overseer at San Gabriel, who clipped off the ears of the renegades. In the chapter on San Gabriel is related B. D. Wilson's account of his campaigns against these renegades. There is no doubt that too stern treatment occasionally drove some of the Indians to desperation; then they fled to the mountains, became outlaws and had to be proceeded against as such.

All Southern California Indians have a dread of earthquakes. The great *temblor* of 1812 which slew thirty-nine Indians in the great new Mission at San Juan Capistrano was another reminder of the instability of the ground and served to keep alive their fears. They seemed to be an inheritance. In the chapter "Was there a Real Ramona?" it will be recalled that Doña Victoria, Hugo Reid's Indian wife, would never go upstairs on account of her fears of earthquake.

I well remember being at Warner's Ranch after an earthquake a few years ago which shook down the wall of an adobe house in Saboba and killed several Indians. In all my conversations with the Indians they would not come into the adobe school-house. They were afraid. It had been somewhat shaken. They dreaded sending their children to school, lest another *temblor* should come and tumble the heavy bricks and the roof down upon their boys and girls to their injury or death.

The Hot Springs referred to in Chapter XXII are existent not far from San Jacinto. Of late years they have become very popular amongst the whites, as also have many other similar springs. There are those at Arrowhead, Palm Springs, Elsinore, and Warner's Ranch, and these are but few of the many that used to be prized by the Indians of Ramona's country for the benefit they were to them when sick or diseased.

Mrs. Jackson's keen observation is revealed in many pages of ***Ramona,*** and in Chapter XXV is another illustration of it. As Aunt Ri and Felipe go up to see the sick Ramona at Cahuilla they pass many pines on Mt. San Jacinto and "on many of them the bark had been riddled from root to top, as by myriads of bullet-holes. In each hole had been cunningly stored away an acorn,—the woodpecker's granaries." To thousands of visitors to Southern California this is an interesting sight, for it is by no means uncommon to see these acorn-filled trees wherever pines abound.

The "old man" or wild wormwood used by Aunt Ri (Chapter XXV) to restore Ramona to health is very abundant in Southern California. It resembles what in the East is called southernwood, but has a different odor.

When all that I have written above in this chapter is considered, in connection with other chapters dealing with the facts used in the story, I think the ingenuous mind will readily concede that ***Ramona*** is a story largely of fact, though its hero and heroine are fiction, and that in the larger truth which lies behind all human life it can truthfully be said that ***Ramona,*** though a work of fiction, is a work of essential truth.

John R. Byers, Jr. (essay date 1975)

SOURCE: "The Indian Matter of Helen Hunt Jackson's *Ramona*: From Fact to Fiction," in *American Indian Quarterly,* Vol. 2, No. 3, Autumn, 1975, pp. 331-46.

[*In the following essay, Byers contends that factual descriptions included in* Ramona, *especially those concerning Ramona and Alessandro's flight and search for security, closely mirror information Jackson had submitted as part of her Mission Indian report.*]

In 1881 Helen Hunt Jackson published her ***A Century of Dishonor,*** one of the most scathing indictments of the United States Government on the treatment of the Indian population, or on any other charges, ever put forth. The work was the outgrowth of a rising feeling, beginning in 1872 when she traveled in California and shortly afterwards to Colorado where she finally made her home, that the American Indian was in worse shape than the slave had been.[1] Mrs. Jackson became extremely conscious of the fact that, according to the surrounding white population, the Indian had no rights whatever and that governmental concern was practically nil. The actual catalyst to her work for the Indians was a lecture in 1879 in Boston, where she heard "Standing Bear" and "Bright Eyes," whom she later met in New York, tell their tales of the mistreatment of the Poncas.[2] After months of gruelling research in the Astor Library in New York, she saw her work come from the press. So great was her faith in the book and so intense were her feelings on the subject that she presented at her own expense a copy to each member of Congress.[3] The indictment did not, however, accomplish what she desired; the situation remained unchanged.

Although Congress did not take any sort of action on Mrs. Jackson's treatise, the Department of the Interior, in 1882, did honor her by appointing her and Mr. Abbot Kinney of Los Angeles to investigate the conditions and needs of the Mission Indian of California. For Mrs. Jackson this appointment was a remarkable opportunity to further her work. To the reading public the appointment was also important, for the record of her travels was to be eventually the source for one of the most popular pieces of literature ever published in America, the novel ***Ramona.***[4]

During the spring of 1883, Mrs. Jackson and Mr. Kinney visited most of the tribes of the Mission Indians. They moved from village to village, often into the mountains, to observe the Indians in their daily life, to hear their stories of woe, and to investigate their treatment by the whites. Sometimes they talked with whole tribes; sometimes with a group of chiefs; sometimes with only individuals. In a few short months they were able to collect enough data to write a comprehensive report. It is a business-like document, filled with cold facts, impressions, descriptions of various sorts, short episodes, and suggestions; and, more important, it is interesting simply as a piece of literature. A quality unusual in a report, it is well-written, being not merely the findings of a person intent on accumulating facts. For Mrs. Jackson, who is said to have written practically the whole report,[5] this was one of the most important tasks in her life. This was the first time that she had worked from primary sources; therefore, she wanted her work to achieve its purpose.

Such, however, was not the case. A new Secretary of the Interior had entered office, and, unfortunately for Mrs. Jackson, he believed in the rapid exploitation of the Western resources. Her report was quietly laid away and forgotten.[6] For the second time, she saw her work fail. Still determined, however, she began another project—to create a work of fiction using her California Indian report as a basis.

When Mrs. Jackson began on December 1, 1883, to write her ***Ramona,*** she was as one possessed. She had a mission to accomplish, and that mission was to lay before the American public, not just a group of legislators, the many and great wrongs done to the American Indian. So burning was this sense of duty and so well did she have the story transfixed in her mind, that she wrote on February 5, 1884, "As soon as I began, it seemed impossible to write fast enough. In spite of myself, I write faster than I would write a letter. I write two thousand to three thousand words in a morning, and I *cannot* help it. It racks me like a struggle with an outside power."[7] And later, from her deathbed in 1884, she wrote, "I did not write ***Ramona;*** it was written through me. My life blood went into it—all I had thought, felt, and suffered for five years on the Indian question."[8]

Although Mrs. Jackson said that she "did not write ***Ramona,***" the statement is not completely true, because she had written only six months earlier in her Mission Indian report the seeds for the whole story as it is found in the novel. The relationship between the novel ***Ramona***[9] and the **"Report of the Conditions and Needs of the Mission Indians of California,"** made by Special Agents Helen Jackson and Abbot Kinney, to the Commissioner of Indian Affairs,[10] is, indeed, a close one.

Mrs. Jackson's **"Report"** is fifty-six ordinary pages in length. The first part (sixteen pages) is the main body of the document, being a history of the Mission Indians, the location of various tribes, their position under both the Mexican and American governments, the general nature of the people, recommendations concerning education, divisions of reservations, rights, agencies, and the purchase of specified tracts of land. In this section Mrs. Jackson presents an overall picture of the Indians, generalizing a great deal and treating individuals only rarely. There are few descriptions of places and almost no definite incidents of mistreatment on the part of the whites. It is as if she had intentionally made this section of the document as cold as possible, as if she had consciously kept out any undue amount of sentimentality.

The second part of the **"Report"** is made up of what Mrs. Jackson called "Exhibits." There are eighteen of these exhibits, lettered "A" through "R." The divisions, whose average length is from two to four pages, treat the various tribes or groups of importance that Mrs. Jackson and Mr. Kinney visited. Included in these sections are descriptions of particular tribal locations, of villages, and individuals, and, most important of all, definite examples of mistreatment. It is chiefly, then, in these exhibits, which are treated in a much more emotional manner than the first sections, that the novel ***Ramona*** was born.

Ramona itself may, in general, be divided into two main scenes of action. The first scene is the ranch of Senora Moreno. It introduces the main characters, presents the basic conflict between races, describes life on one of the few remaining old Spanish haciendas, and prepares the way for the second part. Although this section is an essential part of the novel, it contributes almost nothing toward the campaign that caused Mrs. Jackson to write her masterpiece.

The second part becomes more involved. It deals with the flight of the Indian Alessandro, whose name was probably taken from the main body of the **"Report"** (p. 468), and the half-Scottish, half-Indian Ramona. In their flight and search for security the couple visits the Temecula village, the Pachanga cañon, San Pasquale, the village of Saboba, and finally the secluded cabin in the San Jacinto Mountains. For Mrs. Jackson this part of the novel is her final and best work on behalf of the Indians. Here she succeeded where earlier she had failed.

Since the first half of the novel treats only slightly Mrs. Jackson's problem, it is the second part which is her chief concern.

The misfortunes of Alessandro and Ramona begin when the two vow to become man and wife, and Senora Moreno, although she is a friend of the Indians, forbids the marriage. The couple cannot be dissuaded, and their elopement will take place as soon as Alessandro returns from the home in the Temecula village. He is delayed, however, and upon returning relates his tragic story. It is told in a passionate manner, but still truthfully as Mrs. Jackson knew it.

> "Dearest Senorita! I feel as if I should die when I tell you,—I have no home; my father is dead; my people are driven out of their village. I am only a beggar now, Senorita. . . ."
>
> (***Ramona,*** p. 236).

> "There was no battle. There would have been, if I had had my way; but my father implored me not to resist. He said it would only make it worse for us in the end. The sheriff, too, he begged me to let it all go on peacably, and help him keep the people quiet. . . . They thought there would be trouble; and well they might,—turning a whole village full of men and women and children out of their houses, and driving them off like foxes."
>
> (***Ramona,*** p. 237).

> "[The sheriff] said the judge had said he must take enough of our cattle and horses to pay all it had cost for the suit up in San Francisco. They didn't reckon the cattle at what they were worth, I thought; but they said cattle were selling very low now. There were not enough in all the village to pay it, so we had to make it up in horses; and they took mine."
>
> (***Ramona,*** p. 240).

Mrs. Jackson had written earlier in her **"Report"** concerning the Pachanga Indians who had been evicted from their old homes:

> This little band of Indians is worthy of a special mention. They are San Luisenos, and formerly lived in the Temecula Valley, where they had good adobe houses and a large tract of land under cultivation. The ruins of these houses are still standing there, also their walled graveyard full of graves. There had been a settlement of Indians in this Temecula Valley from time immemorial, and at the time of the Secularization of the missions many of the neophytes of San Luis Rey returned thither to their old homes.
>
> (**"Report,"** Exhibit M, p. 504)

And farther on she says in the **"Report":**

> In 1873 a decree of ejectment against these Indians was obtained in the San Francisco courts without the Indians" knowledge. The San Diego Union of September 23d, 1875, says on the subject:
>
> "For forty years these Indians have been recognized as the most thrifty and industrious Indians in all California. For more than twenty years past these Indians have been yearly told by the United States commissioners and agents, both special and general, as well as by their legal counsel, that they could remain on these lands. Now, without any previous knowledge by them of any proceedings in court, they are ordered to leave their lands and homes. The order of ejectment has been served on them by the sheriff of San Diego County. He is not only commanded to remove these Indians, but to take of their property whatever may be required to pay the costs incurred in the suit."
>
> (**"Report,"** Exhibit M. p. 505).

The words in Mrs. Jackson's **"Report,"** "The ruins of these houses are still standing here, also their walled graveyard full of graves," show to what extent she kept her feelings under control for the purely factual document. In the novel, however, she allowed her emotions to run freely. Of Alessandro's arrival at Temecula, she wrote:

> There Allessandro saw the roofless houses, and the wagons being loaded, and the people running about, the women and children wailing; and then they showed him the place where his father lay on the ground, under the tule . . . (***Ramona,*** pp. 250-251) . . . he turned their horses' heads in the direction of the graveyard. It was surrounded by a low adobe wall, with one small gate of wooden paling. As they reached it, Alessandro exclaimed, "The thieves have taken the gate!" (***Ramona,*** p. 286). The graves were thick, and irregularly placed, each mound marked by a small wooden cross. . . . When they reached the corner, Ramona saw the fresh-piled earth of the new grave. Uttering a wailing cry, Carmena, drawing Ramona to the edge of it, pointed down with her right hand, then laid both hands on her heart, and gazed at Ramona piteously. Ramona burst into weeping, and again clasping Carmena's hand, laid it on her own breast, to show her sympathy. Carmena did not weep.
>
> (***Ramona,*** pp. 287-288).

Earlier, on their way to Temecula, Alessandro and Ramona spend two idyllic days in a small hidden cañon that Mrs. Jackson depopulated for the two days. The essential descriptive elements can be located in two brief passages. They are:

> Alessandro had decided to hide for the day in a cañon he knew, from which a narrow trail led direct to Temecula,—a trail which was known to none but Indians. Once in this cañon, they would be safe from all possible pursuit. (***Ramona,*** pp. 265-266). The cañon at its head was little more than a rift in the rocks, and the stream which had its rise in it was only a trickling spring at the beginning. It was this precious water, as well as the inaccessibility of the spot, which had decided Alessandro to gain the place at all hazards and costs. (***Ramona,*** p. 266).

This scene Mrs. Jackson was completely familiar with. After having observed the Los Coyotes Indians in their secluded home, she wrote in her **"Report:"**

> Five miles up from the head of the San Ysidro Cañon, to be reached only by a steep and narrow trail, lies a

small valley on the desert side of the mountains. It is little more than a pocket on a ledge. . . . Few white men have ever penetrated to it, and the Indians occupying it have been hitherto safe, by reason of the poverty and inaccessibility of their home. (**"Report,"** Exhibit F, p. 490).

Upon finding his home destroyed and his father dying Alessandro assumes the leadership of the tribe and suggests that they move to the Pachanga cañon. Part of the tragedy lies with Carmena, whose husband is buried in the Temecula graveyard and whose child Alessandro helps to bury at Pachanga. In relating the incident after Ramona's question, he describes the place with a hopeless air:

"Where is Pachanga?" asked Ramona.

"About three miles from Temecula, a little sort of cañon. I told the people they'd better move over there; the land did not belong to anybody, and perhaps they could make a living there. There isn't any water; that's the worst of it." (***Ramona,*** p. 242).

Concerning the Indians following their removal, Mrs. Jackson wrote briefly and with no show of emotion in her **"Report"** the whole sorrowful story:

A portion of these Temecula Indians, wishing to remain as near their old homes and the graves of their dead as possible, went over in the Pachanga cañon, only three miles distant. It was a barren, dry spot; but the Indians sunk a well, built new houses, and went to work again. (**"Report,"** Exhibit M, p. 505).

From the Temecula episode Alessandro and Ramona move to San Pasquale, the second of the settings in the flight portion of the novel. In introducing the village for the first time to the reader of ***Ramona,*** Mrs. Jackson commented:

San Pasquale was a regularly established pueblo, founded by a number of the Indian neophytes of the San Luis Rey Mission at the time of the breaking up of the Mission. (***Ramona,*** pp. 272-273).

Mrs. Jackson, feeling that the San Pasquale situation was of such importance (the village had suffered the same fate as Temecula), treated this location in the main body of the "Report." In describing the settlement for the Department of the Interior, she used almost the same words:

This San Pasquale village was a regularly organized Indian pueblo, formed by about one hundred neophytes of the San Luis Rey Mission, under and in accordance with the provisions of the Secularization Act in 1834. (**"Report,"** Main body, 460).

For the purpose of the novel, in picturing a romantic little village, Mrs. Jackson goes into great detail, filling the passage with lyric beauty:

When they rode down into the valley, the whole village was astir. The vintage-time had nearly passed; everywhere were to be seen large, flat baskets of grapes drying in the sun. Old women and children were turning these, or pounding acorns in the deep stone bowls; others were beating the yucca-stalks, and putting them to soak in water; the oldest women were sitting on the ground, weaving baskets. There were not many men in the village now; two large bands were away at work,—one at the autumn sheep-shearing, and one working on a large irrigating ditch at San Bernardino.

In different directions from the village slow-moving herds of goats or of cattle could be seen, being driven to pasture on the hills; some men were ploughing; several groups were at work building houses of bundles of the tule reeds. (***Ramona,*** p. 327).

Describing the village in the **"Report,"** she used only one sentence stripped of all literary merit, but the facts are the same.

These Indians had herds of cattle, horses, and sheep; they raised grains, and orchards and vineyards. (**"Report,"** Main body, p. 460).

Alessandro and Ramona live happily for awhile at San Pasquale, but their happiness is not to be enjoyed for long. The storm clouds begin to gather. This time, Mrs. Jackson does not, however, let the couple suffer the mistreatment; it is Ysidro, their friend, who is the victim of the whites.

Ysidro, it seemed, had the previous year rented a cañon, at the head of the valley, to one Doctor Morong. It was simply as beepasture that the Doctor wanted it, he said. He put his hives there, and built a sort of hut for the man whom he sent up to look after the honey. Ysidro did not need the land, and thought it a good chance to make a little money. He had taken every precaution to make the transaction a safe one. . . . Now, the time of the lease having expired, Ysidro had been to San Diego to ask the Doctor is he wished to renew it for another year; and the Doctor had said that the land was his, and he was coming out there to build a house, and live. (***Ramona,*** p. 345).

Ysidro had gone to Father Gaspara for help, and Father Gaspara had had an angry interview with Doctor Morong; but it had done no good. The Doctor said the land did not belong to Ysidro at all, but to the United States Government; and that he had paid the money for it to the agents in Los Angeles . . . (***Ramona,*** pp. 300-301).

Mrs. Jackson seems to have created this incident from two separate incidents that she had included in her **"Report."** She borrowed slightly from the section on the San Ysidro Indians, in which a cañon is wrested from them by a man named Chatham Helm and which is ultimately used for a bee business (**"Report,"** Exhibit E, p. 489). The main source, however, is an incident which happened on the Cahuilla Reservation and which Mrs. Jackson heard when she visited that place. The incident, as related in the report, reads:

A few rods from the hot spring there stood a good adobe house, shut up unoccupied. The history of this house is worth telling, as an illustration of the sort of troubles to which Indians in these remote regions, unprotected by the Government, and unable to protect themselves, are exposed. Some eight years ago the Cahuillas rented a tract of their land as pasture to two Mexicans named Machado. These Machados, by permission of the Indians, built this adobe house, and lived in it when looking after their stock. At the expiration of the lease the house was to be the property of the Indians. When the Machados left they said to the

> Cahuilla captain, "Here is your house." The next year another man named Thomas rented a pasture tract from the Indians and also rented this house, paying for the use of it for two years six bulls, and putting into it a man named Cushman, who was his overseer. At the end of the two years Thomas said to the Cahuillas, "Here is your house; I now take my cattle away." But the man Cushman refused to move out of the house; said it was on railroad land which he had bought of the railroad company. In spite of the Indians' remonstrances he lived on there for three or four years. Finally he died. After his death his old employer, Thomas, who had once rented this very house from the Indians, came forward, claimed it as his own, and has now sold it to a man named Parks. Through all this time the Indians committed no violence on the trespassers. They journeyed to Los Angeles to find out from the railroad company whether Cushman owned the land as he said, and were told that he did not. They laid the matter before their agent, but he was unable to do anything about it. (**"Report,"** Exhibit C, 482).

Treating the incident in ***Ramona,*** Mrs. Jackson, here, has turned her wrath not upon the Indian agents, but directly upon the government in Washington. Of the agents she said in the novel:

> They were not inhuman, and they felt sincere sympathy for this man, representative of two hundred hard-working, industrious people, in danger of being turned out of house and home. . . . These officials had neither authority nor option in the matter. They were there simply to carry out instructions, and obey orders. (***Ramona,*** p. 348).

After the Ysidro episode it is not long before Alessandro and Ramona are caught in the middle of the storm. A white man comes into the valley and says to Alessandro who is ploughing an extra field in hopes of harvesting a larger crop:

> "Look here! Be off, will you? This is my land, I'm going to build a house here."
>
> Alessandro had replied, "This was my land yesterday. How comes it yours to-day?"
>
> Something in the wording of this answer, or something in Alessandro's tone and bearing, smote the man's conscience, or heart, or what stood to him in the place of conscience and heart, and he said: "Come, now, my good fellow, you look like a reasonable kind of a fellow; you just clear out, will you, and not make me any trouble. You see the land's mine. I've got all this land round here;" and he waved his arm, describing a circle; "three hundred and twenty acres, me and my brother together, and we're coming in here to settle. We got our papers from Washington last week. It's all right, and you may just as well go peaceably, as make a fuss about it. Don't you see?" (***Ramona,*** p. 354).
>
> The man is embarrassed by Alessandro's plight and says:
>
> "Of course, I know it does seem a little rough on fellows like you, that are industrious, and have done some work on the land. But you see the land's in the market; I've paid my money for it." (***Ramona,*** p. 355).

He does agree to pay two hundred dollars for the crops and farm equipment. Alessandro accepts the pittance and with a breaking heart prepares to leave.

In creating this incident Mrs. Jackson has again borrowed from two separate incidents. The matter of the two hundred dollars is probably taken from her record of the Indians living in Los Coyotes Valley, which she had used earlier as the small cañon to which Alessandro and Ramona first fled. She reported:

> About three weeks before our arrival at Warner's Ranch a man named Jim Fane, a comrade of Helm, who usurped the San Ysidro Cañon, having, no doubt, learned through Helm of the existence of the Los Coyotes Valley, appeared in the village and offered the Indians $200 for their place. They refused to sell, upon which he told them that he had filed on the land, should stay in any event, and proceeded to cut down trees and build a corral. (**"Report,"** Exhibit F, p. 491).

The characterization, however, comes from the main body of the **"Report,"** which in one instance concerns the San Pasquale tribe:

> In 1873 one of these special agents, giving an account of the San Pasquale Indians, mentioned the fact that a white man had just pre-empted the land on which the greater part of the village was situated. He paid the price of the land to the register of the district land office, and was daily expecting his patent from Washington. "He owned," the agent says, "that it was hard to wrest from the well disposed and industrious creatures the homes they had built up; but" said he, "if I had not done it, somebody else would; for all agree that the Indian has no right to public lands." (**"Report,"** Main body, pp. 459-460).

From San Pasquale, then, Alessandro, Ramona, and their child move on, this time toward the San Jacinto Mountains. At this point in the novel, Mrs. Jackson must have decided that she had not given full rein to her feelings. The only way in which she could do this was to create a special character whose main duty would be to feel sympathy for the Indians and disgust for the whites. Therefore, she created Aunt Ri, who at first has the typical white attitude toward the couple, but who is won over by the blue-eyed child and who in time comes to love the couple and to begin her personal fight for the Indians. Aunt Ri is undoubtedly Mrs. Jackson, but she also resembles a Mrs. Gregory who is mentioned briefly in the section on the Conejos Indians.

About Mrs. Gregory nothing is presented except her last name, the fact that the Indians were often in the habit of consulting her when they were in trouble, and that she would often ride horseback nine miles to be present at one of their councils. Then follows one of these councils in which a young Indian is being tried by the members of his tribe for having stabbed a white man who had attempted to take the young man's wife by force. Mrs. Gregory at the council presents an interesting picture; she expresses sentiments remarkably like those of Aunt Ri:

> Recounting the facts, the captain said to Mrs. Gregory, "Now what do you think I ought to do?" "Would you think he deserved punishment if it were an Indian he had stabbed under the same circumstances?" asked Mrs. Gregory. "Certainly not," was the reply, "we should

say he did just right." "I think so too," said Mrs. Gregory; "the Irishman deserved to be killed." But the captain said the white people would be angry with him if no punishment were inflicted on the young man; so they whipped him and banished him from the rancheria for one year. Mrs. Gregory said that during the eleven years that they had kept their cattle ranch in the neighborhood of this village, but one cow had ever been stolen by the Indians; and in that instance the Indians themselves assisted in tracking the thief, and punished him severely. (**"Report,"** Exhibit K, p. 501).

The families of Alessandro and Aunt Ri journey toward the San Jacinto Mountains and finally settle at the village of Saboba where Aunt Ri continues to extol the virutes of the Indians and to condemn the actions of the United States Government much as Mrs. Gregory had done earlier in the **"Report."** Alessandro describes the situation at the village:

"There is Saboba," he said, "at the foot of the San Jacinto Mountain . . . Majella [Ramona] would not like to live in it. Neither do I believe it will long be any safer than San Pasquale. There was a kind, good old man who owned all that valley,—Senor Ravallo; he found the village of Saboba there when he came to the country. It is one of the very oldest of all; he was good to all Indians, and he said they should never be disturbed, never. He is dead, but his three sons have the estate yet, and I think they would keep their father's promise to the Indians. But you see, tomorrow, Majella, they may die, or go back to Mexico. . . . " (***Ramona,*** pp. 377-378).

For the **"Report,"** Mrs. Jackson presented Saboba as it actually was after the fears that Alessandro held had in reality come true:

Saboba is the name of a village of Indians of the Serrano tribe, one hundred and fifty-seven in number, living in the San Jacinto Valley, at the base of the San Jacinto Mountains, in San Diego County. The village is within the boundaries of a Mexican grant, patented to the heirs of J. Estudillo, January 17th, 1880. The greater part of the grant had been sold to a company which, in dividing up its lands, allotted the tract where the Saboba village lies to one Mr. R. Byrnes, of San Bernardino, who proposes to eject the Indians unless the United States Government will buy his whole tract of seven hundred acres at an exorbitant price. . . . The Indians have lived in the place for over a hundred years. (**"Report,"** Exhibit B, p. 479).

Saboba cannot, however, offer Alessandro and Ramona safety for long. They find for awhile an uneasy happiness, but Ramona soon becomes conscious of danger which Alessandro has not been made aware of, the value of the water in the village.

One day she had heard a man say, "If there is a drought we shall have the devil to pay with our stock before winter is over." "Yes," said another; "and look at those damned Indians over there in Saboba, with water running all the time in their village! It's a shame they should have that spring!"

. . . . .

When she reached home that day she went down to the spring in the centre of the village, and stood a long time looking at the bubbling water. It was indeed a priceless treasure; a long irrigating ditch led from it down into the bottom, where lay the cultivated fields . . . (***Ramona,*** p. 391).

Mrs. Jackson also took note of these same things in her investigation. She was fully cognizant of the fact that the water actually constituted danger for the Indians. She wrote in the **"Report:"**

They have adobe houses, fenced fields and orchards, and irrigating ditches. There is in the village a never-failing spring, with a flow of about twenty-five miner's inches. It is claimed by the Indians that the first surveys did not take in their village. This is probably true; the resurveying of grants and "floating" their lines so as to take in lands newly discovered to be worthless, being a common practice in California. In a country where water is gold, such a spring as these Saboba Indians owned could not long escape notice or be left long in the undisturbed possession of Indians. (**"Report,"** Exhibit B, p. 479).

After the death of their child, Alessandro and Ramona again flee, this time high into the San Jacinto Mountains, their last hope in the search for security. At last the couple finds a small hidden valley where they build their final home and Ramona gives birth to their second child.

It was a wondrous valley. The mountain seemed to have been cleft to make it. It lay near midway to the top, and ran transversely on the mountain's side, its western or southwestern end being many feet lower than the eastern. Both the upper and lower ends were closed by piles of rocks and tangled fallen trees; the rocky summit of the mountain itself made the southern wall; the northern was a spur, or ridge, nearly vertical, and covered thick with pine-trees. (***Ramona,*** p. 418).

For the location of this scene Mrs. Jackson has used the information which she collected when she visited the Cahuilla Reservation. She seems to have used not only the description of the main valley in which the Cahuilla village was located, but also, perhaps slightly, a spot where the story from which the death of Alessandro is taken actually happened. The **"Report"** is as follows:

The Cahuilla Valley is about forty miles from Saboba, high up among the peaks and spurs of the San Jacinto Mountains; a wild, barren, inaccessible spot. (**"Report,"** Exhibit C, p. 481).

Then, relating the incident of the Indian Juan Diego, she wrote:

A Cahuilla Indian named Juan Diego had built for himself a house and cultivated a small patch of ground on a high mountain ledge a few miles north of the village. Here he lived alone with his wife and baby. (**"Report,"** Exhibit C, p. 483).

The characterization of Alessandro, his death, and the situation that follows are taken directly from the story of Juan Diego, the wording sometimes being the same. Of Alessandro, whose mind has been crushed because of his burdens, Mrs. Jackson says:

Slowly, so slowly that Ramona could not tell on what hour or what day her terrible fears first changed to an

> even more terrible certainty, his brain gave way. . . . He knew that he suddenly came to his consciousness sometimes, and discovered himself in strange and unexplained situations; had no recollection of what had happened for an interval of time, longer or shorter. But he thought it was only a sort of sickness; he did not know that during those intervals his acts were the acts of a madman; never violent, aggressive, or harmful to any one; never destructive. . . .
>
> Everybody in the valley knew him, and knew his condition. (***Ramona,*** pp. 422-423).

The **"Report"** though presented in a simpler manner is almost as vivid:

> He had been for some years what the Indians call a "locoed" Indian, being at times crazy; never dangerous, but yet certainly insane for longer or shorter periods. His condition was known to the agent, who told us that he had feared he would be obliged to shut Juan up if he did not get better. It was also well known throughout the neighboring country, as we found on repeated inquiry. Everybody knew that Juan Diego was "locoed." (**"Report,"** Exhibit C, p. 483).

Concerning the horse taken by Alessandro in a moment of madness, the novel reads:

> As he drew near, she saw to her surprise that he was riding a new horse. "Why, Alessandro!" she cried. "What horse is this?"
>
> He looked at her bewilderedly, then at the horse. True; it was not his own horse! He struck his hand on his forehead, endeavoring to collect his thoughts. "Where is my horse, then?" he said.
>
> "My God! Alessandro," cried Ramona. "Take the horse back instantly. They will say you stole it."
>
> . . . . .
>
> "I will ride back as soon as I have rested. I am heavy with sleep."
>
> . . . . .
>
> When she went into the house, Alessandro was asleep. (***Ramona,*** pp. 426-427).

The **"Report"** is practically the same:

> He came home at night riding a strange horse. His wife exclaimed, "Why, whose horse is that?" Juan looked at the horse, and replied confusedly, "Where is my horse, then?" The woman, much frightened, said, "You must take that horse right back; they will say you stole it." Juan replied that he would as soon as he had rested; threw himself down and fell asleep. (**"Report,"** Exhibit C, p. 483).

Then follows the murder in the novel:

> She was on the point of waking him, when a furious barking from Capitan and the other dogs roused him instantly from his sleep, and springing to his feet, he ran out to see what it meant. In a moment more Ramona followed,—only a moment, hardly a moment; but when she reached the threshold, it was to hear a gun-shot, to see Alessandro fall to the ground, to see, in the same second, a ruffianly man leap from his horse, and standing over Alessandro's body, fire his pistol again, once, twice, into the forehead, cheek. Then with a volley of oaths . . . he untied the black horse from the post where Ramona had fastened him, and leaping into his saddle again, galloped away, leading the horse. (***Ramona,*** p. 427).

And in the **"Report"**:

> From his sleep he was awakened by the barking of the dogs, and ran out of the house to see what it meant. The woman followed, and was the only witness of what then occurred. A white man, named Temple, the owner of the horse which Juan had ridden home, rode up, and on seeing Juan poured out a volley of oaths, levelled his gun and shot him dead. After Juan had fallen on the ground Temple rode closer and fired three more shots in the body, one in the forehead, one in the cheek, and one in the wrist, the woman looking on. (**"Report,"** Exhibit C, p. 483).

The incidents after the murder in the novel follow closely the bare outline in the **"Report."** Both Ramona and the wife of Juan Diego flee to the Cahuilla village for help. Both Temple and Farrar, the murderer in the novel, turn themselves over to officers of the law, and both swear that the Indian claimed the horse in question and that he brandished a knife. Both juries, called to investigate and pronounce judgment, free the murderer since the only witness to the crime is the murdered man's wife.[11]

Mrs. Jackson, with her feeling of a crusader, was not, however, content to let the situation remain as it appeared in the novel and thereby pass up such an opportunity for venting her wrath on the whites of the area. She deliberately brings Aunt Ri back into the picture. Thus, Mrs. Jackson's opinions in the **"Report"** concerning Juan Diego become Aunt Ri's opinions in the novel, but with numerous variations. The author even goes so far as to create a character in the last pages of the book simply to speak a few sentences that she had recorded in her **"Report"** and to present someone with whom Aunt Ri could argue.

Young Merrill, the newly created character, in justifying the murder, says:

> "'Twas a derned mean thing Jim Farrar did, a firin' into the man after he was dead. I don't blame him for killin' the cuss, not a bit; I'd have shot any man livin' that 'ad taken a good horse o' mine up that trail. That's the only law we stock men 've got out in this country. We've got to protect ourselves. But it was mean, low-lived trick to blow the feller's face to pieces after he was dead . . . (***Ramona,*** p. 458).

The lines from the **"Report"** that Mrs. Jackson insisted upon putting into the novel are:

> He not only justified Temple's killing the Indian, but said he would have done the same thing himself. "I don't care whether the Indian had a knife or not," he said; "that didn't cut any figure at all the way I looked at it. Any man that'd take a horse of mine and ride him up that mountain trail, I'd shoot him whenever I found him. Stockmen have just got to protect themselves in this country," . . . The utmost concession that he would make was finally to say, "Well, I'll agree that Temple was to blame for firin' into him after he was dead. That was mean, I'll allow." (**"Report,"** Exhibit C, p. 484).

After a comparison of the descriptions of places, the main actions, and in some instances the conversation in the novel with the **"Report,"** it is obvious that Mrs. Jackson had the document before her as she wrote ***Ramona.*** The **"Report,"** written to impress upon the minds of Congress the many wrongs done to the Indians, contained, without a doubt, the stories which were best suited to her purpose. One may also assume that the author knew more individual incidents than she chose to include in the document, but in choosing only the more vivid examples of mistreatment she more nearly accomplished the task that she set out to perform, i. e., to speak for the Indians. These vivid examples, then, are almost all transferred to the novel, given highly romantic settings and characters, and aimed at the United States Government whether that body was directly responsible or not.

Perhaps one of the most glittering facets of Mrs. Jackson's artistry lies in the skill with which Alessandro and Ramona are made to represent not simply individuals or even tribes of Indians, but all Indians. In their trials, they become the personification of all the unfortunate wards of the government. It is much as if Alessandro and Ramona had lived in or near all the villages that the author visited during her investigation and had been the principal protagonists in all the stories that she had heard. By placing the suffering on an individual basis, however, Mrs. Jackson has succeeded in making the action more intense and more condemnatory. In each case she has subordinated the total action to the action of one family or even of one man. In the novel the individual is always presented in the foreground, which presentation reduces a much larger wrong to a needle-sharp treatment of that wrong. Constructing her novel in this manner, Mrs. Jackson made it a work that spoke for the Indian as *Uncle Tom's Cabin* had earlier spoken for the Negro.

In general, the author remained true to her **"Report"** in all matters of importance. She did, however, modify or illuminate any scene or action that would add to the over-all effect of the novel. Without any hesitation she moved a whole tribe from a valley, because that particular valley was perfect for another scene. She followed the facts of the various incidents, but she had no compunction about shuffling those facts about a bit to obtain the desired picture. Considering the fact that Mrs. Jackson was a woman with a battle to fight, it is to her credit, then, that the story is essentially an accurate account of the Indian in his dealings with the government.

Ramona was an instant success. In 1886 it was declared "the best novel yet produced by an American woman," and there was doubt "whether in clearness of conception, purity of tone, individuality and pleasing contrast of character and intensity of emotion," it was excelled by an American writer.[11] Mrs. Jackson had started to write principally a novel with a purpose, or as Aunt Ri said, " . . . I jest wish the hull world could see what I've seen!" (***Ramona,*** p. 408). Instead, she became known as the author of one of the most moving love stories ever produced with a purely American setting.

Notes

1. Sarah A. Hubbard, "Helen Hunt Jackson," *Dial,* 6 (September, 1885), 110.
2. Elizabeth Porter Gould, "The Author of *Ramona,*" *Education,* 21 (November, 1900), 182-183.
3. ———, "How *Ramona* was Written," *Atlantic Monthly,* 86 (November, 1900), 712.
4. *Publishers' Weekly,* 120 (October 10, 1931), 1701-1702, records that *Ramona,* "since its original publication in 1884, has sold over 400,000 copies, without any low-priced popular editions" and "is still the then thousand per year class." Carey McWilliams, "Southern California: Ersatz Mythology," *Common Ground,* 6 (Winter, 1946), 29-38, cites the effect of the novel on Southern California and notes that between 1884 and 1946 the novel had sold 601,636 copies with the Los Angeles Public Library alone having purchased over a thousand copies. Andrew F. Rolle, ed., "Introduction," *A Century of Dishonor* (New York, 1965), xx, notes that *Ramona* has undergone three hundred printings and "countless stage and screen versions."
5. ———, "Mrs. Helen Jackson ("H. H.")," *Century Magazine,* 31 (December, 1885), 255.
6. Allan Nevins, "Helen Hunt Jackson, Sentimentalist vs. Realist," *American Scholar,* 10 (Summer, 1941), 276.
7. Cited in "How *Ramona* was Written," *Atlantic Monthly,* 86 (November, 1900), 713.
8. W. J. Harsha, "How *Ramona* Wrote Itself," *Southern Workman,* 59 (August, 1930), p. 370.
9. Helen Hunt Jackson, *Ramona* (Boston, 1885), pp. 1-490. Cited hereafter in the body of this paper.
10. "Report on the Condition and Needs of the Mission Indians of California, made by Special Agents Helen Jackson and Abbot Kinney, to the Commissioner of Indian Affairs," sent from Colorado Springs, Colorado on July 13th, 1883, appears as Appendix XV in Mrs. Jackson's *A Century of Dishonor* (Boston, 1890), pp. 458-514. Referred to hereafter as "Report" and cited in the body of the paper.
11. Albion W. Tourgee, "Study in Civilization," *North American Review,* 143 (September, 1886), p. 246.

Michael T. Marsden (essay date 1980)

SOURCE: "Helen Hunt Jackson: Docudramatist of The American Indian," in *The Markham Review,* Vol. 10, Fall, 1980, pp. 15-19.

[*In the following essay, Marsden presents a brief overview of Jackson's life and works and comments that it wasn't until Jackson became involved with Native American affairs that her remarkable writing abilities found an adequate outlet.*]

ToThe Memory of Helen Hunt Jackson: The Most Brilliant, Impetuous and Thoroughly Individual Woman of American Literature

What songs found voice upon those lips,
What magic dwelt within the pen,
Whose music into silence slips,
Whose spell lives not again!

For her the clamorous to-day
The dreamful yesterday became;
The brands upon dead hearths that lay
Leaped into living flame.

Clear ring the silvery Mission bells
Their calls to vesper and to mass;
O'er the vineyard slopes, thro' fruited dells,
The long processions pass.

The pale Franciscan lifts in air
The cross above the kneeling throng;
Their simple world how sweet with prayer,
With chant and matin song!

There, with her dimpled, lifted hands,
Parting the mustard's golden plumes,
The dusky maid, Ramona, stands,
Amid the sea of blooms.

And Allesandro, type of all
His broken tribe, for evermore
An exile, hears the stranger call
Within his father's door.

The visions vanish and are not,
Still are the sounds of peace and strife,
Passed with the earnest heart and thought
Which lured them back to life.

O, sunset land! O, land of vine,
And rose, and bay! in silence here
Let fall one little leaf of thine,
With love, upon her bier.[1]

"Helen Hunt Jackson," by Ina Coolbrith

We do not have to be reminded that Emerson once enthusiastically greeted a young, new poet by the name of Walt Whitman at the beginning of what he thought would be a promising career. But we have conveniently forgotten that the same Ralph Waldo Emerson once hailed Helen Hunt Jackson as "the greatest American woman poet."[2] Unlike Emerson, a number of her significant literary contemporaries, such as Nathaniel Hawthorne and Henry James, found her work worthy of severe criticism. Nonetheless, this woman writer, who became known affectionately as "Helen of Colorado," while not occupying a place in the various lists of major American authors, does have a secure place in the American imagination. To provide the critical light for a reconsideration of her contribution to American life and letters, one may compare her career to that of Harriet Beecher Stowe, whose literary and political reputation far outstripped Jackson's.

Helen Hunt Jackson was born in 1830 in Amherst, Massachusetts to Nathan Welbe Fiske (a professor of classics, moral philosophy, and metaphysics at Amherst College), and Deborah Vinal Fiske. After the death of her mother when Helen was fourteen, she was sent to live with an aunt who arranged her education at both the Ispwich Female Academy in Massachusetts and at the Abbott brothers' school in New York City. During these school years, Helen gained the lifelong friendship of schoolmate Emily Dickinson.

Early 1852 found Helen in attendance at the Inaugural Ball for the Governor of New York, where she met and subsequently was courted by the Governor's brother, Edward Bissell Hunt, an officer in the Army Corps of Engineers. They were married in the fall of that year and spent the majority of their subsequent eleven married years separated, partly because of her husband's far-flung military assignments and partly, according to some speculative sources, because of their differing temperaments. According to one of Helen's biographers, Minerva Louise Martin, Edward Hunt was hostile to the topic or person of abolitionists and forbade his wife from defending Harriet Beecher Stowe whenever she heard the famous author referred to in conversation as "that talented fiend in human shape."[3]

The Hunts had two sons, the first of whom was born in 1853 and died before his first birthday. Their second son was born in 1856 and died at the age of nine in 1865. Edward Hunt met with a fatal accident in 1863 while on duty. After the death of her first son and her husband, and shortly before the death of her second son, the widow apparently turned to literary pursuits to escape her grief. In 1864 she moved to Newport and there began to work more steadily at her literary efforts under the guidance of Colonel Thomas Wentworth Higginson, a nineteenth century American counterpart of Gertrude Stein. He emphasized writing as a lifestyle, and his one dictum was quantity.[4] Hunt's career was launched with the publication of her first prose piece in the *New York Evening Post* on October 18, 1865.

From 1865 until she published her now famous plea for Indian rights, ***A Century of Dishonor,*** in 1881, Hunt labored in various literary genres from children's stories to magazine essays, fiction, and poetry. She was a productive writer determined to make a living at it during a time when even the President of the United States found little to admire in women's writings:

> During his Presidency, Andrew Jackson entered his protest, assuring the world that the whole of the disturbances of his day had their origin in a source no larger than the nib of the pen of a lady.[5]

It was estimated that despite her reception by the literati, she earned an average of between $3,000 and $4,000 a year.[6]

During her early years as a writer, she developed, as Ruth Odell puts it, "a zest for a kind of game of anonymity,"[7] adopting such pen names as "Marah," "H. H.," "Rip Van

Winkle," and "Saxe Holm" at various points in her career. While a good part of her desire for anonymity can be traced to the contemporary opposition to women writers, the other part of the desire must be traced to her personality, which demanded a separation between her private and public selves until there came a time when a large enough cause, the rights of the American Indian, forced the two selves to become completely public.

From about 1865 until the first part of the 1880s, she traveled a great deal both in America and abroad, using those travels as was the literary habit as subject matter for essays, poems, and even book-length collections of essays, such as ***Bits of Travel.***[8]

A major change occurred in her life when, during the winter of 1873-74, on one of her trips she visited Colorado Springs, Colorado, for reasons of health, and there met William Sharpless Jackson, whom her biographers describe as a frontier gentleman and entrepreneur, involved in banking, railroading, and community development. They were married late in October of 1875, and Colorado Springs remained Helen's home until her death, thus earning her the affectionate title of "Helen of Colorado."

Unlike her first husband, William Sharpless Jackson encouraged her in her literary and social and political concerns. In fact, he apparently enjoyed sharing the limelight with such a famous woman. And Mrs. Jackson continued to travel with and without William.

In 1879, while on a trip to Boston, she discovered the cause that she had been seeking for so long, the cause that was to shape the remaining years of her life into a definite pattern. She heard a presentation by two Ponca Indians, Standing Bear and Bright Eyes, who were on a tour to arouse sympathy for their tribal plight: as a result of governmental error, the land of the peaceful Ponca Indians, who were farmers, was given to the Sioux. In New York in 1881 an acquaintance, J. B. Gilder, suggested to Jackson that "after the unsuccessful attempt by William Justin Horsha's Indian novel *Ploughed Under,* . . . she was the proper person to undertake such a story that would do for the Indian what Harriet Beecher Stowe's novel did for the negroes."[9]

From 1875 to 1880 Helen Hunt Jackson continued to write juvenile and magazine literature and even found time to write two novels in the famous "No Name Series" (so-called because as the published stated, "No name will help the novel, or the story to success"), ***Mercy Philbrick's Choice***[10] and ***Hetty's Strange History.***[11] In 1881 she postponed J. B. Gilder's proposal for an Indian novel and instead began working in the Astor Library in New York during the day and writing at a rapid pace at home at night on a non-fiction project which eventually became the 457-page ***A Century of Dishonor.***[12]

She turned to non-fiction to document for the American public the serious wrongs of the American government and people in past and present dealings with the American Indian. The volume carried a preface by Bishop H. B. Whipple of Minnesota and an introduction by Julius H. Seelye, President of Amherst College, both of which added to its already serious tone. When Congress convened in 1881, Congressmen were surprised to find on their desks copies of the volume bound in blood-red cloth and carrying the following quotation from Benjamin Franklin:

> "Look upon your hands! They are stained with the blood of your relations."[13]

Jackson was inundated with letters from readers testifying, much to her disappointment, to the brutality of the Indians whom they claimed did indeed massacre whites.

In his Preface to ***Century of Dishonor,*** Bishop Whipple reminded readers of the illogic of the Indian wars. More specifically, he repeated the battle statistics which were becoming popular: in the Indian wars ten white men were killed for every Indian, and the slain Indians cost the United States government $100,000 each.[14] But in that same preface, Whipple focused on an issue that, ironically, was the cause of the lack of success of ***Century of Dishonor,*** He wrote:

> No permanent reform can be secured until the heart of the people is touched. In 1862 I visited Washington, to lay before the Administration the causes which had desolated our fair State with the blood of those slain by Indian massacre. After pleading in vain, and finding no redress, Secretary Stanton said to a friend, "What does Bishop want? If he came here to tell us that our Indian system is a sink of iniquity, tell him we all know it. Tell him the United States never cures a wrong until the people demand it; and when the hearts of the people are reached the Indian will be saved."[15]

As Allan Nevins has written, "The literature of knowledge can never compete with the literature of power—if it really has power."[16] A year after the publication of ***A Century of Dishonor,*** the Indian Rights Association was created to rally public opinion around the Indian problem.[17] No causal connection can be made between the two events, however, and ***A Century of Dishonor*** remained a less-than-successful effort to alter national thinking and feeling on the question of Indian rights.

The publication of the volume did lead to Jackson's appointment by the federal government as a special commissioner, along with Mr. Abbot Kinney of Los Angeles, to study the condition and problems of the California mission Indians. By 1883, the commissioners had prepared a report of what they had learned. But even in this case, the political response was not positive enough to satisfy Jackson, and she began to look elsewhere for the vehicle to translate her concern for Indian rights into a national concern.

It was not surprising that she focused on the novel as a political vehicle, as had been suggested by her New York friend J. B. Gilder several years before and by the huge success Harriet Beecher Stowe had enjoyed. In 1883 Jackson wrote to her publisher:

> If I were to write a story with that title ("In The Name Of The Law")—all Indian—would you print it? I have never before felt that I could write an Indian story. I have not got the background. Now I have, and sooner or later I shall write the story. . . . If I could write a story that would do for the Indian a thousandth part of what Uncle Tom's Cabin did for the Negro, I would be thankful the rest of my life. . . . [18]

She realized, as did many other popular writers, that "felt history" was simply more successful, both politically and financially, than "understood" history, which did not have the power that personality-centered fiction could lend it. Her exhortation to the Congress in 1881 did little more than provide her with an effective title for her documented history of the denial of rights to the American Indian.

> What an opportunity for the Congress of 1880 to cover itself with a lustre of glory, as the first to cut short our nation's record of cruelties and perjuries! The first to attempt to redeem the name of the United States from the stain of a century of dishonor![19]

But her novel, ***Ramona,*** was to have a significant effect upon the American imagination.

Ramona was published the same year as *Huckleberry Finn, The Rise of Silas Lapham,* and *The Bostonians*—1885. To date there have been over three hundred printings of ***Ramona.***[20] One contemporary critic referred to the novel not "primarily as a novel with a purpose, but as a sweet and mournful poetic story" and "a prose Evangeline."[21]

Once Jackson had found her cause, she began to use her real name openly in connection with her writing, and for her ***Ramona*** certainly had a purpose. Critical response has been curious. For J. Frank Dobie, ***Ramona*** merely romanticized the Indian missions for tourists; the novel did not have an effect on the Indian problem.[22] Others, such as Carey McWilliams, have pointed out how the Chambers of Commerce in Southern California have helped to promote "Ramona country."[23] Louis Stellman referred to ***Ramona*** as "the *Uncle Tom's Cabin* of the Red Man, and the *Romeo and Juliet* of the Indian race."[24] For Dobie, Helen Hunt Jackson was "more dedicated to a cause than to craftsmanship."[25] Dobie seems to sum up a number of varying critical responses in two separate but related statements:

> Yet ***Ramona*** is authentic. No more authentic chapter exists in the great American determination to get away from reality than the ***Ramona*** legend. Her passion against wrong and for right will make her book live a long, long while yet. Called a historical novel, now it belongs to history.[26]

Yet one thing most critics will concede about the novel is that it has power, or in Allan Nevins's words, "it hit the mark."[27] Nevins argues that before she discovered her cause of Indian rights, Jackson lacked adequate outlet for her remarkable energies. The following passage from her correspondence would certainly seem to substantiate this claim:

> I did not write ***Ramona.*** It was written *through* me. My lifeblood went into it—all I had thought, felt, and suffered for five years on the Indian question. I shall never write another novel.[28]

For Nevins the book has "vitality." He writes:

> As a piece of local-color fiction ***Ramona*** still occupies a unique place in our literature and for a *tour de force* in its field still has remarkable power. Moreover Mrs. Jackson was a born storyteller, and in this swift, impetuous tale she keeps suspense at a high level. But the principal factor in the book's vitality is the poignancy of many of its pages. They were written from an overflowing heart; she was aflame with eagerness to expose wrongs, and despite passages of confusion and unreality the book as a whole leaves an impression of fiery truth.[29]

He credits her novel with being "largely responsible for the ease" with which, in 1887, the Dawes Act was enacted, the first really comprehensive and positive legislation to protect and advance the Indians.[30] Nevins suggests that she did accomplish with ***Ramona*** what she had intended to accomplish with ***A Century of Dishonor:***

> In looking back on the long, sad history of error and oppression marking our relationship with the Indian from the days of the Pequot War, we can point to her volume as eloquent evidence that at one period in our history a large body of Americans began to care, a large body began to be ashamed.[31]

But one easily senses that the social and political implications of the novel do not alone account for its success. Abigail Ann Hamblen, in her excellent "Ramona: A Story of Passion," comes somewhat closer to the whole truth when she writes:

> No one has recognized, apparently, that ***Ramona*** may be viewed as something more than a propaganda novel, or a piece of interesting local color. It may be seen as a poignant love story, a celebration of unabashed sexual passion. . . . But, express it or not, her novel is not casual about sex, either. Passion is there, deep and vibrant, and it is emphasized to the extent that for the modern reader it seems to take over the whole story.[32]

I would argue that ***Ramona,*** written and read within a clearly established sentimental tradition, allowed Helen Hunt Jackson to resolve several tensions existing in her own life as well as in American culture. She was able, finally, to allow her public and private selves to merge and display a deep human passion for unity with her fellow human beings, to share her sorrows and to acclaim, in less bold ways than Walt Whitman, the human body as well as the human spirit. It is impossible to read ***Ramona*** without experiencing the deep, sensual relationship between the lovers. This sensual passion is first prepared for through the story of Ramona's father, Angus Phail: denied in his passionate love for Ramona Gonzaga, Phail seeks solace with an Indian woman with whom he has a child, the Ramona of the novel. Jackson writes of Angus Phail's passion:

> Mad with love from the first to the last was Angus Phail; and there were many who believed that if he had

> ever seen the hour when he called Ramona Gonzaga his own, his reason would have fled forever at that moment, and he would have killed either her or himself as men thus mad have been known to do.[33]

This same "mad" passion exists between the young Ramona and her Indian lover, Alessandro, who is at one with nature. Animals trust him, and human beings respect him. Even their horses recognize the harmony in the passionate rhythms between Ramona and Alessandro:

> The horses were walking slowly, and very close side by side. Baba and Benito were now such friends they liked to pace closely side by side; and Baba and Benito were by no means without instinctive recognitions of the sympathy between their riders. Already Benito knew Ramona's voice, and answered it with pleasure; and Baba had long ago learned to stop when his mistress laid her hand on Alessandro's shoulder.[34]

Even Ramona and Alessandro's first born was a living example of their loving passion:

> . . . in this cradle, on soft white wool fleeces, covered with white homespun blankets, lay Ramona's baby, six months old, lusty, strong, and beautiful, as only children born of great love and under healthful conditions can be.[35]

One is tempted to comment upon the autobiographical significance of such passages, but that might obscure the real thrust of the novel—to humanize the American Indian, a prerequisite to any successful struggle for rights.

Locating the story in the California missions area was a wise and inevitable choice for Jackson. It was wise because it provided the distance in space, and to some extent in time, for the telling of a parallel story that her eastern readers would be otherwise reluctant to accept, even within the sentimental tradition, in its direct form. Making the enemy abstract governmental policy and not the settlers and focusing the story on particular families allowed readers to feel real, and often intense, empathy. The cruelty of Senora Moreno toward the young, innocent Ramona, the love of her foster brother Felipe for Ramona, the dedication of the mission priests, the passion and oneness with nature Alessandro displays, and the plight of the displaced Indians, all result in the reader's identification of himself with particular people caught up in a large, national problem. This process is none other than the one followed by docudramatists as they strive to record epic human moments in terms that can be strongly felt as well as understood. What Senora Moreno fears is not Ramona's marrying an Indian when she knows that Ramona is half-Indian herself, or even marrying below her state in life, but rather Ramona's giving herself to a passionate love affair. Helen Hunt Jackson is suggesting that Senora Moreno fears life itself, as perhaps the writer herself did. The epic nature of ***Ramona*** is clearly suggested in the final paragraph, which describes the future of Felipe and Ramona after they marry and move to Mexico following Alessandro's murder:

> Sons and daughters came to bear his name. The daughters were all beautiful; but the most beautiful of them all, and it was said, the most beloved by both father and mother, was the eldest one: the one who bore the mother's name, and was only step-daughter to the Senor,—Ramona,—Ramona, daughter of Alessandro the Indian.[36]

Ramona did not succeed in righting the wrongs against the American Indians. And in all fairness to the comparison with Harriet Beecher Stowe, we should remember that Stowe did have the Civil War to lend additional power to her "little book." But ***Ramona*** did move generations of Americans. The novel has remained a steady seller over the last hundred years, marking perhaps a century of developing honor for the American Indian. It is still widely read today, has been made into a motion picture four times, into an unsuccessful play once, and is the basis for an annual pageant in Hemet, California.[37]

But Helen Hunt Jackson died believing that she had not really succeeded in her mission. A few days before her death, she wrote the following letter:

> August 8, 1885
>
> To Grover Cleveland, President of the United States
>
> Dear Sir:
>
> From my deathbed I send you message of the heartfelt thanks for what you have already done for the Indians. I ask you to read my ***Century of Dishonor.*** I am dying happier for the belief I have that it is your hand that is destined to strike the first blow toward lifting this burden of infamy from our country and righting the wrongs of the Indian race.
>
> With respect and gratitude,
>
> Helen Jackson[38]

Helen Hunt Jackson may have turned to the profession of writing out of grief and a lack of purpose in her life. She was for more than a decade a writer in search of a cause, which, when she finally found it, consumed her. In the passionate process of her writing, she produced under her own name a volume of documentary evidence and a fictional docudrama of "fiery truth" which she thought would focus the national spirit on the Indian problem. Almost without being conscious of it, in ***Ramona*** Jackson gave us a human solution, a passionate love story. Helen Hunt Jackson is not a curious, minor American woman writer; she is an important American author whose power only her readers seem to be able to remember. On the eve of the hundredth anniversary of the publication of her ***A Century of Dishonor,*** Helen Hunt Jackson's work deserves a serious re-evaluation to determine if she has not in fact helped to give the American Indian and the American people a century of developing honor in the area of Indian rights.

Notes

1. Rpt. in Carlyle Channing Davis and William A. Alderson, *The True Story of "Ramona"* (New York: Dodge Publishing Company, 1914), pp. 259-260.

(They, in turn, cite as their source "Songs from the Golden Gate.")

2. Louise Pound, "Biographical Accuracy and 'H. H.'" (Notes And Queries), *American Literature,* II (January 1931), p. 418.
3. Minerva Louise Martin, *Helen Hunt Jackson In Relation To Her Times* (Unpublished Doctoral Dissertation, Louisiana State University and Agricultural and Mechanical College, 1940), p. 11.
4. Martin, p. 15.
5. Ruth Odell, *Helen Hunt Jackson: H. H.* (New York: D. Appleton-Century Company, 1939), p. 64.
6. Odell, p. 56.
7. Odell, p. 65.
8. (Boston: J. R. Osgood and Co., 1872).
9. Martin, p. 29.
10. (Boston: Roberts Brothers, 1876).
11. (Boston: Roberts Brothers, 1877).
12. Allan Nevins, "Helen Hunt Jackson, Sentimentalist vs. Realist," *American Scholar,* X (1941), p. 274.
13. J. Frank Dobie, "Helen Hunt Jackson and Ramona," *Southwest Review,* Volume XLIV (Spring 1959), p. 95.
14. Helen Hunt Jackson, *A Century of Dishonor* (Minneapolis: Ross & Haines, Inc.) (Reprint), pp. vi-vii.
15. *A Century of Dishonor,* pp. viii-ix.
16. Nevins, p. 278.
17. Nevins, p. 283.
18. Martin, p. 150 (from a letter to Thomas Bailey Aldrich, Los Angeles, May 4, 1883).
19. *A Century of Dishonor,* p. 31.
20. John R. Byers, Jr., "Helen Hunt Jackson (1830-1885)," *American Literary Realism, 1870-1910,* II (Summer 1969), p. 146.
21. Byers, p. 144.
22. Dobie, p. 94.
23. "Southern California: Ersatz Mythology," *Common Ground,* 6 (Winter 1946), pp. 29-38.
24. Martin, p. 164.
25. Dobie, p. 94.
26. Dobie, pp. 96, 98.
27. Nevins, p. 270.
28. Quoted in Nevins, p. 275.
29. Nevins, p. 281.
30. Nevins, p. 284.
31. Nevins, p. 285.
32. *Western Review,* Volume VIII (Spring 1971), pp. 22, 23.
33. *Ramona* (New York: Avon Books, 1970), p. 28.
34. *Ramona,* p. 234.
35. *Ramona,* p. 242.
36. *Ramona,* p. 349.
37. Martin, pp. 164-5.
38. Martin, p. 35. (The author's source, in turn, was A. N. Rollins, *Critic,* VII (1885), p. 193.)

Rosemary Whitaker (essay date 1987)

SOURCE: *Helen Hunt Jackson,* Boise State University, 1987, pp. 24–39.

[*In the following excerpt, Whitaker traces the beginnings of the author's interest in the Native American political cause, providing an overview of Jackson's nonfiction writing on the subject, including* A Century of Dishonor.]

By 1879 Jackson was restless and uncertain about the direction her writing should take. Late in the year she decided to return to the East to see if a change of environment would revitalize her. Her future was decided by a chance encounter. While visiting in Boston, she went to a reception sponsored by a group of prominent citizens who were alive with indignation over the U.S. government's treatment of the Indians. Their sentiment had been aroused by Thomas H. Tibbles, a reporter for the Omaha *Daily Herald* and founder of the Omaha Indian Commission. He had persuaded Ponca Chief Standing Bear and two Omaha Indians, the brother and sister Susette (Bright Eyes) and Frank LaFlesche, to join him on a lecture tour to educate Americans about injustices and to raise money specifically for the Ponca tribe.

Jackson heard at the reception that in 1817 the United States government had moved the Poncas from their ancient lands in the East to the mouth of the Niobrara River in Nebraska. In 1858 a second treaty had reduced their lands. Then soon after gold was discovered in the Black Hills, they were ordered to give up all their remaining land and move to Indian Territory 1,000 miles south. The tribal leaders were able to get one concession from the government: ten chiefs would go to look at the land, and if they were not satisfied, they could have an audience with the President of the United States. The chiefs traveled to Indian Territory, where they found land they considered barren and untillable; but when they asked to see the President, their request was denied and they were abandoned in Indian Territory without food or money.

In the meantime soldiers had forced the tribe to begin the journey south. Chief Standing Bear and his brother, who had remained with the tribe, refused and were jailed, then forced onto the wagons. Many of the tribe died on the way south. Finally Standing Bear and thirty others ran away and headed back to Nebraska, where they were arrested. Through his newspaper, Tibbles informed the world. He also obtained a writ of habeus corpus and freed the jailed Indians by arguing their rights as free citizens. However, having been recognized as free, no longer wards of the government, the Indians faced starvation. Tibbles then set out to raise survival funds.

While in California and Colorado, Jackson had not shown any interest in the Indians. As her travel sketches show, she regarded the few she had seen as "abject" and "loathly." But suddenly she underwent a remarkable transformation. She wrote to her friend Moncure Conway:

> I have done now, I believe, the last of the things I have said I would never do. I have become what I have said a thousand times was the most odious thing in the world, "a woman with a hobby." I cannot help it. I think I feel as you must have felt in the old abolition days. . . . I believe the time is drawing near for a great change in our policy toward the Indians. (Banning, *Jackson* 149)

No cause had ever before received Jackson's support. She had been openly critical of women who appeared on lecture platforms, had no sympathy for suffrage, and not even Higginson had been able to enlist her on the side of liberal causes. Yet suddenly she had a crusade, and it became the dominant force of her life. She helped form the Boston Indian Citizenship Association, traveled with Tibbles, Standing Bear, and the LaFlesches, and began to gather data about government treatment of the Indians. As her essays espousing the Indian cause appeared in newspapers and magazines, she became embroiled in letter wars, notably with William N. Byers, a former editor of the Denver *Rocky Mountain News,* who took exception to her description of the Sand Creek Massacre, and with Carl Schurz, United States Secretary of the Interior, who was aroused by her attacks on government policy and practice. The government position was that, though the Poncas' loss of land was an injustice, returning them to Nebraska was not the solution; rather they should be helped to make a suitable home in Indian Territory. Opponents, including Jackson, vigorously attacked all policies of resettlement to alien territories.

Jackson's prominence led to a contract with Harper and Brothers for a factual exposé of Indian mistreatment. She did exhaustive research in the Astor Library in New York City, which held John Jacob Astor's collection of Western resources. She told Charles Dudley Warner that her book would be "simply and *curtly* a record of our Broken Treaties," and concluded, "I never so much as dreamed what we had been guilty of" (Mathes, "Jackson" 64).

Jackson's ***A Century of Dishonor*** was published in 1881. Two distinguished men contributed prefatory essays. H. B. Whipple, bishop of the Episcopal Church of Minnesota and a long-time advocate of Indian policy reform, calls the Bureau of Indian Affairs "a blunder and a crime" and the Indian Wars "needless and wicked." He lauds Jackson for attempting to secure justice for "a noble and a wronged race," and espouses Christianity as the hope for the Indians' future; for though noble, they are still heathen: the wigwam must be replaced by the Christian home. Julius H. Seelye, the president of Amherst College, blames the government for not civilizing the Indians, for treating them as wards and taking their means of subsistence while shutting them off on reservations. He, too, believes the solution is "an entire change of these people from savage to a civilized life," accomplished through "wise and Christian treatment."

In her own introduction Jackson states her purpose as to give sketches of the history of a few tribes "to show the repeated broken faith of the United States Government toward them." She wants to appeal to the "heart and conscience of the American people," for "What the people demand, Congress will do" (30). Jackson described the first chapter to a friend as "simply a lawyer's brief on the original right of occupancy. . . . I have been through all the law authorities in the Astor Library on these points . . . and I have read this chapter to two lawyers who say there is not a waste word in it and that it is a strong brief" (Odell, *Jackson* 167). Her argument is that the United States has rights under the theory of sovereignty and the Indians under the theory of occupancy. Thus the United States is obligated to treat the occupants without oppression, develop "firm and binding" treaties, and ultimately bring the occupying peoples into the nation as "subjects and citizens."

She then focuses on seven tribes—the Delawares, Cheyennes, Nez Perces, Sioux, Poncas, Winnebagoes, and Cherokees—and describes in detail the government's treatment of each tribe. The chapters are a litany of treaties made in bad faith by the government, of tribes driven to alien and barren lands, of inevitable bloody clashes. Jackson repeatedly condemns the indifference, ignorance, and greed which she cites as the motivations for the ill treatment. She is especially harsh toward agents and the military who, in her view, used their power to subjugate rather than help and defend. In her chapter on the Sioux, her indignation breaks forth in scathing sarcasm. In describing the treaty to remove them from Minnesota, she states that the government instructed the agents to offer two to two and a half cents an acre, defending the offer as the "desire to give these Indians an equivalent of their possessions" but no more than an equivalent, for "it is the government's humanity and duty . . . not to place much money at their direction." Jackson sharply replies, "The government is beginning very well in this direction, it must be admitted, when it proposes to pay for Mississippi Valley lands in Minnesota only two and a half cents per acre. 'Humanity and duty' allied could hardly do more at one stroke than that" (148).

In a chapter following those on the seven tribes, Jackson describes four massacres of Indians by whites, her purpose being to show that the Indian had not always been the aggressor. Then in a final, brief chapter she sums up the needed remedies: punish injustice, whether Indian or white, and protect the just; give Indians citizenship "as fast as they are fit"; and stop "cheating, robbing, and breaking promises."

Though stylistically flawed by hasty writing with little revision, ***A Century of Dishonor*** is a strong, convincing indictment of government policy and practice. In style as well as content, it is a marked departure from anything Jackson had written before. Largely a compilation of facts, it nevertheless conveys not only her personal indignation but her conviction that the government and its citizens owed the Indians immediate compensation for the injustices committed against them. Jackson sent copies at her own expense to every member of Congress and followed up with personal interviews. She answered every letter to the press, taking great care to respond with facts to those who attempted to prove her wrong or to justify government action. Some respondents feared the book would have harmful effects, as the reviewer in *Nation* pointed out: "The influence will work toward disunion among philanthropic people when there ought to be the utmost solidarity of effect" (Banning, *Jackson* 158). All indications were that no one in her home state of Colorado was in sympathy with her. But Jackson's only fear was that the influence would not be strong enough. Immediately after completing the book, she took a trip to Europe to rest. While abroad she wrote to a friend, "Nothing puts the Indians out of my mind. Except that I know there is nothing to be done this summer, I could not be contented to be away, but in the autumn I will take hold again unless Mr. Jackson objects. I propose to fight it out on that line till something is accomplished" (Banning, *Jackson* 154).

On 27 January 1881 a President's Commission gave a report favorable to the Indian cause. Jackson was elated; perhaps her efforts would help to bring justice. She was further encouraged when in March a bill was passed which allowed each member of the Ponca tribe to choose land either in Indian Territory or in Nebraska, and which promised reimbursement for losses and funds for houses and schools. With these small victories to encourage her, she decided to return to California to study the Mission Indians, supported by a commission from *Century Magazine* for articles on the California missions.

In December 1881 she took up temporary residence in Los Angeles and sought out government and church officials as well as descendants of the Spanish settlers who could tell her about the history of California and help her make contact with some of the approximately 5,000 Indians still living in and around the missions. To *Century Magazine* she sent, first, an essay titled **"Echoes in the City of the Angels,"** in which she describes the city's founding by the Spanish, the period of change and instability under the Mexicans after they won their independence, and, finally, the making of a prosperous North American city. She emphasizes the city's special charm resulting from its history—the fluid sounds of the Spanish language and the Spanish influence in architecture and dress—and describes with delight the flowers and fruits growing year round in all the gardens. In her final statement she sums up her reaction to Los Angeles: "Fables are prophecies. The Hesperides have come" (*Glimpses of California and the Missions* 209).

In succeeding articles she turned to the history of the missions, especially the life of the Franciscan, Father Junipero Serra, who founded nine coastal missions from 1769 to his death in 1784. Though inclined to anti-Catholic sentiment, Jackson writes with admiration of the Franciscan friar who first converted the Indians and then taught them the occupations and behaviors of civilization. She also traces the problems over land titles as the church, military, and civil authorities vied for control, and describes the downfall of the mission system with the Secularization Act of 1834 which made the lands around the missions state property. Jackson's sense of injustice does not encompass Spanish dominance over the Indians; she sees only the advantages of civilization over heathen ignorance. Her indignation breaks forth over the fact that Indian communities formed after secularization had no legal possession rights; settlers could simply file pre-emption claims. Jackson charges: "The Americans wanted every rod of his land, every drop of water on it; his schemes were boundless, his greed insatiable; he had no use for Indians. His plan did not embrace them, and could not enlarge itself to take them in. They must go" (112).

At this point in her career Jackson was doing her best writing. Her graceful, clear style is enlivened by the wit and vitality generated by her absorption in her subject. Whether exploding with indignation over injustices or expressing her delight over the wondrous features of the locale, she depicts a vivid and fascinating land. She writes as one who is privileged to see unusual lands and wants her readers to share the experience as fully as possible. The chapters which relate the history of the missions and their place in the development of California are valuable historical documents made more arresting by her personal involvement. She chastizes the Catholic Church and the state for letting the missions fall into ruins, and pleads that they recognize and preserve what is left of the civilization the Franciscans founded.

In 1882 Jackson traveled throughout southern California in the company of various individuals who could serve as historians and guides. Along on some of the journeys was Henry Sandham, an artist *Century Magazine* sent to draw illustrations for her articles. Another companion was Abbot Kinney, a wealthy Californian who offered his help to Jackson because she was expressing concerns he had long held. In July of 1882 she received a government appointment as a Special Commissioner of Indian Affairs, charged "To visit the Mission Indians of California, and ascertain the location and condition of various bands . . . and what, if any lands should be purchased for their use" (Mathes, "Jackson" 68). Gratefully accepting the appointment, she requested only that Abbot Kinney be appointed her coagent and interpreter. Now she could not only prepare a special report that would continue to educate policy makers as she had begun in ***A Century of Dishonor,*** but she would also gather new material for future articles.

One year later Jackson returned to Colorado Springs and on 13 July 1883 submitted to the government the **"Report on the Conditions and Needs of the Mission Indians,"** authored by her and Kinney. After descriptions of conditions among the tribes, the report lists eleven specific recommendations, among them resurveying present reservations, removing whites from reservations, establishing more schools, establishing funds to provide for the elderly, and establishing new reservations. Four months later Jackson wrote friends, "Our report has been favorably received and its recommendations incorporated in a bill before Congress this winter" (Banning, *Jackson* 196). The Commissioner of Indian Affairs had submitted a draft of legislation which would have implemented most of the recommendations; however, though the bill passed the Senate, it did not win approval in the House of Representatives. Jackson could take solace only in some small victories: an Indian agent with whom she had feuded had been forced to resign, and the government had cancelled some homestead claims filed on Indian lands. But dispossessions continued throughout the area.

Discouraged by the little effect her efforts had thus far had on government policy, Jackson was nevertheless intrigued by a suggestion from the editor of *Century Magazine,* Richard Watson Gilder, that she consider writing an Indian novel. Gilder was editing a commissioned novel, *Ploughed Under* by William Justin Harsha with an introduction by Susette LaFlesche; but finding it disappointing, he told Jackson that she was the person to write a novel that would do for the Indians what Harriet Beecher Stowe had done for the Negroes. As she pondered the suggestion, Jackson began to realize how much she had seen and heard that she could use in a novel. In late 1882 she wrote California friends that she had decided to try a different strategy: "I am going to write a novel, in which will be set forth some Indian experiences in a way to move people's hearts. . . . People will read a novel when they will not read serious books" (Banning, *Jackson* 200). To her friend Thomas Bailey Aldrich she wrote that she wanted "to draw a picture so winning and alluring in the beginning of the story, that the reader would become thoroughly interested in the characters before he dreamed of what was before him—and would have swallowed a big dose of information on the Indian question without knowing it" (Mathes, "Jackson" 74).

Her interest in the project quickened still more when, as she told Higginson, she awoke one morning and the whole plot flashed through her mind. To many of her California friends and allies she sent letters asking for information or for verification of her memory. The comparison that Gilder had made to Stowe's book kept coming to her mind. To an Eastern friend she wrote, "If I can do one hundredth part for the Indian that Mrs. Stowe did for the Negro, I will be thankful" (Mathes, "Jackson" 75).

Jackson decided that she could not write the story in Colorado Springs and late in 1883 left for New York City, where she felt she could have total privacy. From December 1883 to March 1884, writing with unusual speed, she composed her novel ***Ramona.*** She confessed to Higginson:

> I wrote faster than I would write a letter . . . two thousand to three thousand words in a morning, and I cannot help it. It racks me like a struggle with an outside power. . . . Twice, since beginning it I have broken down utterly for a week. What I have to endure in holding myself away from it, no words can tell. It is like keeping away from a lover, whose hand I can reach. (Mathes 15; and Banning 202-03)

Jackson had correctly assessed what the public would read, for ***Ramona*** was an instant success. First serialized in the *Christian Union* beginning in May 1884, it appeared in book form in November 1884 and sold 15,000 copies in the first year. For the first time, except for the government report, Helen Hunt Jackson used her own name as author.

Ramona is the story of a half-white, half-Indian girl who, when orphaned, is raised by a Spanish family named Moreno because of her father's connection with the family. The Morenos were deeded vast estates by the Mexican government; and though by the time of the story their holdings had been greatly reduced by U.S. government policy, they still had the original hacienda and considerable wealth in land and sheep. Though not fully accepted by the widowed Señora Moreno because of her Indian blood, the beautiful Ramona wins everyone else's heart, including that of Felipe, the Señora's son. But Ramona falls in love with Alessandro, an Indian who comes to the Moreno ranch at sheepshearing time. At this point Jackson begins to rely on the accounts she had so carefully collected. Ramona is forced to run away with Alessandro and endure the hardships inflicted upon his tribe. The court allows settlers to dispossess them and also rules they must pay the costs of the court suit. With no other assets, they are forced to relinquish their sheep and horses. Completely impoverished, Ramona and Alessandro are driven from place to place. Whenever they start to establish a home, to plant crops and raise sheep, the land is seized and their crops are harvested by invaders. In a scene modeled after a story told to Jackson by the victims, Ramona and Alessandro's baby dies because a government surgeon assigned to serve the Indians will not go to the village to see the sick child. Finally Alessandro's reason is affected by so much hardship, and he has periodic spells when he is out of touch with reality. Again drawing on an account she was told, Jackson describes Alessandro's death. In the grip of one of the spells, he takes a horse he mistakenly believes to be his own and is shot for horsestealing. In the meantime Felipe has been hunting for Ramona. He finds her after Alessandro's death, takes her back to the ranch, and eventually marries her. They ride off, not into the sunset but to Mexico City, where in Jackson's words, "The beautiful young Señora Moreno was the theme of the city" (***Ramona*** 424).

So successful was Jackson in drawing the "winning and alluring" picture she believed necessary to attract readers that the reviewers of ***Ramona*** seldom made reference to her crusading purpose. Instead they emphasized her rich presentation of the Hispanic civilization in the twilight of its history in California. The consensus was that the novel was an entertaining historical romance, a "charming creation of modern fiction." The best that the critics who noted a serious theme at all could say was that it was "a novel with a very exciting purpose" and a work in which "generous indignation . . . glows in the impressive pages." Though pleased with the novel's reception (except in California, where many readers thought it one-sided), Jackson was dismayed by the focus of the reviews. To Charles Dudley Warner she wrote, "Not one word for the Indians; I put my heart and soul in the book for them. It is a dead failure" (Banning, *Jackson* 216).

As Jackson had stated earlier, she would measure her success by whether ***Ramona*** made "one hundredth part" as much difference for the Indians as *Uncle Tom's Cabin* had for the Negroes. Perhaps the major obstacle she faced was that the Indian cause in the 1880s, though certainly a national issue, was not of the magnitude of the slavery issue of the 1850s. Nor was it an issue on which the public could be appealed to from a similar moral perspective to that used by Stowe. Aroused by reports of violence and massacre, especially the annihilation of Custer and his force in 1876, the general public was not receptive to appeals from Indian sympathizers. The phenomenon that was *Uncle Tom's Cabin,* which sold 300,000 copies in its first year compared to ***Ramona***'s 15,000, suggests the difference in the level of public sensibility toward the two issues.

The contrast between the authors' writing techniques may also have contributed to the difference in the public's reaction to the books. Nina Baym points out that Stowe's interests set her apart from the other American women writing fiction and led her away from the genre of women's fiction:

> Stowe's is not woman's fiction . . . because the good women are not engaged in their own cause, either as individuals or in the interest of their sex, but in a cause where their own welfare is not directly involved or may even be endangered. . . . They possess a kind of childish simplicity coupled with spiritual sensitivity that separates them from ordinary people. . . . Perfected beings, they have no functions to perform vis-a-vis themselves; their purpose is to validate religious belief and the spiritual world for others, including the audience. (*Woman's Fiction* 233).

In contrast, Jackson's ***Ramona*** remains true to the genre of women's fiction. Though a half-breed whose hardships necessarily differ markedly from those of Jackson's other heroines, Ramona is still of the type. She possesses the same Victorian moralities of self-control and sacrifice essential to ultimate triumph. Again the romantic interest is central. It is Ramona's love for Alessandro that draws her from the protection of the Moreno household. Initially she looks to Alessandro for support, but as he deteriorates under the stress of persecution, she gains strength and becomes the dominant figure. Jackson must of course show that the forces of injustice are too strong for anyone, no matter how heroic, to overcome them; however, she remains true to the genre: Ramona remains a victim as long as she is on American soil, but she triumphs by choosing to live in Mexico for the rest of her life.

Jackson's adherence to the genre may finally have been the major obstacle to public understanding of her purpose. Perhaps more readers would have been aroused by her social protest if instead of leaving them with the image of Ramona as Felipe's wife, happy and rewarded, she had allowed the tragedy of Ramona and Alessandro to run its course, if the couple had remained in their memories as representatives of a race for whom justice had not been achieved. The marriage is an anticlimax even in terms of structure, an epilogue rather than a naturally motivated conclusion. The loss of the tragic effect has a serious, perhaps fatal influence on the impact of the book. Even so, Ramona's voluntary exile to Mexico could have been as effective a statement about American bigotry as is Huck Finn's decision to "light out for the Territory" if it were not for the image left in the reader's mind of Ramona as the belle of Mexico City.

Stylistically ***Ramona*** is a better book than *Uncle Tom's Cabin.* With her careful eye for detail, Jackson was best in the descriptive passages. At a time when most readers regarded California as an exotic foreign land, her use of local color must have lent interest and authenticity to the book. The first chapter begins: "It was sheep-shearing time in Southern California, but sheep-shearing was late at the Morenos." Thus Jackson begins the plot but also suggests the unique place and way of life that she will describe. Typical of the first part set at the Moreno ranch are the scenes which emphasize the Spanish culture of the household, such as the awakening ceremony. Whichever member of the family awoke first would begin to sing a hymn, and each one upon being awakened would join in until all the family members, visitors, and servants were standing at their open windows celebrating the new morning. Then they would join in a procession to culminate the ceremony with mass at their private chapel.

Jackson also describes with rich effect the attractions of the Santa Clara Valley: the ranch with its vast orchards and fields, the missions and their gardens. With loving detail she describes beautiful and unusual vegetation, as in this fine passage about a wild mustard patch near the Moreno house:

> The wild mustard in Southern California is like that spoken of in the New Testament, in the branches of which the birds of the air may rest. Coming up out of the earth, so slender a stem that dozens can find starting-point in an inch, it darts up, a slender straight shoot, five, ten, twenty feet, with hundreds of fine feathery branches locking and interlocking with all the other hundreds around it, till it is an inextricable network like lace. Then it bursts into yellow bloom still finer,

> more feathery and lacelike. The stems are so infinitesimally small, and of so dark a green, that at a short distance they do not show, and the cloud of blossom seems floating in the air; at times it looks like golden dust. With a clear blue sky behind it, as it is often seen, it looks like a golden snowstorm. The plant is a tyrant and a nuisance—the terror of the farmer; it takes riotous possession of a whole field in a season; once in, never out; for one plant this year, a million the next; but it is impossible to wish that the land were freed from it. Its gold is as distinct a value to the eye as the nugget gold is in the pocket. (44)

Though character development is slight, as is often true in novels with a social purpose, and certainly true in women's fiction, the narrative moves rapidly. This is especially apparent in the section based upon historical accounts, as Jackson weaves into the story the many incidents of injustice that she wants to impress upon her readers. But it is chiefly in the exercise of restraint where Jackson's work is superior to Stowe's. To a large extent Jackson lets the story make her point. In establishing her setting she allows some authorial comment, most notably when after a lengthy description of the Moreno ranch, she compares its original boundaries to those imposed by U.S. government policy and concludes:

> The people of the United States have never in the least realized that the taking possession of California was not only a conquering of Mexico, but a conquering of California as well; that the real bitterness of the surrender was not so much to the empire which gave up the country, as to the country itself which was given up. Provinces passed back and forth in that way, helpless in the hands of great powers, have all the ignominy and humiliation of defeat, with none of the dignities or compensations of the transaction. (15)

But once into the story, she keeps her distance and controls the dialogue so that characters do not seem to be mounting a platform. Only late in the story, when she introduces Aunt Ri, a frontier woman from Tennessee who befriends Ramona, does Jackson allow a character to preach. At times it seems that Aunt Ri must carry the burden of serving as the white conscience. Stowe, on the other hand, hangs a thin story on a heavy and continuous sermon. Again and again characters belabor her mixture of Christianity and emancipation, as in the maudlin death scenes of both Little Eva and Uncle Tom. Given the expectations of nineteenth-century readers of popular fiction, Jackson's book is commendable for the focus on the plot as the vehicle for carrying the message. . . .

Valerie Sherer Mathes (essay date 1990)

SOURCE: "*Ramona,* Its Successes and Failures," in *Helen Hunt Jackson and Her Indian Reform Legacy,* University of Texas Press, 1990, pp. 76-94.

[*In the following essay, Mathes explains that while the author intended to use* Ramona *as a means to awaken pubic interest in the condition of Native Americans, the work has enjoyed far greater success as a love story.*]

By November 1883, with the report and her *Independent* articles completed, Jackson could reflect upon a job well done. She and Kinney had saved several tracts of land and had removed what they believed to be an immoral teacher. In addition, much to Jackson's pleasure, Lawson had resigned as agent. Her critical exchange of letters to government officials may well have been one of the reasons for his leaving government service.

Lawson's replacement, J. G. McCallum, took office on October 1, 1883. Unfortunately, not only was he inefficient but time would prove him dishonest as well. In December, while Jackson was busy writing her Indian novel ***Ramona,*** McCallum traveled nearly three hundred miles to visit at Temecula, Cahuilla, and Agua Caliente and to see about building schools at Rincon and Santa Ysabel, as recommended by the Jackson/Kinney report. He found Santa Ysabel to be a beautifully located village with 159 Indians, 80 of whom were children. Because it was too late in the season to build an adobe school, he decided on a frame building instead. The Indians agreed to haul the necessary lumber.

Away from his office a week, McCallum had no time to visit the village of Rincon but did meet with the captain, who had to consult with his villagers before committing them to building the school. A month later McCallum wrote Commissioner Price requesting authority to rent a suitable house for the Rincon school and employ a female teacher. The school at Rincon was finally established on April 1, 1884.

Leaving the village and school of Agua Caliente, located within the grant belonging to Downey, McCallum unexpectedly met him the following day. Downey informed the agent that he fully intended to have the Indians removed within the next year. Returning to his agency, McCallum visited the offices of the United States surveyor general to look at Downey's grant. He found it to contain the usual protective clause favoring the Indians. The agent was also well aware that Byrnes, the claimant at Saboba, had hired a lawyer and begun proceedings to eject the Indians from their village.[1]

As McCallum began his visit to the various Mission reservations, Jackson pondered what more she could do for their inhabitants. Perhaps a novel—one that presented the true picture of the Indian—as Jackson viewed it. In 1881 *Ploughed Under* by William Justin Harsha had been written with that purpose in mind. Jackson had not only seen the manuscript but had helped Thomas Henry Tibbles make corrections. She remarked to Joseph B. Gilder that it was a pity the first novel on the Indian question was such a bad one.[2] Gilder immediately suggested she write one, but Jackson reluctantly replied that she lacked the local color necessary to do the job adequately.[3] Now she realized she had more than enough background material.

After completing the month-long tour with Kinney in May 1883, she had written Thomas Bailey Aldrich about the fraud and cruelty they had unearthed. "If I could write a story that would do for the Indian a thousandth part that Uncle Tom's Cabin did for the negro, I would be thankful the rest of my life,"[4] she wistfully commented. Following the publication of ***Ramona,*** she wrote Aldrich that she only hoped the novel would make his heart ache. She wanted to create such a winning and alluring picture through her characterization that the reader "would have swallowed a big dose of information on the Indian question without knowing it."[5]

Now in November 1883, home again in Colorado Springs, her thoughts again turned to creating a novel. She asked Ephraim W. Morse of San Diego for additional information on the Temecula removal as well as the theft of a large number of sheep from the Pala or San Luis Rey Indians by Major Cave J. Couts. She wanted to write a story set in Southern California that would influence public sentiment in behalf of the Indians, something ***A Century of Dishonor*** had not accomplished. Only her intimate literary friends would be privy to this project, and she urged him to keep it secret.

In her ending postscript to Morse she mentioned Lawson's resignation and an editorial from the *San Luis Rey Star* that contained "slurring and contemptuous references to . . . [her] in connection with this charge." "It is plain that the Indians have some bitter enemies in San Luis Rey," she concluded.[6] In his editorial column, Francis H. Whaley of the *Star* had called for Jackson's removal. Describing her as a "busy body" and a "meddlesome feminine pet of the Hon. Secretary," he concluded that "no woman should occupy the position of Indian Commissioner; it is no place for any member of the feminine gender."[7]

Writing to the Coronels, she remarked that her government report had been favorably received and the recommendations were to be included in a bill coming up before Congress in winter. Realizing that most people would be more apt to read a fictionalized account, however, she was currently writing a novel setting "forth some Indian experiences in a way to move people's hearts."[8] She was especially interested in everything Mr. Coronel could remember of the Temecula village while he was marking off the Indian boundaries. She lamented not writing a novel while in Los Angeles, but now, with the report finished, she felt able to undertake such a task.

A letter to Mary Sheriff requested information about the murder of Juan Diego by Sam Temple. Jackson had written a detailed account in her *Independent* article, **"Justifiable Homicide in Southern California."** Now she wanted information about the jury, the proceedings, and the judge. In reply to Sheriff's letter, Jackson remarked that cities all over the country were organizing branches of the Indian Rights Association, so work on behalf of the Indian was progressing. The captain at Saboba may not see an improvement, but his children would.[9]

Her annual bout of bronchitis forced her to move to New York in late November where she settled in at the Berkeley Hotel. Shortly thereafter, she informed Aldrich she was going to write a long story which would take three to four months. She inquired if anybody had ever written a book entitled "In the Name of the Law." The story was all planned—so well thought out that it was practically half done.[10]

As the new year dawned, Jackson was still busily working on ***Ramona,*** while her hand-picked lawyers, Brunson and Wells, worked equally hard defending Indian land titles. In the case of the Indians of Capitán Grande, the lawyers had found that the homestead entries of Mead, Hensley, and Strong were valid while that of Knowles was fraudulent. The attorneys recommended to Commissioner Price that the improvements and interests of the three legal entries be purchased by the government. They agreed to await instructions as to whether or not the government would prosecute Knowles.[11]

Three weeks later Commissioner Price informed Brunson and Wells that the entries of Mead and Hensley had been cancelled by the General Land Office on January 8 because the Indians had resided on the land for thirty-one years. Although Colonel Magruder had not legally created a reservation, he had determined the Indian occupancy, therefore removing the tract from jurisdiction of land laws. Knowles' entry was cancelled because of fraud while that of Strong had already passed to the patent stage, and no action had been taken. Furthermore, the commissioner believed that these cancellations would be sustained.[12] However, not until November 3, 1886, almost three years later, did Secretary of the Interior Lucius Q. C. Lamar write the new commissioner, John D. C. Atkins, that the interior department had authorized the "immediate and summary removal" of Hensley, Mead, and Knowles from the Capitán Grande Reservation.[13]

In the meantime, Jackson was busy on her novel. After completing twenty chapters, she wrote to Kinney, asking if it would be improper to rearrange events chronologically. She also informed him there was a bill of some sort prepared and placed before Congress.[14] Next, she requested a copy of this bill from Commissioner Price so she could write supporting letters to newspaper editors, much as she had done when working in behalf of the Ponca, Cheyenne, and Ute Indians.[15]

The first word of ***Ramona*** was written on December 1, 1883, in the Berkeley Hotel in New York City. The plot had flashed through her mind in less than five minutes the previous October. Frightened by the power of the story, she had rushed into her husband's room to tell it to him. Haunted ever since, she wrote two thousand to three thousand words a morning as if engaged in a struggle with an outside power. It was impossible to write fast enough. Twice stricken by a persistent cold and a case of "nervous prostration," she found being kept away from the writing was "like keeping away from a lover, whose hand . . . [she could] reach." The strain became so hard that she occasionally forced herself to stop and write a bit of verse or prose. Never before had she written half that amount in the same period of time, and it was her best work ever. Then she mused—she had turned fifty-two in October and was not "a bit steadier-headed!"[16]

Warner, a frequent visitor, observed that she seemed completely possessed and that "chapter after chapter flowed from her pen as easily as one would write a letter to a friend."[17] On the night of March 9, 1884, only about ten pages remained. And although she generally never wrote anything more than a letter in the evening, she continued working until eleven.[18] When she finished the last sentence, she put her head down on her desk and cried: "My life-blood went into it—all I had thought, felt, and suffered for *five* years on the Indian Question."[19]

Ironically, two weeks later, the *San Diego Union* carried an article about the county sheriff who had been ordered to serve notice of ejectment upon the Saboba Indians on the San Jacinto grant. The paper was sympathetic to Byrnes, who was described as having honestly purchased the land with no desire to upset the Indians. If the government wished to use the land as a home for the Indians, it should pay him. The author of the article concluded that his view, however, would hardly meet with Helen Hunt Jackson's approval. In addition, the paper accused Jackson of believing that the government had the right to take private property for public use without any compensation.[20] Unfortunately, no letters written by Jackson for that time period have been found, and therefore her reaction to the formal ejection of the Saboba Indians or to the newspaper article remains unknown.

About the time the *San Diego Union* published the article on the ejectment of the Saboba village, two members of the Board of Indian Commissioners were busy visiting various agencies in New Mexico, Arizona, and California. The California leg of their tour was a direct response to the Jackson/Kinney report.

Albert K. Smiley and General E. Whittlesey arrived in Los Angeles on March 19 and met first with the law firm of Brunson and Wells. They later conferred with Kinney who filled them in on the problems he and Jackson had encountered during their investigative work. Smiley and Whittlesey then met with Rust of Pasadena regarding the site for an Indian industrial school and traveled to San Bernardino to confer with Mission Agent McCallum.

Unexpected spring rains and flooding made it impossible for the two commissioners to visit many of the San Diego County Indian villages. However, after a visit to the day school in the village of El Potrero near Banning, they were convinced that the Mission Indians had been wronged. Justice demanded their lands be defended.[21]

In mid-April, the Indian Office informed Brunson and Wells of the status of the Byrnes case against the Saboba village. In reply, the two lawyers, serving as special assistants to United States Attorney S. G. Hillborn, noted that Byrnes had begun an action in the Superior Court of San Diego County in early April. They immediately wrote the United States district attorney in San Francisco, suggesting that this was the proper case to have transferred to the United States Court. On May 12 the district attorney advised Brunson and Wells that Attorney General Benjamin Harris Brewster was in agreement. Therefore, the two attorneys immediately filed a petition to have the case transferred to the federal court as a test case.[22]

The original title that Jackson had chosen for her novel was "In the Name of the Law," but for unknown reasons, she changed the name to ***Ramona.*** Writing to Aldrich, she vowed someday to write a long story without a purpose in mind and maybe then he would print it in the *Atlantic.* "This one, [***Ramona***] is not for *myself.*"[23]

Ramona, first serialized in the *Christian Union* in May 1884, was published in book form by Roberts Brothers the following November. It was a historical novel, combining both fact and fiction. Kinney remarked that he and Jackson had met with many of the "characters whose pictures were afterwards drawn with fidelity . . . in the pages of her book."[24] Jackson herself informed Aldrich that the incidents in the book were all true. "A Cahuilla Indian was shot two years ago exactly as Alessandro is—and his wife's name was Ramona and I never knew this last fact until Ramona was half written," she confessed.[25]

But Jackson was to face yet another disappointment in public acceptance of her Indian writings. ***A Century of Dishonor*** and her government report did not result in the passage of reforms or awaken the public's concern for the Indians—at least during her lifetime. ***Ramona*** as the *Uncle Tom's Cabin* of Indian history failed partially because times and issues were different. *Uncle Tom* represented four million slaves in fifteen southern states. The issue of human bondage was so explosive that a war resulted. The Indian population at most, however, was in the low hundreds of thousands. Furthermore, the vast majority of westerners living near Indian communities were not sympathetic; they only wanted Indian land. Those few Indian supporters were eastern humanitarians who still retained a romanticized vision of the "noble savage." The Indian issue would not result in a war for their freedom and rights. Still, it was a significant issue and occupied the attention of politicians and reformers.

Although *Ramona* sold fifteen thousand copies before her death, seven thousand of those within the first three months of publication,[26] Jackson did not live long enough to see its impact. ***Ramona*** was in print only ten months before she died. Since its initial publication by Roberts Brothers in November 1884, however, it has gone through more than three hundred reprintings and inspired numerous stage and screen versions as well as a score of books written by authors claiming to have discovered the real Ramona, or the real Alessandro, or the real rancho where the story took place.

George Wharton James, for example, after carefully retracing Jackson's steps for his book *Through Ramona's Coun-*

try, commented that in a pigeonhole in a baggage room of a railway station in 1910 he saw a well-worn copy of ***Ramona.*** The book's owner informed James it was "the bulliest story [he had] ever read in [his] life." James firmly believed that the "humanizing influence" of the novel continued to be felt by readers. Thus Jackson's good work continued.[27]

Jackson would, no doubt, have been pleased to learn this for she had put her heart and soul into the writing of ***Ramona,*** hoping it would accomplish what her other writings had not. She had no idea it would be her last novel; the illness which she continually attributed to various other problems was in fact cancer of the stomach. To her despair, ***Ramona*** did not achieve her expectations of immediately awakening public interest in the condition of the Indians.

Interestingly, ***Ramona***'s impact has been stronger in the field of literature, as a love story, than in the Indian reform arena, as a condemnation of avaricious white settlers.[28] In *Inventing the Dream,* Kevin Starr remarked that the popular appeal of the novel as "one of America's persistent bestsellers—is not that it translates fact into fiction, but that it translates fact into romantic myth." He believed that Jackson "collapsed American Southern California back onto the Spanish past" and created an enduring myth about the Southern California experience—a myth used as late as the 1930s.[29] According to Starr, the benefit to Jackson of her Southern California experience was two-fold: in Southern California, she found both an escape from her always uncomfortable orthodox Calvinist background and a sense of belonging she had missed while moving from hotel to hotel and city to city. Her sympathy for mission Catholicism became apparent in her articles on California, and she returned to Southern California to regain her health.

While Kevin Starr saw ***Ramona*** as a romantic myth, a contemporary reviewer in the *Critic* called it "one of the most tender and touching [love stories] we have read for a considerable period."[30] Another referred to it as a poet's novel, "a prose Evangeline . . . a sweet and mournful poetic story."[31] A third described ***Ramona*** as an intensively alive novel of reform with artistic distinction, standing "as the most finished, though not the most striking, example that what American women have done notably in literature they have done nobly."[32]

Jackson failed to create a sympathetic feeling for the Indians among many of her readers, who instead saw only a tender love story. One reviewer described ***Ramona*** as a successful love story, "a little over-weighted with misery," but totally inadequate in presenting the Indian problem.[33] Although calling ***Ramona*** the best California novel yet written, the reviewer in the March 1885 issue of the *Overland Monthly* noted that more poet than reformer emerged. It possessed "no burning appeal, no crushing arraignment, no such book as 'Uncle Tom's Cabin.'" It was "an idyl—sorrowful, yet never harsh."[34]

As reviews appeared, Jackson soon realized that some readers had missed her whole purpose. "I am sick of hearing that the flight of Alessandro & Ramona is an 'exquisite ideal,' & not even an allusion to the ejectment of the Temecula band from their homes," she wrote Warner. The *New York Evening Telegram* review had called it dull reading with no end. Jackson felt that only Warner and the *New York Daily Tribune* "seemed to care a straw for the Indian history in it."[35]

Even her dear friend Aldrich seemed to have missed the point. Thanking him on January 10 for his review, she remarked she only wished he had felt the "Indian side of the story" more deeply. "I care more for making one soul burn with indignation and protest against our wrongs to the Indians," she exclaimed, "than I do even for having you praise the quality of my work."[36]

Jackson wrote to another friend that she feared as a story the novel had been too interesting. She complained that critics were more impressed by its literary excellence than by its message.[37] Particularly disturbed by the unflattering review in the *Nation,* Jackson wrote Aldrich to see if there was such a thing as a review of a review. She found it strange that such prominent critics as Warner, Higginson, and others praised it so highly while a reviewer, clever enough to be on the staff of the *Nation,* should disagree. Later, when she discovered the reviewer was a woman, she no longer cared. Looking through the list of female reviewers for the *Nation,* she suspected the identity of the author and why she had written the review. Then Jackson poked fun at Aldrich's review for comparing her to the Spanish artist [Bartolomé Esteban] Murillo. The worst of it was that most Americans would not even know who the artist was.[38]

Fortunately, not every reviewer missed the reform message in her novel. Writing for the *Atlantic Monthly,* H. E. Scudder praised the novel, comparing Jackson's beautiful narrative to the work of an artist. Importantly, he felt, the story never became an open plea for the Indians. The reader, although indignant, never lost interest in the enfolding story. "The result is that the wrongs sink deeper into the mind than if they had been the subject of the most eloquent diatribe."[39] That Alessandro was portrayed as superior to the other Indians did not lessen the injustice done to all Indians by the whites.

Another positive review, by Albion W. Tourgée, appeared in the *North American Review* a year after Jackson's death. Tourgée, calling the book "unquestionably the best novel yet produced by an American woman," also recognized her plea for the American Indian. "A strain of angry, tender, hopeless protest against wrong pervades" the book, he noted, as Jackson presented "the cry of the poor and the weak borne down by the rich and the strong—the cry of the half-converted Indian ground beneath the feet of civilized saints!"[40]

Unfortunately, the failure of ***Ramona*** to become for the Indian what *Uncle Tom's Cabin* was for the slave was par-

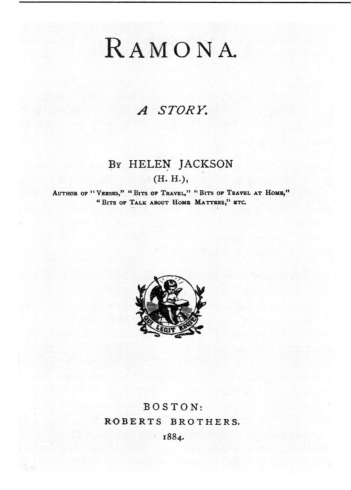

RAMONA.

A STORY.

BY HELEN JACKSON
(H. H.),
AUTHOR OF "VERSES," "BITS OF TRAVEL," "BITS OF TRAVEL AT HOME,"
"BITS OF TALK ABOUT HOME MATTERS," ETC.

BOSTON:
ROBERTS BROTHERS.
1884.

tially the result of characterization. Alessandro, the hero, was not portrayed as a typical Indian, at least not what the public perceived as the stereotype, unlike Uncle Tom. Instead, he was presented as a Christian with a position almost as high as a high-caste Mexican—his Indianism was ignored. Even Ramona did not see him as an Indian. Also Ramona, only half Indian, was more Mexican in her upbringing.[41]

According to historian Allan Nevins, Jackson erred by having the faithful cousin Felipe rescue the heroine after the death of her husband and her tragic flight from the village. Ramona, instead, should have been forced to live in misery and squalor. This happy ending ruined Jackson's effect of portraying a wronged people.[42]

Warner would not have agreed with Nevins's criticism. In a newspaper article written two years after Jackson's death, he noted that in only one point did she give in to her artistic sensibility—in the conclusion. But he agreed with her choice of an ending. "There is as much truth to life in a happy conclusion as in a tragic one," he noted.[43]

Unfortunately, not only did Jackson not live long enough to see the positive reviews, but also she was unable even to carry out her next project which was to have been a child's story on Indians for the *Youth's Companion*. She wanted to educate children "to grow up ready to be just." She had grown up with the "sole idea of the Indian derived from the accounts of massacres." "It was one of my childish terrors," she wrote, "that Indians would come in the night and kill us."[44]

Returning home from New York to Colorado Springs, she enthusiastically set about making renovations to her little house. Three weeks later on June 28, 1884, she caught her foot and fell down the stairs, severely breaking her left leg in three places.[45] Her keen sense of humor continued to be reflected in letters despite the injury and the resulting confinement. When asked by Warner if she thought of frescoing her leg cast, she replied she was going to be content to print "L. E. G." on it in pencil for the doctor. When asked if her husband was able to lift her and help her about, she exclaimed, "It took *four* men to lift me from the floor to the lounge—& all that into the bed!"[46] She now weighed 170 pounds. Her husband, Will, not only was unable to lift her but also, unfortunately, was too busy as receiver of the bankrupt Denver and Rio Grande Railroad to miss her companionship during the week. She particularly hated seeing him wandering around the house in misery on Sundays, missing their usual drives in the country.

She also missed her sojourns in the countryside. Although her bed was in the dining room and she had a view of the top of Cheyenne Mountain, it was not the same. According to her good friend Sarah Chauncey Woolsey, Jackson had a passion for nature and especially loved mountains.[47] In a poem written after Jackson's death, Woolsey noted that her dear friend gave "man the slip to seek in nature truest comradeship."[48]

Therefore, in early October when Jackson finally got out of the house for a drive, she described the experience as opening up "a new Heaven and a new earth!" The effort that it required was great. In a humorous letter to Warner she described the spectacle she made: "carriage driven up on sidewalk close to my gate—I sitting down *flat* on its floor backwards, and hoisting my 170 pounds of body in by my hands—dragging the *LEG* after me."[49] Even her dear maid Effie laughed at the sight. However, Jackson was determined to get out and drive daily.

Her confinement did not stop her from thinking about the Indians and writing letters in their behalf. In late August she informed Senator Dawes that she was glad he was coming to California to look after the Indians of Round Valley. She was sure they could not be any more deserving than the Mission Indians, whom she implored he not overlook.

By this time she probably was well aware that the Mission Indian bill, proposed by Price and accepted by Secretary Teller and the president, had not passed Congress. She explained to Dawes that the greatest disappointment of her life was that all her work and the report had accomplished nothing. She had just received word via Mr. Coronel from the captain of the Rincon ranchería who complained that the destruction of their lands continued. The new agent claimed he had no power to help them; therefore, they came to Mr. Coronel to have him write to Jackson, whom they called the Queen. They were awaiting her answer, believing it their only salvation. Her letter to Dawes reflected her depression. She would never go there again. "I am sick at heart, and discouraged," she noted. "I see nothing more I can do or write."[50] She enclosed a copy of the government report and letters of introduction to Kinney and the Coronels.

In late October she wrote a long, breezy letter to Moncure D. Conway who had recently returned to America from Europe. She informed him the relief bill had passed the Senate but lost in the House. "If I were the Lord I'd rain fire & brimstone on these United States," she commented. The treasury was full of money, wheat was piled up in Chicago, and "bands of Indians that we *promised to feed,* dying of starvation, north & south."[51] She was referring to something she had read earlier about a surplus of wheat that would result in the overstocking of the market. In the same paper an item appeared about the Piegan Indians who were dying at the rate of one a day. They were starving to death because Congress reduced the appropriations for the Indian Office. These two conditions, plenty and want, existing side by side haunted her so much that she wrote a poem about it.[52]

In November, Jackson wrote twice to Secretary of the Interior Teller. The day before she left for Los Angeles, she inquired if Ticknor, former teacher at Cahuilla, could be rehired by the department. The schoolteacher had been so worn out that she had resigned. The new agent, McCallum, regretting Ticknor's departure, informed her numerous times that she could have a position again either at Cahuilla or at the two new schools he had been authorized to establish. But when Ticknor finally wrote for a job, she was informed there were no openings.

Jackson also informed Teller that Coronel had written about the captain of the Rincon ranchería who reported the continued despoliation of their lands. The agent had explained that he had no power to set aside lands for pasture. Jackson described the agent as grossly inefficient since Brunson and Wells were authorized to look after land questions. She added, it was no wonder that the Indians distrusted all that was said to them. Disappointed that the Mission Indian relief bill had not included the recommendation of the purchase of the Pauma Ranch, she requested that such a recommendation be added, if possible. She also suggested that the government purchase the lands of the Rincon, Pala, and La Jolla Indians.[53]

Without knowing Agent McCallum, Jackson believed he was inefficient. After her death it became apparent that he was not only inefficient but more than likely involved in an attempt to defraud the Indians, using his former position to further his own finances. Before McCallum left office, a number of entries under the Desert Land Act had been cancelled. Late in 1885, once out of office and aware of these cancellations, he served as attorney for white applicants attempting to re-enter these lands, even filing most of their applications. His replacement, John S. Ward, described it as a land-grabbing scheme.[54]

Jackson's second letter to Teller from Los Angeles dealt with the Ponca. Apparently, Standing Bear and his followers in Nebraska were better off than those Ponca in Indian Territory. Several of the Indian Territory band had already traveled to Nebraska. She inquired if it would be possible for them to remain there. With sarcastic wit, she wrote that she would like to see all those contented Ponca from Indian Territory returned to Nebraska, "as a final settling of scores on one point, with that hypocrite, Carl Schurz."[55] She prayed daily he would not be given another cabinet position. Illness, confinement, and the passing of five years had not improved her opinion of the former secretary of the interior.

When the leg failed to heal properly, unable to undertake the long train journey to New York or Boston, Jackson moved instead to the warmer climate of Los Angeles in November.[56] Once settled, she again began her letter writing in behalf of the Indians. She suggested to a certain Mr. Frisbie that he read ***Ramona,*** which she hoped would strike "a stronger blow for the Indian cause than . . . [the] ***Century of Dishonor*** did."[57]

Believing she had contracted poisonous malaria, Jackson fled to San Francisco in mid-March.[58] Less than two weeks later she wrote to her husband to bid him goodbye while her mind was still clear. She was dying, but she was ready. Her only regret was not having accomplished more. She hoped that ***Ramona*** and ***A Century of Dishonor*** had helped the Indian cause. "They will tell in the long run," she wrote. "The thought of this is my only consolation as I look back over the last ten years."[59]

Jackson realized she had failed as a wife, although she informed her husband that she "loved him as few men are ever loved in this world." To make her point even clearer, she emphatically wrote: "*Nobody* will ever love you so well."[60] She encouraged him to marry her niece Helen, who was her beneficiary, and raise a family.

Unable to eat at all, Jackson shed some forty pounds. She seemed to improve a bit under the care of a homeopathic doctor. Her illness, however, did not force the condition of the Saboba Indians far from her mind. Writing to Brunson and Wells, she inquired about the case. G. Wiley Wells' reply was probably not too reassuring to the ailing woman. He carefully explained that the ejectment suit by Byrnes had been brought against the village. Wells had personally consulted with the United States attorney in San Francisco twice while his partner, Brunson, journeyed to San Diego to interview witnesses.

The partners decided to have the case removed to the federal court. In the meantime, they had spent their own money on expenses. When they presented their bill to government officials, it was disallowed. Despite this setback, they continued their efforts in behalf of the Indians, preparing the petition and papers necessary to have the case removed from San Diego County to the circuit court. Wells assured Jackson that he still believed the legal right to the land was vested in the resident Indians, but he was appalled that the government took such little interest in their welfare. Both lawyers intended to file the papers and assist the United States attorney in San Francisco. But they would not travel north unless reimbursed by the government.[61]

Wells' letter to Jackson in March had merely scratched the surface of problems the firm was having with the government. By June, Wells was furious. Although he and his partner had undertaken the work without any stipulated fee, leaving it up to the Department of Justice to decide compensation, they believed the Byrnes case would be a test case for all Mission Indians. Therefore, they enthusiastically began their work. The attorney general of the United States had authorized them to proceed as long as expenses did not exceed $200. When they finally sent in their bill, they were informed it was disallowed.

Personally committed and believing that the Indians had been "robbed, abused and mistreated," the two lawyers continued because they felt duty bound. The removal of the case to the federal court required the posting of a bond which the Mission Indians did not have. Therefore, Brunson and Wells located a wealthy individual willing to put up the money. By that time, the Indians had lost by default, and the two lawyers again plunged into the case, preparing papers and affidavits and a motion to set aside the recent judgment.

At this point they decided they could no longer go on unless treated with decency and civility by the government. In the meantime, the Indians continually came to them for help. Caught between their clients, who were being driven from their land like so many gophers, and the government, which was so weak and inattentive that it did nothing to prevent such outrages, Brunson & Wells felt totally powerless.[62]

Not only did Jackson have the problems facing Brunson and Wells on her mind, but also another situation, totally unrelated to the Indians, had emerged. Although bedridden by what she called malaria and an additional case of nervous prostration, her spunk in the face of criticism would not allow her to lie back and do nothing. She was angered about the publication of a biographical sketch by Alice Wellington Rollins in the April 1885 issue of the *Critic*. Rollins, who had already done a sketch on Whittier, visited the Jacksons in Colorado Springs in August 1882.

Disliking gossip about her private life, Jackson preferred not to be interviewed, but her husband, whom she called "the life & soul of the hospitality of [their] house," invited Rollins and her husband to be their guests. When the article appeared, Rollins never mentioned the presence of Will Jackson except as the man who harnessed the horses. Several times in May, Jackson wrote emotional letters to Joseph B. Gilder, of the *Critic*. "The cruel *idiotic* hurt of this picture of me & my life there without any allusion to my husband, is something which it passes my patience to bear, or my utmost thinking to understand!" she remarked.[63] She wanted to know how Rollins would like an article without recognition of her husband who made everything possible and was the center of her life. She requested that Gilder omit her biographical sketch when they were published in a single volume.

Two weeks later she again wrote Gilder. If he did not withdraw the sketch, she would personally write the author and request its withdrawal. In addition to the total absence of any mention of her husband, she was upset about the mention of her picnicking thirteen Sundays in a row. Jackson retorted that the world did not need to know she was a "champion Sabbath breaker." Already, the local people were about ready to stone her for her outings on Sunday; now mere strangers would have the same feeling. She pleaded with him to withdraw the article. Possibly to gain sympathy, she wrote she was growing steadily worse for nine weeks and was living for the last three days only on orange juice and iced champagne—how could he refuse her?[64] He finally relented and the article was omitted from the final copy of *Authors at Home* when it was published in 1888.

Inadvertently, Rollins' sketch revealed that Jackson did not regularly attend church. As a matter of fact, she did not speak of religion in her correspondence nor was she affiliated with any church. She did, however, marry her second husband in a Quaker ceremony. Still, the majority of nineteenth-century Indian reformers, both men and women, were imbued with an almost fanatical sense of evangelical Christianity which Jackson appeared not to possess.[65] Instead she was driven by something other than a strong Protestant obligation to engage in missionary activities.

In addition, most Indian reformers, including those who subsequently carried on in her behalf, had engaged previously in other reforms such as abolition or temperance or the foreign missionary movement. For example, Mary Bonney, founder of the Women's National Indian Association, was also founder of the Chestnut Street Female Seminary and an active member of the Woman's Union Missionary Society of Americans for Heathen Lands. Amelia Stone Quinton, besides various activities in New York City, was a state organizer of the Women's Christian Temperance Union.[66] Jackson, though, had no previous history of any humanitarian work. Somehow, her first glimpse of Standing Bear and the knowledge of the difficult situation of his tribe had troubled her deeply. Possibly, her failure to become involved in reform issues earlier resulted from time spent raising two boys and catering to a husband. Maybe the fact that she no longer had children to care for or was looking for something more important to do with her life caused her to become involved. And once involved, the condition of other tribes including the Saboba kept her continually active in their behalf.

Shortly before her death, tired of confinement and needing fresh air, Jackson wrote naturalist John Muir for assistance. She wanted to be slowly drawn along through the woods to see trees and tumbling brooks; she wanted to find a cool, moist area among the trees. Her party would consist of an ambulance, two camp wagons, four servants, and a maid and a doctor. Could he suggest an itinerary?[67] His kind and delightful letter pleased her, but he really had no suggestions. He sympathetically pointed out that her large party would scare the squirrels and bears but nevertheless encouraged her to go to the mountains. She wrote again asking numerous questions about various areas.[68]

Her concern for the Indians consumed the remaining weeks of her life. In mid-July she wrote Mary Sheriff inquiring if the copy of ***Ramona*** had arrived. She was glad it was causing such a stir in San Diego County. Touched by a message from the captain of Saboba, she told Mary to inform him that over a hundred thousand had read ***Ramona*** and many were working in the Indians' behalf. Also, the new president and the secretary of the interior were friends to the Indians. Further, Charles C. Painter, lobbyist for the Indian Rights Association, had just paid her a visit, so others were now interested in the Mission Indians.[69]

She remarked to Higginson in late July that her work was done, and she was honestly and cheerfully ready to go. "My ***Century of Dishonor*** and ***Ramona*** are the only things I have done of which I am glad. . . . They will live, and . . . bear fruit."[70] Her only regret was that she had not accomplished more. Four days before her death she asked President Grover Cleveland to read ***A Century of Dishonor.*** She informed the president she was dying happier in the belief that it would be his hand that was "destined to strike the first steady blow toward lifting this burden of infamy from our country, and righting the wrongs of the Indian race."[71]

On August 7 she wrote a poem entitled **"Habeas Corpus."** The last line reflected no fear of death, only the realization that there was still work for her to do—somewhere.

> Ah, well, friend Death, good friend thou art;
> I shall be free when thou art through.
> Take all there is—take hand and heart;
> There must be somewhere work to do.[72]

Just five days later, at four in the afternoon on August 12, 1885, Helen Hunt Jackson died of cancer. Her husband was at her side.[73] She was buried on her beloved Cheyenne Mountain. Her Amherst friend Emily Dickinson wrote: "Helen of Troy will die, but Helen of Colorado, never. Dear friend, can you walk, were the last words that I wrote her. Dear friend, I can fly—her immortal reply."[74]

Jackson's death inspired numerous poems and eulogies. Higginson in the August issue of the *Critic* described his dearly departed friend as brilliant, impetuous, and individualistic, "one whose very temperament seemed mingled of sunshine and fire."[75] She met death, he wrote, "with fearlessness . . . in the hope of immortality," because she saw "positive evidence that she had done good by her work."[76] He was, of course, referring to ***A Century of Dishonor*** and ***Ramona.***

Flora Haines Apponyi, a frequent visitor in San Francisco, wrote a touching sketch for the September issue of the *Overland Monthly.* Although Apponyi saw the usual dignity and nobility in Jackson's blue eyes, she also saw "the gentle solemnity of a soul approaching the throne of its Maker."[77] Joaquin Miller, in his tribute, called her "the bravest of all brave women in History."[78] Jackson was someone who had taken up the cause of the weak, the despised savage, and made it her life's work. Sarah Chauncey Woolsey believed her fullness of life would be most remembered. To Woolsey, when Jackson died, "the world seems to have parted with a great piece of its vital force, its vital heat, a loss which it can ill afford to bear."[79]

Jackson's death touched many. Those in the literary world remembered her for her prose and poetry, but those in the field of Indian reform remembered her best for her crusade in behalf of the American Indian. Her influence was probably the greatest upon the upper-and middle-class members of the Women's National Indian Association. When she became a member of the organization is unknown. However, as early as April 1880 she had corresponded with Bonney.[80] At one point she visited organizational offices in Philadelphia[81] and in the WNIA's fourth annual report was listed as an honorary member, contributing fifty dollars. The same report described her as wielding a "vigorous pen" and ranked her as an effective pleader for the Indians.[82]

Quinton, long-time president of WNIA, mourned her loss, insisting that Jackson's soul was marching on, rallying, and inspiring "unselfish souls to the cause she died for."[83] The earnest and hard-working women of the WNIA kept Jackson's memory alive with the establishment of their Ramona Mission among the Cahuilla. Seven of the California branches of the national association paid for the missionary and the furnished cottage. Other missions were soon established among the Mission Indians to whom Jackson had dedicated her life.[84]

Another WNIA member stirred by Jackson's writings was Mrs. Osia Jane Joslyn Hiles of the Wisconsin Women's Indian Association. Hiles set out to preserve the remaining lands of the Mission Indians, investigated their condition first-hand, reported her findings to reformers and government officials, and appealed to the secretary of the interior in their behalf.[85]

Members of the male-dominated Indian Rights Association also took note. Their full-time lobbyist in Washington, Painter, visited Jackson several times before her death. She implored him not to forget the Indians but to give constant attention to their rights and interests.[86] He had been profoundly impressed by his June 27, 1885, visit with the dying woman who warmly welcomed him, declaring there was no one else she so wanted to see. Painter described her as possessing a "face radiant as the face of an angel with the glow of earth's sunset, and the ruddy flush of heaven's sunrise."[87] He believed that one of the comforts of her last days was her realization that the IRA was undertaking the investigation of the Indians whose story she had written in "***Ramona*** with such moving pathos, and whose wretched and hopeless condition weighed so heavily upon her heart."[88] Painter was so strongly influenced by Jackson that he undertook several more extensive tours through the Mission country. He continually praised Jackson's efforts in every pamphlet he wrote, often quoting liberally from the Jackson/Kinney report.

Although his activities among the Mission Indians did not impress Father Ubach, the cleric who met with Painter in California, also believed that the Jackson/Kinney report would be "an eternal monument of truth, justice and fair play," receiving the admiration and applause of everyone reading it.[89]

In addition to her influence upon the WNIA, the IRA, and those they worked with, Jackson influenced various members of the Board of Indian Commissioners, the semi-official group of philanthropists created in April 1869 by Congress to share in the administration of Indian affairs. Their 1885 report included a lengthy tribute to her. Her death brought strong reactions from many board members and other reformers who regularly attended the Lake Mohonk Conference, including: Merrill E. Gates, president of Rutgers College, who was not only a member of the Board of Indian Commissioners, but also presided over the Lake Mohonk Conference; General Clinton B. Fisk, agent of the Freedmen's Bureau and founder of Fisk University; and Alice Cunningham Fletcher, noted anthropologist. Fletcher was deeply moved by Jackson's death. "I feel that the Mission Indians are the bequest of Helen Hunt Jackson," she noted, "and if we love her and honor her let us be faithful, and complete what she has left us to do." President Fisk lamented: "We cannot fathom that Providence that takes such a one from us in the strength of her powers and influence." Finally, President Gates noted: "The supreme significance of Mrs. Jackson's death was the consecration of her life."[90]

Mrs. Electa S. Dawes, the wife of Senator Dawes, also attended the 1885 Lake Mohonk Conference. In a letter to her daughter Anna, she mentioned that these tributes to Helen Hunt Jackson were sweet and touching.[91] Conference members not only paid Jackson a lasting tribute but resolved "to continue and complete the work inspired by her pen, and labored for to the end of her life."[92] They diligently worked in behalf of the Mission Indian bill first proposed after the publication of her report. In addition, Lake Mohonk members worked in behalf of the Saboba village, supporting the court case until it was successfully decided in favor of the Indians.

Jackson's death removed a diligent defender of the Mission Indians. She had achieved numerous successes. Several small parcels of Indian land had been protected, and she had forged a congenial working relationship with both the secretary of the interior, Henry Teller, and Indian Commissioner Hiram Price. Price, who was more sympathetic to the situation of the Indians than many government officials, was replaced by a Democrat in March, 1885, five months before Jackson's death.[93] The appointment of this new commissioner occurred about the time that Brunson and Wells were having difficulties with the government. Possibly, had Price remained in office longer, these special assistants to the United States attorney may have been more successful with their test case.

Jackson did not live long enough to see her beloved Saboba village saved nor to witness the passage of Dawes's Mission Indian bill based on the findings of the Jackson/Kinney report. Nevertheless, because of her inspirational writings, her legacy lived on as the Women's National Indian Association, the Indian Rights Association, and members of the Lake Mohonk Conference took up the fight where she had left off.

Notes

1. J. C. McCallum to Price, monthly report for November 1883, 10 December 1883 (NA, RG 75, OIA, SC 31, LR, #23116—1883). See "Report of Agents in California," U.S. Department of the Interior, Office of Indian Affairs, *Annual Report of the Commissioner of Indian Affairs to the Secretary of the Interior for the Year 1884*, pp. 12-15, and McCallum to Price, 12 January 1884 (NA, RG 75, OIA, SC 31, LR, #1441—1884).
2. Jackson to Gilder, 11 February 1881, Personal—Miscellaneous (Jackson), New York Public Library.
3. J. B. Gilder, "The Lounger," *Critic* NS 4 (22 August 1885): 91.
4. Jackson to Aldrich, 4 May 1883, Aldrich Papers, Houghton Library, Harvard University. She used the same comparison in Jackson to Ward, 1 January 1884, Jackson manuscripts (HM 14197), Huntington Library. See also Valerie Sherer Mathes, "Parallel Calls to Conscience: Reformers Helen Hunt Jackson and Harriet Beecher Stowe," *Californians* 1 (July-August 1983): 32-40.
5. Jackson to Aldrich, 1 December 1884, Aldrich Papers, Houghton Library, Harvard University.
6. Jackson to Morse, 3 November 1883, Ephraim W. Morse Collection, Research Archives, San Diego Historical Society. See also Jackson to Morse, 7 February 1884, Phelan Collection, San Francisco Public Library. For Morse's reply to the 3 November 1883 letter see Morse to Jackson, 22 January 1884, Morse Letter Book, pp. 311-312, Research Archives, San Diego Historical Society.
7. Francis H. Whaley, "The Indian Agency," *San Luis Rey Star,* 4 August 1883. Clipping found in the Research Archives, San Diego Historical Society.

8. Jackson to the Coronels, 8 November 1883, in James, *Through Ramona's Country,* pp. 18-20. The text of this letter is reprinted in George Wharton James, "The Tender Heroine of Indian Friendship, Helen Hunt Jackson," in *Heroes of California,* pp. 367-370.
9. Jackson to Sheriff, 1 December 1883 and 20 January 1884, Jackson manuscripts (HM 14214, 14215), Huntington Library.
10. Jackson to Aldrich, 24 November 1883, Aldrich Papers, Houghton Library, Harvard University.
11. Brunson and Wells to Price, 8 January 1884 (NA, RG 75, OIA, SC 31, LR, #848—1884).
12. Price to Brunson and Wells, 29 January 1884 (NA, RG 75, OIA, LS, Land Division, Volume 61-LB 121, pp. 247-250).
13. Lamar to John D. C. Atkins, commissioner of Indian affairs, 3 November 1886 (NA, RG 75, OIA, SC 31, LR, #14110—1886).
14. Jackson to Kinney, 20 February 1884, in James, *Through Ramona's Country,* pp. 336-337.
15. Jackson to Price, 27 February 1884 (NA, RG 75, OIA, SC 31, LR, #4038—1884).
16. All quotes Thomas Wentworth Higginson, "How Ramona was Written," *Atlantic Monthly* 86 (November 1900): 712-714. This letter written in New York at the Berkeley Hotel on 5 February 1884 was, according to Evelyn Banning, *Helen Hunt Jackson,* p. 198, to Colonel Higginson. In a 4 December 1883 letter to Aldrich, Aldrich Papers, Houghton Library, Harvard University, Jackson noted the book was so predestined in her mind that she wrote one thousand to fifteen hundred words a day, which for her was miraculous. See also W. J. Harsha, "How 'Ramona' Wrote Itself," *Southern Workman* 59 (August 1930): 370-375, found in Hampton Institute Archives, Hampton, Virginia.
17. Charles Dudley Warner, "'H. H.' in Southern California," in *Fashions in Literature and Other Literary and Social Essays & Addresses,* p. 321. See also "Warner in Southern California made 'an estimate' of Ramona," *San Diego Union,* 18 March 1887; "Ramona: How the Book Was Written in a Burst of Inspiration," *San Francisco Call,* 20 March 1887; James, *Through Ramona's Country,* p. 335; and Elaine Goodale Eastman, "Spinner in the Sun: The Story of Helen Hunt Jackson," unpublished, unpaged, typed manuscript in the Sophia Smith Collection, Women's History Archive, Smith College, Northampton, Massachusetts. Eastman also wrote a short sketch on Jackson entitled "The Author of Ramona," *Classmate* (21 January 1939): 6-7.
18. Jackson to Aldrich, 10 March 1884, Aldrich Papers, Houghton Library, Harvard University.
19. "Helen Hunt Jackson's Life and Writings," *Literary News,* p. 100. Copy in Special Collections, Milton S. Eisenhower Library, Johns Hopkins University. This statement was written to Mr. Niles at Roberts Brothers Publishers.
20. "A Case for Mrs. Helen Hunt Jackson," *San Diego Union,* 23 March 1884.
21. "Albert K. Smiley and General E. Whittlesey to Clinton B. Fisk, Chairman, Board of Indian Commissioners, May 1, 1884," in *Sixteenth Annual Report of the Board of Indian Commissioners, 1884,* pp. 18-19.
22. Brunson and Wells to E. S. Stevens, acting commissioner of Indian affairs, 24 May 1884 (NA, RG 75, OIA, SC 31, LR, #10477—1884).
23. Jackson to Aldrich, 10 March 1884, Aldrich Papers, Houghton Library, Harvard University.
24. James, *Through Ramona's Country,* p. 318.
25. Jackson to Aldrich, 1 December 1884, Aldrich Papers, Houghton Library, Harvard University.
26. Jackson to Scribner, 21 February 1885, Archives of Charles Scribner's Sons, Princeton University Library.
27. James, *Heroes of California,* p. 373.
28. This study does not attempt to be a literary analysis of *Ramona* or a discussion of the multitude of books and articles on the subject. For a complete analysis, see James, *Through Ramona's Country* (clearly one of the best studies); Carlyle Channing Davis and William A. Alderson, *The True Story of Ramona;* A. C. Vroman and T. F. Barnes, *The Genesis of the Story of Ramona;* Louis J. Stellman, "The Man who Inspired 'Ramona,'" *Overland Monthly* 50 (September 1907): 2-5; D. A. Hufford, *The Real Ramona of Helen Hunt Jackson's Famous Novel* (clearly apocryphal); Margaret V. Allen, *Ramona's Homeland* (one of the better studies); and Carter, *Some By-Ways,* pp. 57-76.

    For additional information, see also Nevins, "Sentimentalist vs. Realist," pp. 269-285, and J. Frank Dobie, "Helen Hunt Jackson and Ramona," *Southwest Review* 44 (Spring 1959): 93-98 (written as an introduction to a limited-edition printing of *Ramona* in 1959). For an interesting comparison of *Ramona* and the Jackson/Kinney report, see John R. Byers, Jr., "The Indian Matter of Helen Hunt Jackson's *Ramona:* From Fact to Fiction," *American Indian Quarterly* 2 (Winter 1975-1976): 331-346. See also Edward B. Howell, "A Tragic Sequel to 'Ramona,'" *Review of Reviews* 10 (November 1894): 507-513, and *The Annotated Ramona,* intro. and notes by Antoinette May. Illustrations include original drawings by Henry Sandham who had accompanied Jackson on her tours, contemporary photographs, and scenes from various productions of the Ramona Pageant.
29. Starr, *Inventing the Dream,* pp. 60-61; see also pp. 55-63.
30. "Current Criticism: Something Very Rare," *Critic* NS 3 (10 January 1885): 22.
31. Milicent W. Shinn, "The Verse and Prose of 'H. H.,'" *Overland Monthly* 2d S, 6 (September 1885): 323.

32. Helen Gray Cone, "Women in American Literature," *Century Magazine* 40 (October 1890): 927-928.
33. *Southern Workman* (February 1885): 19.
34. "Book Reviews," *Overland Monthly* 2d S, 5 (March 1885): 330.
35. All quotes from Jackson to Warner, 25 December 1884, Warner Collection, Watkinson Library.
36. All quotes Jackson to Aldrich, 10 January 1885, Aldrich Papers, Houghton Library, Harvard University. For an interesting review, see Lawrence Clark Powell, "California Classics Reread: Ramona," *Westways* 60 (July 1968): 13-15.
37. Jackson to Frank Jewett Mather, 13 January 1885, Frank Jewett Mather Autograph Collection (Leaf 34), Princeton University Library, Princeton, New Jersey.
38. Jackson to Aldrich, 9 February 1885, Aldrich Papers, Houghton Library, Harvard University. The letter about the identity of the reviewer was Jackson to Aldrich, 8 March 1885, ibid.
39. "Recent American Fiction," *Atlantic Monthly* 55 (January 1885): 130.
40. All quotes Albion W. Tourgée, "Study in Civilization," *North American Review* 143 (August 1886): pp. 246, 251.
41. Minerva Louise Martin, "Helen Hunt Jackson in Relation to her Time" (Ph.D. dissertation, Louisiana State University, 1940), pp. 160-167. See also Raymond William Stedman, *Shadows of the Indian Stereotypes in American Culture,* pp. 194-196, 259, and William Oandasan, "*Ramona:* Reflected through Indigenous Eyes," *California Historical Courier,* February/March 1986, p. 7.
42. Nevins, "Sentimentalist vs. Realist," p. 280, and Albert Keiser, "The Mission Indians as Viewed by a Woman," in *The Indian in American Literature,* p. 251.
43. "Warner in Southern California . . .," *San Diego Union,* 18 March 1887.
44. Jackson to Warner, 2 October 1884, Warner Collection, Watkinson Library. See also Jackson to Aldrich, 1 December 1884, Aldrich Papers, Houghton Library, Harvard University.
45. Jackson to Warner, 7 July 1884, Warner Collection, Watkinson Library; Jackson to Kinney, 16 July 1884, in James, *Through Ramona's Country,* pp. 337-338; Jackson to Aldrich, 22 September 1884, Aldrich Papers, Houghton Library, Harvard University; Jackson to Gilder, 23 July 1884, Personal—Miscellaneous, (Jackson) New York Public Library; Jackson to Mrs. Pratt, 6 August 1884, Morristown National Historical Park (LWS 2563), Morristown, New Jersey; Jackson to Dawes, 27 August 1884, Dawes Papers (Box 26), Library of Congress; and Jackson to Conway, 28 October 1884, Conway Papers, Butler Library, Columbia University.
46. Jackson to Warner, 19 July 1884, Warner Collection, Watkinson Library. See also Jackson to her sister Ann, 25 July 1884, Jackson Family Papers (Part II, Box 3, fd. 31), Charles Leaming Tutt Library.
47. Sarah Chauncey [Susan Coolidge], "Biographical Sketch of H. H.," Jackson Collection (#7080-a), Clifton Waller Barrett Library.
48. Susan Coolidge, "H. H.," *Critic* NS 4 (3 October 1885): 164; this poem originally appeared in the 17 September 1885 issue of *Christian Union.*
49. All quotes from Jackson to Warner, 2 October 1884, Warner Collection, Watkinson Library. For a reminiscence of Jackson's love for the outdoors see "A. W. R. Writes from Monte Carneire Ranch," *Critic* NS 4 (19 September 1885): 139.
50. Jackson to Dawes, 27 August 1884, Dawes Papers (Box 26), Library of Congress.
51. Jackson to Conway, 28 October 1884, Conway Papers, Butler Library.
52. Jackson to Bowen, 15 October 1884, Jackson Collection (#7080-b), Clifton Waller Barrett Library.
53. Jackson to Teller, 14 November 1884 (NA, RG 75, OIA, SC 31, LR, #22736—1884). For the resignation of Ticknor, see McCallum to Price, 12 January 1884 (NA, RG 75, OIA, SC 31, LR, #1441—1884).
54. John S. Ward to A. B. Upshaw, acting commissioner of Indian affairs, 4 November 1885 (NA, RG 75, OIA, SC 31, LR, #26498—1885). See also Ward to Upshaw, 5 November 1885 (NA, RG 75, OIA, SC 31, LR, #26670—1885).
55. Jackson to Teller, 27 November 1884 (NA, RG 75, OIA, LR, #3278—1884).
56. Jackson to Kinney, 28 September 1884, James, *Through Ramona's Country,* p. 338.
57. Jackson to Alvah L. Frisbie, 28 December 1884, Miscellaneous Manuscripts, Amherst College Library, Amherst, Massachusetts.
58. Jackson to Aldrich, 8 to 21 March 1885, Aldrich Papers, Houghton Library, Harvard University. This letter begun in Los Angeles was completed in San Francisco. See also Jackson to Kinney, 1 April 1885, James *Through Ramona's Country,* p. 343; and Jackson to Edward Abbott, 22 June 1885, Abbott Memorial Collection: Edward Abbott *Literary World,* Lowell Tribute Scrapbook, Bowdoin College Library.
59. Jackson to William Sharpless Jackson, 29 March [1885], Jackson Family Papers (Part I, Box 1, fd. 5), Charles Leaming Tutt Library.
60. Ibid. Will Jackson does marry his wife's niece and does raise a family.
61. G. Wiley Wells to Jackson, 31 March 1885, in James, *Through Ramona's Country,* pp. 331-334.
62. Brunson and Wells to Hon. H. H. Markham, 20 June 1885 (NA, RG 75, OIA, SC 31, LR, #15095—1885).

See also C. C. Painter, *A Visit to the Mission Indians of Southern California and other Western Tribes,* p. 17.

63. Jackson to Gilder, 6 May 1885, Personal—Miscellaneous (Jackson), New York Public Library.
64. Jackson to Gilder, 20 May 1885, Personal Miscellaneous (Jackson), New York Public Library. In her 3 June 1884 letter to Gilder, she thanked him for agreeing to withdraw the article.
65. This theme of evangelical Christianity permeates all of the books on nineteenth-century Indian reform. See Francis Paul Prucha, "Policy Reform and American Protestantism," and "Decline of the Christian Reforms," both in *Indian Policy in the United States,* pp. 229-262.
66. Wanken, "Woman's Sphere and Indian Reform," pp. 7-8, 9-11.
67. Jackson to John Muir, 8 June 1884, John Muir Papers, Holt-Atherton Pacific Center for Western Studies, University of the Pacific, Stockton, California. See also Jackson to Carr, 8 and 14 June 1885, Carr Collection (CA 195, 196), Huntington Library.
68. Muir to Jackson, 16 June 1885, William Frederick Bade, *The Life and Letters of John Muir,* II: 198-202. See her reply, Jackson to Muir, 20 June 1885, Muir Papers, Holt-Atherton Pacific Center for Western Studies.
69. Jackson to Sheriff, 17 July 1885, Jackson manuscripts (HM 14216), Huntington Library. To the Coronels, 27 June 1885, Coronel Collection, Seaver Center, Los Angeles County Museum, she noted that she had "been much cheered by an interview with Prof. Painter." See also C. C. Painter, *A Visit to the Mission Indians of Southern California and other Western Tribes,* pp. 11-12.
70. Jackson to Higginson, 27 July 1885, in Thomas Wentworth Higginson, "Helen Hunt Jackson," *Nation* 41 (20 August 1885): 151.
71. Jackson to Grover Cleveland, 8 August 1885, General Manuscripts (Boxes JA-JE, Folder: Jackson, H. H. 1830-1885, sub folder 2, H. H.), Princeton University Library. This letter has been reprinted in *Critic* NS 4 (3 October 1885): 167, and in *Century of Dishonor,* p. 515. See also Odell, *Helen Hunt Jackson (H. H.),* p. 219, and E. Banning, *Helen Hunt Jackson,* p. 225.
72. Higginson, "The Last poems of Helen Jackson (H. H.), *Century Magazine* NS 31 (November 1885): 258.
73. William S. Jackson to Mrs. E. C. Banfield (Helen's sister), 12 August 1885, Jackson Family Papers (Part I, Box 1, fd. 5), Charles Leaming Tutt Library. For notices of her illness and death see *San Francisco Morning Call,* 5 August 1885, p. 3, and 12 August 1885, p. 13.
74. *The Letters of Emily Dickinson,* ed. Thomas H. Johnson, p. 889; Martha Dickinson Bianchi, *The Life and Letters of Emily Dickinson,* p. 373; and *Letters of Emily Dickinson,* ed. Mabel Loomis Todd, p. 363.

    For an interesting description of her grave at Cheyenne Mountain, see *Critic* NS 4 (21 November 1885): 251-252.
75. Higginson, *Contemporaries,* p. 142.
76. Higginson, "Helen Jackson," *Critic* NS 4 (22 August 1885): 86.
77. Flora Haines Apponyi, "Last Days of Mrs. Helen Hunt Jackson," *Overland Monthly* 2d S, 6 (September 1885): 310. For a mention of this touching story, see *Critic* NS 4 (19 September 1885): 144.
78. Joaquin Miller, "Helen Hunt Jackson: The Life Work of One of Our Most Gifted Writers," *San Francisco Morning Call,* 18 September 1892.
79. Susan Coolidge, "H. H.," *New York Independent,* 3 September 1885. For a moving tribute, see "Helen Jackson," *Southern Workman,* October 1885.
80. Jackson to Reid, 4 April 1880, Papers of Whitelaw Reid, Library of Congress.
81. Quinton, "Care of the Indians," p. 374.
82. WNIA, *Fourth Annual Report* [1884], p. 63 for the honorary membership and p. 9 for the quotation.
83. Quinton, "Care of the Indian," p. 375.
84. Wanken, "Woman's Sphere and Indian Reform," pp. 310-321; and the WNIA, *The Ramona Mission and the Mission Indians.*
85. Francis Paul Prucha, "A 'Friend of the Indian' in Milwaukee: Mrs. O. J. Hiles and the Wisconsin Indian Association," *Historical Messenger of the Milwaukee County Historical Society* 29 (Autumn 1973): 80-84. Reprinted in Prucha, *Indian Policy in the United States,* pp. 214-228.
86. BIC, *Seventeenth Annual Report of the Board of Indian Commissioners for the Year 1885,* pp. 73, 105; Lake Mohonk Conference, *Proceedings of the Third Annual Meeting of the Mohonk Conference of the Friends of the Indians.* [1885], p. 69; and IRA, *Third Annual Report 1885,* p. 10.
87. Painter, *A Visit to the Mission Indians of Southern California,* p. 11.
88. Ibid.
89. Ubach to General W. S. Rosencrans, 4 September 1885 (NA, RG 75, OIA, SC 31, LR, #21068—1885).
90. These three quotes BIC, *Seventeenth Annual Report 1885,* pp. 104-106, and Lake Mohonk, *Third Annual Meeting* [1885], pp. 70-71. For Fletcher, see p. 105, for Fisk see pp. 106 and 71, and for Gates, see pp. 105 and 70.
91. Electa S. Dawes to Anna Dawes, 11 October 1885, Dawes Papers (Box 27), Library of Congress.
92. BIC "Third Annual Meeting of the Lake Mohonk Conference," *Seventeenth Annual Report 1885,* p. 104.

93. Floyd A. O'Neil, "Hiram Price, 1881-1885," in *The Commissioners of Indian Affairs, 1824-1977,* ed. Robert M. Kvasnicka and Herman J. Viola, pp. 176-178.

Carol E. Schmudde (essay date 1993)

SOURCE: "Sincerity, Secrecy, and Lies: Helen Hunt Jackson's No Name Novels," in *Studies in American Fiction,* Vol. 21, No. 1, Spring, 1993, pp. 51-66.

[In the following essay, Schmudde contends that although Jackson was an accomplished essayist, poet and short story writer, she did not realize the full potential and power of her writing abilities until she began publishing her work under her own name. The essay also contains an overview of Jackson's early novels, concluding with a brief analysis of Jackson's eventual involvement with the Native American cause.]

Until the last six years of her life, Helen Hunt Jackson's career as a nineteenth-century American women writer was in so many ways conventional that most contemporary critics conclude, as Cheryl Walker does in *The Nightingale's Burden,* that "for Jackson the culturally determined literary sensibility she inherited was definitive."[1] She turned to writing only after the deaths of her first husband and two sons denied her her first role choice of wife and mother; she published most of her work—poetry, travel essays, domestic advice, children's books, and fiction—pseudonymously or anonymously; while she had a sharp eye for local color and realistic detail, frequently her tone is didactic, her plots improbable, and her characters sentimentally idealized. Today she is remembered as a minor character in the biography of her friend Emily Dickinson and, most importantly, as one of the earliest activists in reforming the United States government's treatment of the American Indian. She is best known for her 1884 novel ***Ramona,*** written in the year and a half before her death. Though ***Ramona*** achieved tremendous popular success as a romance of the American West, Jackson intended it as a protest novel to promote the cause of the American Indian in the way that *Uncle Tom's Cabin* had promoted abolition.[2]

Why Jackson, at the age of forty-nine, suddenly devoted herself to the cause of the American Indian has been essentially inexplicable to her biographers. She was indifferent to abolition and to women's suffrage, though many of her friends, including Thomas Wentworth Higginson and his circle, were active in both causes. Most of her biographers assume she had simply become bored with her life and needed a new interest.[3] Higginson and others have seen continuity in the fact that many of her poems and essays "were written with a distinct moral purpose."[4] Jackson's letters and the comments of her contemporaries leave no doubt that despite being a capable businesswoman, she saw her role as a writer in conventional moral terms. Like the nineteenth-century women writers Mary Kelley discusses in *Private Woman, Public Stage,* she "exemplified the 'habit of feeling for others' by writing for the good of humanity."[5] I propose, however, that her apparently sudden interest in Indian reform has even more specific roots in a particular moral problem with which she had wrestled for the past few years in writing the two anonymous novels she published in Roberts Brothers' No Name Series, ***Mercy Philbrick's Choice*** in 1876, followed by ***Hetty's Strange History*** in 1877. In these two novels Jackson problematized the sentimental convention of "sincerity" in order to examine her society's ambivalence about the meaning of "confidence," thereby demonstrating the potential hypocrisy of sincere intention, the deceptive possibilities of social forms and language, and the moral ambiguity of secrecy and silence. Her exploration of this problem shook her own sense of identity, resulting in the rejection of anonymous authorship with which she publicly became "what I have said a thousand times was the most odious thing in life—'a woman with a hobby.'"[6]

Both ***Mercy Philbrick's Choice*** and ***Hetty's Strange History*** are out of print today, although they sold fairly well in the nineteenth century. In the lives of their heroines, both novels demonstrate what Karen Halttunen in *Confidence Men and Painted Women* identifies as the central premise of sentimental fiction, namely the moral superiority of private sensibility to public action.[7] Mercy and Hetty, both intensely private women, feel experience deeply, make moral judgments of excruciating sensitivity, and choose lives of service to others. Both exemplify the sincerity which Halttunen says sentimentalists saw as society's defense against deceptive evil in the realm of public action; women of the truest sensibility were thought to be "constitutionally transparent, incapable of disguising their feelings."[8]

The heroines of Jackson's No Name novels demonstrate such transparent sincerity: Mercy's face "was not merely a record of her thoughts: it was a photograph of them,"[9] and Hetty is blunt and outspoken, with "expressive features."[10] Strong, determined, cheerful, though widowed at eighteen, Mercy comes as close as humanly possible, the narrator tells us, to "organic honesty,—an honesty which makes a lie not difficult, but impossible" (***Mercy Philbrick's Choice,*** p. 81). She hates compliments, partly from shyness, partly from "an instinctive antagonism in her straightforward nature to any thing which could be even suspected of not being true" (***MPC,*** p. 62). At the climax of the novel's main conflict, Mercy's lover Stephen White finds and keeps a large sum of money to which he has a legal right but, Mercy is convinced, not a moral right. From the perspective of what the narrator calls her "stronger and finer organization" (***MPC,*** p. 241), Mercy pleads with Stephen (***MPC,*** p. 259): "I feel, darling, as if you were color-blind, and I saw you about to pick a most deadly fruit, whose color ought to warn every one from touching it. . . . How can I make you see the truth?"

For Hetty, a sincere commitment to the welfare of her husband leads her to sacrifice her own happiness for what she believes will be his. The narrator insists that Hetty is to be judged on the basis of her sincerity: "call it morbid, call it unnatural, call it wicked if you will, in Hetty Williams to [believe that she alone stood in the way of her husband's best interests]: you must judge her conduct from its standpoint, and from no other. . . . Given this belief, then her whole conduct is lifted to a plane of heroism, takes rank with the grand martyrdoms" (***Hetty's Strange History,*** pp. 184-85).

However, Jackson's novels also reflect her society's profound, if not always acknowledged, ambivalence about the efficacy of sincerity. Karen Halttunen analyzes how the pressure of changing social and economic conditions brought about a painfully self-conscious transformation of the sentimental tradition of the 1830s and 1840s in which Jackson grew up. Antebellum society in America, still largely contained within the institutions of family, church, and local community where "confidence might be offered or denied to another on the basis of long-term mutual knowledge," emphasized sincerity as the basis for human interaction.[11] But greater mobility and the growth of cities and factories were bringing more and more people into contact with strangers. Advice literature of the period was full of warnings to young men leaving home to beware of deceivers, recognizable by their failure to observe the formalized, ritualized sincerity of sentimental fashion and etiquette, of which women were exemplars and guardians. Ironically, the ritualizing of sincerity into social codes heightened fears that such forms could be exploited by hypocrites. "Confidence" became a double-edged word. The game of the "confidence man," a term probably first used in the New York press in 1849[12] and probably most familiarly exemplified for twentieth-century readers in Herman Melville's 1857 novel *The Confidence Man,* was to create trust in order to betray it. "To Victorian Americans," Halttunen writes, "hypocrisy was not merely a personal sin; it was a social offense that threatened to dissolve the ties of mutual confidence binding men together" and "threatened ultimately . . . to reduce the American republic to social chaos."[13]

In *Lying: Moral Choice in Public and Private Life,* philosopher Sisela Bok points out that confidence always depends on the assumption of truth. She argues that unlike truth, deception always requires justification, because of the inhibitions undiscovered lies impose on the choices of both deceived and deceiver and "the impact of discovered and suspected lies on trust and social cooperation."[14] There are situations in which most people would consider a lie justified, and defenses of lies most commonly appeal to "four principles: that of avoiding harm, that of producing benefits, that of fairness, and that of veracity."[15] Bok's terminology is helpful in analyzing Jackson's demonstration that sincerity is not an adequate measure of truth, especially within the conventional constraints on conduct and expression that the sentimental tradition imposed on women.

Mercy's life is an increasingly complex tangle of deception despite a lie's being "impossible" for her. The young woman's sensibility is so acutely conflicted that Mr. Allen, her friend and minister, thinks her "simply morbid" in her reluctance to tell even white lies for the sake of courtesy (***MPC,*** p. 84). The author's voice tells us that Parson Dorrance, a white-haired, intellectually gifted professor, brings "a spiritual vision far keener than her own" to Mercy's "old doubts and perplexities" (***MPC,*** p. 193), but in fact the novel demonstrates that he is unable to distinguish truth from sincere deception.

Mercy begins with a secret, "a secret so harmless in itself, that she was ashamed of having any feeling of guilt in keeping it a secret" (***MPC,*** p. 81): the fact that she earns money publishing her poetry. Because her mother is unreasonably prejudiced against her daughter's working for pay, Mercy uneasily accepts Mr. Allen's argument that it would be "a pity to trouble the feeble old heart with a needless perplexity and pain" (***MPC,*** p. 98). Thus she accommodates herself to accepting the avoidance of pain as a justification for deception. Moving to Penfield for the sake of her mother's health, Mercy meets Stephen White, whose aged mother is bedridden, jealous, and demanding. Stephen feels loyally obligated to his mother, and knows that marriage is impossible for him in her lifetime. Nevertheless he offers Mercy his love, asking nothing but hers, in a relationship which must remain unconsummated and totally secret. The narrator says that if Mercy "had listened dispassionately to such words, spoken to any other woman, her native honesty of soul would have repelled them as unfair" (***MPC,*** p. 162). But motives of love and compassion (to produce benefits and avoid causing pain) thrust Mercy into a deception about the very essence of her identity. Privacy may be necessary to protect identity (Bok argues that "secrecy guards . . . the central aspects of identity"[16]), but Mercy must define privacy so narrowly that silence becomes synonymous with deception. She and Stephen must act like mere acquaintances in public. Mercy eases her conscience by omitting all references to Stephen from her conversation. She cannot tell Parson Dorrance about her secret love. This silence puts both of them in a false position; when she refuses Dorrance's proposal of marriage, he assumes it is because he is too old for her, and though she "can't bear" to have him think that, she cannot tell him she loves another man (***MPC,*** p. 211). This misunderstanding persists throughout Dorrance's life.

Mercy deceives herself as well as others. She is "blinded by her profound sympathy for [Stephen's] suffering" (***MPC,*** p. 162). In fact, the great love that justifies her deceptive silence is itself based on a lie: "she did not in the least suspect that her affection and her loyalty were centring [sic] around an ideal personality, to which she gave his name, but which had in reality never existed" (***MPC,*** p. 242). Thus, to see Mercy as incarnating a sentimentally ideal sincerity is to see only part of what the text reveals. While assuring us that "truth, truth, truth, was still the war-cry of her soul" (***MPC,*** p. 284), the novel shows that Mercy cannot achieve sincerity without compromising behaviors her society required of women: maintaining an unblemished reputation and private identity, and not causing pain for others.

Hetty's Strange History also explores a tricky borderline between sincerity and deception. Hetty Gunn, thirty-five years old, practical and straightforward, the independent owner and manager of her inherited family farm, falls in love for the first time and marries Dr. Eben Williams. Unselfish love for him absorbs her so totally that when she becomes convinced (erroneously) that he would be happier with a younger and more conventionally feminine woman, she contrives her own apparent death by drowning, and disappears to a Canadian village where she dedicates herself, under the name Hibba Smailli, to nursing. Ten years later Eben, a devastated and prematurely aged widower, arrives by chance in the village; misunderstandings are dispelled, and Hetty, under her assumed name, remarries her husband.

Hetty sincerely undertakes to live a lie, not so much to avoid giving pain as to bring about a positive benefit for one she loves. Most nineteenth-century readers apparently accepted the justification. Thomas Wentworth Higginson, reviewing the novel for *The Woman's Journal,* summed up: "it would not be right that Hetty should not suffer profoundly, inasmuch as her act involved many persons in suffering, and might have involved them in a legal crime [bigamy]. . . . On the other hand, it would not be right that she should not be restored to partial happiness at last, because the action, however wrong in form and consequences, was in its motive as profoundly unselfish as any ever done by a human being."[17]

The resolution of the novel nevertheless undermines the distinction between truth and deception. Though forgiven, Hetty is literally trapped in a lie. Reunited with Eben, she balks at remarrying him under her new name: "it would be a lie" (***HSH,*** p. 281). Eben convinces her that her former lie is irreversible (she has been declared legally dead) and "if your love for me bore you up through that lie, it can bear you up through this" (***HSH,*** p. 282). Eben thus appeals, in Bok's terms, to the principle of veracity; the "lie to undo the effect of another lie" is a "lie for the sake of the truth."[18] Only when Hetty concedes that her former bond has been irrevocably "desecrated" by her "long, sad ten years' mistake" can she again find happiness with Eben (***HSH,*** p. 283).

In plot and characterization, Jackson's No Name novels thus demonstrate that sincerity and the preservation of privacy may lead not to moral high ground but rather into a swamp of secrecy and deception. Less overtly, the novels also demonstrate that the privacy-protecting convention of anonymous authorship creates a similar problem. Throughout her writing career, Jackson had followed conventional practice for nineteenth-century women writers in publishing pseudonymously or anonymously. Her earliest published poems were signed "Marah" and her earliest essays "Rip Van Winkle," but within a year of her first publication, she adopted her own initials, "H. H.," as the pseudonym under which her poetry, essays, and children's books appeared for the rest of her life. Her fiction, except for ***Ramona,*** was published under the pseudonym "Saxe Holm" or anonymously. It was widely assumed that the No Name novels' author was Saxe Holm, whose stories had been appearing in *Scribner's Monthly Magazine* since 1871—but only three or four people, sworn to secrecy, knew who Saxe Holm was. While the identity of H. H. was not a secret, Jackson adamantly denied being Saxe Holm.[19]

But unlike the "literary domestics" whom Mary Kelley discusses in *Private Woman, Public Stage,* Jackson did not adopt anonymity to provide "a sense of psychological security" or a "tenuous hold on social propriety."[20] Though she jealously guarded details of her personal life from public scrutiny and used pseudonymity and anonymity to protect her privacy, there is no evidence that Jackson felt any personal inhibitions about being a writer, or thought that public identification of herself as a writer posed any threat to her sense of identity. She intended, she told a correspondent in 1867, to "make my initials a recognized and marketable signature."[21] Using "Saxe Holm" as the pseudonym for her fiction, which generally received more mixed reviews than her poetry, was a way to protect the reputation of the poet H. H.; at the same time, the mystery of the writer's identity caused ten years of controversial attributions, analyses, claims, and counter-claims, enhancing the marketability of the stories, a situation which she gleefully manipulated.[22]

Ruth E. Friend, among other Jackson biographers, attributes Jackson's secrecy to the presence in her fiction of "autobiographical details that might prove embarrassing to herself or to friends who were the originals for numerous characters."[23] For example, Odell sees Hetty's reaction to growing old as "a picture of Helen's own state of mind, evidenced for several years past in her letters. Hetty, like Helen, had a husband younger than herself, whom she felt she was defrauding by giving him no children."[24] At least one of Thomas Wentworth Higginson's biographers and one of Jackson's suggest that Higginson and the newly widowed Helen Hunt were in love while they both (along with Higginson's invalid wife) lived in the same Newport boardinghouse in the late 1860s.[25] Thus Jackson's theme of self-sacrifice for impossible love has been attributed to a secret love for Higginson. Higginson also shares many of Parson Dorrance's characteristics, including devotion to the welfare of freedmen, an invalid wife, and a mentoring relationship to the heroine. Some critics have seen Mercy Philbrick as a portrait of Emily Dickinson. According to Friend, Lavinia Dickinson started a rumor that "Helen Hunt spent two weeks at the Dickinson home and solicited Emily's help on a novel; when Emily refused, H. H. retaliated by putting her into the story."[26] George Whicher attempts to demonstrate that "some circumstances in Emily Dickinson's life are quite literally transcribed" in Jackson's representation of an impossible secret love, though he admits that Mercy "also resembles her creator in that she is represented as a young widow who after passing through fires of suffering becomes a famous poetess."[27]

Surely it is no surprise that like any artist Jackson imaginatively combined and transformed elements of her own experience into new fictional configurations. Nor is it surprising that she should seek anonymity to protect the privacy of her own personal life and that of her friends, though it must have been apparent to her that the ironic result was to intensify the public's interest in confirming parallels between those lives and her fiction. But beyond merely serving to protect the author's privacy, anonymity functions as an integral but ambiguous aspect of the voice of the implied author in the No Name novels. Jackson foregrounds this aspect in ***Hetty's Strange History*** by deliberately raising the question of the reliability of the narrator. The novel's title gives readers warning that they may find it hard to believe; "strange" is the narrator's acknowledgement and containment of the problem, saying, in effect, "I know what I'm doing." Also, the novel is called a "history," a term that makes a truth claim and implies verifiability. But how can this "strange history" be verified?

When the novel appeared in 1877, reviewers generally applied two kinds of criteria they were accustomed to applying to fiction: moral truth and verisimilitude. Higginson's previously quoted comments on the novel's satisfactory resolution subscribe to the tradition that, in Wallace Martin's words, "a narrative true to fact would be considered ethically 'false' if the immoral or illegal acts it represented were not punished. One filled with improbabilities and coincidences might on the other hand be 'true' to the laws of poetic justice, punishing the guilty."[28] But Higginson, like other reviewers, also justified Hetty's strange behavior and the incredible coincidence that resolves the plot as, in effect, fiction no stranger than truth. He argues that Hetty's characterization is psychologically plausible, that improbabilities occur in life and in literature (he describes Hetty's story as "Hawthorne's 'Wakefield' . . . with a motive"), and that because one can imagine carrying out an action like Hetty's, "it is legitimate for the artist to trace it one step farther, and depict it as done." Thus the "strange history" can be verified by giving evidence of both moral truth and verisimilitude.

But the comments the narrator addresses to any "who find the history incredible" do not plead its moral truth or verisimilitude. Instead, they offer the testimony of an eyewitness to presumably verifiable data, the kind of evidence that history, as opposed to fiction, requires. The narrator attests that "I myself have seen" Henrietta Gunn's tombstone, and quotes its inscription, except for "dates, which I have my own reasons for not giving" and "a verse of the Bible, which I will not quote." Secondly, "I" have seen the announcement in a Canadian newspaper of the marriage of Eben Williams and Hibba Smailli. And "thirdly: Since neither of these facts proves my 'Strange History' true, I add one more. I know Hetty Williams" (***HSH,*** p. 289-91). Thus the truth claim made for this history must rest, finally, on the reader's confidence in the testimony of the narrator. But because the author is anonymous, there is no way to judge the narrator's reliability.

Five years earlier in ***Bits of Travel,*** writing as H. H., Jackson had made fun of this kind of "evidence": "we went to church at San Pietro in Montorio. . . . into the little temple which somebody built over the very spot on which Peter was crucified. You don't doubt about that spot, do you? . . . then wait till you hear the circumstantial evidence, i.e., we saw the very hole in which the cross rested! What more could one have!"[29] A woman known to test her acquaintances' understanding by their responses to Hawthorne,[30] Jackson had an unusually modern awareness of the inevitable irony in the perspective of the narrative voice of the implied author. Probably she enjoyed the "confidence game" she was playing with her readers, and expected the more perceptive of them to enjoy it too, assuming, as Bok says, that one excuse for deception is that "the supposed lie is not really a lie, but a joke, perhaps, or an evasion, an exaggeration, a flight of fancy"; such a lie is akin to "a game where both partners know the rules and play by them."[31] Many reviewers, not questioning the convention of anonymous authorship, saw no problem with the reliability of the narrator. Gail Hamilton (the pseudonym of Mary Abigail Dodge) thought that "there is real life in the book" and that Hetty "seems to have some existence outside of the author's mind." A reviewer for *The New York Weekly* rejoiced that "best of all, it is a true story, and the heroine, who for ten years was believed to be dead, is alive, and happy." But other readers objected strenuously. The reviewer for *The Republican,* for example, found the novel wanting in respect to all truth claims—moral truth, verisimilitude, and reliability of the testimony of the narrator:

> The plot is a monstrous one, and some faint glimpse of how monstrous it is seems to come to the author now and then,—but not long enough to produce conviction. . . . I will not touch upon the much-mystified subject of who the author is, but simply remark in passing that a woman who could conceive and applaud such a character as Hetty would find no scruple about denying the authorship of any book she ever wrote, if she had a strong reason for so doing. It is very plain that the ordinary notions of mankind about truth and falsehood have no [meaning] for her.

This reaction, so apparently excessive to a twentieth-century reader, makes more sense if we remember that the demands on nineteenth-century women writers were, as Paula Bennett puts it, "singularly contradictory. On the one hand, as women, they were supposed to live private (domestic) lives. On the other hand, their 'privacy' was what they were supposed to write about."[32]

Though Jackson made no direct comment on this double bind, the No Name novels can be read as her conscious or unconscious probing of it. In *Writing a Woman's Life,* twentieth-century academic Carolyn Heilbrun discusses her choice to write mystery novels under the pseudonym "Amanda Cross." Protection of her identity as a scholar was one reason, but "the most important reason . . . is that the woman author is, consciously or not, creating an alter ego as she writes, another possibility of female destiny."[33] Simply by creating fictional characters, she imaginatively enacts alternate lives, but by attributing that enactment to an implied author whose identity is secret, she frees herself from any public responsibility for them.

Following Heilbrun, it is possible to go further than demonstrating that the characters Mercy Philbrick and Hetty Williams act out some elements of Jackson's personal experience. A close reader of Jackson's No Name novels finds evidence of alternate lives which made some of her contemporaries uneasy enough to call the novels "morbid" and "unnatural." Rachel Blau DuPlessis notes that plots by nineteenth-century women writers frequently represent conflicts between love and the heroine's development as an individual; the conventional result is a subordinating of quest to love, even though such resolutions reveal "much tension" and consign to silence the issues raised by the heroine's individual quest.[34] Though the conflict between love and quest is central to Jackson's fiction, the resolutions of her No Name novels do not subordinate the heroines' quests to love. Though Mercy is said by the narrator to look forward to reunion in heaven with Parson Dorrance, no earthly marriage resolves her quest for self-development. Her life culminates in the spiritual satisfaction, not to mention the fame and fortune, of being a professional poet. The progress of Hetty's quest is more complicated than Mercy's. Hetty's marriage to Eben halfway through the novel apparently offers new opportunity for self-realization to a woman who has financial independence and work she loves, but who is lonely and emotionally underdeveloped. The opportunity, however, proves deceptive. Love so distorts her sense of reality that she mistakenly sacrifices both her own happiness and that of her husband. While nineteenth-century convention glorified women's self-sacrifice for love, and while Jackson herself treated this theme unironically in many of her poems, her representation of it in Hetty's action convincingly illustrates the futility and absurdity of such a sacrifice. Unlike ***Mercy Philbrick's Choice, Hetty's Strange History*** does end in marriage, but all parties recognize that the remarriage of Hetty and Eben brings only partial resolution to the novel's conflicts.

Jackson's novels clearly go further than most of her contemporaries' in demonstrating that a woman's individual development is as important as, or even more important than, marriage. But if we temporarily bracket the novels' discourse (the language of the implied author either in represented dialogue or in narration) and concentrate instead on the novels' stories (the sequence of represented events and their interconnections), an even more subversive modification of the conventional love versus quest resolution becomes apparent. Both novels tell us that marriage in fact impedes or prevents the heroine's quest. The range of experience necessary for Mercy's development as a poet requires that she renounce marriage. Such reasoning would have been offensive to Jackson's contemporaries because it would attribute to Mercy a "selfishness" incompatible with the womanly sensitivity her poetic vocation requires, and would make her moral and social status suspect. Therefore the novel provides Mercy with three conventionally incontrovertible reasons for remaining single: her first husband dies; by the time her second lover is free to marry her, he has proved unworthy; her third lover dies before she is free to love him.[35] For Hetty, marriage has an unexpectedly disastrous effect on self-development. She loses her self, literally, in her husband. Though the discourse of the novel attributes her disappearance to loving self-sacrifice, the story illustrates that Hetty's flight to Canada (many of Jackson's friends had been abolitionists, and that image carried great symbolic freight in antebellum America) is a desperate escape necessary to reassert control over her own life. No longer a wife, she successfully assumes her husband's profession as a healer. When they are reunited, they do not return to his life; he is forced to join her in the life she has made for herself.[36]

Heilbrun writes that pseudonymity "permitted me, as other women have found ways to permit themselves, to write my own life on a level far below consciousness, making it possible for me to experience what I would not have had the courage to undertake in full awareness."[37] I suggest that Jackson's creation of Mercy and Hetty taps into her ambivalence not only about the relationship between marriage and literary career, but also about the relationship between secrecy and deceit in the truth-telling mission of the nineteenth-century woman writer. It is possible to see Mercy and Hetty as imagined lives of Jackson's two pseudonymous identities, H. H. and Saxe Holm.

Mercy Philbrick's Choice was written by Saxe Holm,[38] but the poems represented as written by Mercy Philbrick are indistinguishable from H. H.'s poems. Like Jackson, Mercy begins to publish poems only after being widowed, and the ambitions Jackson ascribed to her fictional heroine—"to do a little towards making people glad, towards making them kind to one another, towards opening their eyes to the omnipresent beauty" (***MPC,*** p. 284)—were her own. But Mercy's experience is not Jackson's. Mercy writes under her own name, not pseudonymously or anonymously, a detail which makes sense if we see Mercy's as the imagined life not of Jackson but of the poet H. H., the implied author of Jackson's poems. Paradoxically, it is only in her poetry, that "secret so harmless in itself, that she was ashamed of having any feeling of guilt in keeping it a secret," that the poet speaks publicly. Mercy's poems have an intensity which reveals that they "had sprung out of the depths of the profoundest experiences" (***MPC,*** p. 284), but she attributes their truth to verisimilitude rather than to fact: "oh, it was purely dramatic! I just fancied how anybody would feel under such circumstances" (***MPC,*** p. 270). Thus poetry as public expression may be "dramatic" truth rather than historical truth. Secrecy is justified to protect identity, but its depths are plumbed and its danger recognized: the sentimental conventions of publicly sincere poetic expression may result from a private deception.

If Mercy is the imagined life of the implied author H. H., it is also possible to see Hetty as the imagined life of Saxe Holm. Because Hetty, unlike Mercy, is not a writer herself, her connection with the implied author of Jackson's fiction lies further beneath the surface. Hetty's decision to step out of her husband's life to enable him to marry a younger woman may have been a fantasy of Jackson's; it is tempting to read "I know Hetty Williams" as self-referential. But while Jackson, unlike Hetty, never literally disappeared into another life, she did disappear into another identity in the pseudonym of Saxe Holm. Is it coincidence that Hetty's adopted pseudonym "Hibba Smailli" has the same initials as Saxe Holm? Jackson was both amused and annoyed when other claimants to the name Saxe Holm appeared, but found that her lie had closed off her options; her fiance Will expressed her dilemma in a letter to her two months before their marriage in 1875: "that Saxe Holm matter is very funny . . . I wouldn't bother about their dear Ruth Ellis or the swing side of thirty or anybody in Texas unless she really did begin writing under the name Saxe Holm & then I don't see what you are to do since you have so positively denied the work."[39] Like Hetty in Canada, Jackson as Saxe Holm is trapped in her own pseudonym. The anonymous author of ***Hetty's Strange History*** who testifies as an eyewitness that the story is true is in the same anomalous position as Jackson writing letters to newspapers as Saxe Holm testifying that other claimants to the name are lying.

The No Name novels show that Jackson was acutely sensitive to such paradoxes as sincere hypocrisy, public secrecy, and deceptive silence. In these novels, even well-intentioned lies and secrets can harm deceiver, deceived, and their social communities. Thus, on that night in October 1879 when Jackson listened to Standing Bear and Bright Eyes tell of the wrongs done to the Poncas, she found an egregious illustration of the moral problem that had occupied her for the last several years. In four months of extensive research on the government's dealings with the Indians, she uncovered evidence of hypocrisy on a grand political scale: the Indians' trust violated by white men's confidence games; treaties, purporting to protect Indian rights, flagrantly broken; and an absence of public discourse about the dishonorable gap between policy as enunciated and policy as implemented. She saw it as hypocrisy so corrupt that, to recall Halttunen's words, it "threatened ultimately, by undermining social confidence . . . to reduce the American republic to social chaos." ***A Century of Dishonor,*** Jackson's documentation of the country's mistreatment of the Indian, contains recurrent references to sincerity and hypocrisy, secrecy and silence, truth and lies. The following sentences, for example, are all found on one page of her concluding chapter: "the United States Government breaks promises now as deftly as [in 1795], and with an added ingenuity from long practice"; "there are hundreds of pages of unimpeachable testimony on the side of the Indian; but it goes for nothing, is set down as sentimentalism or partisanship, tossed aside and forgotten"; "it would probably be no exaggeration to say that not one American citizen out of ten thousand ever sees [the factual reports commissioned by the government] or knows that they exist, and yet any one of them, circulated throughout the country . . . would initiate a revolution which would not subside until the Indians' wrongs were, so far as is now left possible, righted."[40]

Rather than being the secret creator of alternate lives told by an anonymous narrative voice, Jackson suddenly found *herself* become a narrative voice engaged in a truth-telling mission that was no longer a game. When her husband questioned her authority by pointing out that as a woman she lacked the expertise to run the Indian Bureau, she hotly defended the reliability of her narrative voice: "because I am not able—as I most certainly am not,—to 'outline' . . . a detailed system for the management of 220,000 Indians—is there any reason why I should not be qualified to protest against *broken* treaties—cruel massacres—& *unjust laws.* A woman does not need to be a statesman to know that it is base to break promises—to oppress the helpless!"[41] As she was beginning work on ***A Century of Dishonor,*** she wrote to her husband that she felt an irresistible impulse "to say special words & phrases—as if they were put into my mind from outside! I know—if my own consciousness is any evidence of anything, that I write these Indian things in a totally different way from my ordinary habit of composition—I write these sentences—which would ordinarily cost me much effort & work, to get them so condensed—as fast as I can write the words."[42] Writing ***Ramona,*** she told Higginson, "racks me like a struggle with an outside power."[43] It was essential to her purpose that her testimony not only be reliable, but be perceived to be reliable. Of ***A Century of Dishonor,*** she stressed: "I am not writing—& shall not write one word as a sentimentalist! *Statistical records*—verbatim reports *officially* authenticated, are what I wish to get before the American people."[44] "Every word of the Indian history in ***Ramona*** is literally true," she told Higginson.[45] When historical truth rather than "dramatic truth" was really at issue, an anonymous narrative voice would not do. With the first edition of ***A Century of Dishonor,*** signed by H. H., she put the moral authority of that well-respected poet and essayist on the line. Then she went one step further. The ***Report on the Conditions and Needs of the Mission Indians*** which she submitted to Congress in her role as Indian Commissioner (1883), her novel ***Ramona*** (1884), and the second edition of ***A Century of Dishonor*** (1885) were by Helen Jackson.

Notes

1. Cheryl Walker, *The Nightingale's Burden: Women Poets and American Culture before 1900* (Bloomington: Indiana Univ. Press, 1982), p. 93.

2. The letter to Thomas Bailey Aldrich in which Jackson expressed this intention is cited by many of her biographers and critics, but it is perhaps best examined in the context of Valerie Sherer Mathes' *Helen Hunt Jackson and Her Indian Reform Legacy* (Austin: Univ. of Texas Press, 1990), p. 77, which gives a thorough and balanced analysis of the positive and negative effects of Jackson's efforts on behalf of Native Americans.

3. See Ruth Odell, *Helen Hunt Jackson* (New York: D. Appleton Century, 1939), pp. 151-3; Antoinette May, *Helen Hunt Jackson: A Lonely Voice of Conscience* (San Francisco: Chronicle Books, 1987), pp. 57-60; and Rosemary Whitaker, *Helen Hunt Jackson* (Boise, Idaho: Boise State Univ. Press, 1987), p. 24.

4. Thomas Wentworth Higginson, *Contemporaries* (Boston: Houghton Mifflin, 1899), pp. 156-7, and Joanne Dobson, *Dickinson and the Strategies of Reticence: The Woman Writer in Nineteenth-Century America* (Bloomington: Indiana Univ. Press, 1989), p. 95.

5. Mary Kelley, *Private Woman, Public Stage: Literary Domesticity in Nineteenth Century America* (New York: Oxford Univ. Press, 1984), p. 287.

6. Quoted in Higginson, p. 155.

7. Karen Halttunen, *Confidence Men and Painted Women: A Study of Middle-class Culture in America, 1830-1870* (New Haven: Yale Univ. Press, 1982), pp. 56-57.

8. Halttunen, p. 57.

9. *Mercy Philbrick's Choice* (Boston: Roberts Brothers, 1876), p. 64. Subsequent references to this work (as *MCP*) will be in the text.

10. *Hetty's Strange History* (Boston: Roberts Brothers, 1877), p. 47. Subsequent references to this work (as *HSH*) will be in the text.

11. Halttunen, p. 193.

12. Halttunen, p. 6.

13. Halttunen, pp. 34, xv.

14. Sisela Bok, *Lying: Moral Choice in Public and Private Life* (New York: Vintage, 1979), p. 32. See especially Chapter 2, "Truthfulness, Deceit, and Trust."

15. *Lying,* p. 80.

16. Sisela Bok, *Secrets: On the Ethics of Concealment and Revelation* (New York: Pantheon, 1982), p. 13.

17. Helen Hunt Jackson Papers, Part I, Ms. 0020, Bx 6, Fd 14, Tutt Library, Colorado College, Colorado Springs, Colorado. This folder contains clippings of reviews of *Mercy Philbrick's Choice* and *Hetty's Strange History.* Subsequent references to nineteenth-century reviews of these novels are from this source. Permission to quote from the Helen Hunt Jackson papers has been granted by Tutt library.

18. Bok, *Lying,* p. 88.

19. Jackson's friend Thomas Wentworth Higginson wrote that her authorship of the No Name novels "was no secret" at the time of her death (*Contemporaries,* p. 161). According to Ruth Odell, Jackson told her friend Moncure Daniel Conway that she wanted the truth about Saxe Holm known only after her death (Odell, p. 136). Her publishers brought out her posthumous publications, including *Zeph* and *Between Whiles,* both of which had been intended as Saxe Holm works, under the name Helen Jackson (H. H.).

20. Kelley, p. 125.

21. Quoted in Odell, pp. 65.

22. Susan Coultrap-McQuin's *Doing Literary Business: American Women Writers in the Nineteenth Century* (Chapel Hill: Univ. of North Carolina Press, 1990) contains an entire chapter on Jackson which explores in detail Jackson's motives for pseudonymity and anonymity, and their effect on her sales and reputation. See especially pages 158-64. Also helpful is Ruth Friend's summary of the Saxe Holm controversy in *Helen Hunt Jackson: A Critical Study,* unpublished dissertation, Kent State University, 1985, pp. 183-88.

23. Friend, pp. 184-85.

24. Odell, p. 148.

25. Anna Mary Wells, *Dear Preceptor: The Life and Times of Thomas Wentworth Higginson* (Boston: Houghton Mifflin, 1963), pp. 201-11, and Antoinette May, pp. 28-29.

26. Friend, p. 201. For an assessment of the various attributions that have been made about the novel, see pages 201-05.

27. George Whicher, *This Was A Poet* (Ann Arbor: Univ. of Michigan Press, 1965), p. 128.

28. Wallace Martin, *Recent Theories of Narrative* (Ithaca: Cornell Univ. Press, 1986), p. 46.

29. "H. H." [Helen Hunt Jackson], *Bits of Travel* (1872; repr. Boston: Roberts Brothers, 1885), p. 173.

30. Odell, p. 51.

31. Bok, *Lying,* pp. 78, 137.

32. Paula Bennett, *Emily Dickinson: Woman Poet* (Iowa City: Univ. of Iowa Press, 1990), p. 134.

33. Carolyn Heilbrun, *Writing a Woman's Life* (New York: Norton, 1988), p. 110.

34. Rachel Blau DuPlessis, *Writing Beyond the Ending: Narrative Strategies of Twentieth Century Woman Writers* (Bloomington: Indiana Univ. Press, 1985), pp. 3-7. Though DuPlessis' book focusses on twentieth-century women writers, her initial chapter provides a helpful discussion of the situation of nineteenth-century women writers as well.

35. Titles of Jackson's fiction frequently acquire multiple meanings as the narrative progresses, and resolutions frequently involve a reinterpretation of the title. Mercy Philbrick's "choice" would seem to be Stephen White; when she realizes she loved the wrong man and devotes herself in spirit to her dead mentor, her "choice" would seem to be, belatedly, Dorrance. Jackson may or may not have intended a careful reader to observe at the resolution that what Mercy has actually chosen is the life of an independent, dedicated, professional writer.

36. In "Dandy Steve," a story published posthumously in *Between Whiles* (Boston: Roberts Brothers, 1887), Jackson inverts sex roles in a similar plot: Steve leaves his wife Helen, and after many years is accidentally reunited with her. But the narrator tells us that Steve's wife had money, while he had only a little, and when she couldn't help throwing it up to

him, he left. Apparently Jackson felt that self-esteem as a motive for male action, if not for female action, could be acknowledged in the story's discourse.

37. Heilbrun, p. 120.

38. See Odell, p. 140. Jackson intended *Mercy Philbrick's Choice* as a Saxe Holm novelette, but when *Scribner's* rejected it, she expanded it for the No Name Series. According to its title page, *Hetty's Strange History* was written "By the Author of *Mercy Philbrick's Choice.*"

39. William S. Jackson Family Papers, Part I, Ms. 0241 Bx 1, Fd 8, Tutt Library, Colorado College, Colorado Springs, Colorado. Permission to quote from the William S. Jackson Family Papers has been granted by Tutt library.

40. "H. H." (Helen Hunt Jackson), *A Century of Dishonor: The Early Crusade for Indian Reform* (1881), ed. Andrew F. Rolle (New York: Harper Torchbooks, 1965), p. 338.

41. William S. Jackson Family Papers, Part I, Ms 0241 Bx 1, Fd 7. To Will Jackson's credit, it should be noted that she apparently convinced him; in 1880, he wrote to her that the "publication in England [of *A Century of Dishonor*] may be a means of awakening our public men to some sense of the degradation that we as a nation should feel in the true history of our dealings with a comparatively defenceless race" (William S. Jackson Family Papers, Papers, Part I, Ms. 0241, Bx 1, Fd 9).

42. William S. Jackson Family Papers, Part I, Ms. 0241, Bx 1, Fd 7.

43. Whitaker, p. 33.

44. William S. Jackson Family Papers, Part I, Ms 0241, Bx 1, Fd 7.

45. Higginson, *Contemporaries,* p. 167.

David Luis-Brown (essay date 1997)

SOURCE: "'White Slaves' and the 'Arrogant *Mestiza*': Reconfiguring Whiteness in *The Squatter and the Don* and *Ramona,*" in *American Literature,* Vol. 69, No. 4, December, 1997, pp. 813-39.

[*In the following essay about* Ramona *and* The Squatter and the Don, *Luis-Brown theorizes that through their use of sentimentality, both works attempt to shape the reader's politics and to question white male authority over marginalized groups.*]

Helen Hunt Jackson's ***Ramona*** (1884) and *The Squatter and the Don* (1885) by María Amparo Ruiz de Burton are indisputably political novels, representing conflicts over land, class position, and racial status in California in the 1870s. These novels represent Anglos, *Californios,* and Indians as struggling for social position following the U.S. annexation of one-half of Mexico as a result of the Mexican War of 1846-1848.[1] However, although most critics view these texts as political, their insufficient historicization of narrative form has led them to misconstrue as antagonistic the relationship between form and reform in these novels. Despite the canon-expanding feminist criticism of Lauren Berlant, Ann Douglas, Jane Tompkins, and others, which has allowed us to read as politically engaged the previously marginalized genres of melodrama and romance, Michael Dorris associates melodrama in ***Ramona*** with improbable events, simplistic characterization, and chaste love; Rosaura Sánchez and Beatrice Pita split *Squatter* into "two tracks, one historical and one romantic."[2] Sánchez and Pita view the romance as a love story inadequate to *Squatter*'s historical content—conflicts over racial caste.[3] According to the logic of such constricting definitions of romance, a politically engaged, protofeminist nineteenth-century sentimental text would be a contradiction in terms, a clearly untenable conclusion given recent feminist scholarship.

Feminist scholarship on sentimentalism has allowed us to grasp the point of view expressed by José Martí, an early admirer of ***Ramona.*** In the prologue to his 1888 translation of ***Ramona,*** Martí argues that ***Ramona***'s sentimental qualities constitute its political strength.[4] He compares the novel favorably to *Uncle Tom's Cabin,* whose sentimental qualities he had earlier recognized, praising it as "a tear that has something to say."[5] As this metaphor suggests, nineteenth-century sentimentalism appeals to readers' emotions and morals in an effort to shape their politics, often through tropes of family separation.[6] Martí claims that he found in ***Ramona*** "*our* novel," a model full of "fire and knowledge" for what he would call "Our America," a racially egalitarian Latin America opposing both Spanish and U.S. imperialism. Martí celebrates Ramona as "*la mestiza arrogante,*" implying she is the ideal subject of the revolutionary interracial movement he calls "our *mestiza* America."[7] Martí represents this collectivity as embodied by the product of interracial love, a *mestiza* of mixed Indian and white heritage; he thus fuses politics and romance, the racial question and the gender/genre question, elements assumed to be opposed by most critics.[8]

Both Ruiz de Burton and Jackson corroborate Martí's insights by describing their own texts as indebted to sentimental antislavery novels such as *Uncle Tom's Cabin.*[9] As Lauren Berlant has argued, sentimentalism provided Northern white women authors with a way of morally transforming "the values and practices of domination" in patriarchy without having their activities stigmatized as "political"—and hence unladylike.[10] Sentimentalism thus comprises not only strategies of "emasculation" (as in the account of Sánchez and Pita) but also a cluster of more proactive tactics by which women authors effect reform by representing the public sphere in terms of domestic tropes—emotions, love, and family—and thereby claim moral authority in an arena that routinely excluded them.[11]

The use of sentimentalism as protofeminist moral critique in Jackson and Ruiz de Burton is structured by the discourse of romantic racialism/feminism used in reformist writings from Stowe to W. E. B. DuBois.[12] Romantic racialism is most often intertwined with its double, romantic feminism, the pair equating blacks and women as pious victims of—and hence morally superior to—white men.[13] Depending on how the author uses romantic racialism, the groups defined as victimized by race, gender, or region can be white women and Indians, as in ***Ramona,*** or, in a reversal of Stowe's vision, landed white Southerners and elite *Californios,* as in *Squatter.*[14] Romantic racialism provided women authors with a vocabulary to yoke their protofeminism to the more legitimized traditions of racial reform. Hence sentimentalism intervenes in politics by specifying morally superior, exploited groups who should rule.

The mechanisms by which these novels simultaneously affirm and rework dominant discourses can be explained in relation to their allegorical structures. Rather than separating romance and history, ***Ramona*** and *Squatter* fuse them through melodrama. The key strategy of their melodrama is to resolve social conflict imaginatively through the allegorical union of differing national constituencies in marriage.[15] These allegorical unions at once expand and contract the privileged sphere of whiteness, both including and excluding groups other than Anglo-Saxons. In 1870s California, recently conquered by the predominantly Anglo U.S., being identified as white conferred a social and economic advantage quickly solidifying into law. In this essay I join a growing body of scholars focusing on the ways in which white identity, understood as a socially constructed category, has been assumed or rejected in the process of redefining a socio-economic order. Minority characters in ***Ramona*** and *Squatter* exploit the protean character of whiteness, reconfiguring its bounds and meanings so as to realize differing political aims. Sentimentalism in these novels thus redefines the bounds of whiteness in order to undermine the cultural authority of male Anglo-Saxons, condemning the allegedly materialistic tendencies of whites, particularly squatters, as immoral.[16] These forces of "immorality" are arrayed against the virtue of the marginalized, whether white women, *Californios,* or Indians.[17]

To briefly summarize, *Squatter* and ***Ramona*** both endorse the infusion of the virtues of the victimized into the white male-identified dominant culture through their use of sentimentalism, a women's form of *engagé* writing constituted through the narrative strategies of melodrama: defending morally superior victims, adopting conciliatory approaches to avoid violent conflict, and forging alliances among the elite of different cultures and regions through marital and other unions that expand whiteness. In my analysis of *Squatter* and ***Ramona,*** I will examine the tension between the exclusionary logic of whiteness and the cross-cultural alliances that alternately reinforce and undermine it. By exploring how these novels contract, expand, and sometimes even disrupt the ideology of whiteness, we can explain their very different political aims.

The "Double Loop": Uniting "White Slaves" in *Squatter*

Struggles over land dominated the maneuvering for racial caste position in late nineteenth-century California. The California State Land Law of 1851 called for a thorough examination of *Californio* land titles on the fictitious grounds that such titles were confused, but the desire to make *ranchero* land available to Anglos through squatting, or homesteading, actually motivated the law. Costly legal fees forced the *Californios* to sell their land, and squatters took advantage of the legal irresolution to stake their claims on *Californio* ranchos. The *Californios* engaged "in relentless backyard guerrilla warfare with settlers bent on outright confiscation."[18] From 1851 to 1875, Anglos took control of "thousands of acres" of *Californio* land by a variety of legal and illegal methods.[19] Such conflicts over land, class and racial status, and male privilege take center stage in *The Squatter and the Don,* as its title suggests.

Squatter's intervention in such conflicts is structured by the moral oppositions within its sentimental discourse. The novel contrasts two means of securing class position: a conciliatory style characterized by the cross-cultural alliance politics of Mrs. Darrell, her son Clarence, and Don Mariano Alamar; and a violent, confrontational style characteristic of William Darrell and other Anglo squatters. When Mr. Darrell insists on staking a claim on Don Mariano's land, Mrs. Darrell responds by instructing her wealthy son Clarence to purchase the property against her husband's will, thereby avoiding conflict and channeling male agency.[20] When he learns of the transaction, Mr. Darrell accuses Don Mariano of "bribing" Clarence with the offer of Mercedes, the Don's daughter. "Livid with rage," Darrell attempts to strike the Don with his horsewhip, but before he can do so Gabriel Alamar tosses a *reata* around Darrell, physically containing his movement (*S,* 248). To this *reata* of violent conflict, *Squatter* counterposes its morally upright, sentimental alternative, the "double loop" of marital union, which later unites Clarence and Mercedes, thus joining Anglo and Californio elites (*S,* 123). The double loop refers to the ceremonial *lasso* tossed over the heads of bride and groom in traditional Mexican Catholic wedding ceremonies.[21]

Don Mariano takes a similarly conciliatory approach in his dealings with the squatters. Although they routinely destroy his property and refuse to cooperate, he proposes a compromise: he offers his cattle to the squatters so that they will stop killing them (as is their legal right), and he advises them to grow fruit rather than grains, suggesting the change that made California agriculture more profitable in the 1880s.[22] If the squatters cooperate, the Don promises to help pay for their irrigation and to drop his appeal against their land claims. The Don's plan for peaceful coexistence represents a shrewder, more rational capitalism than that enacted by the squatters, a capitalism that avoids conflict to ensure higher productivity. The *Californios*' conciliatory manner of interacting with both sympathetic and antagonistic Anglos reflects the influence of sentimental culture.

Ruiz de Burton represents characters from differing cultures as embodying morally desirable qualities in order to suggest political compatibilities, as in the parallel between the *Californios* and the white Southerner Mary Moreneau Darrell, the mother of Clarence. The narration implicitly compares the restraint, manners, and Catholicism of Mary and the white South she represents to similar qualities in Don Mariano, contrasting these traits with the Protestant, violent temper of William and the Northeast (*S,* 60). Mary's refined manners signal a potential alliance between the Southern and *Californio* elites.

Moreover, the South and California are both represented as sectional victims of the corrupt monopolies and the lower classes: "Well, the poor South is in pretty much the same fix that we are," George Mechlin says to his wife Elvira (*S,* 297). The novel calls for these victimized regional classes, white Southerners and *Californios,* both of whom embody old money, honor, traditional values, and a stable social hierarchy, to redeem the nation morally by displacing the monopoly capitalists. The North-South alliance creates an entrepreneurial finance capitalism that offers paternalistic control of the lower classes, whereas unfettered monopoly capitalism symbolizes chaos at both ends of the class hierarchy.

This North-South alliance marks Ruiz de Burton's departure from the antislavery version of sentimental politics found in Stowe, as is clear in the description of the Texas Pacific Railroad scheme. Southerner Tom Scott's proposed Texas Pacific Railroad would actualize an economic alliance between elite *Californios* and white Southerners.[23] Indeed, Gabriel Alamar and Clarence plan to start a bank in San Diego once the Texas Pacific railway has been constructed (*S,* 296). Their unsuccessful fight to bring the railroad to San Diego reveals that they hope to transform southern California and the South into the leaders of an expanding capitalist economy, with white Southerners, *Californios,* and sympathetic Northeasterners like Clarence at its helm.[24] By establishing commerce between the elites of different cultures and regions, the railroad epitomizes *Squatter*'s political project of postbellum sectional reconciliation.

At the end of the novel, Ruiz de Burton again emphasizes that the South and southern California are suffering a common plight—both "must wait and pray for a Redeemer who will emancipate the white slaves of California" from monopoly capitalists (*S,* 372). The phrase "white slaves" turns Stowe's antebellum brand of romantic racialism on its head, portraying a white elite rather than black slaves as oppressed. While Mr. Darrell was courting Mary Moreneau in Washington, D.C., she kept a black servant named Letitia, who "was devotedly attached to her" (*S,* 59). This brief reference to black-white race relations in the South marks Southern institutions as benevolent, allowing Ruiz de Burton to elide race and class hierarchies.[25] Whereas Stowe reconciles the races through antislavery sentimentalism, Ruiz de Burton promotes a racially homogeneous reconciliation between white representatives of the South and California. In Ruiz de Burton's paradoxical logic, the expansion of whiteness via the *Californio*/white South alliance depends on an expansion and inversion of the meaning of slavery. Sánchez and Pita, in claiming that the "Redeemer" longed for by the "white slaves" of California is both Christ-like and Lincoln-like, miss the historical irony that the white slaves, if redeemed, would go on enslaving Indians and blacks.

Calling the white upper classes slaves is possible in part because of what Immanuel Wallerstein has termed the dual appropriation of surplus in the capitalist world system: its appropriation by an owner from a laborer and its appropriation in peripheral zones by core zones.[26] Ruiz de Burton's inverted romantic racialism represents the relationship of "unequal exchange" between European and U.S. capitalist core zones and their underdeveloped peripheries and regional semiperipheries. Indeed, Almaguer has shown that California was a semiperipheral zone in the 1870s and 1880s. Thus the story Ruiz de Burton tells is not merely a provincial one but rather a regional variation of a global pattern of capitalist core-periphery disparities. Ruiz de Burton strategically emphasizes regional exploitation in the capitalist world system so as to create a discourse of white unity that obscures exploitation by race and class.

The South provides an ideal model for the strategy of downplaying race and class inequality. After the U.S. defeated California and the South in the Mexican American and Civil Wars, both could claim regional victim status.[27] The ideology of the "prostrate South" mistakenly held that physical damage to the South during the Civil War had devastated the Southern economy, thereby articulating a discourse of reunion on Southern terms.[28] Northerners bought into this ideology in the 1870s, expressing a new sympathy for the white Southern upper classes allegedly victimized by Reconstruction. California Governor Henry Haight draws upon this ideology in his 1867 victory speech, blaming nonwhites for the ills of both California and the South:

> I will simply say that in this result we protest . . . against populating this fair state with a race of Asiatics—against sharing with inferior races the Government of our country . . . and this protest of ours will be re-echoed in thunder tones by the great central states until the Southern States are emancipated from negro domination, and restored to their proper place as equals and sisters in the great Federal family.[29]

Haight uses the South as a model for white unity at the expense of nonwhites, just as Ruiz de Burton uses the discourse of the prostrate South in an attempt to secure a stable foothold for elite *Californios* in a racially hostile climate.

As the parallel between elite *Californios* and Southerners makes clear, Ruiz de Burton's alliance between these regions would not lead to a more egalitarian social order. Rather, portraying themselves as morally righteous victims enables the *Californios* to preserve their challenged status. The class status of *Californios* and Anglos depends on the exploitation of *mestizos,* Indians, and blacks. Clarence becomes a multimillionaire partly by speculating in western mines, mines that in California exploited primarily Mexican *mestizo* labor in supplying raw materials for the capitalist world system.[30] Their common exploitation of nonwhites links the squatters and dons, otherwise separated by culture and class. When Don Mariano proposes that the squatters raise cattle instead of growing grain, a squatter protests, "I ain't no '*vacquero,*'" implying that his white racial status precludes his working as a cowboy. Don Mariano, white in caste himself, attempts to reassure the squatter by responding that one can "hire an Indian boy" to perform such work (*S,* 94).[31]

Following the annexation of California by the United States, most Indians worked under a condition of peonage, coerced into remaining with a single employer by a creditor-debtor relationship. James Rawls likens such peonage to the Black Codes of the post-Reconstruction South. Indian peons composed most of the labor on *Californio* cattle farms like the Alamars' during their boom in the 1850s. Moreover, both *Californios* and Anglos participated in the kidnapping and slave trade of 4,000 Indian women and children between 1852 and 1867.[32] The enslavement of Indians thus persisted in this ostensibly union state even after the end of the Civil War, revealing yet another commonality between the nineteenth-century elites of California and the South.[33]

Indeed, *Squatter* proposes a race and class hierarchy only slightly different from that proposed by the squatters and monopoly capitalists. The squatters' hierarchy would racialize all Anglos as white and all *Californios*—regardless of class status—as nonwhite "greasers" (*S,* 73). By contrast, the novel proposes a hierarchy on the terms of the elite *Californios,* racializing both the Anglo and *Californio* elites at the top of the social order as white, while grouping at the bottom the Anglo "riff-raff," the squatters, other alleged "thieves," the Indians, *mestizos,* and African Americans (*S,* 67, 315).[34] In both systems the subordinate position of those racialized as nonwhite remains constant.

The novel's cultural work of maintaining racial hierarchies signals the necessity of shoring up the *Californios*' shaky elite status. The *Californios*' class status is unstable because the squatters threaten to dispossess them not only of their land and wealth but also of their racialization as white. Similarly, Clarence worries that his father's attack on Don Mariano has made the Darrell family "lose caste" (*S,* 274). As in ***Ramona,*** the *Californio* mother's prohibition of a cross-cultural union results from her fear that it will diminish her family's social standing. Before sanctioning the union, Doña Josefa demands that Clarence demonstrate his superiority to the squatters by distancing himself from his father's behavior. The union between Clarence and Mercedes offers a potential resolution of the two families' social instability. Clarence offers the Alamars wealth, business savvy, and financial ties; the *Californios* offer Clarence land, aristocratic traditions, and an elite status commensurate with his fortune.

The alliance proposed through the marriage plot is, however, destabilized by a sexual tension in the structure of the melodrama. The mother's prohibition shows that erotic attraction between groups must be tempered and legitimated by the mother's moral authority. The allegorical expansion from the individual to the collective involves a sublimation of disruptive sexual energies and interracial ties.[35] The nation as a sentimental imagined community needs the mother to secure its respectability, a respectability threatened by the culturally and racially diverse elements it must consolidate ideologically in order to maintain its authority.[36]

The representation of the Alamars as blue-eyed Spaniards similarly legitimates the proposed national alliance, in this case by strategically concealing the sexually charged issue of *mestizaje* (racial mixing). Historically speaking, money did tend to "whiten" Mexican families in formerly Mexican territory, but only in terms of class status.[37] Portraying the Alamars as resembling fair Europeans physically enables Ruiz de Burton to avoid figuring the union between Mercedes and Clarence as miscegenation, which would have been distasteful to the intended Anglo readership of C. Loyal, Ruiz de Burton's pseudonym. The shadow plot of miscegenation may explain why so many readers have tried to keep history and romance separate in these novels: the ostensibly cross-cultural unions covertly blur the racial bounds of the national community imagined as white Anglo-Saxon; the "white slaves of California" to be redeemed include both Anglos and "half-savage" *Californios.* The elements marking *Squatter* as a sentimental melodrama are thus crucial to its political project: unmasking the Big Four monopoly capitalists as the true "invaders" of California (rather than Anglo U.S. imperialists) and promoting an alliance of *Californios* and sympathetic Anglos in an effort to reconfigure whiteness.

Squatter's romantic racialism integrates the *Californios*—ostensibly white yet racially ambiguous—into whiteness as caste through marital union, overtly expanding whiteness yet covertly subverting concepts of racial purity. By contrast, ***Ramona***'s romantic racialism, through its overt plot of marital union, views the marginalized—Indians and *Californios*—as excluded from whiteness and rule, relegated to the nation's exploited lower classes. Even more so than *Squatter*'s, ***Ramona***'s overt plot is shadowed by a plot of racial ambiguity and homoerotics figuring a multiracial alliance that unsettles the nation's claims to racial and sexual propriety. If forgetting "is a crucial factor in the creation of a nation,"[38] then what is most forgotten is the sexual underside of sentimental plots focusing on maternal authority, marital union, and homoerotics (a countercultural form of national fraternity). Such shadow plots constitute what Raymond Williams has termed an "emergent structure of feeling": a new practice or experience "at the very edge of semantic availability" because it serves as an alternative to dominant understandings.[39] What I term the overt plot reinforces dominant discourses, while the covert or shadow plot subverts them by revealing their undersides and contradictions. In contrasting overt and shadow plots, I am distinguishing between the successful allegorical marital unions composing the Sommerian romance and other modes of allegorical union that fall out of her discussion because she privileges the term *romance* over the more neutral *melodrama.*[40]

The "Arrogant Mestiza" and Whiteness in Ramona

In *Squatter* Indians are represented as lowly "thieves" to be enslaved by Southerners and *Californios.* ***Ramona*** takes seriously Indians' struggles for rights in its portrayal of the consequences of Anglo expansion for the Indian Alessandro and his *mestiza* lover Ramona, even though it is set at a time when Indians no longer posed a threat to white expansion. The novel takes us on a California version of the "Trail of Tears," as Euro-American squatters, reviled as "thieves and liars" (***R,*** 177), lay claim to entire Indian villages, forcing Ramona, Alessandro, and his fellow villagers to undergo a series of removals to less and less desirable land.

The dire condition of Indians in California resulted from the 1849 California Constitution and the subsequent white aggression against Indians. Drafted by forty Anglos and eight *Californios,* this Constitution deprived Indians of the right to vote and other rights accorded "whites," a category comprising both Anglos and elite *Californios* (as in *Squatter*). Between 1850 and 1870, Indians were considered obstacles to Anglo settlement. Indeed, in 1851 Governor Peter Burnet endorsed a policy of exterminating the Indians. During the 1850s Indian villages suffered repeated assaults by volunteer military companies and by U.S. army troops, often ending in the destruction of entire villages.[41] In 1856 U.S. Army Captain Henry S. Burton, the husband of Ruiz de Burton, led his troops in a confrontation with the Indians portrayed in Jackson's novel—the Luiseño Indians of Temecula, in San Diego County.[42] As a result of such policies, the population of Native Americans in California plunged from 100,000 in 1850, to 20,000 in 1870, to 17,500 in 1900. Only in the 1870s, when Indians no longer posed a direct threat to Anglo settlement, were they granted basic civil rights by California, gaining the right to testify in court in 1872 and the right to vote in 1879. Nevertheless, as if confirming the relevance of ***Ramona***'s indictment of whites' mistreatment of Indians, as late as 1886 the California Supreme Court, in *Thompson v. Doaksum,* ruled that Indians had no legal claim to land they had previously occupied, a decision upheld by the U.S. Supreme Court in 1889. Indians were not granted U.S. citizenship until 1924.[43]

Despite the importance of the history of white-Indian race relations in ***Ramona,*** I would argue that we should not read the figure of the Indian in the novel only as the embodiment of systemic racial oppression of diverse Indian populations in California; rather, we should also attempt to understand the character of the *mestizo* or mixed-race American future that Ramona embodies. I thus shift from the political-economic analysis of my reading of *Squatter* to a more speculative tack in my analysis of ***Ramona.*** In my reading of *Squatter* it was necessary to provide considerable historical detail to demonstrate the specific political resonances of the term "white slave." Gauging the import of Ramona's contestation of whiteness as an "arrogant *mestiza*" calls for a different approach: here I spell out the narrative techniques by which the novel blurs racial boundaries, proposing novel conceptions of North American racial identity in the domain of common sense. Common sense, of course, is no less a political realm than the economic, as the theory of hegemony has shown. ***Ramona*** responds to the political and economic conditions of capitalist expansion—national consolidation and displacement of indigenous peoples—with an anguished, tragic narrative, but also with a shrewd reconfiguration of whiteness.

Ramona's shadow plot calls into question the racial hierarchy endorsed by *Squatter.* ***Ramona*** undermines whiteness by proposing cross-racial alliances through the ambiguous figure of the blue-eyed Ramona, the daughter of an Anglo and an Indian, who, as Martí suggests, chooses a politicized Indian identity, and through Ramona's successive marriages to Alessandro, an Indian, and Felipe, a *Californio.* ***Ramona*** also disrupts whiteness through the homoerotic relationship between Alessandro and Felipe. Both novels construct national identity as marked by racial oppression and interracial desire. The shadow of fraternity as the basis for national imagining is interracial homoeroticism, and the shadow of maternity and sibling affection is incest. These national/narrative "shadows" cast a pall over national respectability. Exploring the divisions of the national imaginary in more detail will show the extent to which Jackson undermines whiteness from within.

While *Squatter* portrays a marital union linking two cultures, in ***Ramona*** the ostensibly racially homogeneous marriage between Alessandro and Ramona solicits the reader's sympathies.[44] Their union constitutes the core of the novel's political strategy, which aims to turn its readers into reformists through sentimental discourse. Exemplifying the aims of this strategy, the Iserian implied reader of the novel, Aunt Ri Hyer, a white migrant from Tennessee, gains "heaps er new ideas inter [her] head"—and a newly conciliatory reformist stance—as a result of her acquaintance with the Indian couple (349).[45] The couple's devotion to their baby gradually warms Aunt Ri's heart, until "the last vestige of her prejudice against Indians had melted and gone" (***R,*** 347). Aunt Ri's change of heart suggests how the reader can similarly empathize with Indians.

The transformative potential of women's religious and moral influence is brought home even more dramatically in the description of Sam Merrill, an Anglo settler in Indian territory and a neighbor of the Hyers. After Aunt Ri criticizes Sam's callous assumption that murdering any Indian is justified, invoking, in typical sentimental fashion, the higher "law o' God," the narrator describes Merrill as a typical frontiersman. In a passage reminiscent of Stowe's description of Augustine St. Clare in *Uncle Tom's Cabin,*

Jackson portrays Merrill as a man whose violent experiences on the western "frontier" bury his virtuous New England heart:

> Young Merrill listened with unwonted gravity to Aunt Ri's earnest words. They reached a depth in his nature which had been long untouched; a stratum . . . which lay far beneath the surface. . . . Underneath the exterior crust of the most hardened and ruffianly nature often remains—its forms not yet quite fossilized—a realm full of the devout customs, doctrines, religious influences, which the boy knew, and the man remembers. . . . The wild frontier life had drawn him in and under, as in a whirlpool; but he was a New Englander yet at heart. (***R,*** 346)

This "romantic feminist" passage opposes the restraint and religious morality purportedly characteristic of women, New England, and the South to the "wild frontier life of men."[46] In ***Ramona,*** as in other sentimental novels, the job of women is to restore morality to men: Aunt Ri and the wife of the Anglo usurper of Alessandro's house perform the same function as Mrs. Darrell in *Squatter* and Mrs. Bird and Aunt Ophelia in *Uncle Tom's Cabin.* Thus Jackson's sentimental project, like Ruiz de Burton's, revives national morality, in the case of ***Ramona*** by according greater cultural authority and influence to the maternal sphere.

The novel attempts to achieve sentimental reform by countering racial ideologies that portray Indians as inherently criminal. Alessandro argues that Indians are not born thieves but rather are sometimes compelled by hunger to steal (***R,*** 308). Aunt Ri attacks another pillar of white supremacy when she argues that killing an Indian—despite California law—is indeed murder (***R,*** 345-46). Jackson thus aims to reinstate the personhood of Indians in the minds of Euro-American readers.

But in ***Ramona*** Indians are also lower-class laborers and "human ruins" to be pitied with imperialist nostalgia (***R,*** 324).[47] ***Ramona*** thereby replaces the "male" policy of displacing and exterminating Indians with the sentimental policy of seeing them as exploited members of the empire. The last name of Pablo and Alessandro, Assis, associates them with Saint Francis of Assisi and might be read as signifying that Indians must take a vow of poverty to be included in the nation. The overt reformist plot invites Indians into the imagined national community as long as they remain subordinate.

Since Alessandro is a "natural" man, "not a civilized man," who experiences "only simple, primitive, uneducated instincts and impulses," he needs to prove himself worthy of citizenship (54). Alessandro wins the favor of Señora Moreno through what she calls his "devotion" to her son (***R,*** 96). When Felipe faints while packing sheep's wool, Alessandro rushes to his rescue, proclaiming "I am very strong" (***R,*** 58). Alessandro plays a key role in Felipe's recovery, singing him to sleep and then keeping vigil. Their relationship embodies an opposition between savagery and civilization. Alessandro is associated with the body and nature, exemplified by his physical strength, singing talent, and motherly nurturing, while Felipe is associated with "training" (***R,*** 74). Alessandro paradoxically provides Felipe with both a strong father's physical support and the healing caress of a loving mother. Felipe alludes to the homoerotic character of their relationship when he remarks that when Alessandro sang, "I thought the Virgin had reached down and put her hand on my head and cooled it" (***R,*** 74).

Portrayals of homoeroticism and racial ambiguity provide a way for Jackson to both maintain and transcend national racial and sexual respectability. Racial ambiguity—exemplified both by Ramona's blue eyes and by the *Californios'* anomalous status as upper-class yet different from the Anglo norm in culture and color—seduces the reader into contemplating illicit affective and political unions, both homoerotic and cross-racial. Homoerotic and cross-racial unions do not, however, earn the national sanction figured in the mother's approval—neither Doña Josefa's in *Squatter* or Señora Moreno's in ***Ramona.*** Accordingly, the discourse of moral reform, in relying on the authority of the nation conceived of as family, must overtly satisfy expectations of racial and sexual homogeneity: Ruiz de Burton represents the *Californios* as white, and Ramona's Indian husband Alessandro dies. Egalitarian longings are relegated to the subterfuges of the shadow plot. Overtly Alessandro is a faithful member of the U.S. empire, but covertly he provides a symbol of resistance, one that Martí recognized, though few others have.

Ramona simultaneously forbids and invites its shadow plot, which is more fully developed than *Squatter*'s. Through the shadow plot the reader swallows "a big dose of information on the Indian question, without knowing it," as Jackson once described her project.[48] ***Ramona*** proposes a cross-racial alliance more implicitly than explicitly, operating on the hegemonic terrain of transforming common sense. To the extent that the homoerotic relationship between Felipe and Alessandro functions as an allegorical union in the covert plot, it undermines the dominant racial hierarchy. Moreover, Felipe's ambiguous racialization as a "half barbaric, half civilized" *Californio* invites white readers to indulge a transgression of race and gender norms without fully implicating themselves (***R,*** 11). After all, the *Californios* are only part white. Similarly, although Jackson marks the union between Ramona and Alessandro as racially homogeneous, Ramona's blue eyes suggest that she is also a site of identification for whites.

By soliciting the identification of readers with racially ambiguous subjects, the covert plot undermines racial discourses of absolute difference. Ramona is physically whitened, inviting white readers' identification, but emotionally, intellectually, and spiritually Indianized. Señora Moreno gives Ramona the chance of "marrying worthily" with a non-Indian, but Ramona refuses, rejecting the lure of whiteness to cast her lot with Indians (***R,*** 132). Ramona's love for Alessandro makes her lose her "race feeling," and she ceases to think of him in a racially marked way (***R,*** 75). Here Ramona provides a model for the white reader's disavowal of whiteness. Perhaps Ramona's rejection of whiteness explains why Martí celebrates her as an "arrogant *mestiza.*" For Martí, as for Ramona, Indianness is not merely a biological identity, a given, but also an identification, a choice.[49] Señora Moreno's contradictory racialization of Ramona also undermines racialist discourses of blood: she marks Ramona as predominantly white until her affair with Alessandro, after which she is viewed as predominantly Indian. As an alternative to such racialism, ***Ramona*** emphasizes upbringing; Alessandro's manners prove him worthy of associating with whites.

As in *Squatter,* national respectability is secured via the sanction of the mother; but while in *Squatter* Mercedes obeys her mother, Ramona defies Señora Moreno. Conflicts between the mother's desire for whiteness and the daughter's desire for Indianness come to a head when Señora Moreno strikes Ramona on the mouth upon encountering Ramona and Alessandro in an embrace. "The story of Ramona the Señora never told" (***R,*** 24), because to reveal Ramona as racially mixed would threaten her family's social standing as white, a fact that confirms my argument that national respectability is secured through both racial homogeneity and sexual propriety. Ramona's racial identity threatens Señora Moreno's sense of family propriety; when she catches the lovers kissing, she suspects a "disgraceful intrigue" involving sexual intercourse (***R,*** 114). Moreover, because Ramona is racially mixed, Señora Moreno can't bring herself to love her: "I like not these crosses. It is the worst, and not the best of each, that remains" (***R,*** 30). Señora Moreno only tolerates Ramona as a family member because she can pass for white. Thus when Ramona falls in love with an Indian, it is as if the repressed has returned—and speaks: "Terror for herself had stricken her dumb; terror for Alessandro gave her a voice" (***R,*** 112). It is the Indian that allows the *mestiza* to speak in her own voice, a voice marked as distinctively American, female, and part Indian. Thus while *Squatter* is concerned with carving out a space for *Californios* in whiteness, ***Ramona***'s protofeminism enacts a reformist project upsetting racial norms and establishing the personhood of Indians.

In stark contrast to Señora Moreno's sexist and anti-Indian politics, Ramona adapts creole nationalist ideologies to stake her claim to a uniquely *mestiza* American and women-oriented culture.[50] Ramona symbolizes the libidinal and collective possibilities of a racially "crossed" America that has been suppressed. Indeed, Ramona's simplicity signifies an American identity that contrasts with the Señora's European complexity: "She was a simple, joyous, gentle, clinging, faithful nature . . . as unlike as possible to the Señora's" (***R,*** 31). In contrast to the Señora's incestuous feelings for her son, Ramona's love for Alessandro is simple and desexualized:

> nothing could have been farther removed from anything like love-making. . . . This is a common mistake on the part of those who have never felt love's true bonds. . . . They are made as the great iron cables are made, on which bridges are swung across the widest water-channels,—not of single huge rods, or bars, which would be stronger, perhaps, to look at; but of myriads of the finest wires, each one by itself so fine, so frail, it would barely hold a child's kite in the wind. . . . Such cables do not break. (***R,*** 162)

While the Señora's love is selfish and mired in the past, Ramona's asexual yet productive love symbolizes the novel's sentimental, romantic racialist project for rule: exploited groups—Indians, *Californios,* and women—making "common cause" against tyrants (***R,*** 165).[51] The "myriads of the finest wires" of love elicit a cross-racial alliance between Anglo readers identifying with Ramona and Indians. However, the allegedly Indian qualities that compose the wires that bind the nation together—kindness, generosity, fidelity, and obedience—also construct Indians as subordinates, thereby contracting whiteness to exclude them. Even so, Jackson's project of white-Indian national reconciliation sharply contrasts with the intercultural but racially homogeneous national reconciliation in Ruiz de Burton.

Toward the end of Jackson's novel, the overt and shadow Ramonas approach each other in the representation of her multiracial family in Mexico. The overt Ramona is Indian by blood, while the shadow Ramona is ironically a blue-eyed model for Anglo readers. Whether Ramona is viewed as primarily Indian or European, her marriage to Felipe creates an explicitly multiracial family. By the end of the novel, the mantle of Americanness passes from the U.S. to Mexico. Felipe and Ramona's decision to move to Mexico expresses their disgust with the U.S. as dominated by greed and their willingness to consider alternative models of racially egalitarian rule.[52] Foreshadowing Martí's "Our America," Jackson even hints at a potential Indian and *mestizo* anti-imperialist uprising against the U.S. Alessandro says that the Indians would join the Mexicans if they were to "rise against" the U.S. (***R,*** 238). For Jackson, as for Martí, Señora Moreno represents the tyranny not only of Europe but also of the United States. While North America "drowns its Indians in blood," "Our America" will be "saved by its Indians," as Martí writes.[53] Both Jackson and Martí find in Latin America a polemical alternative to U.S. race relations.

The Enduring Hegemony of Whiteness

If ***Ramona*** and *Squatter* deserve to be read and reread because of their complex allegorical engagement with U.S. race relations and imperialism, as critics have shown, their politics must be viewed as shaped by their use of sentimentalism as an ethical discourse. Their engagement with social issues through sentimentalism thrusts us into a confusing thicket of contradictory political stances exemplified by the simultaneous expansion and contraction of whiteness. Stuart Hall has recently described such contradictory politics as exemplifying cultures of imperialism.[54] Conquerors and conquered cannot always be easily distinguished. This was especially the case with elite *Californios,* conquered with the annexation of California yet still conquerors in terms of race and class. Such "simultaneous contradictory conflicts," in Hall's phrase, are flattened out in Sánchez and Pita's assertion that the elite *Californios* in *Squatter* can be viewed as an "oppressed and marginalized . . . subaltern" collectivity.[55]

Even as *Squatter* and ***Ramona*** attempt to secure an expansion of opportunities for certain non-Anglos by expanding whiteness culturally in the overt plot and racially in the shadow plot, they simultaneously contract whiteness in a variety of ways. In *Squatter* the incorporation of the *Californios* into whiteness through allegorical union produces an elite-class discourse that subordinates nonwhites, as the comment "I ain't no *vacquero*" indicates. In ***Ramona*** the contraction of whiteness—the Indians' obligatory low-class status—is countered with an expansion or undermining of whiteness; Ramona's blue eyes signal her racial ambiguity and the possibility of multiracial alliances. This tension between the expansion and contraction of whiteness can be understood dialectically as its alternately assimilative and exclusionary operations.[56]

The expansion of whiteness in *Squatter* requires concealing the shadow plot of miscegenation implicit in cross-cultural union by representing Mercedes as Nordic rather than *mestiza*. By contrast, ***Ramona*** teases out the contradictions inherent in the dominant construction of the nation as sexually respectable and racially homogeneous through its treatment of homoeroticism, racial ambiguity, and miscegenation, and through its suggestion of the possibility of a multiracial uprising against the U.S. Moreover, ***Ramona*** further challenges the bounds of whiteness by allowing its readers to identify only with marginalized or displaced subjects: the Hyers, a poor white migrant family from Tennessee; the racially ambiguous Morenos; and Ramona, an Indian made more palatable through *mestizaje*.[57] These emergent structures of feeling constructing a politics of interracial alliance were waiting to be explicated by contemporary readers such as Martí.

As a romantic racialist/romantic feminist strategy of vindicating groups exploited on the basis of region, race, culture, class, or gender, sentimentalism links gender politics to racial caste politics. While *Squatter*'s female characters confirm their husbands' attempts to maintain white elite caste privilege, ***Ramona***'s rejection of whiteness enhances the power of women who choose to upset U.S. imperialism's racial hierarchies; its critique of whites' hostility towards Indians shapes its dismantling of whiteness as a strategy of sectional reconciliation and racial and gender oppression.[58]

I have focused on whiteness as the central point of contention in these texts for several reasons. First, whiteness has long shaped the subjective experience of class in the U.S., as David Roediger has argued. Thus maintaining or upsetting class hierarchies necessitates a reinforcement or dismantling of whiteness, as in Ruiz de Burton's and Jackson's nineteenth-century California. Second, since the dismantling of whiteness is directly related to women's political agency in these texts, whiteness provides a way of linking gender and racial oppression. Finally, in the current context of rollbacks against affirmative action in California and Texas, gutted inner cities, and attacks on Mexican and other immigrants, intellectuals can play a role in forming what Gramsci calls an "ideological bloc" aimed at dismantling whiteness.[59]

Notes

I would like to thank Stuart Christie, Susan Gillman, John González, José Saldívar, Roz Spafford, and Gene Ulansky for their comments on previous versions of this essay. I am also grateful to the anonymous readers for *American Literature* for their helpful suggestions.

1. See Tomás Almaguer, *Racial Fault Lines* (Berkeley and Los Angeles: Univ. of California Press, 1994), passim.

2. Michael Dorris, introduction to *Ramona* (New York: Signet Classics, 1988), xv; Rosaura Sánchez and Beatrice Pita, introduction to *The Squatter and the Don* (Houston: Arte Público Press, 1992), 5. (All quotations from *Ramona* and *The Squatter and the Don* are from these editions and are cited parenthetically in the text as *R* and *S*, respectively.) In an otherwise brilliant reading of *Ramona* in terms of legal discourse, Carl Gutiérrez-Jones argues similarly that *Ramona*'s romance betrays a politics more patriarchal than protofeminist: "Ultimately, the family romance may have overtaken Jackson's political intentions because her involvement in reform was continually subjected to patriarchal definitions of her project, definitions that always returned to the familial" (*Rethinking the Borderlands: Between Chicano Culture and Legal Discourse* [Berkeley and Los Angeles: Univ. of California Press, 1995], 65). For the canon-expanding feminist criticism on sentimentalism and the romance, see especially Ann Douglas, *The Feminization of American Culture* (New York: Knopf, 1977); Jane Tompkins, *Sensational Designs: The Cultural Work of American Fiction, 1790-1860* (New York: Oxford Univ. Press, 1985); Lauren Berlant, "The Female Woman: Fanny Fern and the Form of Sentiment," in *The Culture of Sentiment*, ed. Shirley Samuels (New York: Oxford Univ. Press, 1992); and Karen Sánchez-Eppler, *Touching Liberty: Abolition, Feminism, and the Politics of the Body* (Berkeley and Los Angeles: Univ. of California Press, 1993).

3. At times Sánchez and Pita define "romance" as a masculine quest narrative that attempts to transform reality, but elsewhere they speak of romance as a Harlequin-style formulaic love plot. Thus they view the relationship between history and romance as a "tension" between "two tracks" and are forced to rely on George Dekker's notion of the historical romance as a politicization of the romance. The fact that Dekker focuses on the "predominantly masculine genre" of the historical romance reveals to what

extent Sánchez and Pita end up at odds with feminist scholarship on the gender politics of genre; see George Dekker, *The American Historical Romance* (Cambridge: Cambridge Univ. Press, 1987).

4. See José Martí, introduction to Helen Hunt Jackson, *Ramona: Novela Americana,* trans. José Martí (New York: Jose Martí, 1888). For a reprint, see José Martí, *Obras Completas,* vol. 24 (Havana: Editorial Nacional de Cuba, 1965), 203-05. Martí was a poet, essayist, and Cuban independence leader who spent fifteen years in exile in New York before his death on a battlefield in Cuba in 1895.

5. José Martí, "The Indians in the United States," in *Inside the Monster by José Martí: Writings on the United States and American Imperialism,* ed. Philip S. Foner, trans. Elinor Randall et al. (New York: Monthly Review Press, 1975), 216. The tear is a defining trope of sentimentalism, writes Karen Sánchez-Eppler: "Reading sentimental fiction is . . . a bodily act, and the success of a story is gauged, in part, by its ability to translate words into heartbeats and sobs" (*Touching Liberty,* 26-27). I find Sánchez-Eppler's definition of sentimentalism useful here, even though I disagree with her overly pessimistic conclusions on white women's abolitionism.

6. The longstanding critical dismissal of the sentimental has worked to conceal an important inter-American cultural circuit: the antislavery and Indian reformism in Stowe and Jackson furnished Martí with a repertoire of sentimental rhetorical strategies for his revolutionary writings. My argument that Martí recognizes the power of *Ramona*'s sentimental strategies is corroborated by the fact that he himself employs sentimentalism in important essays in an effort to forge a revolutionary consensus among the Cuban exile communities. Martí adopts sentimental tropes in two of his key writings: the imprisoned son longing to see his mother in "Madre América" ("Mother America," 1889); and the son who disowns his sick Indian mother in "Nuestra América" ("Our America," 1891). Translations of both essays are included in José Martí, *Our America: Writings on Latin America and the Struggle for Cuban Independence,* ed. Philip Foner, trans. Elinor Randall (New York: Monthly Review Press, 1977).

7. José Martí, "Nuestra América" in *José Martí: Sus Mejores Páginas,* ed. Raimundo Lazo (México: Editorial Porrúa, 1970), 89. Martí's reading of *Ramona* in terms of "Our America" thus extends the term to include racialized groups in the U.S.

8. For the Easterner Albion Tourgée, like Martí a contemporary reviewer of *Ramona,* the novel's focus on *Californio* culture provokes reflection on what constitutes "our Anglo Saxon" culture. While Martí sees Ramona as the harbinger of an emerging civilization, Tourgée views her as embodying "two decaying civilizations," the Indian and the Spanish. Nevertheless, drawing on a study by the historian Hubert Bancroft, Tourgée argues that U.S. Indian policy was much harsher than Spanish treatment of Indians, and he condemns the annexation of California. Tourgée, like Martí, reads *Ramona* as an anti-imperialist text: "fiction and history have put in our hands the means of refuting error and rebuking wrong" ("A Study in Civilization," *The North American Review,* September 1886, 261).

9. When Ruiz de Burton proclaims "we . . . must wait and pray for a Redeemer who will emancipate the white slaves of California," she is drawing upon sentimentalism's rhetoric of Christian millenial commitment (*S,* 372). Similarly, Jackson claims that writing *Ramona* fulfilled God's designs: "I did not write *Ramona.* It was written through me" (quoted in Antoinette May, *Helen Hunt Jackson: A Lonely Voice of Conscience* [San Francisco: Chronicle Books, 1987], 135). She says that she modeled her novel on Stowe's exemplar of sentimentalist reform novels: "If I could write a story that would do for the Indian a thousandth part of what *Uncle Tom's Cabin* did for the Negro, I would be thankful the rest of my life" (quoted in Michael T. Marsden, "Helen Hunt Jackson: Docudramatist of the American Indian," *Markham Review* 10 [fall/winter 1980-81]: 17, 18).

10. Berlant, "The Female Woman," 268, 270.

11. What Sánchez and Pita term "feminization" serves only in the "handicapping of male agency . . . a corollary to emasculation" (introduction to *Squatter and the Don,* 46); it exposes the constraints on women rather than their resistance to such limits. The term *feminization* comes, of course, from Ann Douglas, who regards sentimentalism as "fakery" and as "anti-intellectual." Sánchez and Pita apparently accept Douglas's pessimistic conclusion that "Sentimentalism . . . never exists except in tandem with failed political consciousness" (*Feminization of American Culture,* 12-13, 254.

12. Romantic racialism is a more benign version of racialist thought than scientific racial determinism because it holds that various national and cultural groups are fundamentally different, with distinct racial "gifts," but that blacks and women are inherently superior rather than inherently inferior because they allegedly possess a greater degree of Christian morality and reverence and more deeply felt emotions than white men. DuBois's famous formulation of the "*souls* of black folk" reveals his indebtedness to this tradition; see George Fredrickson, "Uncle Tom and the Anglo-Saxons: Romantic Racialism in the North," in his *The Black Image in the White Mind: The Debate on Afro-American Character and Destiny, 1817-1914* (New York: Harper & Row, 1971), 97-129.

13. The widespread pairing of romantic racialism and romantic feminism is reflected in the multitude of antislavery advocates who also struggled on behalf of women's rights and in the widespread view that "the negro race is the feminine race of the world"

(Theodore Tilton, "The Negro: A Speech at Cooper Institute, New York, May 12, 1863," quoted in Fredrickson, *The Black Image in the White Mind,* 115).

14. In the postbellum era of what Nina Silber terms the "romance of reunion," a strain of Northern sentimental discourse made an about-face in extending sympathies to former slaveholders. By 1868, even Stowe had reversed her earlier position on Southern race relations, defending the former slaveholders as "poor, weak and defeated"; see Silber, *The Romance of Reunion: Northerners and the South, 1865-1900* (Chapel Hill: Univ. of North Carolina Press, 1993), 47-53.

15. I use the term *melodrama* because it is defined by its allegorical structure: characters embody "primal ethical forces" (Peter Brooks, *The Melodramatic Imagination* [New York: Columbia Univ. Press, 1985], ix). Jesús Martín Barbero argues that melodrama consists of a narrative mixing of ethics and aesthetics that we are taught to ignore as popular and vulgar; see his *Communication, Culture, and Hegemony* (London: Sage, 1993), 112-19, 224-28. On the allegorical "national romance," see Doris Sommer, *Foundational Fictions: The National Romances of Latin America* (Berkeley and Los Angeles: Univ. of California Press, 1991), 5-6. For an analysis of melodrama as an allegorical narrative of U.S. race relations, see Susan Gillman, "The Mulatto, Tragic or Triumphant? The Nineteenth-Century American Race Melodrama," in Samuels, *The Culture of Sentiment,* 221-43.

16. Here I hope to contribute to a growing body of scholarship on whiteness from a wide range of disciplines. Especially relevant to my study is Alexander Saxton's historicization of whiteness in the nineteenth-century U.S., *The Rise and Fall of the White Republic* (New York: Verso, 1991). Saxton argues that white racism repeatedly served as a means of creating a cross-class alliance of whites who stood to benefit materially from the oppression and exploitation of nonwhites. Other key studies of whiteness include Richard Dyer, "White," in his *The Matter of Images: Essays on Representations* (New York: Routledge, 1993); bell hooks, "Representing Whiteness in the Black Imagination," in *Cultural Studies,* ed. Lawrence Grossberg and Cary Nelson (New York: Routledge, 1992); George Lipsitz, "The Possessive Investment in Whiteness," *American Quarterly* 47 (September 1995): 369-87; Eric Lott, "White Like Me: Racial Cross-Dressing and the Construction of American Whiteness," in *Cultures of United States Imperialism,* ed. Amy Kaplan and Donald E. Pease (Durham: Duke Univ. Press, 1993); Toni Morrison, *Playing in the Dark: Whiteness in the Literary Imagination* (Cambridge: Harvard Univ. Press, 1992); and David Roediger, *Towards the Abolition of Whiteness* (New York: Verso, 1994).

17. According to Tomás Almaguer, the integration of regions into a national economy, in part through the construction of a vast railway network, allowed the U.S. to move from a semiperipheral to a core position in the capitalist world system. Thus the very form of these two novels—whether viewed as "regional novels" or allegorical melodramas—participates in the logic of capitalism by performing cultural work on behalf of national consolidation; see Almaguer, "Interpreting Chicano History: The World-System Approach to Nineteenth-Century California," *Review* 4 (winter 1981): 471, 491.

18. Leonard Pitt, *The Decline of the Californios* (Berkeley and Los Angeles: Univ. of California Press, 1965), 95. The breakup of the ranchos occurred more quickly in northern California than in southern California. Anglos controlled a great many northern ranchos by 1856 but didn't make substantial inroads into southern ranchos until 1875.

19. Almaguer, "Interpreting Chicano History," 492.

20. The narration emphasizes the important moral role the wife and mother play in the politicized familial sphere by employing war metaphors in describing Mr. and Mrs. Darrell's debate over the ethics of squatterism. Acknowledged by her husband to be a "comandante," Mrs. Darrell fights the holy war on behalf of virtue (*S,* 57).

21. At this point in *Squatter,* the families forging an alliance are the *Californio* Alamars and the Mechlins, Anglos associated with banking interests in New York. Gabriel Alamar marries Lizzie Mechlin, and Elvira Alamar marries George Mechlin.

22. Agriculture in California actually took the course prescribed by Don Mariano, shifting from small-scale grain farming in the 1870s to large-scale capitalist cultivation of fruits and vegetables in the 1880s and 1890s; see Almaguer, *Racial Fault Lines,* 31.

23. Thomas Scott, the president of the Texas and Pacific, was also the president of the Pennsylvania Railroad, "the biggest freight carrier in the world and probably the most powerful corporation in America at the time" (C. Vann Woodward, *Origins of the New South, 1877-1913* [Baton Rouge: Louisiana State Univ. Press, 1951], 31). Scott has the dubious honor of having called for federal army suppression of the first general strike in U.S. history, the St. Louis General Strike of 1877. Scott's railroad proposal challenged the monopoly of the Union Pacific and Central Pacific on transcontinental routes and to some symbolized an alliance between the South and West. In 1877 Congressman Lucius Lamar of Mississippi praised the bill for its promotion of a sectional reconciliation, but that year President Hayes announced his opposition to the bill. Southern Democrats called for a Western alliance in 1878, proclaiming their defiance "of Eastern capitalism, its banks, monetary system, railroads, and monopolies" (Woodward, 48). But by the end of 1878, the conservatives prevailed, and the South courted northeastern economic interests instead. On Scott's role in the St. Louis General Strike, see Roediger, *Towards the Abolition of Whiteness,* 92.

24. Following a depression in 1879, northeastern U.S. and English capital began investing heavily in the South and in the West; see Woodward, *Origins of the New South,* 113.

25. While Ruiz de Burton presents capitalism in the context of the South in euphemistic terms, she criticizes the inequities of capitalism on a global scale: "In the meanwhile, the money earned in California (as Californians only know how) is taken to build roads in Guatemala. Towns are crushed and sacrificed in California to carry prosperity to other countries" (*S,* 371).

26. See Immanuel Wallerstein, *The Capitalist World Economy* (New York: Cambridge Univ. Press, 1979): 18-19, 29. After 1873, core zones (Northern Europe, for example) engaged primarily in manufacturing and were characterized by strong state systems and wage labor. By contrast, the primarily agricultural peripheral zones were characterized by slave labor or other forms of coerced labor. Almaguer has shown that as early as the first decade of the 1800s California participated in the world system not only as a remote outpost during the Spanish (1769-1821) and Mexican (1821-1848) periods, but as an important source of raw materials (furs, hides, cattle) for New England merchants; see "Interpreting Chicano History," 469-80.

27. Following the Civil War, white Southerners seized on the image of the South as female—used by Northerners to justify their control over the allegedly helpless South—to create a counter-discourse of Southern victimization by the North; see Silber, *The Romance of Reunion,* 4-7.

28. Later historians have found that the South underwent a swift recovery in manufacturing and transportation following the Civil War, contradicting Southern claims of wholesale devastation. In addition, the slow growth of Southern agriculture was due primarily to blacks' withdrawal of labor following emancipation—their choice to work fewer days and fewer hours; see Roger Ransom and Richard Sutch, *One Kind of Freedom: The Economic Consequences of Emancipation* (New York: Cambridge Univ. Press, 1977), 41-51.

29. Quoted in Saxton, *The Rise and Fall of the White Republic,* 296.

30. One measure of mining's importance to the global economy is that "until 1887 more than half of the world's mercury supply came from California, the greater proportion of it from the New Almaden Quicksilver Mine near Santa Clara" (Pitt, *The Decline of the Californios,* 255).

31. The Treaty of Guadalupe Hidalgo marked a dramatic shift in the rule of California, but the condition of Indians as exploited and unfree labor remained the same or worsened. The 1849 California State Constitutional Convention in Monterey, attended by both Anglos and Californios, adopted a white supremacist policy of depriving Indians of political rights and according them inferior legal rights and a subordinate status as laborers; see James J. Rawls, *Indians of California* (Norman: Univ. of Oklahoma Press, 1984), 81-82, 86.

32. Rawls, *Indians of California,* 95.

33. Although northern California was pro-Union, as late as 1859 Los Angeles was a Democratic and proslavery town; see Pitt, *The Decline of the Californios,* 194.

34. According to Don Mariano, "Unfortunately . . . the discovery of gold brought to California the riff-raff of the world" (*S,* 67).

35. For a concise definition of allegory, see Fredric Jameson, *The Political Unconscious: Narrative as a Socially Symbolic Act* (Ithaca: Cornell Univ. Press), 30.

36. For Benedict Anderson fraternity is the key to national imaginings: "the nation is always conceived as a deep, horizontal comradeship" (*Imagined Communities: Reflections on the Origin and Spread of Nationalism* [New York: Verso, 1983], 7). By contrast, in melodrama maternity and sexuality are also central.

37. David Montejano argues that Mexicans in the late nineteenth-century U.S. were racialized according to their class status: landowners were considered Spanish; laborers were considered "half-breeds"; see Montejano, *Anglos and Mexicans in the Making of Texas, 1836-1986* (Austin: Univ. of Texas Press, 1987), 315.

38. Ernest Renan, "What is a Nation," in *Nation and Narration,* ed. Homi K. Bhabha (New York: Routledge, 1990), 11. See also Homi K. Bhabha, "DissemiNation: Time, Narrative, and the Margins of the Modern Nation," in *Nation and Narration,* 291-322.

39. Raymond Williams, *Marxism and Literature* (New York: Oxford Univ. Press, 1977), 130-32.

40. See Doris Sommer, *Foundational Fictions,* passim.

41. See Rawls, *Indians of California,* 86, 29, 121, 130-33.

42. Burton's march to Temecula in 1856 occurred at a time of especially great hostility between whites and Indians; see George Harwood Phillips, *Chiefs and Challengers: Indian Resistance and Cooperation in Southern California* (Berkeley and Los Angeles: Univ. of California Press, 1975), 132-34.

43. Both political-economic factors and extreme racial antagonism contributed to the declining population of Indians: sixty percent of deaths were due to disease, thirty percent to malnutrition and starvation, and ten percent to violent attacks by Anglos; see Almaguer, *Racial Fault Lines,* 130.

44. The intimate familial alliance that *Squatter* proposes between Anglos and Californios is not possible between *Ramona*'s Anglos and Indians because even in romantic racialist ideology Indians were racialized as

nonwhite. Since the Californios were deemed half-civilized, they were the only other cultural group Euro-Americans would marry in late nineteenth-century California. Native Americans were considered savage, so Indian women—or "squaws," as Anglos called them—were available only for illicit unions. The infrequency of formal marriage between Anglos and Indians meant that Jackson would have had difficulty winning sympathy for the plight of Indians had she chosen a white suitor for Ramona; see Almaguer, *Racial Fault Lines,* 58, 108, 120.

45. Michele Moylan identifies Aunt Ri as the Iserian implied reader in "Reading the Indians: The Ramona Myth in American Culture," *Prospects* 18 (1993): 155.

46. For discussions of "romantic feminism," see my comments above and Fredrickson, "Uncle Tom and the Anglo-Saxons," 114-15.

47. "Imperialist nostalgia" is a phrase coined by Renato Rosaldo in *Culture and Truth: The Remaking of Social Analysis* (Boston: Beacon Press, 1989), 68-90.

48. Moylan, "Reading the Indians," 154.

49. Marti, *Obras Completas,* 204.

50. Here "creole" refers not to black-Spanish and black-French mixtures in New Orleans but to Americans descended from the European peoples who subjected their states to colonial rule. Brazil, the colonies of Spain, and the U.S. were all "creole states, formed and led by people who shared a common language and common descent with those against whom they fought" (Anderson, *Imagined Communities,* 47). Creole nationalists distinguished themselves from the *peninsulares,* or colonial loyalists to Spain, by developing ideologies contrasting the Americas with Europe.

51. Marti argues similarly: "Common cause must be made with the oppressed, so as to secure the system against the interests and customs of the oppressors" ("Our America," 90).

52. *Ramona* thus enacts the "myth of Latin American racial democracy," a myth in tension with Jackson's portrayal of Señora Moreno as a corrupt Spaniard in the tradition of the "black legend." On the ideology of Latin American racial democracy, see Aline Helg, *Our Rightful Share: The Afro-Cuban Struggle for Equality, 1886-1912* (Chapel Hill: Univ. of North Carolina Press, 1995), 6-7 and passim; on the "black legend," see Michael Hunt, *Ideology and U.S. Foreign Policy* (New Haven: Yale Univ. Press, 1987), 58.

53. Martí, "Our America," 85.

54. According to Stuart Hall, postcolonial analysis is valuable for its refusal to construct imperial conflicts along stark lines of opposition; see Hall, "When Was 'The Post-Colonial'? Thinking at the Limit," in *The Post-Colonial Question: Common Skies, Divided Horizons,* ed. Iain Chambers and Lidia Curti (New York: Routledge, 1996), 242-60.

55. Sánchez and Pita, introduction to *Squatter,* 7-8.

56. I am indebted to Stuart Christie for this formulation.

57. Jackson's representation of Hartsell's "Mongrel establishment" as at once a tavern, a den of vice and white supremacy, and a life-sustaining farm readying itself for the harvest of a utopian interracial society best captures the emergent structure of feeling in Ramona, her Jamesonian "protopolitical impulses" that attempt to create a more egalitarian social order despite cultural limitations. On the emergent as the incipient crystalization of an alternative hegemony, see Williams, *Marxism and Literature,* 121-27; on "protopolitical impulses," see Jameson, *The Political Unconscious,* 287.

58. I have used whiteness as an analytical term rather than merely stressing the more abstract notion of the social construction of race because whiteness is more suited to describing hegemony, relations of power maintained by constituting and reconstituting "common sense," as David Roediger has argued (*Towards the Abolition of Whiteness,* 4-5). George Lipsitz has recently demonstrated the destructiveness of whiteness in its institutionalized form: government subsidies for racial suburbanization have constituted a massive "possessive investment" in whiteness, creating a systematic economic advantage for whites at the expense of people of color ("The Possessive Investment in Whiteness," passim). This investment in whiteness has fueled conservative and neoliberal attacks on public education, the universal health care plan, education, the inner city, and mass transportation, depriving poor and middle-class people of all races of access to much-needed services and human rights. My analysis of whiteness in nineteenth-century California attempts to contribute to the dismantling of whiteness by revealing its historically contingent workings. On hegemony, see Williams, *Marxism and Literature,* 108-14.

59. Antonio Gramsci, *Marxism: Essential Writings,* ed. David McLellan (New York: Oxford Univ. Press, 1988), 268.

FURTHER READING

Bibliographies

Byers, John R., Jr. and Elizabeth S. Byers. "Helen Hunt Jackson (1830-1885): A Critical Bibliography of Secondary Comment." In *American Literary Realism* 6, No. 3 (1973): 197-241.

Comprehensive bibliography of Jackson's writings, including brief annotations.

Olson, Kelli. "Helen Hunt Jackson." In *Nineteenth-Century American Women Writers: A Bio-Bibliographical Critical Sourcebook,* edited by Denise D. Knight, pp. 253-61. Westport: Greenwood Press, 1997.

Sourcebook for biographical and bibliographical information on Jackson.

Biographies

Banning, Evelyn I. *Helen Hunt Jackson.* New York: The Vanguard Press, 1973, 248 p.

Biographical survey of Jackson's life, with special emphasis on the circumstances surrounding the writing of *A Century of Dishonor* and *Ramona.*

Odell, Ruth. *Helen Hunt Jackson (H. H).* New York: Appleton-Century, 1939, 326 p.

A comprehensive biography of Jackson's life and works.

Criticism

Delany, Martin Robison. *The Condition, Elevation, Emigration, and Destiny of the Colored People of the United States.* New York: Arno Press and the New York Times, 1968, 215 p.

Provides historical and sociological information about minorities in the United States during the 1800s.

James, George Wharton. "Why Ramona Was Written." In his *Through Ramona's Country,* pp. 1-21, Boston: Little, Brown and Company, 1913.

James examines the reasons that led Jackson to write *Ramona.*

Mathes, Valerie Sherer. *The Indian Reform Letters of Helen Hunt Jackson, 1879-1885.* Norman: University of Oklahoma Press, 1998, 372 p.

Reprinted letters written by Helen Hunt Jackson during her involvement with the Native American cause, including two introductory essays on her works related to that subject.

Polanich, Judith K. "*Ramona's* Baskets: Romance and Reality." In *American Indian Culture and Research Journal* 21, No. 3 (1997): 145-62.

An overview of the art of basket-weaving during the late 1880s, with a comparison to baskets featured in *Ramona.*

Additional coverage of Jackson's life and career is contained in the following source published by the Gale Group: *Dictionary of Literary Biography,* Volumes 42, 47, 186, and 189.

James Russell Lowell
1819-1891

American poet, critic, essayist, and editor. The following entry presents recent criticism of Lowell's works. For further discussion of Lowell's life and career, see *NCLC,* Volume 2.

INTRODUCTION

Lowell is considered one of the most erudite and versatile American authors of the nineteenth century. In his earnest, formal verse, he sought to advance liberal causes and establish an American aesthetic. While such poems as *Ode Recited at the Commemoration of the Living and Dead Soldiers of Harvard University, July 21, 1865* (commonly referred to as the *Commemoration Ode*), and *The Vision of Sir Launfal* (1848) were widely admired in his day, Lowell's poetry is now considered diffuse and dated and is seldom read. Modern critics generally agree that his outstanding literary contributions were in the areas of satire and criticism in such works as *A Fable for Critics: A Glance at a Few of Our Literary Progenies* (1848) and *The Biglow Papers* (1848).

BIOGRAPHICAL INFORMATION

Lowell was born in Cambridge, Massachusetts to a wealthy and influential Boston family. His privileged ancestry and Harvard education provided Lowell with access to the New England literati, and as a young man he became acquainted with Ralph Waldo Emerson, Henry David Thoreau, and Henry Wadsworth Longfellow. A natural conservative, Lowell turned increasingly toward liberal humanitarianism after his marriage to Maria White, a poet and abolitionist who encouraged her husband to contribute poetry to the *National Anti-Slavery Standard* and the *Pennsylvania Freeman.* In 1848, Lowell achieved national acclaim with the publication of three of his best-known works: *Poems: Second Series, A Fable for Critics,* and *The Biglow Papers.* After his wife's death in 1853, Lowell concerned himself more with editing, scholarship, and criticism than with poetry. In 1855, he succeeded Longfellow as Smith Professor of Modern Languages at Harvard, a post which allowed him to travel abroad and study European languages and literature. Two years later, Lowell assumed additional responsibilities as first editor of the *Atlantic Monthly* and later joined Charles Eliot Norton as coeditor of the *North American Review.* In 1877, President Rutherford B. Hayes appointed Lowell minister to Spain. James Garfield, in 1880, transferred Lowell to England where the diplomat made himself known among London literary society. Lowell died in Cambridge in 1891.

MAJOR WORKS

Representative of his early poetry, *A Year's Life* (1841) demonstrates numerous technical flaws and a didactic tone that was to mar much of Lowell's later lyrical work. In contrast, many of the selections in his *Poems: Second Series* are political in nature, and represent Lowell's strengths as a public poet. *A Fable for Critics,* a witty diatribe written in lively though sometimes careless verse, is remarkable for its numerous critical appraisals of American literary figures which have endured through time and changing styles. An ingenious combination of humor, poetry, and trenchant satire written in a brisk Yankee dialect, the first volume of *The Biglow Papers* records the sardonic observations of Hosea Biglow, a New England farmer, and his neighbors as the United States enters the Mexican War. Lowell's popular verse fantasy *The Vision of Sir Launfal* follows an Arthurian knight in his search for the Holy Grail. Melancholy in tone, *The Cathedral* (1870) meditates on the subject of faith and was prompted by Lowell's visit to Chartres. His 1865 *Commemoration Ode* is considered among Lowell's most significant works of public poetry, and speaks to the enduring qualities of the American mind.

CRITICAL RECEPTION

During his lifetime, Lowell earned wide esteem as an arbiter of American literary tastes. Since his death, however, his reputation as a poet has declined significantly, though many continue to view his critical work favorably. Modern scholars have generally regarded the satirical *Biglow Papers* as Lowell's masterpiece. Additionally, the astuteness and scope of Lowell's criticism, despite some charges that it is merely impressionistic, has moved literary historians to consider him a major nineteenth-century American critic on a par with Edgar Allan Poe. He has been praised as well for his general prose pieces, personal essays that exhibit a wryness absent from his verse. Critics have also recently begun to focus on Lowell's relationship to the New England Transcendentalists, specifically Emerson and Thoreau. Overall, while acknowledging Lowell's numerous shortcomings as a poet, commentators have maintained a steady interest in his importance and contribution to nineteenth-century American literature as a satirist, journalist, and critic.

PRINCIPAL WORKS

A Year's Life (poetry) 1841
Poems (poetry) 1844
Conversations on Some of the Old Poets (criticism) 1845
The Biglow Papers (poetry) 1848
A Fable for Critics: A Glance at a Few of Our Literary Progenies (verse criticism) 1848
Poems: Second Series (poetry) 1848
The Vision of Sir Launfal (poetry) 1848
Fireside Travels (essays) 1864
Ode Recited at the Commemoration of the Living and Dead Soldiers of Harvard University, July 21, 1865 (poetry) 1865
The Biglow Papers: Second Series (poetry) 1867
Under the Willows and Other Poems (poetry) 1868
Among My Books (criticism) 1870
The Cathedral (poetry) 1870
My Study Windows (criticism) 1871
Among My Books: Second Series (criticism) 1876
Democracy and Other Addresses (essays) 1886
The Old English Dramatists (criticism) 1892
Letters (letters) 1893
Last Poems (poetry) 1895

CRITICISM

Robert A. Rees (essay date 1971)

SOURCE: "James Russell Lowell," in *Fifteen American Authors Before 1900: Bibliographic Essays on Research and Criticism,* edited by Robert A. Rees and Earl N. Harbert, University of Wisconsin Press, 1971, pp. 285-305.

[*In the following excerpt, Rees surveys biographical and critical assessments of Lowell, noting "that the definitive study of Lowell has not yet been written."*]

Biography

Though Lowell is extensively discussed in literary histories and critical works and though he is mentioned in biographies of other great men of his time, there are relatively few biographies of Lowell. Of these only two qualify as full-scale historical biographies: Horace Scudder's *James Russell Lowell: A Biography* and Martin Duberman's *James Russell Lowell.*

Scudder's book was preceded by such works as Francis H. Underwood's *The Poet and the Man: Recollections and Appreciations of James Russell Lowell* (Boston, 1892) and Edward Everett Hale, Jr.'s *James Russell Lowell and His Friends* (Boston, 1899). Written shortly after his death by those who saw him as the dominant literary figure of America, these books have little to recommend them to the modern scholar. Both authors are more interested in praising than in portraying and evaluating Lowell. An anonymous reviewer lamented particularly the superficiality of Hale's biography since Hale was "perhaps the one surviving man best acquainted with Lowell and his career from the brilliant start to the honored close." He saw Hale's book as "a series of gossipy reminiscences" which were "interesting . . . but also disappointing" ("Littérateur, Ambassador, Patriot, Cosmopolite," *Academy,* 29 July, 1899).

Two noteworthy views by Lowell's later contemporaries are those of Henry James and William Dean Howells, both of whom had long and intimate associations with Lowell. In his "Studies of Lowell" (a reprint of an essay in the September 1900 issue of *Scribner's*) in *Literary Friends and Acquaintance* (New York, 1900), Howells warmly recalls many visits with Lowell, especially at Elmwood. He concludes, "I believe neither in heroes nor in saints; but I believe in great and good men, and among such men Lowell was the richest nature I have known. His nature was not always serene and pellucid; it was sometimes roiled by the currents that counter and cross in all of us; but it was without the least alloy of insincerity, and it was never darkened by the shadow of a selfish fear. His genius was an instrument that responded in affluent harmony to the power that made him a humorist and that made him a poet, and appointed him rarely to be quite either alone."

Henry James recalled his long friendship with Lowell in two *Atlantic Monthly* essays (Jan. 1892 and Jan. 1897; the first was reprinted in *Essays in London and Elsewhere,* New York, 1893). James, who certainly was not blind to Lowell's shortcomings, considered him "completely representative." After rereading Lowell, James says, "He looms, in such a renewed impression, very large and ripe and sane, and if he was an admirable man of letters there should be no want of emphasis on the first term of the title." He concludes, "He was strong without narrowness; he was wise without bitterness and bright without folly. That appears for the most part the clearest ideal of those who handle the English form, and he was altogether in the straight tradition. This tradition will surely not forfeit its great part in the world so long as we continue occasionally to know it by what is so solid in performance and so stainless in character."

Scudder's two-volume study is a surprisingly competent work for its time. Scudder was the first scholar to use letters and manuscripts in telling the story of Lowell's life, and he is the first to suggest the complexities of the man. While Scudder, like Norton, is cautious and conservative when it comes to the proprieties of biography, one must credit him at least with an attempt at objectivity. It is a tribute to Scudder that subsequent biographers have been indebted to him and that his work was the standard biography for over sixty years.

Ferris Greenslet, *James Russell Lowell: His Life and Work* (Boston, 1905), proposed to write "a biography of the mind," but Greenslet, like others before him in the nineteenth century, set limitations which precluded any presentation of a viable image of the mind or the man. In his introduction Greenslet says, "In this narrative . . . there will be little occasion to adduce any piece of 'bare truth' that the man himself in his essays, his poems, and his letters has not made a part of the record." In spite of these limitations, and in spite of the fact that his work is derivative, Greenslet is at times accurate and perceptive about some aspects of Lowell's life. His chapter on Lowell's poetry is especially penetrating. Greenslet's later study, *The Lowells and Their Seven Worlds* (Boston, 1946), which is devoted to the Lowell family, adds little to his picture of Lowell. Perhaps the best brief biography of Lowell was that written for the *Dictionary of American Biography* (1933) by M. A. de Wolfe Howe, who makes a masterful summary of Lowell's life and an estimate of his place in American literature.

Only two major biographical studies of Lowell appeared between Greenslet's work and Duberman's: Richmond Croom Beatty's *James Russell Lowell* (Nashville, Tenn., 1942) and Leon Howard's *Victorian Knight-Errant: A Study of the Early Literary Career of James Russell Lowell.* Both studies are limited. In his preface Beatty admits to a bias ("almost everybody appears to have one") and then proceeds to manifest that bias on almost every page. As a southerner, Beatty seems incapable of forgiving Lowell for being a northerner and an abolitionist. He says Lowell "never understood history, . . . never comprehended politics. . . . Moreover, Harvard scholar though he was, he never made any effort worth mentioning to understand the civilization of the South. He proved himself, from his undergraduate days, a dupe of the most irresponsible propaganda his age afforded." Nor does Beatty give Lowell much credit as a thinker and a critic: "For the central facts about [Lowell's] mind were its discursiveness, its self-conscious irrelevance, and inner certainty, the compulsion of which was always present to disperse his meditations. . . . The evidence is unmistakable that any basic coherence in his thinking about literature appears to have come to him only at intervals, and by happy though sadly infrequent accidents." At times Beatty shows enough insight into Lowell to suggest he might have written a far better book.

Beatty's view on Lowell and the South does not jibe with that of Howells, who said of Lowell, in his reminiscence mentioned above (*Scribner's,* Sept. 1900): "He had a great tenderness for the broken and ruined South, whose sins he felt that he had had his share in visiting upon her, and he was willing to do what he could to ease her sorrows in the case of any particular Southerner." Howells's view is supported by Max L. Griffin's "Lowell and the South" (*Tulane Studies in English,* 1950). Griffin feels that Lowell's abolitionism was moral and philosophical rather than political and sectional, and that it did not affect his personal friendships with southerners.

Leon Howard's study is limited by design. Howard did not intend to write a full or a conventional biography; instead he wanted "to discover the extent to which a meticulous examination of an individual's entire literary output, within the human context of its origin, could improve one's understanding of the individual himself and of the age in which he lived." Howard's book is an interesting study in literary research; it is also the most comprehensive view we have of Lowell's life and times through his literature. Howard may give more information than some readers would wish, but he draws extensively and intelligently upon the canon of Lowell's creative work to provide us with many new biographical insights. One should not quibble with the limits stipulated by Howard, but one cannot help but wish he had carried his study past the year 1857 when, for him, Lowell reached a state of arrested development; the success of Howard's approach to the early Lowell makes us want to see all of Lowell in such a context.

Although written earlier than Howard's book, H. H. Clark's biographical introduction to *James Russell Lowell: Representative Selections* presents an interesting view that differs from Howard's premise. For Clark, Lowell's life underwent progressive change from beginning to end. Clark traces the development of Lowell's life and career through three major stages—the Humanitarian (to 1850), the Nationalist (1850 to 1867), and the Natural Aristocrat (1867 to 1891)—and makes a convincing argument that the evolution from one to the other was organic. This argument is based on Clark's earlier study, "Lowell—Humanitarian, Nationalist, or Humanist?" (*Studies in Philology,* July 1930), in which he argued that Lowell's life was "an essentially progressive and symmetrical expansion from a center, a steady widening of circles."

Duberman's intended scope was all-inclusive, and he had access to practically every manuscript relevant to Lowell's life. He made good use of those materials in filling in the gaps and fleshing out the details of Lowell's life and in correcting errors that have accumulated over the years. Duberman states that his purpose in writing the book was not "to restore Lowell's stature as a Renaissance figure or a literary giant" (he feels that Lowell was neither), but "to restore him as a man." Duberman is interested in Lowell as a virtuous man, as a man of character, and not as a man of letters. One has the feeling that part of the real Lowell is still missing and that Duberman's easy dismissal of Lowell as an artist ("There are many moments in his poetry, long sections in his essays, which deserve respect, . . . but they remain incidental; rather than high-lighting a consolidated achievement, they call attention to its absence.") suggests that he does not fully understand Lowell. But Duberman's study is likely to be the best that we will have for some time. Perhaps it need disappoint only those who still consider Lowell primarily as a litterateur, as a man who gave American letters a dignity that it has seldom had in our history.

A biographical study of Lowell which has appeared since Duberman's, Claire McGlinchee's Twayne's United States Authors Series *James Russell Lowell* (New York, 1967), is hardly worthy of mention. A glib and superficial study, it contributes nothing to our understanding of Lowell.

One of the difficulties that have faced his biographers and one of the reasons why the essential Lowell has in one way or another eluded all of his biographers, is that he was so diverse and so versatile. If comparison often places him second in some category of literary or other endeavors, rarely has one man demonstrated excellence in so many facets. He was: poet, essayist, humorist, letter-writer, linguist, critic. He was also: abolitionist, journalist, crusader for political and other reform, diplomat, teacher of modern foreign languages and literatures, public lecturer, after-dinner speaker, and editor (*The Pioneer, The Atlantic Monthly,* and *The North American Review*). As Frank R. Stockton said in a "Personal Tribute to Lowell" written at the time of Lowell's death, "Without occupying the highest rank in any of his vocations, he stood in front of his fellow citizens because he held so high a rank in so many of them" (*The Writer,* Sept. 1891).

There are areas of Lowell's life which need further attention. Though a great deal is known of Lowell and Lowell's thinking from the time of his youth, his letters are revelatory on some matters and carefully silent on others. These areas of reverberating silence involve his relationships with his family and his feeling about his mother's insanity. The silence is entirely in keeping with nineteenth-century reticence; it indicates no scandal, but it cuts off a means of insight into Lowell as a creative artist. That he had a morbid streak far deeper than his contemporaries realized or reported can be deduced from many *passim* remarks. And no one has satisfactorily come to terms with Lowell's mysticism, an aspect of his life on which there is a good deal of divided opinion. Psychoanalysis, applied through the veil of over a century and based on fragmentary evidence, would be foolish and dangerous, but some new attempt to evaluate and to interpret all of Lowell's character and personality is needed.

Another area that needs further exploration is the influence of Lowell's wives upon his moral and intellectual patterns. There is speculation that Maria was more devoted to abolition than he was and that she was more creative. There are also indications that Frances did not like Lowell's dialect poetry; since moderns consider this one of his strongest areas, did she inhibit him from developing further along this line?

Perhaps there are parts of the Lowell puzzle which we will never find, but until we understand more about the complexities of his personality we will never completely understand him as a creative artist. Perhaps the key to the puzzle lies in the works themselves. And until a biographer comes along who has a greater interest in Lowell's total creative output—bad as well as good—we are not likely to get the story of Lowell's life which we need and which he deserves.

Criticism

James Russell Lowell's critical reputation has never been very secure. In almost every decade since he started writing, he has been praised by some critics and damned by others—sometimes for the same thing. One could generalize, however, that before his death Lowell was praised for things that were not true of him and after his death damned for things that were.

Lowell's critics seem always to lament that he was not something other than he was: a more disciplined poet, less a dilettante, more patriotic, less a Puritan, more a scholar, less an Anglophile, more an abolitionist, and so on. Critics wishing that Lowell were not himself seem to reflect Poe's sentiment on first meeting Lowell: "He is not half the noble looking person I expected to see."

While a good deal of nineteenth-century criticism is essentially effusive and of little critical worth to modern readers, there have been from the beginning a few critics who have tried to be objective about Lowell. Of Lowell's early contemporaries, perhaps the views of Edgar Allan Poe and Margaret Fuller are most significant. Poe felt that Lowell was the best poet in America with the exception of Longfellow and "perhaps one other" (presumably Poe himself), essentially because of the vigor of Lowell's imagination. Poe, however, felt that Lowell's ear for rhythm was imperfect and his artistic ability of second rank. Poe was less than enthusiastic about ***A Fable for Critics,*** which he found "essentially 'loose'—ill conceived and feebly executed as well in detail as in general" and lacking polish (*Southern Literary Messenger,* Mar. 1849). Poe's estimate may have been colored by Lowell's finding him "two-fifths sheer fudge" in the ***Fable.***

Margaret Fuller was more sharply critical of Lowell and, in her estimate of his reputation, almost prophetic. Speaking of Longfellow, she says, "Though imitative, his [poetry] is not mechanical. We cannot say as much for Lowell, who, we must declare it, though to the grief of some friends, and the disgust of more, is absolutely wanting in the true spirit and tone of poesy. His interest in the moral questions of the day has supplied the want of vitality in himself; his great facility at versification has enabled him to fill the ear with a copious stream of pleasant sound. But his verse is stereotyped; his thought sounds no depth, and posterity will not remember him." In retaliation, Lowell painted a most unflattering portrait of Miss Fuller in the ***Fable*** and refused to remove or soften it in later editions.

Lowell's death in 1891 stimulated some of the most vigorous criticism of him in the nineteenth century. Thomas Wentworth Higginson is perhaps representative of those who were extravagant in their evaluations of Lowell. Higginson (*Nation,* 13 August 1891) called the ***Commemoration Ode*** "the finest single poem yet produced in this country"; and Lowell himself "our foremost critic." If Higginson is close to the mark in these estimates, he was clearly off the mark in stating that "no American author, unless it be Emerson, has achieved a securer hold upon a lasting fame."

An opposite, almost violent reaction to Lowell is found in an anonymous review of his ***Last Poems*** (1895) in the *Athenaeum* (4 January 1896). The reviewer considers Lowell a third-rate poet primarily because of his inability to use metaphor properly: "The figure of speech was to him speech at its finest elevation; and he laid violent and indiscriminate hands on everything that could be compared to anything else." He adds, "But after all it is not the prevalence of bad lines, of false metaphors, of any other external blemish, that forbids us to assign Lowell any place among the conspicuous poets of his time; it is his radically prosaic attitude of mind and his radically prosaic construction of verse. . . . He gets the right number of syllables in his lines, but he seems to get them by counting on his fingers." He concludes, "That he should ever have seemed to the American critic or the American public a poet of national importance is, perhaps, the severest criticism on itself that the American nation has ever made."

A more rational and perceptive English view is that in "An English Estimate of Lowell" (*Forum New York,* Oct. 1891) by Frederic William Farrar. Farrar points out that Lowell "might have been greater, had he in some respects been less. He might have done more, had he not known so much." Farrar felt that ***A Fable for Critics*** had been underestimated, that it had "a very unusual power of seeing the real men through the glamour of temporary popularity and the cloud of passing dislike." Farrar is just as perceptive when it comes to Lowell's poetry: "The chief element of his strength, and not of his weakness, was the intensity of that moral sympathy which makes his best poetry distinctly didactic. The best chords of his lyre are exactly those in which he means to preach." Farrar sees Lowell's poetry as being too imitative; "sometimes defective in distinctness, and sometimes in symmetry, as well as sometimes in melody"; and lacking "a clear, definite impression."

A final nineteenth-century estimate worthy of mention is that of Henry James in Charles Dudley Warner's edition of *A Library of the World's Best Literature, Ancient and Modern* (New York, 1897). James was impressed with Lowell's learning and his versatility, which gave him "among Americans of his time, the supreme right to wear the title of a man of letters." James praises ***The Biglow Papers*** as "an extraordinary performance and a rare work of art" which established Lowell as "the master and the real authority" of dialect and colloquial writing. Of Lowell's poetry, James remarks, "The chords of his lyre were of the precious metal, but not perhaps always of the last lyric tenuity. He struck them with a hand not idle enough for mere moods, and yet not impulsive enough for the great reverberations. He was sometimes too ingenious, as well as too reasonable and responsible."

While others criticized Lowell for his Puritanism, James praised him for it: "It is the recognition of the eternal difference between right and wrong that gives the ring to his earliest melodies, the point to his satire, the standard to his critical judgments, the sublimity to his ***Commemoration Ode***" (*Atlantic Monthly,* Jan. 1897).

Ferris Greenslet's biography of Lowell did not add much to Scudder's in terms of biographical fact, but he far surpassed Scudder in his critical evaluation of Lowell as a writer. In speaking of Lowell's weakness as a poet, Greenslet observes, "The expression of his views and opinions meant more to him—in all save his most ecstatic poetic moods—than the production of a perfect poem; and he was never steadily able to distinguish between the stress of opinions seeking utterance and the pure poetic impulse." In spite of these shortcomings, Greenslet feels that much of Lowell's poetry succeeds because of "the utter and fervent sincerity of the moods expressed in it"; "the amount of mind that lay back of it"; and "the constant ideality, which was both root and branch of his sincerity and of his abounding intellectual life."

Like others before and after him, Greenslet found the best and the worst of Lowell's prose related to Lowell's conversational style. It is loosely structured and lacking in intellectual unity, but full of learning and emotionally convincing.

An important early twentieth-century essay on Lowell was that by William C. Brownell in his *American Prose Mas-*

ters (New York, 1909).[1] For Brownell, Lowell had a "representative rather than individual turn of mind" and "was not an original but an independent thinker" whose chief qualities were his poise; his passion for patriotism, books, and nature; his "ingrained cleverness" and "his extraordinary personal charm." Brownell feels that, although Lowell's prose "has the piquancy of Pegasus in harness, . . . at least it is never prose poetry. It is masculine, direct, flexible, and energetic prose." While he feels that Lowell wrote "a good deal too much verse," Brownell believes that "a great deal of it is very fine, very noble and at times very beautiful, and it discloses the distinctly poetic faculty of which rhythmic and figurative is native expression." Brownell is of the opinion that Lowell's "patriotic poetry is altogether unmatched—even unrivalled."

Bliss Perry took the occasion of the commemoration of the centenary of Lowell's birth to answer some of Brownell's charges against Lowell. In "James Russell Lowell" (*Harvard Graduate Magazine,* June 1919), Perry felt that Brownell failed to answer the question as to why, in spite of his defects, Lowell's essays were read "with such pleasure by so many intelligent" people. Perry felt that Lowell's greatness was due to the fact that he wrote in a great tradition of literary essays and that he was so much a man of learning and culture. If Lowell was not a great poet, Perry feels, it was because "his was a divided nature, so variously endowed that complete integration was difficult."

In *The Spirit of American Literature* (Garden City, N.Y., 1913), John Albert Macy states that, with the exception of ***The Biglow Papers,*** Lowell's poetry is not successful, "the music simply does not happen." ***The Biglow Papers,*** however, "have no rivals. . . . Occasional poems, they have wings that lift them above occasion to immortality. In them Lowell is possessed by his genius, by a genius that never visited anyone else in the same shape." Macy is one of the few who considers the second series of ***The Biglow Papers*** superior to the first.

Further praise of ***The Biglow Papers*** is found in Edward M. Chapman's "***The Biglow Papers*** Fifty Years After" (*Yale Review,* Oct. 1916). Chapman sees ***The Biglow Papers*** as Lowell's chief contribution to literature because they are written "in a field [humorous wit] where his learning was most profound and his heart most enlisted."

The most extravagant praise of ***The Biglow Papers*** is found in Lewis H. Chrisman's "Permanent Values in ***The Biglow Papers***" in his *John Ruskin, Preacher, and Other Essays* (New York, 1921). Chrisman feels that "in American literature in the field of satire we have nothing better to show than Lowell's ***Biglow Papers***." He adds, "No other writer has written in dialect lines so pathetically beautiful and enchantingly melodious." ***The Biglow Papers*** contain "some of the ripest, richest, and most virile thoughts in American literature." Less hyperbolic but as appreciative is Jenette Reid Tandy's estimate in her *Crackerbox Philosophers in American Humor and Satire* (New York, 1925): "Lowell's range and penetration in satirical portraiture are unsurpassed in America. As a piece of sustained irony ***The Biglow Papers*** has escaped the careful study of present-day critics. We have no other satirist at once so witty and so racy."

An opposite view of ***The Biglow Papers*** is seen in V. L. Parrington's *The Romantic Revolution in America* (New York, 1927). Parrington says, "The native clutter of Lowell's mind is there laid bare—the grotesque mixture of homely satire, moral aphorisms, Yankee linguistics, literary criticism—an unwieldy mass that he could neither simplify nor reduce to order. The machinery spoils the propaganda and weighs down the satire." This is characteristic of Parrington's entire estimate of Lowell. He sees Lowell as limited by his Brahmin and Puritan background and to the last "extraordinarily parochial." For Parrington, Lowell "never speculated widely or analyzed critically. Ideas, systems of thought, intellectual and social movements, he had no interest in; he was content to remain a bookish amateur in letters, loitering over old volumes for the pleasure of finding apt phrases and verbal curiosities. With all his reading, history remained a blank to him; and science he would have none of."

H. H. Clark offered another view of Lowell's Puritanism in his essay on "Lowell's Criticism of Romantic Literature" (*PMLA,* Mar. 1925): "Lowell's refusal to divorce art from ethics goes far deeper than puritanism; it is part of the humanistic creed. Although Lowell appears to stress the ethical side of art, he is very far from slighting beauty; he simply asks that beauty be disciplined to some centre of universal human experience."

In his essay on Lowell in *Nature in American Literature* (New York, 1923), Norman Foerster says that "although nature is the theme or background of most of the poems, [Lowell] never writes of her with sustained spontaneity." Foerster ponders why Lowell's poetry of nature is not better than it is and concludes that it is due to Lowell's failure as an artist to revise and polish his verse and to "the paralyzing effect of the spirit of the times" which confused Lowell's heart and mind.

In the thirties and forties there was a general critical reaction against Lowell. Writing with a definite Marxist bias, Granville Hicks, in *The Great Tradition* (New York, 1933), sees Lowell as inexorably locked into his Brahminism to the extent that he always looked backwards. For Hicks, Lowell belonged to a class of writers who were "kindly men, well-informed, well-intentioned, full of eloquent professions of patriotic and literary zeal, but they were nevertheless parasites—parasites upon the past, upon foreign culture, upon an industrial order that they did not try to understand, did not think of reforming, and did not even venture to defend and advance."

Hicks's point of view is echoed in Percy Boynton's *Literature and American Life* (Boston, 1936) and, to a lesser extent, in Van Wyck Brooks's *The Flowering of New England* (New York, 1936).

In his *American Prosody* (New York, 1935), Gay Wilson Allen found no system or theory of prosody in Lowell's poetry. He concludes, "We must decide that Lowell made no direct contribution to American prosodic thought, but his versification introduced into American poetry the freedom which we find in the first two or three decades of nineteenth-century English poetry."

The anti-Lowell sentiment of the thirties and forties can perhaps best be summarized by quoting the conclusion of Arthur W. M. Voss's 1949 essay on "James Russell Lowell" (*University of Kansas City Review,* Spring 1949): "He was a significant force in furthering our cultural development and is therefore a worthy subject of study for the literary scholar and historian. But he wrote no books which have true literary power. A volume of considerable literary merit might be culled from his writings, but it would be made up of passages and parts, not wholes. Lowell served the cause of humane letters well, but whoever holds that only the best of intellects, the greatest of literary artists, are worthy of the reader's serious attention may ignore him."

Although Leon Howard's interest in Lowell's writings is essentially biographical, his study nevertheless contains a good deal of astute critical commentary. For Howard, the main value of the poems and essays is not in the literary merit they possess, but in the insight they give into Lowell's life and the age he lived in: "Lowell never achieved the quality of excellence which makes some literature so great that it possesses a life of its own, independent of time and place. He was intimately a part of nineteenth-century America, and his importance is determined by that intimacy rather than by the inherent quality of his writings."

Howard sees Lowell's early poetry as his best because Lowell was "fighting wholeheartedly for a poet's place in a difficult world." For Howard, Lowell became less a true poet in middle and later life, because he confused the role of the poet with that of the preacher or moralist and because he "accepted the wisdom of the market place instead of pursuing something less tangible. . . . As a poet, he applied his craftsmanship to writing up to the occasion which called forth his verses, instead of trying to compete with the best that had been thought and said in the world before him."

In spite of such sentiments, Lowell has continued to have his defenders. In his *The Conservative Mind from Burke to Santayana* (Chicago, 1953), Russell Kirk notes that it had become fashionable to belittle Lowell. Kirk answers such critics as Parrington and Harold Laski (*The American Democracy,* New York, 1948) in saying of Lowell: "But how civilized a man, and how versatile! Whoever reads Lowell's letters is not likely to dismiss him summarily. . . . Lowell founded the major American school of literary criticism; he was a poet of high, if limited talent; and he represented the best in Brahmin culture."

George Arms believes that part of the decline in Lowell's reputation is related to the fact that he has been so poorly represented in anthologies, something Arms attempts to correct in the selections of Lowell's poetry he includes in *The Fields Were Green* (Stanford, Calif., 1953). Though Arms feels that Lowell is essentially a failure as a poet ("These closing pages are not written with the hope of making the reader forget the enormously disheartening effect that Lowell's verses as a whole produce."), he feels his best poetry has been wrongly judged by association with his worst. For Arms, Lowell "had a real genius for a certain kind of poem" and Lowell's reputation as a poet must rest on a handful of poems (in addition to ***The Biglow Papers*** and ***A Fable for Critics***): **"Agassiz," "Fitz Adam's Story," "To the Dandelion," "Auspex," "The Cathedral,"** and ***Ode Recited at the Harvard Commemoration.***

In *The Continuity of American Poetry* (Princeton, N.J., 1961), Roy Harvey Pearce sees Lowell as the poet of the ideal, who wrote poetry "to give direction and coherence to men living in the real world and save them from their temptation to take seriously the natural world." As such, Lowell is the "poet as patriarch" and preacher, who writes good public but not good private poems, who sings Songs of Ourselves, but no Song of Myself.

In "The Craftsmanship of Lowell: Revisions in ***The Cathedral***" (*Bulletin of the New York Public Library,* Jan. 1966), G. Thomas Tanselle demonstrates that Lowell was a better craftsman than he is usually accounted.

The matter of Lowell's reputation as a critic deserves special mention if for no other reason than that it has been given special attention by critics and literary historians. Lowell was considered by his contemporaries to be the foremost critic in American letters. This was undoubtedly due in part to his astute appraisal of his contemporaries (and himself) in ***A Fable for Critics*** and to the fact that he expressed his critical views on a variety of subjects over a long period of time.

Although Lowell's reputation as a critic was relatively more secure in the nineteenth century, there were those who belittled that reputation. Two early essays point to the weaknesses that twentieth-century critics were to emphasize. In "Professor Lowell as Critic" (*Lippincott's Monthly Magazine,* June 1871), John Foster Kirk feels that Lowell is "narrow, shallow, and hard, destitute of the insight, the comprehension, the sympathy, by which the true critic, the true poet, searches the domain of thought and the recesses of the mind, illumines the emotions and kindles them." In a long article on "Mr. Lowell's Prose" (*Scribner's,* May, June, July 1872), William Cleaver Wilkinson grants Lowell the wide literary background, the ability to empathize with other writers, and the artistry requisite to the good critic, but feels that Lowell fails as a critic because he has no basic and systematic critical position.

While admiring Lowell as a scholar and man of culture, William C. Brownell, in *American Prose Masters,* feels that Lowell was deficient as a critic because "he occupied himself mainly with genius. As a subject . . . the best was good enough for him." This, according to Brownell, led to Lowell's proclivity to rank poets rather than to evaluate and describe them. Lowell's failure as critic was related to three characteristics, according to Brownell: his criticism grew out of his reading and not out of his thought; he was insensitive to the plastic arts; and he had "no philosophic view to advocate or express."

In the first comprehensive treatment of Lowell as critic (*James Russell Lowell as a Critic,* New York, 1915), Joseph J. Reilly expands on Brownell's view. He considers Lowell a failure because he was limited in his critical interest; he was deficient in his knowledge of art and history; he lacked sympathy for science and classical art; and he had little interest in drama and fiction. According to Reilly, "If Lowell is to survive, it must be frankly as an impressionist, for so far as criticism approaches a science, so far as it depends to any serious extent on ultimate principles, so far, in a word, as it is something more fundamental and abiding than the *ipse dixit* of an appreciator, Lowell is not a critic."

George E. De Mille in "The Critic from Cambridge" (*Sewanee Review,* Oct. 1924) does not try to determine how good a critic Lowell is, but what kind of critic. If Lowell is measured by the standards of the scientific critic "we can hardly say that Lowell is a critic at all. If, on the other hand, we accept Professor Brewster's definition . . . that criticism is simply 'talk about books,' . . . Lowell takes a very high rank indeed."

In *The Romantic Revolution in America* V. L. Parrington takes Reilly's first definition and finds Lowell sorely wanting: "He had no standards other than ethical, only likes and dislikes; no interest in ideas, only a pottering concern for the text; no historical backgrounds, only isolated figures dwelling in a vacuum. He was puzzled over new schools and unfamiliar technic, and was at ease only in praising established reputations and confirming approved judgments."

The best defense of Lowell as critic has been made by Norman Foerster. In "The Creed of Lowell as Literary Critic" (*Studies in Philology,* July 1927), Foerster counters Brownell's contention that Lowell's criticism "lacks the unity of a body of doctrine." In a fuller treatment published the following year in his *American Criticism: A Study in Literary Theory from Poe to the Present* (Boston and New York, 1928), Foerster calls Lowell "our most distinguished literary critic," and defends him against the charge of being merely an impressionist. Foerster feels that Lowell had a "comprehensive vision of the task of the critic. It involves sensitiveness to impressions, historical understanding, and an aesthetic-ethical judgment." If Foerster's views seem at times too much influenced by New Humanism, his defense of Lowell helped to pave the way for a more balanced view of Lowell as critic.

Although generally appreciative of Lowell's critical ability, Bernard Smith (*Forces in American Criticism,* New York, 1939) points out that Lowell did not understand or sympathize with contemporary literary movements after the Civil War. He had nothing to say about Twain and little about James, Howells, or Whitman. Nevertheless, Smith feels Lowell is the "*beau idéal* of gentlemanly critics."

Richard D. Altick defends Lowell against earlier critics (Reilly, Clark, Parrington, and others) who charged that Lowell was unaware of the importance of historical perspective in formulating his critical judgment. In fact, Altick accuses these critics with the same charges they had raised against Lowell, for they failed to evaluate correctly the resources available to Lowell and thus judged him by modern standards. According to Altick, Lowell "was by no means ignorant of the value or the nature of historical criticism, and . . . his critical essays abound with evidences of his awareness of the power exerted by contemporary circumstance upon the literature of a given era" ("Was Lowell an Historical Critic?" *American Literature,* Nov. 1942).

In "Lowell's Criticism of Romantic Literature" (*PMLA,* Mar. 1925), H. H. Clark says that Lowell did not like romantic literature "because it failed to fulfill the requirements of his poetic creed." C. M. Lombard argues that Clark and others were incorrect in their judgment of Lowell's attitude toward the Romantics and that Lowell gave the Romantics reasonable praise ("Lowell and French Romanticism," *Revue de Littérature Comparée,* Oct.-Dec. 1964). In "Lowell on Thoreau" (*Studies in Philology,* July 1930), Austin Warren feels that in his infamous essay Lowell as humanist reacts more to romanticism than to Thoreau.

The culmination of the discussion of Lowell as critic is seen in two well-balanced views. Although John Paul Pritchard (*Criticism in America,* Norman, Okla., 1965) is realistic about Lowell's shortcomings as critic—"His ignorance of America south of Philadelphia and west of the Alleghenies narrowed considerably his capacity to speak for and of the whole country; his aristocratic point of view . . . made him unable to *feel* the nobility of toil; his inability to adapt himself to the age of science restricted his understanding of later writers; and he was too much Man Reading"—he still sees him as at times surprisingly modern, as in his theory of the lyric: "Here eighty years before the relation of poetic texture and structure were discussed by John Crowe Ransom and Allen Tate, Lowell adumbrated the approach to lyric poetry which these well-known New Critics have amplified."

Richard H. Fogle in "Organic Form in American Criticism: 1840-1870" (in *The Development of American Literary Criticism,* edited by Floyd Stovall, Chapel Hill, N.C., 1955) sees Lowell's conservatism and his inhospitality to new writers as having two causes: "He comes at the end of a *great tradition* [the organic tradition of Herder, Goethe, and Coleridge], which at the last failed in energy to revitalize itself; and there really was much in the new generations which Lowell did well to reject." Fogle feels that "Lowell's criticism is eclectic, but organicist in its very eclecticism. . . . He shows the organicist willingness to sympathize, to assimilate, to absorb before he passes judgment. And his judgments generally stand up well. His essay on Keats, for example, written in 1854, contains in the germ all that modern scholarship has fathomed of Keats's identity, his unique fusion of experience and thought, his sensuous power and his idealism."

Influence on Lowell's thinking and writing have been traced by a number of scholars. In his chapter on Lowell in *Return to the Fountains* (Durham, N.C., 1942), John Paul Pritchard finds a significant indebtedness to classical literature, an indebtedness he explored in two earlier essays, "Lowell's Debt to Horace's *Ars Poetica*" (*American Literature,* Nov. 1931) and "James Russell Lowell and Aristotle's Poetics" (*Classical Weekly,* 15 January 1934). Of Aristotle's influence on Lowell, Pritchard says, "It is not too much to say that Lowell's important position in American letters and criticism is based largely upon his knowledge of the principles advocated by Aristotle in the Poetics and his adherence to them." In two later studies, "Lowell and Longinus" (*Transactions of the American Philological Association,* 1945) and "A Glance at Lowell's Classical Reading" (*American Literature,* Jan. 1950), Pritchard adds Longinus, Plato, and Plutarch to the list of Lowell's classical mentors.

Related to Pritchard's work is George P. Clark's Ph.D. dissertation on "Classical Influences and Background in the Writings of James Russell Lowell" (Yale, 1948), and his "James Russell Lowell's Study of the Classics Before Entering Harvard" (*Jahrbuch für Amerikastudien,* 1963).

In "James Russell Lowell's Interest in Dante," J. Chesley Mathews documents Lowell's lifelong preoccupation with Dante but concludes that Dante's influence on Lowell's poetry was slight (*Italica,* June 1959). According to Lawrence H. Klibbe, the Spanish influence on Lowell was not great except for Cervantes and Calderón, both of whom "are vital to the analysis of Lowell's literary theories" (*James Russell Lowell's Residence in Spain, 1877-1880,* New York, 1964). The Spanish influence on Lowell is further explored by Stanley T. Williams in *The Spanish Background of American Literature* (2 vols., New Haven, Conn., 1955).

Charles Oran Stewart's *Lowell and France* (Nashville, Tenn., 1951) examines the influence of French culture and literature in a number of Lowell's works, showing that they provided him with both subject matter and inspiration.

Like many of his contemporaries, Lowell rejected the Bible as a religious text early, but used it extensively in his writing throughout his life. William J. De Saegher concludes his study of "James Russell Lowell and the Bible" (Ph.D. dissertation, U.C.L.A., 1964) by remarking that Lowell understood the Bible well and used it often and variously in his writing, so that "biblical material pervades every facet of his work."

The winds of criticism, notoriously capricious, have left Lowell becalmed in the decade of the sixties, when others of his contemporaries enjoyed revivals of interest. Judging from present trends, it seems ironically unlikely that the Modern Language Association's new annual "James Russell Lowell Prize" for outstanding literary studies will soon be awarded for a study on Lowell, in spite of the fact that the definitive study of Lowell has not yet been written. But no one as richly versatile and influential as Lowell will forever remain unattractive or unrewarding to scholars. The years to come may produce the biographer and critic who will give us the whole artist and the whole man.

Notes

1. A new edition of Brownell's study was edited by Howard Mumford Jones in 1963 (Cambridge, Mass.). Jones's introduction to the text is valuable for the information it provides on Brownell as a literary critic.

Edward Wagenknecht (essay date 1971)

SOURCE: "The Creative Life," in *James Russell Lowell: Portrait of a Many-Sided Man,* Oxford University Press, 1971, pp. 104-26.

[*In the following essay, Wagenknecht analyzes Lowell's literary aesthetic.*]

> Be sure and don't leave anything out because it seems trifling, for it is out of these trifles only that it is possible to reconstruct character.
>
> JRL, to James T. Fields, 1871

I

Though Lowell never confined his activities to writing poetry, he still thought of himself as essentially a poet. He chose this goal for himself early in life, even while his father still regarded it as a species of vagabondage, and he planned a course of study in the laws of English verse preparatory to it. In his law office days he wrote,

> They tell me I must study law,
> They say I have dreamed, and dreamed too long;
> That I must rouse and seek for fame and gold;
> That I must scorn this idle gift of song,
> And mingle with the vain and proud and cold.
> Is, then, this petty strife
> The end and aim of life,
> All that is worth the living for below?
> *O God! then call me hence, for I would gladly go!*

And George William Curtis quotes him at twenty-seven:

> If I have any vocation it is the making of verse. When I take my pen in hand for that, the world opens itself ungrudgingly before me; everything seems clear and

> easy. . . . But when I do prose it is *invita Minerva.* I feel as if I were wasting time and keeping back my message. My true place is to serve the cause as a poet. Then my heart leaps before me into the conflict.

He never really changed his mind about all this, and in later life he thought of his other activities as a kind of infidelity. When Minot J. Savage regretted that he had not given all his time to poetry, Lowell replied, "You have given substantial expression to my own feeling. I have been haunted by the idea that it might have been better if I had devoted myself more exclusively to my literary work." At other times, however, he was not so sure that what was good for the poet would also have been good for the man. Perhaps he was thinking of Goethe's statement that a talent was formed in isolation but a character in the stream of the world.[1]

Lowell wrote rapidly, though often only after long brooding, nearly always on a pasteboard pad on his knee. He began comparatively late for a poet, essentially during his college years. He cherished spontaneity, sometimes even irregularity ("you must write easily," he wrote Henry James, "for you are read with pleasure"), and his writing could be cathartic, for he said he could get rid of something which troubled him by shutting it within covers. His visual imagination was keen ("I always see what I describe while I am thinking of it"), and he wrote, in response to an "inner light," what he "needed" to write, and when he "felt" like it.

He claimed to be able to write verse faster than prose, and in 1838 he told Longfellow he was not going on with poetry for the time being because he could not write slowly enough. The verses in Beatrice Müller's album were dashed off on the spur of the moment in response to her request for an autograph, and he once sent six letter-paper sides of verse to Charles Hazen Dorr, praising the cheese he had sent him.

Yet he could not write to order. For him Dr. Johnson's "setting doggedly about it" just did not work. Though emotional crises could sometimes stimulate him, he often had to wait upon moods and even weather before he could so much as complete an enterprise in hand. Trying to write while serving as ambassador in London was, he said, like trying to be a setting hen who should also have to answer the doorbell. Sometimes he would labor diligently at a composition and be obliged to give it up. Naturally, it was especially hard to try to be humorous to order, and in 1854 he tried to revive ***Biglow*** and failed. In 1889, having attempted a poem for Aldrich's *Atlantic,* he found that "cold molasses is swift as a weaver's shuttle compared with my wits."[2]

As he grew older, the spontaneity was less and the craftsmanship more,[3] but not even large offers could draw a poem out of him when the inner impulse was lacking. Even when he could write with as great enthusiasm as ever, he would print with less confidence. During forty years he only managed to bring out two collections of verses.

To be sure, happy accidents sometimes occurred. **"The Courtin',"** certainly one of his finest poems, was originally a six-stanza space filler, of which he kept no copy. He added six more for a later edition of ***Biglow,*** and ultimately there were twenty-four.[4] With poems like ***The Vision of Sir Launfal,*** **"Agassiz,** and the ***Commemoration Ode,*** it was more inspiration than improvisation, however; at least Lowell was, as it were, rapt clean out of himself, composing at high speed, and in a keen state of excitement which drained his energy and left him limp and doubting afterwards. ("Like a boy I mistook my excitement for inspiration, and here I am in the mud.") He says **"The Cathedral"** absorbed him to such an extent that it made his wife jealous. To a lesser degree, he depended upon such excitement when he wrote prose also, and he thought his essay on Rousseau second-rate because it had not kept him awake at night. The fullest description of such an experience he achieved, however, in connection with the **"Agassiz"** Ode:

> I had gone out of myself entirely. I was in the dining-room at Parker's, and when I came back to self-consciousness and solitude, it was in another world that I awoke, and I was puzzled to say which. It was a case of possession but not self-possession. I was cold, but my brain was full of warm light, and the passage came to me in its completeness without any seeming intervention of mine. I was delighted, I confess, with this renewal of imagination in me after so many blank years. . . . The only part I *composed* was the concluding verses which I suspect to be the weakest part.

And he adds: "I have a respect for things that are *given me,* as the greater part of this was."

Occasionally Lowell cites a source for one of his poems, as Schoolcraft's *Algic Researches* for **"A Chippewa Legend,"** a Breton story of Souvestre's for **"The Washers of the Shroud,"** and Burns's "The Twa Brigs" for the Mason and Slidell piece in ***Biglow.*** In his early life at least, he considered echoing the old poets he had loved as a tribute he owed them. There is reason to believe that Samuel Worcester Rowse was the model for one of his best characters, Fitz Adam.[5] Once at least he dreamed a poem, and though he says, justly on the whole, that he did not belong with those "that hawk their sorrows in the market-place," he did use family griefs in such poems as **"The First Snow-Fall"** and **"After the Burial."** On the whole, however, sources were much less important for him than they were for either Whittier or Longfellow. He understood, and stated felicitously, the conditions under which literary source material may be effectively used: "If a poet take his subject (or plot) from history (or in any other way ready made to his hand), just in proportion to the amount of matter furnished must be that which he supplies out of himself."

Lowell himself said that he liked conceiving a poem but not working it up, and he told Mrs. Herrick that "my temper of mind is such that I never have the patience to read over again what I have once printed." He was, however, much given to suggesting emendations between the acceptance of a poem and its publication. Once at least he revised to avoid the unfair appearance of plagiarism. Actually, revision does not seem to have been a very profitable business for him. When he attempted it conscientiously, as he did with **"The Cathedral,"** which he went over carefully as with a file, he was likely in the end to restore nearly all the original readings.[6]

II

For Lowell, poetry was "made up of Imagination, Experience, Indiscretion, and Art." The first and the third were "the good fairy's gifts." Experience came with years, Art with many years. By Indiscretion he meant "not want of judgment but the faculty of keeping green in despite of Experience." Poetry differed from prose not merely in degree but in kind, and it should concern itself with matters of fact only as they were "embodied by imagination," which was "the everlasting resurrection of the soul from the body." To a prose writer the dictionary was a forest or a quarry, but the poet entered it "like Orpheus" and made "its wild inmates sing and dance and keep joyous time to every wavering fancy of his lyre." And he who possessed an imagination had no need to sigh with Alexander for new worlds to conquer.[7]

Lowell was classical in his insistence upon universal appeal in literature of quality, and this caused him to condemn both the provinciality which is nationalism and the sentimentalism and subjectivism encouraged by Romanticism. As he saw it, the unity of a poem was not "a thing of manufacture like that of a brick" but one "of growth like the rooted and various and waving unity of a tree."

> Its shape, its law of growth, its limit, is irrevocably fore-ordained in the seed. There is nothing haphazard in the matter, from beginning to end. The germ once planted, everything then tends simply to the bringing about of one end,—perfection in its kind. The plot which it has to fill out is definite and rigid. The characters and incidents balance each other like the branches, and every part, from the minutest fibre of the root to the last leaf, conspires to nourishment and so to beauty.

Once he seems to be bringing himself within hailing distance of Poe by declaring that the *Odyssey* is the only long poem that will bear consecutive reading, but when he goes on to distinguish between poetic sense and poetic faculty, he parts company from him. In such poems as *The Divine Comedy* and *Paradise Lost,* one recognizes in every verse, even if detached, a part of the whole, much as one may recognize a friend by his walk. "Perfect in themselves," the parts also contribute to "totality of effect." This evidences poetic faculty, or "the shaping spirit," which is what Poe seems to have ignored in long poems. As for Poe's idea that man cannot create but can only combine previously existent materials, this Lowell dismisses as irrelevant nonsense:

> Suppose by an exertion of my will I could create a black cat here on the desk, would it be less a creation because black cats were invented so long ago, and every boy has flung his boot at some Romeo of the tribe on a moonlight night? Now if I could by my will give every one of you the impression of one sitting here on the desk, how would you decide that it was not a real Grimalkin? This is the way in which the Imagination creates—by magnetising all the senses till they see, hear, taste, feel and smell only what it chooses.

Like Aristotle, Lowell knew that literature must give aesthetic pleasure. "The first duty of the Muse is to be delightful." He praised Howells for having known from the beginning of his career how to be entertaining, for this, he thought, was generally one of the last things a writer learns, and "without it, a man may have all the cardinal virtues, but they are nothing to the purpose."[8] Moreover, a literary work must be judged as literature, not as a system of law or morality.

However much Lowell might be indebted to classical standards, he was not enslaved by them; neither did he neglect later writers when they had something to contribute to his purpose. He was impressed by Goethe's three questions: "What did the author propose to himself? Is what he proposes reasonable and comprehensible? and how far has he succeeded in carrying it out?" He also responded affirmatively to Milton's demand for poetry as simple, sensuous, and passionate.

> It should be simple as being clear, not obvious, as dealing with primary emotions and not with metaphysical refinements upon them; it should be sensuous as not making its appeal to the intellect but to that finer sense to which language is still not the mere vehicle for conveying thought but is a part of it—its very flesh and blood; and it should be passionate not in any sense of wildness or waywardness but simply because [it] can saturate words with all the meaning of its own intenser mood.

Poetry for Lowell was not quite the "pure" thing to which Poe gave his allegiance. Many references scattered through his poems show what he conceived the poet's function to be. His eye is clearer than other men's. He can heal desolate hearts and cause men to hear the songs of the angels and catch golden glimpses of a more glorious future to be. In **"The Shepherd of King Admetus"** he serves God's Kingdom on earth even when he appears to be doing nothing. In **"An Incident in a Railroad Car"** he finds his message in the common heart of humanity, though its ultimate source is God.[9] Humor in poetry, "which consists in a perception of the invincible contradiction between the Imagination and the understanding, between soul and sense," is the result of qualifying Imagination "by the understanding instead of the sense of Beauty." Fancy, which is inferior to the Imagination, combines with sentiment to produce poetry or with experience to produce wit.

Theoretically Lowell realized that a very good case might be made for the thesis that a poet should concern himself only with beauty, but in times like those in which he lived, he believed that in actual practice the poet must also be "a Schoolmaster," a "John the Baptist, a voice crying in the wilderness, preparing for the simply Beautiful, for Art in its highest sense, a wider and more universal reception in a future age." After he himself had served his apprenticeship at making bricks without straw, he wrote Mrs. Horace Mann, he hoped also "to be led to the promised land of Song, and to have my Sinais and my waters from the rock by the way." This was the more important because in the evolution—or devolution—of society, the poet, though not claiming "immediate inspiration," had so largely taken the place of the prophet, "by force of seeing the heart of those mysteries whose shell only is visible to others."[10] The poet, therefore, had become forerunner and prophet "of changes in the moral world." To behold only the "body" of his thought and its "outward grace" was to miss half. Even his lightest fantasies had two meanings—"one of the flesh and of the spirit one." In Lowell's poem about him, Columbus "believed" the poets and thought they spoke for God. Moreover prophetism was one with humanitarianism. "I have made it *radical,*" Lowell writes Charles Briggs of **"Prometheus,"** "and I believe that no poet in this age can write much that is good unless he give himself up to this tendency." In ***Conversations*** he makes Philip say, "You forget that I believe the poetical sentiment and what we call the sentiment of natural religion to be identical. Both of them are life-members of the New England Anti-Slavery Society." He might not have put it quite that way in later years, but his essential point of view never substantially changed.

Lowell judged writers both absolutely, by reference to his own formulated and unchanging standards of what constituted excellence in literature, and relatively, considering the writer's position in the literary history of his country and the special conditions affecting the creation of literature in his generation. Neglect the second criterion, and you will not understand the factors which conditioned his talent nor judge him fairly, but if you neglect the first, you will find it impossible to choose between, say, Milton and Samuel Butler, since both were highly representative figures. A critic must know what he believes and bring his writers to the bar of his own standards, but if he is too rigid and inflexible about this, he will cut himself off from the relish and fair evaluation of many kinds of excellence.

Lowell also insisted that writers must be accepted for what they are. "Because continuity is a merit in some kinds of writing, shall we refuse ourselves to the authentic charm of Montaigne's want of it?" Surely this would be a "schoolboy blunder," for "there never has been a great work of art which did not in some particular transcend the old rules and establish new ones of its own."

> A true scholar should be able to value Wordsworth for his depth of sympathy with nature, without therefore losing all power to enjoy the sparkling shallowness of Pope; he should be able to feel the beauty of Herbert's puritanism, the naked picturesqueness of his style, and yet not refuse to be delighted with the sensuous paganism of Herrick.

He adds that "'In my father's house are many mansions' conveys a lesson of criticism no less than of charity." Even form, which might almost be said to *make* literature, is not absolutely indispensable, for "there have been men of genius, like Emerson, richly seminative for other minds; like Browning, full of wholesome ferment for other minds, though wholly destitute of any proper sense of form."

With such an emphasis as this, the richly sympathetic Lowell inevitably made criticism in large measure a matter of appreciation; as he saw it, the critic's highest function was to think the poet's thoughts after him and not merely to point out where he had failed to express them adequately. Philip of the ***Conversations*** admitted that "for whatever I love, my delight mounts to an extravagance. There are verses which I cannot read without tears of exultation, which to others are merely indifferent," and he doubted that any really convincing reason for such a passion could be communicated to a mind not already predisposed to share it. Lowell himself disliked disenchantment as a critical function. The critic must not "make war on men's little loves and faiths, but endeavor to show how far, and in what sense, they are justifiable. When disenchantment was necessary, it must always be performed "with a kindly tenderness," for "life is too sad and too serious for one to wish to undeceive those who are so lucky as to be happy by mistake."

He also insisted that there was room in the world for much besides great art.

> We cannot breathe the thin air of that Pepysian self-denial, that Himalayan selectness, which, content with one bookcase, would have no tomes in it but *porphyrogeniti,* books of the bluest blood, making room for choicer newcomers by a continuous ostracism to the garret of present incumbents.

If man cannot live by bread alone, he cannot live by spices and stimulants alone either, nor yet by nectar and ambrosia. He must not be told that it is wrong to enjoy Gray or Cowper or Scott because they are not Wordsworth or Shelley. A definition of poetry too narrow to embrace Horace and Crabbe "and whoever else prefers the familiar scenery of life and the habitual to the exceptional motives of happiness and misery would not do." There is a great deal in literature which must be accepted as Mercutio accepted his death-wound: "No, 'tis not so deep as a well, nor so wide as a church-door; but 'tis enough, 'twill serve."

There is far more generous and liberal humanism in these pronouncements that can be found in the official "line" followed by any "school" of criticism nowadays, or, for that matter, illustrated in the practices of many art museums. Yet they have often been attacked as illustrating Lowell's vagueness and uncertainty, his tendency to find his standards in the subject of his essay rather than bringing them to it. This is not altogether unjust. Lowell understood as Keats did—and Keats helped him to learn it—that the poet can *become* that of which he writes, and there are even times when he seems disposed to extend this privilege to the critic. It is hardly unfair to say that he wrote of the Puritans in **"New England Two Centuries Ago"** not as an historian but as an apologist, and the very title of **"A**

Good Word for Winter" is characteristic of both his method and his type of mind. His criteria for choosing **"The Five Indispensable Authors"**[11] have some arbitrariness and inconsistency about them, and he is quite capable of today hitting over-subtlety in criticism and the searching out of hidden motives, so that the critic may be glorified by demonstrating that he has been able to perceive something nobody else has ever seen,[12] yet tomorrow he might tolerate those who read their own ideas (if one can call them that) into a book instead of getting the author's out of it, and of thus (to take an extreme example), encouraging the lunatics who find Napoleon, the Kaiser, or Mussolini, or whoever happens to be the current villain of the moment, in the Book of Daniel and The Revelation of St. John.[13] When he writes about Spenser he praises him for his stylistic lavishness ("in poetry enough is not only not so good as a feast, but is a beggarly parsimony"), but it never occurs to him that, when he writes of Dante, he must not feel quite free to praise him for having discovered "the secret of that magical word too few, which not only distinguishes his verse from all other, but so strikingly from his own prose."

It would be stupid not to perceive these things, but it is even more stupid to make more of them that they deserve. Lowell has a way of being right in both places, as Shakespeare was right when he ran contradictory time-schemes through *Othello* and *The Merchant of Venice,* for this is a much less logical world—the humanist's world at any rate—than the partisans of most critical systems are willing to allow. As a matter of fact, Lowell is much more likely to get into trouble when he does *not* take his tone from his subject, for then he can be as imperceptive as he was about Thoreau or as cruel as he was when flogging a dead horse in his essay on Percival. He applied both historical knowledge and a formulated set of standards to his subjects; only a fool could call him an impressionist. But he would be a considerably bigger fool who should leave his readers with the impression that Lowell's being an impressionist would have left his critical writings worthless. For until criticism comes to be written by machines (and a number of experiments seem to be under way in this area), the impressionistic element must remain the life-giving element in the work of any critic, no matter what he may be called. Of course he must have standards; otherwise he will have no frame of reference, and his sun may well rise in the west and set in the north. But unless he manages, even within the bounds of his "system," to express something which is himself and no other human being, how on earth can he expect us to continue to read him instead of turning for our fodder to newer and better machines?

III

Much too much has been made of Lowell's alleged dislike of realism in literature. Insofar as this existed, it was based upon sound aesthetic, as well as moral, grounds; he did not believe that the literal reproduction of nature or of fact was possible in a work of art, and he disliked lingering upon physical detail for its own sake as a distraction from the theme under consideration and, ultimately, a confession of unreality.[14] Few of us today could be expected to agree with his classification of Trollope's novels, along with the sculpture of John Rogers, as matter-of-fact rather than real, but we ought not to forget his advice to Harriet Beecher Stowe to "stick to Nature and avoid what people commonly call the ideal," his encouragement, as editor of the *Atlantic,* of a whole host of local color writers who did just this, or the admiration which such writers as Edward Eggleston and Joel Chandler Harris felt for him.

Higginson notes that in Lowell's youth Cambridge families employed hired men from the country, to whom the boys liked to talk. Their conversation was "usually harmless, often profitable, sometimes racy; and every trait of Hosea, or even of Bidofredum Sawin could be matched in them." Lowell hated allegory and literary metaphysics, disliked the melodramatic, overblown, dishonestly glorified heroes and heroines of Bulwer and Disraeli, and tried to consider chivalric graces in the metrical romances from the lamb's point of view. He forgave *Gammer Gurton's Needle* its coarseness and earthiness because the author was "at least a man among men, and not a humbug among humbugs." The hackneyed, "refined," conventionalized poetic diction of poets like Thomas Young he found quite destitute of force and vitality, but Chaucer's Pegasus "ambles along, preferring the sunny vales to the thunder-daunting cliffs," and Shakespeare uses a "low" word whenever he needs it. "His pen ennobled them all, and we feel as if they had been knighted for good service in the field."

What Lowell rejected, in other words, was that same surface realism to which, in their own way, expressionists and other aesthetic revolutionaries were later to take exception. He was sure that "all great poetry must smack of the soil, for it must be rooted in it, must suck life and substance from it." But it must grow out of, not in, the soil, like a pine rather than a potato. Otherwise, it will lack idealism (which is a moral objection), but it will also be parochial (which is an aesthetic objection). Truth to nature is not truth to fact, and "the facts of life" must be distinguished from "the accidental and transitory phenomena of life." Only "art's absolution" can "purge" the "polluting" stain of life and grasp "ideal grace." When Lowell compares the reading of cheap fiction to opium eating, or permits one of the speakers in ***Conversations*** to declare that "nothing that God has not thought it beneath him to make" can be considered unworthy of a writer's attention, he is using almost exactly the same language that William Dean Howells was to use. Lowell found the kind of realism he believed in in Howells,[15] but not only there. He found it also in James, Fredrika Bremer, Hawthorne, Sylvester Judd, even J. G. Holland, but for his supreme examples of it, he, not unsurprisingly, went to Shakespeare and Cervantes:

> Give me the writers who take me for a while out of myself and . . . away from my neighbors! I do not ask that characters should be real; I need but go into the street to find such abundance. I ask only that they should be possible, that they should be typical, because

> these I find in myself, and with these I can sympathize. Hector and Achilles, Clytemnestra and Antigone, Roland and Oliver, Macbeth and Lear, move about, if not in worlds not realized, at least in worlds not realized to any eye but that of the imagination. . . . Don Quixote and his Squire are inhabitants of this world, in spite of the prosaic and often vulgar stage on which their tragicomedy is acted, because they are symbolical, because they represent the two great factors of human character and springs of human action—the Imagination and the Understanding.

The writer must use the materials which lie ready to his hand, but he must treat them so as to bring out their universal qualities. "The true ideal is not opposed to the real, nor is it any artificial heightening thereof, but lies in it, and blessed are the eyes that find it!" Not "something out of and beyond Nature," it is rather "Nature as seen through the eye of the Artist," but its visibility depends upon the presence of that eye.

IV

Though Lowell may sometimes have indulged in direct moralizing in literature, he did not approve of it, any more than Howells did. Indeed he praised Howells's *Hazard of New Fortunes* precisely because Howells had avoided it. He urged Mrs. Stowe to deal with theology in her New England fictions only where it came naturally to the surface in the life she described, and he warned himself that, having grown up in a New England that was "all meeting-house," he would never be a real poet until he got out of the pulpit.

The relationship between the quality of a work of art and the character of the man that produced it gave him considerable difficulty. He was unwilling to claim any immunities for poets, and he found it hard to believe that a man could create anything greater than his own soul. But he knew too that aesthetic creativity was more complicated than human logic, perhaps even more complicated than man's moral codes. So he calls Rousseau "a quack of genius" and declares that "whatever he was or did, somehow or other God let him be worthy to write *this,* and that is enough for us." He is not entirely consistent in these matters; he shows Rousseau much more charity than is accorded either Petrarch or Victor Hugo. He believed that if the moral sense predominated in a man over the aesthetic, he became a reformer or a fanatic rather than an artist, and his imagination expressed itself in his life (Bunyan would never have written *The Pilgrim's Progress* without being shut up in jail and cut off from his usual activities). Yet, even though it was the writer's function to stimulate thinking in his readers rather than to do their thinking for them, creativity itself withered without faith, moral and aesthetic faults and virtues were much more closely associated than most people realized, and if an ideal world did not exist, then all the greater was the need that the poet should create one. Nevertheless, beauty involves and embraces its moral; it does not need to be "stuck on," and "poetry is a criticism of life only in the sense that it furnishes us with the standard of a more ideal felicity, of calmer Beauty." "No verse, the chief end of which is not the representation of the beautiful, and whose moral is not included in that, can be called poetry in the true sense of the word."

At times, in fact, Lowell seems willing to accept only the Shakespearean type of imagination, which he makes almost mediumistic. Shakespeare is only a voice, and "we seek in vain in his plays for any traces of his personal character or history." He is not expressing himself but rather giving voice "to the myriad forms of nature, which, wanting him, were dumb."

> In proportion as the poetical sense is abundant in a man or in other words in proportion as it is the law of his nature to surrender himself to the possession of his sensuous impressions—will he be without what we call *character.* The more poet, the less character. I cannot find that Shakespeare had any at all.[16]

At least, the artist must have the privilege of treating both good and evil—

> Yet let us think, that, as there's naught above
> The all-embracing atmosphere of Art,
> So also there is naught that falls below
> Her generous reach, though grimed with guilt
> and woe—[17]

and sometimes, again with such dazzling talents as Shakespeare's, the two may almost be said, aesthetically speaking, to have coalesced:

> Only Shakespeare had that true sense of humor which, like the universal solvent sought by the alchemists, so fuses together all the elements of a character (as in Falstaff), that any question of good or evil, of dignified or ridiculous, is silenced by the apprehension of its thorough humanity.

V

I know of no other writer of comparable fame who is quite so modest about his achievements as Lowell. He claimed that he always lost interest in a book as soon as it was published. When his 1848 collection appeared, he forgot to possess himself of a copy of it, and in 1885 he told Curtis Guild he could not answer any questions concerning the publishers of his early books as he had no copies on hand. The modest dedication of ***Conversations*** to his father[18] is charming, but he is nearly as diffident about ***My Study Windows*** many years later.[19]

He had a worse opinion of himself than of most authors, considering himself a third-rater compared with the masters. He "hated" his books and would rather be valued for his personal qualities than for them,[20] yet he declared inconsistently that the best of himself went into his books. He often lamented that he had done so little and wasted so much, and once, when a young Englishman was gauche enough to tell him that he had read none of his writings, he replied that he did not regard them as necessary to a liberal education.[21] He did not think he would have cared much for his poems if they had been written by somebody else, and he told Fields he could be mistaken for a lion only by persons not well acquainted with that animal. Making his selections for ***Under the Willows*** he thought what he had to choose from on a level with ordinary newspaper verse. After expression for expression's sake had lost its appeal for him, he had more faith in his insight than his expression. Once he said he thought he had "too many thoughts and too little thought." In later years, when authors' readings came into vogue, his natural dislike of public speaking was reinforced by the fact that he could never find a poem he thought worth reading.

But why, then, did he write at all? Obviously, because he had to and wanted to. In the beginning he desired fame ("it's *in* me and it shall come out!")—

I too am a Maker and Poet;
Through my whole soul I feel it and know it!
My veins are fired with ecstasy!
All-mother Earth
Did ne'er give birth
To one who shall be matched with me;
The lustre of my coronal
Shall cast a dimness over all.

But even then the reaction was swift:

Alas! alas! what have I spoken?
My strong, my eagle wings are broken,
And back again to earth I fall![22]

Perhaps he continued to desire fame, but the number of now meaningless names in Allibone's *Dictionary of Authors* reminded him how heavy the odds were against any particular man's being remembered. "Formerly, a man who wished to withdraw himself from the notice of the world retired into a convent. The simpler modern method is, to publish a volume of poems." And when Beatrice Müller asked him for an autograph, he wrote in her album—

O'er the wet sands an insect crept
Ages ere man on earth was known—
And patient Time, while Nature slept,
The slender tracing turned to stone.
'Twas the first autograph: and ours?
Prithee, how much of prose or song,
In league with the Creative powers,
Shall 'scape Oblivion's broom so long?[23]

By this time, fame had become less a motive than the mere desire to do good work, but alas! this was the most difficult thing of all. How close exaltation lay to discouragement in his mind may be gauged by what he wrote Sydney Gay about the ***Fable.*** In a single paragraph he declared both that "there are not above half a dozen persons who know how good it is" and that "it seems bald and poor enough now, the Lord knows."

The thing to do, he knew, was to strive for a sane, balanced, and objective view of one's own work and one's relationship to it, avoiding the melodramatism of both self-vaunting and self-abasement. You could value your natural gifts even while you disparaged your performance, knowing that you were "better at a *spurt* than a steady pull," and that you had fought as good a fight as many who had claimed more. You could know that you had achieved a great strain now and then, that you were "the first poet who has endeavored to express the American Idea," and that sooner or later this must be recognized, even though you might have to die first. You could be sure that ***Biglow*** II was better than ***Biglow*** I, though it lacked something of the verve of its predecessor, because it was less the work of an improviser and more that of an artist, and when you sent ***Launfal*** to Briggs, you could rather "guess" it was good, though you still planned to write something "gooder and newer." At times you could even stubbornly continue to believe in work of such inferior quality as **"Our Own."** You could, on occasion, deny yourself genius, yet somehow manage to make a merit of the lack. ("A genius has the gift of falling in love with the side-face of truth, going mad for it, sacrificing all for it. But I must see the full face, and then the two sides have such different expressions that I begin to doubt which is the sincere and cannot surrender myself.") In later years, Lowell was capable, in the course of a single letter of giving himself a vote of no confidence as a poet and at the same time half resolving to relinquish all his other activities on the ground that this might help him to become a better poet. But even when he was an old man, he could keep his hopes pinned to the future, always being conscious of greater power than he had yet shown.

Lowell professed to believe that "criticism can at best teach writers without genius what is to be avoided or imitated." Moreover, genius or not, "one can't do his best for a theater that has more than one person in it, and that one himself." Claiming "a self-sustaining nature," he did not need encouragement from others. "I am *teres atque rotundus,* a microcosm in myself, my own author, public, critic, and posterity, and care for no other." Praise might make him doubt himself, but in the long run praise and blame were equally immaterial, since no matter what critics said, a writer of quality must ultimately find his proper place.

Even if you are prepared to grant these premises, however, they will not get you far, for the question still remains: When you *cannot* secure your own approval, what do you do then? And this, as we have seen, was Lowell's condition an uncomfortably large number of times. But he himself made the perfect comment on his own declaration of independence when he wrote, "I never saw a man who did not think himself indifferent to praise, nor one who did not like it."

Actually, his own self-doubts made him more dependent upon the praise of others than he would otherwise have been. Howells sensed that any criticism hurt him, especially from those whose opinions he valued, though he never knew him to alter anything he had written merely because of disapproval expressed, and Mrs. Fields records several instances of his sensitiveness. When Emerson once remarked that his humorous poetry was best, he muttered **"The Washers of the Shroud"** and walked away.

When E. P. Whipple, editing the Boston *Notion,* praised him in 1841, Lowell wrote him warmly, not even knowing his name:

> It was very grateful to me as I took up your paper in a public room, where there was but one face among many that I knew, and saw some kind words about myself, to think that, perchance, the writer was now in the room and that among these strangers I had yet a friend.[24]

The friendship which developed between Lowell and Mrs. S. B. Herrick of Baltimore grew out of a "fan letter" she had written him, and he told Charles Eliot Norton that "what I have done has been due to your partiality more than anything else, for you have given me a kind of faith in it." Sometimes he was even willing to reconsider the claims of a poem he had disparaged because somebody else had liked it. "I need every sort of petting on the back," he told Mrs. Wirt Dexter, "for I myself am never pleased with what I do."

This much remained, however, of his professed indifference to criticism—that he would never argue about anything that mattered to him or about which he had made up his mind. Nothing, I am sure, could have bored him more than what are now called "panel discussions." "I seldom care to discuss anything." He was "contemptuously indifferent about arguing matters that had once become convictions." "A man who is in the right can never reason. He can only affirm." "It fags me to deal with particulars." And again:

> I don't very often look into my books but when I do I seem to find a certain vivacity and suggestiveness that are worth something. My impatience of mind is my bane as a critical essayist. I expect everybody to understand *à demi mot.* Perhaps an enemy would call it indolence and perhaps he would be right.

Different as he was from Emerson in many respects, Lowell resembled him in that both possessed essentially deductive minds. They *perceived* truth, made a priori assumptions, and, like the prophets of Israel, *proclaimed* the will of the Lord. A more prosaic or inductive type of mind feels this tendency as working for weakness in his critical essays, and Lowell himself was very well aware of this reaction.[25] But he knew too that both he and Emerson were essentially poets, almost as much so when they wrote prose as when they were writing verse. "What a true poet says always *proves itself* to our minds, and we cannot dodge it or get away from it."

VI

Obviously all this must be taken into account and allowed for by anyone who would understand the poet Lowell. But though Lowell may have been essentially a poet, he was not all poet. He was a man, with a man's emotional needs and hungers. He lived in a community and in the larger community which is the world, coming in contact with his fellows in many different ways, and affecting and being affected by them even when there were no personal ties. Finally, he was a human soul, living, as we all do, under the necessity of achieving, or failing to achieve, harmony with the universe itself. All these aspects of this experience must be explored before we can take our leave of him, and these quests will fill up the rest of this book.

Notes

1. The essentially poetic quality of L's mind shows clearly in the style of his prose. Jeremy Taylor is "a kind of Spenser in a cassock." Carlyle is forever "calling down fire from Heaven whenever he cannot readily lay his hand on the matchbox." Wordsworth's mind "had not that reach and elemental movement of Milton's which, like the trade wind, gathered to itself thoughts and images like stately fleets from every quarter; some deep with silks and spicery, some brooding over the silent thunders of their battailous armaments, but all swept forward in their destined track, over the long billows of his verse, every inch of canvas strained by the unifying breath of their common epic origin." Except for *Areopagitica,* "Milton's tracts are wearisome reading, and going through them is like a long sea-voyage whose monotony is more than compensated for the moment by a stripe of phosphorescence heaping before you in a drift of star-sown snow, coiling away behind in winking discs of silver, as if the conscious element were giving out all the moonlight it had garnered in its loyal depths since first it gazed upon its pallid regent." It is interesting that this last sentence should be followed by "Which, being interpreted," and an explication in the usual manner of prose.

2. These troubles were not wholly confined to poetry. L would not write a critical essay without reading the subject's whole oeuvre, but he put the actual writing off as long as possible. In 1855 he began delivering a course of Lowell lectures with only the manuscript of one in hand. For his excellent advice about writing, see George Bainton, ed., *The Art of Authorship . . .* (Appleton, 1890), pp. 29-30.

3. See Howard, *Victorian Knight-Errant,* pp. 329-30, and the illustrations following, especially on pp. 334, 338-39, 354-55.

4. See also John C. Broderick's demonstration, "L's 'Sunthin' in the Pastoral Line,'" *American Literature,* XXXI (1959-60), 163-72, that this piece is a "made" poem. "Moreover, that part of the poem which has seemed the most spontaneous—the descriptive introduction—emerges as the most contrived."

5. F. DeWolfe Miller, "An Artist Sits for L," *BPLQ,* II (1950), 378-79.

6. For a detailed study, see G. Thomas Tanselle, "The Craftsmanship of L: Revisions in *The Cathedral,*" *Bulletin of the New York Public Library,* LXX (1966), 60-63. See also Arthur W. M. Voss, "L's 'A Legend of Brittany,'" *Modern Language Notes,* LXI (1946), 343-45, which shows that in revising this poem for the 1849 edition, L omitted much moralizing which had been criticized by Poe and Felton. This "indi-

cates that for once, at least, he was capable of exercising a self-criticism hardly to be expected of a young poet so filled with the urge to preach to mankind."

7. A comprehensive critical examination of L's poetic theory and practice is not called for here, where our interest is in painting a character portrait. The most elaborate attempt to formulate L's critical credo was Norman Foerster's, in his *American Criticism* (1928), reprinted in Clark and Foerster, *JRL: Representative Selections.* This has often been attacked as too schematic, but all its elements are present in L's own writings; see "The Function of the Poet" and "The Imagination," both reprinted in *The Function of the Poet* . . . , and especially the manuscript of his first Lowell lecture, preserved in HL—bMS Am765 (899). (This MS, not in L's hand, is marked "being in large part a rewriting of the first Lecture of the Lowell Institute course.") See also Alexis F. Lange, "JRL as a Critic," *University* [*of California*] *Chronicle,* VIII (1906), 352-64; E. S. Parsons, "L's Conception of Poetry," *Colorado College Publication,* General Series, No. 37, Language Series, II (1908), 67-84; Harry Hayden Clark, "L's Criticism of Romantic Literature," *PMLA,* XLI (1926), 209-28; J. P. Pritchard, "Aristotle's *Poetics* and Certain American Literary Critics, III: JRL and Aristotle's *Poetics,*"*Classical Weekly,* XXVII (1933-34), 89-93. Austin Warren, "L on Thoreau," *Studies in Philology,* XXVII (1930), 442-62, finds L a humanist, allied in spirit to Arnold, Santayana, and Babbitt, citing in his support not only the paper on Thoreau but also those on Lessing, Carlyle, Percival, and Rousseau. "All of these studies imply the same critical background: humanism *versus* romanticism." Richard D. Altick asks, "Was L an Historical Critic?" *America Literature,* XIV (1942-43), 250-59, and answers in the affirmative. More interesting still are two older articles by J. M. Robertson, "L as a Critic," *North American Review,* CCIX (1919), 246-62, and "Criticism and Science," pp. 690-96. Robertson begins by considering Reilly's charges against L, many of which he sustains (he is excellent on L's inconsistencies and contradictions), but if L is not a critic, he wonders who is. At its best, his criticism "is the response of a very fine receptive faculty to a great many forms of literary appeal.. . . Few critics put so much material . . . in their readers' way; and surely no English critic has explored quite so much ground with such vivacity and variety of craftsmanlike observation." He was one of the pathbreakers for a more scientific criticism than his own, and there was no generic gap between his product and that of his successors. Percy H. Boynton, "L in his Times," *New Republic,* XVIII (1919), 113-14, remarks interestingly that L "did little thinking that was original, but much that was independent."

8. Review of *No Love Lost, North American Review,* CVIII (1869), 326.

9. The low doggerel of most so-called religious poetry distressed L deeply. "When we think what religion is and what poetry is, and what their marriage ought to be, a great part of what is published as religious poetry seems to us a scandalous mockery." *NAR,* C (1865), 303-304.

10. Review of Fitz-Greene Halleck's *Alnwick Castle, Broadway Journal,* I (1845), 281-83.

11. See *The Function of the Poet.* . . .

12. L gave Peter Bell credit for perceiving that the primrose was a primrose, not a theophany, and I am sure he would also have accounted it to Peter's credit that he knew it was not a hyacinth nor a tulip.

13. "He reads most wisely who thinks everything into a book that it is capable of holding, and it is the stamp and token of a great book so to incorporate itself with our own being, so to quicken our insight and stimulate our thought, as to make us feel as if we helped to create it while we read. Whatever we can find in a book that aids us in the conduct of life, or to a truer interpretation of it, or to a franker reconcilement with it, we may with a good conscience believe is not there by accident, but that the author meant that we should find it there."—"Don Quixote," *Literary and Political Essays.*

14. In his "Rhymed Lecture" on "The Power of Sound," L wrote:

    And what is Art? 'tis Nature reproduced
    In forms ideal, from the actual loosed;—
    Nature sublimed in life's more gracious hours
    By high Imagination's plastic powers. . . .

    In a *North American Review* review of 1866 (CII, 633-34), he wrote: "Whenever a novelist speaks of the pretty boots, or the white hands, or the 'golden-beaded purple silk purses' of his heroes and heroines, or describes the silver and fruit on their dinner-tables, or the abundance of their breakfasts, that moment he shows either that his characters are not accustomed to such things, and therefore are disproportionately regardful of them, or else that he himself, in so carefully observing them, is wasting his force on non-essential particulars." J. P. Pritchard is right when he points out (*Return to the Fountains,* p. 103) that L's insistence on the superiority of poetry to history is thoroughly Aristotelian. But it is also thoroughly idealistic, and it must be admitted that when it came to autobiography, L showed a somewhat divided mind. On the one hand, he thought that reserved autobiography was useless: "But what do we want of a hospitality that makes strangers of us, or of confidences that keep us at arm's-length?" But when one of his authors does write of himself without reserve, he is hardly pleased. "We think there is getting to be altogether too much unreserve in the world. We doubt if any man have the right to take mankind by the button and tell all about himself, unless, like Dante, he can symbolize his experience. Even Goethe we only half thank, especially when he kisses and tells, and prefer Shakespeare's indifference to the intimacy of the German."—*Atlantic Monthly,* IV (1859), 770-73. In a review of Julia Ward Howe's *A Trip to Cuba*—*Atlantic Monthly,* IV (1860), 510—he says: "Here and there it seems to us a little too personal, and the public is made the confidant of matters in which it has properly no concern." Yet he knew that the only travelers worth reading were those who told what they saw, not what they went to see—see *Atlantic Monthly,* V (1860), 629.

15. In *North American Review,* CXII (1871), 236-37, he gave *Suburban Sketches* a "rave" review: "Yes, truly, these are poems, if the supreme gift of the poet be to rim the trivial things of our ordinary and prosaic experience with an ideal light. Here is something of the gracious ease of Chaucer, which cost him so much pains. . . . Let us make the most of Mr. Howells, for in the midst of our vulgar self-conceits and crudenesses, and noisy contempt of those conventions which are the safeguards of letters, and the best legacy of culture, we have got a gentleman and artist worthy to be ranked with Hawthorne in sensitiveness of observation, with Longfellow in perfection of style." Howard M. Munford, "The Disciple Proves Independent: Howells and L," *PMLA,* LXXIV (1959), 484-87, points out that Howells gives *The Biglow Papers* part of the credit for helping him realize the importance of the commonplace, but I cannot agree when he cites L on *The Lady of the Aroostook* as an example of L's desire to have Howells avoid the colloquial even in dialogue: "No Bostonian ever said, 'Was his wife along?' . . . Change it in a new edition—of which there will be lots." L objected to "Was his wife along" not because it was colloquial but only because it was not a New England colloquialism. And surely "of which there will be lots" should have been sufficient to warn Mr. Munford that L had no objection to colloquialism as such.

16. In bMS Am 765 (899)—HL—lines are drawn through this passage, possibly indicating that L thought he had gone too far. But he expresses essentially the same point of view, though less emphatically, elsewhere.

17. "A Legend of Brittany."

18. "whom if I had not the higher privilege of revering as a parent, I should still have honored as a man and loved as a friend, this volume containing many opinions from which he will wholly, yet with the large charity of a Christian heart, dissent, is inscribed, by his youngest child."

19. "My former volume of Essays has been so kindly received that I am emboldened to make another and more miscellaneous collection." He was shutting them up between covers so that they should haunt him no more and free his mind for new enterprises. "I should have preferred a simpler title, but publishers nowadays are inexorable on this point, and I was too much occupied for happiness of choice." The dedication was to Francis James Child, reminding him that he had liked the essay on Chaucer, "about whom you know so much more than I."

20. Ferris Greenslet's suggestion (*James Russell Lowell: His Life and Work,* p. 272) that L's letters "contain perhaps the very best" of him expresses, I think, a not indefensible point of view.

21. Once when L had written Child that nothing was ever quite so good as it should be "except a rose now and then," Child replied:

    Nothing is good as it should be—
    'Cept now and then a rose"—
    And now and then your poetry—
    And now and then your prose.

22. "Bellerophon," in *A Year's Life.*

23. Max Müller, *Auld Lang Syne,* pp. 180-81.

24. Lilian Whiting, *Boston Days* (LB, 1902), p. 83.

25. The failures of craftsmanship involved in certain structural deficiencies in both writers connect here. In *Conversations* the statement is made: "If some of the topics introduced seem foreign to the subject, I can only say, that they are not so to my mind, and that an author's object in writing criticisms is not only to bring to light the beauties of the works he is considering, but also to express his own opinions upon those and other matters." This is not a fault in *Conversations,* the scheme of the work being what it is, but he would be a bold man who should say that L never did the same thing elsewhere. Van Wyck Brooks (*The Flowering of New England,* Dutton, 1936) found "general ideas" in only two of L's essays, and Reilly declares that "his essays lack a unity which comes from the presence of a dominant idea, a thesis to be supported, or a point of view steadily maintained." But L was not interested in "general ideas" in the Van Wyck Brooks sense, and Reilly's illustrations leave the impression that he was not greatly concerned about the validity or the idea or thesis maintained. Comparing L's comments on Gray with Matthew Arnold's, he remarks, "Whether or not one agree with Arnold's conclusion one comes to realize that there is a difference between that penetration which stops short and that other which seeks to pierce to the heart of things." Seeking is no doubt an excellent thing. But is it as good as finding?

Wesley Mott (essay date 1978)

SOURCE: "Thoreau and Lowell on 'Vacation': *The Maine Woods* and 'A Moosehead Journal'," in *Thoreau Journal Quarterly,* Vol. X, No. 3, July, 1978, pp. 14-24.

[*In the following essay, Mott examines Lowell's satirical estimation of Henry David Thoreau in "A Moosehead Journal."*]

To a man of wholesome constitution the wilderness is well enough for a mood or a vacation, but not for a habit of life.

James Russell Lowell,**"Thoreau,"** 1865.

I

The antagonism between Henry David Thoreau and James Russell Lowell is an integral part of the Thoreau legend. It was Lowell's notorious essay **"Thoreau,"** published in the *North American Review* (October 1865) over three years after Thoreau's death, that reputedly set back for decades a just appreciation of Thoreau's writings both in America and in Europe.[1] The sources of the Lowell-Thoreau antipathy have been amply documented and several theories have been advanced to explain the personal aspect of Lowell's criticism.[2] But what has not been fully understood is the role of the State of Maine in shaping the philosophies, literary careers, and, ultimately, personal relationships of the two men. Both wrote accounts of their trips to Maine: Thoreau's "Chesuncook" brought him into direct conflict with the editor Lowell; and Lowell's **"A Moosehead Journal"** provides valuable clues for understanding the vehemence with which he denounced Thoreau's values in 1865.

There had always been a marked cultural gap between the rustic Thoreau and the Brahmin Lowell.[3] Both were Harvard graduates (HDT Class of 1837; JRL, '38); but as an undergraduate Lowell developed his first impression of Thoreau: that he was a poseur, an imitator of Emerson. He dramatized this charge without naming Thoreau in ***A Fable for Critics*** (October 1848). Still, Lowell wrote a generally favorable review of the *Week* for the *Massachusetts Quarterly Review* (December 1849): although he observed a certain egotism in Thoreau, he admired the *Week*'s felicitous descriptions of nature and the young writer's refreshing outlook.

Then as editor of the *Atlantic Monthly,* Lowell solicited an essay from Thoreau, who sent along "Chesuncook," the account of his 1853 trip to Maine, to be published in installments. The decisive rift between the two men was caused by Lowell's excision of one sentence in the second installment. He apparently considered too foggily pantheistic Thoreau's reference to a pine tree: "It is as immortal as I am, and perchance will go to as high a heaven, there to tower above me still." Thoreau wrote bitterly to Lowell on June 22, 1858, charging that the cutting of the line was done "in a very mean and cowardly manner," and was done by someone—he did not name Lowell—"bigoted & timid."[4] Although the abrasiveness of the letter may have been a hostile overreaction to a common editorial practice, the situation was aggravated by Lowell's failure to reply and by his long delay in paying Thoreau for his work.

We cannot be sure whether or not this encounter influenced Lowell's tone or judgement of Thoreau in the 1865 review. Emerson, for one, believed Lowell held a grudge over the letter (Harding, p. 394). Austin Warren, however, argues persuasively that Lowell's criticism of Thoreau's romantic traits must be viewed in the context of an overall philosophical shift to humanism by the mature editor, professor, and "man of the world" (Warren, pp. 456-58).

But in view both of Lowell's fateful editing of "Chesuncook" and of the substance of his charges against Thoreau in 1865, it is odd that so little attention has been paid to Lowell's own curiously Thoreauvian trip to the Moosehead area of Maine in 1853, just a month before Thoreau's Chesuncook trip. Lowell's Maine account, published first in *Putnam's Monthly* (1853), was collected in ***Fireside Travels*** in 1864, a year before his final attack on Thoreau.[5] The 1865 essay covers the entire corpus of Thoreau's writings; but since so much of Lowell's criticism centers on Thoreau's alleged sentimental addiction to nature, it is significant that nowhere (except in *Cape Cod*) does Thoreau record more bluntly than in *The Maine Woods* his response to raw nature. Lowell's **"A Moosehead Journal"** prompts us to ask, What did *he* see in Maine? In terms of his own experience in Maine, did Lowell fully understand Thoreau's reaction to the wilderness and, indeed, his own profound encounter with nature?

"A Moosehead Journal" has been belittled by Thoreauvians and Lowellites alike. Speculating on Lowell's reasons for cutting Thoreau's pine-tree sentence, Sherman Paul has said, "he may well have been discomfited by the obvious superiority of Thoreau's account. Lowell admitted in his **'A Moosehead Journal'** that there was nothing of Moosehead Lake in it; indeed, reading it today one cannot see the woods for the words."[6] Even Lowell's biographer R. C. Beatty conceded that, compared with a work like the *Week,* "The barrenness of the work is painfully evident." Beatty found Lowell's reproduction of regional dialect and observations of woodsmen all that "redeem his pages from complete monotony" (*JRL,* p. 126). The excursion genre is inherently difficult to judge in terms of organic structure; indeed, *The Maine Woods,* with pages of uninspired cataloguing, is not Thoreau's most carefully crafted work. Beyond this, **"A Moosehead Journal,"** extrinsically interesting as an anti-Thoreauvian's Thoreauvian tour, frequently flowers in observations of historical, cultural, and literary value. And it suggests a further personal motive for the attack on Thoreau in 1865.

II

Lowell approached his rustic trip with Brahmin tongue in cheek. He wrote Edmund Quincy on August 9, 1853, that he was going to "the pathless Orient—in other words I start this afternoon for a week's wilderness at Moosehead Lake. My nephew Charlie goes with me, and, if we don't get the fevernague, we shall probably have a good time. I shall revive all my venatic enthusiasms, and have a plan of shooting a dilemma and bringing home the horns. It is a beast which I fancy may be frequent in those parts, and the antlers hung in my study would have an agreeable effect on disputatious persons."[7]

In the same spirit he begins the essay with exaggeration that, save for the hint of irony and the extended clever literary allusions that follow, might be mistaken for transcendental hyperbole: "Moosehead . . . had never enjoyed the profit of being mirrored in my retina" (***AMJ,*** p. 1). Throughout his account Lowell uses a variety of comic stances to poke fun at rural discomforts and backwardness. In mock-heroic terms he recounts leaving Waterville on August 12, ridiculing the food that confronted "the pioneers of breakfast" (p. 8). Sarcastically he observes rural blight: "Now and then the houses thickened into an unsocial-looking village . . . (The taverns) are to real inns as the skull of Yorick to his face" (p. 9). Occasionally he turns the humor back on himself, as when he says that, like a green tourist, he ventured into the woods carrying all his baggage and keys (p. 28). Sometimes the humor is wistful: "I should have been prouder of a compliment to my paddling, than to have had both my guides suppose me the author of *Hamlet.*" He tries to sound matter-of-fact when he tells of learning that a true woodsman says "birch," not "canoe" (pp. 24-25); but there is a touch of self-defensiveness in his gentle sarcasm that suggests that it matters as much to Lowell to impress the woodsmen as it does to Thoreau to match paddling skills with Joe Polis.

Lowell's variety of comic stances is interesting in light of his claim that Thoreau, always seeking "perversity of thought," displayed "a morbid self-consciousness" and had "no humor" (pp. 372, 374); for Lowell strains harder than Thoreau to find clever things to say about Maine. Furthermore, Thoreau does not celebrate rural Maine with sober-faced reverence. He sees, as does Lowell (though without the satire), the ugly signs of struggling or emerging civilization on the road from Monson to Bangor: "Some of the taverns on this road, which were particularly dirty, were plainly in a transition state from the camp to the house."[8] Nor is Thoreau humorless. He mock-heroically recalls his voyage by steamer to Bangor: "Anxious to get out of the whale's belly, I rose early . . . I was proud to find that I had stood the voyage so well, and was not in the least digested" (*MW,* p. 85). He explains the difficulties of our forebears by means of a funny parable about a dog whose explorations earned him porcupine quills in the nose (p. 127). To be sure, Thoreau more often uses serious epic parallels to express his love of the wild. In a famous passage he declares that trout suggest "the truth of mythology, the fables of Proteus, and all those beautiful sea-monsters." But with typical dry humor he checks his own transcendental flight in the next paragraph, "But there is the rough voice of Uncle George, who commands at the frying-pan, to send over what you've got" (p. 54). Thus for Thoreau does humor often establish a balance between the ideal and the actual in nature.

Thoreau typically achieves balance of vision and structure also through an interplay between the modes of excursion and sermon.[9] Observations of natural phenomena and men in nature provide contexts for pronouncements on human nature and institutions. Men like George McCauslin, Thomas Fowler, and the logger John Morrison are admirable because they are resourceful, self-reliant, and respectful of nature. In his enthusiasm for the woodsmen, Thoreau claims that "the deeper you penetrate into the woods, the more intelligent, and, in one sense, less countrified do you find the inhabitants" (p. 22). A compulsive etymologist, he finds place names indexes of either Indian simplicity or human vanity:

> Tomhegan or *Socatarian* stream . . . The last name . . . had a bogus sound, too much like sectarian for me, as if a missionary had tampered with it; but I know that the Indians were very liberal. I think I should have inclined to the Tomhegan first (p. 183).

But he is too shrewd to deny that even in remote villages one cannot escape the contentiousness of civilization; politics infect even the yokels, such as the "total stranger" who "actually frightened the horse with his asseverations, growing more solemnly positive as there was less in him to be positive about" (p. 8). Because Thoreau is a preacher and observer of the human scene as well as a traveller, he underlines description with aphorisms and didactic sermonettes.

Ironically, Lowell in 1865 preferred Thoreau as a mere chronicler of nature, charging that his accuracy of observation suffered from an "itch of originality" (p. 371). However, Lowell in his own account is less concerned to daguerreotype the Maine landscape than to comment on mankind. Indeed, many of his observations are strikingly Thoreauvian. Lowell ridicules place names that smack of the politician's vanity, preferring (with typical Lowell humor) simple, rugged names: "I am no fanatic for Indian nomenclature,—the name of my native district having been Pigsgusset,—but let us at least agree on names for ten years" (***AMJ,*** p. 14). He spends a great deal of time recreating the humorous dialect of Uncle Zeb, whom he considers a Down East relic comparable to "the Dodo" (p. 17). But Lowell's trek is motivated by an unmistakably Thoreauvian impulse to "go personally down East and see for myself" (p. 4). Though at first expressed with tongue-in-cheek self-consciousness, Lowell's convictions sound Thoreauvian when taken out of context: "The divine faculty is to see what everybody can look at" (p. 4). In Maine he sees several crude bumpkins: a newsboy seemingly delighted to trumpet news of a train-wreck (pp. 4-5), a tavern-keeper who "welcomed us as so many half-dollars" (p. 12). But he also has praise for the rugged directness and skill Thoreau admired in woodsmen. Imagining the camp of loggers he meets on a boat, he implicitly measures himself against their manhood: "there a man would soon find out how much alive he was" (p. 15). In admiring one woodsman he calls "a man really educated," Lowell makes a Thoreauvian pun: "He was A.M. and LL.D. in Woods College,—Axe-master and Doctor of Logs" (p. 32).

Instead of making a satirical thrust at the outpost hotel at Kineo, Lowell confesses a liking for the inn-keeper, "hearty" Squire Barrows. At this point in the narrative Lowell sounds dramatically Thoreauvian on several issues:

> —*On self-reliance:* "In these travelling encounters one is thrown upon his own resources, and is worth just what he carries about him" (p. 19).

—*On the character of genuine men:* "Perhaps the kind of intelligence one gets in these out-of-the-way places is the best,—where one takes a fresh man after breakfast instead of the damp morning paper, and where the magnetic telegraph of human sympathy flashes swift news from brain to brain" (p. 20).

—*On the value of direct experience:* "It is curious . . . how tyrannical the habit of reading is, and what shift we make to escape thinking" (p. 21). (There follows a "fable," the poem "Doctor Lobster," which, aside from displaying Lowell's clever wit, resembles the poetic "digressions" in the *Week.*)

—*On transcendental economy:* "The incidents of our voyage were few, but quite as exciting and profitable as the *items* of the newspapers" (p. 34).

The latter ideal he would later criticize in Thoreau as antisocial.

III

In Maine Lowell feels as does Thoreau a liberation of the spirit by measuring his values against a vast, inhuman standard; he finds the wilderness at once refreshing for man and vulnerable to man's intrusion, at once despoiled by human contact and pleasingly refined by signs of cultivation. Thoreau finds it remarkable that a town-bred person adapts immediately to sleeping in a blanket in the woods even on a cold, rainy night (*MW,* p. 104). But despite occasional pantheistic utterances like the one Lowell excised from the *Atlantic,* Thoreau seldom calls for a return to a Rousseauistic natural state. He finds esthetic delight in the eminently artificial red of the woodsman's traditional flannel shirt, cast in relief against pines and water (pp. 68, 131). Frequently his eye discovers harmony between wilderness and civilization. He describes North Twin Lake: "the lake lay open to the light with even a civilized aspect, as if expecting trade and commerce, and towns and villas" (p. 36). Indeed, he is not shocked at one point to mistake an "islet" and trees for a steamer, "So much do the works of man resemble the works of nature" (p. 175).

The tension between the values of nature and civilization that runs through most of Thoreau's writings suggests the "complex pastoralism" Leo Marx has distinguished from simple "sentimental pastoralism."[10] While Thoreau equates Nature with the Good and imagines moments of inspiration as occurring in rural settings, he is too honest to believe that nature is always conducive to harmony and innocence. In the first place, "explorers, and lumberers generally, are all hirelings" who act not out of "love for wild nature," but love of money (p. 119). The enormous guilt that comes from Thoreau's part in the moose-kill leads him to project his self-loathing onto the very children of nature, the Indians: "What a coarse and imperfect use Indians and hunters make of nature! . . . I already and for weeks afterward felt my nature the coarser for this part of my woodland experience" (p. 120). (Lowell's only moose encounter was comically inept. He "declined" to carry a gun, but waited hours in wet darkness for moose to appear. When at last a moose stumbled upon them, the guns of his companions misfired because of the damp [(***AMJ,*** pp. 35-36.)] Ultimately, Thoreau knew, proper love of nature is a matter not of literal immersion in the woods, but of imaginative preparation. Indeed, "some are nearer the frontiers on feather-beds in the towns than others on fir-twigs in the backwoods" (*MW,* p. 200).

Lowell rarely achieves such a richly complex pastoral stance. He is, first, concerned extensively with his journey *to* Moosehead. After a "dreadful ride," he arrives "like a devilled kidney" at Waterville, an outpost "in a hobbledehoy age" between wilderness and town (p. 5). Mocking the ugly buildings of Waterville (now Colby) College, he perceives that in a crude, growing society architectural efforts go primarily to factories (p. 6). (This leads to a Thoreauvian digression on work: "We snatch an education like a meal at a railroad-station" [p. 7].) The village of Greenville "looks as if it had dripped down from the hills, and settled in the hollow at the foot of the lake" (p. 12). Paradoxically, when Lowell does succumb to the beauty of Maine, it is in terms of unabashed sentimental pastoralism. His coach-driver stops to repair a wheel: "It was a pretty spot, and I was not sorry to lie under a beech-tree (Tityrus-like, meditating over my pipe)" (p. 10). In a moment of mystical rapture, he finds fact and imagination become "one unreal reality": "Sunset and moonrise at once! Adam had no more in Eden—except the head of Eve upon his shoulder" (pp. 33-34).

Lowell discovers, like Thoreau, that a city-dweller quickly learns to sleep in the wild: "I . . . had become in two days such a stoic of the woods, that I went to sleep tranquilly, certain that my bedroom would be in a blaze before morning" (indeed, he slept this night while his hut burned down around him! [p. 37]). Although he despises primitive towns and the truly wild, he likes "the thriving town of Dexter," where prosperous crops, "prettier" houses, and the "pleasant home-look" of flowers and orchards exude picturesque charm. No longer threatened by Maine there, Lowell is moved to a sentimental defense of the pines that surpasses in pantheistic feeling the line he would later cut from Thoreau's essay. He sees "that the war between the white man and the forest was still fierce"; indeed, he seems to "hear a sigh now and then from the immemorial pines, as they stood watching these campfires of the inexorable invader" (p. 11). He goes on to say that he was inspired to recite the opening of *Evangeline.* But wit undercuts growing sentimentality, and he burlesques the lines as they sounded while his coach bounced over a rugged log road (p. 12).

Domestic tameness characterizes Lowell's later glimpses of natural beauty. In a birch "The repose was perfect. Another heaven hallowed and deepened the polished lake" (p. 30). Just as Thoreau found comfort in the wilderness by discovering old newspapers, advertisements, and other human signs, Lowell observes, "The tame hay-cocks in the midst of the wildness gave one a pleasant reminiscence of home, like hearing one's native tongue in a strange country" (p. 31). He is prepared now to look beneath the woodsman's lack of "hard external polish" to discover the "deeper grace which springs only from sincere manliness . . . I have never seen a finer race of men" (p. 38). Still, having found worn-out clothes discarded by woodsmen preparing to go to town, Lowell curiously drifts into a diatribe against this "Ready-made Age" (p. 39). The Carlylean theme and the digressive sermonizing he shares with Thoreau; but coming as it does close on the heels of unbounded praise of the woodmen, the attack seems forced. Perhaps he instinctively senses that his urbane pose has been let down too long in praise of his rugged companions.

Thoreau was not only capable of a richer variety of pastoral stances than Lowell; he was also the only one daring enough, in "Ktaadn," to confront stark, primeval nature. Lowell contemplates Mt. Katahdin at armchair ease: "It was debated whether we saw Katahdin or not, (perhaps more useful as an intellectual exercise than the assured vision would have been)" (p. 13). But Thoreau, probing at nature at her most hostile, created what is doubtless the most famous episode of *The Maine Woods,* the climb and descent of the mountain. The transcendentalist comes face to face with a nature that "was no man's garden, but the unhandselled globe . . . It was Matter, vast, terrific,—not his Mother Earth" (p. 70).

There is no single passage so memorable in **"A Moosehead Journal."** Lowell keeps his distance from nature in her threatening forms through wit and literary posing. But both Thoreau and Lowell cite mountains as standards against which to measure human vanity. Upon finding a tin dipper scratched with names atop Mt. Kineo, Lowell is led to the Thoreauvian reflection, "But, alas! institutions are as changeable as tin-dippers" (p. 40). (Ironically, it is Thoreau who laments after climbing Katahdin that they had not carried a brick to the top "to be left there for our mark"—"It would certainly have been a simple evidence of civilized man" [p. 45].) But only once in the **"Journal"** does Lowell come close to Thoreau's well-known love of mountain-top vigils:

> The forest primeval is best seen from the top of a mountain . . . mere size is hardly an element of grandeur, except in works of man.. . . It is through one or the other pole of vanity that men feel the sublime in mountains. It is either, How small great I am beside it! or, Big as you are, little I's soul will hold a dozen of you. The true idea of a forest is . . . something humanized a little . . . To some moods, it is congenial to look over endless leagues of unbroken savagery without a hint of man (pp. 40-41).

For Lowell mountain-top views are therapeutic both because nature's solid, massive durability remedies that claustrophobic nineteenth-century malady, ennui, and because, paradoxically, man is reassured of the ultimate centrality of mind and spirit in the universe. Direct contact or immersion in primeval matter is not the goal; rather, a man must achieve a vantage point from which he can imaginatively control and tame the wilderness.

A variation on this theme occurs in *The Maine Woods* as Thoreau, who loved mountain-top vigils, comes through dense woods to the shore of a lake, which he finds "liberating and civilizing even . . . The lakes also reveal the mountains, and give ample scope and range to our thought." Here he is moved to see images of civilization in the wilderness: the gulls on the lake remind him of "custom-house officers" (p. 198). The experience on Mt. Katahdin is so terrifyingly different largely because the view, essential to imaginative control, is obscured by heavy mist; deprived of the "liberating" value of fresh visual perspective, Thoreau is momentarily overwhelmed by "contact," the otherness of inanimate matter.

That Lowell could not appreciate Thoreau's honesty and courage in facing primitive nature stripped of illusion is implicit in his remark in the 1865 review, "it will be a positive refreshment to meet a man who is as superbly indifferent to Nature as she is to him" (p. 377). It is true that Thoreau quickly recovers from his terror on the mountain; but he had for a time dared to risk the very assurance of a benign nature that was the core of his transcendental faith.

IV

What is perhaps Lowell's least founded criticism of Thoreau arises from his literal reading of the theme of solitude in *Walden.* The misunderstanding that Thoreau preferred muskrats to men contributed mightily to his reputation as a misanthropic hermit. "I look upon a great deal of the modern sentimentalism about Nature," Lowell declared, "as a mark of disease" (p. 375).

Even in *The Maine Woods,* Thoreau's most unstructured rambles through nature, he is acutely conscious of the dangers of total immersion in the wild. He does not, as Lowell would have us believe, uncritically idealize the Penobscot Indians. At several points he finds the modern Indian, whose noble past is as unrecoverable as a dream, almost as "dirty" as the lumberers (p. 133) and as corrupt, we have seen, in their use of nature. Often the Indians are boring, inarticulate (p. 172). Far from trying to adopt Indian ways, Thoreau finds in their language "startling evidence of their being a distinct and comparatively aboriginal race" (p. 136), a clear awareness of unbridgeable cultural otherness. Thoreau deeply admires much of what survives of genuine Indian culture; yet he is impressed on his final trip to Maine by an Indian who uses the stagecoach to save time on a hunting trip, thus "availing himself cunningly of the advantages of civilization, without losing any of his woodcraft, but proving himself the more successful hunter for it" (p. 201).

Nor does Thoreau leave behind his shrewd Yankee eye when he visits Maine. He is appalled by the waste of improperly tended apple trees (p. 8); tree-cranberries should be cultivated "both for beauty and for food" (p. 132). The urban poor, he suggests, should come to Maine to avail themselves of cheap land and houses (p. 14); felled trees presently left to rot could be used to heat the homes of the poor (p. 17). Indeed, he is not shocked when he contemplates steamers and sailboats in Maine: "These beginnings of commerce on a lake in the wilderness are very interesting" (p. 90).

What, then, are Thoreau's final uses for Maine? Lowell declared in 1865, "To a man of wholesome constitution the wilderness is well enough for a mood or a vacation, but not for a habit of life" (pp. 375-76). Ironically, Thoreau, although capable of a deeper and more complex love of the wild than Lowell, agreed. In the often cited conclusion to "Chesuncook," which Lowell surely knew, Thoreau expresses the fear that Maine might soon suffer from the overdevelopment that afflicts Massachusetts. Yet he is glad to get home, finds it "a relief" to return to Massachusetts (p. 155). Savage-like immersion was not the best use of nature. The wilderness is necessary "for a resource and a background" to our lives. But "The partially cultivated country it is which chiefly has inspired, and will continue to inspire, the strains of poets." In the wild the poet can "drink at some new and more bracing fountain of the Muses" (pp. 155-56). Ultimately the wilderness infuses *civilization* with new spirit and power. Thoreau's final concern is for national preserves and parks, including those within towns and cities, that the greatest number of lives will be refreshed for activity in society through contact with "partially cultivated," protected nature.

V

Intrinsically **"A Moosehead Journal"** is inferior to *The Maine Woods.* But Lowell's own concluding words, turned back on him by Sherman Paul to suggest the dullness of the work, appropriately explain his intention:

> There is very little about Moosehead Lake in it . . . It did not profess to give you an account of the lake; but a journal, and, moreover, my journal, with a little nature, a little human nature, and a great deal of I in it, which last ingredient I take to be the true spirit of this species of writing; all the rest being so much water for tender throats which cannot take it neat (pp. 41-42).

There is a touch of defensiveness in Lowell's tone. But for our purposes it is significant that he is implicitly describing the forte of *Thoreau*—the fashionable combination of excursion, lay sermon, and autobiography. Lowell also admits he has written "in the diffuse Oriental manner" (p. 41); in 1865 he would label this the chief stylistic flaw of Thoreau: "there is no writing comparable with Thoreau's in kind, that is comparable with it in degree where it is best; where it disengages itself, that is, from the tangled roots and dead leaves of a *second-hand Orientalism,* and runs limpid and smooth and broadening as it runs, a mirror for whatever is grand and lovely in both worlds" (p. 379 [my italics].) Thus in **"Thoreau"** Lowell is criticizing not only Thoreau's style, but one in which he himself had briefly indulged and which he now felt to be at least a minor embarrassment.

What does this tell us about the standards by which Lowell judged Thoreau in 1865? **"A Moosehead Journal"** contains much in terms of opinion, method, and style that is Thoreauvian. But even while Lowell continues in his notorious review to respect Thoreau's idealism (p. 379), he makes charges based upon a shallow, selectively literal reading of Thoreau. Lowell was probably motivated in part by spite, as Emerson's recollection suggests, and by a steady shift toward humanistic critical values that simply settled on Thoreau as the obvious whipping-boy, as Austin Warren has demonstrated. He may or may not have been jealous of "the obvious superiority of Thoreau's account" of Maine when he cut out the pine-tree sentence in 1853. But surely by 1865 Lowell was increasingly aware of the inappropriateness of his own past "venatic enthusiasms." This best explains, I think, the conflict between his earlier Thoreauvian impulses and his later allegations of sentimental nature-worship in Thoreau. Published three years after Thoreau's death and a year after **"A Moosehead Journal"** was collected in ***Fireside Travels,*** at a time when Lowell's critical standards had become emphatically humanistic, the **"Thoreau"** review is implicitly *self*-criticism.

Lowell had guarded himself even in **"A Moosehead Journal"** against romantic effusion through witty imitation of regional dialect, dense literary allusions, and satire. Now in 1865 he felt the need to hold that Maine experience and what it represented at full arm's length. In suppressing values he himself had once courted, Lowell distorted, ignored, or simply could not appreciate in Thoreau that which now threatened his new critical posture. In denying that part of himself that he had "outgrown," Lowell missed in Thoreau a richer, more varied response to nature than he had himself been capable of.

Notes

1. *The Recognition of Henry David Thoreau,* ed. Wendell Glick (Ann Arbor: The University of Michigan Press, 1969). Although Lowell was once "the most influential critic of the time," there has been a "reverse correlation in the movement of the reputations of Lowell and Thoreau in this century." pp. ix, xi.
2. See especially Austin Warren, "Lowell on Thoreau," *Studies in Philology,* XXVII (July 1930), 442-61. The standard biographies are Martin Duberman, *James Russell Lowell* (Boston: Beacon Press, 1966), esp. pp. 169-72; and Walter Harding, *The Days of Henry Thoreau* (New York: Alfred A. Knopf, 1970), esp. pp. 392-95.
3. Richmond Croom Beatty observed a "snobbish urbanity" in Lowell's 1865 review, and noted that Thoreau held a "pronounced contempt for Cambridge culture," *James Russell Lowell* (Nashville: Vanderbilt University Press, 1942), pp. 221, 223.
4. *The Correspondence of Henry David Thoreau,* ed. Walter Harding and Carl Bode (New York: New York University Press, 1958), pp. 515, 516.
5. This paper follows the text of "A Moosehead Journal" in *Literary Essays* (Boston: Houghton, Mifflin and Company, 1892), I, 1-42. Cited hereafter as *AMJ.* The "Thoreau" essay is from I, 361-81.
6. *The Shores of America: Thoreau's Inward Exploration* (Urbana: University of Illinois Press, 1958), p. 364, n24.

7. *New Letters of James Russell Lowell,* ed. M. A. DeWolfe Howe (New York: Harper & Brothers Publishers, 1932), p. 45.
8. *The Maine Woods,* ed. Joseph J. Moldenhauer (Princeton: Princeton University Press, 1972), p. 145. Cited hereafter as *MW.*
9. Sidney B. Poger, "Thoreau: Two Modes of Discourse" (unpublished Ph.D. dissertation, Columbia University, 1965).
10. *The Machine in the Garden: Technology and the Pastoral Ideal in America* (New York: Oxford University Press, 1968).

Brian Attebery (essay date 1980)

SOURCE: "The Empty Cathedral: Lowell and Adams," in *The Markham Review,* Vol. 9, Winter, 1980, pp. 29-32.

[*In the following essay, Attebery views Lowell's* The Cathedral *as a significant transitional work thematically linked to the writings of Henry Adams and T. S. Eliot.*]

James Russell Lowell dismissed himself in ***A Fable for Critics*** as a poet "who's striving Parnassus to climb / With a whole bale of *isms* together with rhyme . . . / The top of the hill he will ne're come nigh reaching / Till he learns the distinction 'twixt singing and preaching."[1] Lowell's self-criticism is accurate enough to have become the common critical view: excepting only the ***Fable*** and a few of the dialect poems, his work is passed over as amateurish, didactic, and dated. Yet one other important exception—**"The Cathedral"**—should be added to the list of Lowell's lasting poetic contributions. It deserves to be re-examined by the sympathetic twentieth-century reader for two reasons. First, it presents with imagination and insight many of the themes that typify twentieth-century literature. Second, it is linked historically with at least one of the great writers of the opening of the century, Henry Adams, and through him to others, notably T. S. Eliot.

Lowell's influence on late nineteenth-century American letters has been largely ignored. But, as a friend of Adams, Charles Eliot Norton, Francis James Child, and William and Henry James; as a noted editor and educator; and simply as what George Santayana called one of the "gentle lights really burning" in Boston,[2] Lowell was one of the major shapers of the Harvard environment from which were to emerge, around the turn of the century, Eliot, Frost, Stevens, and other founders of modern literature. The link with Adams is the clearest bridge between Lowell and the new century, and **"The Cathedral,"** of all his works, most demonstrably anticipates the new motifs. Showing both the anticipation and the direct succession should clarify Lowell's role as literary grandfather to a new age and to inspire a fresh reading of his most ambitious creation.

What are the typical motifs of Modern literature? To judge from the early Eliot they are the antitheses of Romantic dogma. There is an attempt to take an unromantic, "scientific" view of reality that leaves mankind "formulated, sprawling on a pin."[3] There is a sense of alienation and mistrust of the natural world that makes April "the cruelest month."[4] There is a feeling of loss—loss of love, of faith, of vitality—that directly counters the old belief in progress: the world is on its way to ending "not with a bang but a whimper."[5] There is a sense of man's, and particularly the artist's, impotence: "Our dried voices, when / We whisper together / Are quiet and meaningless / As wind in dry grass . . . / Paralyzed force, gesture without motion."[6] There is a fear of the common man, Eliot's "Sweeney," and a questioning of the worth of democracy. There is the use of the past, not for its picturesque associations, but as a standard by which the present is measured and found wanting: this is one of the functions of the "mythic method." There is, finally, a need to counter all these things and to find within the poet, through the medium of poetry, a personal solution to the problems that he sees. This solution may be Eliot's mystical Anglo-Catholicism, Wallace Stevens's "supreme fiction," or Robert Frost's protective irony, but each poet must find it for himself. These are themes that pervade the literature of this century, with which all major writers must deal in one way or another. They are also the particular questions that form the substance and thought of **"The Cathedral."**

"The Cathedral" was published simultaneously in the January, 1870, issue of the *Atlantic* and as a separate volume. Lowell made several revisions in subsequent editions of the poem, as described in Thomas Tanselle's article on "The Craftsmanship of Lowell: Revisions in ***The Cathedral.***"[7] The final version, as reprinted in Edwin Cady's *The American Poets: 1800-1900* (Glenview, Illinois: Scott, Foresman and Company, 1966), differs from the first edition primarily in the omission of weak material caricaturing a group of English visitors to the cathedral. This uncharacteristic afterthought and this concern with technical polish are in keeping with the unusual (for Lowell) seriousness and complex ideas expressed within the poem.

Lowell's poem begins indirectly and abstractly, dealing not with his experiences at the cathedral of Chartres, or even with the memory of that experience, but with memory itself. Memory holds a glowing picture of the past, "cloudless of care, down-shod to every sense, / And simply perfect from its own resource."[8] The particular memories that Lowell is concerned with, the ones that "are present still," forming "parts of myself," concern the poet's first impressions of nature. Yet, though he has just established the importance of nature and memory, he begins, like Eliot, to undercut both. Nature, as vital to us as she is, "lets us mistake our longing for her love, / And mocks with various echoes of ourselves." The same duplicity is found in the memories of natural things, the "first sweet frauds upon our consciousness," which color the world ever afterward and rob later experience of its primal power: "Our own breath dims the mirror of the sense, / Looking too long and closely: at a flash / We snatch the essential grace of meaning out, / And that first passion beggars all behind

. . . / So Memory cheats us, glimpsing half-revealed." Because of memory, the poet says, he has known but one true spring, one summer, one autumn, one winter; "and later visions seem but copies pale / From those unfading frescoes of the past." Two of the twentieth-century themes have already appeared: we begin to feel a sense of loss, of expulsion from the innocence of pure sensation, and connected with this loss is a growing mistrust of the natural world that promises and fails to fulfill. The opening of the poem is vague and rhetorical while it pursues the Romantic ideal of communion with memory and nature, but when doubt enters, the writing becomes more immediate and more richly metaphorical. It is precisely the doubt that vitalizes the poem and keeps it above the level of Lowell's more blithe, less interesting lyrics.

"The world's a woman to our shifting mood, / Feeling with us, or making due pretence; / To make all things our thought's confederates. . . ." The poem here expresses a disillusionment with nature directly counter to the common nineteenth-century view developed by Emerson. Emerson wrote confidently that "Nature never wears a mean appearance. Neither does the wisest man extort her secret, and lose his curiosity by finding out all her perfection. Nature never became a toy to wise spirit."[9] Yet the speaker in **"The Cathedral"** has discovered that nature's "secret" is merely the reflection of his own mind. She can offer him neither true sympathy nor new discoveries. All that is left to the poet is "feigned surprise"—a key concept in the poem. At this point the pronoun *she* shifts from Nature to the soul, and thence to the Muse, "Bringer of life, witching each sense to soul, / That sometimes almost gives me to believe / I might have been a poet. . . ." The rapid switching of referent is confusing but significant: the three *she*s are blurred because they share the same relationship to the poet. He woos all three unsuccessfully. Each promises to lift the poet above himself and then abandons him to his own meditation. Their mark is fickleness.

Here begins the main body of the poem. In an effort to win back muse, soul, or nature, he plans an experience that she will not find "a dish warmed over at the feast of life": a trip to the cathedral of Chartres. That it will be only a "feigned surprise" is hinted from the first, when the poet, before approaching the cathedral itself, orders a dinner "with the Saxon's pious care." There is no spontaneity in this solitary meal. The poet's character shows itself as Prufrockian, repressed and impotent, when compared with the simple Frenchmen whom he meets. They are at ease and open, "while we, each pore alert with consciousness, / Hide our best selves as we had stolen them. . . ." The poet ponders his character while he wanders down the equivalent of Prufrock's "streets that follow like a tedious argument / Of insidious intent":[10] these lead the poet suddenly to the looming cathedral. Its initial description is the most vivid passage thus far in the poem:

> Silent and gray as forest-leaguered cliff
> Left inland by the ocean's slow retreat,
> That hears afar the breeze-borne rote and longs,
> Remembering shocks of surf that clomb and fell,
> Spume-sliding down the baffled decuman,
> It rose before me, patiently remote
> From the great tides of life it breasted once,
> Hearing the noise of men as in a dream.

Tied in with the very strength of the cathedral is melancholy. We see that the poet's attempt at fresh experience is foredoomed: he has picked a place as bound by the lost past as himself. The extended ocean simile reminds us of Matthew Arnold's receding sea of faith at "Dover Beach" and also of "The Waste Land," where there is "no water but only rock."[11] The cathedral, like the poet, is unable to capture new experience; it can only remember. "She," the muse or soul, cannot be won in this way, and so the feminine now disappears from the poem like the feminine sea that the cathedral once "breasted." Yet the poet is led to a false hope by the building's "hazardous caprices . . . heavy as nightmare, airy-light as fern, / Imagination's very self in stone." If this fantastic creation is Gothic, then he owns himself "a happy Goth."

There follows a section on the vitality of the German tribes who replaced the dying Rome "of men invirile and disnatured dames / That poison sucked from the Attic bloom decayed." Greece had fallen, and Rome after her, but red blood still flowed in the North, where such a monument could be built. The counter-argument is obvious: where are your powerful builders now? The poet realizes that he is no Goth, but the "child of an age that lectures, not creates, / Plastering our swallow-nests on the awful Past, / And twittering round the work of larger men, / As we had builded what we but deface." Within the mighty edifice are no mighty Goths, only a few peasant women and "a sense of undefined regret, / Irreparable loss, uncertain what. . . ." The poet asks, "Was all this grandeur but anachronism, / A shell divorced of its informing life, / Where the priest housed him like a hermit crab . . . ?" Doubt once again brings forth one of the poem's stronger images.

The poet watches one of the praying women and is first scornful ("she told mechanic beads / Before some shrine of saintly womanhood, / Bribed intercessor with the far-off Judge"), then longing ("Blessed the natures shored on every side / With landmarks of hereditary thought!"), and then skeptical once again ("or was it not mere sympathy of brain? / A sweetness intellectually conceived / In simpler creeds to me impossible"). He toys with his own ideas of God and faith, desiring to believe but unable to find solace in the forms of religion, despite the cathedral's aesthetic appeal. "Let us be thankful when, as I do here, / We can read Bethel on a pile of stones, / And, seeing where God *has* been, trust in him." The thought brings to his mind the contrasting present: "Fagot and stake were desperately sincere: / Our cooler martyrdoms are done in types; / And flames that shine in controversial eyes / Burn out no brains but his who kindles them. / This is no age to get cathedrals built. . . ." But, he asks, why does not Democracy, the ultimate in human progress, accomplish as much? Because of the "Western giant coarse" that it breeds. "What hope for those fine-nerved humanities / That made earth gracious once with gentler arts, / Now the rude hands have caught the trick of thought / And claim an equal suffrage with the brain?" The poet finds himself to be "the born disciple of an elder time," as will Adams and Eliot after him. In the end, "I walked forth saddened; for all thought is sad, / And leaves a bitterish savor in the brain, / Tonic, it may be, not delectable. . . ." The carefully planned feast for the soul turns out to be a bitter medicine.

Outside the building, even the sparrows that fly about the spires, "irreverently happy," like the earlier simple Frenchmen, are shadowed by a hawk. The poet realizes he must confront nature as she really is, "force conservative, / Indifferent to our noisy whims." He no longer expects progress in the world, only change;

> No mortal ever dreams
> That the scant isthmus he encamps upon
> Between two oceans, one, the Stormy, passed,
> And one, the Peaceful, yet to venture on,
> Has been the future whereto prophets yearned
> For the fulfilment of Earth's cheated hope,
> Shall be that past which nerveless poets moan
> As the lost opportunity of song.

Lowell ends the poem, not here with his dark discovery, but with a prayer—his attempt at a personal solution. The optimism of the prayer seems out of keeping with the conclusions reached above, yet it represents Lowell's honest and direct response. The soul reappears: she has not been lost, only "muffled from sight in formal robes of proof." The ending is affirmative, but it attempts to hold in mind the lesson of the cathedral, that we have no logical proof of God and hope, no guarantee but the soul: "While she can only feel herself through Thee, / I fear not Thy withdrawal; more I fear, / Seeing, to know Thee not, hoodwinked with dreams / Of signs and wonders, while, unnoticed, Thou, / Walking Thy garden still, commun'st with men, / Missed in the commonplace of miracle." Lowell comes down to his own belief, having rejected reason, tradition, nature, democracy, and progress as true signs of God or sources of meaning. Such a conclusion is closer in mood (though hardly comparable in technique) to the *Four Quartets* than to "Prufrock" or "The Waste Land": it is to be read, like the *Quartets,* as the record of a search rather than as a moral lesson. Seen as hope rather than as homily, it provides an appropriate and valiant ending to a challenging poem.

The metaphor of the cathedral unifies the poem and establishes its several levels of meaning. It is, first, the object of a pilgrimage that fails. The poet comes seeking faith, renewal, and also, veiled in the triple "she" of soul, muse, and nature, lost love. He finds only a place where these things have been, the high water mark of the vanished flood. Second, the cathedral represents the noble past, which silently condemns the present. Lowell wrote elsewhere, "The age that produced those buildings was not barbarous. That which produces Trinity Church is, because it is an abortion, because the conception of the edifice was never clear in the mind of the builder. The Gothic style is just as fit for a church (meeting-house) as ever; the difficulty is that the Church has shrunk so as not to fill the ancient idea."[12] And with the Church has shrunk mankind. This leads to a third meaning for the cathedral. As a creation of man it is a symbol for all art: the cathedral and **"The Cathedral"** are symbolically the same, and the limitations of the building imply the limitations of the poem. The poet can create a work of beauty and grandeur, but he cannot create by fiat a lasting faith. Lowell, in a letter to William Dean Howells, indicated the symbolic association, describing his poem in architectural terms: "There seems to be a bit of clean carving here and there, a solid buttress or two, and perhaps a gleam through painted glass. . . ."[13] Art, memory, faith, love, progress, nature: all these are brought together in the idea of the great cathedral.

How did Lowell, the facile, cheerful poet of ***The Vision of Sir Launfal,*** come to write such a questioning poem? **"The Cathedral"** was written in 1869, twenty years after ***Sir Launfal***: it is the work of a man of fifty and the product of years of experience, thought, and reading. In addition, the incident that inspired the poem, a day at Chartres, was in 1855, soon after the death of his wife Maria.[14] Discussing an illness of Maria's in 1853, Lowell wrote, "Such a sorrow opens a door clear down into one's deepest nature that he had never suspected before."[15] When Maria died the door opened wider still, and Lowell's meditations at Chartres were profound enough to inspire a poem fourteen years later.

Lowell's pupil and friend, Henry Adams, also fused personal sorrow, historical skepticism, and philosophical inquiry into a work of art centered on the cathedral at Chartres. In *Mont-Saint-Michel and Chartres* and its companion piece *The Education of Henry Adams,* Adams contrasts the cathedral, representing the unity of the thirteenth century, with his own life in the chaotic nineteenth century. It is not certain that Adams picked up the metaphor from Lowell: Robert Mane reports that "There is no copy of the book in Adams's library, and his letters bring no evidence that he ever read it."[16] Yet the lives of Lowell and Adams were too interconnected for Adams to have been unaware of **"The Cathedral."** Lowell introduced Adams to European literature at Harvard and is the only one of Adams's professors to whom he acknowledges a debt in *The Education.* There Adams writes, "James Russell Lowell had brought back from Germany the only new and valuable part of its universities, the habit of allowing students to read with him privately in his study. Adams asked the privilege, and used it to read a little, and to talk a great deal.. . . Lowell was a new element in the boy's life."[17] Lowell represented "Concord"—"feeling, poetry or imagination"[18]—and Adams significantly says that he approached Concord "as he would have entered a Gothic Cathedral, for he knew that the priests regarded him as only a worm."[19]

Adams left Harvard, having absorbed Lowell's method of teaching for his own future use,[20] and went, as had Lowell, to Germany. In Dresden Adams lived with the family Lowell had stayed with years before.[21] When Adams returned to Harvard, the two men were colleagues in teaching and in successively editing the *North American Review*. In 1869 Adams wrote to an English friend listing the few things he considered worthwhile in American literature: he included Lowell's ***Biglow Papers*** and the nature descriptions of ***The Vision of Sir Launfal***.[22] In 1872, two years after the publication of **"The Cathedral,"** Adams sailed to Europe and was pleased to find on the same ship "my confrère, James Russell Lowell,"[23] and Lowell's latest work could have been discussed on board. When Lowell became Ambassador to England, he assumed a position once filled by Charles Francis Adams; the bond of friendship must have been strengthened by this association with Henry's father, who plays an important and admirable role in *The Education*. Adams seems to have looked on Lowell as his mentor long after leaving Harvard. In 1879, Lowell, in Spain, received a letter from him asking Lowell to "teach me to adore Spanish literature, for the more I read of it, the meaner my intelligence seems and the more abject becomes my dependence of English."[24]

A comparison of *Mont-Saint-Michel and Chartres* and Lowell's poem supports the probability of influence. A sense of loss underlies Adams's work, an awareness that after the time of cathedrals, "the world grew cheap, as worlds must."[25] The most important losses are those of love and faith. For Adams, the feminine principle is not scattered among nature, the muse, and the soul; it is gloriously figured by the Virgin of Chartres. Chartres is the palace of the Empress Mary, but "unfortunately she is gone, or comes here now so very rarely that we shall never see her. . . ." (144). Only her image remains, "with her three great prophets on either hand, as calm and confident in their great strength and in God's providence as they were when Saint Louis was born, but looking down from a deserted heaven, into an empty church, on a dead faith" (197).

Mont-Saint-Michel seems to represent the strength of man, Chartres the power of woman: Adams can find neither in his own century. Between the year 1200 and the present, "Unity turned itself into complexity, multiplicity, variety, and even contradiction" (381). The title of one of the chapters, "The Twelfth Century Glass," indicates not only the colored windows, but also the role of the twelfth century's achievement as a looking-glass for the twentieth. "Our age has lost much of its ear for poetry, as it has lost its eye for color and line, and its taste for war and worship, wine and women" (29). Art is beyond us now, says Adams, nor can we expect help from the "bankruptcy of reason" (326). Equally impotent is modern democratic society: "An economic civilization troubles itself about the universe much as a hive of honey-bees troubles about the ocean, only as a region to be avoided" (350). Like Lowell, Adams takes from the cathedral no consolation, only the sense of distant beauty and once-significant emotion: "You can read out of it whatever else pleases your youth and confidence; to me, this is all" (353). Yet Adams does not end his statement here, with the end of the book. Like Lowell, he was compelled to add a prayer, the "Prayer to the Virgin of Chartres," unpublished during his lifetime. In it he prays, like Lowell, for an understanding unclouded by reason: "Help me to know! not with my mocking art— / With you, who knew yourself unbound by laws. . . ."[26] The two prayers are codas in which the lost faith and Femininity are invoked. Adams's demonstrates the same blend of sincere appeal and self-irony as Lowell's, though it is stronger in language and more bitter, and contains a new element in the disturbing "Prayer to the Dynamo."

Although Adams's work is a grander effort than Lowell's, at once more immediate in its detailed descriptions and more rigorously philosophical, the two clearly belong to the same tradition. The next and probably greatest heir to that tradition was T. S. Eliot. We have seen how Lowell anticipates Eliot's themes in his poem; now we can see the possibility of a chain of influence between the two. Eliot reviewed *The Education of Henry Adams*,[27] and was impressed by it enough to make it the primary source of his poem "Gerontion."[28] The traits discussed at the beginning of this paper are clearly shared by all three writers: self-questioning, alienation, a sense of loss and longing, and an ultimate desire to cast away doubt and believe in the faith they saw in the past. Eliot made his pilgrimage to the past in "Little Gidding," where he went, like Lowell and Adams, "to kneel / Where prayer has been valid."[29]

The weaknesses in **"The Cathedral"** are easy to see; though the thought is strong, the expression of it is often limited by outdated rhetoric and conventional imagery. There is a tension between the twentieth-century matter and the nineteenth-century method from which Lowell was unwilling to depart. He believed in the conventions he followed: to him they were "everlasting boundary-stones that mark the limits of a noble reserve and self-restraint, and seem to say, 'Outside of us is Chaos—go there if you like—*we* knew better—it is a dreary realm where moan the ghosts of dead-born children, and where the ghost of mad old Lear is king.'"[30] Lowell's refusal to flirt with chaos and rage with Lear kept him from breaking into the modern mode, leaving his successors to make the leap. But now that the leap has been made, we can look back and try to bridge the gulf. **"The Cathedral"** is linked to both old and new. Our reading of Adams and Eliot has prepared us to find more meaning and unity in Lowell's poem than did his contemporaries. We are prepared to find artistic strength in ambiguity and hesitation, if they are justified. We can see **"The Cathedral"** as an important transitional work, in which the two-way pull of style and subject adds a certain paradoxical interest. Lowell casts light on the origins of Adams and Eliot, and they in turn illuminate his achievement. As Lowell noted, anticipating Eliot's "Tradition and the Individual Talent," "men have their intellectual ancestry, and likeness of some one of them is forever unexpectedly flashing out in the features of a descendent."[31] The fitful gleams in Lowell's work forecast the brilliance of Adams's and Eliot's. **"The Cathedral"** is a flawed but living work, and its author was, in his way, a prophet.

Notes

1. James Russell Lowell, "A Fable for Critics," *The American Poets: 1800-1900,* ed. Edwin H. Cady (Glenview, Illinois: Scott, Foresman and Company, 1966), p. 238.
2. George Santayana, *Persons and Places: The Background of My Life* (New York: Charles Scribner's Sons, 1944), p. 49.
3. T. S. Eliot, "The Love Song of J. Alfred Prufrock," *Collected Poems: 1909-1962* (New York: Harcourt, Brace & World, Inc., 1963), p. 5.
4. T. S. Eliot, "The Waste Land," *Collected Poems,* p. 53.
5. T. S. Eliot, "The Hollow Men," *Collected Poems,* p. 82.
6. "The Hollow Men," p. 79.
7. G. Thomas Tanselle, "The Craftsmanship of Lowell: Revisions in *The Cathedral,*" *Bulletin of The New York Public Library,* 70 (January, 1966), 50-63.
8. This and the following quotes are taken in sequence from "The Cathedral," *The American Poets: 1800-1900,* pp. 253-269.
9. Ralph Waldo Emerson, "Nature," *Selected Prose and Poetry,* 2nd Edition, ed. Reginald L. Cook (New York: Holt, Rinehart & Winston, 1969), p. 5.
10. "The Love Song of J. Alfred Prufrock," p. 3.
11. "The Waste Land," p. 66.
12. Edward Wagenknecht, *James Russell Lowell: Portrait of a Many-Sided Man* (New York: Oxford University Press, 1971), p. 60.
13. Lowell, *Letters of James Russell Lowell,* ed. Charles Eliot Norton (New York: Harper & Brothers Publishers, 1894), II, 35.
14. Robert LeClair, *"Three American Travellers in England: James Russell Lowell, Henry Adams, Henry James,"* Diss. University of Pennsylvania, 1945, p. 15.
15. Lowell, *Letters,* I, 204.
16. Robert Mane, *Henry Adams on the Road to Chartres* (Cambridge, Mass.: Harvard University Press, 1971), p. 37.
17. Henry Adams, *The Education of Henry Adams* (1918; rpt. Boston: Houghton Mifflin Company, 1961), p. 62.
18. *Ibid.*
19. *Ibid.*
20. Ernest Samuels, *The Young Henry Adams* (Cambridge, Mass.: Harvard University Press, 1948), p. 30.
21. *Ibid.,* p. 65.
22. Henry Adams, *Letters of Henry Adams: 1858-1891,* ed. Worthington Chauncey Ford (Boston: Houghton Mifflin Company, 1930), pp. 167-68.
23. *Ibid,* p. 229.
24. Henry Adams, *Henry Adams and His Friends: A Collection of His Unpublished Letters,* comp. Harold Dean Cater (Boston: Houghton Mifflin Co., 1947), p. 91.
25. Henry Adams, *Mont-Saint-Michel and Chartres* (Boston: Houghton Mifflin Company, 1913), p. 9. Textual notes to this edition follow.
26. Henry Adams, "Prayer to the Virgin of Chartres," *The American Poets: 1800-1900,* p. 494.
27. T. S. Eliot, "A Sceptical Patrician," *The Athenaeum,* 23 May 1919, 361-62.
28. F. O. Matthiessen, *The Achievement of T. S. Eliot* (New York: Oxford University Press, 1959), p. 73.
29. T. S. Eliot, "Little Gidding," from *Four Quartets,* in *Collected Poems,* p. 201.
30. Lowell, *Letters,* I, 242.
31. Herbert F. Smith, "Introduction" to *Literary Criticism of James Russell Lowell* (Lincoln, Nb.: University of Nebraska Press, 1969), p. xix.

C. David Heymann (essay date 1980)

SOURCE: "The Humanitarian," in *American Aristocracy: The Lives and Times of James Russell, Amy, and Robert Lowell,* Dodd, Mead & Company, 1980, 71-90.

[*In the following essay, Heymann details Lowell's life and writings of the 1840s, particularly his works of 1848:* Poems, A Fable for Critics, The Biglow Papers, *and* The Vision of Sir Launfal.]

James Russell Lowell's divergent path from "the clan's straight and well-paved highway" was . . . partially the result of his parents' influence. His father, although not an avid abolitionist, placed the emphasis of his spiritual teaching directly upon the mind-broadening straits of humanitarianism—or in James Russell Lowell's words, upon the need for "a wider and wiser humanity." In place of the Puritans' "vertical" love of man for God, "a stress on perfecting one's higher self," the pleasant, cautious minister directed his congregation toward the "horizontal" division of man's love for man. His influence in such worldly concerns can be traced to the moral philosophizing of his former teacher Dugald Stewart and to the Reverend's reading of the works of Benjamin Franklin, whose Deism as stipulated in writing proclaimed that "the most acceptable service of God was the doing good to man." The Reverend maintained for Franklin the same high degree of admiration that James Russell Lowell reserved for his father. Writing to C. F. Briggs in 1844, the poet said of the Reverend:

> He is Dr. Primrose in the comparative degree, the very simplest and charmingest of sexagenarians, and not without a great deal of the truest magnanimity.

The poet was named after his father's maternal grandfather, Judge James Russell, of Charlestown, but it was from his mother's side of the family that he derived much of his talent and charm. His mother's grandfather, Robert Traill, had traveled at a young age from the Orkney Islands to America, had married there and left a daughter, Mrs. Lowell's mother, when he returned to Great Britain with the outbreak of the Revolutionary War. "My grandmother,"[1] Lowell ventured, "was a loyalist to her death, and whenever Independence Day came round, instead of joining in the general rejoicing, she would dress in deep black, fast all day, and loudly lament 'our late unhappy differences with his most gracious Majesty.'" Lowell's mother inherited a touch of her own mother's feeling for "the old country." Full of Orkney Islands imagination and sympathies, she liked to trace her heritage (and in turn her son's) to persons no less portentous than Minna Troil and Sir Patrick Spens, legendary figures in the colorful history of Celtic balladry. Other Traills to descend from the same Orkneys bloodline included Bishop Trayle (author), Alexander Trail (poet), Archbishop Adamson (poet), Henry Duff Traill (author), Dr. Thomas Traill (author), Walter Trail Dennison (author), Thomas Traill (author), David Balfour (poet and essayist), and James Boswell, the celebrated biographer of Samuel Johnson. Family historian Ferris Greenslet notes[2] that Harriet Lowell not only possessed an abundance of the wild beauty of the dwellers of those "windy northern isles," but their irresistible tendency toward poetic occultism. She had revived this propensity by visiting the Orkney Islands in company with her husband early in their married life. Henceforth, until the onset of her mental decrepitude late in 1842, Harriet was "a faerie-seer." Some credited her with an acute sense of "second sight," others merely with the possession of a musical ear for sound lyric verse. From the lips of his mother, Lowell listened with delight to the singing of the old ballads. Her changeable, brooding, fanciful nature—as unrestrained as that of any Gothic heroine's—lived again in the poetic inclinations of her poet son and in his own arrogant, mawkish, humorous, self-contradictory ways.

If his turning to verse was partially the result of his Orkneys background, another important influence was that of the community of his birth. During his adolescence the fashion of Cambridge was predominantly literary. At Harvard, during Lowell's student days, Byron, Shelley, and Keats were much in vogue, with Tennyson fast joining the ranks and Carlyle, that most Teutonic Scot, not far behind. The New England literary tradition, inspired by the dominance of the German universities in the first half of the nineteenth century and filtered through the German Romantic notion of natural self-sufficiency, encountered boundless support. Literary men, among whom Lowell was recognized from the start, were considered Harvard's first citizens. That dowdily intellectual crowd—the Danas, Nortons, and Parkmans, to name a few—was widely read and dedicated in an ardent way to all the humanities. If they lacked anything as a group, it was a firmly developed political conscience, an abiding interest in government as an institution and as an instrument to effect necessary political change.

There were notable exceptions, as for instance the sometime Bostonian John Greenleaf Whittier, who struck the loudest political note of all with his raging pro-abolitionism: "Poetry that won't speak and ring is worse than none. Poetry is the match, the torch of our little field piece, and if it is not fiery, if there is no ignition in it, no explosion, we might as well put an icicle to our priming." In 1843, as a contributor to *The Pioneer,* he encouraged its editor to write the "liberty song" which "shall be to our cause what the song of Rouget de Lisle was to the French Republicans." Of Lowell's early poems, Whittier was partial toward "On Reading Wordsworth's Sonnets in Defence of Capital Punishment," a series of six sonnets directed against Wordworth's old-age philosophy espousing the virtues of capital punishment.

By September 1844 it was decided that Lowell and Maria White would be married on the day after Christmas and depart at once for Philadelphia, where he would accept the position of contributing editor to the *Pennsylvania Freeman,* an abolitionist newspaper. In the hectic weeks and months before their wedding, the author slaved to complete his latest project, ***Conversations on the Old Poets,*** a selection of essays published previously in the *Miscellany* and *The Pioneer.* Chaucer, George Chapman, John Ford, Edward Taylor, Donne, Marvell, and Keats were among the cast members of Lowell's pantheon. ***Conversations*** appeared in December 1844, both in Boston and London, with a dedication to Reverend Charles Lowell followed by a note stipulating that the volume contained "many opinions from which he will wholly, yet with the large charity of a Christian heart, dissent." A "literary" preface anticipated the reader's would-be reservations: "If some of the topics introduced seem foreign to the subject, I can only say that they are not so to my mind, and that an author's subject in writing criticism is not only to bring to light the beauties of the works he is considering, but also to express his own opinions upon those and other matters."

Those "other matters" are unfortunately accorded more than their rightful due. The essays in ***Conversations*** appear to be compiled rather than written, filled with a stream of personal views and impressions with little regard for the works of the authors themselves. The pieces are in fact veritable rewrites of entire sections of Lowell's personal correspondence and portions of his daybook, rambling endlessly, wandering without direction across the page. Moreover, they are laden, as Greenslet has said, with "defects of judgment," such as where we are told that "Ovid is the truest poet among the Latins" or that Alexander Pope was far and away the weakest poet of his generation (other authors are both praised and condemned with equal indiscretion). In mood and style there is too much of the sentimental pap and self-indulgent mawkishness that we find in great globs in Lowell's early verse. What can be said in favor of the book is that the poet's fervent love of literature is manifest on almost every page. The overflow of emotion in no way redeems the manuscript, but it does lend it the authority of literary conviction.

Lowell's arrangement with the *Pennsylvania Freeman* called for a monthly salary of ten dollars, plus an honorarium to help cover moving expenses. In addition, he received a small stipend from home and earned extra income from free-lance literary work. Briggs and Poe were currently editing a small magazine out of New York called *Broadway Journal,* and there Lowell and his bride, who also wrote, found a temporary home for their verse. Briggs took a rather dim view of Lowell's ***Conversations*** and penned an acerbic attack for the *Journal,* taking issue with his friend's "hot and excited" abolitionism, excoriating him for "a certain impudent egotism." What annoyed Lowell more than the review itself was the editor's refusal to publish an essay the poet had recently written decrying the annexation of Texas; in turning it down Briggs claimed that its tone was overly dramatic and severe. Lowell retained sincere affection for Briggs but for a time suspended his contributions to the magazine.[3]

In Philadelphia the couple boarded with the Parkers, abolitionists and Quakers who were active in local political circles. For eight dollars a week they were fed three meals a day and given a small room, third-floor rear,[4] with white muslin curtains trimmed with evergreen. It was quiet and they spent their free time at home, reading and writing, "happy as two mortals can be." Lowell visited Philadelphia's Whister Club, a weekly gathering of scientific and literary minds, but found the town bereft of educational and cultural attractions. Maria was disappointed with Pennsylvania's abolitionists, agreeing with Lydia Maria Child that they were all "fussy, ignorant, old women," too prim and proper to benefit the movement.

Lowell, upon joining its staff, condemned the *Freeman* for its timid editorial policy, its refusal to admonish New England's religious sects, including those that had demonstrated little sympathy for the abolitionists and that supported a "non-extension" policy. The non-extenders believed that slavery must not be allowed to spread beyond the boundaries it presently occupied but that it should not be interfered with in those regions where it already existed. The Lowells, however, were convinced that slavery "posed too great a danger for equivocation"[5] and inactivity; it threatened "the very basis on which the nation rested, the very heart of its professed principles, democratic and Christian," and inasmuch "could not be dealt with 'gradually' or in a 'compromising' spirit." William Garrison had put the matter into terms which even the man on the street could understand: "As leave tell a man to 'go slow' on slavery, as tell him *slowly* to put out a fire destroying the house in which his wife and children lay asleep." Lowell, picking up on Garrison's words, transposed them into his own subdued idiom: "There is something better than Expediency and that is Wisdom, something stronger than Compromise and that is Justice."

The termination of his relationship with the *Freeman,* after five months of incompatibility, left little reason for the Lowells to remain in Philadelphia. By the end of May 1845, they had returned to Cambridge, having stopped briefly in New York to call on Poe; the difference in their background and temperament, coupled with Poe's alcoholism, made communication between the two poets difficult, although they had previously enjoyed a long and warm correspondence.

In Cambridge the Lowells were presently living on the top floor of Elmwood. The deteriorating mental condition of Harriet Lowell forced them to transfer her to McLean's, a private hospital located in Belmont, a suburb of Boston. Although all reason spoke against it, the Reverend refused to give up hope for his wife's eventual recovery. In a letter to James, written while his son was living in Philadelphia, he expressed the futile expectation that "the aberration of mind has its origins in the stomach, and is not an affliction of the brain. I desire to trust in God."

Elmwood became a less grim place when, in December 1845, Maria gave birth to her first child, a daughter named Blanche. That summer the family rented a small farmhouse at Stockbridge, in western Massachusetts. When Longfellow came to visit, he found his Cambridge neighbor "hale as a young farmer" and just as occupied. Isolated from the rest of humanity, the Lowells had turned to subsistence farming; surrounded by dogs and cats, goats (they made their own cheese), chickens (which they were breeding), ducks (purely ornamental), and an occasional hog, they were surviving nicely. They had learned to cope with raccoons, porcupines, and deer in the vegetable garden and were coming to terms with the short and unpredictable growing season in this part of the country. Although husband and wife appeared to be in the best of spirits, something was apparently disturbing the poet; a letter to Briggs that he wrote at about this time belied a troubled interior:

> My sorrows are not literary ones, but those of daily life. I pass through the world and meet with scarcely a response to the affectionateness of my nature. I believe Maria only knows how loving I am truly. Brought up in a very reserved and conventional family, I cannot in society appear what I really am. I go out sometimes with my heart so full of yearning toward my fellows that the indifferent look with which even strangers pass me brings tears into my eyes. And then to be looked upon by those who *do* know me (externally) as "Lowell the poet"—it makes me sick. Why not Lowell the man,—the boy rather,—as Jemmy Lowell, as I was at school?

One source of the poet's depression stemmed from his concern with the apparent lack of interest among his contemporaries in the plight of the abolitionists. In order to gain support for the movement he wrote a series of articles on **"Anti-Slavery in the United States"** for the London *Daily News.* The articles were published anonymously,[6] the author's impression being that they would be better received if not known to be the work of a committed abolitionist. Fully devoted to the cause of humanitarianism, the Brahmin engaged in a furious letter-writing campaign with numerous men of letters, including Oliver Wendell

Holmes, whom he tried to swing over to the side of "abolition, temperance, the claims of the poor, pacifism, and reform and reformers in general." But the future Autocrat would have none of it; he countered Lowell's gibe with a thrust of his own: "I must say, with regard to art and a management of my own poems, I think I shall in the main follow my own judgment and taste rather than mould myself upon those of others. . . . Let me try to impress and please my fellow men after my own fashion at present. When I come to your way of thinking (this may happen) I hope I shall be found worthy of a less qualified approbation than you have felt constrained to give me at this time."[7]

Lowell fought on, accepting a position as a regular contributor to the *National Anti-Slavery Standard,* the Garrisonian-controlled, militant newspaper, whose base was New York. Its editors were Maria Weston Chapman, Edmund Quincy, and Sydney Gay, who were all from the wealthiest, best-bred families of New England. Edmund Quincy was the son of Josiah Quincy, one-time mayor of Boston and president of Harvard. Gay's distinguished bloodline could be traced to John Cotton, Increase Mather, and Governor Bradford of Plymouth, while the Chapmans were of equally highborn origin. Despite the wealth and sobriety of its editorial staff, the *Standard* espoused most of Garrison's hard-fought values; it championed women's rights and the plight of the Northern factory worker, supported temperance and abolition. These four issues became the main concerns of the Garrison-backed Liberation Party.

Lowell, in full agreement with the *Standard*'s basic views concerning abolition, did not on the other hand concur with all of the Liberation Party's tactics, finding some of them too rigid for his own peace-loving blood. Although he admired Garrison and identified with him in an intellectual sense, he disdained the majority of the activist's followers. "They treat ideas," he once wrote, "as ignorant persons do cherries. They think them unwholesome unless they are swallowed, stones and all."

The *Standard* paid Lowell an annual salary of five hundred dollars for a weekly contribution of prose or verse. A number of the poems he contributed, starting with the issue of September 1847, were at once widely circulated and attained a high degree of popularity. Here first appeared the compassionate poem for Garrison—comparing him as an effective reformer with Luther—and a poem for John G. Palfrey (a stalwart of the movement), the stirring stanzas to Freedom, and other lines of poetic repute. Besides the poems that spoke out against slavery, there were those that revealed Lowell's feelings for the great outdoors, the green and natural world as sung by Wordsworth and Coleridge, Keats and Shelley. Best known of this group were **"Eurydice," "The Parting of the Ways,"** and **"Beaver Brook."**

It was in the *Standard* that Lowell published his poem **"The First Snow-Fall,"** a mellow outflow of the grief that overcame the author with the sudden and tragic death of his daughter Blanche in March 1847, and a record of the "tremulous happiness renewed" in the birth of a second daughter, Mabel, in the fall of the same year. "May you never have the key which shall unlock the whole meaning of the poem to you," Lowell wrote to the editors of the antislavery periodical. Writing the poem helped assuage the poet's sorrow:

> I stood and watched by the window
>   The noiseless work of the sky,
> And the sudden flurries of snow-birds,
>   Like brown leaves whirling by.
>
> I thought of a mound in sweet Auburn
>   Where a little headstone stood;
> How the flakes were folding it gently,
>   As did robins the babes in the wood.
>
> Up spoke our own little Mabel,
>   Saying, "Father, who makes it snow?"
> And I told of the good All-father
>   Who cares for us here below.

These fragments point to the poem's final stanza, a quatrain dense with emotion:

> Then, with eyes that saw not, I kissed her,
>   And she, kissing back, could not know
> That *my* kiss was given to her sister,
>   Folded close under deepening snow.

"She Came and Went" and **"The Changeling,"** both written at this time, likewise reflect the sad circumstance of the tiny shoe that for years hung over a picture of Blanche in Lowell's study. As a group the three poems depict the gross and frightening depressions that continued to plague him his entire life. Often these bouts of wallowing and melancholy came upon him without warning and for no apparent reason. They were accompanied by mental torpor, paranoia, unexplainable fears that he was going mad, pangs of guilt. The tumultuous conflicts, guilts, and fears that possessed him seemed to be the result of the incongruities between his personal longings and the actualities of his existence—the eternal conflict in his soul between infantile intensity of passion and profound self-control, between Brahmin conservative roots and romantic impulse. But there was no clinical explanation, only the florid symptoms, the tortured visual signs, the anguished shorthand—talking with his fingers, popping and tapping them, while his nerves constricted and his brain wandered. There was an animal inside his skin, eating away at his mind and marrow. The bouts of depression drove him into seclusion. For weeks he remained bedridden, refusing to see anyone, refusing to eat, unable to work, trapped within the confines of his own skull.

Frequently these episodes of melancholia gave way to their manic counterpart—great gushes of mental activity and physical exertion, as though the melancholy were prerequisite to the flow of energy. After weeks of inactivity he could churn out as many as twelve hundred words of polished prose an hour, or fifty printed pages a day, the equivalent of two medium-length essays, or one-fifth of a finished book. Poems poured out of him at the rate of three or four daily, needing little or no revision. Or else he might take long walks or run or shadowbox, dance, sing, play cards, take sleigh rides, engage in a round of plain buffoonery. He would extemporize long-drawn-out accounts of make-believe figures such as "Mitchell Bonyrooty Angylo," or would compose and execute a full-length opera "entirely unassisted and, à la Beethoven, on a piano without any strings." He could barely contain himself. Words, ideas, and thoughts churned out of him. He became a geyser, spouting theories on literature, quoting endless sections of books that he knew verbatim, imitating brogues and foreign accents, reciting poems, making puns, cracking jokes, insulting friends. His extraordinary mannerisms, his tics and convulsions at these explosive moments were often frightening to behold. On one occasion he hoisted himself up a lamppost, where for hours he perched and crowed like a rooster. Acquaintances recalled Lowell unconcernedly removing and proceeding to eat with knife and fork a bouquet of flowers from the centerpiece at a literary supper in one of Boston's great houses. At an important meeting of poets he astounded everyone by gathering up his coattails and galloping around the room to illustrate the movements of a horse. He was known to accost strangers on the street and swing them about as though they were his closest friends, whom he had not seen in years. Nor was the stone wall built that he could resist mounting and conquering, balancing himself along its edge with the finesse of a tightrope artist. People who knew him took Lowell at these instances for a rowdy show-off or a violent madman, rather than the intellectual hero and cultural ideologue he prided himself on being. Had he been any less accomplished a poet he would surely have been handcuffed and led off, never to be heard from or seen again.

The February 1848 Treaty of Guadalupe Hidalgo marked the end of the bloody, one-sided war between Mexico and the United States. Ratified in October, the treaty enabled the United States to seize Texas and the territory that later became New Mexico, California, Utah, Nevada, Arizona, and parts of Colorado and Wyoming. The Mexican War, as future historians would note, was the major turning point in the country's exploratory trek westward. It was also a watershed event in Lowell's personal campaign for literary recognition; 1848 was his annus mirabilis in terms of creative productivity. During his thirtieth year Lowell produced four major volumes: a new collection of ***Poems; A Fable for Critics***; the first series of ***The Biglow Papers***; and ***The Vision of Sir Launfal.***

In a single year the poet had emerged, overcoming the depressions that were so substantial a part of his nature and that threatened always to lay him low. Included in his latest book of ***Poems*** were many of the selections originally contributed to the *Standard* and other radical organs, among them many purely artistic creations and some that read substantially like political tracts, prophetic diatribes that might better have been composed as prose. **"The Present Crisis,"** dealing with the controversial annexation of Texas ("Careless seems the great avenger; history's pages but record / One death grapple in the darkness 'twixt old systems and the Word"), and **"An Indian-Summer Reverie,"** commemorating the same village smithy celebrated by Longfellow in his poem by that title, are prime examples of the poet striving valiantly to conjoin the sonorous and the inspirational in his verse. The first is moralistic in design, the poetician here at odds with the preacher in him, the poem rising out of the dialectic with a surge of power and persuasion. The second poem is a spiritual hymn to nature, subject to the same schismatic shortcoming as the first, but full of tenderness and resounding with passion and vulnerability:

> The ash her purple drops forgivingly
> And sadly, breaking out the general hush;
> The maple-swamps glow like a sunset sea,
> Each leaf a ripple with its separate flush;
> All round the wood's edge creeps the skirting blaze
> Of bushes low, as when, on cloudy days,
> Ere the rain fall, the cautious farmer burns his brush.

With a few quick strokes the poet draws us beneath the surface of the poem, fusing objective description with atmosphere and feeling as though tentatively reaching out for more than the lines might otherwise yield. Among other poems that come close to matching these are **"Freedom," "On the Capture of Fugitive Slaves Near Washington," "To the Dandelion," "The Pioneer,"** and **"Beaver Brook."**

A Fable for Critics, subtitled "A Glance at a Few of Our Literary Progenies," appeared anonymously as a pamphlet at the beginning of the year. In a prefatory note attached by Lowell to a subsequent edition of the poem, following his identification as its author, he explained the ***Fable***'s origin: "This *jeu d'esprit* was extemporized, I may fairly say, so rapidly was it written, purely for my own amusement and with no thought of publication. I sent daily installments of it to a friend in New York, the late Charles F. Briggs. He urged me to let it be printed, and I at last consented to its anonymous publication. The secret was kept till after several persons had laid claim to its authorship."

The poem created a minor sensation among those whom Lowell singled out for attack; yet the portraits he drew of his contemporaries were sufficiently generalized that even the nonliterary could partake of the fun. In his 1966 biography of the aristocrat, Martin Duberman reflects that Lowell was hardest on those whom posterity also treated unkindly: N. P. Willis, Richard Henry Dana, Sr., John Neal, Cornelius Mathews, and Fitz-Greene Halleck. In their particular poetic form, Lowell's views represented the best spontaneous literary criticism that the nineteenth century would endeavor to produce. The rambling poem featured none of the black-hearted satire we find in great abundance in Melville's short fiction or in parts of Swift or Ben Jonson; instead, the poem is an iconography of caricatures, containing the light ticklish humor but not the political immediacy of Byron's "The Mask of Irony"; equally apt might be a comparison between the Lowell poem and

Byron's "English Bards and Scotch Reviewers." The Brahmin's portrait of Halleck serves as adequate illustration of the technique; dismissed as a poet, he is subsequently taken up by Lowell as a personality:

> Halleck's better, I doubt not, than all he has written;
> In his verse a clear glimpse you will frequently find,
> If not of a great, of a fortunate mind,
> Which contrives to be true to its natural loves
> In a world of back-offices, ledgers, and stoves.

This judgment is made more brutal (but at the same time more palatable) by Lowell's use of restraint, his desire to hold something in reserve. What is not said, or what is said in jest, is ultimately as damaging as anything the poet may offer by way of outright criticism. His qualification of Halleck's literary faults, his use of the phrase "if not of a great, of a fortunate mind," makes Lowell look a bit like the smiling viper, the friendly, accommodating assassin.

Even those writers the poet outwardly admired—Emerson, Longfellow, Bryant, James Fenimore Cooper—were in for a bluff and earthy drenching. Emerson is a case in point. At first, lauding the Transcendentalist, Lowell compares him favorably with Carlyle and then Plato:

> There are persons, mole-blind to the Soul's make
> and style,
> Who insist on a likeness 'twixt him and Carlyle;
> To compare him with Plato would be vastly fairer,
> Carlyle's the more burly, but E. is the rarer;
> He sees fewer objects, but clearlier, truelier,
> If C.'s as original, E.'s more peculiar;
> That he's more of a man you might say of the one,
> Of the other he's more of an Emerson.

But just as quickly, reversing his field, he attempts to portray Emerson as a seething and ornery radical:

> All admire, and yet scarcely six converts he's got
> To I don't (nor they either) exactly know what;
> For though he builds glorious temples, 'tis odd
> He leaves never a doorway to get in a god.

Similarly downgrading is the humorist's comment that Cooper, having invented a new and creative character, had then proceeded to plagiarize himself, endlessly repeating it:

> His Indians, with proper respect be it said,
> Are just Natty Bumppo, daubed over with red,
> And his very Long Toms are the same useful Nat,
> Rigged up in duck pants and a sou'wester hat . . .

By far the author's most vicious attack was reserved for Margaret Fuller, whose negative evaluation of his own early work he had never forgiven. Calling her Miranda in the ***Fable,*** he unleashes the following invective:

> But there comes Miranda, Zeus! where shall I
> flee to?
> She has such a penchant for bothering me too . . .
> One would think, though, a sharp-sighted noter
> she'd be
> Of all that's worth mentioning over the sea,
> For a woman must surely see well, if she try,
> The whole of whose being's a capital I:
> She will take an old notion, and make it her own,
> By saying it o'er in her Sibylline tone,
> Or persuade you 't is something tremendously deep,
> By repeating it so as to put you to sleep;
> And she well may defy any mortal to see through it,
> When once she has mixed up her infinite *me*
> through it.
> There is one thing she owns in her own single right,
> It is native and genuine—namely, her spite . . .

The ***Fable*** elicited a full tableau of responses.[8] John Ruskin labeled the poem "in animal spirit and power . . . almost beyond anything I know." Oliver Wendell Holmes found it "capital—crammed full and rammed down hard—with powder (lots of it)—shot—slugs—very little wadding, and that is guncotton—all crowded into a rusty-looking sort of blunderbuss barrel, as it were—capped with a percussion preface—and cocked with a title page as apropos as a wink to a joke." William Wetmore Story, a member of The Band and a close friend of Lowell's, enjoyed the poem but rejected its bitter characterization of Miss Fuller. Edgar Allan Poe, whom the poet summed up in the ***Fable*** as "three fifths . . . genius and two fifths sheer fudge," resented the whole, blaming Lowell's "distortions" on his misguided and roaring abolitionism. It is probable that Poe was still smarting from his personal meeting with Lowell some years before.

These varied responses gained the ***Fable***'s author the kind of notoriety that helps sell books. Three thousand copies of the first edition were sold immediately. Lowell's sudden "drawing room" popularity was felt by the general reading public as well as by the literary elect. On another level the poem illustrates Lowell's early contempt for tradition ("Forget Europe wholly") and his gradual turn from sentimentalism to the critical temper that was to be developed and broadened in his future work. A final and fitting touch to the poem was provided by the scrivener's probing self-examination:

> There is Lowell, who's striving Parnassus to climb
> With a whole bale of *isms* tied together with rhyme,
> He might get on alone, spite of brambles and boulders,
> But he can't with that bundle he has on his shoulders,
> The top of the hill he will ne'er come nigh reaching
> Till he learns the distinction 'twixt singing and
> preaching;
> His lyre has some chords that would ring pretty well,
> But he'd rather by half make a drum of the shell,
> And rattle away till he's old as Methusalem,
> At the head of a march to the last new Jerusalem.

The Vision of Sir Launfal, published on the heels of the ***Fable,*** proved equally popular. This was a story-poem, a mini-epic, written in the half-mystic, half-mocking language that characterized the medieval Arthurian lai. Lowell's modest but charming version of this talismanic legend recounts the tale of Sir Launfal's search for the Holy Grail. As the gallant knight-errant begins his search he encounters a leper outside his castle gate. Determined to complete his quest, the knight ignores the stranger and passes on into the night. Time elapses; the knight ages. By the time of his return, unsuccessful in his search, he finds that another lord has inherited his earldom. Amidst memories of summer days breaks the voice of the long-forgotten leper: "For Christ's sweet sake, I beg an alm . . ." No longer scornful of the poor stranger, the knight gladly feeds him bread and water. A transformation ensues, the leper metamorphosing into a holy man; the man speaks:

> Lo, it is I, be not afraid!
> In many climes, without avail,
> Thou hast spent thy life for the Holy Grail;
> Behold, it is here,—this cup which thou
> Didst fill at the streamlet for me but now;
> This crust is my body broken for thee,
> This water his blood that died on the tree;
> The Holy Supper is kept, indeed . . .

Appearing at the same time as ***Sir Launfal*** was the collected first edition of ***The Biglow Papers,*** nine poems of varying length, the first five published individually in the Boston *Courier,* the remaining four in the *National Anti-Slavery Standard.* It was in these constructions that Lowell for the first time appeared in his full stature as a humorist of the highest order; satirist, however, may be the preferable term here, for political affairs and social mores underscore the entire sequence.

A dozen years after the volume's appearance, on the eve of the Civil War, Lowell provided the editor of the British edition, Thomas Hughes, with a brief declaration of his political position at the time the ***Papers*** were originally issued:

> I believed our war with Mexico (though we had as just ground for it as a strong nation ever has against a weak one) to be essentially a war of false pretenses, and that it would result in widening the boundaries and so prolong the life of slavery. . . . I believed and still believe that slavery is the Achilles heel of our polity: that it is a temporary and false supremacy of the white races, sure to destroy that supremacy at last, because an enslaved people always prove themselves of more enduring fibre than their enslavers.

Lowell portrays three principal characters in ***The Biglow Papers,*** each representative of a different aspect of American life. The first is Parson Wilbur, resident of the invented village of Jaalam, Massachusetts, whose personality is an amalgam of the qualities of at least three people—the pedantry of Reverend Barzillai Frost, Lowell's Concord tutor during his rustication from Harvard; the sweetness and gentleness of Reverend Charles Lowell; and the moral earnestness of the author himself. Writing a good deal of ***The Biglow Papers*** in dialect, Lowell felt that he "needed on occasion to rise above the level of mere *patois,*" and for this purpose conceived the Reverend Mr. Wilbur, who expressed the more scholarly and erudite element of the New England personality. Second, we have young Hosea Biglow, the unsophisticated, unlettered, independent rustic, who nevertheless represented the "homely common sense" of his region. Scornful of slavery, politicians, and the war with Mexico, it is Hosea who pens the majority of these Papers. Third, we encounter Birdofredum Sawin: "I invented Mr. Sawin for the clown of my little puppet show. I meant to embody in him that half-conscious *un*-morality which I had noticed as the recoil in gross natures from a puritanism that still strove to keep in its creed the intense savor which had long gone out of its faith and life." Sawin as rascal and Southern sympathizer represented the darkly humorous Falstaffian villain, a striking counterpart to the charm and beneficence of the remaining members of the cast. Moreover, Sawin epitomized his country's blind faith in Manifest Destiny, which according to Lowell's standards was unequivocably its archenemy.

The main feature of ***The Biglow Papers*** was Lowell's use of a crackerbarrel drawl or Yankee dialect, a mode of communication whose propriety he soon began to question. Shortly after the appearance of the poem in book format the poet notified a friend: "As for Hosea, I am sorry that I began by making him such a detestable speller. There is no fun in bad spelling of itself, but only where the misspelling suggests something else which is droll per se. You see I am getting him out of it gradually." This statement notwithstanding, the later Papers of the series showed no

THE

BIGLOW PAPERS.

BY

JAMES RUSSELL LOWELL.

Newly Edited,

WITH A PREFACE

BY THE

AUTHOR OF "*TOM BROWN'S SCHOOL-DAYS.*"

REPRINTED,
WITH THE AUTHOR'S SANCTION,
FROM THE FOURTH AMERICAN EDITION.

LONDON:
TRÜBNER & CO. 60, PATERNOSTER ROW
1859.

marked departure from the general scheme of Yankee spelling and phonetics that graced the earlier ones. The overwhelming popularity attained by the successive numbers of the sequence may have convinced Lowell that he had discovered a gimmick worth developing. While he made a number of minor changes, shaping the body of the work and fleshing out several secondary characters, the basic configuration of the series remained intact.

In choosing to write in dialect, Lowell was convinced that the outstanding vice of American literature was a studied want of simplicity. His contemporaries were in danger of coming to look upon English as an archaic language that one sought in the grammar and dictionary rather than in the heart. The writings of the day were obscure, formal, moralistic, unnatural. Lowell noted in his introduction to the second series of ***The Biglow Papers*** that "few American writers or speakers wield their native language with the directness, precision, and force that are common as the day in the mother country."

The poet's ambition to get closer to common man and to the experience of common men by way of their diction and language was possibly an unconscious reaction on his part to the overeducated inhabitants and stifling atmosphere of Cambridge. It was quite conceivably a reaction against the Lowell clan itself, which not only disapproved of his role as a poet but also seemed shocked by and opposed to his outspoken political musings. The two in tandem, the poetry coupled with an unorthodox political philosophy, sufficed to single him out as a patrician renegade, an aristocratic exile. ***The Biglow Papers*** did little to ingratiate him with the wealthier and more conventional members of his family.

The first number of ***The Biglow Papers***—in the form of a letter from Ezekiel Biglow to a newspaper editor, enclosing a poem by his son and a note announcing the circumstances under which it was written—sets the sequence's thematic tone. Hosea Biglow, according to his father's letter, had gone down to Boston the week before and there saw a recruiting "Sarjunt" walking about with twenty rooster tails stuck in his cap and enough brass displayed on his shoulders to make a six-pound cannonball. One look at Hosea, and the "Sarjunt" was convinced that this backwoods lad from Jaalam had the makings of a model recruit to help fight the war against Mexico.

That night, highly agitated, Hosea composed a poem about the officer and the army he represented. The poem repeatedly makes the point that warfare is tantamount to cold-blooded murder: "Ef you take a sword an' dror it, / An go stick a feller thru, / Guv'ment aint to answer to it, / God'll send the bill to you."

Other particulars quickly come into play, from militant editors, whom Lowell glibly derides, to the Bay State itself, which had sunk to its knees before the unhallowed altar of servitude. Let Massachusetts speak out, Hosea's poem reads—let the bells in every steeple toll, let them sing to the South a song of rebellion: "I will not help the Devil make man the curse of man: / I am a tyrant hater and the friend of God and Peace. / I prefer separation to a forced and unholy union of them that / God has no ways jined."

The second Paper consists of a note from Mexico, from Private Sawin, who had enlisted with the Massachusetts Regiment; unlike Hosea, he had been taken in by the sergeant's glitter and fanfare, and as we gradually learn, lived to regret it. We find out why in letter eight, the most humorous epistle of the lot, which recounts in verse form Birdofredum Sawin's wanderings in war. Fate has dealt the Army Private a harsh blow. "I spose you wonder ware I be," his letter to the Parson begins: "I can't tell fer the soul o' me, / Exactly ware I be myself,—meanin' by / thet the holl o' me." A serious wound incurred in battle has resulted in the amputation of Sawin's leg. The soldier's sole consolation is that whisky can't get into the wooden stump.

In addition to the leg, Sawin has lost an eye in battle, to say nothing of his left arm and four fingers of his right hand; a half dozen of his ribs were also fractured. Speaking of ribs reminds him of the one he left behind—his wife. Sawin instructs Wilbur to inform her that one day he will be eligible for a military pension, yet at the same time admits that his previous expectations of wealth never materialized; when he enlisted he expected Mexico to be a Garden of Eden, overflowing with milk and honey, rum and gold. "But sech ideas," he writes, "soon melted down an' didn't / leave a grease spot; / I vow my holl sheer o' the spiles would not / come nigh a V spot."

In the same vein Sawin complains that his sole military souvenir, besides battle scars, is a case of shaking fever. He insists that though the enlisted men fought and won the strategic battles, it was the officers who received all the glory: "We get the licks—we're just the grist that's put into War's hoppers; / Leftenants is the lowest grade that helps pick up the coppers." He drones on about meager rations for the troops, accusing the officers of stuffing themselves like pigs on a fare fit for kings. In the middle of his rant he conceives of a plan: When he returns to the States he will run for political office and use his war record and wooden leg as a platform; whenever his opinion on an issue is solicited, he will simply point to his head and yell, "One Eye Put Out!"

Sawin closes his letter by examining his account with the "Bank of Glory," debiting and crediting such items as the loss of a leg against three cheers in Boston's Faneuil Hall, an evening of band music, a uniform, and a homecooked meal. Attached to the document is a note from its recipient, Parson Wilbur, indicting America's system of "indirect taxation" that was used to finance the war: "If we could know that a part of the money we expend for tea and coffee goes to buy powder and balls, and that it is Mexican blood which makes the clothes on our backs more costly, it would set some of us thinking."[9]

The third Paper, **"What Mr. Robinson Thinks,"** depicts a humorous debate between a Whig and a moderate over a forthcoming gubernatorial election, while Letter Five, **"The Debate in the Sennit,"** delivers a sneering, unsparing attack on John C. Calhoun, the Southern congressman who argued unconvincingly for state sovereignty. With unfaltering ribaldry Lowell, as Wilbur, obliterates the villain, asserting that Calhoun represents the worst sort of bigot, the man who believes in the superiority of race.

The Biglow Papers presented the poet with a vehicle for his iconoclastic views and his vision of New England's dual state—its "common sense and canniness, its poetry and pedantry, its idealism, all minted into something as racy and of the soil as a pine-tree shilling."[10] Although the ***Papers*** effectively transmitted both sides of the New England story, the manuscript was too freighted with Lowell's shrill antiwar rhetoric to serve as an objective account of the events in question. Lowell's "hard sell" campaign was well suited for the political dais but less satisfying as a mode of legitimate literary communication. Lowell had been partially blinded by his eagerness to see the issue of slavery, the annexation of Texas, and the Mexican War in realistic terms. He was convinced that the tragedy of the first two and the catastrophe of the third were intertwined, and he was determined to single out those factions he held responsible for all three.

The poet's use (some claimed "abuse") of dialect became a contentious issue. Proud of his intimacy with the finer shades of the Yankee vernacular—"I reckon myself a good taster of dialects"—Lowell carried to the *n*th degree of phonetic exactness his reproductions of the peculiarities of New England speech. Not unexpectedly, a major disagreement arose over Lowell's employment of language, with half the world's critics castigating him for catering to popular tastes by creating not a poem but a patchwork document, a quilt of notes and asides, an unwieldy mass of homely satire, moral aphorisms, and Yankee dialect, replete with an index, a glossary, and other secondhand devices. The main objection of the critics was that the verse, for all its spontaneity, was weighted down by the excessive machinery of the accompanying prose. The poet was attacked, too, on the grounds that the New England dialect, while satisfactory for a character like Hosea Biglow, was far too limited and confining to allow the author to give adequate expression to his deeper and more serious responses to life. The joking colloquialisms, it was argued, served the poet's wit but not the flow or fabric of his ideas. The poem tried to be too many things to too many people; it was narrative, chronicle, journal, biography, history, obituary, fable, parable, and myth; it was the public memory, the voice of the New England mind, the conscience of the urbanite, all wrapped into one.

Whatever Lowell may or may not have accomplished with this series, he did help liberate the language, expose it to a broader audience, open it to a new mode of expression, while serving the important radical "causes" of his day. The Transcendental radicalism espoused by such poems as ***Prometheus*** and **"A Glance behind the Curtain"** (1843), **"Columbus"** and **"The Present Crisis"** (1844), **"On the Capture of Fugitive Slaves near Washington"** (1845), and **"The Pioneer"** (1847), found its purest and most effective outlet in ***The Biglow Papers.*** With its composition Lowell established himself as a working model for future satirists and dialecticians, not only Mark Twain but men such as William Dean Howells, H. L. Mencken, and Ring Lardner. Although the ***Papers*** created certain negative responses, the book as a whole made a strong impression, and the political philosophy secreted in its lines became a part of household literature. Sections of the work, more than a hundred years after their composition, still seem compacted of the stuff of lasting verse.

Notes

1. Scudder, *James Russell Lowell,* p. 11.
2. Greenslet, *James Russell Lowell,* p. 9.
3. *Ibid.,* 64-67.
4. Duberman, *James Russell Lowell,* p. 69.
5. *Ibid.,* 74.
6. *Ibid.,* 410, *n.* 26.
7. See Charles Eliot Norton, ed., *Letters of James Russell Lowell,* 2 vols. (New York, 1894).
8. Duberman, *James Russell Lowell,* pp. 100-101.
9. Beatty, *James Russell Lowell,* pp. 85-86.
10. Greenslet, *The Lowells and Their Seven Worlds,* p. 255.

Thomas Wortham (essay date 1984)

SOURCE: "James Russell Lowell," in *The Transcendentalists: A Review of Research and Criticism,* edited by Joel Myerson, The Modern Language Association of America, 1984, pp. 336-42.

[*In the following essay, Wortham considers Lowell's writings concerning the New England Transcendentalists.*]

Time and place made James Russell Lowell in many respects one with the Transcendentalists: intellectual temperament—he called it a "Toryism of the nerves"—kept him apart, but the personal associations still weighed heavily. Lowell's respect and admiration for Ralph Waldo Emerson in particular increased over the years until his praise in **"Emerson the Lecturer"** took on messianic dimensions: "Emerson awakened us," Lowell wrote in 1868; he "saved us from the body of this death." Several years later, out of a sense of irreparable debt, Lowell dedicated to Emerson his most distinguished and enduring collection of literary essays, ***Among My Books: Second Series*** (1876). None of the other men and women associated with the Transcendentalist movement fared nearly so well in Lowell's estimation, but he knew them all, both professionally and sometimes even as friends. Personal affection could, in Lowell's judgment, redeem the intellectual excesses of his Harvard friend and original Transcendentalist, Charles Stearns Wheeler, just as later it would in his friendly relations with George William Curtis and John Sullivan Dwight, but toward the likes of Thomas Wentworth Higginson, Moncure D. Conway, F. B. Sanborn, and Elizabeth Palmer Peabody, Lowell's cordiality was never untainted by an ill-disguised sense of amused superiority. With Henry David Thoreau, Margaret Fuller, and Ellery Channing, Lowell's lack of sympathy led him to misrepresent their work, ignore their lasting importance, and attack their character and motives. In short, Lowell's response to the Transcendentalists was as mixed and contradictory as were his attitudes towards most of the great issues and concerns of his times. Like other modern conservatives, he was forced to argue largely in terms of the enemy's formulations, and his ultimate defeat—as well as his intellectual stance—was not unlike that of the New Humanists, Irving Babbitt and Paul Elmer More, a generation after.

Lowell disliked the term "transcendental" when used to describe the philosophical climate in New England during the late 1830s and the 1840s, characterizing it as a "maid of all work for those who could not think." The general index to the ten-volume standard "Riverside Edition" of Lowell's ***Writings*** (1890) shows how rarely he addressed the subject of "Transcendentalism" in his published works. Only two of his essays deal with the movement in detail, and both reflect the response of a mature Lowell no longer impressed, as he once had been, by the vitality of philosophical idealism and romantic mysticism. **"Emerson the Lecturer"** first appeared as **"Mr. Emerson's New Course of Lectures"** in the *Nation* (1868); enlarged by the addition of the greater part of Lowell's review of Emerson's *The Conduct of Life* (1861), it was reprinted in his collection of essays, ***My Study Windows,*** in 1871. **"Thoreau,"** also collected in ***My Study Windows,*** was written as a review of Thoreau's *Letters to Various Persons* (1865), but it is, in fact, Lowell's fullest discussion of the Transcendentalist movement. His earlier review of Thoreau's *A Week on the Concord and Merrimack Rivers* (1849) and his sympathetic essay on Sylvester Judd's poem, *Philo: An Evangeliad* (1850), Lowell's only other prose writings on the Transcendentalists, were never reprinted by him, but they have been edited by Graham H. Duncan in "James Russell Lowell's Reviews of American Belles-Lettres."

Although Transcendentalist principles inspired many of the poems Lowell wrote during the decade following his graduation from Harvard in 1838, he is better remembered for his satiric attacks on the movement in his ***Class Poem*** (1838) and ***A Fable for Critics*** (1848). A more balanced but still unsympathetic poem on Margaret Fuller and Amos Bronson Alcott, **"Studies for Two Heads,"** was frequently reprinted by Lowell after its first appearance in ***Poems: Second Series*** in 1848. Except in his warm tribute to **"Agassiz"** (1874), Lowell left no poetic sketch of Emerson other than in his satiric verses. In an age that tended to memorialize itself in rhyme, this was a curious omission. Emerson, on his part, read some lines "To Lowell, on His Fortieth Birthday" in 1859 but deemed them unworthy of publication; Edward Waldo Emerson and Charles Eliot Norton did not share his misgivings and saw that they were printed (1893) after Emerson and Lowell died. One suspects—and Lowell's extant writings support the impression—that Lowell failed to grasp the fundamental meaning and the far-reaching significance of Emerson and the other Transcendentalists.

At first, this failure was largely deliberate. Lowell's Harvard preceptors had grown increasingly alarmed at his disrespectful attitude towards them, and finally in exasperation they rusticated him to Concord during the glorious final weeks of spring term of his senior year. Ostensibly he went there to read John Locke's *Essay Concerning Human Understanding* and James Mackintosh's *Review of Ethical Philosophy,* neither in any way transcendental, but Lowell thought his time better spent in hating Concord and its country ways and working on his graduation poem. Lowell's tutor in exile was the Reverend Barzillai Frost, a man so witless and self-centered as to prove no match for the worldly-wise adolescent. Emerson's kindly overtures were another matter. Invited by the older man to accompany him on walks and into his household, Lowell remembered ever afterward "the exquisite suavity of his demeanor toward me—a boy of nineteen and very young for my age." But the pride of the moment overcame this favorable impression, especially when Lowell detected an element of foolishness in Emerson's sayings and, worse, in those calling themselves disciples. Frequent reports went out to Cambridge of the curious amusements of Concord. Immediately after his introduction to Emerson's circle, Lowell wrote to his classmate Nathan Hale:

> Emerson is a very pleasant man in private conversation but his "talk" did not increase my opinion of his powers. He seemed to try after effect &—fail. After all I'd heard of him, as an Eagle soaring in pride of place, I was surprised to see a poor little hawk stooping at flies or at best sparrows & groundlings. The "elect" would have pleased you, or I'll lose my guess. There was E[dward]. A[ugustus]. R[enouf]. did naught but ogle. R[ufus]. E[llis]. sat wiping the perspiration off his visage which I came to the conclusion was heated by vicinity of nose. W[endell]. P[hillips]. M. P. scarce said a word, E[dward]. A. W[ashburn]. & G[eorge]. W[arren]. L[ippitt]. did all the talking. I was amused to see that none of the company saving E[merson] & myself made any direct assertion, it was all ?'s—as "Wouldn't it?" & "Isn't it?" &c. (8 July 1838)

Four days later Lowell reported having met Thoreau, and his first impression was never corrected: "It is exquisitely amusing to see how he imitates Emerson's tone & manner. With my eyes shut I shouldn't kn[ow] them apart."

It was during Lowell's unhappy rural retreat that Emerson went down to Cambridge to address the youth of the Divinity College. Lowell did not hear Emerson's attack on historical Christianity, and it would be some months before he could read the words in print, but on the authority of hearsay Lowell entered the theological "storm in a washbowl" intent on defending cloth and gown. Writing to Hale on 23 July 1834, he asked:

> Did you hear R. W. E.'s sermon (if it be not a sin to call it when our Saviour's admirable discourse on the

> mount goes by the same name) . . . ? I hear that it was an abomination. Every divinity student that has crossed my path since have I fixed upon & questioned as to their opinion. . . . They have asked him to publish it—I hope he will, for if it excites any notice (which I very much doubt) it will put the man down—if not, why then—each of his disciples will be by 12½ cents the poorer. . . . They say (I don't know who, but they *do* say) that man sees himself in everything around him, if E. could see *him*self & it didn't drive him crazy (if indeed in that respect he isn't past mending) why—amen. I've talked more about the man than he deserves—but I never can help it.

Happily for Lowell the opportunity to set things right was at hand: his class poem would be printed that year because a public reading was prohibited. In halting pentameters Lowell took after most of the follies of the day—abolitionism, women's rights, temperance, and the new philosophy—but it was Emerson's recent Cambridge performance that elicited his particular disgust:

> Alas! that *Christian ministers* should dare
> To preach the views of Gibbon and Voltaire!
> Alas! that one whose life, and gentle ways,
> E'en hate could find it in its heart to praise,
> Whose intellect is equalled but by few,
> Should strive for what he'd weep to find were true!

Lowell characterized Emerson's confederates in cant as "misty rhapsodists" who

> having made a "universal soul,"
> Forget their own in thinking of the whole;
> Who, seeking nothing, wander on through space,
> Flapping their half-fledged wings in Reason's face,
> And if they chance the vestal flame to find,
> That burns a beacon to the storm-tost mind,
> Like senseless insects dish within the fire,
> And sink forgotten in their funeral pyre.

During the following decade, however, Lowell repented of the reactionary heresies of his youth and penned on the cover of his ***Class Poem***:

> Behold the baby arrows of that wit
> Wherewith I dared assail the woundless Truth!
> Love hath refilled the quiver, and with it
> The man shall win atonement for the youth

The abolition of slavery came to command Lowell's most ardent attention, but on other issues as well he chose the side of the true, good, and beautiful. No doubt Maria White, whom Lowell married in 1844, was a decisive force in his conversion. An earnest thinker and an adherent to Transcendentalism, White had been an early participant in Margaret Fuller's Boston Conversations, and her own poetry spoke to the Ideal in passionately familiar terms. After ***A Year's Life*** (1841), his first book of poems, Lowell's verse also reflected current fashion, both in its romantic phrasing and its idealistic outlook. **"Prometheus"** (1843), **"A Glance behind the Curtain"** (1843), **"Columbus"** (1848), and **"The Present Crisis"** (1845) are typical of the best of Lowell's committed verse of the 1840s, but the accent here is political, not transcendental. Even the several sonnets by Lowell that Emerson and Fuller printed in the *Dial* are, in the words of Leon Howard, "negatively anti-sensuous rather than positively transcendental, misty rather than visionary."

Nobody bothers much nowadays with Lowell's "serious" poetry, understandably. His real achievement was the satire and humor of ***The Biglow Papers*** and ***A Fable for Critics,*** both published in 1848, and the public poetry that occasionally appeared after the Civil War. ***A Fable for Critics*** spoofs Emerson, Fuller, Alcott, Thoreau, Channing, and Theodore Parker, as well as other leading literary figures who were then striving to forge an American literature. Lowell's criticisms are harsh but usually just, at least as just as humorous caricature can allow. Only Fuller is treated unfairly. Called "Miranda" in the verses, she is lampooned by Lowell with the same lack of grace he claims to have found in her:

> She's been travelling now, and will be worse
> than ever;
> One would think, though, a sharp-sighted noter
> she'd be
> Of all that's worth mentioning over the sea,
> For a woman must surely see well, if she try,
> The whole of whose being's a capital I:
> She will take an old notion, and make it her own,
> By saying it o'er in her Sibylline tone,
> Or persuade you 'tis something tremendously deep,
> By repeating it so as to put you to sleep;
> And she well may defy any mortal to see through it,
> When once she has mixed up her infinite *me*
> through it.
> There is one thing she owns in her own single right,
> It is native and genuine—namely, her spite;
> Though, when acting as censor, she privately blows
> A censer of vanity 'neath her own nose.

No doubt Lowell had remembered what Fuller wrote of him two years before in her essay "American Literature" (1846):

> Lowell . . . is absolutely wanting in the true spirit and tone of poesy. His interest in the moral questions of the day has supplied the want of vitality in himself; his great facility at versification has enabled him to fill the ear with a copious stream of pleasant sound. But his verse is stereotyped; his thought sounds no depth, and posterity will not remember him.

All this was long past when the *Atlantic Monthly* was founded under Lowell's editorship in 1857. The "Newness" of the 1840s was by then historic and its proponents were published by Lowell on equal footing with those of other points of view. Thoreau objected to Lowell's unauthorized tampering with one of his essays and never afterward concerned himself with the journal, but the rest bravely bore Lowell's cavalier editing until he was succeeded by James T. Fields in 1861.

After that came time for recollection. Lowell's essays on **"Thoreau"** and **"Emerson the Lecturer"** are important historical documents, but in both he addresses himself to personal matters and not to ideas. Lowell had always fancied himself an idealist, but his idealism was based on the traditions of literature and history, not some transcendent and universal oversoul. He sought to turn the "penetrating ray" of the mind "upon what seemed the confused and wavering cloud-chaos of man's nature and man's experience, and find there the indication of a divine offer." The world of the imagination was not "the world of abstraction and nonentity, as some conceive, but a world formed out of chaos by a sense of the beauty that is in man and the earth on which he dwells." Emerson taught that man was divine; Lowell preferred to bring God down to the level of humanity. William Dean Howells, who came to Cambridge just after the Civil War, later remembered "a saying of Lowell's which he was fond of repeating at the menace of any form of the transcendental, and he liked to warn himself and others with his homely, 'Remember the dinner-bell.'"

Lowell's several biographers have all portrayed his association with the Transcendentalists, but few have considered the movement's powerful attraction on him during his youth. Horace Elisha Scudder writes with the authority of familiar acquaintance in his *James Russell Lowell,* a book that still contains much material of primary importance. Another "intimate" account of value is Edward Everett Hale, *James Russell Lowell and His Friends.* Of the more recent biographical studies, only Leon Howard, *Victorian Knight-Errant,* penetrates the attractive surface of Lowell's life to the complexities of mind and temperament that interest us today. Howard's assessment of Emerson's influence on Lowell is especially commendable, the best statement on the subject we shall probably ever have. Martin Duberman had access to a greater number of unpublished manuscripts and letters, but his reading of them in *James Russell Lowell,* though competent on Lowell's relations with the Transcendentalists, pales in comparison with Howard's earlier study. Austin Warren, "Lowell on Thoreau," is informed and judicious, though Warren confuses references to Channing and Thoreau in ***A Fable for Critics.*** E. J. Nichols is also uncertain about the "Identification of Characters in Lowell's ***A Fable for Critics.***" Fortunately, Lowell's holograph for this section of ***A Fable*** has been preserved (in the Henry E. Huntington Library), and it indicates that it is Ellery Channing who treads "in Emerson's tracks with legs painfully short" and Thoreau who "has picked up all the windfalls" from Emerson's orchards. Howard calls attention to this manuscript in a note to *Victorian Knight-Errant,* but it passed the notice of some: see *Toward the Making of Thoreau's Modern Reputation,* ed. Fritz Oehlschlaeger and George Hendrick, which mislocates the names.

Lowell's early venture in periodical literature, the *Pioneer,* briefly competed with Emerson's *Dial,* and for more than just readers, as Sculley Bradley points out in "Lowell, Emerson, and the *Pioneer.*" In 1947 a facsimile reprint of Lowell's 1843 magazine was published, with a brief introduction by Bradley. Lowell's brief association with the *Dial* is told in interesting detail in Joel Myerson, *The New England Transcendentalists and the* Dial. Lowell's contribution to the *Harbinger,* an organ of the Brook Farm phalanx, provoked a response from John Sullivan Dwight (13 Aug. 1845), a letter ineptly edited by R. Baird Shuman.

Lowell's own letters are the great untapped resource for an understanding of his career and his times. Charles Eliot Norton's edition of the ***Letters of James Russell Lowell*** (1894) is limited by Norton's decorous hesitations. M. A. DeWolfe Howe's edition of ***New Letters of James Russell Lowell*** (1932) is limited by Howe's restricted access to the letters. The need for a much fuller and more faithfully edited volume of Lowell's correspondence is evidenced by the many recent articles that publish selected letters, two of which bear on his relations with the Transcendentalists. Joel Myerson, "Eight Lowell Letters from Concord in 1838," a series of highly amusing and revealing letters Lowell wrote to his Harvard classmate George B. Loring, is nicely complemented by Philip Graham, "Some Lowell Letters," which include letters Lowell wrote at the same time to Nathan Hale. Graham's omission of one of the best of the letters to Hale is corrected in Myerson, "Lowell on Emerson." "The Letters of James Russell Lowell to Robert Carter 1842-1876," replete with important references to various Transcendentalists and especially those who contributed to the *Pioneer,* were the subject of a worthy master's thesis by Quentin G. Johnson. Privately owned at the time of Johnson's work, the forty-seven letters are now in the Berg Collection of the New York Public Library. The valuable correspondence of Lowell's first wife is also more accessible than it was when Hope Jillson Vernon presented *The Poems of Maria Lowell with Unpublished Letters and a Biography.* It is to this area of primary documentation that scholarly attention now needs be turned.

Michael J. Bell (essay date 1995)

SOURCE: "'The Only True Folk Songs We Have in English': James Russell Lowell and the Politics of the Nation," in *Journal of American Folklore,* Vol. 108, No. 428, Spring, 1995, pp. 131-55.

[*In the following essay, Bell studies Lowell's ballad lectures as they outline a Romantic perception of American nationalism.*]

> I am going on with my work in an easy way. I can't say that I care so much about it without J. R. L., who has done so much for me. He would have been so much pleased to have it all nicely finished up. He could talk the fine points in a ballad. They seem stale. I go back to the fine ones at times and sing them and cry over them like the old world.
>
> —Francis James Child[1]

Consider the puzzle offered by these words. Had James Russell Lowell lived to eulogize Francis James Child in this fashion, it might have made better sense. Close friends and colleagues for 50 years, Lowell would have appreciated Child's great service to literary studies in bringing the wealth of English and Scottish popular ballads into a single collection. And given Child's scholarly brilliance, Lowell would have been perfectly justified in feeling that Child's death made the ballads less enjoyable. But for Lowell's death to diminish Child's "care" for the ballads seems inexplicable. Who was Lowell to Child that his passing would bring the great collector to declare that his beloved ballads now "seem stale"?

The question is not an idle one. American intellectual history is quick to admit an intellectual link between the two men. They taught together for 25 years at Harvard, wrote an opera together to raise funds for Civil War Relief, and Lowell's assistance to Child's ballad collecting while he was minister to England is well documented (Duberman 1966:142-145; Howe and Cottrell 1952; Hustvedt 1930).[2] History even acknowledges Lowell's folklore concerns. Biographers have noted his deep interest in tradition, tracing it back to the fact that his mother sang folksongs to him as a child: critics have acknowledged that his writings are full of folk materials; even folklorists have avowed his one contribution to the *Journal of American Folklore* in 1891 (Bell 1988:300; Duberman 1966:11; Howard 1952:22-31; Scudder 1901:14-16; Zumwalt 1988:46). But no historian or folklorist claims that Lowell made any contribution to ballad study that might move Child to weep.

Even when a potential link is supplied, the bond between Child, Lowell, and the ballad remains a puzzle. In 1855, Lowell was invited to deliver a series of lectures at the Lowell Institute. Unbeknownst to him, the invitation had been extended in order that Harvard might consider him as a replacement for Longfellow, who had announced his intention to retire (Dubermann 1966:141; Hale 1899:110; Scudder 1901:300). Lowell's general subject was a history of English poetry, and, in his fourth lecture, he undertook to explicate the ballad. Child, in fact, was in the audience for the entire series, and he wrote to Charles Eliot Norton that he thought the lectures "hasty" but nonetheless "quite the best thing he had ever heard from the 'perverse' Lowell" (quoted in Duberman 1966:140).[3]

Perhaps, however, this lecture provides a place from which to approach Child's tears. It is doubtful that James Russell Lowell taught Child much about ballads. If he had, "stubby, honest" Child would have recorded it, or Charles Eliot Norton, Lowell's posthumous editor, would have felt compelled to honor Lowell. But it is possible that what Child heard that day makes all the rest—their 50-year friendship, the ballads they talked about and sang together, the banter between statesman and scholar, even the weeping—make sense. In addition, if Lowell's speech is typical of his life's work, then, just possibly, the lecture also holds a clue to issues of which the ballads were only one dimension. James Russell Lowell was everything that Francis James Child was not. One of the 19th century's most eminent public intellectuals, opponent of the Mexican War, abolitionist, editor of the *Atlantic Monthly,* ambassador to Spain, minister to England, scourge of Gilded Age politicians, he held the national stage for 50 years, defending or damning nearly every idea of his era. Thus, perhaps this lecture, if it plays on that same stage, might also move the ballad onto the uncommon ground of cultural politics.

. . . . .

According to his biographers (Duberman 1966:140; Hale 1899:112), Lowell approached these—his first public lectures—with a mixture of diffidence and dread. He was a notorious procrastinator, and, with less than a month to go before his lectures at the Lowell Institute were to begin, he had finished only five of the twelve talks. As the final date drew closer and public anticipation surged, his anxiety grew. There had been a run on tickets when his course was announced, and, although the institute added an afternoon series, only one out of every five people who requested tickets received them (Duberman 1966:141; Hale 1899:114).[4] Lowell's fears increased further when he realized who would hear him speak. Since 1839, Lowell Institute audiences had heard such lecturers as Asa Grey, Louis Agassiz, and Charles Lyell, and Lowell knew not only that expectations were high but that some of these former speakers would be in the audience. Lowell had a reputation as a poet and critic (it was not his loose family connections that had brought him the offer to speak), but he had never spoken in public before and he knew that, in this forum, wit alone would not do. Of course, none of this distress prevented him from writing to Charles Briggs that he had chosen to lecture on the English poets in order to retaliate "for the injuries received by one whom the public won't allow among the living" (quoted in Duberman 1966:133).

Lowell joked, but he had a complicated retaliation in mind. For 50 years, English critics had ridiculed American writing. "In the four quarters of the globe, who reads an American book?" Sidney Smith wrote in the *Edinburgh Review,* in 1818 (quoted in Spiller 1929:6; see also Lease 1981:3-12). For those same years, American writers had raged against this onus, seeking to overcome English dismissal by inventing American substitutions for Britain's ancestral weight or by denying that history mattered (see Allen 1959; Anderson 1990; Buell 1973; Lease 1981; Ruland 1981; Spencer 1957; Weisbuch 1986). And Lowell, for all that the floated above the fray, content to turn a poet's gaze or a reviewer's eye on the battles, was fully engaged. As much as any American writer at midcentury, Lowell had struggled with Emerson's call for American scholars to walk on their own feet, to work with their own hands, and to speak with their own mouths. And he was resolved therefore to serve these English critics a very cold dish.

In so doing, however, Lowell intended neither to refuse his inheritance nor to exalt pale copies. Already, in his review of Longfellow's *Kavanaugh: A Tale,* entitled provocatively "Nationality in Literature," he had rebuked "the martinets of nationality" on both sides of the Atlantic

(1913[1849]:22). In his view, the United States could not inherit what it had helped to create and thus should not reject its English roots to satisfy a naive version of cultural independence (see Somkin 1967). It was foolish, he thought, to wonder who Americans were: "It is only geographically that we can call ourselves a new nation. . . . Intellectually we were full-grown at the start. Shakespeare had been dead five years, and Milton was eleven years old, when Mary Chilton leaped ashore on Plymouth Rock" (1913[1849]:15). It was even more foolish to wonder where American literature was. "As if we had been without one," he wrote; "as if Shakespeare, sprung from the race and the class which colonized New England, had not been also ours! As if we had no share in the puritan and republican Milton, we who had cherished in secret for more than a century the idea of the great puritan effort, and at last embodied it in a living commonwealth!" (1913[1849]:18).

More directly, Lowell rejected the basic assumptions of American nationalism. National literatures were "not school exercises in composition to be handed in by a certain day," no more than nationality was "a thing to be won by the sword" (1913[1849]:19, 20). Literatures were national, he believed, insofar as they were local, and the United States, which was only beginning to establish its natural landscape, "never had any proper youth as a nation, never had [a] mythic period either" (1913[1849]:20). Still, he continued, if the truth were told, "no race perishes without intellectual heir" (1913[1849]:24), and he might have added, none rises without ancestors. For Lowell, truly great literature survived precisely because it refused to be circumscribed by provincial boundaries. Echoing Longfellow's declaration in *Kavanaugh* that nationality was good but universality was better, Lowell argued that the "truth" of national literature was

> neither more nor less than this, that authors should use their own eyes and ears, and not those of other people. We ask of them human nature as it appears in man, not in books; and scenery not at second hand from the canvas of painter or poet, but from that unmatched landscape painted by the Great Master on the retina of their own eyes. Let an American author make a living character, even if it be antediluvian, and nationality will take care of itself. [1913(1849):30-31]

Lowell's distrust of the formulas of nationalism went well beyond his resentment of English criticism or amusement with American nativism. Like most of his class, he believed that America had lost sight of the common good (Hietala 1985:95-131). Increasingly divided into high and low, the populace seemed, to his mind, no longer willing to distinguish individual self-interest from civic virtue. Moreover, in the absence of the once secure theological and revolutionary justifications for collective sacrifice, the people seemed to have opted for a coarser understanding of social obligation, in which progress was equated with the acquisition of private property and the satisfaction of individual desires. Of course, this general decline did not surprise Lowell at all. The California gold rush, with its lure of the lucky strike and its substitution of chance for hard work, the annexation of Texas, and the Mexican War, each of which had failed to expand liberty; New England's rapid industrialization, which was creating the first signs of strife between factory workers and owners; and, most of all, the North's accommodation to the Fugitive Slave Act of 1850, had all evidenced the possible disintegration of the republic.

Suddenly, however, that potential seemed frighteningly real. Mass immigration (over four million people entered the United States during the 1850s) was overwhelming the country's resources. The sudden addition of large numbers of German and Irish Catholics severely strained the nation's existing public services and seemed to threaten Protestant hegemony over education and republican government. By 1855, one in five Massachusetts residents was foreign-born, and the vast majority of these immigrants were Irish. Poor and unskilled, seen as harbingers of popish influence and as possible tools of the slavocracy, the majority of these newcomers remained at the bottom of the economic ladder with little hope that the Brahmin classes above were concerned for their lives or their welfare. In addition, recessions in 1851, 1854, and 1855 had produced widespread anxiety and resentment at all levels of the economy. Businessmen saw themselves unfairly manipulated by an emerging national market economy that no longer seemed responsive to local needs or under local control, while workers felt threatened by a factory system that increasingly treated them as commodities and not people. Massachusetts, as the nation's most densly populated urbanized and industrialized state, had been particularly vulnerable to these economic dislocations. Deteriorating conditions and high unemployment only exaggerated the distance between the state's Yankee aristocracy and its working class.

The enactment of the Kansas-Nebraska Act of 1854 had also instigated a furious debate over the political future of the republic. Its extension of slavery through the popular sovereignty provision (settlers, rather than Congress, would determine whether a territory would be slave or free) guaranteed that Kansas would become both the central symbol and actual battlefield of the conflict between the North and the South (Fellman 1979:287-307; Howard 1990:132-155). Abolitionists asserted that, if the act overturned the restriction of slavery to territories south of the 36°30' parallel, as established by the Missouri Compromise, then it also invalidated the Fugitive Slave Act. And when authorities captured escaped slave Anthony Burns in May 1854 and ordered his forcible return to slavery, even the most conservative Massachusetts Brahmins were turned into "stark mad abolitionists" (C. F. Adams, as quoted in Mulkern 1990:78). It seemed certain that only violence could bring about the end of the slave power.

At the moment that Lowell lectured, the most recent local elections seemed to have made this descent into anarchy even more apparent. In 1854, the American (Know-Nothing) Party had carried scores of local elections in the Northeastern and Mid-Atlantic states on an unlikely mix of xenophobia, opposition to slavery, and working-class rage (Beals 1960:227-252; Holt 1992:165-190; Mulkern 1990:61-113; Walters 1976:54-69). In Massachusetts, the Know-Nothings captured full control of the state legislature and were busily replacing the long-standing Whig establishment with a government committed to the expulsion of the Irish. In fact, on the very day that Lowell began his course of lectures, Governor Gardner, in his inaugural address, proposed a crusade to "Americanize America" and promised to institute a national cleansing that was destined to "rank with the great movements that originally found nations" (quoted in Mulkern 1990:78).

Lowell particularly feared this localized version of ultra-American nativism because of its potential to derail the cause of abolition. Several years earlier, in the *Anti-Slavery Standard,* Lowell wrote that the European revolutions of 1848 had been "thwarted in a great measure by foolish disputes about races and nationalities," and he recognized the threat such debates posed to the antislavery cause. "We have no especial interest in these assertions of national nobility, except in as far as they have been the cause or the apology of national oppression. Men are very willing to excuse any unnatural feature of their social system by tracing it up to some inscrutable divine arrangement" (Lowell 1902[1849]:26). Now the Know-Nothing exploitation of the Irish question raised the possibility of an alliance that could easily postpone the end of slavery for decades. If the northern Know-Nothings and southern apologists for slavery succeeded in linking their racist ideologies, then they might so soil the ground of American identity with their intolerance that no diversity or dissent would be possible.

For Lowell, then, his lectures offered the opportunity to move beyond the irony and rage of ***A Fable for Critics*** and ***The Biglow Papers.*** American identity was no longer a topic of genteel discussion or a subject for dialect poetry. Suddenly, the linked causes of American Nationalism, abolition, and Irish imagination that he had so long argued for were at war on the plains of Kansas and the streets of Boston. If his audiences were to overcome the forces threatening their community values, they needed to know not only what a genuine national literature might look like but more so what they might do to create it. Here, in the process of unpacking the history of English literature, he could show his New England audiences how they might refashion existing American nationalism into an identity more compatible with Yankee New England's traditions and desires; and by displaying the nuts and bolts of England's own national literature, he could demonstrate the true character of American national identity.

In assuming this particular "quest for nationality," Lowell stepped back onto familiar territory (Spencer 1957). No one who had followed his career could have had any doubt how little faith he had in the politics of commercialism and compromise that dominated post-Jacksonian America. Like most of New England's historians and critics, he had shown how disturbed he was by the apparent fragmentation of the public sphere and the consequent loss of spiritual identity which it presaged. And, like them, he had sought repeatedly to mediate between the desire of the age for an organically whole civic culture and the brute facts of national life (see Gordon 1942). Unlike the majority of those critics, however, he did not yet believe that the best hope of overcoming the contemporary cultural malaise lay in the struggle of the individual against the state (see Anderson 1990; Bercovitch 1975, 1978; Carafiol 1991; Ellison 1984; Hansen 1990; Martin 1991; Pease 1987; Spengemann 1989). At least in 1855, Lowell was unwilling to preach the aggrandizement of the self at the expense of the community. Rather, he was seeking to write a new idiom through which his fragmented society might renew itself. Accordingly, although he would make as full a use of Romantic epistemology as any Transcendentalist in order to construct his vision of genuine American nationalism, he would do so only to oppose the consequences of that epistemology for American cultural life (Riddel 1991:54-56).

Not surprisingly, then, Lowell preferred to ground his new idiom in the politics of the imagination. Poetry was mind made concrete; its origin was consciousness, and consciousness (no matter what the source of its materials) always moved from inside the poet to the external world of the poem. Lowell's actual language relied heavily on Thomas Coleridge's distinction between fancy and imagination (Howard 1952:341-342). Of the two, he declared in his first lecture, fancy was the "frailer quality which in combination with sentiment produces poetry, with experience, wit." In either association fancy occupied itself with "what may be called *scenery.*" In contrast, imagination was a form of empathy. "Imagination," he said, "would seem to be that breath of sympathy which can include the emotions of some other person within its own, and that energy which can then condense this emotion into a word or phrase so vivid that it shall reproduce the same emotion in the reader" (as quoted in Howard 1952:343). Still, although Lowell would argue for the imagination against tradition, he, nonetheless, would turn to the mythology of tradition to begin his discussion of national identity because, as he began his talks, the figure of the "nation" could only be voiced within that mythos (Riddel 1991:57; see also Linberg 1991:233-235).

. . . . .

By the time that he reached the ballad lecture, Lowell was dispensing criticism with relish. Piers Plowman, he told his audience, might be good cultural history, but its substitution of allegory for imagination made it bad poetry. Likewise he insisted that the authors of the metrical romances were barely able to raise their work to the level of fancy. Given such remarks, the audience might have expected ballads to fare no better, and initially they did not, for Lowell began not with ballad poetry but with ballad politics. Citing first Macbeth's injunction against "Fools, minstrels and bards . . . ," he went on:

> When Virgil said *arms* [*sic*] *virumque cano,* arms and the man I sing, he defined in the strictest manner the

> original office of the poet, and the object of the judicious Macbeth's ordinance was to prevent anyone from singing the wrong arms and the wrong man. For the poet was then what the political newspaper is now, and circulated from ear to ear with satire or panegyric. He it was who first made Public Opinion a power in the state by condensing it in a song.[5]

If this were not enough, Lowell concluded his opening remarks with a flourish: "The fluid sentiment dispersed in the atmosphere he gathered into a flash that could rive and burn. Good and evil fame were with him, the more powerful that they were invisible, for what tyrant could procure the assassination of an epithet or throw a couplet into a dungeon?"

Such explicit political claims are decidedly uncharacteristic in ballad scholarship. Ballad makers are rarely described as political forces to be feared, and ballad critics seldom talk politics when they talk ballads. Yet Lowell began by doing both. His ballad makers were genuine threats to the status quo. They arbitrated public opinion; they threatened or enhanced the power of the state. Moreover, their ballads literally caused their hearers to "rive and burn." The description is overwrought, but Lowell was not. Like Spenser (whose portrayal of the political power of Irish bards he quotes approvingly), Lowell wanted the audience to know that, whatever else they might be, ballads were rhetoric in action and their authors were the reporters and editorial writers of that world where "the copies of a poem were so many living men, and all publication was to the accompaniment of music."

This newspaper metaphor, moreover, allowed Lowell to avoid some of the more pernicious features of 19th-century ballad criticism. Admittedly, he was already turning ballad poets into their poems. Still, even with such reification, he posited no mysterious consciousness to explain the absence of authorial claims in balladry. Ballad poets did not call attention to themselves because disguise was simply the most sensible way of avoiding discovery. "[The ballad's] force was in its impersonality," he said, "for Public Opinion is disenchanted the moment it is individualized, and is terrible only so long as it is the opinion of no one in particular." Likewise, he did not treat orality as a degenerative feature. It was merely another natural consequence of the political context of ballad creation. "A Newspaper may be suppressed, and editor may be silenced, every copy of an obnoxious book may be destroyed in those old days when the minstrels were a power, . . . [but a] verse could wander safely from heart to heart and from hamlet to hamlet as unassailable as music and memory."

Lowell did not intend for his audience to mistake the ballad for a modern poem, however. Foremost, ballads embodied popular memory. "It was on the wings of verse that the names of ancestral heroes could float down securely over broad tracts of desert time, and across the gulf of oblivion. And poets were sometimes made use of by sagacious rulers to make legends serve a political purpose." Pomp aside, the traditional role of the ballad maker as community historian emerges. Popular poets cherished what the rest of the community only vaguely remembered, and their special abilities permitted them to shape what ordinary people knew and thought about their past. Yet such poets accomplished more. Citing the example of the great Persian poet, Firdausi, Lowell argued that "to make a people capable of great things, to multiply an army by two, you must make an alliance with their imaginations. A reinforcement of that will overbear great odds, and it is from the past only that it can be recruited. For this kind of thing any past will do, if you can only make men believe in it."

Lowell's argument to this point has a certain panache. Ballad authors do not merely sing history; they make history. The best of them can literally "make any past do." Moreover, the finest of them can imagine a history with the compliance of their audiences. "The human race," he said, "lives to feel a past behind it, to have its rear guarded by an illustrious ancestry. It will have heroes even if it has only shadows to make them out of, and is obliged to wink a little to believe in them. *For national character is cumulative. It is from the dead centuries that national impulses acquire force and direction, and it is from the silent peaks of the past that man's eye controls the great unknown ocean of the future*" (emphasis added). For Lowell, national politics and national poetics were one. Both ballad makers and ballad audiences knew that a nation's very existence depended upon its ability to define itself, not philosophically by its special values, but materially by its special character. Nations, both knew, might be conceived in liberty, but they rose and fell in legend. And hence, both agreed that it was better to bend under the weight of fiction than to stand upright without a history.

Any doubts about why Lowell raised the imaginary quality of national character were quickly laid to rest. Continuing unabated, he asked his audience to consider the "peculiar" position of the English. Christianity and the importation of the French language had cut Saxon and Norman "wholly off from the past," he asserted, and when the two finally began to become one, the severance was absolute. "The English properly so called were a people who hardly knew their grandfathers." Every god, every hero, every tradition that connected them to their past was "as if they had never been." Anglophiles throughout the audience must have blanched at these words, but Lowell persisted. "English writers," he declared, "demand of us a national literature. But where for thirteen centuries was their own?" New Englanders, at least, he went on "brought a past with them to Plymouth" and could claim the laws, the language, the genius, and the triumphs of ancestral daring "wafted to heaven on the real wings of Martyr-fires" as their legitimate inheritance. The Normans, in contrast, were but "an extemporaneous hoard" as much cut off from the past as the army that arose "at the sowing of the gorgon's teeth." And the Saxons they conquered, he continued, were little better. "For we must remember that though Britain was historically old, England was not, and it was as impossible to piece the histories of the two together to make a national record of, as it would be for us to persuade ourselves into a feeling of continental antiquity by adopting the Mexican Annals."

James Russell Lowell never avoided hyperbole. His leaps from ballads to epics to national character are questionable. His anxiety is unmistakable. But his objective is clear. The English ridiculed American literary efforts. He returned their smugness with savagery. Anglo-America, at least, could lay claim to English tradition at its birth.[6] That tradition might be barely 300 years old, but it was tradition nonetheless. More importantly, if English national culture was forged not in the Norman Conquest but in the Protestant Reformation, then America's English heirs could claim even more. Norman swords might have won a land, but Puritan "martyr-fires" forged a soul. No wonder, he continued, Norman poets wrote awful poems. They lacked a national consciousness. Hawthorne had once told him that he found it painful to live in an old house "for the shadows of former occupants that haunted it," but, he continued, the Normans so desperately required a past that they raised up ghosts to haunt them. "To the Normans, England was such an old house and their poets, having no past of their own, raised the ghosts of Arthur and his knights to walk in it. But they were shadows only, and not names to conjure with like those at which the deepest fibre in the heart and brain, the sentiment of race and country, vibrates and tingles."

To prove his assertions, Lowell set out to convict the English by describing true national literature. Such a literature, he began, cannot be imposed from above. "Uneducated people," he told his audience, "will not stand half as much stuff as educated ones, because they have not so many facetious and artificial associations, the string of which is mistaken for that of the heart. (I think the school boy is right when he resents the greater part of Virgil as an impertinence.) To touch simple men and women your words must cut deep to something real and living—to the national sentiments and hereditary beliefs—to a human and not a class experience." For Lowell, national poetry was poetry without cant or class. Attacking English snobbery once again, he declared that Dr. Adam Smith's rejection of the ballad of Chevy Chase because it was "plainly such as no gentlemen could have written" perfectly exemplified the failure of the British to recognize what made ballads immortal. "The ballads," he asserted, "are the first truly national poetry in our language, and national poetry is not that either of the drawing room or the kitchen. It is the common mother earth of the universal sentiment that the foot of the poet must touch, through which shall steal up to the heart and the brain that fine virtue which puts him in sympathy not with his class but his kind."

Informing an audience of New England gentry that ballad makers were no gentleman is hardly tactful; but telling them that roguery was the life blood of the ballad had nothing to do with untender motives. Rather, Lowell was setting forth what would become a recurring leitmotif. In his view, national poetry stood against the artificiality of caste and the power of material difference. It refused to separate the community into the few with much or the many with little or to claim that drawing rooms and kitchens were populated by different peoples merely because circumstance made them appear different. Instead, national poetry spoke to the whole people by exhalting the natural sympathy between the rich and poor, proving that the two classes might be joined together in spite of their differences if only poets would chronicle kindred desires. And it made its case for the nation by demonstrating that "common mother earth" was far more important than any artificial distinction in wealth, power, or locality.

Lowell's faith in the creativity of national poets was just as impassioned. Resonating the hopes and fears of their communities, such poets captured the immediacy of ordinary life. "Courage, devotion, constancy, the fears, the hopes, the successes, and the tragedies of life—whatever moves the heart and inspires the soul of man—these were themes good enough for the ballad makers and it never occurred to them that they were to be found only in the past, that they were the monopoly of the dead." For Lowell, what moved women and men in the national moment were their common sympathies. Thus national poets were not interested in insight or self-display, and certainly took no pride in irony or disdain. They expressed a people's universal sentiments and collective hopes, and, at their best, discovered a community's true virtue. Most importantly, Lowell continued, such sentiments were not dead. "The present to him who knows how to listen to it is epical," he concluded, "and he hears in it the tones of joy as clear and of wail as deep as ever thrilled him in history or poem. . . . Perhaps the ballads are most interesting as showing how full of poetry and beauty our daily life is, if it only be looked at poetically."

Until this last claim Lowell's enthusiasms are familiar territory to folklorists. His distinction between *Kunstpoesie* and *Volksdichtung* is standard Romantic poetics, and his obscurantism only reinforces the Romantic temper of his arguments (Abrahams 1992; Abrams 1958[1953], 1971; Lovejoy 1924). But to assert that modern poets might make national poetry seems heroically optimistic. He had just finished locating ballad making in the classless, preliterate past, and even he would have acknowledged that a modern poet lived in neither state. Why then offer his contemporaries the hope that they might make national poetry when the possibility was fleeting at best? Serendipity aside, Lowell faced a trap of his own devising. By his own admission, national character demanded a long tradition. It was "cumulative," formed from the "dead centuries" and directed from "the silent peaks of the past." Poets might raise knolls into Alps and audiences might "wink" at their alchemy, but the knolls needed to exist. If the English lacked enough history to produce a national character, then America, with even less history, had no hope. But it is precisely this seeming dead end that makes his claim so liberating and American. Like Emerson, who in *Nature* reproved his contemporaries ("why should we grope among the dry bones of the past, or put the living generation into a masquerade out of its faded wardrobe? The sun shines to-day also" [Emerson 1981(1837):7]), Lowell held as an article of faith that an honest poet might shatter time's stranglehold on inspiration. Admittedly, a past made it easier for poets to listen to their communities, but no amount of past was enough if a nation's poets remained deaf to their songs.

To complete this overthrow of history, Lowell flawlessly narrated the Transcendental fantasy of poetic creativity (see Buell 1973:34-56; Hansen 1990:60-71; Kronick 1984:39-41; for the larger Romantic version, see Abrams 1958[1953], 1971). Ballad makers were not "encumbered with any useless information. They had not wit enough to lose their way." Likewise ballad makers attended exclusively to the close and familiar. They succeeded because "they felt and thought and believed just as their hearers did, and because they never thought about it." Ballads are pathetic, he continued, "because the poet did not try to make them so, and [they] are models of simple and nervous diction because the business of the poet was to tell his story, not to adorn it, and accordingly he went earnestly and straight forwardly to work, and let the rapid thought snatch the words as it ran, feeling quite secure of its getting the right one." For Lowell, blinding energy, not craft, made the ballad possible, and in the end, such wild fire begat fury: "*When a thought gets hold of a man it knows how to make him speak.* The poet does not make the poem, it possesses him and he can no more tell how it was made out of him than the brown earth can guess how the snow drop that looks back at her could create itself out of her dusky bosom" (emphasis added).

Here is Romantic wizardry at its best. Great poets do not think; they are possessed by thought and poetry happens. Here also is the genius of the ballad. No matter that no poet, not even the author of Kubla Khan or of Lady Margaret, ever composed in this way. All that matters is that ballad poets somehow stand above even the greatest of modern poets. Modern poets must overcome their refinement. They have more than enough wit "to lose their way," and that wit guarantees that only the very best among them will "fuse learning into one substance with their own thought and feeling, and so interpenetrate it with themselves that the acquired is as much as the native." Fortunately, ballad poets were saved from such artifice. Lowell reserved some of his strongest anger for those writers who substituted language for feeling. "When in a matter that concerns emotion," he said, "a man begins to contrive what he shall say and how he shall say it, he is going to utter something that is unfit for him to speak and for us to hear." He wanted poetry to be free of the accursed consciousness that allowed individuals to act from motives. He wanted even more for poets to be released from the task of building poems. And in ballads he found all that he desired naturally expressed. "The ballads have this merit in common with the highest poetry that we cannot by any analysis detect the processes by which they were produced. We feel as wide a difference between what is manufactured and what is spontaneous as between the sparks ground out by the dozen from an electrical machine (which a sufficiently muscular professor can grind out by the dozen) and the wild fire of God that writes *mene, mene, mene,* on the crumbling palace walls of a midnight cloud."

These contraries—the manufactured and the spontaneous, electrical sparks and divine fire, muscular professor and almighty God—take us well beyond the literary limits of the lecture. Lowell aspired to create as only a poet might, and even though he recognized that such creation was more properly the province of God, he could barely keep his disappointment hidden. He spurned his mechanized world in which the writing on the palace wall was more likely to produce a scientific explanation than to bring down an empire, and he envied the ballad makers their spontaneity. They were much better off than he and his contemporaries. They "had no books." Their language was not seen but heard. "Language, when it speaks to the eye only, loses half its meaning. It is no longer live thinking and feeling, but the unimpassioned vehicle of these." The metaphor is mixed, but the meaning is clear. Language works best when it is spoken: "For the eye is an outpost of the intellect, and fetches and carries messages for that. But the temperament, the deep human nature, the aboriginal emotions—these utter themselves in the voice."

Lowell was too much the showman to leave his audience breathing the rare air of theory any longer than necessary. Besides, he had finished only 15 of his 51 handwritten pages, and he had a great deal left to say. Still, although he would comment on 15 folk and literary ballads in some depth, his remarks on individual ballads were always intended to establish the declension of modern times. Given, however, the psychology he had outlined thus far, few other themes were possible. Contemporary poets sought to moralize at their worst or to educate at their best; and as edifying as those goals might be, neither produced the ingredients of national poetry. Wordsworth was the greatest modern English poet, Lowell would tell his audience, but "Wordsworth has not in him even a suspicion of the dramatic imagination—he has too much individual character—and when he puts himself beside the older poet he seems not only tame but downright barnyard."

The problem, again, was not in Wordsworth but in Wordsworth's imagination. Modern poets were condemned to preach, he said, and preaching always caused them to think instead of to picture. "I think," he said, "we all have a feeling that what we call the mother-tongue is something which underlies the language of books and writing, and makes the dialect of life as distinguished from that of thought. In English, especially as a composite tongue, it is not hard to draw the line between heart-words and brain-words. The first have come from the people, and the last from the governing class." Again Lowell works by contraries, befitting his nascent jeremiad. Mother tongue opposes writing, life opposes thought, heart opposes brain, the people oppose their rulers. And it is not hard to see these oppositions for the struggle that they are. Speech, here, is alive in its cadences, its shadings, its very words, and because it is, it does not permit nonsense the way writing does. Addressing the veneration of the language of thought by critics, he said: "It is this that has given rise to what has now become the *cant* about Anglosaxon—which has gone so far that I have read a harangue in favor of that language, in which every word but the conjunctions and prepositions was of Latin origin" (emphasis in original).[7]

Hidden within the humor is a serious debate about the nature of English (one that Lowell would take up again several times in his life), and cant is a marvelously economical word for his disgust with the zealousness of the schoolmasters. For Lowell, English had no ancient form. It was a "composite tongue," and its only problem was that educated critics were too busy "striving to keep expression blockaded (or block-headed) within certain trenches of usage or authority" to notice that language was best kept alive by those who trusted themselves. Look to Shakespeare, he challenged the audience. "[He] never thought of getting the tower-stamp on his phrases." Or if Shakespeare was too lofty, then they should look to their own children. "They make action verbs wherever they want them," he said, "because their thoughts are action. Your son tells you that he has greened his white trousers, or black and blued his knee, and neither he nor you are pained by want of precedent." The unarguable truth for Lowell was that language and, by implication, identity prospered only because people spoke from the heart. To be sure consideration and "precedent" were absolutely essential to careful expression. But both were paid for with freshness and warmth. "The words of a backwoodsman are sometimes as keen and sure of their mark as his axe. They have never had the life squeezed out of them by the printing press, nor lost their color by imprisonment in books."

Moreover, when the modern imagination did not preach, it inflated. Ballad singers, he said, "plunge into deep water at once. The[ir] transitions are abrupt. . . . The[ir] passions speak out savagely and without any delicacies of circumlocution." As such, ballad events remained urgent and alive. Real people lived, died, knew joy or sorrow in the ballad world. In contrast, modern life appeared in the newspapers. In another burst of oratorical fervor, Lowell proclaimed: "Our age of steam seems to be like an express train on the railway and we rattle from one piece of news to another so swiftly that we have no time to feel anything deeply and livingly. The scenery of life rushes by us blended into an unmeaning ribbon in which particulars are not to be distinguished." The threat, according to Lowell, was not simply that readers preferred bad writing to good or sensation to sense, though he did tell the audience that "the state should furnish every child born in it with a pistol to blow out its brains at once, as with this subtle means of getting rid of them by degrees." Rather it was the "inevitable dilution of mind, of thought, of feeling, and of language . . . in a country like ours, where the only reading of the mass of the people is the newspapers." In their rush to be novel, newspapers painted every story with the same emotional brush, leaving their readers with no way to distinguish melodrama from tragedy or either from farce. No wonder the modern world was in disarray. What else could be expected, he declared, when words were more valued for their length than for their impact. "We have now no longer any fire but disastrous conflagrations; nobody dies but deceases; men do not fall from houses but are precipitated from mansions or edifices; a convict is not hanged, but suffers the extreme penalty of the offended laws of his country."

All that was left was valediction. Sir Walter Scott was wrong, Lowell said, to apologize for the ballad. "Ballads are the only true folk songs that we have in English," and they needed no defense. No other poetry, he went on, addressed its audience so simply and directly. No other poets clung so certainly to what was grand and permanent. No other poetry opposed so unerringly the metaphysical with the ordinary. No other poets opened themselves so directly to the harmonies of the world. For the ballad makers, their own emotions were enough for any poem, and what they lacked in emotion the world supplied. Indeed, Lowell said, ballads were "the pure poetry of the world." Their deaths deal only in dying; their ghosts do not preach immortality, and their dead carry with them only those terrors with which ordinary citizens face the unknown. Moreover, the ballads were winnowed as no other poetry would ever be. Ballad poets read their reviews in "the faces of [their] ring of hearers," and if a ballad did not touch the people, then it was forgotten or replaced by "new editions . . . struck off by mothers crooning their children to sleep, or by wandering minstrels who went about sowing the seed of courtesy and valor in the cottage and on the hillside." Still, even faced by their critics, ballad singers had the advantage. They lived and worked under "the Arch of Heaven," and they were burdened with no library "but clouds, streams, mountains, woods, and men." They did not create in overheated rooms with "indoor inspiration," or write poetry to sing "the virtues of the fireside [or] teach the ethics of home." Their poetry fed on sunshine, and it gave "color and bloom to the brain as well as to the apple and plum." And therein lay the greatest charm of the ballads, "nobody made them," Lowell concluded. "They seem to have come up like violets and we have only to thank God for them."

. . . . .

To no one's surprise, except perhaps his own, James Russell Lowell got the job (Duberman 1966:142).[8] Scott did a better job of defending the minstrel. Coleridge wrote more eloquently on the imagination. Emerson described the "low and familiar" with greater poetry. But Lowell's pastiche of these represented precisely the comforting blend of common sense and romance that the Harvard overseers had in mind for their students. Moreover, although his language soared to unnatural heights and his ballad theory was outdated, his lecture was precisely the blend of poetics and politics that he intended it to be. Lowell's subject may have been English folksong, but his ballad criticism reached directly to the heart of the war for the American imagination.

At the risk of monotony, Lowell justified his claims on classically Romantic grounds. National identity was founded on language as at once the reflection of material things, the bridge between mind and things, and the product of the mind in response to things. But like his Romantic contemporaries, he recognized that the truthfulness of language simply could not be guaranteed. Language slipped its boundaries too easily, and its uneasy mediation of imagined life in speech and literature made even its most subtle Romantic users suspicious. The ordinary Romantic solution was at once ingenious and elegant. Language, alone, could not be trusted. Tie language to consciousness. Consciousness bound to language might prove false. Tie both to history. History produced by both might be fiction. Anchor all three to nature, and when nature proved too awesome to comprehend and indifferent to human desires, enfold this cobbled trio within a metaphor of individual development. As infancy gives way to youth and adolescence to adulthood in an individual's passage to maturity, so too, it asserted, did savagery give way to tribalism, tribes to nations, and nations to civilizations as the races of the world passed from barbarism to culture.

Such rigid traditionalism, however, could not work for the United States. As Lowell had declared, America lacked the history to establish its national individuality and what little history it had foregrounded precisely the dependence on England and Europe that his criticism was intended to overcome. His originality in this lecture (and this lecture, as will be seen, is crucial to that originality) was to promise America a national identity that was at once rooted in language, founded on real history, and yet unburdened by the past. He did so by arguing the priority of will over history. On every page of the ballad lecture, Lowell stressed that the active mind of the poet mattered above all else. It was the first cause and the transforming agent. And it alone had the power to make singers into nation makers. Countries came and went in the ordinary way of things: but countries were not nations, and no evolution or revolution in itself was enough to make a nation no matter what new borders it established. Nations arose only when their people actively sought to be one in beliefs and values, and only when their poets actively worked to give direction to those impulses.

Nowhere are these claims more explicit than in the lecture's linkage of the ballad poet and national character. As much as anyone ever, Lowell enjoyed attacking contemporary poetic sensibilities, but he was not content to play either the shadow Emerson exhorting his audience to surrender to nature or the shadow Whitman trumpeting the apotheosis of the self. From the opening sentence of the lecture—from that first appearance of the ballad maker who threatens the state with a song, to the Persian poets who create a national poetry from whole cloth, to the Norman poets whose lack of community guaranteed a lack of voice, to the English poets who made both genuine folksongs and an English nation—Lowell challenged his audience to recognize that national poetry and national character were man-made and man-makeable. Unfortunately, locating that creative power in the ballad maker evoked an unavoidable, almost sacramental reverence for the past. In the choice of such poets as analytic subjects, therefore, Lowell risked producing not the forward looking inspiration that he desired but the mournful nostalgia that he feared. Since a Romanticism without nostalgia is no Romanticism at all (see Kammen 1991:40-61; Lears 1981) and since Lowell was determined to be Romantic, nostalgia must be saved from its inevitable backward glances.

Lowell inscribed his revised nostalgia onto American character as a substitution of genuineness for genealogy. In his hands, the analysis of balladry was always concerned with motives and seldom with origins. He was not interested in sources. For Lowell, the substance of a ballad was found in the subjective mental state of its producer. If a speaker, or singer, or poet, or an audience member reached within themselves, and if, like Shakespeare or their own children, their "thoughts [we]re action," then they produced a true article. If anyone, however, paused to check themselves against an external authority or surrendered their immediate passion to future considerations, then they were false to themselves and to their common lives. Honest poets, honest speakers, and honest citizens did not imitate and did not defer, because if they did, their good intentions produced bad poetry, insipid talk, and ineffective government. Importantly, Lowell never demanded transcendence or effacement as the price of authenticity. He did not expect his modern audience to suspend judgment or long to return to a simpler past, and he did not demand a rejection of the present. Rather, he called upon his audience to recognize that, although the production of genuine ballads was not possible, the production of genuine poetry was. The key lay in looking inward and not backward. And it was available, now and in the future, to anyone with the strength of character to choose.

A Romanticism that favored choice was unusual; a Romanticism based on choice was exceptional, but an antebellum American Romanticism founded on choice was hazardous as well. Traditional nationalist models were intentionally undemocratic. Designed to oppose Enlightenment political theories of civil government and revolution by consent, Romantic nationalism asserted communal sovereignty as an unconscious inheritance outside the ken of politics. But as Lowell had made eminently clear throughout his analysis, choice was the only choice for the United States. Unconscious solidarity went against the American grain, if for no other reason than because Englishmen had had to think themselves into becoming Americans. Accordingly, having committed himself to choice, Lowell needed a way to give himself and his audience control over their decisions while at the same time closing the door to choices of the sort that he wished them to avoid. Slaveowners simply could not be allowed to imagine that they might dissolve their participation in the American system of government just because they chose to do so. But neither could Americans be offered a false mythology as the price for preventing disunion.

Ironically, then, but not accidentally, the most Romantic and least American of genres, the ballad, became central to the new American idiom that Lowell so artfully constructed in the ballad lecture. For Lowell, the ballad genre formed the precise, concrete linkage between the spiritual and the material which he needed in order to imagine the practical activity inherent in true nationalism. On the one hand, they were marvelously constructed, so well made in fact that they could not be imitated even by the greatest poets of the modern age. On the other, they were wholly without manufacture, "coming up like violets." A Newtonian impossibility, they occupied the space "between metaphor and metaphysics" absolutely essential to the Transcendentalist idea of poetic creativity (Abrams 1958[1953]:262-297; Buell 1973:15). It did not matter which contemporary dichotomy one chose, past and present, poet and nature, individual self and social world, local interest and universal truth, imagination and reality, ballads were capable of containing both in the same space at the same time and thus of restoring the unity that had been lost as a consequence of what Emerson described as the "key" to modern times: "the mind has become aware of its self" (as quoted in Yoder 1978:xiii).

Even better, ballad makers suffered no ill consequences for their trespass on the ground of divine creation. Contemporary poetics required authors to annihilate the self in their quest to occupy this orphic space (Hartman 1970[1962]:50-51; Wilson 1982:27-50; Yoder 1978:3-30); yet in doing so, they risked falling into solipsism. In Lowell's hands, however, the ballad had become the perfect escape from the trap of self-absorption. Romantic/Transcendentalist ideology sought to enact the "poem as hetrocosm" (Abrams 1958[1953]:263), that is, as the creative space in which the act of writing poetry and that of God creating the universe became isomorphic. Because the ballad, according to Lowell, was poetry without consciousness or craft, ballad makers had none of the contemporary poet's need to transcend the self through the self to experience original creation (Hartman 1970[1962]). Hence, in the ballad, they were able to assume their roles as prophets/poets/seers, as completely public selves, receiving and then communicating their simultaneously national and universal message. In ballad making, they became Emerson's ideal poet who "is made great by means of the predominance of the universal nature: he has only to open his mouth, and it speaks; he has only to be forced to act, and it acts" (as quoted in Wilson 1982:22).[9]

Accordingly, their very improbability made ballads central to the development of an American character. "The present is epical to him who hears it," Lowell challenged his audience and the ballad now gave life to the spirit from which such American hearing might arise. Of course, no contemporary American would make ballads. In fact, Lowell told them it was both futile and vulgar to try. Neither would they make American poetry if they sought their muses in models. Rather, Lowell said, if they wished to make national poetry, American poets must learn to make that poetry the way ballad makers made ballads. Like their ballad counterparts, American poets must learn to make poems that emptied themselves of "thinking" at the very moment that they filled with "the popular heart and memory." Such activity, of course, would necessarily follow the traditional Romantic path. As Geoffrey Hartman has noted, American poets suffered from inescapable modernity, and they would have to overcome the "death-in-life" of consciousness and heroically trace their own road through "a purgatory so to speak, [to] gain access to a cosmic consciousness which brings true union with all mankind" (Hartman 1970[1962]:50). But by studying the ballad, by learning the features of real pathos and genuine sentiment, by learning to separate base language from true speech, and by hearing and seeing and rejecting imitation, American poets might lessen their purgatory and learn how to make without making.

More importantly what held for national poetry held for the nation as well. Lowell had spent a great deal of energy analyzing ballad poetry, but his subject remained nation building. If poets could find a space wherein to create this contemporary national poetics, then their example and, more importantly, the power of their work might lead American democracy itself to realize its potential to develop a new public morality to replace the morality that had been eroded by sectional crisis and ethnic strife. Interestingly, Lowell's valediction of choice gave him exactly the weapon he needed to construct such a morality. English critics delighted in the supposed backwardness of American life because it secured their priority and their superiority, but it was no accident that Coleridge and Wordsworth, for example, plotted England's escape into authentic nationalism by promoting the fantasy of passive surrender to unselfconsciousness rather than submit to the German-inspired Teutonic myth of an ancient tribal past. Like their American counterparts half a century later, these English poets realized that their own spotted history offered small hope of independence and that the Scots to their northern flank threatened their claim to much of British traditional poetry. They promoted transcendent reverie (complete with the proverbial man from Porlock who spoiled it all with a knock at the door) and shared common cause with Lowell's substitution of choice for necessity.

However, as Lowell was at pains to demonstrate, common cause cut the English more deeply than it did the Americans. English claims to a nationhood born in the age of the epic depended on the Anglo-Norman poets' rendering of Arthurian myth. But if the Norman invasion delayed the birth of an English nation, as Lowell argued, so that the ballads were the first "true folk songs" in English, then English national character could as easily be derived from New England as New England's character could be said to spring from Elizabethan Britain. For all his identification of the ballad as medieval in tone, Lowell just as adamantly counted its age from the times of Shakespeare, through the conquest and settlement of North America, through the Glorious Revolution, properly ending only in the French and Indian War. If these years, especially the last 200, were England's true national moment, then such an England was much too young to crow loudly and her America was just old enough to join the chorus.

More crucially, this wonderfully savage twist of the British lion's tail gave Lowell the ammunition that he needed to secure his New England version of American nationalism. At its simplest, it allowed him to defend himself from English attack by making choice essential not only to genuine American character but to genuine English character as well.[10] Lowell's not-so-oblique citation of martyr fires wrote the history of modern England from Henry VIII's "half Popish and half Protestant" church to the Glorious Revolution as a providential narrative in which high and low ceased to be divided, faith overcame politics and class, and English culture was purified and made whole. More importantly, it reminded his audience that Puritan New England had as much to do with the holy war against Charles I and Archbishop Laud as any member of the New Model Army and, hence, was as much responsible for the making of English character as were the English. In fact, Lowell went so far as to imply that American unwillingness to retreat from popular theocracy to restored monarchy marked the difference between true national character and false consciousness. New England, he said, chose differently at a time when that choice was as much about the sharpening of English national character as it was about rulers and religion. And because its "living commonwealth" husbanded what Britain abandoned, English character produced not simply two different Protestantisms with two different politics but two different national characters—one grounded on one side of the ocean in hardships of religion and the other on the other side of the ocean in the comforts of monarchy.

Most crucially, this particular ancestral election justified Lowell's covenant of choice as the heart of a democratic Romantic nationalism. Choice, the covenant says, is the only way to an American community. Yet it says with greater force that just choosing is not sufficient. According to Lowell, it was not enough to substitute an active, internalized American character for the externalized, passive desires of European Romanticism. What mattered was that character choose correctly. For Lowell, the freedom to choose was maintained only because its exercise was circumscribed by the morality of those who did the choosing. It is here also that his choice of the ballad as his defining genre takes on its greatest force. Ballads are "the only true folk songs we have in English," not only because they are authentically national but also because their creators were steadfast to the values of the community and to the desires of the whole. Once more, in the realms of poetry, no one can know what America's true folksongs will be. They will not be ballads, and, although sad, that is fine. But whatever they are, they will nor occur unless America's poets are committed to the virtues that promote true nationalism.

By implication, it is the same in politics, almost. Here also, we cannot know what the final shape of America's true national character will be. That character, and the nation it represents, is still unsung, is still awaiting Americans in the future to realize its potential and to compose (no doubt with a wink) the "only true folk songs" of America. But here we can identify the path most likely to bring Americans to their truest national future. Simply put, for Lowell, true American character would follow the New England way. As much as anyone, Lowell said, New Englanders had helped to make Englishmen into Englishmen. Accordingly, that section's past was a perfect prologue for America's future. By revering New England for its unity and by emulating its steadfast morality, the rest of the nation would discover that its true heritage could only be made by a people who preached harmony instead of selfishness and who valued human dignity over profit. True American nationalism, like true New England piety, would value the morality of kind and not the desires of class or the appetites of section.[11]

. . . . .

We are led back to Child's tears and to the question of why he wept. He cried, I would argue, not simply because it was a proper Victorian act for the proper Victorian gentleman he was but rather because with the death of James Russell Lowell he lost touch with the hope of his youth. If it is anything, James Russell Lowell's ballad lecture is a dream of the American future, and it delights in that promised land as only a lecture spoken to a generation that did not know that the Civil War was inevitable could. James Russell Lowell was Francis James Child's best reminder of those young American dreams unencumbered either by the scholar's reticence or the scientist's gaze. Moreover, Lowell gave a distinctly American cast to what would be, for Child, a lifelong but decidedly un-American activity. Child's American searches elicited only a few ballads and his one mature critical essay (published in 1874) left little room for Americans to create the kind of poetry that Lowell promised them was within their power. But no less than Lowell, Child wrote the conditions of American character, and if his search was less innocent, it was only because history had taught his generation painfully that Lowell's vision cost more than they were willing to pay. Child weeps, then, for his friend, but more, I suggest, for the passing of his friend's version of the American dream.

This is not to suggest that James Russell Lowell's American dream ought to stand as a rediscovered foundation for American ballad scholarship. His faults loom too large for that honor. His Romanticism, his class anxiety, his narrow politics, and his parochialism are all reminders that his writing of New England onto American national character was merely a politely phrased, Anglo-Saxon racism, at once much too comforting and much too useful to the power brokers of the 19th and 20th centuries. His vision of New England as the true beginning of American civic culture provided a model of social class in which everything of value moved in orderly fashion from above simply because those at the top were the most enlightened. And we cannot claim that Lowell's values were merely ancillary to the progress of American folk studies. True, he never pretended to be a folklorist, but his vision is clearly woven into our theory and practice. His models of high and low, his opposition of the backwoodsman and the sophisticated elite, his attempt to reconcile nationalism with a democratic ethos by valorizing the ballad—all reflect the contradictions between history and desire that reside at the heart of American folk studies' persisting appetite for nostalgia without memory.

Still, even so, we owe him a great debt. Had Lowell not lectured, American folklorists might continue to imagine themselves as stateless. Because he spoke, they are reminded that the American study of the ballad was an American response spoken in American terms to an American audience in the hopes of satisfying American needs. James Russell Lowell lectured his audience on the ballad because that was what any Romantic would do to reconstruct the essence of national identity. He preached individualism because that was what any American Romantic would do to convince an audience that a democratic nationalism was possible. He said what he said because he believed that the world of his fellow New Englanders held the best hope for a genuinely American self. Contemporary folklorists need not purchase his false historical consciousness. We need not believe in his ideas, and we must not defend his politics; but we cannot afford to deny either, for both connect us to a history that we have forgotten is ours. Without his lecture, American ballad scholars might think themselves strangers in their own land. With it, they may find themselves, albeit uncomfortably, at home.

Notes

I would like to thank Roger D. Abrahams, Regina Bendix, Thomas Hietala, Jerrold Hirsch, and Donald Irving for their critical responses to this essay.

1. Francis James Child to Emily Tuckerman, 23 August 1891, as quoted in Home and Cottrell 1952:830.
2. Lowell provided invaluable aid to Child in his pursuit of ballad manuscripts, as a jocular request from Child indicates: "As Rector of St. Andrews, thou art naturally Lord of all Scotland. Let thy first decree be that every ballad known to any lady, maidservant, fishwife, dairymaid or nurse be given up under penalties of misprision & praemunire to all that shall be art & part in the withholding of the same" (Howe and Cottrell 1952:68).
3. Child was not the only one of Lowell's contemporaries to be moved by the lectures. Scudder notes that Longfellow wrote in his diary that Lowell's first lecture was an "admirable performance," and that the lecture "on the old English ballads, one of the best of the course." He also mentions that Charles Sumner wrote to Longfellow that "Lowell's lecture on Milton lifted me for a whole day. It was the utterance of genius in honor of genius" (1901:301). Edward Everett Hale echoed these compliments at the end of the century: "It is no wonder that the lectures were so popular. They are of the best reading to this day, full of fun, full of the most serious thought as well. And you find in them at every page, I may say, seeds which he has planted elsewhere for other blossoms and fruit" (1899:114-115).
4. Those unable to attended the lectures were not completely excluded. Robert Carter, Lowell's friend, undertook to transcribe Lowell's words for publication in the *Boston Daily Advertiser.* Carter's transcripts were later privately printed by The Rowfant Club of Cleveland (Lowell 1897).
5. This is from James Russell Lowell's lecture "The Ballads." All quotations, unless otherwise cited, are from the handwritten version of this essay which may be found in the James Russell Lowell Papers, Houghton Library MS, Am 183.33, Harvard University (published by permission of the Houghton Library).
6. Lowell's sensitivity to the issue of American literary independence spanned his entire career. Writing at the end of 1848 to C. F. Briggs, possibly in reference to his "Fable for Critics," published in October of that year, he declared, "I am the first poet who has endeavored to express the American Idea, and I shall be popular by and by" (Lowell to C. F. Briggs, 14 December 1848, in Lowell 1893:104). And in 1869 he reiterated his rejection of England: "We are worth nothing except so far as we have disinfected ourselves of Anglicisms" (Lowell 1870:272). Still, his greatest commentary on the subject can be found in the aforementioned "Fable." "You steal Englishman's books and think Englishmen's thoughts, / With their salt on her tail your wild eagle is caught; / Your literature suits its each whisper and motion / To what will be thought of it over the ocean; / The cast clothes of Europe your statesmanship tries / And mumbles again the old blarney and lies;— / Forget Europe wholly, your veins throb with blood, / To which the dull current in hers is but mud; / Let her sneer, let her say your experiment fails, / In her voice there's a tremble e'en now while she rails, / And your shore will soon be in the nature of things / Covered thick with the gilt driftwood of runaway kings" (Lowell 1978[1848]:136).
7. An interesting continuation of Lowell's arguments against linguistic zealots can be found in his introduction to the second series of *The Biglow Papers,* where he wrote, "In choosing the Yankee dialect, I did not act without forethought. It had long seemed to me that the great vice of American writing and speaking was a studied want of simplicity, that we were in danger of coming to look on our mother-tongue as a dead language, to be sought in the grammar and dictionary rather than in the heart and that our only chance of escape was by seeking it at its living sources among those who were, as Scottowe says of Major-General Gibbons, 'divinely illiterate'" (Lowell 1978[1867]:442). Still, although this valori-

zation of the common people appears remarkably democratic, Lowell's intentions are less beneficent. It is one thing to attack the critics with evidence of their idolatry; it is quite another to burden the common people with unsolicited and dangerous gifts. Lowell may have believed sincerely, as he told his audience in the ballad lecture, both that "the nearer you come to the primitive, natural man, the more full of pith is the speech" and that "it is because men of genius have the great gift of being natural that they have the power to speak livingly," but saying so does more harm than good. Not all backwoodsmen ennoble speech, and not all of Shakespeare is natural. More to the point, Shakespeare will still command the respect of the governing class even if only some of his creations are judged works of genius. But a "natural" man whose speech is dull commands no respect. Like Crevecour's frontiersmen or Huck's Pap, a natural man who does not live up to Romantic expectations may find himself named a barbarian. Accordingly, much of what Lowell argues throughout his talk suffers from what Renato Rosaldo defines as "imperialist nostalgia" wherein, "when the so-called civilizing process destabilizes forms of life, the agents of change experience transformations of other cultures as if they were personal losses" (1989:70).

8. According to Duberman, Lowell was delighted to receive the offer "the place has sought me, not I, it" (Duberman 1966:141). His only hesitation was that he did not feel that he was competent for the post, and his response to the offer was to accept and then to request a leave of absence for a year to go abroad to master Spanish and German.

9. This quality of transparency and the threat that it poses to the solidity of nature and the coherence of the social world is overcome in Emerson, as I have argued it is in Lowell and later American folk-song scholarship, through attention to the arena of folklore, and particularly, to the fable (see Ellison 1984:208-227). Quoting first from Emerson's *Journals*: "Why must . . . the philosopher mince his words & fatigue us with explanation? He speaks from the Reason & being of course contradicted word for word by the Understanding he stops like a cogwheel at every notch to explain. Let him say, I *idealize,* & let that be once for all: or I *sensualize,* & then the Rationalist may stop his ears. . . . Fable avoids the difficulty, is at once exoteric and esoteric, & is clapped by both sides . . ." (Emerson 1965:31, quoted in Ellison 1984:225); she asserts further that fable for Emerson "occupies a special ontological realm where it can evade the strict either/or categorization fostered by the bad Romantic habit of applying the Reason/Understanding dichotomy too strictly. It is both ideal and sensual, 'exoteric' and 'esoteric,' [and] . . . reiterates Coleridge's query, 'Though not *fact,* must it needs be false?'" (Emerson 1966:329, as quoted in Ellison 1984:225).

10. It is worth remembering that Longfellow, whose professorship was his to lose, had written the following dialogue in *Kavanaugh:* "Then you think our literature is never to be any thing but an imitation of the English? Not at all. It is not an imitation, but, as someone has said, a continuation. It seems to me that you take a very narrow view of the subject. On the contrary, a very broad one. No literature is complete until the language in which it is written is dead. We may well be proud of our task and of our position. Let us see if we can build in any way worthy of our forefathers. But I insist upon originality. Yes, but without spasms and convulsions. Authors must not, like Chinese soldiers, expect to win victories by turning somersets in the air. Well, really, the prospect from your point of view is not very brilliant. Pray, what do you think of our national literature? Simply, that a national literature is not the growth of a day. Centuries must contribute their dew and sunshine to it. Our own is growing slowly but surely, striking its roots downward, and its branches upward, as is natural; and I do not wish, for the sake of what some people call originality, to invert it, and try to make it grow with its roots in the air. And as for having it so savage and wild as you want it, I have only to say, that all literature, as well as all art, is the result of culture and intellectual refinement" (Longfellow 1965[1850]:86-87).

11. In foregrounding the morality of choice, Lowell once again linked himself to a central element of Romantic ideology. Consider Hölderlin's rendering of the same belief: "Yet, fellow poets, us it behoves to stand / Bareheaded beneath God's thunderstorms, / To grasp the Father's ray, no less, with our own two hands / And, wrapping in song the beautiful gift / To offer it to the people. / For only if we are pure in heart, / Like children, and our hands are guiltless, / The father's ray, the pure, will not seer our hearts" (Hölderlin 1961, as quoted in Wilson 1982:23).

References Cited

Abrams, Meyer H. 1958[1953]. *The Mirror and the Lamp: Romantic Theory and the Critical Tradition.* New York: Columbia University Press.

———. 1971. *Natural Supernaturalism: Tradition and Revolution in Romantic Literature.* New York: Norton.

Abrahams, Roger D. 1988. Rough Sincerities: William Wells Newell and the Discovery of Folklore in Late-19th Century America. In *Folk Roots, New Roots: Folklore in American Life,* ed. Jane S. Becker and Barbara Franco, pp. 61-75. Lexington, Mass.: Museum of Our National Heritage.

———. 1992. Phantoms of Romantic Nationalism. *Journal of American Folklore* 106:3-37.

Allen, H. C. 1959. *The Anglo-American Relationship since 1783.* London: Adams and Charles Black.

Anderson, Douglas. 1990. *A House Undivided: Domesticity and Community in American Literature.* Cambridge: Cambridge University Press.

Beals, Carleton. 1960. *Brass-Knuckle Crusade: The Great Know-Nothing Conspiracy, 1820-1860.* New York: Hastings House.

Bell, Michael J. 1988. "No Borders to the Ballad Maker's Art": Francis James Child and the Politics of the People. *Western Folklore* 47:285-307.

Bercovitch, Sacvan. 1975. *The Puritan Origins of the American Self.* New Haven, Conn.: Yale University Press.

———. 1978. *The American Jeremiad.* New Haven, Conn.: Yale University Press.

Buell, Lawrence. 1973. *Literary Transcendentalism: Style and Vision in the American Renaissance.* Ithaca, N.Y.: Cornell University Press.

Carafiol, Peter. 1991. *The American Ideal: Literary History as a Worldly Activity.* Oxford: Oxford University Press.

Duberman, Martin. 1966. *James Russell Lowell.* Boston: Houghton Mifflin.

Ellison, Julie. 1984. *Emerson's Romantic Style.* Princeton, N. J.: Princeton University Press.

Emerson, Ralph Waldo. 1965. *The Journals and Miscellaneous Notebooks of Ralph Waldo Emerson,* Vol. 5, ed. Merton M. Sealts, Jr. Cambridge, Mass.: Harvard University Press.

———. 1966. *The Journals and Miscellaneous Notebooks of Ralph Waldo Emerson,* Vol. 6, ed. Ralph A. Orth. Cambridge, Mass.: Harvard University Press.

———. 1981. *The Portable Emerson.* ed. Carl Bode and Malcolm Cowley. New York: Viking Penguin.

Fellman, Michael. 1979. Rehearsal for the Civil War: Antislavery and Proslavery at the Fighting Point Is Kansas, 1854-1856. In *Antislavery Reconsidered,* ed. Lewis Perry and Michael Fellman, pp. 287-307. Baton Rouge: Louisiana University Press.

Gordon, G. S. 1942. *Anglo-American Literary Relations.* London: Oxford University Press.

Hale, E. E. 1899. *James Russell Lowell and His Friends.* Boston: Houghton Mifflin.

Hansen, Olaf. 1990. *Aesthetic Individualism and Practical Intellect: American Allegory in Emerson, Thoreau, Adams and James.* Princeton, N. J.: Princeton University Press.

Hartman, Geoffrey. 1970[1962]. Romanticism and Anti-Self-Consciousness. In *Romanticism and Consciousness: Essays in Criticism,* ed. Harold Bloom, pp. 31-60. Ithaca, N.Y.: Cornell University Press.

Hietala, Thomas R. 1985. *Manifest Design: Anxious Aggrandizement in Late Jacksonian America.* Ithaca, N.Y.: Cornell University Press.

Hölderlin, Friedrich. 1961. Wie wenn am Feiertage. In *Samtliche Werke,* vol. 4, trans. James D. Wilson, p. 153. Stuttgart: W. Kohlhammer.

Holt, Michael F. 1992. *Political Parties and American Political Discontent: From the Age of Jackson to the Age of Lincoln.* Baton Rouge: Louisiana State University Press.

Howard, Leon. 1952. *Victorian Knight-Errant.* Berkeley: University of California Press.

Howard, Victor B. 1990. *Conscience and Slavery: The Evangelistic Calvinist Domestic Missions, 1837-1861.* Kent, Ohio: Kent State University Press.

Howe, DeWolfe, and G. W. Cottrell, Jr., eds. 1952. *The Scholar's Friend: Letters of Francis James Child and James Russell Lowell.* Cambridge, Mass: Harvard University Press.

Hustvedt, Sigurd Bernhard. 1930. *Ballad Books and Ballad Men.* Cambridge, Mass.: Harvard University Press.

Kammen, Michael. 1991. *Mystic Chords of Memory: The Transformation of Tradition in American Culture.* New York: Knopf.

Kronick, Joseph G. 1984. *American Poetics of History: From Emerson to the Moderns.* Baton Rouge: Louisiana State University Press.

Lears, T. J. Jackson. 1981. *No Place of Grace: Antimodernism and the Transformation of American Culture, 1880-1920.* New York: Pantheon Books.

Lease, Benjamin. 1981. *Anglo-American Encounters: England and the Rise of American Literature.* Cambridge: Cambridge University Press.

Linberg, Kathrine V. 1991. Whitman's Convertable Terms: America, Self, Ideology. In *Theorizing American Literature: Hegel, the Sign, and History.* ed. Bainard Cowan and Joseph Kronick, pp. 233-268. Baton Rouge: Louisiana State University Press.

Longfellow, Henry W. 1965[1850]. *Kavanagh: A Tale.* ed. Jean Downey. New Haven, Conn.: College & University Press.

Lovejoy, A. O. 1924. On the Discrimination of Romanticisms. *PMLA* 39:229-253.

Lowell, James Russell. 1870[1869]. On a Certain Condescension in Foreigners. In *The Works of James Russell Lowell. Literary Essays, Vol. III,* pp. 220-254. Boston: Houghton Mifflin.

———. 1893. *Letters of James Russell Lowell.* 2 vols., ed. Charles Eliot Norton. New York: Harper and Bros.

———. 1897. *Lectures on the English Poets.* Transcribed by Robert Carter. Cleveland, Ohio: The Rowfant Club.

———. 1902. *The Anti-Slavery Papers of James Russell Lowell.* 2 vols. Boston: Houghton Mifflin and Company.

———. 1913[1849]. Nationality in Literature. In *The Round Table,* ed. Richard G. Badger, pp. 9-39. Boston: The Gorham Press.

———. 1978[1867]. *The Poetical Works of James Russell Lowell,* revised with a new introduction by Marjorie R. Kaufman. Boston: Houghton Mifflin.

Martin, Ronald E. 1991. *American Literature and the Destruction of Knowledge.* Durham, N.C.: Duke University Press.

Mulkern, John R. 1990. *The Know-Nothing Party in Massachusetts: The Rise and Fall of a People's Movement.* Boston: Northeastern University Press.

Pease, Donald E. 1987. *Visionary Compacts: American Renaissance Writings in Cultural Context.* Madison: University of Wisconsin Press.

Rosaldo, Renato. 1989. *Culture and Truth: The Remaking of Social Analysis.* Boston: Beacon Press.

Riddel, Joseph N. 1991. Thresholds of the Sign: Reflections on "American" Poetics. In *Theorizing American Literature: Hegel, the Sign, and History,* ed. Bainard Cowan and Joseph G. Kronick, pp. 53-82. Baton Rouge: Louisiana State University Press.

Ruland, Richard. 1981. The Mission of an American Literary History. In *The American Identity,* ed. Rob Kroes, pp. 46-64. Amsterdam: American Institute of the University of Amsterdam.

Scudder, Horace E. 1901. *James Russell Lowell.* Boston: Houghton Mifflin.

Somkin, Fred. 1967. *Unquiet Eagle: Memory and Desire in the Idea of American Freedom.* Ithaca, N.Y.: Cornell University Press.

Spengemann, William C. 1989. *A Mirror for Americanists: Reflections on the Idea of an American Literature.* Hanover, N.H.: University Press of New England.

Spencer, Benjamin. 1957. *The Quest for Nationality: An American Literary Campaign.* Syracuse, N.Y.: Syracuse University Press.

Spiller, Robert E. 1929. The Verdict of Sidney Smith. *American Literature* 1:3-11.

Walters, Ronald G. 1976. *The Anti-Slavery Appeal: American Abolitionism after 1830.* Baltimore: Johns Hopkins University Press.

Weisbuch, Robert. 1986. *Atlantic Double-Cross: American Literature and British Influence in the Age of Emerson.* Chicago: University of Chicago Press.

Wilson, James D. 1982. *The Romantic Heroic Ideal.* Baton Rouge: Louisiana State University Press.

Yoder, R. A. 1978. *Emerson and the Orphic Poet in America.* Berkeley: University of California Press.

Zumwalt, Rosemary L. 1988. *American Folklore Scholarship: A Dialogue of Dissent.* Bloomington: Indiana University Press.

FURTHER READING

Criticism

Brodie, Edward H., Jr. "Lowell's *Biglow Papers*: No. 1." *The Explicator* 42, No. 4 (Summer 1984): 21-23.

> Attempts to rectify a common misinterpretation of the opening poem of Lowell's *Biglow Papers.*

Gozzi, Raymond D. "Lowell's *The Cathedral* and Frost's 'Happiness Makes Up in Height for What It Lacks in Length.'" *The Explicator* 45, No. 3 (Spring 1987): 28-30.

> Considers the possible influence of Lowell's *The Cathedral* on Robert Frost's poem.

Russo, John Paul. "*Isle of the Dead*: Italy and the Uncanny in Arnold Böcklin, Sheridan Le Fanu, and James Russell Lowell." *Romance Languages Annual* I (1989): 202-209.

> Discusses the image of Italy as a "land of death" in Lowell's travelogues.

Tucker, Edward L. "James Russell Lowell and Robert Carter: The *Pioneer* and Fifty Letters from Lowell to Carter." *Studies in the American Renaissance* (1987): 187-246.

> Details the collaboration of Lowell and Robert Carter on the short-lived literary periodical, the *Pioneer.*

Wortham, Thomas. "William Cullen Bryant and the Fireside Poets." In *Columbia Literary History of the United States,* edited by Emory Elliott, pp. 278-88. New York: Columbia University Press, 1988.

> Includes a brief discussion of Lowell's influence on American literary culture in the 1840s.

Additional coverage of Lowell's life and career is contained in the following sources published by the Gale Group: *Concise Dictionary of American Literary Biography, 1640-1865;* and *Dictionary of Literary Biography,* Vols. 1, 11, 64, 79, 189.

Walter Pater
1839-1894

English essayist, novelist, and fictional portrait writer. For further information on Pater's career, see *NCLC,* Volume 7.

INTRODUCTION

Considered one of the greatest English critics of the nineteenth century, Pater was a major proponent of aestheticism who helped to make Renaissance art appreciated in his era. Distinguished as the first major English writer to formulate an explicitly aesthetic philosophy of life, he promoted the "love of art for art's sake" as the richest way to experience life passionately. In his *Studies in the History of the Renaissance* (1873) and *Marius the Epicurean: His Sensations and Ideas* (1885), Pater is both an original stylist and a highly perceptive critic who notes things others do not. *Marius the Epicurean* has been called the first anti-novel, so unlike most novels is its style and structure. Exalting beauty, art, and the artist, Pater's writings have appealed to and influenced many authors. Oscar Wilde and the young William Butler Yeats are included among his acknowledged disciples, and critics have detected Pater's influence in the work of Virginia Woolf, James Joyce, Wallace Stevens, Joseph Conrad, Ezra Pound, and T. S. Eliot. Pater is recognized as a master prose stylist and a leading exemplar of impressionist criticism.

BIOGRAPHICAL INFORMATION

Pater was born in Shadwell, East London, the second of four children of Richard Pater and Maria Hill. His father, a surgeon, died when Pater was two years old, and the remaining members of the family moved to Enfield, where Pater attended grammar school. He enrolled in King's School in Canterbury in 1853, the year before the death of his mother, and in 1858 won a scholarship to Queen's College at Oxford, where he studied the classics and was inspired by John Ruskin's *Modern Painters.* After taking a degree in humane letters in 1862 and working briefly as a tutor of private pupils, he accepted a fellowship at Brasenose College, Oxford, in 1864—a position he would keep until his death. His first published essay, a work on Samuel Taylor Coleridge, appeared in *Westminster Review* in 1866. Though published anonymously, "Coleridge's Writings," with its promotion of relativism, made Pater's colleagues question his intellectual heterodoxy. Pater lived the last twenty-five years of his life with his two unmarried sisters in both Oxford and London. Much of what is known or thought to be known concerning Pater's life is gleaned from the autobiographical "The Child in the House" (which first appeared in *Macmillan's* in 1878, and was published as *An Imaginary Portrait* in 1894). Indeed, critics have noted that nearly all of Pater's work contains autobiographical elements, and that he often wrote about himself while apparently recounting another's life and career.

MAJOR WORKS

In 1867 Pater published, again anonymously, "Winckelmann," a piece extolling Greek culture and art, followed by "Poems by William Morris" (1868), "Notes on Leonardo da Vinci" (1869), "A Fragment of Sandro Botticelli" (1870), and "The Poetry of Michelangelo" (1871), among others. In these essays Pater eschewed absolute critical standards in favor of his own personal impressions of the artists' works. Pater collected his various writings and included them with other pieces in *Studies in the History of the Renaissance,* a volume which provoked strong objections to his methods. Most notorious is the book's "Conclusion," Pater's boldest statement of his relativist view of art and life. In the "Conclusion" Pater explained that we are here but for a brief interval; that we should strive to expand this interval; and that to do so we need to get "as many pulsations as possible into the given time." Pater asserted that practicing the love of art for art's sake is the best means of multiplying one's consciousness. The essay created a scandal at Oxford and damaged Pater's chances for academic advancement, with critics attacking the piece as antireligious propaganda that could negatively influence impressionable young minds. Conversely, young "aesthetes" such as Oscar Wilde, Lionel Johnson, and Arthur Symons interpreted the "Conclusion" as a manifesto for artistic freedom and became the leading members of his coterie of literary disciples. Pater, the precise reasons for which scholars still argue, withdrew the "Conclusion" from the second edition, retitled *The Renaissance: Studies in Art and Poetry* (1877). His next major work was *Marius the Epicurean,* which was written with the avowed purpose of elucidating the thoughts suggested in the "Conclusion." The ambitious novel follows the career of the fictional character Marius as he searches for a satisfactory philosophy of life in Aurelian Rome. Marius considers but eventually rejects a number of nondeist philosophies but is finally attracted to the ritual and sense of community which he discovers in the early Christian church. *Imaginary Portraits* (1887) is a collection of essays that had been published in *Macmillan's Magazine,* including "Sebastian van Storck," "A Prince of Court Painters: Extracts from an Old French Journal," "Denys l'Auxerrois," and "Duke Carl of Rosenmold." In these essays Pater imaginatively recreated the interaction of various intellectual, artistic, and moral temperaments with the cultures of selected periods of historical transition. The 1888 edition of *The Renaissance* contained the restored but slightly modified "Conclusion" and "The School of Giorgione," which discusses the relationship between form and matter in art. Five chapters of the novel *Gaston de Latour* were published in *Macmillan's* in 1888 (published in book form in 1896) before Pater abandoned the work. Two additional major works were published in Pater's lifetime: *Appreciations: With an Essay on Style* (1889) and *Plato and Platonism* (1893). In *Appreciations* Pater used subjective impressionism to elucidate the qualities informing the genius of Coleridge, William Wordsworth, and others. The essay "Style" concerns itself with the art of writing prose and finding the perfect word to convey a particular mood and meaning. *Plato and Platonism* explored the genius of a culture which, in Pater's eyes, achieved a balance between the physical and the spiritual.

CRITICAL RECEPTION

In general Pater's contemporaries, mollified by his apparent rapprochement with Christianity in *Marius,* praised him in his final years. His reputation faltered, however, after the imprisonment of Wilde in 1895 and the general dissipation of other "aesthetic" disciples of Pater. In recent decades there has been a renewed critical interest in Pater, and scholars continue to find evidence of his profound influence on the works of many twentieth-century critics, poets, and novelists. Much modern interest has also been generated by Pater's possible homosexuality. While some scholars maintain that factual evidence of Pater's personal sexual orientation is at best scant, others have forwarded homoerotic and psychosexual readings of his work. A great deal of attention focuses on *Marius the Epicurean,* portions of which are generally considered autobiographical, and its attempt to, in Richard Dellamora's words, "reconsider Christianity so as to include homosexuality within it." The exact nature of Marius's interest in Christianity and the circumstances surrounding his death have provoked debate, as has the matter of how much of himself Pater wrote into Marius; Pater characteristically remained silent on the subject of his own personal faith. Pater's reputation now appears firmly established. J. Hillis Miller, writing in 1976, called Pater one of the greatest English literary critics of the nineteenth century and a "precursor of what is most vital in contemporary criticism." William E. Buckler asserts that Pater "is still one of a half-dozen indispensable critics in English; from, say, 1880 to 1920, he was without equal."

PRINCIPAL WORKS

Studies in the History of the Renaissance (essays) 1873; also published as *The Renaissance: Studies in Art and Poetry,* 1877
Marius the Epicurean: His Sensations and Ideas. 2 vols. (novel) 1885
Imaginary Portraits (fictional portraits) 1887
Appreciations: With an Essay on Style (essays) 1889
Plato and Platonism: A Series of Lectures (lectures) 1893
An Imaginary Portrait (fictional portrait) 1894; also published as *The Child in the House,* 1895
Greek Studies (essays) 1895
Miscellaneous Studies (essays) 1895
Essays from the "Guardian" (essays) 1896
Gaston de Latour (unfinished novel) 1896
Uncollected Essays (essays) 1903
The Works of Walter Pater. 10 Vols. (essays, novel, unfinished novel, fictional portraits, and lectures) 1910
Walter Pater: Selected Works (essays, novel, fictional portraits, and lecture) 1948
Letters of Walter Pater (letters) 1970

CRITICISM

J. Hillis Miller (essay date 1976)

SOURCE: "Walter Pater: A Partial Portrait" in *Walter Pater (Modern Critical Views),* edited by Harold Bloom, Chelsea House Publishers, 1985, pp. 75-95.

[*In the following essay, originally published in 1976, Miller examines Pater's thoughts on such topics as time, virtue, personality, uniqueness, repetition, form, meaning, and subjectivity; he also contends that the various and contradictory readings of his positions are irreconcilable.*]

Walter Pater is, along with Coleridge, Arnold, and Ruskin, one of the four greatest English literary critics of the nineteenth century. He is also, of the four, the most influential in the twentieth century and the most alive today, although often his influence can be found on writers who deny or are ignorant of what they owe to him. Pater is effective today as a precursor of what is most vital in contemporary criticism.

Pater may be placed in various lines or triangulated on various topographical surfaces. A slightly different perspective on him is gained through each of these various mappings, genealogies, or filiations. He is the nearest thing to Nietzsche England has, as Emerson is Nietzsche's nearest match in America. This could be put less invidiously by saying that Nietzsche is the Pater of the German-speaking world, Emerson the Pater of America. The three together form a constellation, with many consonances and dissonances among the three stars. Toward the past, Pater belongs to the line of English Romanticism, moving from the great Romantics—particularly Wordsworth and Coleridge, in this case—through Tennyson to the Pre-Raphaelites, among whom, along with Ruskin and Swinburne, Pater is a major critical voice. Another affiliation would link Pater to the English Protestant and empirical tradition going back to Locke and to the Puritan autobiographers of the seventeenth century, with their emphasis on private witnessing as the only genuine test of truth. The "aesthetic critic," in Pater's definition of him, must ask first and last, "What is this song or picture, this engaging personality presented in life or in a book, to *me*? What effect does it really produce on me?" Pater is also, however, one of the most important "translators" into Victorian England of Hegelian thought and of German idealism generally. He won his fellowship at Brasenose College, Oxford, as much for his first-hand knowledge of German as for his ability as a classicist. More important than all these associations, perhaps, is the filament that connects Pater with that strand of Western tradition which has been most antithetical to Plato: Heraclitus, the atomists, Epicurus, Lucretius, Joachim of Flora, Bruno, Spinoza, and Goethe.

In the other direction, toward the future, Pater's progeny also form more than one genetic line. Pater's influence on Yeats and, less obviously, on Wallace Stevens was decisive. This influence spread to other poets and novelists of the twentieth century: Joyce, Pound, Eliot, and many others. By way of Proust and the critics of the *Nouvelle Revue Française,* Pater is one of the progenitors of modern subjectivistic, "impressionistic," phenomenological criticism, the so-called "criticism of consciousness" of Georges Poulet and his associates. Another line, however, antithetical to that one, might be called "allegorical" criticism. This line leads from certain aspects of Ruskin through Pater and Wilde to Proust, and beyond Proust to Walter Benjamin and to the rhetorical or "deconstructive" criticism of our own moment in literary criticism. Jacques Derrida, Paul de Man, and Harold Bloom in their different ways exemplify this.

How Pater could produce such diverse "children," like a genetic pool containing potentially both blue-eyed and brown-eyed offspring, my reading of Pater will attempt to indicate. It must be remembered, however, that the figure of genetic "lines" is a trope. Like all figures it is not innocent; it begs the question it assists in raising. In literature, lines of influence go by leaps and swerves, with gaps and deviations. Sudden unpredictable mutation is the law, not the exception. That all reading is misreading is as true of the traditions of criticism as of literature itself. Influence works by opposition, so that the child is a "white" parody or travesty of the father, a mocking "double" or "second." Pater uses this figure in a curious passage at the beginning of Chapter Two of ***Marius the Epicurean*** (1885). The red rose, he says, came first, the white rose later, as its pale repetition. White things are "ever an after-thought, the doubles, or seconds, of real things, and themselves but half-real, half-material" (***Marius the Epicurean,*** 2 vols. London, 1892. I, 14). The question of the relation between the uniqueness of the individual entity and the way it exists as the recurrence of elements which have already been configured in previous ones is one of Pater's pervading concerns. Pater's own work may provide his interpreter with assistance in formulating his multiple relations to those who came before and after.

The remarkable early pages of ***Marius the Epicurean*** are half autobiographical no doubt, but autobiography veiled, displaced. Pater's early life is translated figuratively into the life of a Roman boy of the second century after Christ. Among the first things the reader learns of Marius is that the "old country-house, half farm, half villa" (***ME*** 5), where he passed his childhood, was famous for a "head of Medusa" (***ME*** 21) found nearby. The head was Greek work in bronze with golden *laminae.* An emblem there? The reader also remembers the passage in the essay on Leonardo da Vinci in ***The Renaissance*** (1873) where Pater cites Vasari's disturbing anecdote of the Medusa "painted on a wooden shield" (***The Renaissance: Studies in Art and Poetry.*** London, 1922. 105), which the young Leonardo prepared as a "surprise" for his father. This "childish" work was proleptic, Pater says, of the great Medusa of Leonardo's adult years:

> It was not in play that he painted that other Medusa, the one great picture which he left behind him in Florence. . . . What may be called the fascination of corruption penetrates in every touch its exquisitely finished beauty. About the dainty lines of the cheek the bat flits unheeded. The delicate snakes seem literally strangling each other in terrified struggle to escape from the Medusa brain. The hue which violent death always brings with it is in the features; features singularly massive and grand, as we catch them inverted, in a dexterous foreshortening, crown foremost, like a great calm stone against which the wave of serpents breaks.
>
> (***R*** 106)

What Sigmund Freud made of the Medusa one knows from "Das Medusenhaupt," written in 1922 and first published posthumously in 1940. The Medusa, says Freud, is hieroglyph for the fear of castration and for its veiling or supplementary assuaging. The Medusa head is a sign for the discovery of the absence of the maternal phallus. It also offers in the snakey locks of the Medusa frightening yet secretly reassuring proofs for the existence of that phallus. The Medusa's power to petrify, to turn a man into a column of stone, also offers frightening yet secretly reassuring proof of the spectator's masculinity. As Pater says, the Madusa of Leonardo is "the head of a corpse, exercising its powers through all the circumstances of death" (***R*** 106). All of Pater's most characteristic "portraits," including ***Marius,*** are of gifted young men doomed to an early death which is also somehow a fulfillment. Was Pater "phallogocentric," frozen like Leonardo himself at a Narcissistic or adolescent homosexual stage? Or did he liberate himself, accommodate himself to the absence of the Logos, head or chief source of meaning and power? Such a Logos fathers all later power but also renders it impotent. Did Pater remain fascinated with longing for a lost completeness which can only be obtained metaleptically, replacing early with late, the lost bliss that never was with the death that he imagines over and over for his various *personae?* Is Pater's work centered or acentered, and, if centered, what is its center, its origin, ground, or end?

A cluster of motifs in the early pages of ***Marius the Epicurean*** reinforces the motif of the Medusa head to form a hieroglyph of Pater's own. This composite emblem gathers many of the elements that recur throughout his work. Marius, the reader is told, had lost his father in early childhood, as did Pater himself. Marius's sorrow was "crossed at times by a not unpleasant sense of liberty, as he could but confess to himself, pondering, in the actual absence of so weighty and continual a restraint, upon the arbitrary power which Roman law gave to the parent over the son" (***ME*** 18). Alas, the sense of liberty was only a momentary illusion, for the dead father has become one of the many genii of the place, "a *genius* a little cold and severe" (***ME*** 11). The dead father, along with many other local gods, is the object of a religion of fear for Marius. Such a religion of propitiation and superstitious awe is still alive among children today, as in the singsong of urban sidewalk taboo: "If you step on a crack you'll break your mother's back; if you step on a line you'll break your father's spine." "A sense of conscious powers external to ourselves, pleased or displeased by the right or wrong conduct of every circumstance of daily life—that *conscience,* of which the old Roman religion was a formal, habitual recognition, was become in him a powerful current of feeling and observance" (***ME*** 5). Conscience becomes *ascêsis,* an instinctive habit of renunciation, a dainty fastidiousness, a willingness to give up, even a masochism, a pleasure in self-imposed suffering, with apotropaic motives. "Had the Romans a word for *unworldly?*" asks the narrator.

> The beautiful word *umbratilis* perhaps comes nearest to it; and, with that precise sense, might describe the spirit in which [Marius] prepared himself for the sacerdotal function hereditary in his family—the sort of mystic enjoyment he had in the abstinence, the strenuous self-control and *ascêsis,* which such preparation involved.
>
> (***ME*** 27)

Marius's mother had devoted herself to keeping her dead husband alive in her memory, and the boy Marius loves her devotedly. There is an odd episode, however, at the time of her death, which occurs, as did the death of Pater's mother, while the son is still a schoolboy, the mother going away from home to die. "For it happened," says the narrator, "that through some sudden incomprehensible petulance there had been an angry childish gesture, and a slighting word, at the very moment of her departure, actually for the last time" (***ME*** 45).

Fear of the dead father and a universalization of that fear in an uncanny sense of unseen powers requiring constant propitiation and love for the mother combined with some inexplicable resentment of her—these come together disguised as Marius's fear of snakes. This odd fear is described but not wholly explained. Fear of snakes is the embodiment of Marius's "sense of some unexplored evil, ever dogging his footsteps" (***ME*** 25). Its primal version is in fact a primal scene: "One fierce day in early summer, as he walked along a narrow road, he had seen the snakes breeding, and ever afterwards he avoided that place and its ugly associations, for there was something in the incident which made food distasteful and his sleep uneasy for many days afterwards" (***ME*** 25). The same sense of uncanny distaste recurs when, sometime later in Pisa, Marius sees "an African showman exhibiting a great reptile" (***ME*** 25), and later still in Rome, "a second time," he sees "a showman with his serpents" (***ME*** 26). The motif recurs once more, in case the reader has not already perceived its importance, in Marius's fear of the "great sallow-hued snakes" kept in the temple of the healing god Aesculapius (***ME*** 33).

Why did Marius, or, one guesses, Pater himself, so irrationally fear snakes? And why snakes coupling? Why did this disturb his pleasure in food and sleep? The narrator's answer is oblique:

> He wondered at himself indeed, trying to puzzle out the secret of that repugnance, having no particular dread of a snake's bite, like one of his companions, who had put his hand into the mouth of an old garden-god and roused there a sluggish viper. A kind of pity even mingled with his aversion, and he could hardly have killed or injured the animals, which seemed already to suffer by the very circumstances of their life, being what they were.
>
> (***ME*** 25-26)

The elements associated with the Medusa head recur here and are covertly interpreted. Parents coupling become snakes coupling, viewed with a combination of fascination, aversion, and pity. It is the pity of unawakened sexuality for the burden of the bestiality of sex combined with fear of the absent father and of his power of reprisal. The "unexplored" evil dogging Marius's footsteps becomes embodied in the snakes' breeding. This scene is proof that the phallus is still there, though the father is dead, as with the snakes on the Medusa's head. The phallus is there even as an attribute of the mother, for in the mouth of the old garden-god there is a sluggish viper, as there are snakes surrounding the open mouth and the dead face of the Medusa in the painting in the Uffizi. This repugnant yet somehow pleasurable discovery is displaced from Marius to "one of his companions," who, like Marius, has "no particular dread of a snake's bite." The act of impiety toward the god or of violation of the mother is not performed directly by the hero, except in that moment of petulance and in that slighting word at the time of her death. Presence and absence of an original fathering power, a paternal potency which yet must be an attribute of the mother, presence and absence both feared and desired in the tension of a double double bind—these are the pervasive Paterian elements brought evasively and unostentatiously together in the account of the childhood of Marius.

Is such a reading of a few fragments of ***Marius the Epicurean*** a clue to the rest of Pater? Is this cluster a valid synecdoche for the whole, standing in the same relation to all his work as, in Pater's own criticism, a representative figure such as Leonardo or Michelangelo stands to the Renaissance as a whole? What relation might there be between this repugnance for the coupling snakes, yet pleasure in rousing the viper in the mouth of the garden god, and Pater's methods as a critic, the themes and ideas which organize his work? Is all his work oriented by the dread and desire for a proof that the lost father is not really lost? Only a reading of the whole work could tell. The complexity and suggestiveness of the bits examined so far indicate that Pater must be read not so much for what he tells the reader about the artists and works he criticizes but a literary text demanding the same scrupulous decipherment, phrase by phrase, as the texts of Marcel Proust or of Walter Benjamin, two later writers in Pater's line who similarly require interrogation.

Pater's writing offers the same fascination to the reader as that of any major author, the fascination of a complexity which *works,* which hangs together, which may be "figured out" or resolved. His work has that consonance, those unexpected echoes of this passage with that passage, those hidden resonances and harmonies which Pater saw as the ideal of a musical form that would have absorbed all its matter into that form. Nevertheless, if, as Charles Rosen affirms, the basis of musical expression is dissonance, the critic must, in Pater's case, take note also of disharmonies, contradictions, omissions, hiatuses, incongruous elements which precisely do not "work." In such places the words seem to have exceeded the writer's apparent intention. Such dissonances may be the most important aspect of Pater's work, in spite of his claim in **"Style"** that the fire of a unified "sense of the world" will in the great writers have burned away such *surplusage* (***Appreciations.*** London, 1889. 16). In the something too much, the something left over, the odd detail which may not be evened in a musical form, the snake in the mouth of the garden god, the critic may find the clue and loose the thread that will unravel all that fine fabric of Pater's prose, with its decorous echo of pattern by pattern. The secret revealed by this unraveling may be not so much the hidden center of a personality as an enigma exceeding personality, a secret intrinsic to the materials Pater worked with—language and its concepts, figures, and narrative forms, myths or legends, *legenda,* "things for reading."

The apparent beginning of spiritual life for Pater is the moment, the intense and wholly individual instant of experience. As Pater says in the famous passage in the Conclusion to ***The Renaissance,*** each momentary experience, each "impression," is cut off by virtue of its uniqueness from all moments before and after. It is also entirely private: "Every one of those impressions is the impression of the individual in his isolation, each mind keeping as a solitary prisoner its own dream of a world" (***R*** 235). Moreover, each moment lasts but a moment, the blink of an eye, and then is gone. Time is flux, an endless stream "of impressions, unstable, flickering, inconsistent, which burn and are extinguished with our consciousness of them" (***R*** 235). The inevitable goal of each sequence is death, a final end anticipated and rehearsed in the little death of each moment as it flies. For Pater, the imminence of death and the intensity of experience are always only two sides of the same coin, "the sense of death and the desire of beauty: the desire of beauty quickened by the sense of death" (***A*** 227), as he puts it in the admirable essay on William Morris, **"Aesthetic Poetry."**

It would seem that the entire program of Pater's criticism follows from these solipsistic premises. Each man must concentrate all his attention on each moment as it passes, for that moment is all there is and all he has. He must purge by that effort of refinement or *ascêsis,* as essential in Pater's procedure as in the lives of those whose portraits he sketches, all impurities in the moment, all irrelevant associations, all false idealisms, such as those which, in Pater's understanding of Coleridge, weakened that great poet-critic's force (see **"Coleridge,"** ***A*** 64-106). The moment in its uniqueness or the critic in his experience of it may, then, shed all dross, burn with that "hard, gemlike flame" (***R*** 236). Criticism is the exact recording of what Pater calls the unique "virtue" of each moment, meaning by "virtue" the power or energy specific to the elements concentrated in that moment. Virtue is "the property each [moment] has of affecting one with a special, a unique, impression of pleasure" (***R*** ix), as Pater puts it in the Preface to ***The Renaissance,*** where such a strategy for criticism is most eloquently and exactly defined.

The function of aesthetic criticism is clear. The true critic has sharper impressions than others. He is more able than other people to discriminate the exact "virtue" of a given personality or work of art. He is also more gifted than others in his power of expression, as gifted, ideally, as the great writers themselves. He uses his gift of expression not to transmit the truth of his own personality, but to translate into his own language the unique virtue of the work or person he criticizes. He thereby transmits to his readers impressions they might otherwise miss, or, rather, he transmits subtly displaced repetitions of those impressions. Far from being, as is sometimes said, at liberty to make the work mean anything one likes, impressionism is rigorously bound by the work it describes. It is bound as much as the work itself by that truth of correspondence to a particular personality which Pater makes his ideal in **"Style."** The writer must translate accurately his inner vision. The critic must translate accurately that translation, as is done by that ideal translator of Plato who reproduces him "by an exact following, with no variation in structure, of word after word, as the pencil follows a drawing under tracing-paper" (***A*** 11). The goal of this translation, however, is the transmission of the exact flavor or quality of the consciousness behind the work.

The focus of all Pater's writing is personality, the personalities of Botticelli, Michelangelo, Leonardo, Wordsworth, Coleridge, and others in ***The Renaissance*** or in ***Appreciations*** (1889), the personalities of fictional characters in ***Marius the Epicurean, Imaginary Portraits*** (1887), and ***Gaston de Latour*** (1896), the personalities of mythological figures in certain of the ***Greek Studies*** (1895). Subjectivity—the self—is, it seems, the beginning, the end, and the persisting basis in all Pater's writings. In Pater's work, as in one important strand of the Western tradition generally, subjectivity is the name given to the *Logos,* paternal origin, goal, and supporting ground. Subjectivity is the measure, *ratio,* or "reason" for all the interchanges of person with person, by means of art, which Pater's work explores. As the word itself suggests, subjectivity, the subject, is what is 'thrown under' and therefore underlies all the fleeting impressions which make up what is. There is, after all, a snake in the mouth of the garden god. Pater's religious moments, for example in ***Marius the Epicurean,*** are an extrapolation from his positing of personality as a reassuring, ubiquitous *Logos.* His religion is "a sense of *conscious* powers external to ourselves" (***ME*** 5, emphasis added).

The critic's effort to identify precisely the unique virtue of a single impression or personality leads to an unexpected discovery. This discovery makes of Pater's criticism something quite different from what his stress on personality would make it seem to be. The moment, it turns out, though unique, is not single. Each "impression" is in fact "infinitely divisible" (***R*** 235). It is divisible because it is self-divided, an *Andersstreben,* or striving to be other than itself, as he calls it in **"The School of Giorgione"** (***R*** 134). The moment is in battle against itself in a way that recalls the Heraclitean flux, cited as an epigraph for the Conclusion, or the Parmenidean *polemos,* cosmic warfare. Perhaps it is also to be associated with that sadomasochistic element so evident in Pater's sense of human life and of relations between people.

The flame produced by the purification of an *ascêsis* is kindled by the bringing together of divided forces which burst into flame by their antagonistic proximity. That flame is "the focus where the greatest number of vital forces unite in their purest energy" (***R*** 236). The first example Pater gives in the Conclusion of the intense instant of sensation is "the moment . . . of delicious recoil from the flood of water in summer heat" (***R*** 233). Such a conjunction is the locus "of forces parting sooner or later on their ways" (***R*** 234), as brilliancy of gifts in an individual arises from "some tragic dividing of forces on their ways" (***R*** 237).

The uniqueness of each momentary impression is a result not of its singleness but of its special combination of contradictory forces. These flow into it from the past and are destined to divide again, each to go its separate way into the future. This means that the moment, which was at first seemingly so isolated, is in fact connected by multiple strands to past and future. Pater speaks of this, sometimes using a metaphor of streams meeting and dividing and sometimes of weaving and unweaving. If the moment is the meeting place of divided forces—the forces of a whole life, of an age, or of all the ages in their sequence (as in Pater's celebrated interpretation of *La Gioconda*)—then that moment in all its sensible vividness and uniqueness can stand for the life, for the age, or for all history. It can stand for these because it contains in concentrated essence forces universally distributed in time and space, meeting and dividing and meeting again. The validity of synecdoche is based on substantial participation. This conception of the moment as both individual and representative lies behind a splendid passage from **"The School of Giorgione,"** anticipating both Joyce's "epiphany" and certain passages in T. S. Eliot:

> Now it is part of the ideality of the highest sort of dramatic poetry, that it presents us with a kind of profoundly significant and animated instant, a mere gesture, a look, a smile, perhaps—some brief and wholly concrete moment, into which, however, all the motives, all the interest and effects of a long history, have condensed themselves, and which seem to absorb past and future in an intense consciousness of the present . . . exquisite pauses in time, in which, arrested thus, we seem to be spectators of all the fulness of existence, and which are like some consummate extract or quintessence of life.
>
> (***R*** 150)

Pater's materialist notion of impersonal forces underlying each personality involves a specific theory of repetition. This theory denies the possibility of finding any fixed origin for any person or impression. Such denial has important consequences for criticism. It means that the critic can never find an inaugural point for any idea or for any given hieroglyph of forces. There are no fathers, each apparent father being himself, often unwittingly, the heir of forces that have come together and then separated many times in the past. Whatever the critic reaches as an apparent beginning, a solid ground on which to base an interpretation, dissolves on inspection into a repetition. It is another gathering of elements of immemorial antiquity. As in Nietzsche, so in Pater, a sense of vertigo is generated by this infinite regression into the past, each "source" having another "source" behind it, and so on ad infinitum. No doctrine, no seemingly unique collocation of elements in a personality can be said to be a beginning or to have one.

The notion that the singular personality is Pater's version of the *Logos* is, it seems, exploded by his concept of repetition. What is, is the perpetually woven and rewoven anonymous elements or atoms, forces that have divided and come together for all eternity and that have an eternal future of rebirth and death. In place of the subject as *Logos,* Pater seems to put another equally traditional idea of the metaphysical ground. This idea, too, goes back to the Greeks, though more to Heraclitus, to the atomists, to Lucretius, or even to Aristotle than to Plato. The *Logos* is a ubiquitous and multiple force, energy, *energeia.* This energy is that paternal snake at the originless origin, perpetually born and reborn in the mouth of the god.

Paradoxically, it is apropos of Plato that Pater, in a splendidly eloquent passage at the beginning of ***Plato and Platonism*** (1893), most fully expresses his intuition of a universe without determinable origin. In such a universe, atoms are combined and recombined, world without end, in perpetual repetition in difference. "Plato's achievement," says Pater, "may well seem an absolutely fresh thing in the morning of the mind's history," but "in the history of philosophy there are no absolute beginnings" (***Plato and Platonism.*** London, 1893. 2, 1). Far from being a beginning, Plato, in Pater's view, was a decadent, or at least he lived in a decadent world. Its decadence is defined, in phrases characteristically Paterian in their weary cadence, as the presence everywhere of already used atoms of thought. There was a kind of intellectual pollution of the Greek air at the moment of its greatest cultural splendor:

> Yet in truth the world Plato had entered into was already almost weary of philosophical debate, bewildered by the oppositions of sects, the claims of rival schools. Language and the processes of thought were already become sophisticated, the very air he breathed sickly with off-cast speculative atoms.
>
> (***PP*** 2)

Pater uses four different metaphors to express the way these "off-cast atoms" of thought enter into the intimate texture of Plato's language. All these figures express the notion of tiny particles which make the, so to speak, cellular structure of Plato's thought. These are in no sense superficial borrowings which could conceivably be detached. One metaphor is of the grain of stone, another of parchment with multiple layers of writing, another of woven fabric, another of an organic body, but a similar structural image is in question in each case:

> Some of the results of patient earlier thinkers, even then dead and gone, are of the structure of his philosophy. They are everywhere in it, not as the stray carved corner of some older edifice, to be found here or there amid the new, but rather like minute relics of earlier organic life in the very stone he builds with . . . [I]n Plato, in spite of his wonderful savour of literary freshness, there is nothing absolutely new: or rather, as in many other very original productions of human genius, the seemingly new is old also, a palimpsest, a tapestry of which the actual threads have served before, or like the animal frame itself, every particle of which has already lived and died many times.
>
> (***PP*** 2, 3)

This image of a repetition not exterior but woven into the genetic structure of Plato's thinking leads to a powerful vision of an infinite regression back in time and outward beyond Western culture in an ever wider and deeper unsuccessful search for the beginnings of ideas whose immemorial antiquity deny Plato any status as an origin. Plato was not the inaugurator of an Occidental civilization merely, as Whitehead said, a "footnote" to his work. He was himself already a latecomer, an after-thought. He was a belated footnote to still earlier footnotes, themselves footnotes to footnotes, with nowhere an original text as such:

> The central and most intimate principles of [Plato's] teaching challenge us to go back beyond them, not merely to his own immediate, somewhat enigmatic master—to Socrates, who survives chiefly in his pages—but to various precedent schools of speculative thought, in Greece, in Ionia, in Italy; beyond these into that age of poetry, in which the first efforts of philosophic apprehension had hardly understood themselves; beyond that unconscious philosophy again, to certain constitutional tendencies, persuasions, forecasts of the intellect itself, such as had given birth, it would seem, to thoughts akin to Plato's in the older civilisations of India and of Egypt, as they still exercise their authority over ourselves.
>
> (***PP*** 2-3)

No element in Plato is new, not one speculative atom. What is new is the way of putting these elements together. In Pater's doctrine of recurrence, repetition is always with a difference. The difference lies in the way old forces are brought together once more in a slightly changed way and under new conditions. Pater's term for this novel way of assembling new materials is "form." Plato's originality lies in his brilliant novelty of form:

> Nothing but the life-giving principle of cohesion is new; the new perspective, the resultant complexion, the expressiveness which familiar thoughts attain by novel juxtaposition. In other words, the *form* is new. But then, in the creation of philosophical literature, as in all other products of art, *form,* in the full signification of that word, is everything, and the mere matter is nothing.
>
> (***PP*** 4-5)

Form is everything, matter nothing. Here is another point of overlapping with Nietzsche, who in the preface of 1886 to the second edition of *Die fröhliche Wissenschaft* (1882) praises the Greeks for stopping at the surface (*bei der Oberfläche*) and for believing in forms, tones, words (*an Formen, an Töne, an Worte*). What is Pater's concept of form? What is his critic to make of the abundance of metaphors which are essential to his expression of his thought—threads, forces, writing, and so on? What is the exact status of these figures, and why does he need more than one to express the "same" idea? In **"Style,"** Pater attempts to deny insofar as it is possible the figurative basis of language. He wants language to be the transparent reflection of a personal thought which preceded it and which could, or so it seems, exist without it. He wants the word to be identical with its meaning or with the thought it transmits. In ***The Renaissance,*** he several times praises the subjects of his essays for creating images that are saturated with their meaning, so that there is no discernible difference between sign and referent, word and meaning. In Greek art, for example, "[t]he mind begins and ends with the finite image, yet loses no part of the spiritual motive. That motive is not lightly and loosely attached to the sensuous form, as its meaning to an allegory, but saturates and is identical with it" (***R*** 205-06). The material basis of spiritual meaning is wholly sublimated in that meaning.

Nevertheless, the full exploration of Pater's concept of form will deconstruct once more the apparent end point reached in the interpretation of his work. Such an exploration puts in question both the notion that for Pater subjectivity is the *Logos* and the notion that for him material energy is the *Logos*. Alongside those ideas, overlapping them, folded inextricably into them, contradicting them, and yet necessary to their expression is a notion that is properly literary or semiotic. This incipient theory of signs is a thread which will unravel all the fastidiously patterned fabric of Pater's thought. It can hardly be called a fully developed "theory." It is more an implicit assumption in all Pater's practice with words. This "theory" in all its dimensions involves the categories of difference and discontinuity.

Meaning or significance in a personality, in a gem, a song, a painting, a piece of music is always defined by Pater as a force, as the power to make an impression. This power is not single, nor is it a harmonious collocation of energies making a unity. A "virtue" always results from antagonistic forces, sweetness against strength in the case of Michelangelo, strangeness against the desire for beauty in Leonardo, and so on. The meaning is in neither of the two forces separately, nor in their sum. It arises in the space between them, out of the economy of their difference.

The sign thus constituted by two enemy forces does not draw its meaning solely from its own internal differentiation. It also carries within itself the echo, across the gap of a further difference, of earlier similar gatherings of forces. These lateral resonances form that "chain of secret influences" of which Pater speaks in the essay on Leonardo (***R*** 116). Each virtue is an assemblage of divided energies, and it draws its meaning from its reference to other virtues of which it is the rebirth. The present moment, which, in the Conclusion to ***The Renaissance,*** seems, in its evanescence, to be all there is, carries "a sense in it, a relic more or less fleeting, of such moments gone by" (***R*** 236). The vestige in the present sign of past signs, as the passage quoted from ***Plato and Platonism*** confirms, is intrinsic to the form of the present sign. The past is an inextricable part of the meaning of the present. The rejection of fixed origin is a necessary component of this insight. The past moment of which the present moment contains the relics was itself a system of differentiated traces referring back to a still earlier moment of division, and so on.

Another discontinuity in each sign or virtue is the relation of meaning to its material embodiment. Pater always insists, correctly enough, on the necessity of a material carrier for artistic meaning. "All art," he says, "has a sensuous element, colour, form, sound" (***R*** 209). In spite of his desire to have this material basis saturated with its meaning, Pater recognizes a perpetual residue of non-saturation in the sign. There is always a margin of incongruity between the meaning and its sensuous embodiment.

This distance reveals itself in various ways in Pater's work. It is present in his occasionally explicit recognition of figure, as in the assertion in **"Style"** that each word carries its weight of metaphor and so is a displaced expression of its meaning. "A lover of words for their own sake," says Pater,

> to whom nothing about them is unimportant, a minute and constant observer of their physiognomy, [the writer] will be on the alert not only for obviously mixed metaphors of course, but for the metaphor that is mixed in all our speech, though a rapid use may involve no cognition of it. Currently recognising the incident, the colour, the physical elements or particles in words like *absorb, consider, extract,* to take the first that occur, he will avail himself of them, as further adding to the resources of expression.
>
> (***A*** 17)

A word has a virtue, and like any such power it is made of antagonistic particles in combination. These minute forces make up "all that latent figurative texture in speech" (***A*** 17). This *Andersstreben* means that we cannot say what we mean without being in danger of saying something else implicit in the elementary particles or self-contained tropes in the words we use. Pater's own writing is heavily dependent on figures which are obviously figures: the images of the gemlike flame, of woven fabric, of the relics of long-dead minute organic life in stone, and so on. In all such cases, Pater's "literal" meaning is some linguistic or artistic expression, not fire, cloth, or stone at all. In a similar way, all his work depends on the problematic validity of the trope of synecdoche, a momentary confluence of "forces" in Pico, for example, standing for the whole *Zeitgeist* of the Renaissance. Pico is only in figure a "quintessence." Even the apparently objective word "force" is a figure, since there is no energy as such in the innocent black marks on a page of Wordsworth or Hugo.

The discrepancy between embodiment and meaning is also present in Pater's notion that each form of art attempts to transcend itself, to sublimate the matter in which it is forced to work by that striving to be other than itself whereby each form of art borrows from others, "a partial alienation from its limitations, through which the arts are able, not indeed to supply the place of each other, but reciprocally to lend each other new forces" (***R*** 133-34). It is through this effort that all art, in Pater's famous phrase, "constantly aspires towards the condition of music" (***R*** 135). The condition of music is pure form, the spiritualization of the material substratum so that no referential dimension is left. In music the meaning arises entirely out of the differential relation between note and note, element and element, force and force. In the condition of music, matter has become form, or the form *is* the matter:

> That the mere matter of a poem, for instance, its subject, namely, its given incidents or situation—that the mere matter of a picture, the actual circumstances of an event, the actual topography of a landscape—should be nothing without the form, the spirit, of the handling, that this form, this mode of handling, should become an end in itself, should penetrate every part of the matter: this is what all art constantly strives after, and achieves in different degrees.
>
> (***R*** 135)

Nevertheless, insofar as this *Andersstreben* remains an aspiration, not an achievement, as Pater implies it always does, some element of unspiritualized matter remains.

This discrepancy between incarnation and meaning is, finally, present in all those imaginary portraits of men born out of their time, an Apollo or a Dionysus in Christian Europe, as in **"Apollo in Picardy"** or **"Denys l'Auxerrois,"** a presage of the Enlightenment in still half-barbaric Germany, as in **"Duke Carl of Rosenmold."** The tragedy of all these figures is in the incompatibility between the meanings they carry and the material conditions within which they are forced to embody them. This incompatibility, as much as the tragic division of forces within themselves, destines them to obscurity and early death. Their triumph is that they do reenact the old pattern, for the gods in exile are gods still, and the story works itself out anew in the changed conditions. Even so, Pater's portraits are always of those who do not wholly embody their meaning. They are gods born out of their time. This incongruity dramatizes a universal condition of artistic expression in Pater's view of it.

A remnant of non-saturation is always present, a part of the body left over, some matter not wholly absorbed into form. Its existence leads to the recognition that art for Pater is generated only in the interval between forces. This is not that other kind of Logocentrism which sees the Logos as energy rather than as subject. It involves a different notion, more difficult to grasp, in fact ungraspable. It is the ungraspable as such, an ungraspable which for Pater, with his sense for nuance, is essential to literature and to art generally. This notion is ungraspable because it cannot be thematized or conceptualized. It can only be glimpsed fleetingly, out of the corner of the eye, in the interplay between images. This non-conceptual insight, perpetually in flight, is the notion of meaning constituted by difference. Such meaning is not a correlate of force, whether that force is subjective or objective, self or matter. Such meaning is always in excess of the material substratum which embodies it. It appears momentarily in the openings between, and it is always in league with death. Such a notion might be called the uncanny, but it is not the uncanny as the occult presence of some *ur*-force which has differentiated itself and works as fate. It is the uncanny as the absence of origin. It is the mouth of the garden god with no snake in it.

Is this not that idea of "the disembodied spirit," rather than some more conventional notion of immortality, which Pater formulates in a splendid passage about Michelangelo's "predilection" for those who die young and for all the imagery of death? Here the absence of any definable origin becomes transferred, in a metalepsis, to the absence of any fixable image for that future which is created by life but which lies beyond death. The relation of a dead body to the meaning it contains by not containing it is the most extreme form of that discrepancy between the material image and its meaning which governs all Pater's insight into artistic signs. Here for once Pater is oriented not toward the past but toward the future, though the structure of material signs creating something which exceeds them, a "new body," body not body yet possible only in relation to some body, remains the same. To call Michelangelo's four famous sculptured figures *Night, Day, The Twilight,* and *The Dawn,* says Pater, is far too definite for them. Rather they "concentrate and express,"

> less by way of definite conceptions than by the touches, the promptings of a piece of music, all those vague fancies, misgivings, presentiments, which shift and mix and are defined and fade again, whenever the thoughts try to fix themselves with sincerity on the conditions and surroundings of the disembodied spirit.
>
> (***R*** 95)

Then follows an extraordinary description of the "range of sentiment" in relation to death, of which, says Pater, Michelangelo is "the poet still alive, and in possession of our inmost thoughts" (***R*** 95-96), as if Michelangelo's "new body" were, by some kind of transmigration, our own:

> —dumb inquiry over the relapse after death into the formlessness which preceded life, the change, the revolt from that change, then the correcting, hallowing, consoling rush of pity; at last, far off, thin and vague, yet not more vague than the most definite thoughts men have had through three centuries on a matter that has been so near their hearts, the new body—a passing light, a mere intangible, external effect, over those too rigid, or too formless faces; a dream that lingers a moment, retreating in the dawn, incomplete, aimless, helpless; a thing with faint hearing, faint memory, faint power of touch; a breath, a flame in the doorway, a feather in the wind.
>
> (***R*** 95-96)

The most fully conceptualized expression of this third aspect of Pater's work, implicit denial and deconstruction of the other two, is a passage in the key essay of ***Greek Studies,*** **"The Myth of Demeter and Persephone."** This essay was written in 1875, in the poise between euhemeristic, cosmological, and linguistic theories of myth, in such scholars as Max Müller, and the appearance in 1890 of the first two volumes of Frazer's *The Golden Bough.* Pater's essay is almost exactly contemporary with Nietzsche's *The Birth of Tragedy* (1872). Like Nietzsche's essay it has both a particular interest in relation to the thought of its author and a more general importance as the expression and exemplification of a theory of interpretation. The passage also, by way of its reference to Giotto's frescoes in Padua depicting Virtues and Vices, links itself to a "chain of secret influences" that binds together a series of crucial texts. This series extends from the places where Ruskin discusses those paintings by Giotto through Pater to a passage in Proust, which echoes Ruskin, to critical essays by Walter Benjamin and Paul de Man on Proust.

Pater begins by distinguishing between the abstract personification by modern artists of such entities as "wealth" or "commerce" and the "profoundly poetical and impressive" personifications of Giotto and other early masters. The reader may expect that Pater is going to discriminate between modern concoctions in which there is no intrinsic relation between the meaning and its embodiment, "mere transparent allegory, or figure of speech" (***Greek Studies.*** London, 1895. 98), and, on the other hand, genuine symbolism, in which the meaning saturates its material vehicle. Matters are not so simple in this passage. Giotto, or other artists like him in the modern period, Blake or Burne-Jones, or that old artist who designed the stained glass of the Apocalypse at Bourges, produce "something more than mere symbolism" (***GS*** 98). This is achieved by "some peculiarly sympathetic penetration, on the part of the artist, into the subjects he intended to depict" (***GS*** 98). The word "subject" here has an odd and unexpected meaning. It refers not to that "ethical" or "allegorical" theme of the work but to the material carrier of that theme. The artist's sympathetic penetration is into that embodiment in its peculiar relation to its ethical meaning. This carrier is presented literally, with full mimetic specificity. It is pictured as "realistically" as a Victorian novelist copies, with scrupulous fidelity, the details of daily life:

> Symbolism as intense as this is the creation of special temper, in which a certain simplicity, taking all things literally, *au pied de la lettre,* is united to a vivid preoccupation with the aesthetic beauty of the image itself, the *figured* side of figurative expression, the *form* of the metaphor. When it is said, "Out of his mouth goeth a sharp sword," that temper is ready to deal directly and boldly with that difficult image, like that old designer of the fourteenth century, who has depicted this, and other images of the Apocalypse, in a coloured window at Bourges. Such symbolism cares a great deal for the hair of Temperance, discreetly bound, for some subtler likeness to the colour of the sky in the girdle of *Hope,* for the inwoven flames in the red garment of *Charity.*
>
> (***GS*** 98-99)

This admirable passage, like the similar passages in Ruskin, in Proust, in Benjamin, and in De Man, calls attention to the paradoxical self-cancelling effects of such literalism in allegorical representation. On the one hand, as Proust observes, the intense literalism of such allegory greatly increases the "aesthetic beauty" of the work of art which employs it.

> [P]lus tard j'ai compris [says Marcel] que l'étrangété saisissante, la beauté spéciale de ces fresques tenait à la grande place que le symbole y occupait, et que le fait qu'il fût représenté non comme un symbole puisque la pensée symbolisée n'était pas exprimée, mais comme réel, comme effectivement subi ou matériellement manié, donnait à la signification de l'oeuvre quelque chose de plus littéral et de plus précis.

On the other hand, an exactly opposite effect is produced by taking literally what is after all "only" a figure of speech, so that a sword literally goes out of the mouth of the Christ of the Apocalypse or, in the curiously parallel example Proust gives, Giotto represents Envy with a swollen protruding tongue like an illustration in a medical text for some ghastly disease. Whether or not the parallel here would support a claim that Proust had read the passage in Pater has little importance, but the examples both give are similar cases of a grotesque literalism incongruous with its abstract significance. Both examples involve the organ of speech, that snake in the mouth of gods and men which is the father of lies, that is, of "figurative expression." In both examples, the realism with which the figured side of the figure is represented only intensifies the incompatibility between tenor and vehicle in the metaphor. It calls attention to the fictive or verbal aspect of the expression, even to its absurdity. There is no substantial similarity between the abstraction and its material embodiment, though they may seem plausibly enough connected in the purely linguistic expression. The embodiment can be represented. The more vividly and literally it is pictured, the more beautiful the work of art. Nevertheless, the more literally it is represented, the more it brings into the open the fact that the "ethical" meaning—Temperance, Hope, or whatever—has, as Proust observes, not been represented at all. It has only been indirectly named in a metaphor. This metaphor confesses in its intense literalism to its inability to be anything but itself, a mouth with a sharp sword going out of it, flames, the blue of the sky, the hair of a discreet woman, neatly bound. At best the painter can translate into visual images the equivalents of verbal metaphor, painting flames on the garment of Charity, the blue of the sky on the girdle of Hope. The allegorical meaning vanishes in the realism with which its vehicle is represented. That meaning is shown to exist only as names, as an interplay of displaced words which are the basis of the visual representation.

Even so, Pater returns at the end of the paragraph to the idea of a people for whom the powers governing the universe were seen as real persons. For such a people the false equations of metaphor were literally true. When they talked of the return of Kore to Demeter, for example, they were "yielding to a real illusion; to which the voice of man 'was really a stream, beauty an effluence, death a mist'" (***GS*** 100). Pater's mode of expression here, however, to turn back to the other side once more, demystifies such ways of seeing and returns them to the verbal figures which they take literally. To a vision of such a temper the "illusion" was "real," hence not an illusion. To Pater it is an illusion, a voice not a stream, beauty not an effluence, death only figuratively a mist.

Back and forth between these various contradictory readings of the passage its reader is forced to go. Each reading depends on others which contradict it and it contradicts the others in its turn. The passage, in its insistence that only a "special temper" is capable of the "real illusion" of allegory *au pied de la lettre,* can be taken as reaffirming Pater's subjectivism. In its suggestion that the stratum below the play of allegorical representation is material forces, flame or sky, the passage may be seen as congruent with Pater's objectivism, his materialism of "inwoven" forces. In its recognition that both of these notions are generated by a play of language, the passage may be taken as congruent with the third reading of Pater I have proposed. The god's mouth is empty or is filled only with that uncanny simulacrum of a snake born and dying and born anew in the interaction of the signs men make. In this third interpretation, the reader is seen as intervening actively in any interpretation. Meaning is produced in an act of deciphering which can never reach the original or intrinsic meaning of any text. An "impression" is as much an act as a passion. It is the stamping of crisscrossing forces with a momentary stillness in one reading. Another critic of another "temper" will produce a different reading of the same text. No judge will be able to arbitrate between them, since the text is "undecidable," incapable of being encompassed in a single total reading.

All three of these readings, and other variations on them, are present not only in this paragraph from **"The Myth of Demeter and Persephone"** but also intertwined throughout Pater's work as a whole. The last reading sees the subject of Pater's writing as ultimately, whatever its ostensible theme, writing and reading themselves. Reading is a further writing, and all writing is a palimpsest. The critic produces an additional inscription over an earlier inscription in the flesh, that necessary material basis of all art, though art always exceeds its fleshly incarnations. This fact, however, may only be experienced in the flesh, in a literalism which defeats itself. The critic is, like Leonardo da Vinci, *homo minister et interpres naturae* (***R*** 98), but the minister and the interpreter are perpetually caught in a dance of antagonism, each denying the other and yet dependent on him. Pater's writings, like those of other major authors in the Occidental tradition, are at once open to interpretation and ultimately indecipherable, unreadable. His texts lead the critic deeper and deeper into a labyrinth until he confronts a final aporia. This does not mean, however, that the reader must give up from the beginning the attempt to understand Pater. Only by going all the way into the labyrinth, following the thread of a given clue, can the critic reach the blind alley, vacant of any Minotaur, that impasse which is the end point of interpretation.

Pater's work, then, is heterogeneous, dialogical, or antilogical. Dialogical and antilogical come, in fact, to the same thing, since the doubling of the Logos is a sign of its absence. Each reading in the interchange of overlapping voices may be worked out with full cogency, though it is impossible to have all at once. All three cannot be simultaneously "true." Moreover, they may not be related to one another dialectically or in some kind of hierarchy. My necessarily narrative or sequential development falsifies their implications upon one another, just as the apparent historical development in Pater's theory of myth makes, as Pater himself says, a fictitious narrative of what are in fact simultaneous members of a single system. In all its dimensions, in Pater's interest in the impressions made or felt by the "unique" personality, in his art of portraiture, in his essays on sculpture, in his studies of mythical figures and of an allegorical art that is "more than mere symbolism," Pater's work can be defined as an exploration and deconstruction of the problematic trope of personification, that turn of language or art which gathers impersonal forces under a human figure. Is subjectivity a fixed point of origin from which all else follows, or is personality a fragile receptacle within which impersonal energies are momentarily brought together, or are both the person and the forces gathered within it linguistic fictions generated by the interchange of sign with sign in the productive workings of art or literature?

My three readings of Pater's use of the trope of personification may not be reconciled in any way. They form a bewildering oscillation in which each reading will lead to the others if it is followed far enough, though the others contradict and cancel it out, while at the same time being necessary to its expression. To put this in Pater's terms: If the magical appearance of unity to which we give the name "person" is always produced differentially, by the division or combat of contradictory forces, and yet exceeds anything which may be identified as in those forces, as the "new body" exceeds the dead body, then the momentary poise in a personification will always be divided against itself, folded, manifold, dialogical rather than monological. It will always be open, like all the master tropes of the great texts in the Western tradition, to multiple contradictory readings in a perpetual fleeing away from any fixed sense.

Paul Barolsky (essay date 1982)

SOURCE: "Walter Pater's Renaissance," in*The Virginia Quarterly Review,* Vol. 58, No. 2, Spring, 1982, pp. 208-20.

[*In the following essay, Barolsky extols* The Renaissance *as a literary work of art that is at once historical, autobiographical, philosophical, and poetical.*]

A flood of publications on the elusive Victorian scholar-aesthete, Walter Pater, has appeared during the last two decades. As plans for a critical edition of his works are now being made, the writings on him continue to flow from the presses, threatening to submerge his achievement in their vastness, as they seek to sustain it. Books, articles, anthologies, Ph.D. dissertations, symposia, and now the May 1981 issue of *Prose Studies*—where the interested reader will find a detailed summary of recent bibliography on Pater—have scrutinized seemingly every facet of the man, from his place in the history of literature to the significance of his moustache. This is not to say that even Pater's best-known works are now conveniently available to a broad audience in paperback editions sold in drugstores and airports. For the Pater boom is largely an academic phenomenon.

Few writers as distinguished as Pater have lived lives as diaphanous as his. Between birth in London in 1839 and death 55 years later, he lived in a quiet reverie among books and works of art, seeking to divine the magical powers of beauty, journeying invisibly among sensations and ideas in quest of their ineffable essences. The center of this private existence was Oxford, where the almost ghostly scholar and writer, a seemingly disembodied consciousness, dwelt more than 20 years as student, fellow, and tutor, gravely and fastidiously measuring the exquisite nuances of aesthetic experience in prose of incomparable refinement. He occasionally traveled without incident in Germany, France, and Italy, imperceptibly absorbing impressions under a dream-like veil. One of the singular, rare facts of Pater's physical existence, if one can even speak of it as such, was the decision to print the first edition of his book ***The Renaissance*** on ribbed paper, thereby giving to his thoughts a certain faintly *tangible* reality. As one of Pater's finest critics has observed, "he seems almost to have succeeded in passing through his times with hardly a trace." Not a flesh and blood historical personage, he appears in retrospect as if a fiction from the labyrinth of Jorge Luis Borges' imagination. Pater chose to live "his true life," it is said, in his art, and, not surprisingly, his most recent biographer has had to acknowledge that "the real reasons for re-examining" Pater lie in his writings. It is hard to say whether the day Walter Pater began to write he came to life or disappeared.

Revisionist scholars always tend to exaggerate the weaknesses of their forebears. And to hear recent Paterians speak, you might think a true understanding of Pater dated from the mid-1960's, even though an extensive body of writings throughout this century, including essays by Arthur Symons, Logan Pearsall Smith, and Maurice Bowra, has offered valuable perceptions concerning the character of his work. The most fashionable aspect of Pater's writings at present is the role they are understood to have played in the emergence of Modernist literature. Literary historians are now beginning to investigate his influence on Woolf, Conrad, Joyce, and Proust; on Yeats, Pound, Eliot, and Stevens. Yet this is a field of investigation still only tentatively explored. More attention might especially be paid to the ways in which Pater influenced T. S. Eliot. Although Eliot's attacks on Pater are supposed to mark the beginnings of the decline of Pater's critical fortunes, Eliot wrote in many respects as his perpetuator. Eliot's critical stance in "Tradition and the Individual Talent," for example, which stresses the impersonal "significant emotion" *in* literary art, depends on Pater's preoccupation with "impersonal" style, or "*form* in all its characteristics."

Of all Pater's works ***The Renaissance*** is probably his greatest single achievement. Fascinating as they are, his more apparently imaginative efforts, ***Marius the Epicurean*** and ***Imaginary Portraits,*** so deficient in dramatic interest, are flawed as fiction. And his other essays—gathered in ***Appreciations, Miscellaneous Studies,*** and ***Greek Studies***—are not so subtly harmonized and orchestrated, individually or integrally, as those in ***The Renaissance,*** which remains the heart of Pater's literary career. The chapter on Winckelmann, one of Pater's first essays to appear in print, was first published in 1867; the essay on Giorgione was not added to the book until 1877; and, continuing to polish its style, Pater made revisions in subsequent printings, down through the 1893 edition, published the year before his death. In recent years ***The Renaissance*** has received considerable philological attention. Not only do we now have an excellent new critical edition of it, with extensive notes by Donald L. Hill, but Billie Andrew Inmann's valuable commentary on Pater's reading during the period of its composition has also just appeared. These scholarly works augment our knowledge of Pater's numerous sources, but, modestly refraining from consideration of larger questions of interpretation, they are written, to use Nietzsche's words, *in usum Delphinorum.* Yet we might ask, what kind of a book is ***The Renaissance***? What are its distinctive characteristics?

Reviewing the first edition, published in 1873 as ***Studies in the History of the Renaissance,*** Mrs. Mark Pattison objected that the "historical element" was lacking, prompting Pater to change the title in the subsequent edition to ***The Renaissance: Studies in Art and Poetry.*** Historians of art and literature alike have since continued to comment on Pater's unhistorical approach to his subject. This claim has been much repeated during the recent period of Pater's "rehabilitation." But it goes unnoticed even by his admirers that Pater's suggestions were the first general indications of the extensive role of Neoplatonism in Renaissance theology, philosophy, poetry, painting, sculpture, and architecture. Of Michelangelo's poetry he observes that the great artist "is always pressing forward from the outward beauty . . . to apprehend the unseen beauty . . . that abstract form of beauty, about which the Platonists reason." And, contemplating the Medici Chapel, he sees Michelangelo here as a "disciple" of the Platonists. These remarks on Michelangelo's poetry, sculpture, and architecture are closely related to Pater's appreciation of Pico della Mirandola's "love of unseen beauty." Appropriately comparing Pico himself to an archangel Raphael or Mercury by Piero di Cosimo or Botticelli, Pater seemingly alludes in part to the Mercury in Botticelli's *Primavera.* This *divinus amator* gazes beyond the clouds toward an "unseen beauty," like that beloved of Pico and Michelangelo.

If we take a broad view of Pater's book, we see that its sustained evocations of Platonism are, as though a form of verbal cartography, an historical outline of the place that Neoplatonism occupied in Renaissance culture. In this respect ***The Renaissance*** prefigured and influenced the more detailed historical account in Nesca Robb's *Neoplatonism* *in the Italian Renaissance* (1935), a work which in turn stimulated the most distinguished art historical scholars of Renaissance Neoplatonism, Erwin Panofsky, Edgar Wind, and E. H. Gombrich, all of whom followed, if distantly, in the wake of Pater and whose work depends on his implicit historical formulation.

Pater's historical intuitions, seminal though they are, lie almost concealed by the poetical form of his prose. It is thus not surprising that, reading ***The Renaissance*** primarily as art rather than as history, scholars have overlooked these *aperçus*. To identify Pater's "errors" of fact or "misrepresentations" is to ignore his fundamental definition in ***Appreciations*** of the "sense of fact." The historian, according to Pater, becomes the author of *fine* art, as he comes to transcribe, not mere fact, but his sense of it. Given his "absolutely truthful intention," the historian "amid the multitude of facts presented to him must needs select, and in selecting, assert something of his own humour, something that comes not of the world without but of a vision within." A distinguished art historian has recently argued that "the historian is not a critic and should not aspire to be one." Pater would not object to this scholar's quest for historical truth. But he would ask: even if it is possible to separate "intention" and "significance" in theory, is it possible in practice for the historian to understand this truth apart from his own critical sense of its significance?

The soundness and longevity of Pater's critical evaluations of Renaissance art should not be forgotten. In an admirable new monograph on Luca della Robbia, John Pope-Hennessy speaks of the aesthetic affinities between the sculptor's work and Greek art, referring to the recent observations on this topic by Italian scholars. But it was Pater who first observed so forcefully that "Luca della Robbia and the other Tuscan sculptors of the fifteenth century" partook "of the *Allgemeinheit* of the Greeks, their way of extracting certain select elements only of pure form and sacrificing all the rest." Speaking of Botticelli as a "poetical painter," Pater was to influence Aby Warburg and subsequent generations of scholars who explored the painter's poetical sources; and dwelling on the artist's mastery "of the medium of abstract painting," he influenced Berenson and Horne, Binyon and Yashiro, and still other, more recent interpreters of Botticelli's form and sensibility.

Similarly, Pater's interpretation of the school of Giorgione remains the foundation of our interpretation of the painter today. Although countless attempts have been made to read various meanings—mythical, biblical, moral, and historical—into such works as Giorgione's *Tempesta,* recent scholars of Renaissance art, despite the current aversion to what is called "formalism," still adhere to Pater's sense of such pictures as "the subordination of mere subject to pictorial design." There are also critical and historical perceptions in Pater's writing that have yet to be properly developed by art historians. Describing the "treacherous smile" of Leonardo's *Saint John the Baptist,* which "would have us understand something far beyond the outward gesture," Pater is not merely recalling Gautier's fascination with Leonardo's strangeness, but he is calling attention to the ambiguity and, ultimately, the irony of the painter's vision. Yet on this discomforting aspect of the painter's vision modern scholars (not surprisingly) remain reticent.

II

Above all, Pater is esteemed as a prose poet. And the most famous example of his poetry is the often quoted description of the *Mona Lisa,* rendered in poetical form by Yeats in *The Oxford Book of Modern Verse.* Possibly the single most familiar passage of 19th-century prose, it has lost none of its sensuous enchantment for those today who find pleasure in a prose that conveys "the sound of lyres and flutes." For Pater, that "presence that rose thus so strangely beside the waters" is expressive of Greece, Rome, the Middle Ages, the Renaissance, and modernity—of "all modes of thought and life." But there is another, related passage which, although usually overlooked, helps us to appreciate more intimately the nature of Pater's book. This is his rendering in the chapter on Winckelmann of another aesthetic experience, this one in Rome.

> In one of the frescoes of the Vatican, Raphael has commemorated the tradition of the Catholic religion. Against a space of tranquil sky, broken in upon by a beatific vision, are ranged the greatest personages of Christian history, with the Sacrament in the midst. Another fresco of Raphael in the same apartment presents a very different company, Dante alone appearing in both. Surrounded by the muses of Greek mythology, under a thicket of laurel, sits Apollo, with the sources of Castalia at his feet. On either side are grouped those on whom the spirit of Apollo descended, the classical and Renaissance poets, to whom the waters of Castalia come down, a river making glad this other "city of God." In this fresco it is the classical tradition, the orthodoxy of taste, that Raphael commemorates. Winckelmann's intellectual history authenticates the claims of this tradition in human culture.

Raphael's frescoes in the Stanza della Segnatura, which also include the *School of Athens* and *Civil and Canon Law,* have been appropriately called "one ideal temple of the human mind." They express the "harmony" and "correspondences" between pagan and religious truths, Greek and Roman, Hebrew and Christian, like those to which Pico aspired. Indeed, the relation between Pico's art and Raphael's, implicit in Pater's text, is yet another example of his vivid sense of historical analogy. Just as Raphael created an ideal harmony among theologians, philosophers, poets, and lawgivers, Pater creates a unified picture of visionary thinkers. Speaking of the "spirit of Apollo," and implicitly of the "new Apollo," Pater observes that the medieval poet Dante participates in "both" visions, as a poet of Christ, and, like the other "classical and Renaissance poets," as a poet inspired by Apollo. When he refers to Castalia as the river "making glad this other 'city of God,'" Pater is not only alluding to the "city of God" of Psalm 46, but aptly to Augustine's City of God. For, seated with a copy of his *City of God,* Augustine is one of the "great personages" beholding the vision of Christ in Raphael's *Disputa.*

What Pater has done here is to delineate a history of what he elsewhere calls "visionariness"—from Apollo and the Old and New Testaments to Augustine, Dante, and finally to Raphael himself. But the history does not stop at this point. The art of Greece, inspired by Apollo, is one of "pure thoughts or ideas"—a Platonic art. And Pater reveals to us a similar Platonic character in Raphael's painting. Speaking of Raphael in ***Miscellaneous Studies,*** he observes that in his work "painted ideas, painted and visible philosophy, are for once as beautiful as Plato thought they must be, if one truly apprehended them." We might recall that in Raphael's fresco, Apollo is inspired by the music of the spheres, painted in the ceiling of the stanza. And appearing in the adjacent *School of Athens* with his *Timaeus,* Plato points toward these heavenly harmonies. In the modern historical scholarship the Platonic meaning of these frescoes has been much discussed, especially by Edgar Wind. And we can now see that these discussions return, as do the Neoplatonic interpretations of Michelangelo, to Pater. Yet whereas scholars of Neoplatonic iconography usually speak of what art illustrates, that is, its Neoplatonic *content,* Pater evokes the manner in which Platonism *informs* Raphael's art.

Pater's visionary history extends further to Winckelmann, the inspired writer on Apollo, whom Pater compares to both Dante and Plato. If Winckelmann's history—a bridge between the Renaissance and the modern age—"authenticates" this classical tradition commemorated by Raphael, Pater's writings in like manner authenticate this tradition. Amidst the flux of modernity, in which "universal culture" is "perhaps a lost art," ***The Renaissance*** is itself self-consciously conceived as a renaissance. And Pater himself, like Heine's gods of an earlier epoch, is an Apollonian "exile" in the modern world.

Although the book is ostensibly about the Renaissance, we find that in various ways Pater relates the period to antiquity, the Middle Ages, the Enlightenment, as well as to the modern or Romantic epoch. Recalling the ancient world, the book begins in 12th-century France, and the impact of the awakening there is pursued to the Quattrocento; the influence of Leonardo (who traveled to France) and that of the Renaissance in general are then traced back to the France of the *Pléiade.* As part of his general cultural history, Pater discusses, notes, or appropriates ideas and forms from principal figures of European literature. The French tradition is traced beyond the Renaissance to Pascal, Rousseau, Hugo, Stendhal, Gautier, and finally, Baudelaire. Just as the allusions to Chaucer, Shakespeare, Milton, Blake, Wordsworth, and Arnold chart the history of English literature, references to Lessing, Kant, and Hegel, not to mention Winckelmann and Goethe, hint, and more than hint, at the story of the new German literature, which is seen as a rebirth or renaissance of the classical tradition. Aspiring to the ideal of the "unity of culture," Pater seeks to define the harmony between the classical and biblical traditions and their unity in European culture.

The poetical structure of Pater's intellectual history is, as we have seen, so overwhelming that its historical value has to be excavated. This structure is also so very intricate that it is almost impossible for the reader to grasp all of the analogies or correspondences as they "cross and recross" his book. Endless affinities are established or suggested, as between Botticelli and Dante, Dante and Michelangelo, Michelangelo and Blake, Blake and Shakespeare, Shakespeare and Giorgione, Giorgione and Du Bellay, Du Bellay and Leonardo, Leonardo and Pico, Leonardo and Paracelsus, Leonardo and Bacon, Leonardo and Goethe, Goethe and Winckelmann, Goethe and Pater himself. The numerous artists and writers referred to by Pater, or who have been shown to have influenced him, are not merely present as sources, but, to use Pater's language, they are artistically "threaded through" the text to establish a coherent pattern of cultural wholeness. To express this *Allgemeinheit,* Pater deploys a veritable thesaurus of interrelated words: connection, affinity, analogue, twin, correspondence, repetition, counterpart, equivalent, combination, reconciliation, resemblance, similitude, identity, congruity, Doppelgänger, double meaning (and reflex), union, unison, wholeness, integrity, centrality, interweaving, interfusing, blending, interpenetration. In their analyses of the continuities of Western culture, the great scholarly books of our own time, Curtius' *European Literature and the Latin Middle Ages,* Seznec's *The Survival of the Pagan Gods,* Bolgar's *The Classical Heritage,* and Panofsky's *Renaissance and Renascences,* all follow the path that Pater first struck.

As critics have always observed, Pater's book is also autobiographical, or at least an intellectual autobiography, in which Pater becomes all of his subjects or their creations. Like Luca della Robbia's, Pater's is "a life of labours and frugality, with no adventure." It is a life of the mind resembling that of Pico and the Neoplatonists, who seek "order and beauty in knowledge." With Leonardo, Pater is primarily motivated by the "desire of beauty," as with Giorgione and Du Bellay he aspires to lyrical purity. But in the modern world Pater is an exile, like Michelangelo, "a ghost out of another age." He shares Winckelmann's "wistful sense of something lost to be regained." His solitary journey as an "alien" is paradoxically that of the knight Tannhäuser or the "knight errant of philosophy," Pico. He is these pilgrims to Rome, just as he is Abelard, Botticelli, Leonardo, Du Bellay, Winckelmann, and Goethe, all journeying to the Eternal City.

The examples of Pater's identification with the subjects of his book can be multiplied indefinitely, but it gradually becomes clear that he is building a series of biographies not merely into a diaphanous autobiography but into an incipient novel. The historical actors merge into a single protagonist in search of beauty and truth. In his different guises, this character is himself handsome. The angelic Pico is "of features and shape seemly and beauteous," Leonardo is noted for his "charm of voice and aspect," and Giorgione is of a "presumably gracious presence." Pater's historical personages are protean manifestations of a single fictionalized self who, however uneventfully, lives through history. Pater later developed this implicitly fictional form in ***Marius the Epicurean;*** and, nourished by it, Virginia Woolf parodied it affectionately in *Orlando.*

The Renaissance is conspicuously about philosophy. Himself a Platonist, Pater constantly writes in pursuit of an ideal beauty. In addition to observing the beauty of scholars and artists, Pater denominates their lovely creations—Botticelli's "comely" persons, Leonardo's "bright and animated" angel, and above all, the "beautiful multitude" of the Parthenon, rendered in Platonizing terms. When Pater describes the comeliness of artists and their works, he proceeds as Plato had in the *Symposium.* For, like his Greek hero, Pater ascends from specific examples of beauty to the more abstract idea of the beautiful, to "pure form." The counterparts to Pater in the visual arts, we might recall, are Botticelli, whose beauteous Mercury gazes toward the Sun, and Raphael, whose suave Apollo turns his eyes toward the heavenly spheres.

III

Works of literary art are invariably written in mixed genres, but in this respect perhaps no work is quite like ***The Renaissance.*** It constantly aspires to history, criticism, biography, and autobiography; to poetry, novel, and philosophy. But all of these forms seem almost to disappear as they fuse in utter unity. At the same time Peter seeks to create an art that transcends literature, becoming a visual art in its very "visionariness." Pater's essay, **"Style,"** in ***Appreciations*** serves as a key to our understanding of this aspiration in ***The Renaissance.*** Here he speaks of a "literary architecture," which "if it is to be rich and expressive, involves not only foresight of the end in the beginning, but also development or growth of design, in the process of execution, with many irregularities, surprises, and after-thoughts; the contingent as well as the necessary being subsumed under the unity of the whole." In this manner is the "architectural design" of Pater's book classically proportioned and ordered. But Pater's is also, antithetically, a romantic architecture analogous to that of Renaissance France, where one "often finds a true poetry, as in those strangely twisted staircases of the châteaux of the country of the Loire, as if it were intended that among their odd turnings the actors in a theatrical mode of life might pass each other unseen."

The prose poetry approaches sculpture in its ambition. For Pater, the clarity of the Greek vision manifests itself in sculpture, so lucid in its incisiveness. In the essay, **"Style,"** Pater defines the writer's quest, like that of the sculptor, to remove "surplusage, from the last finish of the gem-engraver blowing away the last particle of invisible dust, back to the earliest divination of the finished work to be, lying somewhere, according to Michelangelo's fancy, in the rough-hewn block." Pater seeks in a similar way to carve and chisel away in prose in order to embody a Platonic essence in words. Speaking of "those 'Mothers' who, in the second part of *Faust,* mould and remould the typical forms that appear in human history," he is expressing his own goal, to mould and remould sculpturally as he gives birth to the idea of history.

If sculpture is the essence of antiquity, painting is the art form more nearly associated in its abstraction with modernity, especially the paintings of Giorgione and his school, in which one beholds a "perfect interpenetration of the subject with its form." Again in the essay, **"Style,"** Pater implicitly reflects on his own aspiration to paint in words; in the prose of the artistic writer the "elementary particles of language will be realised as colour and light and shade." Thus, writing of Venetian art, Pater becomes a Giorgionesque painter in words: "And it is with gold dust, or gold thread, that these Venetian painters seem to work, spinning its fine filaments, through the solemn human flesh, away into the white plastered walls of the thatched huts."

In the end, for Pater all art aspires to the condition of music, which most completely expresses the modern world. Like Giorgione's painted music, "modulated unisons of landscape and persons," Pater's prose aspires to the condition of the lyric. No less so, his writing is inspired by the "double-music" of Du Bellay's poetry, especially its quality of *poésie chantée.* Pater also admires the lyrical character of Shakespeare's poetry, which in *Measure for Measure* "seems to pass for a moment into an actual strain of music." At times Pater's prose achieves a sensuous abstraction and evocativeness related to musical experience: "A sudden light transforms some trivial thing, a weather-vane, a windmill, a winnowing fan, the dust in the barn-door. A moment—and the thing has vanished, because it was pure effect; but it leaves a relish behind it, a longing that the accident may happen again." In the music of Walter Pater, memory is continuously drawn into play, as it absorbs, one upon another, the sensations of history, condensing these into perfect moments, exquisite pauses in time. The ripple of a faint breeze across a still stream, the wondrous whispering of wind-wafted wheat in soft sunshine, the distant murmur of unfamiliar voices at dusk—these, then, among the vagrant undulations of sound, at once present and past, are refined in Pater's reverie, into purely Platonic music, etherealized, at the last, into ghostly silences of unheard melodies.

Just as Pater attempts, among these so numerous antitheses, to reconcile modernity and the classical tradition, he tries to bring the basic literary genres, indeed all forms of art into synthesis, paradoxically dissolving these forms as he unites them. One can read ***The Renaissance*** as poetry, autobiography, philosophy, or even as the origins of some weird fiction. But for all of these aspects of the work, Pater's omnipresent sense of history is the *point d'appui.* His own efforts he viewed as "scholarly," and I have tried to suggest something of the soundness and significance of his highly suggestive historical scholarship. Even so, ***The Renaissance,*** metaphorically becoming architecture, sculpture, painting, and music, and finally all and none of these, becomes in its perpetual striving beyond limits a network of almost Baudelairean "*correspondances*": "*Comme de longs échos qui de loin se confondent / Dans une ténébreuse et profonde unité.*" As we only dimly perceive these Symbolist ambitions and their realization in ***The Re-***

naissance—at once a perfect synthetic form of all art and a "vanishing away" of form—we begin to sense that our reading of his strange, solitary book has only just begun.

Jerome Bump (essay date 1982)

SOURCE: "Seeing and Hearing in *Marius the Epicurean,*" in *Nineteenth Century Fiction,* Vol. 37, No. 2, September, 1982, pp. 188-206.

[*In the following essay, Bump describes how Pater uses aural imagery and performatives in* Marius the Epicurean *to lead Marius to "the music of Logos" and "a fuller sense of human communication."*]

It would be difficult to overestimate just how pervasive are the spatial paradigms of literature we have inherited from Pater. Sharon Bassett points out that Pater was an important precursor of Edmund Wilson, Kenneth Burke, Northrop Frye, and the American deconstructionists, and demonstrates that the source of Pater's influence on modern literary criticism was his anticipation of what Joseph Frank calls "spatiality": "When, in 1945, Joseph Frank endeavors to articulate those specific qualities that belong to modern literature he unerringly focuses on features that a half century earlier Pater had associated with what he hoped would be the modern critical intelligence . . . the a-temporal forms that Frank so convincingly describes . . . Pater's ultimate resting point seems to be not so much that art aspires to the condition of music but that narrative art aspires to the condition, which is to say, to the immediate impact, of visual or spatial art."[1] Pater was clearly the pivotal figure in the transmission of the spatial orientation of Keats and the Pre-Raphaelites to Wilde and our century. The influence of Pater's spatial paradigms of language is obvious, for instance, in such essays of Wilde's as "The Critic as Artist" and "The Decay of Lying," essays which contain in embryo many essential axioms of formalism and its various permutations in our century, including structuralism and deconstructionism.

The dominance of Pater's seminal, visual models of language is nowhere more obvious than in ***Marius the Epicurean.*** "The sum" of the recommendations of the priest of Aesculapius "was the precept, repeated many times under slightly varied aspects, of a diligent promotion of the capacity of the eye, inasmuch as in the eye would lie for him the determining influence of life: he was of the number of those who, in the words of a poet who came long after, must be 'made perfect by the love of visible beauty.'"[2] The "tyrannous reality" of "things visible" "was borne in upon" Marius (ch. 4), and thus of all the "various religious fantasies" of his day "he could well appreciate the picturesque; that was made easy by his natural Epicureanism, already prompting him to conceive of himself as but the passive spectator of the world around him . . . a materialist, but with something of the temper of a devotee" (ch. 8). Marius's "natural Epicureanism" survives the competing claims of Cyrenaicism and Stoicism because Marius retains his "strong apprehension . . . of the beauty of the visible things around him," and "his natural susceptibility in this direction, enlarged by experience, seems to demand of him an almost exclusive pre-occupation with the *aspects* of things . . . their revelations to the eye" (ch. 16).

As Pater's heirs, we too have adopted an almost exclusive preoccupation with the visual aspects of things. When we read, for instance, we usually assume that we are to read with our eyes only, and we look for images and examples of reading and writing in the text which will confirm our paradigm. For example, Gerald Monsman points out that "in Marius's truant reading of Apuleius's Golden Book" readers encounter "a mirror of their own activity of reading and responding to Pater's novel" in which "the text is clearly depicting the process of its own making and of its being read. . . . The two lads 'half-buried in a heap of dry corn, in an old granary' looked around: 'How like a picture! and it was precisely the scene described in what they were reading.'"[3]

"How like a picture!" has become the subliminal refrain of much of modern criticism. Monsman emphasizes the visual aspects of St. Cecilia's house, for instance: "In Saint Cecilia and the church in her house, Marius finds a relational interplay surpassing Apuleius's fantasies, arranged, 'as if in designed congruity with his favourite precepts of the power of physical vision, into an actual picture.'" Monsman also focuses on the garden which formed "a picture" recalling "the old miniature-painters' work on the walls of the chambers within" and on comparisons of Cecilia to a statue, and of Marius's feelings to those of a painter who sees an opening in the background of his picture.[4]

Yet this almost exclusively visual approach to reading is very recent. Just a hundred years ago there was a much wider variety of models of reading. Philip Collins has demonstrated the popularity of reading aloud in the Victorian age, for instance, and Marshall McLuhan and Walter J. Ong have revealed that auditory paradigms were still more prominent in previous eras. Thus, if we are to avoid a simplistic model of reading based on exclusive preoccupation with a single sense, the eye, do we not need to recover some of these other modes of reading? Just as we have searched texts for visual models of reading and writing, we can become aware of auditory models as well: for example, scripts for the dramatic performance of the text itself.

It is easy enough to reconstruct such a model for the performance of, say, Dickens's novels, but I would argue that auditory models of reading were so pervasive, even in the late nineteenth century, that they can be discovered even in texts apparently completely dominated by visual paradigms, indeed even in the seminal text of "spatiality," ***Marius the Epicurean.***[5] Acknowledgment of the auditory as well as the spatial imagery in the novel affects our sense of the ending and suggests an alternative to our current critical paradigm, an alternative only now beginning to be adumbrated by speech act theories of language.

In ***Marius*** the two lads' truant reading of Apuleius is not the only example of Pater's dramatization of the reading of his own text. Consider, for instance, three more extensive narratives within the novel that suggest how the larger narrative should be read: the Halcyon legend, the story of Cupid and Psyche, and the recitation of the Gospel. At the feast for Apuleius manuscripts are brought out, but they are not read in our sense of the word. They are performed: "a famous reader, choosing his lucky moment, delivered in a *tenor* voice" the tale (ch. 20). Gerald Monsman has shown that this legend is another "allegory, like the story of Cupid and Psyche, of a love stronger than death,"[6] but it is also an allegory in the text itself of how to read a text. Pater stresses the power not of sight but of sound: "What sound was that, Socrates? . . . And how melodious it was! Was it a bird, I wonder. I thought all sea-birds were songless." "Aye! a sea-bird," answered Socrates, "a bird called the Halcyon, and has a note full of plaining and tears." Moreover, the speaker's oral performance of the sounds or "notes" of the text has a powerful effect on a live audience, especially on Apuleius: "The reader's well-turned periods seemed to stimulate, almost uncontrollably, the eloquent stirrings of the eminent man of letters then present. The impulse to speak masterfully was visible, before the recital was well over, in the moving lines about his mouth. . . . One of the company . . . made ready to transcribe what he would say, the sort of things of which a collection was then forming . . . elaborate, carved ivories of speech, drawn, at length, out of the rich treasure-house of a memory stored with such" (ch. 20). Despite the belated and subordinate spatial metaphor ("carved ivories") we are reminded that this kind of oral tradition was the model of communication not only for Socrates but also for Jesus, Buddha, and many other leaders who have changed the course of human history through speaking rather than writing.

Apuleius's tale of Cupid and Psyche in the Golden Book that the truant boys were reading places still more emphasis on the ears, even to the exclusion of the eyes. The story is framed by invocations of the magical power of the spoken word, the power of what we now call performatives, in this case "*Declarations:* Illocutionary acts that bring about the state of affairs they refer to."[7] As Pater writes,

> The scene of the romance was laid in . . . the original land of witchcraft. . . . haunts of magic and incantations. . . .
>
> "You might think that through the murmuring of some cadaverous spell, all things had been changed . . . that the birds you heard singing were feathered men. . . . The statues seemed about to move, the walls to speak, the dumb cattle to break out in prophecy; nay! the very sky and the sunbeams, as if they might suddenly cry out." (ch. 5)

And indeed in the tale which follows not only does an ant, a reed, an eagle, a tower, and a river speak but humans elicit speech from the gods themselves: Psyche speaks with Cupid, Ceres, Juno, Pan, and Venus.

Admittedly, Psyche is originally drawn by the visual beauty of Cupid's palace: "but as she gazed there came a voice—a voice, as it were unclothed by bodily vesture. . . . Still she saw no one: only she heard words falling here and there, and had voices alone to serve her." When darkness descends and her eyes are rendered completely useless, "behold a sound of a certain clemency approache[d] her" and "the sound of the voice grew to be her solace in that condition of loneliness and uncertainty." The God of Love becomes her bridegroom but warns her that if she seeks to use her eyes rather than her ears to know him their marriage will be at an end. Like Marius, however, she is too dependent on her eyes and finally insists on seeing as well as hearing him. He, "beholding the overthrow of her faith, quietly took flight from her embraces." The remainder of the tale tells the story of Venus, who sought "the service of Mercury, the god of speech," admitting, "never at any time have I done anything without thy help" (ch. 5). Venus tests Psyche but she survives with the help of the speech of other creatures, and finally Jupiter commands Mercury to assemble the gods and he blesses their marriage.

If both the story of Cupid and Psyche and the Halcyon legend may be read as Christian allegories we should not be surprised to discover that hearing, as opposed to seeing, is even more strongly emphasized in the explicitly Christian sections. Like the God of Love, Cornelius is introduced as a disembodied voice. Stopping at an inn on the way to Rome, Marius is feeling melancholy: "It was just then that he heard the voice of one, newly arrived at the inn . . . a youthful voice, with a reassuring clearness of note, which completed his cure. He seemed to hear that voice again in dreams, uttering his name" (ch. 10). The stress on a voice in dreams calling his name recalls the Victorian myth of the power of Newman's voice and the emphasis on the voice of God throughout the Bible,[8] especially in the parable of the Good Shepherd: "the sheep hear his voice, one by one he calls his own sheep and leads them out. When he has brought out his flock, he goes ahead of them, and the sheep follow because they know his voice. They never follow a stranger but run away from him: they do not recognise the voice of strangers. . . . And there are other sheep I have that are not of this fold, and these I have to lead as well. They too will listen to my voice" (John 10:3-5, 16). The reference to leading sheep not of this fold, that is, to the conversion of the gentiles, is the subject again when Peter hears the voice of God in a trance telling him, "What God has made clean, you have no right to call profane" (Acts 10:15), but Peter does not understand until he discovers the holiness of the Roman centurion, Cornelius, and authorizes the baptism of the first pagans.[9]

Apparently the appeal is to the eye, however, in the climactic visit to Cecilia's house: "Was he willing to look upon that, the seeing of which might define—yes! define the critical turning-point in his days?" But it is not so much the "seeing" of it as the hearing of it that defines this "critical turning-point": "And from the first they could hear singing . . . and of a new kind" (ch. 21). We discover, as Daniel Hughes puts it, that "a kind of musicalization is the key to the 'Christian' chapters of the book":

> Cecilia, in whose house Marius finds the purest Christian sentiment, is of course the later martyred patron saint of music, and it is to the pure sound of the early mass that we are directed. . . . Unlike Marcus' [Aurelius] rejection of the physical world, Cecilian Christianity restores visual and aural exaltation to their purest operation in the early Mass.[10]

Hughes is the only critic to my knowledge to have placed much emphasis on the aural imagery in ***Marius,*** but the term "pure sound" may need some qualification and the "kind of musicalization" needs to be specified, for the implied association of these terms with Pater's suggestion in the ***Renaissance*** that all art aspires to the condition of music can be misleading. Pure music, at least instrumental music, is not the key to this novel. There are references to instrumental music: the invisible harp, lyre, and pipes in Cupid's palace, Apollo's lyre and Pan's reeds at the marriage of Cupid and Psyche, the flutes in Marcus Aurelius's procession (ch. 12), and the performance of the *acroama* at the feast to honor Apuleius (ch. 20). Moreover, music in the "wider Platonic sense" (ch. 9) is important because it becomes a metaphor for the artistic ordering of life (chs. 9, 15, 16, 28) and for the Logos itself (ch. 8). Yet even as metaphor the term "music" includes song and thus speech as well, as in the references to the "call to play," which was heard all over Rome (ch. 9), and to the evening which itself became audible in the singing of the Christians (ch. 21).

In fact, the "kind of musicalization" that is the key to the novel is singing, that is, a combination of two genres, music and poetry. Moreover, the emphasis is on the human voice, one of the motifs of the novel, repeated in varying contexts ranging from the metaphorical "voice" of philosophy recurring in the Mass "with clearer accent than had ever belonged to it before, as if lifted, above its first intention, into the harmonies of some supreme system of knowledge or doctrine, at length complete" (ch. 23) to a brief epithet such as "the voice of Dante, the hand of Giotto" (ch. 22) implying that the essential difference between literature and art was the difference between an invisible voice and a visible hand.

To be more specific, the "kind of musicalization" that is the key to the novel is a fusion of music and a special kind of poetic speech: prayer. It is the "mystic tone of this praying and singing" (ch. 23) that attracts Marius to Cecilian Christianity, especially "the religious poetry of those Hebrew psalms":

> In the old pagan worship there had been little to call the understanding into play. Here, on the other hand, the utterance, the eloquence, the music of worship conveyed, as Marius readily understood, a fact or series of facts, for intellectual reception. That became evident, more especially, in those lessons, or sacred readings, which, like the singing, in broken vernacular Latin, occurred at certain intervals, amid the silence of the assembly. (ch. 23)

"Music" becomes almost a synonym for "utterance" or "eloquence" in this construction, especially the oral performance of sacred texts.[11]

Perhaps the best examples of music in this sense were hymns. Marius is familiar with various pagan combinations of prayer and song, such as the hymns sung during the *Ambarvalia* (ch. 1), the ancient hymns sung by his paternal relatives (ch. 2), Flavian's mystic hymn to life (ch. 6), the hymn sung by the choir of youths at the pageant for the launching of the *Ship of Isis* (ch. 6), the hymn to Diana in the Roman amphitheatre (ch. 14), the hymns chanted while the body of Lucius Verus lay in state at the Forum (ch. 17), but the Judeo-Christian hymns were different. The most successful ones derived from the Psalms. The Psalms had evolved into the music Marius most admires, the music of the Mass:

> In this way an obscure synagogue was expanded into the catholic church . . . she was already, as we have heard, the house of song—of a wonderful new music and poesy. . . . Singing there had been in abundance from the first; though often it dared only be "of the heart." And it burst forth, when it might, into the beginnings of a true ecclesiastical music; the Jewish psalter, inherited from the synagogue, turning now, gradually, from Greek into Latin—broken Latin, into Italian, as the ritual use of the rich, fresh, expressive vernacular superseded the earlier authorised language of the Church. . . . That hymn sung in the early morning, of which Pliny had heard, was kindling into the service of the Mass. (ch. 22)

The result is a seminal paradigm of its age "like the *Zeus* of Olympia, or the series of frescoes which commemorate *The Acts of Saint Francis*" (ch. 23).

However, there is a crucial difference: this is as much an auditory as a spatial paradigm: "It was not in an image, or series of images, yet still in a sort of dramatic action, and with the unity of a single appeal to eye and ear, that Marius about this time found all his new impressions set forth, regarding what he had already recognised, intellectually, as for him at least the most beautiful thing in the world" (ch. 23). The new paradigm, moreover, is without the advantage of a visible central image; it is what we now call a speech event, integrating many genres of speech: "The entire office, indeed, with its interchange of lessons, hymns, prayer, silence, was itself like a single piece of highly composite, dramatic music; a 'song of degrees,' rising steadily to a climax. Notwithstanding the absence of any central image visible to the eye, the entire ceremonial process, like the place in which it was enacted, was weighty with symbolic significance, seemed to express a single leading motive" (ch. 23). As Flavian had recommended in his literary program, this service draws its strength from the living language, that is the spoken language, the colloquial idiom, the vernacular, and it incorporates within it the basic conversational model, dialogue.

All the previous dialogues—the dialogue of cries in the tale of Cupid and Psyche, the dialogue generated by the performance of the text at the feast for Apuleius, the ongoing dialogue between Marius and Cornelius—are summarized and surpassed by the antiphonies of the service:

> The voices burst out . . . though still of an antiphonal character; the men, the women and children, the deacons, the people, answering one another, somewhat after the manner of a Greek chorus. But again with what a novelty of poetic accent; what a genuine expansion of heart; what profound intimations for the intellect, as the meaning of the words grew upon him! . . . Still in a strain of inspired supplication, the antiphonal singing developed, from this point, into a kind of dialogue between the chief minister and the whole assisting company—(ch. 23)

The result is that the communion hymn becomes a new model of human dialogue: "a hymn like the spontaneous product of two opposed militant companies, contending accordantly together, heightening, accumulating, their witness, provoking one another's worship, in a kind of sacred rivalry" (ch. 23).

Yet the most powerful part of the service is the oral performance of a text more like that of the novel itself, that is, a narrative. Here it is quite clear that what appealed to Marius's ear was not so much music, in the usual sense of the word, as the speaking of words we now call performatives. Marius had encountered performatives before—in the repetitions of a consecrated form of words in old Roman religious usage, such as the exclamation "*Numen Inest*" when passing into a grove of ilex, in the recitation of the old Latin words of the pagan liturgy in the procession of the *Ambarvalia* (ch. 1), in the words of some philter or malison a frantic woman cried out as the travelers passed on the way to Rome (ch. 10), in the spells and blessings recounted in the Cupid and Psyche story, in the forms of incantation recited by Aurelius as the chief religious functionary of the state (ch. 12), in the proclamation of the hour of noon by the *Accensus* in Rome (ch. 11), in the changing of the decree of divine rank for Lucius Verus (ch. 17)—but he found all these surpassed by the performatives inspired by the Christian narrative:[12]

> And last of all came a narrative. . . .
>
> . . . the proper action of the rite itself, like a half-opened book to be read by the duly initiated mind took up those suggestions, and carried them forward into the present, as having reference to a power still efficacious, still after some mystic sense even now in action among the people there assembled. . . .
>
> . . . *Adoramus te Christe, quia per crucem tuam redemisti mundum!*—they cry together. So deep is the emotion that at moments it seems to Marius as if some there present apprehend that prayer prevails, that the very object of this pathetic crying himself draws near. From the first there had been the sense, an increasing assurance, of one coming:—actually with them now, according to the oft-repeated affirmation or petition, *Dominus vobiscum!* . . .
>
> . . . catching therewith a portion of the enthusiasm of those beside him, Marius could discern dimly, behind the solemn recitation which now followed, at once a narrative and a prayer, the most touching image truly that had ever come within the scope of his mental or physical gaze. (ch. 23)

Of course this "image" is produced by an appeal not to his "physical gaze" but to his ears.

Nor is this an isolated incident in the text: "In early spring, he ventured once more to listen to the sweet singing of the Eucharist. It breathed more than ever the spirit of a wonderful hope. . . . As he followed again that mystical dialogue, he felt also again, like a mighty spirit about him, the potency, the half-realised presence, of a great multitude . . . the whole company of mankind. . . . And then, in its place, by way of sacred lection . . . came the *Epistle of the churches of Lyons and Vienne*" calling for a "new order of knighthood," of martyrdom if need be (ch. 26). The epistle thus invokes the biblical sense of the word "perform," a meaning even more powerful than those suggested by the modern concept of performatives. In the biblical model the performance of the words of a text demands the complete participation of the reader; his heart and soul are to embrace the heart and soul of the text: "I have inclined my heart to perform thy statutes always, *even unto* the end" (Psalms 119:112). It is not enough to read the text or even to speak it aloud; one must pour one's whole being into the performance of it: "Now therefore perform the doing *of it;* that as *there was* a readiness to will, so *there may be* a performance also out of that which ye have" (2 Cor. 8:11).[13]

The final chapter takes up the question of whether Marius—until now one of the most passive spectators of life—will be able to respond to this new model of reading. The answer is suggested by the title of the chapter, "Anima Naturaliter Christiana." Marius and Cornelius come to a church associated with the legend of the martyr Hyacinthus. Losing sleep over thoughts of that martyrdom, Marius at last sleeps heavily but awakens to find Cornelius absent. The Christians of the town "were at prayer before the tomb of the martyr; and even as Marius pressed among them to a place beside Cornelius" there is an earthquake. The pagans of the town, blaming the Christians, attack them and take Marius and Cornelius prisoner:

> It was surmised that one of the prisoners was not a Christian . . . and in the night, Marius . . . contrived that Cornelius, as the really innocent person, should be dismissed in safety on his way. . . . We wait for the great crisis which is to try what is in us . . . the "great climacteric point"—has been passed, which changes ourselves or our lives. . . . Marius had taken upon himself all the heavy risk of the position in which Cornelius had then been . . . possibly the danger of death. He had delivered his brother. (ch. 28)

The call to martyrdom in the *Epistle of the churches of Lyons and Vienne* had been truly "heard" by Marius; he "perform[ed] the doing *of it.*"

On his deathbed he recalls his almost exclusive preoccupation with the visual aspects of things: "Even then, just ere his eyes were to be shut for ever, the things they had seen seemed a veritable possession in hand; the persons, the places, above all, the touching image of Jesus, apprehended dimly through the expressive faces, the crying of the children, in that mysterious drama, with a sudden sense of peace and satisfaction now, which he could not explain to himself. . . . And again, as of old, the sense of gratitude seemed to bring with it the sense also of a living person at his side" (ch. 28). Those who emphasize Marius's Epicureanism point out that his "faith, to the end, is in the evidence of things seen," that "at the last Marius still longs to see."[14] But now the most important "image" for him is clearly visionary rather than visualized, one that in fact he never really "sees" except in the symbolic sense that the "body of Christ" is reconstituted by his followers. The "touching image of Jesus," of the "living person at his side" is conveyed to him not by his eyes but by the power of the spoken word, a power again invoked in Marius's final moments. Memories of his life flood in upon him: "He awoke amid the murmuring voices of the people who had kept and tended him so carefully through his sickness. . . . The people around his bed were praying fervently—*Abi! Abi! Anima Christiana!*" The title of the chapter suggests the success of this final performative. As he dies they give him the Eucharist and minister Extreme Unction. Finally they give him a Christian burial, "holding his death, according to their generous view in this matter, to have been of the nature of a martyrdom; and martyrdom, as the church had always said, a kind of sacrament with plenary grace" (ch. 28).

Readers with different interpretations of the terms "Christianity" and "Catholic Church" have not always taken such a generous view of the matter, of course. Many regard Marius's sacrifice of himself for Cornelius as a parody or an irony because once "Marius the spectator had become Marius the actor . . . commitment leads only to self-destruction."[15] While some readers may feel that the initial focus on martyrdom was an unfortunate tendency in early Christianity, there can be little doubt that the act itself is a final revelation of whether or not an individual has become a Christian. Marius obviously passes the ultimate test, one many more "orthodox" Christians would have failed: "This is my commandment, That ye love one another, as I have loved you. Greater love hath no man than this, that a man lay down his life for his friends" (John 15:12-13).[16] In terms of this act alone, Marius has clearly become a Christian in some sense of the word.

Readers can still protest that they remain unconvinced, of course, that Marius's conversion is out of character: he has been so passive up to this point that such a sudden act is not believable. U. C. Knoepflmacher, for example, concedes that "this passivity is meant to characterize a deliberate defect in Marius' mental make-up" but feels that "Marius' sacrifice is far less convincing as an active exercise of the 'heart' than either Dorothea Brooke's vindication of Tertius Lydgate or Daniel Deronda's adoption of his people's cause." In his view Marius's death "parodies, rather than re-enacts, the myth of the self-sacrificing God common to the religions of Christ and Apollo."[17]

Such a view is understandable but does not, it seems to me, give due weight to the power of performatives and the rest of the auditory imagery in the novel, nor to the history and psychology of conversions. Both subjects were dramatized by one of Pater's best pupils:

> We lash with the best or worst
> Word last! How a lush-kept plush-capped sloe
> Will, mouthed to flesh-burst,
> Gush!—flush the man, the being with it, sour or sweet,
> Brim, in a flash, full!—Hither then, last or first,
> To hero of Calvary, Christ's feet—
> Never ask if meaning it, wanting it, warned of it—
> men go.

Because sloes can be sour or sweet, it is only when we crush them that we find which they are. Similarly, a man can be good or bad and it is only when his back is to the wall and he lashes out with his best or worst word last that his true being will be revealed. Hopkins goes on to relate this drama to the history of conversions:

> With an anvil-ding
> And with fire in him forge thy will
> Or rather, rather then, stealing as Spring
> Through him, melt him but master him still:
> Whether at once, as once at a crash Paul,
> Or as Austin, a lingering-out swéet skíll. . . .[18]

Marius's conversion is ultimately more in the tradition of the surprising, sudden conversions typified by "as once at a crash Paul" rather than by Augustine. Hence we should not be surprised when the narrator goes on to ask if meaning it, wanting it, warned of it, Marius sought martyrdom, and we learn that even that glory was not sought by him, that, like Jesus in Gethsemane, he would have preferred that this cup of bitterness had been removed.

Although the gospels are clearly invoked in this way in an historical novel about the second century, one can still protest that it remains a Victorian novel and, compared to a realistic Victorian novel such as *Middlemarch,* that the conversion of Marius comes as too much of a surprise. Pater probably did not intend to be as realistic as George Eliot, but Marius's sudden action need not be dismissed as simply unrealistic if we consider the remarks of perhaps the greatest modern critic of realism, George Lukács:

> Situations arise in which a man is confronted with a choice; and in the act of choice a man's character may reveal itself in a light that surprises even himself. In literature . . . the denouement often consists in the realization of just such a potentiality, which circumstances have kept from coming to the fore. . . . The fate of the character depends upon the potentiality in question, even if it should condemn him to a tragic end. . . . It may even be buried away so completely that, before the moment of decision, it has never entered his mind even as an abstract potentiality. The subject, after taking his decision, may be unconscious

> of his own motives. Thus Richard Dudgeon, Shaw's Devil's Disciple, having sacrificed himself as Pastor Andersen, confesses: "I have often asked myself for the motive, but I find no good reason to explain why I acted as I did." Yet it is a decision which has altered the direction of his life . . . the qualitative leap of the denouement, cancelling and at the same time renewing the continuity of individual consciousness, can never be predicted. . . . The literature of realism, aiming at a truthful reflection of reality, must demonstrate both the concrete and abstract potentialities of human beings in extreme situations of this kind.[19]

Marius's self-defining sacrifice demonstrates that finally his most concrete potentiality is Christianity. Yet, partly because the title of the book is ***Marius the Epicurean,*** many readers prefer to stress the Epicurean potentiality. William Sharp, for example, in his review for the *Athenaeum,* was uncertain "if it has been Mr. Pater's intention to offer an apology for the higher Epicureanism."[20] Yet Pater wrote immediately to Sharp: "As regards the ethical drift of Marius, I should like to talk to you, if you were here. I *did* mean it to be more anti-Epicurean than it has struck you as being." While Pater made it clear that he was not "pleading for a formal thesis, or 'parti pris,'"[21] his own statement suggests that he would find some irony in modern arguments that Marius remains Epicurean or even "uncertain" about his potentialities.

Thus Harold Bloom is certainly correct to argue that "currently fashionable sensibility, two-thirds of the way through the century, is perhaps another ironic disordering of Paterian sensibility."[22] But there may be some difference of opinion about the definition of that irony. Bloom's description of Pater, for instance, as one who "makes . . . available to the coming age" the moment "when the mind will know neither itself nor the object but only the dumbfoundering abyss that comes between"[23] suggests how Pater's account of Heraclitus's reputation in the second century ironically foreshadowed his own reputation in the twentieth century: "Heracliteanism has grown to be almost identical with the famous doctrine of the sophist Protagoras, that the momentary, sensible apprehension of the individual was the only standard of what is or is not, and each one the measure of all things to himself. The impressive name of Heraclitus had become but an authority for a philosophy of the despair of knowledge" (ch. 8).

Yet if we heed Pater's auditory as well as his visual metaphors we can reconstruct a more balanced model of his theory of language and literature. Heraclitus's "negative doctrine," Pater reminds us, "had been, as originally conceived, but the preliminary step towards a large positive system of almost religious philosophy." We have overlooked this perhaps because that "almost religious philosophy" is expressed best in auditory rather than in visual images: in Heraclitus's "perpetual flux" there is a "continuance" of "orderly intelligible relationships, like the harmony of musical notes . . . ordinances of the divine reason" (ch. 8). In ***Plato and Platonism*** Pater again emphasizes that there was "another side to the doctrine of Heraclitus; an attempt on his part, after all, to reduce that world of chaotic mutation to *cosmos,* to the unity of a reasonable order, by the search for and the notation, if there be such, of an antiphonal rhythm, or logic, which, proceeding uniformly from movement to movement, as in some intricate musical theme, might link together in one those contending, infinitely diverse impulses."[24] Pater's musical imagery reminds us that despite Marius's initial sense of "the eye, the visual faculty of the mind," as the "unchangeable law of his temperament" (ch. 21), it is the ear which leads him to the music of the Logos.

The appeal of that music, moreover, is precisely that it is the opposite of a philosophy of despair. For Marius, in particular, the divine service was "contrasting itself . . . very forcibly, with the imperial philosopher's so heavy burden of unrelieved melancholy" (ch. 22). In comparison with the merely visual, written words of Marcus Aurelius, which stimulated only an inner dialogue, the oral performance of the script of the divine service provides Marius with a model of a dramatic, external dialogue with others. Thus his ear not only led him to the music of the Logos, but also to a fuller sense of human communication.

Speech is a more inclusive model because, as linguistic pragmatics has shown, it includes forms which writing usually avoids, such as those whose meaning depends on gesture, intonation, speech styles, or other vocal qualifiers, and more informal expressions drawn from the living language so frequently praised in ***Marius,*** the colloquial idiom as it was actually spoken. In spoken discourse, moreover, knowledge of the audience is usually more precise than in writing, and hence the relationships can be more personal and flexible. While written composition, once delivered to the recipient, is regarded as relatively fixed, not subject to further revision, oral composition has the advantage of revision and clarification in response to the audience.[25] The audience in turn has the additional information of the kinesis or para-language of the speaker. A speech act theory of literature, therefore, "offers the important possibility of integrating literary discourse into the same basic model of language as all our other communicative activities," for, unlike structuralist poetics, it need not associate "'literariness' directly with formal textual properties."[26] Moreover, the emphasis on the impact of "performatives" in speech act theory offers a more positive paradigm of language, one that can act as a counterpoise for spatial models, which if stressed too exclusively can lead to a philosophy of the despair of knowledge.

On the other hand, we do not really need a new theory to remind us that part of our experience of a text should be the living human voice. Victorian novels, after all, were often read aloud to families and larger audiences, and Philip Collins reminds us that a hundred years ago "much current literature was apprehended in this way—was indeed written with such a reception in mind," and thus "many people met contemporary literature as a group or communal, rather than an individual experience."[27]

The pervasiveness of auditory imagery even in the seminal text of "spatiality," ***Marius the Epicurean,*** suggests the importance of sound and voice in other texts. Take, for example, the novel we have already mentioned, *Middlemarch.* For Pater, George Eliot's most remarkable passage was Piero di Cosimo's remark in chapter 8 of *Romola* that "the only passionate life is in form and colour," and David DeLaura has demonstrated the influence of that novel on ***Marius the Epicurean.***[28] Pater's remark suggests that one of the key influences of Eliot on ***Marius*** was her visual imagery. The artistic associations of her Dorothea, for instance, suggest that she may be regarded as a prototype for Cecilia in ***Marius.*** The names of both heroines are allusions to saints famous in painting and sculpture. In fact both Dorothea and Cecilia were Latin virgin martyrs who were able to convert men partly because their guardian angels brought fresh flowers gathered in Paradise. Hence both were represented in painting with the palm of victory, a crown of red and white roses, and an angel, and were therefore sometimes difficult to distinguish.

Moreover, the cult of Dorothea among the Pre-Raphaelites endowed her with contemporary artistic associations as well. By the time Eliot wrote *Middlemarch* Dante Gabriel Rossetti had painted his *Dorothy and Theophilus,* Christina Rossetti had completed her "A Shadow of Dorothea," Hopkins had composed two versions of his "For a Picture of St. Dorothea," Swinburne had finished his "St. Dorothy," Burne-Jones had completed his design for an embroidery of her, and Morris had begun a poem on her for *The Earthly Paradise.*[29] These representations of her lend support to the suggestion that the opening sentence of *Middlemarch* "makes of Dorothea a genuinely Pre-Raphaelite Madonna."[30] Moreover, the original nineteenth-century Pre-Raphaelites, the Nazarenes, play an important role in the novel.

Yet it is particularly significant for the auditory imagery of ***Marius,*** especially that associated with St. Cecilia, as well as for our sense of how language and literature work, that the hero of *Middlemarch* finally rejects the visual arts because he discovers, as he tells the leader of the Nazarenes, that only language can begin to convey the ideal which Dorothea represents:

> "And what is a portrait of a woman? Your painting and Plastik are poor stuff after all. They perturb and dull conceptions instead of raising them. Language is a finer medium. . . . Language gives a fuller image, which is all the better for being vague. After all, the true seeing is within; and painting stares at you with an insistent imperfection. I feel that especially about representations of women. . . . This woman whom you have just seen, for example: how would you paint her voice, pray? But her voice is much diviner than anything you have seen of her."[31]

Ladislaw's comments about Dorothea may well have recalled for Pater the descriptions of responses to paintings of Cecilia by Anna Jameson, the founder of the Victorian cult of St. Dorothea. She reported that in one painting Cecilia was "listening with an entranced expression to the song of invisible angels" and in another a friend of hers "was struck by the peculiar expression in the eyes of St. Cecilia, which he said he had often remarked as characteristic of musicians by profession, or those devoted to music,—an expression of *listening* rather than *seeing.*"[32]

Notes

1. "The Uncanny Critic of Brasenose: Walter Pater and Modernisms," *Victorian Newsletter,* No. 58 (1980), pp. 12-13; for examples of the modern emphasis on the visual paradigm see Wallace Stevens, *The Necessary Angel* (New York: Knopf, 1951), p. 159; René Wellek and Austin Warren, *Theory of Literature,* 3rd ed. (New York: Harcourt, Brace, 1956), p. 126; Robert Scholes, *Structuralism in Literature* (New Haven: Yale Univ. Press, 1974), p. 29; Jacques Derrida, *Of Grammatology,* trans. Gayatri Chakravorty Spivak (Baltimore: Johns Hopkins Univ. Press, 1976), p. 7, and Derrida, *Speech and Phenomena,* trans. David B. Allison (Evanston: Northwestern Univ. Press, 1973), p. 76; Jeffrey R. Smitten and Ann Daghistany, eds., *Spatial Form in Narrative* (Ithaca: Cornell Univ. Press, 1981).
2. *Marius the Epicurean: His Sensations and Ideas,* Library Edition, 2 vols. (London: Macmillan, 1914), ch. 3; subsequent citations in my text are to this edition.
3. *Walter Pater's Art of Autobiography* (New Haven: Yale Univ. Press, 1980), p. 52.
4. Ibid., pp. 65-66.
5. On *Marius the Epicurean* as Pater's seminal text see Blanche Winder, "A Master of Aesthetic," *Spectator,* 11 Aug. 1928, p. 186; Joseph Sagmaster, ed., *Marius the Epicurean* (Garden City, N.Y.: Doubleday, Doran, 1935), pp. xix-xxii; David J. DeLaura, *Hebrew and Hellene in Victorian England: Newman, Arnold, and Pater* (Austin: Univ. of Texas Press, 1969), pp. 263, 285; and Graham Hough, *The Last Romantics* (1949; rpt. New York: Barnes and Noble, 1961), p. 145.
6. *Pater's Portraits* (Baltimore: Johns Hopkins Press, 1967), p. 86; cf. pp. 66, 71-74.
7. Elizabeth Closs Traugott and Mary Louise Pratt, *Linguistics for Students of Literature* (New York: Harcourt, Brace, 1980), p. 229.
8. See David J. DeLaura, "'O Unforgotten Voice': The Memory of Newman in the Nineteenth Century," in *Sources for Reinterpretation: The Use of Nineteenth-Century Literary Documents: Essays in Honor of C. L. Cline* (Austin: Dept. of English and Humanities Research Center, Univ. of Texas, 1975), pp. 23-55; James Nohrnberg, "Literature and the Bible," *Centrum,* 2, No. 2 (1974), 19-20, 22-37, 30; and Donald D. Evans, *The Logic of Self-Involvement* (London: SCM Press, 1963).
9. *The Jerusalem Bible,* ed. Alexander Jones et al. (Garden City, N.Y.: Doubleday, 1966), pp. 168, 217.
10. "*Marius* and the Diaphane," *Novel,* 9 (1975), 63.
11. On eloquence as music see DeLaura, "'O Unforgotten Voice,'" pp. 23, 26-27, 41, 43.

12. See Nohrnberg, "Literature and the Bible," and Evans, *The Logic of Self-Involvement;* for the relationship between the divine service and performatives see A. P. Martinich, "Sacraments and Speech Acts," *Heythrop Journal,* 16 (1975), 289-303, 405-417; for a connection with literature see James Leggio, "Hopkins and Alchemy," *Renascence,* 29 (1977), 115-30.
13. King James Authorized version of the Bible.
14. Harold Bloom, *The Ringers in the Tower: Studies in Romantic Tradition* (Chicago: Univ. of Chicago Press, 1971), pp. 189, 194.
15. Ian Fletcher, *Walter Pater* (London: Longmans, Green, 1959), p. 27; a number of other readers find Marius's attraction to Christianity a "movement toward death" and "a surrender of reason," as Avrom Fleishman puts it in *The English Historical Novel: Walter Scott to Virginia Woolf* (Baltimore: Johns Hopkins Univ. Press, 1971), pp. 173-75.
16. Authorized King James Version of the Bible.
17. *Religious Humanism and the Victorian Novel* (Princeton: Princeton Univ. Press, 1965), p. 221.
18. Gerard Manley Hopkins, "The Wreck of the Deutschland," *The Poems of Gerard Manley Hopkins,* ed. W. H. Gardner and N. H. MacKenzie, 4th ed. (London: Oxford Univ. Press, 1967), p. 54. On the power of performatives in the poem see W. David Shaw, "Mill on Poetic Truth: Are Intuitive Inferences Valid?" *Texas Studies in Literature and Language,* 23 (1981), 30-35; for the relationship between Pater and Hopkins see Bernard Duffey, "The Religion of Pater's *Marius,*" *Texas Studies in Literature and Language,* 2 (1960), 103-14; David Anthony Downes, *Victorian Portraits: Hopkins and Pater* (New York: Bookman, 1965); and Jerome Bump, "Hopkins, Pater, and Medievalism," *Victorian Newsletter,* No. 50 (1976), pp. 10-15, which focuses on Pater's initial antagonism to Christianity.
19. "The Ideology of Modernism," *The Meaning of Contemporary Realism,* trans. John and Necke Mander (London: Merlin Press, 1963), pp. 22-23; rpt. in *Twentieth Century Literary Criticism,* ed. David Lodge (London: Longman, 1972), p. 478.
20. Unsigned review of *Marius the Epicurean, Athenaeum,* 28 Feb. 1885, p. 272.
21. Pater to William Sharp, 1 Mar. 1885, *Letters of Walter Pater,* ed. Lawrence Evans (Oxford: Clarendon Press, 1970), pp. 58-59.
22. Bloom, *The Ringers in the Tower,* p. 186.
23. Harold Bloom, "Walter Pater: The Intoxication of Belatedness," *Yale French Studies,* No. 50 (1974), p. 172.
24. *Plato and Platonism,* New Library Edition (London: Macmillan, 1912), pp. 17-18.
25. Traugott and Pratt, *Linguistics for Students of Literature,* pp. 41-46, 260-62.
26. Mary Louise Pratt, *Toward a Speech Act Theory of Literary Discourse* (Bloomington: Indiana Univ. Press, 1977), pp. 88, 87; see also Richard Ohmann, "Literature as Act," in *Approaches to Poetics,* ed. Seymour Chatman (New York: Columbia Univ. Press, 1973), pp. 81-107. For a sense of the debate between writing and speech models of literature see Jacques Derrida, "Signature Event Context," and John R. Searle, "Reiterating the Differences: A Reply to Derrida," both in *Glyph,* No. 1 (1977), pp. 172-208; Jacques Derrida, "Limited Inc.," *Glyph,* No. 2 (1977), pp. 162-254; E. D. Hirsch, "What's the Use of Speech-Act Theory?" *Centrum,* 3, No. 2 (1975), 122-23; Avrom Fleishman, "Speech and Writing in *Under Western Eyes,*" in *Fiction and the Ways of Knowing* (Austin: Univ. of Texas Press, 1978), pp. 123-35; and Jerome Bump, "Reading Hopkins: Visual vs. Auditory Paradigms," *Bucknell Review,* 26, No. 2 (1982), 119-45.
27. *Reading Aloud: A Victorian Métier,* Tennyson Society Monographs, No. 5 (Lincoln, England: Tennyson Research Centre, 1972), pp. 10, 27.
28. "*Romola* and the Origin of the Paterian View of Life," *NCF [Nineteenth-Century Fiction],* 21 (1966), 225-26, 230, 233.
29. For more on the Pre-Raphaelite cult of St. Dorothy see Jerome Bump, "Reading Hopkins: Visual vs. Auditory Paradigms," pp. 122-30.
30. Gillian Beer, "Myth and the Single Consciousness: *Middlemarch* and *The Lifted Veil*" in *This Particular Web,* ed. Ian Adam (Toronto: Univ. of Toronto Press, 1975), p. 102.
31. George Eliot, *Middlemarch,* ed. Gordon S. Haight, Riverside ed. (Boston: Houghton, 1956), ch. 19, p. 142.
32. *Sacred and Legendary Art,* 2 vols. (1896; rpt. AMS Press, 1970), II, 594, and II, 594, n. 6.

Nathan A. Scott, Jr. (essay date 1983)

SOURCE: "Pater's Imperative—To Dwell Poetically," in *New Literary History,* Vol. XV, No. 1, Autumn, 1983, pp. 93-118.

[*In the following essay, Scott describes the plot of* Marius the Epicurean *and defends Pater against critics who, he contends, misread his appeal in "the central statement of his career."*]

> I require of you only to look.
>
> St. Teresa of Avila
>
> . . . yet poetically, dwells
> Man on this earth.
>
> Friedrich Hölderlin

When Walter Pater went up to Oxford in 1858, he was intending to take orders in the Church of England and soon fell much under the influence of the kind of theological liberalism represented by Arthur Penrhyn Stanley and Frederick Denison Maurice and Benjamin Jowett. But by 1866 he was finding it necessary to remark in his essay on Coleridge (the anonymous appearance of which in *The Westminster Review* in January of that year marked his first publication) that "modern thought is distinguished from ancient by its cultivation of the 'relative' spirit in place of the 'absolute.'" And, very clearly, he had traveled a great distance indeed since his matriculation at Queen's College eight years earlier, for his intention in the essay on Coleridge to speak as a champion of "the 'relative' spirit" cannot be mistaken. His great charge is that Coleridge, in his role as metaphysician and theologian, had had too great a lust for the Absolute: his "chief offense" lay in "an excess of seriousness . . . arising . . . from a misconception of the perfect manner." One does not "weep" or "shriek" over the collapse of a received tradition: what is requisite is "a kind of humour"[1] that permits one urbanely to remark the passing of what must pass—and this Coleridge did not have. So the plaintiveness expressed by many of his contemporaries regarding the erosion of the religious terrain Pater would not, on principle, allow himself: since he conceived "metaphysical questions . . . [to be] unprofitable,"[2] he chose rather to embrace "the wholesome scepticism of Hume and Mill."[3]

Yet though Pater himself was prepared to speak of the wholesomeness of that skepticism which he found in Hume and Mill, he was in so doing surely by way of misrepresenting himself in no small measure. For the essential tonality of his mind bears hardly any resemblance at all to that of so thoroughly secular a man as Stuart Mill. True, by the time he had reached his full maturity he appears to have become persuaded that that whole structure of thought denominated in our own period by Martin Heidegger as "onto-theo-logy" was just so much metaphysical lumber that one could quite easily do without. And the more purely theoretical passages in ***The Renaissance*** make clear, as do many of his other writings, a deep temperamental attachment to English empiricism, for he remained always convinced that the noumenality of the world—what things are *in themselves*—must forever surpass the reach of the human mind. But he despised as heartily as did the Arnold of *Culture and Anarchy* the new secular ethos of his time that seemed everywhere to be in the ascendancy and to be promoting the superstition that human welfare lay in some new arrangement of "the mere machinery of life," in some new mode of *doing* rather than *being*.[4] And he had no sympathy at all for the Mr. Gradgrinds of the world—those who (in Dickens's account in *Hard Times*) proceed "upon the principle that two and two are four, and nothing over," who keep always the multiplication table in their pockets, "ready to weigh and measure any parcel of human nature, and tell you exactly what it comes to," supposing that it is all "a mere question of figures, a case of simple arithmetic." For in such an apprehension of the world, so lacking in "breadth" and "centrality" and "repose,"[5] there was for such a man as Pater a fearsome kind of godlessness, and against this *trahison* of the age he (as he said in a letter to Vernon Lee [Violet Paget]) saw it as a matter of "duty" to chart "a . . . sort of religious phase possible for the modern mind . . . the conditions of which phase it is the main object of my design to convey."[6]

Now, in taking the measure of this design, one needs to begin at the very beginning, with an essay entitled **"Diaphanéité"**[7] which Pater wrote, when he was not yet quite twenty-five, in the early summer of 1864, and which he is thought to have read that July before a little Oxford literary society called "Old Mortality." "There are some unworldly types of character," he suggests, "which the world is able to estimate. It recognises certain moral types, or categories, and regards whatever falls within them as having a right to exist. The saint, the artist, even the speculative thinker, out of the world's order as they are, yet work, so far as they work at all, in and by means of the main current of the world's energy," and the world can manage, therefore, to find "room for them in its scheme of life." But there is another type of character for which it has "no place ready in its affections" and with which it does not easily reckon. This is the Diaphanous Personality, which is distinguished by its concern "to value everything at its eternal worth" and to see "external circumstances as they are." It approaches the world with an utter "simplicity in purpose and act" and is untainted by any kind of predatoriness or desire to master and control and manipulate: it is an adept in the discipline of what the late Martin Heidegger called "letting-be,"[8] and it does not value "things and persons as marks or counters of something to be gained, or achieved, beyond them." The "guilelessness" of this "clear crystal nature" is sometimes mistakenly thought to be merely a sort of "indifferentism," but its guiding motive is *disponibilité,* or what Pater terms "receptivity": it wants to be *open* and intransitively attentive to all the things and creatures of earth, not just as so many appurtenances of the human enterprise but as having, each in its own way, such an inherent dignity as results from each having (as Pater's friend Gerard Manley Hopkins phrased it) its own "pitch of self," its own "instress" and "inscape." "All things," says Hopkins, "are upheld by instress and are meaningless without it."[9] And by "instress" he means that *élan* or ontological energy wherewith a bird or a flower or a cloud in the sky is assembled into the given *gestalt* which it constitutes and is made to be what it is—rather than another thing—whereas "inscape" is simply the pattern or the form which a thing's instress makes. And it is this dimension of the natural and the human order—the dimension of instresses and inscapes, of quiddities and hecceities—that fascinates the Diaphanous Man. Moreover, though Pater never quite gets round clearly to saying so, one finds it difficult to resist the surmise that what is presupposed by the ethic of *diaphanéité* (of openness, of transparency, of what Heidegger calls *Gelassenheit*)[10] is a kind of sacramentalism, a sense of a "dearest freshness deep down things"[11] that charges the world with a grandeur we ignore at a very great cost to ourselves. "He who is ever looking for the breaking of a light he knows not whence about him, notes with a strange heedfulness the faintest paleness in the sky."[12] And it is the *pietas* that may be called forth by this "deepest freshness," this breaking of light, that forms perhaps the essential element in what Pater conceived to be the "religious phase possible for the modern mind."

He never published this "Old Mortality" paper, however, and, apparently, the only remaining copy at the time of his death was that in the possession of Charles Lancelot Shadwell (his former pupil and, later, Provost of Oriel College, Oxford), who, as his literary executor, issued it in the posthumous collection ***Miscellaneous Studies,*** which first appeared in 1895. But though Pater himself never sought an audience for it, it yet provides the essential preparation for a reading of the first masterpiece of his career, the book that Macmillan published in March of 1873 under the title ***Studies in the History of the Renaissance.***[13]

Indeed, it is the Crystal Man[14] who is really the central focus of ***The Renaissance.*** By reason of its splendidly cadenced and remarkably eloquent prose the book, of course, remains one of the great modern classics. Yet with all its misattributions of artworks, its misrenderings of historical fact, and its derivativeness from such historians as Giorgio Vasari and Jules Michelet and Giovanni Battista Cavalcaselle and Cesare Guasti and Carlo Amoretti and Otto Jahn, we do not go to ***The Renaissance*** for instruction about Pico della Mirandola, Botticelli, Luca della Robbia, Michelangelo, Leonardo da Vinci, the school of Giorgione, Joachim du Bellay, and the eighteenth-century German Hellenist Johann Joachim Winckelmann (these figures being Pater's main subjects). True, the book is filled with brilliant *aperçus* and carries many occasional insights into particular works of art that are astonishing in their cogency and penetration. But what is bound to be most captivating for a contemporary reader is the ethic, the discipline, of diaphaneity that is being adumbrated at the beginning of the volume in its "Preface," at the end in its "Conclusion," and at numerous other points in the main body of the text.

Pater's commitment to the phenomenalist interpretation of experience advanced by the classic English empiricists is, of course, made evident again and again throughout the book. "At first sight experience," he says, "seems to bury us under a flood of external objects, pressing upon us with a sharp and importunate reality, calling us out of ourselves in a thousand forms of action. But when reflexion begins to play upon those objects they are dissipated under its influence; the cohesive force seems suspended like some trick of magic; each object is loosed into a group of impressions—colour, odour, texture—in the mind of the observer" (p. 187). So though he is quite as eager as Arnold that we should "see the object as in itself it really is," he wants to lay it down that "the first step towards seeing one's object as it really is, is to know one's own impression as it really is" (p. xix), for this is the one residue that our contact with the world deposits in the mind. In short, to know one's impressions and to discriminate and realize them as distinctly as one possibly can is to *see*—and *seeing* (in the sense not primarily of riveting the eye but of *playing heed*) is our only way of *receiving* the manifold richness of Creation.

But each impression or intuition is an affair of a single moment—and, of course, it is of the nature of each moment to be in perpetual flight. Early and late, indeed, Pater follows one of his great masters Heraclitus in viewing the world as everywhere pervaded by ceaseless flux. In, for example, his book of 1893, ***Plato and Platonism,*** he tells us that "the most modern metaphysical, and the most modern empirical philosophies alike have illustrated emphatically, justified, expanded, the divination . . . of the ancient theorist of Ephesus [Heraclitus]" (p. 19). Yet he felt very strongly that Heraclitus's teaching is misconstrued when it is identified wholly with an emphasis on the transiency and inconstancy of things. In ***Marius the Epicurean*** (1885) he suggests that Heraclitus's doctrine about perpetual change was "but the preliminary step towards a large positive system of almost religious philosophy," since he conceived continual change to be an "indicator of a subtler but all-pervading motion—the sleepless, ever-sustained, inexhaustible energy of the divine reason itself, proceeding always by its own rhythmical logic, and lending to all mind and matter, in turn, what life they had."[15] And he makes a similar point in ***Plato and Platonism,*** where, again, he insists that Heraclitus wanted, finally, to identify a principle of order amidst this "world of chaotic mutation" and that, above all else, he was searching for "an antiphonal rhythm, or logic, which, proceeding uniformly from movement to movement, as in some intricate musical theme, might link together in one those contending, infinitely diverse impulses." He believed, in other words, that even amidst all the flux of universal change, there is a "Wisdom . . . [that] 'reacheth from end to end, sweetly and strongly ordering all things'" (pp. 17-18).

Now, even if Pater himself is not to be found invoking such "an antiphonal rhythm" as he descried in the Heraclitean scheme, he was nevertheless most certainly wanting to propose the possibility of a kind of transcendence of sheer motion and flux—and this, in his view, lay in such a strict attentiveness to each moment as will redeem it from all extraneousness and irrelevancy and permit it to be ignited with a "hard, gem-like flame" (***Renaissance,*** p. 189). We are situated in the immense theater of the world—as the Psalmist says, of the sun and moon, of fire and hail, of mountains and hills, of beasts and flying fowl, of young men and maidens, and old men and children[16]—and only a certain number of experiences (or impressions) are given to us. Which means that if we are in any deep way to be leavened by the rich bounteousness represented by all the marvelous variety of existence, we must, as Pater urges, by way of a most stringent discipline or *ascêsis* cultivate a very careful kind of attentiveness to the "virtue" (i.e., the radically distinctive property) of each passing moment and to what it brings (***Renaissance,*** pp. xx-xxi)—of a sort of family relationship with the things and creatures of earth. "To burn always with this hard, gem-like flame . . . is success in life. . . . Not to discriminate every moment

. . . is, on this short day of frost and sun, to sleep before evening" (p. 189).

Indeed, the chief reason why the Crystal Man is prepared to make large room in his life for art is because "the picture, the landscape, the engaging personality . . . in a book, *La Gioconda* . . . are valuable for their virtues, as we say, in speaking of a herb, a wine, a gem. . . . Our education becomes complete in proportion as our susceptibility to these impressions increases in depth and variety" (p. xx). Which is to say that, his misgivings about what he calls "heavy realism" (p. 52) notwithstanding, Pater takes it as axiomatic that authentic art bears a referential relationship to the actual world. True, the artist transcribes not "mere fact, but . . . his sense of it."[17] Yet finally he does not create *ex nihilo* if he wants to exert a serious claim upon us. For we have only "an interval, and then our place knows us no more," so that "our one chance lies in expanding that interval, in getting as many pulsations as possible into the given time"(p. 190)—and this in turn means that any art, literary or visual,[18] which is to engage us deeply must make our attentiveness to *actual* things more wakeful. In this connection it is significant that the major heroes of ***The Renaissance***—Botticelli and Michelangelo and Leonardo and Giorgione and, most especially, Winckelmann—are all presented as exemplars of Pater's special sort of *ascêsis* by reason of the extraordinary *receptivity* they represent toward the manifold influxions of reality; and this is to say that they are conceived to be examples of the Crystal Man, of him who embodies in a singular way *diaphanéité,* an openness and a transparency vis-à-vis the world, something like Heidegger's *Gelassenheit.*

The essential logic, then, of the book of 1873 would hardly seem to be of the kind suggested by the traditional view of Pater as an effete connoisseur of the rare and the strange, as a mandarin self-indulgently specializing in a hedonistic sensualism. For his refusal of that myth of the world as merely a huge *res extensa,* silent and lifeless; his conviction of its bidding us indeed at every point to join it in a relationship of reciprocity that requires us to cultivate the virtue of *diaphanéité,* of "constant and eager observation" (p. 188); his vision of "the splendour of our experience" (p. 189) within our inherited universe—all this belongs to a basic pattern of ideas which, in its tendency to invest the things of earth with a radical kind of holiness, appears to reflect an *anima naturaliter religiosa* (and one for whom religious value is not subsumed under but does itself subsume aesthetic experience).

But already in the weeks immediately following the first appearance of ***The Renaissance,*** the misreading of Pater's intentions began. For the word carried by the "Conclusion" about "getting as many pulsations as possible into the given time" strangely gave the entire book "the insidious appeal of some prose *Fleurs du Mal,*"[19] and difficult as it may now be to imagine, in conservative Oxford it quickly made an occasion of scandal. The Chaplain of Brasenose College, John Wordsworth, who as a colleague had been on friendly terms with Pater, sent him a brusque letter warning that "it may be my duty to oppose you":

> After a perusal of the book I cannot disguise from myself that the concluding pages adequately sum up the philosophy of the whole; and that the philosophy is an assertion, that no fixed principles either of religion or morality can be regarded as certain, that the only thing worth living for is momentary enjoyment and that probably or certainly the soul dissolves at death into elements which are destined never to reunite. . . . My object in writing is not to attempt argument on these conclusions, nor simply to let you know the pain they have caused me and I know also many others. Could you indeed have known the dangers into which you were likely to lead minds weaker than your own, you would, I believe, have paused. Could you have known the grief your words would be to many of your Oxford contemporaries you might even have found no ignoble pleasure in refraining from uttering them.[20]

And the letter ends by begging Pater not henceforth to participate as an examiner in the College's divinity examinations. But within Oxford, Wordsworth's renunciation was only one of many rebuffs that came Pater's way. In, for example, 1874, the year as it so happened when it was the prerogative of Brasenose to name a Proctor for the University, Pater, who had been assured of the nomination, was in the event turned aside, this resulting at least in part (as Thomas Wright suggests)[21] from the opposition of Benjamin Jowett, the distinguished Master of Balliol, in whom ***The Renaissance*** had excited a considerable repugnance. Again, in the following year John Fielder Mackarness, the Bishop of Oxford, denounced Pater's book in a pastoral letter to his clergy.[22] And outside Oxford, Mrs. (Margaret Wilson) Oliphant spoke for many when, in her review of the book in *Blackwood's Magazine* (November 1873), she declared that

> Mr. Pater's volume, though there are bits of very pretty writing in it, and here and there a saying which is worth quoting, is full of so much 'windy suspiration of forced breath', and solemn assumption of an oracular importance, that the critic scarcely knows whether to laugh or frown at the loftiness of the intention. . . . The book is *rococo* from beginning to end,—in its new version of that coarse old refrain of the Epicureans' gay despair, 'Let us eat and drink, for tomorrow we die'—as well as in its prettiness of phrase and graceful but far-fetched fancies.[23]

And this philippic prompted George Eliot, a few days after its appearance, to send a letter to the Editor of *Blackwood's* informing him that she "agreed very warmly with the remarks made by your contributor this month on Mr. Pater's book, which seems to me quite poisonous in its false principles of criticism and false conceptions of life."[24]

Now the responses of the mid-1870s to ***The Renaissance,*** in all their wrongheadedness and miscomprehension, did indeed, in projecting an image of Pater as a mannered proficient in *sensualité,* have a decisive effect on the shaping of the canonical verdict, not only about the book of 1873 but about the drift of his work as a whole. And this represents one of the more unfortunate miscarriages of modern literary and intellectual life, since the canonical verdict does so egregiously distort his real message. For what he most wanted to enunciate was his conviction that, if we are to come into our full human stature, we must (in Hölderlin's phrase) dwell "poetically . . . on this earth."[25]

This phrase of Hölderlin's fascinated Martin Heidegger, the last great genius of modern philosophy, and one of his more remarkable essays of the early 1950s—which is entitled ". . . dichterisch wohnet der Mensch . . ."[26]—is devoted to a lengthy meditation on what he took to be implied by Hölderlin's notion of "poetic dwelling." But this essay is only one of many he produced in the forties and fifties on similar themes.[27] For in his later years, he became convinced that "the poet" (*der Dichter*) presents us with the purest and most instructive example of "the thinker" (*der Denker*), since he, insofar as he truly keeps faith with his primary vocation, is an unexampled adept at "paying heed" to the sheer specificity of all the various things with which the world is furnished. For Heidegger, in other words, the true poet is preoccupied never with the light that never was on land or sea but always with the light of ordinary day, and he solicits our attention to the concrete particularity of lived experience. And thus, as Heidegger says in one of the *Holzwege* essays, poetry brings "beings as such for the first time into the Open."

Normally, of course, we move through the world from day to day, paying only so much attention to this or that as the necessities of one or another occasion allow, and the things and persons making up our environment are no more than cues for action or signals of desire, offering not even the merest approximation of what would be there were we to take the trouble of paying heed. So everything is gross and banal and full of dead spots. Which is why we do not have a "world" in which to "dwell," for to have a world is to have a unified matrix of meanings and relations—and this one does not have until "beings as such . . . [are brought] into the Open." Which is in turn to say, for Heidegger, that one can have a world only insofar as one manages to be a "poet" (the chief differentia of the poet being not so much an affair of his versifying as of his performing a certain kind of attentive act before the things of earth).

So on Heidegger's reckoning, really to inhabit this earth is to *dwell poetically,* for it is only in this way that we can be rescued—as *Pater* puts it—from "the fatal, irresistible, mechanic play of circumstance."[28] And this is why the author of *Erläuterungen zu Hölderlins Dichtung* says that it is the poet who *names* "the gods" (meaning by "gods" whatever it is that "assembles" things into the aspect of stability and trustworthiness) and thus mediates "the Holy."

Now it is, of course, a hazardous thing to do to speak of this German master of our own century in relation to the Victorian don who produced ***The Renaissance,*** since one is bound to invite the demurrer, so distant do they at first seem from each other, that a very strange brew is being arranged. But the lesson that long ago Eliot was laying down in his famous essay of 1917 on "Tradition and the Individual Talent" deserves still to be remembered, that intellectual and literary history presents us not with just so many silent monuments but with something like a forum that is very much astir, a forum in which no single figure "has his complete meaning alone," since that meaning stands constantly to be modified or illumined not only by those who have gone before but also by those who come after.[29] Which means that Emerson may be found to comment on Nietzsche, and Proust on Augustine, and Sterne on Joyce, and so on *ad infinitum.* So for all their differences of lineage and idiom, there is no impropriety at all in juxtaposing (as I have done) Pater and Heidegger, most especially since Heidegger's whole concept of *der Dichter* and "poetic dwelling" does so closely parallel and clarify Pater's vision of the Crystal Man and *diaphanéité,* these latter being the conceptions that are at bottom regulating the structure of thought which we confront in ***The Renaissance.***

The pattern of ideas that was most truly essential to this book went by and large, however, unrecognized, and Pater had to endure a critical response that was absurdly wide of the mark. Indeed, it is very probably the bruising effect of the general reception of ***The Renaissance*** that explains the halting tentativeness of Pater's literary efforts over the next several years. In April of 1874 he published in *The Fortnightly Review* a fine essay on Wordsworth, which, in its account of how the poet of *The Prelude* could be lifted from the natural order to a sense of "the brooding power of one universal spirit," presents an exact estimate of Wordsworth's genius, and which at the same time, in its defense of that "impassioned contemplation" whereby life may be approached "in the spirit of art," continues his meditation on the ethic of *diaphanéité.*[30] Then, again, in November of 1874 *The Fortnightly Review* published his fine essay on Shakespeare's *Measure for Measure.* And in the following years in *The Fortnightly* and *Macmillan's Magazine* he issued a few things—the first of his "imaginary portraits" (**"The Child in the House"**), the first of his Greek studies (**"The Myth of Demeter and Persephone"**), and various other pieces—but none of this was major work. In 1878 the Macmillan firm warmly endorsed his proposal to bring out a new collection of his essays, but no sooner was he faced with his proofs than he lost heart altogether, and he wrote to Alexander Macmillan to say (30 November 1878): "I hope you will forgive me all the trouble I have given you. But, sincerely, I think it would be a mistake to publish the essays in their present form; some day they may take a better and more complete form. Please send me a line of assent at once."[31] And a few days later he sent Macmillan "a cheque" for thirty-five pounds to cover the costs of typesetting, requesting in the note that accompanied it that the type be broken up.

Pater's habits of restraint and reticence never, of course, allowed him to express any sort of regret or complaint about the reception of his work: only "those nearest to him," says A. C. Benson (meaning no doubt his sisters Hester and Clara), knew his "dark moods of discouragement."[32] Yet the record of his literary life surely suggests that in the years immediately after the first edition of ***The Renaissance*** he was a deeply wounded man.

Gradually, however, as it would seem, he recovered some firmness of spirit, for by the spring of 1881 he had a new project well in hand, and one that was to prove so exacting that in 1883 he felt obliged, though retaining his Fellowship, to resign his Brasenose tutorship, despite the considerable inconvenience entailed by the consequent loss of a sizable portion of his income. Pater's own sense of the significance of this project—a novel, with its setting in the Roman Italy of the Antonines in the second century A.D., which was to be called ***Marius the Epicurean***—is perhaps most clearly indicated by the footnote he prepared for the "Conclusion" of ***The Renaissance,*** when, after having suppressed it in the second edition of 1877, he restored it in the third edition of 1888. The footnote says: "This brief 'Conclusion' was omitted in the second edition of this book, as I conceived it might possibly mislead some of those young men into whose hands it might fall. On the whole, I have thought it best to reprint it here, with some slight changes which bring it closer to my original meaning. I have dealt more fully in ***Marius the Epicurean*** with the thoughts suggested by it" (p. 186).

More clearly perhaps than anything else that may be cited, the final sentence of this note suggests something of what it was that prompted Pater to undertake the writing of the book that did at last appear in 1885 and that requires to be thought of as the central statement of his career. Though deeply responsive to Catholic Christianity in its Anglican expressions,[33] "the wholesome scepticism" he had learned from Hume and Mill made it impossible, as his essay on Coleridge indicates, for him to accept "vague scholastic abstractions" or any sort of "absolute." Like an American theologian of our own period, he felt that "if we are to have any transcendence . . . it must be in and through the secular," that "if we are to find grace it is to be found in the world and not overhead."[34] Which meant for him that, if whatever it is that gives ultimate meaning and dignity to the human order is to be found (as a later writer was to phrase it) in "the actual landscape with its actual horns / Of baker and butcher blowing,"[35] the highest discipline to be cultivated is that of keeping oneself *receptive* and *open* and *attentive* to the things of this world. "I require of you only to look," says St. Teresa of Avila, and it is a similar exaction that is being held up by the "Conclusion" of ***The Renaissance*** as having a primary claim upon us. And since in Pater's view the principal office of art is to cleanse and stimulate and refine our vision, it was natural that he should accord it the kind of propaedeutic role that he conceived it to have in that whole process whereby transcendence is relocated in the dimension of immanence and we learn to "dwell poetically" on this earth. But by many of his contemporaries all this was impatiently dismissed as "art for art's sake" and "neopaganism" and hedonistic sensualism. And thus, as it seems, there came a time when he (like Newman, after the gratuitous attack upon him by Charles Kingsley) felt obliged to produce an apologia that might have the effect of finally clarifying his real motives. As his letter of 22 July 1883 to Violet Paget about this crucial project said (in a previously quoted passage), "I regard this present matter as a sort of duty. For . . . there is a . . . sort of religious phase possible for the modern mind . . . the conditions of which phase it is the main object of my design to convey." His great hope, in other words, was that by casting his position in the form of prose fiction, he might more fully disclose the emphatically religious intention controlling his fundamental endeavor and thereby put to rest the charges that taxed him with a frivolous aestheticism.

The novel that Pater had completed by the end of the summer of 1884 and that Macmillan published in the following year is, of course, a book so much straining against the limits of its genre that many readers are doubtless inclined to wonder if in any sense it can be called a novel at all, and it may well be that we ought indeed to think of ***Marius the Epicurean*** as the first "antinovel" in English literature of the modern period. As Percy Lubbock long ago remarked, "In ***Marius*** probably, if it is to be called a novel, the art of drama is renounced as thoroughly as it has ever occurred to a novelist to dispense with it." So little is brought into the foreground. Virtually nothing is dramatized in action. "The scenes of the story reach the reader by refraction, as it were, through the medium of Pater's harmonious murmur."[36] And that murmur is very nearly all that we *hear,* for the personages of the novel seem never to be engaged in the kind of talk that enlivens *Mansfield Park* and *Middlemarch* and *Bleak House* and *Women in Love*: Marius seems never to be spoken to or himself to engage another in genuine conversation. Everything is oblique, is presented retrospectively, and the remarkable paucity of character and incident and dialogue is bound to try the patience of those who come to the book with the kinds of expectations that are conventionally satisfied by realistic prose narrative.

Yet demanding of his reader as Pater is, ***Marius*** reflects at every point a "meticulous discipline of thought and expression,"[37] and nothing could be further from the truth than T. S. Eliot's exasperated complaint that it is simply "incoherent."[38] On the contrary: as Harold Bloom rightly says, it "is a surprisingly unified narrative"—or, as Mr. Bloom more precisely puts it, it is "a unified reverie" whose "four parts are four stages on the life's way" of its protagonist.[39] And Marius—more centrally than the figures at the fore in the other "imaginary portraits" (Florian Deleal of **"The Child in the House,"** Sebastian van Storck, the Watteau of **"A Prince of Court Painters,"** Gaston de Latour)[40]—is Pater's type and example of the Diaphanous Personality, of the Crystal Man, of openness and *disponibilité* and "poetic dwelling." For he is one whose "whole nature . . . [is] one complex medium of reception, towards the vision . . . of our actual experience in the world."[41] And thus he represents the "sort of entire transparency of nature that lets through unconsciously all that is really life-giving in the established order of things."[42] Which is to say that Marius, as Diaphanous Man, is dedicated to *seeing*. And of course what he comes ultimately to *see* is the *promise* of "a perfect humanity, in a perfect world,"[43] this leading him in turn, given the circumstances in which it is beheld, to embrace the Christian faith. But as Auden says in "For the Time Being," though "the garden is the only place there is, . . . you will not find it / Until you have looked for it everywhere and found nowhere that is not a desert."[44] So Marius has to go the long way round—which involves for him a pilgrimage that will lead from his inherited pagan religion ("the religion of Numa") to, first, Cyrenaicism and then to Stoicism and ultimately to the new Christian movement that is sweeping across the Graeco-Roman world.

The opening chapters beautifully describe the atmosphere enveloping the remote country estate and its fine old villa called *White-nights* where Marius grows up, under the careful guardianship of his adored mother. And here the decisive influence is the simple patriarchal religion of ancient Rome—the religion of the field and the hearth and the household gods—which it is the tradition of the place scrupulously to observe. Even as a boy, Marius, since his father is dead, is obliged, as the last male of his line, to be the president of the various liturgies followed by all the servants and retainers on the family estate, and to this priestly office in all its aspects he brings a gravely punctilious devotion, for he conceives the world to be "touched of heaven" and has a great sense of "the sacredness of time, of life and its events, and the circumstances of family fellowship; of such gifts to men as fire, water, the earth . . ." (I, 6). So the prayers and ceremonies that belong to the daily round and the urns of the dead in the family chapel all receive from him a quiet, reverent service, this being of a piece with "many another homely and old-fashioned trait" (I, 15) in his nature. The "*conscience,* of which the old Roman religion was a formal, habitual recognition, [has] . . . become in him a powerful current of feeling and observance" (I, 5), and he wants not to "fall short at any point of the demand upon him of anything in which deity . . . [is] concerned" (I, 17-18).

But then, with his mother's death, the time comes when this young Tuscan must leave his estate to complete his education in a distinguished rhetorician's school in Pisa modeled on Plato's Academy. And this juncture marks an important turning point, for not only is he a nestling leaving the house of his forebears, but the shock of his mother's death has "turned seriousness of feeling into a matter of the intelligence," has "made him a questioner" (I, 43), and has somehow led him to think of the "much cherished religion of the villa . . . as but one voice, in a world where there [are] . . . many voices it would be a moral weakness not to listen to" (I, 44). So he takes off to Pisa a great new susceptibility—and there he falls under the influence of a prodigiously brilliant and charming schoolmate, a young man named Flavian, who quickly gains an easy dominion over him.

Pisa, which is a fashionable bathing center, is, with its gay and bustling streets, marked by all the "urbanities . . . [and] graceful follies" that one might expect to find in such a town, and Marius is greatly stirred by its promise of freedom and adventure. The excitement and glamor of this urban world present a scene quite different from that of the "gray monastic tranquillity" (I, 47) of *White-nights,* and the capricious waywardness of Marius's new friend Flavian makes him a fine exemplar of the moral climate of the place. Three years older than Marius, Flavian is a young dandy who loves "dress, and dainty food, and flowers" and who cultivates "that foppery of words . . . which was common among the *élite* spirits of that day" (I, 51). There will come a time indeed when, for Marius, "evil things present themselves in malign association with the memory of that beautiful head," and when he will consider Flavian to be "an epitome of the whole pagan world, the depth of its corruption, and its perfection of form" (I, 53).

Meanwhile, Flavian having been appointed to help Marius in his studies, the two are constantly together, and Flavian's intellectual sophistications enable him to introduce Marius to a range of literature and ideas that he has had no previous chance to encounter. It is Flavian who introduces him to Lucian and to Apuleius, and it makes a small irony that one afternoon he should be reading with Marius the tale of Cupid and Psyche in Apuleius's *Metamorphoses,* for (as Gerald Monsman has rightly remarked)[45] the story of Psyche's "love of Love" presents, within the design of the novel, a kind of parable of a similar yearning in Marius that will ultimately lead him to embrace that *Urbs Beata* whose founder is none other than Christ himself.

Flavian, however, locked up as he is within the chambers of his own restless mind, is in no way "touched of heaven," and it seems, therefore, not inappropriate that the stern morality of the novel should ordain that he die in the delirium resulting from the fever that possesses him, once he is stricken by the plague brought into the region from abroad by the Emperor's returning armies. Marius tenderly nurses him through the final days of his illness, and on his last morning Marius, at about daybreak, asks, "Is it a comfort that I shall often come and weep over you?" To which his dying friend says only, "Not unless I be aware, and hear you weeping!" (I, 119). And with this scene of young Flavian's refusing to go gently into the night ahead, the first part of the novel is brought to a close.

"To Marius, greatly agitated by that event, the earthly end of Flavian," as we are told in the opening paragraph of Part II, comes "like a final revelation of nothing less than the soul's extinction" (I, 123). He is so overborne by the spectacle of Flavian's perished body and, after its cremation, of "the little marble chest" carrying the remains of ash that the likelihood of "further stages of being still possible for the soul in some dim journey hence" is suddenly blasted. And the collapse in him of the old hope for some fulfillment beyond the grave brings at last a sense of the untenability of "almost all that remained of the religion of his childhood" (I, 123).

Now it is at this point that Marius, at the age of eighteen, begins his journey in quest of some system of meaning wherewith his broken world may once again be knit together, and this is a journey which is to take him from first one and then to another of the great alternatives proposed by the ancient world. He has a natural antipathy toward Platonism, for the indifference it would have the soul cultivate with respect to "its bodily house" strikes him as essentially "inhuman" (I, 125). But he has an equally natural inclination to embrace Epicureanism, and thus at first he feels prompted to go back from Epicurus and Lucretius to "the writer who was in a certain sense the teacher of both, Heraclitus of Ionia" (I, 128), as well as to Aristippus of Cyrene, who developed and clarified at the level of conduct the practical import of the Heraclitean doctrine of perpetual flux. From Heraclitus he learns that, though "the uncorrected sense gives . . . a false impression of permanence or fixity in things," the world "is in reality full of animation, of vigour, of the fire of life" (I, 129), and that the eternal flux controlling all things is but an expression of "the sleepless, ever-sustained, inexhaustible energy of the divine reason itself." Then, from Aristippus of Cyrene, he learns that, since all "things are but shadows, and . . . [since] we, even as they, never continue in one stay" (I, 135), we "must maintain a harmony with that soul of motion in things, by constantly renewed mobility of character" (I, 139). We must rid ourselves of all such "abstractions as are but the ghosts of bygone impressions" (I, 141), approaching experience, as it were, virginally. "Liberty of soul, freedom from all partial and misrepresentative doctrine which does but relieve one element in our experience at the cost of another, freedom from all embarrassment alike of regret for the past and of calculation on the future: this would be but preliminary to the real business of education—insight, insight through culture, into all that the present moment holds in trust for us, as we stand so briefly in its presence" (I, 142). In short, "*Be perfect in regard to what is here and now*" (I, 145).

Now it is under the influence of this "New Cyrenaicism" that Marius, about a year after Flavian's death, sets out for Rome, a friend of his late father having arranged a secretarial post for him on the staff of the Emperor Marcus Aurelius. And on the seventh evening of his journey, as he is working his way up "the long windings by which the road ascended to the place where that day's stage was to end," a heavy mass of rock is suddenly detached from the steep slope bordering his path and falls to the road, so close behind him that he feels its touch on his heel. By the merest hairsbreadth he has escaped being crushed to death, and the shock of the moment, as it discloses how cruelly exposed we are to the buffetings of sheer contingency, makes him realize in the instant the incompetence of his revisionist Epicureanism in relation to such emergencies of life. "His elaborate philosophy had not put beneath his feet the terror of mere bodily evil; much less of 'inexorable fate, and the noise of greedy Acheron'" (I, 166).

Then, on the following morning as he is leaving the inn where he has spent the night, scheduled now to take the coming day's journey on horseback, he overtakes shortly after his departure a young Roman soldier of the Twelfth Legion whose name is Cornelius. Marius does not know that Cornelius is a Christian: he knows only that there is in this young man a blitheness of spirit, a comeliness of manner, an austere kind of dignity that makes him feel as if he is "face to face, for the first time, with some new knighthood or chivalry, just then coming into the world" (I, 170). And once they arrive in Rome ("The Most Religious City in the World"), Marius remarks his friend's indifference not only to all the various foreign cults and religions to which the city offers hospitality, but also to the effigies and rituals of Roman religion as well.

No sooner does Marius take up his new situation as an amanuensis on the Imperial staff than he finds himself deeply attracted to the majestic figure of Marcus Aurelius, whose Stoicism, in its emphasis on the brevity of our span and the consequent vanity of all ambition, appears to offer a kind of invincible nonchalance wherewith to face all the vicissitudes of life. There is something powerfully appealing in the very fervor of his disillusion, in the asceticism written not unpleasantly into the character of his face, in the genial composure of his general demeanor, and in his habit of seeming never "too much occupied with important affairs to concede what life with others may hourly demand" (I, 217). There is, in other words, an allure about the man himself that makes it inevitable that Marius should feel required seriously to reckon with the body of doctrine to which Aurelius gives his suffrage. And he is led to do so perhaps all the more by the sharpness of its difference from his former creed. For Cyrenaicism says: "The world, within me and without, flows away like a river; therefore let me make the most of what is here and now." But Stoicism says: "The world and the thinker upon it are consumed like a flame; therefore will I turn away my eyes from vanity: renounce: withdraw myself alike from all affections" (I, 201).

There comes a time, however, when this young voyager begins once again to be doubtful about that which bids for his allegiance. For when he finds the Emperor sponsoring the terrible spectacles in the city's amphitheater that involve the torture and slaughter of animals and the fearfully bloody contests between gladiators, he is repelled. Moreover, he finds that when Aurelius is himself afflicted with adversity, his *apatheia* fails and quite deserts him. His little son, Annius Verus, is fatally stricken by some obscure illness, and the child's death plunges him into a desolation which is inconsolable, his air being "less of a sanguine and self-reliant leader than of one . . . defeated" (II, 59). So Marius cannot resist concluding that the Stoic scheme must surely rest on "some flaw of vision," and he feels "a strange pathos" in this whole gospel.

As the third part of the novel gets under way, then, Marius is one for whom both Epicureanism and Stoicism have run aground. And it is the central event in this section of the narrative—the discourse of Cornelius Fronto—that prepares him for the next stage of his progress. It is in the chapter entitled "Stoicism at Court" that Fronto, the Emperor's most trusted counselor and the favorite teacher of his youth, presents a discourse on the nature of morality. Fronto, who is generally regarded as Rome's most distinguished rhetorician, makes this presentation on his birthday—to celebrate which Marcus Aurelius has assembled a fashionable audience of "elegant blue-stockings" to savor the old gentleman's ripened wisdom and his exquisite language. And what he wants chiefly to propose is that the moral life has its true foundation in the idea of the world as one great commonwealth or city the conscience of which becomes explicit in "a visible or invisible aristocracy . . . whose actual manners, whose preferences from of old, become now a weighty tradition as to the way in which things should or should not be done" (II, 10).

As Marius listens to this urbane old Stoic, his reflections quickly move beyond the actual intentions of the speaker, "not in the direction of any clearer theoretic or abstract definition of that ideal commonwealth, but rather as if in search of its visible locality and abiding-place" (II, 11). Fronto, of course, is echoing a theme of Marcus Aurelius himself, who has often spoken of men as holding citizenship in a "*City on high,* of which all other cities are but single habitations" (II, 37). And quite apart from Fronto's particular line of argument, it is simply with this idea of a New Rome, of a Celestial City, an *Urbs Beata* that Marius suddenly finds himself enchanted. Though, like Aurelius, he suspects that this city on high is "incorporate somehow with the actual city whose goodly stones were lying beneath his gaze" (II, 37), given his disenchantment now with Stoicism, he is not inclined to expect that it offers any kind of access to this ideal commonwealth. So as he leaves the assembly that Fronto has addressed, he is haunted by the question as to where this "comely order" may be found. Surely it must have some local habitation, but where? "Where were those elect souls in whom the claim of Humanity became so amiable, winning, persuasive . . .?" (II, 12).

It is Marius's search for the answer to this question that constitutes the central action of the fourth part of the novel, and here, as it turns out, the principal role of Cornelius is to be that of befriending his steps unto that Good Place which is the object of his heart's desire. These two have become good friends in the years that have gone by since Marius first came to Rome, and one afternoon, as they are returning to the city from a visit to a country house, the natural fatigue of the long journey overcomes them quite suddenly about two miles outside the city limits, at which point, "just where a cross-road from the *Latin Way* fell into the *Appian*" (II, 94), Cornelius halts at a doorway and, "as if at liberty to enter," opens the door and takes Marius into the garden of a beautiful villa. Throughout these splendidly ordered precincts "the quiet signs of wealth and of a noble taste" (II, 95) are to be noticed. The whole place—which belongs to the Roman matron Cecilia—is "like a bride adorned for her husband" (II, 97): everywhere there is simplicity, order, peace, and an "air of venerable beauty," especially in the family burial place of the Cecilii which causes Marius to marvel at these people who do not consign their dead to the funeral fire but who bury them, as if by some heavenly alchemy the perished body may be expected to be reconstructed. And wherever they go on the estate, a most wonderful singing of hymns is to be heard: it is, of course, an underground church assembled for something like a service of evensong.

Now from this point on the pace of the novel noticeably quickens, as it moves toward its imminent climax. Marius has a consuming eagerness to ferret out as much information as he can possibly win about this Christian congregation that meets in Cecilia's house. And gradually, as he learns more and more, he comes to feel "the stirring of some wonderful new hope within himself," for, as it seems to him, this new movement is by way of bringing into existence a "regenerate type of humanity" (II, 110). Never, he tells himself, has old Rome so cherished the family as do these people. And what a remarkable solicitousness they represent with respect to children! Moreover, they are a people who cherish industry and honest workmanship. Nor do they harbor any ascetical contempt for the life of the body and the natural order: on the contrary, they declare the sensuous world to be created of God. And he is deeply impressed by the generously humanistic kind of hospitality with which the Church adopts "many of the graces of pagan feeling and pagan custom" (II, 125) and gratefully acknowledges its evolution from and indebtedness to the great traditions of Jewish spirituality. At every point, as he feels, this is a community touched by a quite remarkable kind of gaiety and "debonair grace" and (most important of all) chasteness of life.

But perhaps beyond all else, what Marius is most moved by in the life of the Church is its "unparalleled genius for worship" (II, 123). Indeed, it is his experience of a Christmas Mass that seals his commitment to the People of the Catacombs. On a certain winter morning—which he does not know to be the Feast of the Nativity—having decided to leave Rome for a time and wanting Cornelius to know of his whereabouts, he goes to his friend's lodgings. Not finding him in, he then goes to the Cecilian villa, thinking that Cornelius may be there. He passes through the empty courtyard and into "the vast *Lararium,* or domestic sanctuary, of the Cecilian family," where, as he discovers, a great company of people, "at that moment in absolute silence," is assembled. Then the silence is broken by cries of *Kyrie Eleison! Christe Eleison!,* and the Eucharistic office proceeds on through the *Pro-Anaphora* to the *Anaphora,* the immense absorption and dignity with which the entire company participates in the service suggesting to Marius that "a cleansing and kindling flame" (II, 131) is indeed at work amongst them. The local bishop is the celebrant, and, when he begins to recite the great central prayer of consecration, it is "as if he alone possessed the words of the office, and they flowed anew from some permanent source of inspiration within him" (II, 136). At its conclusion the faithful approach the altar (which is in fact "the tomb of a youthful 'witness' of the family of the Cecilii") for the administration of the sacrament. Then "the remnants of the feast are borne away" to be administered to the sick. A hymn is sung—after which the young deacons cry out *Ite! Missa est!* And as the people depart, Marius feels "that he must hereafter experience . . . a kind of thirst for all this, over again" (II, 140), for the figure of Christ "towards whom this whole act of worship . . . turned . . . seemed to have absorbed, like some rich tincture in his garment, all that was deep-felt and impassioned in the experiences of the past" (II, 134). In short, he is now convinced that here at last in this community he has found that *Urbs Beata,* that wholly inclusive society for which he has been searching.[46]

This *anima naturaliter Christiana* (as the novel speaks of Marius, echoing the famous phrase in Tertullian's *Apologeticum*) has now reached what is essentially the end of his journey, and it is not at all surprising that his thoughts should begin to turn back to *White-nights.* "Home is where one starts from," says Eliot's "East Coker": "In my beginning is my end." But certain things must transpire before he returns to his old Tuscan estate. First, he has a long conversation one morning with the writer Lucian, who, confirmed skeptic that he is, insists on the relativity of all doctrines and philosophies. But though Marius can appreciate a certain cogency in Lucian's agnosticism, it does not finally meet what is for him the crucial exigency—which is (as he says in his diary) that "there is a certain grief in things as they are, in man as he has come to be, as he certainly is, over and above those griefs of circumstance which are in a measure removable" (II, 181), and what we need, therefore, for the withstanding of the tragic things in life is not so much schemes of metaphysics (which are all without profit, on Lucian's account) as the assurance that "a certain permanent and general power of compassion" is the "elementary ingredient" of our world. And since it is the promise of this "ingredient" that he has found in Cecilia's house, he finds himself drawn back again to the underground Church: he listens once more to "the sweet singing of the Eucharist," and, as he follows again the "mystical dialogue" of the Mass, he feels himself to be a part of a great company which, having heard "the sentence of its release from prison," represents now "the whole company of mankind" (II, 190). In the course of the service an Epistle from the Churches of Lyons and Vienne to "their sister" the Church of Rome is read, this Epistle recounting the martyrdoms amongst these Christians that Aurelius's legions have exacted. Marius is greatly moved, and it occurs to him that here, indeed, in the kind of testimony made by the willingness of these people to lay down their lives for their faith and for one another, is "that absolute ground amid all the changes of phenomena, such as our philosophers have of late confessed themselves quite unable to discover" (II, 184).

Shortly afterward he returns to *White-nights,* his childhood home, and spends eight days there. As he wanders through the family mausoleum, he is distressed by the "odd air of neglect," the faded flowers and the thickness of the fallen dust; and being struck by a "yearning . . . still to be able to do something for" his own dead, he arranges for the burial of his ancestors' remains in the Christian way. While he is overseeing this work, his friend Cornelius, having found himself in the neighborhood, stops at *White-nights,* and the two resolve to return to Rome together. But on their way, they are of a sudden caught in an earthquake at Lucca. The inhabitants superstitiously conceive these strangers, along with certain others, to be the cause of the event, and they are arrested. Marius bribes the guards, however, to release Cornelius, who blithely proceeds on to Rome, it having been so arranged as for him to suppose that Marius will immediately follow. And before his captors can dispose of him, Marius himself falls ill and is left to die at a farmhouse, under the care of some country people who, as it turns out, are Christians. As he lies on the rough bed provided him, his life rapidly ebbing away, this hierarch of the spirit devotes his last hours to "a conscious effort of recollection." In accord with the ethic of *diaphanéité* he is, of course, one who has always set *seeing* "above the *having,* or even the *doing,* of anything. For, such vision, if received with due attitude on his part, was, in reality, the *being* something" (II, 218). And now he thinks "how goodly" the vision has been:

> Throughout that elaborate and lifelong education of his receptive powers, he had ever kept in view the purpose of preparing himself . . . towards some ampler vision. . . . At this moment, his unclouded receptivity of soul, grown so steadily through all those years, from experience to experience, was at its height; the house ready for the possible guest; the tablet of the mind white and smooth, for whatsoever divine fingers might choose to write there. And was not this precisely the condition, the attitude of mind, to which something higher than he, yet akin to him, would be likely to reveal itself; to which that influence he had felt now and again like a friendly hand upon his shoulder, amid the actual obscurities of the world, would be likely to make a further explanation. (II, 219-20)

He has not, in other words, directly beheld the naked glory of God himself—which must perhaps remain beyond the reach and ken of any mortal creature—so there are "further explanations," further visions to be awaited, possibly in some "brave new world" wherein there "is no unrest, no travel, no shipwreck." But within the range of what is possible in this life, he has had the great thing, for in the New Israel, amidst the People of the Catacombs, he has beheld "Heaven . . . come down among men" (II, 214). Which makes it by no means unaccountable that, as he gives up the ghost, the people around his bed should be "praying fervently—*Abi! Abi! Anima Christiana!*" (II, 224), for he has surely undergone what the old doctors of the Church called "baptism of desire."

But though Pater wanted in this book to chart "a . . . sort of religious phase possible for the modern mind," he trifles not at all with anything resembling such an "aesthetic religion" as A. C. Benson imputed to ***Marius the Epicurean.*** Benson claimed that "the weakness of the case [made by the novel] is, that instead of emphasising the power of sympathy, the Christian conception of Love, which differentiates Christianity from all other religious systems, Marius is after all converted, or brought near to the threshold of the faith, more by its sensuous appeal, its liturgical solemnities; the element, that is to say, which Christianity has in common with all religions, and which is essentially human in character."[47] But nothing could be further from the truth, for that which most convinces Marius that the "*City on high*" for which he has been searching is incorporate within the Church is just the certainty he gradually wins that here, amongst the people he first encounters in the villa of the Cecilii, is a community indwelt by *agape.*

Benson says that "the sensuous element triumphs over the intellectual,"[48] and this is simply a gross misstatement of things. True, Pater hardly presents at all any explication of Marius's conversion in terms of what his protagonist conceived to be at stake in the way of formal doctrine. And for this there are, I think, two explanations, the first being that, since "Marius attains to Christianity within the primitive church of the apostles and martyrs, not the church of the *Summa Theologiae,* it would be unhistorical to expect from him a theologically reasoned [argument]"[49] of a piece with the expositions of a Calvin or a Schleiermacher or a Newman. But then secondly, what it is no doubt even more important to recall in this connection is that "wholesome scepticism" for which Pater gratefully acknowledged his indebtedness to Hume and Mill. Like so many other Victorian intellectuals, he took for granted what Matthew Arnold had enunciated in his book of 1875, *God and the Bible,* that "two things about the Christian religion must surely be clear to anybody with eyes in his head"—the one being that "men cannot do without it; the other, that they cannot do with it as it is."[50] And that which was no longer negotiable was nothing other than the old supernaturalist postulates of classical theism, with their projection of an immutable, impassive, immaterial, self-subsistent Being "up there"—the *ens realissimum*—who, like the elder Lord Shaftesbury, thinks and acts and who governs the universe, intervening here and there to move it in one direction or another. Pater was not himself, of course, a theologian, nor did he have ready at hand, even in the more advanced theology of his time, a language calculated to offer incisive definition of what it was that needed reformulation. So, as in his essay on Coleridge, he could only speak somewhat darkly about the irrelevance of "the absolute" and of "vague scholastic abstractions." But however awkwardly the essayist may have expressed it, the novelist knew that the *sensus divinitatis* is mediated by way not of dubious metaphysical propositions but of precisely that which A. C. Benson mistakenly declared him to be unmindful of—namely, the encounter with *agape.* He knew, in other words, that "Love is the unfamiliar name"[51] behind the design of the *civitas terrena,* and thus Marius's conversion to the Christian faith is accounted for not in formal doctrinal terms (since none of those available to Pater, as he in all likelihood felt, were wholly satisfactory) but in terms rather, as Graham Hough says, of "an actual experience, the experience of a society which he can see, whose atmosphere he can feel, in which he has some hope of participating,"[52] and which, in its consecration to the *caritas* made manifest in Christ, represents (as the novel says) "the whole company of mankind." And as Pater wanted to suggest, a faith thus grounded is of a sort "possible for the modern mind."

It was by way, then, of the elaborate stratagem involved in the writing of ***Marius the Epicurean*** that Pater hoped to "correct" or to clarify the "Conclusion" of ***The Renaissance.*** Which is to say that ***Marius*** was intended to be his full statement of where a true *diaphanéité* may be expected to lead. Many had concluded that his earlier plea for "openness" to and "receptivity" of what experience brings represented nothing more than a somewhat oblique apology for a program of hedonistic self-indulgence, and having suffered at once surprise and distress at this miscomprehension of what he was aiming at, he had withdrawn the "Conclusion" from the second edition of ***The Renaissance.*** But then restoring it in the third edition of 1888, he said: "I have thought it best to reprint it here. . . . I have dealt more fully in ***Marius the Epicurean*** with the thoughts suggested by it." And what he trusted his more attentive readers to realize was that ***Marius*** had indeed made it clear that the ethic of *diaphanéité,* of openness and receptivity, when seriously pursued in relation to *the grief in things,* leads not—far from it!—to any sort of unprincipled *sensualité* but rather to a search for that which, in releasing us from "the prison" of the single ego's solitariness, confers the kind of beatitude that is found only in a community of Love. In short, to "dwell poetically" is to be poised toward that universal commonwealth which some call "the Kingdom of Christ." So to state the matter is to put it in terms which Pater's reserve would not perhaps have allowed him. (In his "reserve" how much like Keble he is!)[53] But his real intention is fully disclosed in ***Marius the Epicurean,*** which surely deserves to be accounted amongst the few great religious classics of the modern period.

To speak of ***Marius*** as a religious classic is not, of course, to foreclose the possibility of its being regarded in its "doctrine" as something more religiously ambiguous than I have been inclined to suggest. (Indeed, many of those in recent years who have undertaken to deal with it in a serious way have been so eager to multiply ambiguity that their renderings often in no way at all "prove" themselves in relation to one's *immediate* experience of the novel.) It is only to say that—like the poems of Hopkins, like Martin Buber's *I and Thou,* like the books of Simone Weil, like Eliot's *Quartets*—it causes us to question the authenticity of our present mode of being in the world in such a way as, in effect, to make us "retrieve" the religious *possibility;* and thus it makes "a nonviolent appeal to our minds, hearts and imaginations, and through them to our wills."[54] Which is in turn to say that Pater's legacy deserves to be accorded a status rather different from that of dusty *school* classics.

Notes

1. [Walter Pater], "Coleridge's Writings," *The Westminster Review,* American Edition, 85 (January 1866), 49-50.

2. Walter Pater, "Preface" to *The Renaissance: Studies in Art and Poetry,* the 1893 text, ed. Donald L. Hill (Berkeley and Los Angeles, 1980), p. xx.

3. Walter Pater, *Plato and Platonism* (London, 1925), p. 31.

4. Walter Pater, "Wordsworth," in *Appreciations* (New York, 1910), pp. 62, 61.
5. Pater, *Renaissance,* p. 181. Hereafter cited in text.
6. *Letters of Walter Pater,* ed. Lawrence Evans (Oxford, 1970), p. 52.
7. Strangely, Pater, despite his excellent command of French, omitted the acute accent over the first *e* and placed a grave accent over the second *e.*
8. See Martin Heidegger, "On the Essence of Truth," in *Existence and Being,* ed. Werner Brock, tr. R. F. C. Hull et al. (Chicago, 1949), pp. 319-51.
9. *The Journals and Papers of Gerard Manley Hopkins,* ed. Humphry House and Graham Storey (London, 1959), p. 127.
10. In Heidegger's lexicon the term *Gelassenheit* speaks of a meditative openness and surrender to that mysterious surplusage of meaning that indwells all things: see his *Gelassenheit* (Pfullingen, 1959), which is available in an English translation by John M. Anderson and E. Hans Freund under the title *Discourse on Thinking* (New York, 1966).
11. "God's Grandeur," in *The Poems of Gerard Manley Hopkins,* ed. W. H. Gardner and N. H. Mackenzie, 4th ed. (London, 1967), p. 66.
12. See Walter Pater, "Diaphaneitè [sic]," in *Miscellaneous Studies* (New York, 1900), pp. 215-22.
13. In her review prepared for the April 1873 issue of *The Westminster Review,* Mrs. Mark Pattison insisted that the title was "misleading," rightly maintaining that the book does not in any real way present a *history* of the Renaissance but rather simply a series of studies of a few representative figures. Pater quickly took her point, and from 1877 on, all subsequent editions have borne the title *The Renaissance: Studies in Art and Poetry.*
14. This is the term used by Thomas Wright, Pater's first biographer, for the Diaphanous Personality: see his *Life of Walter Pater* (1907; rpt. New York, 1969), I, 216-18.
15. Walter Pater, *Marius the Epicurean* (London, 1910), I, 130-31.
16. Psalm 148 (King James Version).
17. *Appreciations,* p. 6.
18. In *The Renaissance* Pater speaks of music only to say that all art, in its desire to obliterate the distinction between matter and form, "aspires towards the condition of music" (p. 106).
19. Michael Levey, *The Case of Walter Pater* (London, 1978), p. 141.
20. The letter (dated 17 March 1873) is in *Walter Pater: The Critical Heritage,* ed. R. M. Seiler (London, 1980), pp. 61-62.
21. Wright, I, 255-56.
22. Levey, p. 143.
23. *The Critical Heritage,* ed. Seiler, pp. 86, 91.
24. *The Critical Heritage,* ed. Seiler, p. 92.
25. Friedrich Hölderlin, "In Lieblicher Bläue," in *Sämtliche Werke,* II, pt. 1 (Stuttgart, 1951), 372—"Voll Verdienst, doch dichterisch, wohnet der Mensch auf dieser Erde" ("Full of merit, yet poetically, dwells / Man on this earth").
26. Martin Heidegger, *Vorträge und Aufsätze* (Pfullingen, 1954). The essay is available in English in *Poetry, Language, Thought,* tr. Albert Hofstadter (New York, 1971).
27. See his *Erläuterungen zu Hölderlins Dichtung* (Frankfurt-am-Main, 1944) and his *Holzwege* (Frankfurt-am-Main, 1950).
28. *Plato and Platonism,* p. 124.
29. See T. S. Eliot, "Tradition and the Individual Talent," in *Selected Essays: 1917-1932* (New York, 1932), pp. 3-11.
30. Pater, "Wordsworth," in *Appreciations,* pp. 37-63.
31. *Letters,* ed. Evans, p. 34.
32. A. C. Benson, *Walter Pater* (London, 1906), p. 209.
33. Pater over many years was unfailingly regular in his attendance at the Chapel of Brasenose College, being present for both the morning and evening services. And outside Oxford, he sought out such centers of Catholic liturgical life in London as St. Alban's, Holborn, and St. Austin's Priory, Walworth. Mrs. Humphry Ward's story (in her book *A Writer's Recollections* [New York, 1918], I, 161-62) about his having once scandalized over his dinner table the wife of a distinguished Oxford professor by denying that any reasonable person could govern his life by the opinions of a man (Jesus) who had died eighteen centuries ago is sometimes cited as evidence of agnosticism. But such badinage is not unknown even amongst professional theologians, particularly when they may feel it appropriate to administer a shock to some kind of smug and unthinking orthodoxy. And it would seem that, on the occasion recounted by Mrs. Ward, Pater felt that such a shock needed to be served out: Mrs. Ward was present, and she says that he "had been . . . pressed controversially beyond the point of wisdom. . . . The Professor and his wife . . . departed hurriedly, in agitation. . . ."
34. Amos N. Wilder, *The New Voice: Religion, Literature, Hermeneutics* (New York, 1969), p. 236.
35. Wallace Stevens, "An Ordinary Evening in New Haven," in *The Collected Poems of Wallace Stevens* (New York, 1955), p. 475.
36. Percy Lubbock, *The Craft of Fiction* (London, 1926), p. 195.
37. R. V. Osbourn, "*Marius the Epicurean,*" *Essays in Criticism,* 1, No. 4 (October 1951), 387.

38. T. S. Eliot, "Arnold and Pater," in *Selected Essays,* p. 355.
39. Harold Bloom, *The Ringers in the Tower: Studies in Romantic Tradition* (Chicago, 1971), pp. 188, 192.
40. See Walter Pater, *Imaginary Portraits* (London, 1894) and *Gaston de Latour* (London, 1897).
41. Pater, *Marius the Epicurean,* I, 143.
42. "Diaphaneitè," in *Miscellaneous Studies,* p. 219.
43. *Marius the Epicurean,* II, 218. Hereafter cited in text.
44. W. H. Auden, "For the Time Being," in *The Collected Poetry of W. H. Auden* (New York, 1945), p. 412.
45. Gerald Monsman, *Pater's Portraits* (Baltimore, 1967), pp. 71-74.
46. In his book *Hebrew and Hellene in Victorian England* (Austin, Tex., 1969), p. 325, David J. DeLaura says that "there can be little doubt" that Pater's insistent use of a *universal commonwealth* as an image for the Church "is a version of the 'great association of nations' . . . described by Newman" in the lecture on "Christianity and Letters" that belongs to the second half of the *Idea of a University.* And it may be that Mr. DeLaura is right in part, but I should think that anyone who knows Frederick Denison Maurice's *The Kingdom of Christ* (London, 1842) would find it difficult not to feel that in this matter, Pater is *far more* echoing Maurice's view of the Church as the universal family of man *qua* man.
47. Benson, p. 111.
48. Benson, p. 106.
49. Monsman, p. 102.
50. Matthew Arnold, *God and the Bible* (New York, 1913), p. xi.
51. T. S. Eliot, "Little Gidding," in *Four Quartets* (New York, 1943), p. 38.
52. Graham Hough, *The Last Romantics* (London, 1949), p. 151.
53. Among the great men of the Oxford Movement, John Keble was, of course, notable in part for his strong and constant emphasis on "reserve," on the necessity of keeping Christian faith and practice pure of all ostentation and display and lust for immediate effect. Pater met Keble on only one occasion, in the period when he was a pupil at the King's School in Canterbury, probably at some point in 1855; and it would seem that each was profoundly impressed by the other. At this time one of Pater's closest friends was his schoolmate John Rainier McQueen, he and McQueen and one other boy, Henry Dombrain, being known at the King's School as "The Three Inseparables." And Thomas Wright reports (*Life of Pater,* I, 132) that a relation of the McQueen family, Mary Ann Virginia Gabriel, expected the young Pater to prove to be in time "a second Keble," an expectation supported in some measure perhaps by the verse of Pater's that survives from this period of his life and from his early days at Oxford and that suggests how much he was then under the influence of *The Christian Year.*
54. David Tracy, *The Analogical Imagination* (New York, 1981), p. 177. Chapters 3, 4, and 5 of this book present a suggestive interpretation of "the classic" and "the religious classic."

Austin Warren (essay date 1983)

SOURCE: "Pondering Pater: Aesthete and Master" in *The Sewanee Review,* Vol. XCI, No. 4, Fall, 1983, pp. 643-54.

[*In the following essay, Warren describes some characteristics of the aesthetic type, comments on the ways in which they do and do not apply to Pater, and speculates on Pater's religious faith.*]

The aesthete is a late-appearing, a decadent type of man—a man who, having the practical basis of life provided, the economic basis, and security, not for the day or the year but for a vague perpetuity, is free to enjoy. The aesthete is one kind of hedonist, of man who can, and does, live for pleasure. But his pleasures are not of the cruder sort, such as gluttony or debauchery, are not indeed sensual, but sensuous—the pleasures of discrimination (Huysmans's *À rebours*), the epicure's pleasures, those of the gourmet in any form, but most especially the pleasures of the connoisseur of the arts—of painting, music, ballet (addiction to which is almost a hallmark), of "pure poetry," of art for art's sake. The aesthete is the specialized consumer of the arts, who may spend his daytime resting in order that he may be fresh to receive in all their delicacy the impressions an evening performance, of whatever kind, may give.

Definitions of the aesthete are best neither too brief nor too rigid. There are exclusions, but there are also linkages and overlaps. The aesthete as such is not an artist, a maker, a craftsman, a producer of the beautiful, but a consumer; yet of course the same man may be producer and consumer—e.g. the readers of a writer's writer (a term that today means chiefly a writer regarded by critics as serious) are other writers: Joyce is almost entirely a writer's writer.

Sexually the aesthete generally proves to be a lover, passive or active, of his own kind—a lover of young men. He is an introvert as well as an invert; an indoors, and most likely also a nighttime, man (night being the time when ideas and dreams best flower, with the exclusion of extroverted sunlight and the optional addition of alcohol and drugs).

The aesthete is a dandy in dress and manners (Baudelaire, Wilde, Max Beerbohm); a dandy in literary style even if not in personal décor (Wallace Stevens: the dandy as poet;

Firbank: the dandy as writer of daintily elegant dialogue). And the aesthete's dandyism is pride, not vanity: he dresses, talks, writes, performs for his own mirror-image—his own delectation. He cares no more to impress than to instruct or edify.

The aesthete is, proudly, a dilettante. He shrinks from being professional—which means partly being so good at something that one can earn his living by it. If that is how one defines a dilettante, then obviously most of the serious writers of our time are dilettantes: they earn their livelihood by editing or teaching or the reading circuit, not by their writing.

The aesthete is often identified with the hedonist—that is, with one who identifies the good with pleasure, not with, say, duty, or with social usefulness or utility. But the aesthete may hold out for eudaimonism—for happiness as his goal. He is likely to be a solipsist, for whom the only demonstration of existence is his own consciousness, his own sensations and ideas.

He loves artifacts rather than Nature, thinks indeed that it is the artist who gives value to Nature; we see only what art has taught us to see. He is likely to collect artifacts (books, pictures, phonograph records) and to find the meaning of his private existence, his leisure, his solitude, in selecting from among his treasures the single work upon which he is, at this time, to concentrate.

Perception, appreciation, vision, contemplation: these are, in ascending order, the names for the aesthetic experience. As Pater said, it is not the fruit of experience (the generalization, the moral, the wisdom) but the experience itself that is to be prized.

So much for a type portrait of the aesthete, the man who lives for, and in, his sensibility; and whose sensibility is most gratified not by natural objects, but by objects of art and persons. Of course no one is ever perfectly the type; and those aesthetes whose names occur to me are, in addition to their enjoyment of the beautiful, also either collectors and patrons of art and artists, or art experts and curators like Bernard Berenson and Sir Kenneth Clark, or critics of art like Roger Fry and Clive Bell, or writers about art (the highest category) like Ruskin and Pater. Ruskin was also a moralist and an economist, rather a good one; and Pater was a thinker and writer of high distinction, a master in kind.

Now, I turn from the type to Pater, first as a Man and then as a Writer, two portraits that almost merge yet gain from being not quite merged.

Pater as a man is best outlined in the early (1908) two-volume life by Thomas Wright, a stupid, crude, and essentially hostile book, yet one that preserves early stances of Pater otherwise unnoticed: especially the adolescent Anglo-Catholic ritualistic and orthodox piety, that of his Canterbury schooldays, and of his friendship with Dombrain and MacQueen, schoolfriends whose very existence was unknown to A. C. Benson, Pater's authorized biographer; then the Oxford undergraduate period of religious skepticism followed by the young Oxford don's period of flippant yet serious gibing at Christianity in social gatherings of faculty and their wives; finally Pater's late return to ritualistic religion, a religion without the dogma, but flamboyantly represented by Pater's acquaintance with Richard C. Jackson and the St. Austin Friars.

Pater signally tried to suppress, cover up, the overtly, sophisticatedly skeptical period in his life. No critic before me has remarked that; and indeed in ***Marius the Epicurean,*** the intellectual and affective autobiography which so closely follows the general intellectual outlines and the destined patterns of Pater's own development, there is no skeptical, no *blasé* period. Nearest would come the friendship with Flavian (who is called "corrupt"—in unspecified ways); but this friendship is at least dominantly aesthetic, literary. And—a correlative observation—the wit and irony which characterized Pater's conversation in early middle life are completely absent from all periods of his writing. He never learned how to unite the two sharply separate sides of his nature; perhaps he was even repelled by the idea of doing so. This is not a late development but true from the start; the writings, even the earliest (**"Diaphanéité"** and the early essay on Coleridge), are utterly serious and sincere. This is perhaps to be regretted: a tincture of Wilde's levity would have helped a prose that can become clogged and sweetly cloying, as that of ***Marius,*** for example, sometimes becomes.

The boy Pater was strict and pious (he loved to play the priest, and to arrange holy processions; and he loved "holy lights, flowers, and incense," his sacred trinity). In **"The Child in the House,"** the first and the germ of his Imaginary Portraits, he sketches the sensitive, chiefly solitary boy he was, perceptively aware of delicate impression, of light and shadow and fragrances. And he notes the two dominances that go through his life and his writing: beauty and pain, or beauty and death—notes the fugitive character, the fragility of all beauty. In Pater's nature, as we see increasingly in late writings like **"Denys l'Auxerrois"** and **"Apollo in Picardy,"** there is an element of algolagnia, the love of pain, a sadomasochism, one side of his passive sensibility. What in Swinburne (an early teacher of Pater's) is overt—what Mario Praz calls the Romantic Agony—is so clearly present that I cannot doubt Pater's awareness of this element in his nature. At any event he certainly makes no effort, in those latest "portraits" of his, to try to conceal it.

About Pater's sexual nature I think there can be no doubt. He was by temperament a lover (in the Greek style of Socrates, another physically plain man) of young men, especially young athletes and soldiers (like Emerald Uthwart and Cornelius). It is highly improbable that he was a practicing homosexual: in the Oxford of his time, that would have been virtually impossible, and so retired a nature as his would almost certainly, at that point or any near it, have shrunk from such a display of appetite. Another of this kind was A. C. Benson, whose 1907 book on Pater I think far superior to the current estimate of it. David Newsome's excellent *On the Edge of Paradise: A. C. Benson, the Diarist* (1980) makes clear how much the men had the same problems. Benson is never (save for the limits of his period and his profession) evasive. Of Pater, if Benson speaks with great reserve, it is on his own account as well as Pater's—but, as he says accurately, Pater's "secret is told for those that can read it in his writings."

The set, the pattern, the direction of Pater's mind was unique. It was little attracted to things or models English—that is, to literary or artistic monuments. He likes a certain kind of almost dumbly inarticulate and unconscious young Englishman of character (Emerald Uthwart, or the type of Shadwell, the model for **"Diaphanéité"**); Santayana felt the same attraction: compare his *Soliloquies in England* and *The Last Puritan.* But how strangely absent from Pater is any attraction to the English cathedrals, or to places like Bemerton or Little Gidding, or, for that matter, to men like George Herbert who were at once unneurotic and unique, artists particularly English.

For Pater, devotee of Culture, the models were—as they were, intellectually, for Arnold also (in some ways, along with Ruskin, Pater's distinguished predecessor as proselyte and prosateur)—Germany and France. To them Pater significantly adds Italy—not, however, the Italy of the present but of antiquity and the Renaissance, and not the Italy of literature but of painting, sculpture, and architecture.

Pater began as a scholar of philosophy, centrally of Hegel (so often quoted in the initiatory essay by Pater, the long one on Winckelmann). But then he breaks dramatically, almost histrionically, with the abstractions of philosophy. **"Winckelmann,"** the nearest to an intellectual autobiography Pater ever wrote, describes that predecessor and guide of Goethe as he turns away from the few "colorless books" upon which he has "hungrily fed" at school, and turns toward the plastic, the concrete, the particular, and the sensuous. ***Plato and Platonism*** (1893), the last book by Pater to be published in his lifetime, is a strange attempt to press even Plato (whose dialogues grow more and more abstract and bloodless) into the cause of the concrete. Pater pleads that the only value of abstractions is to know the relief granted their greyness and bleakness by the delicacy of a rose petal.

The new developments of the physical sciences, including Darwinian evolution, certainly played a significant part in shattering Pater's early development. He read Huxley, Renan, and Comte; became an unawed positivist and contributed to the *Westminster Review.* He also became aware of his solipsism: that man can never really get outside his own consciousness. As he wrote in his famous Conclusion to ***The Renaissance,*** "experience, already reduced to a group of impressions, is ringed round for each one of us by that thick wall of personality through which no real voice has ever pierced on its way to us, or from us to that which we can only conjecture to be without." His solipsistic conviction finally destroyed for him the validity of any metaphysical system. Epistemology and Ethics remain to him; he is in effect an existential philosopher, to be grouped with Kierkegaard, Nietzsche, and William James: it is to me strange that Pater has not so been recognized. His writings are not—are far from being—just exercises in style; Pater is always painstakingly, painfully saying something really momentous about consciousness and conscientiousness, or observation and meditation.

Pater intensely meant all he said, and meant it with an intensity hard to take in, since his "message" is not something doctrinal, and is even less some call to action. (Action is as absent from Pater's contemplative and solipsistic world as dialogue, except dialogue with oneself.) When Pater calls himself an aesthetic critic and calls for the production of such criticism, he is sharply dissociating himself from any moral or social criticism, with the call of such criticism to do or reform something. Aesthetic criticism expresses the critic's "enjoyment" of a work of art and seeks to share that enjoyment.

Pater also overtly contrasts aesthetic with historic criticism: the former detaches from a work done by past standards its current value, what we can call either its timeless value or its value for the present moment. Pater stresses the latter element, feeling that as soon as one talks about the timeless, as a classicist is wont to do, one is likely to stray away from the immediate direct confrontation of and delectation in the work of art. Pater's aesthetic essays, like his ***Marius,*** are all, amazingly, written from *now,* and the reader is not allowed to forget that.

To see an object as it is (the Arnoldian phrase quoted in the preface to ***The Renaissance***) is to see and feel a work of art as Pater, in his time and with his sensibility, sees it. He is dealing with impressions, facts to sensibility; and his desire is to find, in his turn, a "formula" that will sum up in speech the unique quality that his refined sensibility discovers in a painter or a poet or a painting or a poem.

The search for the unique: that is almost the central term for Pater's quest. Of uniqueness he is a connoisseur. Habits and routine dull our perceptions. In this brief life we have time beyond our minimum duties (in Pater's case the don's reception of his scholars and their essays) only for the unique of this moment—a completely hedonistic doctrine. The end of these unique precious experiences is not to use them: "not the fruit of experience but experience itself."

The most famous part of ***The Renaissance*** (1873), the freshest, most boldly written, brilliant, and influential of Pater's books, is the Conclusion. Though half of the reviewers did not mention it, it struck the attention and the discussion of Sidney Colvin, for example. Before long the chaplain of Brasenose College, John Wordsworth, wrote Pater a frank letter telling him that the Conclusion was contrary to all Christian doctrine and would have a bad influence on the young who read it. The book, especially the heretical Conclusion, was ill received in Oxford, and Pater's Oxford reputation suffered. He was passed over in all the relevant academic promotions, including the professorships of poetry and the fine arts. Pater professed not to feel pain at his rejection; such professions his personal decorum required; but of course he felt them keenly, as he did the satire of him as Mr. Rose in Mallock's *The New Republic* (1876).

What had happened? Was he unaware what bold doctrine he had avowed? Could he possibly have supposed that his real meaning would not be grasped? Had he been brave without properly counting the cost to his academic career? I cannot answer clearly. He had never fitted well into the academic world; later he moved to London to further his other and dearer pursuit, his literary career. But London life didn't quite suit him either: he was too literary for Oxford, and too donnish for London.

Pater withdrew the Conclusion from the second edition of his book, fearing that it might "mislead" some of the young men who read it; his subsequent note, when it was returned to later editions, stated that he had, in ***Marius,*** made his original meaning clear. This is untrue. In ***Marius*** a different doctrine is preached. For hedonism is substituted eudaimonism, the search for happiness as the chief goal; and that happiness, that completeness of experience, is indeed so interpreted as to include an undogmatic reception of religion.

Published in 1885, ***Marius*** was the work of six or seven years, and shows it. Benson, who in his milder way shared something of Pater's dilemma, has written much the best exposition and appraisal of this overlong and overlabored book. Pater meant it as a correction and wiser statement of the bold doctrine he, in his thirty-year-old self-confidence, had brilliantly blurted forth in ***The Renaissance.*** Pater intended ***Marius*** to be his masterpiece, but I think it is not. This sensitive and brilliant essayist could not manage a long book. Why should he? The very delicacy, subtlety, and precision with which he writes a sentence, or a paragraph, or at the most a chapter show his talents misplaced in this ampler genre.

Try to summarize the arguments of ***Marius,*** his book-length essay, and you fail to reproduce all that is characteristic of its best perceptions, thinking, and writing. Even the four parts are too crude as divisions: part 1, Marius's boyhood ancient (pagan) religion, his schooling at Pisa, his early literary preciosity ("Euphuism"), and his friendship with Flavian, the young poet, who (like a true Pater hero) dies young; part 2, Marius's secretaryship to Marcus Aurelius—his Cyrenaic phase, his study of the emperor's Stoicism; part 3, "Second Thoughts," about the adequacy, as life-guides, of the two philosophies—the reaching toward wisdom; part 4, the movement to the way, Christianity.

In ***Marius*** Pater carries on two historical sequences at once. As he says, early in "Second Thoughts," ***Marius*** is about Marius-like young men at the end of the nineteenth century, whether they be in Paris, London, or Rome. Pater is not a historicist; he is a cyclical thinker, who is drawn to interpret his own time, a fin de siècle time of termination and transition, in terms of parallel times in the past: if he did not anticipate a Fall of the British Empire to parallel the Decline and Fall of the earlier empire, still he did see the parallel religious situation, the slow transition from paganism to Christianity (in Pater's time, the reverse was beginning to take place), the many intermediaries and relations. In Elizabethan euphuism he sees the parallel to his own fine art-writing (artistic prose).

It seems impossible to follow securely Pater's serpentine wanderings and reflections. Does Marius cease being an Epicurean (1) as he has "second thoughts" or (2) as he almost becomes Christian? Though I can't answer either question with certainty, I am inclined to say No to both. And (3) in ***Marius*** has Pater changed his position from that of ***The Renaissance*** or has he, as he asserts, merely stated more fully what he had meant in the earlier work? Though again I waver in my view, I think Pater has changed—at least widened or amplified his position. "Transcend by including" is, I'm sure, what Pater thought he was doing. In all this there was a certain insincerity or hypocrisy, whether Pater recognized this in himself or not. Certainly Pater, the brilliant young don, had falsely estimated what he could get away with at Oxford, and was pulled up short. But I think that he was really led to reconsider his brash hedonistic Conclusion to ***The Renaissance*** and to substitute "enlargement of consciousness" for intensity of single vivid experiences.

Part 4 of ***Marius*** ends with a version of Pater's own final ritualism. From reading his two biographers, Benson and Wright, I cannot decide whether Pater really returned to the faith of his high-church childhood, which would mean that he went to the altar rail in Brasenose Chapel and received the sacrament, or whether he just sat in his decanal stall, or kneeled at least ceremonially, reverently. Most probably the latter. I infer that Pater never regained—never after he became an adult held—any intellectual literal faith in the Apostles' Creed, never accepted the dogmas (existence of God, Incarnation, Trinity, personal immortality). Such an inference is quite compatible with supposing (as I do) that Pater's whole attitude toward religion and the "historic Church," as he characteristically calls it, did substantially change, over the years—after the writing of ***The Renaissance.***

Pater observed to a friend that ***Marius*** was written "to show the necessity of religion." And to Violet Paget, who had written an article outlining three types of rationalistic unbelief—optimistic, pessimistic, and humanitarian—Pater testified that writing ***Marius*** was "a sort of duty" to him, because "I think that there is a fourth sort of religious phase possible for the modern mind." This fourth phase one might call reverent and hopeful agnosticism—agnosticism which does not close the door to a faith which it cannot prove.

Tradition would be the best single word to express what, in popular culture—and to a certain extent in high culture also—Pater valued. *Continuity* would be another word, and *comprehensiveness* another. This whole tendency in Pater seems inconsistent with his early emphasis on the intensity of an individual aesthetic experience; it represents change and development. They are united only by being (both) aesthetic—in one aspect sensuous. Liturgy, the Christian ritual, is, like the pagan ritual of Marius's childhood, like the ritual of Pater's boyhood, a matter of processions, lights, flowers, and incense. (Why not add music? Apparently because, despite his generalization in aesthetics that all arts aspire to the condition of music, Pater himself lacked interest in music.)

Pater's view of the relation between ritual and religion can almost be summed up as this: Let the ritual persist, while the myth behind it can, may—and will—change. The continuity of society (precious to those sensitive souls who need for their well-being even an external continuity) means stability of the social order, security—quite compatible with shifting of dogmas or (those less potent things) philosophical systems.

It is common—and natural—to accuse people who like ritual in church (candles, incense, flowers, colored priestly vestments, and altar hangings) of being, at best, concerned with the externals of religion; and if you think, as Arnold did, that religion is only morality "touched with emotion," these ecclesiastical trappings may seem even antireligious: in one way this is the age-long fight between the prophet and the priest. But there is, I believe, an aesthetic approach to religion which is not only valid so far as it goes but the only one available to some, probably many, people. In his "Symposium" Plato teaches the ascent from beautiful bodies to the idea of the beautiful; through intermediate degrees the sensuous can lead to the supersensuous, the Idea of the Beautiful. And Catholic Christianity is sacramental and incarnational: the divine is incarnate in man; in the sacraments an ideal reality assumes material manifestation. What is the whole religion of symbolism but an expansion, an extension, of the sacramental system? Every material object is a correspondence of some spiritual essence. The soul never appears, is never known, naked: it is always clothed, vested. We approach the soul through the body, through the senses.

I put all this flatly, matter-of-factly. But to Pater all this was flaming, fighting doctrine. Having started his intellectual life as a student of Greek and especially of German philosophy, and having then (probably during that memorable first tour of Italy) turned from the philosophy of Germany to the visual art of Italy, he felt a kind of anger at having been so long misled. When Pater returns, from his youthful skepticism and irony, to some kind of acceptance of religion, he thinks of religion as an orderly sequence of sensuous objects dimly symbolizing spiritual truths, but not to be skipped over as though they were mere signs.

Why could Pater not entirely dismiss the Church and churchly religion for very long—not for more than ten or fifteen years? First of all I have to think of the solipsistic doctrine so painfully put in the famous Conclusion—that memorable passage about how walled in, how insulated each of us is. We can't prove the existence of anything outside of our own consciousness—not even the "existence of other selves" (to cite F. H. Bradley). Solipsism is an epistemological problem: how do we know, how can we know, anything outside the self? And, as Hume will add, how do we know there is a self beneath all our momentary impressions? But solipsism is more than an intellectual problem: it names the emotional chill of feeling isolated, not by passing circumstances, but by the very nature of things.

Pater's deep sense of isolation, of inability to communicate, reaches out for community; and the "historic Church," through its ritual, gave him at least the illusion of belonging to a group, a sense that, for him, neither State nor University offered. And in part 3 of ***Marius*** we see this "hero" reaching out toward a theistic belief that he is not alone in the world, that there is an Unseen Companion (a kind of spiritual double) walking beside him. And then in part 4 I note Pater's emphasis on the "blitheness," the cheerfulness, the gaiety, of the Christians he meets through Cornelius, the ideal young soldier, and the life of Hope which pervades the Christian community. Though Pater never reached that Hope, he envies it, and connects it with the Christian church.

Pater knew of attempts—on the part of the Anglo-Catholic clergy as well as men like Maurice and of course the positivists—to preach and initiate social reform. And, since Pater read and almost began his own career as an aesthetic critic by reading Ruskin's *Modern Painters,* he must have been acquainted with Ruskin's later teachings in *Unto This Last*—and must have known something about the social teachings of William Morris, to whose poetry he had devoted an essay. But really Pater has nothing to say to, or about, economic and social equality. He seems to take it for granted that the poor will always be with us, and he is concerned only with giving the poor the temporary relief of beauty—a flower or a stained-glass window. Pain cannot be abolished: it can only be temporarily assuaged, alleviated.

Pater is so much of an elitist that he never seems to feel any guilt at his standing, however modestly, on what Forster in *Howards End* calls "the gold island," that island on which people who attend concerts and read highbrow books and frequent picture-galleries obviously must stand (unlike Leonard Bast, who vainly hungers for "the best that has been thought and said in the world"). To be sure, to be an aesthete you don't have to be rich (at no time in his life was Pater that), but you have to have a minimal start in the world even to be an Oxford man on a scholarship.

The intellectual progress, the argument, or the dialectic (no one of these terms fits) which occupies the middle section of ***Marius*** (part 3 particularly) is the most serious and engaging part of the book. It's a philosophical discussion of an existential sort. Pater is an antiphilosophical philosopher (like Kierkegaard and Nietzsche): once attracted by philosophy, he seems to feel that it wasted his time, misled him. He now is the foe of abstraction. But you can't talk about silence except in words; nor can you attack philosophy except by being abstract. Pater never really solves this problem: he ends up an amateur.

Pater's *Guardian* reviews—of Amiel's Journal, and of *Robert Elsmere*—try to define what he meant by a fourth phase, a sophisticated modern view which could be taken toward religion. This view invokes sympathy with—a reverent, sympathetic agnosticism toward—"the historic Church," as Pater repeatedly called it. (This reminds me of the phrases I used to hear about the "historic episcopate" and the "historic creed.") The word *historic* here is a weasel word that does not assert the truth or validity; it only suggests a certain—and valued—continuity.

There is a minor but real relation between Pater and Newman, a generation earlier. Like Arnold, Pater admired Newman—as a stylist certainly; but also—for Pater was a thinker as well as a literary man—he admired Newman as a type of original thinker. In his early *Westminster* essay **"Coleridge as a Theologian"** (1866) Pater speaks of Newman: "How often in the higher class of theological writings—writings which really spring from an original religious genius, such as those of Dr. Newman—does the modern aspirant to perfect culture seem to find the expression of the immortal delicacies of his own life, the same yet different." Christian spirituality "has often drawn men on little by little into the broader spiritualities of systems opposed to it—pantheism, or positivism, or a philosophy of indifference." That earlier meaning he found in the sacred we find today in any artist or philosopher.

A possible relation may exist between the *Apologia* and ***Marius:*** for ***Marius*** is Pater's reply to the attacks on ***The Renaissance,*** in which he tries (Newman-like) to review the habits of thought and of feeling that underlie, and lead up to, what seems put dogmatically and too briefly in the famous Conclusion (which in a way stands like the dogmas to which Newman subscribed). In Newman's case Kingsley doubted his sincerity; we may not doubt Pater's, but Pater expressed himself with an uncharacteristic and melodramatic bravado.

Pater's uninvitingly named ***Miscellaneous Studies*** (1895), a posthumous collection, gives the best idea of his scope: Pascal, Raphael, Art Notes in Northern (**"cis-Alpine"**) Italy, but also the delicately autobiographical **"The Child in the House"** and **"Apollo in Picardy."** This book one can pick up at any time and read a few pages in, opening even at random. What does that tell one about Pater, and his characteristic virtues? Much, I think. His characteristic virtue is closeness of attention, concentration, on what he is saying and (but only incidentally) on how he is saying it. (To call him a stylist seems to imply that he has nothing to say, which is untrue.) But what he has to say is not a broad generalization which can be taken in as you speed-read it. The Conclusion, I'm afraid, can—even if improperly—be so read; but it is uncharacteristic.

The kind of thing Pater wants to say is a fabric, a tissue, of qualifications, hesitations, reserves, modulations, hints—something said half, but only half, restricted to what can be said by nuances.

This makes Pater in much of ***Marius***—say, in "Second Thoughts," perhaps the deepest and subtlest chapter of the book—hard to understand. Pater ponders. It is thought-feeling, or felt-thought, intellectual sensibility which is his *métier.* But I apprehend all along that he is trying to be precise, not vague—aiming at precision, though the materials with which he works are filmy and fragile.

Pater teaches one attention, concentration, the scrupulous analysis of one's own mental and affective states. Continuity, the broad long straight line, is not Pater's strength. How can it be? He has the defects of his virtues, his virtues being for the minute, the delicate, the detailed.

Walter Pater was a man born with a Word to utter, and he uttered it. Almost from the start he knew what he wanted to say and how to say it: groping and fumbling are amazingly absent, after he had destroyed his early pious poetry. It is perhaps to be regretted that he didn't find some way of incorporating his satire and irony, his sharp, wry, negative note, into his harmony, but only perhaps. His tone is pure rather than rich, though here words "slip and slide," for in another sense he is a cloyingly rich and sweet writer. This purity, or singleness, was of a richness that had to exclude the tart and the acid. That is his formula, his essence.

Richard Dellamora (essay date 1983)

SOURCE: "An Essay in Sexual Liberation, Victorian Style: Walter Pater's 'Two Early French Stories'" in *Literary Visions of Homosexuality,* edited by Stuart Kellogg, The Haworth Press, 1983, pp. 139-50.

[*In the following essay, Dellamora contends that Pater's revision of the first chapter of* The Renaissance *attempts to reconcile Christianity and homoeroticism.*]

The following essay challenges a common view of the career of Walter Pater: that he criticized Victorian religious beliefs and social mores in his first book, ***Studies in the History of the Renaissance*** (1873), then spent the rest of his life backing down.[1] Such a retreat appears to be evident in his decision to delete the notorious Conclusion from the second edition, now retitled ***The Renaissance*** (1877).[2] Nevertheless, I will argue that his decision was made in order to avoid entangling himself in further arguments with his critics at Oxford, critics who had already shown an ability to damage his academic career. At the same time, he added to the opening chapter an attack on religious and moral bigotry that refers to his own difficulties at Oxford. Writers on Pater have scarcely noticed another major change in the second edition, the addition to the first chapter of passages discussing *The Friendship of Amis and Amile,* a thirteenth-century French romance centered on male friendship.[3] Analysis of the romance and of Pater's interpretation indicates that in adding this discussion, he made both more explicit and more nuanced his view of the value of the body in human relationships and of the importance of libidinal elements in Christianity and in medieval culture. His historical analysis parallels a theoretical analysis whereby Pater argues the necessity and worth of the libidinal aspects of culture generally.[4] The rapprochement with Christianity that a critic like David DeLaura sees in Pater's revision exists, but alongside his continuing opposition to organized religion.

I

In this section I will analyze both the original version of the first chapter of Pater's book and its revision in the second edition. This analysis, though detailed, is necessary to show both the humanist polemic with which Pater began and its extension, in the second edition, to include the claims of male love. Because he offers his analysis as historical, I have also referred to the medieval texts on which he bases his arguments. Pater sees in the texts esteem for the body. In *The Friendship of Amis and Amile* in particular, he sees a rapprochement between eroticism and Christianity, as well as a positive individual and cultural narcissism. My own consideration of the medieval texts further bears out Pater's interpretation.

While critics always remember the suppression of the Conclusion in the 1877 edition of ***The Renaissance,*** much less attention is paid to the other major change in the edition, the revision of the opening chapter. In the first edition the opening chapter had been entitled "Aucassin and Nicolette." It is well known for Pater's suggestion in it that the Renaissance had already begun in the twelfth century in France.[5] Pater associates this "great outbreak" of the human spirit both with philosophic rationalism and with aberrant sexual behavior.[6] He instances the romance of the philosopher Abelard with his young niece Heloïse to exemplify both: "the name of Abelard, the great clerk and the great lover, connects the expression of this liberty of heart with the free play of human intelligence round all subjects presented to it" (***SHR,*** p. 4). Pater associates Heloïse and Abelard both with the courtly-love poetry of Provence and with a thirteenth-century prose and verse romance, *Aucassin and Nicolette,* which he proceeds to discuss, emphasizing its delight in detail and expression for their own sake and its "faint air of overwrought delicacy, almost of wantonness" (***SHR,*** p. 10). Particularly, he notes "this rebellious element, this sinister claim for liberty of heart and thought" (***SHR,*** p. 16). He ends the chapter by quoting the hero Aucassin saying (naturally, in French) that he would rather be in hell with Nicolette than in heaven with monks (***SHR,*** p. 17). In the course of the chapter Pater speaks of the rebirth of Venus as well as of the return of the god Amor in the guise of Aucassin (***SHR,*** pp. 15, 14). This erotic renewal signals the "medieval Renaissance" (***SHR,*** p. 15).

In the 1877 revision of the chapter, now called "Two Early French Stories," Pater has added a new element, *The Friendship of Amis and Amile.* While he describes this work as a thirteenth-century romance, the story exists in one version as early as the late eleventh century; and the version that Pater uses is in form a saints' legend. The essence of the story is "the testing of the fidelity of two friends."[7] In *Christianity, Social Tolerance, and Homosexuality,* John Boswell observes that "there is no hint of sexual interest between the knights, but their love for each other explicitly takes precedence over every other commitment."[8] Pater regards this latter aspect as the antinomian element of the story. In retelling the tale, he emphasizes as well the specifically bodily aspect of the friendship, an aspect that suggests that Boswell may be overly cautious in not noting a "sexual interest" below the religious surface of the legend. Pater observes that in it "that free play of human affection, of the claims of which Abelard's story is an assertion, makes itself felt in the incidents of a great friendship, a friendship pure and generous, pushed to a sort of passionate exaltation."[9] Pater quotes from the romance a long section in which the angel Raphael appears to Amis while he and Amile are sleeping alone together in Amis' sick chamber. The angel informs Amis that his "body shall be made whole" (***R*** 1877, p. 13) only if Amile kills his own children and bathes Amis in their blood. With anguish, Amile does so; and Amis is healed. At the end of the story, after the death of the two men, the body of one miraculously moves to the church in which the body of the other is being kept. Pater uses this passage to end the revised essay. (In the romance there are other mentions of the body, too. Friends from childhood, "the two children fell to loving one another so sorely that one would not eat without the other, they lived of one victual, and lay in one bed."[10] Later, they embrace and kiss when they meet as adults. Though these contacts are not sexual, they are physical. Body is important in their friendship.)

The Friendship of Amis and Amile may be read as a text in which the figure of Christ as supreme Knight is assimilated to a cult of friendship that is almost Greek.[11] Both protagonists are antitypes of Christ in his double aspect of loving and sacrificial friend of whom it may be said, "Greater love than this no man has, that one lay down his life for his friends" (John 15: 13-14). At one point in the romance Amis lays down his life for Amile by agreeing to fight in single combat in his place; Amile in turn lays down his life by proxy by slaying his children so that Amis may be healed. Generally, the knighthood or "chivalry" of the two friends is closely associated with Christ (Morris, pp. 296, 306-07).

In the tale, Christian love, sacrifice, and male friendship are conflated. The writer also stresses the importance of chastity. Though Amis warns Amile not to yield to the daughter of the French king, he does, thereby occasioning the need for Amis to rescue him by combat with a knight who has challenged Amile before the king. Amis then tests Amile a second time by sending him to stay with Amis' own wife. Again he advises Amile not to sleep with the woman. Since the two friends are doubles, Amis' wife mistakes Amile for her husband, nor does he undeceive her. But "a night-time whenas they lay in one bed, then Amile laid his sword betwixt the two of them, and said to the woman: 'Take heed that thou touch me in no manner wise, else diest thou straightway by this sword.' And in likewise did he the other nights, until Amis betook him in disguise to his house to wot if Amile kept faith with him of his wife" (Morris, p. 301).[12] Only after this test does Amis fight and slay Amile's accuser. Later, after Amile's children have been first killed and then miraculously restored to life, Amile and his wife "even unto their death . . . held chastity" (Morris, p. 308). The emphasis on chastity carries a hint of the superiority of male friendship to heterosexual love, even to married love. As well there is a suggestion that Amis and Amile fall short of one another in at times preferring women to each other. I have already mentioned that Amile fails Amis (and Christ) by going to bed with the daughter of the French king. Earlier, Amis had set out to search for Amile; but after meeting and marrying a wife, Amis forgets his quest for a year and a half before remembering and telling his men: "We have done amiss in that we have left seeking of Amile" (Morris, p. 298). This lapse indicates uxoriousness on Amis' part, a shortcoming his wife pays for when he sends Amile to her in disguise and for which he himself pays when, after he has become a leper, his wife "had him in sore hate, and many a time strove to strangle him" (Morris, p. 303).

In the 1877 edition, Pater deploys his quotations from *The Friendship of Amis and Amile* on either side of his discussion of *Aucassin and Nicolette.* Doing so, he suggests sexual connotation in the friendship of Amis and Amile. Pater paraphrases the description in the romance of the golden-haired Aucassin's beauty. Aucassin, "the very image of the Provençal love-god" represents the "ideal intensity of passion" (***R*** 1877, p. 25).[13] At the center of the romance are the secrets of sexual intimacy, imaged in "the little hut of flowers which Nicolette constructs in the forest, whither she has escaped from her enemies" (***R*** 1877, p. 21). The hut is a test of Aucassin's love:

> So she gathered white lilies,
> Oak-leaf, that in green wood is,
> Leaves of many a branch I wis,
> Therewith built a lodge of green,
> Goodlier was never seen,
> Swore by God who may not lie,
> "If my love the lodge should spy,
> He will rest awhile thereby
> If he love me loyally."
>
> (p. 46)[14]

When Aucassin and Nicolette meet in the lodge, "either kissed and clipped the other, and fair joy was between them" (p. 57). It is there too that Nicolette heals Aucassin's shoulder, injured when he fell from his horse.

The attractiveness and intimacy of the two lovers add the element of sexual interest about which the story of Amis and Amile is silent. By associating the works, Pater revives not just Amor but specifically the homoerotic Amor of Greek tradition. The "antinomian" elements of *Aucassin and Nicolette*—Aucassin's rejection of an asexual Christian paradise, his rejection of knightly duty in preference for love (p. 20), his sexual contact with Nicolette before marriage (pp. 63, 72)—indicate nonconformity with the norms of courtly love and suggest that nonconformity underlies *The Friendship of Amis and Amile* as well. Pater also indicates his preference for the intensity of a tale of male friendship by the fact that he has juxtaposed it with a heterosexual romance that parodies "the love theme" of serious romance.[15] At one point, for instance, Aucassin intervenes in a fight in which the only weapons are baked apples, eggs, and fresh cheeses. After he slays many men, he is begged to desist, since "it is nowise our custom to slay each other" (p. 62). Pater has chosen a parodic instance of heterosexual romance to compare with what he calls the "strength" of the tale of Amis and Amile, a strength not only of sworn friendship but also, in the version of the story that Pater is following, of feudal obligations and Christian faith.

Pater makes it clear that he is aware that the rival claims of friendship and love may be claims between two kinds of love. Seeing this conflict also in the later thirteenth-century romance of Chaucer, *The Knight's Tale,* Pater says: "Such comradeship, though instances of it are to be found everywhere, is still especially a classical motive, Chaucer expressing the sentiment of it so strongly in an antique tale, that one knows not whether the love of both Palamon and Arcite for Emelya, or of those two for each other, is the chiefer subject of the *Knight's Tale*" (***R*** 1877, p. 9). His further reference to the "sweet . . . daily offices" of Palamon and Arcite in prison is a coded reference to sexual intimacy. In finding male love in an "antique" tale by a medieval writer, Pater connects medieval, Christian culture with the tradition of homosexual friendship in Greek culture.

II

The ideal of male love that Pater specifically introduces with reference to *The Knight's Tale* is androgynous in character, combining strength with sweetness.[16] The masculine connotation of *strength* is already evident in Pater's application of the term to *The Friendship of Amis and Amile. Sweetness,* his term for *Aucassin and Nicolette,* suggests artistic playfulness, beauty, and sensuality. It also suggests femininity. Pater had borrowed the term *sweetness* from his Oxford contemporary Matthew Arnold; but the addition of a sexual charge is his own. DeLaura notes that Abelard was one of Arnold's heroes too; nevertheless, the "'worship of the body'" with which Pater later inflects and infects Arnold's critical terminology is "emphatically no part of Arnold's proposed pattern of human life" (p. 243).[17]

In infusing the strength of *The Friendship of Amis and Amile* with the sweetness of *Aucassin and Nicolette,* Pater achieves a cultural and erotic synthesis that he identifies with the Renaissance both in its classic sixteenth-century phase and in its earlier manifestation during the Middle Ages (***R*** 1877, pp. 16-17). The medieval Renaissance does not merely juxtapose these terms; they are dialectical, and Pater discovers sweetness within *The Friendship of Amis and Amile* itself.[18] Besides being an act of literary interpretation, this discovery enables Pater to divine the structure of personal relations in a much earlier period. Further, the interpretation is cultural. He regards eros as crucial in an integrated culture. The love of Amis and Amile adds a necessary sweetness to the severe and patriarchal order imaged in the legend. In this way, Pater provides what one might call a model of cultural narcissism. The love of Amis and Amile figures a libidinal aspect of medieval culture without which it would be rigid, brutal, and hysterical. Finally, the synthesis of sweetness and strength in *The Friendship of Amis and Amile* and in the medieval Renaissance itself reaffirms a permanent tendency in human action and culture towards androgyny, a conciliation of "masculine" and "feminine" values. Accordingly, the Christ who stands above and is typified by events in the story of Amis and Amile is feminized in their mutual love.[19]

In referring above to "cultural narcissism," I have in mind Freud's view of the place of narcissism in the mature self. In Freud, opposed terms ultimately include each other in dynamic relations. For instance, in the lecture "The Libido Theory and Narcissism" (1917), he describes narcissism as the libidinal element of the ego and as "the source of the Ego Ideal" though earlier he had opposed the terms *ego* and *libido*.[20] In other words, the "*ideal ego*" or "conscience" derives from libido and has as its object the restoration to the self of primal bliss.[21] When, however, the external object of the libido and this "ego-censor" (p. 429) contradict each other, neurosis may ensue. In the lecture Freud focuses on neuroses that occur precisely when the attraction towards someone of the same sex conflicts with the demands of conscience. Writing forty years before him and with great suppleness, Pater observes the same need for conciliating the object of libido with moral choice. In "Two Early French Stories," he considers the need not only as it affects Amis and Amile individually but as it is fulfilled in their love. In this context, moreover, he goes a step further in seeing androgyny as crucial to the development of a sound culture. Such cultures seldom occur, and Victorian England is not among them; but in his writing Pater repeatedly celebrates their advent. He sees the urge to achieve "the harmony of human interests" (***R*** 1877, p. 29) as a primary impulse in Western culture.

III

Pater's handling of medieval materials as discussed above might be considered wholly profane in spirit, with Christ and Christianity being valued only as both become expressive of androgynous values. Further, Pater's analysis is in a line of nineteenth-century argument, both French and English, that tends to reduce religion to sexuality.[22] In this section, I will discuss the rationalizing, scientific aspect of Pater's approach. In Section IV, however, I will try to explain how Pater's presentation of Christianity combines erotic and religious elements without reducing one to the other.

At the time of Pater, it was commonplace to reduce religious meaning to psychological. For instance, in *Idylls of the King* Tennyson "treats the quest for the Holy Grail as an example of mass hysteria. The whole thing originated, he makes perfectly clear, in the frustrated sexual desires of a young woman who had been disappointed in love and gone into a nunnery."[23] In *Madame Bovary,* Flaubert portrays Madame Bovary's schoolgirl religiosity as a displacement of sentimental erotic yearnings.[24] In "Two Early French Stories" Pater cites Victor Hugo's *Notre Dame de Paris* as exemplifying the "rebellious" tendency of medieval culture (***R*** 1877, p. 27). In that novel the scholarly, devout, and dutiful Archdeacon Claude Frollo pursues his studies into the profane arcana of alchemy and thereafter falls into a wholly destructive passion for the virginal Esmerelda. Pater had plotted a similar trajectory in his early review of William Morris' *The Defence of Guenevere* (1858). Concluding a discussion of the transformation of medieval religion into the "rival religion" of courtly love, Pater observes: "That whole religion of the middle age was but a beautiful disease of [sic] disorder of the senses. . . . Reverie, illusion, delirium; they are the three stages of a fatal descent both in the religion and the loves of the middle age. Nowhere has the impression of this delirium been conveyed as by Victor Hugo."[25] Mariolatry is reduced to the worship of the courtly lady, the idolization of Christ to the idolization of the knight. By the same logic, pious edification is transformed by the clerical author of *The Friendship of Amis and Amile* into homoerotic reverie. "This low descendental view" echoes in turn Pater's biography.[26] A devout adolescent intent on becoming a clergyman, Pater lost his faith while a student at Oxford (1858-62), probably at the same time that he became conscious of his homosexual orientation.

IV

The interpretation of culture proposed here goes beyond the rationalizing aspect of Pater's analysis at the same time that it makes the point that a revisionary view of sexual relations has implications for the understanding and transformation of culture itself. By 1877 Pater had eschewed a positivist approach that offered to explain religion as an epiphenomenon of psychology. Rather, he was now ready to attempt a rapprochement between Christianity and eros that is very much his own. When DeLaura observes a "new welcome extended to Christianity" (p. 261) in "Two Early French Stories," he is referring to passages like the following added in 1877: in "the Renaissance . . . the human mind wins for itself a new kingdom of feeling and sensation and thought, not opposed to, but only beyond and independent of the spiritual system then actually realised" (***R*** 1877, p. 7). Such statements, however, are conciliatory in a highly qualified way. Pater's refusal to oppose Christianity is a refusal to engage in dogmatic disputes, which falsify his sense of "the more sincere and generous play of the forces of human mind and character, which I noted as the secret of Abelard's struggle" (***R*** 1877, p. 28). In the sentence quoted by DeLaura, Pater asserts the independence of culture from the demands of religious orthodoxy. His most positive comment about Christianity is one in which he describes Abelard or, more generally, the humanist as "reaching out to and attaining modes of ideal living, beyond the prescribed limits of that system, though possibly contained in essential germ within it" (***R*** 1877, p. 8). The "essential germ" of humanism may be contained within Christianity. This claim, however, grants little to orthodox belief at the same time as it concedes to humanism, with its "reason and heart and senses quick" (***R*** 1877, p. 8), a basis of Christian authority.

Pater's comments on the Christian "system" have a context in contemporary liberal writing. For instance, at the same time as Pater was writing the essays that would later appear in ***Studies in the History of the Renaissance,*** John Stuart Mill also criticized conventional sexual norms in *On the Subjection of Women* (1869). And in *On Liberty* (1859) he too had contrasted custom, conventional Christianity, and public opinion to individual liberty and growth:

> The creed remains as it were outside the mind, incrusting and petrifying it against all other influences addressed to the higher parts of our nature; manifesting its power by not suffering any fresh and living conviction to get in, but itself doing nothing for the mind or heart, except standing sentinel over them to keep them vacant. To what an extent doctrines intrinsically fitted to make the deepest impression upon the mind may remain in it as dead beliefs, without being ever realised in the imagination, the feelings, or the understanding, is exemplified by the manner in which the majority of believers hold the doctrines of Christianity.[27]

Both Mill and Pater contrast an inert dogmatic Christianity to the life of the individual.

When critics discuss Pater's move toward Christianity in 1877 and later in ***Marius the Epicurean*** (1885), they need to emphasize his understanding of Christianity as valorizing the body, including the homoerotic body. In this regard, the story of Heloïse and Abelard, with which Pater introduces the two romances, provides an instructive point of contact with Pater and suggests that in conflating eros and Christianity he spoke with an understanding of medieval Christianity. The degree to which Heloïse, who eventually became head of a religious house, internally assented to the "system" that she served so well is open to debate. Peter Dronke, however, demonstrates that the intensity of her love for Abelard, and the esteem accorded it by her contemporaries, are not in doubt. In a letter that Pater would have appreciated for its conciliation of religious and erotic feeling, Peter the Venerable, Abbot of Cluny and prince of the Church, wrote to Heloïse at Abelard's death:

> My illustrious and dearest sister in God: this man to whom you cleaved, after the sexual oneness, with the stronger and finer bond of divine love, he with whom and under whom you have long served God—I tell you, God is now cherishing him in his lap, in place of you, or like a replica of you. And at the second coming, at the sound of the archangel and the trumpet heralding God descending from the heavens, God will restore him to you through his grace, having preserved him for you.[28]

It is further worth observing that Abelard himself "explored with great sensitivity and feeling the nature of the love between . . . two men" in his *planctus* of David for Jonathan.[29]

Pater's positive remarks about Christianity occur in a passage in which he sees contemporary opposition to Abelard in the Church as one between "the mere professional, official, hireling ministers of that system, with their ignorant worship of system for its own sake, and the true child of light, the humanist" (***R*** 1877, pp. 7-8). This dichotomy is Pater's riposte to his critics at Oxford, including the bishop there, after publication of ***Studies in the History of the Renaissance.*** The book had also prompted an attack on Pater by a colleague and former student at his Oxford college, John Wordsworth, grandnephew of the poet. As a result, Pater missed a routine promotion that instead went to Wordsworth. The setback was a shock that would in itself adequately account for Pater's decision to withdraw the Conclusion from the second edition (1877). He had additional reason, however, in that the Conclusion had been parodied by "the horrid undergraduate" W. H. Mallock in his successful satirical novel of 1876, *The New Republic* (Brake, p. 50). By deleting the Conclusion and rewriting Chapter i, Pater for the moment regained control of his meaning.

He made his decision to delete that Conclusion no later than November 1876 (***Letters,*** p. 17). That same year, he decided to stand for Professor of Poetry at Oxford. Though he was aware that he would be strongly opposed, he knew that he merited the position. Nonetheless, opposition took an unexpected turn when Benjamin Jowett, Master of Balliol College and chief political power in Oxford at the time, blackmailed Pater by threatening to disclose some incriminating letters. According to rumor, it was Mallock who gave the letters to Jowett (Brake, p. 48). While no evidence for the specific date of Jowett's showdown with Pater has yet been discovered, it likely occurred between February 1877, when a student publication opposed Pater's candidacy, and April, when he withdrew his name (Brake, p. 48; Small, pp. 314-315).[30] In the meantime, Pater was also attacked in an article in the March issue of *The Contemporary Review* (Small, p. 315).

In the same month that saw his humiliation, the second edition of ***The Renaissance*** was being bound (Small, p. 314). In suppressing the original Conclusion, Pater had tried to avoid "well-recognised controversy, with rigidly defined opposites, exhausting the intelligence and limiting one's sympathies" (***R*** 1877, p. 28); but he added a polemic against what his biographer would later refer to as "vile little opportunists" (Brake, p. 48). As well, he also now took the opportunity to celebrate male friendship, a celebration that elaborates his view of the libidinal element of culture and at the same time extends the claims for "liberty of the heart" to male love. Doing so, he was willing to reconsider Christianity so as to include homosexuality within it, a process he continued in ***Marius the Epicurean.***

Writing the essay was an act of courage that also illuminated homoeroticism in Western culture. On these grounds, Pater was an important originator of homosexual criticism. He saw homoerotic interpretation as a means of affiliation whereby homosexuals in different times and places may confirm their experience and use it as a means of access to alien cultures. A century before John Boswell wrote of "The Triumph of Ganymede" in the literature of 1050 to 1150, Pater had already divined and written about it in **"Two Early French Stories,"** though he did not write about the specifically homosexual texts that Boswell adduces.[31] It is worth keeping in mind, moreover, that Pater's homosexual polemic coincided with a general polemic in praise of the diversity of erotic and other experience. As well, he was always concerned to see eros and personal freedom in relation to cultural formation and change. This plurality of concerns in Pater recommends itself well to critics today.

Notes

1. U. C. Knoepflmacher, *Religious Humanism and the Victorian Novel: George Eliot, Walter Pater, and Samuel Butler* (Princeton: Princeton Univ. Press, 1965), pp. 7-8, 153-55. Geoffrey Tillotson, "Pater, Mr. Rose and the 'Conclusion' of *The Renaissance,*" in *Criticism and the Nineteenth Century* (London, 1951; rpt. Hamden, Conn.: Archon Books, 1967), pp. 124-46.
2. For Pater and Oxford politics, see Laurel Brake, "Judas and the Widow: Thomas Wright and A. C. Benson as Biographers of Walter Pater: The Widow," *PSt,* 4 (May 1981), 39-54. See also Walter Pater, *Letters,* ed. Lawrence Evans (Oxford: The Clarendon Press, 1970), pp. xxi-xxii, but see also p. 13n; hereafter cited in text as *Letters.* For a debate on Pater's reasons for deleting the Conclusion, see Lawrence F. Schuetz, "The Suppressed 'Conclusion' to *The Renaissance* and Pater's Modern Image," *ELT,* 17 (1974), 251-59; and "Pater and the Suppressed 'Conclusion' to *The Renaissance:* Comment and Reply," *ELT,* 19 (1976), 313-21. See also Michael Levey, *The Case of Walter Pater* (London: Thames and Hudson, 1978), pp. 141-44.
3. For an exception, see Richard L. Stein, "The Private Themes of Pater's *Renaissance,*" *Psychoanalysis and Literary Process,* ed. Frederick Crews (Cambridge, Mass.: Winthrop, 1970), pp. 175-177.
4. See, for instance, Robert L. Caserio, *Plot, Story, and the Novel: From Dickens and Poe to the Modern Period* (Princeton: Princeton Univ. Press, 1979), pp. 50-56.
5. He drew the suggestion from French writers. See Walter Pater, *The Renaissance: Studies in Art and Poetry: The 1893 Text,* ed. Donald L. Hill (Berkeley: Univ. of California Press, 1980), pp. 304-05; hereafter cited in notes as *R* 1893.
6. Walter Pater, *Studies in the History of the Renaissance* (London: Macmillan, 1873), p. 2; hereafter cited in text as *SHR.*
7. MacEdward Leach, ed., *Amis and Amiloun,* Early English Text Society, O. S. no. 203 (1937; rpt. London: Oxford Univ. Press, 1960), p. xx. See also Ojars Kratins, "The Middle English *Amis and Amiloun:* Chivalric Romance or Secular Hagiography?" *PMLA,* 81 (1966), 347-54; Dale Kramer, "Structural Artistry in *Amis and Amiloun,*" *Annuale Mediaevale,* 9 (1968), 103-22; Kathryn Hume, "Structure and Perspective: Romance and Hagiographic Features in the Amicus and Amelius Story," *JEGP [Journal of English and Germanic Philology],* 69 (1970), 89-107; Kathryn Hume, "*Amis and Amiloun* and the Aesthetics of Middle English Romance," *SP [Studies in Philology],* 70 (1973), 19-41; and Diana T. Childress, "Between Romance and Legend: 'Secular Hagiography' in Middle English Literature," *PQ [Philological Quarterly],* 57 (1978), 311-22, esp. 318-19.
8. John Boswell, *Christianity, Social Tolerance, and Homosexuality: Gay People in Western Europe from the Beginning of the Christian Era to the Fourteenth Century* (Chicago: Univ. of Chicago Press, 1980), p. 240.
9. Walter Pater, *The Renaissance: Studies in Art and Poetry,* 2nd ed. (London: Macmillan, 1877), p. 9; hereafter cited in text as *R* 1877.
10. I quote from the translation of William Morris, *The Friendship of Amis and Amile,* in *The Collected Works,* introd. May Morris (New York: Russell and Russell, 1966), XVII, 295.
11. For sexuality in Greek male friendship, see Richard J. Hoffman, "Some Cultural Aspects of Greek Male Sexuality," *Journal of Homosexuality,* 5 (1980), 217-25; K. J. Dover, *Greek Homosexuality* (London: Duckworth, 1978), p. 170 et passim; Boswell, chs. i and ii passim; John Addington Symonds, *Studies in Sexual Inversion* (n.p.: privately printed, 1928), p. 19. Gervase Mathew touches on the relation of sexuality to medieval friendship though he makes no use of the gay literature that John Boswell discusses ("Ideals of Friendship," in *Patterns of Love and Courtesy,* ed. John Lawlor [London: Edward Arnold, 1966], pp. 46, 49).
12. Leach, discussing *Amis and Amiloun,* an English version of the tale, remarks: "The motivation of the incident is the common one used throughout the story: it is as much a test of Amis' friendship for Amiloun as the judicial combat is a test of Amiloun's friendship for Amis" (pp. xlvi-xlvii).
13. The appeal of this figure to homoerotic sensibility is indicated as well in that the poem attributed to Pierre

Vidal which Pater refers to at this point is one that he knew from John Addington Symonds' *An Introduction to Dante* (1872). Symonds, a bisexual, rhapsodizes over the image of "Chivalrous Love" (*R* 1893, pp. 316-17).

14. References to *Aucassin and Nicolette* in the text are to Andrew Lang, *Aucassin and Nicolette* (New York: Barse and Hopkins, n.d.).
15. D. H. Green, *Irony in the Medieval Romance* (Cambridge: Cambridge Univ. Press, 1979), p. 99.
16. For a discussion of the importance of these terms in Pater's critical vocabulary, see Billie Andrew Inman, "Pater's Conception of the Renaissance: From Sources to Personal Ideal," *VN [Victorian Newsletter],* 47 (Spring 1975), 22-24.
17. References to DeLaura in the text are to David J. DeLaura, *Hebrew and Hellene in Victorian England: Newman, Arnold, and Pater* (Austin: Univ. of Texas Press, 1969). For a discussion of the relation of Arnold and Pater, see pp. 165-91, 202-22, 240-44 et passim. Michelet also uses the term *sweetness* to characterize Abelard (*R* 1893, p. 308).
18. As well he might. Taking *Amis and Amiloun* as "the medieval English classic on . . . friendship," Mathew notes that the first known Anglo-Norman version (c. 1200) "begins by promising that it will be a song of love, of loyalty, and of great sweetness ('d'amour, de leaute, et de grand doucour')" (p. 45). I have already mentioned the "sweet . . . daily offices" of Palamon and Arcite.
19. For the feminization of Christ in Pater's writing see my essay "Pater's Modernism: The Leonardo Essay," *UTQ [University of Toronto Quarterly],* 47 (Winter 1977/78), 137, 145. I also discuss this process in my current study of *Marius the Epicurean.*
20. Marthe Robert, *The Psychoanalytic Revolution: Sigmund Freud's Life and Achievement,* trans. Kenneth Morgan (New York: Harcourt, 1966), p. 312.
21. Sigmund Freud, *The Standard Edition of the Complete Psychological Works,* trans. James Strachey (London: The Hogarth Press, 1971), XVI, 429.
22. *R* 1893, pp. 308, 317-18. Pater's reading of medieval culture shares attributes with what Herbert Sussman calls "second-generation Pre-Raphaelitism," a phenomenon that he associates with A. C. Swinburne, D. G. Rossetti, and William Morris. Sussman says that the work of these writers "deals openly with wholly non-respectable forms of sexuality, employs a style that often moves toward the evocative and *symboliste,* and is presented as the expression of an adversary culture." See Herbert Sussman, "The Pre-Raphaelite Brotherhood and Their Circle: The Formation of the Victorian Avant-Garde," *VN,* no. 57 (Spring 1980), p. 7. In particular, Swinburne in his *William Blake* (1868) gave Pater the passage from *Aucassin and Nicolette* with which he ends the chapter in the first edition as well as the general idea of "the old Albigensian 'Aucassin' and all its paganism." See Algernon Charles Swinburne, *The Complete Works,* ed. Sir Edmund Gosse and Thomas James Wise (London, 1925; rpt. New York: Russell and Russell, 1968), XVI, 135, 136n. Cf. *R* 1893, p. 303.
23. A Dwight Culler, *The Poetry of Tennyson* (New Haven: Yale Univ. Press, 1977), p. 228.
24. Gustave Flaubert, *Madame Bovary: A Story of Provincial Life,* trans. Alan Russell (Harmondsworth: Penguin, 1967), pp. 48-49, 50-53. See Gerald Monsman, *Walter Pater* (Boston: Twayne, 1977), p. 21.
25. James Sambrook, ed., *Pre-Raphaelitism: A Collection of Critical Essays* (Chicago: Univ. of Chicago Press, 1974), p. 107. In the passage, "of" is an obvious misprint of "or."
26. Culler, p. 229.
27. John Stuart Mill, *On Liberty,* ed. David Spitz (New York: Norton, 1975), p. 40.
28. Peter Dronke, *Abelard and Heloise in Medieval Testimonies* (Glasgow: Univ. of Glasgow Press, 1976), p. 23.
29. Boswell, p. 238. See Peter Dronke, *Poetic Individuality in the Middle Ages: New Departures in Poetry 1000-1150* (Oxford: The Clarendon Press, 1970), p. 116.
30. Although Brake implies that the meeting occurred before Pater decided to delete the Conclusion (p. 51), for the reasons that I adduce in the preceding paragraph, I believe that Pater reached this decision on his own. It is more likely that Jowett would have intervened in 1877 when controversy about Pater was spilling over into the press. I realize, however, the limited worth of inference when a date is in question, and I look forward to more biographical information becoming available.
31. Boswell, pp. 243-266.

Gerald Monsman (essay date 1984)

SOURCE: "'Definite History and Dogmatic Interpretation': The 'White-nights' of Pater's *Marius the Epicurean,*" in *Criticism,* Vol. 26, No. 2, Spring, 1984, pp. 171-91.

[*In the following essay, Monsman asserts that Pater's work contains many alternative possible meanings; its ambiguities, variations, and masks defy final meaning, he concludes.*]

"*White-nights*! so you might interpret its old Latin name. 'The red rose came first,' says a quaint German mystic, speaking of 'the mystery of so-called *white* things,' as being 'ever an after-thought—the doubles, or seconds, of real things, and themselves but half-real, half-material' . . . So, white-nights, I suppose, after something like the same analogy, should be nights not of quite blank forgetfulness, but passed in continuous dreaming, only half veiled by sleep. Certainly the place was, in such case, true to its fanciful name in this, that you might very well conceive, in face of it, that dreaming even in the daytime might come to much there" (***Marius,*** 1: 13-14).[1] If the reader is called upon to "interpret" the old Latin of the villa's name as signifying dreaming nights and days (the absence of the original Latin belatedly supplied in a footnote as *Ad Vigilias Albas* had given the "you" an interpretation in the first two editions of the novel without any means of authentication), then Pater's readers as well as Pater's characters and Pater himself are concerned even more with the problematics of interpreting those dreams themselves. There is a great deal about the meaning of sleep, dreams, and vision not only in the chapter describing Marius' home of White-nights but throughout the novel; indeed, the novel's epigraph seems to characterize the whole work as a fantasy in the mind of the author or reader: "A dream in wintertime, when the nights are longest." Long before Joseph was sold into Egyptian slavery and rose by interpreting the Pharoah's dreams, this activity had a venerable tradition. But if Joseph's success lay in what essentially is the technocrat's accurate forecast, Pater's originality is constituted by his realization that meaning always eludes any final form. Every bit as avant-garde as Freud's pioneering work in the interpretation of dreams some fifteen years later, ***Marius the Epicurean*** sponsors a theory of interpretation that denies dreams any definitive meaning but instead offers other dreams as their explanation, one behind another like the layers of a lily bulb without a final core (or much like the pages of the text which at Marius' death has circled back to its opening scenes). So too Freud's or Jung's archetypal myths operate like the meaning of the dream scenes in ***Marius,*** each patient's history is a layer of the bulb's overlapping leaves, a form of the myth which itself is but a story whose explanation depends on and varies with other myths. The process of interpreting the dreamtext itself is, I intend to show, like the activity of interpreting the old Latin name of Marius' villa—a translation or substitution of one name or sign for another without any final closure. Notice in the opening quotation the dubiety expressed by the triple use of "might," of "I suppose," of "something like" which leaves as the only certainty a mere possibility of productive dreaming ("certainly . . . you might")—but productive of what the "you" (always a transparent mask for the authorial "I" behind) is not sure.

Of course, the reader who is familiar with Pater's other works may be aware that this world of dreams between sleep and waking is under the aegis of Persephone who holds "the poppy, emblem of sleep and death by its narcotic juices, of life and resurrection by its innumerable seeds, of the dreams, therefore, that may intervene between falling asleep and waking" (***Greek Studies,*** 148-49). Pater says that the best Latin equivalent for the English *unworldly* is "the beautiful word *umbratilis*" (***Marius,*** 1: 25) which describes Marius' life as shadowy or as remaining in the shade and, when taken together with the "languid and shadowy" (17) existence of his mother, seems to present an underworld abode of the dead—not unlike Swinburne's "Garden of Proserpine" where all life ends "in doubtful dreams of dreams," except that in Pater's novel there is the hope of an awakening. The thrust of ***Marius*** is from dream—"'sometimes those dreams come true'" (228)—to vision, from the "half real" to the seeing of a wholly real embodiment of the early desire for maternal love: "And as his mother became to him the very type of maternity in things, its unfailing pity and protectiveness, and maternity itself the central type of all love;—so, that beautiful dwelling-place lent the reality of concrete outline to a peculiar ideal of home, which throughout the rest of his life he seemed, amid many distractions of spirit, to be ever seeking to regain" (22). Presumably White-nights embodies the realm of the cyclic Persephone in her innocent phase as Kore, united with her mother Demeter as described by Pater in ***Greek Studies,*** before the dream turns to the nightmare of separation and she once again enters the kingdom of Dis. Pater may have been thinking of this cyclic coinherence of modes when he describes how Wordsworth had pondered deeply

> on those strange reminiscences and forebodings, which seem to make our lives stretch before and behind us, beyond where we can see or touch anything, or trace the lines of connexion. . . . It was in this mood that he conceived those oft-reiterated regrets for a half-ideal childhood, when the relics of Paradise still clung about the soul—a childhood, as it seemed, full of the fruits of old age, lost for all, in a degree, in the passing away of the youth of the world, lost for each one, over again, in the passing away of actual youth. (***Appreciations,*** 54-55)

Notwithstanding the novel's repeatedly stated hopes of vision, dreaming is productive only of more dreams of lost love or of nightmare.

As Marius lies dying, sleeping and awakening by turns, he seems primarily prepared for some *written* revelation. Mindful possibly of his life at White-nights that "had been so like the reading of a romance to him" (***Marius,*** 1: 25), Marius in his last hours looks forward to

> some ampler vision, which should take up into itself and explain this world's delightful shows, as the scattered fragments of a poetry, till then but half-understood, might be taken up into the text of a lost epic, recovered at last. At this moment, his unclouded receptivity of soul, grown so steadily through all those years, from experience to experience, was at its height; the house ready for the possible guest; the tablet of the mind white and smooth, for whatsoever divine fingers might choose to write there. (2: 220).

But does the writing of the divine fingers complete the "scattered fragments"? Perhaps, rather, it is akin to the "long-lost text" of the Homeric Hymn recovered in 1780 that Pater will translate in his "attempt to select and weave together" the details of the myth of Demeter: "Portions of the text are missing, and there are probably some additions by later hands. . . . Listen now to a somewhat abbreviated version of it" (***Greek Studies,*** 82-83). Fragmentary by both what still is missing and what here is deleted, a pastiche by virtue of those additions by "hands" that come later, Pater's exquisite story-translation somehow affords a glimpse more revelatory of the original ideal than any text hitherto produced. Yet, Pater observes, all knowledge of truth

> precisely because it resembles some high kind of relationship of persons to persons, depends a good deal on the receiver; and must be, in that degree, elusive, provisional, contingent, a matter of various approximation. . . . The treatise, as the instrument of a dogmatic philosophy *begins* with an axiom or definition: the essay or dialogue, on the other hand, as the instrument of dialectic, does not necessarily so much as conclude in one; like that long dialogue with oneself, that dialectic process, which may be co-extensive with life. It does in truth little more than clear the ground, as we say, or the atmosphere, or the mental tablet, that one may have a fair chance of knowing, or seeing, perhaps. (***Plato,*** 187-88)

Applied to the dying Marius, the "mental tablet" resists the closure of dogmatic inscription; instead, Marius' lifelong "dialectic" or "dialogue" has been like that "of persons to persons"—from Kore to Persephone to Kore, from dream to nightmare and back again. The long-awaited vision is still only a "perhaps" within a Platonic dialogue of search: "every one of Plato's Dialogues is in essence such like that whole, life-long, endless dialogue which dialectic, in its largest scope, does but formulate, and in which truly the last, the infallible word, after all, never gets spoken. Our pilgrimage is meant indeed to end in nothing less than the *vision* of what we seek. But can we ever be quite sure that we are really come to that? By what sign or test?" (192).

One might say that in the shadowy, dreamy world of White-nights signs of the vision remain only signs. The central event in the opening chapters, the spring festival of the *Ambarvalia* and its sacrifice of bull, ram, and pig offered to Mars as an agricultural deity, entails "the old Latin words of the liturgy, to be said as the procession moved on its way, though their precise meaning was long since become unintelligible. . . . But for the monotonous intonation of the liturgy by the priests . . . the procession moved in absolute stillness, all persons, even the children, abstaining from speech . . . lest any words save those proper to the occasion should hinder the religious efficacy of the rite" (***Marius,*** 1: 7-8). Like the scattered poetry figuratively "half-understood" by the dying Marius, the "unintelligible" words of the liturgy have an important implication for the boy:

> in the young Marius, the very absence from those venerable usages of all definite history and dogmatic interpretation, had already awakened much speculative activity; and to-day, starting from the actual details of the divine service, some very lively surmises, though scarcely distinct enough to be thoughts, were moving backwards and forwards in his mind, as the stirring wind had done all day among the trees, and were like the passing of some mysterious influence over all the elements of his nature and experience. (9)

The "unintelligible" liturgy is not mere nonsense; whatever its tenor might be taken to be, the ritual has a very specific organization or differentiated structure: no words are permitted "save those proper to the occasion," no reflections except "upon the scrupulous fulfilment of all the details of the ceremonial" (9). But just as Marius' tablet of the mind resists dogmatic inscription, so here among the fragments of words Marius cannot read (the root sense of "unintelligible" from *inter* + *legere*) any final meaning, any last infallible word. Nevertheless, the awakening of his surmises seems to occur precisely in this absence of "dogmatic interpretation." Ergo, the medium really is the message.

The chief characteristic of the medium is, then, its heterogeneity, its alternative possibilities of meaning which preclude choice. Both language inevitably and art by intention are, Pater would say, "receptacles of so many powers or forces: they possess, like the products of nature, so many virtues or qualities" (***Renaissance,*** viii). But the impression that any specific virtue makes upon the beholder is the result not of some mediated reality, some fixed meaning recoverable by interpretation from within the aesthetic receptacle as wine may be drunk from its cup; rather, the ordering, the juxtapositions of aesthetic forms speak directly as a primary reality in their own right. Notice how in Pater's description of the feast in honor of Apuleius, for example, he calls his readers' attention not merely to the dark red wine but to the more striking image of "the crystal vessels darkened with old wine" (***Marius,*** 2: 78). What is important here is not the contents—this or that shade of reds or whites—but the way the container contains. The fact that the aesthetic object lays claim to no reality "beyond its own victorious fairness" (***Renaissance,*** 205) gives point to Lucian's image of the seekers for ultimate truth who are like temple guards searching among a host of secular cups, flagons, and diadems for a missing sacred vessel—neither shape nor material known, and unfortunately not inscribed with the name of its divine owner. Like the undoubtedly beautiful but unspecified cup, the aesthetic object reduces to no final reality in consequence of a privileged meaning. Thus the importance in ***The Renaissance*** of the cups given to Amis and Amile, doubles like the Dioscuri or Demeter's daughters, lies not in their contents or specific usage but, like the twins themselves, in their doubleness: "two marvelously beautiful cups, also exactly like each other. . . . These two cups, which by their resemblance help to bring the friends together at critical moments, . . . cross and recross very strangely in the narrative" (9). This unity only in multeity is the regnant quality of the aesthetic object. Just as the identical cups "bring the friends together," so each work of art, doubling all others, embodies an infinite host of interchangeable meanings that "cross and recross very strangely in the narrative."

Granting that the doubling of cups, brothers, persons or personae is (or may be) a figure for the way a work of art carries its meanings, let us consider two cupular images associated with the snakes that appear so ominously at the core of the White-nights chapter—the mouth of the garden god and the oval chamber. In particular, I would like to begin with an interpretation by J. Hillis Miller of an incident involving an encounter with breeding snakes and Marius' recollection of an earlier event:

> He wondered at himself indeed, trying to puzzle out the secret of that repugnance, having no particular dread of a snake's bite, like one of his companions, who had put his hand into the mouth of an old garden-god and roused there a sluggish viper. A kind of pity even mingled with his aversion, and he could hardly have killed or injured the animals, which seemed already to suffer by the very circumstance of their life, being what they were. (***Marius,*** 1: 23-24).

Miller speaks of the "pleasure in rousing the viper" and notes that the companion, "like Marius, has 'no particular dread of a snake.'"[2] For Miller, the companion deliberately puts his hand into the mouth of the garden god aware of the sluggish reptile within and with no fear of its bite plays with that phallic creature. Now, my first impulse is to interpret the passage in diametrically opposite terms. I read it as saying that Marius and his companion both disliked snakes but that Marius, never having been bitten, did not particularly fear the snake's bite but that his companion certainly did, owing to the experience of playfully (sacrilegiously perhaps) putting his hand into the mouth of the god not suspecting the presence of a snake—and then getting bit as a nasty surprise. The difference of interpretation turns on whether the connective "like" links Marius and his companion in straightforward similarity or whether "like" compares the "dread" and the companion. In my interpretation "like" really means "unlike"—Marius has "no particular dread" of the sort harbored by one of his companions. Down the page a few lines that "sluggish" snake really does try to bite: "There was a humanity, dusty and sordid and as if far gone in corruption, in the sluggish coil, as it awoke suddenly into one metallic spring of pure enmity against him" (24). Miller's observation that the companion is a displaced version of Marius makes even more sense if we presume the snake struck the companion since here the snake strikes directly at Marius himself. However, I think *both* of our contradictory interpretations inhere in the garden god episode, just as the old Latin words of the *Ambarvalia* permit associations "backwards and forwards." The displacement in the incident with the companion allows Pater to have Marius react to the snake in two ways—literally with "no particular dread" and displaced as his companion with "dread." Marius is both afraid and not afraid of the serpents; he both pities and hates them. Pater's language here does no more than what psychoanalysis has recognized personality itself as sometimes doing; namely, resolving conflicts by multiple, dissociated personalities—contradictory attitudes, opposing emotional drives in which different groups of strivings, attitudes and values are associated with independent self-systems.

Miller's pleasures of the viper have their equivalences elsewhere in the novel's design of recurrent imagery, as in the prick of an arrow for example—and arrows are everywhere present, especially the prick of Cupid at Psyche's first glimpse of the god: "And Psyche, gazing hungrily thereon, draws an arrow from the quiver, and trying the point upon her thumb, tremulous still, drave in the barb, so that a drop of blood came forth. Thus fell she, by her own act, and unaware, into the love of Love" (75). Psyche, of course, originally had dreaded "that evil serpent-thing" (64) but, like the ambiguous interpretations of the snake in the god's mouth, her fear turns to love and "under one bodily form she loathes the monster and loves the bridegroom" (74). Although Cupid's arrow clearly mimics the benign Millerian serpent inasmuch as Psyche bears Voluptas, whose name means "pleasure," the object of Psyche's desire, Cupid, turns out to be simply a vision or personification of *cupido*—"the love of Love" or the desire of forever desiring. By definition Cupid is like the "absent or veiled" image of Zeus in the middle ages, "distracted . . . into a thousand symbols and reflections"[3]; only by imagining Psyche on Olympus can the storyteller award her the final vision. As mortal, Psyche has no more chance of arriving at the determinate vision of her desire than would any viewer of some mythical creature fragmented among the multiple planes of Cubist art. Yet Psyche's story is in sharp contrast to the sad narrative in "The Ceremony of the Dart." Cupid's barb becomes there "the bloodstained spear" (2: 44) the emperor Aurelius casts to insure public victory; he reaps only personal defeat. Desirous of attaining to some inner and permanent spiritual reality, Aurelius doubles the boy thrusting his hand into the face of the garden god, striking through the mask of the phenomenal to seize the reality of the noumenal within. But all he finds is the sting of death, dimly the victim of his own deadly dart.

The ceremonial knife-play and blood-letting with which the chapter opens (echoes of the fertility sacrifices of the *Ambarvalia*) are a prelude to the tragically pathetic repetition and inversion of its close, the knife of the country surgeon and afterwards "a company of pupils pressing in" (56) around the dying child of the emperor, recalling again the slaughter of the *suovetaurilia* and the "frank curiosity in the spectacle" (1: 9). The loss of Aurelius' child contrasts with the expectation and delight of Psyche in recovering her absent lover not by any direct vision (her original error) but indirectly in the form of her child to be born: "'in the face of this little child, at the least, shall I apprehend thine'" (93). Aurelius finds nothing but his own overthrow doubled in the child's misery: "Marius was forced into the privacy of a grief, the desolate face of which went deep into his memory, as he saw the emperor carry the child away—quite conscious at last, but with a touching expression upon it of weakness and defeat—pressed close to his bosom, as if he yearned just then for one thing only, to be united, to be absolutely one with it, in its obscure distress" (2: 56). Aurelius' understandable yearning for absolute unity with his dying son is expressed in the generalized face of grief reflected in both parent and child—a unity of visage owing its radical hopelessness to the emperor's Psyche-like error of desiring to attain directly to a suprahuman reality, to some permanent ideal that excludes renewal because it transcends flux. But as the cupular figure of his furniture-emptied palace ultimately indicates, there is no determinate center within appearances except for the emptiness of the grave. Despiser of the physical body, Aurelius erringly focuses entirely on inner, visionary ideals, on what might be called with a certain irony the furniture of thought rather than on the process itself whereby the palace of thought is replenished with those moveable articles. Since Aurelius does not value the "crystal vessel" for its protean possibilities of endlessly renewed meanings, he cannot turn the loss of his child back onto the hope of a renewal as do the Christians with the child's grave: "treated as, *natalitia*—a birthday" (102). The Christian practice of "burial instead of burning" (99) turns the tomb into a womb and the sting of death into the thrusting through or piercing of the sexual act, a sowing of the seed that the fertility rite of the *Ambarvalia* celebrated. In this sense Cupid revives the sleep-enveloped Psyche, "awaking her with the innocent point of his arrow" (1: 89-90). Having turned her vanished old love back upon the new, death is thus employed against itself to summon the face and renew the pleasure of her absent lord.

Throughout much of his novel Pater seems to be reweaving the familiar words from the fifteenth chapter of the first epistle of Paul to the Corinthians; only Paul's imagery of the body sown in "corruption" that is not quickened and raised in incorruption except it die becomes for Pater an endless process of dying and renewal without final wholeness—other than the innocence concealed as the sting of death momentarily glimpsed in Cupid's "innocent" arrow. Except for G. M. Hopkins, I do not know another of Pater's contemporaries who adapts so subtly and yet so pervasively the thematic motif of the nail and thorn-pierced *crucifixus* in order to portray life concealed within the wound of death. As might be expected, the ramifying image of the serpent in the mouth of the garden god is not fully deployed in the White-nights chapter except by reference to the "chamber, curved ingeniously into oval form" that contains the "head of Medusa, for which the villa was famous" (19). Persephone, of course, had been the goddess of White-night's dreaming; and it is she, Pater states in ***Greek Studies,*** who keeps the gorgon-head of Medusa. Miller is right, as far as he goes, in associating this Medusa with that of Leonardo da Vinci described by Pater in his essay on Leonardo as

> the head of a corpse, exercising its powers through all the circumstances of death. What may be called the fascination of corruption penetrates in every touch its exquisitely finished beauty. . . . The delicate snakes seem literally strangling each other in terrified struggle to escape from the Medusa brain. The hue which violent death always brings with it is in the features; features singularly massive and grand, as we catch them inverted, in a dexterous foreshortening, crown foremost, like a great calm stone against which the wave of serpents breaks.
>
> (***Renaissance,*** 106)

If, as we are told, the traveler pauses "to read the face, as it were, of so beautiful a dwelling-place" (***Marius,*** 1: 18), then in one sense the oval chamber of White-nights is itself the *os* (L face, mouth) of the garden god in which the ophidian form of death lurks; however, since the ovular *pinacotheca* also contains the death masks of Marius' ancestors, as well as the head of Medusa, container and contained once again present themselves as differentiated but interconnected masks for each other. What the traveler "reads," then, is the disguised form of a familiar visage—life hidden in death, death hidden in life.

This ambiguity is clearly present in Marius' friend Flavian who serves as Medusa's double in real life:

> How often, afterwards, did evil things present themselves in malign association with the memory of that beautiful head, and with a kind of borrowed sanction and charm in its natural grace! To Marius, at a later time, he counted for as it were an epitome of the whole pagan world, the depth of its corruption, and its perfection of form. And still, in his mobility, his animation, in his eager capacity for various life, he was so real an object, after that visionary idealism of the villa. His voice, his glance, were like the breaking in of the solid world upon one, amid the flimsy fictions of a dream. A shadow, handling all things as shadows, had felt a sudden real and poignant heat in them. (53)

Flavian's "breaking in" upon the shadowy Marius with "real and poignant" (L *pungere* to prick, sting) heat anticipates his own death "with a fiery pang in the brain, fancying no covering thin or light enough to be applied to his body" (112). As Flavian lies dying, he dictates to Marius a nuptial hymn in which his feverish pangs now are read playfully as priapic ferment: Cupid "'has put his weapons by and will keep holiday. He was bidden go without apparel, that none might be wounded by his bow and arrows. But take care! In truth he is none the less armed than usual, though he be all unclad'" (113). This equivocal flip-flopping between Marius and Flavian, mortal and god, arrow of fever and phallus of lust is precisely what the shape of the Medusa chamber realizes. The curious form of the room, oddly oval, suggests binary foci that make it impossible to place anything truly at its center. Wherever the head of Medusa is placed in the room, at best it can be positioned only at one focus with, perhaps, the beholder standing at the other interchangeable focus—sinister arrangement! This is, of course, exactly the double condition of Persephone and White-nights in which dreams, death, and unreality never quite restate themselves as vision, life, and reality. Like some final meaning within the unintelligible words of the *Ambarvalia,* the presence of vision, life, and reality dwell amidst the alternations of Marius' home but remain invisible, ungraspable. In this, the ovular room can be seen to be a significant foreshadowing of the central episode in the novel, central thematically as well as by actual word count—the butchery of the arena in "Manly Amusement." The rising tiers of seats around the red patches of blood on the sand of the amphitheater gather up into an elliptical image the butchering knives, the bite and barb of fang and arrow, the "poignant heat" of fever and lust. The crowd's "curious interest in the dexterously contrived escape of the young from their mother's torn bosoms" (238) is both a larger setting for the morbidity of the laborers at the *Ambarvalia* and the pupils around Aurelius' child as well as the climatic presentation of the Medusa transformations. As the gestating creatures fall from their torn mothers, so also the young of Leonardo's viviparous mother struggle in terror to escape her brain—images of life concealed by death and death concealed by life. Thus Pater says that in Leonardo's *Medusa* "corruption penetrates . . . beauty" to produce his great Florentine masterpiece—which, we may be sure, Pater then studies with "a certain curious interest" also.

What governs the beholder's involvement with the Medusan head, with "the depth of its corruption, and its perfection of form," is the phenomenon that the necessary precondition to any symbolic (Gk *syn* with + *ballein* to throw) or aesthetic mode of unity is the diabolic (*dyo* two > *dia*- across, apart + *ballein*) polarization of mortal existence. For precisely this reason the Pater-saturated Yeats has his Crazy Jane tell the Bishop that "'nothing can be sole or whole / That has not been rent.'" Beauty without its fallen temporality is no beauty any mortal can apprehend; and if the throw and thrust of coition seems to reverse the stab and sting of death, it does so only by engendering a new mortality. Pater and Pater's heroes, like Baudelaire before them, puzzle over the philosophical conundrum concerning "the entanglement of beauty with evil—to what extent one might succeed in disentangling them or, failing that, how far one may warm and water the dubious, double root, watch for its flower or retain the hope, or the memory, or the mere token of it in one's keeping."[4] To disentangle Flavian's "beautiful head" from its corruption—to clear the snakes from Medusa's brow—is to disavow the very means of renewal by which one arrives at beauty in the first place. Here and there in Pater's work we catch a glimpse of this uncorrupted ideal—most notably in his earliest essay, **"Diaphaneitè,"** in which he observes of this diaphanous figure that "as he comes nearer and nearer to perfection, the veil of an outer life not simply expressive of the inward becomes thinner and thinner. . . . The veil or mask of such a nature would be . . . entire transparency of nature that lets through unconsciously all that is really lifegiving" (***Miscellaneous Studies,*** 249, 251). Beyond "violence" (252) and "sexless" (253), such a "clear crystal nature" (253) notoriously lacks concrete identity—at least until Pater cannibalized parts of his unpublished essay to describe Winckelmann's interest in antique statues. In order "to suggest and interpret a train of feeling," Greek statuary had simplified its resources to only "a little of suggested motion, and much of pure light on its gleaming surfaces, with pure form—only these. And it gains more than it loses by this limitation to its own distinguishing motives; it unveils man in the repose of his unchanging characteristics. That white light, purged from the angry, bloodlike stains of action and passion, reveals, not what is accidental in man, but the tranquil godship in him" (***Renaissance,*** 212-13).

Pater's well-known conclusion to his portrait of Emerald Uthwart which consists of the surgeon's postmortem describing "the extreme purity of the outlines, both of the faces and limbs" (***Miscellaneous Studies,*** 245) of the almost living body of Emerald in death is an English echo of this Greek ideal. Modeling his description on two famous accounts—by Sir Thomas Browne to a friend upon the demise of a common acquaintance and by Johann Peter Eckermann on the beauty of Goethe's face and form in death—Pater implies that although mortals reveal a glimpse of this diaphanous purity, the condition itself does not coexist with life. If applied to Emerald's character, Pater's description of the diaphane must be qualified: "it is that fine edge of light, where the elements of our moral nature refine themselves to the burning point. . . . It is a thread of pure white light that one might disentwine from the tumultuary richness of Goethe's nature" (248-54). The "thread" (OE *thrāwan* to cause to twist or turn; akin to L *terere* and Gk *tetrainein* to bore, pierce) is in its root sense the cycling that twists the filaments into the *syn* + *ballein* of personality; to "disentwine" and isolate the pure white light is to reinstate the diabolic or Medusan dividing of forces. This urge to privilege a single thread is a version of Psyche's error of desiring to behold the divine form, and the hot oil that burns Cupid's shoulder is an image of the *dia* + *ballein,* the "poignant heat" of death's sting. Although the figure of the edge or thread of light refining itself "to the burning point" seems inescapably an anticipation of the "Conclusion" to ***The Renaissance*** where Pater maintains that "to burn always with this hard, gemlike flame, to maintain this ecstasy, is success in life" (***Renaissance,*** 236), the "to" of the burning point to which the diaphanous hero refines his elements functions equivocally to signify either a flame attained or not fully attained. The diaphane seems to but does *not* descend into the arena of the "angry, bloodlike stains of action and passion." In death Emerald, whose name suggests the "gemlike flame," becomes a gem without its vivifying flame, a "clear crystal nature" not unlike those "crystal vessels" at Apuleius' feast but now without the darkening of their old wine. Were it not for his heart-piercing, blood-corroded bullet, Emerald would not have satisfied the necessary precondition for renewal, would not be like the transparent crystal or gem erubesced by wine or flame, nor like Marius' sense of the crucified Christ who seemed "to have absorbed, like some rich tincture in his garment, all that was deep-felt and impassioned in the experiences of the past" (***Marius,*** 1: 134).

A few pages after Pater's description of Leonardo's *Medusa* comes the most sinister and famous head in the whole range of Pater's writing—the Mona Lisa. If the beholder cannot look upon Medusa without petrifaction nor upon Cupid without his vanishing, Mona Lisa also thwarts the urge typified by Aurelius or Psyche to disentwine her meanings and isolate the infallible last word; yet all the time she obscenely weaves and unweaves her sinuous guises before the beholder, tantalizing him with her dark and forbidden knowledge. On one of those small slips on which he habitually scribbled notes to himself, Pater reversed the Aristotelean preeminence of plot, the soul of tragedy, over character by defining his more fanciful instances of portraiture as "imaginary:—and portraits, because they present not an action, a story: but a personality, character—revealed especially in outward detail."[5] In the place of action or story, which suggest in any given work or passage the organic unity or plot closure of a beginning, middle, and end, Pater places the heterogeneous ideal of the old Latin words of the uninterpretable *Ambarvalia.* In Pater's word "character," which derives from a Greek marking instrument and has "engrave" or "scratch" as its basal meaning, one again encounters the serpent's fang and the arrow's barb, as well as Lady Lisa's face which has been "etched" by all the thoughts and experiences of the world (***Renaissance,*** 125). Pater's other term, "personality," derives of course from the Latin for "mask" and suggests that the scratch which erubesces the light is the mask of selfhood. Standing as they do in syntactical apposition to each other, the adjacent nouns, "personality, character," imply that this scratch that constitutes the "fine edge" or "thread of pure white light" cannot be disentwined from its mask because any unveiling or unmasking of personality would entail precisely the filiform abrasion that by erasing away reconstitutes the scratch of character palimpsestically. Psyche's compulsion to see the "godlike" form or the dying Marius' yearning to read some infallible, determinate meaning are errors that nevertheless serve as preconditions for renewal insofar as they cause one sign to be substituted for another—as in Plato's philosophy "the seemingly new is old also, a palimpsest, a tapestry of which the actual threads have served before" (***Plato,*** 8), as in "the old over-written pavement at the great open door" (***Gaston,*** 10) of Saint Hubert's in Pater's unfinished second novel, as in the elaborately carved desk top at Emerald Uthwart's school, or as in Lisa's face on which "all the thoughts and experience of the world have etched" their lust and love, saintliness and sin.

Among the women of Florence, Leonardo "found a vent for his thought in taking one of these languid women"—like Marius' "languid and shadowy" mother—"and raising her . . . to the seventh heaven of symbolical expression" (***Renaissance,*** 123). As "the presence that rose" (124) so strangely and symbolically, Mona Lisa betokens Leonardo's desire to apprehend the ideal face, not unlike Psyche's desire to see the divine form of Cupid:

> We all know the face and hands of the figure, set in its marble chair, in that circle of fantastic rocks, as in some faint light under sea. . . . Present from the first incorporeally in Leonardo's brain, dimly traced in the designs of Verrocchio, she is found present at last in *Il Giocondo's* house. That there is much of mere portraiture in the picture is attested by the legend that by artificial means, the presence of mimes and flute-players, that subtle expression was protracted on the face. Again, was it in four years and by renewed labour never really completed, or in four months and as by stroke of magic, that the image was projected? (123-24)

Her circle or "cirque" of rocks, as the first edition reads, is, like her marble chair and "unfathomable smile," a curve in transit, an oscillating cycle broken into multiplying arcs like the image of Zeus "distracted" in the middle ages "into a thousand symbols and reflections." As the only possible origin of that ideal beauty which—ironically—she resists and disorganizes, Mona Lisa is a function of the losses and imperfections of the Medusan *dia* + *ballein* employed against themselves to generate within or among their dissimilar yet echoing modes or masks the textual *syn* + *ballien.* Suddenly or violently pulled apart or "distracted" among lust, mysticism, ambition, love, and sin, she is nevertheless also the arena, the "cirque" or bowl of the natural mountain amphitheater, that symbolizes "all modes of thought and life."

Present finally in Il Giocondo's house exactly as the Medusa had been present in Marius' villa, Lady Lisa sits for a portrait that the artist either completes with magical dispatch, much as the cathedral of St. Etienne had been finished in Pater's **"Denys l'Auxerrois,"** or that he must finally abandon as fragmentary, much as Flavian put aside his "unfinished manuscript" (***Marius,*** 1: 116) or as Watteau in **"A Prince of Court Painters"** left the portrait of Marie-Marguerite incomplete on the easel. Heterogeneous and without determinate unity, the palimpsestic work will always, short of magic, resist closure while proclaiming its manifold richness. In her play of multiple masks, each of which in turn grounds the other's figure, each of which serves as the crystal vessel for the other's wine, Lisa is like nothing so much as the old Latin words of the *Ambarvalia;* she is "expressive of what in the ways of a thousand years men had come to desire" (***Renaissance,*** 124). Accordingly, Leonardo's portrait will delight not by any appeal to some interpretable or privileged meaning but will "first of all delight the sense, delight it as directly and sensuously as a fragment of Venetian glass; and through this delight alone become the vehicle of whatever poetry or science may lie beyond them in the intention of the composer" (132-33). Notice how the vehicle's tenor is merely a "whatever"—anything or everything the artist may intend—whereas what is important for the beholder is that "outward detail" in which "character, personality" are revealed. "In its primary aspect, a great picture has no more definite message for us than an accidental play of sunlight and shadow for a few moments on the wall or floor: is itself, in truth, a space of such fallen light, caught as the colours are in an Eastern carpet, but refined upon, and dealt with more subtly and exquisitely than by nature itself" (133). The accidental or unintended play of nature becomes in the work of art a more finely woven, cunningly contrived, carefully selected play of rhetorical figures that by substitutions, displacements, and differences approaches the colorless all-color of "transparency in language" (***Appreciations,*** 215); but since no artifact literally includes but only stands in the place of other innumerable and often unnameable sources, the translucence of the symbol is darkened at its source by the cleavage of the diabolic that preceded it. Thus, like the "fragment of Venetian glass," White-nights is itself an "exquisite fragment" (***Marius,*** 1: 18-19); and, of course, the dying Marius who anticipated uniting the "scattered fragments" (2: 220) of some lost epic had aspired earlier to live more modestly in some "fragment of perfect expression" (1: 155).

Given that even the most finely woven artwork cannot hope to reify all possible meanings but can aspire only to symbolize that ultimate wholeness, it remains a fragment of multiple masks perpetually without closure. No solid archetypal model grounds any action or story; no single determinate meaning governs any phrase or passage. Like the traveler who pauses "to read the face" of Marius' villa, the reader of Pater's text also will be concerned with its surface, with what is on its face, because the play of masks is all it offers for interpretation. Accordingly, Pater writes of the way in which "Pascal re-echoes Montaigne" that "one of the leading interests in the study of Pascal is to trace the influence upon him of the typical sceptic of the preceding century. Pascal's 'Thoughts' we shall never understand unless we realise the under-texture in them of Montaigne's very phrases" (***Miscellaneous Studies,*** 84). In the phrases of the not quite consistent skeptic (so Pater elsewhere defines Montaigne), the reader approaches the text of the not quite certain believer (so Pater here describes Pascal); beneath the surface of one text is simply the antithetical surface of an earlier text, itself no less a palimpsestic surface previously engraved or scratched (*palin* - again + *psaō* rub, scratch). Thus the phrases, passages, actions, and stories in Pater's ***Marius*** are to be understood only in terms of similar words in his other works, such as ***The Renaissance,*** or in terms of their echoes in other writers. When in 1873 Pater published his ***Studies in the History of the Renaissance,*** the storm that broke over its "Conclusion" caused him to suppress it in the second edition and not restore it until the third after he had "dealt more fully in ***Marius the Epicurean*** with the thoughts suggested by it" (***Renaissance,*** 233). ***Marius,*** then, was an attempt to explain and develop the doctrine of flux so startlingly appended to Pater's study of the lives and works of the Renaissance artists. And, indeed, the resemblances are extensive. The imprisoned, dreaming mind of the "Conclusion" is everywhere as the undertexture of the dreamy, shadowy life of the lad Marius—both are "chambers" of Persephone's kingdom. If "no real voice has ever pierced" the prison of the solipsistic mind, then only "a single sharp impression"—the serpent's fang and arrow's barb of ***Marius***—will free the imprisoned self; and the child's hand that "roused" the sluggish viper is not unlike the tool of philosophy employed "to rouse, to startle" the human spirit "to a life of constant and eager observation" (235-36). Again, this "eager observation" is dramatized in Psyche's quest actuated by her forbidden glimpse that caused the "clear, perpetual outline of face and limb" to transform itself into nothing less than "that continual vanishing away, that strange, perpetual weaving and unweaving of ourselves" (234, 236) as the "Conclusion" depicts it.

Pater remarked, both of Leonardo's "lost originals" and of those existing originals that are mere thematic fragments to be treated developmentally, that "variations" of these works in the art of others bring out "the purpose, or expression of the original" (118). Thus, when after ***Marius*** Pater restored his "Conclusion" in the third edition of 1888 and mentioned in his footnote that he had made some "slight changes which bring it closer to my original meaning" (233), he well knew that this "original meaning" could be expressed only through an undertexture of re-echoing and open-ended "variations," ***Marius*** being designed to refine and deal "more subtly and exquisitely" with them. So, for example, the quotation in the "Conclusion" from Hugo's *Le dernier jour d'un condamné* is re-echoed and vastly extended in Marius' sense of being "condemned to die" (***Marius,*** 2: 223): "Well! we are all *condamnés* as Victor Hugo says: we are all under sentence of death but with a sort of indefinite reprieve—*les hommes sont tous condamnés à mort avec des sursis indéfinis:* we have an interval, and then our place knows us no more" (***Renaissance,*** 238). Indeed, the reader finds this condemned criminal at the very center of Pater's novel: "Scaevola might watch his own hand, crackling, in the fire, in the person of a culprit, willing to redeem his life by an act so delightful to the eyes, the very ears, of a curious public" (***Marius,*** 1: 239). By repeating the hand-destroying act that saved the Romans, the condemned criminal, impersonating the legendary hero Scaevola, saves his own life. One recognizes with something of a shock that this indeed might be one way to burn with the "hard, gemlike flame," the "one chance" of the *condamné.* Allusively, in Pater's desire to "be present always at the focus where the greatest number of vital forces unite in their purest energy," in his desire "to burn always with this hard, gemlike flame, to maintain this ecstasy" (***Renaissance,*** 236), one half-hears both Bentham's phrase, "the greatest happiness of the greatest number," and Mill's definition of the philosopher's "rapture" and "exalted pleasure" that "lasts only moments . . . and is the occasional brilliant flash of enjoyment, not its permanent and steady flame."[6] Returning Mill's revision of Bentham to the textual arena that de- and reconstructs both Bentham and Mill, Pater insists that the pursuit of ecstasy is the foundation neither of public nor of private morality but of consciousness itself. When in his essay on Leonardo Pater describes the four years' period during which the Mona Lisa was painted as "one of prolonged rapture or ecstasy" (122), he ironically transforms the "occasional" in Mill's "rapture" into the "always" of the "ecstasy" of the "Conclusion."

Given the cruel dilaceration of Bentham and Mill in Pater's text, one suspects the "reprieve" of the "Conclusion" is only a mask for the actual execution of the death sentence. Consider what occurs when "the individual in his isolation, each mind keeping as a solitary prisoner its own dream of a world" (235), attempts his escape. "What more ingenious diversion had stage manager ever contrived," Pater writes in ***Marius*** of the amusement in the amphitheater, "than that incident, itself a practical epigram never to be forgotten, when a criminal, who, like slaves and animals, had no rights, was compelled to present the part of Icarus; and, the wings failing him in due course, had fallen into a pack of hungry bears?" (***Marius,*** 1: 238-39). The prisoner in the first text, escaping, is mangled by bears in the second. Attempting to read every scene in terms of another, one recalls a footnote somewhere to the effect that in the first edition Pater erroneously had written not Icarus, but Daedalus. If the meaning of any scene is dependent on and varies with other scenes to which it refers the reader, then what directions had Pater been giving, consciously or unconsciously, in the first edition? Suddenly, alerted by the strange phrase, "practical epigram," one goes to Marcus Valerius Martialis. And there the scene is, in the eighth epigram of Martial's "On the Spectacles": "Being so mangled by a Lucanian bear, how you must wish, Daedalus, you had your wings now!"[7] So the first edition's Daedalus is indeed the legitimate father of the second edition's Icarus. Moreover, the association of Pater's spectacles with Martial's thin first book of epigrams on the same scenes opens to scrutiny the poet's later epigrams as well. Martial's bear lurks elsewhere in Pater's text, but disguised like the original father in his filial emendation; in his third book, nineteenth epigram, Martial writes: "Next to the Hundred Columns, where figures of wild beasts ornament the grove of sycamore trees, a bear is displayed. While playfully baiting its gaping jaws, fair Hylas plunged his young hand into its mouth. But an evil viper lurked in the shadows of the bronze, animated with a life more deadly than that of the beast. The boy suspected nothing until he felt the sting and died. O what an outrage, that the bear was unreal!" Martial's bear is doubly masked; disguised as the old wooden garden god Priapus (my authority for the deity being yet another epigram of Martial), it conceals itself within itself as the snake, a mask not without its own horticultural associations.

Like Marius among the "scattered fragments" of some "lost epic," the reader searches in vain for an original version that will control all these variants. But precisely because Pater hides the bear of Daedalus inside the bear of Hylas—concealing the real in the unreal, disguising the condemned criminal in the innocent boy—the text offers only a vertiginously arch play of differences without reconciliation. Nesting thus one within the other, these rhetorical fragments are not susceptible to the coadunation of polar opposites; their relationship is surdal, incommensurable, capable only of a perpetual turning back of the one upon the other. For this reason the only final meaning is that there is no final meaning, merely "that continual vanishing away." Like old wine darkening the cup of the textual receptaculum, the pierced hand of the innocent-guilty (he plays most suggestively with Priapus) Hylas is erubesced by the burning hand of the criminal-hero Scaevola (the reader now is hardly surprised to discover that Scaevola himself had been the subject of an epigram or two by Martial) which gathers up into its incandescence Marius' first view of the ambiguous Faustina, "her long fingers lighted up red by the glowing coals" (218), as well as various lightning-struck images of miraculous birth and death (5, 186), and, of course, the burning oil of Psyche's lamp on Cupid's shoulder, his vanishing away and her guilt, sentence, reprieve, and prolonged ecstasy—bringing the reader back to the "Conclusion" and the *condamné* who burns with a gemlike flame.

None of this has yet alluded to the autobiographical level—to the snake, for example, that brother William wound around a doorknob on which the horrified Walter put his hand—or to scission imagery in works other than ***The Renaissance*** and ***Marius,*** as, for example, the missing arm of Apollyon in **"Apollo in Picardy"** or the "sudden, severe pain" of a wasp sting and the analogous burning of the child's hand while making flowers of sealing-wax, both in **"The Child in the House"** (***Miscellaneous Studies,*** 189). Indeed, the most memorable of all such passages belongs to the unpublished pages of Pater's most tantalizing work, the incomparable ***Gaston de Latour.*** It takes the famous image of the metal honeysuckle that in **"An English Poet"** had been Pater's figure for prose style itself and relates it directly to the serpent's ambiguous fang:

> You may read in a certain old Suabian chronicler whose grimy blacksmith's hands handled a pen forcibly, how a famous Italian smith constructed a singular flower of iron. . . . They loved, those genial old Swiss and South German masters, to curb, smooth, and curl their harsh rude metal into trellis work of honeysuckle, spiked lilies, bossy roses: and now here was a cunning Italian more than emulating their art, being determined for once to do the like while retaining under the undulous leaves all iron's native poignancy and defiance. How he contrived, polished, veiled his machinery, you were tempted to try with the finger amid the graceful foliage, touched the hidden spring perchance, and found your wrist imprisoned in a moment in a circle of bristling points, while the central stamen slid through your hand, like a great poignard from its sheath, or the fang of a steely serpent.[8]

The forcible pen in the blacksmith's hand doubles the Italian smith's poniard that pierces the palm of the curious beholder. Here surely is an image of the paralyzing Medusan trap—the "delicate snakes" and their "terrified struggle to escape" now mock the victim whose hand they pierce with their "circle of bristling points."

Like Psyche who would see the god and so reify her dream or like the curious spectators fascinated by the dismemberment in the arena who feel themselves immune, the beholder "tempted to try" the iron lily's "how"—i.e., to interpret absolutely what he himself has touched—looks directly upon the petrifying face of the gorgon. Because the red rose always precedes the white, to privilege any dream as final vision is to lose the symbolic within the diabolic, to become the victim of the Medusa head. Dreaming cannot produce vision; but enriched by the red rose reveries that precede, it can forge more cunningly contrived symbols of the white rose of innocence. Like some departed saint's "relic" spied through the crystal of a medieval reliquary, consciousness, as Pater remarked in the "Conclusion," reduces "to a single sharp impression, with a sense in it, a relic more or less fleeting, of such moments gone by" (***Renaissance,*** 236). Within the present the dead past is still capable of working a miracle, a miracle (L *mirari* to wonder, Skt *smayate* he smiles) reflected in the smile of Lady Lisa who shares the secret of the beholder. This beholder, willing to put all definite histories and dogmatic interpretations back into play, looks upon Medusa's reflection from beyond her enclosing border and glimpses her "virginal beauty" (***Marius,*** 2: 106). He does not exempt himself from the Medusan sting of death; but, knowing her as the goddess who conceals herself within herself, he turns the steely fang that pierces his hand back upon itself to find there the ecstasy of the pen. This is the artist who raises his mortality to the level of symbol in order "to live, perhaps, a little while beyond the allotted hours, if it were but in a fragment of perfect expression" (***Marius,*** 1: 155).

Notes

1. Parenthetical citations made within the text are to the Library Edition of *The Works of Walter Pater,* 10 vols. (London: Macmillan, 1910); these citations are shortened to only the page number if they follow a previous reference to the identical volume.
2. J. Hillis Miller, "Walter Pater: A Partial Portrait," *Daedalus,* 105 (1976), 102-103.
3. Walter Pater, "Poems by William Morris," *Westminster Review,* 34 (October, 1868), 302.
4. Quoted in Germain d'Hangest, *Walter Pater: L'homme et l'oeuvre* (Paris: Didier, 1961), 2: 364 n. 15. This passage is without commas in the MS.
5. d'Hangest, 2: 45, 356 n. 11. Pater's symbol for "because" has been converted into its verbal form.
6. Present throughout Bentham's work, the Greatest Happiness formula first appears in the opening sentences of the Preface of his first book, *A Fragment on Government,* vol. 1 of *The Works of Jeremy Bentham,* ed. John Bowring (New York: Russell and Russell, 1962), p. 227. The quotation from Mill appears in "Utilitarianism," ed. D. P. Dyer in *Essays on Ethics, Religion and Society,* vol. 10 of *The Collected Works of John Stuart Mill,* ed. J. M. Robson (Toronto: Univ. of Toronto Press, 1969), p. 215.
7. Unlike the hypothetical reader, this author is indebted to Roland G. Frean, "Walter Pater's *Marius the Epicurean:* Notes and Commentary Preliminary to a Critical Edition," Diss. University of Toronto 1961, pp. 341-44, 55.
8. Walter Pater, *Gaston de Latour,* Chapter XI, presently being edited by the author for *Gaston de Latour and Criticism,* vol. 5 of the projected *Complete Works of Walter Pater.*

William E. Buckler (essay date 1985)

SOURCE: "The Poetics of Pater's Prose: 'The Child in the House,'" in *Victorian Poetry,* Vol. 23, No. 3, Autumn, 1985, pp. 281-88.

[*In the following essay, Buckler uses* "The Child in the House" *as an example of how Pater combines recollection, insight, and form to make his prose poetic.*]

If one can profitably think of Arnold's key-signature poems as imaginary portraits, as I think one surely can, then the critical instruments appropriate for an exploration of how they work should, with certain obvious adjustments, be suitable for measuring the poetry they share with Pater's key-signature prose pieces. This, I suggest, is the case—that poems like "Stanzas in Memory of the Author of *Obermann,*" "Stanzas from the Grande Chartreuse," and even "Dover Beach," "The Scholar-Gipsy," and *Empedocles on Etna* have an artistic motive very similar to the artistic motive of Pater's imaginary portraits, including, besides the four published under that umbrella-title, **"The Child in the House,"** the "Conclusion" to ***The Renaissance*** and ***Marius the Epicurean.*** That motive is what, in literature, we call poetic, and hence, when I speak of the poetry of Pater's prose as a specific object of critical study, its poetics, I am speaking of an organic, not an ornamental, dimension of the works. Both Arnold and Pater had submitted to the "secret discipline," the *disciplina arcani,* of Wordsworth's influence and had thereby "become able constantly to distinguish in art, speech, feeling, manners, that which is organic, animated, expressive, from that which is only conventional, derivative, inexpressive"[1] and both had learned from Goethe the supreme importance to the writer of "control[ling] his subject-matter and keep[ing] himself beautifully objective."[2] "Through me," Goethe wrote,

> the German poets have become aware that, as man must live from within outwards, so the artist must work from within outwards, seeing that, make what contortions he will, he can only bring to light his own individuality. I can clearly mark where this influence of mine has made itself felt; there arises out of it a kind of poetry of nature, and only in this way is it possible to be original.[3]

It is this "poetry of nature"—"organic, animated, expressive"—that Arnold's poems and Pater's prose pieces have in common.

I begin my remarks at this point for several reasons. First, I am not using the terms of my title—the "poetics" of "prose"—as specialized tropes in a "systematic theory of literature."[4] The poetic qualities that prose and verse share have, in my judgment, little to do with the characteristics of the two conventions of writing. They are imaginative qualities of a very specific though infinitely variable kind having more to do with the peculiar "organization"—the "mental and spiritual constitution"—of the writer and his distinctive way of treating his subject than with the outward appearance of either prose or verse. Subject (action, myth), language in all its inexhaustible varieties, and construction (architecture, shape) are the inner stuff of poetry, and when a writer makes them the sustainers of a prose creation, his prose is poetic and the study of how it works poetics. Second, I want to implant at least the firmly held, easily documented belief that the literary movement from Arnold to Pater was one of the truly creative, exhilarating, exemplary transfers in our literature, received by the one from the other with clear, worthy, open-spirited gratitude and without any of the anxiety and peevish cunning that some commentators have attempted to interject into it. Nothing valuable is added to our labors on behalf of a critical humanism under siege by what Newman called a poisoning of the wells, and an ill-disguised anger at Arnold is not a useful basis for advocacy of Pater. Pater does not need it and, after some initial surprise, would have been quick to dissociate himself from it. Third, as a corollary for which the present occasion does not allow adequate elaboration, I want at least to state the persuasion that there is a fascinating, tentatively groping, circuitous, elusive but real and seemingly inevitable line of development from Arnold's poetry to Pater's imaginary portraits. In the background of both are two monumental imaginative pressures, so persistent and so mutually reinforcing that they become virtual extensions backward in time of the continuity itself and as organically merged as form and content. These two pressures are Wordsworth and Goethe, and if I may distress my metaphor without destroying it, Wordsworth is the pressure of the *what,* the content, and Goethe is the pressure of the *how,* the form; but they coexist, mutually reinforcing, organically fused.

The selection from Pater that I have chosen to illustrate how the poetry of his prose actually works is **"The Child in the House."**[5] It is not only a fine and characteristic piece but also the initiating creation, the imaginative model, from which the other portraits emerge and on which they ring their variations. Moreover, it is the creative outgrowth of Pater's critical writings—a sort of extension of them—and its roots can clearly be identified there. The specific passage out of which **"The Child in the House"** grew occurs just two-thirds of the way through the essay originally entitled **"Romanticism"** and reads, in briefest part, as follows: "The habit of noting and distinguishing one's own most intimate passages of sentiment makes one sympathetic, begetting, as it must, the power of entering, by all sorts of finer ways, into the intimate recesses of other minds." Pater then goes on to connect both the motive and the affect of this procedure with pity, humor, singularity of incident and phrase, and the idea of expressiveness—of "a predominant sense of literary charm," "the secret of exquisite expression," "the gift of exquisite speech" (**"Postscript,"** ***Appreciations,*** pp. 254-255).

One hardly needs to insist on the intimate relevance of this to the imaginary portraits; it is too luminously self-evident. But it is useful to remind oneself that the date of the essay **"Romanticism"** is 1876 and that **"The Child in the House"** was published in *Macmillan's Magazine* in August 1878 under the title **"Imaginary Portrait. The Child in the House."** These facts, together with the lack of any real evidence that Pater retitled **"Romanticism"** and placed it at the end of ***Appreciations*** in 1889 as an oblique signal that it constituted his "critical Credo,"[6] leads me to favor the idea that he saw it rather as a symbolic point of transition from one kind of writing to another, a sort of "movable feast" or "via media" between creative criticism and critical creativity. In that, too, there is a linkage with Arnold, the linkage of a reversed parallel: Arnold's Preface of 1853, particularly as expanded and reinforced by the Preface to *Merope* (1858), is his symbolic point of transition from creativity that turns upon a critical consciousness (his poetry) to criticism suffused with a creative motive (his prose).

Pater concludes **"Romanticism"** with uncharacteristic severity of phrase: "The legitimate contention is, not of one age or school of literary art against another, but of all successive schools alike, against the stupidity which is dead to the substance, and the vulgarity which is dead to form" (**"Postscript,"** ***Appreciations,*** p. 261). Pater obviously felt strongly about the negative effects of contentiousness among various "schools," and one would like to avoid his censure. Nevertheless, it is true that to see **"Romanticism"** as something so bald as a critical manifesto is, to a significant degree, to be "dead to [its] substance," and to see **"The Child in the House"** as merely hidden autobiography is, in like degree, to be "dead to [its] form." Like its successors, **"The Child in the House"** is an imaginary portrait, and unless we are willing to release it into imagination's care, we can hardly expect it to lead us to anything more than a very prosaic result. Goethe's rubric about the "poetry of nature" is crucial here. The artist works "from within outwards" as a poet, not as a historian; his "individuality" or originality is the outgrowth of fidelity to his imagination, not to episodes in his personal history. Memory heightens; perception transforms; structure distances and directs. It is not fact, but an "imaginative sense of fact," that distinguishes art: the finer the distinction, the finer the art.

These three manifestations of the imagination at work—recollection, insight, form—are mutually reinforcing, organically fused, in **"The Child in the House,"** but, for critical purposes, they can be identified individually.

In the first paragraph, the narrator correlates memory and dreams. Florian's dream, occasioned by the initiating incident, "did for him the office of the finer sort of memory, bringing its object to mind with a great clearness, yet, as sometimes happens in dreams, raised a little above itself, and above ordinary retrospect." Dream-memory is raised to something very like dream-vision in the next two sentences: "only, with tints more musically blent on wall and floor, and some finer light and shadow running in and out along its curves and angles, and with all its little carvings daintier," there is "a flutter of pleasure . . . within him at the fair light, as if it were a smile, upon" the place where he had passed his earliest years. This is the premise of how the recollected object and incidents are apprehended by the persona and are to be viewed by the spectator—the key in which they are to be heard, the peculiar wash of light in which they are to be seen. They are not facts but the imagination's idealization of facts, suspended in a medium as a painter or composer or poet might suspend them.

As the narrator recollects in a special way, so also he perceives distinctively. "Thus a constant substitution of the typical for the actual took place in his thoughts." The process by which this distinctive inclination or habit of insight is delineated follows the classic profile of the predominant nineteenth-century idea of the imagination. Whether one takes his basic epistemological image from John Locke or from Aristotle—the *tabula rasa* of the former or the "smooth wax" of the latter[7]—the aesthetic result is the same. Abstractionist ways of perceiving yield almost entirely to sense experience:

> Metaphysical speculation did but reinforce what was instinctive in his way of receiving the world, and for him, everywhere, that sensible vehicle or occasion became, perhaps only too surely, the necessary concomitant of any perception of things, real enough to be of any weight or reckoning, in his house of thought.

Lockean *Sentio, ergo sum* rather than Cartesian *Cogito, ergo sum* defines his character's mode of establishing contact with a reality that is conducted along the senses to a center in the emotional consciousness rather than in the abstractionist mind. There the accident of temperament takes over: he is both an aesthetic empiricist and a muted romantic idealist. Hence his metaphysics has a peculiarly experiential, spiritually tactile bent, like a "great chain" of personal being:

> A place adumbrated itself in his thoughts, wherein those sacred personalities, which are at once the reflex and the pattern of our nobler phases of life, housed themselves; and this region in his intellectual scheme all subsequent experience did but tend still further to realise and define. Some ideal, hieratic persons he would always need to occupy it and keep a warmth there. And he could hardly understand those who felt no such need at all, finding themselves quite happy without such heavenly companionship, and sacred double of their life, beside them.

Anyone familiar with the Pater canon will recognize the idea, language, rhythm, and tone of this passage as quintessentially "Paterian," but it also has a much larger emblematic content which will be discussed below.

One of the privileges and responsibilities of serious poetry is to encompass an enveloping subject in a relatively few words—to mirror man in a miniature, as it were. For that, the engaged reader is willing to suspend his disbelief almost endlessly and still keep the faith. The poetic artifact may be as large as the epic or as small as the cinquain so long as the artist is reaching for an apprehension that he cannot hope to encompass fully, the truth of what he says being "mere imagery on the wall" compared to the truth he intuits and tries to convey. The reader will not be recklessly toyed with, and therefore he demands a "clear, perpetual outline of face and limb," a "firm design in a web." But once he is given that, he is quite willing to accept it as "but an image" "under which we group things," knowing full well that "the actual threads . . . pass out [far] beyond it" ("Conclusion" to ***The Renaissance,*** par. 1).

Though **"The Child in the House"** is only 7000 words long, its subject is as large as life itself, and we know this through form. The speaker is Florian Deleal speaking of himself as if he were not himself in retrospect and prospect—that is, at a peculiarly illumined moment in time. Pater might have used an I-narrator, but this would have sent out two false artistic signals: it would have implied that, in art, there is an essential rather than merely a usable distinction between the first- and third-person points of view, and it would have seemed to subscribe to the notion that poetry can do without "its boundaries and wholesome regulative laws" and that "a true allegory of the state of one's own mind in a representative history . . . is perhaps the highest thing one can attempt in the way of poetry."[8] But Pater is twice-removed from his narration: it is the fictive portrait of an imaginary but representative character named Florian Deleal as related by a narrator whose identity is implicit in the peculiarities—facts, interpretations, attitudes, needs—of what he tells. Thus, it fully qualifies, not as verifiable fact, but as self-verifying myth. The "poor aged man" whom Florian Deleal at approximately 42 helps with his burden along the road "one hot afternoon," the boy Florian Deleal who is "the child in the house" denotatively, the Florian who has grown into middle manhood bearing the unremitting weight of "an agony of home-sickness" that has been the result of an eager anticipation realized "almost thirty years" ago, and the middle-aged man who must look forward to the prospect of an old age weary with the road, burdened with what he carries, and in need of human sympathy—they are all one person, and **"The Child in the House"** is the poetic myth of man in this world whose house is furnished forever in the first twelve years of his life. It is his "material shrine or sanctuary of sentiment" that knits his affections to the earth; it is the paradise from which his very eagerness to depart visits on him a piercing and eternal sense of loss.

That is the poetic subject (action, myth), shaped with the most tasteful delicacy in its formal appointments and realized in language that is at once approximative and firm, reaching for an intuition of great clarity, the "actual threads of which pass out [far] beyond it." The differences between prose and verse have little or nothing to do with it, and certainly Pater had not the least inclination to use "conventional, derivative, inexpressive" techniques of verse in his prose. But so little of what can legitimately be called "poetic" is lost in this literary transaction that one is tempted to see **"The Child in the House"** as an imaginative extension even of the idea of prosody into a new literary form that is at once "organic, animated, expressive."

When one comes to the question of "meaning" or emblematic content in **"The Child in the House,"** it is useful to keep a firm grasp on two crucial considerations: its character as myth and its artistic motive, the former being an organic outgrowth of the latter. The motive, we recall, was to make us "sympathetic, begetting . . . the power of entering, by all sorts of finer ways, into the intimate recesses of other minds"; and the myth—a fictive configuration of such a representative process—is the poetic result. The point of such a process is obviously emblematic, not factual, and the means are emblematic (metaphoric), too. Even if the means should or could be proved to be facts—specific historical incidents from Pater's own life—the poet's, and hence the critic's, problem would be expanded rather than changed in any essential way: one additional stage in the process of transformation would command attention.

Transformation is, I suggest, the emblematic content of **"The Child in the House,"** and for all its markings as a representative example of Romantic Modernism, Pater's first imaginary portrait finds its literary models in *The Golden Ass* of Apuleius and the *Metamorphoses* of Ovid. It is a myth of transformation or metamorphosis, and, as in the works of Pater's classical predecessors, the myth *is* the meaning. Like those of its mythic models, the story line is very simple. A younger man helps a "poor aged man" who is overtasked along the way "one hot afternoon." The old man tells him "his story," and though they are strangers, he finds they have a common place of origin. This has the effect, at once natural and magical, of putting him in mind of the place where he was born and of enabling him to review and penetrate his early life there for the first time. Thus, his reward for having taken pity on the old man's plight is self-knowledge, and although like all Apollonian gifts it has its price—the sorrow born of knowledge born of disposition and need—it better enables him to enter into the joys and pains of others, to feel less caged and abandoned in the "hot afternoon" of his life, and to moderate in his mind the extremes of joy and sorrow to which he seems temperamentally susceptible.

As his psyche undergoes formation in this highly favored retrospect, he begins to understand that rich and curious thing called life as mirrored in his own individuality: the need for order and security; how often the sentiments of beauty and pain are intertwined; that tears may be common to joy as well as to sorrow; how suddenly and intensely one can feel the weight of world-sadness of Weltschmerz in the reiterations of pain and terror, especially as experienced by children and small animals with no means of resistance and as carried to the eye by the concentrated power of pictures or to the ear by music or the devastating cry of a hopeless woman or the "hundred different expressions of voice" of a slowly dying animal; that beauty the most intense releases feelings of mutability the most piercing, and the fear of death in certain temperaments makes one cling to the world of the senses with a vigor that is almost tyrannical; how, again in certain temperaments, the child's "material shrine or sanctuary of sentiment" can be transformed into "a kind of mystical appetite for sacred things" and the love of "comely order" in all one's surroundings converted into noble thoughts of a holy place with heavenly companionship. Thus, the illusion of simplicity in the fictive vehicle or myth of **"The Child in the House"** draws us into a process of "brain-building" or psyche-formation in which "little accidents have their consequence" and such seemingly inconsiderable things as "floating thistledown and chance straws" get themselves compacted as "the house of thought in which we live."

As the myth of **"The Child in the House"** is, through its delicate appointments of form, distanced and directed away from "the state of [the author's] own mind," so is its meaning. It is much larger than the *Bildung* of an authorial house of thought, just as **"Romanticism"** is something much more representative than a personal creed. Pater is personally complicit in both, of course, but only in the generic sense in which Flaubert exclaimed, "*Emma Bovary c'est moi!*" or in which Thomas Hardy might have ruminated, "*Modernisme c'est moi.*"

It has been more customary to read **"The Child in the House"** and other of Pater's works as person-bound (autobiography), or period-bound (*fin de siècle* decadence), or idea-bound (post-Romantic Romanticism). That has not been the emphasis here for two reasons: my subject has been the poetics of prose, or what specifically one means when he says that Pater's prose works poetically; and I am unwilling to yield to biographical, historical, or ideological "fact" the place of unequaled quality that poetry, as both form and idea, occupies in my life.

Notes

1. Walter Pater, "Wordsworth," in *Appreciations* (London, 1901), p. 42.
2. Heinrich Heine, as quoted in Matthew Arnold, "Heinrich Heine," *The Complete Prose Works of Matthew Arnold,* ed. R. H. Super (Univ. of Michigan Press, 1962), III, 109.
3. As quoted by Arnold, *CPW,* III, 110.
4. This is the prescription of Jonathan Culler in his "Foreword" to Tzevtan Todorov's *The Poetics of Prose* (Cornell Univ. Press, 1977).
5. In view of the brevity of the piece, I have omitted pagination. It was included in *Miscellaneous Studies,* and Harold Bloom places it first in his *Selected Writings of Walter Pater* (New York, 1974) as "the largest clue to his work, criticism and imaginary portraits alike" (p. 15).
6. Harold Bloom, in his first note to the essay in *Selected Writings.*
7. The phrases "white paper" and "smooth wax" are Pater's, in "The Child in the House."
8. These are the "false aims" of the modern critic that Arnold rebuts in the Preface to *Poems* (1853).

William E. Buckler (essay date 1987)

SOURCE: "Pater's Apprenticeship in Critical Prose" in *Walter Pater: The Critic as Artist of Ideas,* New York University Press, 1987, pp. 1-35.

[*In the following excerpt, Buckler traces Pater's aesthetic development as evidenced in his works.*]

That Walter Pater is our premier exponent and exemplar of aestheticism has long been generally accepted. In the climactic words of Iain Fletcher, Pater "created himself for us in his *oeuvre* as a permanently significant symbolical figure: the most complete example, the least trivial, of the aesthetic man."[1] What has not been so readily perceived even by some who have written about him with sympathy and insight is that he is much more than that—that in Pater's handling of the subject art becomes as large as human life is in itself capable of being. Pater did not, like some of his more flamboyant disciples, leap prematurely to an art-for-art's-sake creed and then spend his energy and gifts demonstrating with what brilliant virtuosity he could defend it. He was a thoroughly scholarly, serious-minded man who undertook a rigorous regimen of historical, philosophical, and literary study as an integral part of a deliberate process of spiritual or intellectual self-formation that only gradually led him to the conclusion that art considered under its ideal aspect was for him the practical means by which success in life, "at least among 'the children of this world,'"[2] could be achieved.

Once that conclusion assumed a controlling place in his valuation of things, it retained its special potency, but as it had been conscientiously won, it was carefully, even ascetically, used. More than anything else, art enabled Pater to achieve a positive view of life, to see the continuity and promise of human history in the permanent creative constituents of the human mind or spirit.

That Pater resisted too ready a commitment to an art-for-art's-sake position is clear from his earliest extant essay, **"Diaphaneitè,"** a paper he presented before Old Mortality, an Oxford literary society, soon after being elected a probationary fellow at Brasenose College (1864). His effort there is to draw out the lineaments of, to picture to the mind's eye, an ideal that might serve "as a basement [or foundation] type" of humanity, a type that, if it ever gained majority status, would result in "the regeneration of the world."[3] The ideal envisaged in the essay excels art, sanctity, and speculative thought, although the artist, the saint, and the philosopher—indeed, all persons of genius—aspire to it and experience recurrent moments when it has a self-validating presence in their intellectual, moral, and spiritual consciousness. It is the ideal of which Dante created an image in "the Beatrice of the Commedia" and of which Raphael made his very life exemplary; it has close kinship with Plato's imaginative vision of a permanent, preexistent Ideal Reality and partakes of Wordsworth's "wise passiveness."

Such a nature is discontent with the world as it is but invokes no violence against it; it is indifferent to the accidents of time and place, not because it is neutralized by them, but because it recollects the cycle through which life has passed and will pass again. It is possessed of ". . . that pride of life, which was to the Greeks a heavenly grace," and since its goal is simply to fulfill the law of its own being, it "instinctively" keeps itself open or transparent to whatever light from without may contribute to its self-illumination and development and lives in the serene unbroken faith that, undistracted by aggression in any form or degree, the cycle will harmoniously complete itself. Its motto being unity with itself and simplicity, the Christ of the *Imitation* supplies one example, as the Hermaphroditus of Plato supplies another. Though its very "wholeness of nature" may make it appear impotent and ineffectual from a competitive viewpoint, it has "a divine beauty and significance of its own."

One would not claim, of course, that **"Diaphaneitè"** represents Pater as a mature thinker or as a master of style. It is a mood piece in which incantation threatens to take precedence over analysis, and the intellectual dexterity or logical structure that Pater would come to see as indispensable to good prose is subordinated to a degree of free associationism not surprising in a self-conscious young writer's transition from verse that has ceased to work for him to prose that is not yet fully working. One can, however, make several substantial claims for the essay: that the ideal Pater is articulating is sufficiently comprehensible despite its inherent evanescence; that he conceives of the ideal in terms of both a real and an imaginary human type that enables him to make appropriately refined inclusions and exclusions; and that his basic compositional goal is to create a single image around which to order the various implications, the "suggestiveness," of what he has to say. Central to the present argument, moreover, is the careful way in which Pater positions art in relation to this ideal intellectual, moral, spiritual type. The latter is clearly primary, whereas the former is valued for its manifestation of the artist's extraordinary capacity to feel the charm of the human ideal and to aspire to its realization in his work or in himself, even if, as in the case of Goethe, one must "disentwine" it from the "tumultuary richness" of his "nature."[4]

Nothing Pater says in his later works contradicts this order of priorities; indeed, in his last volume, ***Plato and Platonism,*** he so elaborately reconfirms it that the book assumes the symbolic character of a fulfilled myth of the return, Pater acknowledging toward the end of his life the debt he owed to the novice-master of his soul. The inference from this is clear and crucial. The ideal human reality, that is, the highest type of life man in his earthly estate can actually form an image of and aspire to, was the overarching motive for Pater's critical-creative labors—"rather as a longing after what is unattainable, than as a hope to apprehend."[5] To that, even art itself was secondary, an activity in which, paradoxically, means and ends become one in the service of an end of which it is itself only the most approximate example. Through a process of inclusions and exclusions demanded by the nature of his perceptions, Pater concluded that for him and the other "'children of this world'"—those who believe that any paradise they may find will be an earthly paradise with earthly bounds—"the love of art for art's sake" was the activity, among "various forms of enthusiastic activity," that promised most in the way of self-illumination and development and threatened least the openness or transparency upon which the fulfillment of the law of their being depended.[6]

"Diaphaneitè" was not published during Pater's lifetime, and although it is now an important marker in his total career, he was quite right not to offer it to a largely anonymous public. Its style, like its sentiments, is private, self-referential, ruminative rather than expository. One may wonder that he chose to present to a small fellowship of more or less fraternal spirits in Old Mortality its intensely personal self-projection, especially in light of the almost total absence from even his friendliest letters of anything like the confessional quality we find, for example, in Matthew Arnold's letters to Arthur Hugh Clough. Pater treated private, self-reflexive writers like Sir Thomas Browne and Charles Lamb with admirably appreciative critical empathy, and the chief motive of his fictional pieces or imaginary portraits was to enter "by all sort of finer ways, into the intimate recesses of other minds."[7] That is the quality that gives them their extraordinary interest and strength.

But Pater never again wrote anything so directly and transparently personal and self-confessional as **"Diaphaneitè."** He was throughout his works intimate by critical calculation and design—intimate by well-considered strategy, *engagé* for effect—as well as by nature and conviction. The distinctive new quality Pater brought to his criticism and creations was not so much autobiography as self-referentiality. He adopted the classical principle of the primacy of self-knowledge and extrapolated it along classical lines. All knowledge being a form of self-knowledge, one must not only know oneself but also "value" such knowledge "at its eternal worth."[8] That means seeing oneself imaginatively or symbolically rather than literally, seeing oneself *sub specie aeternitatis;* it means seeing "beyond the facts"[9] of the recollected spars and fragments of one's historical existence to their inner significance. Only the imagination can know and make constructive use of that knowledge, and the more unobstructed and successful the process, the more likely even the most historical personal details are to be impersonal, representative, universal. The conversion of personal intimacy into impersonal, imaginative self-referentiality was perhaps the most precarious and rewarding of Pater's critical-creative achievements. By transforming Romantic self-consciousness into classical self-awareness, he opened the history of the human mind to the history of his own mind and freed himself from the impediments of an artificial Romantic-classical dichotomy, enabling him to accept the fact and meet the challenge of modernism without feeling cut off from the master workmen of antiquity and their successors. With the admirable reserve characteristic of him, Pater had the courage to know, accept, and be himself in the belief that only thus could he hope to understand critically and creatively the reism or existential reality of others.

The critical agenda inherent in such a viewpoint began to emerge readily enough, though a critical craftsmanship equal to it took time and much effort. The three essays Pater published anonymously during the next four years—**"Coleridge's Writings"** (1866), **"Winckelmann"** (1867), and **"Poems by William Morris"** (1868)—show him struggling toward rather than fully achieving representative self-objectification. The Coleridge essay is an extraordinary initiation into critical analysis and evaluation, and the essays on Winckelmann and Morris are still the best of their kind substantively. However, the unifying image and formal architecture—the fusion of intuition and treatment—that characterize such masterpieces as **"Leonardo da Vinci"** and **"Wordsworth"** are not fully working yet, and the relationship of the narrator to the narrative is more apparent than transparent, self-conscious rather than fully symbolic. The language is much more specific and the expository lines much firmer than in **"Diaphaneitè,"** and there is a traceable progression through the three essays in making the narrative persona's angle of vision representative as well as idiosyncratic, the Morris essay being notably more successful in this respect than the Coleridge piece. Still, the struggle for authorial self-definition has not yet yielded to artful self-mastery. The three essays are fully characteristic of Pater, but of Pater the conscientious apprentice, and this gives them a special relevance and importance to the student of Pater's emergence as the finest critic of his generation. Pater is still one of a half-dozen indispensable critics in English; from, say, 1880 to 1920, he was without equal.

Implicit in **"Coleridge's Writings"** is the tough-mindedness with which Pater was determined to pursue a career as a critic. Coleridge was an enormous if somewhat vague and shaggy presence in the critical consciousness of the mid-1860s; he was the pedestal figure in the new philosophical criticism introduced early in the century, having contributed more than anyone else to the freeing of literary study from the aesthetic conventions of the previous age. Through him, the revolution launched by the German Romantic philosophers and men of letters had become naturalized in England, and he had restored to contemporary relevance such classical lines of thought as those represented by Plato and Plotinus. It was mandatory, therefore, that a young man with unusual critical ambitions take careful measure of Coleridge and decide to what degree he might serve as a model.[10] Pater was himself an informed student of the German Romantics, and his lifelong interest in Plato was already well advanced. Hence, he no doubt brought to his investigation of Coleridge the expectation that he would find there qualities of considerable practical value to himself.

The fact that Pater found little in Coleridge's critical prose to adopt should not distract one from the value to him of the investigation of the subject and the formulations it enabled him to make. He was in the process of determining just what sort of man of letters he was going to be. He had already despaired of being a poet, and he had little sympathy for or interest in, as he had no apparent talent for, the robust, sensational, roughly crafted, intellectually superficial popular "entertainments" called the contemporary novel. He had a highly developed sense of self, and the realistic appraisal of his creative gifts as genuine but distinctive, coupled with a keen interest in the various ways in which generously endowed persons had used their imaginative powers to leave an exemplary mark on human history, made it inevitable, perhaps, that criticism in some form would be his medium. That, however, left the specific premises of his work undetermined, and his study of Coleridge became in large part an exercise in self-definition.

Pater expresses great empathy for the image Coleridge presents to the mind—that of a magnificently gifted "philosophic critic" who, from some inner discord or disease of the spirit, fought a heroic but futile battle against the imperatives of the emergent *Zeitgeist.* Coleridge defended the untenable against the inevitable, and though his subtlety and strength served to refine the issues at the heart of the conflict, he became alienated from his own genius, which was for poetry and insights of a poetic character, and left a prose canon that is philosophically partisan and stylistically chaotic. Coleridge was a great original, and the intuition at the center of his philosophy, fueled largely by his knowledge of, and enthusiasm for, the German Romantics, has correspondences in the Idealist formulations of the pre-Socratic Greeks and in the writings of Plato and Plato's successors. But what remained for Plato and the prephilosophical Greek animists upon whom he drew an endlessly fascinating poetic intuition became for Coleridge a fixed idea that he strove to put into place in defiance of "the lords of change."[11] His idealism had a degree of cold-bloodedness about it that resulted in too rigid, one-sided a view of the complex nature of the intellectual life and lost him his influence on the future while largely depriving him of the personal rewards of his extraordinary gifts.

Pater's evaluation of Coleridge as a "philosophic critic" is historically significant. Along with Arnold's handling of the same subject in *Essays in Criticism,* it is a useful corrective to the general impression left by John Stuart Mill's characterization of Coleridge as one of the two great seminal minds of the century.[12] However strongly one may disagree with Arnold's and Pater's estimates, the fact that neither of them could find in Coleridge the guidance that each sought there cannot be ignored. Both were inclined to adopt serviceable critical direction wherever they found it, and neither found it to any significant degree in Coleridge.

The negative side of Pater's criticism of Coleridge is well compensated for by the positive self-construction he evolved from it. He was himself one of those persons whose thoughts had been clarified, refined, and strengthened by contact with Coleridge's rigorous philosophical reasoning even though he did not admire its manner and was not persuaded by its matter. Pater was enormously attracted to the conception of an Ideal Reality and succumbed very early to the poetic beauty with which Plato had reached imaginatively from the finite forms of things to an image of things as they may be conceived of in their perfect and permanent form, but he resisted the conversion of such an imaginative mode of regard into a definite theory of ideas. Its charm for the philosophic critic lay in the imaginativeness of its initiating intuition and in the artistic process by which it was put into place; once it became an argument in a philosophical treatise, it assumed a secondary order of interest for the philosophic critic, whatever it might be for the professional philosopher.

Thus, he faulted Coleridge for both his matter and his manner. Coleridge had adopted premises that the modern observational sciences were daily making less credible, had asserted an idealist, metaphysical view of life when the particular form of idealism that depends on metaphysics was everywhere being deconstructed. As a philosopher and critic, he had accepted as a fact what was in fact being returned to solution, and because he had become an advocate rather than a scientific or philosophic critic indifferent to particular outcomes, he failed to be attentive enough to the need constantly to clear the organs of observation and analysis. He did what he did brilliantly, and what he did has had so many correspondences in mankind's mind in every age since the pre-Socratic Greeks that it must be seen as representing a constituent or permanent part of the human mind. However, the one-sidedness of Coleridge's view of life and art and the violence of his advocacy of that view make him something of a modern philosophical ruin with whose heroic image one may deeply empathize while taking from it no significant guidance except caution.

As Coleridge had renounced the path to the future being mapped by the observational sciences, Pater embraced it as both inevitable and inherently exciting. It redefined rather than scuttled idealism and made the past available under an entirely new aspect. The modern spirit is a spirit born of the observational sciences according to which nothing can be known "except relatively under conditions."[13] All relations are affected by this relative spirit, "the relations of body and mind, good and evil, freedom and necessity."[14] Our relation to the world thus becomes one of "fine gradations and subtly linked conditions,"[15] we ourselves undergoing perpetual change even as the world we inhabit is perpetually changing. The "subtleties of effect" resulting therefrom are the most "precious" objects of the modern spirit's interest, subtleties that make it essential that the philosophic critic constantly clear "the organs of observation" and be forever attentive to the "perfecting of analysis."[16] Insight and language, truth and expressiveness, are the things the modern critic must be acutely responsive to if he would be truly philosophic, ready to sacrifice classical "precision of form" for modern "intricacy of expression."[17] A willingness to redact one's view of the world is part of it; a willingness to redact one's view of oneself redacting, though not an absolutely greater part, is both indispensable and primary.

The new idealism implicit in Pater's critical position has yielded up all its traditional metaphysical underpinnings. It is an idealism of types, of actual human types. The gods of his idolatry are those persons who have used their unusual gifts to create things both more magnificent and more lasting, namely, images of the heights to which the human spirit can reach in the circumstances in which it finds itself, forms that exceed matter as such by converting matter into imaginatively compelling emblems of an eternity that, though reality-bound, is wholly equal to man's needs in his earthly interval. Thus relieved of all metaphysical necessities, human history assumes a different sort of engagement for the philosophic critic of the type envisioned. The style of an argument becomes more important than its conclusions, to which one becomes essentially indifferent; what one *is* and, under his immediate influence, enables others to become in the here and now merits our best attention. How a poet, philosopher, scientist, or holy man mastered his particular environment being the really significant thing, the environment must be thoroughly understood.[18] But besides the environment, there is also the person, poet, philosopher, scientist, or holy man, and the imaginative process by which, in contradiction to an almost infinite number of failures, he created a simple and unified image of nonmetaphysical transcendence—what he proved about mankind's wholly human possibilities—is the true object of critical fascination. History, like poetry, means "beyond the facts" in such a context; one must bring to it an imaginative sense that largely dissolves the stubborn illusions of time and space and makes the past and present intricate illuminations of each other.

It would probably be easier at the present time to make a credible argument for the soundness of Pater's overall dissatisfaction with Coleridge as a philosophic critic than at any time in the last hundred years. At no previous moment has the critical determination to deconstruct metaphysics been stronger, while much of the Coleridgean revival of the last forty years has, paradoxically, been fueled by a renewed romance with metaphysics among academic critics. However, such an argument would be digressive. The primary inference to be drawn from Pater's maiden essay in criticism is a developmental inference—that it facilitated his own process of critical self-definition in a firm and lasting way. It enabled him to declare fully and enthusiastically his critical alignment with the spirit of the modern observational sciences and to acknowledge a humanistic rather than a fideistic interest in the strong recurrent tendency of the human mind to seek out and subscribe to metaphysical explanations; to endorse unabashedly a relativist epistemology, according to which nothing can be known absolutely and the quality of any observation is so dependent on self-awareness as to make all knowledge essentially a form of self-knowledge; and to postulate the values to be derived from critical indifference to material or substantive outcomes, including especially the freedom to notice the manner rather than the matter, the *how* rather than the *what,* of things and to experience something of that transformation of spirit that an awareness of such exemplary or ideal forms effects in us as perennial imitators of life-styles.

The clear, firm critical advance Pater makes in **"Coleridge's Writings"** over **"Diaphaneitè"** pales somewhat by comparison with the quantum leap he achieves in **"Winckelmann."** All things considered—the singularity of its subject, Pater's youth and relative inexperience at the time of writing it, the far-reaching implications of its critical substance and manner, the inner authority it continues to manifest—**"Winckelmann"** is one of the truly extraordinary critical essays in English. It was placed last among the essays on art history in ***The Renaissance,*** but it is not only much the longest and most critically elaborate of the essays in the book; it is also the essay that establishes the strongest implicit connection between what has been (history) and what may yet be (poetry). To the degree that one can identify with, or participate in, the renewal of the human spirit that these "studies in the history of the Renaissance" implicitly suggest—in their "parabolic drift," so to speak[19]—the self-re-creation of Winckelmann and through him of Goethe is the book's most representative revelation, as, in all probability, it was its initiating intuition and sustaining motive. What we all need most in the "bewildering toils" of modern necessity is the "equivalent for a sense of freedom." That is what Winckelmann needed desperately, and the fact that he achieved it, becoming something that all the forces in his personal circumstances and in the imperious culture of his place and time seemed to dictate that he should not become, makes him "the last fruit of the Renaissance" and his personal history a "striking" explanation of the "motives and tendencies" of Pater's book about it.[20]

The evidence in the **"Winckelmann"** essay that Pater has achieved a quantum leap in his development as a critic goes far beyond the essay's chief substantive movements—Winckelmann's personal history, the relationship between art and religion, the necessary distinctions to be drawn between and among the various arts, the gulf that exists between Hellenism and modernism. The fact that each of these topics is recognized as germane to the essay's essential subject and that each is exemplarily treated would, in ordinary circumstances, be sufficient to sustain such a thesis. The circumspection with which the subject is conceived, the originality with which it is analyzed, the order in which it is displayed, and the language by which it is illuminated and made pleasurable (what Pater called "expressiveness") demonstrate that a critic of unusual courage and capacity is rapidly emerging. He is not only making rapid advances on his critical monitors (on Arnold, for example, and Hegel); he is also making rapid advances on himself. Moreover, he is developing in a direction not ordinarily taken by philosophic critics and certainly not taken by Coleridge. Besides attempting to refine his critical skills, his "organs" of observation and analysis, of insight and language, he is beginning to give criticism itself a new character.

Though **"Winckelmann"** is not itself a work of art of the finely finished kind represented by **"Leonardo da Vinci"** and **"Wordsworth,"** it is artistic in that Pater has conceived of and attempted to execute his subject creatively. It is thoroughly critical in being about something other than itself, but it also has its own subject which that "something other than itself" is made to serve without any sacrifice of its integrity as criticism. In other words, the *critical subject matter,* though wholly intact, has been transformed into a *creative subject,* and criticism has been thereby made a form of literary art with its own special necessities of construction and diction. Fact remains authentically fact, but through imagination it has been made to "mean, beyond the fact, / Suffice the eye and save the soul beside."[21] Moreover, the critic-creator's "imaginative sense of fact"[22] is the decisive factor in the essay's architecture and language.

One quick, practical way of confirming the delicate conversion Pater is effecting in his essay is to stand back and view it as a whole, the way one views a picture. Then its real subject is seen to be not how one comes to terms with art but how one comes to terms with life, how one succeeds in making his life a work of art, complete, serene, indifferent to "the chain of circumstances" that threatened it along the way. This is the force of the metaphor by which Pater firmly justifies his critical enthusiasm for Winckelmann and by which, in the last half-dozen paragraphs, he harvests the fruits of his critical endeavor: "to place Winckelmann in an intellectual perspective, of which Goethe is the foreground."[23] These painterly metaphors are then reinforced by an image eminently visual and stirring—"the beautiful lad Euphorion, as Goethe conceives him, on the crags, in 'splendour of battle and in harness as for victory,' his brows bound with light" (p. 181). This child of the marriage of Faust and Helena is said to be "the art of the nineteenth century," and though art in the specialized formal sense is certainly not excluded, the contextual image is much too large for that; it refers rather more importantly to the art of living on higher ground, above modern life's "fatal combinations" and with a "nobler . . . attitude" (p. 185).

That life is itself the ultimate work of art, its creation the purpose of all the "reflected, refined light" of "a great education" (p. 181), is not only where the essay ends but also where it begins. Goethe speaks of Winckelmann "as of an abstract type of culture, consummate, tranquil, withdrawn already into the region of ideals, yet retaining colour from the incidents of a passionate intellectual life. He classes him with certain works of art . . ." (p. 141). At the heart of the essay, supplying the "key" both to Winckelmann and to Pater's underlying purpose, is a quotation from Hegel's *Aesthetik* that celebrates the Greeks' superb "sense for the consummate modelling of divine and human forms."[24] Their poets and orators, historians and philosophers—Pericles, Phidias, Plato, Sophocles, Thucydides, Xenophon, Socrates, and so forth—"are ideal artists of themselves, cast each in one flawless mould, works of art, which stand before us as an immortal presentment of the gods" (p. 175). On the two sides of this extended quotation from Hegel, who has been cited along with Goethe in the opening paragraph, are two images. On one side is that of "the *adorante* of the museum of Berlin," a work of Hellenic art whose subject is "a youth who has gained the wrestler's prize, with hands lifted and open, in praise for the victory." Like the youths of the Panathenaic frieze, he expresses a supreme "indifference" to all that is "relative or partial."

> Fresh, unperplexed, it is the image of man as he springs first from the sleep of nature, his white light taking no colour from any one-sided experience. He is characterless, so far as *character* involves subjection to the accidental influences of life. (pp. 174-175)

On the other side is Winckelmann. Though he was born into a "tarnished intellectual world," was compelled to accommodate himself to the shabbiest, most judgmental provincialism, compromised even self-respect as ordinarily understood to the higher goal of self-realization, was impeded for what must have seemed a generation by adversity in the form of poverty or in the disguise of respectability, that antique sense seems to have maintained itself deep within him, and when the opportunity came, it sprang forth in a remarkably pure form. Undisturbed by "interests not his, nor meant for him," unattracted by "formal principles, [which are] always hard and one-sided," disinclined to become "one-sidedly self-analytical," Winckelmann devoted himself to "perfecting himself and developing his genius," to "refining his *meaning* into a *form,* express, clear, objective" (pp. 175-176, emphasis added).[25] In short, he crafted a work of art out of his own life.

That is, admittedly, a heightened, symbolic, parabolic way of regarding Winckelmann, but there is no denying the careful logical structure, the intellectual dexterity, with which Pater accomplishes it. In at least a preliminary way, it confirms the judgment that Pater's way of proceeding was informal but not unmethodical and that his primary effort was to express "the irrepressible because almost unconscious poetry" of his critical insights.[26]

As our capacity to see the subtle, reserved, intuitively proportioned way Pater is working increases, so does our sympathy, and this brings us to an additional dimension of the parable of the piece, what can perhaps fairly be called its Goethe-Hegel-Winckelmann-Pater equation. Goethe is clearly Pater's great modern exemplar of "life in the whole," of that spiritual beauty that comes of having divested oneself of partial and relative truths even the most "precious" and of having molded one's life according to an ideal of "artistic perfection," unwilling to settle for the one-sided genius of more limited men. Goethe "illustrates a union of the Romantic spirit, in its adventure, its variety, its profound subjectivity of soul, with Hellenism, in its transparency, its rationality, its desire of beauty," and emphasizes the "preponderance" in that union of Hellenism (p. 181). Goethe, therefore, represents a cultural ideal to which Pater aspires but that he despairs of actually reaching. Hegel, on the other hand, represents a more attainable goal.[27] What Goethe saw in Winckelmann, despite the opaqueness of his prose and such limitations of experience as might have crippled a lesser man, was, in Hopkins's phrase, his "one fetch"—that single-minded, intuitive devotion with which he went straight to the heart of Hellenism and, like a pagan after a long exile returning to his natural home, made of himself an authentic work of art, an embodiment of "an inexhaustible gift of suggestion" (p. 141). What Hegel saw was of a more limited, less poetic order: Winckelmann "'is to be regarded as one of those who, in the sphere of art, have known how to initiate a new organ for the human spirit'" (p. 141). To have done that, says Pater, "is the highest that can be said of any critical effort," and it is on those specific terms that he begins his critical exposition. But while Hegel unquestionably supplies much of the "philosophic" ballast of the essay, much of its "historic" line of argument, he provides none of the spiritual "modelling" that made the study of antiquity so self-transformational for Winckelmann and, through his conversion of its "true essence" into personal "form," made him such a powerful influence on Goethe's own spiritual modeling.

A sentence from the "Conclusion" to ***The Renaissance,*** that part of the work closest in date of composition to the **"Winckelmann"** essay, is relevant here. "What we have to do is to be for ever curiously testing new opinions and courting new impressions, never acquiescing in a facile orthodoxy, of Comte, or of Hegel, or of our own" (p. 189). Coming in so crucial and concentrated a context, Pater's reference to one on whom he had drawn so heavily as representing a "facile orthodoxy" against whose blandishments one must be perpetually on one's guard has perplexed many commentators, but such perplexity on one level may be illumination on another. Pater's inclusion of himself in the list is the clue to be followed up—"facile orthodoxy, of Comte, or of Hegel, or of our own." An important part of him was attracted to Hegel; he frequently found correspondences between the way his mind worked and Hegel's. And from a purely critical point of view, the comparative results were distinctive enough and persuasive enough to be adopted as a characteristic idiom—even sufficient perhaps to enable him, in the England of his day, "to initiate a new organ for the human spirit," as Comte had seemed to do among a certain order of minds. But as the example of Goethe showed, that would be an offense to "the proper instinct of self-culture" and hence to true culture itself and the exigent modern need for it; that would mean to abandon one's quest for "the supreme, artistic view of life" and to settle for "one special gift," one brilliant "form of culture," and to limit thereby one's "capabilities" (p. 183).

In future contexts comparably oblique, Pater will reinforce a reservation about Hegel already implicit in the "Conclusion" and in the **"Winckelmann"** essay: for all his "historic" or "philosophic" gift, Hegel lacked what Goethe and Plato not only had but had full, unfailing faith in, namely, the poetic instinct. Hegel was one of the most brilliant and trustworthy treatise-makers in the arena of modernism, but a treatise-maker nonetheless, the best of the systematists, perhaps, but still a systematist. Orthodoxy is generally thought of as something "out there" among the other conventions of an age, but in its subtlest form it takes place "in here." It takes root within the individual spirit when his ideas become customary and to that degree petrified, routine rather than adventuresome, and he has too easy ("facile") an access to their use. They are to criticism what Parnassianism is to poetry, examined and characteristic rather than continuously reexamined and inspired. Pater seems to have seen his face in Hegel's mirror and to have recognized what could become a personal tendency if he did not keep before his spiritual eye the supreme example of Goethe. By such a standard, the highest of critical goals, that of "initiat[ing] a new organ for the human spirit," was merely a most "precious" impediment to that cultural open-endedness, that perpetual process of becoming, from which one's very successes can distract one.

Many commentators on **"Winckelmann"** have noted a strong current of self-identification in the essay. Kenneth Clark calls it "the decisive piece of self-identification" and elaborates the point as follows:

> The hunger for a golden age, the austere devotion to physical beauty, the feeling of a dedication to art and to the unraveling of its laws, "the desire" as Pater says "to escape from abstract theory to intuitions, to the exercise of sight and touch"—all the characteristics which Winckelmann had united with a burning clarity, Pater recognized as half-smothered fires in his own being. Even those elements in Winckelmann's character which seem more questionable, his formal acceptance of the Catholic faith as the price of a ticket to Rome, and his passionate love affairs with young men, corresponded to impulses which Pater felt in his own character and increased his feelings of sympathy.[28]

The sort of "self-identification" spoken of here is a very different matter from the self-referential aspect of Pater's creative mind and method cited earlier and addressed below, but one can accept without quibble the general proposition that Pater probably had strong autobiographical feelings for the human image of Winckelmann. However, Winckelmann's place in our Goethe-Hegel-Winckelmann-Pater equation is a formal, textual issue, as are Goethe's, Hegel's, *and Pater's.* He is both a historical and a symbolic figure, and he is being formally ordered or processed as a part of a poetic parable.[29]

As Goethe is the maximum modern example of an authentic Hellenism, Winckelmann is the minimum but still genuine example, and therein lies his peculiar virtue for latter-day questers after self-culture like the Pater of the piece and those he is trying to reach. Goethe, of course, was the Olympian modern: "possessing all modern interests, ready to be lost in the perplexed currents of modern thought, he defines, in clearest outline, the eternal problem of culture—balance, unity with one's self, consummate Greek modelling" (p. 182). Winckelmann was "infinitely less" than that (p. 181). He was not modern ("he could hardly have conceived of the subtle and penetrative, yet somewhat grotesque art of the modern world," p. 178), and he had no experience of "that bolder type of [Greek art] which deals confidently and serenely with life, conflict, evil" (p. 178).

And yet, Winckelmann's longing, dedication, talent, and manner were such that "from a few stray antiquarianisms, a few faces cast up sharply from the waves," he "divine[d] the temperament of the antique world," yielded entirely to it and, through his effect on Goethe, tendered self-redemption to the modern world. Winckelmann, then, is an example of how much can be done with how little if one yields to the "demand of the intellect . . . to feel itself alive" and seeks to find even in a fragmentary knowledge of a supreme spiritual culture the sources of one's "own strength" (p. 183). So if Pater despaired of becoming a Goethe and desired to become something different from a Hegel, he had in Winckelmann both the self-modeling and the promise of possible success.

Pater's entry into the complexities of his subject through a deft use of the biographical mode (pp. 141-157) is itself symbolic. He was not an abstractionist, though he constantly searched out and was exhilarated by the discovery of those patterns of the human mind that were continuous at varying levels of visibility both in human history and in himself. Informed intuition was his chosen instrument, and "the exercise of sight and touch" (p. 147) was both his test of authenticity and the source for him of the keenest spiritual pleasure. But as he had early learned to mine his own experience, he had an extraordinarily sympathetic way of mining the experience of others.[30] He wanted to discover things for himself both as to fact and as to form. Therefore, his initial question has three parts—"what kind of man" "under what conditions" led to a particular result?—and though he was not so naive as to suggest that, on the basis of such isolated evidence, one could make an easy inductive leap, he was employing the empirical method symbolically, as a matter of formal structure, rather than quantitatively—imaginatively rather than literally. The authority of Goethe and Hegel was a given as to the result, and that was instructive, but the "kind of man" and "conditions" were at the heart of the struggle for self-realization and were thus the focus of a true humanistic interest and the source of any personal strength one might draw from it.

Moreover, the barely sixteen pages that Pater devotes to Winckelmann's life and works, themselves interspersed with many illuminating general observations along the way, are symbolic, distilled metaphors of a man's contest with adversity rather than a biographical account as such. He prefaced the essay as it appeared in the *Westminster Review* with the titles of two books—Otto Jahn's *Biographische Aufsätze* (1866) and G. H. Lodge's translation of Winckelmann's *Geschichte der Kunst des Altertums* (1850)—but he made no references to them in the essay itself,[31] signaling thereby that, though dependable quantitative erudition lay behind his highly select metaphors, he was engaged in a quite different kind of imaginative undertaking. Still, the biographical symbolism is significant: Winckelmann was, like us, a human being trying to cope with particular conditions, and the fruit his life bore was deeply rooted in his longing for, and recognition of, an ideal of completeness. The essential unity with himself and the simplicity that he preserved in the seed he finally came to enjoy and to see celebrated in the flower.[32]

Pater's motive for the next three movements of the essay—on art and religion, on the necessary distinctions to be drawn between and among the various arts, and on the gulf between Hellenism and modernism—is a fusion of matter and manner, of adequate substance and adequate artistry. He has the "infinite" distance to travel between Winckelmann and Goethe, between an isolated, relatively obscure, even morally suspect eighteenth-century German art historian and the colossus of modern Paneuropean culture whom Matthew Arnold had used throughout *Essays in Criticism* as the "manifest centre" of modern Europe's intellectual and spiritual life—its critical and creative liberator. To accomplish this in a satisfactory way, he must gradually enlarge and deepen his subject matter, must create an imposing historical, philosophic context that takes the eye off Winckelmann, who was inadequate to it, while providing suitable opportunities to show how the gift of nature that Winckelmann so assiduously cultivated—"itself like a relic of classical antiquity"—was relevant to it and in fact "laid [it] open by accident to our alien, modern culture" (p. 175). Thus, Pater brings to his handling of Winckelmann some of the "quick tact," in Arnold's phrase, that he found in Winckelmann.

The formal aspects of this process are further reinforced by the essay form itself. In *Essays in Criticism,* Arnold had used the critical essay in an exploratory, experimental sense—as an "attempt—specimen"[33]—and Pater's use is comparable. However, Pater has provided us with a far more detailed idea of what the essay form meant to him, and though his specific formulation is of a much later date (***Plato and Platonism,*** 1893), there is no reason not to believe that even in the mid-1860s he had so conceived the idea. In the second part of the chapter "The Doctrine of Plato," entitled "Dialectic" (pp. 174-196), Pater comments on the three forms or methods of philosophical writing. "The poem, the treatise, the essay: you see already that these three methods of writing are no mere literary accidents, dependent on the personal choice of this or that particular writer, but necessities of literary form, determined directly by matter, as corresponding to three essentially different ways in which the human mind relates itself to truth."[34] At the heart of the poem is intuition, of the treatise dogma, of the essay tentativeness or experimentation. Pater says that the dialogue as used by Plato is the ancient equivalent of the modern essay, and since he sees all authentic literary dialogue[35] as essentially a dialogue of the mind with itself, as all knowledge is ultimately self-knowledge, it seems fair to apply the conditions he sets for literary dialogue to his ideal of the essay, including his own essays. It is a process; its ultimate means and ends combine in the person involved in the process; the process must be free, varied, elastic, informal, easy, and natural enough really to make the inclusions and exclusions that the nature of the subject suggests to the mind in such an uninhibited "journey" after truth. Its method must be truly "one" and "cover the entire process, all the various processes, of the mind, in pursuit of properly representative ideas, of a reasoned reflex of experience"; thus thoroughly prosecuted, it becomes "co-extensive with life itself—a part of the continuous company we keep with ourselves through life"; rather than a "system of propositions," it forms a "temper" that humbly recognizes the limits of knowledge *(What do I know? Who ever really knows?).*

While it would be extravagant to press such a catalogue on **"Winckelmann"** in a literal-minded way, the spirit of it is there. As the essay ends in the celebration of a very personal process ("self-culture"), so it embodies at an empirical as well as a symbolic level a process. It moves back and forth between the general and the particular, experimenting, testing, verifying. On the one hand, it is conscientiously scientific in its care for distinctions and in the way it makes its inclusions and exclusions. On the other hand, it takes the most adventuresome chances, its boldness of subject and assertion being saved from amateurish dogmatism by its emotional and intellectual dexterity—aptness of illustration, precision of argument, generosity of spirit, ingratiation of language, a tone of exigent reserve, all leading to the sober but inspiriting conclusion that modern man can not only survive but prevail. By having Winckelmann touch Goethe so conversionally and by having Goethe acknowledge that "'One learns nothing from him . . . but one *becomes* something'" (p. 147), Pater opens endless possibilities of spiritual reciprocation between the very great and the relatively small.

The unorthodox argument by which Pater attempts to absolve Winckelmann of the sin of "insincerity"[36] in his profession of Roman Catholicism—that in him "the moral instinct, like the religious or political, was merged in the artistic" (p. 149)—parallels his dissent from the "orthodoxy of taste" (p. 157), the "standard of artistic orthodoxy" (p. 159), of which Raphael is offered as the touchstone and Newman the spokesman.[37] Though Pater was the gentlest, most urbane of dissenters, never appearing to relish controversy as Arnold did and remaining generally faithful to the stern principle of intellectual "indifference," the integrity of his view of Hellenism's relevance to modern man's spiritual plight was so inherent in this issue that one might charge him with being gentle at the cost of clarity and emphasis. Yet he knew how fundamentally subversive his argument was and how easily his effectiveness as a man of letters could be destroyed if, like Nietzsche, he let "the hammer" speak.[38]

The orthodoxy from which Pater was dissenting was both cultural and religious, historical and philosophic, and his choice of Newman as the spokesman for it was strategic. To see "'the classical polytheism'" as "'gay and graceful, as was natural in a civilised age'" (p. 159) was to take a "partial" view of Hellenic culture—to see it, in the orthodox post-Raphaelite way, "on the sharp, bright edge" of its highest point and thus to ignore a large portion of its human representativeness—the "sadness" that filled its mind and tempted it to take refuge in "thoughts beyond itself." It was also to beg the question of its suitability as a solution to the human dilemma and to make medieval Christianity's solution seem cminently more suitable because infinitely more reflective of the human condition and of human nature itself. That is the partial view, the imbalance, Pater undertook to correct. His purpose was not to attack the Christian solution but to give a fairer view of the total Greek experience and thus to rehabilitate its solution. However, the nature of his subject required certain "acts of 'inclusion' and 'exclusion'"[39] that were implicitly critical of Christianity's enormous satisfaction with itself. Those he did not ignore, though he was as agreeable as honesty would allow.

Pater's line of argument is crisp and clear enough. All religions—pagan, Christian, Eastern—grow from human seeds in human soil and represent human efforts to find human solutions to human problems. Their ritualistic systems, despite the sharp differences resulting from the vastly different conditions out of which they grew, are alike natural or "pagan." The essential differences between them—for example, between the Greek religion and Christianity—are determined by the "cycle of poetical conceptions" that become attached to these ritualistic systems and keep them culturally alive. In Greece those conceptions "derived from mythology," which did not have a religious source and developed along purely human lines. In an age earlier than what we think of as the stage of Hellenic culture, Greek religion had its "worship of sorrow": "Scarcely a wild or melancholy note of the medieval church but was anticipated by polytheism!" (p. 162). But the Greeks happily found their solution in the "Dorian worship of Apollo, rational, chastened, debonair" (p. 162), and their religion was thereby enabled "to transform itself into an artistic ideal" (p. 163). As a result, "the thoughts of the Greeks about themselves, and their relation to the world generally, were ever in the happiest readiness to be transformed into objects for the senses" (p. 163).

At a later stage, beyond its zenith, Greek religion became "too inward," began to "boast its independence of the flesh," to absorb "everything with its emotions," to reflect "its own colour everywhere," to move toward an "exaggerated idealism" that would inevitably plunge it "into the depths of religious mysticism" (pp. 164-165). That, too, may have been an inevitable development, mankind being what mankind is, but it does not detract from Pater's central point that Hellenic culture at its height struck "a sharp edge of light across [the world's] gloom" and became thereby a constructive model for modern man.

Pater does not emphasize the implications for Christianity of the contrastive structure of his exposition, but diplomacy does not obscure his criticism. Christianity suffers from an attitudinal problem in its thoughts about itself and its relationship to the world, a vestigial medieval attitude that modern thought is rapidly undercutting and making a part of the modern problem rather than an aid to its solution. Though he is careful not to describe Hellenism as a dispensation, calling it rather a matter of luck, of "some supreme good luck" (p. 165), he presents it as one of man's happiest spiritual achievements that perpetually beckons his return.

The next and last major movement of the essay before the peroration, that on the characteristic differences between and among the arts and on the breaking point between Hellenic and modern art (pp. 167-181), is as analytically "indifferent" as the peroration itself is ardently so, and the paradox is significant. Though Arnold and Pater represent a broad continuity of concern over the issue of modern cultural regeneration that their differences of style, emphasis, and critical-historical perspective do not disturb, Pater shared little if any of Arnold's anxiety over the state of modern poetry or his efforts in the 1850s and 1860s to set it on a new track. More Hegelian in this respect than Arnold, Pater applied the principle of historic, philosophic necessity to the new poetry of the nineteenth century and, having more imaginative sympathy for what it was trying to create out of conditions it had not created, he showed more imaginative capacity than Arnold to understand its constructive aesthetic ideals and to identify both its distinction and its linkages with the poetry of the past. Though many of the metaphors with which he described the modern era were similar to Arnold's and were perhaps borrowed from him,[40] Pater was less spiritually resistant to his times than Arnold was and more critically curious and detached about its art. Rightly or wrongly, he was much less inclined than Arnold to make even an implicit, parabolic case for a true Judeo-Christian renascence.

It would be capricious to emphasize Pater's critical advances on Arnold at the expense of Arnold, ignoring the subtly different *Zeitgeists* in which they flourished and the enormous contribution Arnold had made to the critical climate Pater inherited, but the temperamental differences between them were real, and temperament, as Pater repeatedly asserted, plays a large part in both the making and the liking of literature. Also, Pater's application to criticism of the creative principle of "art for art's sake" enabled him to see an age's spiritual culture mirrored in its poetry at the distance of the individual poet's talent, the poet's distinctive response to the age being in crucial respects very different from the age's more conspicuous demands, while recognizing that poetry, especially the best poetry, has internal laws and legacies that are quite independent of a particular age. On both of these matters, Pater is both more explicit and more insistent than Arnold.

It is useful to refocus one's view of the Arnold-Pater connection as one approaches this celebrated movement in the **"Winckelmann"** essay for two reasons. First, though they read many of the same aesthetic theorists, both were practical critics with little faith in the application of systematic theories of art to art itself. Second, like Goethe, Pater did not allow his advances on, or divergences from, Winckelmann to eclipse his recognition of Winckelmann's importance as a critical founder or of his own enormous spiritual debt to him, and one can reasonably speculate that he felt similarly toward Arnold.

When he called the **"Winckelmann"** essay "the earliest and . . . the most sustained of all [Pater's] writings on aesthetic theory,"[41] Kenneth Clark had in mind this movement on the various arts, and though the general intent of the assertion may seem unexceptionable, it raises one of the subtlest issues the critic working in today's climate must face, namely, the difference between "aesthetic theory" as the term is regularly applied to Pater and theory in its stricter, more systematic sense. In the latter sense, Pater can hardly be said to have had any aesthetic theories. Earlier in the **"Winckelmann"** essay, he had said with unmistakable irony, "Lessing, in the *Laocoon,* has theorised finely on the relation of poetry to sculpture; and philosophy may give us theoretical reasons why not poetry but sculpture should be the most sincere and exact expression of the Greek ideal" (p. 147). However, he himself does not adopt such reasons and goes on to applaud Winckelmann's "happy, unperplexed . . . concrete" way of "*finding* . . . Greek art."[42]

One must be careful, then, not to impose a twentieth-century need for theory on a nineteenth-century need for empirical discovery and verification. Pater's criticism depends, not on abstract theory, but on informed imaginative intuition; though he was fully cognizant of Lessing's theory, he clearly opted for Winckelmann's practice. He formed aesthetic conclusions, not aesthetic theories; his hypotheses or generalizations were the result rather than the condition of his experience of art. Pater viewed art historically in a double sense—the history of its becoming in time ("criticism must never for a moment forget that 'the artist is a child of his time,'" p. 158) and the history of its becoming in his own critical consciousness.

Even if one extracts the irony from "theorised finely" and the scepticism from "may" in the comment on Lessing, the difference is both real and important, as real and important as the potential influence of art on our lives. The finest theory establishes a relationship between us and the art object that is simply different from the relationship cultivated by an empirical approach. What it ends up verifying is the beauty and excitement of the theory rather than of the art; it trains us in abstract system-making, not in practical aesthetics. The "exercise of sight and touch" (p. 147) trains us in art, in the ideal way in which the artist "has gradually sunk his intellectual and spiritual ideas in sensuous form" (p. 176), his "blending and interpenetration of intellectual, spiritual, and physical elements . . . with the possibilities of a whole world closed within it" (p. 174). The strongest impression Pater as an exponent of this informal but not unmethodical approach makes is of having stood before representative works of art and actually looked at them with the kind of spiritual attitude that they could not resist, compelling them, like deep answering to deep, to give up their secrets. An eye, an attitude, and a language monitored by complete loyalty to the object as it really is and to his impression of the object are the instruments he brings to his endeavor. They are also the instruments he passes on.

"The arts," Pater says, "may . . . be ranged in a series, which corresponds to a series of developments in the human mind itself" (p. 167). By "the human mind" Pater means the mind in history and the mind in himself. Therefore, he examines the work of art both objectively, as a historical development, and subjectively, as an object having significance to the degree that he discovers its correspondence in his own imaginative intellect. This has the effect of setting up a perpetual, active exchange between the impersonal past and the personal present with the result that the very highest premium is put on a maximally developed consciousness that, to a critically useful degree, personalizes the past and depersonalizes the present.

Adding to this dismantling of the conventional objective-subjective dichotomy the observation that "different attitudes of the imagination have a native affinity with different types of sensuous form" (p. 167), Pater projects himself along the historical continuum and, by a combination of his own and history's perspectives, concludes that what each age did in the way of art was what it could do best. From this, in an orderly but unschematic progression, he moves to the critical issue of how each age has done or is doing its characteristic work and from representative examples draws a link between antique or classical art and modern or Romantic art as roughly the period of the creation of the late classical or Hellenistic *Laocoon.*

Nor can Pater's analysis of the distinguishing strengths and limitations of the various arts, especially of classical sculpture and modern poetry, be considered theoretical in the current sense. They are brilliant deductions from specific examples—what Bacon called a "Table of Discovery"—and are persuasive only to the degree that the examples are sufficiently inclusive and the deductions adequately drawn. Their critical strength lies in the implicit parameters[43] Pater establishes (e.g., "discourse and action" in poetry, "motion," "pure light," and "pure form" in sculpture), the specific illustrations he uses, and the power of those illustrations to draw to the support of his argument the many unnamed examples that individual readers of the essay may know. Throughout he is being concrete rather than abstract, practical rather than theoretical, and what he says of the complexity of the Browning poem he cites (p. 117) it just as particular as are his comments on the simplicity of the Greek marbles.

In his ascent from the subject of the various arts to the subject of Goethe and Goethe's magnificent regenerative relevance to modernism, Pater acknowledges Winckelmann's inadequacy in an area of Hellenism in which Goethe was supreme—that bold tragic vision that confidently wrought serenity out of terrifying evil and turbulent conflict. In the very act of doing so, however, he takes an oblique, ironic glance at the moralistic rigidities that in a modern Christian culture are customarily associated with evil—the superficial morality that "makes the blood turbid, and frets the flesh, and discredits the actual world about us" (p. 177). That is enough, he says, to make us "regret" ever having "passed beyond" the "Hellenic ideal, in which man is in unity with himself, with this physical nature, with the outward world" (p. 177).

Basically, he is talking about the part the denial of his sexuality plays in modern man's distress, the denial of sexuality being only the most tangible metaphor of a general malaise of the spirit resulting from a refusal to accept the world as it in fact is and to be "complete" on those terms. Even if Winckelmann's experience did not comprehend the grandest achievement of the Greek spirit and he did not, like Goethe, become an Olympian-like victor over the truly terrifying realities of human life, he was yet free of this turbid, feverish, superficial sexual morality; being without "any sense of want, or corruption, or shame" in his contact with sensuous pagan truth, he was rewarded with a paganlike joy, "shameless and childlike" (pp. 176-177).

To be thus subversive of Christian morality as he had been subversive of Christian metaphysics took courage, and Pater has not always been given the credit he deserves for courage. One of the least confrontal of men outwardly, he was one of the most radical inwardly. His career as a critic is roughly contemporaneous with that of Nietzsche, with whom he shared the same classical and modern intellectual legacy. Their temperaments, literary manners, and worldly situations were very different, and there is nothing in Pater's story to correspond with the Continental campaign Nietzsche made of his dissent. Nietzsche, like Luther, posted the grounds for his dissent in public in a spirit of both popular defiance and popular appeal. Pater addressed a much more limited audience even than Newman and Arnold spoke to and depended on a more indirect, subterranean influence. Still, there are many critical parallels between Pater and Nietzsche that need to be studied *in the context of* their temperamental, artistic, rhetorical, and cultural differences. A historian of impeccable conscientiousness, a philosophic critic who was so original that he sometimes seems naive, a lover of art who was "one entire medium of spiritual expression, trembling, blushing, melting into dew, with inward excitement" (p. 168), and, at the same time, a person who so prized reserve that he disciplined himself according to an ascetic ideal of "indifference" or "passionate coldness" at which he could not wholly succeed, Pater's radicalism comes to us almost in the disguise of loyalty to language.

But inherent in that language is a loyalty to subject more than equal to it, and therein lies one of the practical choices facing the contemporary critic of Pater. Even after one has made his fascination with Pater's language adequate to it, something of the subject still remains. At that point, the critic's choice is between staying with the limits of language and going beyond language—between standing firmly on language's outer edge, so to speak, and trying to harvest everything the language itself actually points to or implies, on the one hand, and, on the other, assuming that the really challenging subject is what the language does not point to or imply, does not "say," and giving one's critical attention to that. As usual in criticism, it is a choice between the several varieties of formalism and one of the many alternatives to it.

Pater was himself too much of a self-examined formalist not to be acutely aware of its many fascinating alternatives. Indeed, that is his subject in the "Conclusion" to ***The Renaissance.*** He begins: "To regard all things and principles of things as inconstant modes or fashions has more and more become the tendency of modern thought" (p. 186). He then goes on to admit what both the inward and outward facts of life confirm: "That clear, perpetual outline of face and limb is but an image of ours, under which we group them—a design in a web, the actual threads of which pass out beyond it" (pp. 186-187). Nevertheless, he concludes that, among the alternatives available even to a thoroughly modern consciousness, art in the disciplined, formal sense is the best: "For art comes to you proposing frankly to give nothing but the highest quality to your moments as they pass, and simply for those moments' sake" (p. 190). In other words, simply by being what it is and not something else, art is man's quintessential spiritual resort and refuge, art being defined by an extension of the meaning assigned to poetry as "all [imaginative] production which attains the power of giving pleasure by its form, as distinct from its matter" (p. 184). There is no challenge here to the fact that the "actual threads" with which the artist makes his designs "pass out beyond" those designs and to follow them on their ongoing course can be fascinating, but Pater suggests that we should call them something other than art and the study of them something other than aesthetic or literary criticism.

The reader may wonder why, in the face of so extensive and basically constructive a commentary on the strengths and strategies of the **"Winckelmann"** essay, it is still necessary to insist that it is not a fully finished work of art. The reason can be made sufficiently clear, perhaps, only by a comparative recognition of the aesthetic advances Pater has still to make in **"Leonardo da Vinci"** and **"Wordsworth."** All the conditions of art are present in **"Winckelmann";** it is the actual accomplishment that awaits realization. Pater's problem at this point is not intellectual richness or artistic intention but workmanship, "the translation of ideas into images."[44] Like Leonardo, he is in the midst of his own "struggle between the reason and its ideas, and the senses, the desire of beauty."[45] What he needs and has not quite achieved is a style adequate to an abundance of ideas.

In some respects, **"Winckelmann"** may be called Pater's most varied and comprehensive single critical essay and in that sense his most important. It certainly dwarfs even the positive characteristics of **"Coleridge's Writings,"** introducing a host of quite fresh aesthetic considerations and revealing in a thoroughly exciting way how criticism can reach beyond itself toward independent artistic creation. What he has not quite succeeded in doing is converting ideas to images, discursiveness to autonomous, self-validating form. What Winckelmann achieved under untoward circumstances and passed on to Goethe is the heart of the parable, but the parable is not singularly enough the heart of the essay. The various movements of the essay enlarge and illuminate their creator's subject rather than contributing to a unity of effect that makes its outcome inevitable and complete. Pater's manner of treating Winckelmann in his historical, critical, and spiritual context has not quite proved that he has one subject in hand rather than three or four.

Unity of effect, on the other hand, seems to have been an object of special endeavor in the next essay, **"Poems by William Morris,"** and the curious result enables us to pinpoint an important tension in Pater's struggle to perfect his distinctive style. *Unity of effect* is a term more regularly applied to works of art than to works of criticism. Whatever high claims one might make for the originality, rigor, and fundamental soundness of Coleridge's criticism, one would not, I think, want to fault Pater's judgment that it is written in a fragmentary, discontinuous style that neglects manner in favor of matter—that its style lacks in itself a genuine literary motive. To think of a poem's "unity of effect" is so natural, in fact, that a young writer attempting to bring that quality to criticism would almost inevitably be tempted to write "poetic" prose. Something of this conflict between the proprieties of poetry and prose appears to have been central to Pater's struggle to create artistic criticism, and although he had gradually moved away from the premature poetic style of **"Diaphaneitè,"** he reverted toward it to some degree in **"Poems by William Morris."** Though he may have been reasonably well satisfied with **"Winckelmann"** as a comprehensive statement of his critical position and as an adequate illustration of his ability to bring several diverse topics into logical coherence with each other, he yet recognized it as predominantly discursive rather than experiential, its "mind" being more in evidence than its "soul."[46]

Pater was soon to acknowledge, as he already certainly knew, that the terms *Romantic* and *classical* applied to critical prose as well as to other objects of critical endeavor and therefore that good prose depended on more organic qualities than mood, incantation, verbal mesmerism for its poetic character—that, as in sculpture, "line" took precedence over "color." However, in **"Poems by William Morris"** he suspended what are really quite admirable structural lines in an atmosphere of verbal sound and private association reminiscent of **"Diaphaneitè,"** though the later essay is distinctly superior in depth and clarity of insight and in precision of phrase. Of course, **"Poems by William Morris"** was Pater's first essay in criticism of poetry, and its style can in part be accounted for by the "fine mimicry" he would regularly practice, absorbing into his own style some of the identifying marks of the work being criticized. On the other hand, the style of **"Poems by William Morris"** is one to which he would never return, and the two pieces he mined from it, the "Conclusion" to ***The Renaissance*** and **"Aesthetic Poetry"** in the first edition of ***Appreciations,*** continued ever after to evoke from him ambivalent feelings that may have had as much to do with the style in which they were written as with the thoughts they expressed, "style" including the voice he had used and the way he had positioned himself in relation to their subjects.

"Poems by William Morris" mirrors an important moment of self-illumination and is more ecstatic or epiphanic than Pater usually allows himself to be—franker in its use of artifice, more intense in its self-referentiality. The "Conclusion" to ***The Renaissance*** was the original essay's peroration, and that accounts for its heightened perorative style. **"Aesthetic Poetry,"** on the other hand, records a moment of insight, a perceptual victory, without which ***The Renaissance*** would have lacked a clear and sufficient motive. Thus, one may say that the "Conclusion" has an organic relationship to **"Aesthetic Poetry"** and an emblematic relationship to ***The Renaissance.*** It is a natural outgrowth of the former and was used as a codalike celebration of the personal significance of the latter. **"Aes-**

thetic Poetry" implicitly acknowledges Pater's debt to Morris and the Pre-Raphaelites for their contribution to his emergence as an aesthetic critic. The "Conclusion" is a carefully crafted song of himself, a celebration of self-discovery and affirmation, that is "poetic" by analogy with such dramatic lyrics as *Dover Beach* and *Come into the Garden, Maud.*

"Aesthetic Poetry" describes the poetry that from his incapacity as a poet Pater did not write, aesthetic criticism being the alternative available to his particular talents. Like Morris's (and Rossetti's) poetry, Pater's criticism is dedicated to the art-for-art's-sake principle, accepting frankly the artifice inherent in striving to idealize an ideal in which the spontaneity of so-called natural feeling has already been formalized and distanced, and putting the highest premium on the style in which it is executed. Shared attitudes of so basic a character made Pater an extraordinarily insightful critic of the poetry of Morris and Rossetti. No successor has ever come closer to seeing what their poetic goals were, how those goals worked in the making of their poems, and what the essential difference between them is. Despite the late date officially assigned to the Rossetti critique, it belongs stylistically to the same period as **"Poems by William Morris,"** the intense years between 1867 and 1869 when Pater was experiencing a climax of aesthetic self-discovery. Pater brought to his study of them an enthusiasm excited by his knowledge of Winckelmann's hold on Goethe, an enthusiasm for the liberating effects of the Hellenic ideal. He saw that ideal working in Morris in a poetically salutary way, and through seeing how it worked there, he discovered how it should work, on what terms any imaginative ideal of the past can be brought into the service of present imaginative need. Rossetti, on the other hand, never fully found the secret of the Hellenic ideal. In consequence, he was imprisoned in a refined medieval ideal, and though he crafted out of its weightiness of outlook and "grandeur of literary workmanship" a "great style," he suffered the defect of its quality and was unable to liberate himself from what ultimately became a malignant force in his imaginative life.

Following **"Winckelmann"** by a year, **"Poems by William Morris"** contained an answer to the troublesome question that stood between the very special kind of self-modeling achieved by the eighteenth-century protohellenist Winckelmann and passed on by him to the Olympian Goethe, on the one hand, and, on the other, the more general and widely accessible, the archetypal, renaissance of the spirit that could and finally did supply the motive for ***The Renaissance.*** It was a question of "revival." Past environments could not be revived; nor could the particular ways in which master spirits had dealt with the conditions prevailing in their moments in history. However, the sustaining human *ideal* that they had realized in their lives and works others could also realize if they would identify the choice element in their common humanity instanced there and "be divided against themselves"—that is, struggle against their humanity's baser inclinations—in trying to revive that. "We cannot truly conceive the age: we can conceive the element it has contributed to our culture: we can treat the subjects of the age bringing that into relief."[47] That is what Pater found in Morris's poetry, and it showed him how to open the idealized past to the most thoroughly modern of idealizing presents and gave him a creative mission, in the best sense a religion, to which he could be forever faithful and in that faith flourish. It would require exercises of an Ignatian rigor, but it made a wholly secular ideal clear and worthy, showing him that what he had the greatest sympathy and capacity for could be one with the intellectual and moral meaning of his life.

Notes

1. Iain Fletcher, *Walter Pater* (London: Longmans, Green, 1959), p. 37.
2. "Conclusion," *The Renaissance: Studies in Art and Poetry/The 1893 Text,* ed. Donald L. Hill (Berkeley: University of California Press, 1980), p. 190.
3. "Diaphaneitè," *Miscellaneous Studies* (London: Macmillan, 1910), pp. 247-[254].
4. Ibid., p. [254].
5. Ibid., p. 251.
6. "Conclusion," *The Renaissance,* ed. Hill, p. 190.
7. "Postscript," *Appreciations/With an Essay on Style* (London: Macmillan, 1910), p. 254.
8. "Diaphaneitè," p. 248.
9. Robert Browning, *The Ring and the Book,* ed. Richard D. Altick (New Haven: Yale University Press, 1981), XII, 862.
10. Arnold as Professor of Poetry at Oxford probably played a significant part in turning Pater's attention to Coleridge at this particular time (1864-1866). In his lecture on Joubert, he had described Joubert as "a French Coleridge," and whether or not Pater actually attended the lecture, he certainly read it either in its magazine version or in *Essays in Criticism* (1865).
11. "Diaphaneitè," p. 251.
12. Mill's choice of Bentham and Coleridge as the two great seminal minds of the nineteenth century in England has generally gone unchallenged for almost a century and a half, though the essays—"Bentham" (1838) and "Coleridge" (1840) reveal more about Mill's own mind than about the mind of the century.
13. "Coleridge's Writings," *English Critical Essays of the XIX Century,* ed. Edmund D. Jones (London: Oxford University Press, 1922), p. 493.
14. Ibid., p. 494.
15. Ibid.
16. Ibid.
17. Ibid., pp. 494-495.
18. *Plato and Platonism* (London: Macmillan, 1910), p. 125.
19. The term is one Tennyson created to describe the particular species of allegory at work in *Idylls of the King.*

20. "Preface," *The Renaissance,* ed. Hill, p. xxv. This adaptation of Pater's words on his subject to his treatment of his subject is, I think, implicitly authorized by Pater himself. He is using the essay's very incongruity to "tell a truth / Obliquely, do the thing shall breed the thought, / Nor wrong the thought, missing the mediate word." See Browning, *The Ring and the Book,* ed. Altick, XII, 855-857.
21. Browning, *The Ring and the Book,* ed. Altick, XII, 862-863.
22. Throughout the essay "Style," Pater distinguishes between "the literature of fact" and "the literature of the imaginative sense of fact." See, for example, *Appreciations,* p. 8.
23. Throughout this discussion of "Winckelmann," page references are to the Hill edition of *The Renaissance* and are given in parentheses in the text.
24. I have drawn freely and gratefully on Hill's "Critical and Explanatory Notes" to his edition of *The Renaissance,* which are excellent on Pater's use of Hegel.
25. As used here, "*meaning*" has the extended spiritual content Newman gives it in the "Preface" to the *Apologia* as he ponders Kingsley's question, "*What, then, does Dr. Newman mean?*"
26. *Plato and Platonism,* pp. 159-160.
27. See, besides the several important references to Hegel in the text itself, Hill's "Critical and Explanatory Notes" to the "Winckelmann" essay in *The Renaissance,* pp. 410-441.
28. "Introduction," *The Renaissance,* ed. Kenneth Clark (Cleveland and New York: World Publishing Company, 1961), p. 13. Though Clark's phrasing raises as many critical questions as it seeks to answer, his introduction is fascinating in itself and a landmark in the updating of Pater's reputation among art historians and critics.
29. The role of the audience in Pater's prose is itself a subject of critical interest. Pater was through much of his life a lecturer, and it is customary to note the "lecture effect" on *Plato and Platonism,* the only complete example in his canon of a series of undergraduate lectures given book form. But the audience issue is deeper, more systemic than that. The dialogues of Plato are perhaps the literary model that most influenced him, but the care for an imaginary audience was part of the poetic fabric of his age, and the internal evidence that he absorbed it into his own literary manner is highly suggestive. He did not have the dramatic literary sense of Browning, but he was a monologuist who accepted the interpenetration between his role and that of those he wanted to affect. The issue is also related to Pater's desire to give his life as well as his writing artistic form.
30. In the "Postscript" to *Appreciations* (originally entitled *Romanticism,* 1876), he articulated this as a general principle: "the habit of noting and distinguishing one's own most intimate passages of sentiment makes one sympathetic, begetting, as it must, the power of entering, by all sorts of finer ways, into the intimate recesses of other minds. . . ." See *Appreciations,* p. 254.
31. *The Renaissance,* ed. Hill, pp. 410-411.
32. Pater's characteristic use of the biographical mode—his persistent habit of seeing ideas as emanating from the spirits of various particular kinds of men working under different but specific conditions—has its correspondence in what he describes as Plato's strong temperamental tendency to perceive ideas as something very like "persons," "to be known as persons must be [known]" and "to be loved for the perfections, the visible perfections . . . of their being" (*Plato and Platonism,* p. 166). It is also cognate with his view of the tensions in mankind's spiritual history as the result of different kinds of men working under different conditions as well as with his view that various universal ideas are reflections of patterns and tendencies of the mind itself, to be verified by reference to one's own mind if one can remain sufficiently detached and observant.
33. See *Matthew Arnold's Books: Toward a Publishing Diary,* ed. William E. Buckler (Geneva: E. Droz, 1958), p. 66.
34. *Plato and Platonism,* p. 175.
35. As distinct, that is, from got-up dialogue or dialogue *manqué,* which, as used by such persons as Bruno, Berkeley, and Landor, is merely the giving of a popular form to essentially dogmatic ideas.
36. Though Pater does not actually use the word *sin,* he could hardly have avoided thinking it, and he was quite capable of the buried pun with its sophisticated ironic playfulness.
37. Though Pater does not mention Arnold, Arnold is large in the background. Besides his general position as the age's most articulate spokesman for classical literary ideals, Arnold had delivered a lecture at Oxford, printed in the *Cornhill* in April, entitled "Pagan and Medieval Religious Sentiment." The lecture-essay stimulated both Pater's thinking and his courage on the subject, including the kind of corrective and courageous thinking that Pater often applied to Arnold after close study. David J. DeLaura takes the closely argued but, in my judgment, over-emphatic position that Pater's essay is "centrally a response" to Arnold's. Pater's essays seem to me to have a quite different "center" which is obscured by DeLaura's emphasis. See David J. DeLaura, *Hebrew and Hellene in Victorian England* (Austin: University of Texas Press, 1969), pp. 202-222.
38. Pater's line of thinking here and later in the essay (pp. 177-179) moves in a direction to be passionately developed by Nietzsche in *The Birth of Tragedy out of the Spirit of Music* (1872). From that point of view, Winckelmann, who "did not enter" into "this

stage of Greek achievement" (p. 178), was himself the exponent of the sort of orthodoxy Pater is criticizing, indeed, is said by some to have been its originator.

39. *Plato and Platonism,* pp. 159-160.
40. For example, he seems to echo "The Scholar-Gipsy" when he says, "for us of the modern world, with its conflicting aims, its entangled interests, distracted by so many sorrows, with many preoccupations, so bewildering an experience . . ." (p. 182), though he could also be echoing the beginning of chapter V in Newman's *Apologia.*
41. "Introduction," *The Renaissance,* ed. Clark, p. 14.
42. One is reminded of Arnold's declaration that "the cardinal rule" of his critical inquiry is "*Hypotheses non fingo*" *(I do not invent my hypotheses).* He takes the "rule" from Isaac Newton and means by it that he "finds" his critical hypotheses empirically. See *Literature and Dogma* in *The Complete Prose Works of Matthew Arnold,* ed. R. H. Super (Ann Arbor: University of Michigan Press, 1968), VI, 275.
43. He is much more explicit in this regard in the opening pages of "The School of Giorgione."
44. "Leonardo da Vinci," *The Renaissance,* ed. Hill, p. 88.
45. Ibid.
46. Pater makes the distinction between the "mind" and the "soul" of good prose in his essay "Style." See especially *Appreciations,* pp. 25-27.
47. "Charles Lamb," *Appreciations,* p. 113.

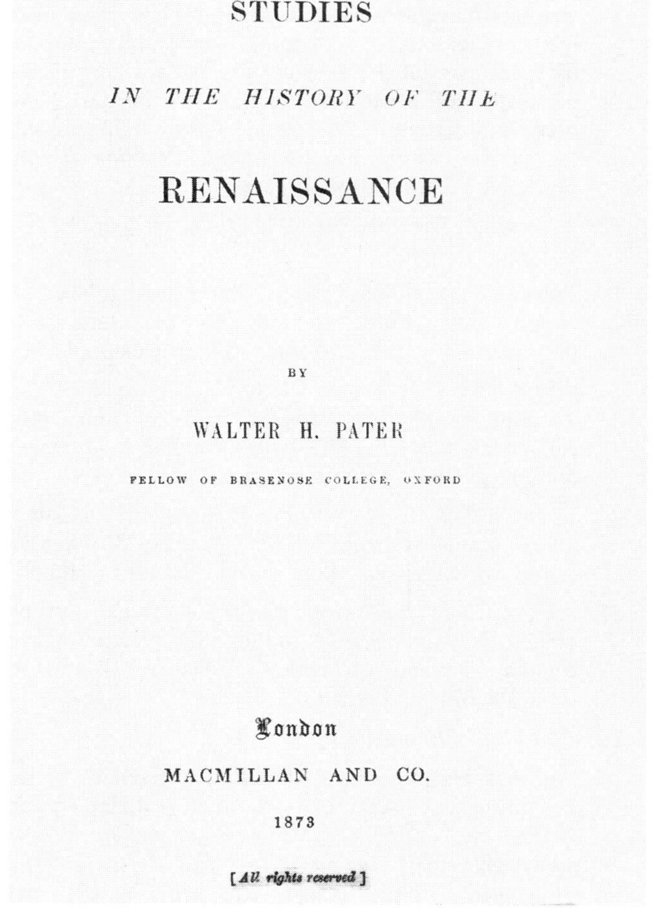
STUDIES

IN THE HISTORY OF THE

RENAISSANCE

BY

WALTER H. PATER

FELLOW OF BRASENOSE COLLEGE, OXFORD

London

MACMILLAN AND CO.

1873

[*All rights reserved*]

Carolyn Williams (essay date 1989)

SOURCE: "Opening Conclusions" in *Transfigured World: Walter Pater's Aesthetic Historicism,* Cornell University Press, 1989, pp. 11-37.

[*In the following excerpt, Williams examines the infamous "Conclusion" to* Studies in the History of the Renaissance *and explains what Pater meant in proposing aesthetic distance as an alternative to prevailing modern thought.*]

My choice to begin with the "Conclusion" is not an empty gesture, though it is a familiar and almost traditional opening gesture in discussions of Pater's work. My reason has little to do with the fact that the "Conclusion" to the 1873 first edition of ***Studies in the History of the Renaissance*** was, and is, Pater's most controversial piece, that it inaugurated the career of public notoriety which he both invited and evaded, and that it established him as the inspiration of an elite counterculture whose further elaborations often shocked him, precipitating his lifelong recoil into less and less vivid restatements of his original positions. The "Conclusion" might have been more readily understood (or at least less radically misunderstood) if it had been positioned as an introduction or invocation to the volume, and therefore I want to begin by exposing the several senses in which the essay serves more properly as an introduction than as a conclusion to the volume.

Of course, the "Conclusion" was never written to conclude ***Studies in the History of the Renaissance***—it was written originally to conclude another work altogether. It first appeared in 1868 as the last few paragraphs of Pater's review essay **"Poems by William Morris"** and was therefore written before all but one of the other essays in the Renaissance volume.[1] But the "Conclusion" should be read as an introduction to Pater's work for reasons more profound than its priority in the chronology of his publication record. Though Pater strategically positions it at the end of his first published volume, and though its title claims the rhetorical function of conveying in summary fashion what has been logically or experientially derived from the volume as a whole, its conclusions instead prefigure and enable all of Pater's "aesthetic criticism," including the Renaissance studies.

It was necessary for Pater to arrive at these conclusions before even beginning the series of "studies" whose fundamental value depends on circumventing certain philosophical problems that threaten to make any study of history virtually impossible. Before approaching a consideration of history, in other words, Pater had to answer several questions raised in his mind by modern physical science and epistemological philosophy. His particular version of aestheticism is then formulated in the "Conclusion" as Pater's answer to the problems posed by what he there calls "modern thought." The volume of Renaissance studies, and the inaugural moment of Pater's literary career, are founded on the theoretical position taken in the "Conclusion": that the problems of modern thought could be solved only by fully acknowledging them, confronting them, and regulating their effects.

Pater's "Conclusion" is still regarded as the major theoretical statement in English of nineteenth-century aestheticism, and yet it is still frequently misunderstood.[2] The stock literary-historical view of Pater's career has always taken his "Conclusion" as if it represented in its entirety Pater's own conclusions, and perhaps this is as good a reason as any for us to begin there. The popular misreading still takes the essay to be Pater's impassioned statement of his belief in relativism, subjectivism, nihilism, and hedonism—when it is nothing of the kind. Instead, in the "Conclusion" Pater briefly but painstakingly outlines the material and epistemological conclusions drawn by "modern thought," and then he devotes the full force of his rhetorical, figurative, and philosophical energies to proposing an alternative stance. His formulation of aestheticism is that alternative stance.

It is an irony of literary history that Pater has been repeatedly accused of propounding the very philosophies he meant to expose and combat, but it is an irony with its own interpretable significance. Pater had so thoroughly assimilated the most dangerous "modern thought" of his day that his vigorous and subtle defenses against it, as well as his profound desire to assimilate it *to* the traditional past of his culture (and therefore to domesticate it), were often missed. In Pater we find a quintessentially "transitional" figure who holds together in an unstable equilibrium ideologies from both sides of what will later come to be seen—and to a great extent was seen even at the time—as a historical divide. Pater is a deeply conservative writer whose conservatism nevertheless had a radical effect, in part because it engaged so closely with its dialectical counterpart. His aestheticism can be fully understood only if we see it in its role as a dialectical response, operating both within and against the forces he outlines in paragraphs one and two of the "Conclusion."

In these initial paragraphs, Pater distills and generalizes two strands of argument within "modern thought," embodies them in lushly figurative language, and takes the implications of each to its extreme limits, to the point where the argument dissolves at the boundaries of the articulate. Pater stages in these paragraphs the "passage and dissolution" of mind, body, soul, self, and text. But the rhetorical position he takes toward these paragraphs is neither straightforward nor even simply ironic, but oblique in another way, for he is engaged in conveying the full entangling force of these "modern" arguments while remaining at a distance from them—representing and at the same time disowning the train of thought represented. As Richard Wollheim has correctly suggested, the first two paragraphs of the "Conclusion" should be read as if they were enclosed in quotation marks.[3] But whom, then, is Pater quoting, or pretending to quote, and to what end? Why is he engaged in this form of ventriloquism, and what do the projected voices say?

The opening paragraphs of the "Conclusion" are known to more readers, perhaps, than any other passage from Pater's work. In the following two sections I pursue a close reading of these paragraphs in order to recall some already-established territory in Pater studies as well as to introduce a few of the central concepts and strategies of reading that will guide this book.

1. "That Which Is Without"

> . . . To regard all things and principles of things as inconstant modes or fashions has more and more become the tendency of modern thought. Let us begin with that which is without—our physical life. Fix upon it in one of its more exquisite intervals, the moment, for instance, of delicious recoil from the flood of water in summer heat. What is the whole physical life in that moment but a combination of natural elements to which science gives their names? But these elements, phosphorus and lime and delicate fibers, are present not in the human body alone: we detect them in places most remote from it. Our physical life is a perpetual motion of them—the passage of the blood, the wasting and repairing of the lenses of the eye, the modification of the tissues of the brain under every ray of light and sound—processes which science reduces to simpler and more elementary forces. Like the elements of which we are composed, the action of these forces extends beyond us: it rusts iron and ripens corn. Far out on every side of us those elements are broadcast, driven in many currents; and birth and gesture and death and the springing of violets from the grave are but a few out of ten thousand resultant combinations. That clear, perpetual outline of face and limb is but an image of ours, under which we group them—a design in a web, the actual threads of which pass out beyond it. This at least of flamelike our life has, that it is but the concurrence, renewed from moment to moment, of forces parting sooner or later on their ways. (***R***, 233-34)

Although it serves generally to frame the essay in its place at the end of the volume, Pater's epigraph, from the *Cratylus,* must be understood more particularly in relation to what it immediately precedes. Plato characteristically represents the words of Socrates, but in this case Socrates's words themselves quote a fragment of Heraclitus: "Heraclitus somewhere says that all things are moving along and that nothing stands still." Pater gives the epigraph in its original Greek, inviting translation by the initiated and implying at the same time that he himself is chief among them, for the first two paragraphs of the "Conclusion" in effect "translate" these words of Heraclitus into their nineteenth-century English equivalent. The dense and explicit intertextuality of the epigraph condenses a whole history of voices: Heraclitus and Socrates subsumed, contextualized, and voiced by Plato, whose words in turn are given by Pater as a prefiguration of his own. In this small prefatory gesture, opening with an ancient fragment in order to interpret "modern" thought, Pater almost ostentatiously displays his command of the entire history of Western philosophy, positioning himself at one and the same time at the latest and at the earliest verge of his tradition's written record.

But even more important than Pater's tacit claim to mastery of the tradition is the hint that "modern" thought is not so thoroughly new, but is in many ways only a "modernization" of the classical tradition. The epigraph quietly shows, to those who read Greek, that Pater believes the threat of "modern" thought to be an ancient, a persistent, even a traditional threat. For the present study, this epigraph will serve as a brief introduction to Pater's habit of finding "mythic" recapitulations in the history of thought, since here the latest findings of science and philosophy suggest to him an analogue in Heraclitus.[4] The epigraph enacts, moreover, one characteristic Paterian strategy of quotation, although the first two paragraphs of the "Conclusion" make use (as we will see) of another, more subtle and pervasive intertextual strategy.

After the first sentence of paragraph one—which briefly and simply announces the subject under scrutiny—Pater begins to explore the extremes of this "tendency of modern thought" by presenting summary arguments meant to characterize entire intellectual disciplines. In the first paragraph, he represents the extreme conclusions of modern physical science, as in the second he will represent the extremes of epistemological philosophy. Here in the first paragraph, life is shown reduced to its "physical basis."[5] Within the terms of this discourse, the complexities of life become mere biological "processes which science reduces to simpler and more elementary forces." Here Pater highlights the relation between the methods of a discourse and its effects: the analytical practices of "science" both mimic and describe the perpetual fragmentation of bodies into their constituent "elements." That sense of perpetual reduction and fragmentation is accompanied by an equally pervasive sense of instability, of constant movement, the Heraclitean "flux" of phenomena in time. The particular form of "perpetual motion" set forth in this first paragraph is the never-ending process of physical bodies "wasting and repairing."

This paragraph represents the discourse of "objectivity." To view "life" as purely physical or material—to view "life" as an object of scientific study—depends upon establishing a certain distance between the viewing subject and the object of observation, a figurative "distance" that expresses in spatial terms the disciplinary practices necessary to establish "factual" or "scientific" knowledge. But here this analytical distance is extended by the "long view" of late Victorian, post-Darwinian science. That extremely distant perspective regards change over such vast periods of time that the solidity of physical objects seems only an illusion of our limited, transitory, and human perspective. Transformations taking a lifetime or more may be imagined as happening incrementally at every moment. Within this view there is no small oasis of stability; each moment rushes by, full of decay. In this particular configuration of space and time, distance and speed, we can perhaps see the clash of classical physics and chemistry with evolutionary geology and biology, each with a different view of the constitution of the object of study, the latter involved in a profound contemporary redefinition of historical change.

From the perspective of Pater's immediate literary tradition, it is as if Wordsworth's visionary image of monumental permanence in continuity, the "woods decaying, never to be decayed," from Book 6 of *The Prelude,* were represented not as a stable visual image but in an accelerated, time-lapsed moving picture, with each momentary frame implicated in the dissolving process of the whole. Looking back at paragraph one from paragraph two, Pater does seem to see the Wordsworthian illusion of permanence preserved within the discourse of objectivity: "the water flows down indeed, though in apparent rest" (***R,*** 234). But here in the midst of paragraph one, Wordsworth's vision is revealed as wishful thinking, the illusion of permanence shattered by a discourse in which physical appearances are not allowed their common deception. Despite "apparent" rest, the truth is "perpetual motion"; all is wastage and dispersal, decomposition and reformation. The elements, forces, "threads" of which each of us is composed, "extend beyond us," for human life is but a "flamelike" and momentary "concurrence" of forces soon to be dispersed. Despite the allusive literary memorialization granted past life by "the springing of violets from the grave,"[6] all of human "gesture" is reduced to the one word lodged between "birth" and "death." Human life occupies a very small space within this view of things; after all, only "a few out of ten thousand combinations" ever result in human form.

The only concept of continuity preserved in the vision of paragraph one lies in the regeneration implicit in nature's constant recycling of elements, but that concept of regeneration makes any particular physical body only an arbitrary and passing combination. The stoic faith—that dead bodies, dispersed into their constituent elements, constantly recombine to form new wholes—can operate as comfort only from a cosmic or a scientific perspective. But from the perspective of Christian humanism—against which this post-Darwinian view contends here—a new body can be no comfort unless it is the *same* body, for reformation implies as well a change or loss of content, and in the realm of incarnational poetics the "content" of a human body is its soul. Like a scientific version of mythic recurrence, this reincarnational vision of continuity involves so much transformation that it undermines the value of individual identity. In this discourse, any notion of the "self" disappears as irrelevant. This discourse, then, represents a crucial destabilization of the incarnational view, for visible bodies are themselves so unstable that they cannot be confidently seen to "contain" selves or souls.

In other words, the scientifically objective view of physical bodies in time has both epistemological and aesthetic consequences, for it implies that visible form can no longer be trusted to mark stable content. The "outline" of an object marks only our mental effort to believe in permanent form, to "group" elements together momentarily while nevertheless "far out on every side of us those elements are broadcast," to "fix" the play of forces in some fictive combination we can recognize, "an image of ours," a figure in the carpet whose "actual threads . . . pass out beyond it." These metaphors attempt to implicate two incompatible forms of incoherence: atomism and inextricable interrelation, one as old as Lucretius, the other a characteristic formulation of late Victorian aesthetics and social analysis.[7] Whether every element or particle is separate from every other, or whether every fiber or thread is woven into an inextricable texture with every other—within the logic, that is, of either metaphor—discrete form is understood to have been imposed by the eye, not to be inherent in the object. Together the metaphors suggest that what the eye can see is the merest mask for the unseen truth: that the chief activity of the world is its speedy decomposition.

With an eye to behold it, the world becomes a text to be read and deciphered, but a text understood to have been written in the very act of reading, composed by the will to envision design. Within the terms of paragraph one, the perception of form has been relegated to the status of personal wish or aesthetic illusion, a myth that modern science dispels with its brutal truth.

2. "The Inward World of Thought and Feeling"

In the objective framework of paragraph one, then, subjectivity is cast in the role of irrelevant illusion, but in paragraph two the tables are turned. There the experience of the individual perceiving self is taken as primary, but the consequences are the same: the object again loses its definition, and the notion of a stable, unified self dissolves as well. Taken together, these opposite and interlocking discourses seem to suggest that "modern thought" in general—regardless of the specific mental processes or the particular disciplinary methods enforced—tends to dissolve subject and object in relation to one another, correlatively. Pater himself made this destructive correlation vividly clear, in a passage that originally followed paragraph two and thus framed his discussion of "modern thought":

> Such thoughts seem desolate at first; at times all the bitterness of life seems concentrated in them. They bring the image of one washed out beyond the bar in a sea at ebb, losing even his personality, as the elements of which he is composed pass into new combinations. Struggling, as he must, to save himself, it is himself that he loses at every moment.[8]

But the correlative relation of the two paragraphs should be clear even at the beginning of the second paragraph, where a rhetorical turn signals that a different position will be taken toward "modern thought" and prefigures Pater's demonstration that another modern discourse leads to essentially the same conclusions. The blatant parallelism opening each paragraph—"Let us begin . . . Or if we begin . . ."—seems unmistakable, yet it has often been missed, along with its important implication that the two opposed discourses present parallel and interlocking hypothetical cases of "passage and dissolution."

> Or if we begin with the inward world of thought and feeling, the whirlpool is still more rapid, the flame more eager and devouring. There it is no longer the gradual darkening of the eye, and fading of color from the wall—the movement of the shoreside, where the water flows down indeed, though in apparent rest—but the race of the midstream, a drift of momentary acts of sight and passion and thought. At first sight experience seems to bury us under a flood of external objects, pressing upon us with a sharp and importunate reality, calling us out of ourselves in a thousand forms of action. But when reflection begins to play upon those objects they are dissipated under its influence; the cohesive force seems suspended like a trick of magic; each object is loosed into a group of impressions—color, odor, texture—in the mind of the observer. And if we continue to dwell in thought on this world, not of objects in the solidity with which language invests them, but of impressions, unstable, flickering, inconsistent, which burn and are extinguished with our consciousness of them, it contracts still further: the whole scope of observation is dwarfed to the narrow chamber of the individual mind. Experience, already reduced to a swarm of impressions, is ringed round for each one of us by that thick wall of personality through which no real voice has ever pierced on its way to us, or from us to that which we can only conjecture to be without. Every one of those impressions is the impression of the individual in his isolation, each mind keeping as a solitary prisoner its own dream of a world. Analysis goes a step farther still, and assures us that those impressions of the individual mind to which, for each one of us, experience dwindles down, are in perpetual flight; that each of them is limited by time, and that as time is infinitely divisible, each of them is infinitely divisible also; all that is actual in it being a single moment, gone while we try to apprehend it, of which it may ever be more truly said that it has ceased to be than that it is. To such a tremulous wisp constantly reforming itself on the stream, to a single sharp impression, with a sense in it, a relic more or less fleeting of such moments gone by, what is real in our life fines itself down. It is with this movement, with the passage and dissolution of impressions, images, sensations, that analysis leaves off—that continual vanishing away, that strange, perpetual weaving and unweaving of ourselves. (***R***, 234-36)

To move us "inward" at the beginning of paragraph two, Pater first stages a loss of distance in relation to physical objects. As distance is lost, the definitive marks of the object's "objectivity"—its externality and its wholeness—are perforce lost as well. Without distance between observer and object, there can be no perceivable definition, no "outline"; nor can there be the sense of a "sharp" and "importunate" external reality "outside," ready to "[call] us out of ourselves." This is the discourse of the "inside," of extreme subjectivity. If paragraph one took the extreme long view, paragraph two takes the extreme close view, in which subject and object are one, as the mind becomes the object of its own self-reflexive regard.

With his usual keen attention to etymological nuance, Pater reminds us of the literal significance of "analysis" and of a certain sense in which the scrutiny of mental operations must always tend to "break up" or "loosen" the coherence of the mind and its objects. When "reflection begins to play upon those objects," they are "loosened" into their separate sensory attributes; their coherence seems to be "suspended like a trick of magic." Again, as in paragraph one, but here even more explicitly, language "invests" objects with a solidity and coherence they would otherwise lack; names counteract "analysis" by creating the illusion of an overarching wholeness even where none can be directly experienced.

Reflection's "trick of magic" is also a trick of time. As in paragraph one, tropes of fragmentation, reduction, and acceleration express the connection Pater draws between the distance taken on an object and the resulting sense of time. In this case the crux of the equation is the notion of "impressions," the middle term between mind and object. United in the notion of the impression are the effects of fragmentation and speed, for like the "elements" of paragraph one, the "impressions" of paragraph two represent parts of objects in the perpetual motion of dissolving and "reforming." And this is a temporal, not spatial, phenomenon: "each of them is limited by time, and . . . as time is infinitely divisible, each of them is infinitely divisible also." Impressions are problematic, in other words, not only because they are mental phenomena rather than physical objects, and not only because they are representatives of parts rather than wholes, but also because they pass so quickly they cannot be grasped. Faster than the "currents" of paragraph one, their passage here is "still more rapid," the "race of the midstream."

Behind the words of this paragraph lie the empiricist epistemologies of Locke and Hume, but also and more immediately the critiques of Berkeley and Kant.[9] Pater seems to grapple here with the difficult notion that the long tradition of empiricist epistemology has undergone a dialectical reversal: a discourse instituted to counteract the classical form of idealism by relying on the evidence of the senses seems to have circled back to enunciate another, subjectivist form of it. And again the clue to this doubleness is the particular notion of the "impression" found in paragraph two. The empiricist sense-impression has been replaced by a subjectivist, idealist "impression" that has only a "relic" of "a sense" left in it, a distant reminder of the sensory experience that stimulated it in the first place. The difference between the empiricist "impression" and the subjectivist "impression" has to do with the one's relative attention to the object and the other's relative absorption in the mind's own processes. Another way to draw this distinction would be to characterize the traditional empiricist project as an attempt to balance the claims of object and mind through the mediating agency of the "sense-impression." But here Pater portrays a notion of "impressions" very far from their stimuli in the world of objects. It is true that elsewhere in Pater the notion of the "impression" retains a greater degree of fidelity to the evidence of the senses. In other words, in Pater's explicit unfolding of his own theory of impressionism, the impression retains its empiricist role as the crucial mechanism of internalization from a real outside.[10] But here in paragraph two, where Pater's goal is to portray the extremes of subjectivism, the impression has accordingly lost touch with its objective source.

This second paragraph presents Pater's famous late romantic restatement of the anxious agonies of solipsism. In attempting to provide another response to this problem, the "Conclusion" falls squarely in the philosophical and literary tradition of Johnson kicking a rock to prove Berkeley wrong, of Wordsworth grasping for dear life at the wall.[11] Once again Pater places his words at the end of a modern tradition (which itself recapitulates a classical tradition, as his epigraph vigilantly insists). As Wordsworth is more anxious than Johnson, Pater is more anxious than Wordsworth, and at the same time Pater is more familiar with the anxieties of self-consciousness, which are by now a traditional part of his late romantic literary culture. He pushes the literary tradition of romantic epistemology further toward its limits by figuratively expressing the danger as even more acute, reflexive, and involuted.

In Pater's representation of "modern thought," the mind can no longer resort to a physical, bodily, or commonsense solution: in the first paragraph the "physical basis of life" provided no solid ground, and here in the second no solid object can even be imagined for long. The Wordsworthian wall cannot be reached for its steadying influence, for it is no longer figured "outside," at the objective distance that makes it available to be grasped. Instead, in the famous Paterian figure, the wall is represented as constitutive of subjectivity, and "personality" has consequently become a figurative prison. The passage in which Pater gives us "the thick wall of personality" behind which each mind keeps "as a solitary prisoner its own dream of a world" probably characterizes the extreme subjectivist position as vividly as any in English literature. But it is therefore crucial to recognize that if Pater uses this paragraph to enact his profound understanding of—perhaps even his temptation toward—the position of epistemological nihilism, he holds that position at a hypothetical distance from his own.

What are the consequences of figuring the "wall" as constitutive of subjectivity? Once the wall is figuratively located inside, its effect is to articulate another inside and outside, both figuratively contained within the internal territory of the mind. In the words of the figure, each individual mind is a walled-off, isolated "narrow chamber," and then inside each already-isolated mind is the solitary figure of a prisoner, a figure for the mind's dream of a world outside. The figure, in other words, is metafigural in structure and content: it depicts multiple and recapitulatory layers of containment, and it represents in spatial form, as a place or "scene," the essentially figural, aesthetic act through which the mind recreates the world. If the usual account of literary figuration represents the metaphorical figure as having an inside and an outside, a meaning conveyed by a linguistic vehicle or contained in a covering layer, Pater's figure (of the chamber) has another figure (of the prisoner) "inside" it, and that inner figure is a figure for the act of figuration (the mind's "dream of a world"). In bringing the Wordsworthian wall "inside," making it constitutive of subjectivity instead of a sign of the stabilizing world of external objects, Pater makes a figure for the mind in the act of constructing itself and the world together: both inside and outside have been recontained, both are now understood to be inside. Mind and object in relation to one another—the mind together with its object—is now the object of the mind's representations. Subject and object together have become the revised content or object of consciousness. This important Paterian figure, in other words, represents the tradition of romantic epistemology as metafigural discourse.

This move of metafiguration—in which the mind figuratively steps outside itself in one further self-reflexive gesture, to represent itself in the act of representing itself and the world—provides Pater with a way to slip out of the "prison" of solipsism. On the level of meaning, the gesture is tantamount to the bracketing admission that every perception as well as every utterance is already an aesthetic creation, and on this level the metafigural figure has frequently been associated with literary modernism. Both paragraphs include this modernist avowal that the perception of form is generated in the eye of the beholder, or by language itself. But the figure of the prisoner is metafigural in a particularly spatial way, a figure of what I will be calling "recontainment." And it will be possible to see why this strategy of recontainment might be appealing when we note that the alternative model of mental activity at work in this paragraph—consciousness figured as "stream"—presents, in several senses, a much graver danger.

Of course, the metaphor of the "stream" of consciousness is the quintessential figure for the temporality of mental experience. As Pater's evocation of Heraclitus reminds us, you cannot step into the same stream twice. But paragraph two of the "Conclusion" gives us the passage of temporal experience in a vastly accelerated version, the "race of the midstream," moments of experience "in perpetual flight." By the end of the paragraph, all of experience has been reduced to "a single moment, gone while we try to apprehend it, of which it may ever be more truly said that it has ceased to be than that it is." Throughout these first two paragraphs, Pater uses the word "passage" to characterize the Heraclitean "flux," the perpetual motion of physical and mental phenomena in time, but when the "passage of the blood" succeeds to the "passage and dissolution of impressions" here in paragraph two, the double and triple implications of the word begin to resonate. Here the word calls attention to the inability of the mind to grasp its own experience as that experience passes into the past.

In a certain sense, the problem is the very opposite of solipsism. When the mind turns to reflect upon itself, all it can observe are these "passages" of impressions, until the mind itself seems nothing more than the site of their passage. What, then, is the mind? Can it exert any control over this "drift"? Or is it capable only of registering the impressions as they pass? Is it a site at all, a location, a place? Are there depths below the surface of the "stream," where invisible things are stored away from the drift? As these questions indicate, this model too has potentially spatial implications as well as temporal ones. Pater described the Kantian issue of the "substantial reality of mind" this way:

> What remained of our actual experience was but a stream of impressions over the (supposed but) wholly unknown mental substratum which no act of intuition or reflexion could ever really detect.[12]

"Substantial" and "substratum" suggest the attempt to rationalize a metaphorics of depth to describe mental process, but those implications are more or less refused in paragraph two of the "Conclusion," where the "relic" of sensory experience floats on the surface of the current as "a tremulous wisp . . . reforming itself on the stream." What is really at issue here is the mind's questionable ability to "grasp" or "apprehend," to "hold" or "contain" anything at all.

Given the problems implied in the figure of the stream in its passage, it may be possible now to see how the figure of the prisoner might be relatively appealing to Pater. Even though that figure represents the "outside" as conjectural, unreal, and dreamlike, still the metafigural logic of the metaphor permits the faith that there *is* an outside into which the dreamer might wake, the prisoner be freed. The discourse of the "outside" in paragraph one admits of no such more objective realm, whereas the alternative metaphor of the stream in paragraph two questions the ability of the mind to hold or to grasp anything at all. By contrast, the figure of the prisoner depicts the mind in the act of holding on to the faith or "dream" of another world, an outside, objective world.[13] If it portrays the mind completely isolated and cut off from the world, it also portrays the mind keeping its dream or faith securely inside, as content.

Of course, the figure of impressions in their passage on the stream of consciousness has its own version of this doubleness: if it portrays the mind with no control over what passes through it, it also portrays the mind free, unrestrained, and mobile—the very opposite of solipsistic, immobilized, and imprisoned. The two metaphorical systems are in many ways incommensurate. As in paragraph one, where we found contradictory figures for the incoherence of the material world—atomism and inextricable interrelation—paragraph two reveals contradictory figures for the impossibility of knowing: solipsism and mania, radical containment and radical noncontainment, the metaphorics of the "prisoner" and those of the "passage." The problem that nothing stays in the mind for very long seems to be the opposite of the problem that nothing can get out, and their juxtaposition and doubleness indicate a confusion about the relation of these models. On the other hand, the ability of each to articulate, at one and the same time, both impediment and capacity suggests the sense in which they may overlap or dialectically interact (on the question of depth, for example). Each model has its aesthetic consequences, but in the largest sense they may be made to work together, each correcting the other in a model of mental activity that escapes the perils of "modern thought." In the next section of this book, I shall show how Pater constructs this alternative model in elaborating his own discourse of aestheticism.

Finally, it must be noted that Pater stresses the inextricable inter-definition of subject and object not only in the figures for self-consciousness that dominate paragraph two, but also in the relationship that obtains between the two paragraphs. There *are* two discourses represented here, but together they form one argument, the parts of which interlock logically as well as rhetorically.[14] By relating every subject to its uneasy grounding in "the physical basis of life," and every object to its uneasy grounding in an isolated and ephemeral subject, Pater presents scientific objectivity and romantic epistemology as two opposing but correlative modes of deriving the radically relativist position at the extremes of "modern thought." The inevitability of material annihilation makes the self irrelevant; epistemological nihilism makes the world of objects—and finally the mind itself—unknowable. Without at least a provisional outside, there is no inside; without solid objects, there can be no subject; without a provisional other, there is no certainty of "our own elusive inscrutable mistakable self."[15] Pater's simultaneously late romantic, late Victorian, and early modern position in the English literary tradition may be seen in this intensified awareness that the problem of "objective" knowledge and the problem of "subjectivity" are intractably one and the same problem.

3. Aestheticism

Many years later, in writing ***Marius the Epicurean,*** Pater attempted to explain more fully the thoughts suggested by his "Conclusion."[16] At that point he wrote into Marius's character the "peculiar strength" of having "apprehended," from the very beginning of his career, the possible consequences of "what is termed 'the subjectivity of knowledge'":

> That is a consideration, indeed, which lies as an element of weakness, like some admitted fault or flaw, at the very foundation of every philosophical account of the universe; which confronts all philosophies at their starting, but with which none have really dealt conclusively, some perhaps not quite sincerely; which those who are not philosophers dissipate by "common," but unphilosophical, sense, or by religious faith. The peculiar strength of Marius was, to have apprehended this weakness on the threshold of human knowledge, in the whole range of its consequences. (***ME*** I, 137-38)

Certainly Pater understood Marius's "peculiar strength" to be his own. In this section of my argument I want to ask how Pater's aestheticism functions as an "apprehension"—both as grasp, or understanding, and as arrest or halting—of this "weakness" and how it responds to this "weakness" with its own "peculiar strength." If the problem of "objective" knowledge and the problem of the "subjectivity" of knowledge are, for Pater, correlative problems, then they must be solved correlatively. That is exactly what his theory of aestheticism attempts to do. And the solution depends upon reconstituting, upon new grounds, a provisional objectivity.

Aestheticism, as the suffix implies, proposes itself as a systematic attitude of self-consciousness, a coherent stance or perspective on things, a method of attention. Whether the word accurately refers to a coherent "movement" or not,[17] a coherent account of the method was propounded in English both by Pater and by Wilde. I want to describe here, as succinctly as possible, how I see the method working. I continue to focus on the "Conclusion," but I shall also begin to range freely among the other essays in which Pater specifically addresses himself to articulating theoretically the function and operation of "aesthetic criticism."

The "Conclusion" presents an extraordinary texture of metaphorical doubleness and transformation. All the dominant figures of paragraphs one and two are reworked and transvalued in paragraphs three through five. This is one way the discourse of aestheticism answers modern thought in its own terms—figuratively—and the instability of figures here is evidence both of the problem and, dialectically, of its solution. In the "Conclusion," the systematic transvaluation of figures enacts on the level of form what has been clearly announced on the level of theme: Pater's commitment to engage with and assimilate "modern thought" and then to turn it against itself under the auspices of aestheticism. In his original introduction to the paragraphs that eventually became the "Conclusion," Pater made it quite clear that the essay would discuss the response provided by "the desire of beauty" to the destructive tendencies of modern philosophy. The "desire of beauty," Pater wrote, in another of his graphic characterizations of modern thought, is "quickened by the sense of death."[18] That phrase resonates with his description at the end of the "Conclusion" of the goal and end of the aesthetic attitude: a "quickened, multiplied consciousness." The essay was framed, then, by phrases describing the aesthetic attitude as "quickened," which Pater uses to mean both "enlivened" and "accelerated." And indeed, quickness (as mental mobility) is closely associated with the sense of "life" promised by aestheticism, just as the rapidity of dissolution was associated in the first two paragraphs with "the sense of death." If we follow a few of these doubling, transformative turns for a moment, we will be able to find out what Pater imagines in a "quickened" and "multiplied" consciousness.

The "moment," for example, which in paragraphs one and two signified only impermanence, temporal fragmentation, and the vertiginous speed of decay, is transformed in paragraph three into the culmination of a temporal sequence in which beauty and, above all, form is finally achieved:

> Every moment some form grows perfect in hand or face; some tone on the hills or the sea is choicer than

> the rest; some mood of passion or insight or intellectual excitement is irresistibly real and attractive to us,—for that moment only. (***R,*** 236)

Here form is taken at its face value, not dismissed as illusion; it may be accurately perceived, but it is alive and changing every moment, so it must be pursued actively. In the terms of modern thought, experience was portrayed as drastically ephemeral, "all that is actual in it being a single moment, gone while we try to apprehend it"; but Pater's aestheticism proposes that we may in fact "apprehend" that moment if we will only speed up and "fasten" our attention:

> How shall we pass most swiftly from point to point, and be present always at the focus where the greatest number of vital forces unite in their purest energy? (***R,*** 236)

Recommended here is a mental "quickening" that would enable us to keep up with moments in their passage by "passing" along with them, so that our attention could coincide with their brief points of focus. But in addition to the rush to "be present"—in spatial and in temporal terms, to be "there" and to be in the present moment—Pater's aestheticism also promises an active, prehensile and formative capacity to grasp and focus those moments as they pass:

> While all melts under our feet, we may well grasp at any exquisite passion or any contribution to knowledge that seems by a lifted horizon to set the spirit free for a moment. (***R,*** 237)

Pater's exhortation here means not only that "we may as well" grasp but also that we may do it well—that is, skillfully—though through the years most readers have heard Pater resignedly making the best of a bad situation and have missed the overtone promising skill and strength. This active, prehensile attention, which "may well grasp" and "fix on" moments before they pass, is one answer to the "passage and dissolution" of modern thought.

This notion of mental attachment in the moment allows for tropes of reduction and contraction to be revalued as concentration and stillness—the answering opposite of the rapid mental dissolution of paragraph two. The famous injunction "to burn always with that hard, gemlike flame" may be seen, then, as the culminating moment in Pater's transvaluation of "modern thought." This figure portrays mental life as intense, concentrated, and pointedly organized, not as fragmentary, chaotic, and dissolute. Because the discourse of modern science in paragraph one had represented the passage of our physical life as "flamelike," and the discourse of modern philosophy in paragraph two had described impressions that "burn and are extinguished with our consciousness of them," this well-known Paterian figure might literally be said to fight fire with fire. Gerald Monsman, wittily recognizing Pater's gesture of responsiveness here, has remarked that the "hard, gemlike flame" evokes "the spirit of the Bunsen burner" no less than "the spirit of the waxen candle in a holy place."[19]

On the other hand, the aesthetic stance promises not only concentration in the "moment" but also—paradoxically—expansion as well. As a response to the brevity of life, "our one chance lies in expanding that interval"; in that attempt "we may well grasp" at anything "that seems by a lifted horizon to set the spirit free for a moment." In this apparent contradiction, we may once again recognize Pater's attempt to imagine a response to the seemingly opposite problems of modern thought: fragmentation and solipsism. Tropes of contraction and intensity respond to the speed of the "stream" in its "passage," while tropes of expansion "set the spirit free" from its figurative imprisonment. The paradoxical joining of contraction and expansion is resolvable only in temporal terms, not in spatial terms, as experience—or as literature—not as philosophical systematics. The key here is mobility or movement, shifts in attention that temporalize what was before, invidiously, conceivable only as the spatial figure of the prison. The mind in the act of passing "swiftly from point to point" constantly moves "outside" or "beyond" its former frame of awareness. There is a sense of freedom in this constant activation of a self-consciousness that is now no longer fixated, immobilized, and spatially "contained," but is constantly moving outside itself, away from one point in time and toward another moment and another point of view.

Pater is proposing a dynamic of attention in which mobility or "quickening" plays off against fixation, "grasp," or "apprehension." What we find here, in the terms of our earlier discussion, amounts to a transvaluation of the "passage" as an activity of the shaping mind, interrupted by moments that have themselves been redefined as moments of active focus. As a description of an epistemological strategy, we can begin now to hear in the word "passage" both its musical and its textual senses, for this mental strategy involves a regulated articulation of time's passage in which extended phrases of play are punctuated by moments of "apprehension" or fixity. Responding to the mental chaos engendered by "modern thought," Pater has created an order by distinguishing the "moments" from their correlative, ongoing, overarching "passages." This model has the double advantage of marking out brief points of stillness and yet also liberating those moments of focus from any sense of permanent immobilization because they are constantly taken up in an overarching mobility. Both "moment" and "passage" are endowed, in this model, with the conscious shaping power of aesthetic formation.[20] And this transvaluation of "moments" and their "passages" (each in itself and in relation to the other) has consequences also for the figure of the "prisoner," as we have just seen. For now the spatial metaphorics of solipsism can be transformed in successive moments of ecstasy, as consciousness evades entrapment by continually moving outside or beyond its former point of view.

"To burn always with this hard, gemlike flame, to maintain this ecstasy, is success in life." The aesthetic "ecstasy" recommended here—in its literal sense of "standing apart from (oneself)"—is as important to "maintain" as the intensity and concentration of the "hard, gemlike flame." We may note in passing that this figure of ecstasy also involves an important metaphorical transvaluation of "modern thought": the essential self as "prisoner" has been succeeded and joined by an overseeing self, standing outside itself. Thus this passage is important because it offers us a way to see what Pater imagined as the "multiplied" consciousness. In one sense I am simply pointing to Pater's embrace of the figure of self-division familiar from romantic epistemology and poetics, but Pater turns it into an active, operating principle with new consequences. Not only does it represent to him a stance that can be actively chosen, taken and retaken moment by moment, rather than suffered, however passionately, but it also creates a space of difference, a figurative gap within consciousness across which an object may be perceivable again. This attempt to recreate a sense of objectivity places Pater directly in the mainstream of Victorian poetics, but his temporalizing of the ecstatic stance represents one of his crucial shifts toward the "modern."

What is at stake here is recreation of the sense of distance—a figurative and internal distance, to be sure, but one that will serve to reconstitute the grounds of a provisional objectivity. In his description of the aesthetically mobile, experimental state of mind, Pater describes a rhythm of identification and detachment that is, in effect, the mobilization of this internal distance. He cautions, for example, against any "interest into which we cannot enter, or some abstract theory we have not identified with ourselves." But he also warns against static fixation on any one object: "what we have to do is to be forever curiously testing new opinions and courting new impressions"; we must "gather up what might otherwise pass unregarded," and then we must pass on, detaching from one object in order to be receptive to another. At first the object, in its state of "identification" with the self, is practically invisible. But through a process of discrimination it can be distinguished from the perceiving consciousness, and it is through these oscillations in internal distance, these successive acts of identification and detachment, that the object is "objectively" perceivable again. Thus aesthetic experience permits a revised form of knowledge.[21]

We may see in this procedure the embrace of further self-consciousness as a dialectical "remedy" for the ills of self-consciousness itself, and in this sense it is a typically romantic gesture—here especially interesting in its historical sequence after one strain of romantic (Carlylean) and Victorian (Arnoldian) anti-self-consciousness.[22] But a better way to specify the literary-historical moment of this strategy would be to take Pater's own cues from the "Conclusion," where aesthetic "ecstasy" appears as an internalization of "objective" distance. Aestheticism, then, appears as an ironic transvaluation of the stance of scientific objectivity. Not only does the distance established by self-division serve, epistemologically speaking, to reconstitute any object as an "aesthetic object," but also historically speaking, Pater has blatantly presented his solution after a summary representation of the specifically contemporary ills it was designed to cure. In other words, he marks this particular "solution" explicitly as a return to rethink romantic self-consciousness and the role of art "after"—meaning "later in time," as well as "in imitation of" and "against or in reaction to"—the specific developments of contemporary science and philosophy.[23] We can see the sense in which his version of "aesthetic distance" is offered as a figurative simulacrum structured on the model of scientific or "objective" distance, and his aesthetic method of representing knowledge of an object is modeled as a cross between the methods offered by skeptical scientific empiricism and epistemological philosophy.

This provisionally objective stance enables an object to be perceived once more, but the object has now been relativized, reconstituted in relation to the subject. According to this model, the "aesthetic object" is "aesthetic" largely because it is admittedly recreated within the perceiving consciousness. This explains the curious circularity of one tenet of aestheticism: that any object can become an "aesthetic object" when regarded in the "aesthetic attitude."[24] We can see all this clearly in the following passage from the "Preface," where Pater's revision of Arnold figures prominently:

> "To see the object as in itself it really is," has been justly said to be the aim of all true criticism whatever; and in aesthetic criticism the first step toward seeing one's object as it really is, is to know one's own impression as it really is, to discriminate it, to realize it distinctly. The objects with which aesthetic criticism deals, music, poetry, artistic and accomplished forms of human life, are indeed receptacles of so many powers or forces; they possess, like natural elements, so many virtues or qualities. What is this song or picture, this engaging personality presented in life or in a book, to *me*? What effect does it really produce on me? . . . How is my nature modified by its presence, and under its influence? The answers to these questions are the original facts with which the aesthetic critic has to do; and, as in the study of light, of morals, of number, one must realize such primary data for oneself, or not at all. . . . The aesthetic critic, then, regards all the objects with which he has to do, all works of art, and the fairer forms of nature and human life, as powers or forces producing pleasurable sensations, each of a more or less peculiar and unique kind. This influence he feels, and wishes to explain, analyzing it, and reducing it to its elements. (***R***, viii-ix)

The sly subversion of Arnold here has frequently, and "justly," been noted as the very linchpin of Pater's revisionary, aesthetic procedure.[25] However, his introductory claim to be following Arnold's dictum is not a simple pretense but a complex and dialectical gesture. For one thing, it is in ways like this that Pater signals his awareness of his own particular historical moment, the proximate source or immediate precursor of his position, and his own critical difference from that precursor. In turning away from the "aim" of objectivity, he does not turn away entirely, and he puts in its place not the subjectivism with which he is continually—and wrongly—associated, but a regulated process, a method of recreating a provisional objectivity through a dynamic of internalization and discrimination within.

To answer the famous question "What is this . . . to *me*?" is not Pater's final "aim," after all, but only the "first step" in a dialectical model of self-consciousness, whose aim is finally to discriminate the object again by analyzing its "influence" within the aesthetic critic:

> The function of the aesthetic critic is to distinguish, analyze, and separate from its adjuncts, the virtue by which a picture, a landscape, a fair personality in life or in a book, produces this special impression of beauty or pleasure, to indicate what the source of that impression is, and under what conditions it is experienced. His end is reached when he has disengaged that virtue, and noted it, as a chemist notes some natural element. (***R***, ix-x)

Those "adjuncts" are partly in the object and partly in its context, which is, in this frame of reference, the mind of the observer. The "disengagement" of the object's "power" or "virtue" is a second-order process: first the aesthetic object must be distinguished from its context in the self—through its "impression" and the way that pressing force shifts the internal shape of things—and only then can one quality of the object be distinguished from another. And if the experiences of its effects on the subject are the "original facts" or "primary data," then the knowledge of the object would be a "secondary" result of this analysis. This process of "disengagement" is modeled here on the process of chemical analysis, and that explicit analogy tacitly assigns to the aesthetic critic the function of answering the "analysis" of one science with a scientific analysis of his own.

This line of thought suggests that Pater's particular "impressionism" should be more rigorously identified as a late romantic model of the correlation of poetic imagination, science, and philosophy. Above all, his impressionism must be understood in the plastic sense of "impression," for it represents a mode of renewed belief in the possibility of internalizing the experience of real objects from a real outside.[26] (One result of this reconstituted and aesthetic "objectivity" may be seen in a related shift in the notion of "content." Though objects are still called "receptacles," they contain not "content" but the "powers or forces" of "influence."[27] Impressed with an object from the outside, the critical consciousness then scrutinizes itself for the "influence" of the object on its own "modified" configurations. Pater will use a wide range of figures for this relation, especially figures of backgrounding and foregrounding, in which the object is figuratively cast into "relief" against the background of an experiencing or observant subject.

Aesthetic "objectivity" remains provisional. It is always to be regarded as figurative, not "given" by the object as data but "made" from the object's effect on the subject, not absolute but relative, and continually in the process of being reconstituted through this dialectic of identification and detachment. By asking the crucial question—"what does it mean to *me*?"—an aesthetic, analytical, observant aspect of the subject differentiates itself from the receptive, vulnerable, "impressed" aspect of the subject laboring in the toils of experience. At any given moment, in other words, the aesthetic stance of self-division stops the uncontrolled "flux" with a sense of fixated attention. And, as we have seen, this very activity also seems to reduce the experience of time to fragments, isolated moments "with no before and after," as T. S. Eliot would later complain. However, when this same stance is mobilized in time, figured in temporal terms, it gains an operational value of another kind, for the aesthetic method is not only a method of positioning attention in such a way as to recreate the object. In Pater the romantic "ecstasy" of self-division also establishes an instrumental position from which an organized and totalized sense of the experiencing consciousness may be restored. The aesthetic, "critical" division within the subject is mobilized in time so that it may precipitate the sense of continuous identity, the sense of "self."

How does this work? With each self-conscious move "outside" or "beyond" itself, the subject establishes a still point, a present moment from which the "passage" of experience will then be regarded in the past. In other words, the gap constructed between one part of the self and another is refigured as the space of difference between present and past. By the time it is discriminated from the subject and perceivable as an object again, the object has already been reconceived, reconstituted, remembered. Analogously, that aspect of the subject which had been "impressed" has now been reformed; the "impression" records a former state of being, now remembered. Mobilized in time, as one moment of self-division succeeds another, the aesthetic position becomes the federating power of memory. In the mobility of these recreative self-divisions, both object and self are correlatively reconstituted as distinct and whole—but in the past and *as* the past.

The interrelated dynamics of attention I have been discussing as the method of Pater's aestheticism—both the dynamic of mobility and fixation (figured as the passage punctuated by moments of focus) and the dynamic of romantic self-division (figured as "impression" followed by detachment or "ecstasy")—reconstitute the self in relation to its objects as a function of retrospection. It should be possible now to see the conservative force of Pater's aestheticism—and to begin an approach to his historicism. When cast in temporal terms, these dynamics of attention project the "passages" of experience into an ideal, overarching continuity of attention, a personal identity in time. Put another way, Pater uses the language of temporality to recontain the self as a whole. Perhaps it is clear that these operations yield not the "substratum" Pater wanted to intuit from Kant, but rather a decentered, "outer" layer of awareness always in the process of reforming. Describing Goethe as the type of his aesthetic attitude, Pater wrote that "such natures rejoice to be away from and past their former selves" (***R***, 229). That "former" self is also the "formed" self, from whom the reforming self, in its continually reconstructed present moment, continually flees away.

Nevertheless, though Pater theorizes this decentering flight into an absolute present, he does so from within the traditional commitment to a central self. In fact, he finally does so in order to conserve its centrality and wholeness in a sense of history or continuity.[28] Surely this is one reason that Pater should be reexamined in our current critical moment. In an effort to preserve its wholeness, this aesthetically or critically divided self is continually in the process of projecting a transcendent identity to oversee its own passages of experience. That the metaphysical implications of this projection are undergoing a rigorous critique today should make Pater more, not less, interesting to us.[29] Pater is explicitly aware of his aesthetic projection of identity—as I shall show in discussing ***Marius the Epicurean***—and aware also that the projection of an overarching history is its necessary corollary. Throughout his work, Pater employs a transformed, secularized version of Bunyan's "House Beautiful" as an image of the transcendent place where disparate moments of individual and cultural time are gathered together and restored. Of course, this end point, the result of Pater's aesthetic dialectic, is Hegelian and sublationary—as is so much of Pater, including all the formal techniques explored in this brief section: his dialectical transvaluation of metaphor, the subsumption of distinct moments in their "passage," the notion of memory as the overarching re-collection of successive moments of self-division.

Pater's attempt to reread the figurative "distance" of self-consciousness as a difference between present and past should remind us that in the nineteenth century the notion of scientific objectivity was often conceived as historical distance. It is within the historical realm that the already-made thing, the work of art, becomes the exemplary instance of Pater's aesthetic solution. As the quintessential relic from the past, the work of art is effective *because* it is definitively and already "different" from the self in the present. . . .

Notes

1. For dating of the essays, see Samuel Wright, *A Bibliography of the Writings of Walter H. Pater* (New York: Garland, 1975). "Winckelmann" was published in 1867 and therefore antedates "Poems by William Morris." Inman has forcefully argued that Pater originally intended to conclude the volume of Renaissance studies with his essay on Wordsworth. See Billie Andrew Inman, *Walter Pater's Reading: A Bibliography of His Library Borrowings and Literary References, 1858-1873* (New York: Garland, 1981), pp. 264-66.
2. For a recent example, see Perry Meisel, *The Absent Father: Virginia Woolf and Walter Pater* (New Haven, Conn.: Yale University Press, 1980), pp. 114-15, and Inman's response to Meisel in "The Intellectual Context of Walter Pater's 'Conclusion,'" *Prose Studies* 4 (May 1981), 13.
3. Richard Wollheim, "Walter Pater as a Critic of the Arts," *On Art and the Mind* (Cambridge, Mass.: Harvard University Press, 1974), pp. 161-64: "Without in any way being seduced by the theory, we are made to feel its seductiveness; and we are made to feel it not the less but the more so for our comparative detachment or distancing. Initially we might take the passage . . . as though it asserted the very theory it was about: but, as we read on, the passage puts itself into inverted commas for us. . . . [W]e do right to take the passage obliquely and not literally. It does not address us, we overhear what it says." See Graham Hough's partial recognition in *The Last Romantics* (1947; reprint, London: Methuen, 1961), p. 140: "But Pater does not really mean it."
4. *Cratylus* 402a. I have used the unidentified translation given by Gerald Monsman in *Pater's Portraits: Mythic Patterns in the Fiction of Walter Pater* (Baltimore, Md.: Johns Hopkins University Press, 1967), p. 4. On Pater's similar response to the *Thaetetus,* see Inman, "The Intellectual Context of Pater's 'Conclusion,'" p. 19. For the figurative comparison of "mythic" recapitulation in the history of thought to "translation," see Herbert N. Schneidau, *Sacred Discontent: The Bible and Western Tradition* (Baton Rouge: Louisiana State University Press, 1976).
5. Huxley's famous essay "On the Physical Basis of Life" was not published until 1869 in the *Fortnightly Review,* but for the sources of Pater's vision of modern science, see Inman, "The Intellectual Context of Pater's 'Conclusion,'" pp. 13-16; Inman, *Pater's Reading,* pp. 182-92; and Donald Hill's textual and explanatory notes to Pater's *The Renaissance: Studies in Art and Poetry, The 1893 Text,* ed. Donald L. Hill (Berkeley: University of California Press, 1980), pp. 451-54 (hereafter, Hill's notes). Inman points out that this scientific vision entailed a redefined understanding of identity.
6. *Hamlet,* 5.1.
7. On atomism, see Harold Bloom, introduction to *Selected Writings of Walter Pater,* ed. Harold Bloom (New York: Columbia University Press, 1982), p. xv: "Pater's strange achievement is to have assimilated Wordsworth to Lucretius, to have compounded an idealistic naturalism with a corrective materialism." On the Victorian concept of inextricable interrelation, see Josephine Miles, *Poetry and Change* (Berkeley: University of California Press, 1974), p. 126; and John Holloway, "Thought, Style, and the Idea of Co-Variance in Some Mid-Nineteenth-Century Prose," *Studies in the Literary Imagination* 8 (Fall 1975), 1-14.
8. Hill's notes, p. 273.
9. And many others. In addition to Locke, Hume, Berkeley, and Kant, Inman mentions Fichte, Bacon, Hegel, and Plato (*Walter Pater's Reading,* pp. 182-92); see also Hill's notes, pp. 454-55.
10. For my reading of Pater's impressionism, see below, Part One, sec. 3; and Part One, sec.7.

11. For a recent treatment of these anecdotes and of the romantic responses to the anxieties of solipsism, see Charles Rzepka, *The Self as Mind* (Cambridge, Mass.: Harvard University Press, 1985).

12. Hill's notes, p. 455.

13. For variations on the figure of imprisonment and the desire for a "sense of escape" or a "sense of freedom," see, e.g., "Aesthetic Poetry" (B, 190, 193) and "Winckelmann" (R, 231).

14. Inman sees here two separate discourses and a "central inconsistency" between them (Inman, "The Intellectual Context of Pater's 'Conclusion,'" p. 13), but Meisel notes their crucial interrelation, though he misses the obliquity of the two paragraphs (Perry Meisel, *The Absent Father* [New Haven: Yale University Press, 1980], pp. 114-15).

15. Pater's formulation, in Hill's notes, p. 455.

16. He makes this clear in the famous footnote restoring the "Conclusion" to the third edition of *The Renaissance,* after its suppression in the second. For the wording of that footnote, see below, Part Three, sec. 2.

17. For the ongoing argument about whether aestheticism should be understood as a "movement," see Ruth Z. Temple, "Truth in Labelling: Pre-Raphaelitism, Aestheticism, Decadence, Fin-de-Siècle," in *English Literature in Transition* 17, no. 4 (1974), 201-22; and Ian Fletcher, "Some Aspects of Aestheticism," in *Twilight of Dawn: Studies in English Literature in Transition* (Tucson: University of Arizona Press, 1987), pp. 1-31. Germain d'Hangest assigns Pater "the decisive role" in the aesthetic movement in "La Place de Walter Pater dans le mouvement esthétique," *Études anglaises* 27 (April-June 1974), 158-71.

18. This passage is rarely seen, having never been reprinted after its 1868 publication in the *Westminster Review,* n.s. 34 [October 1868], 300-312, until Hill's 1980 edition of the 1893 *Renaissance.* Following these words, the first two paragraphs of the "Conclusion" appear quite clearly as an exercise in the ironic ventriloquism of "modern thought": "One characteristic of the pagan spirit these new poems have which is on their surface—the continual suggestion, pensive or passionate, of the shortness of life; this is contrasted with the bloom of the world and gives new seduction to it; the sense of death and the desire of beauty; the desire of beauty quickened by the sense of death. '*Arriéré*!' you say, 'here in a tangible form we have the defect of all poetry like this. The modern world is in possession of truths; what but a passing smile can it have for a kind of poetry which, assuming artistic beauty of form to be an end in itself, passes by those truths and the living interests which are connected with them, to spend a thousand cares in telling once more these pagan fables as if it had but to choose between a more and a less beautiful shadow?' It is a strange transition from the earthly paradise to the sad-coloured world of abstract philosophy. But let us accept the challenge; let us see what modern philosophy, when it is sincere, really does say about human life and the truth we can attain in it, and the relation of this to the desire of beauty" (Hill's notes, p. 272). David DeLaura explained this setting of the "Conclusion" in *Hebrew and Hellene in Victorian England: Newman, Arnold, and Pater* (Austin: University of Texas Press, 1969), pp. 224-25.

19. Monsman, *Pater's Portraits,* p. xvi.

20. The articulation of this systematic relation marks Pater's revision of the Wordsworthian "spots of time." As all revisions are, his revision was both an advance (toward Joyce's "epiphanies" and Woolf's "moments of being") and a return (for this systematic relation is embodied throughout *The Prelude*). For a short history of the epiphanic moment, which unaccountably slights Pater's pivotal role, see M. H. Abrams, "Varieties of the Modern Moment," in his *Natural Supernaturalism* (New York: Norton, 1971), pp. 418-27; and Bloom, introduction to Pater's *Selected Writings,* pp. x-xv. Bloom argues that Pater "de-idealizes" the epiphany by effecting a return to Wordsworth after Ruskin's critique of the pathetic fallacy.

21. This internal distance is related to but different from what is commonly called "aesthetic distance," which is usually taken to mean the adoption of an "aesthetic attitude" toward an object or event that might under most circumstances seem to demand a more practical response. See Edward Bullough's 1912 essay, "'Psychical Distance' as a Factor in Art and an Aesthetic Principle," in Marvin Levich, ed., *Aesthetics and the Philosophy of Criticism* (New York: Random House, 1963), pp. 233-54. Though Bullough mentions the dynamics of internal "distance" or self-division, the essay concentrates on the "outward" consequences of that assumed distance, in the turning away from utilitarian or practical considerations. The initial example given (which incidentally recalls the aesthetics of Ruskin, Turner, and Whistler) involves appreciating a fog at sea for its beauty rather than exerting oneself actively in the pursuit of safety.

22. The *locus classicus* is Geoffrey Hartman's essay "Romanticism and 'Anti-Self-Consciousness,'" revised and expanded in Harold Bloom, ed., *Romanticism and Consciousness: Essays in Criticism* (New York: Norton, 1970), pp. 46-56. For an excellent critique of this romantic self-characterization, see Jerome J. McGann, *The Romantic Ideology* (Chicago: University of Chicago Press, 1983), pp. 40-41.

23. D'Hangest also argues that Pater's aestheticism was "based . . . directly on the contemporary disenchantment; he derived it from that very disenchantment and presented it as a remedy, the only one possible,

for the confusion in which scientific progress had plunged Victorian spirits" (quoted in Hill's notes, p. 451).

24. On this circularity and the general dilemma of the "aesthetic attitude" in relation to the constitution of an "aesthetic object," see Monroe C. Beardsley, "Aesthetic Objects" and "Postscript 1980," in *Aesthetics: Problems in the Philosophy of Criticism* (1958; rpt. Indianapolis, Ind.: Hackett, 1981), pp. xvii-74.

25. On the complex relation of Pater to Arnold, see David DeLaura, *Hebrew and Hellene in Victorian England.* On Pater in relation to Arnold's "object," see Richard Ellmann, *The Critic as Artist: Critical Writings of Oscar Wilde* (New York: Vintage, 1968), pp. xi-xii. "There are not two but three critical phases in the late nineteenth century, with Pater transitional between Arnold and Wilde. . . . In 1864 . . . Arnold declared . . . that the 'aim of criticism is to see the object as in itself it really is.' . . . Nine years later Walter Pater [pretended] . . . to agree with Arnold's definition. . . . But Pater's corollary subtly altered the original proposition; it shifted the center of attention from the rock of the object to the winds of the perceiver's sensations. . . . [E]ighteen years later . . . Wilde rounded on Arnold by asserting that the aim of criticism is to see the object as it really is not." Bloom (introduction to Pater's *Selected Writings,* p. viii) repeats this formulation in 1974 and adds: "Between Arnold's self-deception and Wilde's wit comes Pater's hesitant and skeptical emphasis upon a peculiar kind of vision."

26. The best discussion of critical impressionism in its Swinburnean sense may be found in Jerome J. McGann, *Swinburne: An Experiment in Criticism* (Chicago: University of Chicago Press, 1972), pp. 14-23. Pater's style is deeply influenced by Swinburne throughout, and he does of course engage in famous passages of this sort of impressionism—for example, in his reading of the Mona Lisa. But as Wellek pointed out, these passages are rare in Pater and are not representative of his method (René Wellek, *The History of Modern Criticism: 1750-1950,* vol. 4: *The Later Nineteenth Century* [New Haven, Conn.: Yale University Press, 1965], p. 382).

27. Crinkley points out that the notion of the object in "eternal outline" gives way to the notion of the object as "receptacle." See Richmond Crinkley, *Walter Pater: Humanist* (Lexington: University of Kentucky Press, 1970), p. 9.

28. For a discussion of the conflict between modernity and the concept of history, see Paul de Man, "Literary History and Literary Modernity," in his *Blindness and Insight: Essays in the Rhetoric of Contemporary Criticism* (1971; reprint, Minneapolis: University of Minnesota Press, 1983), pp. 142-65.

29. The names Foucault and Derrida will suffice to indicate the broad outlines of that critique, but I mean specifically to call attention here to their stress on the correlative projections of the unitary subject and of an overarching history. Thus Foucault, in *The Archaeology of Knowledge,* trans. A. M. Sheridan Smith (New York: Pantheon, 1972), p. 12: "Continuous history is the indispensable correlative of the founding function of the subject: the guarantee that everything that has eluded him may be restored to him; the certainty that time will disperse nothing without restoring it in a reconstituted unity; the promise that one day the subject—in the form of historical consciousness—will once again be able to appropriate, to bring back under his sway, all those things that are kept at a distance by difference, and find in them what might be called his abode. Making historical analysis the discourse of the continuous and making human consciousness the original subject of all historical development and all action are the two sides of the same system of thought." Derrida makes a similar argument toward the end of his "Structure, Sign, and Play in the Discourse of the Human Sciences," in *Writing and Difference,* trans. Alan Bass (Chicago: University of Chicago Press, 1978), p. 291: "It could be shown that the concept of *epistèmè* has always called forth that of *historia,* if history is always the unity of a becoming, as the tradition of truth or the development of science or knowledge oriented toward the appropriation of truth in presence and self-presence, toward knowledge in consciousness-of-self."

John J. Conlon (essay date 1990)

SOURCE: "Walter Pater and the Art of Misrepresentation," in *Annals of Scholarship,* Vol. 7, No. 2, 1990, pp. 165-79.

[*In the following essay, Conlon examines several of Pater's "artful misrepresentations" and argues that they were created to more fully present Pater's "imaginative sense of fact."*]

> Oh Galuppi, Baldassaro, this is very sad to find!
> I can hardly misconceive you; it would prove me deaf
>   and blind;
> But although I take your meaning, 'tis with such
>   a heavy mind!
>
> —Browning, "A Toccata of Galuppi's" (1855)

One immediate problem with the issue of representation/misrepresentation in Victorian art and letters is that it is embedded within the ubiquitous question of authority in Victorian culture: who is to decide what, in criticism, is a representation or a misrepresentation of Leonardo's "Mona Lisa" or, in painting, of a rocket falling in the night sky above Cremorne Gardens? In Charles Dickens's *Hard Times* (1854) an approving Inspector of Schools agrees with Bitzer's standard definition of a horse and wrathfully explains to the cowering children of the Gradgrind School why they would not paper a room with representations of horses: "horses do not walk up and down the sides of rooms in reality" and "you are not to see anywhere, what you don't see in fact; you are not to have anywhere, what you don't have in fact. What is called Taste, is only another name for Fact" (Dickens, 51). Such artistic representations of horses and their arrangement in a room are, it seems, misrepresentations.

Dickens here anticipates an aesthetic dogma set down by another Inspector of Schools, Matthew Arnold, in "On Translating Homer" (1862):

> Of the literature of France and Germany, as of the intellect of Europe in general, the main effort, for now many years, has been a critical effort; the endeavour, in all branches of knowledge, theology, philosophy, history, art, science, to see the object as in itself it really is. (Arnold, I, 140)

At the risk of laboring the obvious: criticism following Arnold's tenet presents accurate representations; that which does not, misrepresentations.

Poised against both School Inspectors is Walter Pater (1839-1894) who, subverting Arnold and the School of Fact, asserts:

> "To see the object as in itself it really is," has been justly said to be the aim of all true criticism whatever; and in aesthetic criticism the first step toward seeing one's object as it really is, is to know one's own impression as it really is, to discriminate it, to realise it distinctly. (Pater, ***Renaissance,*** xix)

For Pater, the modification of Arnold's phrase and stance allows for true representation in criticism and Arnold's unmodified posture becomes the vehicle for misrepresentation since it denies the instrumentality of the critic, the role of the critic's personality in shaping a representation, and, as Pater was to outline and Oscar Wilde was to name, the place of the Critic as Artist.

With the decline and near demise of Pater's critical importance and reputation in the first half of the twentieth century, thanks to Paul Elmer More, T. S. Eliot (Arnold's ephebe, in Harold Bloom's locution) and the prophets of the New Criticism, the critical field has gone to Arnold and the illusion of objectivity (Bloom, 13). For decades, then, as Bloom characterizes it, "Most of what the Academy considers acceptable critical style is of course merely a worn-out Neoclassical diction, garlanded with ibids, and civilly purged of all enthusiasm" (Bloom, *ibid.*). In deference to Arnold's victory and conventional, received authority, I will treat Pater's art as one of misrepresentation although it may indeed turn out to be a true or truer representation as we find it approaching the condition of fine art.

Pater's art of misrepresentation has not fared well in the past century. Various writers have expressed consternation, dismay, opprobrium, amusement and condescension upon their discovering lapses, errors and "misrepresentations" in the work of this most important of late Victorian critics. In Pater's own time, to use one representative instance, Mrs. Mark Pattison argued that the title of his first volume, ***Studies in the History of the Renaissance*** (1873), was inappropriate; Pater seems to have inappropriately agreed with her and changed the title, more, perhaps, to avoid argument than to alter his method. This alteration amounts to a self-misrepresentation since his work, historically based, is indeed a series of studies in the history of the Renaissance. When, early in this century, Samuel C. Chew found himself entangled in those of Pater's quotations culled from various sources and presented as unified discourses, he upbraided Pater for misleading his readers and misrepresenting his sources. Helen H. Law, in a monument of philological scholarship, cleared Pater of Chew's charges in his handling of classical Greek texts, although Paul Shorey had earlier noted some "fanciful" translations and interpretations of phrases from Plato's *Republic.* T. S. Eliot, though not at all averse to borrowing key concepts and phrases from Pater, derided him for his alleged misreadings/misrepresentations of Shakespeare and others. More recently, Christopher Ricks joined the chorus of complaint about Pater's quotations as misrepresentations, a complaint Gerald Monsman effectively answered by claiming that Pater's project is a lifelong essay in "criticism-as-creative-self-portraiture" in which he "modifies his readers' conception of the past and creates his precursors anew in his own self-image" (Monsman, *Autobiography,* 13). Without disagreeing with Monsman's persuasive rebuttal of the literal-minded, I would elaborate a parallel project I find in Pater, one that springs from the very starting-place Monsman takes, and assert that in his works Pater is seeking to create artful misrepresentations and to make a high art of misrepresentation, one that extends to the art of self-misrepresentation.

If, as Harold Bloom asserts, all strong reading is misreading, then one ramification of this dictum is that all strong representation is misrepresentation (Bloom, 16). Writing of authentic instances of the voice of the critic Bloom observes: "The great theorist of voice *as voice* remains Oscar Wilde, when he reminds us, following Walter Pater, how important it is that the critical imagination never fall into careless habits of accuracy. We must see the object, the poem, as in itself it really is not, because we must see not only what is missing, but why the poem had to exclude what is missing" (Bloom, 13). As Monsman puts it, "For Pater the act of autobiography begins with a question about his subjective or personal response to artistic presentation: 'What is this song or picture, this engaging personality presented in life or in a book, to *me*? What effect does it really produce on me? Does it give me pleasure? How is my nature modified by its presence and under its influence?'" (Monsman, *Autobiography,* 13; Pater, ***Renaissance,*** xix-xx). Citing Pater on the critical method of Charles Lamb, in particular the interpretation of the charm one feels in considering art or life and conveying that charm, Monsman continues to quote from Pater: "he seeming to himself but to hand on to others, in mere humble ministration, that of which for them he is really the creator—this is the way of criticism" (Monsman, *Autobiography,* 13; Pater, ***Appreciations,*** 112). Criticism, then, in Pater's hands becomes something quite different from the mimetic objectification some would claim for it and indeed becomes a rival creation, a fine art Pater sought to figure forth in **"Style."** In what follows as I examine several instances of Pater's "misrepresentation," one of my objects is to illustrate the unity of his thought in the modifications he brought to bear upon his "objects" as they presented themselves to be modified by him. Another is to point out some instances of revision as self-revision and self-misrepresentation, again in keeping with the unity of his thought.

To trace the history of Pater's art of misrepresentation throughout his thirty-year career as a writer is to attempt to grasp all of Western culture and to relate it to his consistent, determined effort to draw it into his circle of consciousness and to express it in a form of discourse rippling outward from the center of that consciousness. Further, one must grant his premise, as most critics prior to the 1950s did not, that he is bodying forth in language his aesthetic representation of what those things he writes of mean to him. To elaborate Monsman's trope, Pater's work is his song of himself as a consciousness integrating and synthesizing disparate elements of knowledge and experience.

Pater's first volume, ***Studies in the History of the Renaissance*** (1873), implicitly challenged the most prominent and prolific art critic in Victorian England, John Ruskin, who, out of anxious propriety, had dismissed (and thus misrepresented) the Renaissance as a merely pagan, sensuous era. For Pater, however, the luxuriousness was attractive and the sense of decay alluring; both elements present in much Renaissance work seemed important to a right understanding of preceding and subsequent cultural phenomena and of himself. In effect, as Pater makes clear in his "Preface" (***Renaissance,*** xix) the many attempts to define beauty in the abstract as Ruskin, his readers would recall, had done in the early volumes of *Modern Painters* amount to misrepresentations since the only true representation must be a relative one.

Pater's ***Renaissance*** is a curious mix of representations, the "history" of which Mrs. Pattison found lacking because she missed the point of Pater's projects: the studies in history and the history of studies are precisely what Pater had in mind and presented. The "history," culled from the works of Jules Michelet, Giorgio Vasari, Stendhal, Edgar Quinet, Claude Charles Fauriel and others, is not the accumulation of dates, facts and events but their interpretation by a writer who today might be called an historian of ideas, bent upon pursuing those ideas, their representations, trends of emphasis and continuity. Pater's studies in history resemble not the scientific method Jules Michelet had authentically albeit spuriously proclaimed as his object but the actual practice of Michelet as interpreter of history. The lack of what she and the majority of her contemporaries regarded as accurate documentation appeared to Mrs. Pattison to support her judgment that Pater's "history" was misrepresentation; and this judgment itself misrepresents Pater, who is out to transform the presentation of history by writing his interpretation of it, what it means to him. Nonetheless, stung by varied hostile criticism of his work, he changed its title in its second (1877) and subsequent (1888; 1893) editions to ***The Renaissance: Studies in Art and Poetry*** and suppressed its "Conclusion" in 1877, an act he later mis/represented as arising from delicacy.

Among the patent "misrepresentations" in the book's first essay is the tale of Heloise and Abelard, one which Pater treats in typically romantic fashion, allying Abelard and Tannhäuser (a forerunner of Winckelmann, and both of Pater himself) and celebrating the triumph of the human spirit in the letters that pass between Heloise and her teacher/lover. Yet Pater passes lightly over Abelard's punishment, as he does over Tannhäuser's humiliation, as merely the unsympathetic responses of "adherents of the poorer and narrower culture" (***Renaissance,*** 6). A larger, more controversial "misrepresentation" is his celebration of a French "Renaissance in the end of the twelfth and the beginning of the thirteenth century, a Renaissance within the limits of the Middle Age itself" (***Renaissance,*** 1). One clue to Pater's larger design appears in this essay when, in a key passage, he elaborates a scheme of cultural continuity that will recur in the majority of his work:

> But in the *House Beautiful* the saints too have their place; and the student of the Renaissance has this advantage over the student of the emancipation of the human mind in the Reformation, or the French Revolution, that in tracing the footsteps of humanity to higher levels, he is not beset at every turn by the inflexibilities and antagonisms of some well-recognised controversy, with rigidly defined opposites, exhausting the intelligence and limiting one's sympathies. The opposition of the professional defenders of a mere system to that more sincere and generous play of the forces of human mind and character, which I have noted as the secret of Abelard's struggle, is indeed always powerful. But the incompatibility with one another of souls really "fair" is not essential; and within the enchanted region of the Renaissance, one needs not be for ever on one's guard. Here there are no fixed parties, no exclusions: all breathes of that unity of culture in which "whatsoever things are comely" are reconciled, for the elevation and adorning of our spirits. And just in proportion as those who took part in the Renaissance become centrally representative of it, just so much the more is this condition realised in them . . . the painter of the *Last Supper,* with his kindred, lives in a land where controversy has no breathing-place. They refuse to be classified. (***Renaissance,*** 20-21)

Just here is the edifice of art, the *House Beautiful* Pater had already identified in his review (1872) of Sidney Colvin's "Children in Italian and English Design," and repeated it later in his discussion of Wordsworth (1874) and in his wonderful misrepresentation, **"Romanticism"** (1876). This *House Beautiful,* unlike Tennyson's anxiety-filled Palace of Art, is a "home" to the various writers, artists and exemplars of "accomplished forms of human life" Pater sought to represent as living together harmoniously.

It is also a trope for Pater's own consciousness, a consciousness he represents in his essays as it has already "modified" the person or object it has contemplated. These strong representations, of Leonardo, Botticelli, Michelangelo, the Pleiade, Pico, Winckelmann (the subject of the book's last essay, there to close the circle begun with the allusion to Tannhäuser in its first) may, perhaps must, be misrepresentations since Pater has already prepared for them a dwelling place in his *House Beautiful* of consciousness, ringed round, we discover in the "Conclusion," by a "thick wall of personality."

Pater adds to his *House Beautiful* in **"On Wordsworth,"** an essay that had seven iterations, including one in ***Appreciations*** (1889) where it serves as an illustration of criticism as a "fine art" Pater established in that volume's lead essay, **"Style."** In discussing Wordsworth, Pater traces a "chapter in the history of the human mind," the growth of which is typically French—from Rousseau to Chateaubriand to Hugo—and includes writers "as unlike each other as Senancour and Théophile Gautier" and George Sand in a Wordsworthian context (***Appreciations,*** 43; 52). These, surely, are partially appropriate connections, but, as I have observed elsewhere, are less than usual associations and are not without a tinge of the sensational (*Walter Pater and the French Tradition,* ch. 3). When he discourses on the origins of the Romantic tradition, the pagan culture that brought forth the Greek gods, and mentions the many strange aftergrowths of that culture, we begin to see the holistic Pater linking the ancient past to the immediate past and both to the present, the present consciousness representing the link to the past in a proleptically Joycean vicus of recirculation (***Appreciations,*** 47-48). This circle includes, somewhat unexpectedly, "Saint Catherine of Sienna, who made the means to her ends so attractive that she won for herself an undying place in the *House Beautiful,* not by her rectitude of soul only, but by its 'fairness'—by those different qualities which command themselves to the poet and the artist" (***Appreciations,*** 60-61). Well!, as Pater sometimes writes, here is a jumble of mis/representations, of Wordsworth's guilt by association with George Sand and Gautier, of the innocence of all by association with Saint Catherine as we recall the passage from ***The Renaissance*** (cited above) concerning the *House Beautiful* in which "the saints too have their place."

So, too, in **"Romanticism"** we are confronted with manifold mis/representations. In describing the limited utility of distinctions between "classic" and "romantic" for aesthetic criticism, he supports his argument with an appeal to the authority of Sainte-Beuve to demonstrate that the "classic" is healthy and the "romantic" is sick, the former, "*énergique, frais, et dispos,*" the latter, "*faible, maladifs ou malades.*" Pater asserts that

> what in the eighteenth century is but an exceptional phenomenon, breaking through its fair reserve and discretion only at rare intervals, in the habitual guise of the nineteenth, breaking through it perpetually, with a feverishness, an incomprehensible straining and excitement, which all experience to some degree, but yearning also, in the genuine children of the romantic school, to be *énergique, frais, et dispos,* for those qualities of energy, freshness, comely order; and often, in Murger, in Gautier, in Charles Baudelaire, for instance, with singular felicity attaining them. (**"Romanticism,"** 67)

On one level Pater has engaged in a misrepresentation I do not believe is conscious: he has attributed to Sainte-Beuve words that the French critic actually translated from Goethe. This factual misrepresentation, possibly unnoticed by Pater, was not corrected in his later reprinting of **"Romanticism"** as the **"Postscript"** to ***Appreciations,*** a reprinting that I discuss below as an act of self-misrepresentation. A far deeper misrepresentation, of course, is his assertion that the work of Murger (in a later incarnation popularized by Puccini as *La Bohème*), Gautier and Baudelaire are "classic." This misrepresentation is again tied to Pater's pursuit of an appreciation of art and literature that transcends the "opposition of the professional defenders of a mere system" and ends when "all breathes of that unity of culture in which 'whatsoever things are comely' are reconciled" (***Renaissance,*** 20-21). We have returned again to the *House Beautiful.*

One further effort of the 1870s deserves attention in light of Pater's artful misrepresentations, his **"The School of Giorgione"** (1877; included in the third edition of ***The Renaissance***). Here Pater engages in a classic misrepresentation we fuss over today as an "attribution problem." In fact, as Patricia Clements has brilliantly demonstrated and as I have briefly noted, Pater's central focus in the essay is drawn from the writings of Charles Baudelaire in a series of internally undocumented translations from the French writer: he presents Baudelaire's thought and work as his own. Pater's object here, unlike that in **"Romanticism,"** was not to win for Baudelaire an English readership that could regard him as a "classic" writer; instead, his aim was to explore what the paintings he discusses mean "to him" in respect to their musical qualities and as modified by his knowledge of aesthetic theories promulgated by Baudelaire. As in earlier and subsequent "misrepresentations" of his sources, Pater was less concerned about seeing his objects as in themselves they really were and more interested in presenting them as modified by his own consciousness, desiderative, expectant, as he might put it. So, for example, when Pater describes but does not name synesthesia, he is leaning heavily upon Baudelaire's statements as he modified them. And when he writes of all art aspiring to the condition of music, he is applying his knowledge of Baudelaire to announce an aesthetic of harmony he wishes his readers to contemplate.

What are we to make of these associations in the harmonious *House Beautiful*? Who is represented and who is misrepresented by inclusion within it? Who must be misrepresented, traditionally speaking, to gain entry? Again I return to Monsman's idea of "criticism-as-creative-self-portraiture" to help explain what Pater is about, modified by my idea of "criticism-as-creative-misrepresentation" that evolves into creative self-misrepresentation as I trace some of Pater's next steps. While one could easily multiply examples of Paterian misrepresentation in the 1870s and in subsequent decades, four examples from the last several years of his career seem particularly noteworthy as representative of his artistic aims and practice—his handling of **"Style"** and Flaubert's place in it, his singular representation of Plato as the father of "art for art's sake," his odd handling of the "Conclusion" to ***The Renaissance,*** and his revisions in and of ***Appreciations.*** Each is a curious study in misrepresentation from an artistic point of view. Some amount to self-misrepresentation as Pater sought, on the one hand, to soften his public image and, on the other, in ***Plato and Platonism*** (1893), to solidify it through the time-honored appeal to authority.

"Style" provides several keys to Pater's thought and practice since it contains his carefully constructed argument in favor of prose style as a fine art and an articulated example of aesthetic criticism from the perspective he set down in the **"Preface"** to ***The Renaissance.*** In the first of the essay's three sections Pater is again at work blurring distinctions and denying their validity as he argues against treating poetry and prose as mutually exclusive forms of artistic expression. As he had done with "classic" and "romantic," so here he insists on a breadth of perspective that allows for an interpenetration of the realities that those terms seek to isolate. As is his custom, he seeks in his critical method a vehicle for the expression of personal meaning: with a logic internal to his method, he draws a distinction not between prose and verse but between the literature of power and the literature of knowledge, between the former which embodies an imaginative sense of fact and the latter as a mere reproduction of fact.

This expression of an imaginative sense of fact is the basis of his art. In a sentence that is retrospective to his procedure in ***The Renaissance,*** Pater writes: "Your historian, for instance, with absolutely truthful intention, amid the multitude of facts presented to him must needs select, and in selecting assert something of his own humour, something that comes not of the world without but of a vision within" (***Appreciations,*** 9). Further, he writes, "For just in proportion as the writer's aim, consciously or unconsciously, comes to be the transcribing, not of the world, not of mere fact, but of his sense of it, he becomes an artist, his work *fine* art" (***Appreciations,*** 9-10). Once again we are asked to consider the nature of the representation of the self in selecting and transcribing its own sense of phenomena and are made complicit, should we be persuaded by Pater's argument, in substituting self-representations or imaginative senses of facts for Gradgrindian Facts. His formulation of an alternative to the traditional representation of fact he terms "soul-fact." His criterion for judging the worth of literary art is its fidelity to the representation of one's imaginative sense of fact: "It will be good literary art not because it is brilliant or sober, or rich, or impulsive, or severe, but just in proportion as its representation of that sense, that soul-fact, is true, verse being only one department of such literature and imaginative prose, it may be thought, being the special art of the modern world" (***Appreciations,*** 11).

Allied to Pater's sense of the necessity of "soul" in style is his vision of "mind," an "architectural conception of work, which foresees the end in the beginning and never loses sight of it, and in every part is conscious of all the rest, till the last sentence does but, with undiminished vigor, unfold and justify the first . . ." (***Appreciations,*** 21). The unity of work Pater has in mind finds its expression for him in "the word that is associated with its import. The term is right, and has its essential beauty, when it becomes, in a manner, what it signifies, as with the names of simple sensations" (***Appreciations,*** 21). One must recall, nonetheless, that signification in Pater's universe is modified or conditioned signification: what does it signify to *me*?

"By mind," Pater recapitulates in the last paragraph of the essay's first segment, "the literary artist reaches us through static and objective indications of design in his works, legible to all. By soul, he reaches us, somewhat capriciously perhaps, one and not another, through vagrant sympathy and a kind of immediate contact" (***Appreciations,*** 25). This summary and the examples in the discussion that follows it provide a more than adequate basis for considering the whole essay, its subject and its content, as self-reflexive in both Monsman's autobiographical sense and my self-representational sense: as Pater elaborates his critical perspective he presents an example of the special art of the modern world, an example of fine art, in the very text he presents.

The second portion of the essay contains a classic case of mis-representation that involves, as I noted some years back, a conflation of excerpts from Flaubert's letters to several other correspondents (Maxime du Camp, Ernest Chevalier, Alfred le Poittevin) and their presentation as letters to the famous Mme. X., Louise Colet. This is clearly the sort of editorial and authorial practice we would find unacceptable in contemporary research, a practice that would earn a deserved rebuke for its flagrant misrepresentation. Such a modern response would be entirely appropriate in the exposition of shoddy scholarship since we have, as Bloom himself reminded us above, both explicit and implicit expectations of those who engage in academic discourse and of their work. Just here is the telling difference: Pater has prepared us not for fact but for an imaginative sense of fact; and we, as readers, choose an eccentric response should we hold him to the production of the literature of knowledge instead of the literature of power, if we demand of him "mind" without "soul." This, of course, is a common error in reading Pater's prose—it has surely been my error repeated in print over many years—to seek knowledge untempered by an imaginative sense of fact therein. I suggest that Pater's actual misrepresentation of Flaubert's addressees has, must have, another point.

That point, I believe, is embedded in Pater's references not to Louise, whose name he, of course, knew since it was both an "open secret" and also part of Maupassant's biography of Flaubert from which Pater translates and quotes without attribution, but to Mme. X. Subtly, in a way that has escaped detection for a century, Pater is the artist practicing the special art of the modern world by arranging fragments of letters, phrases, sentences, and addressing them from his "soul" to the "soul" reading the essay, the new Mme. X. It is she to whom Flaubert and Pater's sense of him, Pater's creation, "Flaubert," speaks his "mind" through Pater's design and arrangement. We are not, then, to focus upon facts but upon soul-facts: and to do so in no way diminishes either Flaubert's counsel or Pater's integration of it into his art work. That it is, objectively speaking, sheer misrepresentation leads me back to my notion of Pater's developing misrepresentation into an art, the special art of the modern world.

Before turning to what I call Pater's art of self-misrepresentation, the artful concealment of thought by suppressing its expression or altering its expression to further his own ends, it is useful to look at a glaring act of misrepresentation that adds to an appreciation of Pater's art. In ***Plato and Platonism,*** a series of lectures Pater claims were first delivered in 1891-1892 but may have existed prior to that academic year, he expropriates several elements of Plato's thought while attributing to Plato, in the process Monsman has characterized as creating his predecessors anew in his own image, some of his own notions. One idea in particular appears in Pater's **"Plato's Aesthetics"** in which he states that Plato, perhaps a weightier authority for Pater's contemporaries than for succeeding generations, is the ultimate source for the phrase "art for art's sake":

> Before him, you know, there had been no theorizing about the beautiful, its place in life, and the like: and as a matter of fact he is the earliest critic of the fine arts. He anticipates the modern notion that art as such has no end but its own perfection,—"art for art's sake." (*Plato,* 267-268)

Even those only cursorily acquainted with Plato's *Republic* and a vague recollection of its treatment of poets (Book X) would find this odd. Paul Shorey notes this (I, 58) among other of Pater's "fanciful" citations in his translation of the *Republic* and renders Plato's text, "Is there, then, for each of the arts any other advantage than to be as perfect as possible" (I, 59). Is Pater misrepresenting Plato? Literally, his is a fanciful misrepresentation, particularly since the phrase, "art for art's sake" had a very specific connotative burden in Pater's work and in his era. Yet Shorey, an enthusiastic reviewer of ***Plato and Platonism*** upon its publication (*Dial,* April 1893), makes room in his lifelong work on Plato for just such "fanciful" readings/misreadings:

> The right way to read Plato is fairly indicated by casual utterances of such critics as Renan, Pater, Emerson, and Emile Faguet. The captious attitude of mind is illustrated by the set criticism of Aristotle, the Christian Fathers, Zeller, De Quincy, Landor, Spencer, and too large a proportion of professional philologists and commentators. "As the poet too," says Emerson, "he (Plato) is only contemplative. . . . All his painting in the *Republic* must be esteemed mythological with the intent to bring out, sometimes in violent colours, his thought."
>
> This disposes at once of all criticism, hostile or friendly, aesthetic or philological, that scrutinizes the *Republic* as if it were a bill at its second reading in Parliament, or a draft of a constitution presented to an American state convention. (*Republic,* I, xxxii-xxxiii)

In short, Pater's reading of Plato's statement as that of an advocate of art for art's sake, while not explicitly condoned by Shorey, is yet indicative of a direction in the interpretation of Plato's thought Shorey finds acceptable and appropriate. Shorey, like Pater, can allow for an imaginative sense of fact; and Pater, in his commentaries on Plato, is putting that sense of fact to work in the production of the literature of power that makes use of what we recognize in the literature of knowledge as misrepresentation.

Pater's use of Plato as a proponent of art for art's sake in February, 1893 is also a salvo in his Twenty-Five-Years'-War at the barricades of *l'art pour l'art,* the last shot of which he would fire from camouflage as "art for its own sake" in the fourth edition of ***The Renaissance*** (December, 1893). It is the camouflaged version that I take to be one element in his art of self-misrepresentation, a self-defensive art he began to practice immediately after the first publication of ***The Renaissance*** in 1873. Apparently sensitive to adverse criticism, he not only altered the book's title in its second edition (1877) but also eliminated the "Conclusion" in which he had made the case for "art for art's sake." Restored to the third edition (1888) along with what may well be a misleading note, the essay was purged of such words as "religion" and "morality" but still contained the phrase central to the aesthetic creed. In this note Pater wrote that he had omitted the "Conclusion" from the work's second edition "as I conceived it might possibly mislead some of those young men into whose hands it might fall" and had made "some slight changes which bring it closer to my original meaning" (***Renaissance,*** 186). These changes, however, are cosmetic and not substantive except insofar as they remove the essay further from Pater's original meaning by toning down its radicalism and thus contributing to Pater's calculated self-misrepresentation.

Pater's art of self-misrepresentation may well be an attempt to mask himself from hostile criticism, to temper not his thought but its expression, to avoid controversy without sacrificing his aesthetic principles. What had begun with his changes to ***The Renaissance*** in its various forms also occurred, to some extent, in his handling of the novel, ***Marius the Epicurean*** (1885), as he excised segments from the first edition in preparing the second, and, to a greater and more telling extent, in his alterations to ***Appreciations. Appreciations, with an Essay on Style*** is composed of a series of essays on English literature, a subject then under discussion for inclusion in the curricula of Oxford and Cambridge Universities; that is the original plan and the format of the first edition. As noted above, the volume holds within it exercises in artistic misrepresentation; it also embodies Pater's art of self-misrepresentation in at least two notable instances.

Just as **"Romanticism"** set forth misrepresentations of the classic/romantic question, so its edited version as the

"Postscript" to ***Appreciations*** gives further evidence of Pater's art of self-misrepresentation. In the essay's first iteration he had manipulated the words of Goethe and Sainte-Beuve to place Baudelaire in his *House Beautiful.* Baudelaire's was a controversial name in the 1870s and, even though, following Pater's lead, George Saintsbury's first published essay was on Baudelaire, it remained a controversial one on the eve of the nineties. It was also one thing to praise Baudelaire in a literary journal and quite another to include his name in a published volume. Pater, in a frame of mind Monsman identifies and elaborates as something of a crisis at mid-life (*Autobiography*), removed all references to Baudelaire from the revised version of the essay as his "Postscript," at one point substituting Victor Hugo's name for Baudelaire's. This substitution vitiates, in one sense, the burden of Pater's earlier, more daring position and misrepresents, through mis-labeling, his advocacy of the patently shocking Baudelaire by turning it into a polite acceptance of the acceptable Hugo, the writer who had been lionized in death and accorded the highest of public obsequies in 1885.

A second concealment that amounts to a more serious act of self-misrepresentation appears in the differences between the first (November 1889) and the second (May 1890) editions of ***Appreciations.*** The first edition contains a more subdued version of his early review, **"Poems by William Morris"** (1868), as **"Aesthetic Poetry."** In the second, he replaced it with one of his weakest, least inspired reviews, **"Feuillet's *La Morte*"** thereby weakening the design and unity of the volume while, compensatorily, widening it to extend its subjects beyond English writing. One explanation for Pater's alteration of the book comes from Michael Field in the person of Katherine Bradley who noted the change in her journal for August 25, 1890, as reported by Samuel Wright: Pater "has struck out the ***Essay on Aesthetic Poetry in Appreciations*** because it gave offence to some pious person—he is getting hopelessly prudish in literature and defers to the moral weaknesses of everybody. Deplorable!" (Wright, 89). This may well be a self-masking to avoid controversy, a self-misrepresentation not unusual in Pater. The essay may indeed have been mildly off-putting to those with the moral weakness of propriety, though this is doubtful. More to the point, I think, was Pater's conscious decision to dissociate himself from the "aesthetic" production he knew of and would soon see in print in *Lippincot's Monthly Magazine* (July 1890), Oscar Wilde's *The Picture of Dorian Gray.* As Laurel Brake has suggested in speaking of Pater's association with Wilde in the period from 1888 to 1891, they disagreed about the novel and their disagreement may account for Pater's lukewarm review of the republished version (1891), too short on praise and too late to help, may form part of Pater's public retreat from the new aestheticism Wilde promulgated (see Conlon, "Brasenose," 29). My premise is that ***"Aesthetic Poetry"*** was withdrawn from ***Appreciations*** partly for its content and partly for its title. It is not, as I have shown, that Pater retreated from the formulation of "art for art's sake" or "art for its own sake." Rather, he engaged in an evasive self-misrepresentation both in the revised format of ***Appreciations*** and in his tepid review of Wilde's novel for motives that may have involved prudery, a mid-life turning, a sense that Wilde had gone too far in art, a fundamental disagreement over the reality of epicureanism. In any event, Pater muted the possibility of controversy by choosing to alter his public image but not, it seems, his actual intent.

Nearly a quarter of a century ago Gerald Monsman, in bringing a new perspective to the study of Pater's mythic patterns, suggested that we see all of Pater's writing in terms of the ultimate image of the circle (Monsman, *Portraits,* esp. ch. 7). His useful remarks have guided many readings of Pater's works as they help explain the Dionysian/centripetal and Apollonian/centrifugal motifs not only in Pater's fiction but in all of his writing. In this context Pater's image of the self which Monsman had cited early in his study emerges with heightened meaning:

> Experience, already reduced to a group of impressions, is ringed round for each one of us by that thick wall of personality through which no real voice has ever pierced on its way to us, or from us to that which we can only conjecture to be without. Every one of those impressions is the impression of the individual in his isolation, each mind keeping as a solitary prisoner its own dream of a world. (***Renaissance,*** 188)

Monsman also suggested that in fiction "Pater's typical hero traces out a sort of mental pilgrimage through time and space" (*Portraits,* 165), returning spiritually to that first home which he had been "ever seeking to regain" (***Marius,*** I, 22). "That vision of home," Monsman continues, "at which the hero finally arrives is depicted in Pater's thought as the Perfect City—Olympus, Civitas Dei, the Kingdom of Heaven, Utopia, the Personalistic Community of Selves" (*Portraits,* 213).

I suggest that the critic's search for home and centeredness helps account for the reconciliations of opposites and the building of a *House Beautiful* of all the arts ringed round by that thick wall of Pater's own personality. The advocate of public culture, Arnold, would have seen this, as his sons and heirs have seen it, as a futile quest and a building founded upon misrepresentation. For Pater and those who look to him as the original architect of their criticism, this is the only possible way of achieving authentic representation that artfully widens and contracts the circle of consciousness. It is in the artistic representation of his imaginative sense of fact that Pater has created artistic misrepresentations and it is in the act of self-concealment that he applied his art to the creation of self-misrepresentation. To cite another master of misrepresentation:

> One and two are not one; but one and nothing is two;
> Truth can hardly be false, if falsehood cannot be true.
> (Swinburne, "The Higher Pantheism in a Nutshell")

Works Cited

Arnold, Matthew. "On Translating Homer" (1862) in *The Complete Prose Works of Matthew Arnold.* Ed. R. H. Super. Ann Arbor: University of Michigan Press, 1960. Vol I.

Bloom, Harold. *Agon: Towards a Theory of Revisionism.* New York: Oxford University Press, 1982.

Chew, Samuel. "Pater's Quotations." *Nation,* 99 (1914), 404-405.

Clements, Patricia. *Baudelaire and the English Tradition.* Princeton: Princeton University Press, 1985.

Conlon, John J. "Brasenose Revisited: Pater in the Eighties," *ELT [English Literature in Transition, 1880–1920],* 32:1 (1989), 27-32.

———. *Walter Pater and the French Revolution,* Lewisburg: Bucknell University Press, 1982.

Dickens, Charles. *Hard Times* (1854). London: Penguin, 1988.

Law, Helen H. "Pater's Use of Greek Quotations." *MLN,* 58:8 (1943), 575-585.

Monsman, Gerald. *Pater's Portraits: Mythic Pattern in the Fiction of Walter Pater.* Baltimore: Johns Hopkins Press, 1966.

———. *Walter Pater's Art of Autobiography.* New Haven: Yale University Press, 1980.

Pater, Walter. *Appreciations* (1889; 1890). London: Macmillan, 1910.

———. *Marius the Epicurean* (1885). London: Macmillan, 1910.

———. *Plato and Platonism* (1893). London: Macmillan, 1910.

———. *The Renaissance: Studies in Art and Poetry* (1873; 1877; 1888; 1893). Ed. Donald L. Hill. Berkeley: University of California Press, 1980.

———. "Romanticism." *Macmillan's Magazine,* 35 (November 1876), 64-70.

Pattison, E. F. S. "Art." *Westminster Review,* NS 43 (1873), 639-640.

Ricks, Christopher. "Pater, Arnold and Misquotation." *TLS [Times Literary Supplement]* (25 November 1977), p. 1384.

Shorey, Paul. "Plato and Platonism." *Dial,* 14 (1893), 211-214.

———. Trans. *Republic* (1930). Cambridge, MA: Harvard University Press, 1963.

Wright, Samuel. *A Bibliography of the Writings of Walter H. Pater.* New York: Garland, 1975.

J. H. Stape (essay date 1990)

SOURCE: "Comparing Mythologies: Forster's *Maurice* and Pater's *Marius,*" in *English Literature in Transition, 1880-1920,* Vol. 33, No. 2, 1990, pp. 141-53.

[*In the following essay, Stape examines E. M. Forster's debt to Pater, particularly as demonstrated in parallels between* Marius the Epicurean *and Forster's* Maurice.]

I

In her ninetieth birthday tribute to E. M. Forster, Elizabeth Bowen, having acknowledged that no English novelist had influenced her own fiction more than Forster, went on to query "who influenced *him*? One finds no traces."[1] As perhaps befit the occasion, Bowen generously overstated her case: "traces" of Jane Austen, Samuel Butler, George Meredith, to name only the most obvious "influences," are much in evidence. Bowen's comment, however, insightfully emphasizes how subtle and complex Forster's assimilation of his predecessors is, and the extent to which one of these—Walter Pater—informs and influences his fiction has been belatedly, but only partly, recognized.

In a path-breaking analysis of Forster's debts to Pater at the Forster Centenary Conference in Montréal in 1979, Robert K. Martin could rightly summarize that "Forster himself had little to say about Pater, aside from recognizing in *Aspects of the Novel* that any definition of the genre must be able to encompass ***Marius the Epicurean*** as well as *Ulysses* and *Pilgrim's Progress,* among others."[2] Since that occasion, however, the publication of "Nottingham Lace," a novel fragment dating to 1901, and the appearance of Forster's *Selected Letters* reveal that Pater loomed larger as an interest and point of reference. The abandoned novel's allusion to him is wholly deflationary. Confined by a cold, Edgar, the novel's hero (who in some ways rather too obviously resembles its author), wiles away his hours by reading:

> Edgar meanwhile read Walter Pater. He had got a cold and was not allowed to go out and as there was no fire in his own room was immured with his aunt. His aunt bored him, and Pater did not, nor did he see a parallel between the Oxford don who found undergraduates too boorish to speak to and the middle-class lady who was finding the world too vulgar a place to live in.[3]

The accusation of snobbery, the escape from commonplace tedium into literature or art are typical charges laid against Pater, and they set up here a significant opposition between the narrative voice and the characters. Forster some years later again accuses Paterism of snobbery and escapism in the character of Cecil Vyse in *A Room with a View* (1908) and in Tibby Schlegel, a would-be Oxford aesthete, in *Howards End* (1910).

In April and May 1905, a year that he appears later to qualify as marking the apogee of Pater's reputation, Forster read ***Marius the Epicurean,*** recording in his diary on 2 May that the "absence of vulgarity . . . is something like fatal," noting that Pater seemed moved only by death: "any death is wonderful: dead or wounded flesh gives Pater the thrill he can never get from its healthiness."[4] Later references to ***Marius,*** however, show an altered estimation of Pater's interests and achievement. On New Year's Day 1917, Forster, then working for the Red Cross in Alexandria and an observer of much "wounded flesh" himself, copied the end of the *Beata Urbs* chapter into his diary, summarizing it to his aunt, Laura Mary Forster:

> he describes the longing of Marcus Aurelius for the Ideal City that lies even farther from *his* grasp than it had from Plato's because (unlike Plato) A[urelius]. conceived of it as including tenderness and pity; virtue, wisdom, and beauty were not enough.[5]

And a year later, writing to his friend and confidante Florence Barger, he referred to "The Will as Vision" chapter as "touching."[6] Such references complicate coming to terms with Forster's interest in and relationship to Pater's novel: his comments on his earlier reading as well as his fictional portraits reduce Paterism to a clichéd aesthetic pose languidly neglectful of the urgent and passionate problems in human relationships while the later references, focusing on Pater's humanism, reveal a deeply shared yearning for the Ideal City. Precisely why Forster's later re-reading and consequent revaluation were more nuanced and sympathetic remains unclear. Caricature, however, had obviously not served him adequately as a means of coming to terms with and assessing a writer with whom he shared various viewpoints and affinities, and by this stage in his life and writing career Forster had clearly become conscious of how Pater was, in part at least, writing out of his sexuality.

Forster's complexly textured assimilation of Pater extends beyond the early stories and novels hitherto seen as showing this influence more markedly than the later work, and it is his posthumously published *Maurice,* written in 1913-1914 (and revised from time to time for the next fifty years) that Pater most profoundly influenced.[7] The novel develops and sustains a dialogue with Paterian ideas—at times taking issue with them, at times concurring with them. Pater's subtitle, "His Sensations and Ideas," well describes Forster's intentions, and the development of a single consciousness through experience, self-discovery, and self-acceptance parallel Marius's search for a coherent philosophy, for a companion, and for immortality.

In contrast to Pater, however, Forster advocates self-realization not as an end in itself but as a means whereby the individual weds self to society, and he thus opts to depict the coming to awareness of an extroverted sensibility whose confrontation with the world—as that of the Wilcoxes in *Howards End*—occurs with money and business rather than with art and aesthetics. Maurice Hall's "averageness"—his awkward emotions, his blunt mind and spirit—functions, then, as polemic as much as it serves as an antidote to the excessive aestheticism Forster had already criticized in such "Paterian" figures as . . . Cecil Vyse and Tibby Schlegel. By his choice Forster asserts that the "average" man is capable of a range of feeling and sensation that once aroused and developed transforms not only him but also, by implication, his society. Whatever the marked differences in the sensibilities of their main characters, the novels share several structural as well as thematic coincidences: Flavian, the pagan, and Cornelius, the Christian, represent stages towards which Marius moves while in *Maurice* Clive and Scudder represent, respectively, a donnish and moribund Hellenism and the natural man. Echoes of Flavian's illness and death resound in Clive's climactic illness whereby he affirms his allegiance to social norms and conventions, and in both novels symbolic illnesses represent turning points at which earlier visions are outgrown and rejected. Marius moves beyond the paganism Flavian symbolizes, while Maurice is forced to confront the essential incompleteness of platonic love as symbolized by Clive. For Maurice and Clive, "Cambridge" and Plato's *Symposium* play the role that the School of Rhetoric in Pisa and Apuleius's "Golden Book" play in ***Marius.***

Whether such parallels suggest some conscious modelling of *Maurice* on the earlier novel is less important than the suggestion of shared aims and methods. They also highlight the degree to which Forster's novel is a confession and apologia, rather than the simple "fantasy" or "sentimental romance" some reviewers and critics have considered it.[8] As ***Marius*** was both Pater's attempt to explore in fiction some of the ideas of his essays as well as a rebuttal against attacks he suffered from misreadings of his ***Studies in the History of the Renaissance*** (1873), Forster's *Maurice* is similarly an attempt at a coherent explication and a sustained defence of an ethical system and sexual temperament. And like its predecessor, *Maurice,* despite its somewhat greater commitment to traditional formal realism, can be seen as an enquiry into neoplatonic conceptions of beauty and morality, of the nature of love and of the soul, of Utopia and the search for immortality, and for the means of reconciling the absolute with the actual and contingent. As Claude J. Summers has usefully suggested, it is a "thesis novel," but not one confined to the exposition and elaboration of a single idea.[9] Nor does it advocate or undertake the study of a unitary self, for Maurice pursues the discovery of a polyphonic self whose centers lie, he ultimately discovers, beyond societal direction and control. The complexly woven skeins of the novel's thematics have been little appreciated. Criticism has focused on its plotting, which deliberately subverts air-tight definitions of realism. And critical commentary has inadequately assessed the depth and breadth of the novel's ideological positions and commitments.

II

The novel's opening scene pointedly reveals the necessity and validity of constructing a world through one's own experience and sensations. Mr. Ducie's instruction of Maurice into the mysteries of sex by drawing in the sand and repeating with much satisfaction a series of Victorian clichés about the "ideal man" and "the noble woman" (God's being "in his heaven; All's right with the world") becomes a negative initiation into late-Victorian hypocrisy and self-contentment as the schoolmaster agonizes over the possibility that his drawings might offend some casual promenaders on the beach.[10] Maurice's lesson from this substitute father-figure—the boy remains, not surprisingly, unenlightened and even confused about the nature of the sexual act itself—is that concealment and embarrassment are socially linked to sexual expression. While Maurice does learn to conceal his own sexuality, even at the cost of approaching the brink of moral and mental breakdown, this opening scene also subverts its surface meaning as the reader and the protagonist are persuaded of the superiority of the twin goals of truth and of fidelity to the truth of one's own sensations. Thus, Mr. Ducie's revelations are an invitation to the construction of a false "social" self, and Maurice's instinctive rejection of this is confirmed by his later experiences and emotions. His quest for their expression will necessarily liberate him from society as constituted since it requires from him a self carefully regulated by a set of rigid but unspoken rules that are inculcated and sustained by traditional social institutions—Family, School, and the Church—all of which Forster targets as agents of "repression." The self advocated by these institutions must be "unlearned," and in this respect the novel shows its explicit connection with another "influence," Samuel Butler's *The Way of All Flesh* (1903), where the painful "unlearning" of the ways of Victorian perception becomes the only means for self-realization and for healing the split imposed between the true self and the conscious self, the latter "surrounded on every side by lies" and "trained in priggishness."[11]

In *Maurice* and in ***Marius the Epicurean*** the shared theme of education is first articulated by the respective heroes' initiation into a vision of wholeness through dreams and is further advanced and developed by a series of epiphanic moments (usually considered to be Pater's most significant contribution to literary modernism).[12] Marius, during the initiation at the Temple of Aesculapius, awakens from "feverish dreaming" to find in his room "a youthful figure" of "gracious countenance" bearing a light, a prefiguration of the tale of Cupid and Psyche recounted in a later chapter.[13] This first symbolic moment of awakening reveals to Marius the central significance of his quest in conflating, in a specifically religious context, the themes of the unity of body and soul, of the companion, of illumination and transformation—a version of the Platonic ladder of the Renaissance. These themes are embodied in the figure of "the friend," first in Flavian, later in Cornelius, and then finally and transcendentally in the hypothetical "eternal friend to man, just hidden behind the veil of a mechanical and material order, but only just behind it, ready perhaps even now to break through."[14]

Maurice's recurrent "that is your friend" dream similarly prefigures and resumes the eventual unification, à la Plato's myth in the *Symposium* or Whitman's longings in "Passage to India," of his incomplete self with its longed for and sought after other half. Maurice's original and naive interpretation of his dream—he first assumes the "friend" is Christ, then decides he must be a Greek god—evolves and becomes psychologically and philosophically complex in his conclusion that "most probably he was just a man."[15] The final interpretation of this dream establishes the novel's humanist poetics as much as it delineates Maurice's ultimate goal. The interpenetration and intersection of divine and human worlds through dream link Pater and Forster closely, for while Forster uses dream states as articulations of typically Freudian wish fulfillments, they also function in *Maurice* in classical terms as foretelling the future, a further link with Pater in that Marius's dream-vision at the Temple of Aesculapius (the Healer) predicts his future wholeness.

In both novels the theme of initiation into wholeness is explicitly linked to the myth of Eros and Psyche: in ***Marius*** the myth is recounted in its entirety, while in *Maurice* two sequences explicitly recollect Keats's "casement ope at night, / To let the warm Love in" ("Ode to Psyche"). In both novels the retelling of Apuleius's story (itself framed in the *Golden Asse* as a tale of initiation into the mysteries of potential other and future selves related by an old woman to a young girl) prepares the way for later transformations. In Forster's first recollection of the myth, Clive as Psyche welcomes the nocturnal visit of Maurice, an incomplete Eros, as Maurice enters Clive's room through the window; in the second scene, Maurice himself plays Psyche awakening to the presence of Alec Scudder's achieved and complete Eros as Scudder comes to him at night through another open window. Scudder, the gamekeeper mythically linked to the forces of Pan and nature and a radically alternate reading of or a replacement text for Mr. Ducie's diagrams, functions almost exclusively as a symbol of sexual, instinctual, and life-force energies in a novel that otherwise makes realistic gestures and closely focuses on social detailing. In recalling the Psyche myth, Forster, rather than being simply evocative, explodes the novel's realistic texture, intensifying the narrative to engender the reader's own awakening to new perspectives.

In Pater, the reading of Apuleius's tale frames and structures the eventual replacement of traditional and received authorities for the self. In this new dispensation—accommodated and shaped by the then-new myth of Christianity—personal vision and individual consent rather than external authority construct the self. These terms are taken up by the novel's conclusion in which explicitly Christian selves subvert and in their own terms triumph over the hostility of Roman imperial authority, which represents and sustains "the old gods" who "wroth at the presence of this new enemy among them"[16] send down a plague in an attempt to maintain and perpetuate their power.

Whatever the complexities of Marius's own relationship to Christianity, the novel ends with the coming into being of a new, Christian, era. As Christ is a new incarnation of Eros, wounding and finally conquering through Love, the conclusion iconographically unites lover and beloved in a figure reinforced by later tradition with the Church as the Bride of Christ and with the marriage of the individual soul with the godhead. At the end of his novel, then, Pater recuperates and revivifies a central Western myth about the self's poignant longing for its own unification in consciousness. Significantly, the original myth as recounted in *The Golden Asse* also depicts this experience as an essentially hostile act towards established religious authority—the cult of Aphrodite, which wanes as tales of Psyche's human beauty proliferate. The vanquishing of this authority and its replacement by a new awareness both in Apuleius as well as in the versions of the myth considered here demands an encounter with death and a fidelity unto death (the traditional test to which true love is put). And in the myth, as well as in these novels, this confrontation—whether actually present as in ***Marius*** or symbolically evoked as in *Maurice* (where exile or imprisonment hover)—is the moment of crisis in which the individual either wins or loses control over "his sensations and ideas," or, to use another terminology, the self. Clive, for instance, in his symbolic illness resolves his crisis by submerging the self into the communal and later devotes himself to maintaining the social hierarchy, fitting into the mold of the country squire ever eager to maintain class boundaries that bolster a socially invented rather than a "natural" or authentic self. In him, Eros and Psyche never "share"—to use the novel's term—and, consequently, the social and the private self remain separate and at odds. Maurice, on the other hand, in establishing a new social vision commits himself to the destruction of the boundaries Clive jealously maintains and removes himself from the influence of the institutions that support them.

Essentially a comic myth, as it remains in its retelling and reinvigoration by Pater and Forster, the tale of Psyche and Eros champions a new world emergent upon the union of eros and psyche against the old world of form and law. And as in Apuleius, so in Pater's nineteenth-century and Forster's early twentieth-century reshapings and retellings, the achievement of this unity leads to deification: at the conclusion of both novels the protagonists become solar heroes with Marius thought of as a saint in heaven, and Maurice appearing "clothed in the sun."[17] Though Forster's imagery echoes Revelation (and possibly recalls Blake's "Glad Day"), he may also be alluding to his friend Edward Carpenter's concept of the natural man as clothed only with the sun—a by-word for Naturism. The contrast between Clive, whose last words to his friend emphasize rituals connected to formal dress and the de-emphasis of the body—"Dinner-jacket's enough, as you know"[18]—and Maurice, naked and resplendent, is, if anything, too obvious.

But Forster's insistence on the "deity of man" at the end of *Maurice* repeats subtly what in some earlier stories and in *The Longest Journey* was imperfectly assimilated or overly explicit. In "The Tomb of Pletone" (1903-1904), a historical story about a misplaced attempt to revive the gods of ancient Greece in fifteenth-century Italy (a story replete with Paterian echoes), an exchange between two characters reveals a fundamental but significant confusion: "You are a god! Sismondo told him . . . 'I am a man,' he replied stupidly."[19] In a decidedly more mature work, the attempt to establish a viable mythology with a human hero-god at its center is, in part, accomplished by greater narrative and thematic control, but, arguably, Forster more keenly felt the need to connect this personal mythology with "the outer life," as he calls it in *Howards End,* and for this connection Pater serves as provocative and partial model.

Marius the Epicurean and *Maurice* are further linked by their anxiousness about the possibility of connecting the private self with the public and communal. In Pater, Marius's initiatory experience at the Temple of Aesculapius—an intense revelation of his interior world—culminates in a social vision: shown a view of the valley that lies beyond the Temple, he beholds a "new world" revealed as "the very presentment of a land of hope."[20] What Pater claims by this symbol of Utopia is the necessity of connecting the interior and visionary experience with a corollary in external and public space. Forster similarly links private and public destinies since Maurice's self-realization implies a new England peopled by a society no longer constrained or hobbled by class or by puritanism. Faced with exile at the novel's conclusion, Maurice, like Lawrence's Paul Morel in *Sons and Lovers,* turns from death to life as he watches the boat depart that was to take Scudder away from him and England:

> He watched the steamer move, and suddenly she reminded him of the Viking's funeral that had thrilled him as a boy. The parallel was false, yet she was heroic, she was carrying away death . . . she was off at last, a sacrifice, a splendour, leaving smoke that thinned into the sunset, and ripples that died against the wooded shores. For a long time he gazed after her, then turned to England.[21]

This insistence on England—on the here and now—explicitly contradicts Pater, for in the *Beata Urbs* chapter the Blessed City of Plato remains beyond Marcus Aurelius's reach—as it remains, too, beyond the grasp of Pater's hero though it must be his ultimate goal. Forster instead demands Utopia not merely as an ideal incapable of realization but as an actuality, and however offensive to notions of traditional realism his Greenwood might be, it remains a potent symbol of the possibilities of fulfillment and completeness, the modernist corollary to traditional visions of an afterlife but located in the present. In offering a corrective to Pater's version of the Blessed City, Forster insists, then, on the actual transformational power of love. And as in *Howards End,* a novel with a similarly "problematic" conclusion, this is as integral to his personal mythology as much as it is to his sense of the novel as a genre peculiarly capable of re-shaping and altering societal and personal modes of being.[22]

III

Since traditional generic patterns need to be re-shaped in order to express and embody new "sensations" adequately, ***Marius the Epicurean*** and *Maurice* both conclude in a radically redefined comic mode. While comic tradition demands the simultaneous integration of self and society after the individual has moved beyond the death threatened as punishment by the old society, Pater and Forster undermine and carefully qualify the motif of social integration. Marius is claimed by the Christian community as one of their own: they hold "his death, according to their generous view in this matter, to have been of the nature of a martyrdom."[23] Forster's more assertive resolution is double-edged. Clive's complete integration into the existing social order demands that he deny parts of himself, that he remain, in essence, fragmented with one side of himself unrealized; at the end of the novel, he is "fully" socialized yet hardly integrated, the various competing aspects of his nature reduced through social pressure to a single role. His final act, a repetition of Mr. Ducie's duplicity and self-deception, is "to devise some method of concealing the truth" from his wife.[24] Clive thus rejects instinct and the ideal, deliberately choosing falsity, and, consequently, forever excludes love from his life. In Forsterian terms such a choice represents the unforgivable sin: by his act Clive uses Anne, condemning her to the role of a mere social appendage and rejecting her as a true companion. On the other hand, Maurice, Clive's positive mirror image, chooses for himself a new society as yet not wholly defined except that it be based on truth and include love—an Edwardian version of the Theban band, the symbols and images of the classical world offering, characteristically in Forster's fiction, an alternative and contrast to the militant, oppressive certitudes of late-Victorian domestic pieties.

The typical conflation at the conclusion of generic comedy of life and death and new and old orders motivates both Pater and Forster, and, indeed, only at the end of each novel do their multiple generic allegiances become fully felt. At the conclusion of *Maurice,* Forster's "ordinary man" incarnates the life-force itself when Maurice, sprinkled with the pollen of the evening primroses, is transformed into a kind of Boticellian "Primavera," coming to Clive's memory "Out of some eternal Cambridge . . . clothed in the sun, and shaking out the scents and sounds of the May Term."[25] Forster asserts by this image no less than a vision of immortality, the traditional promise at the conclusion of comedy, and a triumph of the new order over the blocking forces of convention, with self-repression and self-censorship doing duty for paternal fiat. The conclusion's imagery and tone connect it, moreover, to an earlier chapter where Mr. Grace, Maurice's grandfather who is facing death, explains the "new religion—or rather a new cosmogony" he has evolved in his old age: "The chief point was that God lives inside the sun, whose bright envelope consists of the spirits of the blessed."[26]

In addition to self-consciously alluding to myths of the solar hero, Forster by his concluding image champions, like Mr. Grace, a new mythology: the Greek pantheon precious to Victorian and Edwardian "Cambridge," and the Christian one, still thought to be valid by Maurice's mother, have been replaced by Maurice's version of a new heaven embodied in himself and Scudder as the novel realizes the meaning of his early "that is your friend" dream. The typically Forsterian humanist vision delineated here gains in emphasis by the allusion to and reinvigoration of the images of traditional mythology. And the search for a mythology with a human face—so anxious in Forster's early short stories, in *The Longest Journey,* and in *Howards End*—finds its culminating moment.

The link with Pater's philosophical and social interests in ***Marius*** is obvious. In sacrificing his life for Cornelius, his friend, Marius (an explicit *imitatio Christi,* dying with the viaticum on his lips) is transformed into a Christian martyr.[27] The conclusion thus recollects the novel's central transformation myths, those of Eros and Psyche and of Christ and his bride, the Church. Pagan versions of immortality as symbolized by "The Ceremony of the Dart" are superseded, but, in the end, even Apuleius's myth is replaced by a humanist one as Marius goes in death to meet a "divine companion," the "eternal friend" earlier hypothesized.

Whatever their vast tonal differences, both novels conclude with their heroes poised for a transformation that on a larger metaphoric scale limns the renewal of time. The climactic change in Pater from the Pagan to the Christian epoch is, in part, a displaced depiction of the transition from Victorianism to Modernism, an alteration of consciousness and spirit that Forster more energetically insists upon in *Maurice.* Forster's realism, while it documents an emerging debate about gender and social status at the end of the Victorian age, is altered and enriched by a denouement opting for the structure and imagery of myth. As Norman Page has suggested in his study of Forster's posthumously published fiction, *Maurice* forms "an experiment in a new mode,"[28] and it is precisely that mode's grammar that critical debate neglected upon the novel's belated publication, for despite manifest weaknesses, *Maurice* is an intense and subtle comedy that derives its thematic richness from its tendency towards generic hybridism. To use Judith Herz's term, it is a characteristically Forsterian example of "cross generic" writing, with traits typical of the "essayistic story" and the "story-like" essay.[29] The novel is obviously and self-consciously modelled on—while it occasionally parodies—the *apologia,* the polemical tract, the manifesto, the *roman à thèse,* and the *Bildungsroman.* It is also partly a coterie text, representing, according to S. P. Rosenbaum, one side of the dialogue amongst the Cambridge Apostles about "the higher sodomy," their code term for platonic homosexuality.[30]

An attentive reading of *Maurice*'s conclusion, however much it might assist in coming to terms with Forster's general aims, simultaneously problematizes them for some readers. The refusal of conventional bliss, and of actual social integration, that disturbed some readers on the novel's publication is wholly consistent with its tone and thematics. Although Forster revealed in an appended "Terminal Note" written in 1960 that he once intended to depict Maurice and Scudder "some years later"[31] (an avowal of the possibility of fidelity and continuance outside conventional social structures), his inability to tag on such a scene underscores the success and completeness of the novel as it stands, for thematically "wholeness" rather than "happiness" is in Forsterian terms the true achievement of the life sensitively and intelligently lived. Moreover, as with the conclusion of *Howards End,* Forster remains true to his declaration, made as early as 1906, that changing mores dictated a new ending to his chosen genre: for the novel in modern times, he stated, marriage was "rather a beginning" than an ending.[32] In such a statement one glimpses Pater's wider influence on late-Victorian and early modernist writing, for the refusal of closure in ***Marius*** serves as a model and challenge to writers concerned with depicting the modernist problematics of the self.

The final scene of *Maurice,* imbued as it is with Pater's sense of the self emergent upon experience and sensation, evidences a technical advance on and a greater maturity of vision than the undermined and anxious conclusion of *Howards End* and moves closer to that of the novel that followed it—*A Passage to India*—where Forster poignantly confronts the individual's ultimate solitude with his never-to-be-satisfied yearning for understanding and for a place in community. *Maurice,* then, is a step on the way to the later novel's density and resonance. And the degree to which it is so is emphasized by recalling that *A Passage to India* was left incomplete—blocked, one could argue—in 1912-1913 and only taken up again in 1922, after Forster's second sojourn to the sub-continent, with *Maurice* written, but unpublished, behind him.

Notes

1. "A Passage to E. M. Forster," *Aspects of E. M. Forster: Essays and Recollections written for his Ninetieth Birthday 1st January 1969,* Oliver Stallybrass, ed. (London: Arnold, 1969), 12.
2. "The Paterian Mode in Forster's Fiction: *The Longest Journey* to *Pharos and Pharillon,*" *E. M. Forster: Centenary Revaluations,* Judith Scherer Herz and Robert K. Martin, eds. (London: Macmillan, 1982), 101.
3. "Nottingham Lace," *Arctic Summer and Other Fiction,* Elizabeth Heine and Oliver Stallybrass, eds. (London: Arnold, 1980), 2.
4. Cited in P. N. Furbank, *E. M. Forster: A Life: Vol. 1 The Growth of the Novelist (1879-1914)* (London: Secker, 1977), 132.
5. *Selected Letters of E. M. Forster: Vol. 1: 1879-1920,* Mary Lago and P. N. Furbank, eds. (London: Collins, 1983), 248-49.
6. *Selected Letters,* 285.
7. On the textual history of the novel, see Philip Gardner, "The Evolution of E. M. Forster's *Maurice,*" *E. M. Forster: Centenary Revaluations,* 204-23.
8. For a representative selection of reviews of *Maurice,* see *E. M. Forster: The Critical Heritage,* Philip Gardner, ed. (London: Routledge, 1973), 428-90. Biases operating in the novel's reception are discussed in Claude J. Summers, *E. M. Forster* (New York: Ungar, 1983), 371-72.
9. Summers, 143.
10. *Maurice,* P. N. Furbank, ed. (London: Arnold, 1971), 8.
11. *Ernest Pontifex, or The Way of All Flesh* (1903), Daniel F. Howard, ed. (London: Methuen, 1964), 115-16.
12. See Jay B. Losey's "Epiphany in Pater's Portraits," *ELT [English Literature in Transition],* 29:3 (1986), 297-308.
13. *Marius the Epicurean* (1885), Michael Levey, ed. (Harmondsworth: Penguin, 1985), 53.
14. Ibid., 208.
15. *Maurice,* 15.
16. *Marius,* 289.
17. *Maurice,* 230-31.
18. Ibid., 230.
19. *Arctic Summer,* 94.
20. *Marius,* 58.
21. *Maurice,* 223.
22. Both societal pressures and self-censorship help explain *Maurice*'s delayed publication: during his mother's lifetime Forster wished to avoid the public and private confrontation its publication would have required, and it needs be recalled that until 1967 homosexual activity was a crime punishable by law in England. Moreover, as social attitudes changed Forster was aware (as he indicates in *Maurice*'s "Terminal Note") that aspects of the novel "dated."
23. *Marius,* 297.
24. *Maurice,* 231.
25. *Maurice,* 230-31. Furbank's edition appears to perpetuate an error in the typescript: "external Cambridge" is most likely a misprint for "eternal Cambridge." Professor Philip Gardner, who has carefully studied the novel's pre-publication states, graciously responded to an enquiry about this and indicated agreement with this supposition.
26. *Maurice,* 127. Forster reveals here his indebtedness to one of his own liberating literary forerunners: in Samuel Butler's *The Way of All Flesh,* Old Mr. Pontifex, Ernest's grandfather, has near the end of his life a special relationship with the sun. Cf. "The old man had a theory about sunsets and had had two steps built up against a wall in the kitchen garden on which he used to stand and watch the sun go down whenever it was clear." *Ernest Pontifex,* 13.
27. The motif of sacrifice for "the friend" plays an important role at the conclusion of Forster's *The Longest Journey* where Rickie Elliot dies for his half-brother Stephen Wonham, and at the conclusion of *Maurice* both Alec and Maurice sacrifice financial security and a position in society in order to be together.
28. *E. M. Forster's Posthumous Fiction,* English Literary Studies 10 (Victoria: University of Victoria, 1977), 69.

29. *The Short Narratives of E. M. Forster* (London: Macmillan, 1988), 1-2.

30. *Victorian Bloomsbury: The Early Literary History of the Bloomsbury Group* (New York: St. Martin's, 1987), 269.

31. "Terminal Note," *Maurice,* 239.

32. "Pessimism in Literature," *Albergo Empedocle and Other Writings,* George H. Thomson, ed. (New York: Liveright, 1971), 135.

Jay Fellows (essay date 1991)

SOURCE: "The Prose Architecture of Mental Abodes: The Presence of Inhabitable Language" in *Tombs, Despoiled and Haunted: "Under-Textures" and "After-Thoughts" in Walter Pater,* Stanford University Press, 1991, pp. 40-55.

[*In the following excerpt, Fellows analyzes the nature of Pater's prose, describing it as stationary yet penetrating.*]

> The wind, persistent, the mantle, purple, the blond hair in the persistent wind against the chiselled features. Like a corpse, a mummy wrapped in a winding sheet, bound against that persistent wind which "for many years . . . had its dwelling among the mountains, [and] came as a stranger, darkly. Persistent now."
>
> —Pater, anonymously unwritten, in an act of sabotage based on baseless animus

> At twilight he came over the frozen snow. As he passed through the stony barriers of the place the world around seemed to curdle to the center—all but himself, fighting his way across it, turning now and then right-about from the persistent wind, which dealt so roughly with his blond hair and the purple mantle whirled about him.
>
> —Pater, **"Denys l'Auxerrois"**

> When you speak of me to cathedrals, I cannot but feel touched at the evidence of an intuition which has led you to guess what I had never mentioned to anyone, and here set down in writing for the first time—that I once planned to give to each part of my book a succession of titles, such as *Porch, Windows in the Apse,* etc. . . . so as to defend myself in advance against the sort of stupid criticism which has been made to the effect that my books lack construction, whereas I hope to prove to you that their sole merit lies in the solidarity of their tiniest parts. I gave up the idea of using these architectural titles because I found them too pretentious, but I am touched at finding that you have dug them up by a sort of intelligent divination.
>
> —Marcel Proust, letter to Comte Jean de Gaigneron

Like the often antithetical Ruskin before (and during) him, Pater is, or would have one believe him to be, a kind of optical system that receives visual impressions and translates them back verbally into what J. Hillis Miller calls "linguistic design"[1] and what Pater calls "pictorial form" (***R,*** 149), as of the Center-Circumference dynamic in ***Plato and Platonism.*** Pater's other sensory apprehensions of the world are significantly more felicitous than Ruskin's, who will live, desire, go mad, and die by the eye, even as he will often, especially later, smell the "mephitic," hear bells that are infernal, and touch, essentially, only shovel and possessions. But with apparent delight, Pater, or his personae, will smell, hear, and touch, even or especially the forbidden. The young, mnemonically revisited Florian, from **"The Child in the House,"** receives impressions or "recognitions of [the] visible, tangible, audible loveliness of things" (***MS,*** 181).

Still, most of all, Pater, even as he hears those urgent and exiled *voices of absence,* is essentially an existential phenomenologist of sight. The autobiography of his linguistic consciousness will be shaped, to an extraordinary degree, by what he sees. As with Raphael, so, though less ambitiously, with his commentator: "By him [Raphael] large theoretic conceptions are addressed, so to speak, to the intelligence of the eye" (***MS,*** 57). With both Pater and Ruskin, the optical "intelligence" is especially worth noting because it is, apparently, uncharacteristic of the English temperament and its sensory bias. Writing ostensibly about Steele, in the essay **"English Literature,"** Pater tells us at least as much about himself: "It was one of his [Steele's] peculiarities, he tells us, to live by the eye far more than any other sense (a peculiarity, perhaps in an Englishman)" (***EG,*** 181).

Yet "peculiar" Englishmen who "live by the eye" do not necessarily possess an optical intelligence. At times, it would seem that what might be an Italian or Greek intelligence translates into an English, perhaps Evangelical, "lust." Such a "lust" leads Florian, the "Child," from his "House" at a considerable, though necessarily inevitable, cost—the cost of loss:

> He could trace two predominant processes of mental change in him—the growth of an almost diseased sensibility to the spectacle of suffering, and, parallel with this, the rapid growth of a certain capacity of fascination by bright colour and choice form—the sweet curvings, for instance, of the lips of those who seemed to him comely persons, modulated in such delicate unison to the things they said or sang—marking early the activity in him of a more than customary sensuousness, "the lust of the eye," as the preacher says, which might lead him, one day, how far! (***MS,*** 181)

From the mnemonic perspective of the adult, the Child might have been pleased, or at least interested, to have seen farther at first—the presbyopia of eventual anteriority that becomes increasingly significant in "after-thoughts." But "prediction," the desired farsightedness of youth, is not often possible even for those whose eyes may already be old. The future may be Pater's most conditional tense—one that frequently slips into a past which "might have been": "Could he [Florian] have foreseen the weariness of the way" (***MS,*** 181). Anticipated, future repetitions can only be seen by later eyes.

Before, as well as later, close to Pater's corrective end, the result of his weary "way," there is an optically informing Plato. If Pater's Plato is neither Pater in the manner of

Marius, nor an autonomous Plato, what emerges from a reading of ***Plato and Platonism*** is a Paterian version of Plato. Pater may in fact be more "at home" in *his* Greece of Plato than in the England of Victoria—an England where it is unusual "to live by the eye," though perhaps more common after Ruskin than in the time of Steele. Discussing **"The Genius of Plato,"** Pater alludes both to visibility and to its receptive audience: "Like all masters of literature, Plato has of course varied excellences; but perhaps none of them has won for him a larger number of friendly readers than this impress of visible reality" (***PP,*** 129).

As Pater understands visible illustration, there is, for example, Plato's version of the end of Socrates:

> Sometimes, even when they are not formally introduced into his work, characters that had interested, impressed, or touched him, inform and colour it, as if with their personal influence, showing what purports to be the wholly abstract analysis of some wholly abstract moral situation. Thus, the form of the dying Socrates himself is visible. . . . When Plato is dealing with the inmost elements of personality, his eye is still on its object, on *character* as seen in *characteristics,* through those details, which make character a sensible fact, the changes of colour in the face as of tone in the voice. . . . What is visibly expressive in, or upon, persons, . . . it is always more than worth his while to make note of these. (***PP,*** 130-31)

Pater's Plato possesses "the delicacy of the artist, the fastidious eye for the subtleties of colour as soul made visibly expressive" (***PP,*** 133). Further, "when Plato speaks of visible things it is as if you saw them" (***PP,*** 135). Essentially, Plato's genius is to make what might be a "chilly abstraction" (***PP,*** 49) visible, perhaps as colored as a soul incarnate: "He gives names to the invisible acts, processes, creations, of old. As Plato speaks of them, we might say, those abstractions too become visible living creatures" (***PP,*** 141).[2] *This* Plato, more phenomenological than Platonic, may not be easily recognized, but he is undeniably Plato the way Pater would have him, and thus an important nexus of the "metamorphoses of . . . [Pater's own] mind." With obvious reluctance, Pater admits the Plato of "harshest dualism": "His aptitude for things visible, with the gift of words, empowers him to express, as if for the eyes, what except to the eye of the mind is strictly invisible, what an acquired asceticism induces him to rank above, sometimes, in terms of harshest dualism, opposed to, the sensible world" (***PP,*** 143).

If the "lust of the eye" takes the Child far ("how far"?) from his House, it is a cultivated and "fastidious eye" that accompanies Plato on his journeys: "A traveller, adventurous for that age, he certainly becomes. After the *Lehrjahre,* the *Wander-jahre*!—all round the Mediterranean coasts as far west as Sicily. Think of what all that must have meant just then, for eyes that could see" (***PP,*** 147). If the Child, impelled by his eyes, quits the House with a mixture of lust and reluctance, Plato, whose eyes see as fully as the Child's, leaves with different emotions: "If those journeys had begun in angry flight from home, it was for the purposes of self-improvement they [the journeys of essentially visual apprehension] were continued" (***PP,*** 147).

Whether fastidious or lusting, Pater's eyes are most "at home" "in" the home, despite his need to make intimacy distant. His Marius will "keep the eye clear [if more experienced than innocent] by a sort of exquisite personal alacrity and cleanliness, extending even to his dwelling place" (***ME1,*** 33). Pater's own favorite observation of the completing or fulfilling return, which will carry him, through his personae, back to that original "dwelling place," is as immaculate as a clear eye devoid of "lust" that has been erased by the act of arrival.

He is ready to explore the perceptions of the eye in a way that, translated to the fine arts, goes against an accepted, single-minded orthodoxy. More specifically, Pater will make the Platonically "visible" something either more or less than a scene for the educated eye, whether that eye be lustful or fastidious. It is a situation he will approach obliquely, with characteristic qualification and subordination. In his essay **"Sandro Botticelli,"** Pater points out that "Botticelli's illustrations are crowded with incident, blending with naive carelessness or pictorial propriety, three phases of the same scene into one plate" (***R,*** 52). Here, it is as if, before the structures of Lessing's *Laocoon,* we were to confront the emblems, for instance, of George Whither (***A,*** 119), with painting aspiring not toward the condition of music so much as toward the condition of narrative. Pater describes Botticelli affectionately as "before all things a poetic painter, blending the charm of the story and sentiment, the medium of the art of poetry, with the charm of line and colour, the medium of abstract painting" (***R,*** 52).

Pater is himself neither naïve nor deaf to those admonitions of Lessing, but he will refer, in his well-known passage from **"The School of Giorgione,"** to other "German critics" whose aesthetics come closer to satisfying his ideals. He makes his case by beginning tentatively, antithetically, as if to guard his flanks, with a sophisticated "but although" that, precluding innocence, is on the opposite side of the sentence's ending and essential point:

> But although each art has thus its own specific order of impression, and an untranslatable charm, while a just apprehension of the ultimate differences of the arts is the beginning of aesthetic criticism; yet it is noticeable that, in its special mode of handling its given material, each art may be observed to pass into the condition of some other art, by what German critics term an *Anders-streben*—a partial alienation from its own limitations, through which the arts are able, not indeed to supply the place of each other, but reciprocally to lend each other new forces. (***R,*** 133-34)[3]

Later, in the same essay, the doubled Pater, perhaps anticipating an instinct toward integration, will have the "twin born . . . imaginative reason" moving toward the unity of a "single effect." It is ironic that one whose final condition is itself a conflict that is more accommodated than resolved should be the one to break down the barriers of categories that may now strike us as false. Nevertheless, it is Pater as "embodied paradox," who points out that

> art, then, is thus always striving to be independent of the mere intelligence, to become a matter of pure perception, to get rid of its responsibilities to its subject or material; the ideal examples of poetry and painting being those in which the constituent elements of the composition are so welded together, that the material or subject no longer strikes the intellect only; nor the form, the eye or the ear only; but form and matter, in their union or identity; present one single effect to the "imaginative reason," that complex faculty for which every thought and feeling is twin-born with its sensible analogue or symbol. (***R,*** 138)

Theory would become the incarnation of presence, as Pater moves from the implicit toward practice and example. The ideal example of vitalizing reciprocity between the visible and the verbal is dependent upon the selection of a subject that will be compatible with "pictorial form":

> It [Giorgione's] is the school of genre, and employs itself mainly with 'painted idylls,' but, in the production of this pictorial poetry, exercises a wonderful tact in the selecting of such matters as lends itself most readily and entirely to pictorial form, to complete expression by drawing and colour. For although its products are painted poems, they belong to a poetry which tells itself without an articulated story. (***R,*** 149)

Employing a "pictorial form" without painting an "articulated story" is a form that itself tends to elude Pater, whose talent with language is other than that of chronological narrative. In fact, as well shall see, Pater is perhaps as picaresque in return as he is not in decentering pilgrimage. **"The School of Giorgione"** predicts the once-erased "Conclusion" to ***The Renaissance*** in its apprehension of a time that is essentially nonsequential:

> Now it is part of the ideality of the highest sort of dramatic poetry, that it presents us with a kind of profoundly significant and animated instant, a mere gesture, a look, a smile, perhaps—some brief and wholly concrete moment—into which, however, all motives, all the interests and effects of a long history, have condensed themselves, and which seem to absorb past and future in an intense consciousness of the present. Such ideal instants the school of Giorgione selects, with its admirable tact, from that feverish, tumultuously coloured world of the old citizens of Venice—exquisite pauses in time, in which, arrested thus, we seem to be spectators of all the fullness of existence, and which are like some consummate extract or quintessence of life. (***R,*** 150)

With **"The School of Giorgione,"** we are far from the "naive carelessness" of Botticelli, who would charmingly flirt with isolated moments of extended serial time, instead of selecting "ideal instants" as privileged, almost epiphanic condensations.

Yet Pater's aesthetics, more phenomenological than metaphysical (though the relics of a discredited logocentricity linger, as in the case of Sebastian, who defies easy dismissal, even as he himself dismisses everything but "nothing"), cannot be reduced by the anthologizing mind that would take aphoristic statement for exclusive meaning. One might affirm that Pater, at least as the early linguistic autobiographer's double creature of "immature radiance," is himself not only "twin-born" but that his later existence, even in a consolidating and condensed present of epiphanic moments, is still double. In his essay on Raphael, first delivered as a lecture some years after the appearance of **"The School of Giorgione,"** Pater, still hunting for origins, though he "must be content to follow faint traces" (***GS,*** 111)—those "faint traces" being like infirm vantage points that would reveal the anteriority of perpetual regression—notes a "narrative power" that is not grounded in those economically "ideal instants": "Now, Raphael, on the other hand, in his final period at Rome, exhibits a wonderful narrative power in painting; and the secret of that power—the sources of developing a story in a picture, or a series of pictures—may be traced back from him to Pinturicchio" (***MS,*** 45).

Still, Pater is not simply a mirror of his Giorgione or Raphael. Perhaps he is "twin-born," and then later of Janusian accommodation. Though capable of the *affiliation* of "appreciation," he is not using a painter's brush to tell a story. Rather, he is writing about looking. His looking, unlike Ruskin's, appears limited to canvases, as if in the reflex of "modern subjectivity" he were anticipating Ortega's regression of the focal point, where the "owned body" of Paul Ricoeur might be owned by a self that had broken from objectivity. Similar to his version of Plato, Pater would make language itself visible. He writes as if he were painting, while avoiding the genre of word pictures, and, significantly, without the "narrative power" that Raphael implicitly borrows from the orthodox usage of language.

Pater's prose, in fact, appears even more stationary than the canvases of the painters he describes. At times his narrative thread might be described as a series of superimposed repetitions surrounding a kind of coil, or concentric palimpsest. (The shrill wind, the harmattan, undoubtedly, whistling down from the mountains, and then, as if never heard before, without truth, utterly, it seemed, triumphant . . . the shock to my auditory canal, my acoustic meatus, my tympanum, my anvil played with arrogance, the whistling, the rutting, the infernal percussion. . . . Inevitable. The Repetitions. As always, and the alien corn ripped by that ruthless wind.) Perhaps with some impulse toward reciprocity or balance, his prose aspires toward a form of illustration that is without essential or convincing movement. Occasionally, as if impelled by a will toward "*Anders-streben*" that defines his own alienated relation to aspects of himself, words become pictures. Those pictures, it is apparent, will be closer to statuary than either murals or Siennese narrative paintings. Beginning **"The Bacchanals of Euripides,"** Pater is content to say, "So far, I have endeavoured to present, with something of the concrete character of a picture . . ." (***GS,*** 53).

Yet if words should contribute to pictures that are as stationary as statues, these pictures/words should also, it seems, be suitable for framing. Often Pater's ***Imaginary Portraits*** appear to possess the impulse of a certain centripetence, as if directed toward a Center that either seems to evade location, as with **"Denys,"** or one that is located firmly in its centricity, as with **"The Child"**—a centripetal movement that is to become characteristic of the fulfilling Pater of "return." This situation is reminiscent of some of the short stories of Ernest Downson, whose "portraits" are themselves enclosed, or framed in a setting that is also a defensive vantage point for a kind of regressive departure—a departure turned toward enclosing spaces of interior liminalities.

If **"The Child"** is mnemonically framed, we recall that, to arrive at a portrait of **"Denys l'Auxerrois,"** both the reader and the reluctant "To me" / "I" are guided, as if by thresholds of spiralling interiorities, through a landscape reminiscent of Turner, to a stained glass window, and finally to a series of tapestries, where, with the "help of certain notes," "the story shaped itself at last" (***IP,*** 54). In the case of **"Denys,"** as has been suggested, the frames may be a cage. The circumferential vitality of relative immediacy, of something approaching the visceral activity of the present tense, has been filtered through concentric layers of a variety of the arts informed by "pictorial form," to become, finally, a subverted narrative of spatial form. This language does not so much work, in an orthodox sense, in its dissonance, as it does in its cultivated idiosyncrasy, precisely because of the juxtaposed, not to say Janusian, spatialized "dissonance"[4] of a kind of "included difference." Dionysian performance, essentially circumferential, is controlled by a framing imprisonment that separates Pater and his reader from the excesses of frenzy. All this may only be the work of a writer engaged in the displacement of certain aspects of linguistic consciousness, who, somewhat equivocally, desires to protect his personae from the full consequences of a dangerous psychic exhibitionism that takes place on the inner surface of a framing Circumference.

Essentially, neither movement nor narrative is encouraged in a language that, as if of concentric repetitions surrounding a cylindrical palimpsest, would achieve the stability, even while describing a world of evanescence, of a framed portraiture that, in turn, would be like, say, the figures on the tombs of Michelangelo's *Night and Day, The Twilight,* and *The Dawn,* as described by Pater (***R,*** 94). "Twin-born" "creatures of immature radiance" might be reborn into stones of immutability. Most often, when there is a primitive form of narrative movement in Pater's fundamentally synchronic fiction, it will be concentrically, which is to say safely, surrounded and removed from the presence, or vitality verging on frenzy, of the present tense of those full, epiphanic moments that, paradoxically (and therefore characteristically), are enthusiastically advertised, especially in **"The School of Giorgione,"** the "New Cyrenaicism" chapter from ***Marius,*** and the "Conclusion" to ***The Renaissance.***

Further, despite the fact that Sebastian van Storck is a kind of "diagonally antithetical" Paterian persona, even for the Amielian or Giorgionesque-informed "twin-born," Sebastian's beginning is caught in space with time an extracted dimension—a condition typical of the Paterian bias for frames that enclose thresholds which themselves both stabilize and effect liminal transition. The exterior world, in this case the world of Sebastian, is defined as an example of art—a world that, caught and framed, only permits an optical exit or entrance which is rendered safe by virtue of its framing: "It was a winter-scene, by Adrian van de Velde, or by Isaac van Ostade" (***IP,*** 81).

Still, the transformation of the arts—Pater's version of "*Anders-streben*" taken to an extreme degree—is, significantly, not complete; it is yet to be frozen in a "winter-scene" that will never thaw. While Pater would freeze the forward motion of an always-weary temporal narrative thread (though not, perhaps, the daemonic energies of the nihilistic circumferential nightmare, "that deep undercurrent of horror which runs below" [***GS,*** 78]) by a variety of framing devices, he would also, with the apparent contradiction we shall come to assume, introduce the Euclidean world of three dimensions. This world of shifting mutability includes the temporal dimension of distance-as-depth (and death), of the "how far" (***MS,*** 173) necessary for the act of return (or arrival, as it will seem)—an act that is, of course, documented even as a form of retrospective-as-narration-as-"after-thought." And even portraits that are imaginary might well cast shadows, as though from the statues examined by Winckelmann: "The art of sculpture records the first naive, unperplexed recognition of man by himself" (***R,*** 213). Those shadows are of the third dimension of a temporally implicated depth.

Pater's language is horizontally frozen or framed, with its lateral, left-to-right narrative element as static or "frozen" as one might expect from a language of "pictorial form" fundamentally outside of the sense of time that it is nevertheless informed by. Still, this language appears to *penetrate* (later we shall see how important that word/concept is to Pater) or invade the limitations of a two-dimensional page—even, perhaps, the canvas as palimpsest, which is the characteristically encrusted Paterian surface. It does this by travelling beyond the page's immediate surface into the territory of distance-as-depth and time, which is the prospective and reflexive territory of "departure" and "return" that is also a version of "loss" and "regain," located "within" the language of the page. This sense of travelling *into* the page helps shape "the relieving interchange" (***ME2,*** 106) of Paterian metalepsis. With the impression that the end is merely superimposed over the beginning, rather than off to the side, substitutions become inevitable to even the stationary eye.

Winckelmann's appreciated statuary, more "concrete" (certainly less diaphanous) than the "character of a picture," can be said to predict, if not living people, concrete living spaces—or "abodes"—for the living. Such "dwelling places," or "homes," reflect a verbal style that has surpassed the "partial alienation from its own limitations" by breaking away from the two-dimensional discourse of lateral narrative to the shadow-casting substance of three dimensions. Here, the third dimension is temporally implicated in the "how far" of a recessional space of almost inevitable reversal. Pater's style, as if aedicularly shaped by statuary that itself predicts both "mental" and "physical" "abodes," reflects the substitution of the depth of Euclidean space, with its superimpositions, in place of the serial procession of the horizontal or lateral in what amounts to a shift of orthodox emphasis in syntactic procession.

Significantly, Pater, in his essay **"English Literature,"** borrows from George Saintsbury the concept of "architecture," with its implicit occupation of Euclidean space, as a model for what he calls "prose structure" (***EG,*** 6). In his "Joachim du Bellay" essay, Pater, bringing shadows to language, establishes a relation between architecture and poetry. He notes that the audiences of the *Pleiad* "love a constant change of rhyme in poetry, and in their houses that strange, fantastic interweaving of thin, reed-like lines, which are a kind of rhetoric of architecture" (***R,*** 170). And with a broader concept of poetry, Pater, as if recalling Ruskin's *The Poetry of Architecture* (1837-38), as well as the effects of those "golden stains of time" from *The Seven Lamps of Architecture*'s (1849) "The Lamp of Memory," observes that there is a "poetry also of memory and of the mere effect of time, by which architecture often profits greatly" (***R,*** 134).

In the essay **"Sir Thomas Browne,"** Pater will observe, with a dubious first glance (and we shall come to know what Pater thinks of "first sights" uninformed by "afterthought"), the absence of precisely that sense of "pictorial form" which becomes an architecture of language: "And all is so oddly mixed, showing, in its entire ignorance of self, how much he, and the sort of literature he represents, really stood in need of technique, of a formed taste in literature, of a literary architecture" (***A,*** 126-27). Nevertheless, Pater, whose "second sights" are more final—and eventually primary—than his "first sights," has immediate second thoughts that result in his considering, as a literary model, the possibility of a highly idiosyncratic "prose structure." This almost inhabitable, aedicular architecture of modular "mental abodes" is, in fact, a home of linguistic consciousness:

> And yet perhaps we could hardly wish the result different in him [Browne], any more than the books of Burton and Fuller, or some other similar writers of that age—mental abodes, we might liken, after their own manner, to the little old private houses of some historic town grouped about its grand public structures, which, when they have survived at all, posterity is loth to part with. (***A,*** 127)

The syntax of "mental abodes" is a "literary architecture" worthy of survival precisely because it is both authentically of a linguistic autobiography and reflective of its context: "For, in their absolute sincerity, not only do these authors clearly exhibit themselves ('the unique peculiarity of the writer's mind,' being, as Johnson says of Browne, 'faithfully reflected in the form and matter of his work') but, even more than merely professionally instructed writers, they belong to, and reflect, the age they live in" (***A,*** 127).

Closer to the architecture of the Paterian home that is itself a model for "literary architecture," Florian Deleal, in **"The Child in the House,"** is an architect of autobiographical consciousness, involved as he is "in that process of brain-building by which we are, each one of us, what we are" (***MS,*** 173). And the Child's "brain-building," part of the "metamorphoses of the mind," is Pater's construction of one of those "mental abodes" that is, in fact, a syntactical place of three dimensions in which to abide. It is as if one—or one's soul—might live within, or "occupy," one's own "prose structure" in a condition of Ricoeur's "owned body" that had transcended objectivity—a "prose structure," at least stylistically, of presence or "grace." As though daydreaming, Florian, in that "half-spiritualized house" of his self-referential consciousness,

> could watch the better, over again, the gradual expansion of the soul which had come to be there—of which indeed, through the law which makes the material objects about them so large an element in children's lives, it had actually become a part, inward and outward being woven through and through each other into one inextricable texture—half, tint and trace and accident of homely colour and form, from the wood and the bricks; half, mere soul-stuff, floated thither from who knows how far. (***MS,*** 173)

The process of leaving, whether for the Child's first time or for the adult's dream-impelled "mental journey" (***MS,*** 174), informed by eyes of memory that are either lustful or fastidious—though, in either case, presumably "intelligent"—is a departure that takes one neither horizontally right nor left, in a series of explicit diachronic narrations. Rather, it ventures "into" the recessional distance/depths of a Euclidean world organized about concentric repetition, in a characteristic act of "penetration." Yet the model architecture-become-"mental abodes"-become-House for a Child is a place, even if origins are problematic, to which one always returns. Florian Deleal, after what amounts to an act of centrifugal decentering from a fictional, if "effective," Center, returns to the framing "prose structure" of the first page. There he greets an awaiting reader who knew that the ending would be in the beginning, as in the repetitions of "a certain distance." The origin is Pater's final destination, though with the implicit rebeginnings of oscillation.

Figuratively, one might reconstruct that first paragraph of **"The Child"** as a model for the Paterian text, just as one takes "the House," less figuratively, as a model for "literary architecture"—a model as a framed page of superimposition, rather than of lateral series, that creates depth for a "literary architecture" that is the result of an extensive transformation in the arts. Language, dissatisfied with itself (perhaps with the burden of meaning-as-information that is less evident in music or architecture), has passed beyond "pictorial form" to construct an "abode" whose exit is its entrance. It is as if the first and last pages have been laminated together in order that they might hold beginnings and endings simultaneously. This page of **"The Child,"** as the text becomes what will later be called an "abiding place," with the Paterian self inhabiting the public texts of his own linguistic autobiography, might be seen as a trope—in Pater's self-divided and reciprocally re-created, frozen world of "*Anders-streben*"—for the hypothetically frozen music of a "literary architecture."

That autobiographical architecture may even have been part of that "winter scene by either Adrian van de Velde or Isaac van Ostade" (***IP,*** 81). (Scum-knelling, closer, a dandy? *le beau* . . . ? of the dandy fever? a handy dandy fever?—or more to the purpose? Scum-belling closer, like thunder and lightning, the leprous here and now. Eventually. Inevitable. In due course. The *evacue.* Ishmael called to be recalled. In undue course? Perhaps an ill wind will in fact blow . . . ill. . . .) Perhaps, in fact, it is a scene of frozen time, as though the day of the winter solstice had been caught in oils, showing unfrosted ice over blood-covered snow—a sense that might turn out to be a version of Pater's imaginary portrait of himself, in his Dionysian aspect, as both "the hunter and the spoil" (***GS,*** 79), doubled in self-alienation to be reintegrated in purposeful, if daemonic, performance as the finally dislocated Apollo of decidedly eccentric centripetence, who inhabits this text's complementary "Post-Face." In that autobiographical "literary architecture," which is the "mental abode" for the autobiography of linguistic consciousness, Pater's essential, if antithetical, self may occupy a textual depth of shadows within the pair of "imaginary portraits" that are of first and final frames. Pater himself becomes more substantial than diaphanous, with the laminations of superimposed "after-thoughts" providing substance if not nourishment. But then, as with a nostalgia that would take a *dis*owned body for home, one remembers that doomed creature of "immature radiance," who may be claimed, perhaps redeemed, if not resurrected, in the immaculately white antecedence of the Paterian self, whose misremembrance is a metamemory, as from the ashes—or rather shards—of a buried urn (***A,*** 152) to be reconstructed, a mosaic or relic that might show the way to a condition, itself a "persistent after-thought" (***GdL,*** 42), that might have been of a paradisiacal anteriority, and might be again, in a world of repetitions both Platonic and uncanny, even if only after the fact.

Pater's shaping impulse, as he might say after the "after-thought," is "*ex post facto*" (***GdL,*** 83), as one might also say, finally, of all of Pater's finished art.

Voice of Conjecture: For a moment—for more than a moment—one wonders whether, "*ex post facto,*" "second sights" would be the "normal" sight of the jaded eye—if, in fact, they can perceive what "might have been" in the reconstitution of paradisiacal relics, traces. But then, in Pater, "loss" is for the sake of "re-gain," just as "departure" will be for the sake of a nostalgically impelled "return": "This, to begin and end with" (***R,*** 140). Is that moment or more of "vain puerilities"? It is not, perhaps, yet of *white indeterminacy.*

The Epistolary Voice:

September 19, 18—

My Silent Confidant: (Mr. X, Esq.?) two cheers for you, who have nothing to lose. Oh, some who see my protest for what it is not may say, sagaciously, what Basilio says of Figaro. Who can blame them? But I, even if not much more than a lackey or two, a leech who was once so much more, of military verticality, reduced to the state of a—lightning, blinding, maddening—an avaricious parasite, have had everything to lose, and though the thunder closes I am not myself (I do not have much faith in this thunderstorm. And just whom have I deceived?). I may not myself entirely be this kowtower, this abject truckler, even if, or especially if, I would write so that only the initiated would understand, like Clement of Alexandria—the thunder even closer. Is it possible, R. > : Reconciliation? A Repetition? Does one dare?

Devotedly and anonymously yours. Soon to be pseudonymously yours, if dares prove too daring. And then, what's the point, anyway?

Notes

1. J. Hillis Miller, "Walter Pater: A Partial Portrait," *Daedalus* (Winter 1976): 97-113.

2. The importance of the audible in conjunction with the visible should be underscored in Plato's perception of the world. There is "the delicacy of eye and ear" (*PP,* 133); further, there is the "secret of the susceptible and diligent eye, the so sensitive ear," as well as "those finer intimations, to eye and ear" (*PP,* 134). Plato's "intimate concern with, his power over, the sensible world" is the result of "indulging, developing, refining, the sensuous capacities, the powers of eye and ear" (*PP,* 135), of "carrying an elaborate cultivation of the bodily senses, of the eye and ear" (*PP,* 139).

3. Previously, I have said that there is an important auditory Pater, and Pater is himself apparently certain that "all art constantly aspires towards the condition of music" (*R,* 135). But the problem is more complicated than the epigrammatic quotation suggests and cannot at length be discussed here. Gerald Monsmon has added an apt corrective, suggesting the spatializing—and pre- or posttemporality—of Pater's usage of language: "Music, for the most part, has a driving, linear movement. It goes places. But Pater's style, with its interminable qualifications and afterthoughts, with its parallelisms and antitheses, with its connotative richness and frequent ambiguity, is certainly anything but fluid. It is static, pictorial. It resembles the highly inflected structure of the classical languages in that it permits a more arbitrary order of words so that the sentence seems to present to the reader all of its parts simultaneously" (*Pater's Portraits* [Baltimore, 1967], p. 57).

   "All art constantly aspires towards the condition of music." The Paterian aphorism repeatedly leads to elaborated footnotes, further qualifications and complications—a densely chiasmal structure. Music, as Pater is very much aware, does more than simply go places. J. Hillis Miller points out that Pater's work "has that consonance, those unexpected echoes of this passage with that passage, those hidden resonances and harmonies which Pater saw as the ideal of a musical form that would have absorbed all its matter into that form. Nevertheless if, as Charles Rosen affirms, the basis of musical expression is dissonance, the critic must, in Pater's case, take note also of disharmonies, contradictions, omissions, hiatuses, incongruous elements which precisely do not 'work.' In such places the words seem to have exceeded the writer's apparent intention. *Such dissonances may be the most important aspect of Pater's work* [italics mine], in spite of his claim in 'Style' that the fire of a unified 'sense of the world' will in the great writers have burned away such *surplusage* (*A*, 16). In the something too much, the something left over, the odd detail which may not be evened in a musical form, the snake in the mouth of the garden god, the critic may find the clue and loose the thread that will unravel all that fine fabric of Pater's prose, with its decorous echo of pattern by pattern" ("Walter Pater," p. 103).

At the least, one might say that Pater's "thread," coiling, is one of echo, rebound, and repetition that, like much music, goes backward even as it goes forward.

4. See Ellen Frank's convincing *Literary Architecture: Essays Toward a Tradition* (Berkeley, 1979), which makes a further case for the embryonic notion of *ut architectura poesis.* The chapter on Pater is excellent and the more theoretical chapter, "The Analogical Tradition of Literary Architecture," is most provocative.

A Note on Sources

Almost all references to the works of Pater refer to what might be called the Library Edition (London, 1910) and will appear in parentheses after quotations. Abbreviations in the text are as follows:

A	*Appreciations*
A/89	*Appreciations* (1889 edition)
EG	*Essays from the "Guardian"*
GdL	*Gaston de Latour*
GS	*Greek Studies*
IP	*Imaginary Portraits*
ME1, ME2	*Marius the Epicurean* (volume 1 or 2)
MS	*Miscellaneous Studies*
PP	*Plato and Platonism*
R	*The Renaissance: Studies in Art and Poetry*

The Letters of Walter Pater, introduced and edited by Lawrence Evans (Oxford, 1970), and *Imaginary Portraits by Walter Pater,* introduced and edited by Eugene J. Brzenk (New York, 1964), which includes the unfinished "An English Poet," are noted without abbreviation. . . .

Anne Marie Candido (essay date 1993)

SOURCE: "Biography and the Objective Fallacy: Pater's Experiment in 'A Prince of Court Painters,'" in *Biography,* Vol. 16, No. 2, Spring, 1993, pp. 147-60.

[*In the following essay, Candido describes Pater's portrait of Jean-Antoine Watteau as radically incorporating multiple layers of perspective. Candido also discusses Pater's inclusion of himself as "editor" in order to demonstrate the impossibility of objective biography.*]

An enlightening though largely unacknowledged essay by Charles Whibley, "The Limits of Biography," appeared in England in 1897 in a periodical entitled *The Nineteenth Century.*[1] The essay reflects new biographical standards which marked a trend in the later part of the century toward an even more inward vision of the biographical subject than either Carlyle or the American Transcendentalists had provided, a vision not essentially moral or metaphysical (as it was for the Transcendentalists), but rather poetic and imaginative. Here is Whibley on the subject:

> the biographer's first necessity is invention rather than knowledge. If he would make a finished portrait of a man, he must treat him as he would treat the hero of a romance; he must imagine the style and habit wherein he lived. He must fill in a thousand blanks from an intuitive sympathy; should he use documents in his study he must suppress them in his work, or pass them by with a hint; thus only will he arrive at a consistent picture, and if he starts from an intelligent point of view is at least likely to approach the truth.[2]

This statement marks a distinctly revolutionary concept of the function of biography. The genre is profoundly redefined as an "imaginary portrait" with "point of view" as preeminent. Such a concept is a telling reflection of a trend during the last decades of the nineteenth century that defied both Victorian pragmatism as regards art and the standards of "objective" realism which were often revered at the expense of beauty and aesthetic form. Walter Pater was among the most radical aesthetic reformers of his time, not only in his theory of artistic form, but particularly in his approach to biographical writing. One could maintain, for example, that the highly impressionistic portraits in ***The Renaissance*** are the full flowering of a special biographical motive which had its embryonic beginnings early in the century in works such as Landor's *Imaginary Conversations* and Gaskell's *Brontë.* Although ***The Renaissance*** is indisputably a literary work of art criticism (and has been generally treated as such), and although Pater never refers to the portraits contained in the work as biographies but rather as "studies" or "essays," it is obvious enough that with the exception of the first essay these "studies" were written in the form of brief lives. The portraits of Pico della Mirandola and Winckelmann in particular are fully rounded biographical records. The others, though less systematic, follow in varying degrees the conventional birth-to-death pattern. Moreover, Pater expressly states in his "Preface" that it is through examination of the lives and personalities of individuals—that is, through biography—rather than through the study of the cultural habits, ideas, or artistic movements of an age that the identity and *Weltanschauung* of that age are most accurately revealed. Pater declares that the questions to be asked are "In *whom* did the stir, the genius, the sentiment of the period find itself? Where was the receptacle of its refinement, its elevation, its taste?"[3]

Pater's aesthetic principles, as he articulates them in the Preface to ***The Renaissance,*** provide an important key to his approach to biography, particularly since he never directly wrote down his thoughts about the genre in his various writings. One must conclude from these principles that, like any artistic work, biography is the heightened expression of the author's personal impression of his subject. Since genuine biography (which seeks the inner life of the subject) is necessarily subjective and personal—like all truth—the biographer's unique and individual perception must be regarded as a given. What makes it convincing and palpable is its expression. The biographer's chief aim is to *make* something of his perception, to capture it in an aesthetically heightened and ordered form. Perception will then become artistic vision; form and substance will become one. For Pater, artistic effect is not a vehicle for reinforcing a larger biographical purpose; it is in itself preeminent. Mode of expression, thematic structure, and tone—all emanating from the biographer's personal perspective—become the biographer's primary concerns and are his chief instruments in depicting his subject.

It is probably because of the strikingly impressionistic quality of Pater's brief lives that critics have shied away from exploring ***The Renaissance*** as biography. Indeed, many modern biographical critics would consider Pater's work too radical to be classified in the genre at all. However, Pater obviously considered his role as biographer to be visionary; he believed his vocation was to convey, in Gerald Monsman's words, "neither an artificial value system nor a set of real-life occurrences, but rather an inner vision, a complete *dramatis personae* of the soul . . . draw[ing] the same distinction as Rossetti between fact and the artist's imaginative sense of fact."[4] Yet, besides shaping the personalities of Pico, du Bellay, or Michelangelo, he also participates in them and in their "spiritual community." Thus he combines the uniqueness of his own personality and of his *empathic* faculties with a *sympathetic* participation in his subject's personality to produce a wholly fresh, synthetic vision. The product is precisely what Whibley was to prescribe: an imagined portrait. Collectively, these imagined Renaissance portraits represent the visible form, the physical embodiment of Pater's ideal spiritual community; they become still points amid the flux, the "consummate type" of Pater's own cultural ideal.

But I would like to consider Pater's brief portrait of Jean-Antoine Watteau (1684-1721) as revealing a further, even more radical step in Pater's contribution to visionary biography. **"A Prince of Court Painters"** first appeared in 1885 as a separate piece in *Macmillan's Magazine* and was then published as the first portrait in ***Imaginary Portraits*** (1887). Monsman argues persuasively that after ***The Renaissance*** Pater felt confined by the facts of historical personalities in expressing his vision of the ideal aesthetic personality. He needed more freedom "both with respect to external events and also inner motives," a synthesis he could achieve more fully in completely imaginary portraits.[5] The life of Pico, for example, has "rough edges and [does] not fit easily into a preconceived fictional pattern of dénouement. Few historical lives do.[6] And so, Pater began to create his own fictional subjects, even though in the process he placed them in distinct historical contexts—an accomplishment reached only by continued laborious historical research. A series of short imaginary portraits ensued, including **"A Child in the House"** (1887), **"An English Poet"** (1878), as well as the full-length historical novel, ***Marius the Epicurean*** (1885), and those portraits contained in ***Gaston Latour*** (1896).

These portraits of fictional personalities bear close resemblance to those in ***Imaginary Portraits,*** which also treats the mythical experience and lives of fictional characters—with the notable exception of the portrait of Watteau, the first in the collection. This portrait is unique in the volume insofar as it represents a genre somewhere between the visionary biographies of the earlier Renaissance lives and the wholly imaginary portraits contained in ***Imaginary Portraits.***[7] And yet, Whibley considered this portrait to be the very model of biographical form and technique. "When Mr. Pater drew his imaginary portrait of Watteau," he writes,

> he excluded from the perfected work all the sketches and experiments which had aided its composition. There was no parade of knowledge or research, and such research as discovered the quality of the artist was held severely in reserve. This, then, is the ideal of biography: an imagined portrait stripped of all that is unessential, into which no detail is introduced without a deliberate choice and a definite intention.[8]

William E. Buckler has remarked that the "essential truth" of Pater's portrait of Watteau "has been confirmed by a century of increasingly sophisticated art history and art criticism,"[9] and Ruth Child has earlier pointed out that despite the obvious fictional elements of the portrait, one need only consult Friedrich Staub's *Das Imaginäre Porträt Walter Paters* to be convinced that Pater had "studied the best sources of information, and woven them together skillfully, adhering closely to the facts, and at the same time trying to penetrate the motives that lay underneath them. He has done exactly what is attempted by writers of the modern school of biography: and . . . has taken scarcely any more liberties than they do."[10] Child's allusion here to the "modern school of biography" undoubtedly refers to a twentieth-century trend toward rigid scholarly research into every external and psychological "fact" available. Yet it is well that Child qualifies her final statement with "scarcely," for Pater has taken one very substantial liberty with biographical fact—one involving a major theme of the portrait which lies at the core of its dramatic structure. Pater had the fond hope and some evidence that he was a descendent of Jean-Baptiste Pater, a protegé of Watteau.[11] Jean-Baptiste is a prominent figure in **"A Prince of Court Painters,"** and more importantly, Jean-Baptiste's sister, Marie-Marguerite, is the author of the imaginary journal that comprises the formal structure of the portrait. Pater assigns to Marie-Marguerite a fictional, unrequited love for Watteau, and in so doing introduces an even more intimate connection between his family and the subject of his—or, that is, Marie-Marguerite's—portrait.

Pater thus chose not to ascribe his portrait of Watteau to himself, but rather to the invented personality of the historically real Marie-Marguerite, whose fictionalized feelings and meditations provide an effective framework for a unique perspective of what Pater himself obviously thought to be a pattern of Watteau's character. With a curious double perspective, Pater publicly relegates his own role merely to editor of the journal—the full title of the portrait being **"A Prince of Court Painters: Extracts from an Old French Journal."** Although the word "extracts" may imply that the entries of the journal are merely those which remained extant at the time the editor lived, the much stronger implication is that the editor consciously extracted them from a larger body of material, regarding them as most relevant to a fictional point of view, supplanting his own with Marie-Marguerite's; yet as silent and assumed editor he admits his artistic intervention in his contribution toward the fine tuning of that point of view. The portrait thus becomes a kind of visionary biography thrice removed—a biographical portrait of a real person framed by a fictionally edited imaginary journal. Monsman maintains that since Pater makes use of these fictional elements and "distancing" techniques, his primary concern "is not with biography but with the portrayal of an imagined world."[12] Yet it is clear, it seems to me, that Pater's portrait is an important and provocative experiment in genre, radically exploring the possibilities of artistic biography while also testing the limits of biographical truth. Given the premise, perhaps controversial, that we ought to define the limits of biography in terms of what each age has accepted *as biography* rather than to define its limits according to a preconceived set of standards, and given the obvious intention of Pater to demonstrate the complexities of point of view and perspective as they affect any struggle to capture a personality, we should find it useful to examine **"A Prince of Court Painters"** as a genuine attempt to gain insight into the spirit of the subject's life in an ordered, aesthetic form. It is interesting to note that much of the life and personality of Watteau is still shrouded in mystery—even today, despite the fact that we have a fairly complete chronology of the major events of his life. This fact provided Pater a greater challenge and rationale in offering his own version of Watteau's personality in a fashion similar to Whibley's prescription.

Like ***Marius the Epicurean,*** **"A Prince of Court Painters"** depicts its central character as seeking an aesthetic ideal. But unlike Marius' search, which is earnest, thoughtful, and finally consummated, Watteau's is agitated, preoccupied, and never wholly fulfilled. As Marie-Marguerite perceives him, Watteau is continually unable to synthesize the extremes of Valenciennes, his quiet and rather staid Flemish home village, and of the active, convivial, though shallow, life of Paris where he lives most of his adult life as an artist. He eventually becomes aware that great artistic expression, as well as a genuinely happy life for himself, cannot result from his experience in either of these cities alone but must be drawn from his own creative synthesis of the two. So he spends much of his life restlessly darting from one city to the other as if to draw a balance of sustenance from each. Gradually, according to Marie-Marguerite, he begins to invest the shallow elements of Parisian life (i.e., the ornate laces and antiques, the lively social gatherings, the fashionable ladies) with "a wonderful sagacity" inherited from his youthful career as a mason in Valenciennes.[13] He imposes "an air of real superiority on such things" in his pursuit of "his dream—his dream of a better world than the real one."[14]

But intellectually, Marie-Marguerite's Watteau becomes aware that this dream cannot be realized in the depiction of such superficial objects and studies, despite his abilities to deepen them and give them a "representative or borrowed worth" (256). Yet both his temperament and his love of fame have drawn him inexorably to a love of these objects; they have already become a permanent part of him and he cannot let them go. Nor can "he make a reality his long-pondered journey" (250) to Rome—the city where he would have encountered the aesthetically balanced life he sought. There, as Marie-Marguerite suggests, he would have learned how to give form and substance equal value. Instead, he becomes lost in what Monsman calls "the fragmentation of experience."[15] Watteau's unhappiness with his predicament is reflected in the restlessness not only of his life but also of his art. Always discontented with himself, he never seems to paint anything completely. Everything seems half finished. Marie-Marguerite writes in her journal: "It is pleasanter to him to sketch and plan than to paint and finish; and he is often out of humour with himself because he cannot project into a picture the life and spirit of his first thought with the *crayon*" (257).[16]

At last Watteau decides to make a journey—but to England, not Rome. Knowing that England is the "veritable home of the consumptive," Marie-Marguerite regards his move as ominous:

> Ah me! I feel it may be the finishing stroke. To have run into the native country of consumption! Strange caprice of that desire to travel, which he has really indulged so little in life—of the restlessness which, they tell men, is itself a symptom of this terrible disease! (259)

As if in fulfillment of her fears, Watteau falls ill on his return from England. Soon after, he dies "after receiving the last sacraments" and after "he had been at work upon a crucifix for the good curé of Nogent, liking little the very rude one he possessed" (262). Monsman attributes a significance to this crucifix which reflects a kind of final attainment of the Ideal: "It is large enough to encompass the soul and its dreams of a world of immortal love; in it we do not see the forms of sense struggling vainly to contain in the narrow sensuousness of the present moment some unmanageable vision."[17] Yet whatever synthesis Watteau finally does attain, Marie-Marguerite finds that it is inspired solely by the otherworldly, for he has never found contentment in this world. Marie-Marguerite articulates this pathetic fact: "For the rest, bodily exhaustion perhaps, and this new interest in an old friend, have brought him tranquility at last, a tranquility in which he is much occupied with matters of religion. . . . Yet I know not what there is of a pity which strikes deep, at the thought of a man, a while since so strong, turning his face to the wall from the things which most occupy men's lives" (261). Finally, he was able to find happiness only in the denial of the very things to which he had wholly dedicated his life.

Such is the portrait that Marie-Marguerite draws for the reader in her personal journal. It presents the image of Watteau that Pater himself clearly had extracted not only from his research but from his own sympathetic imagination. In order to grasp the more radical elements of Pater's portrait, however—elements that even Whibley would not have acknowledged or grasped as desirable in a biography—it behooves us to analyze the female voice and personality of the narrator as she records her meditations and intermittent encounters with her subject.

In consistently portraying Watteau as too abstractly preoccupied with his quest, too cold and distant in his character to accept close friendships and intimate contact with those around him, Marie-Marguerite suggests that he is temperamentally incapable of accepting the fact that *she* might be the solution to his restless unhappiness with himself, that *she* might be the embodiment of the Ideal for which he is seeking. He is so embroiled in the world of flux that he passes her by, along with everything else. At sudden and erratic intervals he is always departing from or returning to Valenciennes, and Marie-Marguerite poignantly sums up her perception of his fragmented relationship with her in an entry marked July 1714: "My own portrait remains unfinished at his sudden departure" (250). He never does, in fact, finish the portrait but leaves it for his protegé, Jean-Baptiste, to finish. Marie-Marguerite finds that because of his frequent and often long absences, she can observe his life only indirectly: "Well! We shall follow his fortunes . . . at a distance" (240), she laments early on in her diary after Watteau's first departure to Paris. She must base her knowledge of his life in Paris on such inadequate sources as infrequent letters from Watteau himself, rumor, or a few fragmented, second-hand reports from Jean-Baptiste (her vicarious point of contact with her beloved). Indeed, in Watteau's absence, her brother's art becomes "the central interest" (251) of her life. Although it is far inferior to Watteau's art, she finds satisfaction in it because it is her only tangible link to him. Eventually, Marie-Marguerite anticipates her own occasional tragic failures "even in imagination" to recreate what his life must be like in the foreign but convivial and rich life of Paris:

> Antony Watteau returned to Paris yesterday. Yes!—Certainly, great heights of achievement would seem to lie before him; access to regions whither one may find it increasingly hard to follow him even in imagination and figure to one's self after what manner his life moves therein. (244)

Fittingly, whether the result of Pater's fictional editing or because Marie-Marguerite herself has ceased writing for a time, the journal entry which follows this discouraging meditation is separated by a span of four whole years.

Eventually, her frustration is so keen that she begins to express it outright—poignantly and tragically:

> One's journal, here in one's solitude, is of service at least in this, that it affords an escape for vain regrets, angers, impatience. One puts this and that angry spasm into it, and is delivered from it. (259)

It becomes evident that Marie-Marguerite is as unfulfilled as she perceives Watteau to be, increasingly convinced that if Watteau had only chosen to remain with her, away from both his family's cold and impersonal stone residence and away from the lively but shallow life of Paris, he, as well as she, might have found happiness: "It would have been better for him—he would have enjoyed a purer and more real happiness—had he remained here, obscure; as it might have been better for me!" (251-252). It is soon clear that each bit of information we learn about Watteau's personality, his life, and his art is told to us by a frustrated lover. We inevitably conclude that Marie-Marguerite's vision is charged with an empathic imagination, filled with fond rationalizations about the causes of Watteau's unhappiness. Is Marie-Marguerite *really* the "solution" to Watteau's unfulfilled yearnings? One has the strong impression that Marie-Marguerite, taking on the role of "psychobiographer,"[18] on some level *knows* that her portrait is not merely the result of any "objective" observations of Watteau but also, to some extent, the creation and reflection of her private wishes and frustrations, for Pater persistently invests her portrait with all the impressionistic and indeterminate expressions one typically finds in a personal diary:[19]

> "As we understand from him . . ."
>
> "I could fancy myself . . ."
>
> "Can it be that . . .?"
>
> "Methinks I see him there . . ."
>
> "As I may judge . . ."
>
> "It would seem . . ."
>
> "It is as if . . ."
>
> "To persuade myself of that, is my womanly satisfaction . . ."

Through this narrative voice, which reveals what Leon Edel would regard as a dangerous kind of "transference,"[20]

Pater has chosen to depict an aesthetically ordered portrait based on his research of a life only sketchily known by art historians. Yet, Pater would say that what Marie-Marguerite does in her diary is nothing more than what he himself or any biographer does, consciously or unconsciously, given the inevitable subjectiveness of personal perspective and of biographical truth. Hers is a highly personal but resolute and unapologetic attempt to impose some kind of intelligent order, some logical sequence and motive, some meaning on the sporadic events, reports, and contacts which pass by her. The very entries in her diary reveal at least an attempt to define and hold still for a time the flux in which she envisions Watteau entangled. While Watteau seems incapable of completing anything or of finding such still points in his own life and in his art, Marie-Marguerite successfully creates her diary as a psychological and artistic instrument of escape from the flux. But it is a positive instrument insofar as she builds a creative structuring all her own. Her personality is an ordering rather than a self-destructive one. Complementing her sympathetic portrait of Watteau, her empathic imagination shapes the events of Watteau's life in accordance with the requirements and injunctions of her psyche. In shaping these events she represents much more fully than does Watteau a positive, determined, and creative force which captures and interprets moments of time—moments in which Watteau seems so embroiled as to be "distant and preoccupied" (247) when confronting his own opportunity to order them. It is as if Marie-Marguerite were the writer to whom she refers who interprets and lends meaning to the tragedy of a bird caught helplessly fluttering from window to window within the confines of a stone church. Although she too is in a sense caught in a tragic situation in her unrequited love, she finally is able through her personal vision to invest her tragedy, as well as what she perceives to be Watteau's, with the composure of a truly aesthetic personality. While Watteau must rely for his consolation on the rites and sentiments of another world and on the creation of a religious object meant for someone else, she has created *for herself* a permanent, concrete monument of this world from which she can derive sustenance.

Artistically shaping the thematic emphasis, tone, and language of her portrait she lends form and beauty to her perception of Watteau—a perception, though, which the "editor" has further refined. Perhaps the real irony of the portrait is that Marie-Marguerite, an obscure permanent resident of an obscure town, unintentionally portrays herself as the central and most successful artist of the piece rather than the Prince of Court Painters. Her portrait, despite its chronological holes, is at least artistically complete (unlike Watteau's portrait of her), assuming the perhaps justifiable pretense of more palpably revealing Watteau's personality than does his own art.

It is obvious that Pater the "editor" intended the reader of this portrait to feel the kind of illicit thrill one might have in reading a diary meant to be secret—a private vision, teasingly punctuated by long periods of silence. It is a vision whose full meaning only the fictional personality of the narrator can unlock, but which the editor has attempted to interpret for us through his own art of biographical editing and thus through his own sympathetic insight into Watteau. Yet despite its tone and poetic mystery, it also irresistibly invites our own sympathetic participation into the private psyche of the narrator, into the workings of her perception of Watteau's life and personality. Through Pater's portrait, the reader finds a handle, so to speak, on the otherwise historically enigmatic personality and motives of Watteau, but only as they must be filtered through the personality of Marie-Marguerite (who, in turn, often interprets facts filtered by letters and reports from her informant, Jean-Baptiste); the resultant meditations by the narrator are then finally shaped by the supposed "editor" himself. And all of these layers of perspective, of course, are borne out of Pater's own laborious research into the "real," i.e., historical, facts of Watteau's life. Thus, not surprisingly, our sympathetic participation in the narrator's portrait is by no means solely emotional; it is also aesthetic—detached enough from Marie-Marguerite and her subjective depiction of Watteau to leave us with as strong a sense of the work's beauty and ingeniously crafted form as of its tragedy and pathos.[21]

Clearly, Pater's experiment here radically stretches the limits of biographical truth for his time, and even for our own. Yet the portrait is in itself a testimony to and probing into the very real dilemmas of "point of view" and its relation to biographical "truth." Pater seems only to be bringing to our attention the varied and complex layers of point of view involved in the act of capturing an inner or poetic truth. Artistically recording and analyzing the life, personality, and motives of any biographical subject involves two important responsibilities and processes of the biographer. The first is the acquiring of the "facts," through careful research, which may very well turn out to be incomplete, sketchy, or already distilled by very subjective points of view replete with hidden agendas, transferences, or distanced perspectives. The second is the conscious artistic shaping of those distilled facts into a creative "imagined" portrait, one borne inescapably and naturally out of the biographer's own personality and private agendas (i.e., Pater's hope that he was related to Jean-Baptiste), yet one also ordered and synthesized. The editing of a biographical portrait, of course, involves yet more labyrinthine removals from any presumed conception of the "real thing." Finally, Pater seems to want us to conclude that "the real thing" is not something to be grasped at in biography and is indeed not even a realistic *desideratum* of biography. Inherent in the tone of Pater's portrait of Watteau is always the unarticulated but bold assumption that the important thing is that the biographer be true to his own sympathetic and empathic perceptions in his creation of a coherent, ordered, and aesthetic vision. Pater would have considered psychological transference on the part of the biographer as natural and inevitably human—and therefore not at all an obstacle to effective biography or portraiture. On the contrary, if the transference is palpable and obvious to the reader, the human perspective and dimension it would assume would lend a further poignancy and beauty to the portrait.[22]

The great achievement of Pater's experiment in **"A Prince of Court Painters"** is not only the unity, beauty, and poignancy of its vision of Watteau, but also the evocation of the limitless complexities of the human sympathetic and empathic imagination, as well as the layers of human perspective as they are inevitably involved in the biographer's task. As such, it is a portrait that challenges some of our own twentieth-century assumptions regarding the feasibility and even desirability of striving for "objective" or "neutral" biography—a goal which Pater must surely have regarded, finally, as chimerical.

Notes

1. (March 1897): 428-436. Charles Whibley (1859-1930) was a scholar, critic, editor, journalist, and a Tory, who was also much admired during his time as a stylist, conversationalist, and accomplished writer of *belles lettres.* One of his admirers, T. S. Eliot, described him as someone who "wrote chiefly for occasion, either in his monthly commentary on men, events, and current books, or in his essays and prefaces, or sometimes in a lecture" (*Charles Whibley: A Memoir.* The English Association, Pamphlet No. 80, p. 5). Whibley was the author of *Literary Portraits* (1904), *Essays in Biography* [Biographical sketches] (1913), *Political Portraits* (1914), and *Literary Studies* (1919), among other works. Charles A. Le Guin only briefly alludes to Whibley's essay on biography, mentioned here, in his article "The Language of Portraiture" in *Biography* 6:336.
2. "The Limits of Biography," 435. A segment of Whibley's essay is also found in *Biography as an Art,* James Clifford, ed. (New York: Oxford Univ. Press, 1962) 107-110.
3. *The Renaissance Studies in Art and Poetry* in *Walter Pater: Three Major Texts (The Renaissance, Appreciations, Imaginary Portraits).* William E. Buckler, ed. (New York: New York Univ. Press, 1986) 73.
4. *Walter Pater* (Boston, Twayne, 1977) 137.
5. *Pater's Portraits: Mythic Patterns in the Fiction of Walter Pater* (Baltimore: Johns Hopkins Univ. Press, 1967) 63.
6. *Ibid,* 62-63.
7. Pater's eventual impatience with real-life subjects for his portraits is reflected interestingly also in Watteau's own "reticence about the personality of his sitter," which Donald Posner notes in *Antoine Watteau* (Ithaca, N.Y.: Cornell Univ. Press, 1984) "is a reflection of [Watteau's] discomfort with the traditional constraints [i.e., of realism] and demands of portraiture. His imagination was sustained by fantasy, and it was happiest with the fictionalized doings of *types,*" (245) just as Pater seemed most comfortable with creating his personalities as mythical types than as subjects of "realistic" portraits.
8. "The Limits of Biography," 435.
9. *Walter Pater: Three Major Texts,* 42
10. *The Aesthetic of Walter Pater* (New York: Macmillan, 1900) 112.
11. Paul Barolsky, in *Walter Pater's Renaissance* (University Park: The Pennsylvania State Univ. Press, 1987), writes: "When asked if his family was related to that of the painter Jean-Baptiste Pater, [Pater] replied: 'I think so, I believe so, I always say so.' The very tone and structure of this utterance—of which the point is that his speech exceeds his grasp—are a perfect emblem of Pater" (4).
12. *Pater's Portraits,* 100.
13. Posner maintains that it was a popular interpretation of Watteau's works in the nineteenth century to emphasize the melancholy sentiment in his paintings and sketches which "allowed one to attribute a quality of seriousness, of profundity, to images that appear on the surface trivial or pointless in subject. Thus Watteau could be said to have a 'philosophy' . . . which provided the necessary justification for a conviction that the artist has a place among the greatest painters in history" (8).
14. *Imaginary Portraits* in *Walter Pater: Three Major Texts,* 256. Subsequent references to "A Prince of Court Painters" are noted parenthetically in the text.
15. *Walter Pater,* 130.
16. Posner remarks on the erratic nature of Watteau's attempts to complete a work: ". . . Watteau, unable to satisfy himself, would sometimes efface and re-do completely finished parts of pictures. The artist normally must have had several, maybe many, paintings in different states of completion in his studio at one time. A picture begun after another may have been completed before it, and a picture reworked over a period of many months, perhaps years in some cases, as a whole reflects no precise moment in Watteau's career" (10).
17. *Pater's Portraits,* 107.
18. For a discussion of the psychobiographer, see Eva Schepeler's "The Biographer's Transference: A Chapter in Psychobiographical Epistemology." *Biography* 13: 111-129.
19. Note Pater's own palpable tendency to reveal his private wishes concerning his possible familial connection with Jean-Baptiste Pater. Barolsky observes that in Pater's statement regarding this connection (see ff. 11), it is obvious that Pater "both believes and disbelieves what he argues" (4) just as does Marie-Marguerite here. One cannot help but note, moreover, that a number of books on Watteau must inevitably—as a result of the mystery surrounding Watteau's personal life—also make use of this inde-

terminate language. Posner, for example, writes this: "Our knowledge of Watteau's private life is necessarily fragmentary. . . . One might like to imagine him. . . . There is, however, no evidence of this supposition, and it seems very unlikely that . . ." (181), etc.

20. See *Writing Lives: Principia Biographica* (New York and London: Norton, 1984), which includes a chapter entitled "Transference," earlier published as "Transference: The Biographer's Dilemma" in *Biography* 7:283-291.

21. Thomas Wright, in his biography *The Life of Walter Pater* (New York: G. P. Putnam's Sons, 1907), writes: "Pater has wrought into the leading facts of Watteau's career a wistful tenderness, and has clothed them with ethereal beauty, forming a picture as delicate and as dreamy almost as Watteau's own beautiful work" (vol. 2, 184). Posner maintains, however, that this traditionally nineteenth-century perception of Watteau (obviously shared by Pater) is not necessarily wholly true since the core of Watteau's art, he feels, is actually "a joyful affirmation of love. . . . His pictures are robust and virile, full of humour, sometimes bawdy in tone, and the action in them not at all so vague or ambiguous as is usually thought" (8).

22. Leon Edel's premise in his critical writings is, of course, that objective biography *is* a *desideratum* and is essentially within the grasp of a good biographer; less effective biographers have succumbed unconsciously to the pitfalls of transference, which usually produces dangerous obstacles to faithful rendering.

    Eva Schepeler indicates, in her article, that developing transferences is almost inevitable on the part of the psychobiographer, but she suggests various practical steps for "professional" psychobiographers to take as correctives in dealing with their feelings of transference, with the hopeful result that they might attain as faithful a rendering of the subject as possible.

Christopher Coates (essay date 1994)

SOURCE: "Exhumation and Anachronism: Walter Pater and Nineteenth-Century Historicism," in *Victorians Institute Journal,* Vol. 22, 1994, pp. 99-113.

[In the following essay, Coates describes "Duke Carl of Rosenmold" as Pater's treatment of the conflict between historical difference and historical continuity.]

> May it be my part in the future, to have not attained, but marked the goal of history, to have called it a name that no one else had. Thierry called it narration, and M. Guizot analysis. I have named it resurrection, and this name will remain.
>
> Jules Michelet, *Le Peuple*

> In a bright dress he rambled among the graves, in the gay weather, and so came, in one corner, upon an open grave for a child—a dark space on the brilliant grass—the black mould lying heaped up around it, weighing down the little jewelled branches of the dwarf rose-bushes in flower.
>
> Walter Pater, **"The Child in the House"**

A century after they are trampled to death and buried, as the story of Pater's **"Duke Carl of Rosenmold"** goes, the corpses of the Duke and his wife are unexpectedly unearthed when a tree falls during a storm.[1] Thus it happens that the bejeweled remains of the Duke and his wife become exposed at once to the scrutiny of nearby villagers, Pater, and us. During their examination of this singular exhumation, the villagers find that at last they can solve several local mysteries, not the least of which is the story of the Duke's final dispensation. At some point during the act of standing over an opened grave, in other words, Pater's villagers find the ability to resolve a narrative that had been considered unresolvable.

This "face to face" tableau, as I have described it, is one way to characterize historical practice in the nineteenth century. That an understanding of the past demands a physical apprehension, that this evidence in turn creates a liaison between chronologically separated epochs, is a typically nineteenth-century conception that Pater himself "unearths" for evaluation in this portrait.[2] More to the point, Pater's simulation of this tableau serves as his critique of its theoretical underpinnings.[3] Although the villagers' own curiosities may be resolved easily by this striking scene, the questions that Pater uncovers in this, his most sustained discussion of historical exhumation, become increasingly more complex.

One such complication is Pater's extensive discussion of historical anachronism in **"Duke Carl of Rosenmold."** From the beginning, Pater suggests that a rhetorical similarity may exist between the century-old corpses and the people who view them. The fact that the Duke's story has been unresolved for so long, and is therefore perpetually "current," keeps this imagined similarity dynamic and viable. One way "currency" is evidenced, for instance, is in Pater's decision to describe the villagers' reaction to the corpses by recreating the night of the Duke's death: ". . . the disposition of the remains suggested to them a lively picture of a sullen night, the unexpected passing of a great army, and the two lovers rushing forth wildly at the sudden tumult outside their cheerful shelter, caught in the dark and trampled out so, surprised and unseen, among the heroes and the heavy guns" (***IP*** 120-21).

We find later that the villagers share this anachronistic desire to re-enact past narratives with their ancestor, Duke Carl, whose persona in the years leading up to his death had become a patchwork of affected cultural and historical artifacts. Duke Carl, in other words, had become a walking anachronism.

Although it is a term that one hears often, it is not at all clear what is meant by the word *anachronism.* As it is typically used, anachronism implies a judgment—as if the very act of identifying an anachronistic element were also an attempt to return it to its proper, chronological space. For Pater, however, anachronism is not something merely to be corrected, as such an action assumes a "correct" or progressive notion of history. Instead, the concept of anachronism, in Pater's hands, becomes a rhetorical device that exposes the inevitable discrepancies in this progressive notion of history.[4] One of the more prominent such discrepancies is the paradoxical desire to revive an "ancient subject" in the name of progress or enlightenment:

> And yet it is one of the charming anachronisms of a poet, who, while he handles an ancient subject, never becomes an antiquarian, but animates his subject by keeping it always close to himself. . . .
>
> In handling a subject of Greek legend, anything in the way of an actual revival must always be impossible. Such vain antiquarianism is a waste of the poet's power. The composite experience of all the ages is part of each one of us; to deduct from that experience, to obliterate any part of it, to come face to face with the people of a past age, . . . is as impossible as to become a little child, or enter again into the womb and be born. (**"Aesthetic Poetry"** 195-96)

The poet's simple anachronism, like the anachronism that one corrects, is harmless and inconsequential. "Face to face" communion—the kind that appears to be taking place at graveside in **"Duke Carl of Rosenmold"**—however, is as complicated in its cultural implications as the Duke's desire to exhume the Apollonian ideal for modern Germany. Similarly, the poet's anachronism is as "charming" as the Duke's originally benign interest in Celtes, the German poet who inspires his Apollonianism. When his flirtation with this anachronistic power tempts him into effecting a revival, however, the results are the increasingly complex machinations that eventually lead to his self-destruction.[5] The Duke's progress from curiosity to self-annihilation to exhumation, therefore, can be used to identify Pater's own use and critique of this historical problem that achieves such prominence in the nineteenth century.

This so-called progress begins, anachronistically enough, in 1486—the year that Conrad Celtes's own summons for cultural revival is printed: "the young Duke Carl *laid his hand* on an old volume of the year 1486, printed in heavy type, with frontispiece, perhaps, by Albert Durer—*Ars Versificandi: The Art of Versification:* by Conrad Celtes. Crowned poet of the Emperor Frederick the Third, he had the right to speak on that subject; for while he vindicated as best he might old German literature against the charge of barbarism, he did also a man's part towards reviving in the Fatherland the *knowledge* of the poetry of Greece and Rome" (123; emphasis added).[6]

Here and throughout the portrait, Pater situates each historical artifact as specifically as possible so that, in this case, the Duke's touching of the book becomes, as Pater suggests, an attempt to efface chronological history. Duke Carl's "vision," moreover, comes not so much from his reading of the Celtes text as it does from the volume's sensual qualities augmented by other revelatory elements: "Those verses, coming to the boy's hand *at the right moment,* brought a beam of effectual daylight to a whole magazine of observation, fancy, desire, stored up from the first impressions of childhood. To bring Apollo and his lyre to Germany! It was precisely that he, Carl, desired to do—was, as he might flatter himself, actually doing" (123-24; emphasis added).

Pater does not disclose whether this "moment" occurs at the "right" time in the Duke's life, in the continuum of temporarily frozen German culture, or in the happy convergence of historically transcendent elements with cultural desire (i.e. the hand of Apollo). Like the Duke, Pater finds it best to leave the source of this moment mystified. For Duke Carl, this mystification—for him unequivocal and physical evidence of "a world beyond"—becomes carte blanche for his other anachronistic manipulations of culture and history. For Duke Carl, it seems, sensory evidence participates in two worlds: it is the courier of phenomena transcending particular cultures at the same time that it provides a grounding for phenomena inside his own. Physical and intellectual phenomena, for him, do not reside in isolated spheres; so it is to the physical realm that he constantly turns for explanations to intellectual problems. He wonders, for instance, whether "a physical cause might lie beneath [his] strange restlessness, like the imperfect reminiscence of something that had passed in an earlier life" (133).[7] Like the villagers who observe the results of his exhumation, the Duke believes that he can resolve his fragmented nature with unequivocal, physical evidence.

Consequently, in his attempt to bring Apollo to his "candlelit people," the Duke dons and discards cultural artifacts as if these anachronistic maneuvers might resurrect that original, powerful contact with the Celtes volume. To Germany, for instance, he brings "Apollo in the dandified costume of Lewis the Fourteenth" (124); he redecorates his royal residence with "'pavilions' (after the manner of the famous Mansard)" (124); and he stages French plays, such as Marivaux's *Death of Hannibal,* wherein "Duke Carl himself, attired after the newest French fashion, play[s] the part of Hannibal [247-183 BC]" (125).[8] By organizing his life through these artifacts, it might be argued, the Duke succeeds in his goal of suspending the influence of the German culture to which he belongs. Indeed, Pater tells us in the afterword that the *Aufklärung* did spring full blown into German history—not by the Duke but through his spiritual allies: Lessing, Herder, and Goethe.

The "successes" the Duke may have generated, however, should be qualified by the consistent failure of sensual artifacts to achieve his anachronistic ends. None of them seems to satisfy: "One fault only Carl found in his French models, and was resolute to correct. He would have, at least within, real marble in place of stucco, and, if he might, perhaps solid gold for gilding" (125). These costly, decidedly unspiritual materials, in turn, become the fabric of the Duke's "new" self-presentation. As a result of these elaborate attempts, the portrait of Duke Carl becomes not that of a man inhabited by the "spirit of Apollo" or the manifestation of some long-awaited Hellenic Zeitgeist; it becomes the story of a man whose desperation to transcend his culture drives him further into the material economy of that very culture. By extension, anachronism, in its appearance of getting beyond cultural and historical boundaries, fixes one all the more inside those boundaries.

Nonetheless, the Duke sees himself as one who moves freely between cultures and chronologies. "Middle Age" Germany, for example, becomes present and future Germany: "The spirits of distant Hellas would reawake in the men and women of little German towns. Distant times, the most alien thoughts, would come near together, as elements in a great historic symphony. A kind of ardent, new patriotism awoke in him, sensitive for the first time at the words *national* poesy, *national* art and literature, *German* philosophy" (144-45).

It is possible for the Duke to consider such concepts as "patriotism" and "nationalism" precisely because he believes them to be, like himself, disengaged from culture. These formations are the acts of a free, self-determining will, of a mind that can orchestrate a "symphony" of artifacts free from their place in chronology or culture, simply because it has disengaged its interest from it, because it has wrenched itself from culture's hold: "[a] free, open space had been determined, which something now to be created, created by him, must occupy" (145). Convinced that this end has been realized, the Duke imagines himself to be—as villagers confirm with their comments as he passes down the street—Apollo himself.

Since thus to transcend culture is also to transcend the self, this cultural annihilation turns out to entail a kind of self-annihilation.[9] Duke Carl's violent death, then, should not surprise us, especially after Pater speaks of the "Resurgam on Carl's empty coffin" (153). In the end, the Duke and his "beggarmaid" wife, whom he asks to "believe in him," "flee *into* the tumult" (152; emphasis added). But even this last-ditch effort to destroy self, wife, and culture, to achieve some kind of desperate transcendence, is met with a political, historicizing response: the trampling hooves of a very contemporary German army.

Indeed, the Duke's desire for cultural transcendence through cultural revival has the opposite effect in the end: it makes him a prominent cultural figure and figuration of culture. At the time that they are uncovered, for example, the lovers' bodies had been familiar and "contemporary" artifacts for a full century: "for the minds of some long-remembering people their discovery set at rest an old query. It had never been precisely known what was become of the young Duke Carl, who disappeared from the world a century before. . . . Restless, romantic, eccentric, had he passed on with the victorious host, and taken the chances of an obscure soldier's life?" (120).

Other documents contribute to the discursive web that surrounds these bodies: "Certain old letters hinted at a different ending—love letters which provided for a secret meeting, preliminary perhaps to the final departure of the young Duke (who, by the usage of his realm, could only with extreme difficulty go whither, or marry whom, he pleased) to whatever worlds he had chosen, not of his own people" (120).

Instead of being associated with linear intellectual progress, Duke Carl's legacy is a complicated narrative web that has insinuated itself into every villager's life to be passed along, reworked, reconstructed. When the exhumed bodies arrive on the scene a century later, they do not so much function as a corroboration of a single, heroic legend, but as another sensational and vibrant text that feeds the thick network of discourse that prefigures the corpses. The Duke who sought to become pure spirit has instead become the stuff of popular legend. By participating in the Duke's exhumation a century later, the villagers do indeed resolve an ancient narrative. More important, however, or so Pater implies, they create a new, more complicated narrative of their own.

The resolution of this narrative for the villagers is signaled by Pater's entry, deus ex machina, to tell us what really happened to Duke Carl of Rosenmold and his wife. Resolving the story of Duke Carl neatly for the villagers with an act of exhumation allows Pater to examine the complexities and problems with exhumation as a historical practice. Pater sets up the villagers, in other words, as practitioners of a method that calls for his rigorous examination and critique.

Establishing the villagers this way, however, also includes the rhetorically suspect maneuver of making the villagers part of a culture that is "frozen"; the villagers, by implication, are somehow uncomplicated and naive: "Time, at the beginning of the eighteenth century might seem to have been standing still almost since the Middle Age—since the days of the Emperor Charles the Fifth, at which period, . . . a sudden tide of wealth, flowing through the grand-ducal exchequer, had left a kind of golden architectural splendour on the place, always too ample for its population" (121).

Pater's villagers might be expected to react the same way to the exhumed bodies; an inability to absorb "ampleness" is strongly embedded, having had "almost since the Middle Age" to do its work. Consequently, they are easily convinced of the power and finality of the Duke's exhumation. For them, the exhumation is the conclusive, physical resolution to a complex narrative.

Pater's "stepping-in," then, is itself a significant historicizing gesture. It is important for the villagers' narrative to seem resolved, precisely because it allows him to contrast and intensify his own. Since the villagers—in their timeless simplicity—are unable to distinguish historical complexity, Pater must do so for them. Indeed, the catalyst for their curiosity is a "popular fancy," a fairy tale much like the ones that Pater sets up as evidence of a superstitious, pre-*Aufklärung* Germany. It is Pater from his chronologically advantageous position in 1887 who must historically situate the villagers and Duke Carl. Instead of completing any single narrative, Pater suggests, exhumation opens up numerous others and thus makes this kind of historical discourse impossible to resolve or simplify. In their historical naiveté, the villagers are unable to take in the "ampleness" of such complexities.

To these ends, Pater adopts a version of German history wherein he may endorse or dismiss, as it suits him, a progressive or Enlightenment-based history. Thus having it both ways is what Friedrich Nietzsche—in his own critique of nineteenth-century historical practice—might call the act of an *überhistorische,* or "superhistorical," philosopher:

> [the super-historical philosophers] are unanimous in the theory that the past and the present are one and the same, typically alike in all their diversity, and forming together a picture of eternally present imperishable types of unchangeable value and significance. Just as hundreds of different languages respond to the same constant and elemental needs of mankind, and one who understood the needs could learn nothing new from the languages; so the "superhistorical" philosopher sees all the history of nations and individuals from within. He has divine insight into the original meaning of the hieroglyphs. ("Use" 14)

Although it would be wrong to accuse him of what Nietzsche has overstated for rhetorical advantage, Pater does indeed want it both ways: he wants to exhume both the body and the problems of the Duke at the same time that he wants to critique the use and abuse of such exhumations; he wants to point out the need to consider historical difference at the same time that he often operates within a model of historical continuity. One of the more conspicuous such dual positions is Pater's alternate praise and criticism of the Duke. Although the Duke crosses Pater's line between "charming" and "antiquarian" anachronisms, Pater concludes the portrait by praising the legacy of Duke Carl.[10] What Pater sets up as the Duke's naiveté and absurdity is transformed, in the end, into an "aspiring soul" that is finally "effective"—but only in death.

As is so often the case in Pater's work, the figure's death is where one must look for clarification: the noble Marius is granted a peaceful death; the violent Denys l'Auxerrois is torn to shreds; and Duke Carl, finally, is trampled to death and his body disposed under mysterious circumstances. While this is by no means the only instance in which Pater provides grisly ends for his characters,[11] nonetheless, the Duke's death-by-trampling cannot be dismissed as just another Paterian exercise in sadism. Considering the ridiculous ends to which the Duke has sought to recreate himself through anachronism, could there be a historicizing judgment in his death? Certainly, Pater has made the Duke's enterprise a failure: as we have seen, every time he adopts new artifacts the Duke is driven deeper within the material confines of his own culture; even his final desperate attempt to transgress class boundaries by marrying the "beggarmaid" plays into the prevalent fairy tales and myths about nobles and commoners. The final rejection of his desires, one might say, comes by political exigency: the stampeding German Army.

Determining Pater's final judgment, however, may be superfluous: if the Duke's cultural anxiety is manifested in his desire for self-annihilation, then he succeeds. This "natural" closure, however, does not end either Pater's, the villagers', or our reading. The Duke's death, burial, and exhumation are not so much judgments on the Duke as they are complexities designed to preclude such judgments. The post-Duke, post-Enlightenment world, in other words, is not where the spirit of Apollonian reason and light has suddenly appeared, but rather a place where culture becomes discursive and where clear, binary judgments are hard to come by.

From this perspective, the terms *Enlightenment, Aufklärung,* and *Renaissance* are themselves anachronistic conceptions. Such terms—says Michel Foucault in his essay "What is Enlightenment?"—present themselves as harbingers of a historical progress that they cannot deliver. He explains that Immanuel Kant (like the Duke) conceived of *Aufklärung* in terms of a "way out" of "immaturity." Furthermore, this conception is characterized by a notion of historical progress that is difficult to reconcile with the fact that Kant's "way of philosophizing" is, for all intents and purposes, still with us: we still think in terms of progress at a time when such thought must appear anachronistic and anti-progressive. Foucault proposes that instead of being seen in terms of accumulation, knowledge might be "conceived as an attitude, an ethos, a philosophical life in which the critique of what we are is at one and the same time the *historical* analysis of the *limits* that are imposed on us and an experiment with the *possibility of going beyond them"* (50; emphasis added). Attempts to reverse or subvert chronology, history, or culture, in other words, cannot be conceived apart from a recognition that such boundaries are inescapable. Bringing the antiquity of Apollo to contemporary Germany, at the same time that it is in the strictest sense a direct affront to this progressive notion of enlightenment, for Duke Carl, paradoxically exists nonetheless.

Thus, Pater's discussion of anachronism, revival, and Enlightenment in **"Duke Carl of Rosenmold"** is a careful positioning and retreat from judgments based on progressive notions of history. One of the more prevalent stereotypes of pre-*Aufklärung* Germany, for instance, is the people's supposed "belief" in fairy tales, in a mythology at which we, in our historically advantageous position, are supposed to scoff. Although Pater himself includes more than a few references to what we must imagine to be a uniquely German proclivity, his reading of these "fairy tales" is more complex. For example, he speaks of this time in terms of a "hyperborean German darkness," of a time when "there were violent robbers, nay, real live devils, in every German wood" (123). Historical or contextual reading here takes the place of historical judgment. Indeed, Pater presents himself in the act of reading: during his description of pre-*Aufklärung* Germany, he corrects himself in mid-sentence and describes the phenomenon of the German woods in terms of what he perceives to be the contemporary conventional wisdom. Instead of discussing the absurdity of goblins in the German woods, he finds more value in examining how these conceptions are created. For Pater, that history must be textualized gives it its vitality. Thus, to describe the architecture of the town, he historicizes "fairy tales" in terms of those for whom they "lived": "The sloping Gothic roofs for carrying off the heavy snows still indented the sky—a world of tiles, with space uncurtailed for the awkward gambols of that very German goblin, Hans Klapper, on the long, slumberous, northern nights" (121). In his reading, Pater occupies this cultural artifact and imagines the "gambols" of this "goblin" and, by participating in the mythology himself, forgoes judgment.

These moments of historical occupation in **"Duke Carl of Rosenmold"** indicate what for Pater are the most valuable uses of the exhumed artifact. By distancing himself from the unearthing of the artifacts, he proposes an alternative to simplistic models of cultural revival and thus to the actions of Nietzsche's *überhistorische* philosopher. In its various forms, historical practice in the nineteenth century is in part defined by the anachronistic desires that Pater illustrates in this portrait. In the Romantic history of, say, Jules Michelet or Ernest Renan, or in the historical fiction of George Eliot or Walter Scott and others, a desire to transcend beyond by going back cannot be simplified like that of the villagers who see exhumation as final and complete. Michelet, for one, seeks out the exhumatory model of resurrection precisely because it complicates historical discourse. Pater's villagers, however, do not state a case for the efficacy of the exhumatory model. Instead, they represent one side of a complex dialectic whose only resolution is to demonstrate how difficult such things are to reconcile.

Notes

1. All references to "Duke Carl of Rosenmold" are taken from the 1920 edition of *Imaginary Portraits.*
2. This essay is taken from a larger work-in-progress on representations of bodily exhumation in nineteenth-century historical writing. This model, I argue, informs the work of George Eliot, Scott, Dickens, Rossetti, and many others, but is especially important in the work of Jacob Burckhardt, Jules Michelet, and Thomas Carlyle. In *The Civilization of the Renaissance in Italy* (1860), for example, Burckhardt discusses exhumation within the context of the Renaissance's revival of antiquity; as the passage heading this essay suggests, Michelet, who actually attended several exhumations himself, uses the exhumatory model overtly (see *Mother Death* [89-90] for such an account); for Carlyle, this model is implicated in the very process of historical writing and reconstruction. This is particularly evident in his account of the John Stuart Mill episode, when Mill accidently dropped the only copy of Carlyle's *French Revolution* manuscript into the fire. (See Froude 1. 29.)
3. While all of Carolyn Williams's important study, *Transfigured World: Walter Pater's Aesthetic Historicism,* is germane to the issues of historical recovery that I address here, it is especially so in her identification of the Paterian "exhumatory" technique of representing a historical totality through the individual figure and how Pater means this figure to represent the vivid concretion of an original historicity; then all the disparate experiences and productions of that figure are summed up and interpreted as representative of that age (8).
4. Although David DeLaura claims that Pater enthusiastically embraced the evolutionary theories of Hegel and Darwin (174), I find a much more skeptical Pater on issues of progress—historical or otherwise. Whereas history, for Hegel, advances dialectically to its own end, history for Pater cannot even properly be called linear. As this portrait suggests, any notion of progress must take into account the contradictory artifices that mark progress—the most striking of which is the anachronistic model of exhumation.
5. Anachronism plays an important part elsewhere in Pater's work. See, for instance, Chapter 16, "Second Thoughts," of *Marius the Epicurean,* wherein Pater openly acknowledges this "free play": "Let the reader pardon me if here and there I seem to be passing from Marius to his modern representatives—from Rome, to Paris or London" (181). See also "A Prince of Court Painters" wherein Pater's first person narrator refers to a pre-Revolution-era France of 1717 in conspicuously Revolutionary language: "People talk of a new era now dawning upon the world, of *fraternity, liberty, humanity,* of a novel sort of social freedom in which men's natural goodness of heart will blossom at a thousand points hitherto repressed" (*IP* 33; emphasis added).
6. See Konrad Celtis, *Selections,* for examples of Celtes' work. A German who wrote in Latin at a time when there is "one might think, enough writing of that period in German . . ." (*Selections* 5), Celtes is perhaps best known for his ode—*Ars versificandi et carminum*—"*inviting* Phoebus to come to Germany and spread the art of song." Not only did the ode express this desire, but "made available the technical instruction for achieving this aim" (3-4).
7. It is around the time of Pater's writing of this portrait that the Eugenics Movement starts to take form in England. This movement, which would later boast such members as Winston Churchill, Theodore Roosevelt, and Alexander Graham Bell, arose out of the *fin de siècle* anxiety that the collective genetic pool had become seriously "watered down." It is not too difficult to find such anxieties, for example, in Joris-Karl Huysmans' *A rebours* (1884) or in Oscar Wilde's *The Picture of Dorian Gray* (1890). For a

history of the Eugenics Movement, see Farrall. The consequence of physiology is also a recurring concern in much of Nietzsche's work. In *The Will to Power* (1889), for example, he attempts to draw connections between physical and moral pathology and speaks of the same kind of genetic degeneration that Huysmans' Des Esseintes fears is the cause of his malady.

8. Pater refers here to Marivaux's *Annibal,* presented for the first time by Les Comediens Français on 16 December 1720. In the introduction to that volume, Frederic Deloffre writes that to contemporary eyes, "[Marivaux's] principal fault was without a doubt the absence of all salient traits. Treating an historical subject, Marivaux has neither the taste for politics nor the dramatic sense of Corneille . . . in a period when the public is eager for new emotions, Marivaux was unable to play upon any of these provocations" (*Théatre complet* 118; my translation). Apropos to our discussion, the introduction to the play implies that Marivaux was trying to imitate the "voice of the ancients" (120)—much to the dismay of his contemporary audience.

9. Thomas Carlyle discusses this connection between self-denial and culture in terms of "*Selbsttödtung,* Annihilation of Self, justly reckoned the beginning of all virtue: here is the highest form of it, still possible to the lowest man. The voice of Nature this, to a repentant outcast sinner turning again towards the realm of manhood;—and I understand it is the precept of all right Christianity too" (256).

10. In the final "frame" of the portrait, for example, Pater steps out of the carefully constructed historical problems embodied in his portrayal of the Duke and discusses Duke Carl in terms of the actual *Aufklärung* and connects the spirit of the Duke with those "other hands" who "effected" it, namely Lessing, Herder, and Goethe. Seeing this as evidence of Pater's wholesale endorsement of Duke Carl's efforts—as many others have—as well as those of whom Duke Carl is most likely modeled upon, J. J. Winckelmann, is problematic, since such a reading necessarily overlooks the majority of the complex characterization preceding the afterword. We should also note that twenty-one years separate Pater's "Winckelmann" essay and this imaginary portrait and that even in the earlier essay, as laudatory as Pater was towards Winckelmann's similar efforts to resurrect Greek culture, he did not stint in his criticism.

11. See, for instance, the mutilation of Denys L'Auxerrois in the *Imaginary Portrait* of the same name, the account of the St. Bartholomew's Eve massacre in *Gaston de Latour,* the "Manly Amusement" of Roman public torture in *Marius the Epicurean,* and even the delicate rendering of Winckelmann's murder in "Winckelmann," to cite but a few such deaths.

Works Cited

Burckhardt, Jacob. *The Civilization of the Renaissance in Italy.* Vienna: Phaidon, 1937.

Carlyle, Thomas. *Latter-Day Pamphlets.* Freeport, New York: Books for Libraries, 1972.

Celtis, Konrad. *Selections.* Cambridge: Cambridge UP, 1949.

DeLaura, David. *Hebrewand Hellene in Victorian England: Newman, Arnold and Pater.* Austin: U of Texas P, 1969.

Farrall, Lyndsay Andrew. *The Origins of the English Eugenics Movement, 1865-1925.* New York and London: Garland, 1985.

Foucault, Michel. "What is Enlightenment?" *The Foucault Reader.* Ed. Paul Rabinow. New York: Pantheon, 1984. Pp. 32-50.

Froude, James Anthony. *Thomas Carlyle: A History Of His Life in London, 1834-1881.* 2 vols. London, 1897.

Huysmans, Joris-Karl. *A rebours.* Paris: Flammarion, 1978.

Marivaux, Pierre Carlet de Chamblain de. *Théatre complet.* Nouvelle Ed. Paris: Bordas, 1989.

Michelet, Jules. *Le Peuple.* Paris, 1866.

———. *Mother Death: The Journal of Jules Michelet, 1815-1850.* Trans. and Ed. Edward K. Kaplan. Amherst: U of Massachusetts P, 1984.

Nietzsche, Friedrich. "The Use and Abuse of History." *Thoughts Out of Season,* Part II. Trans. Adrian Collins. New York: Russell, 1964. Pp. 3-100.

———. *The Will to Power.* Ed. Walter Kaufmann. Trans. Walter Kaufmann and R. J. Hollingdale. New York: Vintage, 1967.

Pater, Walter. "Aesthetic Poetry." *Selected Writings of Walter Pater.* Ed. Harold Bloom. New York: Columbia UP, 1974. Pp. 190-98.

———. "The Child in the House." *Miscellaneous Studies: A Series of Essays.* London: Macmillan, 1917.

———. "Denys l'Auxerrois." *Imaginary Portraits.* London: Macmillan, 1920.

———. "Duke Carl of Rosenmold." *Imaginary Portraits.* London: Macmillan, 1920.

———. *Gaston de Latour.* London: Macmillan, 1914.

———. *Marius the Epicurean.* Ed. Michael Levey. New York: Penguin, 1985.

———. "A Prince of Court Painters." *Imaginary Portraits.* London: Macmillan, 1920.

———. "Winckelmann." *The Renaissance. Studies in Art and Poetry: The 1893 Text.* Ed. Donald L. Hall. Berkeley: U of California P, 1980. Pp. 141-85.

Wilde, Oscar. *The Picture of Dorian Gray.* Ed. Donald L. Lawler. New York: Norton, 1987.

Williams, Carolyn. *Transfigured World: Walter Pater's Aesthetic Historicism.* Ithaca: Cornell UP, 1989.

FURTHER READING

Biographies

Benson, A. C. *Walter Pater.* 1906. Detroit: Gale Research Co., 1968, 226 p.

Classic biography of Pater.

Monsman, Gerald. *Walter Pater.* Twayne's English Author Series, edited by Sylvia E. Bowman, No. 207. Boston: Twayne Publishers, 1977, 213 p.

Respected introduction to Pater's life and work.

Criticism

Adams, James Eli. "Gentleman, Dandy, Priest: Manliness and Social Authority in Pater's Aestheticism." *ELH* 59, No. 2 (Summer 1992): 441-66.

Discusses Pater's writing as demonstrating the dynamics of "manliness."

Block, Ed, Jr. "Walter Pater's 'Diaphaneitè' and the Pattern of Reader Response in the Portrait Essay." *Texas Studies in Literature and Language* 25, No. 3 (Fall 1983): 427-47.

Examines Pater's "attempts to engage the reader in a reflective dialogue," particularly in "Diaphaneitè."

Brake, Laurel. "Aesthetics in the Affray: Pater's *Appreciations, with an Essay on Style.*" *The Politics of Pleasure: Aesthetics and Cultural Theory,* edited by Stephen Regan, pp. 59-86. Buckingham, England and Philadelphia: Open University Press, 1992.

Addresses questions of style, romanticism, gender, and literature raised by Pater in *Appreciations* in regard to aesthetic criticism.

———. "The 'wicked *Westminster,*' the *Fortnightly,* and Walter Pater's *Renaissance.*" *Literature in the Marketplace: Nineteenth-Century British Publishing and Reading Practices,* edited by John O. Jordan and Robert L. Patten, pp. 289-305. Cambridge: Cambridge University Press, 1995.

Examines how the formats, chief interests, and politics of the journals in which Pater's writings appeared influenced the nature of his essays.

Carroll, Joseph. "Pater's Figures of Perplexity." *Modern Language Quarterly* 52, No. 3 (September 1991): 319-40.

Attempts to ascertain the meaning of *Marius the Epicurean* by separately analyzing the metaphysical and psychosexual aspects of the work.

Connor, Steven. "Myth as Multiplicity in Walter Pater's *Greek Studies* and 'Denys l'Auxerrois'." *The Review of English Studies* 34, No. 133 (February 1983): 28-42.

Examines Pater's mythological fiction, his debt to German mythographer Ludwig Preller, and the combination of conscious and unconscious myth found in Pater's imaginary portrait of Dionysus.

Dowling, Linda. "Walter Pater and Archaeology: The Reconciliation with Earth." *Victorian Studies* 31, No. 2 (Winter 1988): 209-31.

Examines "The Myth of Demeter and Persephone" with emphasis on Pater's controversial three-part division of "the elaboration of myth" and his choice of diction in expressing it.

Lubbock, Jules. "Walter Pater's *Marius the Epicurean*—The Imaginary Portrait as Cultural History." *Journal of the Warburg and Courtland Institutes* 46 (1983): 166-90.

Denies that *Marius the Epicurean* should be viewed as autobiography, arguing instead for a cultural-historical reading.

Matz, Jesse. "Walter Pater's Literary Impression." *Modern Language Quarterly* 56, No. 4 (December 1995): 433-56.

Examines Pater's theories and attitudes concerning the "impression" and explores their links to homoeroticism.

McGowan, John. "From Pater to Wilde to Joyce: Modernist Epiphany and the Soulful Self." *Texas Studies in Literature* 32, No. 3 (Fall 1990): 417-45.

Examines the extremism of Pater's "Conclusion" and its implications concerning knowledge of the self.

Monsman, Gerald. "Pater's 'Child in the House' and the Renovation of the Self." *Texas Studies in Literature and Language* 28, No. 3 (Fall 1986): 281-95.

Analyzes the origins of "Child in the House" and the "dialectic between the author and his textual reflection."

Morgan, Thaïs E. "Reimagining Masculinity in Victorian Criticism: Swinburne and Pater." *Victorian Studies* 36, No. 3 (Spring 1993): 315-32.

Describes the similarities and distinct differences between Algernon Charles Swinburne's and Pater's homoerotic writings.

Shuter, William F. "The 'Outing' of Walter Pater." *Nineteenth Century Literature* 48, No. 4 (March 1994): 480-506.

Analyzes the evidence concerning Pater's homosexuality and the attempts to decode his text, and argues that the conclusions and interpretations reached by certain critics are somewhat dubious.

Williams, Carolyn. "Typology as Narrative Form: The Temporal Logic of *Marius.*" *English Literature in Transition 1880-1920* 27, No. 1 (1984): 11-33.

Considers Pater's use of symbolic representation in *Marius the Epicurean.*

Additional coverage of Pater's life and career is contained in the following sources published by the Gale Group: *Concise Dictionary of British Literary Biography 1832–1890*; and *Dictionary of Literary Biography,* Vols. 57 and 156.

How to Use This Index

The main references

Calvino, Italo
1923-1985 .... **CLC 5, 8, 11, 22, 33, 39, 73; SSC 3**

list all author entries in the following Gale Literary Criticism series:

BLC = *Black Literature Criticism*
CLC = *Contemporary Literary Criticism*
CLR = *Children's Literature Review*
CMLC = *Classical and Medieval Literature Criticism*
DA = *DISCovering Authors*
DAB = *DISCovering Authors: British*
DAC = *DISCovering Authors: Canadian*
DAM = *DISCovering Authors: Modules*
DRAM: *Dramatists Module;* ***MST:*** *Most-Studied Authors Module;*
MULT: *Multicultural Authors Module;* ***NOV:*** *Novelists Module;*
POET: *Poets Module;* ***POP:*** *Popular Fiction and Genre Authors Module*
DC = *Drama Criticism*
HLC = *Hispanic Literature Criticism*
LC = *Literature Criticism from 1400 to 1800*
NCLC = *Nineteenth-Century Literature Criticism*
NNAL = *Native North American Literature*
PC = *Poetry Criticism*
SSC = *Short Story Criticism*
TCLC = *Twentieth-Century Literary Criticism*
WLC = *World Literature Criticism, 1500 to the Present*

The cross-references

See also CANR 23; CA 85-88;
obituary CA116

list all author entries in the following Gale biographical and literary sources:

AAYA = *Authors & Artists for Young Adults*
AITN = *Authors in the News*
BEST = *Bestsellers*
BW = *Black Writers*
CA = *Contemporary Authors*
CAAS = *Contemporary Authors Autobiography Series*
CABS = *Contemporary Authors Bibliographical Series*
CANR = *Contemporary Authors New Revision Series*
CAP = *Contemporary Authors Permanent Series*
CDALB = *Concise Dictionary of American Literary Biography*
CDBLB = *Concise Dictionary of British Literary Biography*
DLB = *Dictionary of Literary Biography*
DLBD = *Dictionary of Literary Biography Documentary Series*
DLBY = *Dictionary of Literary Biography Yearbook*
HW = *Hispanic Writers*
JRDA = *Junior DISCovering Authors*
MAICYA = *Major Authors and Illustrators for Children and Young Adults*
MTCW = *Major 20th-Century Writers*
SAAS = *Something about the Author Autobiography Series*
SATA = *Something about the Author*
YABC = *Yesterday's Authors of Books for Children*

Literary Criticism Series Cumulative Author Index

Akst, Daniel 1956- .... **CLC 109**
See also CA 161
Aksyonov, Vassily (Pavlovich) 1932- .... **CLC 22, 37, 101**
See also CA 53-56; CANR 12, 48, 77
Akutagawa, Ryunosuke 1892-1927 .... **TCLC 16**
See also CA 117; 154
Alain 1868-1951 .... **TCLC 41**
See also CA 163
Alain-Fournier TCLC 6
See also Fournier, Henri Alban
See also DLB 65
Alarcon, Pedro Antonio de 1833-1891 .... **NCLC 1**
Alas (y Urena), Leopoldo (Enrique Garcia) 1852-1901 .... **TCLC 29**
See also CA 113; 131; HW 1
Albee, Edward (Franklin III) 1928- . **CLC 1, 2, 3, 5, 9, 11, 13, 25, 53, 86, 113; DA; DAB; DAC; DAM DRAM, MST; DC 11; WLC**
See also AITN 1; CA 5-8R; CABS 3; CANR 8, 54, 74; CDALB 1941-1968; DA3; DLB 7; INT CANR-8; MTCW 1, 2
Alberti, Rafael 1902-1999 .... **CLC 7**
See also CA 85-88; 185; CANR 81; DLB 108; HW 2
Albert the Great 1200(?)-1280 ...... **CMLC 16**
See also DLB 115
Alcala-Galiano, Juan Valera y
See Valera y Alcala-Galiano, Juan
Alcott, Amos Bronson 1799-1888 .... **NCLC 1**
See also DLB 1, 223
Alcott, Louisa May 1832-1888 . **NCLC 6, 58, 83; DA; DAB; DAC; DAM MST, NOV; SSC 27; WLC**
See also AAYA 20; CDALB 1865-1917; CLR 1, 38; DA3; DLB 1, 42, 79, 223; DLBD 14; JRDA; MAICYA; SATA 100; YABC 1
Aldanov, M. A.
See Aldanov, Mark (Alexandrovich)
Aldanov, Mark (Alexandrovich) 1886(?)-1957 .... **TCLC 23**
See also CA 118; 181
Aldington, Richard 1892-1962 .... **CLC 49**
See also CA 85-88; CANR 45; DLB 20, 36, 100, 149
Aldiss, Brian W(ilson) 1925- . **CLC 5, 14, 40; DAM NOV; SSC 36**
See also CA 5-8R; CAAS 2; CANR 5, 28, 64; DLB 14; MTCW 1, 2; SATA 34
Alegria, Claribel 1924- .... **CLC 75; DAM MULT; HLCS 1; PC 26**
See also CA 131; CAAS 15; CANR 66; DLB 145; HW 1; MTCW 1
Alegria, Fernando 1918- .... **CLC 57**
See also CA 9-12R; CANR 5, 32, 72; HW 1, 2
Aleichem, Sholom TCLC 1, 35; SSC 33
See also Rabinovitch, Sholem
Aleixandre, Vicente 1898-1984
See also CANR 81; HLCS 1; HW 2
Alepoudelis, Odysseus
See Elytis, Odysseus
Aleshkovsky, Joseph 1929-
See Aleshkovsky, Yuz
See also CA 121; 128
Aleshkovsky, Yuz CLC 44
See also Aleshkovsky, Joseph
Alexander, Lloyd (Chudley) 1924- ... **CLC 35**
See also AAYA 1, 27; CA 1-4R; CANR 1, 24, 38, 55; CLR 1, 5, 48; DLB 52; JRDA; MAICYA; MTCW 1; SAAS 19; SATA 3, 49, 81
Alexander, Meena 1951- .... **CLC 121**
See also CA 115; CANR 38, 70
Alexander, Samuel 1859-1938 .... **TCLC 77**
Alexie, Sherman (Joseph, Jr.) 1966- .... **CLC 96; DAM MULT**
See also AAYA 28; CA 138; CANR 65; DA3; DLB 175, 206; MTCW 1; NNAL
Alfau, Felipe 1902- .... **CLC 66**
See also CA 137
Alfred, Jean Gaston
See Ponge, Francis
Alger, Horatio Jr., Jr. 1832-1899 .... **NCLC 8, 83**
See also DLB 42; SATA 16
Algren, Nelson 1909-1981 ..... **CLC 4, 10, 33; SSC 33**
See also CA 13-16R; 103; CANR 20, 61; CDALB 1941-1968; DLB 9; DLBY 81, 82; MTCW 1, 2
Ali, Ahmed 1910- .... **CLC 69**
See also CA 25-28R; CANR 15, 34
Alighieri, Dante
See Dante
Allan, John B.
See Westlake, Donald E(dwin)
Allan, Sidney
See Hartmann, Sadakichi
Allan, Sydney
See Hartmann, Sadakichi
Allen, Edward 1948- .... **CLC 59**
Allen, Fred 1894-1956 .... **TCLC 87**
Allen, Paula Gunn 1939- .... **CLC 84; DAM MULT**
See also CA 112; 143; CANR 63; DA3; DLB 175; MTCW 1; NNAL
Allen, Roland
See Ayckbourn, Alan
Allen, Sarah A.
See Hopkins, Pauline Elizabeth
Allen, Sidney H.
See Hartmann, Sadakichi
Allen, Woody 1935- .... **CLC 16, 52; DAM POP**
See also AAYA 10; CA 33-36R; CANR 27, 38, 63; DLB 44; MTCW 1
Allende, Isabel 1942- . **CLC 39, 57, 97; DAM MULT, NOV; HLC 1; WLCS**
See also AAYA 18; CA 125; 130; CANR 51, 74; DA3; DLB 145; HW 1, 2; INT 130; MTCW 1, 2
Alleyn, Ellen
See Rossetti, Christina (Georgina)
Allingham, Margery (Louise) 1904-1966 .... **CLC 19**
See also CA 5-8R; 25-28R; CANR 4, 58; DLB 77; MTCW 1, 2
Allingham, William 1824-1889 ...... **NCLC 25**
See also DLB 35
Allison, Dorothy E. 1949- .... **CLC 78**
See also CA 140; CANR 66; DA3; MTCW 1
Allston, Washington 1779-1843 .... **NCLC 2**
See also DLB 1
Almedingen, E. M. CLC 12
See also Almedingen, Martha Edith von
See also SATA 3
Almedingen, Martha Edith von 1898-1971
See Almedingen, E. M.
See also CA 1-4R; CANR 1
Almodovar, Pedro 1949(?)- .... **CLC 114; HLCS 1**
See also CA 133; CANR 72; HW 2
Almqvist, Carl Jonas Love 1793-1866 .... **NCLC 42**
Alonso, Damaso 1898-1990 .... **CLC 14**
See also CA 110; 131; 130; CANR 72; DLB 108; HW 1, 2
Alov
See Gogol, Nikolai (Vasilyevich)
Alta 1942- .... **CLC 19**
See also CA 57-60
Alter, Robert B(ernard) 1935- .... **CLC 34**
See also CA 49-52; CANR 1, 47
Alther, Lisa 1944- .... **CLC 7, 41**
See also CA 65-68; CAAS 30; CANR 12, 30, 51; MTCW 1
Althusser, L.
See Althusser, Louis
Althusser, Louis 1918-1990 .... **CLC 106**
See also CA 131; 132
Altman, Robert 1925- .... **CLC 16, 116**
See also CA 73-76; CANR 43
Alurista 1949-
See Urista, Alberto H.
See also DLB 82; HLCS 1
Alvarez, A(lfred) 1929- .... **CLC 5, 13**
See also CA 1-4R; CANR 3, 33, 63; DLB 14, 40
Alvarez, Alejandro Rodriguez 1903-1965
See Casona, Alejandro
See also CA 131; 93-96; HW 1
Alvarez, Julia 1950- .... **CLC 93; HLCS 1**
See also AAYA 25; CA 147; CANR 69; DA3; MTCW 1
Alvaro, Corrado 1896-1956 .... **TCLC 60**
See also CA 163
Amado, Jorge 1912- .... **CLC 13, 40, 106; DAM MULT, NOV; HLC 1**
See also CA 77-80; CANR 35, 74; DLB 113; HW 2; MTCW 1, 2
Ambler, Eric 1909-1998 .... **CLC 4, 6, 9**
See also CA 9-12R; 171; CANR 7, 38, 74; DLB 77; MTCW 1, 2
Amichai, Yehuda 1924- ... **CLC 9, 22, 57, 116**
See also CA 85-88; CANR 46, 60; MTCW 1
Amichai, Yehudah
See Amichai, Yehuda
Amiel, Henri Frederic 1821-1881 .... **NCLC 4**
Amis, Kingsley (William) 1922-1995 ...... **CLC 1, 2, 3, 5, 8, 13, 40, 44, 129; DA; DAB; DAC; DAM MST, NOV**
See also AITN 2; CA 9-12R; 150; CANR 8, 28, 54; CDBLB 1945-1960; DA3; DLB 15, 27, 100, 139; DLBY 96; INT CANR-8; MTCW 1, 2
Amis, Martin (Louis) 1949- .... **CLC 4, 9, 38, 62, 101**
See also BEST 90:3; CA 65-68; CANR 8, 27, 54, 73; DA3; DLB 14, 194; INT CANR-27; MTCW 1
Ammons, A(rchie) R(andolph) 1926- ...... **CLC 2, 3, 5, 8, 9, 25, 57, 108; DAM POET; PC 16**
See also AITN 1; CA 9-12R; CANR 6, 36, 51, 73; DLB 5, 165; MTCW 1, 2
Amo, Tauraatua i
See Adams, Henry (Brooks)
Amory, Thomas 1691(?)-1788 .... **LC 48**
Anand, Mulk Raj 1905- .. **CLC 23, 93; DAM NOV**
See also CA 65-68; CANR 32, 64; MTCW 1, 2
Anatol
See Schnitzler, Arthur
Anaximander c. 610B.C.-c. 546B.C. .... **CMLC 22**
Anaya, Rudolfo A(lfonso) 1937- ...... **CLC 23; DAM MULT, NOV; HLC 1**
See also AAYA 20; CA 45-48; CAAS 4; CANR 1, 32, 51; DLB 82, 206; HW 1; MTCW 1, 2
Andersen, Hans Christian 1805-1875 .... **NCLC 7, 79; DA; DAB; DAC; DAM MST, POP; SSC 6; WLC**
See also CLR 6; DA3; MAICYA; SATA 100; YABC 1

Author Index

Bakhtin, M.
See Bakhtin, Mikhail Mikhailovich
Bakhtin, M. M.
See Bakhtin, Mikhail Mikhailovich
Bakhtin, Mikhail
See Bakhtin, Mikhail Mikhailovich
Bakhtin, Mikhail Mikhailovich 1895-1975 .... **CLC 83**
See also CA 128; 113
Bakshi, Ralph 1938(?)- .... **CLC 26**
See also CA 112; 138
Bakunin, Mikhail (Alexandrovich) 1814-1876 .... **NCLC 25, 58**
Baldwin, James (Arthur) 1924-1987 . **CLC 1, 2, 3, 4, 5, 8, 13, 15, 17, 42, 50, 67, 90, 127; BLC 1; DA; DAB; DAC; DAM MST, MULT, NOV, POP; DC 1; SSC 10, 33; WLC**
See also AAYA 4, 34; BW 1; CA 1-4R; 124; CABS 1; CANR 3, 24; CDALB 1941-1968; DA3; DLB 2, 7, 33; DLBY 87; MTCW 1, 2; SATA 9; SATA-Obit 54
Ballard, J(ames) G(raham) 1930-1964 .... **CLC 3, 6, 14, 36; DAM NOV, POP; SSC 1**
See also AAYA 3; CA 5-8R; CANR 15, 39, 65; DA3; DLB 14, 207; MTCW 1, 2; SATA 93
Balmont, Konstantin (Dmitriyevich) 1867-1943 .... **TCLC 11**
See also CA 109; 155
Baltausis, Vincas
See Mikszath, Kalman
Balzac, Honore de 1799-1850 ... **NCLC 5, 35, 53; DA; DAB; DAC; DAM MST, NOV; SSC 5; WLC**
See also DA3; DLB 119
Bambara, Toni Cade 1939-1995 ...... **CLC 19, 88; BLC 1; DA; DAC; DAM MST, MULT; SSC 35; WLCS**
See also AAYA 5; BW 2, 3; CA 29-32R; 150; CANR 24, 49, 81; CDALBS; DA3; DLB 38; MTCW 1, 2; SATA 112
Bamdad, A.
See Shamlu, Ahmad
Banat, D. R.
See Bradbury, Ray (Douglas)
Bancroft, Laura
See Baum, L(yman) Frank
Banim, John 1798-1842 .... **NCLC 13**
See also DLB 116, 158, 159
Banim, Michael 1796-1874 .... **NCLC 13**
See also DLB 158, 159
Banjo, The
See Paterson, A(ndrew) B(arton)
Banks, Iain
See Banks, Iain M(enzies)
Banks, Iain M(enzies) 1954- .... **CLC 34**
See also CA 123; 128; CANR 61; DLB 194; INT 128
Banks, Lynne Reid CLC 23
See also Reid Banks, Lynne
See also AAYA 6
Banks, Russell 1940- .... **CLC 37, 72**
See also CA 65-68; CAAS 15; CANR 19, 52, 73; DLB 130
Banville, John 1945- .... **CLC 46, 118**
See also CA 117; 128; DLB 14; INT 128
Banville, Theodore (Faullain) de 1832-1891 .... **NCLC 9**
Baraka, Amiri 1934- . **CLC 1, 2, 3, 5, 10, 14, 33, 115; BLC 1; DA; DAC; DAM MST, MULT, POET, POP; DC 6; PC 4; WLCS**
See also Jones, LeRoi
See also BW 2, 3; CA 21-24R; CABS 3; CANR 27, 38, 61; CDALB 1941-1968; DA3; DLB 5, 7, 16, 38; DLBD 8; MTCW 1, 2
Barbauld, Anna Laetitia 1743-1825 .... **NCLC 50**
See also DLB 107, 109, 142, 158
Barbellion, W. N. P. TCLC 24
See also Cummings, Bruce F(rederick)
Barbera, Jack (Vincent) 1945- .... **CLC 44**
See also CA 110; CANR 45
Barbey d'Aurevilly, Jules Amedee 1808-1889 .... **NCLC 1; SSC 17**
See also DLB 119
Barbour, John c. 1316-1395 .... **CMLC 33**
See also DLB 146
Barbusse, Henri 1873-1935 .... **TCLC 5**
See also CA 105; 154; DLB 65
Barclay, Bill
See Moorcock, Michael (John)
Barclay, William Ewert
See Moorcock, Michael (John)
Barea, Arturo 1897-1957 .... **TCLC 14**
See also CA 111
Barfoot, Joan 1946- .... **CLC 18**
See also CA 105
Barham, Richard Harris 1788-1845 .... **NCLC 77**
See also DLB 159
Baring, Maurice 1874-1945 .... **TCLC 8**
See also CA 105; 168; DLB 34
Baring-Gould, Sabine 1834-1924 ... **TCLC 88**
See also DLB 156, 190
Barker, Clive 1952- ...... **CLC 52; DAM POP**
See also AAYA 10; BEST 90:3; CA 121; 129; CANR 71; DA3; INT 129; MTCW 1, 2
Barker, George Granville 1913-1991 .... **CLC 8, 48; DAM POET**
See also CA 9-12R; 135; CANR 7, 38; DLB 20; MTCW 1
Barker, Harley Granville
See Granville-Barker, Harley
See also DLB 10
Barker, Howard 1946- .... **CLC 37**
See also CA 102; DLB 13
Barker, Jane 1652-1732 .... **LC 42**
Barker, Pat(ricia) 1943- .... **CLC 32, 94**
See also CA 117; 122; CANR 50; INT 122
Barlach, Ernst (Heinrich) 1870-1938 .... **TCLC 84**
See also CA 178; DLB 56, 118
Barlow, Joel 1754-1812 .... **NCLC 23**
See also DLB 37
Barnard, Mary (Ethel) 1909- .... **CLC 48**
See also CA 21-22; CAP 2
Barnes, Djuna 1892-1982 .... **CLC 3, 4, 8, 11, 29, 127; SSC 3**
See also CA 9-12R; 107; CANR 16, 55; DLB 4, 9, 45; MTCW 1, 2
Barnes, Julian (Patrick) 1946- .... **CLC 42; DAB**
See also CA 102; CANR 19, 54; DLB 194; DLBY 93; MTCW 1
Barnes, Peter 1931- .... **CLC 5, 56**
See also CA 65-68; CAAS 12; CANR 33, 34, 64; DLB 13; MTCW 1
Barnes, William 1801-1886 .... **NCLC 75**
See also DLB 32
Baroja (y Nessi), Pio 1872-1956 ..... **TCLC 8; HLC 1**
See also CA 104
Baron, David
See Pinter, Harold
Baron Corvo
See Rolfe, Frederick (William Serafino Austin Lewis Mary)
Barondess, Sue K(aufman) 1926-1977 .... **CLC 8**
See also Kaufman, Sue
See also CA 1-4R; 69-72; CANR 1
Baron de Teive
See Pessoa, Fernando (Antonio Nogueira)
Baroness Von S.
See Zangwill, Israel
Barres, (Auguste-) Maurice 1862-1923 .... **TCLC 47**
See also CA 164; DLB 123
Barreto, Afonso Henrique de Lima
See Lima Barreto, Afonso Henrique de
Barrett, (Roger) Syd 1946- .... **CLC 35**
Barrett, William (Christopher) 1913-1992 .... **CLC 27**
See also CA 13-16R; 139; CANR 11, 67; INT CANR-11
Barrie, J(ames) M(atthew) 1860-1937 .... **TCLC 2; DAB; DAM DRAM**
See also CA 104; 136; CANR 77; CDBLB 1890-1914; CLR 16; DA3; DLB 10, 141, 156; MAICYA; MTCW 1; SATA 100; YABC 1
Barrington, Michael
See Moorcock, Michael (John)
Barrol, Grady
See Bograd, Larry
Barry, Mike
See Malzberg, Barry N(athaniel)
Barry, Philip 1896-1949 .... **TCLC 11**
See also CA 109; DLB 7, 228
Bart, Andre Schwarz
See Schwarz-Bart, Andre
Barth, John (Simmons) 1930- ... **CLC 1, 2, 3, 5, 7, 9, 10, 14, 27, 51, 89; DAM NOV; SSC 10**
See also AITN 1, 2; CA 1-4R; CABS 1; CANR 5, 23, 49, 64; DLB 2, 227; MTCW 1
Barthelme, Donald 1931-1989 ... **CLC 1, 2, 3, 5, 6, 8, 13, 23, 46, 59, 115; DAM NOV; SSC 2**
See also CA 21-24R; 129; CANR 20, 58; DA3; DLB 2; DLBY 80, 89; MTCW 1, 2; SATA 7; SATA-Obit 62
Barthelme, Frederick 1943- ...... **CLC 36, 117**
See also CA 114; 122; CANR 77; DLBY 85; INT 122
Barthes, Roland (Gerard) 1915-1980 .... **CLC 24, 83**
See also CA 130; 97-100; CANR 66; MTCW 1, 2
Barzun, Jacques (Martin) 1907- ...... **CLC 51**
See also CA 61-64; CANR 22
Bashevis, Isaac
See Singer, Isaac Bashevis
Bashkirtseff, Marie 1859-1884 .... **NCLC 27**
Basho
See Matsuo Basho
Basil of Caesaria c. 330-379 .... **CMLC 35**
Bass, Kingsley B., Jr.
See Bullins, Ed
Bass, Rick 1958- .... **CLC 79**
See also CA 126; CANR 53; DLB 212
Bassani, Giorgio 1916- .... **CLC 9**
See also CA 65-68; CANR 33; DLB 128, 177; MTCW 1
Bastos, Augusto (Antonio) Roa
See Roa Bastos, Augusto (Antonio)
Bataille, Georges 1897-1962 .... **CLC 29**
See also CA 101; 89-92
Bates, H(erbert) E(rnest) 1905-1974 . **CLC 46; DAB; DAM POP; SSC 10**
See also CA 93-96; 45-48; CANR 34; DA3; DLB 162, 191; MTCW 1, 2
Bauchart
See Camus, Albert

Author Index

Bottoms, David 1949- .... **CLC 53**
See also CA 105; CANR 22; DLB 120; DLBY 83
Boucicault, Dion 1820-1890 .... **NCLC 41**
Bourget, Paul (Charles Joseph) 1852-1935 .... **TCLC 12**
See also CA 107; DLB 123
Bourjaily, Vance (Nye) 1922- .... **CLC 8, 62**
See also CA 1-4R; CAAS 1; CANR 2, 72; DLB 2, 143
Bourne, Randolph S(illiman) 1886-1918 .... **TCLC 16**
See also CA 117; 155; DLB 63
Bova, Ben(jamin William) 1932- ...... **CLC 45**
See also AAYA 16; CA 5-8R; CAAS 18; CANR 11, 56; CLR 3; DLBY 81; INT CANR-11; MAICYA; MTCW 1; SATA 6, 68
Bowen, Elizabeth (Dorothea Cole) 1899-1973 . **CLC 1, 3, 6, 11, 15, 22, 118; DAM NOV; SSC 3, 28**
See also CA 17-18; 41-44R; CANR 35; CAP 2; CDBLB 1945-1960; DA3; DLB 15, 162; MTCW 1, 2
Bowering, George 1935- .... **CLC 15, 47**
See also CA 21-24R; CAAS 16; CANR 10; DLB 53
Bowering, Marilyn R(uthe) 1949- .... **CLC 32**
See also CA 101; CANR 49
Bowers, Edgar 1924-2000 .... **CLC 9**
See also CA 5-8R; CANR 24; DLB 5
Bowie, David CLC 17
See also Jones, David Robert
Bowles, Jane (Sydney) 1917-1973 ..... **CLC 3, 68**
See also CA 19-20; 41-44R; CAP 2
Bowles, Paul (Frederick) 1910-1999 . **CLC 1, 2, 19, 53; SSC 3**
See also CA 1-4R; 186; CAAS 1; CANR 1, 19, 50, 75; DA3; DLB 5, 6; MTCW 1, 2
Box, Edgar
See Vidal, Gore
Boyd, Nancy
See Millay, Edna St. Vincent
Boyd, William 1952- .... **CLC 28, 53, 70**
See also CA 114; 120; CANR 51, 71
Boyle, Kay 1902-1992 .... **CLC 1, 5, 19, 58, 121; SSC 5**
See also CA 13-16R; 140; CAAS 1; CANR 29, 61; DLB 4, 9, 48, 86; DLBY 93; MTCW 1, 2
Boyle, Mark
See Kienzle, William X(avier)
Boyle, Patrick 1905-1982 .... **CLC 19**
See also CA 127
Boyle, T. C. 1948-
See Boyle, T(homas) Coraghessan
Boyle, T(homas) Coraghessan 1948- .... **CLC 36, 55, 90; DAM POP; SSC 16**
See also BEST 90:4; CA 120; CANR 44, 76, 89; DA3; DLBY 86; MTCW 2
Boz
See Dickens, Charles (John Huffam)
Brackenridge, Hugh Henry 1748-1816 .... **NCLC 7**
See also DLB 11, 37
Bradbury, Edward P.
See Moorcock, Michael (John)
See also MTCW 2
Bradbury, Malcolm (Stanley) 1932- .... **CLC 32, 61; DAM NOV**
See also CA 1-4R; CANR 1, 33, 91; DA3; DLB 14, 207; MTCW 1, 2
Bradbury, Ray (Douglas) 1920- .... **CLC 1, 3, 10, 15, 42, 98; DA; DAB; DAC; DAM MST, NOV, POP; SSC 29; WLC**
See also AAYA 15; AITN 1, 2; CA 1-4R; CANR 2, 30, 75; CDALB 1968-1988; DA3; DLB 2, 8; MTCW 1, 2; SATA 11, 64
Bradford, Gamaliel 1863-1932 .... **TCLC 36**
See also CA 160; DLB 17
Bradley, David (Henry), Jr. 1950- ... **CLC 23, 118; BLC 1; DAM MULT**
See also BW 1, 3; CA 104; CANR 26, 81; DLB 33
Bradley, John Ed(mund, Jr.) 1958- . **CLC 55**
See also CA 139
Bradley, Marion Zimmer 1930-1999 .... **CLC 30; DAM POP**
See also AAYA 9; CA 57-60; 185; CAAS 10; CANR 7, 31, 51, 75; DA3; DLB 8; MTCW 1, 2; SATA 90; SATA-Obit 116
Bradstreet, Anne 1612(?)-1672 ...... **LC 4, 30; DA; DAC; DAM MST, POET; PC 10**
See also CDALB 1640-1865; DA3; DLB 24
Brady, Joan 1939- .... **CLC 86**
See also CA 141
Bragg, Melvyn 1939- .... **CLC 10**
See also BEST 89:3; CA 57-60; CANR 10, 48, 89; DLB 14
Brahe, Tycho 1546-1601 .... **LC 45**
Braine, John (Gerard) 1922-1986 . **CLC 1, 3, 41**
See also CA 1-4R; 120; CANR 1, 33; CDBLB 1945-1960; DLB 15; DLBY 86; MTCW 1
Bramah, Ernest 1868-1942 .... **TCLC 72**
See also CA 156; DLB 70
Brammer, William 1930(?)-1978 ...... **CLC 31**
See also CA 77-80
Brancati, Vitaliano 1907-1954 .... **TCLC 12**
See also CA 109
Brancato, Robin F(idler) 1936- .... **CLC 35**
See also AAYA 9; CA 69-72; CANR 11, 45; CLR 32; JRDA; SAAS 9; SATA 97
Brand, Max
See Faust, Frederick (Schiller)
Brand, Millen 1906-1980 .... **CLC 7**
See also CA 21-24R; 97-100; CANR 72
Branden, Barbara CLC 44
See also CA 148
Brandes, Georg (Morris Cohen) 1842-1927 .... **TCLC 10**
See also CA 105
Brandys, Kazimierz 1916- .... **CLC 62**
Branley, Franklyn M(ansfield) 1915- .... **CLC 21**
See also CA 33-36R; CANR 14, 39; CLR 13; MAICYA; SAAS 16; SATA 4, 68
Brathwaite, Edward (Kamau) 1930- ...... **CLC 11; BLCS; DAM POET**
See also BW 2, 3; CA 25-28R; CANR 11, 26, 47; DLB 125
Brautigan, Richard (Gary) 1935-1984 .... **CLC 1, 3, 5, 9, 12, 34, 42; DAM NOV**
See also CA 53-56; 113; CANR 34; DA3; DLB 2, 5, 206; DLBY 80, 84; MTCW 1; SATA 56
Brave Bird, Mary 1953-
See Crow Dog, Mary (Ellen)
See also NNAL
Braverman, Kate 1950- .... **CLC 67**
See also CA 89-92
Brecht, (Eugen) Bertolt (Friedrich) 1898-1956 .... **TCLC 1, 6, 13, 35; DA; DAB; DAC; DAM DRAM, MST; DC 3; WLC**
See also CA 104; 133; CANR 62; DA3; DLB 56, 124; MTCW 1, 2
Brecht, Eugen Berthold Friedrich
See Brecht, (Eugen) Bertolt (Friedrich)
Bremer, Fredrika 1801-1865 .... **NCLC 11**
Brennan, Christopher John 1870-1932 .... **TCLC 17**
See also CA 117
Brennan, Maeve 1917-1993 .... **CLC 5**
See also CA 81-84; CANR 72
Brent, Linda
See Jacobs, Harriet A(nn)
Brentano, Clemens (Maria) 1778-1842 .... **NCLC 1**
See also DLB 90
Brent of Bin Bin
See Franklin, (Stella Maria Sarah) Miles (Lampe)
Brenton, Howard 1942- .... **CLC 31**
See also CA 69-72; CANR 33, 67; DLB 13; MTCW 1
Breslin, James 1930-1996
See Breslin, Jimmy
See also CA 73-76; CANR 31, 75; DAM NOV; MTCW 1, 2
Breslin, Jimmy CLC 4, 43
See also Breslin, James
See also AITN 1; DLB 185; MTCW 2
Bresson, Robert 1901- .... **CLC 16**
See also CA 110; CANR 49
Breton, Andre 1896-1966 .. **CLC 2, 9, 15, 54; PC 15**
See also CA 19-20; 25-28R; CANR 40, 60; CAP 2; DLB 65; MTCW 1, 2
Breytenbach, Breyten 1939(?)- .. **CLC 23, 37, 126; DAM POET**
See also CA 113; 129; CANR 61; DLB 225
Bridgers, Sue Ellen 1942- .... **CLC 26**
See also AAYA 8; CA 65-68; CANR 11, 36; CLR 18; DLB 52; JRDA; MAICYA; SAAS 1; SATA 22, 90; SATA-Essay 109
Bridges, Robert (Seymour) 1844-1930 ... **TCLC 1; DAM POET; PC 28**
See also CA 104; 152; CDBLB 1890-1914; DLB 19, 98
Bridie, James TCLC 3
See also Mavor, Osborne Henry
See also DLB 10
Brin, David 1950- .... **CLC 34**
See also AAYA 21; CA 102; CANR 24, 70; INT CANR-24; SATA 65
Brink, Andre (Philippus) 1935- . **CLC 18, 36, 106**
See also CA 104; CANR 39, 62; DLB 225; INT 103; MTCW 1, 2
Brinsmead, H(esba) F(ay) 1922- ...... **CLC 21**
See also CA 21-24R; CANR 10; CLR 47; MAICYA; SAAS 5; SATA 18, 78
Brittain, Vera (Mary) 1893(?)-1970 . **CLC 23**
See also CA 13-16; 25-28R; CANR 58; CAP 1; DLB 191; MTCW 1, 2
Broch, Hermann 1886-1951 .... **TCLC 20**
See also CA 117; DLB 85, 124
Brock, Rose
See Hansen, Joseph
Brodkey, Harold (Roy) 1930-1996 ... **CLC 56**
See also CA 111; 151; CANR 71; DLB 130
Brodskii, Iosif
See Brodsky, Joseph
Brodsky, Iosif Alexandrovich 1940-1996
See Brodsky, Joseph
See also AITN 1; CA 41-44R; 151; CANR 37; DAM POET; DA3; MTCW 1, 2
Brodsky, Joseph 1940-1996 ..... **CLC 4, 6, 13, 36, 100; PC 9**
See also Brodskii, Iosif; Brodsky, Iosif Alexandrovich
See also MTCW 1
Brodsky, Michael (Mark) 1948- .... **CLC 19**
See also CA 102; CANR 18, 41, 58

Bulgya, Alexander Alexandrovich 1901-1956 .... **TCLC 53**
See also Fadeyev, Alexander
See also CA 117; 181

Bullins, Ed 1935- .... **CLC 1, 5, 7; BLC 1; DAM DRAM, MULT; DC 6**
See also BW 2, 3; CA 49-52; CAAS 16; CANR 24, 46, 73; DLB 7, 38; MTCW 1, 2

Bulwer-Lytton, Edward (George Earle Lytton) 1803-1873 .... **NCLC 1, 45**
See also DLB 21

Bunin, Ivan Alexeyevich 1870-1953 .... **TCLC 6; SSC 5**
See also CA 104

Bunting, Basil 1900-1985 .... **CLC 10, 39, 47; DAM POET**
See also CA 53-56; 115; CANR 7; DLB 20

Bunuel, Luis 1900-1983 .. **CLC 16, 80; DAM MULT; HLC 1**
See also CA 101; 110; CANR 32, 77; HW 1

Bunyan, John 1628-1688 ... **LC 4; DA; DAB; DAC; DAM MST; WLC**
See also CDBLB 1660-1789; DLB 39

Burckhardt, Jacob (Christoph) 1818-1897 .... **NCLC 49**

Burford, Eleanor
See Hibbert, Eleanor Alice Burford

Burgess, Anthony -1993 .... **CLC 1, 2, 4, 5, 8, 10, 13, 15, 22, 40, 62, 81, 94; DAB**
See also Wilson, John (Anthony) Burgess
See also AAYA 25; AITN 1; CDBLB 1960 to Present; DLB 14, 194; DLBY 98; MTCW 1

Burke, Edmund 1729(?)-1797 .... **LC 7, 36; DA; DAB; DAC; DAM MST; WLC**
See also DA3; DLB 104

Burke, Kenneth (Duva) 1897-1993 ... **CLC 2, 24**
See also CA 5-8R; 143; CANR 39, 74; DLB 45, 63; MTCW 1, 2

Burke, Leda
See Garnett, David

Burke, Ralph
See Silverberg, Robert

Burke, Thomas 1886-1945 .... **TCLC 63**
See also CA 113; 155; DLB 197

Burney, Fanny 1752-1840 .. **NCLC 12, 54, 81**
See also DLB 39

Burns, Robert 1759-1796 . **LC 3, 29, 40; DA; DAB; DAC; DAM MST, POET; PC 6; WLC**
See also CDBLB 1789-1832; DA3; DLB 109

Burns, Tex
See L'Amour, Louis (Dearborn)

Burnshaw, Stanley 1906- .... **CLC 3, 13, 44**
See also CA 9-12R; DLB 48; DLBY 97

Burr, Anne 1937- .... **CLC 6**
See also CA 25-28R

Burroughs, Edgar Rice 1875-1950 . **TCLC 2, 32; DAM NOV**
See also AAYA 11; CA 104; 132; DA3; DLB 8; MTCW 1, 2; SATA 41

Burroughs, William S(eward) 1914-1997 .. **CLC 1, 2, 5, 15, 22, 42, 75, 109; DA; DAB; DAC; DAM MST, NOV, POP; WLC**
See also AITN 2; CA 9-12R; 160; CANR 20, 52; DA3; DLB 2, 8, 16, 152; DLBY 81, 97; MTCW 1, 2

Burton, SirRichard F(rancis) 1821-1890 .... **NCLC 42**
See also DLB 55, 166, 184

Busch, Frederick 1941- .... **CLC 7, 10, 18, 47**
See also CA 33-36R; CAAS 1; CANR 45, 73, 92; DLB 6

Bush, Ronald 1946- .... **CLC 34**
See also CA 136

Bustos, F(rancisco)
See Borges, Jorge Luis

Bustos Domecq, H(onorio)
See Bioy Casares, Adolfo; Borges, Jorge Luis

Butler, Octavia E(stelle) 1947- .... **CLC 38, 121; BLCS; DAM MULT, POP**
See also AAYA 18; BW 2, 3; CA 73-76; CANR 12, 24, 38, 73; CLR 65; DA3; DLB 33; MTCW 1, 2; SATA 84

Butler, Robert Olen (Jr.) 1945- .... **CLC 81; DAM POP**
See also CA 112; CANR 66; DLB 173; INT 112; MTCW 1

Butler, Samuel 1612-1680 .... **LC 16, 43**
See also DLB 101, 126

Butler, Samuel 1835-1902 . **TCLC 1, 33; DA; DAB; DAC; DAM MST, NOV; WLC**
See also CA 143; CDBLB 1890-1914; DA3; DLB 18, 57, 174

Butler, Walter C.
See Faust, Frederick (Schiller)

Butor, Michel (Marie Francois) 1926- .... **CLC 1, 3, 8, 11, 15**
See also CA 9-12R; CANR 33, 66; DLB 83; MTCW 1, 2

Butts, Mary 1892(?)-1937 .... **TCLC 77**
See also CA 148

Buzo, Alexander (John) 1944- .... **CLC 61**
See also CA 97-100; CANR 17, 39, 69

Buzzati, Dino 1906-1972 .... **CLC 36**
See also CA 160; 33-36R; DLB 177

Byars, Betsy (Cromer) 1928- .... **CLC 35**
See also AAYA 19; CA 33-36R, 183; CAAE 183; CANR 18, 36, 57; CLR 1, 16; DLB 52; INT CANR-18; JRDA; MAICYA; MTCW 1; SAAS 1; SATA 4, 46, 80; SATA-Essay 108

Byatt, A(ntonia) S(usan Drabble) 1936- .... **CLC 19, 65; DAM NOV, POP**
See also CA 13-16R; CANR 13, 33, 50, 75; DA3; DLB 14, 194; MTCW 1, 2

Byrne, David 1952- .... **CLC 26**
See also CA 127

Byrne, John Keyes 1926-
See Leonard, Hugh
See also CA 102; CANR 78; INT 102

Byron, George Gordon (Noel) 1788-1824 .... **NCLC 2, 12; DA; DAB; DAC; DAM MST, POET; PC 16; WLC**
See also CDBLB 1789-1832; DA3; DLB 96, 110

Byron, Robert 1905-1941 .... **TCLC 67**
See also CA 160; DLB 195

C. 3. 3.
See Wilde, Oscar (Fingal O'Flahertie Wills)

Caballero, Fernan 1796-1877 .... **NCLC 10**

Cabell, Branch
See Cabell, James Branch

Cabell, James Branch 1879-1958 .... **TCLC 6**
See also CA 105; 152; DLB 9, 78; MTCW 1

Cable, George Washington 1844-1925 .... **TCLC 4; SSC 4**
See also CA 104; 155; DLB 12, 74; DLBD 13

Cabral de Melo Neto, Joao 1920- ... **CLC 76; DAM MULT**
See also CA 151

Cabrera Infante, G(uillermo) 1929- . **CLC 5, 25, 45, 120; DAM MULT; HLC 1; SSC 39**
See also CA 85-88; CANR 29, 65; DA3; DLB 113; HW 1, 2; MTCW 1, 2

Cade, Toni
See Bambara, Toni Cade

Cadmus and Harmonia
See Buchan, John

Caedmon fl. 658-680 .... **CMLC 7**
See also DLB 146

Caeiro, Alberto
See Pessoa, Fernando (Antonio Nogueira)

Cage, John (Milton, Jr.) 1912-1992 . **CLC 41**
See also CA 13-16R; 169; CANR 9, 78; DLB 193; INT CANR-9

Cahan, Abraham 1860-1951 .... **TCLC 71**
See also CA 108; 154; DLB 9, 25, 28

Cain, G.
See Cabrera Infante, G(uillermo)

Cain, Guillermo
See Cabrera Infante, G(uillermo)

Cain, James M(allahan) 1892-1977 .. **CLC 3, 11, 28**
See also AITN 1; CA 17-20R; 73-76; CANR 8, 34, 61; DLB 226; MTCW 1

Caine, Hall 1853-1931 .... **TCLC 97**

Caine, Mark
See Raphael, Frederic (Michael)

Calasso, Roberto 1941- .... **CLC 81**
See also CA 143; CANR 89

Calderon de la Barca, Pedro 1600-1681 .... **LC 23; DC 3; HLCS 1**

Caldwell, Erskine (Preston) 1903-1987 .. **CLC 1, 8, 14, 50, 60; DAM NOV; SSC 19**
See also AITN 1; CA 1-4R; 121; CAAS 1; CANR 2, 33; DA3; DLB 9, 86; MTCW 1, 2

Caldwell, (Janet Miriam) Taylor (Holland) 1900-1985 .. **CLC 2, 28, 39; DAM NOV, POP**
See also CA 5-8R; 116; CANR 5; DA3; DLBD 17

Calhoun, John Caldwell 1782-1850 .... **NCLC 15**
See also DLB 3

Calisher, Hortense 1911- .... **CLC 2, 4, 8, 38, 134; DAM NOV; SSC 15**
See also CA 1-4R; CANR 1, 22, 67; DA3; DLB 2; INT CANR-22; MTCW 1, 2

Callaghan, Morley Edward 1903-1990 .... **CLC 3, 14, 41, 65; DAC; DAM MST**
See also CA 9-12R; 132; CANR 33, 73; DLB 68; MTCW 1, 2

Callimachus c. 305B.C.-c. 240B.C. .... **CMLC 18**
See also DLB 176

Calvin, John 1509-1564 .... **LC 37**

Calvino, Italo 1923-1985 .... **CLC 5, 8, 11, 22, 33, 39, 73; DAM NOV; SSC 3**
See also CA 85-88; 116; CANR 23, 61; DLB 196; MTCW 1, 2

Cameron, Carey 1952- .... **CLC 59**
See also CA 135

Cameron, Peter 1959- .... **CLC 44**
See also CA 125; CANR 50

Camoens, Luis Vaz de 1524(?)-1580
See also HLCS 1

Camoes, Luis de 1524(?)-1580 .... **PC 31**
See also HLCS 1

Campana, Dino 1885-1932 .... **TCLC 20**
See also CA 117; DLB 114

Campanella, Tommaso 1568-1639 .... **LC 32**

Campbell, John W(ood, Jr.) 1910-1971 .... **CLC 32**
See also CA 21-22; 29-32R; CANR 34; CAP 2; DLB 8; MTCW 1

Campbell, Joseph 1904-1987 .... **CLC 69**
See also AAYA 3; BEST 89:2; CA 1-4R; 124; CANR 3, 28, 61; DA3; MTCW 1, 2

Campbell, Maria 1940- .... **CLC 85; DAC**
See also CA 102; CANR 54; NNAL

Codrescu, Andrei 1946- .... **CLC 46, 121; DAM POET**
See also CA 33-36R; CAAS 19; CANR 13, 34, 53, 76; DA3; MTCW 2
Coe, Max
See Bourne, Randolph S(illiman)
Coe, Tucker
See Westlake, Donald E(dwin)
Coen, Ethan 1958- .... **CLC 108**
See also CA 126; CANR 85
Coen, Joel 1955- .... **CLC 108**
See also CA 126
The Coen Brothers
See Coen, Ethan; Coen, Joel
Coetzee, J(ohn) M(ichael) 1940- ...... **CLC 23, 33, 66, 117; DAM NOV**
See also CA 77-80; CANR 41, 54, 74; DA3; DLB 225; MTCW 1, 2
Coffey, Brian
See Koontz, Dean R(ay)
Coffin, Robert P(eter) Tristram 1892-1955 .... **TCLC 95**
See also CA 123; 169; DLB 45
Cohan, George M(ichael) 1878-1942 .... **TCLC 60**
See also CA 157
Cohen, Arthur A(llen) 1928-1986 ...... **CLC 7, 31**
See also CA 1-4R; 120; CANR 1, 17, 42; DLB 28
Cohen, Leonard (Norman) 1934- ...... **CLC 3, 38; DAC; DAM MST**
See also CA 21-24R; CANR 14, 69; DLB 53; MTCW 1
Cohen, Matt 1942-1999 .... **CLC 19; DAC**
See also CA 61-64; CAAS 18; CANR 40; DLB 53
Cohen-Solal, Annie 19(?)- .... **CLC 50**
Colegate, Isabel 1931- .... **CLC 36**
See also CA 17-20R; CANR 8, 22, 74; DLB 14; INT CANR-22; MTCW 1
Coleman, Emmett
See Reed, Ishmael
Coleridge, Hartley 1796-1849 .... **NCLC 90**
See also DLB 96
Coleridge, M. E.
See Coleridge, Mary E(lizabeth)
Coleridge, Mary E(lizabeth) 1861-1907 .... **TCLC 73**
See also CA 116; 166; DLB 19, 98
Coleridge, Samuel Taylor 1772-1834 .... **NCLC 9, 54; DA; DAB; DAC; DAM MST, POET; PC 11; WLC**
See also CDBLB 1789-1832; DA3; DLB 93, 107
Coleridge, Sara 1802-1852 .... **NCLC 31**
See also DLB 199
Coles, Don 1928- .... **CLC 46**
See also CA 115; CANR 38
Coles, Robert (Martin) 1929- .... **CLC 108**
See also CA 45-48; CANR 3, 32, 66, 70; INT CANR-32; SATA 23
Colette, (Sidonie-Gabrielle) 1873-1954 . **TCLC 1, 5, 16; DAM NOV; SSC 10**
See also CA 104; 131; DA3; DLB 65; MTCW 1, 2
Collett, (Jacobine) Camilla (Wergeland) 1813-1895 .... **NCLC 22**
Collier, Christopher 1930- .... **CLC 30**
See also AAYA 13; CA 33-36R; CANR 13, 33; JRDA; MAICYA; SATA 16, 70
Collier, James L(incoln) 1928- .... **CLC 30; DAM POP**
See also AAYA 13; CA 9-12R; CANR 4, 33, 60; CLR 3; JRDA; MAICYA; SAAS 21; SATA 8, 70
Collier, Jeremy 1650-1726 .... **LC 6**
Collier, John 1901-1980 .... **SSC 19**
See also CA 65-68; 97-100; CANR 10; DLB 77
Collingwood, R(obin) G(eorge) 1889(?)-1943 .... **TCLC 67**
See also CA 117; 155
Collins, Hunt
See Hunter, Evan
Collins, Linda 1931- .... **CLC 44**
See also CA 125
Collins, (William) Wilkie 1824-1889 .... **NCLC 1, 18**
See also CDBLB 1832-1890; DLB 18, 70, 159
Collins, William 1721-1759 . **LC 4, 40; DAM POET**
See also DLB 109
Collodi, Carlo 1826-1890 .... **NCLC 54**
See also Lorenzini, Carlo
See also CLR 5
Colman, George 1732-1794
See Glassco, John
Colt, Winchester Remington
See Hubbard, L(afayette) Ron(ald)
Colter, Cyrus 1910- .... **CLC 58**
See also BW 1; CA 65-68; CANR 10, 66; DLB 33
Colton, James
See Hansen, Joseph
Colum, Padraic 1881-1972 .... **CLC 28**
See also CA 73-76; 33-36R; CANR 35; CLR 36; MAICYA; MTCW 1; SATA 15
Colvin, James
See Moorcock, Michael (John)
Colwin, Laurie (E.) 1944-1992 .... **CLC 5, 13, 23, 84**
See also CA 89-92; 139; CANR 20, 46; DLBY 80; MTCW 1
Comfort, Alex(ander) 1920- .... **CLC 7; DAM POP**
See also CA 1-4R; CANR 1, 45; MTCW 1
Comfort, Montgomery
See Campbell, (John) Ramsey
Compton-Burnett, I(vy) 1884(?)-1969 .... **CLC 1, 3, 10, 15, 34; DAM NOV**
See also CA 1-4R; 25-28R; CANR 4; DLB 36; MTCW 1
Comstock, Anthony 1844-1915 ...... **TCLC 13**
See also CA 110; 169
Comte, Auguste 1798-1857 .... **NCLC 54**
Conan Doyle, Arthur
See Doyle, Arthur Conan
Conde (Abellan), Carmen 1901-
See also CA 177; DLB 108; HLCS 1; HW 2
Conde, Maryse 1937- .... **CLC 52, 92; BLCS; DAM MULT**
See also BW 2, 3; CA 110; CANR 30, 53, 76; MTCW 1
Condillac, Etienne Bonnot de 1714-1780 .... **LC 26**
Condon, Richard (Thomas) 1915-1996 ...... **CLC 4, 6, 8, 10, 45, 100; DAM NOV**
See also BEST 90:3; CA 1-4R; 151; CAAS 1; CANR 2, 23; INT CANR-23; MTCW 1, 2
Confucius 551B.C.-479B.C. .. **CMLC 19; DA; DAB; DAC; DAM MST; WLCS**
See also DA3
Congreve, William 1670-1729 .... **LC 5, 21; DA; DAB; DAC; DAM DRAM, MST, POET; DC 2; WLC**
See also CDBLB 1660-1789; DLB 39, 84
Connell, Evan S(helby), Jr. 1924- . **CLC 4, 6, 45; DAM NOV**
See also AAYA 7; CA 1-4R; CAAS 2; CANR 2, 39, 76; DLB 2; DLBY 81; MTCW 1, 2
Connelly, Marc(us Cook) 1890-1980 . **CLC 7**
See also CA 85-88; 102; CANR 30; DLB 7; DLBY 80; SATA-Obit 25
Connor, Ralph TCLC 31
See also Gordon, Charles William
See also DLB 92
Conrad, Joseph 1857-1924 .... **TCLC 1, 6, 13, 25, 43, 57; DA; DAB; DAC; DAM MST, NOV; SSC 9; WLC**
See also AAYA 26; CA 104; 131; CANR 60; CDBLB 1890-1914; DA3; DLB 10, 34, 98, 156; MTCW 1, 2; SATA 27
Conrad, Robert Arnold
See Hart, Moss
Conroy, Pat
See Conroy, (Donald) Pat(rick)
See also MTCW 2
Conroy, (Donald) Pat(rick) 1945- ... **CLC 30, 74; DAM NOV, POP**
See also Conroy, Pat
See also AAYA 8; AITN 1; CA 85-88; CANR 24, 53; DA3; DLB 6; MTCW 1
Constant (de Rebecque), (Henri) Benjamin 1767-1830 .... **NCLC 6**
See also DLB 119
Conybeare, Charles Augustus
See Eliot, T(homas) S(tearns)
Cook, Michael 1933- .... **CLC 58**
See also CA 93-96; CANR 68; DLB 53
Cook, Robin 1940- .... **CLC 14; DAM POP**
See also AAYA 32; BEST 90:2; CA 108; 111; CANR 41, 90; DA3; INT 111
Cook, Roy
See Silverberg, Robert
Cooke, Elizabeth 1948- .... **CLC 55**
See also CA 129
Cooke, John Esten 1830-1886 .... **NCLC 5**
See also DLB 3
Cooke, John Estes
See Baum, L(yman) Frank
Cooke, M. E.
See Creasey, John
Cooke, Margaret
See Creasey, John
Cook-Lynn, Elizabeth 1930- . **CLC 93; DAM MULT**
See also CA 133; DLB 175; NNAL
Cooney, Ray CLC 62
Cooper, Douglas 1960- .... **CLC 86**
Cooper, Henry St. John
See Creasey, John
Cooper, J(oan) California (?)- .... **CLC 56; DAM MULT**
See also AAYA 12; BW 1; CA 125; CANR 55; DLB 212
Cooper, James Fenimore 1789-1851 .... **NCLC 1, 27, 54**
See also AAYA 22; CDALB 1640-1865; DA3; DLB 3; SATA 19
Coover, Robert (Lowell) 1932- ...... **CLC 3, 7, 15, 32, 46, 87; DAM NOV; SSC 15**
See also CA 45-48; CANR 3, 37, 58; DLB 2, 227; DLBY 81; MTCW 1, 2
Copeland, Stewart (Armstrong) 1952- .... **CLC 26**
Copernicus, Nicolaus 1473-1543 .... **LC 45**
Coppard, A(lfred) E(dgar) 1878-1957 .... **TCLC 5; SSC 21**
See also CA 114; 167; DLB 162; YABC 1
Coppee, Francois 1842-1908 .... **TCLC 25**
See also CA 170
Coppola, Francis Ford 1939- ... **CLC 16, 126**
See also CA 77-80; CANR 40, 78; DLB 44

Crustt
See Crumb, R(obert)
Cruz, Victor Hernandez 1949-
See also BW 2; CA 65-68; CAAS 17; CANR 14, 32, 74; DAM MULT, POET; DLB 41; HLC 1; HW 1, 2; MTCW 1
Cryer, Gretchen (Kiger) 1935- .... **CLC 21**
See also CA 114; 123
Csath, Geza 1887-1919 .... **TCLC 13**
See also CA 111
Cudlip, David R(ockwell) 1933- .... **CLC 34**
See also CA 177
Cullen, Countee 1903-1946 .... **TCLC 4, 37; BLC 1; DA; DAC; DAM MST, MULT, POET; PC 20; WLCS**
See also BW 1; CA 108; 124; CDALB 1917-1929; DA3; DLB 4, 48, 51; MTCW 1, 2; SATA 18
Cum, R.
See Crumb, R(obert)
Cummings, Bruce F(rederick) 1889-1919
See Barbellion, W. N. P.
See also CA 123
Cummings, E(dward) E(stlin) 1894-1962 .... **CLC 1, 3, 8, 12, 15, 68; DA; DAB; DAC; DAM MST, POET; PC 5; WLC**
See also CA 73-76; CANR 31; CDALB 1929-1941; DA3; DLB 4, 48; MTCW 1, 2
Cunha, Euclides (Rodrigues Pimenta) da 1866-1909 .... **TCLC 24**
See also CA 123
Cunningham, E. V.
See Fast, Howard (Melvin)
Cunningham, J(ames) V(incent) 1911-1985 .... **CLC 3, 31**
See also CA 1-4R; 115; CANR 1, 72; DLB 5
Cunningham, Julia (Woolfolk) 1916- .... **CLC 12**
See also CA 9-12R; CANR 4, 19, 36; JRDA; MAICYA; SAAS 2; SATA 1, 26
Cunningham, Michael 1952- .... **CLC 34**
See also CA 136
Cunninghame Graham, R. B.
See Cunninghame Graham, Robert (Gallnigad) Bontine
Cunninghame Graham, Robert (Gallnigad) Bontine 1852-1936 .... **TCLC 19**
See also Graham, R(obert) B(ontine) Cunninghame
See also CA 119; 184; DLB 98
Currie, Ellen 19(?)- .... **CLC 44**
Curtin, Philip
See Lowndes, Marie Adelaide (Belloc)
Curtis, Price
See Ellison, Harlan (Jay)
Cutrate, Joe
See Spiegelman, Art
Cynewulf c. 770-c. 840 .... **CMLC 23**
Czaczkes, Shmuel Yosef
See Agnon, S(hmuel) Y(osef Halevi)
Dabrowska, Maria (Szumska) 1889-1965 .... **CLC 15**
See also CA 106
Dabydeen, David 1955- .... **CLC 34**
See also BW 1; CA 125; CANR 56, 92
Dacey, Philip 1939- .... **CLC 51**
See also CA 37-40R; CAAS 17; CANR 14, 32, 64; DLB 105
Dagerman, Stig (Halvard) 1923-1954 .... **TCLC 17**
See also CA 117; 155
Dahl, Roald 1916-1990 ...... **CLC 1, 6, 18, 79; DAB; DAC; DAM MST, NOV, POP**
See also AAYA 15; CA 1-4R; 133; CANR 6, 32, 37, 62; CLR 1, 7, 41; DA3; DLB 139; JRDA; MAICYA; MTCW 1, 2; SATA 1, 26, 73; SATA-Obit 65
Dahlberg, Edward 1900-1977 .. **CLC 1, 7, 14**
See also CA 9-12R; 69-72; CANR 31, 62; DLB 48; MTCW 1
Daitch, Susan 1954- .... **CLC 103**
See also CA 161
Dale, Colin TCLC 18
See also Lawrence, T(homas) E(dward)
Dale, George E.
See Asimov, Isaac
Dalton, Roque 1935-1975
See also HLCS 1; HW 2
Daly, Elizabeth 1878-1967 .... **CLC 52**
See also CA 23-24; 25-28R; CANR 60; CAP 2
Daly, Maureen 1921-1983 .... **CLC 17**
See also AAYA 5; CANR 37, 83; JRDA; MAICYA; SAAS 1; SATA 2
Damas, Leon-Gontran 1912-1978 .... **CLC 84**
See also BW 1; CA 125; 73-76
Dana, Richard Henry Sr. 1787-1879 .... **NCLC 53**
Daniel, Samuel 1562(?)-1619 .... **LC 24**
See also DLB 62
Daniels, Brett
See Adler, Renata
Dannay, Frederic 1905-1982 . **CLC 11; DAM POP**
See also Queen, Ellery
See also CA 1-4R; 107; CANR 1, 39; DLB 137; MTCW 1
D'Annunzio, Gabriele 1863-1938 ... **TCLC 6, 40**
See also CA 104; 155
Danois, N. le
See Gourmont, Remy (-Marie-Charles) de
Dante 1265-1321 .... **CMLC 3, 18, 39; DA; DAB; DAC; DAM MST, POET; PC 21; WLCS**
See also Alighieri, Dante
See also DA3
d'Antibes, Germain
See Simenon, Georges (Jacques Christian)
Danticat, Edwidge 1969- .... **CLC 94**
See also AAYA 29; CA 152; CANR 73; MTCW 1
Danvers, Dennis 1947- .... **CLC 70**
Danziger, Paula 1944- .... **CLC 21**
See also AAYA 4; CA 112; 115; CANR 37; CLR 20; JRDA; MAICYA; SATA 36, 63, 102; SATA-Brief 30
Da Ponte, Lorenzo 1749-1838 .... **NCLC 50**
Dario, Ruben 1867-1916 .... **TCLC 4; DAM MULT; HLC 1; PC 15**
See also CA 131; CANR 81; HW 1, 2; MTCW 1, 2
Darley, George 1795-1846 .... **NCLC 2**
See also DLB 96
Darrow, Clarence (Seward) 1857-1938 .... **TCLC 81**
See also CA 164
Darwin, Charles 1809-1882 .... **NCLC 57**
See also DLB 57, 166
Daryush, Elizabeth 1887-1977 ...... **CLC 6, 19**
See also CA 49-52; CANR 3, 81; DLB 20
Dasgupta, Surendranath 1887-1952 .... **TCLC 81**
See also CA 157
Dashwood, Edmee Elizabeth Monica de la Pasture 1890-1943
See Delafield, E. M.
See also CA 119; 154
Daudet, (Louis Marie) Alphonse 1840-1897 .... **NCLC 1**
See also DLB 123
Daumal, Rene 1908-1944 .... **TCLC 14**
See also CA 114
Davenant, William 1606-1668 .... **LC 13**
See also DLB 58, 126
Davenport, Guy (Mattison, Jr.) 1927- .... **CLC 6, 14, 38; SSC 16**
See also CA 33-36R; CANR 23, 73; DLB 130
Davidson, Avram (James) 1923-1993
See Queen, Ellery
See also CA 101; 171; CANR 26; DLB 8
Davidson, Donald (Grady) 1893-1968 .... **CLC 2, 13, 19**
See also CA 5-8R; 25-28R; CANR 4, 84; DLB 45
Davidson, Hugh
See Hamilton, Edmond
Davidson, John 1857-1909 .... **TCLC 24**
See also CA 118; DLB 19
Davidson, Sara 1943- .... **CLC 9**
See also CA 81-84; CANR 44, 68; DLB 185
Davie, Donald (Alfred) 1922-1995 .... **CLC 5, 8, 10, 31; PC 29**
See also CA 1-4R; 149; CAAS 3; CANR 1, 44; DLB 27; MTCW 1
Davies, Ray(mond Douglas) 1944- ... **CLC 21**
See also CA 116; 146; CANR 92
Davies, Rhys 1901-1978 .... **CLC 23**
See also CA 9-12R; 81-84; CANR 4; DLB 139, 191
Davies, (William) Robertson 1913-1995 .... **CLC 2, 7, 13, 25, 42, 75, 91; DA; DAB; DAC; DAM MST, NOV, POP; WLC**
See also BEST 89:2; CA 33-36R; 150; CANR 17, 42; DA3; DLB 68; INT CANR-17; MTCW 1, 2
Davies, Walter C.
See Kornbluth, C(yril) M.
Davies, William Henry 1871-1940 ... **TCLC 5**
See also CA 104; 179; DLB 19, 174
Da Vinci, Leonardo 1452-1519 ..... **LC 12, 57, 60**
Davis, Angela (Yvonne) 1944- .... **CLC 77; DAM MULT**
See also BW 2, 3; CA 57-60; CANR 10, 81; DA3
Davis, B. Lynch
See Bioy Casares, Adolfo; Borges, Jorge Luis
Davis, B. Lynch
See Bioy Casares, Adolfo
Davis, H(arold) L(enoir) 1894-1960 . **CLC 49**
See also CA 178; 89-92; DLB 9, 206; SATA 114
Davis, Rebecca (Blaine) Harding 1831-1910 .... **TCLC 6; SSC 38**
See also CA 104; 179; DLB 74
Davis, Richard Harding 1864-1916 .... **TCLC 24**
See also CA 114; 179; DLB 12, 23, 78, 79, 189; DLBD 13
Davison, Frank Dalby 1893-1970 ..... **CLC 15**
See also CA 116
Davison, Lawrence H.
See Lawrence, D(avid) H(erbert Richards)
Davison, Peter (Hubert) 1928- .... **CLC 28**
See also CA 9-12R; CAAS 4; CANR 3, 43, 84; DLB 5
Davys, Mary 1674-1732 .... **LC 1, 46**
See also DLB 39
Dawson, Fielding 1930- .... **CLC 6**
See also CA 85-88; DLB 130
Dawson, Peter
See Faust, Frederick (Schiller)
Day, Clarence (Shepard, Jr.) 1874-1935 .... **TCLC 25**
See also CA 108; DLB 11
Day, Thomas 1748-1789 .... **LC 1**
See also DLB 39; YABC 1

Day Lewis, C(ecil) 1904-1972 . **CLC 1, 6, 10; DAM POET; PC 11**
See also Blake, Nicholas
See also CA 13-16; 33-36R; CANR 34; CAP 1; DLB 15, 20; MTCW 1, 2
Dazai Osamu 1909-1948 .. **TCLC 11; SSC 41**
See also Tsushima, Shuji
See also CA 164; DLB 182
de Andrade, Carlos Drummond 1892-1945
See Drummond de Andrade, Carlos
Deane, Norman
See Creasey, John
Deane, Seamus (Francis) 1940- ...... **CLC 122**
See also CA 118; CANR 42
de Beauvoir, Simone (Lucie Ernestine Marie Bertrand)
See Beauvoir, Simone (Lucie Ernestine Marie Bertrand) de
de Beer, P.
See Bosman, Herman Charles
de Brissac, Malcolm
See Dickinson, Peter (Malcolm)
de Campos, Alvaro
See Pessoa, Fernando (Antonio Nogueira)
de Chardin, Pierre Teilhard
See Teilhard de Chardin, (Marie Joseph) Pierre
Dee, John 1527-1608 .... **LC 20**
Deer, Sandra 1940- .... **CLC 45**
See also CA 186
De Ferrari, Gabriella 1941- .... **CLC 65**
See also CA 146
Defoe, Daniel 1660(?)-1731 .... **LC 1, 42; DA; DAB; DAC; DAM MST, NOV; WLC**
See also AAYA 27; CDBLB 1660-1789; CLR 61; DA3; DLB 39, 95, 101; JRDA; MAICYA; SATA 22
de Gourmont, Remy(-Marie-Charles)
See Gourmont, Remy (-Marie-Charles) de
de Hartog, Jan 1914- .... **CLC 19**
See also CA 1-4R; CANR 1
de Hostos, E. M.
See Hostos (y Bonilla), Eugenio Maria de
de Hostos, Eugenio M.
See Hostos (y Bonilla), Eugenio Maria de
Deighton, Len CLC 4, 7, 22, 46
See also Deighton, Leonard Cyril
See also AAYA 6; BEST 89:2; CDBLB 1960 to Present; DLB 87
Deighton, Leonard Cyril 1929-
See Deighton, Len
See also CA 9-12R; CANR 19, 33, 68; DAM NOV, POP; DA3; MTCW 1, 2
Dekker, Thomas 1572(?)-1632 . **LC 22; DAM DRAM; DC 12**
See also CDBLB Before 1660; DLB 62, 172
Delafield, E. M. 1890-1943 .... **TCLC 61**
See also Dashwood, Edmee Elizabeth Monica de la Pasture
See also DLB 34
de la Mare, Walter (John) 1873-1956 ..... **TCLC 4, 53; DAB; DAC; DAM MST, POET; SSC 14; WLC**
See also CA 163; CDBLB 1914-1945; CLR 23; DA3; DLB 162; MTCW 1; SATA 16
Delaney, Franey
See O'Hara, John (Henry)
Delaney, Shelagh 1939- .... **CLC 29; DAM DRAM**
See also CA 17-20R; CANR 30, 67; CDBLB 1960 to Present; DLB 13; MTCW 1
Delany, Mary (Granville Pendarves) 1700-1788 .... **LC 12**
Delany, Samuel R(ay, Jr.) 1942- .. **CLC 8, 14, 38; BLC 1; DAM MULT**
See also AAYA 24; BW 2, 3; CA 81-84; CANR 27, 43; DLB 8, 33; MTCW 1, 2
De La Ramee, (Marie) Louise 1839-1908
See Ouida
See also SATA 20
de la Roche, Mazo 1879-1961 .... **CLC 14**
See also CA 85-88; CANR 30; DLB 68; SATA 64
De La Salle, Innocent
See Hartmann, Sadakichi
Delbanco, Nicholas (Franklin) 1942- .... **CLC 6, 13**
See also CA 17-20R; CAAS 2; CANR 29, 55; DLB 6
del Castillo, Michel 1933- .... **CLC 38**
See also CA 109; CANR 77
Deledda, Grazia (Cosima) 1875(?)-1936 .... **TCLC 23**
See also CA 123
Delgado, Abelardo (Lalo) B(arrientos) 1930-
See also CA 131; CAAS 15; CANR 90; DAM MST, MULT; DLB 82; HLC 1; HW 1, 2
Delibes, Miguel CLC 8, 18
See also Delibes Setien, Miguel
Delibes Setien, Miguel 1920-
See Delibes, Miguel
See also CA 45-48; CANR 1, 32; HW 1; MTCW 1
DeLillo, Don 1936- ..... **CLC 8, 10, 13, 27, 39, 54, 76; DAM NOV, POP**
See also BEST 89:1; CA 81-84; CANR 21, 76, 92; DA3; DLB 6, 173; MTCW 1, 2
de Lisser, H. G.
See De Lisser, H(erbert) G(eorge)
See also DLB 117
De Lisser, H(erbert) G(eorge) 1878-1944 .... **TCLC 12**
See also de Lisser, H. G.
See also BW 2; CA 109; 152
Deloney, Thomas 1560(?)-1600 .... **LC 41**
See also DLB 167
Deloria, Vine (Victor), Jr. 1933- ...... **CLC 21, 122; DAM MULT**
See also CA 53-56; CANR 5, 20, 48; DLB 175; MTCW 1; NNAL; SATA 21
Del Vecchio, John M(ichael) 1947- .. **CLC 29**
See also CA 110; DLBD 9
de Man, Paul (Adolph Michel) 1919-1983 .... **CLC 55**
See also CA 128; 111; CANR 61; DLB 67; MTCW 1, 2
DeMarinis, Rick 1934- .... **CLC 54**
See also CA 57-60, 184; CAAE 184; CAAS 24; CANR 9, 25, 50
Dembry, R. Emmet
See Murfree, Mary Noailles
Demby, William 1922- .... **CLC 53; BLC 1; DAM MULT**
See also BW 1, 3; CA 81-84; CANR 81; DLB 33
de Menton, Francisco
See Chin, Frank (Chew, Jr.)
Demetrius of Phalerum c. 307B.C.- .... **CMLC 34**
Demijohn, Thom
See Disch, Thomas M(ichael)
de Molina, Tirso 1584(?)-1648 .... **DC 13**
See also HLCS 2
de Montherlant, Henry (Milon)
See Montherlant, Henry (Milon) de
Demosthenes 384B.C.-322B.C. ...... **CMLC 13**
See also DLB 176
de Natale, Francine
See Malzberg, Barry N(athaniel)
Denby, Edwin (Orr) 1903-1983 .... **CLC 48**
See also CA 138; 110
Denis, Julio
See Cortazar, Julio
Denmark, Harrison
See Zelazny, Roger (Joseph)
Dennis, John 1658-1734 .... **LC 11**
See also DLB 101
Dennis, Nigel (Forbes) 1912-1989 ...... **CLC 8**
See also CA 25-28R; 129; DLB 13, 15; MTCW 1
Dent, Lester 1904(?)-1959 .... **TCLC 72**
See also CA 112; 161
De Palma, Brian (Russell) 1940- ...... **CLC 20**
See also CA 109
De Quincey, Thomas 1785-1859 ..... **NCLC 4, 87**
See also CDBLB 1789-1832; DLB 110; 144
Deren, Eleanora 1908(?)-1961
See Deren, Maya
See also CA 111
Deren, Maya 1917-1961 .... **CLC 16, 102**
See also Deren, Eleanora
Derleth, August (William) 1909-1971 .... **CLC 31**
See also CA 1-4R; 29-32R; CANR 4; DLB 9; DLBD 17; SATA 5
Der Nister 1884-1950 .... **TCLC 56**
de Routisie, Albert
See Aragon, Louis
Derrida, Jacques 1930- .... **CLC 24, 87**
See also CA 124; 127; CANR 76; MTCW 1
Derry Down Derry
See Lear, Edward
Dersonnes, Jacques
See Simenon, Georges (Jacques Christian)
Desai, Anita 1937- ..... **CLC 19, 37, 97; DAB; DAM NOV**
See also CA 81-84; CANR 33, 53; DA3; MTCW 1, 2; SATA 63
Desai, Kiran 1971- .... **CLC 119**
See also CA 171
de Saint-Luc, Jean
See Glassco, John
de Saint Roman, Arnaud
See Aragon, Louis
Descartes, Rene 1596-1650 .... **LC 20, 35**
De Sica, Vittorio 1901(?)-1974 .... **CLC 20**
See also CA 117
Desnos, Robert 1900-1945 .... **TCLC 22**
See also CA 121; 151
de Stael, Germaine 1766-1817 .... **NCLC 91**
See also Stael-Holstein, Anne Louise Germaine Necker Baronn
See also DLB 119
Destouches, Louis-Ferdinand 1894-1961 .... **CLC 9, 15**
See also Celine, Louis-Ferdinand
See also CA 85-88; CANR 28; MTCW 1
de Tolignac, Gaston
See Griffith, D(avid Lewelyn) W(ark)
Deutsch, Babette 1895-1982 .... **CLC 18**
See also CA 1-4R; 108; CANR 4, 79; DLB 45; SATA 1; SATA-Obit 33
Devenant, William 1606-1649 .... **LC 13**
Devkota, Laxmiprasad 1909-1959 . **TCLC 23**
See also CA 123
De Voto, Bernard (Augustine) 1897-1955 .... **TCLC 29**
See also CA 113; 160; DLB 9
De Vries, Peter 1910-1993 ..... **CLC 1, 2, 3, 7, 10, 28, 46; DAM NOV**
See also CA 17-20R; 142; CANR 41; DLB 6; DLBY 82; MTCW 1, 2
Dewey, John 1859-1952 .... **TCLC 95**
See also CA 114; 170
Dexter, John
See Bradley, Marion Zimmer
Dexter, Martin
See Faust, Frederick (Schiller)
Dexter, Pete 1943- .. **CLC 34, 55; DAM POP**
See also BEST 89:2; CA 127; 131; INT 131; MTCW 1

Diamano, Silmang
See Senghor, Leopold Sedar
Diamond, Neil 1941- .... **CLC 30**
See also CA 108
Diaz del Castillo, Bernal 1496-1584 .. **LC 31; HLCS 1**
di Bassetto, Corno
See Shaw, George Bernard
Dick, Philip K(indred) 1928-1982 ... **CLC 10, 30, 72; DAM NOV, POP**
See also AAYA 24; CA 49-52; 106; CANR 2, 16; DA3; DLB 8; MTCW 1, 2
Dickens, Charles (John Huffam) 1812-1870 .... **NCLC 3, 8, 18, 26, 37, 50, 86; DA; DAB; DAC; DAM MST, NOV; SSC 17; WLC**
See also AAYA 23; CDBLB 1832-1890; DA3; DLB 21, 55, 70, 159, 166; JRDA; MAICYA; SATA 15
Dickey, James (Lafayette) 1923-1997 .... **CLC 1, 2, 4, 7, 10, 15, 47, 109; DAM NOV, POET, POP**
See also AITN 1, 2; CA 9-12R; 156; CABS 2; CANR 10, 48, 61; CDALB 1968-1988; DA3; DLB 5, 193; DLBD 7; DLBY 82, 93, 96, 97, 98; INT CANR-10; MTCW 1, 2
Dickey, William 1928-1994 .... **CLC 3, 28**
See also CA 9-12R; 145; CANR 24, 79; DLB 5
Dickinson, Charles 1951- .... **CLC 49**
See also CA 128
Dickinson, Emily (Elizabeth) 1830-1886 ..... **NCLC 21, 77; DA; DAB; DAC; DAM MST, POET; PC 1; WLC**
See also AAYA 22; CDALB 1865-1917; DA3; DLB 1; SATA 29
Dickinson, Peter (Malcolm) 1927- .. **CLC 12, 35**
See also AAYA 9; CA 41-44R; CANR 31, 58, 88; CLR 29; DLB 87, 161; JRDA; MAICYA; SATA 5, 62, 95
Dickson, Carr
See Carr, John Dickson
Dickson, Carter
See Carr, John Dickson
Diderot, Denis 1713-1784 .... **LC 26**
Didion, Joan 1934- .... **CLC 1, 3, 8, 14, 32, 129; DAM NOV**
See also AITN 1; CA 5-8R; CANR 14, 52, 76; CDALB 1968-1988; DA3; DLB 2, 173, 185; DLBY 81, 86; MTCW 1, 2
Dietrich, Robert
See Hunt, E(verette) Howard, (Jr.)
Difusa, Pati
See Almodovar, Pedro
Dillard, Annie 1945- .. **CLC 9, 60, 115; DAM NOV**
See also AAYA 6; CA 49-52; CANR 3, 43, 62, 90; DA3; DLBY 80; MTCW 1, 2; SATA 10
Dillard, R(ichard) H(enry) W(ilde) 1937- .... **CLC 5**
See also CA 21-24R; CAAS 7; CANR 10; DLB 5
Dillon, Eilis 1920-1994 .... **CLC 17**
See also CA 9-12R, 182; 147; CAAE 182; CAAS 3; CANR 4, 38, 78; CLR 26; MAICYA; SATA 2, 74; SATA-Essay 105; SATA-Obit 83
Dimont, Penelope
See Mortimer, Penelope (Ruth)
Dinesen, Isak -1962 .. **CLC 10, 29, 95; SSC 7**
See also Blixen, Karen (Christentze Dinesen)
See also MTCW 1
Ding Ling CLC 68
See also Chiang, Pin-chin
Diphusa, Patty
See Almodovar, Pedro
Disch, Thomas M(ichael) 1940- ... **CLC 7, 36**
See also AAYA 17; CA 21-24R; CAAS 4; CANR 17, 36, 54, 89; CLR 18; DA3; DLB 8; MAICYA; MTCW 1, 2; SAAS 15; SATA 92
Disch, Tom
See Disch, Thomas M(ichael)
d'Isly, Georges
See Simenon, Georges (Jacques Christian)
Disraeli, Benjamin 1804-1881 ... **NCLC 2, 39, 79**
See also DLB 21, 55
Ditcum, Steve
See Crumb, R(obert)
Dixon, Paige
See Corcoran, Barbara
Dixon, Stephen 1936- .... **CLC 52; SSC 16**
See also CA 89-92; CANR 17, 40, 54, 91; DLB 130
Doak, Annie
See Dillard, Annie
Dobell, Sydney Thompson 1824-1874 .... **NCLC 43**
See also DLB 32
Doblin, Alfred TCLC 13
See also Doeblin, Alfred
Dobrolyubov, Nikolai Alexandrovich 1836-1861 .... **NCLC 5**
Dobson, Austin 1840-1921 .... **TCLC 79**
See also DLB 35; 144
Dobyns, Stephen 1941- .... **CLC 37**
See also CA 45-48; CANR 2, 18
Doctorow, E(dgar) L(aurence) 1931- .... **CLC 6, 11, 15, 18, 37, 44, 65, 113; DAM NOV, POP**
See also AAYA 22; AITN 2; BEST 89:3; CA 45-48; CANR 2, 33, 51, 76; CDALB 1968-1988; DA3; DLB 2, 28, 173; DLBY 80; MTCW 1, 2
Dodgson, Charles Lutwidge 1832-1898
See Carroll, Lewis
See also CLR 2; DA; DAB; DAC; DAM MST, NOV, POET; DA3; MAICYA; SATA 100; YABC 2
Dodson, Owen (Vincent) 1914-1983 .... **CLC 79; BLC 1; DAM MULT**
See also BW 1; CA 65-68; 110; CANR 24; DLB 76
Doeblin, Alfred 1878-1957 .... **TCLC 13**
See also Doblin, Alfred
See also CA 110; 141; DLB 66
Doerr, Harriet 1910- .... **CLC 34**
See also CA 117; 122; CANR 47; INT 122
Domecq, H(onorio Bustos)
See Bioy Casares, Adolfo
Domecq, H(onorio) Bustos
See Bioy Casares, Adolfo; Borges, Jorge Luis
Domini, Rey
See Lorde, Audre (Geraldine)
Dominique
See Proust, (Valentin-Louis-George-Eugene-) Marcel
Don, A
See Stephen, SirLeslie
Donaldson, Stephen R. 1947- .... **CLC 46; DAM POP**
See also CA 89-92; CANR 13, 55; INT CANR-13
Donleavy, J(ames) P(atrick) 1926- .... **CLC 1, 4, 6, 10, 45**
See also AITN 2; CA 9-12R; CANR 24, 49, 62, 80; DLB 6, 173; INT CANR-24; MTCW 1, 2
Donne, John 1572-1631 .... **LC 10, 24; DA; DAB; DAC; DAM MST, POET; PC 1; WLC**
See also CDBLB Before 1660; DLB 121, 151
Donnell, David 1939(?)- .... **CLC 34**
Donoghue, P. S.
See Hunt, E(verette) Howard, (Jr.)
Donoso (Yanez), Jose 1924-1996 ... **CLC 4, 8, 11, 32, 99; DAM MULT; HLC 1; SSC 34**
See also CA 81-84; 155; CANR 32, 73; DLB 113; HW 1, 2; MTCW 1, 2
Donovan, John 1928-1992 .... **CLC 35**
See also AAYA 20; CA 97-100; 137; CLR 3; MAICYA; SATA 72; SATA-Brief 29
Don Roberto
See Cunninghame Graham, Robert (Gallnigad) Bontine
Doolittle, Hilda 1886-1961 . **CLC 3, 8, 14, 31, 34, 73; DA; DAC; DAM MST, POET; PC 5; WLC**
See also H. D.
See also CA 97-100; CANR 35; DLB 4, 45; MTCW 1, 2
Dorfman, Ariel 1942- ...... **CLC 48, 77; DAM MULT; HLC 1**
See also CA 124; 130; CANR 67, 70; HW 1, 2; INT 130
Dorn, Edward (Merton) 1929-1999 .... **CLC 10, 18**
See also CA 93-96; CANR 42, 79; DLB 5; INT 93-96
Dorris, Michael (Anthony) 1945-1997 .... **CLC 109; DAM MULT, NOV**
See also AAYA 20; BEST 90:1; CA 102; 157; CANR 19, 46, 75; CLR 58; DA3; DLB 175; MTCW 2; NNAL; SATA 75; SATA-Obit 94
Dorris, Michael A.
See Dorris, Michael (Anthony)
Dorsan, Luc
See Simenon, Georges (Jacques Christian)
Dorsange, Jean
See Simenon, Georges (Jacques Christian)
Dos Passos, John (Roderigo) 1896-1970 ... **CLC 1, 4, 8, 11, 15, 25, 34, 82; DA; DAB; DAC; DAM MST, NOV; WLC**
See also CA 1-4R; 29-32R; CANR 3; CDALB 1929-1941; DA3; DLB 4, 9; DLBD 1, 15; DLBY 96; MTCW 1, 2
Dossage, Jean
See Simenon, Georges (Jacques Christian)
Dostoevsky, Fedor Mikhailovich 1821-1881 . **NCLC 2, 7, 21, 33, 43; DA; DAB; DAC; DAM MST, NOV; SSC 2, 33; WLC**
See also DA3
Doughty, Charles M(ontagu) 1843-1926 .... **TCLC 27**
See also CA 115; 178; DLB 19, 57, 174
Douglas, Ellen CLC 73
See also Haxton, Josephine Ayres; Williamson, Ellen Douglas
Douglas, Gavin 1475(?)-1522 .... **LC 20**
See also DLB 132
Douglas, George
See Brown, George Douglas
Douglas, Keith (Castellain) 1920-1944 .... **TCLC 40**
See also CA 160; DLB 27
Douglas, Leonard
See Bradbury, Ray (Douglas)
Douglas, Michael
See Crichton, (John) Michael

Author Index

Durkheim, Emile 1858-1917 .... **TCLC 55**
Durrell, Lawrence (George) 1912-1990 .... **CLC 1, 4, 6, 8, 13, 27, 41; DAM NOV**
See also CA 9-12R; 132; CANR 40, 77; CDBLB 1945-1960; DLB 15, 27, 204; DLBY 90; MTCW 1, 2
Durrenmatt, Friedrich
See Duerrenmatt, Friedrich
Dutt, Toru 1856-1877 .... **NCLC 29**
Dwight, Timothy 1752-1817 .... **NCLC 13**
See also DLB 37
Dworkin, Andrea 1946- .... **CLC 43**
See also CA 77-80; CAAS 21; CANR 16, 39, 76; INT CANR-16; MTCW 1, 2
Dwyer, Deanna
See Koontz, Dean R(ay)
Dwyer, K. R.
See Koontz, Dean R(ay)
Dwyer, Thomas A. 1923- .... **CLC 114**
See also CA 115
Dye, Richard
See De Voto, Bernard (Augustine)
Dylan, Bob 1941- .... **CLC 3, 4, 6, 12, 77**
See also CA 41-44R; DLB 16
E. V. L.
See Lucas, E(dward) V(errall)
Eagleton, Terence (Francis) 1943- .. **CLC 63, 132**
See also CA 57-60; CANR 7, 23, 68; MTCW 1, 2
Eagleton, Terry
See Eagleton, Terence (Francis)
Early, Jack
See Scoppettone, Sandra
East, Michael
See West, Morris L(anglo)
Eastaway, Edward
See Thomas, (Philip) Edward
Eastlake, William (Derry) 1917-1997 .... **CLC 8**
See also CA 5-8R; 158; CAAS 1; CANR 5, 63; DLB 6, 206; INT CANR-5
Eastman, Charles A(lexander) 1858-1939 .... **TCLC 55; DAM MULT**
See also CA 179; CANR 91; DLB 175; NNAL; YABC 1
Eberhart, Richard (Ghormley) 1904- .. **CLC 3, 11, 19, 56; DAM POET**
See also CA 1-4R; CANR 2; CDALB 1941-1968; DLB 48; MTCW 1
Eberstadt, Fernanda 1960- .... **CLC 39**
See also CA 136; CANR 69
Echegaray (y Eizaguirre), Jose (Maria Waldo) 1832-1916 .... **TCLC 4; HLCS 1**
See also CA 104; CANR 32; HW 1; MTCW 1
Echeverria, (Jose) Esteban (Antonino) 1805-1851 .... **NCLC 18**
Echo
See Proust, (Valentin-Louis-George-Eugene-) Marcel
Eckert, Allan W. 1931- .... **CLC 17**
See also AAYA 18; CA 13-16R; CANR 14, 45; INT CANR-14; SAAS 21; SATA 29, 91; SATA-Brief 27
Eckhart, Meister 1260(?)-1328(?) ... **CMLC 9**
See also DLB 115
Eckmar, F. R.
See de Hartog, Jan
Eco, Umberto 1932- .... **CLC 28, 60; DAM NOV, POP**
See also BEST 90:1; CA 77-80; CANR 12, 33, 55; DA3; DLB 196; MTCW 1, 2
Eddison, E(ric) R(ucker) 1882-1945 .... **TCLC 15**
See also CA 109; 156
Eddy, Mary (Ann Morse) Baker 1821-1910 .... **TCLC 71**
See also CA 113; 174
Edel, (Joseph) Leon 1907-1997 .. **CLC 29, 34**
See also CA 1-4R; 161; CANR 1, 22; DLB 103; INT CANR-22
Eden, Emily 1797-1869 .... **NCLC 10**
Edgar, David 1948- .. **CLC 42; DAM DRAM**
See also CA 57-60; CANR 12, 61; DLB 13; MTCW 1
Edgerton, Clyde (Carlyle) 1944- ...... **CLC 39**
See also AAYA 17; CA 118; 134; CANR 64; INT 134
Edgeworth, Maria 1768-1849 .... **NCLC 1, 51**
See also DLB 116, 159, 163; SATA 21
Edmonds, Paul
See Kuttner, Henry
Edmonds, Walter D(umaux) 1903-1998 .... **CLC 35**
See also CA 5-8R; CANR 2; DLB 9; MAICYA; SAAS 4; SATA 1, 27; SATA-Obit 99
Edmondson, Wallace
See Ellison, Harlan (Jay)
Edson, Russell CLC 13
See also CA 33-36R
Edwards, Bronwen Elizabeth
See Rose, Wendy
Edwards, G(erald) B(asil) 1899-1976 .... **CLC 25**
See also CA 110
Edwards, Gus 1939- .... **CLC 43**
See also CA 108; INT 108
Edwards, Jonathan 1703-1758 .... **LC 7, 54; DA; DAC; DAM MST**
See also DLB 24
Efron, Marina Ivanovna Tsvetaeva
See Tsvetaeva (Efron), Marina (Ivanovna)
Ehle, John (Marsden, Jr.) 1925- ...... **CLC 27**
See also CA 9-12R
Ehrenbourg, Ilya (Grigoryevich)
See Ehrenburg, Ilya (Grigoryevich)
Ehrenburg, Ilya (Grigoryevich) 1891-1967 .... **CLC 18, 34, 62**
See also CA 102; 25-28R
Ehrenburg, Ilyo (Grigoryevich)
See Ehrenburg, Ilya (Grigoryevich)
Ehrenreich, Barbara 1941- .... **CLC 110**
See also BEST 90:4; CA 73-76; CANR 16, 37, 62; MTCW 1, 2
Eich, Guenter 1907-1972 .... **CLC 15**
See also CA 111; 93-96; DLB 69, 124
Eichendorff, Joseph Freiherr von 1788-1857 .... **NCLC 8**
See also DLB 90
Eigner, Larry CLC 9
See also Eigner, Laurence (Joel)
See also CAAS 23; DLB 5
Eigner, Laurence (Joel) 1927-1996
See Eigner, Larry
See also CA 9-12R; 151; CANR 6, 84; DLB 193
Einstein, Albert 1879-1955 .... **TCLC 65**
See also CA 121; 133; MTCW 1, 2
Eiseley, Loren Corey 1907-1977 .... **CLC 7**
See also AAYA 5; CA 1-4R; 73-76; CANR 6; DLBD 17
Eisenstadt, Jill 1963- .... **CLC 50**
See also CA 140
Eisenstein, Sergei (Mikhailovich) 1898-1948 .... **TCLC 57**
See also CA 114; 149
Eisner, Simon
See Kornbluth, C(yril) M.
Ekeloef, (Bengt) Gunnar 1907-1968 ... **CLC 27; DAM POET; PC 23**
See also CA 123; 25-28R
Ekelof, (Bengt) Gunnar
See Ekeloef, (Bengt) Gunnar
Ekelund, Vilhelm 1880-1949 .... **TCLC 75**
Ekwensi, C. O. D.
See Ekwensi, Cyprian (Odiatu Duaka)
Ekwensi, Cyprian (Odiatu Duaka) 1921- ...... **CLC 4; BLC 1; DAM MULT**
See also BW 2, 3; CA 29-32R; CANR 18, 42, 74; DLB 117; MTCW 1, 2; SATA 66
Elaine TCLC 18
See also Leverson, Ada
El Crummo
See Crumb, R(obert)
Elder, Lonne III 1931-1996 .... **DC 8**
See also BLC 1; BW 1, 3; CA 81-84; 152; CANR 25; DAM MULT; DLB 7, 38, 44
Eleanor of Aquitaine 1122-1204 ... **CMLC 39**
Elia
See Lamb, Charles
Eliade, Mircea 1907-1986 .... **CLC 19**
See also CA 65-68; 119; CANR 30, 62; DLB 220; MTCW 1
Eliot, A. D.
See Jewett, (Theodora) Sarah Orne
Eliot, Alice
See Jewett, (Theodora) Sarah Orne
Eliot, Dan
See Silverberg, Robert
Eliot, George 1819- . **NCLC 4, 13, 23, 41, 49, 89; DA; DAB; DAC; DAM MST, NOV; PC 20; WLC**
See also CDBLB 1832-1890; DA3; DLB 21, 35, 55
Eliot, John 1604-1690 .... **LC 5**
See also DLB 24
Eliot, T(homas) S(tearns) 1888-1965 ...... **CLC 1, 2, 3, 6, 9, 10, 13, 15, 24, 34, 41, 55, 57, 113; DA; DAB; DAC; DAM DRAM, MST, POET; PC 5, 31; WLC**
See also AAYA 28; CA 5-8R; 25-28R; CANR 41; CDALB 1929-1941; DA3; DLB 7, 10, 45, 63; DLBY 88; MTCW 1, 2
Elizabeth 1866-1941 .... **TCLC 41**
Elkin, Stanley L(awrence) 1930-1995 .. **CLC 4, 6, 9, 14, 27, 51, 91; DAM NOV, POP; SSC 12**
See also CA 9-12R; 148; CANR 8, 46; DLB 2, 28; DLBY 80; INT CANR-8; MTCW 1, 2
Elledge, Scott CLC 34
Elliot, Don
See Silverberg, Robert
Elliott, Don
See Silverberg, Robert
Elliott, George P(aul) 1918-1980 .... **CLC 2**
See also CA 1-4R; 97-100; CANR 2
Elliott, Janice 1931- .... **CLC 47**
See also CA 13-16R; CANR 8, 29, 84; DLB 14
Elliott, Sumner Locke 1917-1991 ..... **CLC 38**
See also CA 5-8R; 134; CANR 2, 21
Elliott, William
See Bradbury, Ray (Douglas)
Ellis, A. E. CLC 7
Ellis, Alice Thomas CLC 40
See also Haycraft, Anna (Margaret)
See also DLB 194; MTCW 1
Ellis, Bret Easton 1964- ..... **CLC 39, 71, 117; DAM POP**
See also AAYA 2; CA 118; 123; CANR 51, 74; DA3; INT 123; MTCW 1
Ellis, (Henry) Havelock 1859-1939 .... **TCLC 14**
See also CA 109; 169; DLB 190
Ellis, Landon
See Ellison, Harlan (Jay)

Ellis, Trey 1962- .... **CLC 55**
See also CA 146; CANR 92
Ellison, Harlan (Jay) 1934- ... **CLC 1, 13, 42; DAM POP; SSC 14**
See also AAYA 29; CA 5-8R; CANR 5, 46; DLB 8; INT CANR-5; MTCW 1, 2
Ellison, Ralph (Waldo) 1914-1994 .... **CLC 1, 3, 11, 54, 86, 114; BLC 1; DA; DAB; DAC; DAM MST, MULT, NOV; SSC 26; WLC**
See also AAYA 19; BW 1, 3; CA 9-12R; 145; CANR 24, 53; CDALB 1941-1968; DA3; DLB 2, 76, 227; DLBY 94; MTCW 1, 2
Ellmann, Lucy (Elizabeth) 1956- ..... **CLC 61**
See also CA 128
Ellmann, Richard (David) 1918-1987 .... **CLC 50**
See also BEST 89:2; CA 1-4R; 122; CANR 2, 28, 61; DLB 103; DLBY 87; MTCW 1, 2
Elman, Richard (Martin) 1934-1997 .... **CLC 19**
See also CA 17-20R; 163; CAAS 3; CANR 47
Elron
See Hubbard, L(afayette) Ron(ald)
Eluard, Paul TCLC 7, 41
See also Grindel, Eugene
Elyot, Sir Thomas 1490(?)-1546 .... **LC 11**
Elytis, Odysseus 1911-1996 .... **CLC 15, 49, 100; DAM POET; PC 21**
See also CA 102; 151; MTCW 1, 2
Emecheta, (Florence Onye) Buchi 1944- .. **CLC 14, 48, 128; BLC 2; DAM MULT**
See also BW 2, 3; CA 81-84; CANR 27, 81; DA3; DLB 117; MTCW 1, 2; SATA 66
Emerson, Mary Moody 1774-1863 .... **NCLC 66**
Emerson, Ralph Waldo 1803-1882 . **NCLC 1, 38; DA; DAB; DAC; DAM MST, POET; PC 18; WLC**
See also CDALB 1640-1865; DA3; DLB 1, 59, 73, 223
Eminescu, Mihail 1850-1889 .... **NCLC 33**
Empson, William 1906-1984 ... **CLC 3, 8, 19, 33, 34**
See also CA 17-20R; 112; CANR 31, 61; DLB 20; MTCW 1, 2
Enchi, Fumiko (Ueda) 1905-1986 ..... **CLC 31**
See also CA 129; 121; DLB 182
Ende, Michael (Andreas Helmuth) 1929-1995 .... **CLC 31**
See also CA 118; 124; 149; CANR 36; CLR 14; DLB 75; MAICYA; SATA 61; SATA-Brief 42; SATA-Obit 86
Endo, Shusaku 1923-1996 ..... **CLC 7, 14, 19, 54, 99; DAM NOV**
See also CA 29-32R; 153; CANR 21, 54; DA3; DLB 182; MTCW 1, 2
Engel, Marian 1933-1985 .... **CLC 36**
See also CA 25-28R; CANR 12; DLB 53; INT CANR-12
Engelhardt, Frederick
See Hubbard, L(afayette) Ron(ald)
Engels, Friedrich 1820-1895 .... **NCLC 85**
See also DLB 129
Enright, D(ennis) J(oseph) 1920- .. **CLC 4, 8, 31**
See also CA 1-4R; CANR 1, 42, 83; DLB 27; SATA 25
Enzensberger, Hans Magnus 1929- .... **CLC 43; PC 28**
See also CA 116; 119
Ephron, Nora 1941- .... **CLC 17, 31**
See also AITN 2; CA 65-68; CANR 12, 39, 83
Epicurus 341B.C.-270B.C. .... **CMLC 21**
See also DLB 176
Epsilon
See Betjeman, John
Epstein, Daniel Mark 1948- .... **CLC 7**
See also CA 49-52; CANR 2, 53, 90
Epstein, Jacob 1956- .... **CLC 19**
See also CA 114
Epstein, Jean 1897-1953 .... **TCLC 92**
Epstein, Joseph 1937- .... **CLC 39**
See also CA 112; 119; CANR 50, 65
Epstein, Leslie 1938- .... **CLC 27**
See also CA 73-76; CAAS 12; CANR 23, 69
Equiano, Olaudah 1745(?)-1797 .... **LC 16; BLC 2; DAM MULT**
See also DLB 37, 50
ER TCLC 33
See also CA 160; DLB 85
Erasmus, Desiderius 1469(?)-1536 ...... **LC 16**
Erdman, Paul E(mil) 1932- .... **CLC 25**
See also AITN 1; CA 61-64; CANR 13, 43, 84
Erdrich, Louise 1954- .... **CLC 39, 54, 120; DAM MULT, NOV, POP**
See also AAYA 10; BEST 89:1; CA 114; CANR 41, 62; CDALBS; DA3; DLB 152, 175, 206; MTCW 1; NNAL; SATA 94
Erenburg, Ilya (Grigoryevich)
See Ehrenburg, Ilya (Grigoryevich)
Erickson, Stephen Michael 1950-
See Erickson, Steve
See also CA 129
Erickson, Steve 1950- .... **CLC 64**
See also Erickson, Stephen Michael
See also CANR 60, 68
Ericson, Walter
See Fast, Howard (Melvin)
Eriksson, Buntel
See Bergman, (Ernst) Ingmar
Ernaux, Annie 1940- .... **CLC 88**
See also CA 147
Erskine, John 1879-1951 .... **TCLC 84**
See also CA 112; 159; DLB 9, 102
Eschenbach, Wolfram von
See Wolfram von Eschenbach
Eseki, Bruno
See Mphahlele, Ezekiel
Esenin, Sergei (Alexandrovich) 1895-1925 .... **TCLC 4**
See also CA 104
Eshleman, Clayton 1935- .... **CLC 7**
See also CA 33-36R; CAAS 6; DLB 5
Espriella, Don Manuel Alvarez
See Southey, Robert
Espriu, Salvador 1913-1985 .... **CLC 9**
See also CA 154; 115; DLB 134
Espronceda, Jose de 1808-1842 ..... **NCLC 39**
Esquivel, Laura 1951(?)-
See also AAYA 29; CA 143; CANR 68; DA3; HLCS 1; MTCW 1
Esse, James
See Stephens, James
Esterbrook, Tom
See Hubbard, L(afayette) Ron(ald)
Estleman, Loren D. 1952- ..... **CLC 48; DAM NOV, POP**
See also AAYA 27; CA 85-88; CANR 27, 74; DA3; DLB 226; INT CANR-27; MTCW 1, 2
Euclid 306B.C.-283B.C. .... **CMLC 25**
Eugenides, Jeffrey 1960(?)- .... **CLC 81**
See also CA 144
Euripides c. 485B.C.-406B.C. .... **CMLC 23; DA; DAB; DAC; DAM DRAM, MST; DC 4; WLCS**
See also DA3; DLB 176
Evan, Evin
See Faust, Frederick (Schiller)
Evans, Caradoc 1878-1945 .... **TCLC 85**
Evans, Evan
See Faust, Frederick (Schiller)
Evans, Marian
See Eliot, George
Evans, Mary Ann
See Eliot, George
Evarts, Esther
See Benson, Sally
Everett, Percival L. 1956- .... **CLC 57**
See also BW 2; CA 129
Everson, R(onald) G(ilmour) 1903- . **CLC 27**
See also CA 17-20R; DLB 88
Everson, William (Oliver) 1912-1994 .... **CLC 1, 5, 14**
See also CA 9-12R; 145; CANR 20; DLB 212; MTCW 1
Evtushenko, Evgenii Aleksandrovich
See Yevtushenko, Yevgeny (Alexandrovich)
Ewart, Gavin (Buchanan) 1916-1995 .... **CLC 13, 46**
See also CA 89-92; 150; CANR 17, 46; DLB 40; MTCW 1
Ewers, Hanns Heinz 1871-1943 ..... **TCLC 12**
See also CA 109; 149
Ewing, Frederick R.
See Sturgeon, Theodore (Hamilton)
Exley, Frederick (Earl) 1929-1992 .... **CLC 6, 11**
See also AITN 2; CA 81-84; 138; DLB 143; DLBY 81
Eynhardt, Guillermo
See Quiroga, Horacio (Sylvestre)
Ezekiel, Nissim 1924- .... **CLC 61**
See also CA 61-64
Ezekiel, Tish O'Dowd 1943- .... **CLC 34**
See also CA 129
Fadeyev, A.
See Bulgya, Alexander Alexandrovich
Fadeyev, Alexander TCLC 53
See also Bulgya, Alexander Alexandrovich
Fagen, Donald 1948- .... **CLC 26**
Fainzilberg, Ilya Arnoldovich 1897-1937
See Ilf, Ilya
See also CA 120; 165
Fair, Ronald L. 1932- .... **CLC 18**
See also BW 1; CA 69-72; CANR 25; DLB 33
Fairbairn, Roger
See Carr, John Dickson
Fairbairns, Zoe (Ann) 1948- .... **CLC 32**
See also CA 103; CANR 21, 85
Falco, Gian
See Papini, Giovanni
Falconer, James
See Kirkup, James
Falconer, Kenneth
See Kornbluth, C(yril) M.
Falkland, Samuel
See Heijermans, Herman
Fallaci, Oriana 1930- .... **CLC 11, 110**
See also CA 77-80; CANR 15, 58; MTCW 1
Faludy, George 1913- .... **CLC 42**
See also CA 21-24R
Faludy, Gyoergy
See Faludy, George
Fanon, Frantz 1925-1961 ... **CLC 74; BLC 2; DAM MULT**
See also BW 1; CA 116; 89-92
Fanshawe, Ann 1625-1680 .... **LC 11**
Fante, John (Thomas) 1911-1983 ..... **CLC 60**
See also CA 69-72; 109; CANR 23; DLB 130; DLBY 83

Farah, Nuruddin 1945- ...... **CLC 53; BLC 2; DAM MULT**
See also BW 2, 3; CA 106; CANR 81; DLB 125
Fargue, Leon-Paul 1876(?)-1947 .... **TCLC 11**
See also CA 109
Farigoule, Louis
See Romains, Jules
Farina, Richard 1936(?)-1966 .... **CLC 9**
See also CA 81-84; 25-28R
Farley, Walter (Lorimer) 1915-1989 .... **CLC 17**
See also CA 17-20R; CANR 8, 29, 84; DLB 22; JRDA; MAICYA; SATA 2, 43
Farmer, Philip Jose 1918- .... **CLC 1, 19**
See also AAYA 28; CA 1-4R; CANR 4, 35; DLB 8; MTCW 1; SATA 93
Farquhar, George 1677-1707 ... **LC 21; DAM DRAM**
See also DLB 84
Farrell, J(ames) G(ordon) 1935-1979 .... **CLC 6**
See also CA 73-76; 89-92; CANR 36; DLB 14; MTCW 1
Farrell, James T(homas) 1904-1979 . **CLC 1, 4, 8, 11, 66; SSC 28**
See also CA 5-8R; 89-92; CANR 9, 61; DLB 4, 9, 86; DLBD 2; MTCW 1, 2
Farren, Richard J.
See Betjeman, John
Farren, Richard M.
See Betjeman, John
Fassbinder, Rainer Werner 1946-1982 .... **CLC 20**
See also CA 93-96; 106; CANR 31
Fast, Howard (Melvin) 1914- .. **CLC 23, 131; DAM NOV**
See also AAYA 16; CA 1-4R, 181; CAAE 181; CAAS 18; CANR 1, 33, 54, 75; DLB 9; INT CANR-33; MTCW 1; SATA 7; SATA-Essay 107
Faulcon, Robert
See Holdstock, Robert P.
Faulkner, William (Cuthbert) 1897-1962 .... **CLC 1, 3, 6, 8, 9, 11, 14, 18, 28, 52, 68; DA; DAB; DAC; DAM MST, NOV; SSC 1, 35; WLC**
See also AAYA 7; CA 81-84; CANR 33; CDALB 1929-1941; DA3; DLB 9, 11, 44, 102; DLBD 2; DLBY 86, 97; MTCW 1, 2
Fauset, Jessie Redmon 1884(?)-1961 .... **CLC 19, 54; BLC 2; DAM MULT**
See also BW 1; CA 109; CANR 83; DLB 51
Faust, Frederick (Schiller) 1892-1944(?) .... **TCLC 49; DAM POP**
See also CA 108; 152
Faust, Irvin 1924- .... **CLC 8**
See also CA 33-36R; CANR 28, 67; DLB 2, 28; DLBY 80
Fawkes, Guy
See Benchley, Robert (Charles)
Fearing, Kenneth (Flexner) 1902-1961 .... **CLC 51**
See also CA 93-96; CANR 59; DLB 9
Fecamps, Elise
See Creasey, John
Federman, Raymond 1928- .... **CLC 6, 47**
See also CA 17-20R; CAAS 8; CANR 10, 43, 83; DLBY 80
Federspiel, J(uerg) F. 1931- .... **CLC 42**
See also CA 146
Feiffer, Jules (Ralph) 1929- ..... **CLC 2, 8, 64; DAM DRAM**
See also AAYA 3; CA 17-20R; CANR 30, 59; DLB 7, 44; INT CANR-30; MTCW 1; SATA 8, 61, 111
Feige, Hermann Albert Otto Maximilian
See Traven, B.
Feinberg, David B. 1956-1994 .... **CLC 59**
See also CA 135; 147
Feinstein, Elaine 1930- .... **CLC 36**
See also CA 69-72; CAAS 1; CANR 31, 68; DLB 14, 40; MTCW 1
Feldman, Irving (Mordecai) 1928- ..... **CLC 7**
See also CA 1-4R; CANR 1; DLB 169
Felix-Tchicaya, Gerald
See Tchicaya, Gerald Felix
Fellini, Federico 1920-1993 .... **CLC 16, 85**
See also CA 65-68; 143; CANR 33
Felsen, Henry Gregor 1916-1995 ..... **CLC 17**
See also CA 1-4R; 180; CANR 1; SAAS 2; SATA 1
Fenno, Jack
See Calisher, Hortense
Fenollosa, Ernest (Francisco) 1853-1908 .... **TCLC 91**
Fenton, James Martin 1949- .... **CLC 32**
See also CA 102; DLB 40
Ferber, Edna 1887-1968 .... **CLC 18, 93**
See also AITN 1; CA 5-8R; 25-28R; CANR 68; DLB 9, 28, 86; MTCW 1, 2; SATA 7
Ferguson, Helen
See Kavan, Anna
Ferguson, Niall 1967- .... **CLC 134**
Ferguson, Samuel 1810-1886 .... **NCLC 33**
See also DLB 32
Fergusson, Robert 1750-1774 .... **LC 29**
See also DLB 109
Ferling, Lawrence
See Ferlinghetti, Lawrence (Monsanto)
Ferlinghetti, Lawrence (Monsanto) 1919(?)- .... **CLC 2, 6, 10, 27, 111; DAM POET; PC 1**
See also CA 5-8R; CANR 3, 41, 73; CDALB 1941-1968; DA3; DLB 5, 16; MTCW 1, 2
Fern, Fanny 1811-1872
See Parton, Sara Payson Willis
Fernandez, Vicente Garcia Huidobro
See Huidobro Fernandez, Vicente Garcia
Ferre, Rosario 1942- .... **SSC 36; HLCS 1**
See also CA 131; CANR 55, 81; DLB 145; HW 1, 2; MTCW 1
Ferrer, Gabriel (Francisco Victor) Miro
See Miro (Ferrer), Gabriel (Francisco Victor)
Ferrier, Susan (Edmonstone) 1782-1854 .... **NCLC 8**
See also DLB 116
Ferrigno, Robert 1948(?)- .... **CLC 65**
See also CA 140
Ferron, Jacques 1921-1985 .... **CLC 94; DAC**
See also CA 117; 129; DLB 60
Feuchtwanger, Lion 1884-1958 .... **TCLC 3**
See also CA 104; DLB 66
Feuillet, Octave 1821-1890 .... **NCLC 45**
See also DLB 192
Feydeau, Georges (Leon Jules Marie) 1862-1921 .... **TCLC 22; DAM DRAM**
See also CA 113; 152; CANR 84; DLB 192
Fichte, Johann Gottlieb 1762-1814 .... **NCLC 62**
See also DLB 90
Ficino, Marsilio 1433-1499 .... **LC 12**
Fiedeler, Hans
See Doeblin, Alfred
Fiedler, Leslie A(aron) 1917- .. **CLC 4, 13, 24**
See also CA 9-12R; CANR 7, 63; DLB 28, 67; MTCW 1, 2
Field, Andrew 1938- .... **CLC 44**
See also CA 97-100; CANR 25
Field, Eugene 1850-1895 .... **NCLC 3**
See also DLB 23, 42, 140; DLBD 13; MAICYA; SATA 16
Field, Gans T.
See Wellman, Manly Wade
Field, Michael 1915-1971 .... **TCLC 43**
See also CA 29-32R
Field, Peter
See Hobson, Laura Z(ametkin)
Fielding, Henry 1707-1754 ..... **LC 1, 46; DA; DAB; DAC; DAM DRAM, MST, NOV; WLC**
See also CDBLB 1660-1789; DA3; DLB 39, 84, 101
Fielding, Sarah 1710-1768 .... **LC 1, 44**
See also DLB 39
Fields, W. C. 1880-1946 .... **TCLC 80**
See also DLB 44
Fierstein, Harvey (Forbes) 1954- .... **CLC 33; DAM DRAM, POP**
See also CA 123; 129; DA3
Figes, Eva 1932- .... **CLC 31**
See also CA 53-56; CANR 4, 44, 83; DLB 14
Finch, Anne 1661-1720 .... **LC 3; PC 21**
See also DLB 95
Finch, Robert (Duer Claydon) 1900- .... **CLC 18**
See also CA 57-60; CANR 9, 24, 49; DLB 88
Findley, Timothy 1930- . **CLC 27, 102; DAC; DAM MST**
See also CA 25-28R; CANR 12, 42, 69; DLB 53
Fink, William
See Mencken, H(enry) L(ouis)
Firbank, Louis 1942-
See Reed, Lou
See also CA 117
Firbank, (Arthur Annesley) Ronald 1886-1926 .... **TCLC 1**
See also CA 104; 177; DLB 36
Fisher, Dorothy (Frances) Canfield 1879-1958 .... **TCLC 87**
See also CA 114; 136; CANR 80; DLB 9, 102; MAICYA; YABC 1
Fisher, M(ary) F(rances) K(ennedy) 1908-1992 .... **CLC 76, 87**
See also CA 77-80; 138; CANR 44; MTCW 1
Fisher, Roy 1930- .... **CLC 25**
See also CA 81-84; CAAS 10; CANR 16; DLB 40
Fisher, Rudolph 1897-1934 .. **TCLC 11; BLC 2; DAM MULT; SSC 25**
See also BW 1, 3; CA 107; 124; CANR 80; DLB 51, 102
Fisher, Vardis (Alvero) 1895-1968 ...... **CLC 7**
See also CA 5-8R; 25-28R; CANR 68; DLB 9, 206
Fiske, Tarleton
See Bloch, Robert (Albert)
Fitch, Clarke
See Sinclair, Upton (Beall)
Fitch, John IV
See Cormier, Robert (Edmund)
Fitzgerald, Captain Hugh
See Baum, L(yman) Frank
FitzGerald, Edward 1809-1883 .... **NCLC 9**
See also DLB 32
Fitzgerald, F(rancis) Scott (Key) 1896-1940 .. **TCLC 1, 6, 14, 28, 55; DA; DAB; DAC; DAM MST, NOV; SSC 6, 31; WLC**
See also AAYA 24; AITN 1; CA 110; 123; CDALB 1917-1929; DA3; DLB 4, 9, 86; DLBD 1, 15, 16; DLBY 81, 96; MTCW 1, 2
Fitzgerald, Penelope 1916- ... **CLC 19, 51, 61**
See also CA 85-88; CAAS 10; CANR 56, 86; DLB 14, 194; MTCW 2

Fitzgerald, Robert (Stuart) 1910-1985 .... **CLC 39**
See also CA 1-4R; 114; CANR 1; DLBY 80

FitzGerald, Robert D(avid) 1902-1987 .... **CLC 19**
See also CA 17-20R

Fitzgerald, Zelda (Sayre) 1900-1948 .... **TCLC 52**
See also CA 117; 126; DLBY 84

Flanagan, Thomas (James Bonner) 1923- .... **CLC 25, 52**
See also CA 108; CANR 55; DLBY 80; INT 108; MTCW 1

Flaubert, Gustave 1821-1880 .... **NCLC 2, 10, 19, 62, 66; DA; DAB; DAC; DAM MST, NOV; SSC 11; WLC**
See also DA3; DLB 119

Flecker, Herman Elroy
See Flecker, (Herman) James Elroy

Flecker, (Herman) James Elroy 1884-1915 .... **TCLC 43**
See also CA 109; 150; DLB 10, 19

Fleming, Ian (Lancaster) 1908-1964 . **CLC 3, 30; DAM POP**
See also AAYA 26; CA 5-8R; CANR 59; CDBLB 1945-1960; DA3; DLB 87, 201; MTCW 1, 2; SATA 9

Fleming, Thomas (James) 1927- ...... **CLC 37**
See also CA 5-8R; CANR 10; INT CANR-10; SATA 8

Fletcher, John 1579-1625 .... **LC 33; DC 6**
See also CDBLB Before 1660; DLB 58

Fletcher, John Gould 1886-1950 .... **TCLC 35**
See also CA 107; 167; DLB 4, 45

Fleur, Paul
See Pohl, Frederik

Flooglebuckle, Al
See Spiegelman, Art

Flying Officer X
See Bates, H(erbert) E(rnest)

Fo, Dario 1926- .... **CLC 32, 109; DAM DRAM; DC 10**
See also CA 116; 128; CANR 68; DA3; DLBY 97; MTCW 1, 2

Fogarty, Jonathan Titulescu Esq.
See Farrell, James T(homas)

Follett, Ken(neth Martin) 1949- ..... **CLC 18; DAM NOV, POP**
See also AAYA 6; BEST 89:4; CA 81-84; CANR 13, 33, 54; DA3; DLB 87; DLBY 81; INT CANR-33; MTCW 1

Fontane, Theodor 1819-1898 .... **NCLC 26**
See also DLB 129

Foote, Horton 1916- .... **CLC 51, 91; DAM DRAM**
See also CA 73-76; CANR 34, 51; DA3; DLB 26; INT CANR-34

Foote, Shelby 1916- ..... **CLC 75; DAM NOV, POP**
See also CA 5-8R; CANR 3, 45, 74; DA3; DLB 2, 17; MTCW 2

Forbes, Esther 1891-1967 .... **CLC 12**
See also AAYA 17; CA 13-14; 25-28R; CAP 1; CLR 27; DLB 22; JRDA; MAICYA; SATA 2, 100

Forche, Carolyn (Louise) 1950- .... **CLC 25, 83, 86; DAM POET; PC 10**
See also CA 109; 117; CANR 50, 74; DA3; DLB 5, 193; INT 117; MTCW 1

Ford, Elbur
See Hibbert, Eleanor Alice Burford

Ford, Ford Madox 1873-1939 ... **TCLC 1, 15, 39, 57; DAM NOV**
See also Chaucer, Daniel
See also CA 104; 132; CANR 74; CDBLB 1914-1945; DA3; DLB 162; MTCW 1, 2

Ford, Henry 1863-1947 .... **TCLC 73**
See also CA 115; 148

Ford, John 1586-(?) .... **DC 8**
See also CDBLB Before 1660; DAM DRAM; DA3; DLB 58

Ford, John 1895-1973 .... **CLC 16**
See also CA 45-48

Ford, Richard 1944- .... **CLC 46, 99**
See also CA 69-72; CANR 11, 47, 86; DLB 227; MTCW 1

Ford, Webster
See Masters, Edgar Lee

Foreman, Richard 1937- .... **CLC 50**
See also CA 65-68; CANR 32, 63

Forester, C(ecil) S(cott) 1899-1966 ... **CLC 35**
See also CA 73-76; 25-28R; CANR 83; DLB 191; SATA 13

Forez
See Mauriac, Francois (Charles)

Forman, James Douglas 1932- .... **CLC 21**
See also AAYA 17; CA 9-12R; CANR 4, 19, 42; JRDA; MAICYA; SATA 8, 70

Fornes, Maria Irene 1930- . **CLC 39, 61; DC 10; HLCS 1**
See also CA 25-28R; CANR 28, 81; DLB 7; HW 1, 2; INT CANR-28; MTCW 1

Forrest, Leon (Richard) 1937-1997 .. **CLC 4; BLCS**
See also BW 2; CA 89-92; 162; CAAS 7; CANR 25, 52, 87; DLB 33

Forster, E(dward) M(organ) 1879-1970 ...... **CLC 1, 2, 3, 4, 9, 10, 13, 15, 22, 45, 77; DA; DAB; DAC; DAM MST, NOV; SSC 27; WLC**
See also AAYA 2; CA 13-14; 25-28R; CANR 45; CAP 1; CDBLB 1914-1945; DA3; DLB 34, 98, 162, 178, 195; DLBD 10; MTCW 1, 2; SATA 57

Forster, John 1812-1876 .... **NCLC 11**
See also DLB 144, 184

Forsyth, Frederick 1938- .... **CLC 2, 5, 36; DAM NOV, POP**
See also BEST 89:4; CA 85-88; CANR 38, 62; DLB 87; MTCW 1, 2

Forten, Charlotte L. TCLC 16; BLC 2
See also Grimke, Charlotte L(ottie) Forten
See also DLB 50

Foscolo, Ugo 1778-1827 .... **NCLC 8**

Fosse, Bob CLC 20
See also Fosse, Robert Louis

Fosse, Robert Louis 1927-1987
See Fosse, Bob
See also CA 110; 123

Foster, Stephen Collins 1826-1864 .... **NCLC 26**

Foucault, Michel 1926-1984 . **CLC 31, 34, 69**
See also CA 105; 113; CANR 34; MTCW 1, 2

Fouque, Friedrich (Heinrich Karl) de la Motte 1777-1843 .... **NCLC 2**
See also DLB 90

Fourier, Charles 1772-1837 .... **NCLC 51**

Fournier, Pierre 1916- .... **CLC 11**
See also Gascar, Pierre
See also CA 89-92; CANR 16, 40

Fowles, John (Philip) 1926- .. **CLC 1, 2, 3, 4, 6, 9, 10, 15, 33, 87; DAB; DAC; DAM MST; SSC 33**
See also CA 5-8R; CANR 25, 71; CDBLB 1960 to Present; DA3; DLB 14, 139, 207; MTCW 1, 2; SATA 22

Fox, Paula 1923- .... **CLC 2, 8, 121**
See also AAYA 3; CA 73-76; CANR 20, 36, 62; CLR 1, 44; DLB 52; JRDA; MAICYA; MTCW 1; SATA 17, 60

Fox, William Price (Jr.) 1926- .... **CLC 22**
See also CA 17-20R; CAAS 19; CANR 11; DLB 2; DLBY 81

Foxe, John 1516(?)-1587 .... **LC 14**
See also DLB 132

Frame, Janet 1924- . **CLC 2, 3, 6, 22, 66, 96; SSC 29**
See also Clutha, Janet Paterson Frame

France, Anatole TCLC 9
See also Thibault, Jacques Anatole Francois
See also DLB 123; MTCW 1

Francis, Claude 19(?)- .... **CLC 50**

Francis, Dick 1920- .... **CLC 2, 22, 42, 102; DAM POP**
See also AAYA 5, 21; BEST 89:3; CA 5-8R; CANR 9, 42, 68; CDBLB 1960 to Present; DA3; DLB 87; INT CANR-9; MTCW 1, 2

Francis, Robert (Churchill) 1901-1987 .... **CLC 15**
See also CA 1-4R; 123; CANR 1

Frank, Anne(lies Marie) 1929-1945 . **TCLC 17; DA; DAB; DAC; DAM MST; WLC**
See also AAYA 12; CA 113; 133; CANR 68; DA3; MTCW 1, 2; SATA 87; SATA-Brief 42

Frank, Bruno 1887-1945 .... **TCLC 81**
See also DLB 118

Frank, Elizabeth 1945- .... **CLC 39**
See also CA 121; 126; CANR 78; INT 126

Frankl, Viktor E(mil) 1905-1997 ...... **CLC 93**
See also CA 65-68; 161

Franklin, Benjamin
See Hasek, Jaroslav (Matej Frantisek)

Franklin, Benjamin 1706-1790 .. **LC 25; DA; DAB; DAC; DAM MST; WLCS**
See also CDALB 1640-1865; DA3; DLB 24, 43, 73

Franklin, (Stella Maria Sarah) Miles (Lampe) 1879-1954 .... **TCLC 7**
See also CA 104; 164

Fraser, (Lady) Antonia (Pakenham) 1932- .... **CLC 32, 107**
See also CA 85-88; CANR 44, 65; MTCW 1, 2; SATA-Brief 32

Fraser, George MacDonald 1925- ...... **CLC 7**
See also CA 45-48, 180; CAAE 180; CANR 2, 48, 74; MTCW 1

Fraser, Sylvia 1935- .... **CLC 64**
See also CA 45-48; CANR 1, 16, 60

Frayn, Michael 1933- .... **CLC 3, 7, 31, 47; DAM DRAM, NOV**
See also CA 5-8R; CANR 30, 69; DLB 13, 14, 194; MTCW 1, 2

Fraze, Candida (Merrill) 1945- .... **CLC 50**
See also CA 126

Frazer, J(ames) G(eorge) 1854-1941 .... **TCLC 32**
See also CA 118

Frazer, Robert Caine
See Creasey, John

Frazer, Sir James George
See Frazer, J(ames) G(eorge)

Frazier, Charles 1950- .... **CLC 109**
See also AAYA 34; CA 161

Frazier, Ian 1951- .... **CLC 46**
See also CA 130; CANR 54

Frederic, Harold 1856-1898 .... **NCLC 10**
See also DLB 12, 23; DLBD 13

Frederick, John
See Faust, Frederick (Schiller)

Frederick the Great 1712-1786 .... **LC 14**

Fredro, Aleksander 1793-1876 .... **NCLC 8**

Freeling, Nicolas 1927- .... **CLC 38**
See also CA 49-52; CAAS 12; CANR 1, 17, 50, 84; DLB 87

Freeman, Douglas Southall 1886-1953 .... **TCLC 11**
See also CA 109; DLB 17; DLBD 17

Freeman, Judith 1946- .... **CLC 55**
See also CA 148

Author Index

Graduate of Oxford, A
See Ruskin, John
Grafton, Garth
See Duncan, Sara Jeannette
Graham, John
See Phillips, David Graham
Graham, Jorie 1951- .... **CLC 48, 118**
See also CA 111; CANR 63; DLB 120
Graham, R(obert) B(ontine) Cunninghame
See Cunninghame Graham, Robert (Gallnigad) Bontine
See also DLB 98, 135, 174
Graham, Robert
See Haldeman, Joe (William)
Graham, Tom
See Lewis, (Harry) Sinclair
Graham, W(illiam) S(ydney)
1918-1986 .... **CLC 29**
See also CA 73-76; 118; DLB 20
Graham, Winston (Mawdsley)
1910- .... **CLC 23**
See also CA 49-52; CANR 2, 22, 45, 66; DLB 77
Grahame, Kenneth 1859-1932 ...... **TCLC 64; DAB**
See also CA 108; 136; CANR 80; CLR 5; DA3; DLB 34, 141, 178; MAICYA; MTCW 2; SATA 100; YABC 1
Granovsky, Timofei Nikolaevich
1813-1855 .... **NCLC 75**
See also DLB 198
Grant, Skeeter
See Spiegelman, Art
Granville-Barker, Harley
1877-1946 .... **TCLC 2; DAM DRAM**
See also Barker, Harley Granville
See also CA 104
Grass, Guenter (Wilhelm) 1927- ... **CLC 1, 2, 4, 6, 11, 15, 22, 32, 49, 88; DA; DAB; DAC; DAM MST, NOV; WLC**
See also CA 13-16R; CANR 20, 75; DA3; DLB 75, 124; MTCW 1, 2
Gratton, Thomas
See Hulme, T(homas) E(rnest)
Grau, Shirley Ann 1929- . **CLC 4, 9; SSC 15**
See also CA 89-92; CANR 22, 69; DLB 2; INT CANR-22; MTCW 1
Gravel, Fern
See Hall, James Norman
Graver, Elizabeth 1964- .... **CLC 70**
See also CA 135; CANR 71
Graves, Richard Perceval 1945- .... **CLC 44**
See also CA 65-68; CANR 9, 26, 51
Graves, Robert (von Ranke)
1895-1985 .. **CLC 1, 2, 6, 11, 39, 44, 45; DAB; DAC; DAM MST, POET; PC 6**
See also CA 5-8R; 117; CANR 5, 36; CDBLB 1914-1945; DA3; DLB 20, 100, 191; DLBD 18; DLBY 85; MTCW 1, 2; SATA 45
Graves, Valerie
See Bradley, Marion Zimmer
Gray, Alasdair (James) 1934- .... **CLC 41**
See also CA 126; CANR 47, 69; DLB 194; INT 126; MTCW 1, 2
Gray, Amlin 1946- .... **CLC 29**
See also CA 138
Gray, Francine du Plessix 1930- ..... **CLC 22; DAM NOV**
See also BEST 90:3; CA 61-64; CAAS 2; CANR 11, 33, 75, 81; INT CANR-11; MTCW 1, 2
Gray, John (Henry) 1866-1934 ...... **TCLC 19**
See also CA 119; 162
Gray, Simon (James Holliday)
1936- .... **CLC 9, 14, 36**
See also AITN 1; CA 21-24R; CAAS 3; CANR 32, 69; DLB 13; MTCW 1
Gray, Spalding 1941- ..... **CLC 49, 112; DAM POP; DC 7**
See also CA 128; CANR 74; MTCW 2
Gray, Thomas 1716-1771 .... **LC 4, 40; DA; DAB; DAC; DAM MST; PC 2; WLC**
See also CDBLB 1660-1789; DA3; DLB 109
Grayson, David
See Baker, Ray Stannard
Grayson, Richard (A.) 1951- .... **CLC 38**
See also CA 85-88; CANR 14, 31, 57
Greeley, Andrew M(oran) 1928- ..... **CLC 28; DAM POP**
See also CA 5-8R; CAAS 7; CANR 7, 43, 69; DA3; MTCW 1, 2
Green, Anna Katharine
1846-1935 .... **TCLC 63**
See also CA 112; 159; DLB 202, 221
Green, Brian
See Card, Orson Scott
Green, Hannah
See Greenberg, Joanne (Goldenberg)
Green, Hannah 1927(?)-1996 .... **CLC 3**
See also CA 73-76; CANR 59
Green, Henry 1905-1973 .... **CLC 2, 13, 97**
See also Yorke, Henry Vincent
See also CA 175; DLB 15
Green, Julian (Hartridge) 1900-1998
See Green, Julien
See also CA 21-24R; 169; CANR 33, 87; DLB 4, 72; MTCW 1
Green, Julien CLC 3, 11, 77
See also Green, Julian (Hartridge)
See also MTCW 2
Green, Paul (Eliot) 1894-1981 .... **CLC 25; DAM DRAM**
See also AITN 1; CA 5-8R; 103; CANR 3; DLB 7, 9; DLBY 81
Greenberg, Ivan 1908-1973
See Rahv, Philip
See also CA 85-88
Greenberg, Joanne (Goldenberg)
1932- .... **CLC 7, 30**
See also AAYA 12; CA 5-8R; CANR 14, 32, 69; SATA 25
Greenberg, Richard 1959(?)- .... **CLC 57**
See also CA 138
Greene, Bette 1934- .... **CLC 30**
See also AAYA 7; CA 53-56; CANR 4; CLR 2; JRDA; MAICYA; SAAS 16; SATA 8, 102
Greene, Gael CLC 8
See also CA 13-16R; CANR 10
Greene, Graham (Henry)
1904-1991 .... **CLC 1, 3, 6, 9, 14, 18, 27, 37, 70, 72, 125; DA; DAB; DAC; DAM MST, NOV; SSC 29; WLC**
See also AITN 2; CA 13-16R; 133; CANR 35, 61; CDBLB 1945-1960; DA3; DLB 13, 15, 77, 100, 162, 201, 204; DLBY 91; MTCW 1, 2; SATA 20
Greene, Robert 1558-1592 .... **LC 41**
See also DLB 62, 167
Greer, Germaine 1939- .... **CLC 131**
See also AITN 1; CA 81-84; CANR 33, 70; MTCW 1, 2
Greer, Richard
See Silverberg, Robert
Gregor, Arthur 1923- .... **CLC 9**
See also CA 25-28R; CAAS 10; CANR 11; SATA 36
Gregor, Lee
See Pohl, Frederik
Gregory, Isabella Augusta (Persse)
1852-1932 .... **TCLC 1**
See also CA 104; 184; DLB 10
Gregory, J. Dennis
See Williams, John A(lfred)
Grendon, Stephen
See Derleth, August (William)
Grenville, Kate 1950- .... **CLC 61**
See also CA 118; CANR 53
Grenville, Pelham
See Wodehouse, P(elham) G(renville)
Greve, Felix Paul (Berthold Friedrich)
1879-1948
See Grove, Frederick Philip
See also CA 104; 141, 175; CANR 79; DAC; DAM MST
Grey, Zane 1872-1939 . **TCLC 6; DAM POP**
See also CA 104; 132; DA3; DLB 212; MTCW 1, 2
Grieg, (Johan) Nordahl (Brun)
1902-1943 .... **TCLC 10**
See also CA 107
Grieve, C(hristopher) M(urray)
1892-1978 ..... **CLC 11, 19; DAM POET**
See also MacDiarmid, Hugh; Pteleon
See also CA 5-8R; 85-88; CANR 33; MTCW 1
Griffin, Gerald 1803-1840 .... **NCLC 7**
See also DLB 159
Griffin, John Howard 1920-1980 ..... **CLC 68**
See also AITN 1; CA 1-4R; 101; CANR 2
Griffin, Peter 1942- .... **CLC 39**
See also CA 136
Griffith, D(avid Lewelyn) W(ark)
1875(?)-1948 .... **TCLC 68**
See also CA 119; 150; CANR 80
Griffith, Lawrence
See Griffith, D(avid Lewelyn) W(ark)
Griffiths, Trevor 1935- .... **CLC 13, 52**
See also CA 97-100; CANR 45; DLB 13
Griggs, Sutton (Elbert)
1872-1930 .... **TCLC 77**
See also CA 123; 186; DLB 50
Grigson, Geoffrey (Edward Harvey)
1905-1985 .... **CLC 7, 39**
See also CA 25-28R; 118; CANR 20, 33; DLB 27; MTCW 1, 2
Grillparzer, Franz 1791-1872 .... **NCLC 1; SSC 37**
See also DLB 133
Grimble, Reverend Charles James
See Eliot, T(homas) S(tearns)
Grimke, Charlotte L(ottie) Forten
1837(?)-1914
See Forten, Charlotte L.
See also BW 1; CA 117; 124; DAM MULT, POET
Grimm, Jacob Ludwig Karl
1785-1863 .... **NCLC 3, 77; SSC 36**
See also DLB 90; MAICYA; SATA 22
Grimm, Wilhelm Karl 1786-1859 .. **NCLC 3, 77; SSC 36**
See also DLB 90; MAICYA; SATA 22
Grimmelshausen, Johann Jakob Christoffel von 1621-1676 .... **LC 6**
See also DLB 168
Grindel, Eugene 1895-1952
See Eluard, Paul
See also CA 104
Grisham, John 1955- .... **CLC 84; DAM POP**
See also AAYA 14; CA 138; CANR 47, 69; DA3; MTCW 2
Grossman, David 1954- .... **CLC 67**
See also CA 138
Grossman, Vasily (Semenovich)
1905-1964 .... **CLC 41**
See also CA 124; 130; MTCW 1
Grove, Frederick Philip TCLC 4
See also Greve, Felix Paul (Berthold Friedrich)
See also DLB 92
Grubb
See Crumb, R(obert)

Grumbach, Doris (Isaac) 1918- . **CLC 13, 22, 64**
See also CA 5-8R; CAAS 2; CANR 9, 42, 70; INT CANR-9; MTCW 2
Grundtvig, Nicolai Frederik Severin 1783-1872 .... **NCLC 1**
Grunge
See Crumb, R(obert)
Grunwald, Lisa 1959- .... **CLC 44**
See also CA 120
Guare, John 1938- .... **CLC 8, 14, 29, 67; DAM DRAM**
See also CA 73-76; CANR 21, 69; DLB 7; MTCW 1, 2
Gudjonsson, Halldor Kiljan 1902-1998
See Laxness, Halldor
See also CA 103; 164
Guenter, Erich
See Eich, Guenter
Guest, Barbara 1920- .... **CLC 34**
See also CA 25-28R; CANR 11, 44, 84; DLB 5, 193
Guest, Edgar A(lbert) 1881-1959 ... **TCLC 95**
See also CA 112; 168
Guest, Judith (Ann) 1936- .... **CLC 8, 30; DAM NOV, POP**
See also AAYA 7; CA 77-80; CANR 15, 75; DA3; INT CANR-15; MTCW 1, 2
Guevara, Che CLC 87; HLC 1
See also Guevara (Serna), Ernesto
Guevara (Serna), Ernesto 1928-1967 .... **CLC 87; DAM MULT; HLC 1**
See also Guevara, Che
See also CA 127; 111; CANR 56; HW 1
Guicciardini, Francesco 1483-1540 ..... **LC 49**
Guild, Nicholas M. 1944- .... **CLC 33**
See also CA 93-96
Guillemin, Jacques
See Sartre, Jean-Paul
Guillen, Jorge 1893-1984 .... **CLC 11; DAM MULT, POET; HLCS 1**
See also CA 89-92; 112; DLB 108; HW 1
Guillen, Nicolas (Cristobal) 1902-1989 ... **CLC 48, 79; BLC 2; DAM MST, MULT, POET; HLC 1; PC 23**
See also BW 2; CA 116; 125; 129; CANR 84; HW 1
Guillevic, (Eugene) 1907- .... **CLC 33**
See also CA 93-96
Guillois
See Desnos, Robert
Guillois, Valentin
See Desnos, Robert
Guimaraes Rosa, Joao 1908-1967
See also CA 175; HLCS 2
Guiney, Louise Imogen 1861-1920 .... **TCLC 41**
See also CA 160; DLB 54
Guiraldes, Ricardo (Guillermo) 1886-1927 .... **TCLC 39**
See also CA 131; HW 1; MTCW 1
Gumilev, Nikolai (Stepanovich) 1886-1921 .... **TCLC 60**
See also CA 165
Gunesekera, Romesh 1954- .... **CLC 91**
See also CA 159
Gunn, Bill CLC 5
See also Gunn, William Harrison
See also DLB 38
Gunn, Thom(son William) 1929- .. **CLC 3, 6, 18, 32, 81; DAM POET; PC 26**
See also CA 17-20R; CANR 9, 33; CDBLB 1960 to Present; DLB 27; INT CANR-33; MTCW 1
Gunn, William Harrison 1934(?)-1989
See Gunn, Bill
See also AITN 1; BW 1, 3; CA 13-16R; 128; CANR 12, 25, 76
Gunnars, Kristjana 1948- .... **CLC 69**
See also CA 113; DLB 60
Gurdjieff, G(eorgei) I(vanovich) 1877(?)-1949 .... **TCLC 71**
See also CA 157
Gurganus, Allan 1947- . **CLC 70; DAM POP**
See also BEST 90:1; CA 135
Gurney, A(lbert) R(amsdell), Jr. 1930- ..... **CLC 32, 50, 54; DAM DRAM**
See also CA 77-80; CANR 32, 64
Gurney, Ivor (Bertie) 1890-1937 ... **TCLC 33**
See also CA 167
Gurney, Peter
See Gurney, A(lbert) R(amsdell), Jr.
Guro, Elena 1877-1913 .... **TCLC 56**
Gustafson, James M(oody) 1925- ... **CLC 100**
See also CA 25-28R; CANR 37
Gustafson, Ralph (Barker) 1909- ..... **CLC 36**
See also CA 21-24R; CANR 8, 45, 84; DLB 88
Gut, Gom
See Simenon, Georges (Jacques Christian)
Guterson, David 1956- .... **CLC 91**
See also CA 132; CANR 73; MTCW 2
Guthrie, A(lfred) B(ertram), Jr. 1901-1991 .... **CLC 23**
See also CA 57-60; 134; CANR 24; DLB 212; SATA 62; SATA-Obit 67
Guthrie, Isobel
See Grieve, C(hristopher) M(urray)
Guthrie, Woodrow Wilson 1912-1967
See Guthrie, Woody
See also CA 113; 93-96
Guthrie, Woody CLC 35
See also Guthrie, Woodrow Wilson
Gutierrez Najera, Manuel 1859-1895
See also HLCS 2
Guy, Rosa (Cuthbert) 1928- .... **CLC 26**
See also AAYA 4; BW 2; CA 17-20R; CANR 14, 34, 83; CLR 13; DLB 33; JRDA; MAICYA; SATA 14, 62
Gwendolyn
See Bennett, (Enoch) Arnold
H. D. CLC 3, 8, 14, 31, 34, 73; PC 5
See also Doolittle, Hilda
H. de V.
See Buchan, John
Haavikko, Paavo Juhani 1931- .. **CLC 18, 34**
See also CA 106
Habbema, Koos
See Heijermans, Herman
Habermas, Juergen 1929- .... **CLC 104**
See also CA 109; CANR 85
Habermas, Jurgen
See Habermas, Juergen
Hacker, Marilyn 1942- ...... **CLC 5, 9, 23, 72, 91; DAM POET**
See also CA 77-80; CANR 68; DLB 120
Haeckel, Ernst Heinrich (Philipp August) 1834-1919 .... **TCLC 83**
See also CA 157
Hafiz c. 1326-1389(?) .... **CMLC 34**
Hafiz c. 1326-1389 .... **CMLC 34**
Haggard, H(enry) Rider 1856-1925 .... **TCLC 11**
See also CA 108; 148; DLB 70, 156, 174, 178; MTCW 2; SATA 16
Hagiosy, L.
See Larbaud, Valery (Nicolas)
Hagiwara Sakutaro 1886-1942 ..... **TCLC 60; PC 18**
Haig, Fenil
See Ford, Ford Madox
Haig-Brown, Roderick (Langmere) 1908-1976 .... **CLC 21**
See also CA 5-8R; 69-72; CANR 4, 38, 83; CLR 31; DLB 88; MAICYA; SATA 12
Hailey, Arthur 1920- ..... **CLC 5; DAM NOV, POP**
See also AITN 2; BEST 90:3; CA 1-4R; CANR 2, 36, 75; DLB 88; DLBY 82; MTCW 1, 2
Hailey, Elizabeth Forsythe 1938- ..... **CLC 40**
See also CA 93-96; CAAS 1; CANR 15, 48; INT CANR-15
Haines, John (Meade) 1924- .... **CLC 58**
See also CA 17-20R; CANR 13, 34; DLB 212
Hakluyt, Richard 1552-1616 .... **LC 31**
Haldeman, Joe (William) 1943- .... **CLC 61**
See also Graham, Robert
See also CA 53-56, 179; CAAE 179; CAAS 25; CANR 6, 70, 72; DLB 8; INT CANR-6
Hale, Sarah Josepha (Buell) 1788-1879 .... **NCLC 75**
See also DLB 1, 42, 73
Haley, Alex(ander Murray Palmer) 1921-1992 . **CLC 8, 12, 76; BLC 2; DA; DAB; DAC; DAM MST, MULT, POP**
See also AAYA 26; BW 2, 3; CA 77-80; 136; CANR 61; CDALBS; DA3; DLB 38; MTCW 1, 2
Haliburton, Thomas Chandler 1796-1865 .... **NCLC 15**
See also DLB 11, 99
Hall, Donald (Andrew, Jr.) 1928- ...... **CLC 1, 13, 37, 59; DAM POET**
See also CA 5-8R; CAAS 7; CANR 2, 44, 64; DLB 5; MTCW 1; SATA 23, 97
Hall, Frederic Sauser
See Sauser-Hall, Frederic
Hall, James
See Kuttner, Henry
Hall, James Norman 1887-1951 ..... **TCLC 23**
See also CA 123; 173; SATA 21
Hall, Radclyffe -1943
See Hall, (Marguerite) Radclyffe
See also MTCW 2
Hall, (Marguerite) Radclyffe 1886-1943 .... **TCLC 12**
See also CA 110; 150; CANR 83; DLB 191
Hall, Rodney 1935- .... **CLC 51**
See also CA 109; CANR 69
Halleck, Fitz-Greene 1790-1867 .... **NCLC 47**
See also DLB 3
Halliday, Michael
See Creasey, John
Halpern, Daniel 1945- .... **CLC 14**
See also CA 33-36R
Hamburger, Michael (Peter Leopold) 1924- .... **CLC 5, 14**
See also CA 5-8R; CAAS 4; CANR 2, 47; DLB 27
Hamill, Pete 1935- .... **CLC 10**
See also CA 25-28R; CANR 18, 71
Hamilton, Alexander 1755(?)-1804 .... **NCLC 49**
See also DLB 37
Hamilton, Clive
See Lewis, C(live) S(taples)
Hamilton, Edmond 1904-1977 .... **CLC 1**
See also CA 1-4R; CANR 3, 84; DLB 8
Hamilton, Eugene (Jacob) Lee
See Lee-Hamilton, Eugene (Jacob)
Hamilton, Franklin
See Silverberg, Robert
Hamilton, Gail
See Corcoran, Barbara
Hamilton, Mollie
See Kaye, M(ary) M(argaret)
Hamilton, (Anthony Walter) Patrick 1904-1962 .... **CLC 51**
See also CA 176; 113; DLB 191

King, Thomas 1943- ... **CLC 89; DAC; DAM MULT**
See also CA 144; DLB 175; NNAL; SATA 96

Kingman, Lee CLC 17
See also Natti, (Mary) Lee
See also SAAS 3; SATA 1, 67

Kingsley, Charles 1819-1875 .... **NCLC 35**
See also DLB 21, 32, 163, 190; YABC 2

Kingsley, Sidney 1906-1995 .... **CLC 44**
See also CA 85-88; 147; DLB 7

Kingsolver, Barbara 1955- .... **CLC 55, 81, 130; DAM POP**
See also AAYA 15; CA 129; 134; CANR 60; CDALBS; DA3; DLB 206; INT 134; MTCW 2

Kingston, Maxine (Ting Ting) Hong 1940- .... **CLC 12, 19, 58, 121; DAM MULT, NOV; WLCS**
See also AAYA 8; CA 69-72; CANR 13, 38, 74, 87; CDALBS; DA3; DLB 173, 212; DLBY 80; INT CANR-13; MTCW 1, 2; SATA 53

Kinnell, Galway 1927- ..... **CLC 1, 2, 3, 5, 13, 29, 129; PC 26**
See also CA 9-12R; CANR 10, 34, 66; DLB 5; DLBY 87; INT CANR-34; MTCW 1, 2

Kinsella, Thomas 1928- .... **CLC 4, 19**
See also CA 17-20R; CANR 15; DLB 27; MTCW 1, 2

Kinsella, W(illiam) P(atrick) 1935- . **CLC 27, 43; DAC; DAM NOV, POP**
See also AAYA 7; CA 97-100; CAAS 7; CANR 21, 35, 66, 75; INT CANR-21; MTCW 1, 2

Kinsey, Alfred C(harles) 1894-1956 .... **TCLC 91**
See also CA 115; 170; MTCW 2

Kipling, (Joseph) Rudyard 1865-1936 .... **TCLC 8, 17; DA; DAB; DAC; DAM MST, POET; PC 3; SSC 5; WLC**
See also AAYA 32; CA 105; 120; CANR 33; CDBLB 1890-1914; CLR 39, 65; DA3; DLB 19, 34, 141, 156; MAICYA; MTCW 1, 2; SATA 100; YABC 2

Kirkland, Caroline M. 1801-1864 . **NCLC 85**
See also DLB 3, 73, 74; DLBD 13

Kirkup, James 1918- .... **CLC 1**
See also CA 1-4R; CAAS 4; CANR 2; DLB 27; SATA 12

Kirkwood, James 1930(?)-1989 .... **CLC 9**
See also AITN 2; CA 1-4R; 128; CANR 6, 40

Kirshner, Sidney
See Kingsley, Sidney

Kis, Danilo 1935-1989 .... **CLC 57**
See also CA 109; 118; 129; CANR 61; DLB 181; MTCW 1

Kivi, Aleksis 1834-1872 .... **NCLC 30**

Kizer, Carolyn (Ashley) 1925- ... **CLC 15, 39, 80; DAM POET**
See also CA 65-68; CAAS 5; CANR 24, 70; DLB 5, 169; MTCW 2

Klabund 1890-1928 .... **TCLC 44**
See also CA 162; DLB 66

Klappert, Peter 1942- .... **CLC 57**
See also CA 33-36R; DLB 5

Klein, A(braham) M(oses) 1909-1972 . **CLC 19; DAB; DAC; DAM MST**
See also CA 101; 37-40R; DLB 68

Klein, Norma 1938-1989 .... **CLC 30**
See also AAYA 2; CA 41-44R; 128; CANR 15, 37; CLR 2, 19; INT CANR-15; JRDA; MAICYA; SAAS 1; SATA 7, 57

Klein, T(heodore) E(ibon) D(onald) 1947- .... **CLC 34**
See also CA 119; CANR 44, 75

Kleist, Heinrich von 1777-1811 ...... **NCLC 2, 37; DAM DRAM; SSC 22**
See also DLB 90

Klima, Ivan 1931- .... **CLC 56; DAM NOV**
See also CA 25-28R; CANR 17, 50, 91

Klimentov, Andrei Platonovich 1899-1951 .... **TCLC 14**
See also CA 108

Klinger, Friedrich Maximilian von 1752-1831 .... **NCLC 1**
See also DLB 94

Klingsor the Magician
See Hartmann, Sadakichi

Klopstock, Friedrich Gottlieb 1724-1803 .... **NCLC 11**
See also DLB 97

Knapp, Caroline 1959- .... **CLC 99**
See also CA 154

Knebel, Fletcher 1911-1993 .... **CLC 14**
See also AITN 1; CA 1-4R; 140; CAAS 3; CANR 1, 36; SATA 36; SATA-Obit 75

Knickerbocker, Diedrich
See Irving, Washington

Knight, Etheridge 1931-1991 . **CLC 40; BLC 2; DAM POET; PC 14**
See also BW 1, 3; CA 21-24R; 133; CANR 23, 82; DLB 41; MTCW 2

Knight, Sarah Kemble 1666-1727 .... **LC 7**
See also DLB 24, 200

Knister, Raymond 1899-1932 .... **TCLC 56**
See also CA 186; DLB 68

Knowles, John 1926- . **CLC 1, 4, 10, 26; DA; DAC; DAM MST, NOV**
See also AAYA 10; CA 17-20R; CANR 40, 74, 76; CDALB 1968-1988; DLB 6; MTCW 1, 2; SATA 8, 89

Knox, Calvin M.
See Silverberg, Robert

Knox, John c. 1505-1572 .... **LC 37**
See also DLB 132

Knye, Cassandra
See Disch, Thomas M(ichael)

Koch, C(hristopher) J(ohn) 1932- .... **CLC 42**
See also CA 127; CANR 84

Koch, Christopher
See Koch, C(hristopher) J(ohn)

Koch, Kenneth 1925- .... **CLC 5, 8, 44; DAM POET**
See also CA 1-4R; CANR 6, 36, 57; DLB 5; INT CANR-36; MTCW 2; SATA 65

Kochanowski, Jan 1530-1584 .... **LC 10**

Kock, Charles Paul de 1794-1871 . **NCLC 16**

Koda Rohan 1867-
See Koda Shigeyuki

Koda Shigeyuki 1867-1947 .... **TCLC 22**
See also CA 121; 183; DLB 180

Koestler, Arthur 1905-1983 ... **CLC 1, 3, 6, 8, 15, 33**
See also CA 1-4R; 109; CANR 1, 33; CDBLB 1945-1960; DLBY 83; MTCW 1, 2

Kogawa, Joy Nozomi 1935- ..... **CLC 78, 129; DAC; DAM MST, MULT**
See also CA 101; CANR 19, 62; MTCW 2; SATA 99

Kohout, Pavel 1928- .... **CLC 13**
See also CA 45-48; CANR 3

Koizumi, Yakumo
See Hearn, (Patricio) Lafcadio (Tessima Carlos)

Kolmar, Gertrud 1894-1943 .... **TCLC 40**
See also CA 167

Komunyakaa, Yusef 1947- .... **CLC 86, 94; BLCS**
See also CA 147; CANR 83; DLB 120

Konrad, George
See Konrad, Gyoergy

Konrad, Gyoergy 1933- .... **CLC 4, 10, 73**
See also CA 85-88

Konwicki, Tadeusz 1926- .... **CLC 8, 28, 54, 117**
See also CA 101; CAAS 9; CANR 39, 59; MTCW 1

Koontz, Dean R(ay) 1945- .... **CLC 78; DAM NOV, POP**
See also AAYA 9, 31; BEST 89:3, 90:2; CA 108; CANR 19, 36, 52; DA3; MTCW 1; SATA 92

Kopernik, Mikolaj
See Copernicus, Nicolaus

Kopit, Arthur (Lee) 1937- ..... **CLC 1, 18, 33; DAM DRAM**
See also AITN 1; CA 81-84; CABS 3; DLB 7; MTCW 1

Kops, Bernard 1926- .... **CLC 4**
See also CA 5-8R; CANR 84; DLB 13

Kornbluth, C(yril) M. 1923-1958 .... **TCLC 8**
See also CA 105; 160; DLB 8

Korolenko, V. G.
See Korolenko, Vladimir Galaktionovich

Korolenko, Vladimir
See Korolenko, Vladimir Galaktionovich

Korolenko, Vladimir G.
See Korolenko, Vladimir Galaktionovich

Korolenko, Vladimir Galaktionovich 1853-1921 .... **TCLC 22**
See also CA 121

Korzybski, Alfred (Habdank Skarbek) 1879-1950 .... **TCLC 61**
See also CA 123; 160

Kosinski, Jerzy (Nikodem) 1933-1991 .... **CLC 1, 2, 3, 6, 10, 15, 53, 70; DAM NOV**
See also CA 17-20R; 134; CANR 9, 46; DA3; DLB 2; DLBY 82; MTCW 1, 2

Kostelanetz, Richard (Cory) 1940- .. **CLC 28**
See also CA 13-16R; CAAS 8; CANR 38, 77

Kostrowitzki, Wilhelm Apollinaris de 1880-1918
See Apollinaire, Guillaume
See also CA 104

Kotlowitz, Robert 1924- .... **CLC 4**
See also CA 33-36R; CANR 36

Kotzebue, August (Friedrich Ferdinand) von 1761-1819 .... **NCLC 25**
See also DLB 94

Kotzwinkle, William 1938- ..... **CLC 5, 14, 35**
See also CA 45-48; CANR 3, 44, 84; CLR 6; DLB 173; MAICYA; SATA 24, 70

Kowna, Stancy
See Szymborska, Wislawa

Kozol, Jonathan 1936- .... **CLC 17**
See also CA 61-64; CANR 16, 45

Kozoll, Michael 1940(?)- .... **CLC 35**

Kramer, Kathryn 19(?)- .... **CLC 34**

Kramer, Larry 1935- .. **CLC 42; DAM POP; DC 8**
See also CA 124; 126; CANR 60

Krasicki, Ignacy 1735-1801 .... **NCLC 8**

Krasinski, Zygmunt 1812-1859 .... **NCLC 4**

Kraus, Karl 1874-1936 .... **TCLC 5**
See also CA 104; DLB 118

Kreve (Mickevicius), Vincas 1882-1954 .... **TCLC 27**
See also CA 170; DLB 220

Kristeva, Julia 1941- .... **CLC 77**
See also CA 154

Kristofferson, Kris 1936- .... **CLC 26**
See also CA 104

Krizanc, John 1956- .... **CLC 57**

Krleza, Miroslav 1893-1981 .... **CLC 8, 114**
See also CA 97-100; 105; CANR 50; DLB 147

Leiber, Fritz (Reuter, Jr.) 1910-1992 .... **CLC 25**
See also CA 45-48; 139; CANR 2, 40, 86; DLB 8; MTCW 1, 2; SATA 45; SATA-Obit 73

Leibniz, Gottfried Wilhelm von 1646-1716 .... **LC 35**
See also DLB 168

Leimbach, Martha 1963-
See Leimbach, Marti
See also CA 130

Leimbach, Marti CLC 65
See also Leimbach, Martha

Leino, Eino TCLC 24
See also Loennbohm, Armas Eino Leopold

Leiris, Michel (Julien) 1901-1990 ..... **CLC 61**
See also CA 119; 128; 132

Leithauser, Brad 1953- .... **CLC 27**
See also CA 107; CANR 27, 81; DLB 120

Lelchuk, Alan 1938- .... **CLC 5**
See also CA 45-48; CAAS 20; CANR 1, 70

Lem, Stanislaw 1921- .... **CLC 8, 15, 40**
See also CA 105; CAAS 1; CANR 32; MTCW 1

Lemann, Nancy 1956- .... **CLC 39**
See also CA 118; 136

Lemonnier, (Antoine Louis) Camille 1844-1913 .... **TCLC 22**
See also CA 121

Lenau, Nikolaus 1802-1850 .... **NCLC 16**

L'Engle, Madeleine (Camp Franklin) 1918- .... **CLC 12; DAM POP**
See also AAYA 28; AITN 2; CA 1-4R; CANR 3, 21, 39, 66; CLR 1, 14, 57; DA3; DLB 52; JRDA; MAICYA; MTCW 1, 2; SAAS 15; SATA 1, 27, 75

Lengyel, Jozsef 1896-1975 .... **CLC 7**
See also CA 85-88; 57-60; CANR 71

Lenin 1870-1924
See Lenin, V. I.
See also CA 121; 168

Lenin, V. I. TCLC 67
See also Lenin

Lennon, John (Ono) 1940-1980 .. **CLC 12, 35**
See also CA 102; SATA 114

Lennox, Charlotte Ramsay 1729(?)-1804 .... **NCLC 23**
See also DLB 39

Lentricchia, Frank (Jr.) 1940- .... **CLC 34**
See also CA 25-28R; CANR 19

Lenz, Siegfried 1926- .... **CLC 27; SSC 33**
See also CA 89-92; CANR 80; DLB 75

Leonard, Elmore (John, Jr.) 1925- . **CLC 28, 34, 71, 120; DAM POP**
See also AAYA 22; AITN 1; BEST 89:1, 90:4; CA 81-84; CANR 12, 28, 53, 76; DA3; DLB 173, 226; INT CANR-28; MTCW 1, 2

Leonard, Hugh CLC 19
See also Byrne, John Keyes
See also DLB 13

Leonov, Leonid (Maximovich) 1899-1994 .... **CLC 92; DAM NOV**
See also CA 129; CANR 74, 76; MTCW 1, 2

Leopardi, (Conte) Giacomo 1798-1837 .... **NCLC 22**

Le Reveler
See Artaud, Antonin (Marie Joseph)

Lerman, Eleanor 1952- .... **CLC 9**
See also CA 85-88; CANR 69

Lerman, Rhoda 1936- .... **CLC 56**
See also CA 49-52; CANR 70

Lermontov, Mikhail Yuryevich 1814-1841 .... **NCLC 47; PC 18**
See also DLB 205

Leroux, Gaston 1868-1927 .... **TCLC 25**
See also CA 108; 136; CANR 69; SATA 65

Lesage, Alain-Rene 1668-1747 .... **LC 2, 28**

Leskov, Nikolai (Semyonovich) 1831-1895 .... **NCLC 25; SSC 34**

Lessing, Doris (May) 1919- ... **CLC 1, 2, 3, 6, 10, 15, 22, 40, 94; DA; DAB; DAC; DAM MST, NOV; SSC 6; WLCS**
See also CA 9-12R; CAAS 14; CANR 33, 54, 76; CDBLB 1960 to Present; DA3; DLB 15, 139; DLBY 85; MTCW 1, 2

Lessing, Gotthold Ephraim 1729-1781 . **LC 8**
See also DLB 97

Lester, Richard 1932- .... **CLC 20**

Lever, Charles (James) 1806-1872 .... **NCLC 23**
See also DLB 21

Leverson, Ada 1865(?)-1936(?) .... **TCLC 18**
See also Elaine
See also CA 117; DLB 153

Levertov, Denise 1923-1997 .. **CLC 1, 2, 3, 5, 8, 15, 28, 66; DAM POET; PC 11**
See also CA 1-4R, 178; 163; CAAE 178; CAAS 19; CANR 3, 29, 50; CDALBS; DLB 5, 165; INT CANR-29; MTCW 1, 2

Levi, Jonathan CLC 76

Levi, Peter (Chad Tigar) 1931- .... **CLC 41**
See also CA 5-8R; CANR 34, 80; DLB 40

Levi, Primo 1919-1987 . **CLC 37, 50; SSC 12**
See also CA 13-16R; 122; CANR 12, 33, 61, 70; DLB 177; MTCW 1, 2

Levin, Ira 1929- .... **CLC 3, 6; DAM POP**
See also CA 21-24R; CANR 17, 44, 74; DA3; MTCW 1, 2; SATA 66

Levin, Meyer 1905-1981 .... **CLC 7; DAM POP**
See also AITN 1; CA 9-12R; 104; CANR 15; DLB 9, 28; DLBY 81; SATA 21; SATA-Obit 27

Levine, Norman 1924- .... **CLC 54**
See also CA 73-76; CAAS 23; CANR 14, 70; DLB 88

Levine, Philip 1928- .. **CLC 2, 4, 5, 9, 14, 33, 118; DAM POET; PC 22**
See also CA 9-12R; CANR 9, 37, 52; DLB 5

Levinson, Deirdre 1931- .... **CLC 49**
See also CA 73-76; CANR 70

Levi-Strauss, Claude 1908- .... **CLC 38**
See also CA 1-4R; CANR 6, 32, 57; MTCW 1, 2

Levitin, Sonia (Wolff) 1934- .... **CLC 17**
See also AAYA 13; CA 29-32R; CANR 14, 32, 79; CLR 53; JRDA; MAICYA; SAAS 2; SATA 4, 68

Levon, O. U.
See Kesey, Ken (Elton)

Levy, Amy 1861-1889 .... **NCLC 59**
See also DLB 156

Lewes, George Henry 1817-1878 ... **NCLC 25**
See also DLB 55, 144

Lewis, Alun 1915-1944 .... **TCLC 3; SSC 40**
See also CA 104; DLB 20, 162

Lewis, C. Day
See Day Lewis, C(ecil)

Lewis, C(live) S(taples) 1898-1963 .... **CLC 1, 3, 6, 14, 27, 124; DA; DAB; DAC; DAM MST, NOV, POP; WLC**
See also AAYA 3; CA 81-84; CANR 33, 71; CDBLB 1945-1960; CLR 3, 27; DA3; DLB 15, 100, 160; JRDA; MAICYA; MTCW 1, 2; SATA 13, 100

Lewis, Janet 1899-1998 .... **CLC 41**
See also Winters, Janet Lewis
See also CA 9-12R; 172; CANR 29, 63; CAP 1; DLBY 87

Lewis, Matthew Gregory 1775-1818 .... **NCLC 11, 62**
See also DLB 39, 158, 178

Lewis, (Harry) Sinclair 1885-1951 . **TCLC 4, 13, 23, 39; DA; DAB; DAC; DAM MST, NOV; WLC**
See also CA 104; 133; CDALB 1917-1929; DA3; DLB 9, 102; DLBD 1; MTCW 1, 2

Lewis, (Percy) Wyndham 1882(?)-1957 .... **TCLC 2, 9; SSC 34**
See also CA 104; 157; DLB 15; MTCW 2

Lewisohn, Ludwig 1883-1955 .... **TCLC 19**
See also CA 107; DLB 4, 9, 28, 102

Lewton, Val 1904-1951 .... **TCLC 76**

Leyner, Mark 1956- .... **CLC 92**
See also CA 110; CANR 28, 53; DA3; MTCW 2

Lezama Lima, Jose 1910-1976 .... **CLC 4, 10, 101; DAM MULT; HLCS 2**
See also CA 77-80; CANR 71; DLB 113; HW 1, 2

L'Heureux, John (Clarke) 1934- ...... **CLC 52**
See also CA 13-16R; CANR 23, 45, 88

Liddell, C. H.
See Kuttner, Henry

Lie, Jonas (Lauritz Idemil) 1833-1908(?) .... **TCLC 5**
See also CA 115

Lieber, Joel 1937-1971 .... **CLC 6**
See also CA 73-76; 29-32R

Lieber, Stanley Martin
See Lee, Stan

Lieberman, Laurence (James) 1935- .... **CLC 4, 36**
See also CA 17-20R; CANR 8, 36, 89

Lieh Tzu fl. 7th cent. B.C.-5th cent. B.C. .... **CMLC 27**

Lieksman, Anders
See Haavikko, Paavo Juhani

Li Fei-kan 1904-
See Pa Chin
See also CA 105

Lifton, Robert Jay 1926- .... **CLC 67**
See also CA 17-20R; CANR 27, 78; INT CANR-27; SATA 66

Lightfoot, Gordon 1938- .... **CLC 26**
See also CA 109

Lightman, Alan P(aige) 1948- .... **CLC 81**
See also CA 141; CANR 63

Ligotti, Thomas (Robert) 1953- ...... **CLC 44; SSC 16**
See also CA 123; CANR 49

Li Ho 791-817 .... **PC 13**

Liliencron, (Friedrich Adolf Axel) Detlev von 1844-1909 .... **TCLC 18**
See also CA 117

Lilly, William 1602-1681 .... **LC 27**

Lima, Jose Lezama
See Lezama Lima, Jose

Lima Barreto, Afonso Henrique de 1881-1922 .... **TCLC 23**
See also CA 117; 181

Limonov, Edward 1944- .... **CLC 67**
See also CA 137

Lin, Frank
See Atherton, Gertrude (Franklin Horn)

Lincoln, Abraham 1809-1865 .... **NCLC 18**

Lind, Jakov CLC 1, 2, 4, 27, 82
See also Landwirth, Heinz
See also CAAS 4

Lindbergh, Anne (Spencer) Morrow 1906- .... **CLC 82; DAM NOV**
See also CA 17-20R; CANR 16, 73; MTCW 1, 2; SATA 33

Lindsay, David 1876(?)-1945 .... **TCLC 15**
See also CA 113

Lindsay, (Nicholas) Vachel 1879-1931 . **TCLC 17; DA; DAC; DAM MST, POET; PC 23; WLC**
See also CA 114; 135; CANR 79; CDALB 1865-1917; DA3; DLB 54; SATA 40

Ludlam, Charles 1943-1987 .... **CLC 46, 50**
See also CA 85-88; 122; CANR 72, 86
Ludlum, Robert 1927- .... **CLC 22, 43; DAM NOV, POP**
See also AAYA 10; BEST 89:1, 90:3; CA 33-36R; CANR 25, 41, 68; DA3; DLBY 82; MTCW 1, 2
Ludwig, Ken CLC 60
Ludwig, Otto 1813-1865 .... **NCLC 4**
See also DLB 129
Lugones, Leopoldo 1874-1938 ...... **TCLC 15; HLCS 2**
See also CA 116; 131; HW 1
Lu Hsun 1881-1936 .... **TCLC 3; SSC 20**
See also Shu-Jen, Chou
Lukacs, George CLC 24
See also Lukacs, Gyorgy (Szegeny von)
Lukacs, Gyorgy (Szegeny von) 1885-1971
See Lukacs, George
See also CA 101; 29-32R; CANR 62; MTCW 2
Luke, Peter (Ambrose Cyprian) 1919-1995 .... **CLC 38**
See also CA 81-84; 147; CANR 72; DLB 13
Lunar, Dennis
See Mungo, Raymond
Lurie, Alison 1926- .... **CLC 4, 5, 18, 39**
See also CA 1-4R; CANR 2, 17, 50, 88; DLB 2; MTCW 1; SATA 46, 112
Lustig, Arnost 1926- .... **CLC 56**
See also AAYA 3; CA 69-72; CANR 47; SATA 56
Luther, Martin 1483-1546 .... **LC 9, 37**
See also DLB 179
Luxemburg, Rosa 1870(?)-1919 ..... **TCLC 63**
See also CA 118
Luzi, Mario 1914- .... **CLC 13**
See also CA 61-64; CANR 9, 70; DLB 128
Lyly, John 1554(?)-1606 .... **LC 41; DAM DRAM; DC 7**
See also DLB 62, 167
L'Ymagier
See Gourmont, Remy (-Marie-Charles) de
Lynch, B. Suarez
See Bioy Casares, Adolfo; Borges, Jorge Luis
Lynch, B. Suarez
See Bioy Casares, Adolfo
Lynch, David (K.) 1946- .... **CLC 66**
See also CA 124; 129
Lynch, James
See Andreyev, Leonid (Nikolaevich)
Lynch Davis, B.
See Bioy Casares, Adolfo; Borges, Jorge Luis
Lyndsay, Sir David 1490-1555 .... **LC 20**
Lynn, Kenneth S(chuyler) 1923- ...... **CLC 50**
See also CA 1-4R; CANR 3, 27, 65
Lynx
See West, Rebecca
Lyons, Marcus
See Blish, James (Benjamin)
Lyre, Pinchbeck
See Sassoon, Siegfried (Lorraine)
Lytle, Andrew (Nelson) 1902-1995 ... **CLC 22**
See also CA 9-12R; 150; CANR 70; DLB 6; DLBY 95
Lyttelton, George 1709-1773 .... **LC 10**
Maas, Peter 1929- .... **CLC 29**
See also CA 93-96; INT 93-96; MTCW 2
Macaulay, Rose 1881-1958 .... **TCLC 7, 44**
See also CA 104; DLB 36
Macaulay, Thomas Babington 1800-1859 .... **NCLC 42**
See also CDBLB 1832-1890; DLB 32, 55
MacBeth, George (Mann) 1932-1992 .... **CLC 2, 5, 9**
See also CA 25-28R; 136; CANR 61, 66; DLB 40; MTCW 1; SATA 4; SATA-Obit 70
MacCaig, Norman (Alexander) 1910- .... **CLC 36; DAB; DAM POET**
See also CA 9-12R; CANR 3, 34; DLB 27
MacCarthy, Sir(Charles Otto) Desmond 1877-1952 .... **TCLC 36**
See also CA 167
MacDiarmid, Hugh CLC 2, 4, 11, 19, 63; PC 9
See also Grieve, C(hristopher) M(urray)
See also CDBLB 1945-1960; DLB 20
MacDonald, Anson
See Heinlein, Robert A(nson)
Macdonald, Cynthia 1928- .... **CLC 13, 19**
See also CA 49-52; CANR 4, 44; DLB 105
MacDonald, George 1824-1905 .... **TCLC 9**
See also CA 106; 137; CANR 80; DLB 18, 163, 178; MAICYA; SATA 33, 100
Macdonald, John
See Millar, Kenneth
MacDonald, John D(ann) 1916-1986 .. **CLC 3, 27, 44; DAM NOV, POP**
See also CA 1-4R; 121; CANR 1, 19, 60; DLB 8; DLBY 86; MTCW 1, 2
Macdonald, John Ross
See Millar, Kenneth
Macdonald, Ross CLC 1, 2, 3, 14, 34, 41
See also Millar, Kenneth
See also DLBD 6
MacDougal, John
See Blish, James (Benjamin)
MacDougal, John
See Blish, James (Benjamin)
MacEwen, Gwendolyn (Margaret) 1941-1987 .... **CLC 13, 55**
See also CA 9-12R; 124; CANR 7, 22; DLB 53; SATA 50; SATA-Obit 55
Macha, Karel Hynek 1810-1846 .... **NCLC 46**
Machado (y Ruiz), Antonio 1875-1939 .... **TCLC 3**
See also CA 104; 174; DLB 108; HW 2
Machado de Assis, Joaquim Maria 1839-1908 ..... **TCLC 10; BLC 2; HLCS 2; SSC 24**
See also CA 107; 153; CANR 91
Machen, Arthur TCLC 4; SSC 20
See also Jones, Arthur Llewellyn
See also CA 179; DLB 36, 156, 178
Machiavelli, Niccolo 1469-1527 ..... **LC 8, 36; DA; DAB; DAC; DAM MST; WLCS**
MacInnes, Colin 1914-1976 .... **CLC 4, 23**
See also CA 69-72; 65-68; CANR 21; DLB 14; MTCW 1, 2
MacInnes, Helen (Clark) 1907-1985 .... **CLC 27, 39; DAM POP**
See also CA 1-4R; 117; CANR 1, 28, 58; DLB 87; MTCW 1, 2; SATA 22; SATA-Obit 44
Mackenzie, Compton (Edward Montague) 1883-1972 .... **CLC 18**
See also CA 21-22; 37-40R; CAP 2; DLB 34, 100
Mackenzie, Henry 1745-1831 .... **NCLC 41**
See also DLB 39
Mackintosh, Elizabeth 1896(?)-1952
See Tey, Josephine
See also CA 110
MacLaren, James
See Grieve, C(hristopher) M(urray)
Mac Laverty, Bernard 1942- .... **CLC 31**
See also CA 116; 118; CANR 43, 88; INT 118
MacLean, Alistair (Stuart) 1922(?)-1987 .. **CLC 3, 13, 50, 63; DAM POP**
See also CA 57-60; 121; CANR 28, 61; MTCW 1; SATA 23; SATA-Obit 50
Maclean, Norman (Fitzroy) 1902-1990 .... **CLC 78; DAM POP; SSC 13**
See also CA 102; 132; CANR 49; DLB 206
MacLeish, Archibald 1892-1982 ... **CLC 3, 8, 14, 68; DAM POET**
See also CA 9-12R; 106; CANR 33, 63; CDALBS; DLB 4, 7, 45; DLBY 82; MTCW 1, 2
MacLennan, (John) Hugh 1907-1990 . **CLC 2, 14, 92; DAC; DAM MST**
See also CA 5-8R; 142; CANR 33; DLB 68; MTCW 1, 2
MacLeod, Alistair 1936- .... **CLC 56; DAC; DAM MST**
See also CA 123; DLB 60; MTCW 2
Macleod, Fiona
See Sharp, William
MacNeice, (Frederick) Louis 1907-1963 .... **CLC 1, 4, 10, 53; DAB; DAM POET**
See also CA 85-88; CANR 61; DLB 10, 20; MTCW 1, 2
MacNeill, Dand
See Fraser, George MacDonald
Macpherson, James 1736-1796 .... **LC 29**
See also Ossian
See also DLB 109
Macpherson, (Jean) Jay 1931- .... **CLC 14**
See also CA 5-8R; CANR 90; DLB 53
MacShane, Frank 1927-1999 .... **CLC 39**
See also CA 9-12R; 186; CANR 3, 33; DLB 111
Macumber, Mari
See Sandoz, Mari(e Susette)
Madach, Imre 1823-1864 .... **NCLC 19**
Madden, (Jerry) David 1933- .... **CLC 5, 15**
See also CA 1-4R; CAAS 3; CANR 4, 45; DLB 6; MTCW 1
Maddern, Al(an)
See Ellison, Harlan (Jay)
Madhubuti, Haki R. 1942- . **CLC 6, 73; BLC 2; DAM MULT, POET; PC 5**
See also Lee, Don L.
See also BW 2, 3; CA 73-76; CANR 24, 51, 73; DLB 5, 41; DLBD 8; MTCW 2
Maepenn, Hugh
See Kuttner, Henry
Maepenn, K. H.
See Kuttner, Henry
Maeterlinck, Maurice 1862-1949 ... **TCLC 3; DAM DRAM**
See also CA 104; 136; CANR 80; DLB 192; SATA 66
Maginn, William 1794-1842 .... **NCLC 8**
See also DLB 110, 159
Mahapatra, Jayanta 1928- .... **CLC 33; DAM MULT**
See also CA 73-76; CAAS 9; CANR 15, 33, 66, 87
Mahfouz, Naguib (Abdel Aziz Al-Sabilgi) 1911(?)-
See Mahfuz, Najib
See also BEST 89:2; CA 128; CANR 55; DAM NOV; DA3; MTCW 1, 2
Mahfuz, Najib CLC 52, 55
See also Mahfouz, Naguib (Abdel Aziz Al-Sabilgi)
See also DLBY 88
Mahon, Derek 1941- .... **CLC 27**
See also CA 113; 128; CANR 88; DLB 40

Marsten, Richard
See Hunter, Evan
Marston, John 1576-1634 .... **LC 33; DAM DRAM**
See also DLB 58, 172
Martha, Henry
See Harris, Mark
Marti (y Perez), Jose (Julian) 1853-1895 ...... **NCLC 63; DAM MULT; HLC 2**
See also HW 2
Martial c. 40-c. 104 .... **CMLC 35; PC 10**
See also DLB 211
Martin, Ken
See Hubbard, L(afayette) Ron(ald)
Martin, Richard
See Creasey, John
Martin, Steve 1945- .... **CLC 30**
See also CA 97-100; CANR 30; MTCW 1
Martin, Valerie 1948- .... **CLC 89**
See also BEST 90:2; CA 85-88; CANR 49, 89
Martin, Violet Florence 1862-1915 .... **TCLC 51**
Martin, Webber
See Silverberg, Robert
Martindale, Patrick Victor
See White, Patrick (Victor Martindale)
Martin du Gard, Roger 1881-1958 .... **TCLC 24**
See also CA 118; DLB 65
Martineau, Harriet 1802-1876 .... **NCLC 26**
See also DLB 21, 55, 159, 163, 166, 190; YABC 2
Martines, Julia
See O'Faolain, Julia
Martinez, Enrique Gonzalez
See Gonzalez Martinez, Enrique
Martinez, Jacinto Benavente y
See Benavente (y Martinez), Jacinto
Martinez Ruiz, Jose 1873-1967
See Azorin; Ruiz, Jose Martinez
See also CA 93-96; HW 1
Martinez Sierra, Gregorio 1881-1947 .... **TCLC 6**
See also CA 115
Martinez Sierra, Maria (de la O'LeJarraga) 1874-1974 .... **TCLC 6**
See also CA 115
Martinsen, Martin
See Follett, Ken(neth Martin)
Martinson, Harry (Edmund) 1904-1978 .... **CLC 14**
See also CA 77-80; CANR 34
Marut, Ret
See Traven, B.
Marut, Robert
See Traven, B.
Marvell, Andrew 1621-1678 .. **LC 4, 43; DA; DAB; DAC; DAM MST, POET; PC 10; WLC**
See also CDBLB 1660-1789; DLB 131
Marx, Karl (Heinrich) 1818-1883 . **NCLC 17**
See also DLB 129
Masaoka Shiki TCLC 18
See also Masaoka Tsunenori
Masaoka Tsunenori 1867-1902
See Masaoka Shiki
See also CA 117
Masefield, John (Edward) 1878-1967 ..... **CLC 11, 47; DAM POET**
See also CA 19-20; 25-28R; CANR 33; CAP 2; CDBLB 1890-1914; DLB 10, 19, 153, 160; MTCW 1, 2; SATA 19
Maso, Carole 19(?)- .... **CLC 44**
See also CA 170
Mason, Bobbie Ann 1940- ... **CLC 28, 43, 82; SSC 4**
See also AAYA 5; CA 53-56; CANR 11, 31, 58, 83; CDALBS; DA3; DLB 173; DLBY 87; INT CANR-31; MTCW 1, 2
Mason, Ernst
See Pohl, Frederik
Mason, Lee W.
See Malzberg, Barry N(athaniel)
Mason, Nick 1945- .... **CLC 35**
Mason, Tally
See Derleth, August (William)
Mass, William
See Gibson, William
Master Lao
See Lao Tzu
Masters, Edgar Lee 1868-1950 .... **TCLC 2, 25; DA; DAC; DAM MST, POET; PC 1; WLCS**
See also CA 104; 133; CDALB 1865-1917; DLB 54; MTCW 1, 2
Masters, Hilary 1928- .... **CLC 48**
See also CA 25-28R; CANR 13, 47
Mastrosimone, William 19(?)- .... **CLC 36**
See also CA 186
Mathe, Albert
See Camus, Albert
Mather, Cotton 1663-1728 .... **LC 38**
See also CDALB 1640-1865; DLB 24, 30, 140
Mather, Increase 1639-1723 .... **LC 38**
See also DLB 24
Matheson, Richard Burton 1926- .... **CLC 37**
See also AAYA 31; CA 97-100; CANR 88; DLB 8, 44; INT 97-100
Mathews, Harry 1930- .... **CLC 6, 52**
See also CA 21-24R; CAAS 6; CANR 18, 40
Mathews, John Joseph 1894-1979 .. **CLC 84; DAM MULT**
See also CA 19-20; 142; CANR 45; CAP 2; DLB 175; NNAL
Mathias, Roland (Glyn) 1915- .... **CLC 45**
See also CA 97-100; CANR 19, 41; DLB 27
Matsuo Basho 1644-1694 .... **PC 3**
See also DAM POET
Mattheson, Rodney
See Creasey, John
Matthews, (James) Brander 1852-1929 .... **TCLC 95**
See also DLB 71, 78; DLBD 13
Matthews, Greg 1949- .... **CLC 45**
See also CA 135
Matthews, William (Procter, III) 1942-1997 .... **CLC 40**
See also CA 29-32R; 162; CAAS 18; CANR 12, 57; DLB 5
Matthias, John (Edward) 1941- .... **CLC 9**
See also CA 33-36R; CANR 56
Matthiessen, F(rancis) O(tto) 1902-1950 .... **TCLC 100**
See also CA 185; DLB 63
Matthiessen, Peter 1927- ... **CLC 5, 7, 11, 32, 64; DAM NOV**
See also AAYA 6; BEST 90:4; CA 9-12R; CANR 21, 50, 73; DA3; DLB 6, 173; MTCW 1, 2; SATA 27
Maturin, Charles Robert 1780(?)-1824 .... **NCLC 6**
See also DLB 178
Matute (Ausejo), Ana Maria 1925- .. **CLC 11**
See also CA 89-92; MTCW 1
Maugham, W. S.
See Maugham, W(illiam) Somerset
Maugham, W(illiam) Somerset 1874-1965 ... **CLC 1, 11, 15, 67, 93; DA; DAB; DAC; DAM DRAM, MST, NOV; SSC 8; WLC**
See also CA 5-8R; 25-28R; CANR 40; CDBLB 1914-1945; DA3; DLB 10, 36, 77, 100, 162, 195; MTCW 1, 2; SATA 54
Maugham, William Somerset
See Maugham, W(illiam) Somerset
Maupassant, (Henri Rene Albert) Guy de 1850-1893 . **NCLC 1, 42, 83; DA; DAB; DAC; DAM MST; SSC 1; WLC**
See also DA3; DLB 123
Maupin, Armistead 1944- ..... **CLC 95; DAM POP**
See also CA 125; 130; CANR 58; DA3; INT 130; MTCW 2
Maurhut, Richard
See Traven, B.
Mauriac, Claude 1914-1996 .... **CLC 9**
See also CA 89-92; 152; DLB 83
Mauriac, Francois (Charles) 1885-1970 .... **CLC 4, 9, 56; SSC 24**
See also CA 25-28; CAP 2; DLB 65; MTCW 1, 2
Mavor, Osborne Henry 1888-1951
See Bridie, James
See also CA 104
Maxwell, William (Keepers, Jr.) 1908- .... **CLC 19**
See also CA 93-96; CANR 54; DLBY 80; INT 93-96
May, Elaine 1932- .... **CLC 16**
See also CA 124; 142; DLB 44
Mayakovski, Vladimir (Vladimirovich) 1893-1930 .... **TCLC 4, 18**
See also CA 104; 158; MTCW 2
Mayhew, Henry 1812-1887 .... **NCLC 31**
See also DLB 18, 55, 190
Mayle, Peter 1939(?)- .... **CLC 89**
See also CA 139; CANR 64
Maynard, Joyce 1953- .... **CLC 23**
See also CA 111; 129; CANR 64
Mayne, William (James Carter) 1928- .... **CLC 12**
See also AAYA 20; CA 9-12R; CANR 37, 80; CLR 25; JRDA; MAICYA; SAAS 11; SATA 6, 68
Mayo, Jim
See L'Amour, Louis (Dearborn)
Maysles, Albert 1926- .... **CLC 16**
See also CA 29-32R
Maysles, David 1932- .... **CLC 16**
Mazer, Norma Fox 1931- .... **CLC 26**
See also AAYA 5; CA 69-72; CANR 12, 32, 66; CLR 23; JRDA; MAICYA; SAAS 1; SATA 24, 67, 105
Mazzini, Guiseppe 1805-1872 .... **NCLC 34**
McAlmon, Robert (Menzies) 1895-1956 .... **TCLC 97**
See also CA 107; 168; DLB 4, 45; DLBD 15
McAuley, James Phillip 1917-1976 .. **CLC 45**
See also CA 97-100
McBain, Ed
See Hunter, Evan
McBrien, William (Augustine) 1930- .... **CLC 44**
See also CA 107; CANR 90
McCabe, Patrick 1955- .... **CLC 133**
See also CA 130; CANR 50, 90; DLB 194
McCaffrey, Anne (Inez) 1926- .... **CLC 17; DAM NOV, POP**
See also AAYA 6, 34; AITN 2; BEST 89:2; CA 25-28R; CANR 15, 35, 55; CLR 49; DA3; DLB 8; JRDA; MAICYA; MTCW 1, 2; SAAS 11; SATA 8, 70, 116
McCall, Nathan 1955(?)- .... **CLC 86**
See also BW 3; CA 146; CANR 88

McCann, Arthur
See Campbell, John W(ood, Jr.)
McCann, Edson
See Pohl, Frederik
McCarthy, Charles, Jr. 1933-
See McCarthy, Cormac
See also CANR 42, 69; DAM POP; DA3; MTCW 2
McCarthy, Cormac 1933- ...... **CLC 4, 57, 59, 101**
See also McCarthy, Charles, Jr.
See also DLB 6, 143; MTCW 2
McCarthy, Mary (Therese) 1912-1989 .. **CLC 1, 3, 5, 14, 24, 39, 59; SSC 24**
See also CA 5-8R; 129; CANR 16, 50, 64; DA3; DLB 2; DLBY 81; INT CANR-16; MTCW 1, 2
McCartney, (James) Paul 1942- . **CLC 12, 35**
See also CA 146
McCauley, Stephen (D.) 1955- .... **CLC 50**
See also CA 141
McClure, Michael (Thomas) 1932- ... **CLC 6, 10**
See also CA 21-24R; CANR 17, 46, 77; DLB 16
McCorkle, Jill (Collins) 1958- .... **CLC 51**
See also CA 121; DLBY 87
McCourt, Frank 1930- .... **CLC 109**
See also CA 157
McCourt, James 1941- .... **CLC 5**
See also CA 57-60
McCourt, Malachy 1932- .... **CLC 119**
McCoy, Horace (Stanley) 1897-1955 .... **TCLC 28**
See also CA 108; 155; DLB 9
McCrae, John 1872-1918 .... **TCLC 12**
See also CA 109; DLB 92
McCreigh, James
See Pohl, Frederik
McCullers, (Lula) Carson (Smith) 1917-1967 .... **CLC 1, 4, 10, 12, 48, 100; DA; DAB; DAC; DAM MST, NOV; SSC 9, 24; WLC**
See also AAYA 21; CA 5-8R; 25-28R; CABS 1, 3; CANR 18; CDALB 1941-1968; DA3; DLB 2, 7, 173, 228; MTCW 1, 2; SATA 27
McCulloch, John Tyler
See Burroughs, Edgar Rice
McCullough, Colleen 1938(?)- .... **CLC 27, 107; DAM NOV, POP**
See also CA 81-84; CANR 17, 46, 67; DA3; MTCW 1, 2
McDermott, Alice 1953- .... **CLC 90**
See also CA 109; CANR 40, 90
McElroy, Joseph 1930- .... **CLC 5, 47**
See also CA 17-20R
McEwan, Ian (Russell) 1948- .... **CLC 13, 66; DAM NOV**
See also BEST 90:4; CA 61-64; CANR 14, 41, 69, 87; DLB 14, 194; MTCW 1, 2
McFadden, David 1940- .... **CLC 48**
See also CA 104; DLB 60; INT 104
McFarland, Dennis 1950- .... **CLC 65**
See also CA 165
McGahern, John 1934- ... **CLC 5, 9, 48; SSC 17**
See also CA 17-20R; CANR 29, 68; DLB 14; MTCW 1
McGinley, Patrick (Anthony) 1937- . **CLC 41**
See also CA 120; 127; CANR 56; INT 127
McGinley, Phyllis 1905-1978 .... **CLC 14**
See also CA 9-12R; 77-80; CANR 19; DLB 11, 48; SATA 2, 44; SATA-Obit 24
McGinniss, Joe 1942- .... **CLC 32**
See also AITN 2; BEST 89:2; CA 25-28R; CANR 26, 70; DLB 185; INT CANR-26
McGivern, Maureen Daly
See Daly, Maureen
McGrath, Patrick 1950- .... **CLC 55**
See also CA 136; CANR 65
McGrath, Thomas (Matthew) 1916-1990 ..... **CLC 28, 59; DAM POET**
See also CA 9-12R; 132; CANR 6, 33; MTCW 1; SATA 41; SATA-Obit 66
McGuane, Thomas (Francis III) 1939- .... **CLC 3, 7, 18, 45, 127**
See also AITN 2; CA 49-52; CANR 5, 24, 49; DLB 2, 212; DLBY 80; INT CANR-24; MTCW 1
McGuckian, Medbh 1950- .... **CLC 48; DAM POET; PC 27**
See also CA 143; DLB 40
McHale, Tom 1942(?)-1982 .... **CLC 3, 5**
See also AITN 1; CA 77-80; 106
McIlvanney, William 1936- .... **CLC 42**
See also CA 25-28R; CANR 61; DLB 14, 207
McIlwraith, Maureen Mollie Hunter
See Hunter, Mollie
See also SATA 2
McInerney, Jay 1955- .... **CLC 34, 112; DAM POP**
See also AAYA 18; CA 116; 123; CANR 45, 68; DA3; INT 123; MTCW 2
McIntyre, Vonda N(eel) 1948- .... **CLC 18**
See also CA 81-84; CANR 17, 34, 69; MTCW 1
McKay, Claude TCLC 7, 41; BLC 3; DAB; PC 2
See also McKay, Festus Claudius
See also DLB 4, 45, 51, 117
McKay, Festus Claudius 1889-1948
See McKay, Claude
See also BW 1, 3; CA 104; 124; CANR 73; DA; DAC; DAM MST, MULT, NOV, POET; MTCW 1, 2; WLC
McKuen, Rod 1933- .... **CLC 1, 3**
See also AITN 1; CA 41-44R; CANR 40
McLoughlin, R. B.
See Mencken, H(enry) L(ouis)
McLuhan, (Herbert) Marshall 1911-1980 .... **CLC 37, 83**
See also CA 9-12R; 102; CANR 12, 34, 61; DLB 88; INT CANR-12; MTCW 1, 2
McMillan, Terry (L.) 1951- .... **CLC 50, 61, 112; BLCS; DAM MULT, NOV, POP**
See also AAYA 21; BW 2, 3; CA 140; CANR 60; DA3; MTCW 2
McMurtry, Larry (Jeff) 1936- .. **CLC 2, 3, 7, 11, 27, 44, 127; DAM NOV, POP**
See also AAYA 15; AITN 2; BEST 89:2; CA 5-8R; CANR 19, 43, 64; CDALB 1968-1988; DA3; DLB 2, 143; DLBY 80, 87; MTCW 1, 2
McNally, T. M. 1961- .... **CLC 82**
McNally, Terrence 1939- ... **CLC 4, 7, 41, 91; DAM DRAM**
See also CA 45-48; CANR 2, 56; DA3; DLB 7; MTCW 2
McNamer, Deirdre 1950- .... **CLC 70**
McNeal, Tom CLC 119
McNeile, Herman Cyril 1888-1937
See Sapper
See also CA 184; DLB 77
McNickle, (William) D'Arcy 1904-1977 .... **CLC 89; DAM MULT**
See also CA 9-12R; 85-88; CANR 5, 45; DLB 175, 212; NNAL; SATA-Obit 22
McPhee, John (Angus) 1931- .... **CLC 36**
See also BEST 90:1; CA 65-68; CANR 20, 46, 64, 69; DLB 185; MTCW 1, 2
McPherson, James Alan 1943- .. **CLC 19, 77; BLCS**
See also BW 1, 3; CA 25-28R; CAAS 17; CANR 24, 74; DLB 38; MTCW 1, 2
McPherson, William (Alexander) 1933- .... **CLC 34**
See also CA 69-72; CANR 28; INT CANR-28
Mead, George Herbert 1873-1958 . **TCLC 89**
Mead, Margaret 1901-1978 .... **CLC 37**
See also AITN 1; CA 1-4R; 81-84; CANR 4; DA3; MTCW 1, 2; SATA-Obit 20
Meaker, Marijane (Agnes) 1927-
See Kerr, M. E.
See also CA 107; CANR 37, 63; INT 107; JRDA; MAICYA; MTCW 1; SATA 20, 61, 99; SATA-Essay 111
Medoff, Mark (Howard) 1940- ... **CLC 6, 23; DAM DRAM**
See also AITN 1; CA 53-56; CANR 5; DLB 7; INT CANR-5
Medvedev, P. N.
See Bakhtin, Mikhail Mikhailovich
Meged, Aharon
See Megged, Aharon
Meged, Aron
See Megged, Aharon
Megged, Aharon 1920- .... **CLC 9**
See also CA 49-52; CAAS 13; CANR 1
Mehta, Ved (Parkash) 1934- .... **CLC 37**
See also CA 1-4R; CANR 2, 23, 69; MTCW 1
Melanter
See Blackmore, R(ichard) D(oddridge)
Melies, Georges 1861-1938 .... **TCLC 81**
Melikow, Loris
See Hofmannsthal, Hugo von
Melmoth, Sebastian
See Wilde, Oscar (Fingal O'Flahertie Wills)
Meltzer, Milton 1915- .... **CLC 26**
See also AAYA 8; CA 13-16R; CANR 38, 92; CLR 13; DLB 61; JRDA; MAICYA; SAAS 1; SATA 1, 50, 80
Melville, Herman 1819-1891 ..... **NCLC 3, 12, 29, 45, 49, 91; DA; DAB; DAC; DAM MST, NOV; SSC 1, 17; WLC**
See also AAYA 25; CDALB 1640-1865; DA3; DLB 3, 74; SATA 59
Menander c. 342B.C.-c. 292B.C. ... **CMLC 9; DAM DRAM; DC 3**
See also DLB 176
Menchu, Rigoberta 1959-
See also HLCS 2
Menchu, Rigoberta 1959-
See also CA 175; HLCS 2
Mencken, H(enry) L(ouis) 1880-1956 .... **TCLC 13**
See also CA 105; 125; CDALB 1917-1929; DLB 11, 29, 63, 137; MTCW 1, 2
Mendelsohn, Jane 1965(?)- .... **CLC 99**
See also CA 154
Mercer, David 1928-1980 .... **CLC 5; DAM DRAM**
See also CA 9-12R; 102; CANR 23; DLB 13; MTCW 1
Merchant, Paul
See Ellison, Harlan (Jay)
Meredith, George 1828-1909 .. **TCLC 17, 43; DAM POET**
See also CA 117; 153; CANR 80; CDBLB 1832-1890; DLB 18, 35, 57, 159
Meredith, William (Morris) 1919- .... **CLC 4, 13, 22, 55; DAM POET; PC 28**
See also CA 9-12R; CAAS 14; CANR 6, 40; DLB 5
Merezhkovsky, Dmitry Sergeyevich 1865-1941 .... **TCLC 29**
See also CA 169
Merimee, Prosper 1803-1870 ... **NCLC 6, 65; SSC 7**
See also DLB 119, 192
Merkin, Daphne 1954- .... **CLC 44**
See also CA 123

Merlin, Arthur
See Blish, James (Benjamin)
Merrill, James (Ingram) 1926-1995 .. **CLC 2, 3, 6, 8, 13, 18, 34, 91; DAM POET; PC 28**
See also CA 13-16R; 147; CANR 10, 49, 63; DA3; DLB 5, 165; DLBY 85; INT CANR-10; MTCW 1, 2
Merriman, Alex
See Silverberg, Robert
Merriman, Brian 1747-1805 .... **NCLC 70**
Merritt, E. B.
See Waddington, Miriam
Merton, Thomas 1915-1968 ..... **CLC 1, 3, 11, 34, 83; PC 10**
See also CA 5-8R; 25-28R; CANR 22, 53; DA3; DLB 48; DLBY 81; MTCW 1, 2
Merwin, W(illiam) S(tanley) 1927- ... **CLC 1, 2, 3, 5, 8, 13, 18, 45, 88; DAM POET**
See also CA 13-16R; CANR 15, 51; DA3; DLB 5, 169; INT CANR-15; MTCW 1, 2
Metcalf, John 1938- .... **CLC 37**
See also CA 113; DLB 60
Metcalf, Suzanne
See Baum, L(yman) Frank
Mew, Charlotte (Mary) 1870-1928 .. **TCLC 8**
See also CA 105; DLB 19, 135
Mewshaw, Michael 1943- .... **CLC 9**
See also CA 53-56; CANR 7, 47; DLBY 80
Meyer, Conrad Ferdinand 1825-1905 .... **NCLC 81**
See also DLB 129
Meyer, June
See Jordan, June
Meyer, Lynn
See Slavitt, David R(ytman)
Meyer-Meyrink, Gustav 1868-1932
See Meyrink, Gustav
See also CA 117
Meyers, Jeffrey 1939- .... **CLC 39**
See also CA 73-76; CAAE 186; CANR 54; DLB 111
Meynell, Alice (Christina Gertrude Thompson) 1847-1922 .... **TCLC 6**
See also CA 104; 177; DLB 19, 98
Meyrink, Gustav TCLC 21
See also Meyer-Meyrink, Gustav
See also DLB 81
Michaels, Leonard 1933- .... **CLC 6, 25; SSC 16**
See also CA 61-64; CANR 21, 62; DLB 130; MTCW 1
Michaux, Henri 1899-1984 .... **CLC 8, 19**
See also CA 85-88; 114
Micheaux, Oscar (Devereaux) 1884-1951 .... **TCLC 76**
See also BW 3; CA 174; DLB 50
Michelangelo 1475-1564 .... **LC 12**
Michelet, Jules 1798-1874 .... **NCLC 31**
Michels, Robert 1876-1936 .... **TCLC 88**
Michener, James A(lbert) 1907(?)-1997 .... **CLC 1, 5, 11, 29, 60, 109; DAM NOV, POP**
See also AAYA 27; AITN 1; BEST 90:1; CA 5-8R; 161; CANR 21, 45, 68; DA3; DLB 6; MTCW 1, 2
Mickiewicz, Adam 1798-1855 .... **NCLC 3**
Middleton, Christopher 1926- .... **CLC 13**
See also CA 13-16R; CANR 29, 54; DLB 40
Middleton, Richard (Barham) 1882-1911 .... **TCLC 56**
See also DLB 156
Middleton, Stanley 1919- .... **CLC 7, 38**
See also CA 25-28R; CAAS 23; CANR 21, 46, 81; DLB 14
Middleton, Thomas 1580-1627 .... **LC 33; DAM DRAM, MST; DC 5**
See also DLB 58
Migueis, Jose Rodrigues 1901- .... **CLC 10**
Mikszath, Kalman 1847-1910 .... **TCLC 31**
See also CA 170
Miles, Jack CLC 100
Miles, Josephine (Louise) 1911-1985 .. **CLC 1, 2, 14, 34, 39; DAM POET**
See also CA 1-4R; 116; CANR 2, 55; DLB 48
Militant
See Sandburg, Carl (August)
Mill, John Stuart 1806-1873 .... **NCLC 11, 58**
See also CDBLB 1832-1890; DLB 55, 190
Millar, Kenneth 1915-1983 ... **CLC 14; DAM POP**
See also Macdonald, Ross
See also CA 9-12R; 110; CANR 16, 63; DA3; DLB 2, 226; DLBD 6; DLBY 83; MTCW 1, 2
Millay, E. Vincent
See Millay, Edna St. Vincent
Millay, Edna St. Vincent 1892-1950 .... **TCLC 4, 49; DA; DAB; DAC; DAM MST, POET; PC 6; WLCS**
See also CA 104; 130; CDALB 1917-1929; DA3; DLB 45; MTCW 1, 2
Miller, Arthur 1915- ...... **CLC 1, 2, 6, 10, 15, 26, 47, 78; DA; DAB; DAC; DAM DRAM, MST; DC 1; WLC**
See also AAYA 15; AITN 1; CA 1-4R; CABS 3; CANR 2, 30, 54, 76; CDALB 1941-1968; DA3; DLB 7; MTCW 1, 2
Miller, Henry (Valentine) 1891-1980 .... **CLC 1, 2, 4, 9, 14, 43, 84; DA; DAB; DAC; DAM MST, NOV; WLC**
See also CA 9-12R; 97-100; CANR 33, 64; CDALB 1929-1941; DA3; DLB 4, 9; DLBY 80; MTCW 1, 2
Miller, Jason 1939(?)- .... **CLC 2**
See also AITN 1; CA 73-76; DLB 7
Miller, Sue 1943- .... **CLC 44; DAM POP**
See also BEST 90:3; CA 139; CANR 59, 91; DA3; DLB 143
Miller, Walter M(ichael, Jr.) 1923- ... **CLC 4, 30**
See also CA 85-88; DLB 8
Millett, Kate 1934- .... **CLC 67**
See also AITN 1; CA 73-76; CANR 32, 53, 76; DA3; MTCW 1, 2
Millhauser, Steven (Lewis) 1943- .... **CLC 21, 54, 109**
See also CA 110; 111; CANR 63; DA3; DLB 2; INT 111; MTCW 2
Millin, Sarah Gertrude 1889-1968 ... **CLC 49**
See also CA 102; 93-96; DLB 225
Milne, A(lan) A(lexander) 1882-1956 ..... **TCLC 6, 88; DAB; DAC; DAM MST**
See also CA 104; 133; CLR 1, 26; DA3; DLB 10, 77, 100, 160; MAICYA; MTCW 1, 2; SATA 100; YABC 1
Milner, Ron(ald) 1938- .... **CLC 56; BLC 3; DAM MULT**
See also AITN 1; BW 1; CA 73-76; CANR 24, 81; DLB 38; MTCW 1
Milnes, Richard Monckton 1809-1885 .... **NCLC 61**
See also DLB 32, 184
Milosz, Czeslaw 1911- ...... **CLC 5, 11, 22, 31, 56, 82; DAM MST, POET; PC 8; WLCS**
See also CA 81-84; CANR 23, 51, 91; DA3; MTCW 1, 2
Milton, John 1608-1674 .... **LC 9, 43; DA; DAB; DAC; DAM MST, POET; PC 19, 29; WLC**
See also CDBLB 1660-1789; DA3; DLB 131, 151
Min, Anchee 1957- .... **CLC 86**
See also CA 146
Minehaha, Cornelius
See Wedekind, (Benjamin) Frank(lin)
Miner, Valerie 1947- .... **CLC 40**
See also CA 97-100; CANR 59
Minimo, Duca
See D'Annunzio, Gabriele
Minot, Susan 1956- .... **CLC 44**
See also CA 134
Minus, Ed 1938- .... **CLC 39**
See also CA 185
Miranda, Javier
See Bioy Casares, Adolfo
Miranda, Javier
See Bioy Casares, Adolfo
Mirbeau, Octave 1848-1917 .... **TCLC 55**
See also DLB 123, 192
Miro (Ferrer), Gabriel (Francisco Victor) 1879-1930 .... **TCLC 5**
See also CA 104; 185
Mishima, Yukio 1925-1970 .... **CLC 2, 4, 6, 9, 27; DC 1; SSC 4**
See also Hiraoka, Kimitake
See also DLB 182; MTCW 2
Mistral, Frederic 1830-1914 .... **TCLC 51**
See also CA 122
Mistral, Gabriela TCLC 2; HLC 2
See also Godoy Alcayaga, Lucila
See also MTCW 2
Mistry, Rohinton 1952- .... **CLC 71; DAC**
See also CA 141; CANR 86
Mitchell, Clyde
See Ellison, Harlan (Jay); Silverberg, Robert
Mitchell, James Leslie 1901-1935
See Gibbon, Lewis Grassic
See also CA 104; DLB 15
Mitchell, Joni 1943- .... **CLC 12**
See also CA 112
Mitchell, Joseph (Quincy) 1908-1996 .... **CLC 98**
See also CA 77-80; 152; CANR 69; DLB 185; DLBY 96
Mitchell, Margaret (Munnerlyn) 1900-1949 . **TCLC 11; DAM NOV, POP**
See also AAYA 23; CA 109; 125; CANR 55; CDALBS; DA3; DLB 9; MTCW 1, 2
Mitchell, Peggy
See Mitchell, Margaret (Munnerlyn)
Mitchell, S(ilas) Weir 1829-1914 .... **TCLC 36**
See also CA 165; DLB 202
Mitchell, W(illiam) O(rmond) 1914-1998 .. **CLC 25; DAC; DAM MST**
See also CA 77-80; 165; CANR 15, 43; DLB 88
Mitchell, William 1879-1936 .... **TCLC 81**
Mitford, Mary Russell 1787-1855 ... **NCLC 4**
See also DLB 110, 116
Mitford, Nancy 1904-1973 .... **CLC 44**
See also CA 9-12R; DLB 191
Miyamoto, (Chujo) Yuriko 1899-1951 .... **TCLC 37**
See also CA 170, 174; DLB 180
Miyazawa, Kenji 1896-1933 .... **TCLC 76**
See also CA 157
Mizoguchi, Kenji 1898-1956 .... **TCLC 72**
See also CA 167
Mo, Timothy (Peter) 1950(?)- ... **CLC 46, 134**
See also CA 117; DLB 194; MTCW 1
Modarressi, Taghi (M.) 1931- .... **CLC 44**
See also CA 121; 134; INT 134

Author Index

Modiano, Patrick (Jean) 1945- .... **CLC 18**
See also CA 85-88; CANR 17, 40; DLB 83
Moerck, Paal
See Roelvaag, O(le) E(dvart)
Mofolo, Thomas (Mokopu)
1875(?)-1948 .. **TCLC 22; BLC 3; DAM MULT**
See also CA 121; 153; CANR 83; DLB 225; MTCW 2
Mohr, Nicholasa 1938- .... **CLC 12; DAM MULT; HLC 2**
See also AAYA 8; CA 49-52; CANR 1, 32, 64; CLR 22; DLB 145; HW 1, 2; JRDA; SAAS 8; SATA 8, 97; SATA-Essay 113
Mojtabai, A(nn) G(race) 1938- ..... **CLC 5, 9, 15, 29**
See also CA 85-88; CANR 88
Moliere 1622-1673 ..... **LC 10, 28; DA; DAB; DAC; DAM DRAM, MST; DC 13; WLC**
See also DA3
Molin, Charles
See Mayne, William (James Carter)
Molnar, Ferenc 1878-1952 .. **TCLC 20; DAM DRAM**
See also CA 109; 153; CANR 83
Momaday, N(avarre) Scott 1934- ...... **CLC 2, 19, 85, 95; DA; DAB; DAC; DAM MST, MULT, NOV, POP; PC 25; WLCS**
See also AAYA 11; CA 25-28R; CANR 14, 34, 68; CDALBS; DA3; DLB 143, 175; INT CANR-14; MTCW 1, 2; NNAL; SATA 48; SATA-Brief 30
Monette, Paul 1945-1995 .... **CLC 82**
See also CA 139; 147
Monroe, Harriet 1860-1936 .... **TCLC 12**
See also CA 109; DLB 54, 91
Monroe, Lyle
See Heinlein, Robert A(nson)
Montagu, Elizabeth 1720-1800 .... **NCLC 7**
Montagu, Elizabeth 1917- .... **NCLC 7**
See also CA 9-12R
Montagu, Mary (Pierrepont) Wortley
1689-1762 .... **LC 9, 57; PC 16**
See also DLB 95, 101
Montagu, W. H.
See Coleridge, Samuel Taylor
Montague, John (Patrick) 1929- ..... **CLC 13, 46**
See also CA 9-12R; CANR 9, 69; DLB 40; MTCW 1
Montaigne, Michel (Eyquem) de
1533-1592 .... **LC 8; DA; DAB; DAC; DAM MST; WLC**
Montale, Eugenio 1896-1981 ... **CLC 7, 9, 18; PC 13**
See also CA 17-20R; 104; CANR 30; DLB 114; MTCW 1
Montesquieu, Charles-Louis de Secondat
1689-1755 .... **LC 7**
Montgomery, (Robert) Bruce 1921(?)-1978
See Crispin, Edmund
See also CA 179; 104
Montgomery, L(ucy) M(aud)
1874-1942 .... **TCLC 51; DAC; DAM MST**
See also AAYA 12; CA 108; 137; CLR 8; DA3; DLB 92; DLBD 14; JRDA; MAICYA; MTCW 2; SATA 100; YABC 1
Montgomery, Marion H., Jr. 1925- .... **CLC 7**
See also AITN 1; CA 1-4R; CANR 3, 48; DLB 6
Montgomery, Max
See Davenport, Guy (Mattison, Jr.)
Montherlant, Henry (Milon) de
1896-1972 ..... **CLC 8, 19; DAM DRAM**
See also CA 85-88; 37-40R; DLB 72; MTCW 1
Monty Python
See Chapman, Graham; Cleese, John (Marwood); Gilliam, Terry (Vance); Idle, Eric; Jones, Terence Graham Parry; Palin, Michael (Edward)
See also AAYA 7
Moodie, Susanna (Strickland)
1803-1885 .... **NCLC 14**
See also DLB 99
Mooney, Edward 1951-
See Mooney, Ted
See also CA 130
Mooney, Ted CLC 25
See also Mooney, Edward
Moorcock, Michael (John) 1939- ...... **CLC 5, 27, 58**
See also Bradbury, Edward P.
See also AAYA 26; CA 45-48; CAAS 5; CANR 2, 17, 38, 64; DLB 14; MTCW 1, 2; SATA 93
Moore, Brian 1921-1999 ... **CLC 1, 3, 5, 7, 8, 19, 32, 90; DAB; DAC; DAM MST**
See also CA 1-4R; 174; CANR 1, 25, 42, 63; MTCW 1, 2
Moore, Edward
See Muir, Edwin
Moore, G. E. 1873-1958 .... **TCLC 89**
Moore, George Augustus
1852-1933 .... **TCLC 7; SSC 19**
See also CA 104; 177; DLB 10, 18, 57, 135
Moore, Lorrie CLC 39, 45, 68
See also Moore, Marie Lorena
Moore, Marianne (Craig)
1887-1972 .... **CLC 1, 2, 4, 8, 10, 13, 19, 47; DA; DAB; DAC; DAM MST, POET; PC 4; WLCS**
See also CA 1-4R; 33-36R; CANR 3, 61; CDALB 1929-1941; DA3; DLB 45; DLBD 7; MTCW 1, 2; SATA 20
Moore, Marie Lorena 1957-
See Moore, Lorrie
See also CA 116; CANR 39, 83
Moore, Thomas 1779-1852 .... **NCLC 6**
See also DLB 96, 144
Moorhouse, Frank 1938- .... **SSC 40**
See also CA 118; CANR 92
Mora, Pat(ricia) 1942-
See also CA 129; CANR 57, 81; CLR 58; DAM MULT; DLB 209; HLC 2; HW 1, 2; SATA 92
Moraga, Cherrie 1952- .... **CLC 126; DAM MULT**
See also CA 131; CANR 66; DLB 82; HW 1, 2
Morand, Paul 1888-1976 .... **CLC 41; SSC 22**
See also CA 184; 69-72; DLB 65
Morante, Elsa 1918-1985 .... **CLC 8, 47**
See also CA 85-88; 117; CANR 35; DLB 177; MTCW 1, 2
Moravia, Alberto 1907-1990 .... **CLC 2, 7, 11, 27, 46; SSC 26**
See also Pincherle, Alberto
See also DLB 177; MTCW 2
More, Hannah 1745-1833 .... **NCLC 27**
See also DLB 107, 109, 116, 158
More, Henry 1614-1687 .... **LC 9**
See also DLB 126
More, Sir Thomas 1478-1535 .... **LC 10, 32**
Moreas, Jean TCLC 18
See also Papadiamantopoulos, Johannes
Morgan, Berry 1919- .... **CLC 6**
See also CA 49-52; DLB 6
Morgan, Claire
See Highsmith, (Mary) Patricia
Morgan, Edwin (George) 1920- .... **CLC 31**
See also CA 5-8R; CANR 3, 43, 90; DLB 27
Morgan, (George) Frederick 1922- .. **CLC 23**
See also CA 17-20R; CANR 21
Morgan, Harriet
See Mencken, H(enry) L(ouis)
Morgan, Jane
See Cooper, James Fenimore
Morgan, Janet 1945- .... **CLC 39**
See also CA 65-68
Morgan, Lady 1776(?)-1859 .... **NCLC 29**
See also DLB 116, 158
Morgan, Robin (Evonne) 1941- .... **CLC 2**
See also CA 69-72; CANR 29, 68; MTCW 1; SATA 80
Morgan, Scott
See Kuttner, Henry
Morgan, Seth 1949(?)-1990 .... **CLC 65**
See also CA 185; 132
Morgenstern, Christian 1871-1914 .. **TCLC 8**
See also CA 105
Morgenstern, S.
See Goldman, William (W.)
Moricz, Zsigmond 1879-1942 .... **TCLC 33**
See also CA 165
Morike, Eduard (Friedrich)
1804-1875 .... **NCLC 10**
See also DLB 133
Moritz, Karl Philipp 1756-1793 .... **LC 2**
See also DLB 94
Morland, Peter Henry
See Faust, Frederick (Schiller)
Morley, Christopher (Darlington)
1890-1957 .... **TCLC 87**
See also CA 112; DLB 9
Morren, Theophil
See Hofmannsthal, Hugo von
Morris, Bill 1952- .... **CLC 76**
Morris, Julian
See West, Morris L(anglo)
Morris, Steveland Judkins 1950(?)-
See Wonder, Stevie
See also CA 111
Morris, William 1834-1896 .... **NCLC 4**
See also CDBLB 1832-1890; DLB 18, 35, 57, 156, 178, 184
Morris, Wright 1910-1998 .. **CLC 1, 3, 7, 18, 37**
See also CA 9-12R; 167; CANR 21, 81; DLB 2, 206; DLBY 81; MTCW 1, 2
Morrison, Arthur 1863-1945 .... **TCLC 72; SSC 40**
See also CA 120; 157; DLB 70, 135, 197
Morrison, Chloe Anthony Wofford
See Morrison, Toni
Morrison, James Douglas 1943-1971
See Morrison, Jim
See also CA 73-76; CANR 40
Morrison, Jim CLC 17
See also Morrison, James Douglas
Morrison, Toni 1931- . **CLC 4, 10, 22, 55, 81, 87; BLC 3; DA; DAB; DAC; DAM MST, MULT, NOV, POP**
See also AAYA 1, 22; BW 2, 3; CA 29-32R; CANR 27, 42, 67; CDALB 1968-1988; DA3; DLB 6, 33, 143; DLBY 81; MTCW 1, 2; SATA 57
Morrison, Van 1945- .... **CLC 21**
See also CA 116; 168
Morrissy, Mary 1958- .... **CLC 99**
Mortimer, John (Clifford) 1923- ..... **CLC 28, 43; DAM DRAM, POP**
See also CA 13-16R; CANR 21, 69; CDBLB 1960 to Present; DA3; DLB 13; INT CANR-21; MTCW 1, 2
Mortimer, Penelope (Ruth)
1918-1999 .... **CLC 5**
See also CA 57-60; CANR 45, 88
Morton, Anthony
See Creasey, John

Ovid 43B.C.-17 . **CMLC 7; DAM POET; PC 2**
See also DA3; DLB 211
Owen, Hugh
See Faust, Frederick (Schiller)
Owen, Wilfred (Edward Salter) 1893-1918 .... **TCLC 5, 27; DA; DAB; DAC; DAM MST, POET; PC 19; WLC**
See also CA 104; 141; CDBLB 1914-1945; DLB 20; MTCW 2
Owens, Rochelle 1936- .... **CLC 8**
See also CA 17-20R; CAAS 2; CANR 39
Oz, Amos 1939- ...... **CLC 5, 8, 11, 27, 33, 54; DAM NOV**
See also CA 53-56; CANR 27, 47, 65; MTCW 1, 2
Ozick, Cynthia 1928- .... **CLC 3, 7, 28, 62; DAM NOV, POP; SSC 15**
See also BEST 90:1; CA 17-20R; CANR 23, 58; DA3; DLB 28, 152; DLBY 82; INT CANR-23; MTCW 1, 2
Ozu, Yasujiro 1903-1963 .... **CLC 16**
See also CA 112
Pacheco, C.
See Pessoa, Fernando (Antonio Nogueira)
Pacheco, Jose Emilio 1939-
See also CA 111; 131; CANR 65; DAM MULT; HLC 2; HW 1, 2
Pa Chin CLC 18
See also Li Fei-kan
Pack, Robert 1929- .... **CLC 13**
See also CA 1-4R; CANR 3, 44, 82; DLB 5
Padgett, Lewis
See Kuttner, Henry
Padilla (Lorenzo), Heberto 1932- ..... **CLC 38**
See also AITN 1; CA 123; 131; HW 1
Page, Jimmy 1944- .... **CLC 12**
Page, Louise 1955- .... **CLC 40**
See also CA 140; CANR 76
Page, P(atricia) K(athleen) 1916- ...... **CLC 7, 18; DAC; DAM MST; PC 12**
See also CA 53-56; CANR 4, 22, 65; DLB 68; MTCW 1
Page, Thomas Nelson 1853-1922 .... **SSC 23**
See also CA 118; 177; DLB 12, 78; DLBD 13
Pagels, Elaine Hiesey 1943- .... **CLC 104**
See also CA 45-48; CANR 2, 24, 51
Paget, Violet 1856-1935
See Lee, Vernon
See also CA 104; 166
Paget-Lowe, Henry
See Lovecraft, H(oward) P(hillips)
Paglia, Camille (Anna) 1947- .... **CLC 68**
See also CA 140; CANR 72; MTCW 2
Paige, Richard
See Koontz, Dean R(ay)
Paine, Thomas 1737-1809 .... **NCLC 62**
See also CDALB 1640-1865; DLB 31, 43, 73, 158
Pakenham, Antonia
See Fraser, (Lady) Antonia (Pakenham)
Palamas, Kostes 1859-1943 .... **TCLC 5**
See also CA 105
Palazzeschi, Aldo 1885-1974 .... **CLC 11**
See also CA 89-92; 53-56; DLB 114
Pales Matos, Luis 1898-1959
See also HLCS 2; HW 1
Paley, Grace 1922- .... **CLC 4, 6, 37; DAM POP; SSC 8**
See also CA 25-28R; CANR 13, 46, 74; DA3; DLB 28; INT CANR-13; MTCW 1, 2
Palin, Michael (Edward) 1943- .... **CLC 21**
See also Monty Python
See also CA 107; CANR 35; SATA 67
Palliser, Charles 1947- .... **CLC 65**
See also CA 136; CANR 76
Palma, Ricardo 1833-1919 .... **TCLC 29**
See also CA 168
Pancake, Breece Dexter 1952-1979
See Pancake, Breece D'J
See also CA 123; 109
Pancake, Breece D'J CLC 29
See also Pancake, Breece Dexter
See also DLB 130
Pankhurst, Emmeline (Goulden) 1858-1928 .... **TCLC 100**
See also CA 116
Panko, Rudy
See Gogol, Nikolai (Vasilyevich)
Papadiamantis, Alexandros 1851-1911 .... **TCLC 29**
See also CA 168
Papadiamantopoulos, Johannes 1856-1910
See Moreas, Jean
See also CA 117
Papini, Giovanni 1881-1956 .... **TCLC 22**
See also CA 121; 180
Paracelsus 1493-1541 .... **LC 14**
See also DLB 179
Parasol, Peter
See Stevens, Wallace
Pardo Bazan, Emilia 1851-1921 .... **SSC 30**
Pareto, Vilfredo 1848-1923 .... **TCLC 69**
See also CA 175
Parfenie, Maria
See Codrescu, Andrei
Parini, Jay (Lee) 1948- .... **CLC 54, 133**
See also CA 97-100; CAAS 16; CANR 32, 87
Park, Jordan
See Kornbluth, C(yril) M.; Pohl, Frederik
Park, Robert E(zra) 1864-1944 ..... **TCLC 73**
See also CA 122; 165
Parker, Bert
See Ellison, Harlan (Jay)
Parker, Dorothy (Rothschild) 1893-1967 .... **CLC 15, 68; DAM POET; PC 28; SSC 2**
See also CA 19-20; 25-28R; CAP 2; DA3; DLB 11, 45, 86; MTCW 1, 2
Parker, Robert B(rown) 1932- .... **CLC 27; DAM NOV, POP**
See also AAYA 28; BEST 89:4; CA 49-52; CANR 1, 26, 52, 89; INT CANR-26; MTCW 1
Parkin, Frank 1940- .... **CLC 43**
See also CA 147
Parkman, Francis Jr., Jr. 1823-1893 .... **NCLC 12**
See also DLB 1, 30, 186
Parks, Gordon (Alexander Buchanan) 1912- .... **CLC 1, 16; BLC 3; DAM MULT**
See also AITN 2; BW 2, 3; CA 41-44R; CANR 26, 66; DA3; DLB 33; MTCW 2; SATA 8, 108
Parmenides c. 515B.C.-c. 450B.C. .... **CMLC 22**
See also DLB 176
Parnell, Thomas 1679-1718 .... **LC 3**
See also DLB 94
Parra, Nicanor 1914- ...... **CLC 2, 102; DAM MULT; HLC 2**
See also CA 85-88; CANR 32; HW 1; MTCW 1
Parra Sanojo, Ana Teresa de la 1890-1936
See also HLCS 2
Parrish, Mary Frances
See Fisher, M(ary) F(rances) K(ennedy)
Parson
See Coleridge, Samuel Taylor
Parson Lot
See Kingsley, Charles
Parton, Sara Payson Willis 1811-1872 .... **NCLC 86**
See also DLB 43, 74
Partridge, Anthony
See Oppenheim, E(dward) Phillips
Pascal, Blaise 1623-1662 .... **LC 35**
Pascoli, Giovanni 1855-1912 .... **TCLC 45**
See also CA 170
Pasolini, Pier Paolo 1922-1975 .. **CLC 20, 37, 106; PC 17**
See also CA 93-96; 61-64; CANR 63; DLB 128, 177; MTCW 1
Pasquini
See Silone, Ignazio
Pastan, Linda (Olenik) 1932- .... **CLC 27; DAM POET**
See also CA 61-64; CANR 18, 40, 61; DLB 5
Pasternak, Boris (Leonidovich) 1890-1960 .... **CLC 7, 10, 18, 63; DA; DAB; DAC; DAM MST, NOV, POET; PC 6; SSC 31; WLC**
See also CA 127; 116; DA3; MTCW 1, 2
Patchen, Kenneth 1911-1972 .. **CLC 1, 2, 18; DAM POET**
See also CA 1-4R; 33-36R; CANR 3, 35; DLB 16, 48; MTCW 1
Pater, Walter (Horatio) 1839-1894 . **NCLC 7, 90**
See also CDBLB 1832-1890; DLB 57, 156
Paterson, A(ndrew) B(arton) 1864-1941 .... **TCLC 32**
See also CA 155; SATA 97
Paterson, Katherine (Womeldorf) 1932- .... **CLC 12, 30**
See also AAYA 1, 31; CA 21-24R; CANR 28, 59; CLR 7, 50; DLB 52; JRDA; MAICYA; MTCW 1; SATA 13, 53, 92
Patmore, Coventry Kersey Dighton 1823-1896 .... **NCLC 9**
See also DLB 35, 98
Paton, Alan (Stewart) 1903-1988 ...... **CLC 4, 10, 25, 55, 106; DA; DAB; DAC; DAM MST, NOV; WLC**
See also AAYA 26; CA 13-16; 125; CANR 22; CAP 1; DA3; DLB 225; DLBD 17; MTCW 1, 2; SATA 11; SATA-Obit 56
Paton Walsh, Gillian 1937- .... **CLC 35**
See also Walsh, Jill Paton
See also AAYA 11; CANR 38, 83; CLR 2, 65; DLB 161; JRDA; MAICYA; SAAS 3; SATA 4, 72, 109
Paton Walsh, Jill
See Paton Walsh, Gillian
Patton, George S. 1885-1945 .... **TCLC 79**
Paulding, James Kirke 1778-1860 ... **NCLC 2**
See also DLB 3, 59, 74
Paulin, Thomas Neilson 1949-
See Paulin, Tom
See also CA 123; 128
Paulin, Tom CLC 37
See also Paulin, Thomas Neilson
See also DLB 40
Pausanias c. 1st cent. - .... **CMLC 36**
Paustovsky, Konstantin (Georgievich) 1892-1968 .... **CLC 40**
See also CA 93-96; 25-28R
Pavese, Cesare 1908-1950 .. **TCLC 3; PC 13; SSC 19**
See also CA 104; 169; DLB 128, 177
Pavic, Milorad 1929- .... **CLC 60**
See also CA 136; DLB 181
Pavlov, Ivan Petrovich 1849-1936 . **TCLC 91**
See also CA 118; 180
Payne, Alan
See Jakes, John (William)
Paz, Gil
See Lugones, Leopoldo

Paz, Octavio 1914-1998 . **CLC 3, 4, 6, 10, 19, 51, 65, 119; DA; DAB; DAC; DAM MST, MULT, POET; HLC 2; PC 1; WLC**
See also CA 73-76; 165; CANR 32, 65; DA3; DLBY 90, 98; HW 1, 2; MTCW 1, 2
p'Bitek, Okot 1931-1982 .... **CLC 96; BLC 3; DAM MULT**
See also BW 2, 3; CA 124; 107; CANR 82; DLB 125; MTCW 1, 2
Peacock, Molly 1947- .... **CLC 60**
See also CA 103; CAAS 21; CANR 52, 84; DLB 120
Peacock, Thomas Love 1785-1866 .... **NCLC 22**
See also DLB 96, 116
Peake, Mervyn 1911-1968 .... **CLC 7, 54**
See also CA 5-8R; 25-28R; CANR 3; DLB 15, 160; MTCW 1; SATA 23
Pearce, Philippa CLC 21
See also Christie, (Ann) Philippa
See also CLR 9; DLB 161; MAICYA; SATA 1, 67
Pearl, Eric
See Elman, Richard (Martin)
Pearson, T(homas) R(eid) 1956- .... **CLC 39**
See also CA 120; 130; INT 130
Peck, Dale 1967- .... **CLC 81**
See also CA 146; CANR 72
Peck, John 1941- .... **CLC 3**
See also CA 49-52; CANR 3
Peck, Richard (Wayne) 1934- .... **CLC 21**
See also AAYA 1, 24; CA 85-88; CANR 19, 38; CLR 15; INT CANR-19; JRDA; MAICYA; SAAS 2; SATA 18, 55, 97; SATA-Essay 110
Peck, Robert Newton 1928- .... **CLC 17; DA; DAC; DAM MST**
See also AAYA 3; CA 81-84, 182; CAAE 182; CANR 31, 63; CLR 45; JRDA; MAICYA; SAAS 1; SATA 21, 62, 111; SATA-Essay 108
Peckinpah, (David) Sam(uel) 1925-1984 .... **CLC 20**
See also CA 109; 114; CANR 82
Pedersen, Knut 1859-1952
See Hamsun, Knut
See also CA 104; 119; CANR 63; MTCW 1, 2
Peeslake, Gaffer
See Durrell, Lawrence (George)
Peguy, Charles Pierre 1873-1914 ... **TCLC 10**
See also CA 107
Peirce, Charles Sanders 1839-1914 .... **TCLC 81**
Pellicer, Carlos 1900(?)-1977
See also CA 153; 69-72; HLCS 2; HW 1
Pena, Ramon del Valle y
See Valle-Inclan, Ramon (Maria) del
Pendennis, Arthur Esquir
See Thackeray, William Makepeace
Penn, William 1644-1718 .... **LC 25**
See also DLB 24
PEPECE
See Prado (Calvo), Pedro
Pepys, Samuel 1633-1703 ..... **LC 11, 58; DA; DAB; DAC; DAM MST; WLC**
See also CDBLB 1660-1789; DA3; DLB 101
Percy, Walker 1916-1990 .... **CLC 2, 3, 6, 8, 14, 18, 47, 65; DAM NOV, POP**
See also CA 1-4R; 131; CANR 1, 23, 64; DA3; DLB 2; DLBY 80, 90; MTCW 1, 2
Percy, William Alexander 1885-1942 .... **TCLC 84**
See also CA 163; MTCW 2
Perec, Georges 1936-1982 .... **CLC 56, 116**
See also CA 141; DLB 83
Pereda (y Sanchez de Porrua), Jose Maria de 1833-1906 .... **TCLC 16**
See also CA 117
Pereda y Porrua, Jose Maria de
See Pereda (y Sanchez de Porrua), Jose Maria de
Peregoy, George Weems
See Mencken, H(enry) L(ouis)
Perelman, S(idney) J(oseph) 1904-1979 .. **CLC 3, 5, 9, 15, 23, 44, 49; DAM DRAM; SSC 32**
See also AITN 1, 2; CA 73-76; 89-92; CANR 18; DLB 11, 44; MTCW 1, 2
Peret, Benjamin 1899-1959 .... **TCLC 20**
See also CA 117; 186
Peretz, Isaac Loeb 1851(?)-1915 ... **TCLC 16; SSC 26**
See also CA 109
Peretz, Yitzkhok Leibush
See Peretz, Isaac Loeb
Perez Galdos, Benito 1843-1920 ... **TCLC 27; HLCS 2**
See also CA 125; 153; HW 1
Peri Rossi, Cristina 1941-
See also CA 131; CANR 59, 81; DLB 145; HLCS 2; HW 1, 2
Perlata
See Peret, Benjamin
Perrault, Charles 1628-1703 ... **LC 3, 52; DC 12**
See also MAICYA; SATA 25
Perry, Anne 1938- .... **CLC 126**
See also CA 101; CANR 22, 50, 84
Perry, Brighton
See Sherwood, Robert E(mmet)
Perse, St.-John
See Leger, (Marie-Rene Auguste) Alexis Saint-Leger
Perutz, Leo(pold) 1882-1957 .... **TCLC 60**
See also CA 147; DLB 81
Peseenz, Tulio F.
See Lopez y Fuentes, Gregorio
Pesetsky, Bette 1932- .... **CLC 28**
See also CA 133; DLB 130
Peshkov, Alexei Maximovich 1868-1936
See Gorky, Maxim
See also CA 105; 141; CANR 83; DA; DAC; DAM DRAM, MST, NOV; MTCW 2
Pessoa, Fernando (Antonio Nogueira) 1888-1935 .... **TCLC 27; DAM MULT; HLC 2; PC 20**
See also CA 125; 183
Peterkin, Julia Mood 1880-1961 ...... **CLC 31**
See also CA 102; DLB 9
Peters, Joan K(aren) 1945- .... **CLC 39**
See also CA 158
Peters, Robert L(ouis) 1924- .... **CLC 7**
See also CA 13-16R; CAAS 8; DLB 105
Petofi, Sandor 1823-1849 .... **NCLC 21**
Petrakis, Harry Mark 1923- .... **CLC 3**
See also CA 9-12R; CANR 4, 30, 85
Petrarch 1304-1374 .... **CMLC 20; DAM POET; PC 8**
See also DA3
Petronius c. 20-66 .... **CMLC 34**
See also DLB 211
Petrov, Evgeny TCLC 21
See also Kataev, Evgeny Petrovich
Petry, Ann (Lane) 1908-1997 ... **CLC 1, 7, 18**
See also BW 1, 3; CA 5-8R; 157; CAAS 6; CANR 4, 46; CLR 12; DLB 76; JRDA; MAICYA; MTCW 1; SATA 5; SATA-Obit 94
Petursson, Halligrimur 1614-1674 .... **LC 8**
Peychinovich
See Vazov, Ivan (Minchov)
Phaedrus c. 18B.C.-c. 50 .... **CMLC 25**
See also DLB 211
Philips, Katherine 1632-1664 .... **LC 30**
See also DLB 131
Philipson, Morris H. 1926- .... **CLC 53**
See also CA 1-4R; CANR 4
Phillips, Caryl 1958- . **CLC 96; BLCS; DAM MULT**
See also BW 2; CA 141; CANR 63; DA3; DLB 157; MTCW 2
Phillips, David Graham 1867-1911 .... **TCLC 44**
See also CA 108; 176; DLB 9, 12
Phillips, Jack
See Sandburg, Carl (August)
Phillips, Jayne Anne 1952- .... **CLC 15, 33; SSC 16**
See also CA 101; CANR 24, 50; DLBY 80; INT CANR-24; MTCW 1, 2
Phillips, Richard
See Dick, Philip K(indred)
Phillips, Robert (Schaeffer) 1938- .... **CLC 28**
See also CA 17-20R; CAAS 13; CANR 8; DLB 105
Phillips, Ward
See Lovecraft, H(oward) P(hillips)
Piccolo, Lucio 1901-1969 .... **CLC 13**
See also CA 97-100; DLB 114
Pickthall, Marjorie L(owry) C(hristie) 1883-1922 .... **TCLC 21**
See also CA 107; DLB 92
Pico della Mirandola, Giovanni 1463-1494 .... **LC 15**
Piercy, Marge 1936- .... **CLC 3, 6, 14, 18, 27, 62, 128; PC 29**
See also CA 21-24R; CAAS 1; CANR 13, 43, 66; DLB 120, 227; MTCW 1, 2
Piers, Robert
See Anthony, Piers
Pieyre de Mandiargues, Andre 1909-1991
See Mandiargues, Andre Pieyre de
See also CA 103; 136; CANR 22, 82
Pilnyak, Boris TCLC 23
See also Vogau, Boris Andreyevich
Pincherle, Alberto 1907-1990 .... **CLC 11, 18; DAM NOV**
See also Moravia, Alberto
See also CA 25-28R; 132; CANR 33, 63; MTCW 1
Pinckney, Darryl 1953- .... **CLC 76**
See also BW 2, 3; CA 143; CANR 79
Pindar 518B.C.-446B.C. .... **CMLC 12; PC 19**
See also DLB 176
Pineda, Cecile 1942- .... **CLC 39**
See also CA 118
Pinero, Arthur Wing 1855-1934 ... **TCLC 32; DAM DRAM**
See also CA 110; 153; DLB 10
Pinero, Miguel (Antonio Gomez) 1946-1988 .... **CLC 4, 55**
See also CA 61-64; 125; CANR 29, 90; HW 1
Pinget, Robert 1919-1997 .... **CLC 7, 13, 37**
See also CA 85-88; 160; DLB 83
Pink Floyd
See Barrett, (Roger) Syd; Gilmour, David; Mason, Nick; Waters, Roger; Wright, Rick
Pinkney, Edward 1802-1828 .... **NCLC 31**
Pinkwater, Daniel Manus 1941- .... **CLC 35**
See also Pinkwater, Manus
See also AAYA 1; CA 29-32R; CANR 12, 38, 89; CLR 4; JRDA; MAICYA; SAAS 3; SATA 46, 76, 114
Pinkwater, Manus
See Pinkwater, Daniel Manus
See also SATA 8

Author Index

Author Index

Rich, Adrienne (Cecile) 1929- ... **CLC 3, 6, 7, 11, 18, 36, 73, 76, 125; DAM POET; PC 5**
See also CA 9-12R; CANR 20, 53, 74; CDALBS; DA3; DLB 5, 67; MTCW 1, 2
Rich, Barbara
See Graves, Robert (von Ranke)
Rich, Robert
See Trumbo, Dalton
Richard, Keith CLC 17
See also Richards, Keith
Richards, David Adams 1950- .... **CLC 59; DAC**
See also CA 93-96; CANR 60; DLB 53
Richards, I(vor) A(rmstrong) 1893-1979 .... **CLC 14, 24**
See also CA 41-44R; 89-92; CANR 34, 74; DLB 27; MTCW 2
Richards, Keith 1943-
See Richard, Keith
See also CA 107; CANR 77
Richardson, Anne
See Roiphe, Anne (Richardson)
Richardson, Dorothy Miller 1873-1957 .... **TCLC 3**
See also CA 104; DLB 36
Richardson, Ethel Florence (Lindesay) 1870-1946
See Richardson, Henry Handel
See also CA 105
Richardson, Henry Handel TCLC 4
See also Richardson, Ethel Florence (Lindesay)
See also DLB 197
Richardson, John 1796-1852 .... **NCLC 55; DAC**
See also DLB 99
Richardson, Samuel 1689-1761 ...... **LC 1, 44; DA; DAB; DAC; DAM MST, NOV; WLC**
See also CDBLB 1660-1789; DLB 39
Richler, Mordecai 1931- ...... **CLC 3, 5, 9, 13, 18, 46, 70; DAC; DAM MST, NOV**
See also AITN 1; CA 65-68; CANR 31, 62; CLR 17; DLB 53; MAICYA; MTCW 1, 2; SATA 44, 98; SATA-Brief 27
Richter, Conrad (Michael) 1890-1968 .... **CLC 30**
See also AAYA 21; CA 5-8R; 25-28R; CANR 23; DLB 9, 212; MTCW 1, 2; SATA 3
Ricostranza, Tom
See Ellis, Trey
Riddell, Charlotte 1832-1906 .... **TCLC 40**
See also CA 165; DLB 156
Ridge, John Rollin 1827-1867 ...... **NCLC 82; DAM MULT**
See also CA 144; DLB 175; NNAL
Ridgway, Keith 1965- .... **CLC 119**
See also CA 172
Riding, Laura CLC 3, 7
See also Jackson, Laura (Riding)
Riefenstahl, Berta Helene Amalia 1902-
See Riefenstahl, Leni
See also CA 108
Riefenstahl, Leni CLC 16
See also Riefenstahl, Berta Helene Amalia
Riffe, Ernest
See Bergman, (Ernst) Ingmar
Riggs, (Rolla) Lynn 1899-1954 ..... **TCLC 56; DAM MULT**
See also CA 144; DLB 175; NNAL
Riis, Jacob A(ugust) 1849-1914 ..... **TCLC 80**
See also CA 113; 168; DLB 23
Riley, James Whitcomb 1849-1916 .... **TCLC 51; DAM POET**
See also CA 118; 137; MAICYA; SATA 17
Riley, Tex
See Creasey, John
Rilke, Rainer Maria 1875-1926 .. **TCLC 1, 6, 19; DAM POET; PC 2**
See also CA 104; 132; CANR 62; DA3; DLB 81; MTCW 1, 2
Rimbaud, (Jean Nicolas) Arthur 1854-1891 . **NCLC 4, 35, 82; DA; DAB; DAC; DAM MST, POET; PC 3; WLC**
See also DA3
Rinehart, Mary Roberts 1876-1958 .... **TCLC 52**
See also CA 108; 166
Ringmaster, The
See Mencken, H(enry) L(ouis)
Ringwood, Gwen(dolyn Margaret) Pharis 1910-1984 .... **CLC 48**
See also CA 148; 112; DLB 88
Rio, Michel 19(?)- .... **CLC 43**
Ritsos, Giannes
See Ritsos, Yannis
Ritsos, Yannis 1909-1990 .... **CLC 6, 13, 31**
See also CA 77-80; 133; CANR 39, 61; MTCW 1
Ritter, Erika 1948(?)- .... **CLC 52**
Rivera, Jose Eustasio 1889-1928 ... **TCLC 35**
See also CA 162; HW 1, 2
Rivera, Tomas 1935-1984
See also CA 49-52; CANR 32; DLB 82; HLCS 2; HW 1
Rivers, Conrad Kent 1933-1968 .... **CLC 1**
See also BW 1; CA 85-88; DLB 41
Rivers, Elfrida
See Bradley, Marion Zimmer
Riverside, John
See Heinlein, Robert A(nson)
Rizal, Jose 1861-1896 .... **NCLC 27**
Roa Bastos, Augusto (Antonio) 1917- .... **CLC 45; DAM MULT; HLC 2**
See also CA 131; DLB 113; HW 1
Robbe-Grillet, Alain 1922- .... **CLC 1, 2, 4, 6, 8, 10, 14, 43, 128**
See also CA 9-12R; CANR 33, 65; DLB 83; MTCW 1, 2
Robbins, Harold 1916-1997 .... **CLC 5; DAM NOV**
See also CA 73-76; 162; CANR 26, 54; DA3; MTCW 1, 2
Robbins, Thomas Eugene 1936-
See Robbins, Tom
See also CA 81-84; CANR 29, 59; DAM NOV, POP; DA3; MTCW 1, 2
Robbins, Tom CLC 9, 32, 64
See also Robbins, Thomas Eugene
See also AAYA 32; BEST 90:3; DLBY 80; MTCW 2
Robbins, Trina 1938- .... **CLC 21**
See also CA 128
Roberts, Charles G(eorge) D(ouglas) 1860-1943 .... **TCLC 8**
See also CA 105; CLR 33; DLB 92; SATA 88; SATA-Brief 29
Roberts, Elizabeth Madox 1886-1941 .... **TCLC 68**
See also CA 111; 166; DLB 9, 54, 102; SATA 33; SATA-Brief 27
Roberts, Kate 1891-1985 .... **CLC 15**
See also CA 107; 116
Roberts, Keith (John Kingston) 1935- .... **CLC 14**
See also CA 25-28R; CANR 46
Roberts, Kenneth (Lewis) 1885-1957 .... **TCLC 23**
See also CA 109; DLB 9
Roberts, Michele (B.) 1949- .... **CLC 48**
See also CA 115; CANR 58
Robertson, Ellis
See Ellison, Harlan (Jay); Silverberg, Robert
Robertson, Thomas William 1829-1871 .... **NCLC 35; DAM DRAM**
Robeson, Kenneth
See Dent, Lester
Robinson, Edwin Arlington 1869-1935 ... **TCLC 5; DA; DAC; DAM MST, POET; PC 1**
See also CA 104; 133; CDALB 1865-1917; DLB 54; MTCW 1, 2
Robinson, Henry Crabb 1775-1867 .... **NCLC 15**
See also DLB 107
Robinson, Jill 1936- .... **CLC 10**
See also CA 102; INT 102
Robinson, Kim Stanley 1952- .... **CLC 34**
See also AAYA 26; CA 126; SATA 109
Robinson, Lloyd
See Silverberg, Robert
Robinson, Marilynne 1944- .... **CLC 25**
See also CA 116; CANR 80; DLB 206
Robinson, Smokey CLC 21
See also Robinson, William, Jr.
Robinson, William, Jr. 1940-
See Robinson, Smokey
See also CA 116
Robison, Mary 1949- .... **CLC 42, 98**
See also CA 113; 116; CANR 87; DLB 130; INT 116
Rod, Edouard 1857-1910 .... **TCLC 52**
Roddenberry, Eugene Wesley 1921-1991
See Roddenberry, Gene
See also CA 110; 135; CANR 37; SATA 45; SATA-Obit 69
Roddenberry, Gene CLC 17
See also Roddenberry, Eugene Wesley
See also AAYA 5; SATA-Obit 69
Rodgers, Mary 1931- .... **CLC 12**
See also CA 49-52; CANR 8, 55, 90; CLR 20; INT CANR-8; JRDA; MAICYA; SATA 8
Rodgers, W(illiam) R(obert) 1909-1969 .... **CLC 7**
See also CA 85-88; DLB 20
Rodman, Eric
See Silverberg, Robert
Rodman, Howard 1920(?)-1985 .... **CLC 65**
See also CA 118
Rodman, Maia
See Wojciechowska, Maia (Teresa)
Rodo, Jose Enrique 1872(?)-1917
See also CA 178; HLCS 2; HW 2
Rodriguez, Claudio 1934- .... **CLC 10**
See also DLB 134
Rodriguez, Richard 1944-
See also CA 110; CANR 66; DAM MULT; DLB 82; HLC 2; HW 1, 2
Roelvaag, O(le) E(dvart) 1876-1931 .... **TCLC 17**
See also Rolvaag, O(le) E(dvart)
See also CA 117; 171; DLB 9
Roethke, Theodore (Huebner) 1908-1963 .... **CLC 1, 3, 8, 11, 19, 46, 101; DAM POET; PC 15**
See also CA 81-84; CABS 2; CDALB 1941-1968; DA3; DLB 5, 206; MTCW 1, 2
Rogers, Samuel 1763-1855 .... **NCLC 69**
See also DLB 93
Rogers, Thomas Hunton 1927- .... **CLC 57**
See also CA 89-92; INT 89-92
Rogers, Will(iam Penn Adair) 1879-1935 ... **TCLC 8, 71; DAM MULT**
See also CA 105; 144; DA3; DLB 11; MTCW 2; NNAL
Rogin, Gilbert 1929- .... **CLC 18**
See also CA 65-68; CANR 15
Rohan, Koda
See Koda Shigeyuki

Satyremont
See Peret, Benjamin
Saul, John (W. III) 1942- ...... **CLC 46; DAM NOV, POP**
See also AAYA 10; BEST 90:4; CA 81-84; CANR 16, 40, 81; SATA 98
Saunders, Caleb
See Heinlein, Robert A(nson)
Saura (Atares), Carlos 1932- .... **CLC 20**
See also CA 114; 131; CANR 79; HW 1
Sauser-Hall, Frederic 1887-1961 ...... **CLC 18**
See also Cendrars, Blaise
See also CA 102; 93-96; CANR 36, 62; MTCW 1
Saussure, Ferdinand de 1857-1913 .... **TCLC 49**
Savage, Catharine
See Brosman, Catharine Savage
Savage, Thomas 1915- .... **CLC 40**
See also CA 126; 132; CAAS 15; INT 132
Savan, Glenn 19(?)- .... **CLC 50**
Sayers, Dorothy L(eigh) 1893-1957 .... **TCLC 2, 15; DAM POP**
See also CA 104; 119; CANR 60; CDBLB 1914-1945; DLB 10, 36, 77, 100; MTCW 1, 2
Sayers, Valerie 1952- .... **CLC 50, 122**
See also CA 134; CANR 61
Sayles, John (Thomas) 1950- . **CLC 7, 10, 14**
See also CA 57-60; CANR 41, 84; DLB 44
Scammell, Michael 1935- .... **CLC 34**
See also CA 156
Scannell, Vernon 1922- .... **CLC 49**
See also CA 5-8R; CANR 8, 24, 57; DLB 27; SATA 59
Scarlett, Susan
See Streatfeild, (Mary) Noel
Scarron
See Mikszath, Kalman
Schaeffer, Susan Fromberg 1941- ..... **CLC 6, 11, 22**
See also CA 49-52; CANR 18, 65; DLB 28; MTCW 1, 2; SATA 22
Schary, Jill
See Robinson, Jill
Schell, Jonathan 1943- .... **CLC 35**
See also CA 73-76; CANR 12
Schelling, Friedrich Wilhelm Joseph von 1775-1854 .... **NCLC 30**
See also DLB 90
Schendel, Arthur van 1874-1946 ... **TCLC 56**
Scherer, Jean-Marie Maurice 1920-
See Rohmer, Eric
See also CA 110
Schevill, James (Erwin) 1920- .... **CLC 7**
See also CA 5-8R; CAAS 12
Schiller, Friedrich 1759-1805 . **NCLC 39, 69; DAM DRAM; DC 12**
See also DLB 94
Schisgal, Murray (Joseph) 1926- .... **CLC 6**
See also CA 21-24R; CANR 48, 86
Schlee, Ann 1934- .... **CLC 35**
See also CA 101; CANR 29, 88; SATA 44; SATA-Brief 36
Schlegel, August Wilhelm von 1767-1845 .... **NCLC 15**
See also DLB 94
Schlegel, Friedrich 1772-1829 .... **NCLC 45**
See also DLB 90
Schlegel, Johann Elias (von) 1719(?)-1749 .... **LC 5**
Schlesinger, Arthur M(eier), Jr. 1917- .... **CLC 84**
See also AITN 1; CA 1-4R; CANR 1, 28, 58; DLB 17; INT CANR-28; MTCW 1, 2; SATA 61
Schmidt, Arno (Otto) 1914-1979 ...... **CLC 56**
See also CA 128; 109; DLB 69
Schmitz, Aron Hector 1861-1928
See Svevo, Italo
See also CA 104; 122; MTCW 1
Schnackenberg, Gjertrud 1953- .... **CLC 40**
See also CA 116; DLB 120
Schneider, Leonard Alfred 1925-1966
See Bruce, Lenny
See also CA 89-92
Schnitzler, Arthur 1862-1931 . **TCLC 4; SSC 15**
See also CA 104; DLB 81, 118
Schoenberg, Arnold 1874-1951 ...... **TCLC 75**
See also CA 109
Schonberg, Arnold
See Schoenberg, Arnold
Schopenhauer, Arthur 1788-1860 .. **NCLC 51**
See also DLB 90
Schor, Sandra (M.) 1932(?)-1990 ..... **CLC 65**
See also CA 132
Schorer, Mark 1908-1977 .... **CLC 9**
See also CA 5-8R; 73-76; CANR 7; DLB 103
Schrader, Paul (Joseph) 1946- .... **CLC 26**
See also CA 37-40R; CANR 41; DLB 44
Schreiner, Olive (Emilie Albertina) 1855-1920 .... **TCLC 9**
See also CA 105; 154; DLB 18, 156, 190, 225
Schulberg, Budd (Wilson) 1914- .. **CLC 7, 48**
See also CA 25-28R; CANR 19, 87; DLB 6, 26, 28; DLBY 81
Schulz, Bruno 1892-1942 .. **TCLC 5, 51; SSC 13**
See also CA 115; 123; CANR 86; MTCW 2
Schulz, Charles M(onroe) 1922-2000 .... **CLC 12**
See also CA 9-12R; CANR 6; INT CANR-6; SATA 10
Schumacher, E(rnst) F(riedrich) 1911-1977 .... **CLC 80**
See also CA 81-84; 73-76; CANR 34, 85
Schuyler, James Marcus 1923-1991 .. **CLC 5, 23; DAM POET**
See also CA 101; 134; DLB 5, 169; INT 101
Schwartz, Delmore (David) 1913-1966 ... **CLC 2, 4, 10, 45, 87; PC 8**
See also CA 17-18; 25-28R; CANR 35; CAP 2; DLB 28, 48; MTCW 1, 2
Schwartz, Ernst
See Ozu, Yasujiro
Schwartz, John Burnham 1965- .... **CLC 59**
See also CA 132
Schwartz, Lynne Sharon 1939- .... **CLC 31**
See also CA 103; CANR 44, 89; MTCW 2
Schwartz, Muriel A.
See Eliot, T(homas) S(tearns)
Schwarz-Bart, Andre 1928- .... **CLC 2, 4**
See also CA 89-92
Schwarz-Bart, Simone 1938- . **CLC 7; BLCS**
See also BW 2; CA 97-100
Schwitters, Kurt (Hermann Edward Karl Julius) 1887-1948 .... **TCLC 95**
See also CA 158
Schwob, Marcel (Mayer Andre) 1867-1905 .... **TCLC 20**
See also CA 117; 168; DLB 123
Sciascia, Leonardo 1921-1989 .. **CLC 8, 9, 41**
See also CA 85-88; 130; CANR 35; DLB 177; MTCW 1
Scoppettone, Sandra 1936- .... **CLC 26**
See also AAYA 11; CA 5-8R; CANR 41, 73; SATA 9, 92
Scorsese, Martin 1942- .... **CLC 20, 89**
See also CA 110; 114; CANR 46, 85
Scotland, Jay
See Jakes, John (William)
Scott, Duncan Campbell 1862-1947 .... **TCLC 6; DAC**
See also CA 104; 153; DLB 92
Scott, Evelyn 1893-1963 .... **CLC 43**
See also CA 104; 112; CANR 64; DLB 9, 48
Scott, F(rancis) R(eginald) 1899-1985 .... **CLC 22**
See also CA 101; 114; CANR 87; DLB 88; INT 101
Scott, Frank
See Scott, F(rancis) R(eginald)
Scott, Joanna 1960- .... **CLC 50**
See also CA 126; CANR 53, 92
Scott, Paul (Mark) 1920-1978 ...... **CLC 9, 60**
See also CA 81-84; 77-80; CANR 33; DLB 14, 207; MTCW 1
Scott, Sarah 1723-1795 .... **LC 44**
See also DLB 39
Scott, Walter 1771-1832 . **NCLC 15, 69; DA; DAB; DAC; DAM MST, NOV, POET; PC 13; SSC 32; WLC**
See also AAYA 22; CDBLB 1789-1832; DLB 93, 107, 116, 144, 159; YABC 2
Scribe, (Augustin) Eugene 1791-1861 ..... **NCLC 16; DAM DRAM; DC 5**
See also DLB 192
Scrum, R.
See Crumb, R(obert)
Scudery, Madeleine de 1607-1701 .. **LC 2, 58**
Scum
See Crumb, R(obert)
Scumbag, Little Bobby
See Crumb, R(obert)
Seabrook, John
See Hubbard, L(afayette) Ron(ald)
Sealy, I(rwin) Allan 1951- .... **CLC 55**
See also CA 136
Search, Alexander
See Pessoa, Fernando (Antonio Nogueira)
Sebastian, Lee
See Silverberg, Robert
Sebastian Owl
See Thompson, Hunter S(tockton)
Sebestyen, Ouida 1924- .... **CLC 30**
See also AAYA 8; CA 107; CANR 40; CLR 17; JRDA; MAICYA; SAAS 10; SATA 39
Secundus, H. Scriblerus
See Fielding, Henry
Sedges, John
See Buck, Pearl S(ydenstricker)
Sedgwick, Catharine Maria 1789-1867 .... **NCLC 19**
See also DLB 1, 74
Seelye, John (Douglas) 1931- .... **CLC 7**
See also CA 97-100; CANR 70; INT 97-100
Seferiades, Giorgos Stylianou 1900-1971
See Seferis, George
See also CA 5-8R; 33-36R; CANR 5, 36; MTCW 1
Seferis, George CLC 5, 11
See also Seferiades, Giorgos Stylianou
Segal, Erich (Wolf) 1937- . **CLC 3, 10; DAM POP**
See also BEST 89:1; CA 25-28R; CANR 20, 36, 65; DLBY 86; INT CANR-20; MTCW 1
Seger, Bob 1945- .... **CLC 35**
Seghers, Anna CLC 7
See also Radvanyi, Netty
See also DLB 69
Seidel, Frederick (Lewis) 1936- .... **CLC 18**
See also CA 13-16R; CANR 8; DLBY 84
Seifert, Jaroslav 1901-1986 .. **CLC 34, 44, 93**
See also CA 127; MTCW 1, 2

Sei Shonagon c. 966-1017(?) .... **CMLC 6**
Séjour, Victor 1817-1874 .... **DC 10**
See also DLB 50
Sejour Marcou et Ferrand, Juan Victor
See S
Selby, Hubert, Jr. 1928- .... **CLC 1, 2, 4, 8; SSC 20**
See also CA 13-16R; CANR 33, 85; DLB 2, 227
Selzer, Richard 1928- .... **CLC 74**
See also CA 65-68; CANR 14
Sembene, Ousmane
See Ousmane, Sembene
Senancour, Etienne Pivert de 1770-1846 .... **NCLC 16**
See also DLB 119
Sender, Ramon (Jose) 1902-1982 ...... **CLC 8; DAM MULT; HLC 2**
See also CA 5-8R; 105; CANR 8; HW 1; MTCW 1
Seneca, Lucius Annaeus c. 1-c. 65 .... **CMLC 6; DAM DRAM; DC 5**
See also DLB 211
Senghor, Leopold Sedar 1906- .... **CLC 54, 130; BLC 3; DAM MULT, POET; PC 25**
See also BW 2; CA 116; 125; CANR 47, 74; MTCW 1, 2
Senna, Danzy 1970- .... **CLC 119**
See also CA 169
Serling, (Edward) Rod(man) 1924-1975 .... **CLC 30**
See also AAYA 14; AITN 1; CA 162; 57-60; DLB 26
Serna, Ramon Gomez de la
See Gomez de la Serna, Ramon
Serpieres
See Guillevic, (Eugene)
Service, Robert
See Service, Robert W(illiam)
See also DAB; DLB 92
Service, Robert W(illiam) 1874(?)-1958 .... **TCLC 15; DA; DAC; DAM MST, POET; WLC**
See also Service, Robert
See also CA 115; 140; CANR 84; SATA 20
Seth, Vikram 1952- .... **CLC 43, 90; DAM MULT**
See also CA 121; 127; CANR 50, 74; DA3; DLB 120; INT 127; MTCW 2
Seton, Cynthia Propper 1926-1982 .. **CLC 27**
See also CA 5-8R; 108; CANR 7
Seton, Ernest (Evan) Thompson 1860-1946 .... **TCLC 31**
See also CA 109; CLR 59; DLB 92; DLBD 13; JRDA; SATA 18
Seton-Thompson, Ernest
See Seton, Ernest (Evan) Thompson
Settle, Mary Lee 1918- .... **CLC 19, 61**
See also CA 89-92; CAAS 1; CANR 44, 87; DLB 6; INT 89-92
Seuphor, Michel
See Arp, Jean
Sevigne, Marie (de Rabutin-Chantal) Marquise de 1626-1696 .... **LC 11**
Sewall, Samuel 1652-1730 .... **LC 38**
See also DLB 24
Sexton, Anne (Harvey) 1928-1974 ..... **CLC 2, 4, 6, 8, 10, 15, 53; DA; DAB; DAC; DAM MST, POET; PC 2; WLC**
See also CA 1-4R; 53-56; CABS 2; CANR 3, 36; CDALB 1941-1968; DA3; DLB 5, 169; MTCW 1, 2; SATA 10
Shaara, Jeff 1952- .... **CLC 119**
See also CA 163
Shaara, Michael (Joseph, Jr.) 1929-1988 .... **CLC 15; DAM POP**
See also AITN 1; CA 102; 125; CANR 52, 85; DLBY 83
Shackleton, C. C.
See Aldiss, Brian W(ilson)
Shacochis, Bob CLC 39
See also Shacochis, Robert G.
Shacochis, Robert G. 1951-
See Shacochis, Bob
See also CA 119; 124; INT 124
Shaffer, Anthony (Joshua) 1926- ..... **CLC 19; DAM DRAM**
See also CA 110; 116; DLB 13
Shaffer, Peter (Levin) 1926- .. **CLC 5, 14, 18, 37, 60; DAB; DAM DRAM, MST; DC 7**
See also CA 25-28R; CANR 25, 47, 74; CDBLB 1960 to Present; DA3; DLB 13; MTCW 1, 2
Shakey, Bernard
See Young, Neil
Shalamov, Varlam (Tikhonovich) 1907(?)-1982 .... **CLC 18**
See also CA 129; 105
Shamlu, Ahmad 1925- .... **CLC 10**
Shammas, Anton 1951- .... **CLC 55**
Shandling, Arline
See Berriault, Gina
Shange, Ntozake 1948- .... **CLC 8, 25, 38, 74, 126; BLC 3; DAM DRAM, MULT; DC 3**
See also AAYA 9; BW 2; CA 85-88; CABS 3; CANR 27, 48, 74; DA3; DLB 38; MTCW 1, 2
Shanley, John Patrick 1950- .... **CLC 75**
See also CA 128; 133; CANR 83
Shapcott, Thomas W(illiam) 1935- .. **CLC 38**
See also CA 69-72; CANR 49, 83
Shapiro, Jane CLC 76
Shapiro, Karl (Jay) 1913- . **CLC 4, 8, 15, 53; PC 25**
See also CA 1-4R; CAAS 6; CANR 1, 36, 66; DLB 48; MTCW 1, 2
Sharp, William 1855-1905 .... **TCLC 39**
See also CA 160; DLB 156
Sharpe, Thomas Ridley 1928-
See Sharpe, Tom
See also CA 114; 122; CANR 85; INT 122
Sharpe, Tom CLC 36
See also Sharpe, Thomas Ridley
See also DLB 14
Shaw, Bernard
See Shaw, George Bernard
See also BW 1; MTCW 2
Shaw, G. Bernard
See Shaw, George Bernard
Shaw, George Bernard 1856-1950 .. **TCLC 3, 9, 21, 45; DA; DAB; DAC; DAM DRAM, MST; WLC**
See also Shaw, Bernard
See also CA 104; 128; CDBLB 1914-1945; DA3; DLB 10, 57, 190; MTCW 1, 2
Shaw, Henry Wheeler 1818-1885 .. **NCLC 15**
See also DLB 11
Shaw, Irwin 1913-1984 .... **CLC 7, 23, 34; DAM DRAM, POP**
See also AITN 1; CA 13-16R; 112; CANR 21; CDALB 1941-1968; DLB 6, 102; DLBY 84; MTCW 1, 21
Shaw, Robert 1927-1978 .... **CLC 5**
See also AITN 1; CA 1-4R; 81-84; CANR 4; DLB 13, 14
Shaw, T. E.
See Lawrence, T(homas) E(dward)
Shawn, Wallace 1943- .... **CLC 41**
See also CA 112
Shea, Lisa 1953- .... **CLC 86**
See also CA 147
Sheed, Wilfrid (John Joseph) 1930- . **CLC 2, 4, 10, 53**
See also CA 65-68; CANR 30, 66; DLB 6; MTCW 1, 2
Sheldon, Alice Hastings Bradley 1915(?)-1987
See Tiptree, James, Jr.
See also CA 108; 122; CANR 34; INT 108; MTCW 1
Sheldon, John
See Bloch, Robert (Albert)
Shelley, Mary Wollstonecraft (Godwin) 1797-1851 ..... **NCLC 14, 59; DA; DAB; DAC; DAM MST, NOV; WLC**
See also AAYA 20; CDBLB 1789-1832; DA3; DLB 110, 116, 159, 178; SATA 29
Shelley, Percy Bysshe 1792-1822 .. **NCLC 18; DA; DAB; DAC; DAM MST, POET; PC 14; WLC**
See also CDBLB 1789-1832; DA3; DLB 96, 110, 158
Shepard, Jim 1956- .... **CLC 36**
See also CA 137; CANR 59; SATA 90
Shepard, Lucius 1947- .... **CLC 34**
See also CA 128; 141; CANR 81
Shepard, Sam 1943- .... **CLC 4, 6, 17, 34, 41, 44; DAM DRAM; DC 5**
See also AAYA 1; CA 69-72; CABS 3; CANR 22; DA3; DLB 7, 212; MTCW 1, 2
Shepherd, Michael
See Ludlum, Robert
Sherburne, Zoa (Lillian Morin) 1912-1995 .... **CLC 30**
See also AAYA 13; CA 1-4R; 176; CANR 3, 37; MAICYA; SAAS 18; SATA 3
Sheridan, Frances 1724-1766 .... **LC 7**
See also DLB 39, 84
Sheridan, Richard Brinsley 1751-1816 .... **NCLC 5, 91; DA; DAB; DAC; DAM DRAM, MST; DC 1; WLC**
See also CDBLB 1660-1789; DLB 89
Sherman, Jonathan Marc CLC 55
Sherman, Martin 1941(?)- .... **CLC 19**
See also CA 116; 123; CANR 86
Sherwin, Judith Johnson 1936-
See Johnson, Judith (Emlyn)
See also CANR 85
Sherwood, Frances 1940- .... **CLC 81**
See also CA 146
Sherwood, Robert E(mmet) 1896-1955 .... **TCLC 3; DAM DRAM**
See also CA 104; 153; CANR 86; DLB 7, 26
Shestov, Lev 1866-1938 .... **TCLC 56**
Shevchenko, Taras 1814-1861 .... **NCLC 54**
Shiel, M(atthew) P(hipps) 1865-1947 .... **TCLC 8**
See also Holmes, Gordon
See also CA 106; 160; DLB 153; MTCW 2
Shields, Carol 1935- .... **CLC 91, 113; DAC**
See also CA 81-84; CANR 51, 74; DA3; MTCW 2
Shields, David 1956- .... **CLC 97**
See also CA 124; CANR 48
Shiga, Naoya 1883-1971 ..... **CLC 33; SSC 23**
See also CA 101; 33-36R; DLB 180
Shikibu, Murasaki c. 978-c. 1014 ... **CMLC 1**
Shilts, Randy 1951-1994 .... **CLC 85**
See also AAYA 19; CA 115; 127; 144; CANR 45; DA3; INT 127; MTCW 2
Shimazaki, Haruki 1872-1943
See Shimazaki Toson
See also CA 105; 134; CANR 84
Shimazaki Toson 1872-1943 .... **TCLC 5**
See also Shimazaki, Haruki
See also DLB 180
Sholokhov, Mikhail (Aleksandrovich) 1905-1984 .... **CLC 7, 15**
See also CA 101; 112; MTCW 1, 2; SATA-Obit 36

Shone, Patric
See Hanley, James
Shreve, Susan Richards 1939- .... **CLC 23**
See also CA 49-52; CAAS 5; CANR 5, 38, 69; MAICYA; SATA 46, 95; SATA-Brief 41
Shue, Larry 1946-1985 .... **CLC 52; DAM DRAM**
See also CA 145; 117
Shu-Jen, Chou 1881-1936
See Lu Hsun
See also CA 104
Shulman, Alix Kates 1932- .... **CLC 2, 10**
See also CA 29-32R; CANR 43; SATA 7
Shuster, Joe 1914- .... **CLC 21**
Shute, Nevil CLC 30
See also Norway, Nevil Shute
See also MTCW 2
Shuttle, Penelope (Diane) 1947- .... **CLC 7**
See also CA 93-96; CANR 39, 84, 92; DLB 14, 40
Sidney, Mary 1561-1621 .... **LC 19, 39**
Sidney, SirPhilip 1554-1586 . **LC 19, 39; DA; DAB; DAC; DAM MST, POET**
See also CDBLB Before 1660; DA3; DLB 167
Siegel, Jerome 1914-1996 .... **CLC 21**
See also CA 116; 169; 151
Siegel, Jerry
See Siegel, Jerome
Sienkiewicz, Henryk (Adam Alexander Pius) 1846-1916 .... **TCLC 3**
See also CA 104; 134; CANR 84
Sierra, Gregorio Martinez
See Martinez Sierra, Gregorio
Sierra, Maria (de la O'LeJarraga) Martinez
See Martinez Sierra, Maria (de la O'LeJarraga)
Sigal, Clancy 1926- .... **CLC 7**
See also CA 1-4R; CANR 85
Sigourney, Lydia Howard (Huntley) 1791-1865 .... **NCLC 21, 87**
See also DLB 1, 42, 73
Siguenza y Gongora, Carlos de 1645-1700 .... **LC 8; HLCS 2**
Sigurjonsson, Johann 1880-1919 ... **TCLC 27**
See also CA 170
Sikelianos, Angelos 1884-1951 ...... **TCLC 39; PC 29**
Silkin, Jon 1930- .... **CLC 2, 6, 43**
See also CA 5-8R; CAAS 5; CANR 89; DLB 27
Silko, Leslie (Marmon) 1948- .... **CLC 23, 74, 114; DA; DAC; DAM MST, MULT, POP; SSC 37; WLCS**
See also AAYA 14; CA 115; 122; CANR 45, 65; DA3; DLB 143, 175; MTCW 2; NNAL
Sillanpaa, Frans Eemil 1888-1964 ... **CLC 19**
See also CA 129; 93-96; MTCW 1
Sillitoe, Alan 1928- ... **CLC 1, 3, 6, 10, 19, 57**
See also AITN 1; CA 9-12R; CAAS 2; CANR 8, 26, 55; CDBLB 1960 to Present; DLB 14, 139; MTCW 1, 2; SATA 61
Silone, Ignazio 1900-1978 .... **CLC 4**
See also CA 25-28; 81-84; CANR 34; CAP 2; MTCW 1
Silver, Joan Micklin 1935- .... **CLC 20**
See also CA 114; 121; INT 121
Silver, Nicholas
See Faust, Frederick (Schiller)
Silverberg, Robert 1935- .... **CLC 7; DAM POP**
See also AAYA 24; CA 1-4R, 186; CAAE 186; CAAS 3; CANR 1, 20, 36, 85; CLR 59; DLB 8; INT CANR-20; MAICYA; MTCW 1, 2; SATA 13, 91; SATA-Essay 104
Silverstein, Alvin 1933- .... **CLC 17**
See also CA 49-52; CANR 2; CLR 25; JRDA; MAICYA; SATA 8, 69
Silverstein, Virginia B(arbara Opshelor) 1937- .... **CLC 17**
See also CA 49-52; CANR 2; CLR 25; JRDA; MAICYA; SATA 8, 69
Sim, Georges
See Simenon, Georges (Jacques Christian)
Simak, Clifford D(onald) 1904-1988 . **CLC 1, 55**
See also CA 1-4R; 125; CANR 1, 35; DLB 8; MTCW 1; SATA-Obit 56
Simenon, Georges (Jacques Christian) 1903-1989 .... **CLC 1, 2, 3, 8, 18, 47; DAM POP**
See also CA 85-88; 129; CANR 35; DA3; DLB 72; DLBY 89; MTCW 1, 2
Simic, Charles 1938- .... **CLC 6, 9, 22, 49, 68, 130; DAM POET**
See also CA 29-32R; CAAS 4; CANR 12, 33, 52, 61; DA3; DLB 105; MTCW 2
Simmel, Georg 1858-1918 .... **TCLC 64**
See also CA 157
Simmons, Charles (Paul) 1924- .... **CLC 57**
See also CA 89-92; INT 89-92
Simmons, Dan 1948- .... **CLC 44; DAM POP**
See also AAYA 16; CA 138; CANR 53, 81
Simmons, James (Stewart Alexander) 1933- .... **CLC 43**
See also CA 105; CAAS 21; DLB 40
Simms, William Gilmore 1806-1870 .... **NCLC 3**
See also DLB 3, 30, 59, 73
Simon, Carly 1945- .... **CLC 26**
See also CA 105
Simon, Claude 1913- .... **CLC 4, 9, 15, 39; DAM NOV**
See also CA 89-92; CANR 33; DLB 83; MTCW 1
Simon, (Marvin) Neil 1927- ... **CLC 6, 11, 31, 39, 70; DAM DRAM**
See also AAYA 32; AITN 1; CA 21-24R; CANR 26, 54, 87; DA3; DLB 7; MTCW 1, 2
Simon, Paul (Frederick) 1941(?)- ..... **CLC 17**
See also CA 116; 153
Simonon, Paul 1956(?)- .... **CLC 30**
Simpson, Harriette
See Arnow, Harriette (Louisa) Simpson
Simpson, Louis (Aston Marantz) 1923- ...... **CLC 4, 7, 9, 32; DAM POET**
See also CA 1-4R; CAAS 4; CANR 1, 61; DLB 5; MTCW 1, 2
Simpson, Mona (Elizabeth) 1957- .... **CLC 44**
See also CA 122; 135; CANR 68
Simpson, N(orman) F(rederick) 1919- .... **CLC 29**
See also CA 13-16R; DLB 13
Sinclair, Andrew (Annandale) 1935- . **CLC 2, 14**
See also CA 9-12R; CAAS 5; CANR 14, 38, 91; DLB 14; MTCW 1
Sinclair, Emil
See Hesse, Hermann
Sinclair, Iain 1943- .... **CLC 76**
See also CA 132; CANR 81
Sinclair, Iain MacGregor
See Sinclair, Iain
Sinclair, Irene
See Griffith, D(avid Lewelyn) W(ark)
Sinclair, Mary Amelia St. Clair 1865(?)-1946
See Sinclair, May
See also CA 104
Sinclair, May 1863-1946 .... **TCLC 3, 11**
See also Sinclair, Mary Amelia St. Clair
See also CA 166; DLB 36, 135
Sinclair, Roy
See Griffith, D(avid Lewelyn) W(ark)
Sinclair, Upton (Beall) 1878-1968 ..... **CLC 1, 11, 15, 63; DA; DAB; DAC; DAM MST, NOV; WLC**
See also CA 5-8R; 25-28R; CANR 7; CDALB 1929-1941; DA3; DLB 9; INT CANR-7; MTCW 1, 2; SATA 9
Singer, Isaac
See Singer, Isaac Bashevis
Singer, Isaac Bashevis 1904-1991 .. **CLC 1, 3, 6, 9, 11, 15, 23, 38, 69, 111; DA; DAB; DAC; DAM MST, NOV; SSC 3; WLC**
See also AAYA 32; AITN 1, 2; CA 1-4R; 134; CANR 1, 39; CDALB 1941-1968; CLR 1; DA3; DLB 6, 28, 52; DLBY 91; JRDA; MAICYA; MTCW 1, 2; SATA 3, 27; SATA-Obit 68
Singer, Israel Joshua 1893-1944 .... **TCLC 33**
See also CA 169
Singh, Khushwant 1915- .... **CLC 11**
See also CA 9-12R; CAAS 9; CANR 6, 84
Singleton, Ann
See Benedict, Ruth (Fulton)
Sinjohn, John
See Galsworthy, John
Sinyavsky, Andrei (Donatevich) 1925-1997 .... **CLC 8**
See also CA 85-88; 159
Sirin, V.
See Nabokov, Vladimir (Vladimirovich)
Sissman, L(ouis) E(dward) 1928-1976 .... **CLC 9, 18**
See also CA 21-24R; 65-68; CANR 13; DLB 5
Sisson, C(harles) H(ubert) 1914- .... **CLC 8**
See also CA 1-4R; CAAS 3; CANR 3, 48, 84; DLB 27
Sitwell, Dame Edith 1887-1964 ..... **CLC 2, 9, 67; DAM POET; PC 3**
See also CA 9-12R; CANR 35; CDBLB 1945-1960; DLB 20; MTCW 1, 2
Siwaarmill, H. P.
See Sharp, William
Sjoewall, Maj 1935- .... **CLC 7**
See also Sjowall, Maj
See also CA 65-68; CANR 73
Sjowall, Maj
See Sjoewall, Maj
Skelton, John 1463-1529 .... **PC 25**
Skelton, Robin 1925-1997 .... **CLC 13**
See also AITN 2; CA 5-8R; 160; CAAS 5; CANR 28, 89; DLB 27, 53
Skolimowski, Jerzy 1938- .... **CLC 20**
See also CA 128
Skram, Amalie (Bertha) 1847-1905 .... **TCLC 25**
See also CA 165
Skvorecky, Josef (Vaclav) 1924- ...... **CLC 15, 39, 69; DAC; DAM NOV**
See also CA 61-64; CAAS 1; CANR 10, 34, 63; DA3; MTCW 1, 2
Slade, Bernard CLC 11, 46
See also Newbound, Bernard Slade
See also CAAS 9; DLB 53
Slaughter, Carolyn 1946- .... **CLC 56**
See also CA 85-88; CANR 85
Slaughter, Frank G(ill) 1908- .... **CLC 29**
See also AITN 2; CA 5-8R; CANR 5, 85; INT CANR-5
Slavitt, David R(ytman) 1935- ..... **CLC 5, 14**
See also CA 21-24R; CAAS 3; CANR 41, 83; DLB 5, 6
Slesinger, Tess 1905-1945 .... **TCLC 10**
See also CA 107; DLB 102
Slessor, Kenneth 1901-1971 .... **CLC 14**
See also CA 102; 89-92
Slowacki, Juliusz 1809-1849 .... **NCLC 15**
Smart, Christopher 1722-1771 .. **LC 3; DAM POET; PC 13**
See also DLB 109

Smart, Elizabeth 1913-1986 .... **CLC 54**
See also CA 81-84; 118; DLB 88
Smiley, Jane (Graves) 1949- ...... **CLC 53, 76; DAM POP**
See also CA 104; CANR 30, 50, 74; DA3; DLB 227; INT CANR-30
Smith, A(rthur) J(ames) M(arshall) 1902-1980 .... **CLC 15; DAC**
See also CA 1-4R; 102; CANR 4; DLB 88
Smith, Adam 1723-1790 .... **LC 36**
See also DLB 104
Smith, Alexander 1829-1867 .... **NCLC 59**
See also DLB 32, 55
Smith, Anna Deavere 1950- .... **CLC 86**
See also CA 133
Smith, Betty (Wehner) 1896-1972 .... **CLC 19**
See also CA 5-8R; 33-36R; DLBY 82; SATA 6
Smith, Charlotte (Turner) 1749-1806 .... **NCLC 23**
See also DLB 39, 109
Smith, Clark Ashton 1893-1961 .... **CLC 43**
See also CA 143; CANR 81; MTCW 2
Smith, Dave CLC 22, 42
See also Smith, David (Jeddie)
See also CAAS 7; DLB 5
Smith, David (Jeddie) 1942-
See Smith, Dave
See also CA 49-52; CANR 1, 59; DAM POET
Smith, Florence Margaret 1902-1971
See Smith, Stevie
See also CA 17-18; 29-32R; CANR 35; CAP 2; DAM POET; MTCW 1, 2
Smith, Iain Crichton 1928-1998 .... **CLC 64**
See also CA 21-24R; 171; DLB 40, 139
Smith, John 1580(?)-1631 .... **LC 9**
See also DLB 24, 30
Smith, Johnston
See Crane, Stephen (Townley)
Smith, Joseph, Jr. 1805-1844 .... **NCLC 53**
Smith, Lee 1944- .... **CLC 25, 73**
See also CA 114; 119; CANR 46; DLB 143; DLBY 83; INT 119
Smith, Martin
See Smith, Martin Cruz
Smith, Martin Cruz 1942- .... **CLC 25; DAM MULT, POP**
See also BEST 89:4; CA 85-88; CANR 6, 23, 43, 65; INT CANR-23; MTCW 2; NNAL
Smith, Mary-Ann Tirone 1944- .... **CLC 39**
See also CA 118; 136
Smith, Patti 1946- .... **CLC 12**
See also CA 93-96; CANR 63
Smith, Pauline (Urmson) 1882-1959 .... **TCLC 25**
See also DLB 225
Smith, Rosamond
See Oates, Joyce Carol
Smith, Sheila Kaye
See Kaye-Smith, Sheila
Smith, Stevie CLC 3, 8, 25, 44; PC 12
See also Smith, Florence Margaret
See also DLB 20; MTCW 2
Smith, Wilbur (Addison) 1933- .... **CLC 33**
See also CA 13-16R; CANR 7, 46, 66; MTCW 1, 2
Smith, William Jay 1918- .... **CLC 6**
See also CA 5-8R; CANR 44; DLB 5; MAICYA; SAAS 22; SATA 2, 68
Smith, Woodrow Wilson
See Kuttner, Henry
Smolenskin, Peretz 1842-1885 .... **NCLC 30**
Smollett, Tobias (George) 1721-1771 ... **LC 2, 46**
See also CDBLB 1660-1789; DLB 39, 104
Snodgrass, W(illiam) D(e Witt) 1926- .... **CLC 2, 6, 10, 18, 68; DAM POET**
See also CA 1-4R; CANR 6, 36, 65, 85; DLB 5; MTCW 1, 2
Snow, C(harles) P(ercy) 1905-1980 ... **CLC 1, 4, 6, 9, 13, 19; DAM NOV**
See also CA 5-8R; 101; CANR 28; CDBLB 1945-1960; DLB 15, 77; DLBD 17; MTCW 1, 2
Snow, Frances Compton
See Adams, Henry (Brooks)
Snyder, Gary (Sherman) 1930- . **CLC 1, 2, 5, 9, 32, 120; DAM POET; PC 21**
See also CA 17-20R; CANR 30, 60; DA3; DLB 5, 16, 165, 212; MTCW 2
Snyder, Zilpha Keatley 1927- .... **CLC 17**
See also AAYA 15; CA 9-12R; CANR 38; CLR 31; JRDA; MAICYA; SAAS 2; SATA 1, 28, 75, 110; SATA-Essay 112
Soares, Bernardo
See Pessoa, Fernando (Antonio Nogueira)
Sobh, A.
See Shamlu, Ahmad
Sobol, Joshua CLC 60
Socrates 469B.C.-399B.C. .... **CMLC 27**
Soderberg, Hjalmar 1869-1941 ...... **TCLC 39**
Sodergran, Edith (Irene)
See Soedergran, Edith (Irene)
Soedergran, Edith (Irene) 1892-1923 .... **TCLC 31**
Softly, Edgar
See Lovecraft, H(oward) P(hillips)
Softly, Edward
See Lovecraft, H(oward) P(hillips)
Sokolov, Raymond 1941- .... **CLC 7**
See also CA 85-88
Solo, Jay
See Ellison, Harlan (Jay)
Sologub, Fyodor TCLC 9
See also Teternikov, Fyodor Kuzmich
Solomons, Ikey Esquir
See Thackeray, William Makepeace
Solomos, Dionysios 1798-1857 .... **NCLC 15**
Solwoska, Mara
See French, Marilyn
Solzhenitsyn, Aleksandr I(sayevich) 1918- .. **CLC 1, 2, 4, 7, 9, 10, 18, 26, 34, 78, 134; DA; DAB; DAC; DAM MST, NOV; SSC 32; WLC**
See also AITN 1; CA 69-72; CANR 40, 65; DA3; MTCW 1, 2
Somers, Jane
See Lessing, Doris (May)
Somerville, Edith 1858-1949 .... **TCLC 51**
See also DLB 135
Somerville & Ross
See Martin, Violet Florence; Somerville, Edith
Sommer, Scott 1951- .... **CLC 25**
See also CA 106
Sondheim, Stephen (Joshua) 1930- . **CLC 30, 39; DAM DRAM**
See also AAYA 11; CA 103; CANR 47, 68
Song, Cathy 1955- .... **PC 21**
See also CA 154; DLB 169
Sontag, Susan 1933- .... **CLC 1, 2, 10, 13, 31, 105; DAM POP**
See also CA 17-20R; CANR 25, 51, 74; DA3; DLB 2, 67; MTCW 1, 2
Sophocles 496(?)B.C.-406(?)B.C. .... **CMLC 2; DA; DAB; DAC; DAM DRAM, MST; DC 1; WLCS**
See also DA3; DLB 176
Sordello 1189-1269 .... **CMLC 15**
Sorel, Georges 1847-1922 .... **TCLC 91**
See also CA 118
Sorel, Julia
See Drexler, Rosalyn
Sorrentino, Gilbert 1929- .. **CLC 3, 7, 14, 22, 40**
See also CA 77-80; CANR 14, 33; DLB 5, 173; DLBY 80; INT CANR-14
Soto, Gary 1952- .... **CLC 32, 80; DAM MULT; HLC 2; PC 28**
See also AAYA 10; CA 119; 125; CANR 50, 74; CLR 38; DLB 82; HW 1, 2; INT 125; JRDA; MTCW 2; SATA 80
Soupault, Philippe 1897-1990 .... **CLC 68**
See also CA 116; 147; 131
Souster, (Holmes) Raymond 1921- .... **CLC 5, 14; DAC; DAM POET**
See also CA 13-16R; CAAS 14; CANR 13, 29, 53; DA3; DLB 88; SATA 63
Southern, Terry 1924(?)-1995 .... **CLC 7**
See also CA 1-4R; 150; CANR 1, 55; DLB 2
Southey, Robert 1774-1843 .... **NCLC 8**
See also DLB 93, 107, 142; SATA 54
Southworth, Emma Dorothy Eliza Nevitte 1819-1899 .... **NCLC 26**
Souza, Ernest
See Scott, Evelyn
Soyinka, Wole 1934- .... **CLC 3, 5, 14, 36, 44; BLC 3; DA; DAB; DAC; DAM DRAM, MST, MULT; DC 2; WLC**
See also BW 2, 3; CA 13-16R; CANR 27, 39, 82; DA3; DLB 125; MTCW 1, 2
Spackman, W(illiam) M(ode) 1905-1990 .... **CLC 46**
See also CA 81-84; 132
Spacks, Barry (Bernard) 1931- .... **CLC 14**
See also CA 154; CANR 33; DLB 105
Spanidou, Irini 1946- .... **CLC 44**
See also CA 185
Spark, Muriel (Sarah) 1918- ..... **CLC 2, 3, 5, 8, 13, 18, 40, 94; DAB; DAC; DAM MST, NOV; SSC 10**
See also CA 5-8R; CANR 12, 36, 76, 89; CDBLB 1945-1960; DA3; DLB 15, 139; INT CANR-12; MTCW 1, 2
Spaulding, Douglas
See Bradbury, Ray (Douglas)
Spaulding, Leonard
See Bradbury, Ray (Douglas)
Spence, J. A. D.
See Eliot, T(homas) S(tearns)
Spencer, Elizabeth 1921- .... **CLC 22**
See also CA 13-16R; CANR 32, 65, 87; DLB 6; MTCW 1; SATA 14
Spencer, Leonard G.
See Silverberg, Robert
Spencer, Scott 1945- .... **CLC 30**
See also CA 113; CANR 51; DLBY 86
Spender, Stephen (Harold) 1909-1995 .... **CLC 1, 2, 5, 10, 41, 91; DAM POET**
See also CA 9-12R; 149; CANR 31, 54; CDBLB 1945-1960; DA3; DLB 20; MTCW 1, 2
Spengler, Oswald (Arnold Gottfried) 1880-1936 .... **TCLC 25**
See also CA 118
Spenser, Edmund 1552(?)-1599 ..... **LC 5, 39; DA; DAB; DAC; DAM MST, POET; PC 8; WLC**
See also CDBLB Before 1660; DA3; DLB 167
Spicer, Jack 1925-1965 .... **CLC 8, 18, 72; DAM POET**
See also CA 85-88; DLB 5, 16, 193
Spiegelman, Art 1948- .... **CLC 76**
See also AAYA 10; CA 125; CANR 41, 55, 74; MTCW 2; SATA 109
Spielberg, Peter 1929- .... **CLC 6**
See also CA 5-8R; CANR 4, 48; DLBY 81

Stone, Robert (Anthony) 1937- ... **CLC 5, 23, 42**
See also CA 85-88; CANR 23, 66; DLB 152; INT CANR-23; MTCW 1
Stone, Zachary
See Follett, Ken(neth Martin)
Stoppard, Tom 1937- ... **CLC 1, 3, 4, 5, 8, 15, 29, 34, 63, 91; DA; DAB; DAC; DAM DRAM, MST; DC 6; WLC**
See also CA 81-84; CANR 39, 67; CDBLB 1960 to Present; DA3; DLB 13; DLBY 85; MTCW 1, 2
Storey, David (Malcolm) 1933- . **CLC 2, 4, 5, 8; DAM DRAM**
See also CA 81-84; CANR 36; DLB 13, 14, 207; MTCW 1
Storm, Hyemeyohsts 1935- ..... **CLC 3; DAM MULT**
See also CA 81-84; CANR 45; NNAL
Storm, Theodor 1817-1888 .... **SSC 27**
Storm, (Hans) Theodor (Woldsen) 1817-1888 .... **NCLC 1; SSC 27**
See also DLB 129
Storni, Alfonsina 1892-1938 . **TCLC 5; DAM MULT; HLC 2**
See also CA 104; 131; HW 1
Stoughton, William 1631-1701 .... **LC 38**
See also DLB 24
Stout, Rex (Todhunter) 1886-1975 ..... **CLC 3**
See also AITN 2; CA 61-64; CANR 71
Stow, (Julian) Randolph 1935- ... **CLC 23, 48**
See also CA 13-16R; CANR 33; MTCW 1
Stowe, Harriet (Elizabeth) Beecher 1811-1896 .... **NCLC 3, 50; DA; DAB; DAC; DAM MST, NOV; WLC**
See also CDALB 1865-1917; DA3; DLB 1, 12, 42, 74, 189; JRDA; MAICYA; YABC 1
Strabo c. 64B.C.-c. 25 .... **CMLC 37**
See also DLB 176
Strachey, (Giles) Lytton 1880-1932 .... **TCLC 12**
See also CA 110; 178; DLB 149; DLBD 10; MTCW 2
Strand, Mark 1934- .... **CLC 6, 18, 41, 71; DAM POET**
See also CA 21-24R; CANR 40, 65; DLB 5; SATA 41
Straub, Peter (Francis) 1943- . **CLC 28, 107; DAM POP**
See also BEST 89:1; CA 85-88; CANR 28, 65; DLBY 84; MTCW 1, 2
Strauss, Botho 1944- .... **CLC 22**
See also CA 157; DLB 124
Streatfeild, (Mary) Noel 1895(?)-1986 .... **CLC 21**
See also CA 81-84; 120; CANR 31; CLR 17; DLB 160; MAICYA; SATA 20; SATA-Obit 48
Stribling, T(homas) S(igismund) 1881-1965 .... **CLC 23**
See also CA 107; DLB 9
Strindberg, (Johan) August 1849-1912 .... **TCLC 1, 8, 21, 47; DA; DAB; DAC; DAM DRAM, MST; WLC**
See also CA 104; 135; DA3; MTCW 2
Stringer, Arthur 1874-1950 .... **TCLC 37**
See also CA 161; DLB 92
Stringer, David
See Roberts, Keith (John Kingston)
Stroheim, Erich von 1885-1957 ..... **TCLC 71**
Strugatskii, Arkadii (Natanovich) 1925-1991 .... **CLC 27**
See also CA 106; 135
Strugatskii, Boris (Natanovich) 1933- .... **CLC 27**
See also CA 106
Strummer, Joe 1953(?)- .... **CLC 30**
Strunk, William, Jr. 1869-1946 ...... **TCLC 92**
See also CA 118; 164
Stryk, Lucien 1924- .... **PC 27**
See also CA 13-16R; CANR 10, 28, 55
Stuart, Don A.
See Campbell, John W(ood, Jr.)
Stuart, Ian
See MacLean, Alistair (Stuart)
Stuart, Jesse (Hilton) 1906-1984 ... **CLC 1, 8, 11, 14, 34; SSC 31**
See also CA 5-8R; 112; CANR 31; DLB 9, 48, 102; DLBY 84; SATA 2; SATA-Obit 36
Sturgeon, Theodore (Hamilton) 1918-1985 .... **CLC 22, 39**
See also Queen, Ellery
See also CA 81-84; 116; CANR 32; DLB 8; DLBY 85; MTCW 1, 2
Sturges, Preston 1898-1959 .... **TCLC 48**
See also CA 114; 149; DLB 26
Styron, William 1925- .... **CLC 1, 3, 5, 11, 15, 60; DAM NOV, POP; SSC 25**
See also BEST 90:4; CA 5-8R; CANR 6, 33, 74; CDALB 1968-1988; DA3; DLB 2, 143; DLBY 80; INT CANR-6; MTCW 1, 2
Su, Chien 1884-1918
See Su Man-shu
See also CA 123
Suarez Lynch, B.
See Bioy Casares, Adolfo; Borges, Jorge Luis
Suassuna, Ariano Vilar 1927-
See also CA 178; HLCS 1; HW 2
Suckling, John 1609-1641 .... **PC 30**
See also DAM POET; DLB 58, 126
Suckow, Ruth 1892-1960 .... **SSC 18**
See also CA 113; DLB 9, 102
Sudermann, Hermann 1857-1928 .. **TCLC 15**
See also CA 107; DLB 118
Sue, Eugene 1804-1857 .... **NCLC 1**
See also DLB 119
Sueskind, Patrick 1949- .... **CLC 44**
See also Suskind, Patrick
Sukenick, Ronald 1932- .... **CLC 3, 4, 6, 48**
See also CA 25-28R; CAAS 8; CANR 32, 89; DLB 173; DLBY 81
Suknaski, Andrew 1942- .... **CLC 19**
See also CA 101; DLB 53
Sullivan, Vernon
See Vian, Boris
Sully Prudhomme 1839-1907 .... **TCLC 31**
Su Man-shu TCLC 24
See also Su, Chien
Summerforest, Ivy B.
See Kirkup, James
Summers, Andrew James 1942- .... **CLC 26**
Summers, Andy
See Summers, Andrew James
Summers, Hollis (Spurgeon, Jr.) 1916- .... **CLC 10**
See also CA 5-8R; CANR 3; DLB 6
Summers, (Alphonsus Joseph-Mary Augustus) Montague 1880-1948 .... **TCLC 16**
See also CA 118; 163
Sumner, Gordon Matthew CLC 26
See also Sting
Surtees, Robert Smith 1803-1864 .. **NCLC 14**
See also DLB 21
Susann, Jacqueline 1921-1974 .... **CLC 3**
See also AITN 1; CA 65-68; 53-56; MTCW 1, 2
Su Shih 1036-1101 .... **CMLC 15**
Suskind, Patrick
See Sueskind, Patrick
See also CA 145
Sutcliff, Rosemary 1920-1992 .... **CLC 26; DAB; DAC; DAM MST, POP**
See also AAYA 10; CA 5-8R; 139; CANR 37; CLR 1, 37; JRDA; MAICYA; SATA 6, 44, 78; SATA-Obit 73
Sutro, Alfred 1863-1933 .... **TCLC 6**
See also CA 105; 185; DLB 10
Sutton, Henry
See Slavitt, David R(ytman)
Svevo, Italo 1861-1928 ...... **TCLC 2, 35; SSC 25**
See also Schmitz, Aron Hector
Swados, Elizabeth (A.) 1951- .... **CLC 12**
See also CA 97-100; CANR 49; INT 97-100
Swados, Harvey 1920-1972 .... **CLC 5**
See also CA 5-8R; 37-40R; CANR 6; DLB 2
Swan, Gladys 1934- .... **CLC 69**
See also CA 101; CANR 17, 39
Swanson, Logan
See Matheson, Richard Burton
Swarthout, Glendon (Fred) 1918-1992 .... **CLC 35**
See also CA 1-4R; 139; CANR 1, 47; SATA 26
Sweet, Sarah C.
See Jewett, (Theodora) Sarah Orne
Swenson, May 1919-1989 ...... **CLC 4, 14, 61, 106; DA; DAB; DAC; DAM MST, POET; PC 14**
See also CA 5-8R; 130; CANR 36, 61; DLB 5; MTCW 1, 2; SATA 15
Swift, Augustus
See Lovecraft, H(oward) P(hillips)
Swift, Graham (Colin) 1949- ...... **CLC 41, 88**
See also CA 117; 122; CANR 46, 71; DLB 194; MTCW 2
Swift, Jonathan 1667-1745 ..... **LC 1, 42; DA; DAB; DAC; DAM MST, NOV, POET; PC 9; WLC**
See also CDBLB 1660-1789; CLR 53; DA3; DLB 39, 95, 101; SATA 19
Swinburne, Algernon Charles 1837-1909 .... **TCLC 8, 36; DA; DAB; DAC; DAM MST, POET; PC 24; WLC**
See also CA 105; 140; CDBLB 1832-1890; DA3; DLB 35, 57
Swinfen, Ann CLC 34
Swinnerton, Frank Arthur 1884-1982 .... **CLC 31**
See also CA 108; DLB 34
Swithen, John
See King, Stephen (Edwin)
Sylvia
See Ashton-Warner, Sylvia (Constance)
Symmes, Robert Edward
See Duncan, Robert (Edward)
Symonds, John Addington 1840-1893 .... **NCLC 34**
See also DLB 57, 144
Symons, Arthur 1865-1945 .... **TCLC 11**
See also CA 107; DLB 19, 57, 149
Symons, Julian (Gustave) 1912-1994 .... **CLC 2, 14, 32**
See also CA 49-52; 147; CAAS 3; CANR 3, 33, 59; DLB 87, 155; DLBY 92; MTCW 1
Synge, (Edmund) J(ohn) M(illington) 1871-1909 . **TCLC 6, 37; DAM DRAM; DC 2**
See also CA 104; 141; CDBLB 1890-1914; DLB 10, 19
Syruc, J.
See Milosz, Czeslaw
Szirtes, George 1948- .... **CLC 46**
See also CA 109; CANR 27, 61

Szymborska, Wislawa 1923- .... **CLC 99**
See also CA 154; CANR 91; DA3; DLBY 96; MTCW 2

T. O., Nik
See Annensky, Innokenty (Fyodorovich)

Tabori, George 1914- .... **CLC 19**
See also CA 49-52; CANR 4, 69

Tagore, Rabindranath 1861-1941 ... **TCLC 3, 53; DAM DRAM, POET; PC 8**
See also CA 104; 120; DA3; MTCW 1, 2

Taine, Hippolyte Adolphe 1828-1893 .... **NCLC 15**

Talese, Gay 1932- .... **CLC 37**
See also AITN 1; CA 1-4R; CANR 9, 58; DLB 185; INT CANR-9; MTCW 1, 2

Tallent, Elizabeth (Ann) 1954- .... **CLC 45**
See also CA 117; CANR 72; DLB 130

Tally, Ted 1952- .... **CLC 42**
See also CA 120; 124; INT 124

Talvik, Heiti 1904-1947 .... **TCLC 87**

Tamayo y Baus, Manuel 1829-1898 .... **NCLC 1**

Tammsaare, A(nton) H(ansen) 1878-1940 .... **TCLC 27**
See also CA 164; DLB 220

Tam'si, Tchicaya U
See Tchicaya, Gerald Felix

Tan, Amy (Ruth) 1952- . **CLC 59, 120; DAM MULT, NOV, POP**
See also AAYA 9; BEST 89:3; CA 136; CANR 54; CDALBS; DA3; DLB 173; MTCW 2; SATA 75

Tandem, Felix
See Spitteler, Carl (Friedrich Georg)

Tanizaki, Jun'ichiro 1886-1965 ... **CLC 8, 14, 28; SSC 21**
See also CA 93-96; 25-28R; DLB 180; MTCW 2

Tanner, William
See Amis, Kingsley (William)

Tao Lao
See Storni, Alfonsina

Tarantino, Quentin (Jerome) 1963- .... **CLC 125**
See also CA 171

Tarassoff, Lev
See Troyat, Henri

Tarbell, Ida M(inerva) 1857-1944 . **TCLC 40**
See also CA 122; 181; DLB 47

Tarkington, (Newton) Booth 1869-1946 .... **TCLC 9**
See also CA 110; 143; DLB 9, 102; MTCW 2; SATA 17

Tarkovsky, Andrei (Arsenyevich) 1932-1986 .... **CLC 75**
See also CA 127

Tartt, Donna 1964(?)- .... **CLC 76**
See also CA 142

Tasso, Torquato 1544-1595 .... **LC 5**

Tate, (John Orley) Allen 1899-1979 .. **CLC 2, 4, 6, 9, 11, 14, 24**
See also CA 5-8R; 85-88; CANR 32; DLB 4, 45, 63; DLBD 17; MTCW 1, 2

Tate, Ellalice
See Hibbert, Eleanor Alice Burford

Tate, James (Vincent) 1943- ..... **CLC 2, 6, 25**
See also CA 21-24R; CANR 29, 57; DLB 5, 169

Tauler, Johannes c. 1300-1361 ...... **CMLC 37**
See also DLB 179

Tavel, Ronald 1940- .... **CLC 6**
See also CA 21-24R; CANR 33

Taylor, Bayard 1825-1878 .... **NCLC 89**
See also DLB 3, 189

Taylor, C(ecil) P(hilip) 1929-1981 .... **CLC 27**
See also CA 25-28R; 105; CANR 47

Taylor, Edward 1642(?)-1729 ..... **LC 11; DA; DAB; DAC; DAM MST, POET**
See also DLB 24

Taylor, Eleanor Ross 1920- .... **CLC 5**
See also CA 81-84; CANR 70

Taylor, Elizabeth 1912-1975 ..... **CLC 2, 4, 29**
See also CA 13-16R; CANR 9, 70; DLB 139; MTCW 1; SATA 13

Taylor, Frederick Winslow 1856-1915 .... **TCLC 76**

Taylor, Henry (Splawn) 1942- .... **CLC 44**
See also CA 33-36R; CAAS 7; CANR 31; DLB 5

Taylor, Kamala (Purnaiya) 1924-
See Markandaya, Kamala
See also CA 77-80

Taylor, Mildred D. CLC 21
See also AAYA 10; BW 1; CA 85-88; CANR 25; CLR 9, 59; DLB 52; JRDA; MAICYA; SAAS 5; SATA 15, 70

Taylor, Peter (Hillsman) 1917-1994 .. **CLC 1, 4, 18, 37, 44, 50, 71; SSC 10**
See also CA 13-16R; 147; CANR 9, 50; DLBY 81, 94; INT CANR-9; MTCW 1, 2

Taylor, Robert Lewis 1912-1998 .... **CLC 14**
See also CA 1-4R; 170; CANR 3, 64; SATA 10

Tchekhov, Anton
See Chekhov, Anton (Pavlovich)

Tchicaya, Gerald Felix 1931-1988 .. **CLC 101**
See also CA 129; 125; CANR 81

Tchicaya U Tam'si
See Tchicaya, Gerald Felix

Teasdale, Sara 1884-1933 .... **TCLC 4; PC 31**
See also CA 104; 163; DLB 45; SATA 32

Tegner, Esaias 1782-1846 .... **NCLC 2**

Teilhard de Chardin, (Marie Joseph) Pierre 1881-1955 .... **TCLC 9**
See also CA 105

Temple, Ann
See Mortimer, Penelope (Ruth)

Tennant, Emma (Christina) 1937- .. **CLC 13, 52**
See also CA 65-68; CAAS 9; CANR 10, 38, 59, 88; DLB 14

Tenneshaw, S. M.
See Silverberg, Robert

Tennyson, Alfred 1809-1892 ... **NCLC 30, 65; DA; DAB; DAC; DAM MST, POET; PC 6; WLC**
See also CDBLB 1832-1890; DA3; DLB 32

Teran, Lisa St. Aubin de CLC 36
See also St. Aubin de Teran, Lisa

Terence c. 184B.C.-c. 159B.C. ...... **CMLC 14; DC 7**
See also DLB 211

Teresa de Jesus, St. 1515-1582 .... **LC 18**

Terkel, Louis 1912-
See Terkel, Studs
See also CA 57-60; CANR 18, 45, 67; DA3; MTCW 1, 2

Terkel, Studs CLC 38
See also Terkel, Louis
See also AAYA 32; AITN 1; MTCW 2

Terry, C. V.
See Slaughter, Frank G(ill)

Terry, Megan 1932- .... **CLC 19; DC 13**
See also CA 77-80; CABS 3; CANR 43; DLB 7

Tertullian c. 155-c. 245 .... **CMLC 29**

Tertz, Abram
See Sinyavsky, Andrei (Donatevich)

Tesich, Steve 1943(?)-1996 .... **CLC 40, 69**
See also CA 105; 152; DLBY 83

Tesla, Nikola 1856-1943 .... **TCLC 88**

Teternikov, Fyodor Kuzmich 1863-1927
See Sologub, Fyodor
See also CA 104

Tevis, Walter 1928-1984 .... **CLC 42**
See also CA 113

Tey, Josephine TCLC 14
See also Mackintosh, Elizabeth
See also DLB 77

Thackeray, William Makepeace 1811-1863 ...... **NCLC 5, 14, 22, 43; DA; DAB; DAC; DAM MST, NOV; WLC**
See also CDBLB 1832-1890; DA3; DLB 21, 55, 159, 163; SATA 23

Thakura, Ravindranatha
See Tagore, Rabindranath

Tharoor, Shashi 1956- .... **CLC 70**
See also CA 141; CANR 91

Thelwell, Michael Miles 1939- .... **CLC 22**
See also BW 2; CA 101

Theobald, Lewis, Jr.
See Lovecraft, H(oward) P(hillips)

Theodorescu, Ion N. 1880-1967
See Arghezi, Tudor
See also CA 116; DLB 220

Theriault, Yves 1915-1983 .... **CLC 79; DAC; DAM MST**
See also CA 102; DLB 88

Theroux, Alexander (Louis) 1939- .... **CLC 2, 25**
See also CA 85-88; CANR 20, 63

Theroux, Paul (Edward) 1941- ..... **CLC 5, 8, 11, 15, 28, 46; DAM POP**
See also AAYA 28; BEST 89:4; CA 33-36R; CANR 20, 45, 74; CDALBS; DA3; DLB 2; MTCW 1, 2; SATA 44, 109

Thesen, Sharon 1946- .... **CLC 56**
See also CA 163

Thevenin, Denis
See Duhamel, Georges

Thibault, Jacques Anatole Francois 1844-1924
See France, Anatole
See also CA 106; 127; DAM NOV; DA3; MTCW 1, 2

Thiele, Colin (Milton) 1920- .... **CLC 17**
See also CA 29-32R; CANR 12, 28, 53; CLR 27; MAICYA; SAAS 2; SATA 14, 72

Thomas, Audrey (Callahan) 1935- .... **CLC 7, 13, 37, 107; SSC 20**
See also AITN 2; CA 21-24R; CAAS 19; CANR 36, 58; DLB 60; MTCW 1

Thomas, Augustus 1857-1934 .... **TCLC 97**

Thomas, D(onald) M(ichael) 1935- . **CLC 13, 22, 31, 132**
See also CA 61-64; CAAS 11; CANR 17, 45, 75; CDBLB 1960 to Present; DA3; DLB 40, 207; INT CANR-17; MTCW 1, 2

Thomas, Dylan (Marlais) 1914-1953 ... **TCLC 1, 8, 45; DA; DAB; DAC; DAM DRAM, MST, POET; PC 2; SSC 3; WLC**
See also CA 104; 120; CANR 65; CDBLB 1945-1960; DA3; DLB 13, 20, 139; MTCW 1, 2; SATA 60

Thomas, (Philip) Edward 1878-1917 .... **TCLC 10; DAM POET**
See also CA 106; 153; DLB 98

Thomas, Joyce Carol 1938- .... **CLC 35**
See also AAYA 12; BW 2, 3; CA 113; 116; CANR 48; CLR 19; DLB 33; INT 116; JRDA; MAICYA; MTCW 1, 2; SAAS 7; SATA 40, 78

Thomas, Lewis 1913-1993 .... **CLC 35**
See also CA 85-88; 143; CANR 38, 60; MTCW 1, 2

Thomas, M. Carey 1857-1935 .... **TCLC 89**
Thomas, Paul
See Mann, (Paul) Thomas
Thomas, Piri 1928- .... **CLC 17; HLCS 2**
See also CA 73-76; HW 1
Thomas, R(onald) S(tuart) 1913- ...... **CLC 6, 13, 48; DAB; DAM POET**
See also CA 89-92; CAAS 4; CANR 30; CDBLB 1960 to Present; DLB 27; MTCW 1
Thomas, Ross (Elmore) 1926-1995 .. **CLC 39**
See also CA 33-36R; 150; CANR 22, 63
Thompson, Francis Clegg
See Mencken, H(enry) L(ouis)
Thompson, Francis Joseph 1859-1907 .... **TCLC 4**
See also CA 104; CDBLB 1890-1914; DLB 19
Thompson, Hunter S(tockton) 1939- ... **CLC 9, 17, 40, 104; DAM POP**
See also BEST 89:1; CA 17-20R; CANR 23, 46, 74, 77; DA3; DLB 185; MTCW 1, 2
Thompson, James Myers
See Thompson, Jim (Myers)
Thompson, Jim (Myers) 1906-1977(?) .... **CLC 69**
See also CA 140; DLB 226
Thompson, Judith CLC 39
Thomson, James 1700-1748 ... **LC 16, 29, 40; DAM POET**
See also DLB 95
Thomson, James 1834-1882 .... **NCLC 18; DAM POET**
See also DLB 35
Thoreau, Henry David 1817-1862 .. **NCLC 7, 21, 61; DA; DAB; DAC; DAM MST; PC 30; WLC**
See also CDALB 1640-1865; DA3; DLB 1, 223
Thornton, Hall
See Silverberg, Robert
Thucydides c. 455B.C.-399B.C. ..... **CMLC 17**
See also DLB 176
Thumboo, Edwin 1933- .... **PC 30**
Thurber, James (Grover) 1894-1961 .... **CLC 5, 11, 25, 125; DA; DAB; DAC; DAM DRAM, MST, NOV; SSC 1**
See also CA 73-76; CANR 17, 39; CDALB 1929-1941; DA3; DLB 4, 11, 22, 102; MAICYA; MTCW 1, 2; SATA 13
Thurman, Wallace (Henry) 1902-1934 .... **TCLC 6; BLC 3; DAM MULT**
See also BW 1, 3; CA 104; 124; CANR 81; DLB 51
Tibullus, Albius c. 54B.C.-c. 19B.C. .... **CMLC 36**
See also DLB 211
Ticheburn, Cheviot
See Ainsworth, William Harrison
Tieck, (Johann) Ludwig 1773-1853 .... **NCLC 5, 46; SSC 31**
See also DLB 90
Tiger, Derry
See Ellison, Harlan (Jay)
Tilghman, Christopher 1948(?)- .... **CLC 65**
See also CA 159
Tillich, Paul (Johannes) 1886-1965 .... **CLC 131**
See also CA 5-8R; 25-28R; CANR 33; MTCW 1, 2
Tillinghast, Richard (Williford) 1940- .... **CLC 29**
See also CA 29-32R; CAAS 23; CANR 26, 51
Timrod, Henry 1828-1867 .... **NCLC 25**
See also DLB 3
Tindall, Gillian (Elizabeth) 1938- ...... **CLC 7**
See also CA 21-24R; CANR 11, 65
Tiptree, James, Jr. CLC 48, 50
See also Sheldon, Alice Hastings Bradley
See also DLB 8
Titmarsh, Michael Angelo
See Thackeray, William Makepeace
Tocqueville, Alexis (Charles Henri Maurice Clerel, Comte) de 1805-1859 . **NCLC 7, 63**
Tolkien, J(ohn) R(onald) R(euel) 1892-1973 .. **CLC 1, 2, 3, 8, 12, 38; DA; DAB; DAC; DAM MST, NOV, POP; WLC**
See also AAYA 10; AITN 1; CA 17-18; 45-48; CANR 36; CAP 2; CDBLB 1914-1945; CLR 56; DA3; DLB 15, 160; JRDA; MAICYA; MTCW 1, 2; SATA 2, 32, 100; SATA-Obit 24
Toller, Ernst 1893-1939 .... **TCLC 10**
See also CA 107; 186; DLB 124
Tolson, M. B.
See Tolson, Melvin B(eaunorus)
Tolson, Melvin B(eaunorus) 1898(?)-1966 .... **CLC 36, 105; BLC 3; DAM MULT, POET**
See also BW 1, 3; CA 124; 89-92; CANR 80; DLB 48, 76
Tolstoi, Aleksei Nikolaevich
See Tolstoy, Alexey Nikolaevich
Tolstoy, Alexey Nikolaevich 1882-1945 .... **TCLC 18**
See also CA 107; 158
Tolstoy, Count Leo
See Tolstoy, Leo (Nikolaevich)
Tolstoy, Leo (Nikolaevich) 1828-1910 .. **TCLC 4, 11, 17, 28, 44, 79; DA; DAB; DAC; DAM MST, NOV; SSC 9, 30; WLC**
See also CA 104; 123; DA3; SATA 26
Tomasi di Lampedusa, Giuseppe 1896-1957
See Lampedusa, Giuseppe (Tomasi) di
See also CA 111
Tomlin, Lily CLC 17
See also Tomlin, Mary Jean
Tomlin, Mary Jean 1939(?)-
See Tomlin, Lily
See also CA 117
Tomlinson, (Alfred) Charles 1927- .... **CLC 2, 4, 6, 13, 45; DAM POET; PC 17**
See also CA 5-8R; CANR 33; DLB 40
Tomlinson, H(enry) M(ajor) 1873-1958 .... **TCLC 71**
See also CA 118; 161; DLB 36, 100, 195
Tonson, Jacob
See Bennett, (Enoch) Arnold
Toole, John Kennedy 1937-1969 ..... **CLC 19, 64**
See also CA 104; DLBY 81; MTCW 2
Toomer, Jean 1894-1967 .... **CLC 1, 4, 13, 22; BLC 3; DAM MULT; PC 7; SSC 1; WLCS**
See also BW 1; CA 85-88; CDALB 1917-1929; DA3; DLB 45, 51; MTCW 1, 2
Torley, Luke
See Blish, James (Benjamin)
Tornimparte, Alessandra
See Ginzburg, Natalia
Torre, Raoul della
See Mencken, H(enry) L(ouis)
Torrence, Ridgely 1874-1950 .... **TCLC 97**
See also DLB 54
Torrey, E(dwin) Fuller 1937- .... **CLC 34**
See also CA 119; CANR 71
Torsvan, Ben Traven
See Traven, B.
Torsvan, Benno Traven
See Traven, B.
Torsvan, Berick Traven
See Traven, B.
Torsvan, Berwick Traven
See Traven, B.
Torsvan, Bruno Traven
See Traven, B.
Torsvan, Traven
See Traven, B.
Tournier, Michel (Edouard) 1924- .... **CLC 6, 23, 36, 95**
See also CA 49-52; CANR 3, 36, 74; DLB 83; MTCW 1, 2; SATA 23
Tournimparte, Alessandra
See Ginzburg, Natalia
Towers, Ivar
See Kornbluth, C(yril) M.
Towne, Robert (Burton) 1936(?)- ..... **CLC 87**
See also CA 108; DLB 44
Townsend, Sue CLC 61
See also Townsend, Susan Elaine
See also AAYA 28; SATA 55, 93; SATA-Brief 48
Townsend, Susan Elaine 1946-
See Townsend, Sue
See also CA 119; 127; CANR 65; DAB; DAC; DAM MST
Townshend, Peter (Dennis Blandford) 1945- .... **CLC 17, 42**
See also CA 107
Tozzi, Federigo 1883-1920 .... **TCLC 31**
See also CA 160
Traill, Catharine Parr 1802-1899 .. **NCLC 31**
See also DLB 99
Trakl, Georg 1887-1914 .... **TCLC 5; PC 20**
See also CA 104; 165; MTCW 2
Transtroemer, Tomas (Goesta) 1931- .... **CLC 52, 65; DAM POET**
See also CA 117; 129; CAAS 17
Transtromer, Tomas Gosta
See Transtroemer, Tomas (Goesta)
Traven, B. (?)-1969 .... **CLC 8, 11**
See also CA 19-20; 25-28R; CAP 2; DLB 9, 56; MTCW 1
Treitel, Jonathan 1959- .... **CLC 70**
Trelawny, Edward John 1792-1881 .... **NCLC 85**
See also DLB 110, 116, 144
Tremain, Rose 1943- .... **CLC 42**
See also CA 97-100; CANR 44; DLB 14
Tremblay, Michel 1942- .... **CLC 29, 102; DAC; DAM MST**
See also CA 116; 128; DLB 60; MTCW 1, 2
Trevanian CLC 29
See also Whitaker, Rod(ney)
Trevor, Glen
See Hilton, James
Trevor, William 1928- .. **CLC 7, 9, 14, 25, 71, 116; SSC 21**
See also Cox, William Trevor
See also DLB 14, 139; MTCW 2
Trifonov, Yuri (Valentinovich) 1925-1981 .... **CLC 45**
See also CA 126; 103; MTCW 1
Trilling, Diana (Rubin) 1905-1996 . **CLC 129**
See also CA 5-8R; 154; CANR 10, 46; INT CANR-10; MTCW 1, 2
Trilling, Lionel 1905-1975 .... **CLC 9, 11, 24**
See also CA 9-12R; 61-64; CANR 10; DLB 28, 63; INT CANR-10; MTCW 1, 2
Trimball, W. H.
See Mencken, H(enry) L(ouis)
Tristan
See Gomez de la Serna, Ramon
Tristram
See Housman, A(lfred) E(dward)

Waugh, Evelyn (Arthur St. John) 1903-1966 .. **CLC 1, 3, 8, 13, 19, 27, 44, 107; DA; DAB; DAC; DAM MST, NOV, POP; SSC 41; WLC**
See also CA 85-88; 25-28R; CANR 22; CDBLB 1914-1945; DA3; DLB 15, 162, 195; MTCW 1, 2
Waugh, Harriet 1944- .... **CLC 6**
See also CA 85-88; CANR 22
Ways, C. R.
See Blount, Roy (Alton), Jr.
Waystaff, Simon
See Swift, Jonathan
Webb, Beatrice (Martha Potter) 1858-1943 .... **TCLC 22**
See also CA 117; 162; DLB 190
Webb, Charles (Richard) 1939- .... **CLC 7**
See also CA 25-28R
Webb, James H(enry), Jr. 1946- ...... **CLC 22**
See also CA 81-84
Webb, Mary Gladys (Meredith) 1881-1927 .... **TCLC 24**
See also CA 182; 123; DLB 34
Webb, Mrs. Sidney
See Webb, Beatrice (Martha Potter)
Webb, Phyllis 1927- .... **CLC 18**
See also CA 104; CANR 23; DLB 53
Webb, Sidney (James) 1859-1947 .. **TCLC 22**
See also CA 117; 163; DLB 190
Webber, Andrew Lloyd CLC 21
See also Lloyd Webber, Andrew
Weber, Lenora Mattingly 1895-1971 .... **CLC 12**
See also CA 19-20; 29-32R; CAP 1; SATA 2; SATA-Obit 26
Weber, Max 1864-1920 .... **TCLC 69**
See also CA 109
Webster, John 1579(?)-1634(?) ... **LC 33; DA; DAB; DAC; DAM DRAM, MST; DC 2; WLC**
See also CDBLB Before 1660; DLB 58
Webster, Noah 1758-1843 .... **NCLC 30**
See also DLB 1, 37, 42, 43, 73
Wedekind, (Benjamin) Frank(lin) 1864-1918 .... **TCLC 7; DAM DRAM**
See also CA 104; 153; DLB 118
Weidman, Jerome 1913-1998 .... **CLC 7**
See also AITN 2; CA 1-4R; 171; CANR 1; DLB 28
Weil, Simone (Adolphine) 1909-1943 .... **TCLC 23**
See also CA 117; 159; MTCW 2
Weininger, Otto 1880-1903 .... **TCLC 84**
Weinstein, Nathan
See West, Nathanael
Weinstein, Nathan von Wallenstein
See West, Nathanael
Weir, Peter (Lindsay) 1944- .... **CLC 20**
See also CA 113; 123
Weiss, Peter (Ulrich) 1916-1982 .. **CLC 3, 15, 51; DAM DRAM**
See also CA 45-48; 106; CANR 3; DLB 69, 124
Weiss, Theodore (Russell) 1916- ... **CLC 3, 8, 14**
See also CA 9-12R; CAAS 2; CANR 46; DLB 5
Welch, (Maurice) Denton 1915-1948 .... **TCLC 22**
See also CA 121; 148
Welch, James 1940- ..... **CLC 6, 14, 52; DAM MULT, POP**
See also CA 85-88; CANR 42, 66; DLB 175; NNAL
Weldon, Fay 1931- . **CLC 6, 9, 11, 19, 36, 59, 122; DAM POP**
See also CA 21-24R; CANR 16, 46, 63; CDBLB 1960 to Present; DLB 14, 194; INT CANR-16; MTCW 1, 2
Wellek, Rene 1903-1995 .... **CLC 28**
See also CA 5-8R; 150; CAAS 7; CANR 8; DLB 63; INT CANR-8
Weller, Michael 1942- .... **CLC 10, 53**
See also CA 85-88
Weller, Paul 1958- .... **CLC 26**
Wellershoff, Dieter 1925- .... **CLC 46**
See also CA 89-92; CANR 16, 37
Welles, (George) Orson 1915-1985 .. **CLC 20, 80**
See also CA 93-96; 117
Wellman, John McDowell 1945-
See Wellman, Mac
See also CA 166
Wellman, Mac 1945- .... **CLC 65**
See also Wellman, John McDowell; Wellman, John McDowell
Wellman, Manly Wade 1903-1986 ... **CLC 49**
See also CA 1-4R; 118; CANR 6, 16, 44; SATA 6; SATA-Obit 47
Wells, Carolyn 1869(?)-1942 .... **TCLC 35**
See also CA 113; 185; DLB 11
Wells, H(erbert) G(eorge) 1866-1946 . **TCLC 6, 12, 19; DA; DAB; DAC; DAM MST, NOV; SSC 6; WLC**
See also AAYA 18; CA 110; 121; CDBLB 1914-1945; CLR 64; DA3; DLB 34, 70, 156, 178; MTCW 1, 2; SATA 20
Wells, Rosemary 1943- .... **CLC 12**
See also AAYA 13; CA 85-88; CANR 48; CLR 16; MAICYA; SAAS 1; SATA 18, 69, 114
Welty, Eudora 1909- ...... **CLC 1, 2, 5, 14, 22, 33, 105; DA; DAB; DAC; DAM MST, NOV; SSC 1, 27; WLC**
See also CA 9-12R; CABS 1; CANR 32, 65; CDALB 1941-1968; DA3; DLB 2, 102, 143; DLBD 12; DLBY 87; MTCW 1, 2
Wen I-to 1899-1946 .... **TCLC 28**
Wentworth, Robert
See Hamilton, Edmond
Werfel, Franz (Viktor) 1890-1945 ... **TCLC 8**
See also CA 104; 161; DLB 81, 124
Wergeland, Henrik Arnold 1808-1845 .... **NCLC 5**
Wersba, Barbara 1932- .... **CLC 30**
See also AAYA 2, 30; CA 29-32R, 182; CAAE 182; CANR 16, 38; CLR 3; DLB 52; JRDA; MAICYA; SAAS 2; SATA 1, 58; SATA-Essay 103
Wertmueller, Lina 1928- .... **CLC 16**
See also CA 97-100; CANR 39, 78
Wescott, Glenway 1901-1987 .. **CLC 13; SSC 35**
See also CA 13-16R; 121; CANR 23, 70; DLB 4, 9, 102
Wesker, Arnold 1932- ... **CLC 3, 5, 42; DAB; DAM DRAM**
See also CA 1-4R; CAAS 7; CANR 1, 33; CDBLB 1960 to Present; DLB 13; MTCW 1
Wesley, Richard (Errol) 1945- .... **CLC 7**
See also BW 1; CA 57-60; CANR 27; DLB 38
Wessel, Johan Herman 1742-1785 .... **LC 7**
West, Anthony (Panther) 1914-1987 .... **CLC 50**
See also CA 45-48; 124; CANR 3, 19; DLB 15
West, C. P.
See Wodehouse, P(elham) G(renville)
West, Cornel (Ronald) 1953- .... **CLC 134; BLCS**
See also CA 144; CANR 91
West, (Mary) Jessamyn 1902-1984 ... **CLC 7, 17**
See also CA 9-12R; 112; CANR 27; DLB 6; DLBY 84; MTCW 1, 2; SATA-Obit 37
West, Morris L(anglo) 1916-1999 ..... **CLC 6, 33**
See also CA 5-8R; CANR 24, 49, 64; MTCW 1, 2
West, Nathanael 1903-1940 .... **TCLC 1, 14, 44; SSC 16**
See also CA 104; 125; CDALB 1929-1941; DA3; DLB 4, 9, 28; MTCW 1, 2
West, Owen
See Koontz, Dean R(ay)
West, Paul 1930- .... **CLC 7, 14, 96**
See also CA 13-16R; CAAS 7; CANR 22, 53, 76, 89; DLB 14; INT CANR-22; MTCW 2
West, Rebecca 1892-1983 ... **CLC 7, 9, 31, 50**
See also CA 5-8R; 109; CANR 19; DLB 36; DLBY 83; MTCW 1, 2
Westall, Robert (Atkinson) 1929-1993 .... **CLC 17**
See also AAYA 12; CA 69-72; 141; CANR 18, 68; CLR 13; JRDA; MAICYA; SAAS 2; SATA 23, 69; SATA-Obit 75
Westermarck, Edward 1862-1939 . **TCLC 87**
Westlake, Donald E(dwin) 1933- .... **CLC 7, 33; DAM POP**
See also CA 17-20R; CAAS 13; CANR 16, 44, 65; INT CANR-16; MTCW 2
Westmacott, Mary
See Christie, Agatha (Mary Clarissa)
Weston, Allen
See Norton, Andre
Wetcheek, J. L.
See Feuchtwanger, Lion
Wetering, Janwillem van de
See van de Wetering, Janwillem
Wetherald, Agnes Ethelwyn 1857-1940 .... **TCLC 81**
See also DLB 99
Wetherell, Elizabeth
See Warner, Susan (Bogert)
Whale, James 1889-1957 .... **TCLC 63**
Whalen, Philip 1923- .... **CLC 6, 29**
See also CA 9-12R; CANR 5, 39; DLB 16
Wharton, Edith (Newbold Jones) 1862-1937 .... **TCLC 3, 9, 27, 53; DA; DAB; DAC; DAM MST, NOV; SSC 6; WLC**
See also AAYA 25; CA 104; 132; CDALB 1865-1917; DA3; DLB 4, 9, 12, 78, 189; DLBD 13; MTCW 1, 2
Wharton, James
See Mencken, H(enry) L(ouis)
Wharton, William (a pseudonym) CLC 18, 37
See also CA 93-96; DLBY 80; INT 93-96
Wheatley (Peters), Phillis 1754(?)-1784 ...... **LC 3, 50; BLC 3; DA; DAC; DAM MST, MULT, POET; PC 3; WLC**
See also CDALB 1640-1865; DA3; DLB 31, 50
Wheelock, John Hall 1886-1978 .... **CLC 14**
See also CA 13-16R; 77-80; CANR 14; DLB 45
White, E(lwyn) B(rooks) 1899-1985 . **CLC 10, 34, 39; DAM POP**
See also AITN 2; CA 13-16R; 116; CANR 16, 37; CDALBS; CLR 1, 21; DA3; DLB 11, 22; MAICYA; MTCW 1, 2; SATA 2, 29, 100; SATA-Obit 44
White, Edmund (Valentine III) 1940- .... **CLC 27, 110; DAM POP**
See also AAYA 7; CA 45-48; CANR 3, 19, 36, 62; DA3; DLB 227; MTCW 1, 2
White, Patrick (Victor Martindale) 1912-1990 ...... **CLC 3, 4, 5, 7, 9, 18, 65, 69; SSC 39**
See also CA 81-84; 132; CANR 43; MTCW 1

White, Phyllis Dorothy James 1920-
See James, P. D.
See also CA 21-24R; CANR 17, 43, 65; DAM POP; DA3; MTCW 1, 2
White, T(erence) H(anbury) 1906-1964 .... **CLC 30**
See also AAYA 22; CA 73-76; CANR 37; DLB 160; JRDA; MAICYA; SATA 12
White, Terence de Vere 1912-1994 ... **CLC 49**
See also CA 49-52; 145; CANR 3
White, Walter
See White, Walter F(rancis)
See also BLC; DAM MULT
White, Walter F(rancis) 1893-1955 .... **TCLC 15**
See also White, Walter
See also BW 1; CA 115; 124; DLB 51
White, William Hale 1831-1913
See Rutherford, Mark
See also CA 121
Whitehead, Alfred North 1861-1947 .... **TCLC 97**
See also CA 117; 165; DLB 100
Whitehead, E(dward) A(nthony) 1933- .... **CLC 5**
See also CA 65-68; CANR 58
Whitemore, Hugh (John) 1936- .... **CLC 37**
See also CA 132; CANR 77; INT 132
Whitman, Sarah Helen (Power) 1803-1878 .... **NCLC 19**
See also DLB 1
Whitman, Walt(er) 1819-1892 .. **NCLC 4, 31, 81; DA; DAB; DAC; DAM MST, POET; PC 3; WLC**
See also CDALB 1640-1865; DA3; DLB 3, 64; SATA 20
Whitney, Phyllis A(yame) 1903- ...... **CLC 42; DAM POP**
See also AITN 2; BEST 90:3; CA 1-4R; CANR 3, 25, 38, 60; CLR 59; DA3; JRDA; MAICYA; MTCW 2; SATA 1, 30
Whittemore, (Edward) Reed (Jr.) 1919- .... **CLC 4**
See also CA 9-12R; CAAS 8; CANR 4; DLB 5
Whittier, John Greenleaf 1807-1892 .... **NCLC 8, 59**
See also DLB 1
Whittlebot, Hernia
See Coward, Noel (Peirce)
Wicker, Thomas Grey 1926-
See Wicker, Tom
See also CA 65-68; CANR 21, 46
Wicker, Tom CLC 7
See also Wicker, Thomas Grey
Wideman, John Edgar 1941- ...... **CLC 5, 34, 36, 67, 122; BLC 3; DAM MULT**
See also BW 2, 3; CA 85-88; CANR 14, 42, 67; DLB 33, 143; MTCW 2
Wiebe, Rudy (Henry) 1934- .. **CLC 6, 11, 14; DAC; DAM MST**
See also CA 37-40R; CANR 42, 67; DLB 60
Wieland, Christoph Martin 1733-1813 .... **NCLC 17**
See also DLB 97
Wiene, Robert 1881-1938 .... **TCLC 56**
Wieners, John 1934- .... **CLC 7**
See also CA 13-16R; DLB 16
Wiesel, Elie(zer) 1928- .... **CLC 3, 5, 11, 37; DA; DAB; DAC; DAM MST, NOV; WLCS**
See also AAYA 7; AITN 1; CA 5-8R; CAAS 4; CANR 8, 40, 65; CDALBS; DA3; DLB 83; DLBY 87; INT CANR-8; MTCW 1, 2; SATA 56
Wiggins, Marianne 1947- .... **CLC 57**
See also BEST 89:3; CA 130; CANR 60
Wight, James Alfred 1916-1995
See Herriot, James
See also CA 77-80; SATA 55; SATA-Brief 44
Wilbur, Richard (Purdy) 1921- ..... **CLC 3, 6, 9, 14, 53, 110; DA; DAB; DAC; DAM MST, POET**
See also CA 1-4R; CABS 2; CANR 2, 29, 76; CDALBS; DLB 5, 169; INT CANR-29; MTCW 1, 2; SATA 9, 108
Wild, Peter 1940- .... **CLC 14**
See also CA 37-40R; DLB 5
Wilde, Oscar (Fingal O'Flahertie Wills) 1854(?)-1900 .... **TCLC 1, 8, 23, 41; DA; DAB; DAC; DAM DRAM, MST, NOV; SSC 11; WLC**
See also CA 104; 119; CDBLB 1890-1914; DA3; DLB 10, 19, 34, 57, 141, 156, 190; SATA 24
Wilder, Billy CLC 20
See also Wilder, Samuel
See also DLB 26
Wilder, Samuel 1906-
See Wilder, Billy
See also CA 89-92
Wilder, Thornton (Niven) 1897-1975 .. **CLC 1, 5, 6, 10, 15, 35, 82; DA; DAB; DAC; DAM DRAM, MST, NOV; DC 1; WLC**
See also AAYA 29; AITN 2; CA 13-16R; 61-64; CANR 40; CDALBS; DA3; DLB 4, 7, 9, 228; DLBY 97; MTCW 1, 2
Wilding, Michael 1942- .... **CLC 73**
See also CA 104; CANR 24, 49
Wiley, Richard 1944- .... **CLC 44**
See also CA 121; 129; CANR 71
Wilhelm, Kate CLC 7
See also Wilhelm, Katie Gertrude
See also AAYA 20; CAAS 5; DLB 8; INT CANR-17
Wilhelm, Katie Gertrude 1928-
See Wilhelm, Kate
See also CA 37-40R; CANR 17, 36, 60; MTCW 1
Wilkins, Mary
See Freeman, Mary E(leanor) Wilkins
Willard, Nancy 1936- .... **CLC 7, 37**
See also CA 89-92; CANR 10, 39, 68; CLR 5; DLB 5, 52; MAICYA; MTCW 1; SATA 37, 71; SATA-Brief 30
William of Ockham 1285-1347 ..... **CMLC 32**
Williams, Ben Ames 1889-1953 ..... **TCLC 89**
See also CA 183; DLB 102
Williams, C(harles) K(enneth) 1936- .... **CLC 33, 56; DAM POET**
See also CA 37-40R; CAAS 26; CANR 57; DLB 5
Williams, Charles
See Collier, James L(incoln)
Williams, Charles (Walter Stansby) 1886-1945 .... **TCLC 1, 11**
See also CA 104; 163; DLB 100, 153
Williams, (George) Emlyn 1905-1987 .... **CLC 15; DAM DRAM**
See also CA 104; 123; CANR 36; DLB 10, 77; MTCW 1
Williams, Hank 1923-1953 .... **TCLC 81**
Williams, Hugo 1942- .... **CLC 42**
See also CA 17-20R; CANR 45; DLB 40
Williams, J. Walker
See Wodehouse, P(elham) G(renville)
Williams, John A(lfred) 1925- ..... **CLC 5, 13; BLC 3; DAM MULT**
See also BW 2, 3; CA 53-56; CAAS 3; CANR 6, 26, 51; DLB 2, 33; INT CANR-6
Williams, Jonathan (Chamberlain) 1929- .... **CLC 13**
See also CA 9-12R; CAAS 12; CANR 8; DLB 5
Williams, Joy 1944- .... **CLC 31**
See also CA 41-44R; CANR 22, 48
Williams, Norman 1952- .... **CLC 39**
See also CA 118
Williams, Sherley Anne 1944-1999 . **CLC 89; BLC 3; DAM MULT, POET**
See also BW 2, 3; CA 73-76; 185; CANR 25, 82; DLB 41; INT CANR-25; SATA 78; SATA-Obit 116
Williams, Shirley
See Williams, Sherley Anne
Williams, Tennessee 1911-1983 . **CLC 1, 2, 5, 7, 8, 11, 15, 19, 30, 39, 45, 71, 111; DA; DAB; DAC; DAM DRAM, MST; DC 4; WLC**
See also AAYA 31; AITN 1, 2; CA 5-8R; 108; CABS 3; CANR 31; CDALB 1941-1968; DA3; DLB 7; DLBD 4; DLBY 83; MTCW 1, 2
Williams, Thomas (Alonzo) 1926-1990 .... **CLC 14**
See also CA 1-4R; 132; CANR 2
Williams, William C.
See Williams, William Carlos
Williams, William Carlos 1883-1963 .... **CLC 1, 2, 5, 9, 13, 22, 42, 67; DA; DAB; DAC; DAM MST, POET; PC 7; SSC 31**
See also CA 89-92; CANR 34; CDALB 1917-1929; DA3; DLB 4, 16, 54, 86; MTCW 1, 2
Williamson, David (Keith) 1942- ..... **CLC 56**
See also CA 103; CANR 41
Williamson, Ellen Douglas 1905-1984
See Douglas, Ellen
See also CA 17-20R; 114; CANR 39
Williamson, Jack CLC 29
See also Williamson, John Stewart
See also CAAS 8; DLB 8
Williamson, John Stewart 1908-
See Williamson, Jack
See also CA 17-20R; CANR 23, 70
Willie, Frederick
See Lovecraft, H(oward) P(hillips)
Willingham, Calder (Baynard, Jr.) 1922-1995 .... **CLC 5, 51**
See also CA 5-8R; 147; CANR 3; DLB 2, 44; MTCW 1
Willis, Charles
See Clarke, Arthur C(harles)
Willy
See Colette, (Sidonie-Gabrielle)
Willy, Colette
See Colette, (Sidonie-Gabrielle)
Wilson, A(ndrew) N(orman) 1950- .. **CLC 33**
See also CA 112; 122; DLB 14, 155, 194; MTCW 2
Wilson, Angus (Frank Johnstone) 1913-1991 . **CLC 2, 3, 5, 25, 34; SSC 21**
See also CA 5-8R; 134; CANR 21; DLB 15, 139, 155; MTCW 1, 2
Wilson, August 1945- ... **CLC 39, 50, 63, 118; BLC 3; DA; DAB; DAC; DAM DRAM, MST, MULT; DC 2; WLCS**
See also AAYA 16; BW 2, 3; CA 115; 122; CANR 42, 54, 76; DA3; DLB 228; MTCW 1, 2
Wilson, Brian 1942- .... **CLC 12**
Wilson, Colin 1931- .... **CLC 3, 14**
See also CA 1-4R; CAAS 5; CANR 1, 22, 33, 77; DLB 14, 194; MTCW 1
Wilson, Dirk
See Pohl, Frederik

Wilson, Edmund 1895-1972 .. **CLC 1, 2, 3, 8, 24**
See also CA 1-4R; 37-40R; CANR 1, 46; DLB 63; MTCW 1, 2
Wilson, Ethel Davis (Bryant) 1888(?)-1980 .... **CLC 13; DAC; DAM POET**
See also CA 102; DLB 68; MTCW 1
Wilson, John 1785-1854 .... **NCLC 5**
Wilson, John (Anthony) Burgess 1917-1993
See Burgess, Anthony
See also CA 1-4R; 143; CANR 2, 46; DAC; DAM NOV; DA3; MTCW 1, 2
Wilson, Lanford 1937- .... **CLC 7, 14, 36; DAM DRAM**
See also CA 17-20R; CABS 3; CANR 45; DLB 7
Wilson, Robert M. 1944- .... **CLC 7, 9**
See also CA 49-52; CANR 2, 41; MTCW 1
Wilson, Robert McLiam 1964- .... **CLC 59**
See also CA 132
Wilson, Sloan 1920- .... **CLC 32**
See also CA 1-4R; CANR 1, 44
Wilson, Snoo 1948- .... **CLC 33**
See also CA 69-72
Wilson, William S(mith) 1932- .... **CLC 49**
See also CA 81-84
Wilson, (Thomas) Woodrow 1856-1924 .... **TCLC 79**
See also CA 166; DLB 47
Winchilsea, Anne (Kingsmill) Finch Counte 1661-1720
See Finch, Anne
Windham, Basil
See Wodehouse, P(elham) G(renville)
Wingrove, David (John) 1954- .... **CLC 68**
See also CA 133
Winnemucca, Sarah 1844-1891 ..... **NCLC 79**
Winstanley, Gerrard 1609-1676 .... **LC 52**
Wintergreen, Jane
See Duncan, Sara Jeannette
Winters, Janet Lewis CLC 41
See also Lewis, Janet
See also DLBY 87
Winters, (Arthur) Yvor 1900-1968 .... **CLC 4, 8, 32**
See also CA 11-12; 25-28R; CAP 1; DLB 48; MTCW 1
Winterson, Jeanette 1959- .... **CLC 64; DAM POP**
See also CA 136; CANR 58; DA3; DLB 207; MTCW 2
Winthrop, John 1588-1649 .... **LC 31**
See also DLB 24, 30
Wirth, Louis 1897-1952 .... **TCLC 92**
Wiseman, Frederick 1930- .... **CLC 20**
See also CA 159
Wister, Owen 1860-1938 .... **TCLC 21**
See also CA 108; 162; DLB 9, 78, 186; SATA 62
Witkacy
See Witkiewicz, Stanislaw Ignacy
Witkiewicz, Stanislaw Ignacy 1885-1939 .... **TCLC 8**
See also CA 105; 162
Wittgenstein, Ludwig (Josef Johann) 1889-1951 .... **TCLC 59**
See also CA 113; 164; MTCW 2
Wittig, Monique 1935(?)- .... **CLC 22**
See also CA 116; 135; DLB 83
Wittlin, Jozef 1896-1976 .... **CLC 25**
See also CA 49-52; 65-68; CANR 3
Wodehouse, P(elham) G(renville) 1881-1975 .... **CLC 1, 2, 5, 10, 22; DAB; DAC; DAM NOV; SSC 2**
See also AITN 2; CA 45-48; 57-60; CANR 3, 33; CDBLB 1914-1945; DA3; DLB 34, 162; MTCW 1, 2; SATA 22
Woiwode, L.
See Woiwode, Larry (Alfred)
Woiwode, Larry (Alfred) 1941- ... **CLC 6, 10**
See also CA 73-76; CANR 16; DLB 6; INT CANR-16
Wojciechowska, Maia (Teresa) 1927- .... **CLC 26**
See also AAYA 8; CA 9-12R, 183; CAAE 183; CANR 4, 41; CLR 1; JRDA; MAICYA; SAAS 1; SATA 1, 28, 83; SATA-Essay 104
Wojtyla, Karol
See John Paul II, Pope
Wolf, Christa 1929- .... **CLC 14, 29, 58**
See also CA 85-88; CANR 45; DLB 75; MTCW 1
Wolfe, Gene (Rodman) 1931- .... **CLC 25; DAM POP**
See also CA 57-60; CAAS 9; CANR 6, 32, 60; DLB 8; MTCW 2
Wolfe, George C. 1954- .... **CLC 49; BLCS**
See also CA 149
Wolfe, Thomas (Clayton) 1900-1938 ...... **TCLC 4, 13, 29, 61; DA; DAB; DAC; DAM MST, NOV; SSC 33; WLC**
See also CA 104; 132; CDALB 1929-1941; DA3; DLB 9, 102; DLBD 2, 16; DLBY 85, 97; MTCW 1, 2
Wolfe, Thomas Kennerly, Jr. 1930-
See Wolfe, Tom
See also CA 13-16R; CANR 9, 33, 70; DAM POP; DA3; DLB 185; INT CANR-9; MTCW 1, 2
Wolfe, Tom CLC 1, 2, 9, 15, 35, 51
See also Wolfe, Thomas Kennerly, Jr.
See also AAYA 8; AITN 2; BEST 89:1; DLB 152
Wolff, Geoffrey (Ansell) 1937- .... **CLC 41**
See also CA 29-32R; CANR 29, 43, 78
Wolff, Sonia
See Levitin, Sonia (Wolff)
Wolff, Tobias (Jonathan Ansell) 1945- .... **CLC 39, 64**
See also AAYA 16; BEST 90:2; CA 114; 117; CAAS 22; CANR 54, 76; DA3; DLB 130; INT 117; MTCW 2
Wolfram von Eschenbach c. 1170-c. 1220 .... **CMLC 5**
See also DLB 138
Wolitzer, Hilma 1930- .... **CLC 17**
See also CA 65-68; CANR 18, 40; INT CANR-18; SATA 31
Wollstonecraft, Mary 1759-1797 ..... **LC 5, 50**
See also CDBLB 1789-1832; DLB 39, 104, 158
Wonder, Stevie CLC 12
See also Morris, Steveland Judkins
Wong, Jade Snow 1922- .... **CLC 17**
See also CA 109; CANR 91; SATA 112
Woodberry, George Edward 1855-1930 .... **TCLC 73**
See also CA 165; DLB 71, 103
Woodcott, Keith
See Brunner, John (Kilian Houston)
Woodruff, Robert W.
See Mencken, H(enry) L(ouis)
Woolf, (Adeline) Virginia 1882-1941 .. **TCLC 1, 5, 20, 43, 56; DA; DAB; DAC; DAM MST, NOV; SSC 7; WLC**
See also Woolf, Virginia Adeline
See also CA 104; 130; CANR 64; CDBLB 1914-1945; DA3; DLB 36, 100, 162; DLBD 10; MTCW 1
Woolf, Virginia Adeline
See Woolf, (Adeline) Virginia
See also MTCW 2
Woollcott, Alexander (Humphreys) 1887-1943 .... **TCLC 5**
See also CA 105; 161; DLB 29
Woolrich, Cornell 1903-1968 .... **CLC 77**
See also Hopley-Woolrich, Cornell George
Woolson, Constance Fenimore 1840-1894 .... **NCLC 82**
See also DLB 12, 74, 189, 221
Wordsworth, Dorothy 1771-1855 .. **NCLC 25**
See also DLB 107
Wordsworth, William 1770-1850 .. **NCLC 12, 38; DA; DAB; DAC; DAM MST, POET; PC 4; WLC**
See also CDBLB 1789-1832; DA3; DLB 93, 107
Wouk, Herman 1915- ... **CLC 1, 9, 38; DAM NOV, POP**
See also CA 5-8R; CANR 6, 33, 67; CDALBS; DA3; DLBY 82; INT CANR-6; MTCW 1, 2
Wright, Charles (Penzel, Jr.) 1935- .. **CLC 6, 13, 28, 119**
See also CA 29-32R; CAAS 7; CANR 23, 36, 62, 88; DLB 165; DLBY 82; MTCW 1, 2
Wright, Charles Stevenson 1932- ... **CLC 49; BLC 3; DAM MULT, POET**
See also BW 1; CA 9-12R; CANR 26; DLB 33
Wright, Frances 1795-1852 .... **NCLC 74**
See also DLB 73
Wright, Frank Lloyd 1867-1959 .... **TCLC 95**
See also AAYA 33; CA 174
Wright, Jack R.
See Harris, Mark
Wright, James (Arlington) 1927-1980 .... **CLC 3, 5, 10, 28; DAM POET**
See also AITN 2; CA 49-52; 97-100; CANR 4, 34, 64; CDALBS; DLB 5, 169; MTCW 1, 2
Wright, Judith (Arundell) 1915-2000 .... **CLC 11, 53; PC 14**
See also CA 13-16R; CANR 31, 76; MTCW 1, 2; SATA 14
Wright, L(aurali) R. 1939- .... **CLC 44**
See also CA 138
Wright, Richard (Nathaniel) 1908-1960 .... **CLC 1, 3, 4, 9, 14, 21, 48, 74; BLC 3; DA; DAB; DAC; DAM MST, MULT, NOV; SSC 2; WLC**
See also AAYA 5; BW 1; CA 108; CANR 64; CDALB 1929-1941; DA3; DLB 76, 102; DLBD 2; MTCW 1, 2
Wright, Richard B(ruce) 1937- .... **CLC 6**
See also CA 85-88; DLB 53
Wright, Rick 1945- .... **CLC 35**
Wright, Rowland
See Wells, Carolyn
Wright, Stephen 1946- .... **CLC 33**
Wright, Willard Huntington 1888-1939
See Van Dine, S. S.
See also CA 115; DLBD 16
Wright, William 1930- .... **CLC 44**
See also CA 53-56; CANR 7, 23
Wroth, LadyMary 1587-1653(?) .... **LC 30**
See also DLB 121
Wu Ch'eng-en 1500(?)-1582(?) .... **LC 7**
Wu Ching-tzu 1701-1754 .... **LC 2**
Wurlitzer, Rudolph 1938(?)- .... **CLC 2, 4, 15**
See also CA 85-88; DLB 173
Wyatt, Thomas c. 1503-1542 .... **PC 27**
See also DLB 132
Wycherley, William 1641-1715 ...... **LC 8, 21; DAM DRAM**
See also CDBLB 1660-1789; DLB 80
Wylie, Elinor (Morton Hoyt) 1885-1928 .... **TCLC 8; PC 23**
See also CA 105; 162; DLB 9, 45

Literary Criticism Series Cumulative Topic Index

This index lists all topic entries in Gale's *Classical and Medieval Literature Criticism, Contemporary Literary Criticism, Literature Criticism from 1400 to 1800, Nineteenth-Century Literature Criticism,* and *Twentieth-Century Literary Criticism.*

NCLC Cumulative Nationality Index

FILIPINO

FINNISH

FRENCH

GERMAN

GREEK

HUNGARIAN

INDIAN

IRISH

ITALIAN

JAPANESE

NCLC-90 Title Index

ISBN 0-7876-4545-1
90000
9 780787 645458